The Hero Within Us

The Hero Within Us

A History of Track and Field in the Twentieth Century from a Michigan Perspective

By Keith McClellan

Eastern Michigan Press, Inc.
Oak Park, MI 48237

Library of Congress Cataloging-in-Publication Data

McClellan, Keith.
    The hero within us : a history of track and field in
the twentieth century from a Michigan perspective / by
Keith McClellan.—1st ed.
    p. cm.
    Includes bibliographical references and index.
    ISBN: 0-9708822-0-3

    1. Track-athletics—Michigan—History.
2. Track-athletics—History—20th century.   I. Title.

GV1060.62.M5M33 2001   796.42'09774
                        QB101-200366

Contents

Pictures on the cover

William DeHart Hubbard (1922), University of Michigan, *(Photo University of Michigan, Bentley Library)*

Tom Ottey (1934) Michigan State College *(Photo Michigan State University Archives)*

Lee Bartlett (1928) Albion College *(Photo courtesy of Cheryl Procter)*

Harvey Woodstra, Michigan State College *(Photo courtesy of Barbara Woodstra)*

John T. Smith (1926) Michigan Normal College *(Photo courtesy of Eastern Michigan University Archives)*

Leon Gaylor (1926) Michigan Normal College *(Photo courtesy of Eastern Michigan University Archives)*

Bernard Otto (1925) Michigan Normal College *(Photo courtesy of Eastern Michigan University Archives)*

Jeanne Bocci (1972/1988) Wayne State University *(Photo courtesy of Jeanne Bocci)*

Gary Morgan (1992) New York Athletic Club *(Photo courtesy of Gary Morgan)*

Charles Eugene Beatty (1932) Michigan Normal College *(Photo Eastern Michigan University Archives)*

Back Cover: Paul Wesley Jones (1959) Eastern Michigan University *(Photo courtesy of Paul Jones)*

Introduction

"**When you're competing at the Olympics,** you are really competing against yourself and within yourself. You're trying to get your body and mind to work at their optimal. . . . The very best competitors are the ones who can resist distractions, and can focus on the feedback their body and mind is giving them." [Mike Wenden, Australian swimmer, 1968.] "When you really start to hurt . . . then it comes down to who's got the mental capacity to push through all those pain barriers. And you have to do it alone. There's no one else out there. You're all by yourself." [Bill Koch, USA Nordic skier.] That is when the hero within you must rise to the top if you hope to be a champion.

Track athletes run the full spectrum of human characteristics. Some are tall, while others are short. Some are hefty, some are lean. Some have difficulty learning, some have extraordinary intellect. Some are blessed with good mental health, others are plagued by mental illness. Nevertheless, all great track stars have certain traits in common. They have the inner drive to excel, and the persistence and courage to keep working in the face of adversity. No track athlete, regardless of how talented he or she may be, goes through a season, much less an entire career, without experiencing adversity, defeat, and failure. It is the willingness and determination "to pick yourself up, dust yourself off and start all over again," as the song suggests, that defines the true champion. Most world class track and field athletes experience severe setbacks and disappointments that would discourage the average person. But, the champion athlete refuses to quit. He or she sends themselves positive messages, focuses on the future, and keeps going. They draw on the inner strength that is within all of us to define the hero within us.

As a historian I have attempted to draw upon the remnants of the past to produce a narrative explanation of what happened, in hopes that my narrative offers insights that will be valuable to those who make decisions that affect the present and the future of sport in America. This narrative is very much concerned with preserving and understanding a part of the record of Michigan's track and field experience in the past century, and not in proving a thesis.

Acknowledgments

I give a special thanks to Erin Davis, Rare Book and Special Collection Librarian, Irwin Library, the Track and Field Hall of Fame Archives at Butler University in Indianapolis, Indiana. The library of Congress was useful, although its newspaper collection, microfilm reading equipment, and speed of service are far too limited for the nation's library. Unfortunately, the Library of Congress reflects twenty years of neglected public investment.

I appreciate the assistance of Diane Windham Shaw, the Special Collections Librarian and College Archivist at Lafayette College. Robert Pruter of Elmhurst (IL) offered suggestions early on in the project. I also appreciate the access I was given to the AIAW Collection, McKeldin Library, University of Maryland at College Park, Maryland; the University of Texas Archives; the Bowling Green University (OH) Library, and the University of Missouri Archives. The yearbook collections at the following Detroit Public Schools: Central HS, Northwestern HS, Southwestern HS, Southeastern HS, Pershing HS, and Northern HS. I appreciate the use of the Wayne State University Library, the State of Michigan Historical Society Library, the University of Michigan Libraries, the Michigan State University Library, University of Detroit-Mercy Library, the Oakland Community College Library, the Eastern Michigan University, and the Western Michigan University. The libraries at the University of Akron, the University of Virginia, Windsor University, Yale University, Hood College, and Central Michigan University. Shirley J. Campbell, Assistant Curator at the Western Michigan University Archives, and Paulette Martis, Office Assistant at Sports Information, Division of University Relations, Michigan State University, were particularly helpful.

I thank the Oak Park Public Library, the Royal Oak Public Library, the Birmingham Public Library, the Southfield Public Library, the Pontiac Public Library, and the Detroit Public Library. I also thank the public libraries in the following Michigan communities: Taylor, Clarkston, Dearborn, Saginaw, Flint, Livonia, Milan, Mount Morris, St. Claire Shores, Warren, and Wyandotte. The public libraries in Cadillac [MI], Cedar Rapids [Iowa], Chattanooga [Tennessee], Chicago [IL], Toledo [Ohio], Fort Wayne [Indiana], Atlanta, [GA], and Windsor [Ontario] also yielded unique information.

The Sports Information Departments at the University of Michigan, Michigan State University, Adrian College, Saginaw Valley State University, Eastern Michigan University, Western Michigan University, Calvin College, University of Iowa, University of Kentucky, LSU, University of Tennessee, and the University of Georgia were helpful. The sports information offices at the University of Michigan and Michigan State University were the most helpful and best organized: those at Eastern Michigan University and Saginaw Valley State University were the least helpful and most poorly organized.

I interviewed Bob Parks, David L. Holmes, Jr., George Dales, Hiram Badia, Cheryl Procter (daughter of Lee Bartlett), Jim Bibbs, Reginald Bradford, Ricky Brown, Roy Fehr, David Foley, and George Gaines. I also interviewed Francie Kraker Goodrich, Aaron Z. Gordon, Cliff Hatcher, Hayes Wendell Jones, Myra Jones, Paul Wesley Jones, Fred La Plante, Bob Luby, and Gary Morgan. I interviewed Rosalie Crosbie, Doug and Theresa McMullen, Benita Fitzgerald Mosley, David Meyers, Sue Parks, Irving "Pete" Petross, Jr., James Podoley, Abraham Rosenkrantz, Hugo Apt, Kenneth "Red" Simmons, and Lou Scott. I spoke at length with Liggett School Archivist Jean Dautenhoff. Finally, I interviewed Mark H. Smith, Jr., Richard A. Swanson, Lynn Telford, John Perry Telford, Allan W. Tellis, Adolf Weinacker, Bernard Wells, Courtney Wenzel, Robert Wingo, Mrs. Harvey H. Woodstra, Keela Yount, Billy Zepp, and Billy Zepp, Jr. In addition, I spoke to Evelyn M. Alix, Jean Dautenhoff, Allan Tolmich, Kathi Harris-Rounds, Frank Soby, Carl Schuler, Greg Richardson, Wendy Truvillion, Randy Williams, Jeanne and Gerry Bocci, William H. Freeman, and Dorothy Frances Anderson Merena.

I would like to give a special acknowledgement to my wife Marian whose love and caring have made my life worth living. I also thank her for the many contributions to this book, including her father's recollections of education at Detroit University School in the years 1917–21. Allow me to thank my brother-in-law, State College of Iowa half-miler Doug Smith. Doug gathered most of the information on Drake Relay results. I also wish to thank my high school history teacher and friend of fifty years, high school quarter-miler Robert Hilsabeck, who read a draft of much of this book and offered helpful suggestions and encouragement. Finally, I must credit the members of the executive board of the Detroit Track and Field Old-Timers for encouraging me to write this book: most notably spiked-shoe stars, John Telford (an All-American friend of our family for thirty years), Aaron Gordon, George Gaines, Al Tellis, Cliff Hatcher, Mark Smith, Paul Wesley Jones, Richard Brown, David Badger, Reggie Bradford, Stan Fields, and Tommy Sledge.

Prologue: The Roots for Modern Track and Field

September 19, 1888 was a red-letter day for Detroit athletics. The very first Amateur Athletic Union (AAU) of the United States national track and field championship was being held, and it was being held in Detroit. Preparations for the meet began in the spring, when the Detroit Athletic Club set about the arduous task of upgrading its athletic field and building a new stand for spectators.[1] Laying out a new running track appropriate for holding a national AAU meet was a considerable undertaking. According to the *AAU Handbook of 1888*, "The first thing to be done in laying out a field is the building of a cinder path"[2]

The *Handbook* offered the following advice:

After the course has been surveyed and staked off, a circle should be chalked or whitewashed on the ground, representing the exact circumference of the track. Then a second circle should be similarly made, eighteen inches inside of the first circle all around. This will represent the inside circle of the track. The proposed width of the track is to be measured outward from the inside curb and a third circle drawn to represent the outside curb.

Dig out the earth to a depth of six inches. The excavation thus made is to be filled in with three different substances: ashes, clay and cinders and each must be manipulated with care and judgement. The ordinary rough ashes form the first layer, and they should be spread over to a depth of four inches. All large pieces and foreign substances should be removed and the ashes carefully raked and leveled over. Then the second layer is to be put on, and for this nothing but rich loam should be used: no sand or street dirt will do. The loam is to be filled in until the track is level with the surrounding ground. In other words, two inches of loam should be spread over. Before the ashes and loam are put down, however, the curbs are to be constructed, and for this purpose seasoned lumber, one inch thick and eight inches wide, should be used. This will allow two inches to project above the surface.

After the loam is put down it should be cleared of every minute particle of stone or pebble, and rolled and watered as often as possible until thoroughly hardened. Three to four weeks are usually devoted to hardening the loam. The top dressing is now put on it. It consists of cinders, sifted very fine and spread over the track just thick enough to entirely cover the surface. Continual rolling, and, if possible, watering is now necessary to make the track perfect. At the end of three months' time it should be firm, hard, springy, and dry, the ashes acting as a drain and the loam furnishing its elastic qualities.

Two "runaways" are needed for the jumping ground. One should be thirty-yards long; the other about forty feet long. Both are to be four feet wide. No curbs are necessary, although the longer broad jump runaway should end with a five inch-wide joist flush with the ground. The shorter high jump runway will also benefit from a joist at the end of the run way. A round, sunken wooden curb is recommended for the weight circle. For the hurdle races, it is more practical to have small individual hurdles than for long hurdles covering all lanes, because the latter may trip a competitor and cause injury when another runner knocks the hurdle over [3]

The Detroit Athletic Club completed its track for the club's July 14 Field Day.[4] Amid reports of deaths in Gainesville and Jacksonville, Florida, from yellow fever,[5] several members of the Detroit Athletic Club began preparing for the First National AAU meet to be held September 19, 1888. In late August of that year, Horace Walker won the cup in several 100-yard handicap races he started from "scratch," meaning that he ran the full distance, while his competitors ran lessor distances.[6] He also won the Phil Sanderson Medal for the quarter-miler, which he ran from scratch. John Lodge was in training for the mile and the one-half mile runs, and W. A. Chope was in training for the 220-yard low-hurdles and the running high jump. All three of these men entered a regional meet held in September by the Chicago Athletic Association.[7]

Excursion cars on trains from New York City, Chicago, Grand Rapids, and Port Huron were arranged for the great championship races. Newspaper readers were not only told that this was the most important athletic meet of the century, but that it would not return to Detroit for at least five years because of AAU rules that prohibited a return engagement for that period of time. Handsome three-sheet posters announcing the meet were printed and posted, and J. B. Field & Co. was authorized to print neat and complete programs for the meet.[8]

The only athletic club west of Detroit to enter the meet was Chicago. V. E. Schefferstein from the Olympic Athletic Club of San Francisco attempted to enter the meet, but was declared ineligible because he had recently taken part in a track meet in St. Louis "in violation of AAU rules." After a lengthy discussion with the executive committee of the Amateur Athletic Union, the misunderstanding was cleared up. After showing appropriate signs of contrition (for example, Schefferstein commended the AAU executive board for sticking to their rules), he was to be allowed to participate in future meets.[9]

More than half of the 17 athletic clubs that played a prominent role in the first national AAU track and field championships were from metropolitan New York City. The athletes representing each club wore track gear displaying its colors and symbol. The Manhattan Athletic Club wore white shirts with a cherry colored diamond as its distinguishing mark. The New York Athletic Club (NYAC) runners wore white shirts with a red winged foot of Mercury on the breast. The Brooklyn Athletic Club wore blue and old gold with a bee as their logo. The Staten Island Club colors were yellow and black with the emblem of a horse head with a fish tail, denoting speed on land and water. The Schuylkill Navy Athletic Club wore white, bearing a design of a club and an oar. The New Jersey Athletic Club wore maroon. The Olympic Athletic Club of New York wore cherry colored shirts with a black badge containing an old English "O", and the Pastime Athletic Club of New York wore blue with a blue Brazilian star in blue on a white background.[10]

Detroit Athletic Club runners wore blue shirts with black lettering, and the Chicago Athletic Association wore white shirts with a blue circle and C in the center of the circle.[11]

It rained on the Sunday before "the greatest athletic meet ever held" in America in that era with clear beneficial effect on the cider track. On Monday, New York City runners declared the Detroit Athletic Club Park cinder path "a dandy."[12] All day on Tuesday the weather was threatening, and it rained again in the evening. After the rain, however, the sky cleared and by midnight there were signs that the next day would be a great day for running.[13]

"Everything in connection with the meet was perfect. There was perfect weather, perfect track and field, perfect arrangements and a perfect jam of spectators." On Wednesday afternoon at 2 p.m. between 5,000 and 6,000 of Detroit's most prominent people honored the occasion with their presence. The members of the Detroit and Boston major league baseball teams were part of the crowd, as were several hundred out-of-town spectators brought to the meet by special excursion trains. Three hundred or so track athletes were on hand as participants in the meet.[14]

The meet featured 17 events, including the two-mile bike ride and the tug-of-war. It was a foregone conclusion that the "muscular marvels" of the rich New York City Clubs would dominate the meet. The Manhattan Athletic Club won the meet. However, because the Manhattan Athletic Club was not a member of the AAU, the Bailey prize trophy—a solid silver plaque bearing the figures of athletes engaged in various track events—was taken home by the New York Athletic Club. The Detroit Athletic Club won two third place finishes-one by H. F. Walker in the 220-yard dash and the other by W. A. Chope in the 220-yard low-hurdles. These were the only two points won by athletes representing clubs located west of the Appalachian Mountains.[15]

For most of the twentieth century the United States dominated men's track and field internationally. However, at the close of the twentieth century, U.S. men held only four of 34 world records in individual events, and U.S. women held four of 33 world records in women's events. Most U.S. world records were set abroad. Moreover, most American newspapers provided virtually no coverage of track and field. Indeed, *The New York Times* did not even list track on its internet page on sports. Surely, American track and field had fallen on hard times.

In the nineteenth century, "athletics" referred specifically to track and field, and it was under that heading that news about the sport could be found in newspapers and magazines. It is still listed that way on the sports pages of English and Scottish newspapers. At the start of the nineteenth century, European society considered running an activity suitable only for the poor or marginalized groups.[16] However, during the first half of the nineteenth century, academic interest in all things Greek revived interest in the Olympic games and helped to transform running into a sport worthy of gentlemen and one that appealed to the socially elite.

Modern track and field in the United States has its roots in the professional foot racing or pedestrianism that flourished in eastern cities and at county fairs from the 1820's through the mid-1880s. Pedestrian races offered cash prizes to distance walkers and runners, who ran ten miles in less than an hour or covered long distances over a six day period.[17] The first major running event held in the United States was a ten-mile run with a $1,000 prize staged at Beacon Raceway outside Hoboken, New Jersey in 1844. Between 25,000 and 30,000 people turned out to watch the race.[18] In the 1880s, interest in professional foot racing declined rapidly, in part, because bettors feared that races were fixed. Pedestrianism was replaced by amateur track and field contests that were said to prohibit betting. The influential metropolitan athletic clubs sponsored amateur meets.

The Scottish Caledonian clubs, first formed before the American Civil War, were an important ethnic influence on the growth of track and field in North America. The Boston Caledonian Club held their first meet in 1853.[19] Caledonian clubs restricted membership to persons of Scottish birth or decent and were designed to perpetuate Scottish manners, customs, costume, and athletic games. The forerunners of modern "Highland Games," Caledonian Club Games drew large crowds to view competition in foot racing, tug o' war, hurdling, jumping, pole vaulting, throwing the hammer and the 56-pound stone, and putting the shot.[20] These contests contributed several events to modern track and field meets, including the hurdles, hammer throw, pole vault, and 56-pound weight throw. Caledonian Clubs sponsored track meets well into the 1930s.[21]

Commercialized racing (or pedestrianism) was a huge success through the 1850s, particularly in New York City, where, for a dime, urban workers, gamblers, prostitutes, and hustlers could see the swiftest runners from Britain and America. Immigrant and working-class athletes, most notably those of the New York Caledonian Society, promoted pedestrianism and awarded substantial cash prizes to the winners.[22]

Masculinity underwent a profound transformation in the nineteenth century, as industrialism and its attendant social disruptions altered personal relationships. Upper-class males felt a loss of power and influence, middle-class males lost independence in the workplace and faced conflicting demands for aggression and self-restraint. Working-class males found authority diminished both at home and at work. As physical prowess became largely irrelevant to real economic power, there was, ironically, growing interest in muscular manliness. Sports became a rite of passage for males in the 1890s.[23]

"Muscular Christianity" was imported from England and emerged in the United States in the 1850s. Thomas Wentworth Higginson wrote an influential article about muscular Christianity in *Atlantic Magazine* in 1858 in which physical fitness and spirituality were linked. The YMCA movement became a visible outgrowth of this movement.

The New York Athletic Club was organized in 1868, just 16 years after the first intercollegiate athletic contest was held. Originally it was a socially fluid, player centered organization that catered to the manly concerns of urban males concerned with the need to maintain masculinity. The club had a locker room in the old Mair's Gymnasium. On September 8, 1868 it was formally incorporated at the Knickerbocker Cottage, Sixth Avenue between 27th and 28th Street. Two months later the New York Athletic Club sponsored their first indoor track meet at the Empire City Skating Rink, 63rd Street and Third Avenue.[24]

The Club built a boathouse on the Harlem River in 1870. On October 21, 1871 they held what they claimed to be the first outdoor amateur meet in the United States.[25] The meet was held on the club's first track, at 130th and Harlem River.[26] In 1874 the New York Athletic Club opened new club grounds at Mott Haven on the banks of the Harlem River. On September 30, 1876 the first amateur championship track meet of America was held on the Mott Haven grounds, under the auspice of the New York Athletic Club.[27] The New York Athletic Club built the first cinder-track in America at Mott Haven. Club member, William B. Curtis, introduced spiked shoes in 1868, and in 1876 the club sponsored the first national amateur championships in track and field.[28]

By the 1880s, when the crouching start was introduced to American sprinters by Bobby MacDonald—a Scotch-Maori from New Zealand—the club underwent a transformation.[29] The original members were growing older and the club needed improvements. A palatial clubhouse was erected at great cost and money was spent on adorning it. In 1883 the initiation fee to the New York Athletic Club was raised from $10 to $25 and a trainer was hired. That November the first cross-country championships were held under NYAC auspice. The new clubhouse at 55th Street and Sixth Avenue was opened February 5, 1885. Membership became a status symbol and helped define the upper status set in the city.

In 1887 the New York Athletic Club purchased Travers Island, the country home of the club, and erected a clubhouse on Travers Island in 1889. In 1892 the initiation fee was increased to $100. In 1892, the NYAC had the most palatial clubhouse in the world.

Voluntary associations were a way for groups to counter the impersonality of urban life, or, in some instances, to demonstrate their achievements and "superior" family connections by withdrawal and exclusion. By the 1880s there were a sufficient number of well-to-do families in cities like New York, Philadelphia, Chicago, and Boston to form exclusive athletic clubs. Within a decade, cities like Detroit, Cleveland, Pittsburgh, Milwaukee, and even Seattle also had exclusive athletic clubs. Ethnic groups mimicked the wealthy and formed athletic clubs of their own. Often these clubs reflected the battle lines of the incessant class warfare and struggle between those who sought a homogenous society and those who wanted to maintain their ethnic identity.[30]

The first groups, other than the Caledonian Clubs, to sponsor track and field events that went beyond pedestrian races were class-based sporting clubs for the socially elite, such as the New York Athletic Club, the Chicago Athletic Association, and the Detroit Athletic Club. Other less prestigious private clubs included the Irish-American Athletic Club, the Millrose Athletic Association, the Standard Club, and the Cornell-Hamburg Athletic Club.[31]

Sports were often introduced into the public high schools as a way to deter frequent pranks and mischief by limiting or controlling informal and otherwise unregulated leisure time activities. The Detroit Central High

School Athletic Club organized its first school field day for athletics [track and field] in June 1886.[32]

Employers also endorsed sports as a way of channeling the leisure time activities of their workers, perhaps on the assumption that unregulated idle time made labor union organizing activities easier. As late as 1935 General Motors sponsored annual field day and athletic meets.[33] It is ironic that years later, while imprisoned, the African National Conference (ANC) in South Africa used a soccer league as the mechanism for organizing their shadow government in exile.

John Wanamaker (1838–1922), founder of the Wanamaker Department Stores, founded the Millrose Athletic Association for his employees in 1908. From the beginning, John Wanamaker sought to promote amateur sports and related benefits in health and welfare for its members. His son, Rodman (1863–1928), developed the Millrose Games to display the talents of the company's track team. He also donated the cup for the Wanamaker mile at the Millrose Games in 1916.

The name "Millrose" was taken from the name of Rodman Wana- maker's country home. In 1910 his athletic club was given a charter by the New York Metropolitan Association of the AAU and functioned under their auspices. The 1908–1911 Millrose track meets took place on the roof of the Wanamaker Lafayette Street warehouse and on the roof of the Philadel- phia store. There also were bucolic Millrose outings to the Manor House where employees assembled en masse. The Manor House at Bath, Brook- lyn was a luxurious clubhouse made available by John Wanamaker. In addition to a first-rate track, there were tennis courts, acres of green fields and a private bathing beach. It was here that the first outdoor track meet for employees was held in July 1913.

The first major Millrose indoor invitation meet was held in 1914 at Madison Square Garden, then located at 26th Street and Fourth Avenue. The meet has been held annually since then. For 86 years whenever the Garden changed locations, the Millrose Games moved with it.[34]

Fred Schmertz joined the Wanamaker organization as a delivery boy on January 23, 1907 and remained with the company for a half a century. He attended evening classes at the Law School of New York University and received a degree in 1914. In 1916 he joined the Wanamaker legal depart- ment. He worked with the Millrose Games for 63 years.[35]

Short-distance foot racing was perhaps one of the first sports known to man. The earliest event in the Olympic program in ancient Greece was the stadium race. A foot race the length of the stadium, a distance of about 210 yards, was one of the first Olympic events. The problem of how to start the race, plagued foot racing for much of the history of the sport. Starting by mutual consent was common, but caused much inconvenience and controversy. The drum roll, used in early American indoor meets, was the best solution until a revolver came to be used sometime in the middle of the 19th century. Races were first timed with some accuracy in the mid-1860s, and experimentation with electrical timing was tried in England in 1892. The world's first recorded sub-10-second 100-yard dash was run by Detroit Athletic Club champion John Owen at age 30 on October 11,1890 at the AAU Championships on Analostan Island, Washington, D.C.[36]

One of the first to run the 220-yard dash in less than 22 seconds was Harry M. Jewett of the Detroit Athletic Club.[37] In 1892 Jewett beat 22 seconds on two occasions—once at the AAU Championships, aided by wind, and in Montreal on a course with only a slight turn.[38]

Prior to the twentieth century, track meets often included bicycle races and other unusual events. For example, a track meet at the University of Wisconsin in 1898 included a drop kick contest in which Pat O'Dea set the world record of 180 feet 11 inches for that event.[39] Private athletic associations frequently ran handicap races. In these events, the best runners ran the full distance "from scratch," while other runners were allowed to start ahead of the "scratch line" in order make the race more even and exciting. Harry M. Jewett of the Detroit Athletic Club was one of the great scratch runners of the era. He was the fastest man in America in the 100-yard dash.[40]

Most of the weight events practiced in modern track meets originated as tests of strength among the Scots and the Irish before the Christian era. The 56-pound throw was enjoyed in the time of Henry the Eighth. King Henry threw the stone.[41] But, it was only toward the middle of the nineteenth century that these events were molded into their present form. In the middle of the 19th century the 16-pound iron ball (shot put) appeared and was thrown from a 7-foot square, the boundaries of which were sunk flush with the ground. "The present 7-foot circle was introduced near the turn of the century."[42]

When the modern Olympics began in 1896 track and field was called "athletics," and there were just six running events: the 100-meter dash, 110-meter hurdles, 400 meter dash, 800-meter run, 1,500-meter run, and the marathon. Trials and finals were held in all events, except the 1,500-meter and marathon. There were also six field events: the discus, high jump, hop-step-and-jump, long jump, pole vault, and shot put. Of these twelve "athletic events," only four would have been familiar to the ancient Greeks, while fully that many events had Scotch roots. In 1900, eleven new events were added to the track and field portion of the games, eight of them had Scotch highland games roots.

Most of the American track athletes who participated in the first modern Olympic Games in Athens in 1896 were members of the Boston Athletic Association formed in 1888. After participating in the 1896 Olympic Games they brought back the idea for staging the Boston Marathon. The Boston Athletic Association held the first Boston Marathon in 1897.[43]

The discus was thrown outside of Greece for the first time at the first amateur athletic meet held in Liverpool in 1862. That meet also featured foot races, hurdles, the triple jump, high jump, and the pole vault.[44] When Robert Garrett, from Princeton University, won the discus at the 1896 Olympic Games in Athens, Greece, the event was unfamiliar to Americans. This turned out to be an advantage because the Greeks mistakenly believed that they should keep their feet planted in a particular way, which inhibited them from shifting the weight of their body into their throw. They threw almost entirely with their arm. By naturally shifting his weight, Garrett added impetus and centrifugal force to the discus throw that gave him the advantage that permitted him to win the event.[45]

There are inherent problems in selecting the best athletes in any sport for purposes of an all-star team, such as an Olympic team or the 100-best of the century. On any given day, some athletes are hurt or perform poorly. Training and running conditions over time are vastly different. As Yale University coach and 1976 chairman of the men's Olympic Track and Field committee, Bob Giegengack, put it: "If we ran a meet every day for two weeks, we would have different results."[46]

History is, in part, the telling of a story with an implicit or explicit message. Inevitably interpretations of human experience, personal values, and public policy are involved. These decisions require the selection of subjects, a focus on particular experiences, an interpretation of biased original sources, and an understanding of the choices involved. The book centers on the experiences of some 200 male and 45 female United States nationals who were born in Michigan or attended college in Michigan. The distribution between male and female subjects reflects the difference in the period of time male and female athletes were involved in interscholastic and intercollegiate track and field in Michigan during the twentieth century.

The book focuses on many of the great practitioners of an individual sport and on the values, the innovations in technology, and the political influences that shaped the sport over the course of a century. Dominant values in Michigan changed several times during the twentieth century, and sports both influenced and reflected those changes. Class-conscious exclusiveness,

racial prejudice, communal values, ethnic inclusiveness, and corporate pro-
motion/advertising, at one time or another, have had a significant influence
on the history of track and field. This book makes an effort to identify the
consequences of those influences on the sport.

The track and field greats in this book were selected on the basis of their
peak performances in national and international meets, and were judged
in comparison with their contemporaries. Some critics will complain that
the book contains too much detail about too many track athletes. There is
some validity to this criticism. However, the 100 year history of an individual sport, with events for men and women, and more than 18 separate
skilled activities cannot be adequately told without reference to many great
athletes, whose personal history provides insight into their motivation. A
decision was made to place an emphasis on individual track athletes and
their contributions rather than on institutional and corporate influences,
which are discussed but not allowed to dominate.

As the twentieth century approached, there was considerable interest in
southeast Michigan track and field. As the *Detroit Free Press* put it:

At present there is quite a healthy movement on to revive the old-time enthusiasm over track and field athletics. About a dozen men are training, most of
them quite regularly, and a number more are expected to begin work right
away. Ed Ryan, the club's secretary, is taking charge of the work and gets out
every day at 5 o'clock with the men. He says that the club's idea is to get the
thing started this year, so that there will be real, genuine interest in track and
field sports manifested in Detroit next year. The club would like to see if Detroit
can furnish some more champions in the national arena, such as were Owen,
Luce, Jewett, Ducharme and others. A club field day will be given on Saturday,
September 4, when most of the championship events will be represented on
the program. In addition, there will be a 100-yard dash and a half-mile bicycle
race for boys. If a good showing is made during the training and in this field
day, about half a dozen men will be sent to Chicago to compete in the central
state championships, to be held there September 21. Detroit may possibly be
represented in the national championships in New York.[47]

The Hero Within Us

1. Being Recognized as "The Best in The West"

(How the University of Michigan used track and field to gain recognition from the social elite)

A **new elitist sports movement** emerged in Great Britain during the last half of the nineteenth century. It came to be called "amateurism." Amateurism was a natural extension of the traditions of British aristocracy, and the prerogatives often claimed by pre-industrial aristocrats. Amateurism was a standard created to separate mechanics, peasants, and other social inferiors from participation in athletic contests with "gentlemen" or members of the leisure-class. In fact, many early statements of rules for amateur events contained a "mechanics clause", which excluded laborers even if they had never accepted financial compensation for their athletic involvement.

The British aristocracy had long held that qualitative superiority resulted from heredity, not the fruit of individually acquired merit. From their point of view, the gentleman-aristocrat was not expected to put forth too great an effort in any single direction. Instead, a gentleman should strive for excellence, but not in a single activity or as a consequence of prolonged training. The aristocrat took great pains to distance himself from the highly trained professional. Investing too much time and effort in one specialized activity was considered plebeian.[1]

Those who espoused amateurism did not want sports to be transformed from recreation to a full-time occupation. Central to the new "amateur" ethos was the belief that leisure activities are superior to those associated with making a living or whose motive is material gain.

The first intercollegiate athletic contest ever held was a 1827 cricket match between Oxford and Cambridge students.[2] A casualness and dislike for organized training characterized British public school athletic contests in the nineteenth century. There were vague feelings that rigid training programs were unsportsman-like. British undergraduates felt strongly that sports were recreational activities in which one participated, not exhibitions to be watched. This player-centered approach was at the heart of the amateur ideal that was institutionalized by the London-based Amateur Athletic Club. The Amateur Athletic Club defined *amateur* synonymously with *gentleman*. As upper-class British sportsmen, they alleged that their "social inferiors" could not comprehend the ethos of amateurism and fair play. They proclaimed that exclusion was "the only way to keep . . . sport pure from the elements of corruption; . . . [specifically], the average workman has no idea of sport for its own sake."

The English apostles of amateurism created a myth that their new ideas had roots in ancient Greece. They argued that the Greeks had initiated competitive athletics out of a deep, genuine love of sport for sport's sake. These claims had no historical support. The ancient Greeks neither distinguished between amateurs and professionals, nor entertained such novel Victorian goals as fair play.[3] The line between a nineteenth-century amateur and professional appears to have been mainly a line between aristocrats and the unpaid members of an underprivileged class.[4]

In the early 1870s, amateurism quickly spread to elite American colleges. Influential spokesmen for the view that American intercollegiate sports should remain strictly amateur events solidified this doctrine for the public through their writings and speeches. Walter Camp, Yale's unofficial football coach and the father of the American game, promoted the English-gentleman model as the preferred exemplar for American collegiate sports. "A gentleman does not make his living from his athletic prowess," Camp proselytized. "He does not earn anything from his victories except glory and satisfaction . . . A gentleman never competes for money, directly or indirectly"[5]

In the United States, as in Great Britain, amateurism represented an attempt to draw class lines against the masses, and to develop a new lifestyle as a badge of middle-and upper-class identity. Initially, the spokesmen for this movement used amateurism to direct their social prejudices against the professional, immigrant, working-class sport of track and field, and then, in the 1880s, toward shaping the more familiar environs of collegiate athletics. Finally, by the last decade of the century, the amateurs were enlisted to support the emergent Olympic movement.[6]

In the United States, a country characterized by exceptional social fluidity, even unschooled athletes recognized the potential of sports clubs as agencies of status ascription. Participating in sport, even if only as a "social" member of an athletic club, was seen as an asset in becoming part of an upper-status group. By 1885 the use of sports as a status enhancing mechanism was well established in the urban Northeast, and the social elite already controlled sports clubs in most metropolitan areas. In 1886 William B. Curtis, a founder of the New York Athletic Club, recognized that the amateur-professional distinction discriminated against lower class groups. He asserted, however,

the practical point is that under existing laws there has grown up a system of clubs and associations whose best interests, pecuniary and social, would partially or wholly lose their value were the amateur fence to be taken down or even materially lowered. So that, in advocating any radical change, one must fight—not abstract right or wrong—but those interests[7]

The major American, metropolitan athletic clubs were involved in such intense rivalries that from the outset they commonly circumvented their own rules of amateurism to field the strongest possible track teams. A superior athlete had little difficulty finding a club that would grant him a free membership and perhaps valuable perquisites as well. Unless he was African-American, a recent immigrant, or too crude in social demeanor for polite company, ways were found to recruit the best athletes. These athletes commonly pawned medals or received under-the-table payments or both, in the same way modern day college football and basketball players are given money or other perquisites. Since these same clubs controlled the board of directors of the AAU, they used the rules as a weapon; not dissimilar to the way the NCAA has functioned, at times, in the second half of the twentieth century.

In 1888 all pretense of a player centered ethos in amateur sports was abandoned when the National Association of Amateur Athletes of America, which had been formed in 1879 by the most exclusive clubs in the East, was replaced by the Amateur Athletic Union (AAU), managed by clubs now controlled by the socially elite who, for the most part, made no pretense of being athletes. In mid-August 1888, with support assured from clubs in Philadelphia, Detroit, Chicago, and St. Louis, the Amateur Athletic Union Board of Managers made its move, which amounted to one of the most successful power grabs in sport history. They declared that "effective immediately . . . any amateur athlete competing in any open amateur games in the United States not governed by rules approved by the Amateur Athletic Union shall be debarred from competing in any games held under the rules of the Amateur Athletic Union." Their arrow was aimed at two members of the Olympic Athletic Association of San Francisco, California, who were leaders of a group of athletic clubs that was resisting efforts to make their activities subject to the "Eastern athletic fraternity."[8]

The AAU represented the greatest and most enduring legacy of the early amateur movement. Now, all athletic club and college runners, jumpers and throwers were obliged to register with the AAU. The Intercollegiate Association of Amateur Athletes of America (IC4A), formed in 1876 by colleges located along the Atlantic seaboard, remained the country's premiere collegiate athletic organization, but was now subordinate to the AAU.

While clocking their actions in the ideology of amateurism, the AAU did not significantly change how Americans practiced a form of professionalism. From the beginning of the movement, a handful of self-interested, power-hungry men were behind the amateur movement. The best athletes were often paid "under the table" or with valuable gifts. Gold "stock" watches were sometimes used. They were called "stock" watches because they went back into the jeweler's stock in return for cash. AAU officials handled the watches and knew both their origin and destination. No sooner had the dominant athletic clubs created rules for amateurism when they started circumventing those rules when it was to their advantage to do so. The hypocrisy was undeniable to all those who cared to look closely.

Nevertheless, the social and economic elite, particularly on the East Coast, followed the English example and subscribed to the principals of amateurism as practiced by the AAU. By 1890, track and field, once the bastion of working class Americans, had been successfully co-opted by the well to do. Presidents and trustees of colleges and universities seeking the attention of would-be students and families who could afford endowments soon discovered that athletics, particularly football and track and field, where a short-cut to the pocketbooks of wealthy male patrons.

At the beginning of the twentieth century, athletics were already playing a vital role in attracting students and endowments to colleges and universities. In an era that offered greater college student capacity than qualified paying students, the closing years of the 19th century were characterized by "cut-throat" competition for students and financial support, and college sports was already a successful commercial enterprise. Franklin Field was built at the University of Pennsylvania in 1895. Harvard built a $300,000 stadium in 1903, Princeton opened

Palmer Stadium in 1914, and in that same year Yale followed with a stadium that seated 75,000.

Imitating Boola-Boola

William Rainy Harper, the first President of the modern University of Chicago, was a pioneer in the use sports to advertise for students. When John D. Rockefeller selected him to create a "great Baptist university" in the heartland of America, Harper inherited a bankrupted college on Chicago's South-side and several million dollars of Standard Oil money.[9] He did not, however, have alumni or a constituency from which to draw students. Moreover, after spending Rockefeller's endowment hiring faculty and building the Quadrangle, he did not have enough money to pay faculty and equip the school.[10]

Harper needed a commodity of proven success to establish his new university at a location where one had already failed and in a city not yet noted for its culture. Harper understood that a bridge that spanned the gap between the high culture of his university and the mass culture espoused by his potential support base would help achieve his goals. Businessmen could understand and would pay for winning athletic teams, even if they were skeptical of "Ivy Tower" intellectuals. Sports gave his new university the public visibility it needed to survive and prosper as "the Harvard of the West." It also gave a few economically deprived young men an opportunity for a college education at a time when "charity funds" for college tuition were inadequately supported. Local merchants and wealthy patrons were willing to subsidize the education of a promising athlete, although they were usually unwilling to subsidize the education of promising teachers or musicians. Consequently, in 1892 Harper hired Amos Alonzo Stagg and told him to build an athletic powerhouse.[11]

Muscular Christianity, with its strong, upper class English bias, deeply influenced Stagg, a former divinity student and star athlete at Yale. It gave him an intense missionary zeal for college athletics. Stagg believed that athletics should be employed to instill good Christian character in the men who were expected to become model citizens and the future leaders of the nation. Stagg believed that Christian character should reflect manly achievement, generous rivalry, good sportsmanship, fidelity to amateurism, and loyalty to the university.[12] While a Christian man, Stagg's view of Christianity did not include suffering fools gladly. He had an enormous ego and no tolerance for things he believed inappropriate. Ignoring the self-evident fact that he was making a handsome living as a well paid coach, he intensely disliked "professionalism" in sports. He also was blind to the reality that not every good athlete has the ability to lead wisely, and that many who lead wisely have little or no athletic talent.

Stagg engineered four critical and calculated decisions at the outset of his tenure as athletic director at the University of Chicago. When Harper persuaded department store magnate Marshall Field to donate land, Stagg expropriated a portion of it for an athletic field. Stagg Field (originally Marshall Field) was built in 1893 and refurbished in 1914. Next, Stagg helped to orchestrate the formation of the Western Intercollegiate Conference, which later became the Big Ten Conference. He scheduled every University of Chicago Western Conference football game at home, making certain that the lion's share of game receipts stayed in Chicago. Finally, he established the Western Intercollegiate Track and Field Championships to be held at the new Marshall Field.[13]

The first Western Collegiate Amateur Athletes Association Track and Field Championships was held in Chicago in 1895. The University of California won the championship, and the University of Michigan placed second in the meet. University of Iowa sprinter John V. Crum, who won the 100 and the 220-yard dashes, was the meet's outstanding athlete.[14] Two weeks later, the Chicago Athletic Association enlisted Crum to defeat the University of California in a track meet held on June 15.[15]

Five year's later, in an effort to place the University of Chicago in the company of Harvard and Yale, Amos Alonzo Stagg personally raised $2,500 to take the stars of the University of Chicago's track team to Paris to participate in the 1900 Olympic Games.[16]

University of Michigan Athletics

Competitive athletics began at the University of Michigan in 1837 when clubs were formed so that students could compete against each other, as in English and European universities. By 1860 clubs, led by the "Pioneer Cricket Club," were competing against similar student organizations from other schools.[17] In 1890 the students formed the Athletic Association of the University of Michigan. It brought the various clubs at the university under one authority, and allowed any student who paid $3 to participate in the management of athletics. Five officers and nine directors were elected to carry on the duties of the Association. In 1891 the Athletic Association hired the University's first football coach.

Problems arose in 1893 when it was discovered that several athletes were competing on University teams without enrolling in school. So, in December 1893, the regents created the Board in Control of Athletics to govern eligibility, the hiring of trainers and coaches, scheduling, "suppress evil tendencies," and handle accusations of misconduct. With this board, control of University of Michigan athletics rested in the hands of the faculty for the first time. The first faculty board participated in creating the Western Intercollegiate Conference, when representatives of seven institutions—the Universities of Chicago, Illinois, Michigan, Minnesota, Northwestern, Purdue, and Wisconsin—met in Chicago on February 8, 1896. The Western Conference became known as the Big Ten Conference in 1912, when Indiana, Iowa and Ohio State were added to the group. In 1898, the faculty board created the position of Graduate Manager of Athletics, the school's first athletic director.

In 1890, University of Michigan football and baseball practice games were played on the campus (in the location where Waterman gymnasium was later built), and games for which the school's athletic association charged admission took place on the county fair grounds. The fair ground fields were rough and rocky, and were a poor place to play championship contests.

"In October 1890, the regents appropriated $3,000 to purchase the plot of ground which now constitutes the south ten acres of Ferry Field." The following year a deal was closed to secure the land and $5,000 was appropriated to put the field in shape for athletic use. The north half of the new grounds were leveled off and a quarter mile cinder track was built. It was called 'The Athletic Field,' placed under the control of the directors of the athletic association, and first used in 1893. Subsequently the association changed the name to 'Regent's Field.' It was known by that name until 1902.

It was the success that Keene Fitzpatrick brought to the University of Michigan athletic program that helped open the door to the acquisition and development of Ferry Field. In 1902 D. M. Ferry of Detroit, Michigan, purchased twenty-one acres lying between the old field and Edwin Street and extending west of State Street for a distance of about one thousand feet. He gave the property to the University, under the condition that it be used exclusively for athletic purposes. In accepting this donation, the regents joined the new ground to the old and gave it all the name of Ferry Field. After 1903 the Athletic Association purchased several small parcels of land and extended the field to the railroad track. By 1907 Ferry Field contained about thirty-eight acres of land.[18]

A little covered stand seating about four hundred people was erected on the athletic field in 1893, but burned down two years later. In 1896 the Regents moved the house used by the groundskeeper on to Ferry Field and built a covered stand on the field, which seated eight hundred spectators. Mr. Ferry also provided the funds to erect gates and ticket offices at the new entrance. All other buildings, stands and improvements on Ferry Field were paid for out of the funds of the athletic association. Between 1900 and 1907 the association spent about seventy thousand dollars on permanent improvements to the field. Between 1902 and 1907 Mr. Ferry spent over thirty thousand and prior to 1900, the board of regents spent between ten and twelve thousand dollars on improvements.

In 1907 Ferry Field had about twenty acres under grass. Besides the old covered stand seating eight hundred, it had football bleachers seating about seventeen thousand people. There was still no grandstand for the new baseball diamond, and a clubhouse with lockers and bathing facilities was needed.[19]

The Real Goods

The University of Michigan hired Keene Fitzpatrick in 1894–5 and rehired him 1898–1914 to make them competitive with Ivy League universities in track and football. Fitzpatrick grew up in Boston and became the athletic trainer at Yale University before accepting a position with the Michigan Athletic Club of Detroit. Fitzpatrick transformed the University of Michigan into a track and field powerhouse, and trained a number of Olympic champions at the University. He scheduled meets with the First Regiment of Chicago and established regular track meets with Cornell University that continued for nearly half a century. These matches signaled to the socially elite that the University of Michigan was allied with what they considered to be appropriate interests.

Keene Fitzpatrick was born in Boston in 1865. He attended the common schools [elementary schools] of that city, and beyond that was self-educated. Keene was a natural athlete, and spent much of his youth as an all-round athlete. He was the best sprinter in the country and a member of a world-champion fire brigade. In 1890 he was appointed athletic trainer at Yale University, and was engaged by the Michigan Athletic Club of Detroit two years later.[20] While with the Michigan Athletic Club, "Fitz" trained several athletes who later attended the University of Michigan. In 1894 "Fitz" was engaged as the gymnasium and athletic instructor at the University of Michigan under the direction of Dr. Fitzgerald, who was the general director of athletics. In 1896 "Fitz" went back to Yale, and the quality of Michigan athletic teams declined. So, in 1898 "Fitz" was brought back to the University of Michigan as acting director of the gymnasium. By 1901, the year radio signals first spanned the Atlantic Ocean, "Fitz" and Yost were fielding championship teams in football and track. Between 1896 and 1910 Keene Fitzpatrick established Michigan as a powerhouse in track. During that period, he won 92 percent of his meets.

From 1894 to 1900 there was little good track material in the University owing to lack of previous development. However, Michigan made a fine showing in the inter-collegiate meets. In 1900 our athletic management sent a team to compete at the Paris Exposition [Olympic Games]. Our team was composed of Hayes (Captain), McLean, Leiblee, and Dvorak, who had to compete with the best athletes in the world. We won three seconds and one third. In this year, we also won the Western Intercollegiate meet. In 1901 the Conference was organized, consisting originally of nine Western universities, and now open to all Western colleges. Our teams have won every Conference meet. However, our victories have not been confined to the West. In 1897, we sent an unsuccessful mile relay team to Philadelphia, but in 1903 our four-mile relay team easily won first place, and Archie Hahn secured second place in the dashes. In 1904, we startled the East by winning the four-mile relay race, the dashes, the hurdles, and the shot put. Yale was again second in the relay race. In indoor meets our teams have been even more successful, as they never have been beaten.

Keene Fitzpatrick is a trainer and a gentleman. One cannot long talk with Mr. Fitzpatrick without being impressed by a certain air of gentlemanliness which is all too rarely found in connection with many men whose business it is to develop the physical sports of young men. It is this quality in Mr. Fitzpatrick, which, more than anything else, endears him to all who know him, be they athlete or not. It is this quality, as much as his athletic ability, which makes him an ideal trainer. He is, in habits, in personality, in general bearing, a worthy and influential example for all who come in contact with him. He is the sort of man under whose charge a father would be glad to place his son.[21]

Keene Fitzpatrick inaugurated the University of Michigan Interscholastic meet in 1898.[22] While promoting high school track and field, the interscholastic meet soon became an important tool for recruiting athletic talent for the University of Michigan's football and track teams. Other Western Conference Universities soon adopted this shrewd device. Among the Universities that followed Michigan's lead were the University of Illinois, the University of Wisconsin, and Northwestern University.[23] In 1901 A. A. Stagg mimicked Fitzpatrick and did him one

Coach Keene Fitzpatrick and Archie Hahn, the runner on the right, 1904
(Photo University of Michigan, Bentley Library)

better by creating the National Interscholastic Track and Field Championships at Marshall Field in Chicago. The National Interscholastic Meet
was also an unabashed recruiting tool. As the *Chicago Tribune* observed,
"A commission of members at of the [the University of Chicago's]
Reynolds Club has charge of the plans for making the lads have such a
good time that they will want to come back to Chicago as freshmen."
The entertainment for visiting high school athletes included automobile rides, a reception, dinner and dance. The Reynolds Club furnished
college co-eds to accompany visiting young men to the dance.[24] On
these occasions fraternities sometimes made future arrangements for
providing free housing, food, or both to athletes who attended their
University and represented it on the athletic fields.[25]

   In 1898, "Fitz" and Charles Baird also played a prominent role in a
dissident association—comprised of Michigan, Wisconsin, and Illinois—that threatened to boycott athletic competition with the Univer-

sity of Chicago in 1899 unless Stagg agreed to both alternate football games on home grounds and an equal division of gate receipts.[26]

Hail to the Victor Valiant

In 1897 J. M. Thomas, a 100-yard and 220-yard dash runner from Douglas, Michigan, was elected captain of the 1898 University of Michigan Track team.[27] One of his teammates was Louis Elbel. Louis came from a family steeped in music. In 1851 when his father moved to South Bend, Indiana from Arzberg, Germany, he set out to establish himself in the music business. In 1860 Louis' father formed the Elbel Band and Orchestra. Louis' older brother joined his father in operating a music store in South Bend, and his older sister married a musician and moved to the Englewood district on Chicago's South-side about a mile and a half from the University of Chicago.

In 1896 Louis Elbel enrolled at the University of Michigan as a part of the class of 1900 to study music. As was so often the pattern of the nineteenth century college student, Louis felt that it was important to develop both body and mind, so he decided to try his hand at athletics. In January 1897 he joined the University of Michigan Union track team, and ran the 40-yard dash. He met and became friends with Jack McLean, one of the best athletes in the class of 1900. The 5'-1", Louis Elbel even won the 40-yard dash at the indoor varsity day track meet in 1897.[28]

During his sophomore year at the University of Michigan, Louis decided to visit his sister in Chicago and attend the University of Michigan vs. University of Chicago football game on Thanksgiving Day. The game would decide the championship of the newly formed Western Conference, and several of his track and field buddies, including Jack McLean, were on the football team.

The game was a close, exciting battle that tested the will and spirit of both teams. In the first half, McLean and Bill Caley were injured, but the trainer was able to patch them up so that they could reenter the fray in the second half. In the closing minutes of the game, Michigan came from behind to tie the score, and Bill Caley kicked goal to win the contest 12 to 11. The 600 or so Michigan fans that attended the game went wild with excitement. For more than an hour, they snake danced up and down Hyde Park Boulevard near the University of Chicago singing and yelling in delight and shear joy. Still pumped up with adrenaline and the vicarious thrill of winning the first conference championship in the history of the school, Louis began hearing a rousing melody in his head as he walked back to his sister's house. He continued to work on the music the next day on the South Shore Interurban travelling to South Bend. He even touched up the piece on the piano when he got home.

When he showed his finished creation to his brother, who was in the music publishing business, his brother insisted that it be orchestrated in Detroit and properly published. The completed song arrived at the University of Michigan from the printers on March 23, 1899. By then, Louis Elbel and his friend had already performed the song on several occasions. When the noted brass band leader, John Philip Sousa, gave a concert before a large crowd at University Hall in Ann Arbor on April 8 he included Elbel's "Victor's March" in his program. The ringing words

> Hail to the victor valiant,
> Hail to the conquering heroes,
> Hail, hail to Michigan,
> The champions of the West

soon became synonymous with University of Michigan and its athletic program.[29]

Elbel's "Victor's March" had a profound impact on the University of Michigan. The words to his fight song became a self full-filling prophecy. Like the University of Chicago, the University of Michigan set out to be Harvard of the West or "the best in the West." The leadership of the University of Michigan implicitly sought the acceptance and accepted the judgement of the eastern social and economic elite as the criteria for being "the best." In doing so, they competed head-to-head with the University of Chicago for this honor during the first third of the twentieth century.

Success against Ivy League teams in sports—particularly football and track—was one of the popular yardsticks used by such gurus as Walter Camp and Caspar Whitney in the first decade of the twentieth century to measures who was "best in the west." Their judgement was often a sign of acceptance by the elite sporting crowd as well as by the balance of the socially elite.

Ironically, Louis Elbel never graduated from the University of Michigan. After his junior year at Michigan, he spent a year studying in Leipzig, Germany, then went on to a career as a concert pianist and music instructor. In 1920, at the age of 43, he married Maud Biggs, a

South Bend social worker. He retained close ties with the University of Michigan, and in the fall of 1958, shortly before his death at age 81, directed the Michigan Marching Band to his "Victor's March."[30]

President of the United States and former Wolverine football player Gerald R. Ford recalls that "to stand on the turf in Michigan's Stadium and hear 'The Victors' played by that great Michigan band . . . was an unbelievable thrill."[31]

John Philip Sousa made several trips to Ann Arbor. His Marching Band was a popular fund raiser for the University of Michigan Athletic Board.[32]

Training to Be Champions

Despite an impressive string of victories on the cinder paths, Michigan was not an ideal place to train, nor were the training schedules as rigorous as three-quarters of a century later. University of Michigan trackmen generally worked out for an hour three or four days a week from early October through the indoor track season, took a couple of weeks off, and trained about four or five hours a week until the season ended. By the standards of the day, "Fitz" worked his trackmen more than most trainers.[33] Few Michigan high schools and colleges had decent tracks, and the spring weather rarely cooperated with the trainer's plan for attaining peak fitness by season's end. Cold or rainy weather frequently halted track practice, and in those days there were no sheltered facilities for training.[34] At times, the bad weather even caused illness that interfered with conditioning, as was the case with Archie Hahn in early March 1903.[35]

Travel also took its toll on Michigan trackmen. Most of the important meets were held in New York City, Philadelphia, or Boston. At the beginning of the twentieth century, a trip east could be an arduous journey. For example, on May 22, 1901 four members of the Michigan track team, including Dvorak and Fishleigh accompanied Coach Fitzpatrick to New York City for the IC4A Meet, also known as the Eastern Intercollegiate Meet. They left Ann Arbor by train at 4:58 p.m. on May 22 for a meet held May 24 and 25. They traveled all night and checked into the Murray Hill Hotel in New York City on the afternoon of May 23. On Sunday they returned to Buffalo, where they spent the night, before returning to Ann Arbor Monday afternoon.[36] A trip that can now be made in two or three hours each way and consumes two or three days took no more than sixteen hours each way by train and consumed five days a century ago.

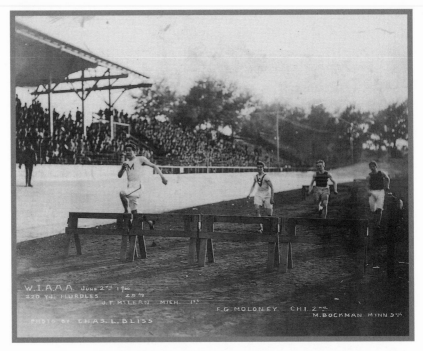

John McLean, Captain of the 1899 U of Michigan track team, enroute to a win in the 220-yard low-hurdles that ensured the U of Michigan a ½ point victory over the U of Chicago at the Western Intercollegiate Meet Amateur Athletic at Marshall Field in Chicago on June 2, 1900.
(Photo University of Michigan, Bentley Library)

Getting a Tradition Started

One of the first track stars at the University of Michigan was John Frederick McLean, whose primary event was the 110-meter high-hurdles. McLean was born in Menominee, Michigan on January 10, 1878. He was captain of the 1899 Michigan track team and a member of the 1897 and 1898 Michigan varsity football teams. Keene Fitzpatrick helped McLean take full advantage of his athletic talent. On May 22, 1897 John set the University of Michigan 120-yard high hurdles record, and reset it (15.25) on May 20, 1899.[37]

Despite "glowering clouds, chilly winds, and a spongy track," John McLean's victory in the 220-yard low-hurdles on June 2, 1900 was the deciding factor in the University of Michigan's win over the University of Chicago by a half a point in the Western Intercollegiate Meet. McLean also placed second in the 120-yard high hurdles and the running high jump at Marshall Field that day in Chicago.[38]

On June 9, 1900 McLean, outfitted in the blue and black colors of the Detroit Athletic Club, won the 220-yard low-hurdles (26.8) and placed second in the running broad jump (20–31/2) at the Central Athletic Association Championships held at the Detroit Athletic Club Field in Detroit. According to the *Detroit Free Press*, the Detroit Athletic Club field track was "in splendid condition [for the meet]. The new cinder path for the 100 and 220-yard dashes and hurdle events [was] pronounced the best in the west. . . ." The meet pitted the University of Michigan against the Milwaukee Athletic Club as the principal antagonists. According to the *Free Press* reporter, "the championships [were] really of more importance than a big college meet, as it [gave] graduate athletes, independent clubs and unattached men a chance to try conclusions with each other." The reporter went on to say, it is "well known that there are many men out of college who are still able to compete with the rising generation of performers on the cinder path."[39] With attitudes like this, it is easy to see why the Amateur Athletic Union (AAU) was gaining influence.

The AAU saw the 1900 Olympic Games as an opportunity to extend their power. The organization appointed William Sloane and James Hyde from Princeton and Casper Whitney, an ardent Anglophile and supporter of the amateur athletic movement to American Olympic Committee (AOC).[40] Whitney had serious reservations about the French sport venues being readied for the Olympic games. The first cinder track ever constructed in France was built for the 1900 Games, and no one was certain that it would be a satisfactory running surface.[41] Six American universities sent teams to the Paris Olympics: the University of Pennsylvania, Princeton, Georgetown, Syracuse, the University of Michigan, and the University of Chicago. The New York Athletic Club and the New England Track Club also sent teams. Each club and university provided its own funding for the trip to Paris.[42] All the athletes who made the journey were registered and in good standing with the AAU. Even though they had not selected the American team, the AOC controlled the expedition to Paris.[43]

Shortly after McLean graduated from the University he accompanied the University of Michigan delegation to the second Olympiad in Paris. The 110-meter hurdles was the first track and field final event contested in the 1900 Olympics. All of the top hurdlers were present. John McLean was fortunate enough to get a flying start, and was feet ahead of Alvin Kraenzlein at the first hurdle. But, Kraenzlein was the superior runner and caught McLean at the eighth hurdle. McLean held on to win the silver medal three yards behind Kraenzlein and just a foot ahead of Frederick Moloney. McLean also placed sixth in the long jump and standing triple jump, and eighth in the running triple jump, at Paris.[44] John taught and coached at Knox College for many years before returning to Detroit to become a bond broker.[45]

In addition to John McLean, Keene Fitzpatrick tutored a number of athletes who were among America's all-time best track and field stars. By the beginning of the new century, as pictures replaced drawings in newspaper stories, the University was reaching into Stagg's own back-yard to recruit athletic talent. Charles Edwards Dvorak was born in Chicago on November 27, 1878. He attended high school at Lewis Institute in Chicago. Dvorak was the first vaulter to use a bamboo pole instead of the ash or hickory pole used by his predecessors.[46] He was an outstanding pole-vaulter before enrolling at the University of Michigan in the fall of 1899. On June 2, 1900 we set the Western Conference Intercollegiate Conference record in the pole vault in Chicago with a jump of 11 feet 6 inches.[47]

On June 9, 1900, with the famous Admiral Dewey watching, Dvorak placed second in the pole vault at the Central Athletic Association Championships held on the Detroit Athletic Club Field in Detroit. "After Dvorak had missed the chance for first place he vaulted off the tie for second and made a most marvelous exhibition, clearing at least twelve feet and going clear over the uprights."[48] Like McLean, Charles Dvorak was a member of the five-member team Fitzpatrick took to 1900 Olympic Games in Paris.

The pole vault contest at the1900 Olympics in Paris was marred by the indecision on the part of the officials in charge. Three of the leading American entries in the pole vault objected to the scheduling of their event on Sunday. Charles Dvorak, Bascom Johnson, and Daniel Horton showed up anyway and were told that the event would be rescheduled, so they left. After they left, the officials changed their minds, and went ahead with the contest without the three Americans. The event was held and Irving Baxter, of the USA won the pole vault with a modest vault of 10 feet 10 inches. The following day a "consolation" event was held, which Horton won with a vault of 11–3¾ inches. Dvorak took second with a vault of 11–3¾.[49]

The following year indoor track meets began to attract relatively large audiences. The growing popularity of track, the addition of "circus seats" at Waterman Gym, and the reduction of ticket prices from fifty cents to twenty-five cents aided the improved turnout.[50] Fitzpatrick was determined to make the Michigan track program "the best in the west." As the University student newspaper put it:

> Last year she [the University of Michigan] sent a team to Paris, and it is thought that, in order to keep her prestige as a leader of college athletics of the west, she should be represented in the annual [Eastern Intercollegiate] games at New York.[51]

That spring, Dvorak tied for first in the pole vault at the IC4A Meet held at Berkeley Ovah in New York City. Under less than ideal conditions, he placed second in a jump off.[52]

On June 12, 1901 Dvorak carried his pole aboard the late evening Michigan Central passenger train bound for Buffalo.[53] He represented the Detroit Athletic Club three days later and won the pole vault (11–3) at the National Senior AAU Outdoor Championships held at the Pan-American Exposition.[54] President McKinley was assassinated on September 6 at the Exposition by Detroit born Leon Czolgosz.[55]

In addition to athletics, Dvorak tried his hand at writing while at the University of Michigan. He was athletic editor of the *University of Michigan Daily* in 1901.[56]

On September 11, 1903 Dvorak represented the First Regiment of Chicago and won the pole vault (11–0) at the National Senior AAU Outdoor Track and Field Championships held at the State Fair Park in Milwaukee.[57] In March 1903 Archie Hahn had accompanied the Chicago First Regiment to the Metropolitan AAU indoor meet held in New York City.[58] The First Regiment of Chicago had a special relationship with the industrial and commercial elite of the "windy city." It was formed in August 1874, three years before state law provided for such a military group, to respond to perceived threats to the industrial and commercial interests of the City of Chicago. Chicago industrialist and commercial magnates, such as Philip Armour, Marshall Field, and Cyrus McCormick, feared riots and labor actions from the largely foreign speaking working class of the city, who it was feared were radical socialists. They purchased a Gattling gun and a machine gun for use by the First Regiment to put down any possible labor unrest, including that that caused by reductions in wages.[59]

Keene Fitzpatrick's predilection for the wealthy was nowhere more evident than in the teams he chose to compete against. Aside from teams in the Western Conference, his track team regularly competed against the First Regiment of Chicago, Cornell University, and Syracuse University.[60] While the First Regiment of Chicago had an excellent amateur track team, so did various Young Men's Christian Associations (YMCA) and Bohemian Turner Track Clubs in Chicago and Detroit.[61]

Dvorak competed for the University of Michigan for five years. Shortly after graduating from Michigan, on September 3, 1904 Dvorak won a gold medal in the pole vault (11–6) at the third Olympiad held in St. Louis. After college, Charles Dvorak was a high school athletic director. He died December 18, 1969.

Amos Alonzo Stagg Locks Horns with James Edward Sullivan

In May 1901 it was announced that the 1904 Olympics would be held in Chicago.[62] However, the announcement proved to be pre-mature. The Chicago committee, lead by Henry J. Furber Jr., William Rainey Harper, and Amos Alonzo Stagg underestimated James Edward Sullivan, the son of Irish immigrants and the powerful secretary of the Amateur Athletic Union. They negotiated directly with Baron de Coubertin, rather than with Sullivan and the eastern amateur sport establishment. Sullivan and Coubertin disliked each other intensely. Sullivan wanted to strip aristocratic influence from the Olympic movement. As in 1900, the AAU controlled the American IOC representatives. Sullivan, Whitney and Sloane were the new delegates. In May 1901 the IOC met in Paris to name a host city for the 1904 games. The IOC unanimously awarded the games of the Third Olympiad to Chicago. "University of Chicago students celebrated with a weeklong party."[63]

Sullivan and the officials of the Louisiana Purchase Exposition in St. Louis wielded considerable power over amateur athletic contests in the USA, and with the help of A.G. Spalding, who had a sports equipment marketing arrangement with the AAU, pushed Chicago to yield to St. Louis. Unable to guarantee that American athletes would participate in Olympic Games held in Chicago, Coubertin waved the white flag on February 10, 1903. Without much consultation from the IOC, he announced that the IOC had shifted the Olympics to St. Louis.[64] It would not be the last time that an Irishman would humiliate a prominent Protestant in the tangled politics of Chicago and, no doubt this added to Stagg's anti-Catholicism. In 1908, when Notre Dame applied for admission to the Western Conference, its application for membership was rejected on what many believed to be theological rather than athletic grounds. The behind the scene efforts of the University of Chicago and A. A. Stagg were central to the rejection of Notre Dame's application.[65]

Since there was no love lost between Stagg and the powerful Executive Secretary of the AAU, it should come as no surprise that when the National Collegiate Athletic Association (NCAA) was formed in 1906 Stagg was in the forefront of the new organization. According to *American Physical Education Review,* February 1911, Amos Alonzo Stagg headed a committee of three coaches that was attempting to consolidate the five existing sets of track and field rules and records for men's college track and field into a single system. It was hoped that this effort would result in a single association for men's track and field that would avoid AAU control over colleges in the sport. By the mid-1920s, in large measure because of the efforts of Stagg, the NCAA would become a viable alternative to the AAU for intercollegiate track athletes.

At the NCAA's first annual convention in 1906, "the offering of inducements to players to enter colleges or universities because of their athletic abilities, or supporting and maintaining players while students because of their athletic abilities," was prohibited.[66]

Another Michigan Man

Fitzpatrick brought several trackmen to national prominence during the first decade of the new century. Among them was Walter Turner Fishleigh, who was born in Chicago in 1880. On May 21, 1898, while attending Lake View High School, Walt placed second in the pole vault at the Sixth Annual Illinois Interscholastic Athletic Association Championships in Champaign.[67] His father was the Assistant Cook County Treasurer in Chicago at the time he attended the University of Michigan, and later became Clerk of Cook County.[68] Walter was a world-class track athlete as a freshman at the University of Michigan. After he enrolled at the University of Michigan the school newspaper remarked, "Fishleigh is a promising young athlete, and made the team for the first time last year. His events are the broad jump, pole vault and hurdles."[69]

During the course of the track season, he broad jumped over 23 feet, and demonstrated competence in the pole vault and high hurdles as well. On May 24–25, 1901 Fishleigh tied for first in the pole vault before placing third in the jump off, which was held in muddy conditions before 1,500 wet, chilly fans at the IC4A meet held at Berkeley Ovah in New York City. He also placed third in the broad jump, and fourth in the 120-yard high hurdles in the meet that was used to establish national collegiate championships.[70] It is important to note that from 1876 until 1904 IC4A meet records were almost the exclusive domain of the Ivy League.[71]

A week later on June 1, 1901 he placed third in the broad jump at the Western Conference Intercollegiate Conference Meet in Chicago. On June 14, while representing the Detroit Athletic Club, Fishleigh set the meet record for the 120-yard high-hurdles (16.8) at the National AAU Junior Outdoor Championships held at Pan-American Exposition in Buffalo, New York. The following day, he won the 120-yard high-hurdles (16.1) and placed third in the pole vault (11–0) and the running broad jump (21–10½) at the National AAU Senior Championships in Buffalo.[72]

On May 13, 1902 the *Michigan Daily News* lamented, " Fishleigh has not been practicing the pole vault and fell out of competition at 10 feet 6 inches, but in the broad jump redeemed himself with a jump of 21 feet 3 inches."[73] Walter, who was considered a versatile track athlete, lettered at Michigan in 1901 and 1902. After graduating with an AB degree in 1902, he became a math teacher in Battle Creek, Michigan from September 1902 through the 1903–04 academic year. In 1905–06 he earned a Bachelor of Science in electrical engineering and joined the faculty of the University of Michigan as an instructor and became an Associate Professor of Automotive Engineering by 1916. When World War I was declared, Professor Fishleigh became a Major in the Sanitation Corps of the United States Army in charge of the use and maintenance of automobiles. While in the Army, he established a school for ambulance drivers and mechanics, then was appointed a member of the Board for Standardization of Motor Vehicles.[74]

After the First World War, Walter Fishleigh left teaching and became an experimental engineer for the Ford Motor Company. He became production manager of the Airplane Division of Ford, before forming his own consulting engineer company in Detroit.[75]

The Milwaukee Meteor

The best sprinter of the era and one of the greatest track athletes in Michigan history was born at Dodgeville, Wisconsin on September 13, 1880. In 1898 Archie Hahn was a state high school track champion and football star at Portage High School. Hahn was the original 'Mr. Five-by-five.' He stood 5'6" tall with shoulders of a bull and the legs of a wrestler. Called the "Milwaukee Meteor," Hahn was sought out by University of Michigan alumni, who helped underwrite his university expenses. He entered law school at Michigan in 1901.

Under the tutelage of Fitzpatrick, Hahn won the Western Conference sprint championships in 1901–02–03–04. In April 1901, Hahn returned to Wisconsin for several days because of his mother's illness, yet won the 100-yard dash at the Western Intercollegiate Meet.[76] In 1904 Hahn nursed an injured foot going into the Western Conference Championships, yet won the sprints.[77] He was national IC4A champion in the 100-yard dash in 1904–05–06. He also won the Canadian sprint title in 1903.[78]

In 1903, as a representative of the Milwaukee Athletic Club, he won the AAU national 100 and 220-yard championships and repeated in the 220 in 1905.[79] But, he did not fare so well in the 100-yard dash. According to Walter H. Liginger, president of the Central AAU, who was in charge of the Milwaukee Athletic Club's track team at the 1905 Portland Exposition, "the change of climate undoubtedly had a great deal to do with the defeat of Archie Hahn in the 100-yard dash, as the little sprinter complained of not feeling well shortly before the event." Hahn lost by about of a half a yard.[80] The great Olympic sprinter, Charles Paddock, later wrote, "Hahn brought to sprinting the great value of a competitive heart. His remarkable powers of endurance, coupled with his never-say-die spirit made it possible for him to be the foremost sprinter of his particular time."[81]

Hahn reached the peak of his popularity in the 1904 St. Louis Olympics when he won the 60, 100 and 200-meter sprint championships for the USA. Among his notable achievements was setting the world and Olympic record for 200-meter straightaway run (21.6). His Olympic record stood for twenty-eight years, until Eddie Tolan broke it in 1932. To cap off his accomplishments, he again won the 100-meter dash in the 1906 Olympics in Athens.[82] In doing so he become the only man in the Olympic movement to win that title in two different Olympic Games until Carl Lewis duplicated the feat in 1984 and 1988.

Although, he won four Olympic gold medals, Hahn's best-known accomplishment occurred in 1910 when he out ran a racehorse in a 50-yard dash at a country fair in Burlington, Wisconsin, after he turned professional.

Hahn graduated with an LL.B. from the University of Michigan in 1904., but never practiced law. Hahn's first coaching position came immediately after his graduation, when he took a teaching-coaching job at Ironwood, Michigan. He stayed at Ironwood High School and competed for the Milwaukee Athletic Club until the summer of 1907.

In the fall of 1907, he began coaching for Pacific University in Oregon. Subsequently he held posts at Monmouth College in Illinois, and Whitman College in Oregon. He became head track coach and football backfield coach at Brown University in 1915. Five years later, he returned to the University of Michigan as assistant track coach to Steve Farrell.[83] Coach Hahn went to Princeton in 1923 as assistant to his former college track coach and mentor, Keene Fitzpatrick. Archie assisted Fitzpatrick at the University of Princeton for several years before accepting the track coach and trainer position at the University of Virginia in 1929.[84]

"Pop" Lannigan, trainer and coach in several sports at the University of Virginia for a quarter of a century, died at the end of 1930 after a lingering illness. In 1929 Archie Hahn replaced Lannigan as head trainer for varsity and freshman football, and head track coach.[85]

Hahn was head coach and athletic trainer at the University of Virginia for 21 years. Under his direction, the Cavalier track team had a superb record. During his coaching tenure, the Cavaliers won 17 state track titles. He considered his 1932 team, which lost the Southern Conference championship to Tulane University, his best track team.[86]

At the AAU national outdoor track and field championships in 1931, Archie "donned his track suit and showed that 'there was life in the old dog yet.'" He held the country's best sprinters even for the first dozen yards, despite the fact that many of them are twenty-five years his junior. "And, Mr. Hahn didn't attribute his firm hold on Youth to the use of any particular soap. He credited his associations with young athletes for keeping him young."[87]

Hahn was one of the first serious students of sprinting and author of one of the best books on running technique, *How to Sprint* [88] distributed by Spaulding's Athletic Library. His book is considered by many to be a classic of track literature. Hahn's prescription for developing top sprinters and hurdlers—and his teams had many—was "lots of work, especially repetitive 300-yard sprints to develop strong finishes." He said great sprinters "can't be made: they're born."[89]

In 1911 he married Sarah Abernathy of Portland, Maryland. He and Sarah had three children.[90] Archie retired from coaching in 1951, and died at his home at the age of 74 on January 21, 1955.[91]

Detroit's Best 100-years Ago

While the University of Michigan was recruiting athletes from far and wide, Keene Fitzpatrick also was attracting track stars from nearby Detroit. In 1903 he recruited two young men from Detroit: John Garrels and Ralph Keeler. Keeler's father, Hiram, was Secretary-Treasurer of the American Insurance Company.[92] Ralph attended Central High School in Detroit in 1901 and 1902. It was there that he gained the attention of trackmen in southeast Michigan when he won the 100-yard dash and the 880-yard relay and placed second in the 220-yard dash at the second annual meet of the Detroit Interscholastic Athletic League on May 18, 1901.[93] Keeler also distinguished himself at the University of Michigan Interscholastic on May 24.[94] Ralph Whittlesey Keeler graduated from Detroit University School in 1903.

Keeler went on to earn letters from Coach Fitzpatrick in 1904 and 1905, before transferring to Cornell University. On June 6, 1903 he placed second in 220-yard dash in the rain at the Central AAU championships held at the Detroit Athletic Club Field.[95] In 1904 Keeler generally ran behind the great Archie Hahn in the sprints, but managed to beat him in the 40-yard dash in a duel meet against the Chicago First Regiment, and placed fourth in the 100-yard dash at the Western Conference Meet in Chicago.[96] After Keeler graduated from Cornell in 1907, he sold Hupp Automobiles. During the 1920s Ralph was a partner in a successful plumbing-contracting firm in New Smyrna, Florida. When his father died, he returned to Detroit and once again became an auto distributor. He died suddenly on June 20, 1932 at the age of 47, still a bachelor.[97]

Not Everyone Attended the University of Michigan

Of course, not all of state's track stars attended the University of Michigan. Sprinter Harry Moon dominated the Michigan Intercollegiate Athletic Association track and field championships held at Albion College in June 1903.[98] In 1904 Harry was the first Michigan Agricultural College track star to try out for the Olympics.

Michigan Agricultural College began formal participation in intercollegiate sports when it entered the Michigan Intercollegiate Athletic Association in 1888. Its first annual field day was held in 1888. Intercollegiate athletics was the responsibility of the Department of Physical Culture until 1904 when the Department of Athletics was formed. In 1945, the Department of Athletics became the Department of Intercollegiate Athletics at what had become Michigan State College.

Perennial Western Conference Champions

In 1903 the University of Michigan won the Western Conference Track and Field Championship for the third straight year, and thereby earned permanent possession of the Spalding trophy. Hahn, Dvorak, and Stewart lead the maize and blue to the championship. Even football star Willie Heston contributed a point in the discus.[99] Raymond G. Stewart, from Ann Arbor High School, established an unofficial world's record (16.4) in the 120-yard high-hurdles.[100]

The 1904 track season was an even greater triumph for Michigan. At the beginning of the second semester, Ralph Rose entered the University of Michigan law school.[101] He turned out to be one of the greatest weight men in the history of track and field. At the Penn Relays the University of Michigan emerged for the shadows of Eastern colleges by winning more first places than any other university, then Michigan won all of its duel meets and the Western Conference Meet. Lead by Archie Hahn, Ralph Rose, Ray Stewart, Ralph Keeler, and Johnny Garrels Michigan beat all comers. In 1904 five University of Michigan track men (Archie Hahn, Charles Dvorak, Ralph Rose, Frederick Schule, and William Coe) won medals at the St. Louis Olympics.

The Weed Commissioner

John Carlyle Garrels was born in Bay City, Michigan on November 18, 1885. His father was a printer. John graduated from Detroit Central High School.[102] While in high school he won the discus throw (92–0) at the Annual Michigan Interscholastic Outdoor Meet in Ann Arbor on May 17, 1902.[103] On June 6, 1903, before attending college, he won the discus (103–2) at the Central Association AAU Championships held in Detroit.

Garrels enrolled at the University of Michigan in the fall of 1903. In June 1904 he anchored the winning mile relay team and placed third in the 440-yard dash (51.6) at the Western Intercollegiate Conference Championships.[104] He was an all-around athlete. He was a star halfback on the University of Michigan football team in 1905 and 1906. In the winter of 1904–1905 Coach Fitzpatrick taught Garrels to run the low-hurdles.[105] Soon, the football star could run the 110-meter high-hurdles, the 220-yard low-hurdles or a quarter-mile and could chalk up points in the discus, shot put, and the hammer throw. On June 2, 1906 he broke the University of Michigan 120-yard high hurdles record set by John McLean in 1899 with his 15.15 effort.[106]

"John C. Garrels, champion discus thrower of the United States, and prominent as an athlete of the Michigan University, was appointed yesterday by Commissioner Haarer to the position of weed commissioner, a job provided for by the Michigan states, and under the supervision of the department of works. Commissioner Garrels has undertaken to give noxious weeds a chase that will put them out of business and the city will pay him $3 per day during the summer for doing it."[107] On June 1, 1907 he won the 120-yard high-hurdles (15.2) and 220-yard low-hurdles (24.0) and second in the shot put (45–2) at the Eastern Collegiate Championships held in Cambridge, Massachusetts. Garrels graduated from the University of Michigan in 1907. He was one of only four chemical engineers who graduated that year.

On July 16, 1908 he won a bronze medal in the shot put (43–3) at the London Olympic Games, but on July 16 failed to place in the discus (133–6½). On July 23 he rallied to win his heat in the 110-meter high-hurdles, and on July 25 won a silver medal in the high-hurdles (16.2). He participated in an international track meet in Paris, France on August 1, and on September 13, 1908 placed third in the discus at the Central AAU Championships at Marshall Field in Chicago.

After the Olympics he went to work as assistant manager for a Canadian mining company in Amherstburg, Ontario, and became manager of the Oxford Sand and Gravel Company in Michigan before becoming President of the Alkali Company in Wyandotte, Michigan. He was married and had three children. He died on October 21, 1956 in Grosse Isle, Michigan.[108]

A Wink at Eligibility

Ralph Rose had an immediate impact on the Wolverine track program when he enrolled at Michigan for the second semester of the 1903–04 academic year. On February 20, 1904 he tossed the shot 45–1, a distance greater than the Western Intercollegiate outdoor meet record.[109] During the indoor season, Rose put the shot 47–6½ against the Chicago First Regiment team, to set the American Intercollegiate record. Presidential candidate, William Jennings Bryan, was in the crowd to enjoy the triumph.[110] However, when Cornell University traveled to Ann Arbor for a meet with the Wolverines, Rose was not allowed to compete because he had not attended classes the first semester and was ineligible according to intercollegiate rules.[111] So "Fitz" had Rose put on a shot put exhibition for the 2,000 people who paid to see the meet. Rose obliged by unofficially putting the shot the unbelievable distance of 48–9.[112]

At the Penn Relays, where AAU eligibility and not collegiate eligibility determined a competitor's standing, Ralph Rose set the meet and world record for the shot put with a toss of 48 feet 2 inches.[113] At the Western Intercollegiate Meet in Chicago, Rose became the first weight man to win the medal for being the most valuable athlete at the meet.

Rose set new conference records in the shot put (47-½) and discus (125–3¼), and placed second in the hammer throw (151–3).[114]

> It is safe to say that the season of 1904 was the greatest track season that Michigan ever had. We won everything; not only did we come out ahead in the Western Conference and all our duel meets, but Michigan clearly showed her superior over the Eastern colleges by winning more firsts at the Penn Relay Carnival than any big school in the country. . . . At the beginning of the second semester, Ralph Rose came to us from California. He is probably the greatest weight man in the country ever produced and helped Michigan win more than one meet by his splendid work.[115]

According to the *Detroit Free Press*, Ralph Rose "quit" the University of Michigan in an "unprofessional" manner after just one semester with the epitaph that "no more unpopular athlete ever left Ann Arbor."[116] It is more likely that University of Michigan authorities "kicked him from their midst because of his unruliness."[117] Although there was discussion of readmitting him, Rose did not return to the services of the blue and maize.[118] In August-September 1904, Rose won four medals at the Olympic Games in St. Louis, and in 1905 he represented the Chicago Athletic Association at the AAU Championships held at the Portland Exposition.[119]

Much to the delight of Michigan men, Wesley Coe, a new University of Michigan recruit, defeated Ralph Rose in the 1905 AAU. According to W.W. Coe:

> I was feeling fine when I made the performance and was satisfied before leaving here [Portland] that I could do more than I had ever done. I owe much to Keene Fitzpatrick of the U. of M. who improved me at least a foot in my practice before I went west. By changing my style just a little under his coaching I was enabled to gain distance in my throws"[120]

In the Pink with "Pinky"

High jumper John Neil "Pat" ["Pinky"] Patterson was one of a half-dozen, world-class athletes who attended Detroit University High School during the first fifteen years of the twentieth century.

Detroit University School was a private, independent college preparatory school organized by Henry Gray Sherrard and Frederick Leroy Bliss, the head of the Classical Department and Principal, respectively, at Detroit Central High School. The school was formed because of overcrowding at Central High School and fear of political interference in the curriculum. The initial location of the school was the Michigan Athletic

Association Building, where Keene Fitzpatrick had been employed in 1892–4. Located on Elwood between Larned and Congress Streets, the building had ample classroom space, a well-equipped gymnasium, and a good cinder track. The school opened with 18 faculty members on September 25, 1899. From the outset the school had a strong athletic program.[121]

The school was later located on Parkview Avenue near the Detroit River. Today the Nubian mansion, where recent Mayors of Detroit have resided, is located near the spot where this school was once housed. In February 1916 the school's new gym and dining room burned in a fire and the school nearly closed altogether. It was reorganized under the leadership of headmaster Daniel H. Fletcher, from Loomis School, Winsor, Connecticut, and in 1918 moved to the property of the Parkview Athletic Club, which now functions as a bed and breakfast.[122] Throughout its history, the school was open to young men from wealthy families of all religious denominations, although, at times, Jewish students felt uncomfortable at the school.[123] Among the young men who attended University School in those days were Edsel Ford, Archibald Trowbridge (later a charter member of Alcoholic Anonymous), Henry C. Buhl (son of the President of the Chambers Motor Car Company), Ralph Keeler, Frank Nelson, and Joseph E. Malcomson.[124] University School is now incorporated into Liggett School, which is located in Grosse Pointe.

Track was considered a major sport at Detroit University School. In 1902 the school won the fifth Michigan Interscholastic meet and placed second in that meet the following year.[125] On May 17, 1902 "Pat" Patterson was second in the 120-yard high hurdles and the high jump at the University of Michigan Interscholastic Meet.[126] On May 28, 1904 Patterson, who was captain of the Detroit University School track team, won the high-jump (5–8) and placed second in the 120-yard high-hurdles at the University of Michigan Interscholastic Outdoor Meet.[127] On August 7, 1905, while representing the Chicago Athletic Association, Patterson was third in the high jump (5–11) at the National AAU Championship at the Lewis and Clark Exposition in Portland, Oregon. It was reported that "Pat" was somewhat handicapped in Portland by the smoke that filled the air because of forest fires in the region.[128]

On September 7, 1906 "Pat" represented the Chicago Athletic Association at the Junior AAU Championships on Travers Island in New York City. He placed third in the running high jump (5–6¾) at the Junior Championships and came back to win the running high jump

(5–11½) at the Senior AAU Championships the next day. After this triumph, he attended the University of Michigan in 1906 and 1907. At Michigan, "Pat" was hazed by being required to carry Johnny Garrels' suitcase to the train for the Penn Relays. The University of Michigan student newspaper reported:

> 'Johnny' Garrels not only carried a discus and a shot in his suitcase, but several large stones that his friends placed there as good luck. This discovery was made by 'Pinky' Patterson, who, after attempting to carry the suitcase, demanded an investigation.[129]

In 1908 "Pinky" dropped out of college and accompanied the Chicago Athletic Association to London to participate in the Olympic Games.[130] "Pinky" placed seventh at the London Olympics with a jump of six feet.[131] After a stint as an automobile salesman in Detroit, he followed his parents to Pasadena, California in 1912. In 1913, "Pat" became a *good roads* enthusiast and made one of the first transcontinental automobile trips on the route of the Lincoln highway. He carried a jug of water from the Pacific Ocean to pour into the Atlantic Ocean. He served as a Captain and District Manager of Aircraft Production in San Francisco during World War I. In later years, he was an apartment manager, a real estate promoter, and good friends with Charley Paddock and Gary Cooper. In 1940 he married Mrs. Mildred Morgan in Beverly Hills. "Pinky" died on December 20, 1948.[132]

Just What the Doctor Ordered

Joseph was son of William G. Malcomson and Jennie McKinlay Malcomson. He had three younger sisters and a younger brother.[133] William G. Malcomson was an architect and President of Malcomson and Higginbotham Architects. He also was President of the Detroit Steam Engine Company.[134] Joseph E. Malcomson attended Detroit University School. On September 7, 1906 Joe represented the Chicago Athletic Association in the Junior AAU Championships in New York City. He placed third in the 220-yard low-hurdles (26.8), then came back the next day to place second in the 220-yard low-hurdles (26.4) at the Senior AAU Championships. In 1907 he wore the red and blue colors of Detroit University School as a member of their 880-yard relay team.[135] His greatest accomplishment in track and field came on August 14, 1909 when he won the National AAU Senior 220-yard low-hurdles championship (25.0) in Seattle as a member of the Seattle Athletic Club.[136]

In 1915 Joseph Malcomson was an assistant coach and trainer for the Detroit Heralds Professional Football team.[137] During World War I he apparently joined the United States Navy. According to the Polk's *Detroit City Directory, 1927–28*,[138] Malcomson & Higginbotham Architects were still in business, and Joseph E. "Vonnie" Malcomson was listed as a doctor in the United States Navy.

Limiting the Influence of A.A. Stagg in the Western Conference

In 1905 "Fitz" and Charles Baird staged another skirmish with Amos Alonzo Stagg, "the would-be dictator of western athletics." On April 22, Charles Baird was in Chicago for a meeting of the athletic directors of the Western Conference. During the course of that meeting, he told the representatives of the conference colleges that Ferry Field in Ann Arbor was "at their disposal whenever they deemed it advantageous to change the place of meeting [for the Western Intercollegiate Track and Field Championship]." The report stated, "this was a diplomatic way of putting it up to Chicago to see if Stagg would be willing to make the meet on a circuit plan." The move was obviously designed to reduce the athletic power of the University of Chicago. As the *Detroit Free Press* correspondent put it, "The dehorning of Stagg may be the consequence." But, all Baird would say was "There is considerable sentiment among the several representatives of the conference colleges favorable to holding the championship meets at different universities each year."[139]

The President of the University Is Unable to Control the Athletic Department

In 1905–6 University of Michigan President James B. Angell attempted to limit the University of Michigan football program and control Fielding Yost and his supporters by calling a meeting of faculty leaders from around the Western Conference to institute changes in the rules governing the conference. Angell was a highly regarded academician, who had been President of the University of Michigan since 1871. He held honorary degrees from nine prestigious universities and took his academic responsibilities seriously.[140]

Yost had won a reputation for his recruiting talents, and he liked experienced players. The star of his undefeated Kansas team of 1899, for example, had played five years at the University of West Virginia and one year as a professional before joining the Jayhawks. A Kansas "purity" campaign resulted in Yost's ouster after the 1899 season. Then Yost went to Stanford, where he recruited a "student-athlete" who failed in his studies and was dropped. Yost carried this man with him to the University of Michigan, where he played some fifteen games, despite his lack of academic success.

At the University of Michigan, Yost recruited several big strong fellows from the iron mines who had more brawn than brains. He also brought in Willie Heston, who was already a graduate of San Jose State College. Willie finally retired after playing college football for seven years. The enthusiastic alumni of Michigan cooperated fully with Yost in recruiting, keeping the football players eligible, and providing sub rosa subsidies to star athletes, all of which violated the spirit of Western Conference rules and the player-centered tradition. It was said, "newspapers regarded the whole institution as the backdrop for the football squad."[141]

Before the "Angell meeting" of the Western Intercollegiate Conference faculty representatives could be held, Fielding Yost urged University trustees, lead by Republican stalwarts Arthur Hume Sawyer, Arthur Hill, and Peter White, to reject the changes. He persuaded them to overrule President Angell and to replace the reformers on the school's athletic committee with faculty amenable to the will of the trustees. Angell tendered his resignation as a result of the affront, but the Regents unanimously refused it.[142]

At the special meeting of the university representatives of the Western Conference, eleven rules were passed without the approval of the University of Michigan. The Conference limited the football schedule to 5 games, did not allow freshmen to play outside games, prohibited pre-season training, limited ticket costs to 50¢, outlawed the training table, and did not allow games after the second Saturday before Thanksgiving. Yost, with the support of the Board of Trustees, objected to these rules.

Yost countered pressure from President Angell to accept the conference rules by appealing in person and through the press directly to students, alumni, and the Board of Regents' to recommend to the Board of Control of Athletics that the University of Michigan withdraw from the Western Conference. When the faculty on the Board of Control sided with President Angell, the regents abolished the Board of Control of Athletics. The regents replaced the Board of Control of Athletics with a new Board of Intercollegiate Athletics that ended faculty control.[143] Although no official action was taken until February 1908, Michigan became a pariah, and dropped out of the conference in 1908 rather than submit to faculty control of athletics.[144]

Between 1908 and 1913 the issues boiled down to the question of faculty control and the maintenance of the training table, which was a surrogate for sub rosa support for football players.[145] In 1915, the regents bowed to faculty and alumni pressure and again allowed the faculty senate to make all decisions regarding intercollegiate athletics, but in point of fact Fielding Yost stayed in full control of the football program, with only modest changes. James B. Angell died on April 2, 1916. In 1917 the University of Michigan returned to the Western Conference, known popularly as the Big Ten.

The Board of Control of Intercollegiate Athletics was never under the control of the President of the University of Michigan or even under the direct control of the University's Board of Regents. This lack of accountability permitted the Athletic Department to operate without appropriate accountability to the University or the community at-large.

Unlike Fielding Yost, Keene Fitzpatrick knew the difference between winning and excellence, and pursued the latter. In the summer of 1910 "Fitz" accepted the position of track coach at Princeton University and extracted himself from the mess associated with athletics at Michigan.[146] Keene Fitzpatrick was at the University of Michigan 16 years and would coach track at Princeton for 22 years.[147] During his tenure at Michigan, "Fitz" won the Western Intercollegiate Conference Track and Field Championship five of the six years Michigan was in the Conference and the meet was held. But, most of all he championed excellence.[148]

The Western Conference Indoor Track and Field Championships were launched in 1910 at the University of Chicago Fieldhouse. Between 1917, when the University of Michigan returned to the Big Ten, and 1936 the University of Michigan won the indoor Big Ten championship seven times (1918, 1919, 1923, 1925, 1931, 1934, and 1936.)

In 1912 soccer was introduced as a U of M sport, while not yet an intercollegiate sport, it was popular among the students. Its adoption came on the heals of a "blanket tax" paid by all students into the coffers of the athletic association to support sports at the University.[149] As the University incorporated more and more intercollegiate sports, support for the track program was diluted. Nevertheless, in 1912 track was one of the three most popular intercollegiate sports at the University of Michigan, and generally rank behind football and on par with baseball. Hence, it was not surprising that during the 1912–13 academic year, work on improving the indoor track and training facilities was underway. Firm and adjustable, new starting cleats were built with the aid of Mr. Thomas, Ferry Field grounds keeper.[150]

Between 1909 and 1921 when Philip Bartelme was athletic director at the University of Michigan, Fielding Yost was frequently self-serving and less than forthright with him. Yost frequently forced his agenda on Bartelme by placing him in a position where he was required to support a project already underway. Yost also engineered the pressure that resulted in Bartelme's resignation. Furthermore, Yost often took credit for events or shifted blame when it was to his advantage. When sports writer Ring Lardner was asked "Do you ever talk to Fielding Yost?" He answered, "No. My father taught me never to interrupt."[151]

After Bartelme's resignation, there was some discussion of making Keene Fitzpatrick Athletic Director. The *Chicago Tribune* reported:

> According to a rumor, which will not die, Keene Fitzpatrick, former track and field coach and trainer of all teams at the University of Michigan, may be the next director of athletics at the Ann Arbor institution, to succeed Phil Bartelme, who resigned. The rumor has it that a Michigan man has gone east to see Fitzpatrick at Princeton, where he has been track and field coach and trainer ever since he left Michigan in the early nineteen hundreds. Fitzpatrick is one of the most respected coaches Ann Arbor ever had. From the time he left that university his loss has been felt, and alumni always have contended Michigan made a grave mistake when he was permitted to go east. During the time Fitzpatrick was at Michigan he developed some wonderful athletes. He groomed Archie Hahn for the sprints and this great little flyer, who is present trainer of teams at Michigan, was one of the most reliable point winners on the team. Nelson Kellogg, present athletic director at Purdue, who was one of the first men to ever run two miles under ten minutes in the west, was another of Keene's products. Johnny Garrels, rated by many Michigan alumni as the greatest all-around athlete ever developed at Ann Arbor, was brought out by Fitzpatrick. Dvorak, the pole vaulter, Niel Snow, and Ralph Rose were among other great athletes who came to the front under Fitzpatrick's teachings.[152]

However, because of his influence with the regents, Yost was named Athletic Director at Michigan. He governed with energy and enthusiasm until 1941. He added six varsity sports and built one of the best football stadiums and the best sports complex in the nation. His engineering background led him to overbuild. In doing so, Michigan laid the foundation for an expansive, well-funded athletic empire. While Fielding Yost deserves credit for his foresight in investing in the buildings and stadiums that would serve the University of Michigan's athletic program for more than a half century into the future, his narcissism, personal prejudices, and imperial view of college athletics had destructive consequences.

Bigotry Reigns

In September 1902, the University of Michigan took a small step in an effort to counteract the "surprising amount of ill-feeling there is here against colored students." For the first time, a building owned by the University was turned into a rooming, boarding and clubhouse to accommodate ten "colored students."[153] Despite efforts to accommodate "students of color" at the University of Michigan, the atmosphere remained hostile to African-American students on the Ann Arbor campus for the next fifty years.[154]

University of Michigan football coach Fielding Yost never even allowed an African-American athlete to tryout for the football team during his tenure as coach, 1901–1923 and 1925–28, and made no apologies or explanations. He did, however, allow the track team to recruit William DeHart Hubbard. Hubbard was clearly enroute to becoming a "world beater," when he graduated from Walnut Hills High School in Cincinnati. Other schools, including Harvard and Rutgers, already had one or two Negro athletes on their track teams, so Michigan would not be creating waves and needed a great track athlete like Hubbard to keep pace with the competition. It seems likely that Yost also was sensitive to suggestions that the track program under the leadership of Keene Fitzpatrick was in decline, and might have feared criticism from Fitzpatrick supporters at the beginning of his tenure as Athletic Director.

Yost's prejudices against persons of color were a hallmark of his administration, as the Willis Ward incident would later demonstrate. Before World War II it was rare for the University of Michigan or other main line colleges to have more than one or two African-American athletes on campus. Few African-Americans played football, and none played basketball in the Big Ten during that era. So, Yost was not alone in his bigotry.

Under Yost's leadership as Athletic Director, the University of Michigan also disdained competition with Catholic colleges such as Notre Dame. In 1909 Michigan agreed to play Notre Dame, because they needed games to fill in for those vacated by dropping out of the Western Conference, and expected to beat the small Catholic school handily. However, Notre Dame recovered two on-side kicks and defeated the Wolverines 11 to 3, while Walter Camp watched. Fielding Yost was embittered by the loss, calling Notre Dame, "the dirty Irish."[155] In 1910 almost on the eve of the game, Yost cancelled the Michigan-Notre Dame football game claiming that Notre Dame had two players who had played college football on the West Coast. While this was true enough, Yost also had two such players and had dropped out of the Western Conference so that he could continue to play them.[156] In 1919 the Wolverines stopped scheduling Notre Dame in track and did not revive the cinder squad competition for 20 years.[157] Yost's bitterness grew when the Walter Camp All-American selection group dropped Yost as a selector and kept Knute Rockne.

When Notre Dame again requested admission to the Big Ten in 1926, Yost spread preposterous stories about Rockne hiding and training player for five to six years before suiting them up for three varsity seasons.[158] A Notre Dame faculty representative recalled his meeting with Yost, "I was engaged but for a moment in a hand clasp of hatred and a glance of defiance." Anti-Catholicism played an important role in the campaign against Notre Dame.[159] Football games between Michigan and Notre Dame did not resume on a regular basis until 1978.[160]

This bitter relationship, borne out of social-economic conflict, had far reaching consequences. Michigan's stance over the years forced Knute Rockne to team up with Michigan State's Athletic Director Ralph Young,[161] and Lloyd Olds of Michigan Normal in 1922 to form the Central Collegiate Conference track meet. The CCC meet opened a pathway to the NCAA championships, which were inaugurated in 1921 and were limited to conference champions.

The bitter relationship between the University of Michigan and Notre Dame affected principles of amateurism and college recruiting. It promulgated a moral crisis in college sports, placed limitations on reform in college sports, and promoted the evolution of sports into big time entertainment.[162]

Track's Contribution to Michigan's Rise to Prominence

Track played a significant role in the University of Michigan's drive to be accepted as a socially elite university on a par with Ivy League universities. Its performance in duel meets with Eastern Universities and at the Penn Relays, the IC4A meet, and the Olympics provided visible proof of Michigan's status. Because of the Wolverine's early example, the State's high schools, colleges and universities produced more America Olympians over the first 65 years of the twentieth century than any other state in the Union. Moreover, this does not include the more than 100 foreign nationals who attended Michigan universities and colleges and participated, often very successfully, in Olympic track and field events.

Yet, the popular support garnered by Fielding Yost among the anti-intellectual, sporting crowd also influenced the course of Michigan athletics. His actions created statewide support that continued for the balance of the twentieth century. A statewide opinion survey undertaken by the *Detroit Free Press* in 1997 found that support for the Michigan Wolverines athletic program was stronger among those who had never attended college than among the college educated. Of particular interest, popular support among those who had never attended college extended to nearly every University of Michigan function.[163]

As for the University of Chicago, despite ending participation in major intercollegiate athletics in 1936, Stagg held the National Collegiate Athletic Association (NCAA) career record for football victories for more than 50 years. At the close of the twentieth century, the University of Chicago still claimed more Big Ten athletic titles (72) than Nobel Prize awards (71).[164]

2. "This Flag Dips for No Earthly King" [1908–1920]

In the first decade of the twentieth century American spokesmen were fixated on the country's relationship with Great Britain. President Theodore Roosevelt wanted to assert America's status as Great Britain's equal. Mayor William H. "Big Bill" Thompson of Chicago investigated school textbooks to make certain that they were not too pro-British.[1] Wealthy Americans emulated the British aristocracy. American colleges and athletic clubs copied English institutions and precedents. And, competition against English athletes drew large crowds in the United States.

American participants in the first three Olympiads were generally well to do self-selected athletes, who attended the games at their own expense or that of wealthy sponsors. Both the second Olympic Games of the modern era held in Paris in 1900 and the third held in St. Louis in 1904 were poorly organized and sparely attended. Some of the athletes were unaware that they were taking part in the Olympic Games.[2]

By contrast, after two straight disasters the Interim Games of 1906, which were opposed by Baron de Coubertin, were quite successful and probably saved the Olympic movement. Held in Athens, the only Michigan athlete of note to participate in these games was Archie Hahn, who won a gold medal in the 100-meter dash. James Lightbody of the Chicago Athletic Association won the 1,500-meter run and placed second in the 800-meter run. Following Melvin Sheppard's win in 1908 no American would again win the 1,500-meter run in the Olympics in the twentieth century. The Athens Games of 1906 were the only intercalated summer Olympic games ever held, and are now considered unofficial by the International Olympic Committee (IOC).

It was not until the 1906 Olympic Games in Athens that the U.S. Olympic Committee sent a national track team to compete. Expenses for travel costs to Athens were still underwritten principally by wealthy Easterners. The New York Athletic Club, the Amateur Athletic Association, the Greater New York Irish American Athletic Association, and New York millionaires S. R. Guggenheim, August Belmont, J. P. Morgan, and George Pratt provided nearly all of the financial support for the venture.[3]

Baron Pierre de Coubertin wanted to hold the 1908 Olympics in Rome, but the 1906 eruption of Mount Vesuvius made the Roman venture untenable. In an effort to win greater cooperation from the British for the Olympic movement, the French aristocrat selected London as the site for the 1908 Games. For the first time, U. S. Olympic officials chose their track team in tryouts held in Philadelphia.[4] As a result, the 1908 U. S. Olympic track team was the most egalitarian squad yet assembled. It included an African-American—John Baxter Taylor, two native Americans, as well as a broad range of European-American ethnic nationals.

The Carlisle Contingent

Native-American athletes attracted national attention in 1905 when more than 10,000 spectators and 1,000 athletes watched as Frank Mount Pleasant, "a full-blooded Indian from the Carlisle school," won the running broad jump at the Penn Relays. "The Indian cleared twenty-three feet one and one-half inches, nearly a foot and a half better than the nearest white competitors."[5] Two weeks later, the Carlisle Indians, lead by Frank Mount Pleasant, beat the Lafayette College track team 53–43 in Easton, Pennsylvania. Mount Pleasant won the 100-yard dash, the 440-yard dash, and the broad jump (22–8½).[6] The following year Mount Pleasant again lead Carlisle to a victory over Lafayette. In 1906 he and Albert Exendine, who would later coach football and track at Georgetown University, won four events and came in second in two events.[7]

Years later, it was reported that in 1908 Frank Mount Pleasant, Louis Tewanima, and Jim Thorpe made up the entire Carlisle Institute track team at duel meets with Lafayette College and Syracuse. They were said to have triumphed over a 20-man track team at Lafayette College and within a week defeated the entire Syracuse University track team.[8] The veracity of this story is questionable. Lafayette College did not meet Carlyle Institute in track in 1907 and there was no duel meet between the schools in 1908, the only years that Mount Pleasant, Tewanima, and Thorpe could have run together.[9] It is more likely that the story had its origins in the 1951 film "Jim Thorpe-All American."

In that film a two-man team comprised of Thorpe and Tewanima defeat Lafayette College in a duel track meet in Easton, Pennsylvania.

The actual events are somewhat different. On May 15, 1909 Carlisle Institute, Dickinson College and Lafayette College met in a triangular meet in Carlisle, Pennsylvania. While several Carlisle athletes participated in the meet, only Thorpe and Tewanima scored points for Carlisle. Thorpe won five events and Tewanima won the two-mile run and placed second in the mile run. Carlisle won the meet with 63 points. Lafayette College earned 48½ points, and Dickinson College 5½ points.[10] On May 30, 1908 Jim Thorpe, Thomas, Two-Hearts, and Tewarie scored all of Carlisle's points when they won the Pennsylvania Intercollegiate Athletic Association Championships in Harrisburg in front of a crowd of 8,000. In that meet, Thorpe won the high jump and placed second in the 220-yard low-hurdles and the shot put.[11] On May 29, 1909 Jim Thorpe won the shot put (42–2½), the high jump, and the broad jump (22–9) at the Pennsylvania Intercollegiate Track and Field Championships in Harrisburg.[12]

At the 1908 Olympic games in London, Frank Mount Pleasant placed sixth in the long jump and the triple jump.[13] Louis Tewanima placed ninth in the marathon. It was reported that Tewanima, a Hopi, trained for the Olympics by chasing rabbits, wild horses, and antelopes.[14] Tewanima reflected a long-heritage of distance running by native-Americans. In 1844, in the first major running event in the United States, native-American John Gildersleeve won the race and earned $10,000 by beating the famed English runner John Barlow in a ten-mile run. Barlow could cover the distance in 54 minutes twenty-one seconds, suggesting that Gildersleeve was indeed a splendid distance runner. Seneca tribe member, Louis Bennett, also was a famous pedestrian competitor, and Tom Longboat, an Onondaga Indian, won the 1907 Boston Marathon.[15]

British-American Antipathy

Athletic competition between the United States and England started early and continued for well over 150-years. Intense rivalry between American and British track teams began in 1844, when promoters of pedestrian races learned that "English vs. American" contests drew large crowds.[16] While wealthy Americans were apt to ape the English, lower-class Americans were more likely to hold the English in contempt, for past injuries and their attitude of superiority.

In June 1888, members of the Manhattan Athletic Club of New York competed in the English Athletic Championships in London, winning the 100-yard dash, the one-mile flat race, the long jump, and the seven mile walk.[17] During the 1890's when Harvard and Yale track teams challenged the track primacy of Oxford and Cambridge, there was a sizable wave of interest on both sides of the Atlantic. At the quadrennial Olympiad in London in 1908 the English were pursuing glory and their arrogance aroused American ire. During the Games, tensions between the American and English athletes were heightened by a variety of actions, and these tensions were fanned by the America press and public. The British countered with arrogance, boasting, and self-glorification of their own. Because many of the American athletes were of Scotch and Irish descent, the confrontation built on generations of conflict and bitterness.

Biased Officials

Proof that the animosity between the United States and Great Britain carried over into the games came when British officials openly cheated John Carpenter of Cornell University out of the victory in the 400-meter dash. Coming down the homestretch of the 400-meter run, Carpenter passed the British favorite, Lieutenant Wyndham Halswelle. Halswelle then attempted to go by Carpenter on the outside, but the American ran wide and kept Halswelle from taking the lead. British officials yelled "foul" and "no race." After a thirty-minute argument, British officials disqualified Carpenter and ordered that the race be rerun. When the Americans refused to rerun the race, Halswelle ran alone and was awarded the gold medal.[18]

British officials also assisted Dorando Pietri, a collapsing Italian runner in the marathon, across the finish line in an attempt to keep an American, John Hayes, from winning that event. Pietri, however, was disqualified.[19] After the London Olympics, America claimed victory based on the number of track and field medals won, although Great Britain earned more points.

The Irish-Americans Show No Love for the English

Irish-American James Sullivan, president of the America Sports Publishing Company, was the most important American amateur-sports leader from 1900 until his death in 1914. In 1888 he was elected the first secretary of the AAU, and, between 1906 and 1914, he served as president and secretary-treasurer of the organization. He headed the

1904 St. Louis Exposition Committee, which hosted the third Olympiad. In 1908 Sullivan was Chairman of the American Olympic Committee, and made Theodore Roosevelt the honorary chairman of the Committee to gain the reflected influence of the White House. Both men were ardent nationalists, and Sullivan declared that "national honor was at stake in the Games."

As if by design, the 1908 London Olympic Games were rife with nationalistic conflict. When the American athletes were boarding for the Trans-Atlantic voyage, the *New York Times* fueled the conflict with headlines like: "American Athletes Sure of Success" and "British Fear Yankee Athletes." By-the-same token, members of the British middle and upper classes, concerned that the empire's prestige was steadily declining, saw the opening ceremonial as a means for promulgating respect for the British aristocracy. A powerful group of the British elite insisted that the athletes parade before the British Monarch during the opening ceremonies. The *London Times* asserted, "there is no one living more fitted to open and in one sense preside over the fourth Olympiad than King Edward the Peacemaker."

Raw conflict between the Americans and the British began during the opening ceremonies on July 13. Shortly before the ceremonies, the U. S. contingent discovered that their flag was missing from the many banners of the competitor nations on display at the stadium. The American athletes were angry. When British officials claimed that a suitable American flag could not be found, the excuse seemed lame and the anger intensified. Ralph Rose, the American standard-bearer who was an Irish-American with a short fuse, refused to dip the flag while passing the royal box in which King Edward and Queen Alexandra sat during the open-ceremony. He later quipped, "This flag dips to no earthly king." Rose's exclamation, which no doubt reflected both the situation and the Irish dislike for the British, gave birth to an American legend and set the tone for the London Games.[20]

The tradition of not lowering the American flag for foreign dignitaries started by Ralph Rose continued in 1928 when Lemuel Clarence "Bud" Houser carried the American flag in the opening ceremonies in Amsterdam. When Houser asked General MacArthur what to do, MacArthur answered by asking, "Well, Bud, how does the flag look best to you?" Bud responded "I like it straight up in the air, and he says, 'You keep it straight up, and if you get in any trouble, I'll be right with you.' So that's what I did." "It was just a tradition that we Americans don't dip the flag for any ruler." [21]

The American Rose

Ralph Rose was born on March 17, 1884 in Louisville, Kentucky. He grew up in Healdsburg, California. His world shot put record of 51 feet on August 21, 1909 stood for 19 years. He won the AAU shot put championship seven times, the discus championship in 1905 and 1909, and the AAU javelin throw in 1909 (141.7 feet). His best discus throw was 131.8 feet. [22]

Dennis Horgan, "an Irish giant", held the world record for the shot put at the beginning of the twentieth century (48–2). After dropping out of the University of Michigan in early summer 1904, Ralph Rose participated in the Olympic Games. At the St. Louis Olympics two Americans, the 6–6, 235 pound Ralph Rose and the more squat 5–10, 210 pound Wesley Coe vided for the shot put championship. Rose won the day with a world record throw of 48–7. Coe came in second with a throw of 47–3. According to an eye witness, "carefully poising the weight in the palm of his high-lifted hand, where it fitted like a marble in the hand of a small boy, leaning back as far as he could without losing his balance, and lifting his leg up to his waist, Rose made one mighty move, throwing his body forward, the shot flew from his hand." He was said to have had tremendous uncultivated potential.[23]

In addition to the gold medal for the shot put (48–7), Rose won a silver medal in the discus (128–10½) and a bronze medal in the hammer throw (150–0) at the St. Louis Olympics. He also placed sixth in the 56-pound weight throw.[24] Rose was the most versatile of the 'big men' operating during this period. He only lost the Olympic discus title to Martin Sheridan in a 'throw-off.'[25] Dennis Horgan responded on September 18, 1904 with a throw of 48–10. After the St. Louis Olympic Games, Rose returned to California to work for a bank.

In 1905 the Chicago Athletic Association brought Rose out of retirement to represent them at the AAU Championships in Portland, Oregon. His first day in training for the 1905 AAU Championships was reported:

Ralph Rose, giant, 'Cyclops,' champion weight lifter, former Michigan athlete, holder of one world's record and prospective possessor of enough records to last him for a few years, was tired when he stalked out on Marshall field wearing the cherry circle track team suit.

"Oh, I'm so very tired," he murmured and his gape was enough to frighten Trainer Mike Butler. Then he tugged a moment at the 16-pound hammer, whirled it as of yore, released the weight and it struck the ground 162 feet away.

"Yes, I'm tired. That trip from California was not quite as exciting as was that of Scotty," continued the Golden Gate State boy. "I've got to get rested."

A few moments later, while still showing that he was tired, in his own great ungainly way, the big athlete carelessly fixed the official A.A.U. discus in the palm of his hand and sent the ancient missile hurling, skimming and *dishing* through the air for a throw of 130 feet.

"Is that all?" he queried when the measurers told the big Chicago athlete association fellow the distance. "I must get rested; that's all there is to it."

While still so very tired that conversation seemed to worry him. Rose took some exercise and hurled the shot about 48 feet.

If Ralph is so strenuous now that he has just resumed training with the C. A. A. team candidates at Marshall field for the national meet at the Lewis and Clark exposition, what will he do when he is 'rested?'

"Seriously, old man," remarked Rose, "while I was home in California the hardest work I did was to cast up columns—of figures, of course. I worked in a bank, and it was terribly confining. You will have to bear with me in practice for a time, until I get around the 170-mark with the hammer, the 145-foot mark with the discus and the 51-foot mark with the shot. These golfers who talk about their *choice score* cards—meaning, I think, the best scores for each hole added—often make a course in 62, many strokes below bogey. If I could get three best marks, I have made in practice for the hammer, shot and discus in the competition at Portland there would be nothing to it but Ralphie the world's champion for years."

Rose was the magnet that attracted quite a few keen critics to Marshall field today. Weather conditions were favorable for all of the cherry circle [Chicago Athletic Association] athletes and Trainer Butler did not overlook any chances"[26]

Wesley Coe established the world record with a 49–6 toss at the AAU meet in Portland. When Rose failed to win the shot put in Portland, more than one Wolverine fan cheered. According to the *Detroit Free Press*,

Among the fans in Ann Arbor who follow athletic dope there could be found no more pleasing news than that from Portland, Ore., where Ralph Rose was dethroned as champion shot putter of the world on Saturday by Cox, the young Easterner, who tossed the weight 49 feet 6 inches. It is all the more gratifying in that Rose was in the contest and got his bumps in competition. Since the young giant from California quit Michigan in such a "professional" manner the Ann Arbor men have been hopeful that someone would bob up and take the wind out of him and the enthusiasts are as much pleased as if Coe was a Michigan man. No more unpopular athlete at Michigan ever left Ann Arbor than Ralph Rose.[27]

Rose, a giant of a man by contemporary standards, won the AAU discus championship in 1905. On September 7, 1907 he broke the shot put record at the Jamestown AAU meet to regain the national championship.[28] In 1908 Rose successfully defended his Olympic title, and proved over the long run to be the strongest of the three rivals. After the Games in London, he took a victory tour in Ireland.[29]

On August 21, 1909 during a triangular meeting between the San Francisco Olympic Club, the New York Athletic Club, and the Chicago Athletic Association, Rose became "the first man to project the 16-pound shot beyond the 50-foot line." His 51-¾ put at San Francisco in 1909 (officially approved at 51 feet) stood as a world record for 19 years. He continued to hold the AAU shot put title until 1911, and won the AAU discus title again in 1909. He won the Olympic shot put title twice (1904 and 1908), and placed second in 1912. He also won the both hands shot put champion in 1912.[30] Altogether, Ralph Rose won six medals—three gold, a silver, and a bronze-over three Olympiads— 1904, 1908, and 1912. He died of typhoid fever on October 16, 1913 in San Francisco at the age of 29.

He too was a Michigan Man for a Short Time

Wesley W. Coe, University of Michigan 1906, began college studies at Oxford University in the fall of 1900. He won the British Amateur Athletic Association title in the shot put and the hammer throw in 1901 and 1902. In 1902 he won the shot put and hammer throw in Oxford-Cambridge meet. Coe returned to the USA in the summer of 1902 and entered Yale, but did not compete for them.

In 1904 Wesley Coe placed second to Ralph Rose in the shot put at the St. Louis Olympic Games. In the summer of 1905 he trained with Keene Fitzpatrick and Wesley attended the University of Michigan as an undergraduate in 1906. In 1908 John Garrels of the University of Michigan placed third in the shot put at the London Olympic Games, and Wesley Coe placed fourth in the shot put at that meet. Coe lived in England from 1920–1926. In 1926 he moved to Montana in response to bad health. He died six months later of Hodgkin's disease at age 47.[31]

When Dull was not dull

Another Michigan man participated in the London Olympiad. Gayle Albert Dull was born on May 4, 1883 in Galion, Ohio and graduated from Galion High School in 1903. His father was a trainmaster and moved to Stratford, Ontario in 1904. Gayle attended the University of Michigan during the 1905 through 1909 academic years.

Gayle Dull's primary events were the mile-run, two-mile run, and three mile run. On June 1, 1907 he placed third in the two-mile run at the Eastern Intercollegiate (IC4A) Championships in Cambridge, Massachusetts. On April 25, 1908 he was on the winning four-mile and the two-mile relay teams at the Penn Relays, and June 6 he placed second in the two-mile run (9:30.2) at the IC4A Outdoor Championships in Boston. His performance in Boston won him a place on the 1908 Olympic team.

On July 13, 1908, at the tryouts for the three-mile team race at the Olympic Games in London, Dull placed second.[32] On July 15 he placed tenth in the three-mile team race at the London Games. [33] Two days later Dull placed third in the fourth heat of the 3,200-meter steeplechase (11:10) but did not qualify for the Olympic finals.[34]

Dull earned an AB degree from the University of Michigan in 1908, and took graduate courses in 1908 and 1909, while living in Detroit. G. A. Dull was Captain of the 1909 University of Michigan track team. On April 24, 1909 he placed second in the four-mile relay at the Penn Relays.

On May 29, 1909 the University of Michigan distinguished itself by performing "somewhat better than anticipated" at the IC4A meet in Boston. They finished fifth. Among the Wolverines present, G. A. Dull impressed the eastern establishment the most by his two-mile run. "Jaques of Harvard; Dull of Michigan; and Taylor of Cornell were the favorites in the race." At the beginning of the race, three University of Michigan runners, including Dull, took the lead with Jaques and Taylor "in easy hailing distance, and the field very well bunched. This was the order until the end of the first mile, which was run in 4 minutes, 47 seconds. Then Taylor jumped into the lead with Dull a stride behind. This pair made the going so fast that at a mile and a half they had a lead of 25 yards over Jaques of Harvard, who was in third place. Dull was satisfied to let the Ithacan make the pace, until the last 400 yards when these two began a fierce struggle for victory. For nearly three hundred yards the Wolverine stuck to the Cornellian's shoulder, but at that point Taylor's superior strength began to count, and he gradually pulled away and sprinted home with a lead of six yards. Jaques was ten yards further back, and West of Michigan, who came out of the ruck [indistinguishable gathering] with a rush in the last 200 yards, was a good fourth." Ralph C. Craig placed second in the 100-yard dash, and J. J. Horner placed third in the shot put. Detroit native Frank Nelson placed second in the pole vault for Yale.[35] Dull ran the two-mile in 9:57.2.

After college, G. A. Dull became a railway agent for Bell Telephone

Company of Pennsylvania in Pittsburgh and ran for the Pittsburgh Athletic Association. Following an operation he died in Franklin, Pennsylvania on October 16, 1918 at the age of 35.[36]

Forgoing the Olympics

In 1912 the Olympics had not yet achieved the status that impelled nearly all great athletes to postpone their professional careers to become an Olympian. Joseph J. Horner, Jr.'s story illustrates that situation.

Joseph J. Horner, Jr.'s grandfather was a Methodist minister born in England. He migrated to the United States for religious freedom. J. J. was the son of Joseph and Sara Elizabeth Knowlson Horner. Joseph Horner, Sr. was founder of the Consumer Ice Company in Grand Rapids. He managed the company until his death in May 1957.[37]

Joseph J. Horner, Jr. was born in Grand Rapids on November 21, 1887. He attended high school at Grand Rapids Central, where he was captain of the track team. On May 23, 1904 Horner placed third in the 440-yard run at the University of Michigan Interscholastic Meet in Ann Arbor. He won the 12-pound shot put at the University of Michigan Interscholastic Meet in May 1906. On May 25, 1907 Horner won the 12 pound shot put (50–4), pole vault (11–3), tied for first in the 220-yard low-hurdles, placed second in the 120-yard high-hurdles, and third in the discus (109–0) at the University of Michigan Interscholastic Meet. On June 1 of that year he won the shot put and pole vault at the Northwestern University Interscholastic Meet.

In 1908 Horner attended the University of Michigan. In 1910, he represented the Chicago Athletic Association at Pittsburgh, Seattle, the World's Fair, and San Francisco. He received a B. A. Degree from Michigan in 1911. Upon graduation from college, Horner gave up sports competition and a chance to be an Olympian to work as circulation manager for the *Saginaw News*. Horner became circulation manager of the *Green Bay Press-Gazette* in 1915. During World War I, he attended the Naval Aviation Ground School at the Massachusetts Institute of Technology; Flying School in Key West, Florida; and became a commissioned officer. In doing so, he was one of the first Navy fliers. He was discharged on December 6, 1918.

After the War Horner returned to Wisconsin, where he became Circulation and National Advertising Manager for *Green Bay Press-Gazette*. In 1927, he became part owner of the Appleton Post-Crescent. He and his wife had two children.[38] He was promoted to Business Manager of the *Green Bay Press-Gazette* in 1930, and became General Manager and Vice-President in 1953. He later became President of the Corporation and was responsible for the company's newspaper and radio station. During the 1950s, he also managed the Post Publishing Company in Appleton, Wisconsin. Horner died on September 12, 1960, a week after brain surgery.[39]

Marketing Relay Races

In 1909 the Penn Relays continued to classify its mile-relay races, as they had done for at least fifteen years, to allow for more equal competition among groups and to permit more winners. College mile relay teams were divided into six separate groups, and in 1909, for the first time, the two-mile relay was divided into two groups. Yale, Princeton, Pennsylvania, Columbia and Dartmouth were placed in a college group for the two-mile relay, while a university group was also scheduled. In addition, a select group, comprised of Pennsylvania, Michigan, Ohio State, Yale, and Cornell, was allowed to compete in the four-mile relay championship.[40]

A Great American Hero

In 1912, both Jim Thorpe and Louis Tewanima were so good that they were selected for the U.S. Olympic team without undergoing trials.[41] The Fifth Olympiad of the modern era was held from May 5 to July 22 in Stockholm. More than 2,500 athletes representing 28 nations participated in the Games. For the first time, the 5- and 10-kilometer runs— sometimes referred to as the "Woolworth double" (the five and ten) were added to the track and field program. These races replaced the five-mile run, and were immediately dominated by a Finnish runner. The twenty-two-year old Johan "Hannes" Kolehmainen, a vegetarian bricklayer, won both races. Louis Tewanima placed second in the 10-K run (32:06.6), trailing the Finn by 45 seconds. Timing to the tenth of a second was used for the time in the Olympics at Stockholm.[42]

Tewanima was the only American to win an Olympic medal at this distance until Billy Mills, another Native-American, won the 10-K run in 1964 in Tokyo.[43] Until 1948 the Finns dominated both the 5-K and 10-K runs. During the 1920s, Paavo Nurmi and Vilho Ritola became known worldwide for their feats in distance running by placing first or second in these events in 1920, 1924, and 1928, for a total of nine medals.[44] America's two native sons were the only two North Americans to win a medal in the 10-K run in the twentieth century.

The real hero of the American Olympic team in 1912 was Native-American, James Francis Thorpe, who won the decathlon and pentathlon.[45] The 1912 Olympics were a severe test of Thorpe's athletic ability. He passed it with the highest possible marks. There was a pentathlon on the program, which Jim won easily, with first places in four of the five events. Then he took the decathlon crown with about 700 points to spare on his nearest opponent, Hugo Wieslander of Sweden. His total points under the 1952 scoring table would have been good enough to win the 1962 British decathlon and would have earned him a silver medal in the 1948 Olympics.

In Stockholm the decathlon stretched over three days, while it is done in two days now. Thorpe ran the 100-meters in 11.2; long-jumped 22–3¼ inches, high-jumped 6–1¾,[46] threw the discus 121–4; pole vaulted 10–8, and ran the 1,500-meter in 4:40.1. His personal best in the 110-meter high-hurdles was 15.0.[47] Thorpe also placed fourth in the high jump and seventh in the long jump in regular competition at Stockholm. In 1913 it was claimed that Thorpe had been a professional before the 1912 Olympics, and his medals were taken from him. After successful careers in professional baseball and football, and a stint in the Merchant Marine, Jim Thorpe died of a heart attack in Lomita California on March 28, 1953.

The Most Dangerous Event in Track and Field

The pole vault is the most dangerous event in track. Sprained ankles, bruised heels, and broken arms and legs are common. In rare instances, catastrophic injuries, such as head concussions, paralysis, and even death, confront the pole-vaulter.[48] Most injuries occur in front of the vault standards in the area of the planting box. Vaulters who do not get enough depth on an attempt sometimes land on the box or on the runway. The higher a vaulter goes, the more problems he confronts. Even an experienced vaulter faces danger on every jump. At the beginning of the twentieth century, unstable bamboo poles were used to vault, and the landing area was a mixture of sand and sawdust. If the pole did not break and place the jumper in danger of falling on the runway or the plant box, he was faced with falling a dozen feet onto a relatively hard surface.

Even sixty years later, when steel poles replaced bamboo poles, there were dangers. The heavier pole could fall on the jumper or propel him out instead of up. Even the lighter and more flexible Fiberglas pole did not end the danger inherent in pole vaulting. Fiberglas poles would

often snap at takeoff or would veer to the side once the vaulter was air-
borne. So, it has always taken courage to pole vault.

In the first two decades of the twentieth century, pole vaulting was
a particularly difficult art, which found two of its most skilled practitioners in Michigan. Charles Dvorak, who attended the University of
Michigan, was the gold medal winner in the pole vault in the 1904
Olympic Games. Frank T. Nelson, a Detroit University High School
graduate and member of one of the city's most prominent families, was
the silver medal winner in the pole vault in the 1912 Olympic Games.[49]

A Blue-Blood Faces Danger

Pole vaulter, Frank Thayer Nelson was born in Detroit on May 22,
1887. Frank was born into what could be considered the aristocratic
class of late nineteenth century Detroit. He was the only son of Edwin
Horatio Nelson and Anna Louise Gilkeson Nelson, who were listed
in the Detroit Society Blue Book. He had a younger sister, Nathalie G.
Nelson.

His father, Edwin Nelson, was President of Nelson, Baker & Company, a chemical company, in Detroit. The elder Nelson was a member
of the Country Club of Detroit, the Detroit Athletic Club, the Detroit
Board of Commerce, the Detroit Boat Club, the Detroit Club, and the
Society of Colonial Wars.[50] Edwin Nelson, was born in Toronto, Canada
in 1859 and graduated from Belleville College and the Ontario College
of Pharmacy in about 1875. After graduating from college, Edwin Nelson became a retail pharmacist, and in 1880 joined with W. C. Johnson
and H. C. Baker to establish Johnson, Nelson & Company in Detroit to
manufacture chemical and pharmaceutical supplies. In the early years
of the business, Edwin Nelson was a "banner salesman" who often
traveled and was Secretary and Treasurer of the firm. By 1890, Johnson, Nelson & Company was one of the leading firms in Detroit.[51]

Frank prepared for college at Detroit University School, where bud-
ding track stars J. N. "Pat" Patterson, Joseph E. Malcomson, and Edsel
Ford were on the school's track team. However, Frank "did little in athletics until he reached college" and did not go out for the school's track
team. Moreover, he left the Detroit University School in his senior year
of high school to attend Lawrenceville Preparatory School.[52]

Once he matriculated at Yale College, as part of the class of 1910,
Frank joined the Yale track team, and became a pole-vaulter under the
tutorage of teammates such as Alfred Gilbert, who later invented the

Erector Set and the Gilbert chemistry set for kids. In 1908 Frank tied for first in the pole vault at the IC4A Championships, and won the event outright in 1910. On June 7, 1908 he also tied for second in the pole vault (12–2½) at the Olympic trials in Philadelphia,[53] but did not attend the Olympics in London. In 1909 and 1910 he won the pole vault at the Penn Relay Carnival in Philadelphia. He tied for second in the pole vault in 1909 at the IC4A outdoor in Boston.[54] In 1910, he was elected captain of the track team.[55]

After graduating from Yale, he attended Harvard Law School. Seven years later he wrote,

> The only matter of autobiographical interest during these . . . [years] was a rather sudden determination on my part to make a trip to Stockholm on the Olympic Team's specially chartered Red Star steamship *Finland*, a boat of about eleven thousand tons, I believe. At the time we were informed that this was the largest ship ever to have found its way through the narrow channels into this port. In the harbor there I remember on several occasions watching some smaller German men-of-war drilling their "green" crews during the day, especially in managing the oars in small boats. At Stockholm, I ran across . . . [a classmate] who proposed to spend the chief part of his summer in Russia. The remaining portion of the six years since graduation is scarcely worth reference. . . . At the present writing I am pursuing the legal profession in Detroit, Michigan.[56]

Frank Nelson won the silver medal for the pole vault in the 1912 Olympics with a vault of 12–7½. All three medals in the pole vault went to Ivy League athletes: Harry Babcock of Columbia won the gold, and Marc Wright from Dartmouth the bronze.

Upon graduating from Harvard Law School, Frank Nelson became an attorney in the office of Lucking, Helfman, Lucking & Halon, attorneys-at-law, of Detroit. Before long he was a member of the Detroit Club, the Country Club, the Racquet Club, and the Grosse Ise Country Club, and was made a director of his father's company, now called Nelson, Baker & Company. Still unmarried, the Blue Book crowd considered him one of the best catches in Detroit.

Shortly after America entered World War I, Nelson attempted to join the Army, but was rejected because of defective vision. In December 1917, he entered Government service as a member of the Legal Committee of the War Industries Board in Washington, D. C. On October 27, 1918, he was commissioned as a Second Lieutenant in the Motor Transport Corps, with assignment to Newport News, Virginia. At the conclusion of the war he was given an honorable discharge and returned to the law offices of Lucking, Hanlon, Lucking & Van Auken.[57] On June 22, 1927, at the age of forty, Frank married Sally Ammerman in Buffalo, New York.

The R. L. Polk, *Detroit City Directory, 1927–28* [58] lists Frank's wife as Sally, and he was still an attorney with the same firm. When his father died in 1932, Frank Nelson became Vice-President of Nelson, Baker & Company. As he grew older, his politics became more conservative, and he spoke out against the New Deal.[59]

By 1950, Frank was still Vice-President of the company his father started, but more and more his thoughts turned to the philosophy of ethics. He retired from the legal profession, and, in English tradition became a gentlemen farmer. He and his wife moved to a large rural estate north of Detroit to become dairy farmers. A decade later, he was still enjoying the camaraderie his friends at the Detroit Athletic Club.[60] He died July 16, 1970. Frank passed away unremembered for his athletic skills during the first dozen years of the twentieth century.

Flying High from a Standing Start

The standing high jump and the standing broad jump was added to AAU meets in 1893. In 1894 both events were dropped until 1898, when they were held for one year, then dropped again in 1899. They were added in 1906 and were held as indoor events until about 1930.

In 1912 one of the country's best all-around athletes was attending Adrian College, in Adrian, Michigan. Nineteen-year old Richard Leslie Byrd, son of a United Brethren Church minister, was a "strong rugged farm lad" and a superior athlete. Born in Shilo, Indiana, on May 19, 1892. Richard attended school in Milford, Illinois. In high school, he and classmate H. Wilmoth won the Iroquois County Track Meet and placed third in the Illinois State Meet. The following year, in 1909, he gained national recognition when he alone placed third in team points at the University of Chicago National Interscholastic Meet, and was awarded a silver cup as the meet's outstanding athlete.[61] In 1910 he set the national scholastic record in the discus and was salutatorian of his seven person graduating class.[62]

Richard Leslie Byrd spent his freshman year at the University of Illinois. In the fall of 1911 he transferred to Adrian College, where it was easier to work his way through school because there was less competition for available jobs.[63] At Adrian College, he played football, and, as in high school, was nearly a one-man track team. In a duel meet with Defiance College, one month after the sinking of the *Titanic*, Byrd won six events. He placed first in the running high jump (5–6), the running broad jump (18–9¾), the discus (124–6), the pole vault (10–0), the shot put (38–8), and the hammer throw (112–8).[64] Byrd's personal best field performance marks in May 1912 were: discus (143–0), shot put (44–9), javelin (150–0), pole vault (10–9), high jump (6–3), and broad jump (21–4). In track they were: 100-yard dash (10.4), 120-yard high-hurdles (16.8), 440-yard dash (56.0), and mile run (5:32).[65]

Richard Byrd exuded confidence and optimism, despite difficulties. When he was invited to the Olympic tryouts, *The Adrian Daily Times* started a fund to raise the $20 necessary for the trip to Evanston, Illinois.[66] He arrived at the Olympic trials with a bad case of stomach flu, and did poorly in the discus throw. He did, however, make the Olympic team in the standing high jump.

After making the team and about the time Wilber Wright, one of the inventors of the airplane, was dying of typhoid fever,[67] Adrian merchants raised $25 to pay Byrd's train ticket to New York City, where he was to catch a Red Star Line ship to Stockholm. When Byrd arrived in New York City on June 11, he had only seventy-five cents in his pocket. He went to the Olympic team headquarters at New York Athletic Club and was told they had no room for him and that they would not have a boat ticket for him. They advised him not even to go to the dock the next day.[68]

Richard walked across the street to Central Park and tried to sleep on a bench, but a policeman ran him out. He went back later and the same policeman came along and out he went again. After a bit, the policeman in a big Irish brogue asked what he was doing. Byrd told him the whole story. It turned out that several members of the Olympic team were Irish members of the New York Police Department. The Irish cop bought him a meal, got him a hotel room, and gave him a dollar.

The next day Byrd went to the dock, but still did not have a ticket or a promise of one. Fellow discus thrower and football player, Arlie Mucks from the University of Wisconsin came by and when he heard Byrd's story, told the Adrian College athlete to get behind him and follow him up the gangplank. Once aboard, Martin Delancy, representing the American Olympic Committee, responded to pressure from the New York Police Department and the press, and got him a ticket.[69]

At the 1912 Olympics Byrd placed second in the discus, tied for fourth in the standing high jump, and placed sixth in the standing broad jump. As a side-note, the all-time American standing high jump and broad jump champion, Raymond Ewry, did not compete in the

1912 Olympics. After winning Olympic gold medals in these events in the 1900, 1904, 1906, and 1908, and two gold medals in the standing triple jump (1900 and 1904), Ewry retired from competition with ten Olympic gold medals. Ewry was born on October 18, 1873 in Lafayette, Indiana. He contracted polio as a small boy and was confined to a wheelchair for several years. Ray began to exercise on his own, and not only regained the use of his legs but became a great athlete. Ewry also held the amateur record for the backward standing long jump (9–3).[70]

In September 1912 Byrd returned to Adrian College and in the first football game of the season against Notre Dame broke his leg. With a broken leg, he was unable to earn the money to stay in college. When his leg healed, Richard L. Byrd went to work for the Ford Motor Company in Detroit. He served as a lieutenant in the Marine Corps in the First World War, and competed in the Inter-Allied Games in Paris at the end of the war. He placed second in the discus at that meet. In 1935 he was a member of the Automotive Labor Board.[71]

A Model Dash Man

Not all of the great trackmen of the period went to the Olympics. Harold Leroy Smith was born on May 9, 1897 in Grand Rapids. His father, Samuel R. Smith, was a druggist. Harold attended the University of Michigan and Grand Rapids Junior College, off and on from 1913 to 1924, when he earned a teacher's certificate. Harold was noted for proper use of his arms to deliver the force in his running style. His arms were always well flexed at the elbows. On May 30, 1914 he placed fourth in the 100-yard dash and second in the 220-yard dash in the IC4A Meet in Boston. In 1915 he placed second in the 100-yard dash at the Penn Relays and won the 100-yard dash (10.0) and the 220-yard dash (22.0) at the IC4A in Philadelphia. In 1924 Harold Smith began teaching English and social studies in the Wyandotte Public Schools. He earned a master's degree from the University of Michigan in 1928 and rose to Department Chairman at Roosevelt High School. He died on June 9, 1961 still a bachelor.[72]

An Olympian Twice

One of the notable Olympians at the Stockholm Games was Ralph Cook Craig, a natural athlete. Ralph was the son of William and Alice Blodgett Craig. He played football and hockey at Detroit Central High School, as well as running in track. His running style was characterized by "intense vigorous momentum with a minimum of body tension."

While at the U of M as a member of the class of 1911, Ralph placed second in the mile-relay at the Penn Relay in 1909, and on May 29, 1909 placed second in the 100-yard dash at the 34th Annual IC4A Meet.[73] On May 28, 1910 he won the 220-yard dash (21.2 wind aided) and placed second in the 100-yard dash (10.0) at the IC4A Championships held in Philadelphia. He tied the world record in 200-meter run (21.2) at that meet. In 1911 he won the 100-yard dash (9.8) and the 220-yard dash (22.2), equaling the meet record in both events, at the IC4A Championships.

In 1912 Ralph was a handsome, erect young man with a thick shock of brown hair when he represented the Detroit YMCA at the Olympic trials. His trip to the Olympics in Stockholm was paid for by the Detroit Y. When Ralph Rose slurred Michigan enroute to the Games, Craig drew the line. The two did not get along well after that incident. It seems likely that Craig was also put off by Rose's excessive drinking, rowdiness, and boasting retorts.[74] While this behavior was welcome in the atmosphere surrounding the Games in London, it was not welcomed by many of the American athletes in Stockholm.

In the Fifth Olympiad, R. C. Craig was in the seventeenth and final heat of round one of the 100-meter flat dash, held on Saturday July 6, 1912. He won his heat and ran in heat four of the second round that day. He won his second round heat in the time of 10.7, and qualified for the finals held on Sunday, July 7, 1912. Howard Drew, a top U.S. sprinter, pulled up lame in the semifinals, putting pressure on Ralph Craig and D. F. Lippincott to carry the day for the USA.[75] There were seven false starts in the 100-meter race on Sunday. Ralph Craig made one of them, and Don Lippincott made another. The officials were totally incompetent, and the American runners were afraid not to keep running even when they fired the recall gun. "I was told, don't take a chance—go!—So I did," Craig later recalled.[76] Both Craig and Lippincott ran the entire race after a false start and had to run again. Finally, there was an absolutely a fair start, and Craig won the finals in the time of 10.7, 60 centimeters ahead of Alvah Meyer, the American AAU 100-meter champion. "Craig ran brilliantly and with enormous power."

The co-holder of the world record for the 200-meter and 220-yard dashes on a straight track had little trouble becoming only the second of the eight men in Olympic history to win both the 100 and 200-meter dashes.[77] On July 10, he won the second heat of round one of the 200-meter flat dash with a time of 22.6. Later that day he won the first heat of round two with a time of 21.9. On the following day, in the finals of the 200-meter flat race, R. C. Craig got "a rapid start and maintained a hard pace of the whole distance" to win his second gold medal in a time of (21.7).[78]

They gave the medals at the end of the games in 1912. "We all marched in, and the King of Sweden gave us the gold medals. Jim Thorpe lined up in front of me, and came back with this big bust of the King of Sweden. He said what do I do with this dang thing?"[79]

Ralph Craig became a State of New York administrator, an industrial engineer, photographer, sportswriter, and cattle judge. At age 59, he was a member of the 1948 U.S. Olympic yachting team. As an alternate for the Dragon Class, he did not get an opportunity to compete, but did carry the American flag in the opening ceremonies. Fourteen years later, Ralph Craig still had the Olympic "bug." *Track and Field News* reported:

> Ralph Craig, 1912 Olympic sprint champion, would like to compete in his third Olympic Games. Craig, now 72, won both sprints at Stockholm and then made the Olympic team again 36 years later in 1948 as a member of the yachting team. 'I'd like to be in the 1964 Games but I guess I won't make it unless they add something new to the program,' Craig said.[80]

Before he died at age 83 on July 21, 1972 in Lake George, New York, Ralph C. Craig was inducted into the in the Helms Track and Field Hall of Fame.

Ralph's younger brother, James Blodgett Craig, attended Detroit Central High School, where he played football; and ran track in 1909–10. Jim was an All-American in both football and track at the University of Michigan. Jim lettered in track in 1912 and 1913, and named to the AAU All-American track team for 1912, after winning the 220-yard low-hurdles at the Eastern Collegiates that year.[81] J. B. was on the University of Michigan football team from 1911 to 1913 and was selected All-American at halfback in 1913. After receiving a bachelors' degree in 1914, he coached football at Mercersburg Academy, served in France as a first lieutenant in the United States Army during World War I, and then coached football and track coach at the University of Arkansas. In 1928 he owned Bonnie Brace Farm near Ann Arbor.[82]

The Cheerleader from Kansas

Another, but less well-known Michigan track Olympian in 1912 was Carroll Barse "Hap" Haff, who was born on February 19, 1892 in

Kansas City, Missouri. His father, Delbert J. Haff was a University of Michigan alumnus, class of 1884. Carroll attended Kansas City Central High School, before enrolling at the University of Michigan in 1910. May 27, 1911 "Hap" placed fourth in the 440-yard dash at the Eastern Intercollegiate Championships (IC4A). He was also a varsity cheerleader from 1911 through 1915.

In 1912 C. B. Haff qualified for the American Olympic team as one of four Americans entered in the 400-meter run. On July 12 "Hap" won the seventh heat (50.4) of the first round of the 400-meter flat run in Stockholm. Later that day, he won the fourth heat of the second round (49.7) to qualify for the finals. On July 13, "Hap" ran his best race (49.5), but came in fifth to Charles D. Reidpath, a Native-American attending the University of Syracuse.[83]

Haff was elected Captain of the 1913 University of Michigan track team. During the indoor track season, he proved his medal by running injured. "Though the captain [Haff] strained a tendon in his leg Thursday afternoon, and was believed to be in unfit condition to run the race, Trainer Farrell allowed him to run, and 'Hap' stood up under the strain in fine shape."[84]

On April 26, 1913 at the Penn Relays he was part of the winning two-mile relay team. Injuries continued to plague him, however. According to the *Michigan Daily*, "Captain Haff injured a tendon in the trials before the Maize and Blue left Ann Arbor, and was prevented from running."[85] He apparently recovered because later that spring, at the 36th Annual IC4A Championships at Harvard, he won the 440-yard dash (48.6) "Hap" followed this by winning the 440-yard dash (48.2) at the Western Intercollegiate Championships in Chicago. On July 4, 1913 while representing the Chicago Athletic Association he became the national champion in the 440-yard dash (51.2) at the AAU Championships in Chicago.[86]

On April 25, 1914, in a rainstorm, Haff's relay team placed second in the two-mile relay at the Penn Relays. On March 14, 1914 he ran in a special collegiate 880-yard race at the Missouri Athletic Association Annual Indoor Athletic Carnival in St. Louis. A week later, he placed second in the two-mile relay at the Fourth Annual Pittsburgh Athletic Association Indoor Championships.

During World War I Carroll Haff was a major in the Field Artillery and Acting Assistant Inspector of the Port of Embarkation in Hoboken, New Jersey. After the war and until 1923 he was in the leather business in

Philadelphia. Thereafter, he became a member of the New York Stock Exchange. He married, had four children, and died April 10, 1947.[87]

A Hammer Thrower

Arthur W. Kohler, weight man from Lansing, Michigan, was Captain of the 1914 U of M track team. Kohler emerged as the Western Intercollegiate champion hammer thrower in 1913, after placing third in the shot put (46–4⅞) and fourth in the hammer throw (147–9½) at the 36th Annual IC4A Championships at Harvard. On July 4, 1913 he placed second in the shot put at the National AAU Senior Championships in Chicago.[88]

In 1914 he placed second in the shot put and was third in the hammer throw at the Penn Relays. He ended his college track career by winning the hammer throw (157–2½) and placing fifth in the shot put (44–3⅛) at the IC4A meet. He was toastmaster of the senior literature class "M" dinner.[89]

Seeking Acceptance as a Member of the Elite

Avery Brundage was born in Detroit in 1887. He was the descendant of Scotch-English ancestors who settled in New England and New York in the sixteenth and seventeenth centuries. He was the son of Charles and Amelia (Lloyd) Brundage. Brundage spent the first eleven years of his life in the motor city, although he spent some time in Chicago with his father, who was a construction contractor at the Chicago Columbian Exposition. However, when his father abandoned him and his mother, he was sent to Chicago to live with his uncle, a prominent Republican corporate lawyer with close ties to Medill McCormick of the *Chicago Tribune* family. His Chicago relatives were people of some means. His uncle served as the Illinois Attorney General from 1921 to 1925. The young Avery Brundage was sent to English High School (now Crane Tech). He then attended the University of Illinois, where he became an all-around track athlete.[90]

Avery was a good scholar. In addition, he edited a college magazine, managed the varsity track team, and participated in basketball and track. On June 6, 1908 he placed second in the discus throw (121–1¼) at the Eighth Western Conference Championships in Chicago. At the 1909 Western Conference Intercollegiates he won the discus. He placed third in the discus at the Central AAU Championships in 1910.[91] During this period, he also began to specialize in the heel-and-toe walk, the high jump, and the shot put.

When he graduated in 1909 with a degree in civil engineering, the brown hair and brown eyed Brundage was six feet tall and weighed 195 pounds. He spent the six years between college graduation and 1915, as a construction superintendent on Chicago skyscrapers. During World War I he was a construction engineer in the Army. After the war his relatives staked him to the capital needed to start his own construction company, and in the early 1920s he apparently received construction contracts that were likely influenced by his uncle's friends and political connections.[92] Later, he became a member of the Glenview Country Club and the conservative Chicago Athletic Association. He married Elizabeth Dunlap in 1927.

In 1912 he specialized in the decathlon, which was known as the "All-Around Championship." In those days because all ten events were often held in the same day. Brundage soon found himself competing against athletes like Jim Thorpe. He had none of the grace and little of the natural ability of Jim Thorpe. Thorpe earned letters in eleven different sports, and even won the 1912 intercollegiate ballroom dancing championship.

Thorpe began his competition at Stockholm by winning in the pentathlon. Unlike the decathlon, the pentathlon was decided according to placement points. After the fourth event only the top six could continue. Thorpe won four of the five events in the pentathlon. He placed third in the javelin throw. He had thrown the javelin for the first time just two months earlier. Brundage placed sixth in the pentathlon, but failed to finish the 1,500-meter run because he was exhausted. While Brundage and the other pentathletes rested the day after the pentathlon, Jim Thorpe finished seventh in the long jump. Without a day of rest, Thorpe then set a world record in the decathlon. By contrast, Brundage ranked fifteenth after 8 events, and dropped out of the decathlon. Thorpe won 9 of 10 events.[93]

After Jim Thorpe turned to professional baseball, Brundage won the American all-around amateur championships in 1914, 1916, and 1918, while representing the Chicago Athletic Association. He ran the 100-yard dash (10.0), high jumped (5–11), put the 6-pound shot (42–0), ran the 120-yard high hurdles (16.0), broad jumped (21–7), pole vaulted (10–6), threw the 56-pound weight (29–4), walked the 880-yards (3:03.75), threw the hammer (125–2½), and ran the mile in 5:17.

As for the effort to deprive Jim Thorpe of his Olympic medals, beneath the moralistic posturing, it is clear that Thorpe was singled out for punishment because of his race. He was vulnerable because he was on the wrong side of a summer baseball controversy that had bedeviled American amateur sport for forty years. For nearly half a century, colleges had condemned semiprofessional summer baseball. Yet, hundreds of college athletes from all over the nation had played semipro baseball for money, and none had been disqualified from college eligibility. Thorpe, in fact, competed in AAU sanctioned track meets after receiving $25 in 1909 for playing semiprofessional baseball. Furthermore, the AAU did not condemn college athletes who were given scholarships, room-and-board, and under-the-table favors. When the issue of Thorpe's eligibility was raised, those who raised it knew full well that Thorpe had done nothing tens of the other American Olympians had not done. Nevertheless, the International Olympic Committee removed his Olympic honors. Without a doubt, Thorpe should have been allowed to keep the honors he clearly won.

A movement to reinstate Thorpe's records and trophies began in1943. Brundage refused to support the effort, and said, "Jim Thorpe was the greatest athlete of our time. Why does he need medals to prove it?"[94] His comments ignored their common desire to be recognized and accepted for their accomplishments. After both Thorpe and Brundage were dead, Thorpe's medals were finally restored on January 18, 1983.

Outstanding Talent, Shortchanged by Skin color

The effort to strip Jim Thorpe of his Olympic records and medals was in many ways a reflection of the prevailing Anglo-American effort to "keep persons of color in their place." Nevertheless, track and field, once the private preserve of the wealthy, was rapidly becoming the sport of opportunity for those who were being short-changed because of the color of their skin.

During the first two decades of the century, half-dozen African-American athletes established themselves as world-class track athletes. George Poage won a bronze medal in the 400-meter hurdles in the 1904 Olympics. John Baxter Taylor won a gold medal in the 1908 Olympics as a member of the 1,600-meter relay team, and Howard Drew was on the 1912 Olympic team. Drew, born in Lexington, Virginia on 28 June 1890 reached his peak in February–March 1914, when he equaled the world records for the 100 (9.6) and the 220-yard (21.2) dashes. On April 27, 1918 Edward Solomon Butler of Dubuque [Iowa] Seminary single-handedly won more points than the entire La Crosse Normal College track team in a duel meet between the two schools. Butler won five events and tied for second in the high jump.

In the process, he set a new meet record in the long jump (21–11½).[95] In 1920 he made the Olympic team as a long jumper and later played professional football. Frederick "Duke" Slater was a shot putter with the University of Iowa and J. A. Shellburne of Dartmouth College ran the 40-yard dash and was a shot putter.[96] In 1921 R. E. Johnson of the Thompson Steel Works Athletic Association in Pittsburgh won the five mile run at the National AAU Senior Championships.[97]

A Change of Heart

The antagonism between the United States and Great Britain so evident in the 1908 Olympic Games began to dissipate in 1912, and after World War I nearly disappeared. The Olympic flag with its five interlocking and multicolored circles, one for each of the five great land masses participating in the Games, was first unfurled in 1920.[98] In many ways it symbolized the decline of the British Empire and the rise of a new world order in which ethnic groups, many believed to be inferior, would ultimately take their place on the victory stand at the world's greatest sporting event.

3. Movies Improve on Real Life [1924, 1928 and 1932 Olympics]

Bring me my bow of burning gold:
Bring me my arrows of desire:
Bring me my spear: O clouds, unfold!
Bring me my Chariot of Fire."

—*hymn by William Blake.*

The decade of the 1920s would be christened "the golden age of sports," but, in truth, it was a period of fundamental social change that was reflected in sports.

Automobiles and Electricity Changes The Life-style of Most Americans

By 1925 nearly twenty million Americans owned an automobile. Indeed, Americans, who represented only six percent of the world's population, owned eighty-one per cent of the world's automobiles. Detroit's Ford Motor Company sold about half of all the motor vehicles registered in the United States. Ford cars sold for about $450 each. The average cost of a competitor's vehicle was $825.[1]

The automobile and motor truck revolutionized how the nation worked and played. By 1927 the industry itself employed 375,000 men directly in the manufacture of automobiles, and an additional three million 325 thousand individuals were indirectly employed in automobile related businesses. New and expanded occupations, such as manufacturing automobile accessories and supplies, automobile salesmen, used car resale, chauffeurs, truck drivers, oil refinery workers, highway construction and maintenance, highway patrolmen, gas station and garage attendants, were created by the motor car.[2] The automobile expanded markets for other products. Farmers were no longer as isolated as they had been for centuries and rural schools and churches could be consolidated. Motor vehicles opened opportunities for the rapid movement of perishable farm and orchard products, eating out, romantic interludes, attending motion pictures and sporting events, taking vacations, getting access to health care and new housing options, and even committing crimes, such as bootlegging and bank robbery.

Electric lighting also was changing the way Americans lived. Between 1913 and 1928 the number of customers for electric light and power increased by 465 per cent. In 1912 only sixteen per cent of American families lived in dwelling with electric lighting; by 1927 sixty-three per cent had electric lights.[3] Electric light and power brought electric irons, vacuum cleaners, clothes washers, and toasters, all of which altered the American life-style. Electric lights also made indoor track meets possible.

In 1903 the University of Michigan used a cork track in their gymnasium for indoor meets.[4] Regularly scheduled indoor championships, however, did not begin until 1906. In that year the AAU Indoor Championship Meet was held New York City, and the Millrose Games were held indoors for the first time in 1914. The Western Conference (Big Ten) and Boston Athletic Association indoor track and field championships were started in 1911, and the Illinois Relays were launched in 1918. But, most multi-team indoor championships, including the Michigan Intercollegiate indoor, the Central Collegiate Indoor Championships [1927], the Michigan State Relays [1920], and the Illinois Tech Relays [1928] were first held during the 1920s when larger structures with good lighting became more common. Yost Fieldhouse indoor track was completed in 1924.[5] Prior to that, University of Michigan indoor track meets were held in Waterman Gym on the basketball court.

The Homogenization of America

Chain-stores began to appear in 1914 when the Great Atlantic and Pacific Tea Company, better known as A & P, began to open stores across the nation. By 1928 A & P had 17,500 branch grocery stores. Kroger, Safeway, and Piggley-Wiggley soon followed A & P's lead, with slight variations, in the grocery business. Five-and-ten cent stores, like Woolworth's and S. S. Kresge, also pioneered in the chain store system before World War I, but expanded rapidly after the *Great Crusade*.[6]

The newspaper chains of William Randolph Hearst, Knight-Ridder, and others were also standardizing news coverage and popularized the crossword puzzle craze. Secretary of Commerce Herbert Hoover would even lead an effort to standardize the threads and sizes of nuts and bolts.

In addition to chain-stores, advertising and mass production accelerated the trend toward nation-wide use of the same brands of clothing, cars, food, and sources of entertainment.[7] Sinclair Lewis observed in his book *Main Street* (1920) "nine-tenths of America towns are so alike that it is complete boredom to wander from one to another." During the last half of the decade, the radio would accelerate the homogenization of national experiences, tastes, values, and speech.

Standardization, among other things, would establish the dates for major relay meets and would affect the medley relay races and other events to be held at those meets.[8] Also, scientific knowledge would be used to improve the soil used in making the tracks on which runners would compete.[9]

Working Conditions

On August 27, 1919 Judge Elbert Gary, for whom Gary, Indiana was named, refused to negotiate with the American Federation of Labor's Amalgamated Association of Iron, Steel, and Tin Workers of North America. After Judge Gary ignored a deadline for negotiating, a strike was called at several mills.[10] The steel strike of 1919, according to the Interchurch World Movement's Commission of Inquiry, resulted from the long working day and work week demanded by employers of its employees. Approximately half of all the employees of the striking mills were subject to twelve-hour work-days, and one half of these workers were, in turn, subject to a seven day work-week. Moreover, when a worker on the replacement shift was absent, workers were sometimes compelled to work twenty-four hours without a rest or an increase in the hourly wage. On average the work week for laborers in the steel mills was 68.7 hours per week.[11] In October Federal troops intervened on behalf of United States Steel. While the strike dragged on until January, Federal intervention made the outcome in favor of management a foregone conclusion. In August 1923 the United States Steel Company finally gave in to pressure from President Harding and instituted an 8-hour day for its workers.[12]

The average annual wage in the United States for all factory workers in 1914 was $580 or about $2 for a ten-hour workday. By 1927 the average wage had risen to $1301 per year or about $4.35 per day for an eight-hour workday. Farm workers were not as fortunate. Their average wage of $1.40 plus meals for a twelve hour day rose relatively little during the "roaring twenties."[13] More leisure time and more disposable income for working Americans would expand the market for sports as entertainment.

Expanded Schooling Contributed to Expanded Participation in Sports

In 1914 there were less than half a million high school students. The gap in school achievement between the children of white, American-born and immigrant parents was appalling. Few foreign-born or African-American students attended school beyond the eighth grade. In 1920 only marginal progress had been made in improving the education of immigrant and African-American children. Nevertheless, by 1927 four million children were enrolled in high school: they constituted half of American children of high school age. Nearly all of the expansion in high school attendance was in the public schools. Overcrowded schools were common and sports and physical education facilities and faculty were frequently inadequate.[14] In 1925 longshoremen made more money than did schoolteachers. In Detroit the lack of athletic facilities was particularly noticeable. In 1924, for example, City College, Northern High School, Central High School, and Cass Tech practiced and held meets on Codd Field to the detriment of all.[15]

Higher education showed a proportionate increase in enrollment. In 1928 the United States had nearly as many high school and college students as the rest of the world. In 1910 there were 226,654 young men and women enrolled in schools of higher education. By 1920 there were 462,445 students in the nation's 950 schools of higher education, and the number had grown to 767,263 by 1926.[16] In 1920–1 academic year the enrollment at the University of Michigan increased by 12½ per cent over the prior year to a total of 10,623 students, against 9,400 for 1919–20.[17] In 1927 the average cost of a college education was $800 per year; $1,500 for private colleges.[18]

As more children attended high school and college, a greater variety of students from more diverse backgrounds participated in interscholastic and intercollegiate sports, as well as field days. In 1914 the Detroit Public Schools sponsored its first annual field day for elementary school children, where running, jumping, throwing and even hurdling skills were tested and rewarded with ribbons and other prizes. By 1926, 200,000 parents and relatives would watch 20,000 kids participate in field day.[19] As more and more of these youngsters attended high school and college, competition became more intense at all levels of participation.

The Inter-Allied Games

American Expeditionary Forces staged an Inter-Allied Games in 1919 at the close of the First World War. Eighteen nations and 1,500 athletes participated at sites in and around Paris. These games, coordinated by Elwood S. Brown, director of the athletic department of the YMCA, were the largest athletic event of the still young twentieth century. An eighteen-year old second lieutenant of the artillery named Charles W. Paddock, from southern California, made his debut in international competition at the Inter-Allied games.

Paddock was born in Gainesville, Texas, on August 11, 1900. He was a sickly child, weighing only 7½ pounds at seven months of age. His parents moved to southern California for his health, eventually settling in Pasadena. Charlie's father sparked his interest in running. Charlie had a peculiar waddle in his walk, and a high-pitched voice that sometimes broke into a falsetto, particularly when he laughed. He had a high knee action, with bouncing stride, and tremendous leg drive. He also had what he referred to as a jump or "freak finish." He took off 10 to 14 feet from the tape, which he broke with both feet off the ground, both arms flung up and outward. It was a finish that was only useful to an exaggerated high, bouncing stride. With it, Paddock would soon be proclaimed the world's fastest human.[20] His life-long competitor would be Jackson Scholz.

Pulp Fiction Runner

Jackson Volney Scholz was born in Buchanan, Michigan on March 15, 1897.[21] The Scholz family moved to St. Louis prior to 1915. In September 1915, Jackson "Jack" Scholz enrolled at the University of Missouri, in the School of Agriculture at Columbia, Missouri. When Scholz entered the University of Missouri, Bob Simpson was the track team's star runner, and Henry F. Schulte was the track coach. Scholz, who was a thin reed of a fellow weighing less than 135 pounds and standing 5 feet 8 inches, did not look the part of a sprinter. Running during a period when America had truly great dashmen, he met them all and at one time or another trounced all of them.

As a freshman, Scholz was the only man on the track team to beat Bob Simpson in the 50-yard dash.[22] He was nicknamed "Germany," earned a varsity letter, and was named an All-American in the 100-yard dash in track in 1917. Scholz ran the 100-yard dash, the 220-yard dash, and the 220-yard low-hurdles as a college sophomore, but he began his career primarily as a 100-yard sprinter. According to the college yearbook,

> Soon after the Christmas holidays, the Rothwell gymnasium floor was occupied during the late hours of every afternoon with many eager to represent Missouri University in the meets this spring. A board track was built west of the gymnasium, with the tearing out of the old indoor track inside to enlarge the basketball court. As soon as the weather permitted, daily practices in the dashes, hurdles, and middle distance runs, were held outside. As a result, the later indoor meets proved that the conditioning of the men in this way was far in advance of the preparation made by any of the other Valley teams.[23]

Scholz won the 100-yard dash at both the 1918 Penn and Drake Relays. On February 10, 1920 he won the 70-yard dash (7.4) at the Millrose Games. In that race he defeated Loren Murchison and Charlie Paddock. Twenty-two years later Paddock recalled:

> Racing Loren Murchison in the winter of 1920 for seventy yards, I was lucky to finish against that comet of the boards. Murchison was at his peak and in his glory at the Millrose Games in 1920.[24]

In 1920 Scholz was named AAU All-American for the 60-yard dash during the indoor season. That spring he again won the 100-yard dash at the Drake Relays and the 220-yard dash at the IC4A.[25] He went on to place fourth to Paddock in the finals of the Olympic 100-meter in Antwerp, Belgium. "Charlie" Paddock recalled,

> It was raining at Antwerp when the six of us lined up for the start of the classic 100 Meters: Loren Murchison, Jack Scholz and Morris Kirksey of the United States; Ali Kahn of France, Harry Edwards of Great Britain and myself.
>
> It was my first Olympic meet. I was more surprised than anybody else that I had been fortunate enough to reach the finals, but when I found that Kirksey, my old rival, was still in the race, my confidence returned. Kirksey said to me before the start, "I can beat anybody else in the world except you," and the thought flashed through my mind that I could beat Kirksey.
>
> Murchison stumbled at the start due to the fact that he did not understand the French instructions that were given us. The rest of the field was closely bunched. At the halfway mark, Kirksey led. Scholz, Edwards and I were about even. Kirksey still led 5 meters from the tape, but as was his custom he turned his head to lunge at the string and as he turned, I jumped for the tape. I thought my jump had won the race and the moments were almost unendurable until the announcement had been made. No other minute in my life will ever be quite so thrilling as the one in which the American flag was raised in the center of the Antwerp Olympic Stadium symbolic of America's victory, as well as my own.

The time was not exceptionally fast, but I do not believe the athletes of today are any better than those who competed in Antwerp in 1920. There are more competitors and conditions are more favorable for record breaking, but human speed has not been materially increased.[26]

Scholz ran the second leg on the 4 × 100-meter relay team that set a world record while winning a gold medal in Antwerp.

Jackson V. Scholz received a Degree of Bachelor of Journalism in absentia in April 1921 as a part of the class of 1920.[27] In 1921 Scholz began writing pulp fiction for a living but continued running as a member of the New York Athletic Club.

University of Michigan Track Star Earns Silver at the Olympics

During the war years, the University of Michigan track coach Stephen Farrell had discovered one of the school's athletic greats. Carl Edward Johnson was born in Genesee County, Michigan on May 21, 1898. His father was a physician and surgeon. When Carl was an infant his family moved to Spokane, Washington, where he later attended Lewis and Clark High School. In 1915 Carl competed as a one-man track team at the National Interscholastic Meet in Chicago, winning second place for his school.[28]

Carl, nicknamed "Heine," enrolled at the University of Michigan in 1917. He lettered in track in 1918, 1919, and 1920. During the War he served as a private in the Student Army Training Corps on the Michigan campus. He was Phi Beta Kappa and President of the University's student body. In 1919 he won four first places at the Western Conference Outdoor Championships, and set a new conference record in the long jump. However, he wrenched a knee at that meet and was never again at peak performance.[29] Nevertheless, Carl earned a silver medal in the long jump (23–3½) at the 1920 Antwerp Olympic Games, just missing first place by six inches, a mark he had reached on several occasions before his knee was injured.

Incidently, Ivan C. Dresser from Burr Oak, Michigan, who had attended Cornell University, was a member of the 3,000-meter team race that won a gold medal at the Antwerp Games. Dresser was the sixth place runner in that event.[30] He, Jackson Scholz, and Carl Johnson were the only Michigan representatives on the 1920 U. S. Olympic track team. Dresser joined General Motors in 1925 and became one of the top executives at GM. He received the honor of Office of the Order of Leopold II from the King of Belgium in 1955, and was a member of the Board of Governors of the New York Symphony Orchestra.[31]

Carl Johnson graduated from the U of M in 1920 with a certificate in Business Administration. At that time, The University of Michigan with over 9,000 students was one of the largest institutions of higher education in the United States. After the Antwerp Olympic Games, Johnson got married and entered the investment business selling bonds for Cray, McFawn and Company in Detroit. He frequently officiated at track meets for the Detroit Police Department, and promoted YMCA activities, including their track program. He died on September 13, 1932 at the age of 34 when a ruptured appendix resulted in peritonitis.[32]

Coach Farrell's Flock

In the fall of 1912, Stephen J. Farrell joined the University of Michigan staff as track and cross-country coach. Farrell had graduated from the University of Maine, where he was a middle distance runner. He received a Masters Degree from Ohio State University. Between 1913 and 1921 Coach Farrell trained six national collegiate champions: Carroll Haff, James E. "Chink" Bond, Arthur W. Kohler, Howard H. Seward, Harold L. Smith, and Carl E. Johnson. Between 1920 and his retirement in 1929 he would produce fourteen additional All-Americans.

In 1921 the pressure to expand the number of sports sponsored by the University was already underway. A student advisory committee at the University of Michigan was formed to make swimming a varsity sport.[33] Some would later argue that the proliferation of intercollegiate sports was robbing track and field of the financial support it needed to thrive.

The 1921 indoor track season got underway at 1:23 p.m. on March 4 when Coach Steve Farrell and 15 members of the Wolverine thinclads boarded the train for Chicago enroute to the fourth annual Illinois Relays in Champaign-Urbana. The trip coincided with the inauguration of Warren G. Harding as President of the United States. The Michigan track team would arrive in Chicago at 7:40 p.m. and change trains for a midnight arrival in Urbana for the Illinois Relays the next morning.[34] The entire one-way trip would take twelve hours.

Prohibition was designed primarily to save America from "the bad habits of its foreign born residents." Italians wanted their Chianti, the German their beer, and the Irishman their whisky. The prohibitionists were determined to keep them from having it and the problems caused by drunkenness. Michigan was one of the states hesitant about, if not downright hostile to, the new law. When Harding became President, prohibition, as a result of the Eighteenth Amendment to the Constitution, had been the law for eight months. In 1919, Congress passed the Volstead Act to enforce the law, but President Wilson vetoed it. Then Congress passed the Act again over the President's veto. The Volstead Act went into effect at midnight, January 16, 1921.[35] Illegal trafficking in alcoholic beverages began immediately, and triggered the biggest crime wave in the nation's history.[36] While prohibition had no direct bearing on track and field, its indirect influence changed the nation.

The indoor track at the University of Illinois Armory measured six laps to the mile. The 290-yard dirt track was laid-out in a building constructed in preparation for World War I. Avery Brundage was the referee for the all-around at the Illinois Relays in 1921.[37] The featured performers at the 1921 Illinois Relays were Brutus Hamilton from the University of Missouri in the all-around, Gus Desch of Notre Dame in the hurdles, and Dave Brown of Illinois in the 1,000-yard run.[38]

The star of the University of Michigan track team in 1921 did not surface until the outdoor track season. Javelin thrower Howard B. Hoffman started to come into his own in April when the University of Michigan track team took the train to Berkeley, California to participate in a meet with the University of California. On May 7 Hoffman won the javelin throw (175–7) and set the Ferry Field record in that event in a duel meet with Ohio State University. Two weeks later he won the javelin throw in a duel meet with the University of Chicago at Ferry Field. According to *The Michiganensian*,[39] Hoffman "jumped into prominence" on June 4 by setting a new Conference javelin record (172–10) at the Western Conference Championships held in Chicago. "A week before he was unknown to track fame."

The 1921 University track season ended on June 18 at the University of Chicago, with the first annual NCAA outdoor track and field championships. The first and top second place winners from the Eastern Conference, the Rocky Mountain, Pacific Coast, Western and other major conferences were invited. The purpose of the NCAA meet was to determine the national college championships for the first time.[40] Hoffman placed third in the javelin throw at that meet.[41]

The following year Hoffman set a meet record in the javelin (182–8) against Ohio State University in Columbus.[42] On June 17, 1922 he set the NCAA record for the javelin (202–3) at the organization's Second Annual Championships in Chicago.[43] His record stood until 1928.

In 1923 under Coach Farrell's leadership, the University of Michigan won the NCAA outdoor track and field championship for its first time and only time. The addition of William DeHart Hubbard in 1921 was a

In 1924, Long-jumper and sprinter William DeHart Hubbard was the first African-American to win an individual Olympic gold medal. *(Photo University of Michigan, Bentley Library)*

major factor in Michigan's 1923 National Championship. Between 1918 and his retirement in 1929, Coach Farrell won four indoor and five outdoor Big Ten Track Championships.

A Bit of Racial Progress

The great tradition of Negro long-jumpers was inaugurated in the early post-war days by Sol Butler, an American who distinguished himself on both sides of the Atlantic. At the Inter-Allied Games in Paris, in 1919,

Butler showed a fine 24 feet 9½ inch (7.557 meters) jump. Curiously enough, officials at that meet not only went to the trouble of taking millimeters into account, but also ruled out the mark with a previously unheard of verdict: 'wind-assisted.' Ken Greenberg, a keen statistical student of the event, claimed that few great long-jump marks, past and present, would come out unscathed if subjected to the same close scrutiny. The present wind limit (2 meters per second or 4.47 miles per hour) was only fixed in 1936, but even today little attention is normally paid to the wind factor in the horizontal jumps. Butler was good enough at the U.S. final trials to make the Antwerp Olympics. He was considered the favorite for the 1920 Olympic title, but pulled a tendon on his first jump in the Belgium arena and placed seventh.[44]

Edward Orval "Ned" Gourdin of Jacksonville, Florida took up track at Harvard University and captured third in the 300-yard dash at the National Senior AAU Indoor Meet on March 19, 1921.[45] On July 23, 1921 he beat Harold Abrahams of Britain in the 100-yard dash and long-jumped 25-3 at the Anglo-American Inter-Varsity meet held at Harvard. Moreover, Gourdin won the AAU Pentathlon Championship in 1921 and 1922, before winning a silver medal in the long jump at the 1924 Olympics.[46] Gourdin, who became the first African-American member of the Massachusetts Supreme Court, was one of a large group of track athletes who reached their peak in non-Olympic years.

William DeHart Hubbard was destined to become the outstanding long-jumper of the decade. A man of medium build with great speed and stamina, Hubbard won six consecutive AAU long-jump titles, an outstanding achievement in such a nerve-racking event.[47] Hubbard, who attended Walnut Hills High School in Cincinnati, Ohio, was a flat chested, spindly thin kid of 16 when he was discovered by Hunter H. Johnson, a black man from Pittsburgh who was looking for a young black with championship potential. Johnson traveled to Cincinnati to scout Hubbard, who was being touted as an athletic prodigy. When he saw Hubbard, Johnson assumed that his trip was a waste of time and money. However, after seeing Hubbard broad jump a couple of times, Johnson became convinced of Hubbard's potential and took him back to Pittsburgh. In Pittsburgh, he introduced the young DeHart Hubbard to Frederick Rubea, Secretary of the AAU by saying, "meet the greatest broad jumper in the world."[48] It was Rubea who brought Hubbard to the attention of Lon Barringer.

University of Michigan alumnus, Lon Barringer, was responsible for getting Hubbard a full scholarship at the U of M. Barringer lived in nearby West Virginia and became familiar with Hubbard's talents both as a student and as an athlete by reading the Cincinnati papers.[49] As a result, Barringer contacted his good friend and fellow West Virginian, Fielding Yost, to see if he was interested in the young athlete. Yost, who was the new Athletic Director at the University of Michigan, was receptive, so Barringer arranged to have Hubbard enter a subscription contest being run by the *Cincinnati Enquirer*. Under the terms of the contest, the 10 area high school students who collected the most new subscriptions would get a $3,000 college scholarship to attend the school of their choice. In 1921 that sum would easily put a kid through four years of college. Barringer told Hubbard that if he would attend Michigan, every effort would be made to help him win the subscription contest. When Hubbard agreed, Barringer got alumni from all around the country to subscribe to the *Enquirer* on behalf of Hubbard. Hubbard was among the contest's winners and enrolled at Michigan the following September.[50]

When asked why he had attended the University of Michigan, Hubbard said, "It wasn't very fashionable for blacks to attend college [in those days], and they got me a scholarship. Very few of my boyhood playmates and high school chums went past high school. I was the only black on the Michigan track team those four years and rarely competed against others, even in national meets." In Hubbard's University of Michigan class there were eight blacks among 1,456 graduates. William DeHart Hubbard married Audrey, his 18-year old high school sweetheart, and started a family while still a student at Michigan.[51]

On September 8, 1922 Hubbard, representing the Cincinnati Gym and Athletic Club, won the long jump (24–3½) at the national AAU Junior Division meet in Newark, New Jersey, to qualify for the senior division titles in the long jump and the hop, step, and jump, which he won. He set a new meet record for the broad jump in the junior division.[52] As a result, he was named to *Spaulding's Guide* All-American track team as a college freshman. He won All-American honors five separate years. In 1923 he was NCAA long-jump champion.

Hubbard is one of fewer than 100 individuals during the twentieth century who won two or more individual events in the same meet at the Drake Relays. In 1924 he won both the long jump and the triple jump at the Relays.[53]

Hubbard became one of the greatest long jumpers in history. He consistency jumped in the neighborhood of 25-feet, at a time when other leading jumpers could *guarantee* a 24-foot jump. He won the AAU long jump title for six consecutive years (1922–27); the last three times with marks exceeding 25-feet. In 1924 Hubbard won the AAU long jump despite being injured, and went on to became the first African American to win an individual gold medal in the Olympics, when he won the long jump in the Paris games. At the 1924 Olympics DeHart Hubbard was more modest than James Connolly had been in the triple jump at the International Olympic Committee's Athens Games in 1896. According to one source, Connolly, a Harvard dropout, threw his hat a meter beyond the longest jump to that point in the competition and then jumped on his hat and won.[54]

Hubbard won the 50-yard dash (5.2) on April 6, 1925 at the Michigan AAU Invitational Indoor Carnival held at the State Fair Coliseum in Detroit. In doing so, he defeated Jackson V. Scholz, George Hester, and Cyril Coafee of the Illinois Athletic Club—joint holder of the world indoor record in the event. That spring, Hubbard set a world record of 25 feet 10⅞ inches in the long jump at the NCAA championships on the same day he won the 100-yard dash title. At the time Hubbard set the word record, an Associated Press report called Hubbard's jump "a record that experts say may stand for all time." However, the record was eclipsed in 1928. Hubbard was at one time a co-holder of the world's 100-yard dash record (9.6), although his mark came three weeks after Paddock's 9.5 (converted to 9.6). A 48-foot plus triple jumper, he won this event twice (1922–23) in the AAU championships.[55]

Hubbard was an All-American for the running broad jump in 1926 as a member of the Century Athletic Club.[56] In 1927 Hubbard set his personal best in the long jump (26–2¼) but his jump was not accepted as a world record because the take-off board was one inch higher than the landing pit.[57] He jumped more than 25 feet on 11 occasions, the best record by anyone before Jesse Owens. His six AAU long jump titles are unequaled.[58] In 1928 Hubbard again made the American Olympic team, but injured his jumping foot and placed eleventh.[59]

DeHart graduated with a degree in physical education. In 1925 he became a "colored worker" for the Cincinnati Recreation Department, where he served until 1941. In 1941 he joined the Federal Housing Authority (FHA), where he remained until his retirement. Hubbard moved to Cleveland in 1943 to become race relations' advisor to the FHA.[60] He was inducted into the Drake Relays Hall of Fame in 1973.

Hubbard died in Cleveland on June 23, 1976 and was buried at Highland Park Cemetery virtually unnoticed. His wife and three children survived him.[61]

The Art of Coaching Track in the "Roaring Twenties"

During the first two decades of the twentieth century, training for track and field was usually based on folklore and local trial-and-error experience. By modern standards preparation was minimal. There was no concept of year around training. Track athletes generally practiced only an hour or so three or four days a week for about four months. In many cases, this practice time was divided among several events. There was no strength training. Everyone believed that strength training reduced muscle quickness, and it was believed that muscle quickness was all-important. In those years, "training" was concerned primarily with prohibitions and taboos. Athletes were told not to drink alcoholic beverages, stay up late at night, have sex, or lift weights. Almost nothing was said about positive, developmental exercise.

Knowledge of kinesiology or the art of movement was in its infancy and effective communication about successful performance strategies was nearly non-existent. During the first half of the twentieth century, most track athletes performed with minimal coaching. Almost no one had any concept of pacing in a race. Fellows just ran. Moreover, the running surface and shoes were often a hindrance to good performance. Officially-recognized world records were started in 1912, but were not published annually until 1932.[62]

Communication among coaches and between athletes was rare, except at national events like the IC4A meet initiated in 1876, the Pennsylvania Relay Carnival starting in 1895, the Western Intercollegiate Meet starting in 1896, and the Drake Relays beginning in 1909. The NCAA Track and Field Championships did not start until 1921, and there was limited interest in the Olympics until they were held in Los Angeles in 1932. American athletes held international championships in most forms of running, leaping, and weight throwing, but were compelled to yield the honors to Europeans in distance events.

Scholz Returns to The Olympics

On June 13, 1924 in the preliminary heats of the 100- and 200-meter dashes at the United States Olympic final track and field tryouts at Harvard Stadium, Jackson Scholz beat Charles Paddock. Scholz, the New

York Athletic Club sprinter, equaled the Olympic record in the 100-meter dash and set a new, world record in the 200-meter dash (21.0).[63] In the rain on the following day, Scholz again shattered the world record for the 200-meter dash (20.9) on a wet track.[64]

At noon on Monday July 16 Scholz and the rest of the American Olympic team embarked on the chartered steamship *America* for Paris where the track and field championships would be held July 6 to 13. On July 7 Scholz finished second to Harold Abrahams in the 100-meter dash in Colombes Stadium. [65]

Jackson Scholz's teammate and rival, Charlie Paddock, who placed fifth in the 100-meter dash on July 7, was convinced that he was washed up as a sprinter. Movie star Douglas Fairbanks asked Paddock to come back to his residence in Paris in hopes of ridding the sprinter of his dark mood. At dinner, Maurice Chevalier entertained Paddock, Mary Pickford, and Douglas Fairbanks with imitations of Paavo Nurmi and of Harold Abrahams, who had defeated Paddock in the 100-meter finals and the first round of the 200-meter preliminaries earlier that day. After dinner Mary Pickford gave Charlie an inspirational pep talk.[66] "Bud" Houser, the winner of two gold medals in 1924, believed that "you have to have emotion to win. You have to have something that little something that gives you the extra zip that has to be there to win."[67] Mary Pickford gave that emotion back to Charlie Paddock. Paddock took her advice to heart, and won a silver medal the following day. Captain Charles W. Paddock, a member of the U. S. Marine Corps, died in an airplane crash in Alaska on July 21, 1943 during World War II.[68]

Meanwhile, Scholz faced his own demons. While at the University of Missouri, he had not believed that he had the speed or the strength to successfully negotiate 200-meters. Now four years later, the New York Athletic Club ace had to find the vision needed to win the 200-meter dash at the Olympics. He did just that, on July 8 when he tied the Olympic record and won the gold medal, nosing out a reinvigorated Charlie Paddock, and defeating third place Eric Liddell and Harold Abrahams who faded to sixth.

Jackson Scholz made the sprint finals in three successive Olympic Games. Scholz beat Charles Paddock five times in ten duels, one of which ended in a tie. "According to the clock, Scholz was credited with an official 20.9 for 200 meters in 1924 and had an unaccepted 9.5 for 100 yards the following year."[69] Paddock, who competed with Scholz many times, observed that Jackson had a peculiar running form all his own. "He knew how to 'turn on the heat' as no other sprinter did. Watching him you realized when he put on the pressure because he had a habit of laying his head over on his right shoulder as he started the drive for the string. Though it spoiled the beauty of his form, it never interfered with his running." As sprinters before him contributed specific elements of style to the art of sprinting, such as competitive ability, stride rhythm, or smoothness of form, Paddock asserted in 1935 that Scholz made a contribution in judgment of pace, which has never since been equaled. According to Paddock,

> He knew exactly what he could do and at the same time he had a very definite estimation of the speed of every competitor he faced and knew the right moment in which to make his drive for victory. In his hundreds of races, Scholz hardly, if ever, displayed bad judgment in the matter of pace.[70]

Scholz was the first to officially to run 100-yards in 9.5 without the aid of wind. He accomplished this neat feat at Greensboro, North Carolina on May 9, 1925. Tenth-second timing was not given recognition in those days, so Jackson's mark was not recorded as a world record. In 1927 Westbrook Pegler, a reporter for the *Chicago Tribune*, wrote:

> Old Jack Scholz, who has been sprinting man and boy since Woodrow Wilson's first administration, was positively frisky today and outran . . . the younger and supposedly faster Henry Russell in the 100-yard special race at the Penn Relays.[71]

In 1928, at the age of 31, Scholz ran a dead heat for third place in the 200-meter dash at the Amsterdam Olympics. A rerun between the two was ordered. Scholz, who had already had an alcoholic drink, forfeited the runoff and was given fourth place. An examination of the photo finish showed that Scholz had indeed placed fourth.[72]

In 1981 Scholz said that he would like to be remembered "as a winner, a successful runner, a decent writer and a gentleman. And one other thing . . . I was fast. I hope they remember I was fast."[73] Scholz became a member of the Helms Hall of Fame and was named to the Drake Relays Hall of Fame (1961) and the New York Athletic Club Hall of Fame (1982). He died October 26, 1986.

Invented Glamour

The 1981 movie "Chariots of Fire" about the 1924 Olympic sprints had several flaws. Eric Liddell was not surprised to learn that his specialty, the 100-meter dash, would be held on Sunday. He was informed of that decision six months in advance, and had plenty of time to adjust his training to the 200 and 400-meter dashes. The cinematic version suggested that Lord Burghley offered his spot on the 400-meter dash to Liddell has little basis in fact. One of the primary reasons that University of Edinburgh star Eric Liddell did not run in the 100-meter dash at the Paris Olympic Games was his experience at the Penn Relays on April 25–6, 1924. Forty thousand spectators watched the Scottish star place fourth in the 100-yard dash at the Penn Relays. One observer wrote, "It wasn't even a close race."[74]

Liddell finished third in the 200-meter behind Jackson Scholz and Charlie Paddock. He won the 400-meter dash in an unorthodox and electrifying manner. Running in the outside lane, Liddell took off as if he was running a short dash, and ran the first 200-meters in 22.2, only 0.3 seconds slower than he had run the 200-meter, and increased his lead in the second half of the race. Liddell set an Olympic record with a 47.6 performance.[75]

Jackson V. Scholz recalled in 1948:

The 1924 Olympic Games, held in Paris, were colorful, thrilling and splendidly organized. Those of us who were fortunate enough to be selected for the United States team have reason to be grateful for the quiet, peaceful setting of the 'Olympic Village' which had been especially constructed in Roquencourt for the temporary convenience of the American team. The games themselves were a whirlwind of action in which Paavo Nurmi of Finland was easily the outstanding performer. He set a new standard for distance running in those fast-moving days, and established himself firmly in the honest admiration of all those who enjoyed the privilege of watching him compete. The most spectacular race, in my estimation, was the 400 meter run, in which Eric Liddell of Scotland, having already placed third in the 200 meter, came through with a magnificent victory. It was a display of stark courage that I have never surpassed upon any track.[76]

Truth Loses to Fantasy

Harold Abrahams, the youngest of six children, was the son of a Lithuanian Jew who earned his living as a banker. Harold was born in Bedford, England on December 15, 1899, and was reared in luxury, but with discipline. He had two brothers who were athletes.[77] Unlike the story in the movie "Chariots of Fire," Abrahams did not race around the great courtyard of Trinity College at Cambridge. It was Lord Burghley who did that. Nor did he look at the 100-meter contest as a chance to redeem himself after his failure in the 200, since the 100-meter dash preceded the 200. Although Abrahams did feel himself an outsider because he was Jewish, a much more important motivating factor was his desire to do better than his two older brothers, who were well-known athletes. One had represented Great Britain in the long jump in the 1906 and 1912 Olympics. Moreover, Harold Abrahams had competed in the 100-meter and 200-meter dashes in the 1920 Antwerp Olympics, but had been eliminated in the quarterfinals.

In 1923 Abrahams came under the direction of Sam Mussabini. Abrahams went to the Paris Olympics in 1924 as Britain's reigning 100-yards champion (9.9) as well as national record-holder in the long jump (24–2½). Few experts imagined him beating the best American sprinters. On the Colombes track, he showed his hidden potential, running the distance three times in 10.6. He peaked at exactly the right moment.[78] The measured paces introduced by Mussabini were the key to Abraham's victory.[79] The medals at the Paris Olympics were sent in the mail, not handed out in ceremonies.[80]

Rhodes Scholar Celebrates with Abrahams

Arthur E. Porritt, who was at the time a Rhodes Scholar at Oxford, won the bronze medal in the 100-meter dash at the 1924 Olympic Games, and became a minor character in the movie "Chariots of Fire." Porritt went on to become the surgeon to Britain's royal family for 35 years. He represented New Zealand on the International Olympic Committee from 1934 until 1967, when Queen Elizabeth II appointed him Governor General of New Zealand.

In 1984 Porritt recalled himself as a casual runner.

I hardly trained at all. I tottered down to the track two or three times a week. Harold Abrahams did train hard. In that, he was ahead of his time. He spent one year training for that race. Until his death [in 1978], Abrahams and his wife and I had dinner at 7 P.M. on July 7 every year, on the day and at the hour when the race was held.[81]

Arthur Porritt never expected to make the finals of the 100-meter dash. A medal was beyond his imagination. He became the only New Zealand sprinter who has ever won a medal. "Halfway through the race, I was exactly where I expected to be—last. Then something happened. I beat the three people who beaten me in the previous rounds. Another yard and I'd have beaten Jackson Scholz for the silver, but I would never have caught Abrahams." After the race, Sam Mussabini, Harold Abraham's cockney trainer, said to Lord Porritt: "Well, young fellow, I guess I've got to congratulate you, but you're the worst runner I've ever seen in my life." "He asked me to train with him, and I did, and I took a full one-tenth of a second off my time. And I beat Harold Abrahams. But it was no fun."

In 1924, Abrahams won the 100-meters in 10.6 seconds, an Olympic record. Carl Lewis won the same race in 1984 in 9.99 seconds. "We wouldn't even qualify now," said Lord Porritt. "And yet, if we had had the training and the facilities . . . perhaps. We dug holes in the track with our little trowels. There were no Olympic villages. We stayed in a miserable little hotel in Paris." He felt that "Chariots of Fire" was more or less accurate, although "the movie slightly over-did Harold's Jewishness. He didn't win the race for Zionism. He won it for Abrahams. He was highly intelligent, pretty well liked, a very good lawyer who was wasted as a civil servant in the department of environment." "It was a great event in our lives, but not the most important event."[82]

Postage Stamp Hero

Coach Lawson Robertson drilled the American 400-meter relay team for two weeks preceding the Olympic event that pitted 13 nations against one another. The U.S. team learned to judge the speed of the approaching sprinter, and start down the track at full speed at just the right moment without even a glance behind. In the finals of the relay, the United States drew the inside lane, often considered the worse draw. Great Britain drew the more favorable third lane.

Although Francis Hussey was still in high school, he was a well-tested sprinter, but new to relay running. Coach Robertson placed Hussey in the led-off position to minimize his chances of mishandling the baton. No one expected him to outrun Harold Abrahams, who had just established himself as the fastest man at 100-meters in the Olympics. Louis Clarke, a dependable sprinter at all times, was placed second to make a sure pass. Because the track at Colombes was 500-meters in length, approximately 107 yards longer than the usual track found in the United States, the third leg of the race was run entirely on a curve. Loren Murchison, who had been part of the world record setting American 400-meter relay team in Antwerp in 1920, was assigned this leg of the race. Alfred Le Coney ran the final leg of the race.

The baton was passed from Hussey to Clarke without a flaw, as Le Coney watched so tense and excited that he could hardly stand still, yet telling himself that he must remain calm and steady to receive the baton properly. When Murchison passed the baton to Le Coney, the USA had a two-yard led. With the indistinguishable roar of the crowd in the grandstand ringing in his ears, Le Coney saw the finish tape and then felt it break across his chest. The American team had set a new world-record of 41.0 seconds.

To the surprise of nearly everyone, Francis Hussey of Stuyvesant High School in New York led off the American team's effort by beating 100-meter gold medalist Harold Abrahams by two yards. J. Alfred Le Coney, a Lafayette College student who had tied Ralph C. Craig's American record for the 100-meter dash, had anchored the American relay team. Now, both of them had won a gold medal in the Olympics and a share of a world record, while Harold Abrahams and his British relay mates had to settle for second place.[83]

When the U. S. Postal Service printed a three-cent stamp in 1932 to commemorate the tenth Olympiad in Los Angeles, engraver Victor McCloskey, Jr. used a picture of intercollegiate sprint champion J. Alfred Le Coney as the model for the stamp.[84]

Another Wolverine Vaulter Goes to the Olympics

In 1921 James K. Brooker attended Michigan State College for one year before transferring to the University of Michigan to major in law.[85] On April 29, 1923 Michigan's James K. Brooker tied for first in the pole vault (12–6) at the Penn Relays. In June 1923 he tied for first in the pole vault at the NCAA Outdoor Championships.

In the following year, on April 26 James K. Brooker won the pole vault (12–10¾) at the Penn Relays. On May 31, 1924 he placed second in the pole vault (12–6) at the regional Olympic trials in Ann Arbor, and on June 14, 1924 he finished in a four-way tie for first in the pole vault (13–0) at the final Olympics trials at Harvard Stadium. Finally, on July 10, 1924 Brooker tied for third in the pole vault (3.90 meters) and won a bronze medal at the Olympic Games in Paris. The winner of the pole vault in the 1924 Olympics, Lee Barnes, a student at Hollywood High School in Los Angeles, appeared in the film *College* as a stand-in for Buster Keaton in a scene that required him to pole vault into a second-story window.[86]

On April 24, 1925 James Kent Brooker, the elected captain of the University of Michigan track team, was declared ineligible for the balance of the 1925 season because he had run one race while enrolled at Michigan State.[87]

Bad Luck Is My Best Friend

George B. Hester, son of William B. and Christine McLean Hester, was born in Toronto, Ontario on August 20, 1902. He lettered in track all four years of high school, was captain of the track team and president of his senior class at Detroit Northern High School. He was also considered an outstanding quarterback on the football team and played basketball and baseball at Northern.[88] George set state high school records for the 100-yard (9.8) and 220-yard (21.7) dashes. Those records stood until 1951.[89]

George attended Mercersburg Academy in 1924, before entering the University of Michigan. He received an A. B. degree from Michigan in 1928.[90]

G. B. Hester moved to Toronto in June 1924 to tryout for the Canadian Olympic team. On June 14 he qualified for the final tryouts when he placed second to Cyril Coaffee, from Winnipeg, who had starred for the University of Iowa in the dashes before running for the Illinois Athletic Club. At the Ontario Canadian Olympic trials held in the University of Toronto Stadium, Hester made it clear that he was one of Canada's best dashmen. On June 17, 1924 he won the 100-meter dash (10.8) and was again second the 200-meter dash at the final Canadian Olympic trials, Molson Stadium in Montreal. His time in the 100-meter dash tied the Canadian record at that distance.[91] On June 20,1924 Hester and twenty-two other Canadian track athletes sailed for Paris on the *Montclair*.

Faced with a rainy day and a muddy track, Hester ran in one of the 17 qualifying heats for the semifinals of the 100-meter dash at the Paris Olympics on July 6. He did not qualify for the semi-finals. On July 9 he ran the qualifying heats of the 200-meter dash, but did not place in the semifinals. A few days later, on July 12, in his last Olympic appearance in 1924, he ran in the 400-meter relay for Canada but again failed to place.

When the Canadian National train "The Inter-City" left Union Station in Toronto on the afternoon of July 10, 1928 to embark on the White Star liner *Albertic* at daybreak on Wednesday July 11, George Hester was full of anticipation.[92] As a seasoned Olympian, great things were expected of him and he expected to do great things at the Olympic Games in Amsterdam later that month. On July 25 the Canadian team, "wearing overcoats, vivid pullover sweaters, and straw hats . . . dashed across London at night from Waterloo station to catch the boat train for Holland. 'We are taking a look at London on our way back. We cannot spare the time now, because we want to be in Amsterdam for the parade before the games on Friday," explained a member of the Canadian Olympic team.[93]

Detroit Northern High School graduate and University of Michigan student, George B. "Buck" Hester represented Canada in the 1924 and 1936 Olympic Games. *(Photo Detroit Northern HS Public School Yearbook, 1923)*

Once in Amsterdam bad luck plagued "Buck" Hester. On the opening day of Olympic competition "Hester might have won his heat [in the 100-meter dash] if he had not mistaken a post six feet from the finish line for the winning post."[94] He eased up too soon and was eliminated in the preliminaries. Although he ran second in his 200-meter dash heat on July 31—fast enough to qualify for the semifinals—Hester was disqualified for not keeping in his proper lane.[95] Finally, on August 4, the Canadian team, of which Hester was a member, qualified for the finals of the 400-meter relay and appearing to be destined for a silver medal. However, the next day during the finals, the lead off runner dropped the baton and the team was as disqualified.[96]

George Hester secretly married Isabel Kelley a Detroit, schoolteacher while still in college. After college he worked for a paper company in Indianapolis, Indiana. He died in Indianapolis on December 8, 1951 at the age of 49.[97]

The Flying Finn Tours America

Paavo Nurmi was one of the heroes of the Paris Olympics. The Finnish distance runner won four, gold medals at the 1924 Olympic games and held six world records. In 1925 the Amateur Athletic Association of the United States sponsored Nurmi on a tour of America. One of Nurmi's first stops was the White House, where on February 25 he was given a photo opportunity with President Coolidge. On April 6–7 the AAU tour brought "the greatest distance runner of all time" to Detroit. At the time of his appearance in Detroit, Nurmi held 18 indoor track records ranging from 1,500-meters to 4,000-yards.[98]

Nurmi's Detroit appearance was originally scheduled for the Olympia, the venue that featured boxing and the Detroit Red Wings for more than three decades. But, the demand for tickets to see Nurmi was so great that the Michigan AAU Indoor Championships were moved to the exhibition building at the State Fair grounds eight miles north of downtown Detroit where 15,000 fans could be accommodated.

Dumping loose, fine cinders on the dirt floor of the exhibition hall, wetting them down and rolling them created a makeshift track that required 12-laps for a mile. The results were not good. After a few races the track had the consistency of beach sand. When Nurmi saw the track he refused to run on a surface where the rankest palooka might beat him. The local AAU committee panicked. They had spent thousands of dollars on the event, and would be bankrupted if the meet did not go on. Finally, Nurmi agreed to run a 1,000-yard race, but not a mile race.[99]

The AAU organizing committee for the event continued to have bad luck when a foot and a half of new snow fell the day of the race. Nevertheless, 4,000 fans managed to make it to the Fair Grounds.[100]

One of the runners selected to run against the "Flying Finn" was Gordon T. Hill, a member of the Detroit City College track team coached by David L. Holmes. Hill, who would work as investigator at Detroit Receiving Hospital for forty years, found himself thirty-yards behind Nurmi after the first lap. However, Hill had good sprint speed and closed to within a few feet of Nurmi on the last lap. Hill later recalled, "The greatest sound I ever heard in my life was that huge crow screaming its lungs out when they thought the local boy was going to catch Nurmi."[101]

Nurmi left Detroit and ran four meets over the balance of the month, including a race against eight Hopi Indians in Los Angeles on April 25.[102] No promotional gimmick seemed too bazaar during the "roaring twenties."

The NCAA Championships in 1927

Fifteen events were held at the sixth annual NCAA meet at Soldier Field in Chicago on June 10–11, 1927. Athletes from 70 colleges and universities qualified for the meet. Seven of these institutions were located in Michigan—Albion College, College of the City of Detroit, Hillsdale College, Kalamazoo College, Michigan State College, Michigan State Normal College, and the University of Michigan. Only Illinois, with Bradley Institute, DePaul, Illinois College, Illinois Wesleyan, Monmouth College, Northwestern University, the University of Chicago, and the University of Illinois, had equal representation, although Iowa and Ohio also were represented by six institutions. However, Michigan qualified 43 athletes, while Illinois qualified 63, Iowa qualified 44, Indiana qualified 37, Wisconsin qualified 22,and Ohio qualified 35. These states accounted for 52% of the participants.[103]

Edward O. Spence, from Detroit Western High School, who was attending Detroit City College set an NCAA record while winning the 220-yard low-hurdles (23.4), and his team-mate J. Kenneth Doherty was a finalist in the javelin throw. Frederick Pitt Alderman from Lansing High School, who was attending Michigan State College, won the 100-yard dash (9.9) and 220-yard dash (21.1). Holly E. Campbell and Wilford H. Ketz from the University of Michigan placed second (149–3) and fourth, respectively, in the hammer throw (140–7). Last, but not least, Lee Marion Bartlett, who was attending Albion College, placed third in the javelin throw (191–6½).[104]

From Failure to Olympian

John Kenneth Doherty's first attempts to become a track athlete met with failure. During his four years at Detroit's Western High School he failed to earn a single letter in the sport. The son of a laborer, Corbert W. Doherty and his wife Elizabeth, J. Kenneth was usually called Ken. The would be athlete graduated from Western High School in 1923; and enrolled that fall at Detroit City College were he became a member of the Honor Society. He majored in education, specialized in English, and won the Howard Donnelly Award for Scholarship and Excellence in Student Activities. He also was elected President of the Student Council.

As a student in the College of the City of Detroit, Ken finally received recognition for his track and field work. He set a number of varsity team records and held the State Intercollegiate record for the high jump (6–1). On February 26–27, 1927 Ken was second in the all-around at the Illinois Relays in Champaign-Urbana, Illinois. According to the *Chicago Tribune*, "Doherty showed well in all events." He won the broad jump, and came in second in all of the other six events.[105]

In 1928 Ken enrolled at the University of Michigan and prepared for his teacher's certificate. As a student at the University of Michigan, Ken availed himself of the athletic facilities and trained for the Olympic Games under the direction of Steve Farrell and of Charles B. Hoyt, who had set a world record for the 220 around a turn while attending Grinnell College.[106]

The 1928 AAU decathlon championships were held over three days at Franklin Field in Philadelphia starting July 3 and served as the Olympic final trials. Doherty won the event by a margin of less than 70 points, and was not considered a likely medalist. In Amsterdam he vastly improved his score to 7,706 points, and took third place behind two Finns. He set a one-day decathlon mark that stood until broken by Bill Watson in 1940. Ken came within nine points of the world record. His feat earned him a bronze medal and All-American status.[107]

Ken taught mathematics and coached track and field at Detroit's Southwestern High School during the 1928–29 academic year. He married Lucile Mason of Detroit in 1929, the same year he set a new AAU record in the decathlon with 7,784 points in winning his second national AAU decathlon championship and All-America honors. That fall he became assistant track coach to Keene Fitzpatrick at Princeton University. After one academic year at Princeton, Ken came back to Detroit. During the summer of 1930 he was a Detroit policeman. When Steve Farrell retired, he was hired as an assistant coach at the University of Michigan.[108]

Ken and his wife had two boys.[109] During the depression years, he ran a summer boy's camp in Ontario. He earned a Masters Degree from Michigan in 1938 and a Ph. D. in 1948. He became a member of Phi Kappa Phi, a national scholastic honor society, and Phi Delta Kappa, national education society. Doherty was a keen student of track and field technique, and was the theorist of the University of Michigan's track team during the 1930s. He helped develop such stars as Sam Stoller, Bob Osgood, Willis Ward, and Bill Watson.

When Charles Hoyt accepted an appointment at Yale in 1939 and Doherty was named head track coach at the University of Michigan.[110] He went on to become one of the world's most distinguished and respected track coaches. Doherty wrote *Modern Track and Field*[111] and *Track and Field Omibook*.[112] His *Track and Field Omnibus* was one of the top instructional books ever written on track and field. His four coaching textbooks were translated into Russian, Finnish, Spanish, and Japanese. During his 18 years at the U of M, the track team won 20 Big Ten team Championships. In his nine years as head coach (1939–48) the Wolverines won 7 conference team championships.

Doherty was introspective. He constantly analyzed life, athletes, and people's reactions to situations. He had more knowledge about track and field techniques than any man of his generation. In 1957–8 Ken developed a new method of teaching track and field. He combined, on paper, the simplicity and clarity of the movie "loop" film with a minimum of verbal explanations. Doherty took loop films and robot sequence photographs of world and Olympic record-holders, projected them by single frames and traced the exact figures for each detail of form.[113]

He was Director of the Pennsylvania Relay Carnival, *Philadelphia Inquirer* Charities Meet, the first USA-USSR duel meet,[114] and the 1935 Big Ten Championships, where Jesse Owens had his greatest day. Doherty was President of the National Track Coaches Association, and was inducted into the U. S. Track and Field Hall of Fame in 1976. He was given the Wayne State University Alumni Citation, and is in the

Wayne State University Sports Hall of Fame. Ken Doherty died in Lancaster, Pennsylvania on April 17, 1996.[115]

Pulling Teeth

The Detroit Public Schools sired another track star in the early twenties. Philip Munro Northrop was born on March 12, 1904 in Detroit, and attended the city's Northwestern High School. On May 18, 1923 Phil won the broad jump (21–1) and the javelin throw (155–4) at the Michigan Interscholastic Championships in Ann Arbor.[116] A few days later he set Metropolitan Scholastic League Record for those two events. He entered the University of Michigan in the fall of 1924.[117]

On May 29, 1926 Phil set the University of Michigan record for the javelin throw (207–7⅝). On June 12 Northrop won the javelin throw (200–10) and placed second in the broad jump at the NCAA outdoor championships in Chicago. On June 19 he won the pole vault (12–0), broad jump (22–10), and the javelin throw (208–10) at the Western Michigan AAU meet in Grand Rapids. In 1927 Philip was captain of the U of M Track team. He was a Phi Kappa Phi his senior year. Northrop graduated with a DDS in 1928. After graduating from the U of M, Phil often functioned as a timer at duel meets held at Yost Fieldhouse.[118]

Philip became an instructor in Clinical Dentistry at the U of M in 1928, the year penicillin was discovered. He earned a Master of Science degree in 1931. He married North Dakota beauty Loraine Jennes in 1932. The marriage begets two children. From 1929 through 1934, Philip was an oral surgeon at Blodgett Memorial Hospital in Grand Rapids. In 1935 Dr. Northrop was appointed Assistant Professor of Oral Surgery at the U of M, and was promoted to Associate Professor in 1941. He was also a member of the staff at Beyer Memorial Hospital in Ypsilanti. He took a retirement furlough on May 18, 1963 and died at age of 59 in Grand Rapids on September 28.[119]

Michigan State's First Olympian

Michigan Agricultural College sprinter, Harry Moon tried out for the Olympics in 1904, but the first track athlete from Michigan State College [now Michigan State University] to participate in the Olympic Games was Frederick Pitt Alderman.

Fred was born on June 24, 1905 in East Lansing, Michigan. His brother, A. L. Alderman, set the freshman Michigan Agricultural College 100-yard dash record in 1913. Fred attended Lansing High School.

Fred Alderman was the first Michigan State College All-American and Olympian. He was 1927 NCAA 100-yard and 220-yard sprint champion and 1928 Olympic gold medal winner in the 4 × 400 meter relay. *(Photo Michigan State University Archives.)*

In 1922 he placed second in the 220-yard dash at the University of Michigan Interscholastic Games in Ann Arbor. His 1922 high school yearbook, *The Oracle*, quoted Fred as saying "It's natural energy that makes me run so fast."

In 1922 former professional football star Ralph Young, who coached at Kalamazoo College in 1921, became the track coach at Michigan Agricultural College. Fortunately, the arrival of Coach Young coincided with Fred Alderman's matriculation at State College. Ralph Young was a good coach, and Fred Alderman emerged as the school's first great track star. As a freshman, Fred broke his brother's record in the 100-yard dash with a 10.0 run. At Michigan Agricultural College, re-christened Michigan State College in 1925, it was not an easy to excel in track. During the indoor season, Fred was forced to run in the old gym, which was 110-yards long. Jenison Field House was not built until after Fred graduated. The outdoor track also was a mediocre facility during the 1920s. Nevertheless, Fred was soon on his way to being a national champion. He also was given an award of a slide rule and $100 for his good grades as a freshman, engineering student.

On May 24, 1924, as a sophomore, Alderman won the 100-yard dash (10.0), the 220-yard dash (21.7), and the broad jump (23–2½) at the Michigan Intercollegiate Outdoor Championships held in East Lansing.[120] A week later, he placed third in the 100-meter dash and fourth in the 200-meter dash at the regional Olympic trials held in Ann Arbor.[121]

In 1925 Fred Alderman placed second in the 300-yard run at the Michigan AAU Indoor Invitational Relay Carnival at State Fair Coliseum meet where Paavo Nurmi ran. Later that spring, Fred won the 100-yard dash (9.7), the 220-yard dash (21.2), and the running broad jump (23–⅜) at the Michigan State Intercollegiate Meet, and won the 220-yard dash (21.12) at the Western Intercollegiate Conference Athletic Association Championships.

On February 25, 1926 Fred Alderman won the 300-yard race (31.2) at the Ninth Annual Illinois Indoor Relays. His medley relay team won the College Division III sprint medley relay at the Third Annual Ohio Relays, before heading to the Drake Relays. In late May, Fred won the 100-yard dash (10.2), the 220-yard dash (22.7), and the broad jump (22–6) at the 11th Annual Michigan State Intercollegiate Outdoor Championships. He then won 100-yard dash (10.2), the 220-yard dash (22.4), and the broad jump (22–9¼) at the Central Collegiate Conference Outdoor Championships. He completed the 1926 track season by winning the 220-yard dash (21.1) and placing fourth in the 100-yard dash at the NCAA Outdoor Championships.

Fred was captain of the 1927 Michigan State track team. During the indoor season, however, Alderman was defeated in the 50-yard dash by a Cass Tech High School student named T. "Eddie" Tolan at the National Town and Country Club Indoor Meet in Detroit. Fred rebounded, and on April 30, 1927, at the Penn Relays, Westbrook Pegler of the *Chicago Tribune* wrote:

> Four mudded lathered young fellows who came from Michigan State College bearing no credentials as wonder men, came within one second of a world record in winning the half mile college relay number described as the Championship of America. The Michigan team, Lang., Henson, Grim, and Alderman, coached by a stout man named Ralph Young, ran that muddy half mile in 1:28.4 to win plenty from Penn State, which was a full second longer on the way.

The Michigan State College relay team also won the one-mile Class B relay in the very good time of 3:20. Pegler mused, "Young's foot runners have won 14 of their last 7 starts, or something like that."[122] At the IC4A in 1927 Fred beat Ray Barbuti in the 440. The following year Barbuti won the Olympic 400-meter run. While Fred won the 100-yard dash and the 220-yard dash at the 1927 NCAA Championships, he pulled a muscle. In 1928 Fred Alderman was selected for the 1,600-meter American Olympic relay team.

After graduating from Michigan State College and winning a gold medal in Amsterdam Olympic games, Fred Alderman became a mechanical engineer for Michigan Federated Utilities. In 1929 he was transferred to their affiliate, the Atlanta Gas and Light Company, for whom he worked until 1945. In 1945 he went into sales at Gaylord Container Corporation, and lived in East Point, Georgia. He retired on June 30, 1970.

After the 1928 Olympics he did no organized running. From 1933 until 1936 he pitched in a softball league in Atlanta. He was an official starter for Georgia Tech track meets from 1933 through 1965, when his hearing problem became a handicap in that role. In the 1950s he also was a starter at several South Carolina State track meets held at Presbyterian College in Clinton, South Carolina.[123]

Frederick Alderman helped to carry the torch in the 1996 Olympic Games in Atlanta. At the time, he was the oldest living U. S. Olympic gold medalist. Fred died in Social Circle, a suburb of Atlanta, on September 15, 1998 at the age of 93.[124]

Denied Opportunity by a General's Orders

Many Americans were disappointed by the track team's performance in the 1924 Olympics, and felt that the team must taken the games more seriously. These critics felt that more discipline was needed, so in 1928 they selected General Douglas MacArthur to head the Olympic Committee. MacArthur was an ardent believer in the value of sport as a builder of manly character. While superintendent of the United States Military Academy, he had ordered that the Duke of Wellington's quotation about the Battle of Waterloo having been won on the playing fields of Eton be carved into the stone portals of the West Point gymnasium.[125] He also was an ambitious man with great political ambitions. MacArthur was eager to become President of the United States and wanted as many non-military hooks to hang his presidential aspirations on as possible.[126]

When MacArthur boarded the *SS President Roosevelt* for Holland, he bragged that the 1928 U.S. Olympic team "is the greatest team ever assembled in our history." He went on to declare that the team is in such "superb condition for the great test [that] Americans can rest serene and assured."[127]

The U.S. Olympic track team picked eight quarter-milers for their team. Two, Fred Alderman and John W. Lewis, were from Michigan. In the Olympic trials Alderman ran faster than Lewis, but after winning the 400-meter run at the central regional Olympic trials in Ann Arbor with a career best 48.0, Alderman withdrew from the Olympic finals. Nevertheless, he was selected for the 1,600-meter relay team.

As it turned out, the American men's track team performed much worse than expected. Raymond Barbuti, a quarter-miler from Syracuse University, was the only American male runner to win an individual event in the 1928 Olympic games. Ray Barbuti recalled:

Most of the joys and heartaches that I've experienced during my thirty years of life are not vastly different than the average person's. Like most other people I have lost and gained in the material things of life. But I am slightly different from most people—in the respect that I possess one thing that can never be taken from me. That is the memory of representing my country in the 1928 Olympic games at Amsterdam, Holland. The memory of winning the 400 Meter championship and of standing alone in the center of the stadium, following the victory, while every person of the fifty thousand present stood bareheaded, while the Dutch band played the 'Star Spangled Banner' and the American flag was raised in the breeze. This memory is a dear one and will always be cherished among my most valuable possessions.[128]

After celebrating his victory in the 400-meter dash, Barbuti returned to the *SS President Roosevelt*. When Barbuti boarded the ship, an army officer notified General MacArthur. Within minutes MacArthur came to Barbuti's cabin. He congratulated the quarter-miler, and told Barbuti that the committee had just met and decided that, as world champion, he would the anchor the 1,600-meter relay the next day. Barbuti protested that he had already run four tough races. MacArthur refused to listen, responding, "You're going to run. That's it!" Barbuti countered, "Well, General, I'm not in the army." But, upon being pressed he admitted that he was a team player, and asked whom the General was going to drop from the relay team. MacArthur said, "Lewis." In Europe Lewis, who was a freshman at Detroit City College [now Wayne State University], was posting faster times than Fred Alderman.

Lewis, an African-American who later was the national AAU 300-yard champion on two occasions, was a nice guy, according to Barbuti, and did not deserve this treatment. So, Barbuti demanded that MacArthur confront Lewis with the decision to replace him on the relay team. MacArthur told Fleming, who later became Superintendent of the Military Academy at West Point, to go and get Lewis, who was eating dinner. The General told Lewis, who had the hopes of Detroit's entire African-American community riding on his slim shoulders, "We have to win, and the only way we figure we can is with Barbuti at anchor, and we're dropping you." According to Barbuti, "The kid started to cry, and I said to him, 'Do you understand that I had nothing to do with this?' That's how I got on the relay team."[129]

The next day the American four by 400-meter relay won the gold medal in world record time, but Fred Alderman ran poorly (49.4) in the finals. He lost ground to both Werner Storz (GER) and John Rinkel (GBR).[130]

As an African-American, Lewis had already learned the lesson preached by Canadian writer Robertson Davies, "There is a time to talk about God and a time to trust God and keep your mouth shut."[131] He kept his mouth shut, despite his deep disappointment in not being allowed to participate in the Olympic Games. On August 13, 1928 Lewis was allowed to run at an international track meet in Ghent, Belgium. He won the 200-meter dash and was on the winning 1,600-meter relay in that meet.

In spite of the poor showing by American trackmen, using American AAU rules the United States outscored all other countries in the Ninth Olympiad in Amsterdam. In the official report on the 1928 Olympics

General MacArthur, an anti-black, Southern elitist, deflected criticism of his leadership of the Olympic team by calling for Americans to lead a more strenuous life. He wrapped himself in the American flag and declared victory, even though the facts did not support his claims.[132] He would repeat this public relations strategy in the future. For example, after burning out the bonus marchers in 1932, he would claim that most of the penniless protesters were fakes and a danger to the republic, even though 94 percent of the bonus marchers had army or navy records, 67 percent had served overseas, and 20 percent were disabled.[133] Later, he spin-doctored the tactical blunders that allowed quick Japanese conquest of the Philippines.[134,135]

Spear chucker

The only Michigan athlete ever to qualify for the Olympics in the javelin throw is Lee Marion Bartlett. The javelin throw was an event from the original Greek Olympics, along with the discus, long jump, foot races, wrestling and chariot races. The javelin-throw at a target and for distance were events in the Athens Olympic revival of mid-October 1859. The javelin throw also was one of the events at the Wenlock Olympics of 1860.[136] During the "roaring twenties," America's best javelin thrower was from a small town in Michigan.

Lee Marion Bartlett and his twin brother, Lynn, were born on March 30, 1907 in Hillsdale, Michigan, where C. E. Singer and Son employed their father, Charles Bartlett, in the retail furniture and undertaking business. Their mother, Gertrude, attended Hillsdale College and taught in the rural schools of Hillsdale County for nearly five years before marrying Charles Bartlett on August 14, 1901.

In 1909 the Bartlett family moved to Union City, located in Branch County north of Coldwater, where Charles Bartlett had purchased a furniture store and undertaking business. Charles and Gertrude became involved in the activities of the Methodist Church.[137]

In 1912 the twins accompanied their father and a couple of local civic leaders to Battle Creek in a model T Ford to hear "Teddy" Roosevelt, who was running for President on the Bull Moose ticket, give a campaign speech.[138]

About the time he was graduating from high school, Lee fell in love with a Union City schoolteacher, Leda Cross, and his mother had to talk him out of marrying her. According to Lee's diaries, the flame of the romance burned for several years.

Influenced by the minister of the Methodist Church, Lee and his twin brother Lynn entered Albion College in the fall of 1925. At Albion Lynn Bartlett found success as the center on the Albion College football team that defeated Michigan State College 2–0 on October 6, 1928. But, Lee had difficulty finding a niche in sports. He had medium muscularity and did not feel comfortable playing college football. He tried out for track, but could not sprint or run distances. He was a flop in the pole vault and the shot put. The coach was about to give up on him when Lee began to show promise in the javelin throw.

According to the AAU rules in effect in the 1920s, a javelin must weigh a minimum of 800 grams (1 pound 12¼ oz.) and measure between 2.6 meters and 2.7 meters.[139] For the throw to be considered valid the pointed metal head must break the turf. The javelin is thrown on the run and must be released above the shoulder. The runway is between 30 meters and 36.5 meters long.[140]

The javelin throw is considered to be a dangerous event. It requires constant, careful supervision and a great deal of a coach's time. As a result, many secondary schools have banned the event. Javelin is what the coaches call a "freak event." The skill required hurling the spear 200-feet or more varies from athlete to athlete. It is an event an athlete can not go out and learn in an afternoon. Indeed, the training routine is 98 percent practice in form. The best javelin throwers in the world fear using all their strength in throwing the shaft more than 10 times a day, and then only when they are in top condition.

Fortunately for Lee Bartlett, he came under the influence of Coach R. R. "Bud" Daugherty, who later became a nationally known football coach at Michigan State University. Daugherty took the time and gave the attention required to turn a small town athlete into a world class track star in the javelin throw. On June 3–4, 1927 Lee threw the javelin (174–6) at the MIAA Championships at Alumni Field at Albion College to win the conference championship. Then, he and Coach Daugherty drove to East Lansing, Michigan to compete in the second Annual Central Intercollegiate Track and Field Meet Saturday afternoon, June 4.[141] Lee won the javelin throw (173–8) in the East Lansing meet, and qualified for the NCAA National Championships held June 10–11, 1927. Lee placed third at the NCAA championships, and established himself as a contender for an Olympic spot in 1928.

In 1928 Lee set the intercollegiate record in the javelin throw (216–7). As a result, Lee was invited to the Fifth Annual Texas Relays in Austin on March 29, 1929. Lee was captain of the Albion College track team in 1928 and 1929.

Both Lee and his brother studied to become science teachers and were awarded BA degrees at Albion College in June 1929. Lee's javelin record at Albion stood for 35 years. Both he and his brother were later inducted into the Albion College Sports Hall of Fame. Lee lived in Detroit for a time during the summer of 1929, and taught in Marlette, Michigan from 1929 until 1932. He qualified for and participated in three Olympiads.

Lee Bartlett was six feet tall, weighted 165 pounds, had a 32 inch waste, size 8½ shoes, a 15½ collar, and 15½ inch shirt sleeves. He won the javelin throw at the Ohio Relays, was second at the Drake Relays, and won both the Michigan State Intercollegiate Championship and the MIAA Conference Championship for the javelin throw. Lee was clearly a candidate for the United State Olympic team.

Lee's diary began on June 8–9, 1928 while hitching a ride with friends to Boston in their Cadillac. They drove through Canada to Buffalo, and on to Harvard, where the final Olympic trials were held. Lee placed fourth in the javelin throw and made the team. He had his picture taken with Charley Paddock, Lee Barnes, and others. After celebrating with his brother and others, he took the train to New York City, where he roomed with Ken Doherty. He and Ken went to Coney Island and to the top of the Woolworth Building, the tallest building in New York City.

On July 11 Lee, Ken, and Fred Alderman boarded the *U.S.S. President Roosevelt* together, and were assigned to the same dining room table for meals during the trip to Europe. After getting sea sick, Lee and the other members of the Olympic team arrived in Amsterdam. They stayed aboard the ship for board and meals while in Holland. The first thing that Lee observed about the Dutch was "they wear wooden-shoes and funny clothes." John W. Lewis was in the group of guys that included Lee Bartlett when walked together around Amsterdam shortly after arrival. On the first day, Lee "met two good looking Dutch girls." During the Olympics, Lee went to a cabaret where American jazz was being played.

After the opening ceremony, where Clarence "Bud" Houser carried the American flag, Lee, Fred Alderman, and Ken Doherty watched the opening track and field events. Charlie Paddock sat immediately in front of Bartlett. Herman Brix, the Washington State University shot putter, won a silver medal. In 1935 Brix would have a starring role in the movie, *New Adventures of Tarzan*, and later would be featured in *Mildred Pierce* and the *The Treasure of Sierra Madre*.[142]

On July 30, Frank J. "Babe" Cuhel from the University of Iowa placed second to Lord David Burghley in the 400-meter hurdles. On May 25, 1924 Cuhel, while at Washington High School in Cedar Rapids, Iowa, won the 220-yard low-hurdles and placed second in the high hurdles ahead of Edward O. Spence in the University of Michigan Interscholastic Meet in Ann Arbor.[143]

Bartlett placed tenth in the javelin at the Amsterdam Games. After appearing in meets in Paris and London, Bartlett returned to the United States aboard the *U.S.S. President Roosevelt*. He, Fred Alderman, Ken Doherty, and two Olympians from Chicago then caught a train back to Michigan.[144]

Unbeknownst to all but the most careful observers, a little known German shoe company, owned by Adi Dassler and located in the small Bavarian mill town of Herzogenaurach, received a major boost when their athletic shoes were worn by German athletes in the Amsterdam Olympics. During the 1930s demand for Dassler athletic shoes mushroomed.[145]

Bartlett Makes the 1932 Olympic Team

On July 2, 1932 Lee Bartlett won the javelin throw (210–7) at the Olympic semi-finals at Dyche Stadium. He was awarded $105 to underwrite expenses to Palo Alto, where the Olympic finals were held. The award did not cover expenses, so "Dan" Clarence Hartung, a former Albion College classmate, drove him to California, helped underwrite Lee's expenses, and acted as his manager. He also accompanied Lee to the Los Angeles Olympics.

On July 16, 1932 Lee placed third in the javelin throw in the Olympic trial finals at Palo Alto to become a member of the Olympic team. On August 4 Bartlett placed fifth in the javelin throw (211–6) at the Los Angeles Olympics.[146] Eugene Oberst, who placed third in 1924 with a throw of 191–5, was the only American Olympic medal winner in the javelin throw prior to 1948. With the exception of Oberst, Lee Bartlett gave the best showing in this event by an American in the first half-century of modern Olympic competition.

Southeastern High School Star Makes Good

When Wilford Herman Ketz graduated from Detroit's Southeastern High School in June 1924, there were 80 graduating seniors. None were people of color. Ketz earned letters in baseball, basketball, and track his junior and senior years in high school, was on the yearbook staff, the Hunter Club, and the Student Council. His nickname was

"Willy," he disliked his big feet, was kidded about his "dainty appetite" and his ambition to be a "dancing instructor."[147] Nordstrom High School was renamed Southeastern High School in 1922. On May 17, 1924 "Willy" won the hammer throw and placed second in the javelin throw at the Detroit Metropolitan League Championships. A week later he won the hammer throw (124–1) at the Michigan Interscholastic Meet in Ann Arbor.

After working for a year to earn money for college expenses, in the fall of 1925 Willy attended the University of Michigan. Between 1927 and 1929, he won top honors in the hammer throw fifteen times, including the NCAA National Championship in 1928, and Drake Relay victories 1927 through 1929. Ketz placed second in the Big Ten Championships in 1927, and won the hammer throw at the Big Ten Outdoor Championships in 1928 and 29. Willy closed the 1927 track season by placing fourth in the hammer throw (140–7) at the Sixth Annual NCAA Championships.

Ketz was a finalist in the hammer throw at the 1928 U. S. Olympic trials in Philadelphia. In 1929 he set the meet record in the hammer (157–8⅔) in the rain at the Drake Relays.[148] On May 4, 1929 he also set the Ferry Field and University of Michigan varsity record in the hammer throw (165–10), and on June 8 he placed second in the hammer (159–9⅝) at the NCAA Championships.

Ketz won the Michigan AAU Championship in the hammer in 1928 and 1929. On July 4, 1929 he set the Michigan AAU record for the 16-pound hammer throw (158–4½), and won the javelin throw, and the 56-pound weight throw. Willy was Captain of the University of Michigan track team in 1929. He became track coach at Union College and was a representative for the Adirondack AAU Association.

Tom Ottey Makes the Olympic Team

Tom Ottey attended high school in Philadelphia and in 1930 emerged as a distance running star for the Meadowbrook Club of Philadelphia. In May 1930 he placed second in the National AAU ten-mile run championships held in Norwich, Connecticut. In August Tom won the National AAU six-mile run, and was named to the American three-mile team race group that defeated the British Empire team at the U.S.A. vs. British Empire meet held at Soldier's Field in Chicago on August 27. In November Ottey placed 26th in the National AAU Senior cross-country championships.

In 1931 Tom Ottey enrolled as a Business Administration major at Michigan State College. On July 1 1932 Ottey won the 10-K run at the

Michigan State College distance runner, Clark Chamberlain, was IC4A cross-country champion in 1930 and National NCAA two-mile champion in 1931. He did not start running until after he entered college. *(Photo Michigan State University Archives)*

National Senior AAU Championships. On July 2, 1932 the NCAA allocated $115 to him to underwrite his expenses for participating in the final Olympics trials in Palo Alto, California.[149] Two weeks later he won the final U. S. Olympic trials in the 10-K run by 40 yards in the respectable time of 32:18.2.

While Ottey made the 1932 Olympic team, he did not place among the top ten in the 10-K run in Los Angeles. Nevertheless, he was an All-American in the 10-K run for 1932.[150] He was again named All-American in cross-country for 1933.[151] In mid-June 1935, Tom missed the National Collegiate Championships in Berkeley, CA, because he was required to spend six weeks at a regular Army camp at the time of the meet.[152] Tom Ottey was named All-American for the second time in the 10,000-meter run in 1936.[153]

Edwin "Ned" Turner of the University of Michigan placed fifth in the 800-meter run (1:52.5) at the Los Angeles Olympics.[154] There were five trackmen representing the State of Michigan in the 1932 Los Angeles Olympic Games: Eddie Tolan, Ned Turner, Lee Bartlett, Tom Ottey, and race-walker Ernest Crosbie. Between 1920 and 1932 the State of Michigan produced 15 Olympians in track and field.[155] Over the first one-third of the twentieth century the State of Michigan could claim thirty-three Olympians in track and field.

4. Breaking Down Barriers: Impact of Track and Field Within the City of Detroit, 1917–1950

"The problem of the twentieth century is the problem of the color line," W. E. B. Du Bois declared at the first Pan-American Congress in 1900.[1] Few predictions for the twentieth century were so prophetic. The century would struggle with colonialism in Africa and Asia, apartheid in the American and South Africa, and a never-ending series of race-based wars, ethnic cleansings, and domestic civil conflicts. As in the rest of the world, the color line was at the core of much of the civil and political strife in Detroit and across the State of Michigan. Participation in track and field was one of the barrier breakers on behalf of racial equality in the United States.

For most of the twentieth century, the people of Michigan considered track and field a major sport. The state, and particularly the City of Detroit, produced many of the best track athletes in the world, including a gold medal winner in track and field in every Olympiad in the first half of the twentieth century. Early in the century, track was primarily a northern sport. Prior to 1935, few segregated Southern schools offered anything resembling a track and field program. Black southern colleges were particularly lacking in even rudimentary track facilities. Conference competition in track and field by the Colored Intercollegiate Athletic Association did not begin until 1924. In the south, track was considered a secondary sport, in part, because the track season competed with the much more popular sport of baseball. The Southern tourist and planting seasons also siphoned off both participants and fan support.[2]

Track and field and boxing were the first sports that were truly open, at all levels of competition, to black athletes. Even then, there were racial barriers. Despite the success of Jack Johnson at the beginning of the twentieth century, the promoters who controlled professional prizefighting denied title bouts to a number of legitimate Negro contenders.[3] Likewise, there are well-documented complaints that schools, like the University of Michigan, denied access to all black athletes, except those with extraordinary talent.[4] Indeed, only four black athletes earned a varsity letter at the University of Michigan prior to 1930, and three of the four were trackmen (De Hart Hubbard, Eddie Tolan, and Booker Brooks). Nevertheless, track offered greater opportunity to the ambitious, black athlete than most sports.

The Question of Color in Detroit

The first racial incident in sports in the Detroit Public Schools occurred on Saturday, May 17, 1909, when five Eastern High School boys quit the team rather than play with John W. Roxborough, the team's Negro catcher.[5] Roxborough, the son of a New Orleans lawyer, had moved to Detroit in 1899 when he was seven years old. He dropped out of the University of Detroit and became a bail bondsman and a numbers operator when he concluded that little was to be gained by a college education. In the 1930s Roxborough became Joe Louis' boxing promoter/manager, and in later years served as President of the Superior Life Insurance Company.[6]

In 1921, when the first racial census of the Detroit Public Schools was taken, there were 5,680 Negro students in the Detroit Public School system and few, if any African-American teachers.[7] At that time, Negroes comprised 4.4% of the student body of the Detroit Public Schools. The environment for race relations in Michigan during the 1920s was far from good. Symbolically, a bill was introduced in the Michigan legislature in 1925 to make interracial marriage illegal.[8] By 1929, the year when a Ku Klux Klan supported candidate was elected mayor of Detroit, the number of Negro children in the Detroit Public Schools had doubled, but so had the school enrollment.[9] Consequently, the proportion of black students in the Detroit Public Schools remained unchanged from the beginning of the decade.

The Sour Smell of Poverty

During the 1920s, Detroit's African-American families were, for the most part, poor and isolated from the rest of the city's population. Nestled in a ghetto, known as "black bottom," named in the eighteenth century for the black topsoil found in the area and not for the color of its twentieth century inhabitants, the city's African-American population had a per family income of only $2,627 per year in 1929 and an

unemployment rate of nearly fifty percent.[10] Less than half of one percent of the enrollment of the state's colleges and universities were people of color, and there were few local Negro heroes, other than the
members of John Roesink's Detroit Stars of the Negro National League,
who played baseball at Mack Park during the summer months.[11]

Between 1917 and 1950, no fewer than fifty African-American
trackmen from the Detroit Public Schools used their track and field skills
to obtain a college education and pursue a professional career in education, recreation, or the law. Their accomplishments occurred before the
first wave of civil rights initiatives—launched by Thurgood Marshall,
Harry Truman, and Hubert Humphrey—began, tentatively, to open
opportunities to black Americans. This elite group of Detroit trackmen
included some of the best track athletes the nation has ever seen.

Adventurous Spirits in the Face of Adversity

The trailblazer for most of these extraordinary athletes was John W.
Lewis. Born in 1908, Lewis trod paths rarely taken before his efforts.
On May 18, 1924, at the age of 15, Lewis was the only person from
Northeastern High School and one of only a dozen or so black athletes
to compete in the Detroit City League Track and Field Championships.
To make thing even more difficult, his school had no track on which to
practice. He took second in the 220-yard dash. A year later, he won the
Detroit High School Championship in the 220-yard dash. On July 4,
1926 he won the State AAU 440-yard dash. In 1927,when he was a
senior in high school, he became the Michigan High School State
Champion in the 220 yard dash and was a member of State Champion
880-yard relay team that set a new national interscholastic record in
that event. A few days later, he won the 440-yard dash at the National
Interscholastic Championships in Chicago.[12]

When he graduated from high school he was without a job or any
prospects for the future, but he was determined to seek new paths. On
June 8, 1927, he vowed to walk from Detroit to San Francisco.[13] But,
David L. Holmes, coach of track and field at Detroit City College, inter-
ceded. He offered John Lewis a scholarship at City College and helped
him get a job to earn money to attend college. Consequently, on July
4, 1927 Lewis successfully defended his Michigan AAU 440-yard dash
championship.

As a freshman, John Lewis could not compete on the varsity track
team, but was a candidate for the U. S. Olympic team that would compete in Amsterdam. To help Lewis prepare for the Olympic trials, Coach

On July 4, 1926 the African-American Detroit Athletic Association won the State of Michigan AAU team championship held at Bell Isle. Leon "Toy" Wheeler, a Detroit Junior College graduate, coached the team and is shown in a suit and bow tie. The members of his team were (front row, left to right) Withe, Gene Beatty, Hartman, Edward Gaines, Graham, John W. Lewis, Bob Sampson. (back row left to right) Thad Dennis, McMaman, Coach Wheeler, Nuthall, Eddie Tolan. This was one of the greatest track teams in Michigan history. *(Photo Aaron Gordon Collection)*

Holmes arranged a special 300-yard race against Fred Alderman of Michigan State College, the NCAA and co-world record holder at that distance. The race was held on May 5, 1928, during a duel meet held at Belle Isle between the freshmen of Michigan State Normal College[14] and Detroit City College. Lewis lost the 300-yard match race to Alderman by less than a yard, but captured the 100-yard dash, 220-yard low hurdles, and 440-yard dash against the Ypsilanti freshmen.

The following month, both John W. Lewis and Fred Alderman qualified for the U. S. Olympic team.[15] Lewis, who was scheduled to run on the 4 × 400-meter relay team, was one of only three black athletes on the country's Olympic track and field squad. On the night before he was to run in the 1,600-meter relay, General MacArthur, President of the U. S. Olympic Committee in 1928, pulled John Lewis from the relay team, and replaced him with Raymond Barbuti.

After returning from Europe, Lewis excelled in track and completed his college education. At the Michigan Intercollegiate Conference Championships in May 1929, he won the 100-yard dash, the 220-yard low hurdles, and the mile relay. On June 9, 1929 he placed fourth in the 440-yard dash at the National NCAA Championships. In 1930, Lewis set the U. S. record for the indoor 40-yard dash, and won the 300-yard dash at the National AAU Senior Indoor Championships. However, on February 25, 1931, when Lewis ran to defend his title in the 300-yard dash at the National AAU Senior indoor meet, he was lost a very close decision. He was forced to run the 300-yards five times, before losing the decision to Bill Carr of the University of Pennsylvania. Lewis ran thrice to qualify for the finals, then fought the deciding race to a dead heat. In the run off, Carr nipped Lewis at the tape.[16]

John W. Lewis graduated from Detroit City College in 1932. He was an All-American in track in 1928, 1929, and 1930.[17] At the National NCAA Outdoor Championships in 1932, Lewis took second in the 440-yard dash. On July 2 the Chicago selection committee for the U.S. Olympic Committee allocated $105 to John Lewis to underwrite his expenses for participating in the final Olympics trials in Palo Alto, California.[18] He joined Leroy Dues and Albert King for the trip west in a 1930 Ford with a rumble seat. He did not, however, make the 1932 Olympic team,but he did watch the Olympic games before returning to Detroit.

The Detroit Public Schools refused to hire him when he graduated from college, and he was forced into a series of odd jobs. In the late 1930s Lewis took the gold medals he won at the AAU Indoor Championships in 1930 and 1931 and had them melted down to use in repairing his teeth.[19] From 1954 through 1970 Lewis was District Recreation Supervisor for the City of Detroit. In that position, he gave part-time and summer jobs to the generation of Wayne State University track team members that rose to coaching and administrative positions in the Detroit Public Schools during the 1970s and 1980s. In 1979, Lewis was inducted into the Wayne State University Sports Hall of Fame.

The Loving Brothers

William C. and Alvin D. Loving were members of the Detroit Cass Tech High School class of 1927. On May 17, 1924, when he was a sophomore at Cass Tech, Bill Loving won the high jump and placed second in both the 120-yard high and the 120-yard low-hurdles at the Detroit Metropolitan League Championships. The following year, he won the 60-yard low (7.2) and the 60-yard high-hurdles (8.5), as well as the high jump (5–9¼) at the First Annual University of Michigan Indoor Interscholastic Invitational Meet held on March 21. On April 6, 1925 he and his brother Al were on the winning high school mile relay team (3:56) and Bill won the 50-yard high-hurdles (.07) at the Michigan AAU Invitational Indoor Carnival held at the State Fair Coliseum in Detroit.

During the 1925 outdoor track season, Bill won the 120-yard high and the 220-yard low-hurdles (24.8), and placed fourth in the 880-yard relay at the University of Michigan Interscholastic Meet in Ann Arbor. He closed the season by winning the 120-yard high-hurdles (16.5) and the 220-yard low-hurdles (25.5), tying for first in the high jump, and placing second in the 880-yard relay at the Michigan Athletic Association Class A State High School Championships.[20]

As a high school senior, Bill Loving continued his amazing track career. On March 23, 1926 Bill Loving and Eddie Tolan traveled together to the National Interscholastic Indoor Championships at Northwestern University in Evanston. On March 25 Bill won the 60-yard high-hurdles and tied for first in the high jump at the National Interscholastic Meet, Northwestern University. On May 29 Bill won the 120-yard high hurdles (16.1), the 220-yard low-hurdles (25.6), tied for second in the high jump, and placed third in the discus throw at the Michigan Class A State High School Championships.

Alvin Loving was also on the track team at Cass Tech (Detroit) and while not as good as his twin brother Bill, was a four-year letter winner and City champion in track. Bill and Alvin enrolled at Western State Teacher's College in Kalamazoo in the fall of 1926. Both boys qualified for scholarships, and both went out for track at Western.

Bill majored in Physical Education. He was the only African-American member of Sigma Theta Gamma, the honorary physical education fraternity, and was the only African-American member of the W Club (letterman's club).[21] Bill was co-captain of the Western State Teacher's College 1930 track team. After the 1927–28 school year, Alvin D. Loving dropped out of track to focus on the Men's Glee Club, the College Choir, and the YMCA Club. Alvin was the only black in the Men's Glee Club.[22]

William C. Loving graduated from Western State Teachers College in 1930. After graduation, he worked for the Detroit Department of

Recreation and the YMCA in Detroit for a year, while his brother finished college. In 1931 Alvin D. Loving, Sr., graduated from Western and got married. The Loving brothers started teaching in River Rouge, because the Detroit Public Schools did not hire African-American high school teachers. They acted as critic teachers for Wayne University from 1937 through 1940. Finally in the fall of 1943, they were given contracts to teach at the nearly all-black Miller High School, joining Leroy Dues, who was hired in 1942.

Bill Loving was the first African-American faculty member at Detroit's Northern High School, his brother, Alvin, was the first African-American faculty member at Detroit's Northwestern High School in 1949. At that time, the student bodies of both High Schools were predominately African-American. Bill died in Detroit on May 22, 1976 at the age of 70. Alvin received a master's degree from Wayne University in 1940, worked for the U.S. Department of Health, Education, and Welfare, and was the first African-American Professor of Education at the University of Michigan. He was given a civic award by President Roosevelt and served on a Governor's Committee for Higher Education. He was a Fulbright scholar, an exchange professor in India, Dean of Students at the University of Nigeria, and President of the National Association for Supervision and Curriculum Development. Western Michigan University awarded him several honors.[23] He lived in Flint in 1982, and died in the last decade of the century.

The "Midnight Express"

Thomas Edward Tolan was born on September 29, 1908 in Salt Lake City, Utah,[24] the same year John W. Lewis was born in Detroit. The Tolan family moved to Detroit in the summer of 1924. Eddie and his brother enrolled at Cass Tech in September 1924. According to one account, "Little Eddie" and his brother got interested in track because of a newspaper sponsored contest that awarded prizes:

Tolan's training began years ago when he was a little boy in a Detroit grammar school. He was a Decathlon athlete. The Decathlon is the annual event staged for schoolboy athletes by the health education department of the public school systems. It is sponsored and financed by the *Free Press*.[25]

During his three years at Cass Tech, Eddie Tolan won 17 of 18 City and State individual outdoor championship races in which he participated. He won the City and the State Championship in the 100 and 220 for three years. "Little Eddie" won the University of Michigan Scholastic crown twice and tied for second the other time. He tied the state record in the 100-yard dash and set the city record in the 220-yard dash. In 1927 Eddie won the 100 and 220-yard dashes at the National Interscholastic Championships in Chicago.

The preliminaries for the national interscholastic track meet were held on Friday, June 4, 1927 at the University of Chicago's Stagg Field. "The rain and heavy track made marks in the dash heats the slowest in the history of the meet." No preliminaries were run in the quarter mile, the half-mile, or the mile.[26] Despite unfavorable track conditions the *Chicago Tribune*, the following day, reported:

Yesterday in the twenty-third annual Chicago University interscholastic track meet at Soldiers' Field before 15,000 spectators, . . . Tolan, a dark boy from Technical High of Detroit, tied the world's pep record of 9.8 in the 100 [yard dash] and won the 220-yard dash in 21.5, a fifth of a second behind the interscholastic record.[27]

In the fall of 1927, Eddie Tolan attended the University of Michigan on a scholarship. In 1928, Tolan made the finals in both the 100-meter and 200-meter dashes at the Olympic trials, but failed to make the U. S. Olympic team. Tolan competed for the University of Michigan in 1929 through 1931. On May 11, 1929 he won the 220-yard dash (22.4) and placed second in the 100-yard dash in a duel meet with the University of Minnesota in Minneapolis. "Tolan allowed his team mate [Godsky] to win [the 100-yard dash] as he took a second looking back over his shoulders."[28]

On May 25, 1929 Tolan won the Big Ten Championships in the 100- and 220-yard dashes, while setting the Big Ten and world record in the 100-yard dash (9.5). A few days later, Tolan took second both the 100-yard and 220-yard dashes at the NCAA Championships. Then in a dramatic breakthrough, on July 5 at the National AAU Senior Championships, Tolan, running into a stiff wind, won the 100 (10.0) and 220-yard (21.9) dashes. His national championships earned him a trip to Europe with the American team. According to European reports, "Tolan came to Europe in the summer of 1929 and made a big impression wherever he ran. He equaled Paddock's 100 meter record (10.4) several times and was beaten only once, in a tight finish, by George Lammers of Germany."[29]

The following year, however, Eddie's claim to the title of world's fastest man was again placed in jeopardy. On April 26, the 100-yard dash that pitted Eddie Tolan against George S. Simpson in what was heralded as the "dash of a century."[30] Eddie placed second in the race. He also was second in the 100 and the 220-yard dashes at the Big Ten Championships. Moreover, he was second in the 220 at the NCAA Championships.

Harry Sargent, an 85-year-old retired hog buyer, first hitchhiked to the Drake Relays in 1928. In 1931 Harry, who was a high school runner in Cedar Rapids, Iowa, remembers staying in the same Des Moines hotel as the University of Michigan track team. Sargent recalls spotting "the dapper sprinter Eddie Tolan in the lobby. He had a suit and a Panama hat. At first, I thought he was a preacher. He was one of the smoothest runners I ever saw. You could have put a glass of water on his head and he'd never spill a drop."[31]

There was no wasted motion when Eddie Tolan ran. As Harry put it, "I always thought that watching people who could really run was about the same thing as watching ballet because they are just beautiful in the way they move their bodies. At Drake, it seems, those bodies run a little faster, jump a little higher or longer and throw heavy objects farther than at other track meets, creating a storehouse of memories for longtime relays fans."[32]

In 1931, Tolan won the 100 and 220 at the Big Ten Championships and placed first in the 220 and second in the 100 at the NCAA Championships. He was on the 1931 AAU All-College and AAU Senior All-American teams for the 220-yard dash.[33]

The 5 foot 7 inch sprinter graduated from the University of Michigan in 1931. In 1931–2, Tolan coached and did graduate work at West Virginia State College to stay in shape for the Olympics.[34] Hard pressed for funds in 1932, he needed the aid of a friend to get to Palo Alto by automobile for the final American Olympic tryouts.

A crowd of 85,000 saw the bespectacled Tolan became the first double Olympic sprint champion in 20 years. However, the outcome was in doubt for some time because some judges thought that Ralph Metcalfe won the 100-meter dash in the Olympic final. It took the official motion pictures to convince them that Tolan was victorious in world record time by the shadowy margin of two inches.[35] Tolan, referred to by the newspapers as the "Midnight Express," then won the 200-meter dash (21.2) and broke the Olympic record set 20 years earlier by Archie Hahn.

The 1932 Olympics was the first international track meet in which electrical timers and cameras were used to determine results in close races. The electrical timer played a role in determining three gold medals, including the one for the 100-meter dash. To the Olympic Officials in Los Angeles, the 100-meter dash appeared to be a dead heat. But, the Kirby camera-timer adopted by the AAU for the meet clearly showed that Tolan was in full stride through the tape, while Metcalfe was poised on the push forward foot at the tape. Thus, Tolan crossed the line with the stride pictured, while Metcalfe needed one more stride to finish.[36]

Ralph H. Metcalfe, who later became a Democratic Congressman from Illinois's First District, refused to believe that he had lost the race even when faced with irrefutable evidence. Metcalfe felt double the doubt when he was told that he had finished third to Tolan in the 200-meter dash, in part, because an official had mismeasured his lane and he had run seven yards more than the other contestants.[37]

Photo-finishes

Three Olympic final finishes played a part in the discussion of records at the AAU convention following the Los Angeles Olympics. The first was the 100-meter final, with Ralph Metcalfe and Eddie Tolan, in which Tolan was adjudged the winner. The 80-meter hurdles final for women, in which Mrs. Evelyn Hall was defeated by Miss Mildred Didrikson; and the 5,000 meter final, with Lauri Lehtinen, of Finland, leading Ralph Hill, of the United States, to the tape.

The pictures for the three photo-finishes were taken with a camera-timer, adopted by the AAU as official. They show 10:38 seconds for the 100-meter race against the announced time of 10:3 seconds; 11:82 seconds for the 80-meter hurdles, against the announced time of 11:7 seconds; and 14 minutes, 29:91 seconds for the 5,000-meter run, against the announced time of 14:30.

The picture showed Metcalfe breasting the tape in a time dead heat with Tolan. But he was not given a tie for the first place, because the rule in force read that a contestant finished when his torso crosses the line. The same was not true in the Miss Didrikson—Mrs. Hall finish. Both were in full stride through the tape, but though both breasted the tape together, Miss Didrikson was declared the winner. In the 5,000-meter run Ralph Hill was clocked in 14:30, the same time as made by Lauri Lehtinen, but the pictures show that he was second, a full foot back.[38]

An All-American Goes Home

Tolan was named AAU All-American in the 100 and 200-meter dashes for 1932.[39] He also was named a New York Athletic Club All-American for he performances at the Olympic games.[40]

When Eddie returned home from Los Angeles, his neighbors roped off a few streets on Detroit's west-side so he could run yet another race for them.[41] After winning gold medals in the 1932 Olympic games Tolan was given proclamations, scrolls and speeches praised him for his sportsmanship and prowess. Michigan even declared "Eddie Tolan Day." In the depths of the depression without a job, Tolan, the hero of the Olympics, was forced to ask the mayor of Detroit for a job during the "Tolan Day" parade celebrating him as the local hero. After some foot shuffling, Eddie was offered and accepted a job as a filing clerk in the Wayne County Office of Deeds. He held that position from 1933 until 1935. But he did not get the job until mid-January 1933, nearly six months after the Olympic games. Eddie walked the streets of several cities before finally getting the filing clerk job. He even made a vaudeville appearance with Negro dancer Bill Robinson, to keep from going hungry.[42] Charles Brennan, secretary of the Michigan AAU, added insult to injury by classifying Tolan as a professional because he used his fame to gain personal profit.[43]

As payback for his clerk's job, Eddie served as director of athletic events at the Detroit Democratic Independence Day picnic in 1933. He also ran an exhibition race on the dirt track for the party faithful, before organizing, acting as chief starter, and handing out prizes for children's races at the picnic. Willis Ward also was at the picnic, but was not scheduled to run against Tolan.[44] It was only one of many community services he performed. On May 1934 Tolan was the starter and field referee at the Southeastern Michigan Regional Meet at Jefferson Field in Ferndale.[45]

While working in the filing clerk post, Tolan attended night law school in hopes of becoming a lawyer. In the winter of 1935 he was given a leave of absence to run professionally in Australia and New Zealand. On March 6, 1935 Tolan won the 75-yard and 100-yard (9.9) dashes at the World's Professional Track and Field Championships in Melbourne, Australia. The next day he won the 120-yard and 220-yard dashes.[46]

When Eddie returned, in the fall of 1935, he returned to a job as a municipal filing clerk. During World War II he was a stock clerk at the Packard Motor Company. In 1945 the hero of the 1932 Olympics was arrested for walking across the street too slowly. He pleaded guilty and was given a suspended sentence. In 1946, he was finally given a contract as a physical education teacher at Goldberg Elementary School, but was not allowed to coach high school track despite his prior coaching experience at West Virginia State University and his unquestioned qualifications. He was an elementary gym teacher until, because of a kidney disorder, he was forced to retire in 1966. Eddie died at age 58 of a heart attack in Detroit on January 30, 1967. Tolan's obituary in the *Detroit Times* said, "He deserved better!" and indeed he did.

The Pride of Miller High School

Leroy W. Dues was on the track team at Northwestern High School in Detroit, 1927–29, but was never considered a star. In 1929 as a senior, he won the State track title in the shot put, and that fall attended Detroit City College, the only college to recruit him. As a freshman at City College, he won the shot put in the Junior Division at the National AAU Championships. The following year, he placed fifth in the shot put at the National NCAA Championships, and set a Junior AAU record for the shot put (48–11). Although Dues had not played football in high school, he made the college varsity football team, as a tackle, in the fall of 1931, and lettered twice in football. In 1932, he was Central Collegiate Indoor Championships in the shot put, placed fourth at the National NCAA Championships, and first at the district U. S. Olympic trials. On July 2 the Chicago selection committee for the US Olympic Committee allocated $105 to Leroy Dues to underwrite his expenses for participating in the final Olympics trials in Palo Alto.[47] He placed fourth at he Olympic trial finals in California, missing the Olympic team by inches.

In 1933 during his senior year at Wayne, Leroy Dues was elected Captain of the track team. He won the shot put both at the Central Collegiate Indoor Championships, and at the first annual Butler Indoor Relays.[48] In April he won the shot put at the Penn Relays. Outdoors, he also placed third in the shot put at National NCAA Championships to become an All-American. Dues was awarded letters in track at Wayne, 1931–33, and earned a BS and a teaching certificate in 1933. However, he was not hired by the Detroit Public Schools until he earned his Master's Degree in 1941. In the meantime, he worked for the Ford Motor Company.

In 1941, Dues became the first African-American track coach and one of the first male, Negro teachers in the Detroit Public Schools. During World War II he became Athletic Director and head of the Physical Education Department at Miller High School. He was an active member of the Detroit Federation of Teachers during the 1940s.[49] In 1945, the Miller Trojans won the Metropolitan High School outdoor track and field championship.

As a coach, Leroy Dues inspired track stars Charles Fonville, Lorenzo Wright, Buddy Coleman, Walter B. Jenkins, Adam Haughton, Cleo Caldwell, and Aaron Z. Gordon. In 1948, friends raised the expense money to allow Dues to travel to London to see his protégéé, Lorenzo Wright, perform in the Olympics.[50] In 1967, Dues earned an E. ED. from Wayne State University. He retired from the Detroit Public Schools in 1975 and died in 1987.

The Kansas City Kid

Before the civil rights movement had an impact, African-Americans who attended high school out of state before participating in track at Michigan universities also experienced difficulties translating a college degree into professional opportunities. Booker Brooks, born in Kansas City, on December 5, 1905, enrolled at the University of Michigan in 1928[51] and earned track letters in 1929, 1930 and 1932. In 1929 Booker Brooks placed third at the Big Ten Championships, and made in the finals in the discus at the NCAA Championships. He won the Big Ten discus championship in 1930 and 1932, and placed second in the shot put in 1930. In 1932 he placed second in the discus at the NCAA Championships and qualified for the final Olympic trials.

When he graduated from the University of Michigan in 1932 with a bachelor's degree, he married Thelma Boone, of Clifton, North Carolina. Unable to find a full-time job, he and his wife both worked part-time and he continued his education. Brooks went on to earn a MA in Social Work from the U of M. Armed with the advanced degree, he was offered a full-time job in Akron, Ohio. His son, Booker T. Brooks, Jr. was born there on July 6, 1937. When Booker Brooks, Jr. grew up he become the first African-American assistant coach at Penn State University.[52]

In 1948 Booker Brooks, Sr. and his wife had returned to Ann Arbor and would spent the rest of their lives in Washtenaw Country. He was hired as a casework supervisor by the Washtenaw County Department of Social Services and was assigned to the Ypsilanti Office. In September 1949 Mr. Brooks was appointed head of the Welfare Department Office in Ypsilanti.[53] Booker Brooks died of kidney failure on November 22, 1968 at the age of 62.[54]

There are other examples of how African-American men were affected by limited opportunities. In February 1939 African-American track star Sterling Paris, a 440-yard dash and 880-yard runner at Michigan Normal College, became the third track letterman to drop out of college because of a lack of money and post-graduate prospects for employment. Paris took a secure civil service position in Toledo, Ohio rather than training for a teaching job he was unlikely to get.[55]

Struggling to Break the Color Line

The opportunities for success for African American track stars of the 1920s and 30s were severely limited by the dominant racial prejudice of the era. Furthermore, the track and field facilities throughout the Detroit Public School system, and most particularly in most of the schools attended by African-American children, were woefully inadequate.[56] This makes the achievements of these men, as role models and trailblazers all the more significant.

In 1930, there was a debate between the Metropolitan League and the Michigan High School Athletic Association over who held the right to determine eligibility and forfeiture. On January 12, 1931 the issue was referred to the State Superintendent of Schools, whose anti-Detroit attitudes seemed likely to result in a ruling against the Metropolitan League. Consequently, the Detroit Metropolitan League schools withdrew from the State Athletic Association, and hence from out-state competition, including the state track meet. The Metro League coaches felt that they had enough competition within their own group and wanted to save money at a time when the depression was causing serious budgetary problems. Detroit used the same eligibility rules as out-state schools, except that in some cases they were more restrictive.[57] Years later, many Detroit trackmen felt that they were the victims of a conspiracy to keep Detroit's black athletes from being state champions. These fears were unfounded, as race played no part in the 1931 decisions.

The mid-1930's were difficult for all poor and working class families, but they were particularly bad for African-American men, who were usually "the last hired and the first fired." When the depression drove the Detroit National Negro Baseball League team, the Detroit Stars, out of business in 1933, track and boxing were the only sports that offered local heroes for Detroit blacks to cheer about. This reality was reflected in the number of African-Americans who turned out for the track team. The first track team at Detroit's Pershing High School in 1931 had six black members out of 18 participants. The 1942 Pershing Doughboy track team had six black members and 19 white members. However, the 1954 Doughboy track team was 90% African-American.[58] Pershing

High's track team reflected enrollment trends in the Detroit Public School over the two decades starting in 1931.

Central High School is the oldest public high school in Detroit. In 1912, there were approximately 1,000 students and 157 faculty members at Central High. The student body was 100% white, as was its faculty. By 1939–40, Central High School was known as the Jewish high school, and more than 1,000 students graduated from Central High School that year. The faculty, smaller than in 1912, was still entirely white. During the 1950s, the mass exit of white families from the central city to the suburbs was at its peak. By 1959, 90% of Central High School's student body was African-American. However, the faculty was 93% white. Five years later, the school's student body was entirely African-American and the faculty was still 55% white. Finally, in 1970, 79% of the faculty was African-American.[59]

In 1922 there were 100 teacher at Detroit's Northern High School, none were African-American. The combined January-June graduating class had 290 students. None of graduates were persons of color. Two years later, the school graduated 402 students. In 1930 there were still about 100 faculty members. Persons of color comprised two percent of the graduating class.

A decade later, the faculty had declined to 89 members. There was still not a single African-American on the faculty. In 1940, 545 individuals graduated from Northern High School. African-Americans comprised 11% of the graduating class. By 1948, Northern High School had undergone a dramatic racial change. That year, 397 individuals graduated from Northern High School, only about 13% of them were Caucasians. There was only one African-American on the Northern High School faculty of 78 members. The African-American faculty member was William Loving, who was a counselor and the assistant track coach.

In 1959, 360 individuals graduated from Northern High School, only 5 were Caucasians. However, the faculty was still predominately Caucasian. Only 23% of the faculty were African-American.[60]

Detroit's Northwestern High School graduated its first class in 1914. A decade later, there were two African-American students in the senior class of nearly 150. By 1929–30, there were still only six African-Americans in each senior class,[61] although super athlete Willis Ward was one of the four black in the "N" Club. There were still no African-American faculty members at the start of the great depression.

By 1948, Northwestern High was clearly experiencing racial transition. When the January, June, and summer graduates were combined, there were about 600 graduating students in the senior class: 284 (47%) of them were persons of color. Still, there were no black teachers. In 1949, 51% of the senior class was Black.

A decade later, the year that long time track coach James H. Russell died, the senior class was 99% African-American, but the school faculty was still 78% Caucasian, and there were only four black males on the teaching faculty.[62]

These school profiles clearly demonstrate that the Detroit Public Schools rarely hired African-American teachers prior to the end of World War II and that class sizes were allowed to grow as the number of Jewish and African-American students increased in a school. The records also show that African-American boys generally joined the track team prior to integrating other school activities. For example, The Northern track team had 17 boys on it in 1922. In 1940 eight of 21 members of the Northern High track team were African-American. The 1948 track team had 75 members, all of whom were African-American. In 1951 98% of the graduating senior classes at Central High were white, but the track team was nearly 40% African-American, and 75% of the cross-country team was African-American. Finally, it should be noted that when the faculties of Detroit high schools were finally integrated, the African-American men that were hired were nearly always former track athletes.

During the 1940's there was modest progress in hiring African-American teachers for Detroit's Public Schools. In 1946 there were 286 African-American teachers in the Detroit Public Schools. They constituted 3.9% of the professional personnel in the system, while African-American students comprised 17.3% of the system's enrollment.[63] In 1946, Horace "Hap" Coleman, track star at Western Michigan Teachers College and the University of Michigan, had a bachelor's degree in health education from Western Michigan Teachers College and lacked one course for a master's degree in administration and supervision in health education from the U of M. He applied to the Detroit Board of Education for a teaching and coaching position. In a clear case of discrimination, he was refused the job because he did not have his master's degree, yet several current coaches lacked a master's degree. Likewise, Joseph Hayden, Jr., an African-American track letterman, left the University of Michigan with the hopes of coaching, but was not hired. He took a job in the City Health Department.

There were only two African-American coaches in the Detroit Public Schools in 1948—Will Robinson and Leroy Dues. Both men taught at Miller High School, an all-black high school.[64]

The color line in Detroit and around the nation did not fall quickly or easily. At the close of the century a majority of Americans had moved to the suburbs, in part to segregate themselves by race and class. As late as 1993 the States of South Carolina and Alabama continued to fly the battle flag of the Confederacy over their state capitals with full knowledge that in doing so they were symbolically defining their racial climate.[65]

5. Running for the Man Who Invented Zebra Stripes

Lloyd **Warner Olds** was born on November 23, 1892 in the family home on Geddes Road in Ypsilanti.[1] Both of his parents were graduates of Michigan State Normal College in Ypsilanti. Lloyd attended Ypsilanti North High School[2] before enrolling at Michigan Normal College in the fall of 1913. He spent nearly all of his life in Ypsilanti, the town of his birth, yet his innovations, policies and practices had a nationwide impact.

Michigan Normal College, where Lloyd Olds spent most of his life, was established in Ypsilanti in 1849. The school held its first Field Day in the spring of 1888. In 1892 Joe Jenkins, an outstanding athlete and track enthusiast, organized the school's first official track team. Michigan Normal College built a wooden gym in 1862, but did not constructed their first permanent gym until 1893. The first intercollegiate track meet on the Ypsilanti campus was held in 1895. The home team won. Cross-country became a varsity sport at Michigan Normal in 1911. No doubt, intercollegiate sports helped to counteract the feminine image often associated with normal schools, where the number of female students frequently outnumbered the male students by at least four to one.

Throughout the nineteenth century interest in physical education was limited. The predominately rural population of the nation felt that farm work was exercise enough for their offspring. However, interest in physical education increased considerably when the legislature for the State of Michigan passed a law in 1911 making the teaching of physical training mandatory in all cities with a population of ten thousand. The law required all normal colleges in the state to give courses to prospective leaders in physical education.[3]

A Love for Running

Lloyd Olds started his career in sports as a middle-distance runner. In 1912 he won the half-mile run (2:11) and placed third the two-mile run at the first annual Adrian College Interscholastic Meet.[4] The following year he repeated as winner of the 880-yard run (2:10.8) at that meet.[5] Lloyd lettered in track and cross-country all four years he was in college and was captain of the Michigan State Normal College track team in 1914 and 1915. He majored in Physical Education and studied with Professor Wilber P. Bowen, a pioneer in the subject. At that time, physical education was restricted to formal classes dealing primarily with apparatus. The problem was accommodating large classes in small spaces. Bowen and Olds saw outdoor, intramural sports as the answer to the problem.

War and Marriage

While in college he met Rose, his future wife, who was also a member of the class of 1916. She was from Lima, Ohio and was physically active. She played field hockey while in college and enjoyed social dancing and swimming.

After graduating from Michigan State Normal, Olds went to work as a physical education teacher in the Grand Rapids public schools. In 1917 he joined the U. S. Navy, and was married on June 30, 1918. Olds won the Meritorious Service Award and emerged from the war as a Commander. When discharged from the Navy in 1919, he took a position in physical education with the Ann Arbor public schools and referred interscholastic and intercollegiate athletic contests, while he attended graduate school at the University of Michigan. He earned a Masters of Science Degree in 1921 and that fall returned to Michigan State Normal to teach and coach. In 1939 he earned a Ph.D. in Public Health from the University of Michigan.

Olds went on to (1) train an influential cadre of physical education teachers and coaches, (2) create a track and field dynasty at Michigan Normal College, (3) implement AAU policy in track and field and (4) establish physical fitness criteria for the American armed services during World War II. In the process, Dr. Olds (a) influenced sport rules and governance, (b) helped shape the conduct of interscholastic and intercollegiate athletics in America, (c) influenced recruiting practices for college sports, and (d) helped to define the areas of conflict between AAU and NCAA policies and practices.

Inventing Zebra Stripes

While attending Michigan Normal College, Lloyd earned extra money by refereeing intramural sports. When the newly hired track coach returned to his alma mater in 1921 he was a well-respected inter-

Lloyd Olds wearing the referee's shirt he devised in 1920–1 and persuaded the Wilson Sporting Goods Co. to manufacture and sell. *(Photo Eastern Michigan U Archives)*

scholastic and intercollegiate athletic official. In 1920 Olds discovered that the all-white or all-black attire commonly worn by referees frequently led them to be mistaken for a player. These mistakes caused interruptions in play that often changed the course of the game, whether it was football, basketball or field hockey. He came to believe that a black and white striped shirt would better identify referees and keep them independent of the action. As Olds recalled,

Back around 1920 I was refereeing the Michigan Agricultural College-Arizona football game at East Lansing. The Arizona players were all dressed in white, something we never saw in Michigan due to the usual bad fall weather. I was dressed in white too, as was common for referees in those days. It was a close, tough game and I was keeping my eye on the backs to prevent rough play. We were on the Michigan State three-yard line when the Arizona quarterback accidentally put the ball in my tummy. Of course I dropped it and, thank goodness, he recovered same.

The incident was the catalyst for evolving the striped shirt. I got my idea of the striped shirt from an English soccer team that played an exhibition game in October of 1920 on the playing fields in Detroit. The first time I used the vertically-striped shirt was in Detroit at the 1921 Michigan State High School Basketball Championships, which I worked for twelve consecutive years. Predictably, I was greeted with catcalls. As I continued to wear the long-sleeved wool shirt emblazoned with broad black and white strips people began to call it a "zebra shirt."[6]

He designed the striped shirt himself and had a seamstress sew one for him. He found that the innovation worked well and asked the Wilson Sporting Goods Company to mass-produce the shirts. They agreed to do so, and the idea caught on. It was ultimately incorporated into official rules as the desired attire for referees. The distinctive uniform both altered and clarified the role of the referee.

On one occasion the striped shirt nearly caused him trouble. Lloyd was asked to officiate a football game at the Michigan penitentiary in Jackson. When he walked onto the field with his black and upright stripes, the convicts were wearing their prison outfits with horizontal stripes of the same colors. The visiting professional team demanded assurance Olds was not a prison inmate.[7]

In 1921 when Lloyd Olds was hired by Michigan Normal College to teach health, manage the intramural program, and coach the track team, there were only four members in the Department of Physical Education. At that time, his chief duty was to expand the intramural program. He developed a system for doing that by using 30 to 40 students as managers. As a result, the Michigan Normal intramural program grew rapidly. By 1937–8 it involved 3,503 participants.

Establishing a Track Dynasty

Olds' great love was track and field. Soon after he became track coach, Michigan Normal emerged as a strong center for the sport. In 1922 in one of his first decisions, Lloyd Olds joined with Knute Rockne and Ralph Young to make Michigan Normal a charter member of the Central Collegiate Conference. He also organized the first state interscholastic cross-country tournament in Michigan. The tournament was held at Michigan Normal in the fall of 1922. It staked-out a niche for Michigan Normal as the institution for higher education in Michigan where distance runners were welcome. Michigan Normal would host the state high school cross-country meet for the next fifty years. While Michigan State College would feature distance and cross-country greats Clark Chamberlain and Thomas C. Ottey in the late 1920s and early 1930s, Michigan Normal College could claim John T. Smith, Roger Arnett, Billy Zepp, Harry Werbin, and Abe Rosenkrantz.

Over the 21 years from 1921 to 1942 his track teams won 85% of their meets. From 1923 to 1931 his teams were 63–5 for a .926 winning percentage. At one point Lloyd's track team won 47 meets in a row. He had 14 undefeated seasons and won at least 20 consecutive meets four times. Under his command, Michigan Normal became known as the "Little Giants of the West." Olds served as an associate Olympic track coach in 1932 and as coach and manager of the American team that toured Scandinavia and northern Europe in 1935. He also managed the 35 person track and field team, which included Al Tolmich, for the 1937 Pan-American Games in Dallas.[8]

Coach Lloyd Olds made track "one of the most important of the major sports" at the college.[9] A new track venue at Michigan State Normal College was officially dedicated on Saturday April 25, 1925 with a meet between "Coach Lloyd W. Olds' thinclads and Hillsdale's squad."[10] The new track helped Coach Olds recruit an even stronger team.

A Good Gamble for a Small College

The first great track star at Michigan Normal was Bernard W. Otto. Otto was born in Perrington, Michigan on July 31, 1902. He entered Michigan Normal College in 1921. After dropping out of school, Otto returned to college in 1924–27. During those years, the team often wore a "Y" on its uniform to represent its unofficial name, Ypsilanti Normal. Although the team had no official nickname, the newspapers often referred to the athletes as the "Normality's." By his senior year in college, it was reported that "Otto is rated the best dash man ever to perform at the Normal. He has won many firsts in the 100 and 220-yard dashes during his career and has also run on the relay teams and the crack distance medley quartet."[11] During his enrollment at Michigan Normal, Otto set the State AAU record for the indoor, standing long-jump, and was captain of the track team in 1927. After leaving college for a second time in 1927, Otto spent some time in Chicago and ran for the Chicago Athletic Association, but was plagued by chronic gambling: he would bet on anything and was often in debt.[12] He finally graduated from Michigan Normal in 1931.

Bernard Otto was athletic director in the High School at St. Johns, Michigan for a time during the early years of the great depression, and coached the girl's track team at Elmore, Ohio in the mid-1930s. He

Bernard W. Otto, Michigan Normal sprinter 1924–7, set the state AAU record for the standing long-jump (10′ 3⅜″) on February 27, 1926. *(Photo Eastern Michigan U Archives)*

retired from coaching and teaching in 1940 when other jobs became more plentiful. He established Otto's Variety Store in Toledo, Ohio, which he and his son, Lloyd, operated for more than thirty years. In 1984 he was placed in the Eastern Michigan University Athletic Hall of Fame.

Winning the Handicap Race

Another of the early track stars developed by Lloyd Olds was Roger Paul Arnett, who was born May 1, 1908 in Owosso, Michigan. Roger was a farm boy with great ambition and little cultural heritage. In the fall of 1927 Roger attended Northwestern University for one semester. He struggled to fit in, felt homesick, ran out of money, and returned home. By the fall of 1928 he had accumulated enough money to enroll at Michigan Normal in Ypsilanti. Olds and his assistant, George Marshall, discovered Arnett that fall in a gym class. They asked him to try out for the track team. Despite having little time to train because he was working his way through college, he complied with the request. Before long, this very persistent young man was the team's best distance runner. In the spring of 1929 he won a Michigan AAU handicap two-mile race. That fall, when the Men's Club adopted the nickname the "Hurons" for Michigan Normal sports teams, he helped Normal win the state cross-country championship.

Arnett did not have an ideal running style—he ran flat-footed—but he had a big lung capacity and great determination. In 1930 Roger placed second in the two-mile run at the Drake Relays and at the State Intercollegiate Meet. He was considered by many to be a serious prospect for the 1932 Olympic Games when, in March 1931 while traveling to a track meet in Indiana, an automobile accident left him a paraplegic.

Inspired by the accomplishments of President Franklin Roosevelt, Roger returned to Michigan Normal College in 1934, where he earned his BA degree and teaching certificate. For a time, he worked as a clerk in the State of Michigan Welfare Department. Later, he became a minister to the handicapped of the Ann Arbor District of the Methodist Church and became a research associate at the University of Michigan Research Center at Willow Run Airport. In 1949 he was appointed to the President's Committee on Employment of the Physically Handicapped. He served in that position for two years. Roger was awarded an honorary master's degree by Eastern Michigan University in 1951, and earned a master's degree in special education from Wayne State University in 1957.

Roger Arnett passed away at the age of 65 on August 24, 1973. He was the subject of a 1967 book titled *Handicap Race: The Inspiring Story of Roger Arnett*. Roger, who was a hero and an inspiration to those who knew him, attributed much of his success to his short track career under the guidance of Coach Olds.[13]

Roger Paul Arnett was the State handicap two-mile Champion and a Drake Relays runner-up before becoming a paraplegic as a result of a 1931 auto accident. *(Photo Eastern Michigan U Archives)*

A Credit to His Race

Perhaps Lloyd Olds' greatest track luminary was Charles Eugene Beatty from Detroit's Northeastern High School Class of 1928. Beatty was a spectacular high school runner, who competed with and against a cadre of Detroit track stars that included Eddie Tolan, John W. Lewis, Bill and Al Loving, Clark Haskins, and Leroy Dues.

Beatty was born in Asheville, North Carolina on April 24, 1909. He was the fourteenth child of Monroe and Nellie Orr Beatty. His mother died when he was seven years old. After his father died when he was eleven, Charles moved to Detroit to live with sister, where he enrolled in seventh grade at Miller Intermediate School. Short in stature, but a fine student and a fast runner, at Miller Intermediate he was called Eugene to keep his identity separate from the many boys named Charles.

On March 19, 1927, as a high school junior, Beatty won the 60-yard low-hurdles (7.3) and tied for first in the running broad jump (20–6½) at the Third Annual Indoor Michigan Interscholastic Meet in Ann Arbor. A week later he won the 880-yard run (2:01.7) and placed second to Eddie Tolan in the 50-yard dash at the National Indoor Interscholastic Meet held at Northwestern University. In late May of 1927 he was a member of state champion 880-yard relay team which set a new national interscholastic record at the Michigan Class A High School State Championships. Finally, on June 3–4, 1927 Eugene won his semi-final heat in the100-yard dash, and won the finals in the 220-yard low-hurdles at the National Interscholastic Outdoor Championships being held in Chicago. The *Chicago Tribune* reported:

> Yesterday in the twenty-third annual Chicago University interscholastic track meet at Soldiers' Field before 15,000 spectators, . . . tiny Eugene Beatty, a seventeen year old Negro hurdler from Detroit, who had already won the high hurdles, stepped to world time in the lows with a mark of 24.2 seconds, three-fifths of a second faster than any high school athlete had ever cleared the sticks in an official meet.[14]

As a high school senior, he won the 120-yard high-hurdles (16.5), the 220-yard low-hurdles (25.9), the broad jump (21–3), and the 880-yard relay (1:36.1) at the Michigan State High School Class A Championships in East Lansing. Then he placed second in the 220-yard low hurdles (26.0) and fourth in the 880-yard relay at the National Interscholastic Outdoor Championships in Chicago. The *Detroit Times* declared "Eugene Beatty of Detroit Northeastern is one of the outstanding prep athletes in the nation."[15]

After graduating from high school, Beatty accepted a scholarship at Northwestern University and got a job working in the Ford Motor Co. foundry to make the additional money needed for school. He expected to start at Northwestern in January, but the job ran out just after the beginning of the fall term. When he contacted Northwestern, he was told that freshman orientation was over and must wait until the second semester to start school. On the advice of Lloyd Olds, Michigan Normal gave Eugene Beatty a scholarship and allowed him to enroll. When Beatty enrolled at Michigan Normal, he was one of only seven African-American, male students attending the school.[16]

Gene Beatty, 400 m hurdles (Detroit NE HS); J. McKinley, pole vault; Fred Glickert, high jump (Toledo, OH); Rha Arnold, 800 m run (Detroit); Billy Zepp, 10-K run, (MA.); Kenneth "Red" Simmons, 400 m hurdles (Redford HS). *(Photo Eastern Michigan U Archives)*

In 1931 Beatty won the 400-meter intermediate-hurdles at the Penn Relays. He was named to the 1931 AAU National All-College All-American Track Team for the 440-yard intermediate-hurdles.[17]

In February 1932, the Michigan Normal team attended the Millrose Games in New York City. When they attempted to check into a hotel in Manhattan, near Madison Square Garden, Gene was refused a room. Coach Olds cancelled their reservations and took the entire team to the YMCA, where all could stay.[18] In 1932 Beatty again won the 400-meter hurdles at the Penn Relays and was named All-American in the 440-yard hurdles for the second time.[19]

On May 26, 1932 Ralph H. Young, Director of Athletics at Michigan State College of Agriculture and Applied Science wrote to Lloyd W. Olds:

You have the finest track team ever gotten together in the State of Michigan and I certainly want to congratulate you and your team upon their fine performance last weekend. All of your boys performed to perfection last Saturday.

You made the highest score that has ever been made in the history of the State [Inter-collegiate] meet and this surely is a great feat in view of the fact of the caliber of the athletes at the other colleges.

We [are traveling by automobile and] will stay at the Windermere West Hotel [in Chicago] Thursday night [enroute to the Central Intercollegiate Meet in Milwaukee]. I hope that you can join us in Chicago.[20]

In 1932 Beatty held the world record in the 220-yard low hurdles and the 880-yard dash, and narrowly missed making the U. S. Olympic team. On July 2, 1932 the NCAA allocated $115 to Gene Beatty to underwrite his expenses for participating in the final Olympics trials.[21] At the final Olympic trials in Palo Alto Beatty was considered a favorite to win the 400-meter high-hurdles.[22] But Beatty did not place in the final trials because in the semi-finals he fell over the last hurdle and was disqualified because he was helped to his feet by a spectator.[23] Lloyd Olds was an assistant track coach for the Olympic team in 1932.

In 1933, his senior year at Michigan Normal, Eugene Beatty was named All-American in the 440-yard hurdles for the third time.[24] When Beatty won the Penn Relays 440-yard hurdles for the third straight year, the *Detroit News* wrote:

It will be a long time before Eugene Beatty, stocky Negro hurdler ace from Michigan Normal forgets the scare he got in defending his 440-yard high-hurdles championship.

Taking the lead on the backstretch Beatty, running easily, steadily drew away from the pack. Seventy-five yards from home he glanced back and what he saw made him grin confidently. Nobody was within yards of him.

The next thing he knew he was 15 yards from home and a guy was breathing down his back.

The guy was unknown R. B. Jackson of Lehigh, and if the race had been 441 instead of 440 those students who passed the hat in Ypsilanti to send Beatty to the races would have worked in vain.

This Jackson, if he isn't a senior, is a man to watch. If he ever gets any form (he takes the hurdles now like a burglar hopping a fence) he'll be tough to beat.[25]

The college yearbook had a more positive slant:

During the season, Gene Beatty, nationally known hurdler, went east where he successfully defended his Penn Relay's 400-meter hurdle crown for the third time, and in doing so went down in the books as one of the few individuals who has gained three successive Penn titles.[26]

After college graduation in 1934, Beatty worked at Ford Motor Co. for a year, then landed a job as a teacher at Harriet School in Ypsilanti. In 1940, he became the first full-time African-American principal in the history of State of Michigan. C. E. Beatty was the principal of the Ypsilanti Public Schools' Harriet Elementary School [now Perry Child

Development Center] from 1940 to 1967. From 1967 to 1970, he was the principal of Central Elementary.[27] From 1970 to 1974, he was the principal of the Chapelle Elementary School. He retired in 1974, after 39 years in the Ypsilanti school district. Beatty was inducted into the Michigan Education Hall of Fame in 1985. Beatty was placed in the Eastern Michigan University Hall of Fame in 1976. A bronze statue mounted on a 4-foot marble base was sculpted by an Eastern Michigan University art professor and placed at the Perry Child Development Center in 1989.

When Lloyd Olds died in 1982, Beatty, President of the Ypsilanti Board of Education and Chairman of the Ypsilanti Public Housing Commission recalled,

> Dr. Olds was a super guy, a teacher par excellence who went beyond being just a coach. He treated all of 'his boys just like his sons. Olds would feed and cloth his students," said Beatty, and was instrumental in locating jobs for them after graduation. He even extended approval of my future wife. Thank God for L.W.[28]

"Red" Changes the Course of Track and Field

Gene Beatty's friend and teammate, Kenneth Gordon "Red" Simmons was born in Cleveland, Ohio on January 5, 1909. Ken's grandparents were textile workers in Manchester, England. When Ken's father, Herbert Simmons, was eleven years old, Ken's grandfather, sent Herbert to live with relatives in Canada so he would not have to work in the textile factories of Northwest England. Once in Canada, Ken's father never saw his parents again and had virtually no further contact with them the rest of his life.

Herbert did not like studying or living with his relatives, so when he was 15 he ran off to become a lumberjack. For several years he was on the move, until he met and married Maggie Travis, a hard-working girl who had grown-up on Manitoulin Island in Ontario. Herbert and Maggie moved to Cleveland in 1906, where "Red's" older brother was born in 1908 and where "Red" started his life in 1910. In 1912 the Simmons family moved to Detroit and settled in Redford.

By his senior year in high school in 1927–8, "Red" surfaced as a star football player at Redford High School, but also played basketball and ran track. In high school track he competed and held his own against the Tolan brothers, the Loving brothers, John W. Lewis and Eugene Beatty. On May 27, 1928 "Red" took second in both the 120-yard high and the 220-yard low-hurdles at the Michigan Class A High School

Championships in East Lansing. At that time he was offered a job—there were no scholarships—to attend and run at the University of Michigan. However, "Red" lacked the entrance requirements for the University of Michigan, so he took additional high school classes in 1928–29. When "Red" was ready to attend college, the depression was on and the Michigan Coach withdrew his offer of a job because campus jobs were drying up.

"Red's" friend, Earl Lange, Jr., planned to attend Albion College, and "Red" wanted to attend college too but had no money. Earl Lange, Sr., a District Principal in the Detroit Public Schools, offered to loan "Red" the $18.10 needed for the first semester's tuition at Michigan Normal School. "Red" accepted the offer, and hitch hiked back and forth to Ypsilanti ever day. He had no money for books, so he tried to use the books of other students when they would allow him to do so. The arrangement was not very satisfactory, and by the end of the semester "Red" found himself on probation. On field day, however, "Red" out performed most of the varsity track team, and Coach Olds convinced the Dean that "Red" deserved another chance. They arranged for him to get a campus job that could cover tuition, meals, and a place to stay. "Red" also found a girl friend. She shared her books and tutored him. Simmons became a four-year letter winner in track at Michigan Normal.[29]

On July 4, 1930 "Red" placed third in the 120-yard high-hurdles at the Michigan AAU Outdoor Championships held on Belle Isle in Detroit. He had a natural ability to adjust his steps in the hurdles. In 1931 he won the mile-relay at the Michigan State Intercollegiate Indoor Relay Carnival in East Lansing and placed second in the mile relay, and won the 50-yard low-hurdles at the Central Collegiate Conference indoor meet in South Bend. On April 25 Ken won a special mile-relay contest (3:26.8) at the Penn Relays, and on May 16 he won the mile-relay at the Michigan Intercollegiate Outdoor Championships in East Lansing. Frequently "Red's" greatest competition came from his own teammate, Eugene Beatty.

On June 24, 1932 "Red" qualified for the semi-finals in the 400-meter hurdles, at the Olympic quarterfinals in Ann Arbor. He was eliminated in the 400-meter hurdles in the semi-finals of the U. S. Olympic trials in Evanston on July 2. On February 4, 1933 he placed second in the 1,600-meter college relay at the Millrose Games at Madison Square Garden. Kenneth Gordon Simmons graduated from Normal College in the class of 1933, and started applying the teachings of Lloyd Olds to his own life.

After spending twenty-five years on the Detroit Police Department, where he pioneered in the use of weight training in track and field while running for its track team for eight years, "Red" retired from the police force. In 1959 he began teaching weight training at the University of Michigan, and in 1960 started the first Ann Arbor women's track club—"the Michigammes". The Michigammes evolved into the University of Michigan NCAA Division I women's track team in 1977, and "Red" was the first coach of this team. His use of weight training with the University of Michigan women's track team resulted in profound improvements in athletes such as Francie Kraker (Goodrich). Today, "Red" Simmons is considered the founding father of Women's track at the U of M.

When "Red" retired for a second time he continued to be active. At the age of 80 he won five gold medals in the senior Olympics (high jump, long jump, shot put, javelin, discus), and at the age of 91 was still officiating at intercollegiate track meets.[30]

The Runner from Big Stone Gap

Billy Zepp was the first National AAU champion distance-runner to attend Michigan Normal College. William C. Zepp was born in Big Stone Gap, West Virginia on April 8, 1907. He was one of five children. His father, M. C. Zepp, was a tanner, and moved around a good deal during Billy's youth. The Zepp family lived on Long Island at Glen Cove, New York, in North Carolina and in St. Louis, before moving to Worcester, Massachusetts when Billy was twelve or thirteen years old.

As a child, Billy enjoyed running. To mark his growth, each year on his birthday, his mother had him run as fast as he could from one tree to another in their yard in West Virginia. Although the run was never timed, except by his mother counting out loud—at the age of 91—Billy recalled how little progress he felt some years in his effort to improve his time. When he reached high school, Bill still enjoyed running, but had little success in the sport. In his junior year in high school he finished twelfth in the half-mile run at field day and was sixth in the mile run as a senior.

In addition to running, Billy was a good student and enjoyed reading, but as the son of a factory worker, had no hope of attending college. He started working at the Graton & Knight Company tannery during the summers while in high school and became a production clerk at their when he graduated from South High School in Worcester. He also worked at a steel mill or two when work was slack at the tannery.

National Champion distance runner, Billy Zepp, and Olympian Tommy Ottey in one of their many hotly contested two-mile run matches. *(Photo courtesy of Billy Zepp)*

Lacking exercise during working hours (9 hours at work five days a week and four hours on Saturday), Billy began running early in the morning before work. His father woke him up at 5:30 am and Billy ran four miles before walking four miles to work, which started at 7 am. During this period the young clerk ran for sheer joy and his health. Recollections of his poor performance in high school kept him out of competitive running.

Zepp ran his first competitive road race at the [Worcester] Park Avenue Church meet on July 4, 1927. He finished second in the six-mile run, but still lacked confidence in his ability to run competitively. Nevertheless he continued to run. He did not run another race until he entered the Boston Marathon on April 19, 1929 on a dare from fellow tannery workers. Much to his amazement, he finished 21st out of 185 entries and ran the entire distance without stopping or walking.

Success in the Boston Marathon gave Billy the confidence to start running on the Boston Athletic Association distance running circuit.

By August 1929, Billy was winning races. On August 24, at the Pere Marquette Race in Boston, William McVicar offered him an opportunity to compete for the Dorchester Athletic Association track team. This was a big break because it guaranteed Zepp access, entrance fees, and travel expenses to the major cross-country races in America.

On September 22, 1929, in his first race for the Dorchester Club, Billy was fourth in the Northeastern AAU Junior and Senior six-mile Championship held in Quincy, Massachusetts. After this race, Billy's feet were bleeding. When the team doctor examined his feet it was discovered that Billy had been running in shoes that were a size too small. His problems with sore and bleeding feet were relieved and his running improved when he was given a pair of size nine shoes to replace the size eight's in which he had been running.

On September 29, 1929 Zepp won the Northeastern AAU Junior 10-mile run (58:44.6) held in Paxton, MA. He completed the year by winning the New England AAU Senior 10-mile road race in Lynn, Massachusetts shortly after the stock market crash that launched the great depression.[31]

The following year Billy Zepp won the AAU Junior and Senior New England Ten-mile Running Championships, and on November 29, 1930 he won the National AAU Senior Six-mile Cross-country Championships at Jersey City, New Jersey. Lloyd Olds attended the National AAU cross-country championships in New Jersey and asked William McVicar if Zepp had ever attended college. When he learned that not only had Billy never attended college, but that he was a high school graduate with good grades Olds approached Zepp with an offer to attend Michigan Normal College. In those days athletic scholarships did not exist at most schools, but tuition at Michigan Normal was less than $20 per term, and the coach had a few jobs that could be dispensed among athletes. With food and lodging at an all time low because of the depression, these jobs were almost as good as a scholarship.

Billy Zepp had no idea that his running skills might permit him to go to college. He jumped at the opportunity to attend Michigan Normal. He did, of course, have to apply for admission and raise enough money for tuition and books. In the meantime, he continued to run and earn money for his tuition. Fortunately, he still had a job. On November 22, 1930 Billy Zepp won the National AAU cross-country championship held at Franklin Park, Boston, and was named to the AAU All-American track team. On May 30, 1931, still running for the Dorchester Club, Zepp won the 10-mile race at the National AAU ten-mile race championship in Norwich, Connecticut.[32] Thus, Zepp was an All-American before attending Michigan Normal.

In the fall of 1931, Zepp entered college. It had been seven years since he attended high school, and he had to relearn study habits. His campus job was driving the bus to athletic contests, and this broke into his study time. Furthermore, in the spring the track meets were scheduled during exam week, so he had to take exams at special times. While he found his first year in college difficult, it changed the course of his life. It furthered his athletic career, allowed him to become a college graduate and a teacher, thereby affecting his social status and economic well being. More importantly, it allowed him to meet his wife and contributed to his son's desire to go to college.

Freshmen were ineligible to compete for the college in those days, and this interfered with preparation for the Olympic trials. Nevertheless, Zepp ran the two-mile at the National AAU meet and was again named an All-American. On June 24–25, 1932 Zepp out ran Clark Chamberlain, but was second to Tom Ottey of Michigan State College in the 10-K run at the district Olympic trials in Ann Arbor. But, on the following day, evened the score by winning the 5-K run (15:21.5) and qualifying for the Olympic trial semi-finals.[33] However, despite his celebrated accomplishments, Billy failed to make the Olympic team in 1932. Short of funds and discouraged by reports that competitors were using "pep" pills, he did not make the trip to Olympic finals in Palo Alto.[34]

Zepp was a self-taught runner, and neither Coach McVicar nor Lloyd Olds knew enough about distance running to suggest significant improvements in his running. He was never taught to shorten his stride, or to pace himself. He later said, "I just got out in front and ran." Only in cross-country did he sometimes alter his strategy. On an unfamiliar cross-country course he often found it advantageous to follow the local star to avoid the soft ground and wet spots, before stepping out in front to win. Zepp also learned on his own that when a distance runner tried to draft on him, that he could throw them off stride by altering his step without notice, to throw them off-stride.

Zepp had no academic problems in college, but learned that desire was critical to success. He often looked back on his marathon experience as proof that he could prevail in the face of difficulty. He remembered the marathon as a living "hell." His feet were swollen and bleeding, and he was tired almost beyond belief, yet he finished the race.[35]

MILLROSE TRACK TEAM—1932

1. Harry Werbin. 2. Robert MacInnes. 3. Peter Taylor. 4. James McDade. 5. Max Lamp. 6. Albert Michelsen. 7. Abraham Rosenkrantz. 8. William Ruckel. 9. Harry C. Ledingham. 10. John Winkler. 11. Vincent Rutherford. 12. Raymond Rutherford. 13. Earl D. Foster. 14. William Carr. 15. Fred W. Ward, Jr.. 16. David Innes. 17. Nathan Kramer. 18. Milton A. Lifschitz. 19. Charles Sherman. 20. Ira B. Singer. 21. Sol H. Furth. 22. Victor J. Biesiakiewicz. 23. Fred Titzel. Harry Werbin was a cross-country All-American in 1928 and 1930. Ira Singer was AAU indoor 60-yard dash champion in 1931, and Fred Titzel was an All-American in cross-country in 1933 and 1934. Victor Biesiakiewicz won the National AAU Indoor 300-yard dash title in 1930. (*Photo Millrose Athletic Association Archives*)

On February 8, 1934 Billy Zepp was placed on the National Collegiate Track honor roll [given All-American status.] On May 20, 1933
Billy Zepp won the two-mile run at the Michigan State Intercollegiate,
and the following year at the Michigan Intercollegiate in East Lansing
in May 1934, Ottey attempted to "pace" or "draft" Zepp, but Billy
altered his step and forced Ottey off stride enough to defeat him. On
December 28, 1934 Zepp ran the two-mile in the Sugar Bowl Invitational, and on February 2, 1935 he ran in the Millrose Games. To prepare for the Millrose Games Billy trained on a gym floor that involved
10-laps to the mile. He ran with Harry Werbin, a sophomore from New
York City, who could keep pace with Zepp for a mile, but little more.[36]
However, Billy contracted a cold enroute to New York City and was
unable to cope with the fast pace set by the star runners entered in the
meet, which included Joe McCluskey, Don Lash, and Ray Sears. He finished fifth in the Millrose Games two-mile run.[37] The race was run on
the new board track built for Madison Square Garden in 1934 to attract
the IC4A indoor meet from a New York Armory to Madison Square
Garden.[38]

Billy rebounded from his poor showing in the Millrose Games by
setting a new Yost Fieldhouse record in the two-mile run at the Second
Annual Michigan AAU Relays on February 9, 1935.

One of the most spectacular of the meet [performances] was the two-mile race
staged by the flying Bill Zepp, Normal distance star. He gained 'sweet' revenge
victory over his archrival, Tom Ottey of Michigan State, in a record-breaking
time. Zepp, who ran the fastest two mile outdoors any place in the world at last
summer's [1934 AAU] state meet, finished with a stirring sprint nearly 55 yards
ahead of Ottey in the remarkable time of 9:21.8 for a 220-yard track. Zepp ran
a smart race from the start to finish, allowing Ottey to set the pace for the first
mile and three-quarters. He then overhauled the Spartan ace with a long, swift
stride, continued to pull away from his foe in the next quarter mile and broke
the tape going away from Ottey. The State star finished only 30 yards ahead of
Harry Werbin, Normal sophomore speedster, who also ran a brilliant race.[39]

After running on the winning two-mile relay team at the Michigan
State Intercollegiate indoor Relay Carnival in East Lansing on February
17, 1935, Zepp faced Tom Ottey again in a triangular meet with the
University of Michigan and Michigan State College at Yost Fieldhouse
in Ann Arbor on February 22. The Huron's lanky distance ace again ran
his archrival into the ground. Zepp dogged Ottey's steps for the first
mile. Then, finding the pace too slow, Zepp took the lead and won
going away. In the process, he lowered the Yost Fieldhouse record by

eight-tenths of a second.[40] The anticipated match between Butler University Olympian Ray Sears and Zepp on Saturday February 23 did not transpire because the Butler distance-runner was ill.[41] On March 9 Zepp completed his sweep of Tom Ottey for the 1935 indoor season by beating the Michigan State runner by 15 yards in the two-mile run at the Central Collegiate Conference indoor championships in the Notre Dame Field house.[42] On June 22 Zepp ran in the NCAA outdoor championships in Berkeley, California against Ottey. Ottey placed second and Zepp third.[43]

After he graduated from college in early May 1936, Zepp was faced with accumulated debt for books and meals, so he was forced to work between college graduation and the Olympic trials held six weeks later. His job interfered with his training, and he was not at his peak when he ran in the Olympic semi-final trials at Marquette University. While his college teammate Abe Rosenkrantz qualified for the Olympic final trials at Randall's Island, Billy finished fifth in the 5-K run despite a relatively slow race.[44] His arch-rival Tom Ottey won the 5-K run at the Olympic semi-finals at Harvard in a time four seconds faster than that run by the winner in Milwaukee.[45] Moreover, Billy Zepp's time at Milwaukee was significantly slower than his time for the same event four years earlier.

William Zepp could not find a teaching job in 1936. Nevertheless, on July 11, 1937 Zepp married Eleanor Eisenmann, Michigan Normal Class of 1938. She and Billy met in college. Eleanor, a farmer's daughter, was 10 years younger, and studying to be an elementary school teacher. After farming for his father-in-law, he took a job as an assistant coach at Central Normal College in Mount Pleasant. When hard times ended this job, Zepp took a job with the Boy's Club in downtown Detroit, where, among other things, he taught swimming. Billy did not like his boss at the Boy's Club, and left it for work in a defense factory in 1940, at the outset of World War II. He worked the midnight shift for seven days, then was given a day off. In 1944 he was hired as a teacher at Hazel Park High School. His wife also taught at Hazel Park. William Zepp taught PE, English and history, and at one time or another coached nearly every sport. He taught swimming in the summers. Zepp retired from teaching in 1972.

The Zepp family lived near a park where baseball was frequently played. Very early on Bill, Jr. showed an aptitude for playing baseball. He could hit a street light pole with a snowball and could make the baseball go where he wanted it to go. Billy Zepp also encouraged his son, and played catch with him nearly every night when he came home from teaching and coaching. Bill Zepp, Jr. became such a success in baseball that he was offered an athletic scholarship at the University of Michigan. After college, Bill, Jr. played in the minor leagues in 1968, and pitched in the Major Leagues for Minneapolis and Detroit in 1969–71. His arm went bad in 1971, and he was in marketing for the Daimler-Chrysler Corporation at the end of the century.[46]

Doctor of the Long Distance Run

On June 3, 1928 Harry Werbin placed third in the three-mile run at the New York Metropolitan Junior Track Championships at Governor's Island, and that fall on October 13, running for the Millrose Athletic Association, Harry placed fourth in the six mile run at the National AAU Junior Outdoor Championships on Travers' Island. He was also on the winning national senior AAU cross-country team in 1928 and 1930. A New Yorker from a poor Jewish family, Harry Werbin had a burning desire to become a doctor, but little hope of attending college, but he did have an ability to run long distances fast enough to make a mark for himself in a city full of poor Jews.

All ready out of high school and working, Harry ran for the Millrose Athletic Association. It gave him hope. On August 23, 1930 Harry placed second to future Olympian Joe McCluskey in the two-mile steeplechase at the National AAU Senior outdoor championships at the University of Pittsburgh. Werbin was now an All-American. On November 8, 1930 Harry placed sixth, behind Andrew Lewis of the Detroit YMCA, in the Junior AAU Cross-country in Cincinnati. Three weeks later, on November 29–30, Harry placed sixteenth in cross-country (30:52) at the National AAU Senior Six-mile Cross-country Championships, Lincoln Park, Jersey City, New Jersey.[47] Clearly, Harry Werbin was developing into a world class runner.

At the 1931 National Senior AAU Cross-country Championships in Ypsilanti, Harry learned that out of state tuition at Michigan Normal was only $35 per semester and that, despite the depression, Lloyd Olds had jobs for members of the track team. He did not have the initial tuition payment or the courage to go to Michigan alone. Finally, after placing third in the 3,000-meter steeplechase at the National AAU Senior Championships at Soldier Field in Chicago on June 29, 1933 Harry and his friend Abe Rosenkrantz decided to attend Michigan Normal that fall.

A rare picture of the indoor training facilities at Michigan Normal College circa 1938. *(Photo Eastern Michigan U Archives)*

On June 29, 1934 Harry Werbin placed second in the 3-K run at the National AAU Junior Outdoor Championships, Marquette University Stadium. The next day he placed fourth in the 3-K steeplechase in the AAU Senior Championships. Merrill Hershey, of Michigan Normal placed fourth in the 400-meter run, while he and Abe Rosenkrantz placed fourth in the 1,600-meter relay at the AAU Senior Championships in 1934.[48] On January 25, 1935 Harry Werbin, Charles Eberhard, and Ray Lowry each placed well at the AAU Junior Championships in Buffalo. In February of that year Michigan Normal demonstrated the power of their track team, when Harry Werbin won the 3,000-meter steeplechase, Charles Eberhard won 65-meter hurdles, Ray Lowry tied for first in the pole vault at the Senior AAU Indoor at Madison Square Garden. Moreover, Ray Lowry, from Scott High School in Toledo, tied for first in the pole vault (13–7) on February 22, 1936 at the National AAU Senior Indoor Championships at Madison Square Garden.[49]

In 1935 Harry and his friend Abe Rosenkrantz made the United State track team for the Maccabi Games in Tel Aviv. While Werbin had his moments of triumph at Michigan Normal, his best running days were already behind him when he arrived at Ypsilanti to attend college. He was an understudy to Billy Zepp and Abe Rosenkrantz most of his time at Michigan Normal College. In 1937 Harry won races when Abe was running elsewhere or was shifted to races that would benefit the team. Harry won the two-mile run against Michigan Central, Kalamazoo College, and Western Teachers College.[50] He placed second in the two-mile against Butler and at the Michigan Intercollegiate outdoor.[51]

Werbin graduated from Michigan Normal in 1938 and went on to Kansas City to become an osteopathic doctor. He then set up practice in Long Beach, California.[52] When Lloyd Olds was named to manage of the U. S. Pan American team headed to Mexico in March 1955, he appointed Dr. Werbin, his former distance runner, trainer for the U. S. Pan American track and field team. One of the innovations that Olds and Werbin instituted was the practice of administering oxygen to all athletes immediately after participation, to counteract the ill effects of the high altitude.[53] Harry retired by 1990 and divided his time between Kansas City and El Toro, California. He died during the 1990s.[54]

The "Bronx Bullet"

Abraham "Abe" Rosenkrantz, who came to Ypsilanti with Harry Werbin in 1933, became one the 100 best track athletes in the state's history. Abe's story begins with his grandfather. A disagreement between Abe's father and his grandfather resulted in a lifetime estrangement between the two men. Abe's father, Harry Rosenkrantz was a baker, who came to the USA from Lodz, Russia[55] in the last decade of the nineteenth century to escape his father's influence. Lodz, a city of about a half-million people, was the second largest city in Poland. It was located in the heart of a productive agricultural region. Control of the city shifted back and forth between Prussia and Russia during the nineteenth century.

Although Abe's father was unschooled, he was a regular reader of the *Jewish Daily Forward* and read Shakespeare in Yiddish. Abe's parents met in New York City's Harlem, and married shortly after the turn of the century. Abraham and his twin brother were born in Harlem on December 25, 1909. His twin brother died 13 months later, and before Abe was three years old, his mother fell out of the window for their apartment to her death. As a youngster, Abe enjoyed playing running games, particularly stick ball and ring-a-leev-eo, a New York City tenement version of "capture the flag." As Abe recalls, "Only one boy on his block was faster than me."[56]

While a better than average student, Abe dropped out of high school when he was fifteen years old to work as an errand boy for a printing company. His primary task was to deliver stationary and envelopes to businesses typically located within a mile of the printing shop. For each delivery, his employer gave him a dime for streetcar fare. A nickel going and the same for the return trip. He soon discovered that if he ran back to the shop he could not only beat the streetcar, but could keep a nickel on each delivery without doing harm to his employer. The average delivery was about a half-mile from the print shop, so that distance became a comfortable run for Abe.

Abe entered his first race a year or two later, when he saw an advertisement outside the Glencoe Athletic Club for an open three-mile road race. While the Glencoe Athletic Club was primarily interested in boxing, its leadership apparently felt that the road race would help promote the club. Abe looked upon the race as an opportunity. From his point of view, it was time to put "tuchas affen tisch".[57] Abe was unsure he could run three miles, and tried to persuade a friend to station himself halfway through the race course to bail him out if he could not make the distance, but the friend refused. Nevertheless, Abe started the race with some fifty other runners. He hung just behind the leaders, and to his astonishment finished eighth against experienced runners from the

Millrose Athletic Association and various regimental track groups. Harry Werbin, who ran for the Millrose Athletic Association, won the race.

Abe Rosenkrantz did so well that the Glencoe Athletic Club decided to sponsor him. They gave him a uniform and running shoes. The club also placed him in meets and picked up expenses, but it was not an ideal arrangement since the Glencoe AC had no track coach and little interest in the sport. Abe was soon told that Von Elling, the New York University track coach, would provide training and running tips to serious runners, so he hung around Coach Von Elling for advice.

As Abe got better, his name began to appear on the sports pages of the New York City newspapers, and he was ultimately asked to join the Millrose Athletic Association track team. Abe also joined the army reserves and ran for his regimental team. In 1931 he won the 1,000-yard handicap race at the Caledonian Club games. A year later he won at a handicap race at the Knights of Columbus Meet in Madison Square Garden. In that race, Abe caught the anchor runners for the other three teams at the tape to steal a victory for the Millrose mile relay. Although there was no newspaper coverage of the race, it was a thrilling experience for Abe because of the adulation of the crowd.

His accomplishments against college runners encouraged Abe to think about seeking a track scholarship to college, so he enrolled at New York Evening High School to complete his last two years of high school. When he graduated from high school in 1932, he was twenty-three years old, the country was in the depths of the great depression, and there were no scholarships for track athletes. However, his friend Harry Werbin had visited Michigan Normal College in Ypsilanti on November 27–28, 1931 to participate in the National Senior AAU Cross-country Championships as a member of the Millrose Athletic Association team, and reported that out-of-state tuition at Michigan Normal was only $35 per semester. Moreover, Werbin reported that Coach Lloyd Olds had jobs for track team members that covered room and board.

Armed with this information, Abe applied for admission at Michigan Normal, and hitchhiked to Michigan with less than fifty dollars in his pocket. When he reached Ypsilanti, he discovered that Coach Olds had given out all his jobs, but he urged Abe to enroll and hang on for a few weeks until the coaching staff could find him a job. Abe followed the coach's advice, but soon ran out of money. Just as Abe decided to go to the University of Michigan to see if they could take care of him, Coach

Olds found him a job. Both Abe and Harry Werbin became members of the Michigan Normal class of 1937.[58]

Over the next four years, Rosenkrantz became one of the best half-milers in Michigan Normal history. In late January 1935 he broke the school indoor record for the 880-yard run (2:00.7).[59] On February 2 Abe was a member of the Michigan Normal mile-relay team that won the college division matched relay (3:29) at the Millrose Games.[60] On a night when Cunningham, Venzke and Bonthron staged a spectacular race in the Wanamaker mile, Abe Rosenkrantz also staged a spectacular race. The Michigan Normal relay team, running against tough competition, trailed by nearly 20 yards after the first quarter-mile because James Matthews had slipped on a curve. However, good baton passing helped them narrow the gap, and great races by Harold Baker and Abe sealed the comeback victory by three yards before 16,000 cheering fans.[61]

Abe Rosenkrantz and Billy Zepp were outstanding in the 1935 Michigan AAU Indoor Meet at Yost Fieldhouse. The *Ypsilanti Press* described the scene:

> At the Second Annual Michigan AAU Relays, the brilliant Huron trio of sophomores, James Matthews, Bowman Hall, and Abraham Rosenkrantz, and a junior veteran Harold Baker, gained a lead on the first lap in the mile relay race with Michigan State and Western Michigan and never lost it. Rosenkrantz then stamped himself a coming varsity star by forcing Captain Harvey Smith of the University of Michigan to establish a new Yost Fieldhouse record in the 880 to defeat him. Rosenkrantz finished under the old mark himself, by gaining the lead on the second lap and holding it until the start of the last lap. Smith won by a scant three yards in the time of 1:55.8.[62]

Concurrently, Billy Zepp set a new Yost Fieldhouse record in the two-mile run (9:21.8), while Harry Werbin placed third in the two-mile run, defeating Neree Alix, who placed fourth.[63]

Later in the month (February 22, 1935) Abe set the Yost Field House record for the half mile run (1:55.1), when he beat Smith's replacement in a triangular meet that also included Michigan State. This time, Abe sprinted the entire race for a decisive win.[64] Billy Zepp set a new two-mile record at the triangular meet. On the following day, the Michigan Normal track team scored a one-sided victory over Butler University in an indoor duel meet held at Waterman Gym in Ann Arbor. Again, Zepp set a new record, this time in the mile run.

On Saturday March 16, 1935 Abe Rosenkrantz was scheduled to run on the Michigan Normal mile and two-mile relay teams at the Armour

Tech Relays held at the University of Chicago Fieldhouse. However, early in that week, while attending a guest lecture, Abe was asked over the public address system to take a long distance telephone call from New York. The caller informed Abe that he had been selected for the American track team that would participate in the Maccabi Games in Palestine. Because of difficulty arranging financing for the team's trip, notifications were made late, and Abe was expected to be in New York by Monday morning for the trans-Atlantic ship passage on the *Conti di Savoia* to Naples and thence to Palestine. Abe had to notify Coach Olds and the school administration of his change in plans, pack, and take a train to New York, all in short order. Harry Werbin decided, on impulse, to tag along in hopes of being added to the American team. The two men left for New York on Saturday night, March 16, 1935.[65] The trip was delayed in Naples because of the Italian invasion of Ethiopia. Abe traveled to Italy with the Jewish-American team and after a layover in Italy was put on an marginal, Italian ship that carried a youth group of Jewish students from German. Werbin did not make the initial group, but was sent later and did participate in the Maccabi Games in Palestine.

On March 27, 1935 Hugo Apt, who was born in Niederaula, Germany, and just over a dozen of his classmates from the Jewish Teacher's Seminary in Wurzburg, Bavaria boarded the 33,000-ton Italian ship *Roma*. Because the Nazis were using all available foreign exchange to purchase raw materials for rearming, German citizens traveling abroad were limited to taking 10 Marks out of Germany. Hence, the entourage from Germany was excited about their voyage and full of energy, but strapped for cash.

The Jewish Teacher's Seminary graduates from Wurzburg planned a month's tour of Palestine, the British Mandate that included Jerusalem and the traditional Jewish homeland. Once aboard the *Roma*, the newly graduated teachers discovered that among the passengers was a group of Jewish-American athletes, including Abe Rosenkrantz, which was on its way to Tel Aviv to participate in the Maccabi Games.

The three-day trip to Haifa, aboard the all-to-dirty *Roma*, afforded the young German and American Jews an opportunity to get acquainted, talk and dream about the adventure ahead. Everyone was excited about the long anticipated arrival in the "promised-land." As they approached Palestine, their first glimpse of the "holy-land" was the tip of the high tower at Haifa barely visible at the edge of the blue horizon. Arriving at an exotic foreign destination by ship is by far the most exciting form of travel. Unlike travel by plane or train, the anticipation grows as the shoreline comes into view. Over the next three hours, the passengers crowded the railings of the *Roma*, as the tower and the hills surrounding Haifa came into view.[66]

Abe Rosenkrantz was very successful at the Maccabi Games in Tel Aviv. He won the 1,500-meter run, the 800-meter run, and the 400-meter intermediate-hurdles (and was second in the medley relay). On Adolf Hitler's birthday, April 20, 1935, an Arab newspaper featured a half page picture of the German Fuehrer with the caption, "In another five years Hitler will be here."[67]

On February 1, 1936 Abe won the 880-yard run (1:56.5) at the Millrose Games, Madison Square Gardens, New York City and started his attempt to qualify for the Berlin Olympic games. On May 1 he was on the relay team that won the Normal college championship matched mile relay and the Class B mile-relay Championship at the Penn Relays in Philadelphia. Abe Rosenkrantz qualified for the central regional Olympic semi-finals at Marquette University. According to contemporary reports, "in the 800-meter run, Rosenkrantz set the early pace, but could not match the speed of Ross Bush of Southern California on the stretch." Abe, however, did defeat Glenn Cunningham, and qualified for the Olympic final tryouts.[68] More importantly in early July, he came within inches of qualifying for the 1936 Olympic team, after coming in second to Ben Eastman in the semi-final heats of the final Olympic trials at Randalls Island with a record setting 1:50.3 to Eastman's American record time of 1:49.8.

On June 2, 1936 Abe, the "Bronx Bullet," was chosen captain of the Michigan Normal track team for 1937. He was the 880-yard record holder for the Notre Dame Fieldhouse and Yost Fieldhouse. He also set the State AAU outdoor record (1:54) in Ann Arbor in late May, 1936.[69] Abe also won the 880-yard run at the 1937 Millrose Games at Madison Square Garden. Moreover, he rallied his relay team in the 1937 Penn Relays, when the lead runner bumped another runner and dropped the baton. Abe anchored the race to victory. The *Encyclopedia of Jews in Sports*[70] lists Abe Rosenkrantz as one of the best Jewish middle distance runners of the century.

Abe met Ann B. Gordon, Michigan Normal class of 1933, shortly after he arrived in Ypsilanti. Ann was from Ypsilanti and he married her in 1937. He used the expense money from a track trip to Toronto for their honeymoon. They were still happily married when both were more than 90 years old. Unable to find a teaching position in 1937 and after working for a time in a gas station, Abe took a job as the manager of a grocery co-op. He replaced a poet who was tired of groceries and sought new experiences.

During World War II, Abe worked in the Willow Run Aircraft plant as a utility man, before joining the army to become a gunner in an amphibious tank. He saw action in the Pacific. After World War II Abe became the owner, operator of an independent grocery store, Gordon's Grocery, named for his wife's family. In 1971 the store was fire bombed, and Abe became a substitute teacher and sold real-estate. He also became active in amateur theater. Well into their retirement, his wife was placed in a nursing home with Alzheimer's disease.[71]

Honoring Olds

In 1937 W. O. Briggs donated the fieldhouse, football stadium, and baseball stadium to Michigan Normal College, due in large measure to the activities of Lloyd Olds. In July 1938 more than 60 athletes who helped to build Michigan Normal into a track and field powerhouse meet for a three-day reunion to honor Coach Olds. Since his arrival in Ypsilanti as a coach, Olds' cross-country runners had won 72 duel meets and lost only three. In indoor and outdoor duel track meets, his thinclads won 82 of its 92 scheduled encounters. The titles acquired in state, regional, and national meets were the envy of coaches' all-over America.

Huron track teams had won eight state intercollegiate titles, five Michigan AAU titles, five Western Michigan AAU titles, four MIAA titles, three others in the Michigan Collegiate Conference, two in Central Intercollegiate competition, and one Central Junior AAU indoor title. In cross-country the Ypsilanti college won titles in nine State Intercollegiate, seven Michigan AAU, four Michigan Collegiate Conference, three MIAA, two Central Collegiate Conference, Championship meets, and a national Junior AAU, and a Loyola University Invitational meet. The cross-country men also were runners-up for National Senior AAU titles in 1931 and 1933. Besides this, Olds' relay teams scored impressive victories in the Penn, Drake, Ohio, Illinois, and Cleveland Knights of Columbus Relays, the Millrose Games, the Southern Canadian Meet, and the Canadian International Meet. Ten Michigan Normal trackmen had earned All-American honors, and two had won berths on the Maccabi Games team.[72]

Concurrently, Olds placed former track athletes and men's physical education students in key positions at Amherst College, Massachusetts State College, Oregon State College, the University of Tennessee, the University of China in Shanghai, Western State Teachers College (WMU), the University of California, Michigan Northern Teacher's College, and high schools in Detroit, Jackson, Milwaukee, Yonkers,

Pasadena, Berkeley (CA), Steubenville, Toledo, State College, Lansing, Grand Rapids, Flint, Saginaw, Willamette, and Ann Arbor. He also had trained women's physical education teachers and coaches who headed programs at Central Michigan University, Kent College, Grand Rapids Junior College, a number of YWCAs, and the Detroit Public Schools.[73]

Olds also had written *Track and Field for High Schools* and *Techniques of Teaching Physical Activities,* as well as numerous professional articles. He was a member of the American Physical Directors Society, and a variety of civil groups.

Ypsi Runner Goes Nuclear

Charles "Whitey" Hlad from Saginaw High School Class of 1937 was the last great runner of the Lloyd Olds era of track and field at Michigan Normal. "Whitey" Hlad was a truly great hurdler who had to contend with regular competition with Allan Tolmich. He also had to contend with unusual situations. For example, in the Illinois Relays of 1941, the six foot two inch hurdler from Saginaw was headed to an almost certain win in the 75-yard high hurdles, when an unintentional slap across the chest by Bill Smutz of Nebraska threw Hlad off stride. Bob Wright of Ohio State took advantage of the situation and crossed the finish line a foot ahead of Hlad. "Whitey" came back in the 75-yard low-hurdles and ran a flawless race. A sharp lunge at the tape enabled Hlad to win, but his maneuver sent him skidding along the cinder track. He did not suffer serious injury.[74]

On Friday February 21, 1941, Charles Hlad left for New York City by train with six other Michigan trackman, including the four members of Wayne University's mile relay team (Bob Wingo, Lin Wright, Bob Grant and Charles Doan). Hlad placed third to Allan Tolmich in the 70-yard high-hurdles in the National AAU indoor championships.[75]

On Saturday March 8, 1941 "Whitey" Hlad won the high hurdles at the Central Collegiate Conference indoor meet in South Bend despite a painful foot injury, which forced him to forego entering the 65-yard low hurdles. Hlad strained his arch during the Michigan State Relays on February 28, 1941. Hlad's appearance in the CCC was costly since the pressure he was forced to exert on his left foot further aggravated his injury. In consequence, he was unable to compete in the Butler Relays and the Michigan AAU Relays in 1941.[76] Hlad was twice honored as an All-American.

In March 1942, "Whitey" Hlad defeated Fred Wolcott in the 60-yard high-hurdles at the New York Knights of Columbus Meet in New York

Charles Hlad, Jr. was one of the nation's top indoor hurdlers on the eve of World War I. He became a nuclear biomedical physicist. *(Photo Eastern Michigan U Archives)*

City. Wolcott went on to become a successful insurance man in Texas after serving as an Ensign in the U.S. Navy during World War II. "Whitey" went on to graduated from the University of Chicago in 1943.[77] From 1944 through 1946 he served with the U.S. Army Chemical Welfare Service. After serving in the U.S. Army, Hlad became an instructor at the School of Pharmacy of the University of Colorado in Denver (1946–49). He earned a MA degree from Stanford University in 1949. "Whitey" Hlad became a Hospital Administrator for the Veteran's Administration in Denver and served in that position from 1949 until 1961. Hlad became Chief of a medical research laboratory from 1961 until his death in 1966. At the time of his death, he was the only nuclear biomedical physicist in the State of Colorado.

Professor Olds Joins the Army, Then Completes His Career in Ypsilanti

Dr. Olds authored the AAU Physical Fitness Handbook used in thousands of American high schools and colleges. In January 1940 he was appointed chairman of the AAU Track and Field Committee at the Annual Convention in Miami, Florida. Following the convention, Dr. Olds visited Cuba, where he inspected the athletic facilities. The athletic plant at the University of Havana was found to be on par with most of the plants at American Universities.[78] Olds was chairman of the Track and Field section of the Amateur Athletic Union from 1940–43, and president of the Michigan Chapter of the organization in 1940–41. As an advisor to the Armed Forces he also was a member of the National Physical Education Committee.

In 1942, Olds left Normal to serve in the U.S. Navy. During World War II, he was active in planning the Navy's physical fitness program. From 1942–45 he was commanding officer for the program in the 11th Naval District in San Diego, and from 1945–47 was commander in charge of the Navy's entire physical fitness program.

Assistant Coach George Marshall became head track coach at Michigan Normal when Professor Olds left for the Army in 1942. Marshall extended the Lloyd Olds tradition of outstanding track at Michigan Normal. In 1949 Michigan Normal joined the Interstate Intercollegiate Conference. That year, Michigan Normal dominated the Baldwin-Wallace Relays in Berea, Ohio. Normal scored 161 points while second place Baldwin Wallace managed only 69 2/5 points, and the other six schools in the meet trailed behind. In that meet Michigan Normal won five relay events.[79]

In 1950 Bob Parks ran the lead off quarter-mile on the mile relay that won the first annual Bowling Green Relays.[80] Later, Bob Parks would succeed George Marshall.

Stan McConner from Northwestern High School in Detroit was another post-war track star at what soon became Eastern Michigan University. According to Stan's January 1949 high school yearbook:

Lanky Stan, the all-city man, is known in the sports world as the streak of lightning. Record-setting Stanley broke the old track record for the city quarter-mile in the terrific time of 49.8 seconds. Stan was also an active member of the "N" Club and a powerful weapon on the swimming team.[81]

Stan attended Adrian College then transferred to Eastern Michigan University. In 1952 he qualified in two events, the 440-yard dash and the 440-yard hurdles, for the final Olympic tryouts.[82]

In 1948 Olds returned to Michigan Normal as Athletic Director. He was Head Manager for the 1948 U. S. Olympic track team. In 1952 he was Athletic Committee Chairman of the AAU of the United States. Olds and Ralph Young were on the 1956 Olympic Men's Track and Field Committee.[83] In 1957 he was a consultant and lecturer on physical fitness for the U.S. military forces in Europe, and in 1959 he was elected to the track and field hall of fame of the NCAA.

In 1962 Olds was on the committee that staged the 75th Annual National AAU Convention in Detroit.[84] He was a member of the United States Olympic Committee, and was a member of the Olympic Track and Field Committee for 1968.[85]

Olds played an important role in influencing physical education activities that eventually became the basis of physical training and recreation in teacher's colleges accross the nation. "Once out of school, it is vitally important for people to go on getting enough exercise." Dr. Olds argued that running and swimming are of the most natural and best recreational activities. Olds spent 55 years as a participant, coach, official and director of athletics.

In 1963 he retired and moved to a home in Laguna Hills, California, after serving 42 years on the faculty of Eastern Michigan University. Olds died of cancer on December 2, 1982 at the age of 90. Eugene Beatty, Bernard Otto, and Pastor William Tipton offered tributes at his memorial service in Ypsilanti. At the memorial service, Dean Rockwell who was recruited by Olds in 1930 to run track and became a U.S. Olympic wrestling coach in 1964, remembered of Olds:

> He didn't let personalities invade principals. He influenced every man he came in touch with. He had strong personality and character. He didn't expect any back talk, but it was done in a manner you didn't feel put upon. It was for the good of all. He's a leader with tremendously high character. He made demands on other people to meet his standards and still had warmth and compassion. When I was recruited to Michigan Normal College, Dr. Olds offered me a job in a restaurant three hours and three meals a day. I came and it changed my life dramatically. He was the kind of man who engenders tremendous loyalty to himself and to the institution.[86]

6. The Miler is King, Except in the Detroit Police Department

State lawmakers approved an act in 1865 that established the Metropolitan Police Department of Detroit. A four-member Police Commission appointed by the governor hired 40 officers who made up the force. Charles Wilson, the first African-American police officer in Detroit, was appointed in 1895. Two additional black police officers were hired shortly after the appointment of Wilson.[1] However, African-Americans were rarely appointed to the Detroit Police Department before 1944, and the few who were tended to be track men hired to improve the Department's track team.

Employer financed track teams were common during the first part of the twentieth century. The most famous of these business-sponsored teams was the Millrose Athletic Association, which was formed in 1910. Frederick W. Wilkins, a prominent sprinter from 1909 to 1913, became an executive of the John Wanamaker store in New York, and in 1933 was elected Vice-President and Treasurer of the Millrose Athletic Association.[2] Wilkins was responsible for introducing the Wanamaker mile at the Millrose Games. During the decade of the 1930s, the pursuit of the four-minute mile was launched. It would fuel middle-distance running, the engine behind the popularity of indoor track that grew until Roger Bannister broke the four-minute barrier in the mile run on May 6, 1954.

As with the military, Police Departments have a long tradition of subsidizing track and field. In the mid-1920s, the police in cities like Detroit, Cleveland, New York, Toronto, and Chicago had highly competitive track teams. Track meets between police departments were a method for determining the relative quality of police officers and frequently the occasion for sizable bets. Thus, it comes as no surprise that good track athletes were prized recruits for the "boys in blue." During the 1930s, Joseph P. "Joe" McCluskey, the "flying policeman," worked for the New York Police Department after graduating from Fordham

University. Detroit Police trackmen included such track and field stand-outs as Victor Leschinsky, Harry Van Nortwick, Garral Noah, Marvin Vollmer, William Watson, Bill Streng, Edward Gaines, Ken "Red" Simmons, Clark Haskins, George Huber, William Daly, and Elmer "Buddy" Coleman. Like Joe McCluskey, these Detroit police officers were world-class runners and weight men.

Eastern European Runner

Victor Leschinsky graduated from Detroit's Northwestern High School in 1923. As a junior in high school, he finished third in the 100-yard dash, the 220-yard dash, and the mile-relay at the Michigan High School Class A State Championships. He also placed fourth in the 220-yard dash at the University of Michigan Interscholastic Games in Ann Arbor that year. In 1923 he again qualified for the finals of the state high school championship in the 100-yard and 220-yard dashes.

Victor enrolled at University of Michigan in 1924, but because of poor grades became ineligible at the end of his freshman year.[3] In the preliminaries of the regional Olympic trials in Ann Arbor on May 31, 1924 Victor set the U. S. record for the 200-meter run (21.25). His record, however, was disputed because of a favorable wind. Victor won the regional trials in 200-meter dash (21.4), but lost to Jackson Scholz, Charles Paddock, George Hill and Bayes Norton at the final trials in Boston, and failed to make the U.S. Olympic team.

Although ineligible for varsity competition, Leschinsky won the 300-yard run (37.0) at the Michigan AAU Indoor Carnival in Detroit on April 6, 1925.[4] In the spring of 1926 Leschinsky was finally eligible for varsity competition and ran at the Drake Relays. He won the 220-yard dash and placed second in the 100-yard dash in a duel meet with the University of Illinois, and won the 220-yard dash (22.0) and tied for first in the 100-yard dash (10.2) at the Big 10 Championships in Iowa City. On June 12 Victor placed fifth in the 220-yard dash at the NCAA Outdoor Championships in Chicago. He failed his classes, however, and dropped out of college. He was never awarded a letter at the U of M for his accomplishments.

The Detroit Police Department hired him and he participated in the first field day meet with the Toronto Police Department in 1926 and on July 4, 1927 Leschinsky won the 220-yard dash at the Michigan AAU State Championships. The next year he placed second to Eddie Tolan in the 100 and the 220-yard dashes at the Michigan AAU Outdoor Championships. On August 26, 1928 Victor won the 100 and 200-yard dashes at the Detroit Police Invitational Meet. On July 4, 1930 he placed second in the mile-relay and fourth in the 100-yard dash at the Michigan AAU Championships held on Belle Isle. As his career as a Detroit Policeman progressed, Leschinsky became a finger print specialist.

College Runner Joins the Detroit Police Department During the Depression

William C. Streng graduated from Detroit City College in June 1929, just before the start of the *great depression* and took a job with the Detroit Police Department where he could continue running track. On February 22, 1930 he placed fourth in the 300-yard dash at the National Junior AAU Indoor Meet held in Detroit. On July 4, 1930, as a member of the Detroit Police track team, Streng placed second in the mile relay and third in the 220 and the 440-yard dashes at the Michigan AAU Championships on Belle Isle.

On February 13, 1931 Streng won the 440-yard dash (55.6) and placed second in the 220-yard dash (25.6) in a duel meet between the Detroit Police team and Michigan Normal freshmen held in the Detroit Police Armory. On June 13 he won the 220-yard dash and placed second in the 440 for the Detroit Police, coached by Ernest Wuesthoff, in a duel meet with the Michigan Normal College freshmen in Ypsilanti.[5]

In June 1934 Bill participated in the 400-meter hurdles for the Detroit Police team at the National Junior AAU Championships in Milwaukee, and the next day he placed third in the 1,600-meter relay at the National Senior AAU Championships.

"Fast Eddie" Gaines

Edward Gaines was a member of the Cass Technical High School class of 1926. The Tolan and Loving brothers were high school teammates. In 1924 Eddie tied for second in the high jump and in the broad jump at the Michigan Class A State High School Championships. The following year he defeated future Olympian J. Ken Doherty in the broad jump at the Detroit Open Meet on Belle Isle.[6] Gaines then attended Western Michigan State Teacher's College where he earned distinction in the running broad jump and the 880-yard run. In 1928 he participated in the Ohio Relays in the two-mile relay and the broad jump.[7] On June 7–8, 1929 he qualified for the finals in both the 880-yard run and the broad jump at the NCAA Championships in Chicago, making him one of the eight fastest half-milers in the nation. Eddie graduated from Western in 1930.

When "Eddie" was asked in 1954 about his track career he said:

There is little doubt in my mind that May 31, 1929 was the day and date of my greatest sports thrill. The place was Michigan State College. It was a wonderful day and the weather was just right. Prior to that time, in high school and my early college days, I had always competed in field events [the broad jump] and relays. I was rather new at the [individual] half mile. The credit for this change goes to Earl T. Martineau. Also, my entry at Michigan State's Inter-Collegiate Track and Field Meet.

The 880 was studded with outstanding runners, like Duke Keifer, University of Detroit; Hackney of Michigan State; Arnold of Ypsilanti Normal and several others whose names escape me.

We were off at the crack of the gun. At the end of the first 25 [yards] I was running in third position. Coming into the last lap the race had narrowed down to a two man-competition—Hackney and myself. Turning on a final burst of speed, I was able to hit the tape first. I was clocked at 1.55.5—a new Inter-Collegiate half-mile mark. According to "Dad" Butler, University of Detroit track coach, my race was the fastest ever turned in by an American Negro. Phil Edwards had bested this time but Phil was a British subject. As a result of winning this race I was placed on the All-American Track and Field Honor Roll by J. L. Griffith of the Big Ten. This was one of the fastest half miles run during '29 in the entire United States.[8]

On July 4, 1930 Eddie Gaines won the 880-yard run (1:58.2) and the broad jump (22–5), and placed second in the high jump at the Michigan AAU Championships. Eddie then became the first African-American recruited by the Detroit Police Department for his running ability. Gaines regularly scored points for the Detroit Police track team in critical meets against other big city police departments.[9] In early July 1934 he ran on the police department's 1,600-meter relay team that place third in the National AAU Senior Championships.

On July 24–25, 1934 the Toronto [Canada] Police Games were held at Hanlan's Point Stadium.[10] The Detroit Police track team was invited,[11] and Eddie Gaines was an important factor in the Detroit's domination of its Canadian rivals. Gaines won the 440-yard dash (50.4) and the running high jump (5–9½), and was the anchor man on the winning mile relay team (3:38).[12] Indeed, the exploits of Gaines and Clark Haskins were, no doubt, responsible the absence of the Detroit Police track club from the Toronto Police Games in 1935.[13]

On February 9, 1935 the Police Department relay team won the mile relay at the Second Annual Michigan AAU Indoor Championships at Yost Fieldhouse, and qualified for the finals of the 400-meter run and the 1,600-meter relay at the National AAU Outdoor Championships in

Lincoln, Nebraska. Gaines placed fourth in the 400-meter hurdles at the Western Michigan AAU Meet in 1936 and won points at the annual field day meet with the Toronto Police Department Amateur Athletic team held at the State Fair Grounds in Detroit that August.[14]

In 1954 Edward Gaines was one of the only two African-American detectives in the Detroit Police Department. At that time, only five percent of the department's employees were African-American.

The Great Detroit Police Weight Throwers

During the great depression of the 1930s an appointment to the Detroit Police Department was a plum, particularly for a man without college experience. Three great weight men, Clark C. Haskins, George "Big George" Huber, and Harry Van Nortwick, went directly from high school into the Detroit Police Department. For a decade they were among the best weight throwers in America, and were mainstays on the Detroit Police Athletic Association track team.

In 1904 and in 1920 the 56-pound weight throw was an Olympic event. The first time the event was included in the Olympics, a Montreal policeman won the competition with a throw of 34 feet 4 inches. Etienne Desmarteau had been refused a leave of absence to participate in the St. Louis Olympics, but he went anyway. When he became Canada's first individual Olympic champion, his dismissal papers were not processed. Unfortunately, he died of typhus the following year.[15] From that point on, this event had a special calling for policemen.

The 240-pound Clark C. Haskins was an extraordinary athlete. He was the State AAU heavyweight weight lifting champion, one of the best 56-pound weight throwers in the nation, and a menacing football player who toyed with college All-Americans. He could outrun most men for 30-yards, and was extremely agile for a big man. Haskins represented the Detroit Police Department Athletic Association on July 4, 1928 when he won the shot put (40–11¾) and placed third in the hammer throw at the Michigan AAU Championships.[16] In 1930 Haskins won the 56-pound weight throw (31–10⅛) at the National AAU Outdoor Championships. On February 13, 1931 the big man won the shot put (41–4⅛) in a duel meet between the Detroit Police Department and Michigan Normal freshmen held in the Detroit Police Armory.

Clark's domination of the weight events continued for the balance of the decade. In 1933–1935 he won the 35-pound weight throw at the Michigan AAU Indoor Championships.[17] In 1934 and 1935 he won the

National AAU Championship in the 56-pound weight throw, and placed sixth in the hammer throw in 1935 National Championships. In 1936 and 1937, he placed second in the 56-pound weight throw at the National AAU Championships. In 1938 he placed third and in 1939 he placed fourth in the 56-pound weight throw at the National AAU Championships.

While a great athlete, Clark Haskins was without moral compunctions. He was, without doubt, mentally ill and often compounded his mental state by self-medicating into the "brown bottle flu." There were reports that as a teenager he beat his father to death. It is known for certain that he abandoned he wife and children to run off with a waitress. Haskins was a person who enjoyed hurting others, and was asked to quit the Detroit Police Department after leading fellow policemen on a high-speed chase while drunk and disorderly.[18] Yet, in field events the big man represented sure points for the Detroit Police track team. He was at his best when there was money on the line. At the Toronto Police Athletic Association Games in 1934, Clark Haskins was the runner-up in individual points scored. He won the 56-pound long throw (34–0) and the hammer throw (144–9½), and placed third in the javelin throw and the 56-pound high throw at that meet.[19]

"Big George" Huber, the Detroit Police Department hammer thrower and 56-pound weight man, had a more pleasant disposition. He worked for "Red" Simmons for some time, before dying some fifty years ago.[20] Huber attended Northwestern High School where he set the Detroit Metropolitan High School League discus record (123–3½) in 1929.[21] On May 10–11, 1929 Huber won the hammer throw, placed third in the discus throw, and fourth in the 12-pound shot put (46–1¼) at the 29th Annual U of M Interscholastic Meet.

When George Huber went to work for the Detroit Police Department and began competing with their Athletic Association (AA), he faced the toughest competition in America on his own team. With competition from teammates Clark Hawkins, Harry Van Nortwick, and Marvin Vollmer, Huber had to become a world-class competitor just to qualify for the team. He was often only the third best weight man on the Detroit Police AA team. On July 3, 1935 Huber was given a chance to participate in the hammer and the 56-pound weight throws in the Junior National AAU Championships. His classification had nothing to do with age. He was in the Junior Division because he had not won the National Junior Championship or placed in the National Senior Championships. While he performed well, he did not place in 1935.

In 1936 Huber continued to improve his weight throws. On August 1 George represented the Detroit Police AA in the annual field day meet with the Toronto Police Department AA team held at the State Fair Grounds in Detroit. On July 2, 1937 Huber finally placed third in the hammer throw and the 56-pound weight throw at the National AAU Junior Championships held in Milwaukee. In 1938 Huber won the 56-pound weight throw (31–10⅛) and placed fourth in the hammer throw at the National AAU Junior Outdoor Championships. Huber then became the 1938 National Senior AAU 56-pound weight throw champion, by defeating Clark Haskins among others.[22]

In March 1940 George Huber placed third in the 35-pound weight throw at the Michigan AAU Indoor Championships, and as late as 1941, he placed second in the 56-pound weight throw at the Michigan AAU Indoor Relays. Huber also did well in the 1941 AAU outdoor meet in Ypsilanti. He won the discus throw (138–10), the hammer throw (166–10), the shot put (45–4½), and placed fifth in the 56-pound weight throw. He set the meet record for the hammer throw that year.

The third nationally ranked weight man on the Detroit Police force was Harry Van Nortwick. Harry attended Northwestern High School, where he won the 1924 Detroit Metro-League Championship for the 12-pound shot put (43–11½).[23] In 1934 and 1935 weight men Marvin Vollmer and Harry Van Nortwick were among the Detroit Police Officers participating at the National Junior AAU Outdoor Championships.

At the 1936 National Junior AAU Outdoor Meet at Princeton, New Jersey, Harry Van Nortwick won the 56-pound weight throw, and Marvin Vollmer placed third in that event.[24] Harry placed fourth in the 56-pound weight throw at the 1937 National Senior AAU Outdoor Championships, behind Clark Haskins and George Huber.[25] At the Michigan AAU Indoor in Ann Arbor in March 1940 Harry Van Nortwick won the 35-pound weight throw (18–6).[26] On June 17–18, 1944 at the National AAU Senior Championships in New York City, Van Nortwick placed third in the 56-pound weight throw (33–8) and fifth in the hammer throw (144–7¼).[27]

"Red" Simmons, Runner Extraordinary

While Kenneth "Red" Simmons joined the Detroit Police Department in 1934, he had his first experience with the police in 1932.

Coach Lloyd Olds had given us money for our hotel bill and bus fare, but a student manager and I thought we'd hitch back because we needed our money.

Trying to thumb a ride out of Elkhart, we were picked up by the police. They asked for identification and we had none. They looked in our bags. Having left our track suits with other members of the squad, we had thought our bags were empty. To our sorrow, the police pulled out a starter's gun and some adhesive tape. That settled the matter for the night, for they seemed to think they had caught a couple of desperadoes. They wired Olds in the morning, however, and he wire back identification. The police gave us a meal, so we finally got home with our money. Money was scarce then.[28]

In June 1934, during his first year with the Detroit Police Department, "Red" won the 400-meter intermediate-hurdles (56.7) at the Western Michigan AAU meet in Grand Rapids, and went on to place second in the 400-meter hurdles (54.8) at the National Junior AAU Outdoor Championships. He also ran on the department's 1,600-meter relay team that placed third in at the National AAU Senior Outdoor Championships.

The Detroit Police Department relay team, comprised of Kenneth "Red" Simmons, Albert Langtray, Edward Gaines, and Fred Carlsberg, won the club mile relay at the Michigan AAU Indoor Championship at Yost Fieldhouse on February 9, 1935.[29] On July 3, 1935 "Red" placed fourth in the 400-meter intermediate-hurdles at the Junior National AAU Championships in Nebraska. The next day he ran in the 1,600-meter relay in the Senior National AAU Championships, with Garral Noah filling in for Langtray.

On June 30, 1936 "Red," representing the Detroit Police, placed second in the 400-meter hurdles, third in the low-hurdles, and third in the 1,600-meter relay at the Michigan AAU Outdoor Championships held at University of Detroit Stadium.

In March 1937 Simmons, a slender, red-haired young man wearing a tan hat and a dark gray overcoat, was assigned to the Central Station in Detroit. He was a leading hurdler on the Detroit Police track team, and ran the 440-yard intermediates in about 54 seconds, just as he did while attending college four years before. He looked frail in comparison to the average policeman. That didn't bother "Red," who jokingly told a reporter, "If things ever got too tough, I think I'd be hard to catch."[30]

In 1941 "Red" was still running for the Detroit Police track team. He placed fifth in the 400-meter hurdles at the Michigan AAU outdoor championships held at Briggs Field in Ypsilanti. "Red" retired from the Detroit Police Department in 1959, and was hired at the University of Michigan as an instructor of physical education and freshman track coach later that year.[31] He promptly introduced the weigh-lifting techniques for track and field he had learned from the Detroit Police weight men and had refined with personal use.[32]

In for an Inch: in for a Mile

On February 18, 1933 local barbers in Ann Arbor reduced haircut prices 15 cents to encourage students to have hair cuts at college rather than in their hometown.[33] Michigan communities were also preparing for the legalization of the manufacture and sale of beer. On May 11, 1933, thousands thronged downtown Ann Arbor beer gardens to buy beer legally for the first time since 1918. One Ann Arbor restaurant sold out of beer by 11:30 p.m. [34]

The legalization of alcoholic beverages caused the deputy superintendent of the Detroit Police to adopt rules covering the use of beer while in uniform. On May 20, 1933 it was announced that,

> Because policemen in less than one week relapsed into the quaint old-fashioned habit of dropping in to see the barmaids on the beat an order is going to go through prohibiting "cops" from drinking beer while in uniform. 'It is like being between the devil and the deep,' James E. McCarty, deputy superintendent, said. 'But the officers weren't discreet. It has to be done. Of course this is going to make it difficult. When can a policeman go to eat where they don't serve beer? They can eat in restaurants all right, but they mustn't drink beer.' It appears that several complaints were made to police officials that the policemen were clustered so thick in some beer places that Joseph Average Citizen could not get much service. Several people called up and said, 'it didn't look nice to see a policeman coming out of a place wiping foam off his mouth.[35]

It was in this milieu that the Detroit Police AA track and field team trained and performed during depression years of the 1930s. At the time the sale of alcoholic beverages was becoming legal again and fundamentally changing the nature of police work, the Detroit Police track team continued to emphasize the brawn necessary for weight throwing. Meanwhile, in the rest of the country the effort to run a four-minute mile began to capture the public imagination, making the miler king for track fans.

The first real king of the American mile was William R. "Bonnie Bill" Bonthron, who was born in Detroit on November 1, 1912. As a child growing up in the motor city, Billy Bonthron was severely burned by a high voltage wire that knocked him unconscious from a 60-foot perch. After falling to the ground, he was run over by a truck. When he was taken to the hospital, he begged the surgeon to save his leg. The doctor later said that only Bill's childhood plea saved his leg.[36] Young Billy took up running as a form of rehabilitation, but did not began competing in track until 1929.[37]

By all accounts, "Bonnie Bill" Bonthron was an unselfish, team man who was strongly committed to the training necessary to becoming a great middle-distance runner. However, when he enrolled at Princeton in the fall of 1930, no one had any idea the young Detroiter would become a renowned athlete.

Bonthron ran both cross-country and track at Princeton. In dual meets between Princeton and Yale in 1932 and 1933, he insisted, for the sake of his team's success, upon participation in the three longest running events on the program. In 1932 he won two of them and came in second in the third. In 1933 he won all of them. As a result of his enthusiasm and leadership, Princeton decisively defeated Yale in the 1932 dual meet and gained a tie with a greatly favored Yale team in the 1933 meet.

During the winter of 1933, Bonthron made other personal sacrifices for the benefit of the team. Rather than running individual events during the indoor season, he anchored relay teams. As a result, Princeton won the 2900-meter relay in record time in the AAU indoor championships and the two-mile relay at the IC4A indoor championships.

In 1911 Cornell University middle-distance runner John Paul Jones gained national attention when he won both the half-mile (1:54.8) and the one-mile (4:15.4) runs on the same day at the IC4A Meet. Until William R. Bonthron arrived upon the scene, no cinderpath runner had surpassed that feat. The fifty-seventh intercollegiate championships has go down in history as Bill Bonthron's meet. It was unfortunate that this was the first year the metric system was used in the intercollegiates, for Bonthron had John Paul Jones's abiding IC4A mile record of 4:12.4 at his mercy. It is, however, easy to estimate Bonthron's feats in terms of the better-known yards, and thus set his races alongside those of Jones in 1911 on the same Harvard oval. The 1,500 meters is 120 yards short of a mile, and allowing 19 seconds for this distance, which is very conservative for so powerful a runner as Bonthron, the Princetonian's 3:54 becomes the equivalent of a 4:13 mile. No miler had ever exhibited as much sheer power as Bonthron did on May 27, 1933. Ordinarily, Bonthron would have delayed his so-called "bicycle kick" finish to the last 100 yards. But on this spring afternoon in 1933, he was so confident and had so much in reserve that he left his rivals with 300 yards to go.

Seventy minutes later Bonthron seemed to jog behind the pace of the half milers and, then once again, "exploded his fiery charge down the homestretch" to win the 800-meter run by a comfortable margin of four yards in 1:53.5. His time was equivalent to a shade over 1:54 for the full 880 yards. Incidentally, Bonthron became the second Princetonian to win that rare "half-mile and mile" double in the Inter-Collegiates. James F. Cregan did it in 1898 with a half in 1:58.4 and a mile in 4:23.6.[38]

Bonthron's fighting spirit and courage were further exemplified in the Princeton-Cornell vs. Oxford-Cambridge meet in July 1933, when he forced Jack Lovelock to break the world record in the mile run to defeat him. Bonthron also broke the world record in his losing effort, and came back within an hour's time to win the half-mile in the extraordinary time of 1:53, given the running surface and track conditions.[39] Bonthron was named All-American for the mile-run for 1933.[40]

After the IC4A meet Matt Geis, the Princeton track coach confided to a reporter that '"Bonthron is one of the easiest men to coach I have ever known. He loves to run, has power to burn, is never flustered."[41] In his senior year at Princeton, Bonthron's teammates rewarded him by electing him Captain of both the varsity cross-country and track teams.

In 1934 the now famous rivalry between Glenn Cunningham and Bill Bonthron drew national attention to the mile run. Cunningham, born in Atlanta, Kansas on August 4, 1909, was the most durable American middle-distance runner of the period. Like Bonthron, Glenn Cunningham's legs were badly burnt at the age of eight, yet he overcame this grave handicap and by 1930 he was a 4:24.7 miler at high school. Cunningham became a national track figure in 1932. In 1933 he won the 1,500-meter run at the AAU Championships and made a successful European tour. Usually a strong front runner, Cunningham had trouble at times when opposed by men with a strong finish. Bonthron had a strong finish and beat Cunningham in the mile run at the NCAA Championships and then edged him in their most memorable duel in the AAU Championships at Milwaukee on June 30, 1934. In the AAU 1,500 "Bonny" used his kick to good advantage for a narrow victory. He set a world record that year in the 1,500-meter run.[42] As a result of his victory over Cunningham and record of sportsmanship, William Bonthron was selected to be the 1934 Sullivan Memorial Trophy winner as the amateur athlete of the year. He was a member of the American track team that competed successfully in Europe in 1934.

On February 2, 1935, a crowd of 16,000 watched one of the hardest fought races in the history of the Wanamaker mile at the Millrose Games. The race featured Glenn Cunningham, Bill Bonthron,[43] and

Gene Venzke. Bonthron had defeated Cunningham, the Kansas ace, in this race in 1934, and was favored again, but the idol of the galleries was Gene Venzke, the Penn stylist.

From the first lap to the seventh it was a five-man race: from the seventh on it was strictly a three-man race. Cunningham took the lead at the end of the first lap and Bonthron slipped into second place a half circuit further on. However,

all the drama was packed into the last few turns around the boards. Venzke glided past "Bonny Bill" two laps from the finish, and the spontaneous, vociferous roar of the crowd was deafening. And when Venzke had the temerity to surge past the Kansan a half lap later, the race had the spectators rocking the Garden rafters in their wild acclaim. But the joy in the galleries was premature. For one full lap, the flashing heels of Venzke blazed the trail. Bonthron was definitely out of it, his dynamite sprint blasted out of him by the fury of the pace. On the other hand, as soon as Venzke moved into the backstretch the Jayhawk flier, Cunningham, came on to oust the usurper. For five, for ten strides they ran neck and neck. Anxiously the crowd watched to see if Venzke could hold on. He just could not. So slowly that it was almost imperceptible at first, Cunningham moved ahead and wheeled into the lead at the turn. Cunningham took the banks high and kept opening up the margin until it was seven yards at the tape. The winged foot jersey worn by Bonthron was twenty yards back.[44]

Glenn Cunningham, the "Iron Horse," again demonstrated his mastery of American milers with a smashing victory over Gene Venzke and Bill Bonthron in the Baxter Mile at the New York Athletic Club Meet in Madison Square Garden. Cunningham gained separation from the pack with a spectacular closing sprint. Cunningham won with a time of 4:09.4. Bonthron was third in 4:15.[45] A week later, Cunningham, the "Kansas Clipper," set a new world indoor record in the 1,500-meter run, while defeating Bill Bonthron at the National AAU Indoor Championships.[46]

Bonthron attempted a comeback in 1936 in an effort to make the U.S. Olympic team, but placed fourth in the final Olympic trials. "Bonny Bill" had peaked in 1934 and was relegated to making his living as an accountant after 1936.[47] Bonthron was later inducted into the Helms Hall of Fame for his feats on the cinder paths.

The University of Detroit Miler

The University of Detroit's Michael H. "Dad" Butler had been a trainer and conditioner for nearly half a century when he took Bill Daly under his wing. Butler was in large measure responsible for bringing Bill Daly to world class status as a miler.

Butler was well over six feet tall and "straight as a string." Every summer he traveled west for a vacation of two or three months. He walked up and down mountain, visited lakes and fished in streams. When he got back he was ready for another year of strenuous activity. "Dad" Butler believed that every man should have a hobby that takes him outdoors for exercise. He advocated swimming, walking, and running as great exercises.[48]

William M. Daly graduated from Cass Technical High School in 1933. As a sophomore at Cass, he won the mile run (4:45.8) at the Detroit Metropolitan League Championships. He also won the mile-run (4:29) at the Detroit Public League Championships as a senior. After graduating from Cass, he enrolled at the University of Detroit. In 1934, as a freshman in college, Daly ran a 4:18.8 mile at the Notre Dame Relays. On May 18–19, 1934 Bill won the two-mile run relay for freshmen (7:57.2) and the mile run (4:16.6) at the Michigan State Intercollegiate Meet in East Lansing. These were rare wins for the Catholic university, better known in those years for its football prowess. On June 29, 1934 Daly placed second in the 1,500-meter run at the National Junior AAU Championships in Milwaukee.[49]

In 1935 Bill Daly continued to improve. On February 2, 1935 he placed third in the College 1,500-meter run (4:17) at the Millrose Games, where Glenn Cunningham, Bill Bonthron, and Gene Venzke were featured in the open 1,500-meter run.[50] Daly placed second in the one-mile run (4:22) at the Seventh Annual Armour Tech Relays in Chicago, and placed third in the open mile invitational at the Canadian Indoor Championships at Maple Leaf Gardens in Toronto.[51]

During the outdoor season in 1935, Bill Daly was on the winning the college division distance medley relay team (10:25.1) at the Drake Relays, and won the mile run (4:16.6) at the Michigan State Intercollegiate Championships with the fifteenth fastest mile run in the USA that year. On May 25 Daly placed second in the mile run (4:16.9) at the Central Collegiate Conference Championships at Notre Dame. Four days later he ran a featured one-mile match race against Glenn Cunningham at the University of Detroit May Fair. On June 21–22, 1935 Daly placed fourth in the mile-run at the 14th Annual NCAA Outdoor Championships at the University of California. He finished the season by running the 1,500-meter on July 4 at the National Senior AAU Championships in Lincoln, Nebraska.[52]

As a college senior, Daly placed third in the open 1,500-meter run at the National AAU Indoor Championships. He also defeated Bill Zepp in the three-mile run (14:58) during the indoor season. On May 16, 1936 Daly won the 5-K run (15:23.3) at Michigan Intercollegiate Championships in Ann Arbor.[53]

On June 13, 1936, after graduating from the University of Detroit, Daly placed third in the mile-run before 30,000 fans at the Princeton Invitational at Palmer Stadium in New Jersey. Two weeks later he placed third in the 1,500-meter run at the central regional semi-finals of the Olympic tryouts in Milwaukee. Still hoping to make the Olympic team, Daly persuaded the Detroit Track Club to sponsor a trip back to Princeton. On July 3, 1936 Daly placed second in the 1,500-meter and the 800-meter (1:54.2) runs at the National Junior AAU Meet.[54] The next day he placed seventh in the 1,500-meter run at the AAU Senior Championships. His showing earned an invitation to participate in the final Olympic trials at Randalls Island on July 10, but like Bill Bonthron he failed to make the team.

After the Olympic trials Bill Daly joined the UAW and became a truck driver for the Ford Motor Company. On May 13, 1937 Daly announced that he would participate in a special event at the Twenty-Second Annual Michigan Intercollegiate Outdoor meet in East Lansing in hopes of setting a new record in the four-mile run. Hannes Kolehmainen of Finland had set the existing track record (20:02) in 1913. The successful challenge to the record took place on the new quarter-mile track at Michigan State College.[55] On June 12 Daly won the 10-K run (34:14) and placed second in the 1,500-meter run at the Western Michigan AAU Meet in Grand Rapids. Still running for the Detroit Track Club, Daly ran in the 1,500-meter at the 1937 National Senior AAU Championships in Milwaukee.

In 1938, on "Red" Simmons' recommendation, Bill Daly was hired by the Detroit Police Department and became a member its track team. On July 4 Daly made his national debut with the Detroit Police by placing fourth in the 1,500-meter run at the National AAU Junior Championships in Buffalo. In 1939, Daly again placed fourth in the 1,500-meter run at the National AAU Junior Championships, at a time when Don Lash, an Indiana State Highway patrolman, was one of the nation's premier milers.[56] On May 31, 1941 Daly won the two-mile run (9:34.6) at the Michigan AAU Championships in Ypsilanti. Sometime later, while trying to break up a fight, Bill Daly was accidentally shot by his partner. The bullet lodged in his liver, and could not be removed. Consequently, Daly was given disability and moved to Maine. In 1980 "Red" Simmons visited Daly and his wife in Maine. At that time Daly was still running marathons. In 1984, when in his mid-60s, Bill came home after running a marathon and died of a heart attack.[57] William M. Daly was one of the first members inducted into the University of Detroit Athletic Hall of Fame.

Three years after Bill Daly joined to the Detroit Police, the Department recruited another trackman—University of Michigan All-American, William Watson. The national decathlon champion added to the meager representation of African-Americans on the city's police force. On June 20, 1942 he won the shot put (50–1) and the 56-pound weight throw (31–11), finished third in the discus, and fifth in the broad jump at the National AAU Junior Championships in New York City. The following year the Detroit policeman successfully defended his decathlon title at the National AAU Championships.[58]

Implementation of the Fair Employment Practices mandated by President Roosevelt's Executive Order of June 1941 encountered resistance in cities like Detroit as well as in the South, where the War Manpower Commission "indefinitely postponed" Fair Employment Practices Committee hearings into discriminatory practices by southern railroads.[59] In early June 1943, a hate strike at Packard Motors, where Eddie Tolan was now employed, idled 25,000 workers and halted nearly all of the plant's production of bomber engines. The walkout was precipitated by the upgrading of three black workers.[60] The hate strikers caused the loss of nearly 2.5 million hours of war production.[61]

Throughout June 1943, a series of incidental racial clashes took place in and around Detroit. Then, on Sunday, June 20, as the temperature topped 90 degrees, thousands of blacks and whites crowded into the Belle Isle Park, where several fights broke out on the bridge linking the island to the mainland. The conflicts soon spread into the city. By Monday as many as 10,000 white residents were rampaging against Detroit blacks. Three-fourths of the Detroit police precincts reported riot activity. Finally, Army troops were brought in to quell the disturbances. By then, twenty-five African-Americans and nine Caucasians had been killed and hundreds of people injured.[62] At that time, forty-four percent of the city's population was African-American, but only 5% of the Detroit Police force was African-American.

Following the race riot of 1943, the Detroit's Police Department refused to heed the warning signs and change department policies and hiring practices. Insensitivity to minority needs and feelings continued to place the city at risk of turmoil. In 1945 Mayor Edward Jeffries won reelection by distributing anti-black literature on the eve of the election, and two years after that, conservative businessman Albert Cobo again played the race card to win the Mayor's office.[63]

Meanwhile, on June 17–18, 1944 Detroit police officer Bill Watson placed second in the shot put (49–10½), fourth in the 56-pound weight throw (33-¾), and fifth in the discus (137–6¾) at the National AAU Senior Championships in New York City. In September 1944 Watson won four events in the eighteenth annual meet with the Toronto Police team.[64]

After World War II, Elmer "Buddy" Coleman, a Wayne University track star became a Detroit policeman. On September 3, 1955 "Buddy" won the 220-yard dash (21.6) at the Canadian Open Meet in Toronto. Two days later he won the 100-yard dash (9.6) at the Canadian Olympic Training Invitational in Toronto. The following June "Buddy," as a member of the Detroit Police Athletic Association team, won the hop, step and jump (44–8½) and placed second in the 100-yard dash (9.8) at the Chicago Track Club Open Meet held at Stagg Field. Elmer Coleman died young. He was reputedly killed by a jealous husband.[65]

In 1964 only 166 of the more than 1,000 Detroit police officers were African-Americans. Only one inspector and four uniformed sergeants was Black. Indeed, as late as 1974, when the department adopted affirmative action in hiring to eradicate the effects of past discrimination, only 10 lieutenants of 230 were African-American. The first year that the Department hired more African-Americans than whites was 1975. That year the Detroit Police Officers Association sued Mayor Coleman Young, the Police Chief, and members of the Board of Police Commissioners to halt the affirmative-action policy. The union said better-qualified white officers were passed over for promotion in order for the department to improve its rankings of minorities. Despite court action, the Board of Police Commissioners voted in 1979 to continue affirmative action until about 1990.[66]

During the 1970s, Tracy Smith, a 5-K runner who placed fifth in the Olympic trials in 1972, worked for the Los Angeles Police Department.[67] He was at his peak in 1968 when he qualified for the Mexico City Olympics in the 10-K run. He later experienced an injury to his Achilles tendon. This injury sent him into a "super depression." As a result of inactivity, he would wake-up nights shaking. His "physical withdrawal" ended when he set a world indoor record in the three-mile run (13:07.2) at the AAU indoor meet at Madison Square Garden on February 23, 1973. It was the most satisfying moment in his career. Smith remarked, "I needed something like this."[68]

At the end of the twentieth century, the leadership of the Detroit Police Department showed little interest in the heritage left by the department's track team. The records and accomplishments of the department's runners and weight men were lost or mislaid, its trophies neglected, and stories forgotten. Yet, when most of the nation was focused on trying to break the four-minute mile, the Detroit Police Department was showing the nation how to toss the 56-pound weight farther than anyone else.

7. Olympic Dreams Denied

With so much attention focused on the Olympic Games, it is easy to assume that the track and field athletes who make the Olympic team are better and more notable than those who do not. This common, but false assumption was the natural by-product of the public attention afforded the Olympic movement by the press and amateur athletes during the 1930s. Prior to the 1932 Olympic Games, most American sportsmen thought of the Olympics as an important, but primarily European sports event. While American athletes such as Jim Thorpe, Johnny Weissmuller, and Charlie Paddock got a boost from their participation in the Olympic Games, their reputations were not dependent on the Olympics alone. The Los Angeles Olympiad, however, offered a welcome reprieve from the great depression that had enveloped the country, and indeed the economies of entire western world. It made national heroes of Babe Didrikson, Eddie Tolan, and Ralph Metcalfe, and put them on a par with the European track stars of the 1920s, such as Paavo Nurmi, Willie Ritola, Harold Abrahams, and Eric Liddell. The cost of staging the Olympics and the huge public spectacle created by the games in 1932 and 1936 further distorted public perceptions of track and field. The Olympics drained scarce resources away from regional and national track and field events and concentrated them on the Olympics.

The emphasis on Olympians obscures the careers of those who did not make the Olympic Games. Often these athletes were often every bit as good as most of those who made the Olympic team. Many deserve recognition long denied. There were four primary reasons reason why these men did not make the Olympic team: injury, the timing of their peak performances, the distances or events in which they performed, or the way in which they perceived the growing tide of intolerance.

Done-in By Injury

Distance runner Neree Denis Alix was an American of French-Canadian descent, who grew up in Lockport, New York. His parents moved south and west to escape the ubiquitous prejudice and lack of opportunity in the French-Canada during the first half of the twentieth century. The five foot nine inch Neree did not begin his track career until 1929 when he was a senior in high school. He ran under the direction of Albert E. Gay, track coach and director of physical education at Lockport High School. As a distance runner that year, Neree Alix competed in three meets and amassed sixteen points for Lockport High School.[1] In a meet against Niagara Falls Alix won the mile run (4:55.2) and placed second in the 880 (2:15.2). The following week he won the mile (4:55.2) and placed second in the 880 (2:08) at the Interscholastic in Niagara Falls. Finally, in the sectional meet in Kenmore, New York, Alix placed second in the mile run (4:49). Gay later recalled,

> He was an eager and enthusiastic pupil and learned quickly. One of the out-standing things I remember is that he religiously followed training rules. He did not smoke, kept good sleeping hours and followed good living habits generally. I well remember pacing him with a car on road work and drilling him as to sense of pace for his mile run. He acquired this sense of timing very readily and could come quite close to making the half mile within the time limit set at the pace for a mile. He had a partner, Clyde Allport, and in every case where they ran together they would join hands and cross the tape sharing first and second place points.[2]

On the advice of Coach Gay, Neree enrolled at the University of Michigan in the fall of 1930. Without financial support, Neree "put in one winter as a not-so-promising aspirant for freshman track honors,"[3] although he won the freshman cross-country meet in the fall of 1930 suggesting that he might have untapped talent.

According to University of Michigan freshman track Coach Ken Doherty, Alix came to Michigan no more than a fairly promising dis-tance runner, and ended his freshman year with best times of 10:10 in the two mile, and 4:38.5 in the mile.[4] By the conclusion of his first year, Neree faced insurmountable financial trouble. Discouraged, he dropped out of college and returned home to work for the local civil works administration.[5] While unable to return to school, young Alix did not give up running. He continued to train and ran in competition at local AAU meets whenever possible. Equally as important, he corre-sponded with Michigan Coach Charles B. Hoyt, who provided consid-erable encouragement.[6]

After a two-year absence from college, Neree returned to Ann Arbor in the fall of 1933 to major in civil engineering. The hard work he put in back home, as well as his increased maturity, made Neree an important asset to the University of Michigan track team in the 1934 indoor season. The financial troubles that had kept him out of school for two years were not removed by any "good fairy." Though back on the campus, he had to sandwich his track activities in between classes and 30 to 50 hours of work each week. For two years he maintained the grind.

On January 27, 1934 Neree won a spot on the varsity travel team by coming in first in the varsity trials. "In the two-mile Neree Alix a sophomore from Lockport, New York surprised the crowd by winning the first major indoor race of the season."[7] One week later, on February 3, 1934 Neree Alix faced Michigan State College Olympian Tom Ottey at the Michigan AAU Indoor Championships held at Yost Fieldhouse. As expected, Ottey won the two-mile race, but Neree ran a close second.[8]

On February 17, the University of Michigan faced Big Ten Conference rival, Indiana University, Michigan's strongest rival for the Western Conference Indoor Intercollegiate Championship. Neree proved his worth by winning the two-mile run in this important duel meet.[9] The following Saturday night U of M hosted a triangular meet with Michigan Normal College and Michigan State College [Michigan State University]. The match-up of the meet was the re-paring of Tom Ottey and Neree Alix. That evening Michigan State College pacemaker John Hammer led Alix for the better part of two miles, followed by Tom Ottey close on Alix's heels. In the ninth lap at Yost fieldhouse, Neree spurted ahead to comfortably win the race.[10]

The win over Tom Ottey made Neree Alix a campus celebrity. The *Detroit News* wrote: "Holt is beginning to figure on young Alix as a 'comer'"[11] and his hometown newspaper wrote: "Alix looks like business as track phenom at Michigan."[12]

On March 3 "Neree Alix, a tiny distance runner, won the two-mile in 9:33.6" in a triangular meet with the University of Chicago and Northwestern in Chicago.[13] Finally, Neree won the two-mile run (9:32.9) at the Western Conference Indoor Championships held at the University of Chicago Fieldhouse on March 10. He and Willis Ward were the only Michigan event winners in the University of Michigan's conference winning team effort. A *Detroit News* sports writer described Neree's win:

Neree Alix, running his first big race for Michigan, did everything that was expected of him by winning a brilliantly run race. He did not look good at the end of the first mile, being at the rear of the field of 12, but he was running according to plan, and as he went into the second mile he started to come up, going into the lead at the end of a mile and a half and he was never menaced after that.[14]

The 1934 Western Conference Indoor Championships found Willis Ward winning three events, for 15 points. Ward set a new conference record in the high jump, tied the Big Ten record in the 60-yard dash and won the 70-yard high-hurdles. He and Alix accounted for more than half of Michigan's team points. Minnesota distance runner Wayne Slocum later complained that his decision to wear a new pair of running shoes handicapped his performance.[15] Incidently, Purdue University middle-distance runner Charles Popejoy, the father of Michigan State University miler Ken Popejoy, placing second in the mile run at the 1934 Conference Indoor Championships.[16]

The 1934 outdoor track and field season, however, was peppered with a strong dose of bad luck. Shortly after the Western Conference Indoor meet, Neree experienced a serious case of shin splints. Then, on April 21 he injured his ankle during the outdoor time trials preceding the team's trip to the Drake Relays.[17] Finally, when he returned to training prematurely, he injured a leg muscle. Consequently, Neree was unable to attain top form at any time during the outdoor season.

That spring injuries also befell Willis Ward, Adam Stone, Cass W. Kemp, and Harold T. Ellerby.[18] Needless to say, Michigan did not win the outdoor championship in 1934. Alix placed third in the two-mile run at the Western Conference Outdoor meet, as Charles Popejoy won the race in 9:33, a slower time than the Michigan sophomore had clocked winning the event indoors.[19]

Still favoring his injured leg, Alix reported for the 1934–35 indoor season. Rounding into condition slowly, he took third in the Conference indoor meet behind Don Lash of Indiana and Wayne Slocum of Minnesota, clocking a decent time of 9:30 against Don Lash's winning time of 9:21.3.[20] After the Conference meet, however, Alix again began to improve. He climaxed the indoor season with a brilliant mile leg as part of the Michigan four-mile relay team that set the meet record at the Butler Relays in Indianapolis.[21]

At 3:30 p.m. on April 5, 1935 twenty-two Michigan track men, together with Athletics Board of Controls member Ralph Aigler, Athletic Director Fielding Yost, Coaches Charles Hoyt and Ken Doherty, track team manager Bill Morgan, trainer John Brasovich, and *Detroit News* sports reporter John E. McManis, boarded the Michigan Central passenger train in Ann Arbor bound for Chicago and places beyond.[22] That evening at about 9 p.m. the entourage completed its transfer to the Rock Island Line bound for Los Angeles, with stops in Kansas City, El Paso, and Tucson. By chance, singer and movie star Bing Crosby was on the same train.[23]

When the train stopped in Kansas City, George Cauthen of the *Kansas City Journal-Post* took a picture of the University of Michigan track team that featured Neree Alix, Fielding Yost and team Captain Harvey H. Smith in the foreground. The picture ran in the *Detroit News*, on Sunday April 7. When the train reached Alhambra, California, the whole gang was in a good mood. The track team worked out at Hollywood High School in the morning and UCLA in the afternoon of April 8, 9, and 10. At 6:30 p. m. on April 8 they attended a Michigan Alumni Club dinner at the Hollywood Roosevelt Hotel, where they were staying. At noon the next day they attended a Big Ten luncheon in Los Angeles, and on April 10 they had lunch at one of the movie studios before leaving for San Francisco on the Southern Pacific that evening at 9 p.m. After spending three days in Oakland, the team was to return through Ogden, Utah and Omaha, Nebraska on the Chicago and Northwestern Railroad to Chicago, and thence to Ann Arbor.[24]

In the brief training period outdoors before the trip to California Alix had begun to show the level of performance that had won him the 1934 Big Ten indoor two-mile championship. He was progressing faster than expected, and was running at nearly his best form as the team left for the California for the long awaited duel meet between the Michigan, Big Ten Indoor Champions, and the Golden Bears of California, the Pacific Coast Conference Track Champions.

Following a Big Ten luncheon in San Francisco and a day's rest, Neree was running well ahead of the four other competitors in the two-mile run, at Edwards Stadium on the afternoon of April 13. Rain had made the cinder path heavy and Neree's leg had been slightly stiff for two or three days, but the race was going well for the Wolverine distance runner. He was on a record setting pace and seemed to be an easy winner. It appeared to all present that Alix was on the path to regaining the Big Ten two-mile championship the following month. Then, as he was finishing the seventh lap of the eight-lap race, the even-striding Wolverine star made a sudden spurt to increase his lead. Without warning, he felt all the muscles of his right leg stiffen up and when his right foot hit the ground with a rigid leg behind it, he heard a crack and then he tumbled to the cinders. Walter Stone, who was trailing Alix by two yards, stumbled over his fallen teammate.[25]

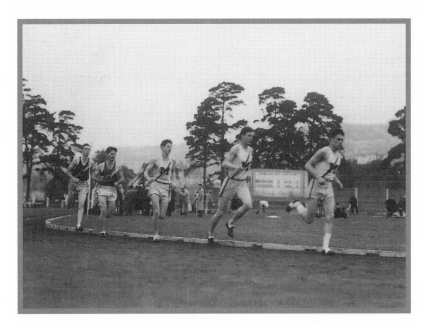

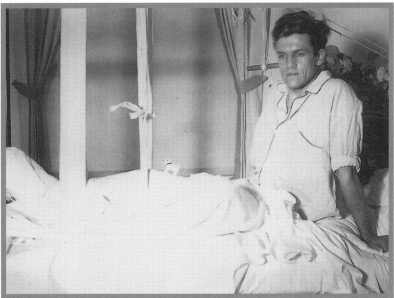

Neree Alix is leading in the two-mile run at the University of California in Berkeley, California. On the next lap his leg bone snapped. The second picture shows Neree recovering in a California hospital. *(Photo courtesy of Evelyn Alix.)*

Bones protruded through the skin and Neree was in a great deal of pain. "Both leg bones [below the knee in the right leg broke had snapped] in three places, the lower fracture projecting through the flesh in a compound wound." Neree was taken to the University of California infirmary and thence to Cowell Memorial Hospital in Berkeley. The serious, unexpected injury to Neree Alix caused considerable gloom in the Wolverine camp. Physicians soon discovered that Alix was the victim of one of the most unique accidents recorded in track and field history. Experts surmised that the chances for a break under such conditions were "one in thousands."[26] Apparently, there was an undetected stress fracture that became an outright break during the course of the hard pounding of race conditions on a hard running surface. The break was probably exacerbated by the fall.[27]

When Neree broke a leg, his Olympic dreams were shattered. A columnist for the *Ann Arbor News* observed:

Material for a contemporary tragedy might be found by the sympathetic dramatist in the case of Neree Alix, the varsity two-miler who is now in the University of California infirmary with a compound leg fracture. Now no one knows what will happen to him when he comes back from California with his leg in a plaster cast. In a sport which demands more than any other patience and concentration, Alix had worked for five years in the face of odds not only in the form of physical injuries but of financial difficulties even more discouraging, to finally reach what his coaches consider the height of his form. Now his serious injury may conclude his running career.[28]

The next day; a letter to the editor asked:

That was great human-interest stuff you had in your column this morning about Neree Alix, but shedding a tear or two over his sad plight isn't going to pay his room and board when he gets out of the hospital. Can't something tangible be done for him?

> Sincerely,
> Track Fan

This letter triggered a spontaneous suggestion by the varsity track team to hold a benefit track meet for the popular, hospitalized runner. A delegation from the track squad took the suggestion to Coach Hoyt. Although Alix's hospital expenses would be fully met by the Michigan Athletic Association, it is understood that after his release from the hospital, Alix would be unable to resume the work that had supported him through his first three years of college.[29] So, they offered to stage a benefit track meet at Ferry Field for Neree on April 30. Coach Hoyt conferred with Lloyd Olds to make certain that such an event would not adversely affect the amateur status of anyone involved. Coach Olds not only offered AAU sanction for the meet but offered to have his track squad, including national champion distance runner Billy Zepp, involved in the benefit meet.[30] Proceeds of the meet were to be turned over to Michigan's injured distance running star, who was still recuperating in Cowell hospital in Berkeley.

Eddie Tolan, former Michigan star and double-winner in the 1932 Olympic sprints, who has just won the world's professional sprint championship in Australia, was invited to give an exhibition if he returned by that date. Members of the freshman varsity squad sold tickets for the benefit meet.[31] While Tolan's schedule did not allow him to make the meet, and rain and wind forced the meet indoors, the benefit was a success. Two-thousand four hundred tickets were sold at 25¢ each, giving the benefit a $600 gross profit, which was a tidy sum of money in 1935.[32]

When Neree returned to Ann Arbor from California in late May, his teammates had won the Big Ten Conference outdoor championship. In the summer of 1935 the University of Michigan Athletic Association arranged a job for Neree checking out caddies on the University golf course. He spent the late hours every day walking over the course. By late August Neree was running again, and Dr. Frank Lynam, physician for the athletic department pronounced the young man fit for further competition, but declared "he will undoubtedly be forced to compete at shorter distances."[33] However, Coach Hoyt advised Alix to take it easy and plan nothing strenuous that year and postpone serious running until the following year.[34] No one had the kind of knowledge in 1935 to be certain what had caused the injury or if it would reoccur, and without better information Neree was afraid of a recurrence of the painful compound fracture. The *Detroit News* told its readers, "Mental hazard of track keeps Alix off '36 team."[35]

Neree Alix reentered track competition March 5, 1937 in a duel meet with the University of Pittsburgh, in which he placed second.[36] Coach Hoyt concluded that Alix was no longer "a strong runner," but was "a steady runner with an uncanny judge of pace."[37] For whatever reason, he never regained his competitive edge. On April 17 the University of Michigan track team traveled again to California to face the University of California. This time Neree placed third the 2-mile run at Edwards Stadium.[38] He earned his third block M letter in 1937. However, he did not win an indoor or outdoor race, except for a staged three-way tie for first in his last race for the University of Michigan.[39]

Walter Stone, a teammate that Neree dominated in 1934–35, placed third in the National AAU 3,000-meter steeplechase in 1937.[40]

In the fall of 1934, Neree Alix met Evelyn Maloy, a Scotch-Irish young-lady who came to the University of Michigan from Kansas City. She was working at the cafeteria at the Michigan League, and training to be a social worker. She had an older brother who was also at the University. In May 1937, Neree Denis Alix graduated from Michigan with a Bachelor of Science degree in civil engineering.[41]

After her graduation from college in 1938, Evelyn and Neree were married in a Catholic ceremony in Kansas City. Alix, now a trained civil engineer and land surveyor, went to work for the Illinois Central Railroad Company and remained with them through 1940. Over those four years he was assigned to several locations between Chicago and New Orleans. In the fall of 1941 he went to work for the Firestone Tire and Rubber Company and was sent to Liberia in November 1941. After completing his work with Firestone, he was loaned to a British research firm doing work in Liberia.[42] Evelyn and Neree already had one child, and she was pregnant with their second child. Instead of accompanying him to Africa as she had hoped, she went back to Kansas City to live with her parents.[43] Pearl Harbor was bombed while Neree was enroute to Africa by boat. He remained in Africa until 1942 to finish the project. He returned to the United States and joined the Navy as a Lieutenant. He was assigned to ordinance in the Pacific in preparation for the invasion of Japan. The atomic bomb may well have saved his life.

When Neree returned from the Pacific, his freshman college track buddy, Dick McManus, offered him a job in Michigan. Alix later became the West Bloomfield Township Engineer, overseeing sewer construction and drainage problems in rapidly growing Oakland County.[44] He quickly became active in civic affairs. By 1954 he was on the budget committee of the West Bloomfield Community Chest[45] and was active in Cub Scouting and the Green School Parent-Teacher's Association.[46]

By 1963–64 Neree had formed the Neree D. Engineering Company of Southfield and was a self-employed, consulting engineer.[47] Neree became West Bloomfield Township engineer in 1963.[48]

As the years passed Neree expanded his community activity, raised six children, including two surveyors and a surgeon, and hosted three exchange students—one each from Argentina, Rhodesia, and Malaysia. Neree was elected Chippewa County Surveyor, as a Republican. However, in the May 1978, his middle son Steve was killed in a freak accident while surveying in Alaska. The death had a noticeable impact on

Neree.[49] On November 30, 1978 Neree Alix died of Cancer in St. Joseph Mercy Hospital in Pontiac.[50]

So Near, Yet So Far

Willis Franklyn Ward attended Northwestern High School in Detroit, where he was an A student and graduated near the top of his class. In 1927, as a 15-year old high school freshman, he won the city high jump title and placed second in the national interscholastic meet in Chicago. There were only four African-Americans on the 1929–30 Northwestern High School track team when he set state records in the high and low hurdles, and set the world interscholastic record in the high jump. The following year, as a senior, he re-set these records. On April 25, 1931 Willis Ward set the national interscholastic record for the running high jump (6–6) in a meet in Detroit.[51] Almost a month later, he won the high jump (6–1½), the 120-yard high-hurdles (15.2), and the 120-yard low-hurdles (12.8) at the Detroit Metropolitan League Championships and led Northwestern High School to the city title. His high jump performance was 3 inches higher than the Michigan Class A Champion's jump that same day, but Detroit stopped competing in the State Meet that year.[52] Noting the occasion, *Detroit Times* observed, "It is Willis Ward, called the greatest athlete to compete in the Detroit schools making his bow at the end of his high school career."[53] It surprised no one that he was named to both the 1931 *Spaulding Almanac* and the AAU National All-Scholastic track team for the running high jump.[54] He also was All-City in football in 1929 and 1930.

Aware that the University of Michigan had not allowed an African-American on its football team in more than thirty-years, Ward planned to accept a scholarship to attend Dartmouth College. With Fielding Yost no longer coaching football at Michigan, prominent Detroit alumni obtained a commitment that Willis Ward would be allowed to play football and participate in track at the U of M. Leaders in the African-American community persuaded Willis to help break down racial barriers in his home state, so he accepted a scholarship at Michigan.

Willis Ward was an instant star at the University of Michigan. He was one of three superlative ends on the football team his first year, alternating with Ivan Williamson and Ted Petoskey. In his freshman year of track, he was allowed to enter the NCAA Outdoor Championship in Chicago to qualify for the Olympic tryouts. On June 11, 1932 he won the high jump (6–7½), but because he was a college freshman he ineligible for NCAA title.[55] Ward's jump was the best of the year and one of the best of any year up to that time. He qualified for the final Olympic trials in Palo Alto. On July 2 the NCAA allocated $115 to Willis Ward to underwrite his expenses for participating in final Olympic trials.[56]

At Palo Alto, Ward was considered a favorite to win the high jump trials for the place on the Olympic team.[57] However, after a long trip in segregated conditions and without prior experience in world class competition, Willis was not quite at his peak in performance. When he arrived on the Pacific Coast, track coaches came from all points to see him jump. Ward, being an obliging and unassuming young man, gave a demonstration to everyone who asked. As a result, when the day of the final tryouts came, he was worn out and finished in a tie for fourth place, with a jump of 6–4.[58] He was too tired to go higher. The Olympic high jump champion that year was Canadian, Duncan McNaughton, with a leap of 6 feet 5⅝ inches. It was a height that Willis Ward had topped as a high school boy.[59]

The following year he was acknowledged to be the most skilled football player on the Michigan team. It was a team that claimed future President Gerald Ford as its center. Ward was named first team end on the AAU All-American football team for 1933.[60] Indeed, he was the best player on two undefeated, top-rated teams.

In 1933 Willis Ward won the high jump (6–4¾) and was second to Ralph Metcalfe in the 100-yard dash at the Drake Relays.[61] A Detroit reporter observed,

Willis Ward . . . has shown great improvement this week in the high-hurdles. Ward has developed a cannon ball start. He takes the first hurdle at full speed as if he were running a 100-yard dash. Ward still waves his right hand awkwardly as he goes over the jumps, but has so much speed, spring and power that he makes up for poor form.[62]

Going into the Big Ten outdoor championships in 1933 a reporter for the *Michigan Daily* stated,

Willis Ward, Michigan's 196-pound Negro all-around star, today led a parade of 15 Wolverines into the finals of the Western Conference 33rd track and field championship meet. Ward, looked upon as the athlete to provide the winning points in the Michigan struggle to retain the title tomorrow, qualified in three events, winning his heats in the 100-yard dash and the 120-yard high-hurdles, and finishing runner-up to another Negro ace, John Brooks of Chicago in the broad jump.[63]

On May 20, 1933 Willis Ward almost single handedly won the Western Conference Championship for the University of Michigan, at Northwestern University's Dyche Stadium. He scored 18 points, with victories in the 100-yard dash and high jump, second place in the broad jump and high-hurdles, fifth in the low-hurdles. He came within two points of equaling the 20-point total that Ivan Fuqua and Charles Hornbostel rang up for Indiana University with two victories each. Ward was the individual point winner in the meet and was awarded the trophy for the best individual performance.[64]

Following the Big Ten Championships, University of Michigan's New England alumni raised funds to bring the Wolverine track squad to the IC4A games at Harvard Stadium. However, Fielding Yost kept them home because of the overall financial situation and forthcoming final examinations.[65]

During the 1933 indoor track season, Ward won the high jump at the Michigan State Relays, the Butler Relays, and the Big Ten Championships. He also placed second in the 60-yard dash at the Big Ten Indoor. He won the high jump and placed second in the 100-yard dash at the Drake Relays, and won the high jump and the 100-yard dash and placed second in the broad jump at the Big Ten Outdoor Championships. Ward finished the season by placing third in high jump at the National NCAA Outdoor Championships in Chicago on June 16–17, 1933.[66]

In 1934 several NCAA rules changes affected track and field competition. Distance penalties were eliminated for false starts and disqualification followed a second false start. In the first round, the contestant was to be allowed four tries rather than three for the shot, hammer, discus, javelin and broad jump. In the high jump it was made clear that at least one foot must precede the body and head across the bar. Finally, the relay baton must be carried in the hand starting in 1934.[67]

In the 1934 Big Ten Indoor meet, Ward won the 60-yard dash, the high jump and the high hurdles. His 15 points went a long way toward allowing Michigan to replace Indiana as the Conference champions. Then came the first blow of fate for Ward. After a remarkable indoor season in which he lost only one event—the 60-yard hurdles at the Butler Relays—he suffered a leg injury and was of little value in the outdoor season.

At the Conference Championships in Evanston, he qualified for the high hurdles, 100-yard dash and broad jump, and was one of the chief reasons why Michigan defeated the University of Illinois. Despite a pulled muscle, Ward was the high scorer for Michigan. He won the broad jump on a single leap in the trials and earned points in the high jump for the leaps he had made before pulling his leg muscle in the finals of the high-hurdles.[68]

Responding to Intolerance

In the fall of 1934, at Athletic Director Fielding Yost's request, football coach Harry Kipke kept Willis Ward from suiting-up for the Georgia Tech football game. Yost, the son of a Confederate Civil War soldier, was honoring the request of Bill Alexander, the Georgia Tech coach and his brother-in-law, Dan McGugin, football coach at Vanderbilt. McGugin had written, "I don't believe you can afford to use colored players as it has never been done in the case of games with teams from this section." After sitting out the Georgia Tech game, the only Michigan victory that season, Ward was so upset he planned to quit the team, and friends were helping him raise the money to pay for his senior year in college, should he quit football. Kipke threatened that if Ward quit that would be the end of opportunities for Negro athletes at Michigan. While it hurt him to stay, he did for the benefit of future black athletes.[69]

Sixty-four years later former President Gerald R. Ford recalled the incident.

I came naturally by my support of [the 1965] Voting Rights Act. Thirty years before Selma, I was a University of Michigan senior, preparing with my Wolverine teammates for a football game against visiting Georgia Tech. Among the best players on that year's Michigan squad was Willis Ward, a close friend of mine whom the Southern school reputedly wanted dropped from our roster because he was black. My classmates were just as adamant that he should take the field. In the end, Willis decided not to play.

His sacrifice led me to question how educational administrators could capitulate to raw prejudice. A university, after all, is both a preserver of tradition and a hotbed of innovation. So long as books are kept open, we tell ourselves, minds can never be closed.

But doors, too, must be kept open. Tolerance, breadth of mind and appreciation for the world beyond our neighborhoods: These can be learned on the football field and in the science lab as well as in the lecture hall; but only if students are exposed to America in all her variety.

For the class of '35, such educational opportunities were diminished by the relative scarcity of African-Americans, women and various ethnic groups on campus. I have often wondered how much different the world might have been in the 1940s, '50s and '60s—how much more humane and just-if my generation had experienced a more representative sampling of the American family. That the indignities visited on Ward would be unimaginable in today's Ann Arbor is a measure of how far we have come toward realizing, however belatedly, the promises we made to each other in declaring our nationhood and professing our love of liberty.

If history has taught us anything in this remarkable century, it is the notion of America as a work in progress. Do we really want to risk turning the clock to an era when the Willis Wards were isolated and penalized for the color of their skin, their economic standing or national ancestry?[70]

While he became an All-American in both football and track, track was Ward's favorite sport, and he was a virtual one-man track team. During his final indoor track season at the University of Michigan, Willis Ward was responsible for the biggest upset in Western Conference history. On March 2, 1935 he defeated Jesse Owens in the 60-yard dash and the 65-yard high hurdles in a duel meet held in Ann Arbor.[71]

Handicapped by his bad leg, Ward did not run well in the 1935 Big Ten Indoor Championships. Nevertheless, he managed to place third in the 60-yard dash and a fourth in the high hurdles. He was kept out of the high jump for fear of a permanent injury to his lame leg. However, the rest of the powerful Michigan team came through to win the Conference title.[72]

Ward appeared to be on a comeback running magnificently in the dual meet with the University of California, and in the high-hurdles at the Penn Relays. But misfortune overtook him in the 100-meters trials at the Penn Relays. Ward again pulled a muscle and was out of competition until the Big Ten Conference met at Ann Arbor, where Jesse Owens would set four world records.

Fearing another muscle injury, Willis lost his confidence and he failed to qualify for the finals of the high-hurdles. Coach Hoyt, also fearing an injury, kept him out of the 100-yard dash, but Willis made the greatest leap of his life, 25–1½ to take second to Jesse Owens' world record-beating broad jump. Ward tied for first in the high jump, again leading all Michigan point winners. Despite the heroics of Jesse Owens, Michigan won the Big Ten title over Ohio State University by a margin of only 4½ points, which shows how important Ward's 8½ points were that Saturday.[73]

Hailed as one of the greatest athletic prospects of all times when he finished at Northwestern High, Ward wound up his collegiate career on June 21–22, 1935. He ended in a three way tie for second in the high jump (6–4) and placed fourth in the broad jump at the 14th Annual NCAA Outdoor Championships held at University of California. After three years as a regular on the football team, three years as high scorer on the track squad, and All-American status in both football and track, this should have been honor enough for any man. Yet, Ward's best football was played with a team so weak that he attracted virtually no national attention. And, although he is one of the greatest trackman ever to wear the maize and blue of Michigan, he did not set a single record on Ferry Field, his home track, and was destined to miss every opportunity for world competition in track and field. Moreover, despite his successes, by standing up for his rights during the Georgia Tech incident, captain honors in track and football were denied, his spirit was destroyed, and he was deprived of the drive needed to make the 1936 Olympic team. He later recalled, "You have to understand the hopelessness of that environment. The good old days were horrible."[74] There was a tradition of disfranchisement of black voters as old as the founding of the nation, and Thurgood Marshall had not even begun his efforts, on behalf of the NAACP, to pass Federal laws making lynching a Federal crime or his efforts to ensue that African-Americans were allowed to sit on juries.[75]

Willis Ward's personal record in the high jump (6–7½) demonstrated what he could have done in this event had he specialized. At Michigan, however, he was not permitted to specialize because the team needed all the points he could make. By 1936, his recurring leg injury raised questions as to whether Willis could ever return to his earlier form in the high jump. In addition, the high jump average in world competition had risen about two inches since 1932, so even if he could shake his injuries he might have had difficulty qualifying for the America's Olympic high jump squad in 1936.

So because Ward was a good fellow and willing to give everything he had for Michigan, he missed the tide of his athletic fortunes, and does not get the credit he deserves. "But," as a *Detroit News* reporter prophesized, "to those who know the inside of affairs at Michigan, and to his coaches, there will be few athletes whose passing will be regretted more than that of Willis Ward—the man who could come up to his greatest performance when the need was the greatest."[76]

Willis Ward was a man of courage and strong convictions. He protested Hitler's Nazism by refusing to participate in the Olympic Games in Germany, and did not participate in the Olympic tryouts in 1936, despite his love for the sport and his desire to perform in the Olympics. Ward's football and track prowess won him a place in four halls of fame, including the State of Michigan Sports Hall of Fame. He also remained a life-time supporter of the University of Michigan and its athletic program.

After college, auto tycoon Henry Ford handpicked Willis Ward to work in the Ford Motor Company personnel department. Ward's primary assignment was recruiting minorities. At night Ward attended the Detroit College of Law. In 1939, he graduated in the top ranks of his class. Following a stint in the Army, he set up private practice in Detroit in 1946.

During the Eisenhower Administration, Ward became Chief of the Civil Division of the U. S. Attorney's office. Next, he became an assistant Wayne County prosecutor. In 1964 Ward was appointed to the Board of Northern Michigan University, and two years later, Governor George Romney appointed him to the Michigan Public Service Commission. He later chaired that Commission. In 1973 Governor William G. Milliken appointed Willis Ward to the Wayne Probate Court. Prior to this appointment, the Wayne Probate Court performed like an exclusive club for a small group of white attorneys. Ward opened the lucrative field of probate work to black attorneys. "He made it fair," Attorney Andrew Perdue noted. "He balanced it. He made sure his staff was integrated and all his appointments were balanced." During his 10-year tenure as a Probate Court judge, Ward settled the contentious, complex, and bitterly contested $44 million estate of auto magnate John F. Dodge.[77]

Willis Ward's first Wife, Alma, was the tragic victim of an automobile accident. After her death in 1969, he married Margaret, who had four children. He was a member of Plymouth Congregational Church in Detroit, a biblical scholar, and a NAACP fund-raiser. Willis Ward died in December 1983.[78]

Poor Timing

Harvey Paul Woodstra was the second son of Mr. and Mrs. Richard Woodstra of Grand Rapids. His brother Donald H. Woodstra was just over a year old, when Harvey was born in Grand Rapids on April 15, 1915. When Harvey was old enough to walk he followed his brother around, and as a teenager he followed Donald into sports. Six foot four inch Don, whose nickname was "Woody", was a three-sport letter winner in high school. Woody, also a talented artist, was an end on the Ottawa Hills High School football team that won the City Championship in 1931, was a hurdler on the track team, and was captain of the basketball team in 1931–2.

Harvey found his first sports success in track and field. In 1931 he won the 120-yard high-hurdles and the high jump, and was second in the 220-yard low-hurdles in a class meet at Ottawa Hills High School,

On June 3, 1938 Harvey Woodstra, Michigan State College, leads (from left to right) Ivy Bledsoe, USC; Leonard Einsidler NYC ; and John R. Gowell, Maine in trials at the IC4A Championships at Randalls Island, New York City. (*Photo courtesy of Barbara Woodstra*)

and the following year led his high school to the City and Class A State High School Track Championships. On May 28, 1932, Harvey, whose nickname was "Bus", won the 220-yard low-hurdles, was fourth in the 120-yard high-hurdles, and ran the second leg of the meet winning 880-yard relay team. In 1933 he attended a fifth year of high school as a post-graduate and worked to earn enough money to go to junior college in 1934.[79]

While at Grand Rapids Junior College, Harvey played end on the football team. He also played amateur basketball with his brother for the Hamburg Packers. More importantly, he won track honors for his school throughout the state and region and qualified for the Olympic trial finals on June 10, 1936 at Randalls Island. He graduated with honors with an associate degree in commerce from Grand Rapids Junior College in June 1936, just days before traveling to Milwaukee to attempt to earn a spot on the Olympic team.

In July 1936 Harvey flew to New York to the Olympic final trials, where he just missed making the team. On July 12, shortly after his disappointing loss of an opportunity to go to Berlin, Harvey wrote his parents the following letter:

Dear Folks:

Arrived in N.Y. ok. Met Palmers at airport. [Lowell Palmer was his high school coach.] I guess I don't go to Berlin so I'll see you soon. Having lots of fun and am being royally entertained. Don't worry!!

"Bus"

Harvey's success on the cinders made him a prize recruit for Athletic Director Ralph H. Young, at Michigan State College. Harvey was an instant success at State College. Although NCAA regulations required Woodstra to compete as a freshman in 1937, he was an immediate point scorer, and in 1938 Harvey was instrumental in making State College a national track powerhouse. Michigan State was runner-up in the IC4A at Randalls Island, where Harvey tied the meet record for the 120-yard high hurdles and also won the 220-yard low-hurdles. A New York newspaper described the events held in wretched weather conditions [in a drizzle]:

In the high hurdles Woodstra of Michigan State, taking the lead at the third hurdle skimmed over the barriers in superb fashion to win by two yards from Jim Humphrey of Southern California in the grand time of 14.4 seconds, this figure equaled . . . the intercollegiate record made in 1920.[80]

On June 13, 1938 Harvey P. Woodstra earned a bachelors' degree in Business Administration from Michigan State College.[81] After graduating, he took a position with the Grand Rapids branch of the Retail Credit Company as an insurance investigator. After seven or eight months, he took a job with the General Electric Company in Schenectady, New York, with the view of staying in condition so that he could qualify for the 1940 Olympics scheduled for Tokyo. General Electric assigned Harvey to a Business Training Course. He played on the Business Training Course basketball team, according to a clipping in Woodstra's scrapbook:

'Twas bandied about at the General A.A. the other night that Harvey Woodstra, a member of the Business Training Course basketball team, did a little hurdling in college. One of our men, more or less for the sake of a conversation, asked Harvey if it were true. And, pals, it was! He won the IC4A 220-yard low hurdle and 120-yard high hurdle championships last year at Randalls Island, equaling the track record of 14.4 for the latter event. Harvey is a likeable young man from Grand Rapids, Mich. He attended Grand Rapids Junior College in 1935 and 1936 and then went to Michigan State College. He may do some hurdling here next Spring.

Oh, yes, about his basketball playing. His basketball experience before coming here was gaining Grand Rapids amateur circles. He doesn't profess to be a standout basketball player and probably won't be in the Works League. But he is a hustler all the way and a good influence on the team. He recently sank a field goal in the last three seconds of play to give Business Training Course a tie with Section E. Then Business Training won in an overtime period.[82]

Harvey never got the opportunity to qualify for the 1940 Olympics. World War II intervened. He entered the Army in July 1942, and was sent to Fort Lee, Virginia. After being commissioned a Second Lieutenant, he was assigned to Boston Harbor, where he was made a Cargo Officer in the Quartermasters Corps. As a Cargo Security Officer and Troop Commander, he made six trips to Europe out of the Boston Port of Embarkation and the New York Port of Entry, accompanying cargo and troops. He met his wife, Barbara J. Connell, who was from Boston, and married her on July 18, 1945. The following year, Pamela Ann, the first of three children was born. After World War II he returned to Schenectady, New York, and worked for General Electric for a year, before moving to Muscatine, Iowa in December 1946.[83]

Harvey worked in Muscatine until he retired as a senior vice-president of the Grain Processing Corporation. Following World War II, Harvey became a Reserve Officer, retiring 20-years later as a Lt. Colonel. He died February 1, 1996.

Bad Luck

As a sophomore in 1935, Bob Osgood became Big Ten champion in the indoor 65-yard high-hurdles. During the outdoor track season, the Cleveland, Ohio mechanical engineering student qualified for the finals of the National AAU Championships in both the 110-meter high-hurdles and the 200-meter low-hurdles. Osgood had all of the qualities to make the Olympic team except good luck.[84]

Because the 200-meter low-hurdles were dropped from international competition after the 1904 Olympiad, Osgood had a choice between the 110-meter high-hurdles and the 400-meter intermediate-hurdles for an attempt to qualify for the 1936 Olympic team. During the 1936 intercollegiate outdoor season, Osgood set three meet records. He set one in the 220-yard low-hurdles (24.2) in a duel meet in Bloomington with Indiana University and two in the 120-yard high hurdles (14.2), including the one in the Big Ten Conference meet. At the Penn Relays in April 1936 Osgood was on the winning mile relay team, demonstrating that he had the quarter-mile speed necessary for the 400-meter intermediate hurdles.[85]

Osgood and Coaches Hoyt and Doherty decided that the Wolverine timber topper should make his try in the 400-meter intermediate hurdles. On June 13, 1936 Osgood placed second in the 400-meter hurdles (53.4) at the Third Annual Princeton Invitational Games in New Jersey. One week later he won the intermediates (53.4) at the NCAA Championships at Stagg Field in Chicago. At the National Senior AAU Championships on July 4 at Palmer Stadium in Princeton, Osgood placed fourth the 400-meter hurdles. Eight days later at the final Olympic trials on Randalls Island, Osgood appeared to have earned a place on the Olympic team when he fell on the last hurdle and lost his opportunity to run in Berlin.[86]

During his senior year, Osgood, Captain of the 1937 University of Michigan track squad, helped set three meet records for the mile relay. On March 5 he helped to set the Yost fieldhouse record for the mile relay (3:19.8) in a duel meet with the University of Pittsburgh. At the Big Ten indoor championships, with a running start he ran his fastest indoor quarter mile (48.2) and made-up a 13-yard deficit in the third leg of the mile relay while setting the conference record for the mile relay (3:20.3).[87] At the Butler Relays the mile relay team set a meet record (3:26.5).[88]

Forrest "Spec" Towns, from Fitzgerald, Georgia, ran the high hurdles at the Bislet track in Oslo, Sweden, in 13.7. However, before the ratification of Towns' 13.7, Bob Osgood ran the first official 14.0 for 120-yard at Ann Arbor, Michigan, on May 22, 1937.[89] Bob Osgood set the American record for the 120-yard high-hurdles in the rain at the Big Ten Conference Championships at Ferry Field in Ann Arbor. A few days later, however, he turned an ankle, so on June 19, 1937 he placed only fifth in the 120-yards high hurdles at the NCAA Championships in Berkeley, California.[90]

After graduating from the University of Michigan in 1937, Bob Osgood became a safety engineer in Detroit. He held similar positions in New York City, Atlanta, Syracuse, and Cleveland, and sold construction equipment before working in the Engineering Department of North Olmsted, Ohio. Osgood retire in 1981.[91]

Wayne University's Fleet Footed Timber Topper Excels In An Event No Longer Featured At The Olympics

Allan Tolmich was born in Detroit on March 30, 1917. He was introduced to track and field by the Detroit Public Schools' elementary school field day that had been introduced, during the World War I era, by Detroit Public Schools athletic director and former Olympian Vonnie Blanchard. Allan tried his skills as a high jumper at the field day without much success. As a sophomore at Central High School, Tolmich was picked out of a gym class and encouraged to try out for the track team. He managed to win a letter, but he did not place in the city meet and did not stick with the sport. Instead, Tolmich went out for the tennis team at Central High. During his junior year he had a run in with the tennis coach, and dropped off the team. Tolmich graduated from Central High School in January 1933, and immediately enrolled at Wayne University. While attending Central High School, Al Tolmich won two athletic letters in track and two in tennis, but he had never placed first in a track and field event before enrolling at Wayne University.[92]

In 1933, Allan went out for the Wayne University tennis team, but when the spring track season started he approach Coach David L. Holmes and asked if he could tryout for track. Holmes had never met Allan Tolmich and knew nothing about the would-be walk-on. Nevertheless, Coach Holmes told Al, "Sure, go get a sweat suit from the athletic office and report back here." That fateful decision, made without much forethought by either party, changed Tolmich's life and produced one of the four best track athletes in Wayne State University history.[93]

In 1936, the year that the *Chicago Daily News* inaugurated its indoor invitational meet at the Chicago stockyards International Amphitheater, Al Tolmich proved himself a world class track athlete, but as John McManis of *The Detroit News* pointed out, his strongest event was no longer included in the Olympic Games.

Tolmich, who entered Wayne University three years ago as a tennis player, with no thought of competing in track, was the sensation of the State intercollegiate meet at Ann Arbor when he ran off with four firsts, winning both dash races and the low and high hurdles. He set a new state record in the high hurdles and he won the sprints easily, but he looked most impressive in the low hurdles, his fourth race of the day. Not at all pressed, and somewhat wearied by his big day on the track, Tolmich ran the race easily, winning much as he pleased. His time was only 23.8 seconds, a fifth of a second from the meet record, . . . but if Tolmich had a chance to train for this race exclusively it is probable it would take a super-runner like Jesse Owens to beat him. . . . Tolmich is not quite tall enough to be a front rank high hurdler, and he has not the speed to run with the very best in the sprints, although he will be a worthy rival for anyone in the 100-yard dash. . . . Tolmich will try for the Olympic team. But it is not likely he will be successful. Good enough in certain competitions [the 200-meter low hurdles, no longer performed in the Olympics] but not those currently in the Olympics.[94]

Meanwhile, on May 13, 1936, members of the Black Legion killed a pregnant Mrs. Rebecca Poole because she threatened to expose them and their tactics. The Black Legion was an anti-Semitic, anti-Catholic organization with strong support in Detroit and its northern suburbs. Her death led to a crackdown on the Black Legion by the Michigan State Police. They discovered that the General of 135,000-member organization was a prison guard in Jackson.[95] This announcement offered tangible proof of the depth of popular support for the anti-Semitic voices of radio broadcaster Father Charles Edward Coughlin of the Shrine of the Little Flower in Royal Oak and automobile magnate Henry Ford, whose anti-Semitic newspaper, the *Dearborn Independent*, was at the peak of its influence. Even the Detroit Southeastern High School students called their yearbook *The Aryan*.

Meanwhile, former Wayne University students and pacifists, Joseph Rosenstein and Roy McQuarrie were in Spain fighting the fascists in a war that for-shadowed the Second World War and the holocaust.[96] Concentration camps for Jews and dissidents were being established in Germany and countries were closing their borders to Jewish refugees all around the world. Concurrently, anti-Communists accused ideological dissenters, particularly Jews, of disloyalty and believed they were a menace to the American way of life.

In this atmosphere of anti-Semitism, a near miracle occurred at Ferry Field in Ann Arbor on the Jewish Sabbath, Saturday, May 16, 1936. Bob Luby, Carl and Fred Culver, and Stan Glazier—the members of the Central High School 880-yard relay team—drove to Ann Arbor's Ferry Field in Stan Glazier's Model A Ford coupe, with a rumble seat, to watch the State Intercollegiate track championships. They were still celebrating of their victory over Cooley High the previous afternoon, and they felt great. It was a perfect spring day. The sun was shining and there was a mild breeze, but best of all Central High School graduate, Al Tolmich, was poised to have one of the best performance's of his all too short track career. Sixty years later, Bob Luby could still experience the thrill of seeing his hero, Al Tolmich, and the barrel-chested Abe

Rosenkrantz ruled the day. Jews were being trashed all around the world, and Jewish heroes were in great demand at Central High.[97]

That day, Tolmich and Rosenkrantz won 7 of 15 regular events at the Michigan Intercollegiate Meet, and Harry Werbin and Rabinowitz added points for Michigan Normal and Western Teachers College. That same day, Sammy Stroller won the 100-yard dash in Bloomington, Indiana. At the twenty-first annual State Intercollegiate held at Ferry Field Allan Tolmich became the first trackman in state history to win four events in the intercollegiate meet.[98] While Tolmich did not make the final Olympic trials, he created a lasting memory for many in 1936.

In 1937 "competing with a slight case of blood poisoning in one leg, Tolmich shattered one meet record and tied another, while winning three events." He ran two preliminaries in each event. He won the 60-yard dash (6.3), the 60-yard high-hurdles (7.5) tying the meet mark, and set the meet record in the 60-yard low-hurdles (7.0) in the Central Collegiate Indoor in South Bend.[99]

After the Central Intercollegiates in South Bend, Allan Tolmich became the talk of Detroit. "Red" Simmons had made the trip to South Bend to watch the meet. "Tolmich appears to be reaching his peak," Simmons said, "and his performances in the spring and summer will stamp him as one of the greatest hurdlers we've seen. He has both speed and strength and will look even better if he tries the longer hurdling distances."[100]

On April 3, 1937, Tolmich ran in the Texas Relays. "It was so sunny and nice down in Texas a couple of weeks ago that I really felt like running," said Tolmich.[101] April 23–24 at the Penn Relays, he placed second in the high-hurdles to Forrest "Spec" Towns, world record-holder and Olympic champion, who defeated him in the 120-yard high-hurdles by four feet. He also placed third to Marty Glickman in the 100-yard dash.[102]

Tolmich rode the train to San Francisco with the University of Michigan delegation of eight track athletes to the NCAA Championships held at Berkeley, California.[103] Bob Osgood, who had just set the American record for the 120-yard high-hurdles "on a track floating in three inches of water" at the Western Conference Championships some three weeks before, was part of the Michigan entourage.[104]

Al attempted to enter all of the events he normally won at the Michigan Intercollegiate or the Central Collegiate Conference Championships. On June 18 he ran preliminaries in the 100-yard dash, the

120-yard high-hurdles and the 220-yard low-hurdles, and had to be talked out of the 220-yard dash preliminaries by Michigan Coach Charles Hoyt. Al qualified for the finals in all three events. He placed third in the first heat of the 100-yard dash, which was won by "Michigan's Olympic Orphan," Sam Stoller. He placed second to "Spec" Towns in the first heat of the 120-yard high-hurdles, and "Iron Man Tolmich of Wayne University" won the 220-yard low-hurdles. Bob Osgood of the University of Michigan, with his ankle heavily taped" because he was suffering from an ankle injury, placed fourth in heat one of the 120-yard high-hurdles.[105] In the 1937 NCAA finals, "Spec" Towns won his fifty-seventh consecutive race in the high-hurdles nosing out Al Tolmich. Bob Osgood grabbed fifth place. Towns was last defeated in 1935 and had not knocked over a hurdle in a meet since his freshman year at the University of Georgia.[106]

In Milwaukee two weeks later, while Bing Crosby was racing his horses at the Del Mar Race Track in Southern California and play-write Eugene O'Neill was planning to build a $40,000 house on his newly acquired ranch in Contra Costa County in northern California, wiry Allan Tolmich, in his black-thatched Wayne University jersey, whipped world champion "Spec" Towns, then came back to set a meet record in the 200-meter low-hurdles. His ten points gave Wayne University fourth place in the National AAU Outdoor Championships. Allan's victory over Towns, in the 110-meter high-hurdles, broke the Georgia champion's fifty-seven race victory string and caused him to kick over the last hurdle in his effort to catch the Detroit timber topper.[107] Tolmich was a track All-American in the 200-meter low-hurdles, 1937.[108] Tolmich also was named to the 1937 AAU All-American track team in the 110-meter hurdles.[109]

After the AAU Championships, Tolmich went to Texas for what was billed as the Pan-American Games, but turned out to be an exhibition meet at the Pan-American portion of the Texas State Fair. The so-called Pan-American Games of 1937 held in Dallas, Texas was a sham. The meet was held on a sand track at the State Fair in Dallas as part of the Pan American Exposition and was more of an exhibition than a true meet involving world class South American athletes.[110] Then on August 5, the AAU champions sailed from San Francisco for Hawaii and Tokyo, where they ran exhibition races.[111] Tolmich took international trips with the AAU in 1937 and in 1938. On the trip to the Orient, he ran at Schofield Barracks in Hawaii and in a half-dozen

Japanese cities, including Nagoya, Tokyo, Kyoto, Osaka, and Niigata. On the other trip he ran in London, Scotland, Germany, and Italy. He recalls being treated well in Nazi Germany and fascist Italy.

Tolmich was a track All-American in 1938 and again in 1939.[112] During his career, he held virtually every indoor hurdle record.

His greatest season over the timbers was in 1938 when he broke or tied indoor records eleven times. He was so versatile that in the 1937 Michigan Intercollegiate Championships he ran 9.7 for 100-yards, 21.5 for 220-yards, 14.8 for the 120-yard high-hurdles, and 23.5 for the 220-yard low-hurdles. The latter was a meet record. Tolmich established a world record of 23.3 for the 200-meter low-hurdles on July 3, 1939.[113]

Tolmich liked to run the indoor circuit. Al recalls that wearing a Wayne University jersey at indoor meets caught people's imagination, particularly out of town sports writers. Moreover, he could work into peak shape with frequent meets and good competition. Meet directors also paid his travel expenses once he had established a reputation, and he liked traveling at other people's expense, staying in nice hotels, and eating good food.. He ran on the boards in Boston Garden and Madison Square Garden, but many indoor meets were held on dirt or cinders. Tolmich did particularly well at the *Chicago Daily News* Relays. They had a three hurdles set and gave a diamond-studded medal for winning all three races. Tolmich won two sets of diamond studs.[114]

Al graduated from Wayne University in 1938 with a teaching certificate. In 1939 he was a substitute teacher, worked on a master's degree in education, and continued to run track. The indoor season was great, but outdoor meets for college graduates were few and far between, Al recalls. It hampered him in AAU outdoor competition. His work history included: one year as a substitute teacher (1938–9) and three years as an elementary school teacher at Barstow Elementary School in Detroit (1939–42), U. S. Army (1942–46), Retail Salesman (1946–48), and lady's apparel sales manager (1949–75).

Throughout his career, Tolmich overcame poor training conditions to win national honors.

Allan Tolmich has frequently referred to as Wayne University's 'one man track team.' It is a wonder that he has been able to win national championships and establish world's records, in view of the fact that all through his indoor track career he practiced in a small gymnasium where he could only set up one hurdle to practice over—in fact, the only time he runs with more than one hurdle is in the Saturday Garden track meets.[115]

Tolmich was named All American for the 65-meter high-hurdles for 1939.[116] He continued to work out in the halls of Wayne University as late as February 1940.[117] He accompanied the Wayne University track team to the AAU Indoor Championships on February 23, 1940.[118] On February 24, 1940 Tolmich shattered a nine-year-old world record for the 70-yard high-hurdles (8.4).[119] Tolmich was named All-American for the 70-yard hurdles for 1940, and on March 15, 1941 won the 45-yard high and low-hurdles at the first annual Knights of Columbus Meet held in Cleveland's Municipal Auditorium.[120] He married a wealthy socialite, was divorced, and remarried to an Episcopalian. At the end of the century he lived near Indianapolis. He was a charter inductee into the Wayne State University Sports Hall of Fame, and was inducted into the Michigan Jewish Sports Hall of Fame in November 1999.

Peaking At the Wrong Time

William Watson was born in Boley, Oklahoma in 1917. His parents moved to Saginaw, Michigan in 1923 when he was six. Bill began his athletic career as a broad jumper for Central Junior High School in 1928. He was already a promising all-around athlete when he entered Saginaw Eastern High School. Quick, strong, and light on his feet, he won the lightweight division Golden Gloves championship in Saginaw as a sophomore in high school. Lured by the accomplishments of such great African-American as "Kid Chocolate," Henry Armstrong, Joe Walcott, and Jack Johnson, Bill wanted to be a boxer. But, after a close pal suffered fatal injuries in the ring, his mother asked him to give up boxing and he bowed to her wishes.[121] Chester R. Stackhouse, the coach at East High in Saginaw, recruited Bill Watson for the track team and added to his versatility. Under Coach Stackhouse, Watson developed into a shot putter, discus thrower, and high jumper, as well as a broad jumper. Watson also played football and basketball at Eastern High.[122]

Between his sophomore and junior year in high school, Watson gained fifty pounds and added strength, but lost none of his foot speed. He rigged up a high jump pit and made a couple of hurdles so he could practice in his own back yard.[123] As a junior in high school, Bill won the 16-pound shot put with a throw of 46 feet at the Western Michigan AAU Outdoor Championships in Grand Rapids in June 1934.[124] It was the first time he had ever picked up a 16-pound shot.[125]

The following year, Watson had a big day in the State Interscholastic Championships. He won the 12-pound shot put (53–10⅜), the high jump (6–1¼), and was only an inch under the broad jump record at 22–5 at the State High School Class A Championships. He also won the

16-pound shot put (45–10) for the second year at the Western Michigan AAU Outdoor Games in Grand Rapids.[126] However, he was not yet ready to make a serious try for the American Olympic team.

When Coach Hoyt recruited Watson for the University of Michigan, he gained more than a weight man. Watson was a sure bet to become one of the most versatile athletes in school history. At Michigan, Watson came under the direction of J. Kenneth Doherty, a bronze medal winner in the Olympic decathlon and twice national champion in that event. It was a great match for Bill Watson, who could now train for the all-around under expert supervision.

It did not take long for Watson to make an impact on the Big Ten. Early in the 1937 indoor season, Watson broke Ralph Rose's Michigan University varsity indoor shot put record.

Bill Watson, the new Wolverine sophomore shot put sensation would rather sing than do most anything else—even heave the iron ball 50 feet. But in as much as Coach Charley Hoyt is no Major Bowes, Bill probably will stick to shot putting, high jumping, and broad jumping, with a little discus throwing on the side.

Although he has participated in only three meets as a Wolverine, Friday night's with Pitt was the third—Watson already has set an all-time Michigan record. When the husky Saginaw Negro tossed the shot 50 feet 1 inch against Ohio State, he was the first U. of M. athlete to pass the 50-foot mark in Ann Arbor annals. And the effort won a gold watch from Hoyt, who had put up the timepiece seven years ago as an incentive to Michigan weight men. No one had come close until Watson used his strong-arm tactics against the Buckeyes. That won the ticker and broke the Ralph Rose all-time Michigan record.[127]

Watson was majoring in Physical Education, but was interested in majoring in voice at the music school. He sang tenor. Singer, athlete Paul Robeson was his hero.[128] His best marks in each of his four specialties were already good enough to win points in any Big Ten Championship Meet. He cleared 6–3½ to win the high jump at the State AAU Championships in 1935 at Detroit.

March 20, 1937 he set the meet and University of Michigan varsity record for the shot put (50–5) at the Butler Relays. Over the next four years he set 14 additional records, and won no fewer than 48 events. Big, strong, and fast, he could long jump 25 feet, high jump 6–5, and throw the shot nearly 55 feet and the discus over 160 feet. Watson was considered the most likely decathlon winner at the 1940 Olympics.

On June 26, 1937 Joe Louis won the world heavyweight boxing title. He was the thirteenth Negro to win a world, boxing crown.[129] In the summer of 1939, Bill Watson, short on money and facing the prospect of dropping out of college, was given a job to act as secretary to heavyweight champion Joe Louis by John Roxborough.[130]

The University of Michigan varsity track captain spent the latter part of the first semester of 1938–39 acting as secretary and companion to Joe Louis. Watson often could be seen mixing a little shadow boxing with his other duties at Yost Fieldhouse. When a student reporter interviewed Watson, Bill remained non-committal about entering the ring when he finished college. "It's a swell game but I'm not going to think very seriously about it until after the Olympics in 1940." There was speculation that "Louis' handlers, Black and Roxborough, can do plenty for Watson and because of his association with them in the past, there is no reason to believe that they wouldn't" help him.[131]

On April 22, 1939 Bill Watson put the shot 54–1¼ against the University of Illinois in a duel meet at Champaign. He also threw the discus 158 feet after only one day of work outdoors. Both were better than the Conference meet record[132] and his shot put was the best collegiate mark in five years and a foot better than the Olympic record.[133]

In the fall of 1939 Doherty became head coach of the University of Michigan track team. Doherty hired Chester Stackhouse from Saginaw, to be assistant track coach at the University of Michigan.[134] On May 31, 1940 Watson won the shot-put (50–0) and the broad jump (23–9¾) at the Michigan AAU Outdoor Championships in Kalamazoo. However, because Chester Stackhouse had car trouble enroute to the meet, Watson did not arrive in time for the discus throw.[135]

Bill Watson won the Big Ten Conference indoor shot put title three times, setting records twice. He also was a three-time Big Ten outdoor champion in three different events, and in his senior year he scored 20 points in the NCAA championships, earning points in four different events. After the 1939 track season, Watson had knee surgery. He was named 1939 AAU All-American for the broad jump.[136] He returned in 1940 to set world records in the decathlon 100-meter dash and the discus while becoming the national decathlon champion and All-American.[137] If World War II had not intervened, there is little doubt that Watson would have become the Olympic decathlon champion in 1940.

Like all African-American athletes during the 1930s and 1940s, Bill Watson often experienced racial discrimination. He was a great basketball player, but until 1948 there was a gentlemen's agreement among Big Ten basketball coaches that no black athlete would be used in intercollegiate competition, so Watson was kept from playing college basketball. Moreover, he experienced numerous humiliations when the team traveled. In 1940, for example, Watson was forced to use the service elevator with the employees, while competing in Chicago when he stayed at the Sherman Hotel in Chicago.[138]

In 1941 Watson joined the Detroit Police Department and competed on their track team through 1945 before experienced serious mental health problems. Watson, who was suffering from manic-depression, went to live with Willis Ward in 1947, because he had no where else to go. Ward tried to help Bill Watson, but had to turn him out when Watson came to Willis' bedroom one night with a gun. On March 2, 1973. while in a drunken state, an armed and dangerous Bill Watson was accidentally killed by his Police partner who was attempting to help him.[139]

8. The Nazis use the Olympics to Promote Racism

Highlights of the 1936 Olympic Games nearly always feature two events: the remarkable performance of Jesse Owens in winning four gold medals in an athletic contest dedicated by Hitler to the superiority of the Aryan race, and the refusal of American track coaches to allow the only two Jews on their team to run in Berlin. An understanding of why these two events are still important sixty-five years later and how they could have occurred is the subject of this chapter.

A Touch of Evil

In 1936 events in Europe were setting the stage for another world war. The stubborn opposition of monarchists and political conservatives to every modicum of change had been poisoning European politics since the French Revolution. Unrequited nationalism, colonialism, and an intransigent aristocracy had fueled the unrest that triggered the First World War. More importantly, the Russian aristocracy made the Bolshevik Revolution possible and foreordained the ferocity of that conflict.

Christian antipathy toward Jews was more than 1,700 years old at the beginning of the twentieth century. Persecution of the Jews by Christians was underway by the reign of Constantine the Great, when Jews were banned from Jerusalem, denied the right to congregate for religious services, and kept from converting others to their faith. Thomas Aquinas, the saint who synthesized Catholic theology held the view that Jews should not be murdered. Instead, friendly persuasion should be used to convert Jews by "allowing them to witness the truth" of Christianity. When this strategy did not work, because of what many in the Catholic Church claimed was the "obstinacy" of Jews (or as some said, "the hard hearts of Jews" or "Jewish blindness"), persecution of Jews by Christians intensified.[1] During the crusades thousands of Jews were killed by Christian missionary armies enroute to the Holy Lands. In the fifteenth and sixteenth centuries the Inquisition tortured, killed, and deported Jews from Europe. Concurrently, Martin Luther called for the destruction of Jewish synagogues and homes. In the sixteenth century Pope Paul IV instituted the Jewish ghetto in Rome and required that Jews wear the yellow Star of David, a practice picked up by the Nazis. Indeed, all of these acts of anti-Semitism laid the foundation for the willing acceptance of anti-Jewish propaganda and acts of violence by Nazis and other hate groups during the 1920s and 1930s. Religion was not an innocent bystander to the forthcoming holocaust, but neither was it the sole cause of anti-Semitism or the only excuse for inhuman personal behavior.

European reformers were concerned with Catholic Church control of over education, culture, and economic development long before the French Revolution. In the 1830s Spanish anti-clerics burned Catholic churches and killed clergy in an effort to reduce church control over the social order. At that time, the Spanish Church lost most of its landed endowments, yet the Catholic clergy fought a rear guard action for the next one-hundred years.[2] Because of the links between the Russian Orthodox Church and the czarist regime, the Bolsheviks attacked Christianity with a vengeance, killing priests, confiscating church property, secularizing education, banning religious orders, and generally uprooting centuries of entrenched vested interests. Fear of communism gripped the Vatican like a bad case of the flu.

Since the reformation, the papacy had been reluctantly adjusting to challenging new ideas and the realities of a fragmented Christendom. Uneasy about liberalism, secularism, science, industrialization, and the evolving nation-state, the papacy set about imposing a top-down power relationship on Catholic clergy and lay-members. In July 1870, for the first time ever, Pope Pius IX espoused "papal infallibility" in an effort to wipe out the "outrageous treason of democracy" in the church. Starting in 1902, work began on the revision of the Code of Canon Law that was promulgated in 1917. This change in church rules centralized authority in the pope over the entire Catholic Church in unprecedented ways and was used by popes in the first half of the twentieth century to oppose modernization, democracy and other changes that might dilute the monarchist or authoritarian model for church and state.

For the advocates of democracy, the emergence and early success in 1931–2 of the Second Republic in Spain was the most unusual and probably the most positive, political event in Europe during the first years of the great depression. Spain embarked on its first complete experience with modern democracy at a time when less developed countries in Southern and Eastern Europe were falling under authoritarian rule.[3] Archbishop Pedro Segura of Toledo responded to the formation of Spain's first democratic government by issuing a pastoral letter praising the fallen monarchy for its respect for the Catholic Church. In doing so, he roused the ire of Republican anti-clerics. The monarchist newspaper added fuel to the fire by insisting that only the monarchy could guarantee Catholic social order. Within days more than 85 Catholic churches were burned. Within a month, Church opposition to democracy produced confrontation, violence, and martial law. The right-wing Catholic Party, the Confederacion Espanola de Derechas Autonomas (CEDA), sabotaged the Republic through a lack of cooperation and insistence on authoritarian policies.[4]

From the standpoint of the popes who dominated the Catholic Church prior to 1958, the Church hierarchy preferred fascism to democracy, and democracy to communism or even socialism, which they mistakenly confused with communism. At the highest levels of the Church, there was a decided preference for governments like those of Franco's Spain and Salazar's Portugal. The idea that Stalin was a far greater long-term threat to world peace than Hitler was widely share by conservatives around the world, and still has proponents.[5]

Hitler's Cult

In September 1919, shortly after the armistice ending World War I was signed, Adolf Hitler, who had a burning hatred for the new German democratic republic, joined the German Worker's Party. The Worker's Party represented a small minority of Germans, and targeted its energies against communism, democratic institutions, and Jews. In the summer of 1920, the German Worker's Party became the National Socialist German Worker's Party. In 1921 Hitler's Party adopted the swastika as the party symbol. The swastika had been the symbol of an anti-Semitic group in Austria, and Hitler liked it. At approximately the same time, the group's "Gymnastic and Sports Division" was used as a cover for the Sturmabteilung or "storm troopers," which soon became the political muscle for the National Socialist Party.[6] It is significant that in this case, and others, sport organization was disguised for the purpose of achieving social and political objectives.

Adolf Hitler's rise to power was facilitated by the devastating consequences of the great depression. Since the Middle Ages, German distrust of Jews had been so intense and so divorced from reality that nearly all calamities were attributed to Jewish malfeasance. Although Jews comprised less than one percent of Germany's population, Hitler's message blaming them for the nation's problems was welcome in Germany, where anti-Semitism and nationalism were inextricably intertwined. His message also coincided with the dominant European belief that Jews were the primary source of disorder and moral decay.[7]

Hitler became Chancellor of Germany on January 30, 1933, five weeks before Franklin Roosevelt was sworn in as President of the United States.[8] The Dachau concentration camp began receiving prisoners as early as March 1933. With unemployment, hunger and poverty at an all time high in Germany, the Vatican felt more comfortable working with a secular authoritarian power than with a democracy. Cardinal Pacelli (who was later Pope Pius XII) and Adolf Hitler negotiated the Reich Concordat, which was signed July 20, 1934. The Concordat dismantled organized Catholic opposition to the Nazis. It also appears that Cardinal Pacelli, with his strong aversion to democratic organizations and popular institutions, was much less aware of what his appeasement involved than was Adolf Hitler, who needed popular support and sought to destroy any source of opposition to his polices. So, while they did not endorse Nazism, Vatican leaders arranged to disband Germany's Catholic Central Party in return for a concordat that strengthened the Vatican's power over German Catholics. This decision also strengthened Hitler's grip on power in Germany and insured him an opportunity to make Jews the scapegoat for Germany's economic problems.[9]

Anti-Semitism and Racism in the United States

"Will America remain Protestant and Anglo-Saxon?" was the overriding question on the minds of American born whites during the "roaring twenties," according to Andre Siegfried, a professor from France, who visited the United States in 1925. The question was particularly salient in states like Michigan, Illinois, New York, New Jersey, and Massachusetts where foreign-born residents and their children outnumbered the "original American" stock.[10]

In 1936 the great majority of all church congregations in the USA were affiliated with six denominations. The Southern Baptists, who claimed 24,671 affiliated churches, and the Negro Baptists, with 23,093 affiliated churches, were the most widespread denominations, but not the largest in aggregate membership. That distinction fell to the Roman

Catholics. There were 18,409 Roman Catholic congregations and their average membership per church was the highest in the country. The Methodist Episcopal Church, with 18,349 affiliated churches, was the fourth largest congregation. The Southern Methodists and the Presbyterians followed on the list. In aggregate, these six denominations accounted for about half of the churches in the United States. In terms of the value of church edifices, the Roman Catholics, Methodist Episcopals, Presbyterians, and Protestant Episcopals, in that order, owned the most valuable church property in America. Average annual church expenditures generally reflected the value of the church edifices occupied.[11]

Michigan, the seventh most populous state in the Union, ranked fourteenth among the 48 states in the number of churches and ninth in church members. The three largest denominations in the state were the Methodists, Roman Catholics, and the Northern Baptists. However, most of the growth in religious affiliation in Detroit was taking place in the Catholic, Jewish, and Negro Baptist denominations. Detroit had 652 churches in 1936. The three most numerous denominations in Detroit were Roman Catholic with 109, Negro Baptist with 62, and Jewish with 47 congregations. Between 1926 and 1936, Jewish congregations had the fifth fastest growth rate in membership among all denominations in the Michigan, and the fastest growth in average expenditures.[12] The number of members in Jewish congregations in Michigan grew from 1,530 in 1906 to 5,383 in 1916, to 83,161 in 1926, to 99, 366 in 1936. Nearly all of this growth took place in Detroit. Meanwhile, overall church membership in Detroit declined from 755,572 members in 1926 to 655,320 members in 1936.[13] Obviously, despite the intense divisions and rivalries within the Jewish community of Detroit during the 1930s, traditional Protestants felt under siege by what they considered to be the religions of foreigners.[14]

Fear of foreigners and "foreign ideas" was already deeply rooted in Detroit and nearby Dearborn early in the twentieth century. Fear often disintegrated into hatred. The attitudes and greed of Detroit's industrial leaders contributed significantly to the mix that fomented racial conflict in Michigan and around the world. In 1916 Rabbi Leo Franklin refused to join President Woodrow Wilson at the Detroit Athletic Club because the DAC refused to accept Jewish members. Ironically, a Jew, Albert Kahn, had designed the building that housed the Detroit Athletic Club. Future Supreme Court Justice Louis Brandeis said of the DAC, "Anti-Semitism seems to have reached its American pinnacle here."[15]

Much of the fear of "foreign ideas" stemmed from opposition to labor unions. In 1917 Henry M. Leland, an engineer and one-time owner of the luxury car works that became the Lincoln Motor Car Company, organized the Employer's Association of Detroit. The Association was a union-wrecking organization that opposed legislation deemed harmful to business interests.[16]

Manufacturers associated labor unions with Jews and "foreign-born radicals," in part, because of earlier strikes in the railroad industry in Chicago and the garment industry in New York City. While business owners were willing to exploit their workers by paying them low wages and requiring them work in unhealthy, dangerous conditions, they were vehemently opposed to labor unions or other efforts to regulate their businesses. They believed that no one should have the right to interfere with their business, and they felt that it was critical for the success of their interests to maintain political control over the state legislature to avoid laws regulating working conditions or minimum wages. One of the ways they did this was by using racism and religious bigotry as a wedge issue to attack African-Americans, Jews, and others considered a challenge to white, Protestant control of American institutions.

Prior to World War I, Henry Ford collaborated with Rabbi Leo Franklin on efforts to Americanize immigrants. Eastern European Jews resented these efforts to force them to assimilate and did not appreciate the patronizing attitudes of Henry Ford and Rabbi Franklin, which they interpreted as efforts to destroy their efforts to live as Jews. Unappreciated, the super-sensitive Henry Ford, who interpreted nearly everything but unqualified praise as criticism, quickly shifted from his assuaging strategy to a virulent attack on Jews. He stopped hiring Jews and in May 1920 Ford began to publish a series with ninety-one parts purporting to expose the "international Jewish conspiracy."[17] There were, of course, a few exceptions to his hiring practices. He employed Albert Kahn to design his Highland Park plant where Ford's automobile assembly line was perfected. Ed Levy, Sr.'s Company was hired to haul slag for the Ford River Rouge Plant, and Morris Itzkoff was hired to tailor Henry Ford's suit jackets, but for the most part Ford stopped hiring Jews and Jews stopped buying Ford automobiles in the early 1920s.

While Henry Ford proved to be a pragmatic borrower of ideas, he had few original ideas of his own. He went to the World's Columbian Exposition in Chicago and mimicked ideas gathered from exhibits by William Morrison, Charles E. Duryea, Elwood Hayes, and Gottlieb Daimler, to build his first automobile.[18] After going broke, he adopted Henry Leland's policies for interchangeable parts, which had been pioneered nearly a century before in the gun and clock industries.[19] Finally, he adopted the assembly line concept used for years by the meat packing industry.[20] In January 1914, in one of his few truly creative moves, Ford confronted his problem with labor retention by offering to pay $5 per day for eight hours of work, at a time when the average wage was $2 per day. The idea brought stability to his work force and fostered a middle-class work force able to purchase his automobiles.

Henry Ford: Hitler's Hero

Racism was to leave a haunting legacy, and Michigan civic leaders made a major contribution to that disturbing heritage. Henry Ford's views contributed directly to the rise of Adolf Hitler. Hitler was an ardent admirer of Ford. Ford's opposition to American entry into World War I was viewed as pro-German, and his ideas about industrial efficiency and public anti-Semitism contributed to Hitler's unbridled anti-Semitism, desire for efficiency at any price, and adamant opposition to labor unions. In 1923 the leader of the newly formed National Socialists (Nazi party) attempted to enlist Ford's support for his beer-hall insurgency. Although rebuffed, Hitler lent ignobility to the Ford name by including it, with adulation, in his autobiographical book, *Mein Kampf*.[21] The energetic Nazi Party Youth Leader, Baldur von Schirach, became an anti-Semite at the age of seventeen after reading Henry Ford's book *Eternal Jew*.[22]

C. C. Little, a geneticist who was president of the University of Michigan; Dr. W. K. Kellogg of Battle Creek; and Henry Ford were just three of the most prominent Michigan civil leaders to contribute to worldwide racism. Little and Kellogg headed the Battle Creek based Race Betterment Society that encouraged eugenics through selective breeding and sterilization. They advocated and supported sterilization of those they labeled as misfits. Michigan was among the first of 39 states to adopt laws allowing authorities to sterilize the mentally ill, mentally retarded, and prisons inmates to prevent the spread of "unfit" characteristics. The American eugenics movement directly inspired Adolf Hitler,[23] and Henry Ford's vision of efficiency inspired Auschwitz—the worst and most efficient act of racial cleansing ever visited by one ethnic group on another.

During the great depression, most Jewish families struggled economically, and shared those struggles with other Jews because they all lived in the same neighborhood. In Detroit it was a neighborhood where a corned beef sandwich in the deli in the Broadway Central Market cost fifteen cents and a glass of Vernors was five cents.[24] Anti-Jewish invective in Michigan and around the world grew more multifaceted and threatening during this period. Groups like the Black Legion, the Ku Klux Klan, and the Silver Shirts (who fashioned themselves after the Nazi SS) began to physically threaten Michigan Jews, and the voices of hate became louder. Led by Father Coughlin and Reverend Gerald K. Smith, Jews were blamed for the spread of communism. Following the signals coming from Pope Pius XII and his American spokesmen Ambassador Joseph P. Kennedy, Fulton J. Sheen, and Cardinal Spellman, Father Coughlin concluded that Hitler stood in defense of the incursion of communism in Europe and North America.[25] Always the cautious politician, and fearful of the power of Southern Democratic politicians and the xenophobic, anti-Semitic mood of the nation, FDR's silence, indifference, and insensitivity to the plight of Jews and Negroes no doubt contributed to the feeling of isolation within these minority groups.

On the other hand, when Eleanor Roosevelt lobbied against the systematic discrimination faced by Negroes and publicly advocated equal justice for black Americans, the FBI placed her under surveillance as a subversive. The more Eleanor became identified with African-American causes, the greater her vilification by conservatives.[26]

During the early years of Congress of Industrial Organizations (CIO) when efforts to organize the auto industry were at their height, Ford and the other automobile manufacturers recruited African-Americans from the rural south in efforts to break strikes and lower employee pay. These efforts also contributed to racial conflict and violence.

Norman Thomas' Socialist Party and The American Communist Party were nearly alone in speaking out against racist policies. In 1936 Norman Thomas told the American public, "How can we either protest Hitlerism with good grace or hope to escape similar ills in America when we chronically carry out a more thoroughgoing discrimination against our colored fellow citizens than he has imposed upon the Jews?" As if in response, in 1938 U. S. Senator Theodore Bilbo from Mississippi introduced legislation in Congress to deport all black Americans to Liberia.[27]

By contrast,

The Berkeley [MI.] city commission has ordered all city employees to sign affidavits stating whether they belong to the Black Legion, the Bullet Club or affiliated organizations. . . . The action was taken at the request of Arend Wickert, Communist party candidate for mayor in 1932, who pointed out Pontiac had taken similar action. City Clerk Edwin J. Johnston was instructed to prepare the affidavits. No penalties for admission of cult membership were specified.[28]

Is it any wonder that W. E. Du Bois, Paul Robeson, and numerous young Jewish radicals had favorable views of the socialists and the communists during this era? For, almost no one else spoke out against racist policies and practices in America.

Racial Policies and Practices in America

In 1936 there was little reason for African-American and Asian-American citizens to think that policies in the United States were substantially better than in Nazi Germany. African-Americans, Asian-Americans, and Jews were refused service in hotels and restaurants on a daily basis. Lynchings of African-Americans were common in the American South.[29] The military services were segregated and racism in the military was rampant.[30] Blacks and Asians were barred from employment in most defense factories, and were excluded from participation in most professional and college sports.

In the American armed services a current Army War College report claimed that:

> In the process of evolution, the American Negro has not progressed as far as other sub-species of the human family. . . . The cranial cavity of the Negro is smaller than whites. . . . The psychology of the Negro, based on heredity derived from mediocre ancestors, cultivated by generations of slavery, is one from which we cannot expect to draw leadership material. . . . In physical courage [he] falls well back of whites. . . . He cannot control himself in fear of danger. . . . He is a rank coward in the dark.[31]

All Blacks were in segregated units, and there were only five African-American officers in the United States Army, three chaplains, a colonel, and a captain. The U. S. Navy only allowed African-American enlisted men to be messmen, and there were no African-American Marines or airmen.[32]

As late as 1940, 82 percent of the defense jobs in Michigan were reserved for whites, and, nation-wide, only one in one-thousand jobs in the aircraft industry were open to blacks or Asians.[33] It was not until Asa Philip Randolph, President of the Brotherhood of Sleeping Car Porters, organized and threatened President Roosevelt with a 100,000-man march on Washington, D.C. that Presidential Order 8802, prohibiting discrimination in hiring on Federal contracts and establishing the Fair Employment Practices Committee, was issued on June 25, 1941. It was the first Federal action protecting the civil rights of minorities in 65 years.[34]

The Planning for the Berlin Olympics

Berlin had been selected as the site for the 1916 Olympic Games, but that Olympiad was cancelled because of World War I. In 1931, before Hitler ascended to power in Germany, Berlin was selected as the site for the XI Olympiad. When Adolf Hitler gained control of the German government on January 30, 1933, the question of whether or not the German government would proceed with the 1936 Olympic Games had to be addressed. There were good reasons to believe that the Fuehrer might cancel the Berlin games. The idea of competing against "inferior non-Aryans" concerned many Nazis. Some German newspapers denounced the Games as "an infamous festival dominated by the Jews." After all, the Germans had not done well in the 1932 Olympics. They had won only four gold metals in Los Angeles. Moreover, there was also the question of whether the Third Reich could afford the cost of the Berlin Olympics.

After stalling for nine months, Hitler overrode internal opposition and announced that the games would be held in Berlin. On October 5, 1933 Adolf Hitler made the decision to build an Olympic Stadium in Berlin that would hold 100,000 spectators. The sight chosen for the new Olympic complex was eight miles west of the city center, the most favorable sight to be found in Berlin. It had a rural look and enjoyed clean air and the prospects for outstanding transportation access. The suburban railway station serving the area was refurbished and enlarged to handle 24 electric trains and six steam trains per hour—a theoretical maximum of 48,000 people each hour could be accommodated.

The Olympic stadium had 71 tiers of seats and descended more than 40 feet below ground. It had 52 changing rooms, several first aid stations, and telephone rooms under the seating, and stood next to broad open fields. The Nazis spent $30,000,000 preparing for the games. In addition to the 100,000-seat track and field stadium, they erected six gyms, a swimming stadium and several smaller arenas. They installed closed circuit television and the Germans even eradicated every mosquito within miles by spraying possible breeding places.

The Nazis built an impressive Olympic village to house more than 3,700 male athletes from forty-nine nations. The Olympic village was constructed near-by at Doberitz, on space that had been used as a train-ing area for the German Army. The Olympic Village consisted of 140 handsome brick-and-stucco cottages for living and sleeping. These houses were considerably superior to those built for the Los Angeles Olympic village. Each house contained 10 or 12 double bedrooms. There were also several large buildings for cooking, eating, and meeting.

Preparations for the Olympics included incentives to homeowners along the routes to the sport venues to make home improvements. The Germans also offered large discounts on the railroads for foreign visi-tors, increased the availability of local transportation, and hired and trained hundreds of guides to help visitors. Yet, the militarism and anti-Semitism of the Nazi government was obvious to anyone who wanted to see it. The only problem was that most people did not want to see what was so easy to observe and to read. They were hell-bent on believing that Germany was a fine country and were easily deceived by Nazi propaganda.

Adolf (Adi) and Rudolph Dassler, joined the Nazi Party and fur-nished athletic shoes for German athletes preparing for the Olympics. Starting in 1938 their factory was commandeered for the production of boots for German soldiers. Adi ran the factory and Rudi joined the Ger-man army.[35]

What was Happening to German Athletes Who were Not Pro-Nazi?

Margaret Lambert was an outstanding Jewish athlete in Nazi Germany. During her years in secondary school, between 1930 and 1933, Mar-garet joined an athletic club and earned a host of medals in the high jump.

In 1933, realizing there was no future for me in Germany [as she was not allowed to enroll at the University of Berlin], my parents and I decided that I should go to England to find a school for my chosen profession. I enrolled in the London Polytechnic to learn English. In the spring of 1934 I started to com-pete for my school and that June I won the British championship in high jump. My father came to watch me and told me that I was ordered back to Germany to try out for the German Olympic team. Refusal would bring repercussions not only to the family but also to all the Jewish clubs and activities. I could not ignore the blackmail and returned to Germany.

Blackmail was a favorite mode of persuasion in those days. For instance our closest friend was approached to join the Elite Storm Troopers, when he refused he was told that, since his father was a civil servant, he had better join or his father would lose his job. He joined.

On my return I was placed on the so-called Olympic nucleus team from which the three best for every event would be chosen. It was ironic that as Jews we were not allowed at restaurants, resorts, movies or concerts, among other places. But Gretel Bergman, as I was known then, was considered for a spot on the German Olympic team. There was a very simple explanation for this "miracle." The United States Olympic Committee had made it clear that unless there was no discrimination of any sort no American team would participate. I was given the Olympic oath to sign and was sent with the rest of the nucleus team to training camp twice a year.

These training sessions were the only opportunities for me to train properly. Converted potato fields were not the place to improve one's potential. It was astonishing that I did as well as my Aryan teammates or better, even though I was rarely allowed to compete because I was not a member of the German Track and Field Association because I was Jewish.

In 1935, the German sports authorities arranged a training session for the best Jewish athletes. Snow White and the Seven Dwarfs had as much chance to make the Olympic team as any of the 30 or so athletes assembled—except myself (not conceit, just fact). On June 30, 1936, I equaled the German record with a high jump of 5 feet 3 inches. That height would have been good enough to win an Olympic silver or bronze medal that summer.

On July 16 I received a letter from the German sports authorities, swastika and all, that my achievements were not good enough. By then the American team was on the high seas and certainly was not expected to turn back, which it didn't.

In 1937 I emigrated to the United States. I won the 1937 American championship in high jump and shot put (weighing all of 112 pounds). In 1938 I again won the American championship in high jump. In 1939, while getting ready to go to another championship, I heard on the radio that war had broken out, and since my family was still in Europe I stopped competing.[36]

Anti-Semitism also was strong in Austria in 1935–36. In 1935 Ruth Langer, a Jewish swimmer, broke the Austrian record for the 100 and 400-meter freestyles and won the Austrian championships at those distances. Although Austrian officials were uncomfortable about choosing Jews for their Olympic team, three Jewish girls, including Ruth, were selected for the team. However, the swimming pools where these girls would do their final training carried signs saying "No entry for dogs and Jews." Heeding the recommendation of the World Federation of Jewish Sports Clubs, the three swimmers refused to take part in the Olympics. "We do not boycott the Olympics, but Berlin," their statement read. In response, the names of all Jewish swimmers were removed from the Austrian record books.

After Germany annexed Austria in 1938, Ruth escaped to Italy by dyeing her hair blonde and carrying a false baptismal certificate. In 1939, she moved to England, where she met and in 1943 married John Lawrence. In 1995, the Federation of Austrian Swimming Clubs finally lifted the lifetime ban imposed on the athletes who refused to serve as window-dressing for the Hitler regime.

Before the 1996 Atlanta Olympics, Mrs. Lawrence told a Reuters' reporter,

Whenever the Games come up again, I get a heartache. It's something that stays with you for the rest of your life. It was a once-in-a-lifetime opportunity. But being Jewish, it was unthinkable to compete in the Games in Nazi Germany, where my people were being persecuted.[37]

The German Catholic sports organization was a popular alternative to the Nazi Youth Movement until Catholic organizations were dismantled as a part of the Reich Concordat in July 1933. Because of his past role and convictions, the group's leader, Adalbert Probst, who was outside the Nazi "sphere of influence," was apparently a significant, potential threat to the totalitarian German State being shaped by the Nazis. For the Nazis, it was not enough that the Catholic sports organization was disbanded. On June 30, 1934, they murdered Probst. His murder was a strong indication of the powerful influence sports was having on popular culture around the world. A man like Probst was simply too threatening for the Nazis to tolerate.[38]

The implications of Probst's murder were lost on International Olympic Committee.

Opposition to the Nazi Olympics

Not all Americans accepted the rosy picture of German life painted by Nazi propaganda. They understood that there was discrimination against and arbitrary imprisonment of Jews, Jehovah's Witnesses, Gypsies, Freemasons, communists, Negroes, and many Catholics, and that these actions were deliberate, relentless and frequently articulated in public by officials of the Nazi Party. James Bausch, winner of the gold-medal in the decathlon in 1932 was one of the most vociferous opponents of the Nazi Olympics. He was among those who urged the Amateur Athletic Union (AAU) to secure a transfer of the Olympics to some other city or to boycott the games, as was J. W. Gerard, the former American Ambassador in Berlin. In 1933, Judge Jeremiah Mahoney, President of the AAU, passed a resolution at their annual convention calling for the International Olympic Committee (IOC) to inform Germany that American athletes would not participate in the Olympic games if Jewish athletes in Germany were not allowed to prepare for and participate in the Games. The AAU was on strong moral ground because it had already twice refused to hold its own championships in southern cities when these cities refused to eliminate barriers to equal treatment for African-American athletes.[39]

The issuing of the Nuremberg Laws in September 1935, depriving Jews of German citizenship and their civil rights, raised a more fundamental problem for many Americans about U.S. participation in the 1936 Olympic games in Berlin.[40] As early as 1933, Avery Brundage, President of the U.S. Olympic Committee, was asked about German anti-Semitism and said, "Frankly I don't think we have any business to meddle in this question. We are a sports group pledged to promote clean competition and sportsmanship. When we let politics, racial questions, religious or social disputes creep into our actions, we're in for trouble." He also remarked on another occasion that "In my club in Chicago, Jews are not permitted either." The *New York Times* replied in an editorial: "When Nazis deliberately and arrogantly offend against our common humanity, sport does not transcend all political and racial considerations."

In the face of criticism, Brundage and the U.S. Olympic Committee became more rigid. General Charles Sherrill of the IOC said, "It does not concern me one bit the way the Jews in Germany are being treated, any more than lynching in the South of our own country." Brundage, who would appear as a speaker for the pro-Nazi American-German Bund in 1939 and 1940, argued that "the persecution of minorities is as old as history . . . Certain Jews must now understand that they cannot use these Games as a weapon in their boycott against the Nazis." But both ignored the fact that the Nazis were using the Olympic Games as a propaganda tool to promote racism. Moreover, the Nazis discriminated against Jews in their Olympic tryouts, and used the Olympics to shield the collection of military intelligence that was used to plan the invasion of several central European counties.

In response to pressure from the AAU, Avery Brundage, President of the American Olympic Committee, was sent to Germany in July 1935. He was, however, narrow in his vision and, to an extraordinary degree, bigoted. Moreover, he sent a statement to be printed on the results of the trip before he left on the trip.[41] When he visited Germany, his tour lasted less than a week and he was always in the presence of German officials. On July 15, 1935, while Brundage was in Germany, "Berlin

Nazis run wild in anti-Jewish riot; streets turned into shambles as Jews beaten," declared *The Toronto Globe*. The *Globe* went on to report, "Nearly 1,000 rabid Nazis turned Kurfuerstendam Street into a shambles [yelling "down with Jews" and "throw the Jews out"] as they pursued and beat up Jews and suspected Jews. The rioting continued for more than two hours. An unestimated number of persons were badly beaten and kicked."[42]

Later, Avery Brundage spoke over the radio and stated that "Germany has given a pledge that there will be no discrimination shown in any way ever in the Olympic Games." On August 2 the *Toronto Globe* took it as final proof that Olympiad officials have no intention of boycotting the Olympiad. It was on the basis of this superficial assessment that Brundage recommended to the American Olympic Committee that America should participate in the Berlin games. The issue came to a head at the beginning of December 1935, when the AAU held its annual convention. It was the stormiest meeting in the organization's history, and ended in great bitterness when a narrow majority favored U.S. participation in the 1936 Olympics in Berlin. As soon as the vote was taken, Judge Mahoney announced that he would not stand for re-election, and Avery Brundage was elected to take Mahoney's place. And so, in spite of severe doubts, the United States decided to support the Nazis Olympics.[43]

Brundage argued that "the politics of a nation is of no concern to the International Olympic Committee," and openly supported Nazi Berlin as the site of the 1936 Olympic games. Furthermore, Brundage was not above profiting from his support for the Nazi Olympics. In 1938 he was selected by the Nazi's to be the contractor for a new German Embassy in Washington, DC.[44] Brundage addressed a German-American [Nazi front] mass meeting at Madison Square Garden in New York that year and again in 1940, when he led the Keep-America-Out-of-War Committee, which sponsored the Chicago rally at which Colonel Charles A. Lindbergh [a pro-Nazi] advised the U. S. to stay out of the European conflict. In 1944, he even declared that German and Japanese athletes would be welcome at coming Olympiads even before the war was settled.[45]

One of the most influential speakers who supported participation in the Berlin Olympics was the British broadcaster, Harold Abrahams, the gold medal sprinter in the 1924 Olympics in Paris. Jewish himself, Abrahams believed that the isolation of Germany would not be good for world peace.[46]

The American Olympic Trials

At the Big Ten Championships held on May 25, 1935 in Ann Arbor, Jesse Owens astonished track and field enthusiasts all around the world by breaking three world records and tying a fourth within the span of one hour. His accomplishments were all the greater because each of the records had been on the books for a number of years. The 12,000 spectators were both stunned to silence and moved to applause by Jesse's almost unbelievable show.

Owens very nearly canceled his appearance at the Big Ten Championships because of an extremely sore back. Yet, after a tub of hot water loosened him up and heat pads and rubdowns, Jesse managed to run the 100-yard dash in 9.3; the 220-yard dash in 20.3; the 220-yard low-hurdles in 22.6; and long-jump 26–8¼. Broke and with no athletic scholarship available in those years, Owens was very nearly disqualified from the 1936 Olympics in the summer of 1935 when he received $159 from the State of Ohio to help him get by.[47]

In 1936, Owens set a new Penn Relays record for the 100-meter dash, won the long jump, and successfully anchored two relay teams. He easily qualified for the Olympics in the 100-meter and 200-meter dashes and the long jump.[48]

In 1931, Sam Stoller, Cincinnati Hughes High School, was named All-Scholastic.[49] Stoller attended the University of Michigan starting in the fall of 1933. At the regional Olympic trials in Milwaukee, "Sam Stoller of Michigan jumped into the lead at the gun, and held it through the first 60-yards, but couldn't stave off the tremendous closing drive with which Ralph Metcalfe finished."[50] He did, nevertheless, qualify for the final Olympic trials.

In 1936 eight Michigan athletes qualified for the final Olympic track and field trials at Randall's Island: Lee Bartlett, Bill Bonthron, Sam Stoller, Bob Osgood, Tom Ottey, Abe Rosenkrantz, Richard Frey and Harvey Woodstra. Frey was sixth in the 5-K, Tom Ottey was tenth in the 5-K. Abe was fourth in the 800-meter, Woodstra was fourth in the 110-meter high hurdles. Bonthron was fifth in the 1500-meters. Only Bartlett and Stoller made the team, along with Michigan State College race walkers Ernest Crosbie and Albert J. Mangan.

Racism was Rife in American Sporting Life

Long before the Civil War promoters learned that the only time most Americans wanted to pay to watch a black man run was when he was racing against one of the hated English. Races drew only a small crowd by having contests between minority-group athletes, but drew a large crowd by featuring an "England vs. American" event.[51] The same principal applied to Jesse Owens and the other black athletes in 1936. They were cheered primarily when they represented America against its adversaries.

African-Americans had been barred from major league baseball since 1887. Starting in 1933 a "gentlemen's agreement," attributed to George Marshall, Art Rooney, and George Halas, excluded African-Americans from professional football. It was rare for blacks to be given title fights in boxing, the Big Ten and most other college conferences kept people of color from playing basketball, and blacks were rarely allowed to play football at white colleges.

During the 1930s, the African-American athlete nearly always endured a double standard. They faced isolation on campus and in social settings. They were unwelcome to nearly all fraternities and social clubs, warned "don't even talk to a white girl," and able to find few friends or support activities. African-American were restricted in housing choice, meals out were commonly limited to second rate restaurants, and they usually endured named calling on a near daily basis.[52] In those days there were no athletic scholarships, so earning the money to attend college was a struggle. Moreover, even after a black athlete graduated from college, he had difficulty finding a job.[53]

The United States had ten-male, African-Americans and two female African-American on their 1936 Olympic track squad. The males were David Albritton, John Brooks, Cornelius Johnson, James LuValle, Ralph Metcalfe, Jesse Owens, Fritz Pollard, Jr, Matthew "Mack" Robinson [older brother of "Jackie" Robinson], Archie Williams, and John Woodruff. The females were Louise Stokes and Tidye Pickett. In addition to the blacks on the track team, there was a black weightlifter, John Terry, and there were three African-American boxers James Clark, Arthur Wilson, and Jackie Wilson. Aside from the Americans, the Canadian Olympic track team had two black athletes: Dr. Phil Edwards, who was third in the 800-meter run, and Sam Richardson, who competed in the hop-step-and-jump. Several members of Brazil's Olympic team were black, as was the sole member of Haiti's athletic team.[54]

Avery Brundage publicly suspended Eleanor Holm Jarrett from the U. S. Olympic team in 1936 because he disapproved of her private behavior onboard the ship enroute to Germany. Once in Germany he also sent two members of the boxing team home under the cover of darkness before the Olympic Games began. It was claimed that, "The boys were homesick and their mental attitude so endangered the morale of the boxing squad that they had to be sent home." In point of fact, they were caught shop lifting. African-American welterweight, Howell King of Detroit, was one of the two boxers sent home in disgrace.[55]

Archie Williams noticed that on board ship they had very careful to put all the black guys in one compartment.[56] Yet, the final report of the U.S. Olympic Committee claimed: "The assignment of the tourist space on the *S. S. Manhattan* to the various team was handed to the satisfaction of all. Each team was assigned a section consisting of inside and outside rooms so that no team had an advantage over another."[57]

Ralph Metcalfe was the senior spokesman for the black trackmen. He looked out for Archie Williams. According to Williams, training with Jesse Owens was like running against a deer. "I got a big kick out of Germany. I had never been out of California. I didn't even know where Germany was."[58]

Someone said to Archie Williams, winner of the gold medal in the 400-meter dash in Berlin, "Just think you were the greatest in the world." A truly modest man, he answered, "Forget about being the greatest in the world. You just beat the ones who showed up that day." Williams went on to say, "We ran the 400-meter race much differently in 1936 than they run that race today. We didn't train as much or as rigorously in those days as today and we didn't do weight training and exercises. We trained four days a week, and took weekends off. They crammed all of our heats into two days."[59]

There was approximately the same number of African-American's on the 1948 U.S. Olympic track team as on the 1936 team. By 1952 black participation on the Olympic track team had doubled. However, in 1956 the number of African-Americans on the Olympic track team stayed at about the same level as 1952, as it did in the Melbourne Olympics in 1960. At the Tokyo Olympics there were 23 Blacks on the squad, and in 1968 thirty-four.[60]

Joseph Goebbels's newspaper *Der Angriff*, referred to the black members of the team as "America's black auxiliaries" and refused to include their winning efforts in its score charts. The ten "black auxiliaries" were truly amazing. Their unofficial point total in track and field events exceeded that of any other nation's track and field team, including their white American teammates. Together they won eight gold, three silver, and two bronze medals.[61]

Olympic Orphans

The 400-meter relay is an episode steeped in accusations of narrow self-interest, ugly anti-Semitism, and petty pride. Sam Stoller, a senior at the University of Michigan, and Marty Glickman, a sophomore at

Syracuse University, were the only two Jews on the American track and field team. Both had resisted the demands of friends and Jewish organizations to boycott the Berlin games. Early in the week of the competition, a trial run was held to decide in what order the 100-meter dash runners would be considered for 400-meter relay. Stoller finished first, Glickman second, and Foy Draper placed third. Stoller proved to be the third fastest 100-meter dash man on the Olympic team behind Jesse Owens and Ralph Metcalfe. However, Draper's mentor, Dean Cromwell of Southern California, was one of the American track coaches. Cromwell was also Frank Wykoff's coach and mentor.[62]

Dean Cromwell was a racist who believed that the Negro athlete excelled because he was "closer to the primitive" than the white athlete. The lead coach, Coach Lawson Robertson of the University of Pennsylvania, shared many of Cromwell's old racial determinist ideas.[63] Dean Cromwell and Avery Brundage were members of the American First Committee, and Nazi sympathizers, who expressed anti-Semitic ideas from time to time.[64]

On August 4, 1936, according to Sam Stoller's Berlin Olympic diary, Coach Robertson assured Sam that, because of his outstanding time trial the day before, even if Metcalfe and Owens were used in the relay Sam would be allowed to run. The day before the 400-meter relays, Coach Robertson announced to the press that Jesse Owens would be added to the 400-meter relay team. Robertson told Owens that the team would consist of Owen, Ralph Metcalfe, Sam Stoller, and Frank Wykoff.

When Foy Draper heard the news he attempted to start an anti-Black revolt to stay on the relay team. The two Jewish runners refused to support the effort. Draper then went to his mentor, Dean Cromwell for a chat about the situation. On August 8, 1936 Stoller and Glickman were denied an opportunity to run in the Olympics. The cover story given to the news reporters as to why Glickman and Stoller were not used on the relay team was that "the time trials of the German quarter led to the belief that only the strongest possible team could win."[65]

The reasons put forth by the Coaches did not hold water. Cromwell later said privately that he wanted an all-white team, and blamed Coach Robertson for the decision. However, it seems more likely that the U.S. Olympic Committee wanted to capitalize on the popularity of Jesse Owens as a way to increase financial support for their Olympic fund, and when Owens and Metcalfe were added, Cromwell went to the mat to keep his USC boys on the relay team. This would not have been possible without the tacit support that resulted from the racism and anti-Semitism that were so deeply rooted within white-Americans in those years.

It is interesting that in 1928 an African-American runner, John W. Lewis was replaced by white runner Raymond Barbuti, and that two Jewish runners were replaced by two black runners, but the U.S. Olympic committee and coaches never replaced a Aryan runner with a Jewish or African-American runner. It seems unlikely that these decisions were purely coincidental. Moreover, Forrest "Spec" Towns, University of Georgia gold medal winner in the 110-meter high hurdles in Berlin, observed that sprint coach, Lawson Robertson, "cost us [the USA] the 4 × 400-meter relay in 1936 because he did not run [African-American] Archie Williams, who had won the 400-meter individual race. He also did not run LuValle or Smallwood, and they and Archie were the top three 400-meter people. He ran Cagle, Young, Fitch, and O'Brien. I don't know why he didn't run the three fastest guys."[66]

In the spring of 1937, the newspapers began to refer to Sam Stoller as Michigan's "Olympic Orphan."[67] "Singin" Sam Stoller, who liked to croon in his spare moments, went on to prove his merit as a 100-meter dash runner.[68] In 1937 he was named NCAA All-American in the 100-yard dash[69] and AAU All-American track team for the 100-meter dash.[70] Stoller continued to run until the Millrose Games in 1940. According to the meet program,

Sam Stoller, who is making his comeback tonight, is indeed a versatile individual. He has traveled over 70,000 miles and has just returned from an extensive tour of the Philippines. He has played in several Hollywood pictures, with many famous screen personalities. He has conducted several radio programs, and is an excellent baritone singer.[71]

At age 56 Sam Stoller was an executive for a radio-TV station in Roanoke, Virginia. He died in Fort Lauderdale in 1983.[72] Foy Draper was killed in action in World War II.

One Man's Observations

As in 1928, Albion College graduate, Lee M. Bartlett kept a personal diary in 1936 covering his Olympic experience. It exposes his preoccupations, interests, and biases, and provides insights into his attitude towards Nazi Germany.

After the 1932 Olympics, Lee M. Bartlett pumped gasoline and did other odd jobs, before accepting a teaching job in Union City, Michigan, his hometown. He taught science and coached football, basketball, and track at Union City, where his father was secretary of the school board.

Lee Bartlett, from Union City, MI, graduated from Albion College in 1928, was an American record holder, and participated in the javelin throw in three consecutive Olympiads. *(Photo courtesy of Cheryl Procter)*

Lee would keep that position from September 1934 until June 1942, when he accepted a science teaching position at Dearborn High School. He stayed at Dearborn High until Edsel Ford High School in Dearborn opened in the fall of 1957. He retired from Edsel High School in 1972.

Lee's father was an undertaker and the owner of a furniture store. His position in the community was helpful in making sure that Lee could continue his athletic career. Lee's mother was concerned about her son's failure to marry and settle down, as his twin brother had done. At twenty-nine years of age, Lee's "wild life" was unsettling to his mother. Lee and his mother had clashed twelve years earlier over Lee's love affair while still in high school with a Union City teacher. The young lady was apparently four years older than Lee, and, more to his mother's sorrow, was Irish-Catholic. From his middle-class, Methodist mother's point of view, an Irish-Catholic girl was unsuitable for marriage to her son.[73]

Since the break-up of that relationship, Lee had dated a long string of girls, but it seemed that "when he was not near the girl that he loved, he loved the girl that he was near." His friends kidded him about his sexual exploits.[74] When Lee traveled to Milwaukee on June 25, 1936, for the semi-final trials for the Olympic team he was corresponding with four girls, each of whom pledged their love for him. One of these young ladies was Dorothy "Nig" Reniger, whose father owned a construction company in Battle Creek.

In Milwaukee Lee met Loraine V. Anson.* After winning the javelin throw at the meet, Lee and Loraine spent the weekend together in Chicago. Lee had fond feelings for Loraine. He called her "pigeon," and wrote of her often in his private diary that summer.

On June 13, 1936 Bartlett won the javelin throw (233–7) at the Western Michigan AAU meet in Grand Rapids. On Friday June 26 he won the qualifying round at the Olympic semi-final meet with a throw of 215–1¼. The following day he won the finals of the javelin (221–11).[75] Representing the Detroit Track Club on June 30, he won the javelin throw (204–0) at the Michigan AAU Championships.

According to Lee M. Bartlett's personal diary:

On Thursday July 9, 1936, after delaying my third Olympic tryouts trip to New York City on account of the hot weather, Lee Kenney drove me to Battle Creek where I caught the 5:05 Wolverine for an air conditioned ride. Rode all night and up till 9:10 Friday morning. Met no exciting people. Slept most of the way in from Poughkeepsie to New York. It was enjoyable along the Hudson and past West Point. Very tired.

*Daughter of Cora Anson, the supervising teacher in the Office of the Grant County Superintendent of Schools in Lancaster, Wisconsin.

July 10, Arrived in New York City and took a taxi to the Lincoln Hotel. Got a room on the 21st floor and it was terrifically hot. The Lincoln is downtown on 44th Street and 8th. Times Square is just 4 blocks away. Broadway is three. The Astor Hotel is directly in back of us and a band plays all the time. Ate at six o'clock and went to bed early. Read the newspapers. [The sports writer,] Abrams has me picked for second and Parker for fifth. They are both crazy.

July 11, Saturday, New York City. Got up at ten o'clock and ate breakfast. Found [Mal] Metcalf in the hotel. We left for Randall Island at 2 o'clock. We ferried across the river. Got dressed and went out on the field. Warmed up plenty. Delay of 30 minutes as Mayor LaGuardia is making a speech. He is standing directly behind me. Started at 3:00 Threw just once for a distance of 223 feet 5¼ inches. [Mal] Metcalf was second and [Alton] Terry was third. Came back at hotel and went to show with Metcalf. Retired at 12 and very happy.

On July 11, 1936, while representing the Detroit Track Club, Lee Bartlett set the United States record for the javelin throw (223–3¼) when qualifying for the finals in that event at the Olympic final trials at Randalls Island in New York City.

July 12, 1936 Friends from Albion College, [Mal] Metcalf, and I went to a show at Minsky's Burlesque.

July 13th, New York City, Monday. Sam [Stoller] of Michigan and I decided to room together. [Ernie] Crosbie came up with [Earnest] Krohler another walker. We toured all-day and bought a lot of things. Start living off the committee tonight. All four of us went to the German-American Athletic Club on Lennox Avenue. Sam and I take a couple of girls home at 3 o'clock. His lived at 100 and mine on 191st Street. We got home very late, but had a good time. Crosbie and Krohler took a couple of German girls home. Thought of pigeon [Loraine V. Anson.]

July 14th, New York City. Slept till noon. Ate and picked up most of our stuff. Found a lumberyard and bought some blocks. Got mixed up on subways and elevated. Ate at six and at eight Sam and I went to the Ford Broadcast of Fred Waring's Pennsylvanians. Had a swell time. He certainly is a wise cracker. Bill Robinson, the tap dancer, did some numbers. Sam [Stoller] and I went to the Parisian at 47th and Broadway. Stayed till 4 o'clock and saw the sun rise over Manhattan. Slept three hours. At 8 a.m. that morning [July 15] we got up and took a taxi down to pier 60 where we sailed on the *S. S. Manhattan* for Germany.

July 15, 1936 [A letter from Lee F. Kinney of Union City, Michigan to
Lee M. Bartlett.]

I heard the last end of the broadcast this morning telling about your sailing.

I got your clippings yesterday and was very delighted that you thought of me.

Yesterday there was a man murdered over by Girard and your father has the job. I imagine that he is glad for a little work.

That reminds me that I might get Carl T. to send you over some rubber goods as a little donation to the cause. I would suggest it to him if I thought you would have any use for them. Of course, I understand that Hitler is trying to enlarge the German army through the birth rate. Here's where you ought to shine.

I read that the two Finns only threw between 220 feet and 228 feet. If this is true, you will have a very good chance to place in the money. I am hoping and for some reason or other have a feeling that if you keep in training you may get another throw over 230 [feet] and that this time it will come when you need it most. We will hope that I am right."

Good luck old man,
Lee

July 19th, 1936, S. S. Manhattan 1993 miles from Ambrose. Helen Hayes emerged from her stateroom and signed autograph books. Played ping pong with Sam [Stoller]. Watched the basketball team work out. Walked a mile on deck. Wrote some more letters. Calm today, but ship is lunging all the time. My head is whirling again. Went to bed at 10:00 with pigeon on my mind.

On July 19, General Francisco Franco stepped out of a de Havilland airplane at the Tetuan airport in Spanish Morocco to lead the revolt that marked the opening of the Spanish Civil War.[76] There is no evidence that Hitler had any hand in the events leading to the civil war, but when Franco asked Hitler for aid on July 22, 1936, it was granted within hours. Over the next three years, Germany sent men and military supplies, including the famous Condor Air Legion, to assist Franco. From the outset, Mussolini also sent assistance to Franco, including 70,000-armed soldiers, to battle the duly elected democratic government of Spain. All of this fascist aid came long before the Republican government turned in desperation to the Soviet Union for help, when the democratic nations of Europe and America refused assistance.[77]

July 20, 1936 [Letter from Adolf Schustermann of Berlin to
Lee Bartlett on board ship.]

We welcome you on your arrival to the Olympic Games in Germany and wish the best success for you. You surely will want to know what the German press reports over your sport success and over your visit in our country. You surely will have no time to collect these reports during the next weeks. We are ready to take over this work for you and send you a collection of press cuttings with reports, notices and photos. The most important newspapers and magazines. If you have special wishes our representative is ready to visit you and receive your wishes. [An] order form [is] enclosed. Rates are 50 Reich marks or 100 Reich marks for the complete package.

*Monday, July 20, 1936 [mailed July 21, 1936, 8 p.m. [On board the S. S.
Manhattan, a letter from Lee M. Bartlett to his parents.]*

Dear Dad and Mother,

Well, we are nearly across now. Thursday we dock at Hamburg and take the
special streamlined train to Berlin, to the Olympic village.

I have stood it pretty well except the first day. The ship was pretty tippsy and
it made my head swim. I guess I get used to it because since then I like it fine.
The waves roll high and the boat swings and heaves, but it doesn't bother me
a bit. In fact, I like it.

There are two Albion men on boat besides me. The head coach from Indiana is from Albion and an Army man who is coaching the pistol team is from
Albion. We are going to send the alumni head a special item on the trip.

We certainly have eaten some awful big meals since we've been here. I'll bet
I've gained ten pounds. You can't exercise too much. The more you exercise
the more you want to eat. Our room is nice and cool. We have air conditioned
rooms with electric fans that make you shiver.

The committee was sure good to the team. Gave us blue serge suits with
white flannels, straw hats and berets, white buck shoes, socks, white shirt, tie,
sweater, and track suit. This is the most we ever got. We haven't got much of a
chance in our event though. There are six or seven Germans and Swedes and
Finns who have hit 240 feet. We play tennis everyday and take pictures. I wish
we would land though. It gets tiresome riding on a shaking boat all the time. I
had a nice time in New York. Two boys from Albion were working there so they
came down to the hotel and we went to shows. There are only 2 or 3 old men
on this team from 1932 and only 2 of us from 1928. . . . Will write when we
land.

Love, Lee

*July 21, 1936 [post-marked July 24, 1936] [Letter to Mr. and Mrs. C. S.
Bartlett from Olympian Lee Bartlett, written on board the United States
Lines, S. S. Manhattan.]*

Dear Dad and Mother—Bi and Petey,

Just about to end of our cruise. We land in another six hours. We're supposed to have been there by now but we're held up at La Havre by the rain and
unloading. We got off boarded for awhile just enough to stand on France. The
German officials came on board and this morning inspected our baggage. We
have "courtesy of the Port," so all they did was to slap stickers on our grips. I
have got to buy another suitcase. Can get them in Berlin for around $2. Have
3 boxes full of clothes that I want to put in something else. They gave us swell
uniforms all right. Double breasted coats, sport cut, with big Olympic buttons
on front and a shield on the pocket. The pants are too long but I'll get them cut
down the flannel pants are pleated sport like and come way up high. The white
shirt is a good one. The tie is terrible, but the sox are Irish linen and the white

shoes are very good. The straw hats are exactly like we had before, but we also got Berets that are swell. Our track suits are the same, but the sweat suit is cotton this time with U. S. A. on front. The belts are the same. We got Oveltine this time and pineapple juice from California. I brought a good diary in New York and keep it everyday. I bought 15 rolls of film at a discount and have taken 3 or 4 rolls already. Ireland and England were so pretty. I was appointed head coach of the javelin team last night by head coach Lawson Robertson. I have to look after transportation and keep the boys in good mood.

The mayor of Hamburg makes us a speech tonight.

Love, Lee

July 23rd, 1936, Arrived Hamburg, Germany in the P.M.

July 24, 1936, Berlin, Germany

Got up at 5:00. Ate breakfast at 6:00. We tipped out steward $6. The boat moved down the Elbe River. The country is so low and green. We became fast on the mud in the river and had to wait for the tide to rise. After two hours of waiting, we started again. Went to shore at 10:00. A German band greeted us. We were taken by bus to the town hall where the mayor made a speech and everyone had a drink of wine. The town hall was beautiful. Kaiser Wilhelm was headman in this place. Gold fixtures trimmings and molding. There are holes in the columns and in the hall that were made in the war of Franco-Prussia. We were put on a train on 11:28. The train was very easy riding. The seats were mohair upholstering and backs too. Air conditioned. Ate on train at 12:30. Passed through several small towns and arrived at Berlin at 12:28. This was the greatest thrill I've ever had. The station house was filled with thousands of people and a large German band. They played the Star and Stripes as we came out of the cars and to the front of the station. Pictures were taken and everything was so exciting, people yelling in English and German and whatnot. Trains whistled and cameras clicked. The official host made a speech followed by Brundage. Then we were taken to the city hall to hear the Burgermeister give his greeting. Traffic was tied up all over Berlin. Thousands of people lined the walks to see the largest delegation ever to enter an Olympic contest. They all seemed very hospitable and gave the Nazi Hitler salute as we passed by. Boys and girls, old men and women and they all waved flags and yelled. We came through the famous Arch Brandenberger, Burgh Thor, and the most famous street in Berlin—Unter den Linden. All the Parliament houses and officials are located here. Fifty boys dressed in white linen uniforms with shorts rode on the busses with us. They ranged between the ages 8 and 16. They spoke both English and German and pointed out the important places to us. The city hall was the most marvelous place I have ever been in and seen. The architecture and paintings are among the most famous in the world. A band was playing when we arrived and German soldiers with guns standing at attention. I had Terry take a picture of me with one. After the ceremony, we were taken on busses to the Olympic Village 20 miles away. [The Olympic Village was located about nine miles from the Olympic Stadium.] The streets are decorated with fir sprigs and flags and pennants and bunting. Everybody seems to be in a happy mood like a big carnival was coming to town. I met Hooper who is now attending Albion College and doing some graduate work, who is representing the Battle Creek, Lansing and Albion newspapers. He came to the village and I introduced him to the boys. When we entered the village which is unbelievable beyond anything I have ever seen. We marched 6 abreast to a 40 piece German band to the Arch of Entrance. Here the American flag was raised to officially show we had arrived and the band played the Star Spangled Banner. Then we marched into the village and up a long winding road past beautiful lawns and lagoons, storks, flamingos, bridges etc. to the top of the hill. Here the band played the Star Spangled Banner again and another flag was raised to officially open the American houses. The name of ours is Chemnitz. [Mal] Metcalf and I are roommates. The house has 20 roommates, a big shower bath and toilet. We ate at six o'clock in the official mess hall. The food was very good. We walked down to the gate, bought some things and came home. Went to bed at 10:30 tired, but very happy. [The female athletes were housed at Frisian House, a new dormitory built for students of the Reich Sports Academy near the Olympic Stadium.]

July 25, 1936, Berlin, Germany. Had a good night's sleep. Went to practice field and had good workout. Wrote some letters. Went downtown and what a town. Everybody is so curious and courteous. We bought several curios. Ate at a fashionable restaurant. Metcalf is the official interpreter. We had milk with water and spoon and sugar, hot dogs and potato salad, and ice cream with wafers. On the way out three girls waved so we got their autographs and ended up with a date for tomorrow afternoon. I wonder if we will really have it.

July 26, 1936
Chemnitz #10 a-R-16
Olympisches Dorf
Berlin, Germany

*[Letter from Olympian Lee Bartlett to his parents. The letter was
written in the Olympic Village.]*

Dear Dad and Mother, "Petey" and "Bi"

This certainly has been a busy day. We have been going all the time. Got up at seven o'clock this morning. We went to the field that is only a block from our house in Olympic Village. We played basketball and worked out for about three hours.

I think the rates are a little high. I bought a few things today downtown. My roommate speaks good German, so we are going to get along all right. We talked with some German girls and tomorrow they are taking us riding in their car. One speaks English and the other two German. The soldiers are marching all the time. Newspaper reporters say Germany will have a war with Czechoslovakia in the next six months.

We had fireworks at the village tonight and what I mean they were really noisy. The rabbits were running in all directions. The storks on the pond were yelling and hollering. Tomorrow we are going to see the city. It rained all day, but stopped about eight o'clock. The fields and grass are very green. They utilize every bit of space for growing things. The rye and oats are being cut now and threshed. They don't raise corn but a grain very similar to make bread out of. The bakeries have the most delicious looking food, so much different from ours though. We bought ice cream today for 5 cents. I think it was made out of water.

Our beds are funny too. No sheets but pads. You have one pad over you and one under you.

The band plays a concert every noon and night at the eating house. They have a very snappy band. We ride all the busses, streetcars and boats free of charge. Will write soon.

Love, Lee

July 26, 1936, Berlin. Ate at 7:30 and then laid around till noon. Took some pictures around the village. Cleaned up. Metcalf called up the gals at 2, 2:30 and 3. Couldn't find a soul. Finally called Sonja's number and found out we were calling wrong number. Called back and talked to Sonja. She told us to meet Edith at the Banuf. Hopped on bus and got down there at 4:30. Met Edith. Shook hands as is the German custom and got in her Essex. She drove us down town and out to her home. We met all the folks and picked up Elaine. We then toured the city. I tried to tell Elaine not to make the fourth lane of traffic but she can't understand English and she did get bawled out. Edith is a beautiful girl, 21 years of age, light hair, tall, slender, small feet, light blue eyes, small mouth with thick lips, fine features. She poses for magazine covers. She certainly has the looks. Sonja is brown haired and brown eyed. She is photographer for poses of Edith. She is well built, smart dresser and drives a nice little car. We had coffee at Koffee-Haus at 6:30. Then we ate in a Hungarian Haus. The goulash was so strange. I could hardly eat it. We certainly were the center of attraction. We drove out to Elaine's relatives and met everybody that came in the front door. The girls drove us to the bus and got home at 12 very tired.

July 27, '36, Berlin. Ate early and then worked out till noon. Had good rub down and hot shower. Ate big lunch. Started raining at one o'clock so went to bed. Bought boomerang at sports store. Ate at early sitting and then cleaned up. Metcalf and I rode to Banuf where we found Ede. Picked up Sonja and decided to go to her apartment. Bought coffee, sugar, cakes, peaches, bananas, plums, milk and vermouth at slot machines. Drove to apartment. Funny thing, the girls ride in the front, and we ride in back. I guess it isn't the custom. Parked in front of apartment and went through front gate. Unlocked another walked through plaza and into third gate. Up two flights of stairs. The apartment was very large and very beautiful. Small kitchen and clothes closet, room 18 feet high, high drapes, bare hard floors, large divan and stools. German women are very bull-headed or else they like to be nice. They want to do everything. I guess it is the custom. We stayed two hours, drank coffee, ate and played American records on a victrola. Germans like American music. We talked about customs, why we do the things we do and we certainly learned a lot. Left about 10:30 and went to nightclub downtown. They play good American music but the price is lousy. Had Bronx and danced with Edith. Had floor show, two Negro tap dancers from Kansas City. Stayed to 2 o'clock. Bought ten liters of gasoline for 3m50 and the girls drove us out to the village. These girls are really very nice. We said goodbye after argument with cop over one headlight. Tried to get in window but was locked. Came in front door. Asleep at 3:00.

July 28, 1936, Berlin. Slept very late. Got ready to work out but was raining. Terry and I decided to go down town. Left on one o'clock train. Bought several things. Got along O.K. Had a big time in ladies shop on Jachalumstrasse. All the women in the shop wanted to wait on us. One had a letter in English from a Japanese [athlete] in the village. We explained to her that he liked her very well. Came home about six o'clock. Ate at six-thirty. I wonder what has become of the mail. No letters since we arrived. Had headache so we went to bed early. Thought of Pigeon.

July 29, 1936, Berlin. Slept twelve hours. Ate breakfast and wrote some letters home. Worked out at ten o'clock. Got rubdown and hot shower. After luncheon, Mal, Terry and I went downtown. Met Eddie Powers from Detroit on bus. I asked about everybody. Rained so we came home. Ate wieners at hot dog stand. Cost ten cents. Max Schmeling was here. Took picture. Sent Ede a telegram. She's sure swell. I wished she could speak English. Ted Huising in broadcasting from village tonight. Met Dr. Martin from Switzerland. Went to bed early.

July 30, 1936 [Letter from R. D. Pendill of Union City, MI to Olympian Lee Bartlett, Olympic Village, Berlin, Germany.]

Mike is putting on a big August sale [at his store]—Jew—Stephens wrote his ads.

July 30, 1936, Berlin. Went down town at Herr Strasse Banuf. Girls were half an hour late. Went to show and saw German picture. Wasn't very good but interesting. Went from show to bus station. Ede sure looked swell tonight. She likes me a little too I know.

July 31, 1936 [mailed August 3, 1936]

[Letter from Olympian Lee Bartlett to his parents from
Olympische Dorf, Berlin, Germany.]

Dear Dad and Mother, "Bi" and "Petey",

Well we are nearly ready for the parade, which starts tomorrow. We practiced marching tonight so we won't look so terribly bad with all these military nations. There are 53 nations here now. The last came in today. This great event will soon be over. It all goes so fast. I'd like to have enough money to stay here for some time. It sure is a marvelous country. Received a card from a girl today in Atlantic City who has the same name as mine. She wished me good luck.

The rain has finally left and the sunshine is sure nice. It gets very cold nights. There are no bugs of any kind. Went to a show last night and got along pretty fair. I have a German girl already. She can't speak a word of English. She has an Opel six with convertible top. We went for a ride Sunday and saw all of Berlin. We went to her home and the folks sure treated us swell. Last night at the show, I never knew when to laugh, so when she laughed, I did. We had an ice cream Sunday that was terrible, but I couldn't tell 'em so.

Max Schmeling came to camp yesterday and I got his picture o.k. I wish I had some sweet corn now and a good malted milk. I get tired of spinach and string beans with the strings.

We leave for London on the 12th. We have a track meet there on the 15th. We start for home on the 19th, which means I will be home close to the 30th. Bought a suitcase today for $2. It will carry all my clothing, I hope. I haven't bought very much yet, but I'll try and get everybody something or other, mostly other. Will write later. Got to make a call for our Fraulines.

Love, Lee

August 1, 1936, Berlin. [Saturday. In the morning the weather was overcast and it was drizzling.] Stayed in bed until ten. Cleaned up and had our pictures taken. Ate an early lunch and took bus down to stadium. [A fleet of 170] Buses carried 7,000 men [male athletes]. [The fleet of buses carrying us from the Olympic Village to the Reich Sports Field was] Over three miles long. [The athletes of 53 nations] Lined up outside of gate. We were 52nd nation, next to the last. [At about 4 p.m.] Adolf Hitler marched in first. [The] Stands were packed. Over one hundred thousand people were there. Track in red as in Amsterdam. Pierre De Coubertin gave short speech followed by Hitler. Torchbearer entered carrying the light from Greece and lit the tower fire. 30,000 carrier pigeons were released and cannons boomed eleven times. [The Zeppelin *Hindenburg*, with big swastika emblems in red, white, and black emblazoned on its tail-fins, flew overhead towing an Olympic flag.] Marched out and came home in buses. There were quite a few Americans at the Stadium and spectacle was very thrilling, but not so much as in Amsterdam. Came home after dinner. Wrote some more letters. Boys came in and we talked a little. Metcalf and I carved on our javelin canes. Went down and got my pictures. They are turning out pretty grand. Listened to Mexican boys play and sing. Sounded very good. Mal opened some of his pineapple juice. It was cool. I turned off the light and went to sleep.

August 2, 1936, Berlin. [Sunday. Unseasonably cold wind and high humidity. Events at the Olympic Stadium started at 10:30 a.m. Late in the morning, Jesse Owen won the twelfth heat of the 100-meter dash preliminaries. In the afternoon he won the second heat of the second round of that event.] Got up at ten o'clock. Went over to the field and watched basketball team workout. Ate early. Went down to the stadium at 2 o'clock. Was filled. We slammed in the high jump [Cornelius Johnson won the gold medal; David Albritton won the silver medal, and Delos Thurber won the bronze medal.] [Jack] Torrance was shut out in the shot. [He finished fifth to German Hans Woelike.] All the girls were shut out in the javelin. Placed three men in [the finals of the] 800 [meter run—John Woodruff, Charles Hornbostel, and Harry Williamson] and three in the 100 [meter dash—Jesse Owens, Ralph Metcalfe, and Frank Wykoff.] [Don] Lash and [Eino] Pentti were shut out in the 10,000. Had hard time getting back from stadium. Hadnutt, Englishman, Mal Wilkins and I hired a taxi. Eats were terrible. Climbed out window at 10:30 and took bus for Banuf Herrstrasse. Met Ede and Sonja at 11:00. Went to Sherbini's place. Had good time. Girls brought us in at 3:30.

August 3, 1936, Chemnitz #106-R-16, Olympische-Dorf. [Monday. Cool cloudy morning with heavy showers at just after noon and at 2 p.m. The cinder track was damp and heavy.] Didn't feel very well this morning so stayed in bed till noon. Ate a big dinner and wrote letters home. Got some pictures and bought an album. Went down to the stadium at 2:30. Stadium filled to capacity. Owens looked good in [the semi-finals and finals of the] 100 [meter dash. He tied the Olympic and word record of 10.3 in the finals.] [Don] Favor and [William] Rowe finished 5th and 6th in the hammer. [Henry] Dreyer got pushed out. Our steeplechase men [Harold Manning and Glen Dawson] looked fair. [Heats for the 400-meter hurdles began at 3 p.m.] Came home at 5:30. Bummed a ride with a German salesman. Mal talked to him about the war. He is just as much against it as we are. Went to bed at ten.

August 3, 1936 [Letter from Loraine V. Anson to Olympian
Lee Bartlett in Berlin.]

Jesse Owens did beautifully today. One can't help admiring him. [Much of the letter concerned their liaison in Chicago.]

August 4, 1936, Chemnitz #106-R-16, Olympische-Dorf [Light rain in the afternoon.] Got up early this morning. Worked out for the last time. Ate dinner at twelve. Wrote letters and then [Bill] Brown [hop, step and jump] and Mal [Metcalf] and I went down to the stadium. Bill and I bummed a ride with meat truck. Owens won 100 [actually the 200.] Stephens 100, Owens [also won] the broad jump. [Don] Lash looked good in 5,000 [meter run]. Virge [Gene Venzke, in the 1500-meter] failed to qualify, came home at six o'clock on the bus. Ate dinner and went to show. Only had American comedies. Went to bed at eleven o'clock.

August 5, 1936 Olympisches Dorf, Berlin, Germany [Cool day.] Stayed in bed this morning. Raining and very cold. Joe E. Brown blew in and put on a little comedy for the boys. Ate at noon. Jim [Gordon G. Dunn] and [W. Kenneth] Carpenter won discus and [Earl] Meadows took the pole vault. "Bing" [Ernie Crosbie] failed in the 50,000-meter walk. Placed one girl hurdler.

*August 5, 1936 [Letter from Lee Bartlett to his family in
Union City, MI. on his mother's birthday.]*

Chemnitz #10a-R-16
Olympisches Dorf
Berlin, Germany

Dear Dad and mother, "Bi" and "Petey"

Well tomorrow is the day for our event so will write tonight. Have been very busy this week attending the games and everything. It has rained every day, but the sun always shines five minutes afterwards. We have to qualify in the morning at 197 feet. The Germans and Finns look awfully good in our event. One of us might slip in 4th, 5th, or 6th place.

I just found out we don't leave 'till the 26th of August. Consequently I won't get home 'till the 6th of September. I will be a week late for school, but have written "Doke" to take care of the football team and also the Superintendent. I don't know who is president of the school board now but you have Dad inform whoever it is to the effect that I will be a few days late, probably 3 or 4. We go to Paris after the meet at London. They changed the program today. We are way ahead in points now and will certainly be world's champions for the third straight time. Had some sweet corn yesterday, but it was fried corn and plenty tough.

Hitler has been there every day and seems to have a big time. I took some pictures of him. We sit about 60 yards from him every day. They give him an awful lot of saluting too.

Haven't seen Teeter as yet so must be he isn't coming. It's so cold now we have to turn the radiators on all day. I guess we aren't used to it. Well will close and get to bed because tomorrow is a big day and will be plenty tired. We have to ride about 40 miles all toll to get too and from the stadium for our event.

Love, Lee

August 6, 1936, Olympic Stadium, Berlin. Ate at 7:30. Took bus for stadium at nine o'clock. There are 34 javelin entries. We had to qualify at 60 meters. All three of us got in on our first throw. Came back to village and ate lunch. Left at one-thirty for stadium. Only 15 qualified for finals. [Gerhard] Stock [of Germany] won at 23 le. [235 feet 8 inches.] [Matti] Jarvinen [of Finland] was pushed out at 220 [officially 227 feet.] [Alton] Terry placed sixth. Pole got 7th and myself 8th [actually he was 9th] at 213. [Mal] Metcalf was about 12th. [John] Lovelock [of New Zealand] beat [Glenn] Cunningham [of Elkhart, Kansas, in the 1,500-meter run.] Came home and sewed my coat up. Tired but stayed up till one o'clock. Mal came in at 3:30.

It is interesting to note that when the blond, blue-eyed Aryan, Gerhard Stock, won the javelin throw, he immediately sprang to attention and gave a rigid Nazi salute, yet his behavior did not evoke any comment from Lee Bartlett.

August 7, 1936, Olympisches Dorf, Berlin. Brown woke me up at ten o'clock and we went downtown. Got to track meet about four o'clock. [Don] Lash didn't place in 5000. [Archie] Williams won the 400 [meter run] and [James] LuValle got third. All three decathlon meets are in [Glenn Morris won the gold medal, Robert Clark won the silver medal, and Jack Parker won the bronze medal.] Came home at 7:30 all tired out.

August 8, 1936 Olympisches Dorf, Berlin. Ate breakfast early. Bill and Romeo and I went to town. Ate lunch in Wertheims. Had wieners, potatoes, ice cream and cakes. Cost 40 cents. Took bus to stadium. [Glenn] Morris won decathlon. Took picture of Hitler. Came home early. Got driven to Herrstrasse Banuf at 9:00. Sonja was upset. Went to picture show. Saw Jean Harlow and Bill Powell in "Reckless". Picked up Ede at Scala's show and went to Sonja's. They drove us home about three o'clock. Had a good time. Went to bed at 4 o'clock.

August 9, 1936 Olympische Dorf, Berlin. Met Sonja and Ede at gate and they drove us to Pottsdam, the home of Fredrick the Great. Country sure was nice. Took pictures and hurried back to get Ede in time for show. Took in Scala's show. Was best I have ever seen. Ede was swell and especially with dogs. Ate at Scala's restaurant where all the players eat. Left Ede and Sonja drove us to Banuf. Took bus home. Met South African boxing referee. Told us all about the country.

August 10, 1936, Olympische Dorf, Berlin. Went to Banuf. Sonja met us there in a taxi. Car was broke so we went to her mother's place and got her Opal. Picked up Ede at 11:30. Went to her studio. Had marvelous time. Ede was very sweet. Had coffee, cakes and buns. Played American pieces on phonograph. Ede has really fallen in love with me. She really has. She talked to me in German all the time. I couldn't understand a word she said. It seems very peculiar to know someone loves you and I know she does and not being able to understand what she is saying. She certainly is very sweet. She cried very much when I kissed her "auf wiedersehen". She didn't want me to leave. I want to see her again but love is like that. Today we leave for London. She gave me her picture. In fact, she gave me four of them. She autographed them too. Sonja told me in English that German girls do not have a string of beaus. If you go with a girl three times the old folks "zinks" you should get married. She wants me to stay so bad but it turned only worse when I did want to go. She has such golden blond hair and blue eyes. I wonder how she keeps from getting married. She is going to write to me. I hope she doesn't forget me but she will. I like her very much in fact too much.

August 10, 1936 [Letter from Olympian Lee Bartlett in Olympisches Dorf, Berlin to his parents in Union City, MI.]

Dear Dad and Mother,

Well the games are over and tomorrow we sail for London. Most of the boys have gone now. The javelin throw came out just as I expected. We just were out-bested. I threw 215 feet or seventh place. I guess its too cold for me over here. I just can't keep warm. The German won it with a throw of 237 feet. Jarvinen was very bad. I beat him on 5 of my throws. He had one great one. The meet as a whole was the best. The stadium was filled to capacity on every morning and afternoon. The figures are about a million and a half people. Three hundred thousand watched the marathon yesterday. Hitler was a spectator every morning and afternoon. It isn't everybody who can throw in front of him. I sat quite close yesterday, but I didn't have my camera. The Germans won a lot of first places and the girls claim they are the winners of the Olympic games, but we got more points.

These last two days have been real nice. The sun is bright and it's been warm. We had an orchestra come up and play last night. It sounded very good. The boys are getting a little homesick. Everybody wants to leave. I'll be glad when we get to England. All we eat is spinach, beans, meat and potatoes. No pie or cake or Jell-O. You can't buy a soda in the city. Nobody likes them so they don't sell them. Well I'm going over to take some lessons from the Finnish coach.

Love, Lee

August 11, 1936, *S. S. Washington*, Hamburg. Went to the train at eleven o'clock. Band was there playing and people gathered. Called Sonja's place but she was out. Her mother was there so Mal told her to tell Sonja and Ede good-bye. We boarded the 12 o'clock train for Hamburg. I never wanted to stay so bad in all my life. I wanted to stay for Ede. I didn't know she meant so much to me. Maybe it's the fact that I never will see her again. It seems just like death to go away from her. I have known her such a short time but she certainly made me want her. Ate on train and got in Hamburg at 4 o'clock. Went to stadium and ate at six. Track meet was swell. We won every event except the hammer. Had a swell dinner and then took buses to *S. S. Washington*. Was glad to get to bed.

August 27, 1936, Boat, train, Le Havre, France. Ate lunch and then settled our cabin. [Stan] Wudyka, [Marty] Glickman, Mal [Metcalf] and I have cabin 103. About 100 of us on board.

September 3, 1936, *S. S. Manhattan*. New York City, U.S.A. Got up at five o'clock to get an early start. Ate breakfast at 5:30 and sat around till nine o'clock. The mayor's secretary Mr. Harve (from Albion) welcomed us and newspaper men came on board. We landed at ten o'clock. I was last one through customs and we grabbed a cab for the parade. Went to Randall Island for a picnic and to get our medals. [Jack] Dempsey (former heavyweight champion), Bill Robinson (black dancer), [Gertrude] Ederle (swam the English Channel), [Gene] Tunney, [Babe] Ruth and Magar were there. Band played and then we marched round the stadium before the school kids that were parked there. After presentation of the medals by Mayor [Fiorello] La Guardia and his force we got back in our car and went to the deck and picked up our grips. Had to tie mine up, as it was broke. Checked my grips at the Central Station and went to the St. Moritz Hotel. Listened to radio and at 10 o'clock went to the train. Got my ticket and my berth looked awful good.

September 3, 1936 [Letter to Lee Bartlett from Ede, the
German girl Bartlett dated.]

My dear Lee,

I thank you very much for your lovely letter. You at least give a little hope in my dark sadness that we shall see each other again. I have often thought how it would be possible to come over to see you in America, but haven't any money and don't know where I'm going to get any and furthermore I don't know whether you have a girl in America or not if you love me and could you be free if I should come to you. I should always love you. Shall never forget you and prey that the opportunity arrives so we can get together again. You are the only and first man in my life who I would have married without knowing what my future would be. It is your fault that I didn't show my love that last morning at the Olympic Village. I could have died from sorrow. I have such a feeling that you enjoyed yourself. I followed your journey to England and Paris and to your own home in my mind, and even today I thank you and please don't forget me and my love. Write me again please and I would like to take you in my arms and kiss you a 1,000 times.

From your Ede.

"Sam Stoller, University of Michigan star, who was denied a place on the 400-meter relay team, said that he was sorry if he leveled too much of a blast against his Olympic track coach. 'Politics kept me off the team,' said Stoller, 'not racial prejudice. But it's all over now. It was a nightmare all the way around, I guess. I intend to go back to Michigan and run my legs off again—if I can get enough money together to get back.'

"All those who could be talked out of shopping and dates with boy and girl friends were taken out to the Yankee Stadium this afternoon to watch the Yankees play the Detroit Tigers. Tonight Jack Dempsey was the host at his restaurant."[78]

The Associated Press reported on September 3, 1936

the second large detachment of the American Olympic delegation, 125 athletes, coaches and committeemen, arrived aboard the Liner Manhattan and was given a noisy welcome. The [New York] mayors' committee went down the bay and greeted the athletes as the boat steamed into the harbor, saluted by fireboats and by a 50-piece band which played abroad one of the welcoming craft. At the pier, a crowd of 5,000 greeted the stars. After baggage inspection, the athletes were driven to the battery where they met their comrades who arrived last week. A parade up Broadway to Randall's Island followed. At

Sammy Stoller was one of two Jewish athletes on the USA Olympic track and field team at the Berlin Olympics. Both were denied participation. *(Photo University of Michigan, Bentley Library)*

Randall's Island, the athletes were guests of the city at a luncheon where commemorative medals were presented.

All the athletes were in good health, reported a smooth crossing and said they were 'broke.'

Glenn Morris of Denver, who set a world decathlon record, said he was so tired after winning that he couldn't sleep for four nights. He will return to Denver where a special "Glenn Morris Day" is to be staged. Morris said his future plans are indefinite but that he is not going to return to his job as an automobile salesman.[79]

The Olympic athlete in Berlin was elevated to a godlike creature. The cinematic artistry of Leni Riefenstahl preserved the best of the Berlin Olympics for future generations. The Germans had even reserved a wooded space near the Olympic Village for those gods. The prettiest handpicked maidens offered themselves to the athletes—especially to the good Aryan types. Olympic babies born out of such encounters were to be cared for by the state. There was every indication that this wooded area for lovemaking was a matter of state policy by the Nazis. The maidens were usually sport teachers or members of Hitler's *Bund deutscher Madchen [German Girl's League]* and they had special passes to enter the Village woods and mingle with the athletes. It was a lovely beech forest that had a pretty little lake, and *Shupos* [Berlin City police] tightly ringed the place by so no one would disturb the sportive couples. Before submitting to the Olympic god of her choice, the girl would request her partner's Olympic badge. In case of pregnancy, she would give this information to state or Red Cross maternity officials to prove the Olympic origin of her baby. Then the state would pay for all her expenses.

"Aryan racial improvement was apparently the object of the young ladies' affection. They avoided blacks and seemed to favor Americans, Scandinavians, Finns, Dutchmen and, of course, Germans."[80] From the Nazi point of view, the German athletes in the 1936 Olympics were "forerunners of new types of Germans, . . . tough, well-formed men and graceful women."[81] Contestants in athletic meets were to be watched and admired not only as sportsmen, but as political troops in a greater struggle.[82]

So Many Did Not Chose to Look for What They Did Not Wish to See

Four thousand athletes from fifty-two nations participated in the Berlin Olympics. Berlin was dressed with a million or more huge swastika banners that fluttered throughout the city. A carnival spirit was created that out did New Orleans during Mardi Gras or New York City on New Year's eve. Carl Diem, a Nazi, created the Olympic flame for use in the Berlin Olympics. The flame was specifically designed to give the proceeding "an ancient aura." The idea was so good that it has become part of Olympic tradition.

Never had a modern Olympiad been to so glittery and gaudy. Flags from the participating nations hang everywhere. Traffic on Unter Den Linden was so heavy it took 15 minutes to walk a couple of blocks. In the midst of such a smothering of decoration and swirl of naval and military display, it was almost impossible to calmly contemplate the actual games despite the fact that they promised the greatest athletic competition ever seen at an Olympiad.

At the Olympic Village there were signs that read "Dogs and Jews not allowed." They were only removed after the IOC president Count Henri de Baillet Latour of Belgium met with Hitler and ordered the Fuehrer to remove the offensive signs.[83]

The Berlin games with all its pomp and ceremony was unlike all the previous Olympiads. It was an expression of a state—a showpiece for the glorification of the third Reich and Adolf Hitler. While the games cost Germany some 60,000,000 marks ($24,200,000) even before the first competing athlete arrived in Berlin, none of that money was spent for intangibles. Every building and stadium erected for the games was a permanent structure for future military and sporting purposes.

The Olympic village on the outskirts of Berlin, for example, was used as barracks for the army. The Olympic stadium, which accommodated 110,000 spectators was later used for Nazi rallies and German sport festivals. For other unestimated millions spent for propaganda purposes, administration of the games and other reasons, the third Reich got back as much in foreign currency. Over 1200 newspaper reporters told the story to the world; more than 350 radio broadcasters carried word pictures daily to all nations and the outstanding events were shown in theaters throughout the world.[84]

Once in Berlin

while the athletes were working out, American Olympic committee announced the official salutes to be used in passing Adolf Hitler during the opening ceremonies. The male athletes will salute Hitler with their straw hats held in their right hands, extended at arm's length and shoulder high midway between straight front and straight right. The decision to include straw hats in the salute makes it certain that no one will misinterpret the gesture as a Nazi salute. The women athletes will give the regulation Olympic salute, with the right arm extended shoulder high and more to the front than to the right [85]

Joseph Goebbels, the Nazi Minister of Propaganda, was a master of misdirection and misrepresentation through the orchestration of events and influence on radio and newsprint reporting. Without question the Nazi presentation of the Olympic Games had much to do with the favorable impression athletes and visitors had of the Berlin Olympics. Goebbels' techniques for influencing public opinion were to have a profound influence on the balance of the twentieth century.

Throughout the Berlin Olympic festival not a single foreign visitor—

Jew or Black—reported being insulted, harassed, or made to feel unwelcome on racial grounds. In terms of athletic performance, the eleventh Olympiad was memorable. In men's track and field seventeen Olympic and five world records were broken, and in women's track and field five Olympic records were set. Nearly everyone who attended came home thinking that rumors about Nazi atrocities were exaggerated or untrue.

The afterglow of the Berlin Olympics was a powerful aphrodisiac. Hitler and the Nazis favorably impressed Charles Lindbergh, who attended the opening ceremonies as a guest of the German government. He wrote a friend, "There is no need for me to tell you that I am not in accord with the Jewish situation in Germany, [but] the undercurrent of feeling [was] that the German Jews had been on the side of the Communists. Hitler is undoubtedly a great man, and I believe has done much for the German people." Anne Morrow Lindbergh, his wife, went even further after their ten-day visit to Germany. She was "perfectly thrilled" with their visit to Berlin, and blamed "Jewish propaganda in the Jewish owned papers" for Hitler's bad image. Her husband would later write:

Europe, and the entire world, is fortunate that a Nazi Germany lies, at present, between Communistic Russia and a demoralized France. With the extremes of government, which now exist, it is more desirable than ever to keep any one of them from sweeping over Europe. But if the choice must be made it can not be Communism.[86]

It is interesting to note that from the time of the "red scare" following World War I to the end of the century, those opposed to change would label anyone or any idea that they opposed as "communist." By using this tactic, they avoided discussing the merits of the proposal or policy and branded their opponents as dangerous radicals.

Olympian Lee Bartlett was one of those people who rejected any information that challenged his beliefs about Nazi Germany. When he returned from the Berlin Olympics, Bartlett made a report to the Coldwater Rotary Club on Tuesday September 16, 1936 about his trip to the Olympics. Howard Teeter of Union City introduced Bartlett to the club. In this presentation, Bartlett reported that:

His opinion of Adolf Hitler rose considerably after he had an opportunity to observe conditions in Germany at close range. . . . Germany is rapidly being built up by Hitler into a prosperous and strong nation. . . . The German people love Hitler. . . . He also exploded another current belief when he claimed that the Jewish population of Germany is not as ill-treated as reported. While Germany has become militaristic under Hitler's regime, the country is hoping for continued peace.

Bartlett's description of the Olympic games, the village where the athletes from all the competing nations were quartered, and the countless other events incident to the recent Olympiad, was so interesting that many of his listeners remaining after the usual hour to press questions."[87]

Lee Bartlett was a sincere man, who reflected the values and prejudices of his small town upbringing. While he willingly roomed with Jewish sprinters Sam Soller and Marty Glickman and admired the performances of Jesse Owens, Ralph Metcalfe, and John Woodruff, he labeled the page of his scrapbook with their pictures on it "Three Crows and Two Jews." The insidious racism that had ascended over Europe and North America had poisoned people's powers of observation as well as their personal relationships.

On March 8, 1937 Lee Bartlett was elected village president of Union City. He held the office for one year. He found it contentious dealing with competing interests and alternative visions of community.[88]

The power of racism did not abate following the 1936 Olympics. On February 25, 1939, following speeches by Adolf Hitler and Paul Joseph Goebbels, the Nazis issued orders requiring the Jewish community in Berlin to furnish to Berlin police authorities the names of 100 persons a day for deportation within two weeks.[89] At the same time, anti-Semitism was a major focus of campus debate at the University of Michigan and elsewhere on college campuses. On February 23, 1939

Two unidentified men, believed to be pranksters, pained three-foot swastikas on the doors of three Jewish fraternity houses at 3:30 a.m. The men, dressed in solid-color mackinaws, were seen walking from one house by two of the fraternity members. Hearing noises on the front porch, they had gone to investigate and saw the men from a front window. Drops of paint were traced a short distance down the street, where they ended suddenly. This was taken as indication that the men had a car waiting. It could not be determined whether they were students."[90]

This generation had yet to learn what Elie Wiesel, a victim of Nazi atrocities, came to understand. Wiesel told the graduates of the Long Island University:

If I shall be insensitive to one pain, I shall be insensitive to all pains. Never be neutral in any situation where human dignity is concerned. The world out there is not always sunny. There is so much suffering, it is easy to give up hope. But if we are not aware and sensitive, then your children will inherit the ruins of the world.[91]

Unlearned Lessons for the 1936 Olympic Games

Baron Pierre de Coubertin, the father of the modern Olympic games, planned the international meet in hopes of reinvigorating French youth. He sought to convince ruling elites that physical education and sport for the masses had paramilitary value. He seemed to be unaware that the supreme levels of athletic excellence manifested in the Olympics might have little relevance to democratic physical education or that democratic physical education, in turn, might have almost no relevance to the skills demanded for modern warfare. The Nazis and military strategists four decades later also missed this point.

In general, athletics did little to promote democracy. Totalitarian governments generally produce as many great athletes as democracies, as the Nazis and later the Soviet Union proved. In 1969 Jack Scott made the point that the most authoritarian methods of training Olympic-class athletes are those used by the United States and the Soviet Union. In both countries training schedules isolated world class athletes with outstanding physical skills from other, less talented youths.[92]

There were lessons to be drawn from the Berlin Olympics. While the superior performance of African-American athletes should have argued against claims of racial superiority, it did not. On the other hand, the Berlin Olympics proved that the Nazis were administratively capable of planning large-scale events with precision, and that athletes from totalitarian nations performed strikingly well. The reinvigorated Germans won more medals than any other country, even though the American team was the largest ever sent abroad.[93]

Even as the thousands of athletes struggled before hundreds of thousands of happy onlookers and millions more reveled in the mass parades, flapping banners, and staged ceremonies, there was ample evidence that the masters of Germany had charted that nation on a collision course with war. According to one sports historian, "the 1936 Olympics were a vast razzle-dazzle that blurred the outlines of a growing threat to Western civilization." The Nazis "disguised the extent to which the diabolical aspects of National Socialist ideology were being used against an unfortunate people."[94]

Despite the success of German athletes, who won more medals than the Americans, the phenomenal performance of African-American athletes in Berlin worried more people than the Nazis. While their successes were a matter of pride in the African-American community, there was a noticeable backlash in parts of the white community.

After the Berlin Olympics, preparations for the 1940 Games were taking place in Sapporo on Hokkaido, the northernmost island in the Japanese archipelago. By the middle of 1937 militarists were clearly in control of the Japanese government, and petitions began to circulate in Sweden, the United States, and Great Britain to move the games to a nation more respectful of Olympic ideals. On January 13, 1938, Avery Brundage, president of the American Olympic Committee, declared in the *New York Times*, "Sport transcends all political and racial situations. Whether our Committee or athletes like or dislike Japan's military policy is beside the point." Brundage clearly missed the lesson taught by the Berlin Olympics, and would continue to turn a blind eye to the uses to which nationalistic political, social, and economic policies were used to subvert athletic competition for national political and economic advantage. While it is true that sports can be an instrument for promoting egalitarian principals, it is also true that sport is often used for less laudable purposes.

Gimmicks Needed to Survive

After winning four, gold medals at the Reich Sports field in the 1936, Jesse Owens was put on board a train to Cologne by the AAU and sent on a grueling European trip. In the next ten days Owens raced eight times and lost 14 pounds. Although exhausted, he was ordered by the AAU to travel to Sweden for more exhibition races, for which he would receive no compensation, as all gate receipts would accrue to the Swedes and the AAU. Owens refused to go and was suspended by the AAU and his amateur status revoked. Despite his accomplishments, Owens was never appointed to a key Olympic Committee or policy-making group.[95]

Even before the 21-year old Jesse Owens, a junior at Ohio State University, won his four gold medals, he was concerned about supporting his wife and family. Jesse told the United Press, "The lure of the dollar is stronger than any desire to prolong my athletic glory. I'm married you know, and I want to earn some money." Owens told reporter he would retire from competition and look for a job.[96]

After the Olympics, Jesse Owens announced that he was prepared to take the stump for Gov. Alfred M. Landon, some say in return for $10,000 given in cash in a brown paper bag.[97] Theatrical agent Marty Perkins, who had recently signed Owens to a one year contract to handle his athletic and business affairs, declared

I absolutely won't allow him to stump for Governor Landon or anybody else to take part in politics. I didn't even know about this statement he gave out. I wouldn't have allowed him to take any side in the political campaign if I had known about it. I don't think he's interested much one way or the other in politics. He told me that he voted the Republican ticket but beyond that he didn't pay much attention to politics. He's in the public hands now and can't be dabbling in political matters.[98]

Like Eddie Tolan, Jesse Owen had difficulty translating athletic achievement into career success, aside from the bribe he received to support Alf Landon. After the Olympic Games Owens, like Tolan before him, struggled to survive. Jesse made a few dollars racing horses at carnivals. The races were rigged by firing the starter's pistol so close to the horse's ear that the startled horse would rear, allowing Owens to break out to an insurmountable head start.[99] During the Second World War Owens ended up in the public relations office at the Ford Motor Company in Detroit, and his daughter graduated with honors from Pershing High School. During those years, Jesse gave encouragement to a number of promising Detroit track athletes.

In the late 1950s he often endured humiliation to make a few dollars giving banquet talks to high school father-son gatherings in suburban Chicago. In 1957, for example, he was arrested when he entered Crete, Illinois to speak to the Crete-Monee High School sports banquet. His only crime was DWB, driving while black, in white suburban Chicago after sundown. My father-in-law, who was the school board President, had to rescue Jesse from the police station so that he could speak to the waiting audience.[100]

Matthew "Mack" Robinson also had difficulty translating an Olympic medal into a job. When he returned to Pasadena from Berlin, he had to take a job sweeping streets to support his wife and two children. He wore his Olympic jacket to and from work not to show off, but because it was all he had to wear. Despite his college education, for years Mack was forced to work at menial jobs. Nevertheless, he helped teach track to pre-teens and teenagers and never expressed bitterness, although he had ample cause.[101]

The Legacy

While Olympic glory in Berlin did not result in financial rewards for most of the black athletes, it did result in greater recognition for African-American athletes than ever before in American history. Jesse Owens received the adulation that had eluded Eddie Tolan. Ironically, the elaborate Olympic extravaganza, purportedly staged to show the success of fascism and the athletic superiority of the Aryan race, had instead gained broad acceptance for African-American athletes. The American press exulted over Owens' triumphs, and declared that their victories were American victories. As the American public began to recognize that fascism was an enemy to democracy, the accomplishments of Jesse Owens became firmly embedded in the folklore of the nation. The need to confront fascism abroad started the slow process of facing up to Jim Crow at home. At long last, the pattern of discrimination had begun to change, and Jesse Owens had opened that gate.

In 1937, Joe Louis, who in June 1936 had suffered his first professional defeat at the hands of German boxer Max Schmeling, came back to defeat Schmeling. In doing so, Louis, who had been earlier considered by many whites to be a black interloper, joined Jesse Owens as a national hero. Owens and Louis did more for black pride than any other action that took place during the great depression.

In an odd way, the denial of opportunity for Sammy Stoller and Marty Glickman highlighted the accomplishments of Jesse Owens all the more. Like the lore of American movies, the stories about Jesse Owens and the superiority of American democracy became a self-fullfilling prophecy. The stories became embodied in the memories of the entire generation and could be called upon as justification for change.

It is perhaps for this reason that in 1939 fascist sympathizer Joseph P. Kennedy traveled to Hollywood to warn the Jewish movie moguls not to produce anti-Nazi films or risk a black lash against Jewish-Americans. Like ordinary Germans, ordinary Americans collaborated with injustice based on race and ethnicity through passivity, denial, and indifference. They even countenanced lynchings. While opposing change, conservatives obviously had learned a thing or two from Joseph Goebbels' approach to the presentation of ideas.[102] After World War II, Joseph McCarthy and Richard Nixon would accuse Jewish leaders in the movie industry of being pro-communist, and would attack them through the House Un-American Activities Committee.[103] Yet, Joe Kennedy's sons were already infected with the new image of America generated by Jesse Owens and Joe Louis, and would part with their father on the issue of race.

9. "The Struggle Against the English Amateur" [1920-1965]

The concept of amateurism was a nineteenth century invention of the British aristocracy. In 1867 London's Amateur Athletic Club (AAC) instituted a rule known as the Henley rule.[1] It was also called "the mechanics clause" as it barred mechanics, artisans, and laborers from competing in amateur athletic contests. Even owners of small businesses and employers were not welcome as athletes, since "engaged in selling goods," they were considered "tradesmen." At the Wenlock Olympian Games held in Wenlock, England in 1867, an amateur oath was introduced requiring the contestants to swear an oath that "I will never compete for money, nor with professionals, nor ever make athletic exercises or contests a means of livelihood." When an oath was to be first administered to athletes at the Olympic Games in Antwerp in 1920 (because of the Jim Thorpe incident), Avery Brundage recommended that the 1867 Wenlock oath—with its denial of even future professionalism—be used.[2]

The British Amateur Athletic Association officially dropped the "mechanics clause" in 1880, but class-elitism continued to be operative in English amateur sport long after the "mechanics clause" was formally abandoned.[3] At the beginning of the twentieth century, American sports publicist Caspar Whitney sought to enforce class-exclusive amateurism in the United States.[4]

Unlike football, nineteenth century American track and field did not develop under the mantle of college institutions and ethos, nor did college officials impose the amateur ethic. The Amateur Athletic Union (AAU) ordained "amateurism" for American track and field. For many, British amateurism was wrong for America. From their point of view, the British elite and their imitators in American, and elsewhere, fought the wrong battle. They pitted the privileged against the poor, instead of pitting the lovers of sport against the exploiters of sport. They offered only an idealized, puritanical view of recreation to combat a variety of pernicious commercial interests, instead of simply offering a practical plan to allow the participants in sports to establish fair rules for sports competition.

If the AAU had focused on the struggle between those who loved athletic competition and those who saw sport primarily as a revenue producing business, they could have used the pride and the joy generated by participation in sports to keep the sports entertainment interests from hijacking the Olympics.

It is interesting to note that pleasure-loving Americans never formed a leisure class in the European sense. Americans carried the same grim seriousness that had served them so well in trade into sports. The desire to excel was as cruelly competitive in sport as in commerce. The sprit of play was lost in the process. In the United States there was never much of a psychological distinction between amateur and professional athlete.[5]

In 1906 the Amateur Athletic Union united the amateur athletic clubs that flourished around the nation into an organization recognized by associations in other parts of the world as being in control of amateur athletics in the USA. In addition, the U.S. Olympic Committee had interlocking leadership with the AAU. Beginning in 1906, American athletes were not allowed to participate in the Olympics or other international track and meets without an AAU card.

Open opposition to the AAU from American colleges and universities surfaced in 1905–6, with the formation of the National Collegiate Athletic Association. Over the next 55 years, prolonged guerilla warfare was waged between the NCAA and the AAU. The feud broke into open war in 1960 and finally ended in June 1978 with the creation of the American Track and Field Association, later re-named the American Track and Field Federation.[6]

Amateur Competition Between Great Britain and the USA

One of the developments that promoted the adoption of the British definition of amateur in the United States was the lasting connection in track and field forged between the elite universities in the two nations starting in the mid-1890s. On June 22, 1895 the Inter-collegiate Athletic Association of Amateur Athletes of America (IC4A) made public correspondence with the President of the Oxford and Cambridge Athletic Association dated March 28. The letter invited Oxford and Cambridge to participate in a track and field meet in England during the coming summer against the first and second place winners of the IC4A Games. It was suggested that the meet be based on the arrangements made between Oxford and Yale in 1894. On June 10 the Oxford and Cambridge Athletic Association expressed regret that it could not accept the challenge. It favored a meet with Harvard and Yale, and gave them right of first refusal. Yale opposed the IC4A plan. The English felt they were under an honorary obligation to Yale.[7] On July 2, 1895 after Harvard backed out of the arrangement negotiations between Yale and Oxford-Cambridge broke down because of timing.[8] In 1895 Yale did return to England to compete against Cambridge.

The Anglo-American Inter-University track and field series, that started in 1894, resumed in 1899 when Harvard joined Yale as partners against Oxford and Cambridge. Except for time out for wars, the series continued practically without suspension for seventy years. The contests were usually held on a home and home basis in June, which often conflicted with the NCAA meet. Meets were not held in competition with the Olympics.[9] Starting in 1920, American and British teams frequently competed in the USA vs. British Empire Games sponsored by the AAU and the British Amateur Athletic Association.

While the Anglo-American Inter-University track and field series began in 1894 with Harvard and Yale, other US schools entered the exchange of competition. In 1921 the New York Athletic Club held a meet in July between Oxford and Cambridge Universities of England and Cornell and Princeton Universities of the USA.[10] Such meets were not without incident. In 1934 the British objected to what they claimed were temporary students

Claiming that some American and British dominion college men enter the university solely with the object of getting coveted athletic honors, the Cambridge University Athletic Club will bar one-year students from the United States and British dominions from competing in inter-university athletics. The decision, unprecedented in college athletics here, will go into effect after the annual athletic meeting between Oxford and Cambridge Universities next March. After that time American and other students, who go into residence at Cambridge for only one year will not be permitted to qualify for athletic honors.[11]

The IC4A track meet began a tentative move away from English standards in 1933. That year their outdoor meet used the metric system for the first time. The IC4A indoor meet was run on the metric system for the first time in 1934.[12]

The Princeton and Cornell partnership competition with Oxford and Cambridge was renewed in 1950. In 1953, Princeton and Harvard withdrew because the meet was not given a high priority. Pennsylvania became Cornell's partner and West Point became the partner of Yale for 1953 and 1955. In 1957 Harvard returned and replaced West Point as Yale's partner. In 1963 the over-all Anglo-American series record stood at twenty wins for the American universities, nineteen for the English, with two meets ending in a tie. The score was calculated strictly on the meet winners, so a typical score might be 9 to 8, as it was in 1963 in favor of the English schools. In 1963 the Oxford-Cambridge vs. Yale-Harvard series, the found English schools leading 10 to 9, with one tie.[13] Some of the individual Anglo-American meet records were fairly respectable performances for universities. For example, 46.9 in the 440-yard dash (Wendell Mottley of Yale), 1:47.8 in the 880-yard run (J. P. Boulter of Oxford), and 25'3" in the broad jump (E. O. Gourdin of Harvard)."[14]

Over three-quarters of a century, elite American colleges competed against the premier English Universities using English rules of engagement. The privileges of social class at Oxford and Cambridge persisted throughout the twentieth century and class distinctions continued to color athletic contests involving those institutions throughout the duration of their competition with American universities. These meets perpetuated support for standards that were sorely in need of change for the future development of the sport of track and field.[15]

The Role of Brundage in American Amateurism

In 1935 Avery Brundage was elected President of the AAU.[16] His reign over the AAU did much to deepen the rift between factions within track and field. Brundage's leadership was marked by a pettiness and unevenness in the enforcement of the rules that created problems over time. An accumulation of these problems created animosities that resulted in open opposition to the AAU. It also produced pressure from track athletes to change the rules to allow more outside financial support for them while participating in track and field competition.

Once he became head track coach at the University of Michigan, Don Canham played a major role in opposing the strict AAU definitions of amateur. During the 1960s, the struggle to control of track and field eligibility rules lead to open warfare between the AAU and the NCAA. The AAU used control over participation in international meets to maintain its influence in college track, while the NCAA attempted to keep post-graduate track athletes from using college facilities. This row resulted in a congressional investigation that started in 1965.

In 1929, Brundage also was elected President of the U. S. Olympic Association and replaced General Douglas MacArthur as chairman of the American Olympic Committee (AOC). In that position he championed a rigid interpretation of the term "amateur" and tried with "religious fervor to keep the games pure and free from commercialism."[17] He would later claim, "In fifty years of sport I have never known or heard of a single athlete who was too poor to participate in the Olympic Games."[18]

One analysis held that

The essence of Avery Brundage's obsession with amateurism in the Olympics is rooted in his own puritanical interpretation of the work ethic—the devout and venerable conviction that man's intrinsic worth is measured in productive work. Sport is a toy. . . . It is offensive to the self-made man in Brundage that people are willing to employ themselves at something so fanciful, so unproductive as a vehicle of fun.[19]

In 1948, Brundage asserted:

Sport is a pastime and a diversion—it is play; and play, according to the dictionary, is action for amusement—opposed to work—free, spontaneous, joyous—for recreation. The minute it becomes any more than this, it is business or work and not sport. Sport is purely incidental and should not be allowed to interfere with the main business of life. It is an avocation not a vocation.[20]

Brundage was contemptuous of professional sports—"They are not sports at all but a segment of the entertainment game—show biz you'd call 'em." ("Show biz" was uttered with a startling sneer.) "An amateur does not rely on sports for his livelihood. . . . If a man has the ability to succeed in another field, he has no business taking part in professional athletics." Brundage also opposed college athletic scholarships—"Why should an education institution have to hire its students?"[21]

On the other hand, it could have been argued, "why should educational institutions be allowed exploit student athletes?" College sports are often big money makers, and, at least in the case of football, endanger the health of the student athlete. They also impinge on the student's study and work time. Moreover, intercollegiate athletics frequently make additional demands on the student's personal resources. Doctor bills, travel costs, and training equipment are common additional expenses.

Avery Brundage's views on amateurism were often combined with other prejudices when questions of eligibility were decided. For example, he once said, after a bitter exchange over his 1933 decision to disqualify Mildred "Babe" Didrikson from amateur competition: "You know, the ancient Greeks kept women out of their athletic games. They wouldn't even let them on the sidelines. I'm not so sure but what they were right."[22] Brundage also held contemptuous views of minorities. During his administration of the AAU and the AOC, Eddie Tolan, Jesse Owens, Bob Ufer, and many others were prohibited from participating in amateur athletics for minor violations of AAU rules. For example, when Eddie Tolan went nearly six months without a job after the 1932 Olympics and made a vaudeville appearance to keep from going hungry, the AAU classified him as a professional "because he had used his fame to gain personal profit."[23]

Like Eddie Tolan, the AAU pursued Jesse Owens with prosecutorial zeal. On March 26, 1937 Jesse Owens charged, "the AAU handling of track is just a racket. Officials discriminate and college boys do not get the breaks that other track stars do." Owens was not very far wrong. He pointed out that 90 percent of trackmen are in college. Owens went on to say that the amateur officials check the college athlete's expense accounts "with a microscope." "But the officials are more lenient with acknowledged stars who have been graduated for several years. They have to make a living and they don't tour the country for the fun of it. As a result, college athletes are becoming dissatisfied." Owens suggested that, "It may come to a point where we will have to go to the sandlots for future Olympic material."[24]

Others were also denied amateur status for frivolous reasons. In 1945 the AAU declared Bob Ufer ineligible "based on the contention that he was cashing in on his athletic abilities by coaching."[25] One runner, Lee Calhoun, faced a ban from the Olympic trials for getting married on the TV program "Bride and Groom" where contestants were chosen on the basis of the love story written by the girl. The TV people did not even know that Lee Calhoun was a runner, yet the AAU forced him to sit out a year of competition [1958] and threatened to ban him from further Olympic competition.[26]

In 1971 Brundage said, "I'm a hundred and ten percent American and an old-fashioned Republican. People like me haven't had anyone to vote for since Hoover and Coolidge."[27] His record leaves little doubt that his political views affected his policy decisions as head of the AOC and the IOC. In 1948 Brundage made a revealing statement:

Other countries have hailed and adopted the ideas of the Olympic Movement proclaimed by Coubertin, have instituted national programs of physical training, and competitive sport for its moral, social, aesthetic, spiritual, and educational values, but in the United States educational institutions' commercialization of the sport program has killed most all of the benefits and led to deplorable conditions. . . . The enemies we have made with our shifting foreign policies are now saying we cannot even play without being paid, that even in sport we are guilty of double dealing, that we are a nation of dollar chasers where gold is God.[28]

Privilege was at the Core of the Olympic Movement

By contrast, from the outset, the International Olympic Committee (IOC) created and maintained an environment of privileges for themselves and their social class. Their personal benefits were in marked contrast to the treatment of Olympic athletes. IOC members nearly always met in luxurious circumstances and were received as dignitaries. By the 1920s, governments, committees, cities, and individuals seeking favors in connection with Olympic events indulged them. Their expenses were often paid by their hosts or underwritten from funds collected from the public in one form or another. Moreover, the IOC was self-perpetuating and functioned without external oversight.

Nevertheless, it is a valid axiom that wealthy people live "high on the hog." In 1948 Brundage claimed that he spent about $50,000 of his own money each year in pursuit of his duties toward the Olympic Games, and it is no doubt true.[29] He loved the role of prince of amateur sports in America and was happy to spend money lavishly on his hobby.

It also must be acknowledged that in the depths of the great depression in1932, when Brundage was president of both the AAU and the American Olympic Committee, he spent much of his time raising funds to underwrite the American Olympic team and to avoid a financial crisis for these organizations.[30]

Brundage, like most IOC members, was a wealthy man. Although he boasted of being a self-made man that was not entirely true. The foundation for his wealth was laid, at least in part, by family political connections and lucrative local government contracts and indulgences. He explained his fortune by saying, "You didn't have to be a wizard to make a fortune during the depression. All you had to do was buy stocks and bonds in depressed corporations for a few cents on the dollar and then wait. I was just lucky."[31] Brundage had a net worth of about $25 million in 1972.[32]

The IOC Shared Brundage's Views

Arthur Porritt represented New Zealand on the IOC from 1934 until 1967, when he was appointed Governor General of New Zealand by

Queen Elizabeth II. Like Avery Brundage, Porritt believed that the Olympians should be part-time athletes without outside assistance. When asked about the athletes in the 1984 Olympic games, he responded,

Their life is athletics. My hobby was athletics. My life was surgery. We were amateurs. There are no amateurs left. There is no way to change the farce of the [Olympic] Games. The Olympic Games suffer from gigantism, commercialism, nationalism, racism, and drugs. It's sad, I still believe in the Games, but I doubt they can be resuscitated. They are trying to do an impossible thing—to keep an Olympic ideal in a modern world.[33]

A majority of those on the executive board of the IOC shared the views of Brundage and Porritt.

The Amateur Code Conflicted with Olympic Goals

The class-bias inherent in the aristocratic concept called amateurism resulted in controversy, resentment and hypocrisy that lasted for more than a hundred years. No where was the bias more clear than in the "mechanics clause." And, the hypocrisy was no more evident than in the eligibility rules for the Olympic Games. By the Eleventh Olympiad (1936), amateurism was fundamentally at odds with the task of winning an Olympic gold medal. As early as 1924, winning a gold medal at the Olympics often required methodical training and an expenditure of time and effort that exceeded the demands of nearly all full-time jobs. In 1936, the Germans won the most medals at the Olympics by subsidizing the training of Olympic athletes so they could devote full-time to training.

While the amateur code required that the athlete continue to work at a regular job to pay living expenses, this was impractical when pursuing sports as an avocation. Such a stand defied practical reality. How was a world-class athlete from an ordinary background supposed to train, travel, and still find time to work at a regular job? The only realistic solution was to compensate athletes for work time missed because of the demands of training. Most world-class athletes needed some form of financial compensation in order to compete successfully.

The Loop-holes in the Amateur Code

During the Brundage years, the guidelines for amateurism used to issue the card needed for AAU, international, and Olympic competition were rigid and uncompromising. More importantly, their application created loop-holes that resulted in uneven application of the rules. The guide-lines during that era stated that an amateur becomes a professional when he:

Enters a competition for money or for prizes of more than $35 in value.

Sells or pawns his prizes.

Accepts a purse of money.

Enters a competition under a false name.

Enters a competition open to a professional, or knowingly competes with a professional

Issues a challenge to compete for money or its equivalent.

Receives reward for becoming or continuing a member of an athletic organ-ization.

Teaches, trains, or coaches in an athletic sport for money or any valuable consideration.

An athlete is disqualified from competing as an amateur who has commit-ted any of the following acts:

Entering or competing against other than registered amateurs in good standing.

Competing from an organization (a) In whose employ he is; (b) In which he is not a member in good standing, (c) When he has competed from another existing organization within a year, except such organization within a year, except such other organization shall have ceased to exist or the athlete taken a bona fide residence in another district of the Union.

Acting in a discourteous or unfair manner.

Competing when knowingly under suspension.

Competing in games not duly authorized.

Entering open games when unregistered.

Refusing to testify [particularly before the House Un-American Activities Committee.]

Allowing his name to be used to advertise or promote the sale on or to act as personal solicitor for the sale, or as the actual salesman of sporting goods, prizes, trophies.

Capitalizes his athletic fame.

A single professional on a team makes the team professional.[34]

There were a number of flaws in the amateur code. Many athletes in the United States and around the world were allowed to train nearly full-time while in the armed services. Paavo Nurmi was in this cate-gory. Paavo entered the Finnish Army in 1918. He found good training facilities and plenty of time for training. Hannes Kolehmainen, who had won the "Woolworth double" in 1912, advised Nurmi to do more speedwork.[35] His flexibility as a soldier assigned to athletic activities made that type of training possible. Other Olympians also benefited from training while in the armed services. Among those who trained nearly full-time while in the army included: Rudolph Harbig, Germany (1936); and Americans, William Mihalo (1944), Willie Atterberry (1954–6), Malvin Whitfield (1948–52), Billy Mills (1964), Warren Druetzler (1956), David Meyers (1956–8), Ira Murchison (1956), Billy Smith (1952–4), Mark H. Smith, Jr. (1956–8), and Adolf Weinacker (1952–1956).

Athletes also were supported by other governmental actions. Allan Tolmich, Hayes Jones, Mal Whitfield, Lorenzo Wright, John Telford, and David Owens were among those who benefited from the State Department which underwrote international competition, sponsored "good will" trips, paid athletes to coach abroad, and supported meets with other countries. In addition, Police Departments subsidized athletes and featured national champions.

The Detroit Police team participated in AAU Meets from 1924–1950, and perhaps longer. While the Detroit Police Department's track team and police department teams in New York, Montreal, Toronto, and Los Angeles were internationally recognized as amateur teams, the departments in all of these cities consistently ignored the spirit of elite amateurism without retribution. Members of police department teams were given preferential treatment in hiring, were paid bonuses that depended on their performance at track meets, allowed time to train during work hours, and were given work assignments based on track and field performances.[36]

Athletic Clubs also subsidized athletes. From the very beginning of so-called amateur sports clubs, such as the New York Athletic Club and the Chicago Athletic Association, assisted many athletes. They paid for both travel expenses and training costs, and in some cases arranged "under-the-table" payments that allowed post-college track athletes to live while taking the time needed to train so they could compete at an "world-class" levels.

The Consequences

The English concept of the amateur athlete did not work in the United States, where a leisure class never developed. In the absence of nobleman or other forms of state sanctioned inherited status, the American model of sport development turned toward the pragmatic and the commercial, rather than toward the elite. Yet, to its credit, for more than half a century "the cloak of amateurism" sheltered track and field from the excesses and adverse consequences of unfettered commercialism.

The sport's modest potential for revenue generation limited its commercial appeal, and amateurism kept track and field athletes from demanding pay for their participation. Low costs allowed the sport to flourish. Track programs, including a growing number of regional and national indoor meets, thrived on limited budgets. Amateurism allowed smaller, less wealthy colleges, such as Detroit City College [Wayne University], Michigan Normal, Michigan Agricultural College, Western Michigan Teacher's College, and even Albion College to produce national champions.

Yet, by 1937 it was becoming clear that without significant subsidies American track and field could not consistently succeed in international competition against government subsidized programs such as the one in Germany. As better records were kept, coaches learned more about pacing and the other subtleties of running, jumping, and throwing. The application of knowledge gained through the study of human kinetics and the mechanics involved in various sports activities also improved competition, and made it clear that achieving human potential in track and field events required better, more intense, and longer periods of training.

In turn, more training required that world class athletes be supported while they developed their talent and skills. Increasingly, secondary education and four years of college proved to be an insufficient period of time for most track athletes to reach the peak of performance necessary to win an Olympic gold medal. This realization caused inevitable conflict with amateur rules. The most gifted athletes could not train enough to reach world class status in track and field without some means of paying for the daily cost of living, much less the cost of travel they needed to face appropriate developmental competition.

National pride also weighed in against the English concept of amateurism. National pride demanded winners, and in many countries government jobs, subsidies, or both offered the path to athletic achievement. Just as Albert Einstein had used his spare time as a civil servant in the Swiss Patient Office to develop his theory of relativity, European athletes were using the army or other government jobs to subsidize their training.

In North America, police departments were among the pioneers in supporting track athletes while they developed their talents. During World War I the American armed services sponsored athletic training, but after the "great crusade" military budgets were cut to the point where such activities became impractical. But, in England and on the

European continent there was a long tradition of men from elite families serving in the army and navy, so the idea of athletic training while in military service was not seen as a violation of amateurism, and it flourished.

The important point, however, is that jobs with the police or the military were used to circumvent amateur codes. Yet, people like Avery Brundage and Arthur Porritt blindly stood against other forms of subsidy. They opposed teaching-coaching position, industrial-recreation assignments, and comparable jobs as violations of amateurism. This stance clearly reflected an elitist bias that was out of synchronization with the development of the sport of track and field.

10. The World War II Generation [1937–50]

Even as the Berlin Olympics were being held, Adolf Hitler was in the process of implementing a far-reaching secret agreement that had been concluded with Austria on July 11, 1936. Concessions to Austrian Nazis in the secret agreement were already undermining the independence of the Austrian nation and making a union with Nazi Germany inevitable. Finally, in March 1938 Nazi Germany would annex Austria. As Jewish scholars living in Germany intensified efforts to leave their home land for a safer environment, a number of them found refuge as professors in African-American colleges in the Jim Crow South and subsequently became ardent supporters of desegregation.

Almost immediately after annexing Austria, Germany began to pressure Czechoslovakia into making concessions that would result in the disappearance of that nation as well. When Neville Chamberlain, Prime Minister of Great Britain, allowed Hitler a free hand in its dealings with the Czechs in return for "peace in our time," the fate of the Czechs was also sealed. In October 1938 Czechoslovakia ceased to exist. The absorption of Czechoslovakia into Germany's growing empire then shifted the focus of European affairs to Poland. After months of threats and pressure against the Polish government, Nazi Germany concluded a treaty with the Soviet Union that essentially divided Poland between the two predators. On September 3, 1939 Germany invaded Poland and Great Britain and France declared war on Germany to start World War II. The German "blitzkrieg" made short work of Poland. On November 30, 1939 the Soviet Union attacked Finland.

After a winter of inaction, known as the "phony war," in April 1940 Germany invaded Denmark and Norway. Finally, on May 10, 1940 Hitler attacked Holland, Luxembourg, Belgium, and France, bringing the "phony war" to an end. Holland fell to the invading Germans in five days. By May 25 the British Expeditionary Force was surrounded at Dunkirk, and it appeared that the war in Europe was over. Only a miraculous evacuation saved Britain from inevitable defeat at the hands of the Nazis. The evacuation, however, left Great Britain without the arms necessary to continue the fight effectively. In the ten days of the Dunkirk evacuation, the British left all but twenty of their tanks in France, lost 82,000 scout cars and motorcycles, 90,000 rifles and an even greater number of machine guns behind for the Germans.[1] At this juncture, the United States became the "arsenal of democracy."

Starting in 1939, American factory production began to increase. The conversion of a peacetime economy to war production was well underway in 1940. As a result, wages began to rise, and unemployment fell. After more than a decade of depression, there was finally light at the end of the tunnel. Slightly better times offered a wider variety of possibilities to depression kids. More teen-agers could finish high school and attend college, so college enrollment increased.

In 1920 only 53,516 college degrees awarded in the USA. In 1940 160,000 college degrees were awarded. Two years later 213,491 college degrees were awarded.[2] During the depression, it was a lucky young man who could attend college. In 1935 a lucky Roy Fehr enrolled at Michigan State College in East Lansing. Like nearly all college men of that era, his father had attended college.

Pre-War Champion

Roy Benner Fehr was born in State College, Pennsylvania, on March 2, 1918. The Fehr family was of German decent, and his father, soon to be a graduate from Penn State University, was a mechanical engineer. The family moved to Royal Oak when Roy was seven, and his younger brother, Bob, was one-year old. When Roy was ten, he attended YMCA summer camp where he ran every day. He soon discovered that he was "the fastest kid on the block," and continued to run just for the fun of it when he returned home. Roy enjoyed running around the block and running down the railroad tracks near his house.[3]

When he was a freshman at Royal Oak High School, Roy went out for track, and found that he was faster than most of the older boys. Roy was an excellent student, as well as an outstanding athlete. He lettered in football, basketball, and track, and was inducted into the National Honor Society. On May 19, 1934, as a junior, Roy qualified for the Michigan Class A State High School Track Championship by winning the 440-yard dash at the Sectional Meet held in Ferndale. The starter and field referee for the meet was Olympic gold medal winner, Eddie Tolan.[4] As a senior, he was a member of the Royal Oak Club and the treasurer of his class. That year, Roy became the first Royal Oak High

Roy Fehr was the first All-State runner from Royal Oak, MI. He became the NCAA and AAU two-mile championship in 1940. *(Photo Michigan State University Archives)*

School athlete to win an event at the State track meet, when he became the Michigan Class A High School quarter-mile Championship.[5]

In the fall of 1935, Roy enrolled at Michigan State College, in East Lansing, with the intention of majoring in Agriculture. He was not recruited for the track team, and did not receive a scholarship. Once at Michigan State, however, Roy went out for the track team as a walk-on, and was welcomed. As a freshman, Roy continued to run the 220 and the 440, as he had done in high school, but discovered that that he was not quick enough to win these events in college competition. As a sophomore, he went out for cross-country and discovered that distance training gave him more endurance, thereby giving him the opportunity to run in longer events during the track season. Roy trained hard. He generally ran two hours a day and walked another hour or so, at least five days a week. Weather permitting, he ran outdoors.

On March 26, 1937 Roy faced 1936 Olympic gold medal winner Johnny Woodruff in the 880 at the West Virginia indoor games. The contest was the highlight of the meet. Although Roy lost by 10 yards in the face of Woodruff's blazing finishing kick, he pushed the long-legged distance runner from the University of Pittsburgh to set a new meet record (1:58.5).[6] Later on the same road trip, Roy acquitted himself well in winning the 880 in a duel meet with Penn State in State College, Pennsylvania, where he defeated Griest, the Nittiney Lion half-miler, in a smartly run contest. However, Roy was not deemed good enough to make coach Young's traveling squad for the April 24 trip to the Drake Relays or the April 30, 1937 trip to Marquette University.[7] Nevertheless, he closed out the track season on May 14, 1937 on the winning two-mile relay team (8:07.9) at the twenty-first annual Michigan State Intercollegiate Outdoor Meet in East Lansing that listed 170 entries.[8]

At the Annual IC4A Cross-country Championship on November 14, 1938, Roy placed eighth with a time of 27:38 over the five mile Van Cortlandt Park course in New York City. "The course was re-routed over the steep hazard of Cemetery Hill for this meet." Michigan State College placed second at the IC4A.[9] A week later, he finished 13th (21:13) over a four mile course in East Lansing at the First NCAA Cross-country Championship.[10] By the standards of the 1940s, his performance in these two meets would have made him an All-American in Cross-country in 1938.

After his sophomore year in college, Roy decided that he was not interested in continuing to study agriculture, and changed his major to chemical engineering. This change in majors added an extra semester or two to Roy's undergraduate education. He was given an athletic scholarship for his final year of study.

By 1939, Roy Fehr was one of the best mile and two mile runners in America. On May 20 at the Michigan State Intercollegiate Meet he won the mile run in a time of 4:18.7, and a week later was fourth in the mile run at the IC4A track meet at Tri-borough Stadium in New York City. This performance made him an All-American candidate. The next fall, Roy traveled west by train to the State of Washington to participate in the National Cross-country Championships. It was a four-day ride, and Roy was not given sleeping accommodations. Nevertheless, he enjoyed the trip and after a couple of days on the West Coast, he felt fine and was ready to run. When he looked over the field, he noticed that few of the really good cross-country runners from east of Chicago had made the trip west. He figured that his chances of doing well at the meet were better than usual.

Roy recalled, nearly sixty years later, that at the cross-country national championships, "I took off fast and got way out ahead of the pack. As I neared the end of the race, I looked back and the fellow from the University of Washington was gaining on me, so I started to sprint and he dropped back. After the race, he told me that he wasn't feeling good that day, but that it was a pleasure to run against me. I have always cherished his comments. It was really nice of him to speak so kindly after such a disappointment on his part."[11]

During the indoor track season, Roy won the mile run at an indoor triangular meet with Michigan Normal College and the University of Michigan,[12] and at the Central Collegiate Indoor Championships in mid-March.[13] At the opening of the outdoor season, Roy continued his winning ways, when he took the train east to the Penn Relays. At the granddaddy of intercollegiate track meets, Roy won the two-mile run. On May 5, 1940, he won the mile run in a duel meet with Marquette University, a week later he ran on the mile relay team that beat Notre Dame, and on May 18, he won the mile run with the respectable time of 4:14.8. He topped off his college career with wins in the two-mile run at the NCAA and the National AAU outdoor finals. On January 1, 1941, Roy Benner Fehr was named to the AAU All-American team for the two-mile run.[14]

After college, Roy ran competitively once or twice, but was more concerned with getting on with his career. He did, however, continue to run for enjoyment for nearly forty years. In 1941 Roy went to work for Du Pont. During World War II he served three years in the U. S. Navy. He and his brother served in the armed services during World War II. Roy's brother, Bob, was killed in action.

After the war, Roy returned to Royal Oak to work with his father on an invention. The project did not work out, but the time with his father was beneficial, and he courted Dorothy J. Lamont, who was six years his junior.[15] Dorothy was a 1942 graduate of Royal Oak High School, who had graduated from Michigan State College in 1946.[16] Following the interlude with his father and his marriage to Dorothy, Roy returned to work with DuPont, and over the next thirty years raised seven children, five of whom were runners. Talk of track and field was normal dinnertime fare at the Fehr household, according to Dorothy.[17]

Roy retired from Du Pont in 1984 and continued to live in West Chester, PA. At the age of 80, Roy was firmly convinced that most people who have not competed do not appreciate how valuable the friendships and experiences derived from track and field can be to the lives of people, like himself.[18]

"Bullet" Bob Poorman Ufer

By contrast, pre-war track champion Bob Ufer did not pass the physical to serve in the armed services during World War II. Bob's father, Clarence E. Ufer, was a Wolverine varsity half-miler in 1916. Clarence set a varsity team record of 1:56.2 in the 880. In 1915, Clarence Ufer won the 880 in duel meets with Notre Dame and Syracuse, and was on the two-mile relay team that set the world's indoor record at Buffalo.[19]

Bob Ufer grew up in Mt. Lebanon, Pennsylvania and attended Mercersburg Academy, where he played halfback in football and ran in track. He played freshman football at the University of Michigan in 1939, but was not big enough to make the varsity team the following year. He was, however, an outstanding quarter-miler and half-miler. In 1940 he broke six freshman records. On March 13, 1940 Bob set the University of Michigan record for the two-mile relay (7:59.5) in a freshman duel meet at Yost fieldhouse.

In 1941, as a sophomore, Robert Ufer began to make a national reputation. On March 19 at the Michigan AAU Relays he set the Yost Fieldhouse and meet record for the mile relay (3:19.7) and three days later helped win the two-mile university relay at the *Chicago Daily News* Relays. On May 3 he set the field record for the mile relay (3:17.0) in a duel meet with the University of Notre Dame held in South Bend.[20]

On February 7, 1942, exactly two months after the bombing of Pearl Harbor and America's entrance into World War II, Ufer was a member of the Michigan relay team that placed third in the mile relay at the Millrose Games. On February 20, while General MacArthur's forces were trapped on the Bataan Peninsula and at Corregidor, Bob Ufer set a meet and Yost fieldhouse record in the 440-yard run (48.8) and the mile relay (3:21) in an indoor duel meet with Notre Dame. One week later he set the meet record for the 440-yard run (49.1) in a duel meet with the University of Pittsburgh. Then, on March 7 "Bullet Bob" set the Conference and American indoor record for the 440-yard dash

(48.1) at the Western Conference [Big Nine] Indoor Meet in Madison. He closed the indoor season five days after it was reported that the Nazis were systematically exterminating Jews in White Russia, when he placed third in the 600-yard run at the *Chicago Daily News* Relays.[21]

In the 1942 outdoor track season, just days before General Jonathan Wainwright surrendered Corregidor and his garrison of 11,500 to the Japanese, Bob Ufer helped win the two-mile relay (7:43.7) and placed fourth in the mile-relay at the Drake Relays. Ufer did some local radio broadcasting in 1941–2 and got started in the broadcast booth for football games by coincidence. In 1942 the publicity director at the athletic department, asked Ufer to be a spotter for a Michigan game being broadcast by Bill Stern. Bob did an outstanding job and was asked to help with other Michigan games whenever Bill Stern needed a spotter for his play-by-play broadcasts.[22]

On February 6, 1943, four days after the Germans surrendered at Stalingrad and as the Battle for Guadalcanal entered its sixth month, Ufer won the two-mile relay (7:47.4) and placed second in 600-yard run at the Millrose Games. Later that month, he won the 600-yard run and the two-mile relay (7:48.8) at the New York City Knights of Columbus Meet. Then, four days after the United States Marines liberated Guadalcanal from the Japanese and at the very time General MacArthur was extolling the value of athletics as a mans of preparing combat troops, "Bullet Bob" set a new meet records in the 300-yard dash (31.4), the sprint medley (3:33.5), and the mile relay (3:22.6) at the Michigan State Relays held in Jenison Fieldhouse. On March 6, 1943 he set the world indoor record for the 440-yard dash (48.1) at the Big Nine Indoor at the University of Chicago Fieldhouse. He closed the 1943 indoor season in April 1943 by setting the American dirt track record for the two-mile relay (7:40.9) at Purdue Relays.[23]

On April 24, 1943, while America troops were fighting in North Africa, Bob Ufer, John W. Roxborough, Robert H. Hume, and H. Ross Hume won the two-mile relay (7:56) at the Penn Relays. Ufer then joined Charles T. Pinney, Leonard W. Alkon and Dave O. Matthews to win the sprint medley relay (3:29.7) and place second in the mile relay at the Penn Relays. In June 1943 Ufer placed second in the 880-yard run at the NCAA championships, and repeated that performance in the 800-meter run at the AAU Outdoor Championships.

Ufer ended his college track career in the winter of 1944, as the Allied Forces in Europe, under the command of General Eisenhower were preparing for the invasion at Normandy. On February 5 he won the two-mile relay (7:53.4) at the Millrose Games. Three weeks later, he won the 600-yard run (1:11.3) and the two-mile relay at the National AAU Senior Indoor Championships. His performance in that race the 12th fastest indoors 600-yards (1:11.2) run in USA for the first half of the twentieth century, and earned him an AAU All-American certificate.[24] On March 18, 1944 Ufer, Roxborough, Ross Hume and Dave Matthews won the two-mile relay and Ufer placed second in the 600-yard open at the *Chicago Daily News* Relays.[25] Since there were no international meets because of World War II, Robert Ufer had reached the highest level of performance possible at the time.

In need of money, Bob took a coaching job at an Ann Arbor high school in the fall of 1945. The AAU declared Ufer ineligible "based on the contention that he was cashing in on his athletic abilities by coaching"[26]

In 1945 WPAG, Ann Arbor's first radio station, hired Bob as its sports director. Ufer started by doing a 15-minute daily sports show for $35 per week. His enthusiasm was infectious. In the fall of 1945 he did his first local broadcast of Michigan football on WPAG. At first his pro-Michigan coverage got him into trouble with the alumni of Michigan State and Ohio State, but since his fans outnumbered his detractors, he was allowed to carry on in his own way. In 1975 WJR recruited Ufer to broadcast Michigan games for them throughout the state. Bob Ufer was the radio voice of University of Michigan football for 362 consecutive games over 37 years.[27]

The Son of Joe Louis' Promoter

In 1941 John W. Roxborough, Jr., whose father was a good high school athlete, a bail bondsman, and Joe Louis' promoter/manager, entered the University of Michigan. A year later, John, Jr. joined Bob Ufer to win the two-mile relay (7:43.7) at the Drake Relays. In the subsequent year, he helped win the two-mile relay (7:47.4) at the Millrose Games, the New York City Knights of Columbus Meet, and the Penn Relays. In April 1943 he also participated in setting the American dirt track record for the two-mile relay (7:40.9) at Purdue Relays.

In 1944 Roxborough won the two-mile relay (7:53.4) at the Millrose Games and at the National AAU Indoor Championships. In addition, he placed second in the 1,000-yard run at the National AAU Indoor. Like Ufer, John Roxborough, Jr. was an AAU All-American in track while at the University of Michigan.

The Hume Twins

In 1942 the Hume twins matriculated into the U of M. H. Ross and Robert H. Hume were from Canonsburg, Pennsylvania, and enrolled at the University of Michigan as pre-med. students, and thus were exempt from the draft until they finished medical school. Both were standout middle-distance runners, and destined to become All-Americans. In 1943 both were members of the championship two-mile relay team, along with Ufer, and Roxborough. In June 1943 Ross placed third in the mile run at the NCAA Championships.

In 1944 Ross and Robert Hume were members of the winning the two-mile relay (7:53.4) at the Millrose Games. Robert also placed fourth in the 600-yard run at that meet. On February 26 Robert placed third in the mile run at the National AAU Senior Indoor Championships. On June 10, 1944 the twins tied for first in the mile run (4:16.6) at the NCAA Outdoor Track and Field Championships at Marquette University in Milwaukee. In 1945 Ross set the meet records for the 880-yard run (1:56.11) and the mile run (4:23.9) in a duel meet with the University of Illinois, the Armory, Champaign. That year, he also participated in setting the U of M varsity distance medley relay record (10:22.8) and the University of Michigan outdoor mile record (4:14.6). However, they did not run well at the *Chicago Daily News* Relays.

Robert Hume was Captain of the 1945 University of Michigan indoor track team. In 1945 he was on the winning the two-mile relay team (7:59.7) and placed third in the 880-yard run at the Millrose Games. In June 1945 Robert won the mile run in the NCAA Finals. In 1946 the Hume brothers, with the help of Horace Coleman, won the university distance medley relay at the Purdue Relays on March 23.[28]

The War Interrupted His Competitive Years

James McNutt "Mac" Umstattd was born in an apartment above Vest's hardware store in Matoaka, West Virginia on March 11, 1922. His mother, Martha Ethel McNutt, from Monroe City, Missouri, was assisted in the birth by her sister, a nurse on leave from Cook County Hospital in Chicago. His father, James G. Umstattd, was a graduate of Kirksville State Normal School and a veteran of the Naval Hospital Corps, who was teaching at Matoaka High School. In the spring of 1924, his father received a master's degree from the University of Missouri and accepted a supervisor position near Beckley, West Virginia, while also teaching at Concord State Normal School in Athens, West Virginia. In the fall of 1928, James G. Umstattd accepted an assistant-ship in the College of Education at the University of Minnesota. He completed his doctorate in June 1930. In 1936 Dr. Umstattd, an ardent supporter of the New Deal, accepted a position with Wayne University and moved his family to Detroit.[29]

The Umtstattd's arrived in Detroit on Labor Day, 1936. They moved into a house at 7345 Kipling Avenue, a mile north of the Fisher Build-ing and about three miles from Wayne University. They had never lived in an industrial city, and in the words of Professor Umstattd, "We were confronted with a mixed society, with an array of people of all races and from all nations, whose religious tenets had come from all religions of the world. And they had been uprooted from the land and suddenly thrown into the confusing whirl of industrial life." As it turned out, the Umstattd family quickly felt the impact of the new environment. The youngest son, Bob, came home from his first morning in school fright-ened and crying, "I'm the only white kid in the third grade. The rest are all Jews." His father had him transferred to another school, where Bob felt more comfortable because his new classmates were "our kind of people."

Mac registered as a ninth grader at Northwestern High School about a mile from his new home. "He made it through the day, but when he came home after school he said, 'Mother, guess who my locker mate is? A great big black nigger.' (In those days neither of our two sons had acquired a great amount of racial tolerance.) Ethel in true Southern style, was horrified. But immediately Mac said he was only kidding, but that about twenty percent of the school population was Negro."[30]

Mac Umtstattd's high school experience in Detroit, which con-tributed significantly to his racial and ethnic tolerance, was filled with success. At age 15 he was elected President of Lincoln House (500 stu-dents) at Northwestern High School, which boasted 4,500 students at the time, and was reelected the following year. Following his father's footsteps, Mac began to participate in sports. Mac's father had played baseball, basketball, and ran track in college. Mac quickly became a track star. According to Bert Maris, the Athletic Director at Northwest-ern High School, "He [Mac] has more natural ability than any high school runner I've ever seen."[31] In 1938, as a junior in high school, Mac won the half-mile run at the Public League Championships by 30-yards.[32] He recorded one of the seven fastest half mile times (1:58.8) in America by a high school student.[33] The following year, James McNutt

Umstattd, a straight A student and valedictorian of his senior class, set the Metro League record in the half-mile run with a 1:56.6 mark that would have placed him in the NCAA finals that year. The *Detroit Free Press* declared Mac Umstattd to be the best high school athlete in Southeast Michigan in 1939.[34]

In 1938 Dr. Umstattd began his long association with the University of Texas, but Mac stayed in Detroit with Professor Soderquist and his wife, who were close family friends, until he graduated from high school. At Christmas time Mac's father sent him a check for a train trip to Austin so that he could spend the holidays with his family. Instead of taking the train, Mac took the bus to save money and proudly handed his father a $20 bill, which his father used to buy a cherished hunting gun.

Mac enrolled at the University of Texas in Austin in the fall of 1939, and was destined to be one of the best middle distance runners in the school's history. In 1941 he had a banner year on the cinders for the Texas Longhorns. He set the conference record for the half-mile run (1.53.8) on May 10 at the Southwest Conference Championships. The record stood for eleven years. He also ran on a sprint medley team that twice broke the world record for that event, with sensational anchor legs of 1:52.1 and 1:51.8 at the Texas and Drake Relays.

At the first of his record setting achievements, Mac thrilled the hometown fans at what has been characterized as "a magnificent show unmatched throughout the United States."[35] On the morning of the Texas Relays *The Daily Texan* reported, "After a Friday full of colorful parade and stupendous revue, ex-students and dads and mothers will spend Saturday, largely by eating, meeting, and greeting."

The relay preliminaries for the 100 teams assembled for the meet started at nine in the morning. By 1:55 p.m., when the finals were scheduled to begin, the sun was bright and a slight breeze was blowing. At slightly after 4:15 p.m., the Longhorn's sprint medley relay team faced similar relay teams from Louisiana State, Kansas University, Oklahoma A & M, Texas A & M, and Kansas State University. When sophomore anchorman Mac Umstattd received the baton, he "almost sprinted through a 52.5 first quarter on his half-mile leg, but he finished in with a 1:52.1 half-mile run, the best of his career, and thus establishing the new [world] record of 3:24 flat." The *Daily Texan* (April 6, 1941) crowed, "For the first time in many moons, the Steers pulled a complete sweep of the university relays—440, 880, sprint medley, and mile."

Three weeks later, the Texas sprint medley team, again led by Mac Umstattd, bettered their world record at the Drake Relays, with a time of 3:23.2.[36] He closed the season by setting the Southwest Conference record for the 880-yard run.

Mac ran cross-country in the fall of 1941, and was active in nearly every aspect of campus life at the University of Texas. He was a member of the Cowboys, an honorary service organization for men, that also had Lloyd Millard Bentsen, Jr. and Dolph Briscoe, Jr. as fellow members that academic year.[37]

Pearl Harbor was bombed during Mac's senior year in college, and in February 1943 he entered the U. S. Army Air Corps. He was commissioned as a Lieutenant on December 24, and for nine months served as a navigator on a B-17 Flying Fortress based in England. He was awarded the Distinguished Flying Cross, the Air Medal with three oak clusters and the Presidential Unit Citation for his bravery in action.[38]

When he returned home on leave after serving his tour of duty, he married Catherine Houston.[39] In 1946 , Mac completed his degree and was admitted to the Texas Bar in 1947. At that time, his a law partner was Dan Moody, who later became Governor of Texas. From 1950 through 1953, Mac was Staff Judge Advocate for the U. S. Air Force. In 1950 he was also made attorney for the Lower Colorado River Authority, and became General Counsel for that agency until his retirement in 1985.[40]

According to a friend of forty years, "Mac was a fun-loving type person, very outgoing. He was a very capable lawyer, who was well thought of by those who knew him."[41] His brother Bob attended the University of Texas and lettered in track, before becoming a physician. Mac's two sons were also trackmen. James McNutt Umstattd died on March 15, 1988, at the age of 66. His brother, wife, three children, and four grandchildren survived him.

Vaulting to Prominence

Theodore Norman Wonch graduated from Lansing East High School in the spring of 1939, and attended Michigan State College that fall. Tom lived at home while attending college.[42] After his fourth year in college, Tom was drafted and entered the armed services. Like so many other athletes of his generation, Ted Wonch had his athletic career interrupted by war. He served in the army from late spring 1943 until 1946. He finally graduated from Michigan State in 1948.

In February 1941 Ted placed second in the pole vault in a triangular meet with the U of M and Michigan Normal College at Jenison Field House. Later that month he won the pole vault (13–0) at the Michigan State Relays. In March he tied for fourth in the pole vault (13–0) at the Central Collegiate Conference indoor meet in South Bend, and in May he won the pole vault (13–2) at the Michigan Intercollegiate Championships.

As the war raged in the Pacific, in February 1942 Ted Wonch tied the meet record for the pole vault (13–0) at the Michigan Relays. On March 7 Ted tied for first in the pole vault (13–4¾) at the Central Collegiate Conference Indoor Championships in East Lansing. A week later he tied for second in the pole vault (13–4) at the Illinois Tech Relays. On the eve of the Battle of the Coral Sea, on May 5 he tied for first the pole vault (12–6) at the 27ᵗʰ Annual Michigan State Intercollegiate Championships. On May 23 Ted tied for first in the pole vault (12–6) in a duel meet with Marquette University.

In his third year of competition, one week after General Eisenhower was appointed commander in chief of all allied forces in North Africa, Wonch tied for fourth in the pole vault (13–0) at the Michigan State Relays. On March 6, 1943 he won the pole vault (13–3⅝) at the Central Collegiate Conference indoor meet.

After serving in the Army in 1944–5, on February 9, 1946 Ted set the Michigan State College varsity indoor track record for the pole vault (13–7¼) in his second place finish at the Michigan State Relays. On March 23 he tied for first in the pole vault (13–1½) at the Purdue Relays. He completed his college eligibility by winning the pole vault (13–0) at the IC4A Outdoor Championships held at Annapolis, MD.

From Hamtramck to the AAU Finals

In 1937, Bob Wingo was part of the Hamtramck High School track team that won the Metropolitan League Indoor Track Championship.[43] Bob attended Wayne University on a tuition scholarship arranged by his high school track coach through Coach David L. Holmes. He was the first person in his family to attend college. Bob took the Baker cross-town west streetcar to Wayne University and the cross-town east home at night. Happy to be in college, Bob did not think about an academic major. In 1941, he decided to become a teacher.

When Bob Wingo attended Wayne, the budget for the track team was so meager that the team drove to all out of town meets by automobile. Often the relay team traveled with the coach in his automobile, and everyone else stayed at home, but sometimes volunteers drove their own cars for the price of gasoline. Usually, the team drove straight through to the meet without stopping except to eat and buy gasoline because they had no money for hotels and were uncertain how African-American and Jewish team members would be treated. Prejudices were strong in those years. Jews were considered to be noisy, cheap, and boisterous people. These same people often considered Blacks to be dumb, dangerous, lazy, and crude. The Penn Relay Programs and nearly all newspaper reports identified "Negro" runners. It was common-place to deny food, toilet, and lodging services to Blacks and Jews, and violent acts against these minorities were not unusual. At the Butler Relays in Indianapolis in 1940, for example, the Wayne University track team was denied rooms in an Indianapolis hotel because of the color of Bob Wingo's skin. Meal service was frequently denied.

Being on a limited budget was a handicap for the Wayne University trackmen in other ways as well. Their track shoes were usually old and not as well suited for field conditions as those athletes representing other colleges, as the Wayne athletes could not change spikes as field conditions changed. Wayne trackmen were not as well rested when they ran out of town meets, because they usually traveled straight through, sleeping in the car, if at all.

In 1942 when Bob Wingo, Linwood Wright, Robert Grant, and Wayne Hatfield qualified for the junior AAU finals at Passaic, New Jersey and the National AAU senior Outdoor Championships at Randalls Island the following day, the AAU sent Coach Holmes $100 to cover expenses. Holmes raised an additional $200 from friends of the University. With the money in hand, they drove to New Jersey straight through in the coach's Hudson. Late the next day, the Wayne relay team ran on a choppy surface in sandy, beach-like conditions in old shoes, and won despite the lack of sleep. In winning the race they set a new AAU record for the 1,600-meter relay (3:24.9). Bob Wingo later recalled that the race was run under the worst conditions he had ever faced. The University of California team did not enter the relay because they did not chose to race on Friday night and then run qualifying and final heats the next day in the senior division individual championships. However, that is exactly what Bob Wingo did. The Wayne relay team stayed over-night in a run down motel in New Jersey on Friday night. Despite the handicap, Bob Wingo took fourth in the 440-

yard dash at the AAU Championships. Immediately after Bob's Saturday race, the team got back into Coach Holmes' car and drove straight back to Detroit without another overnight stay.

Later that summer, Bob Wingo joined the U. S. Army Air Corps, with plans of becoming an aviator. He applied for the Tuskegee Pilot Training program, but was made a truck driver pending his admission. His job as a truck driver was to carry away airplanes that had crashed during pilot training. After one or two such experiences, when all those onboard were killed, he had second thoughts about being a pilot. Instead, he applied for diesel training and was accepted. He was discharged from the Army on points before being sent to the Pacific Theater for combat.

When he returned to college, GIs were given a fifth year of college athletic eligibility. In 1946 he was a member of the Wayne University 1,600-meter relay team that won the Michigan AAU Championship. In September 1947 Bob Wingo started teaching. He was kept as a substitute teacher until 1951, when he was assigned to Cleveland Junior High School. Although he applied for high school teaching and coaching every year, his requests were ignored until 1976 when his brother-in-law, Pete Petross, arranged to have him assigned to Mumford High School. In 1980 Bob Wingo was listed as the cross-country and track coach at Mumford High School.[44] Bob retired in June 1985, but coached track until 1986.[45]

An Olympic Gold Medal

Lorenzo Christopher Wright was born on December 9, 1926 in Detroit and graduated from Detroit's all-black Miller High School as part of the Class of 1942. After working for two years, he enrolled at Wayne University in the fall of 1944 and joined Coach Holmes' track team. In February 1945, in a duel meet with the University of Chicago, Lorenzo Wright won five events and finished third in a sixth. He was a "one-man track team." Lorenzo won the 100- and 220-yard dashes, the 120-yard high-hurdles, the 220-yard low hurdles, the long jump, and anchored the winning 880-yard relay team. He also finished third in the high jump. He contributed to 31 points for Wayne University. Lorenzo Wright served in the U. S. Army from May 23, 1945 to November 8, 1946, and qualified for the GI Bill benefits.

Lorenzo was a humble, calm, good-hearted, and self-assured man. At Wayne University, he practiced long jumping in the gym, with a bamboo high jump bar and a mattress. With meager facilities, but great talent and outstanding coaching, Lorenzo amassed a trunk full of metals. He was a good swimmer and gymnast, as well as a track star.[46] On February 8, 1947 Lorenzo placed second in the 75-yard low-hurdles and the broad jump and third in the college mile relay at the Michigan State Relays. One month later he won the broad jump setting a meet record with a jump of 22–11½. at the Central Collegiate Conference indoor meet. He also placed fourth in the 75-yard dash, and placed fifth in the mile relay at that meet. On May 10 he won the broad jump, and the 100-yard dash at a duel meet with Toledo University held at Kelsey Field in Detroit. On May 24 he won the 100-yard dash (10.1), the 220-yard dash (21.6), the 220-yard low-hurdles (23.2), and the broad jump (24–½) at the Mid-American Conference Meet.

In June 1947 Lorenzo Wright placed second in the long jump (25–9½) at the NCAA finals. On July 4, 1947 Wright won the long jump (24–3¼), placed second in the 100-meter dash (10.4) and the 200-meter hurdles at the National Junior AAU meet in Lincoln, Nebraska.[47] At that meet, Lorenzo was the only entry from Wayne University yet scored sufficient points to win top honors as a "team" over all other colleges and Universities competing. He placed sixth among all teams entered. In 1947 he ranked second in the World in the broad jump and 11th in the low hurdles, according to *Track and Field News*.[48] In 1947–8 Lorenzo was named an All-American by the AAU and by *Track and Field News*.[49]

In the first Olympic year in more than a decade, the Captain of the 1948 Wayne University track team set the school record in the long jump record (25–11). Leading up to the Olympic trials, Lorenzo Wright won the broad jump indoors at the Michigan State Relays (24–9½), the Michigan AAU Indoor (24–6), the New York Athletic Club Games (25–3¾), and the National AAU Indoor meet (25–3¾). After placing third in the 75-yard low-hurdles (8.5), and fifth in the 75-yard dash at the Michigan State Relays, Lorenzo generally restricted himself to the long jump in order not to injure his chances of making the Olympic team. In March, he won the broad jump (24–5¾) at the Illinois Tech Relays, and placed second in the Central Collegiate Conference Championships (24–8½) and the Chicago Relays (24–8½).

During the outdoor season, Lorenzo Wright's march to the Olympic Games continued despite training in inferior facilities. On April 24, 1948 he won the broad jump (24–7⅜) at the Penn Relays, and on June 19 in Minneapolis he placed third (24–5¼) at the NCAA Championships. Then, on July 2–3 he placed second in the long jump (25–2½) and sixth in the 200-meter dash at the National AAU Championships in Milwaukee. On July 9–10 Lorenzo placed third in the broad jump (25–½), sixth in the second heat of the 100-meter dash, and fifth in the 200-meter dash at the final Olympic track tryouts at Dyche Stadium in Evanston. His performance in the broad jump earned him a place on the 1948 Olympic team.

On July 31 Lorenzo fouled on a jump that would have placed him second at the 14th Olympiad in London. Instead, he placed fourth in the broad jump (24–5¼).[50]

Lorenzo's lucky turned for the better when Ed Conwell, a member of the 4 × 100-meter London Olympic relay team, had to be replaced because he was suffering from an asthma attack. On August 6 Wright was substituted for Conwell in the semi-final heat of the 4 × 100-meter relay at Wembley Stadium. On August 7 Lorenzo ran second on the gold medal winning 400-meter relay (40.6) at the 14th Olympiad.

According to the *Track and Field News*[51] the finals went as expected. Norwood "Barney" Ewell and Lorenzo Wright gained very little, but Harrison Dillard, taking the baton on the last curve, shot past everybody in the race and Melvin Patton added another four or five yards to the margin of victory. As the Americans prepared to mount the victory stand to receive their gold medals, they heard the paralyzing announcement that they had been disqualified. A frantic scurrying about disclosed that some obscure official had said he thought perhaps that the first baton pass had been out of bounds.

The Americans had to stand sadly by and see Great Britain honored as champions, but they did not take it quietly. They talked to the newspapers, and to themselves. Mel Patton said, "Go talk to the judges. Go talk to the guy who disqualified us. We can't talk to him." Barney Ewell added, "Let the camera decide, but I'm pretty certain I did not go over the line." Harrison Dillard said, "Wait until the slow motion pictures come out. That will show them. It's just like Joe Jacobs said, "We shoulda stood in bed." Lorenzo Wright said, "Each running lane had three marks in it. They were very dim. In addition, the starting line for a distance race ran through them all. I know we made a legal exchange of the baton, but probably all the marks mixed up the officials. I triple checked the position of my feet while I waited for Barney. I was six inches inside the marker. A judge said to me, "you're not going to step over that line, are you? And I said, "Hell no."

Avery Brundage and Dean Cromwell lodged protests and after viewing the movies a few days later, the Olympic jury awarded the race to the United States. Sportswriter "Red" Smith described consequences,

And now, the Royal Air Force band must return to the desolate forsaken field of Wembley Stadium and unplay 'God Save the King.' Blighty's only track victory in the Olympics, which was presented to Britain last Saturday under the Marshall Plan, fell under the terms of reversed lend-lease today and was restored to the United States, the original copyright holders. It was the most sensational reversal since Serutan.[52]

As "Red" Smith observed this was the first time in international sports history that a decision of the judges that determined the outcome of a sports contest had been reversed because of moving pictures.

On August 13, following the Olympic Games, Lorenzo Wright won the broad jump (24–2½), and placed second in the 440-yard relay at the USA vs. British Empire meet held in London. On August 15–16 he won the broad jump (24–6⅛) and the 400-meter relay, and placed second in the 200-meter dash and third in the 100-meter dash in the USA vs. France meet in Paris.

There was a second Michigan athlete participating in the 1948 Olympic Games. University of Michigan half-miler Herbert O. Barten placed fourth in the 800-meter run.

After the Olympic Games, Lorenzo returned to Wayne University to complete his education. After his gold metal performance, people turned around to see him when he entered class, and would go out of their way to meet him on the streets, yet he never lost his bearings. He was the same unassuming guy he had been before the Olympics.[53] In November 1948 he married Elizabeth Imogene Phillips. According to his college classmates, Lorenzo's Olympic gold medal had little affect on him. On January 28, 1949 he won the broad jump (24–3) at the Michigan AAU Indoor Relays. In February he placed second in the broad jump (24–7) at the Michigan State Indoor Relays, and placed fourth in the broad jump (23–1⅛) at the National AAU Senior Indoor Championships. In March 1949 he won the 220-yard dash and placed second in the 70-yard dash in a duel meet with Illinois Tech.

During the outdoor season, Lorenzo won the 880-yard relay and placed second in the 440-yard relay at the Seton Hall Relays. On April 30, 1949 he won the broad jump (23–8¼), the 440-yard college relay (41.7), the 880-yard college relay (1:26.0), and placed second in the 100-yard dash (9.78) at the Penn Relays. He went on to win the broad jump, the mile relay, and the low-hurdles, while placing second in the 100-yard dash at the State Intercollegiate Meet held in Kalamazoo. Among his best times in 1949 were 9.7 for the 100-yard dash, 21 flat for the 220-yard dash, 23.2 for the 220-yard low-hurdles, and 9.5 for the 75-yard low-hurdles indoor. On June 4 he and his teammates won the 440-yard relay at the Central Collegiate Conference Championships in Milwaukee.

In September 1951, after graduating from Wayne University, Lorenzo taught health and physical education at Cleveland Junior High in Detroit. In September 1952, he transferred to Miller High School to coach football and reserve-basketball, and was assistant track coach to Leroy Dues. He continued to compete until 1952. In 1951 he placed second in the broad jump (22–3½) at the Michigan AAU Indoor and won the broad jump (23–9) at the National AAU Indoor Championships. In 1952 he won the broad jump (23–9) at the National AAU Senior Indoor Championships, but failed to make the Olympic team that year and retired from competition.

In January 1956, Lorenzo transferred to Eastern High School where he coached swimming and track and field. During the 1961–62 school year, Wright was granted a leave of absence to lecture in health and physical education at the University of Nigeria in Nsukka, West Africa. Lorenzo and Mal Whitfield, Olympic champion in 1948 and 1952, coached the track team at the university. They conducted a track and field clinic for the Eastern Region of Nigeria and designed an Olympic size swimming pool, which is still in use at the university. Their work helped to establish the Nigerian National Track Program. Between 1963 and 1965 Wright spoke at clinics sponsored by the Detroit Coaches Association, the Detroit Catholic Coaches Association, the International Coaches Clinic, and the Michigan Interscholastic Track Coaches Association. In 1965 he continued to coach track and swimming at Eastern High.[54] During the 1967–68 school year, Lorenzo Wright was granted a leave of absence to work with the New Detroit Committee, Youth, Recreation and Cultural Affairs Task Force. In 1969 Lorenzo became supervisor of athletics for the Detroit Public Schools.

Lorenzo was one of the great long jumpers in American track and field history, and a world class sprinter. His partner in Nigeria, Mal Whitfield, helped start the Kenyan national track and field program that has come to dominate world class distance running. Lorenzo became one of the first African-American school administrators in the Detroit Public Schools.

Lorenzo's brothers had almost no athletic talent. According to friend Pete Petross, "They couldn't walk across the street without falling over their own feet." Lorenzo was the father of six sons. Lorenzo Wright, Jr. ran on his high school track team at Mumford, but did not have his father's special talent. One of Lorenzo's sons became a Detroit City policeman; another became a Black Muslim.

On March 27, 1972 the Olympic gold medal winner died in his home, during a domestic argument, when his wife stabbed him in the back. Many believe that if a neighbor had not pulled the knife out of his back, he could have been saved. Instead, he bled to death before the ambulance arrived. When Lorenzo's brother called Irving Petross to tell him that Lorenzo was dead, Irving was shocked. Lorenzo's wife later asked Irving for forgiveness, but, as he was not a priest, he did not feel he could give it.

After his death, the track at Martin Luther King High School was named in his honor. In 1973 Lorenzo was inducted into the Michigan Sports Hall of Fame, and in 1976 was made a member of the Wayne State University Sports Hall of Fame.

The GI Bill Underwrote Their College and Living Expenses

In the fall of 1946 a silent revolution was underway that would transform college campuses and create a new suburban society. America was on the verge of becoming the first predominantly middle-class nation in the modern industrial world, largely because of a new government initiative. A generation that had grown up without much money during the great depression and had lived in city tenements, or in modest houses located in small towns or on isolated farms was about to go to college. They were used to houses without central heating or private, indoor plumbing, but would soon discover that they could buy a tract house in the suburbs with indoor plumbing and a dishwasher.

This revolution was the result of the Readjustment Act of 1944, better known as the GI Bill. GI was a catchall abbreviation for "general issue," the name given in the military for all-standard equipment, clothing and weapons, and often applied to enlisted men and women. President Roosevelt signed this Congressional Act into law on June 22, 1944. The law was supported by an improbable coalition that included the American Legion, Republicans, and conservative Southern Democrats. The per capita cost to the public of educating World War II veterans was $1,858 or $14.5 billion. The investment yielded an enormous profit to America taxpayers in terms of future taxes paid. GIs averaged more than $250,00 per person in increased lifetime earning over what they would have made without a college education. Nearly half a million veterans attended college solely because of the GI Bill.[55]

Much to the surprise of its congressional sponsors, the GI Bill over-turned the nation's social and economic structure. It shattered forever the public concept of who should attend college. Few GIs flunked out of college and many made the Dean's list.

Meanwhile, William J. Levitt and his imitators began applying building methods learned in the Seabees to housing construction and grafting those ideas to mortgaging principals pioneered by Homer Hoyt at the Federal Housing Administration. The result was the biggest housing boom in the nation's history. Between 1945 and 1954 more than thirteen million new houses were built, mostly in the suburbs and financed primarily by the Veterans Administration under the GI Bill.[57]

A GI Bill Beneficiary

Irving Petross, Jr. was born in Canton, Illinois on February 21, 1926. He grew up in Kewanee, Illinois, a manufacturing town of 17,100 people on the Chicago, Burlington, and Quincy Railroad near a coal mining region in the west-central part of the state. The Petross family had roots in West Virginia, where Irving's father was born. The family first moved north to Pennsylvania, and then they moved on to the coalfields of Illinois, where Irving was born. Hard times in the coalfields forced Irving's father to leave coal mining to work in a brass foundry in Kewanee. The foundry was even more dangerous than the coal mines, if that is possible, and would ultimately cause health problems that shortened his father's life.

On the other hand, Kewanee was a great place to grow up. Irving and his sisters went to nearly all-white elementary and secondary schools, and received a better education than most African-American children during the great depression.[58] Because he was a quick learner and a good athlete, Irving's best friends in high school were the smartest boys in his class of 39 students. His coach, teachers, and the school principal took a personal interest in him. He played varsity football, basketball, and track, earning nine high school letters on teams that won conference championships in all three sports. Indeed, during his senior year his football team was undefeated and unscored upon. Irving earned extra money as a shoeshine boy, and learned from his Greek boss that Petross means Pete in Greek. After that Irving told people that his name was "Pete." This became the nickname that followed him the rest of his life. During those years his aunt graduated from Western Illinois Normal School and imparted the idea that Pete and his sisters also might someday go to college. While life was not easy in Kewanee, it offered "Pete" a good start.

In May 1943, Irving Petross, Jr. graduated from high school. He worked with his father at the brass foundry until drafted in early 1944. Once in the Navy, Pete chose the Marines, and was sent to Camp Le Jeune to become part of the segregated Marine Corps. He was assigned to a service unit to bury bodies. He was fortunate in his selection of friends. Some of the older fellows took him under their wing, steering him away from the rough, gambling and hard drinking fellows. His behavior gave him his first opportunity for leadership. At the age of 19, Pete was made a platoon leader.

After basic training Pete's unit was sent to Okinawa. His unit missed the battle for Iwo Jima by a week. This bit of luck may well have saved his life, because of the high rate of casualties on Iwo Jima. Pete survived his tour in the Pacific, and was discharged from the Marines in June 1946. Before departing, his Marine buddies demanded that Pete agree to go to college. He tried to brush them off, but they insisted and he agreed.

Meanwhile, Pete's parents moved to Ecorse, Michigan, near Detroit. His dad took a job at Great Lakes Steel, where his uncle was employed. Determined not to work as hard as his father, Pete decided to go to college. Because of his military record, good high school grades, and outstanding character, Irving Petross, Jr. was offered an appointment to the Military Academy at West Point. His mother opposed the appointment on the grounds that it would take her son away from her again, so in September 1946 Pete decided to enroll at Wayne University on the GI Bill to become a high school teacher and coach. His father thought going to college was a waste of time because of the limited opportunities available to college educated African-Americans—"you can become a postman without going to college." At the time Pete enrolled at Wayne University, only seven per cent of the student body was African-American and only 2.5 per cent were African-American males.

Shortly after entering college, track coach, David L. Holmes, saw Pete playing a game of pick-up basketball and suggested that his sport was track, not basketball, and persuaded Pete to join the track team. It was an auspicious decision. He joined Lorenzo Wright ('51), Leon Wingo' ('50), and Elmer "Buddy" Coleman ('50) on a track team that was to be one of the best in school history. At that time, Wayne University had a great track coach, but marginal training facilities and an average outdoor track. In 1947 in East Lansing, Pete ran his first track meet for Wayne. A busload of Wayne athletes were entered in the state intercollegiate meet, but only Lorenzo Wright earned points. Enroute back to Detroit, Pete vowed to Coach Holmes that he would never again enter a meet where he did not score points, and he never did.

Soon, Pete was winning or placing in the 100 yard dash, the 220 yard dash, the long jump, the low-hurdles, and the quarter mile and half mile relays. On April 23, 1949, Irving was on the winning 880-yard relay (1:29.6) and the second place 440-yard relay team at the Seton Hall Relays in Newark.[59] A week later, the Wayne 440 and 880 yard relay teams won the Penn Relays College Division before 30,000 fans at Franklin Field where they recorded the third best time for the 880-yard relay (1:26 flat) in the 55-year history of the track meet. They were just six-tenths over the meet record, and their relay team was just one second off the world's record.[60] Coach Holmes often took just four athletes to big meets. They sometimes had problems with meals and accommodations. They could tell by the Coach's walk if they had problems. If he walked slowly it was all right. If he walked fast, they would move on fast. The coach never deserted them.

Later that year, Lorenzo Wright, Pete's roommate on road trips, won a gold metal at the Olympics. Lorenzo remained one of Pete's best friends as long as he lived. Pete was godfather to Lorenzo's children, and a pallbearer at his funeral.

Pete ran at Wayne University one year after Lorenzo Wright graduated. On May 13, 1950 Pete acquitted himself well at the First Annual Bowling Green Relays on the Whittaker Track in Bowling Green, Ohio. He was on the winning 440-yard relay team, won the individual long jump competition (21–9), and placed second as part of the sprint medley relay and 880-yard relay teams.[61]

Pete also played halfback on the football team at Wayne University, and was offered a tryout with the San Francisco Forty-Niners, but he had no way of getting to the West Coast and no money to get home if he did not make the team. Instead, he played semi-professional football for the Detroit Tars. He also continued to run track through 1958. He had some of his best years in track after graduating from college. He ran unattached for 4 years and practiced alone. In 1957–8 he helped to form the Detroit Track Club. On February 22, 1958, as a member of the Detroit Track Club's sprint medley relay team, he placed second at the National AAU Indoor Championships.

After finishing college, Pete was amateur sprint champion of Michigan five times. The bus strike of 1952 forced him to walk everywhere, which led to his best year in track. He broke 21 seconds for the 220 that year (20.8), and lowered his personal best in the 100-yard dash from 9.8 to 9.6. He had an unofficial 9.5 against Ira Murchison that year. Pete remembers fondly helping Coach Holmes develop theories for teaching techniques to sprinters. He showed Holmes the importance of a level back and well spread fingers in starts.

When Pete graduated from college in 1950, he could not get a teaching job in the Detroit area. He had married the sister of his track buddies, Leon and Bob Wingo, and went to work for the Post Office. In 1951 Pete went to Cleveland in search of a teaching job. Finally, with the help of Mary Malarny, he was allowed to substitute teach in the Detroit Public Schools in the 1951–52 school year. In February 1953 he was made an Emergency Substitute, and in 1954 he was given a full contract. There were few black teachers in the Detroit Public Schools at that time. Lorenzo Wright[62] and Robert Wingo[63] also were required to substitute teach before being given full time teaching contracts.

Pete was given his big break in 1958 when he was allowed to transfer from elementary physical education to a job coaching in football and track at Chadsey High School. He remained in that position until January 1967, when he was promoted to the position of football coach and student counselor at Mumford High School.

In September 1968 he became head of the Physical Education Department at Mumford, where he managed 16 sports. He assigned the football coaching position to someone else, and coached cross-country and track. In 1970 he became Assistant Principal and in 1975 Principal at Mumford High School, a position he held for 11 years. He retired from the Detroit Public Schools in 1986.[64]

Another GI Bill Beneficiary

Fred Daniel Johnson, who was born in 1925, graduated from Grand Rapids High School in the spring of 1942. On June 17, 1944 he represented the Cleveland *Call and Post* at the National AAU Junior Championships held at Randalls Island and placed third in the 200-meter low-hurdles. In the spring of 1946, after serving in the armed service, Fred enrolled at Michigan State College under the GI Bill. He majored in physical education, and was an instant star on the Spartan's track team. On March 9, 1946 he won the broad jump at the Central Collegiate Conference Indoor Meet. The next month he won the broad jump at the Penn Relays.

On February 8, 1947 Fred Johnson won the broad jump (24–6⅝). He also placed third in 75-yard low-hurdles (8.5) and in the 75-yard dash at the Michigan State Relays held at Jenison Fieldhouse. According to the *Chicago Tribune*,

Fred Johnson, Michigan State freshman star, was a duel holder of new records. The Grandville Negro cleared 24 feet 6⅝ inches in the broad jump to better the old mark of 24 feet 2⅝ inches set in 1943. Johnson also established a new mark of 8.5 seconds for the 75-yard low hurdles in the qualifying trials altho he was forced to be satisfied with third place in the finals.[65]

During the spring season, Fred Johnson won the 220-yard low-hurdles (23.7) and the broad jump (24–7⅜), and placed second in the 100-yard dash at the IC4A Championships in Philadelphia. In 1947 Johnson had the second best broad jump mark in the nation.[66]

Johnson had high hopes of making the 1948 Olympic team. In February he won the broad jump (24–8½) at the Michigan AAU Indoor Championships. In March he won the 75-yard dash (7.6) and the 75-yard low-hurdles (8.3) and the broad jump (25–4¾) at the Central Collegiate Championships. He also won the broad jump (25–4¾) and was third in the 50-yard dash (5.2) at the Chicago Relays that month. In late May he won the broad jump (24–1⅝) at the 72nd IC4A Championships. Although his best official jump was 25′ 4¾″, Johnson leaped 25′ 11″ on a foul jump in the 1948 Olympic trials. He was bitterly disappointed in missing the Olympics because of three foul jumps.

In February 1949 Johnson won the broad jump (24–2) at the IC4A indoor Championships. "Johnson, a 24-year-old junior, reversed the tables on his arch rival, Lorenzo Wright of Wayne University, but not without a struggle. Wright had six consecutive jumps over 24 feet, with a best of 24–7, but Johnson reached 24–8½ to win" the Michigan State Relays. Johnson, who is the AAU and IC4A broad jump champion, also won the 75-yard dash in 7.6.[67] Later that year, he won the broad jump (24–6¼) at the IC4A Outdoor Championships and the AAU Championships. He also won the broad jump (25–2½); finished third in his heat of the 100-yard dash (9.69) and won his heat in the 220-yard low-hurdles (22.9). He was injured in the broad jump and scratched from the finals of the low-hurdles at the NCAA Outdoor Championships in the Los Angeles Coliseum. Johnson was named an All-American in the broad jump by *Track and Field News*,[68] as well as earning NCAA All-American honors. Because of a game leg, Johnson was considered by some "too erratic and fragile" to be the world's best broad jumper.[69]

On March 11, 1950 Fred Johnson won the broad jump (24–8¼) at the IC4A Indoor Championships for a final time. In March 1950 *Track and Field News (p. 6)* ranked Fred Johnson the country's top low-hurdler and its second ranked broad jumper, however, repeated injuries kept him from becoming the fourth American to jump 26 feet. Johnson hurt his ankle badly going over the last hurdle as leadoff runner in the shuttle hurdle relay at the Purdue Relays on March 25, and barely crawled on the ground to touch off the next man. A torn tendon ended Fred Johnson's track career.

The tiny, 25-year-old Negro was one of the best broad jumpers of all time, a great low hurdler, and a capable sprinter. War veteran, Johnson, married and a physical education major, is one of five men who have jumped 25 feet in the Los Angeles Coliseum, and the only one to do it three times. But he was almost unbeatable when uninjured. He won five IC4A titles (two indoors) as a well as AAU & NCAA championships. In the low hurdles, he twice ran 22.9, and he won the 1947 IC4A title. His best sprinting feat was finishing less than two feet behind Mel Patton in a 9.6 hundred. He was in top shape last winter, and the latest injury was a sore blow. But now comes the good news that he will recover completely, and will be able to compete in about a year. He may completely, and will be able to compete in about a year. He may yet jump 26 feet . . . and make the Olympic team.[70]

11. "I've Got Plenty of Nothing and Nothing Is Plenty for Me: The Amazing David L. Holmes, Discoverer of Hidden Talent"

The population of the City of Detroit multiplied by a factor of five between 1900 and 1930. Its population rose from 285,000 to 1,568,000.[1] Much of the population growth was due to emigrants from Eastern and Mediterranean Europe. In a 1916 article for *New Outlook* magazine, Gregory Mason wrote that "three out of four persons [you might meet in Detroit] . . . were either born abroad or born here of foreign parents.[2] A survey of immigrants in Detroit based on the 1910 census commissioned by the Detroit Board of Education in 1915 confirmed Mason's observations. It reported that 74 percent of the population of Detroit was either foreign born or were children of at least one foreign born parent. More important, one-half of the males residing in Detroit and of voting age were born on foreign soil, and less than half had been naturalized.[3]

From the viewpoint of public education, the problem of a rapidly expanding population was even more pressing because of increasingly forceful Michigan laws on compulsory school attendance. Originating in 1871, compulsory education laws were strengthened in 1895, 1907 and 1913.[4] It is perhaps no coincidence that Henry Ford started school in 1871, the year the State of Michigan passed its first compulsory school attendance law.[5]

In 1915 a network of streetcars and electric interurban commuter cars made Detroit the hub of urban transportation for some 159 communities within a 75-mile radius.[6] This network favored a central city location for a new college.

In the fall of 1917 Detroit Junior College opened at Central High School with the objective of preserving democracy by bringing education to the masses. The faculty was selected with care and was of university caliber. Three hundred students enrolled for the first semester at Michigan's newest institution of higher learning. By the fall semester of 1923 the enrollment at Detroit Junior College had increased to nearly 2,000 students.[7] The college age population appears to have grown faster in Detroit during the 1920s than elsewhere in Michigan.[8]

The Remarkable Mr. Holmes

David L. Holmes, the first track coach at Detroit City College, was born and raised in Stillwater, Oklahoma. His father-a minister's son—operated the music store in Stillwater, and his parents came from a long line of farmers, circuit riders, and teachers. David was a natural athlete. He began participating in athletics as a sophomore in Oklahoma State University's preparatory school. When he graduated from Oklahoma State in 1908 with a teaching certificate, he had lettered three years in high school and four years in college in football, basketball, and track. In college he was almost a one-man track team, competing in most events and leading his five-man team to its league championship his senior year. His performance records in college track were quite good. He jumped 24 feet 11 inches in the running broad jump and was never defeated. He jumped as far as 25–1 in practice. He ran 10 seconds in the 100-yard dash, 50 seconds in the 440, and threw the discus 134 feet.[9]

After college graduation, David becoming a coach and decided to try out for the 1912 Olympics in both the decathlon and the long jump. In the summers of 1911 and early 1912 he trained at the Chautauqua Institute in upstate New York, one of the citadels of muscular Christianity, which linked physical fitness and spirituality to achieve Christian goals. He met Amos Alonzo Stagg at Chautauqua, and held an idealized, life-time admiration for the University of Chicago Athletic Director. Fate intervened in 1912 to deny Holmes an opportunity to make the U.S. Olympic team. David became violently ill and had to withdraw from the Olympic tryouts. It was one of the low points of his life.

Holmes coached at an Indian academy in Oklahoma, at Bethel College in Kentucky, at Northwestern Military Academy in Lake Geneva [Wisconsin], and at DePauw University in Indiana. Finally, he served as athletic director at Detroit's Cass Technical High School before being recruited to initiate the athletic program at Detroit Junior College in October 1917.[10] The new college was founded on the pattern of City College of New York, but was never as well funded. The Detroit Board of Education operated the college until it became Wayne State in 1956.

City College started in the Detroit Central High School building. There were 103 rooms in Main Building, renamed Old Main in 1950, and because of Detroit's rapid growth it was a promising location. From

The 1949 Wayne University 880-yard relay team that ran the third fastest time in the history of the event at the Penn Relays up to 1950. From left to right Elmer "Buddy" Coleman, Lorenzo Wright, Irving Petross, Leon Wingo, and coach David L. Holmes. *(Photo courtesy of Irving Petross)*

the start, the City College of Detroit, which later became Wayne University and is now Wayne State University, was a working class college, focused primarily on teacher training. It drew its students from Detroit's working class and retail merchant families. Holmes was forced to be a penny-pincher to survive at City College of Detroit. There was never enough money for Detroit's growing elementary and secondary public school population, much less its powerless and often penniless college students.

Holmes was athletic director from 1917 until 1958. He coached basketball until 1929, football until 1936, and track and cross-country until he retired. His first track team in 1918 participated in a single meet which they lost to Normal Michigan.[11] His budget was so meger that his track team rarely traveled by train and the athletic department never owned a bus.

During the 1920s, Coach Holmes depended heavily on trial-and-error learning and the nine American Sports Publishing Company paperback books on track and field technique. These books were ghost written by San Francisco track coach Boyd Comstock and featured advice from such track greats as Archie Hahn. They included a few figure-drawings and pictures indicating proper techniques.

The best athletes in the Detroit schools were offered scholarships or job support to attend the University of Michigan, Michigan State, Michigan Normal College [now Eastern Michigan University], Western Michigan State Teacher's College, the University of Detroit, or the University of Notre Dame. City College got the leftovers. Prior to the Civil Rights movement, many of the good athletes who were not offered scholarships elsewhere were African-Americans, Jews, or kids with academic or personal problems of one kind or another.

As an adult, David L. Holmes stood 5–11, and rippled with muscles. His personality was guileless, upbeat, enthusiastic, and idealistic. He was admired and people liked to be around him. But he had very few close friends or confidants and did not seem to need them, because his work and his athletes absorbed him. According to his son, he sang well, liked classical music, disliked popular music, liked art, and respected scholars. Coach Holmes did not smoke or drink alcohol. He did not swear or enjoy dirty jokes, and was baffled by their allure.

His idea of a good meal was roast beef served at a cafeteria. His Champions were Abraham Lincoln, George Washington Carver, and Amos Alonzo Stagg. He attended a neighborhood Congregationalist Church in Detroit, and would say—quietly—that he was no longer sure of what or whether he believed. Nevertheless, at family gatherings on holidays, he said grace beautifully. He never questioned Christianity as a moral system, and he was a second or third generation advocate of muscular manliness in the service of God.

David L. Holmes was a product of rural America. He was not a sophisticated or particularly cultured man, nor would he have seen these as worthy goals. He took two daily newspapers—at one period, one of them was the *Manchester Guardian*—but read few books, and spent his summers fishing in Canada. He voted Republican, but respected not only Franklin and Eleanor Roosevelt but also Norman Thomas. He was adventurous and was happiest out of doors.

Coach Holmes was neither a political or devious person. He did not know the right people or which levers to pull to get things done, nor was he a great administrator. He simply took the leftovers, put up with primitive facilities, and through the force of his character, his belief in muscular Christianity, and his confidence in the untapped talent found in the offspring of working-class families made his athletes feel like first-rate talent. Even though Wayne University athletes were in a second rate situation, they accomplished great things and left college with a confidence rarely found elsewhere.

While the pioneering work in integration had already been done by the time he entered coaching, Coach Holmes had integrated teams at Detroit Junior College from the outset in 1917–8 when Leon "Toy" Wheeler played football and ran track. "Toy" Wheeler went on to become Director of Brewster Recreation Center in Detroit and coach of the Harlem Globetrotters.[12]

David Holmes was unusual for coaches of his era, as he would not condone separate meals or accommodations for his Negro athletes. A trackman that graduated from City College in 1926 remembered that when all else failed Coach Holmes gave money out of his own pocket to African-Americans to find separate accommodations. But City College and later Wayne University track teams always ate together, and, at least by the 1930s, also stayed together. "On road trips we often didn't go to restaurants. Meals consisted of the team sitting in cars while Holmes argued the price of sandwiches down."[13]

But Coach Holmes gradually developed knowledge of restaurants in the mid-west that would serve African-Americans and would often drive out of his way to go to those restaurants. "Whenever Coach Holmes reconnoitered restaurants in uncharted territory, the team could tell from his walk back from the restaurant whether they would be able to eat there or had to drive on." As for accommodations, former Detroit City College trackmen tell of nights spent in black-operated hotels and even once in a trailer park. The team's integrated status and meager athletic budgets meant that few teams in Coach Holmes' forty-one years of coaching in Detroit ever stayed in an AAA-approved motel or hotel.

Like Amos Alonzo Stagg and Avery Brundage, David L. Holmes was an avid proponent of amateur athletics. However, he never appears to have exhibited the hypocrisy so apparent in the actions of Brundage and Stagg, although he was naive regarding the values of those with other religious or cultural backgrounds.

Hope is the engine that drives most people and no coach in the history of Michigan track and field did a better job of kindling hope than David L. Holmes. Coach Holmes started with acceptance. He accepted his situation, and most of all he accepted the sons of immigrant and African-American families who saw the City of Detroit's commuter college as their only path away from a life of manual labor.

Coach Holmes understood instinctively that a good relationship starts with acceptance. When you accept someone, with all their flaws, you free them to focus on their assets. You give them hope. Coach Holmes was a grand master in his ability to take the young men, ignored by richer and bigger college track programs, and mold them into champions. Coach Holmes wanted his athletic boys to enjoy their sport, and not to be too disappointed when they lost a race, but to take a lesson from the experience and to look forward to the next race. The most important thing was to love the sport and do your best, and then you can be happy with any result. Coach Holmes' secret was that he was really doing what he loved to do.

Holmes assured his athletes that he knew that the road of life is not always easy, but that the hard at times could be balanced by the enjoyment and satisfaction that comes from performing well, and, yes, by winning against the odds. Men often participate in sports for reinforcement of their masculinity. Coach Holmes implicitly understood this, and reinforced their masculine feelings in a positive manner. He also created an atmosphere in which the athlete's need for peer acceptance was satisfied.

Some young men are personal-goal oriented, while others are more task-oriented. Those who have a strong sense of their own strengths and are focused on the tasks necessary to develop their strongest skills generally stay involved in sports and are the most likely to succeed in a sport like track. Those with low-task and low ego-motivation are most likely to drop out of sports. A young man who has internal motivation—a personal love of the sport—will keep running. If they are driven by external motivation they risk dropping out. When an athlete is worried about pleasing the coach, he is less satisfied with his performance, win or lose. Consequently, he is likely drop out to avoid worrying about his performance.[14] Coach Holmes promoted personal goals for his athletes.

City College's 1924 Track Team

The Detroit City College track team was small and rarely had a winning season, but generally spawned a few individual track stars each season.

City College was seriously handicapped by its lack of track facilities. In the 1920s they shared Codd field with the Northern, Central, and Cass High School teams or traveled to Belle Isle to practice. When meets were held by any of the high school teams, the field was tied up.[15]

In 1924, Coach Holmes had half the number of trackmen needed to be affective, when he faced Michigan Agricultural College in East Lansing on May 2. While the Aggies had a 27-man squad, the Munies faced them with a squad of twelve.[16] A heavy rainstorm delayed the meet and turned the track into mire in many places. Very slow times were recorded in the distance races held at the end of the meet. The Munies lost to the Aggies by 3 points, when Kurtz of Michigan Agricultural College beat Don Cooper by ½ inch in the broad jump. The Detroit team did well in field events, but lacked a decent sprinter.[17]

City College of Detroit staged its first home track meet of 1924 at Belle Isle on Friday May 9, against Western Normal of Kalamazoo.[18] The Munies with their small squad, wearing green and gold, were forced to run the same the same men in several events. Seven men, including Cooper, Vincent, Doherty, Brown, Seitz, Blanchard, and Cohen were expected to score as many points as possible.[19] It was the only meet they won that year. The green and gold thinclads then met Ypsilanti [Michigan] State Normal on May 9, 1924, and were overwhelmed 49 to 82.[20]

Early in the 1924 season, Coach Holmes had no thought of entering any of his pupils in the regional Olympic trials, scheduled for May 30–31. Nevertheless, his varsity track squad featured six standout performers: W. Stanley Seitz, Lowell E. Blanchard, Donald Cooper, Reeve Brown, Vincent, and J. Kenneth Doherty. Blanchard, Brown, Doherty, Vincent, and Cooper performed so well he entered them in the Olympic Trials. While none of them made the team, Brown did well in the 880-yard run, Doherty performed adequately, and Don Cooper was competitive in the high and low-hurdles.[21]

Seitz, a native of Monroe, Michigan, graduated from Detroit Western High School and was one of the first prominent pole-vaulters in the state. He finished fourth in the 1924 regional Olympic trials, and won the Michigan Intercollegiate. In 1925, he won the Ohio Relays, placed second in the 1925 Illinois Relays, and fourth at the Penn Relays. He set the Michigan Intercollegiate meet record with a vault of 12–⅞. While that may not sound like much of a vault by today's standards, it should be remembered that in 1925 there was a ground-level landing pit of sand, a small vault box, and heavy and stiff bamboo poles. The winning vault at the 1925 NCAA meet was 12–11.[22]

Lowell E. Blanchard, whose nickname was "Pat," was a good quarter-miler. As sophomore, Blanchard anchored the mile relay team that won the 1924 Michigan AAU mile relay championship. The following year his mile relay team won Michigan State Intercollegiate indoor and outdoor championships, and the teacher's college division of the Penn Relays. Pat Blanchard went on to graduate from the University of Michigan Medical School. He then practiced medicine at Harper Hospital for two years before moving to Hudson, Ohio, where he helped to deliver more than 5,000 babies over a 52-year career.[23]

Donald Cooper, an outstanding hurdler, graduated from Detroit's Eastern High School in 1923. In 1922 at Eastern High School he placed second in the 120-yard high-hurdles at the Michigan University Interscholastic Games. The following year he won the Metropolitan High School League low-hurdles Championship. Don spent one year at Detroit City College before transferring to the University of Michigan. At City College he was a consistent point winner for Coach Holmes, often earning points in four events, as he did against Michigan Agricultural College.

At the University of Michigan, Cooper placed third in 220-yard low hurdles and fifth in the 120-yard high hurdles at the Seventh Annual NCAA Championships in Chicago. In 1930 Don Cooper placed fourth in the standing broad jump at the National Junior AAU Indoor Title Meet held at Olympia Arena in Detroit. After college, Cooper coached and taught at Cass Tech, where one of his prize athletes was Bill Daly, U of Detroit Sports Hall of Fame member. Cooper spent three and a half years during World War II in the Navy as Athletic Director of the San Diego Naval Air Station.[24]

Holmes' First All-American

In 1924 Edward O. Spence graduated from Detroit's Western High School. Spence was one of fifteen boys on the Cowboys track team.[25] In the spring of his senior year, Spence won the 120-yard low-hurdles (13.7) and the 120-yard high-hurdles (16.8) at the Detroit Public League Championships. He also placed second in the 220-yard low-hurdles and third in the 120-yard high-hurdles at the Michigan Interscholastic Meet in Ann Arbor, and was the State Class A High School high-hurdles (16.0) and low-hurdles (24.6) champion.

As a freshman at City College, Edward Spence placed third in the 50-yard high-hurdles at the Michigan AAU Invitational AAU Indoor Carnival in Detroit. In 1925 he beat Michigan Normal in the high-hurdles

(15.8) and the low-hurdles (24.7). The following year, he won the Michigan AAU indoor hurdles championship, the high and low hurdles championship at the Michigan Intercollegiate, and the low-hurdles crown at the at the Central AAU Championships.

Spence achieved All-American status on June 12, 1926 when he won the 220-yard low-hurdles (23:5) at the Fifth Annual NCAA Championships in Chicago,[26] and closed the season by winning the low-hurdles at the Michigan Senior AAU Meet in July and Detroit Open in August.

In 1927 Spence continued his winning ways. He won the 75-yard low-hurdles (8.8) at the Illinois Relays, and won both the high-hurdles and low-hurdles at the Michigan State Intercollegiates and the Michigan Collegiate Conference Championships.[27] For a second time, he won the low-hurdles at the Central AAU Championships and the NCAA Championships. At the NCAA Championships he renewed his head to head battle against Frank Cuhel of Iowa and won in record setting time.[28] Again, Edward Spence was named NCAA All-American in the low-hurdles.

In 1928 the Detroit All-American won the 40-yard hurdles at the Michigan AAU Indoor Championships and the 220-yard low-hurdles (25.8) at the Michigan AAU Senior Outdoor Championships. He finished his college career by placing fourth in the low-hurdles behind Cuhel at both the Seventh Annual NCAA Championships and the National AAU Senior Championships in Denver. Cuhel went on to set a world record in the 400-meter hurdles at the Olympic trials[29] and win a silver medal in the Amsterdam Olympics.

Spence was inducted into the Wayne State University Sports Hall of Fame in 1979.

More Champions

John Kenneth Doherty, Bill Streng, John W. Lewis, and David Beauvais were the next set of champions coached by David L. Holmes. Doherty came to Coach Holmes completely unheralded. He never won a sports letter in high school and there was no reason to believe he would do so in college, except for his determination. John Kenneth Doherty later wrote:

> I remember with some regret but much satisfaction the limited training conditions of my own track career at the City Colleges of Detroit . . . in the 1920s.
> No indoor facility except the college classroom corridors and girl's tiny gym when and if [classes] were finished with it. No outdoor facility except the

Detroit Recreation Department track on Belle Isle [on the Detroit River], six miles from school. No hot showers, no training room or trainer. No locker in which to leave one's track clothes overnight. A seldom-brushed or watered cinder track. Jumping pits that we often spaded ourselves. But, then we had no basis for comparison. So far as we knew, such conditions were quite normal. And in any case, the boundless enthusiasm of Coach David L. Holmes would have soon quieted any team member inclined to gripe. We just made the most of what we had and thought nothing of it.[30]

Coach Holmes took Doherty's determination and added enough enthusiasm, instruction, self-confidence, and opportunity to allow the young man to become an all-around track athlete. In 1925 Doherty set the Michigan AAU indoor high jump record (6 feet).[31] On June 17, 1927 Doherty was one of a class of 96 graduating from Detroit City College with a four-year degree.[32] In 1928 John Kenneth Doherty won the American AAU decathlon championship without winning a single event[33] and won a bronze metal at the Amsterdam Olympics. Doherty's triumphs, however, came a year after graduating from Detroit City College and while training with better equipment at better facilities, and under the tutelage of Steve Farrell and Charles B. Hoyt at the University of Michigan. Bill Streng, on the other hand, achieved stardom at Detroit City College.

William C. "Bill" Streng graduated from Detroit's Eastern High School in 1925. In 1924 he won the 880-yard relay and placed fourth in 220-yard run at the Detroit Public League Outdoor Championships, and in May 1925 placed third in the 220-yard dash in the University of Michigan Interscholastic.[34]

As a freshman at Detroit City College, Streng placed third in the 300-yard run at the Michigan AAU Senior Indoor Championships held in the Detroit Northwestern High School Gym. As a college sophomore, he won the 440-yard dash at the Michigan Collegiate Conference Championships, and as a junior he placed second in the mile relay in the Ohio Relays, won the College Class mile relay at the Penn Relays, and placed fifth in the 440-yard run at the Seventh Annual NCAA Championships in Chicago.[35] Streng, who later became a Detroit policeman, would have been an All-American by modern standards, but was not one by 1928 NCAA standards.

As a senior, Bill Streng placed second in the mile relay, and won the college 880-yard Relay at the Ohio Relays, won the 440-yard dash and was a member of the winning mile relay team at the Michigan Collegiate Conference Championships. He also won the 440-yard dash (49.4) and the mile relay at the Michigan Intercollegiate in 1929.[36] On July 3, 1929 he ran in the 440-yard dash at the National AAU Junior Championships in Denver. Streng was part of the lineage of quarter-milers that won the mile relay at the Penn Relays for six consecutive years from 1926 to 1931.[37]

Because of the color of his skin John W. Lewis was an unwanted track super star. Detroit City College was the only institution of higher education to offer John a scholarship despite the fact that he was a Detroit, State of Michigan, and national interscholastic champion and national interscholastic record holder. Furthermore, he had success-fully competed against such track stars as the Loving brothers, Eddie Gaines, Eddie Tolan and Eugene Beatty. While John W. Lewis found the road to success filled with obstacles, Coach Holmes offered the support lacking in much of John Lewis' life. He guided Lewis onto the 1928 U. S. Olympic team and helped him regain his confidence when it looked like the whole world was stacked against him, after being denied an opportunity to participate in the 1928 Olympics.

Beauvais was one of fifteen members of the Western High School Cowboys track team. There were two African-American members of that team in 1925.[38] In 1927 while a senior at Western High School, David Beauvais was one of the outstanding athletes at the University of Michigan Indoor Interscholastic Meet. He beat Eugene Beatty to win the 60-yard high hurdles, and competed well against Beatty in the low-hurdles and Eddie Tolan in the 50-yard dash.[39] But, like John W. Lewis was not offered college financial assistance anywhere but at Detroit City College.

On February 10, 1928 City College freshman David Beauvais placed fourth in the 40-yard hurdles at the 1928 Michigan AAU Senior Indoor Meet in East Lansing.[40] On May 4, 1928 Beauvais and John W. Lewis were the leading point winners in a freshman Munies loss to Michigan Normal in Ypsilanti. Lewis won the 100-yard dash, the 220-yard low-hurdles, and the 440-yard dash. He placed second in the shot put. Beauvais won the 120-yard high-hurdles and the high jump, placed second in the 220-yard low-hurdles and the broad jump, and tied for third in the pole vault. Swan of Detroit City College won the broad jump and placed third in the high and low-hurdles. Lange of the Munies managed two second places (javelin and 440), while Olowich won the javelin. The other 2 Munies trackmen managed to place second in the 880 and the mile run, and third in the 2-mile run. Holmes had only seven freshmen on his team, to compete against Michigan Normal's 18-man squad. The Munies won 7 events and Normal won 6 events, yet the Ypsilanti team won the meet.[41]

The following year, Beauvais, John Lewis, and Bill Streng were members of the winning 880-yard relay at the Sixth Ohio Relays.[42] Beauvais also placed third in the broad jump at the Michigan Intercollegiate Championships in East Lansing, where "Lewis was largely responsible for Detroit's points with three firsts [the 100, 220, and low-hurdles] and membership on the victorious one-mile relay team."[43]

In 1929 and 1930, Beauvais was co-captain of the Detroit City College track team. As a junior at City College, Beauvais won the 50-yard low-hurdles (6.4) and the 8-lap relay in a duel meet with Michigan Normal College; won the 60-yard high-hurdles at the Illinois Relays, and was a member of winning 440-yard relay team at the Ohio Relays. On April 19, 1930 he won the broad jump (21–10) in a duel meet with Michigan State College. A mediocre senior year followed. After college David became a referee at a number of important national meets. He was a referee and head starter for NCAA Indoor Championships, 1965–77, the Big Ten Indoor and Outdoor Championships, the Big Eight Conference Outdoor Championships, and the U. S. Track and Field Championships. In 1978 David Beauvais was inducted into the Wayne State University Athletic Hall of Fame, as much for his football play and officiating as for his college accomplishments in track and field.[44]

James Russell, Detroit City College, 1929–31, was second in the running broad jump and was a member of the winning mile relay team for the Cadillac Athletic Club at the Michigan AAU Championships in Detroit on July 4, 1929. On April 26, 1930 Russell was on the winning (college division) mile relay team anchored by John Lewis at the Penn Relays, and on May 18, 1930 Russell was on the mile-relay team that set the meet record (3:23.2) at the Michigan Intercollegiate Outdoor Championships. Jimmy Russell went on to become the track coach at Detroit's Northwestern High School, where he coached track greats such as Stan McConner, Billy Smith, and Henry Carr.[45]

The Parade of Champions Continued

Leroy Dues was in the next wave of track champions at Detroit City College. Dues participated in track at Detroit's Northwestern High School, but did not make much of a mark until his senior year. Dues was not recruited for college track. As so often happened, Coach Holmes transformed an "also ran" into an All-American. As a freshman, in 1930, he won the shot put in the Junior Division at the National AAU Championships, and was named an AAU collegiate All-American. He won the State AAU outdoor shot put in 1930 while representing the YMCA. In 1932 Dues missed making the U. S. Olympic team at the final Olympic trials by inches.

In 1932 Coach Holmes experienced another low-point in his life. After being interviewed for the position of Athletic Director and Track and Field Coach at the University of California, he was turned down for the position. It was an appointment he desperately wanted, and his failure to get that job deeply disappointed him.[46] Holmes decided to publish an article in *The Amateur Athlete* to demonstrate to his peers his knowledge of track and field.[47]

In the spring of 1933 Detroit City College nearly cancelled its track, tennis, and golf schedules because of a lack of funds. City College was forced to open its outdoor track season late. They cancelled their annual meet with Michigan State College because funds for the athletic program were not released until April 21, late in the week of the scheduled meet, and City College athletes were in no condition for stiff competition.[48] While Leroy Dues was allowed to participate in the Penn Relays on April 28–89 the balance of the track team did not open their season until May 13.[49]

On April 29, 1933 Dues won the shot put at the Penn Relays with a put of 48–5.[50] Frank Davis, a Hillsdale College sophomore from East Tech High School in Cleveland, who threw the 16-pound ball 48 feet, was the chief shot put rival to Leroy Dues within Michigan.[51] Dues was the last Detroit City College AAU track and field All-American.

A Street-Car College

While the country club set generally attended the University of Michigan or an Eastern college, a wide-variety of individuals from families headed by salesmen, clerks and other retail workers, factory workers, and small businessmen attended Detroit City College. A future metallurgist (Norman V. Smith), trucking firm owner (Walter F. Carey), and bank president (Raymond Perring) were members of the class of 1926.[52] Walter Reuther, who left his Pennsylvania high school to apprentice as a tool and die maker at the Ford Motor Company, completed high school in Detroit by studying at night. During the early years of the depression, Walter, Roy, and Victor Reuther were students at the College of the City of Detroit from 1929 to 1932, both absorbing and adding to the institution's heady intellectual ferment, before playing key roles in organizing the United Auto Workers Labor Union.[53] However, because of the depression, enrollment at Detroit City College-Teachers College fell from a peak of 11,343 in 1929–30 to 8,365 in 1932–33.[54]

City College Becomes Wayne University; and Tolmich Its First All-American

In the fall of 1933, Detroit City College became Wayne University. In depression-stunned Detroit, entertainment was whatever people found to do as a distraction from the ordinary. Winter evenings were spent at a vaudeville show or cinema, at an indoor track meet, and even at the public library. There was an enormous desire among young adults to attend college, but most could not afford to attend Wayne University when the tuition was only $15 a semester. Federal aid allowed enrollment to increase slightly in 1934. Wayne benefited from Federal Relief Administration funds starting in 1933 and from National Youth Administration funds starting in 1935. In 1937 Wayne University received financial support from Wayne County as well as the Detroit Board of Education. Wayne University's pre-World War II enrollment peaked at 16,961 during the 1938–39 academic year.[55]

It was in this environment that Coach Holmes discovered the talented Allan Tolmich. Tolmich was hardly noticed by the track coach at Central High in Detroit. While he lettered as a sophomore, Tolmich never won an event and did not even go out for track his junior and senior years in high school.[56] In February 1934, Allan enrolled at Wayne University. When the spring track season started Tolmich approached Coach David L. Holmes and asked if he could tryout for the track team. Holmes had never met Allan Tolmich and knew nothing about the would-be walk-on, yet he immediately agreed to add the young man to the team. According to a 1940 newspaper story:

> Successful track coaches are smart judges of material. Almost at a glance, David L. Holmes, widely known athletic director and track coach of Wayne University, can spot potential point getters by a brief study of physical make-up, posture and action. Holmes saw that the freshman did not have much of the hurdler qualification about him but that he did have considerable of the sprint qualities—and in addition the youth appeared to be a competitor.[57]

A consultation followed, at which Coach Holmes told his freshman that he could be a track star and travel all over America in that capacity if he so desired. Tolmich had that desire. "Work began. Holmes began building the foundation, first for speed. But the work hadn't gone on long before the coach found that in addition to speed and competitive spirit, the freshman took readily to hurdling technique. There was much more work."[58]

Tolmich soon became the best indoor track athlete in the school's history despite nearly intolerable indoor training facilities. The Tartar track team ran on the tile floors of the halls of Main Building, and in an almost circular track that required 22 laps to the mile. Wayne lacked space for practicing the broad jump, and substituted a jump onto a mattress for authentic practice conditions.[59] Allan Tolmich depended on participation in indoor track meets on the road to work himself into shape.

Al Tolmich surprised the Michigan track and field establishment by placing third to Willis Ward and Bob Osgood in the open 65-yard high-hurdles at the Michigan AAU Indoor Track and Field Championships on February 9, 1935 at Yost Fieldhouse. Tolmich came back to help the Wayne University mile relay-team win the college mile relay. Albert King also tied Willis Ward for first place in the high jump at the meet,[60] Coach Holmes was unable to attend.[61]

The Underrated Tartars Showed Their Fighting Spirit

As a Wayne University sophomore, Tolmich captured fifteen first places, three seconds and six third places in a pretty tough league. As a junior, Tolmich hit his stride. He earned 27 first places, and set a new state intercollegiate indoor meet record of 5.3 for the 50-yard low-hurdles and another new mark in the 120-yard high-hurdles (14.7) outdoors.[62]

Tolmich teammates Albert King, Don McElroy, and Connie Eizak also contributed points at Wayne University track meets in the mid-1930s. On June 25, 1932, when Albert King was a student at Detroit's Pershing High School, he placed second in the high jump (6–2) at the district Olympic trials in Ann Arbor. On July 2, 1932 King tied for first in the high jump (6–4) at the Olympic semi-finals at Dyche Stadium in Evanston, and was awarded $105 to underwrite expenses to the final Olympic trials in Palo Alto. He cleared 6–5¼ at Palo Alto and barely missed 6–6. While the high school junior did not make the Olympic team, he placed second to Willis Ward in the high jump at the 1933 Michigan AAU Indoor Championships at Yost Field House. On May 20, 1933 he won the Detroit Public League high jump championship (6–2).[63] On June 29–30, 1933 Albert King set the National Junior AAU running high jump record (6–5¼) and the following day placed seventh in the high jump at the forty-sixth Annual National Senior AAU Outdoor Championships in Chicago. While attending Wayne University, King won the 1936 Michigan Intercollegiate outdoor high jump championship (6–3½).[64] He also tied for second at the Central Collegiate Conference Outdoor Meet on June 5, 1936 in Milwaukee. In November 1936 he began 36 years of employment at the Ford Motor Company.

McElroy had no right hand, but this did not keep him from consistently placing second to Tolmich in the high and low-hurdles. Constantine "Connie" Eizak, a Greek-American, was a Detroit Pershing High School Metropolitan League shot put champion and All-City Tackle in football, who became Wayne University's weight-man. "Too small for big time field competition,"[65] Eizak, nevertheless, won the shot put (45–1⅛) and the discus (136–7¾) at the 1936 Michigan Intercollegiate Championships in Ann Arbor. On May 8, 1937 he set the track record at the University of Akron in the shot put (42–3½) and the discus (125–10).[66]

Tolmich ran away with first places in the 100-yard dash, the high-hurdles, and low-hurdles at the Armour Tech Relays in 1936. At that year's Penn Relays, only Ohio State's great Jesse Owens and Michigan's Sam Stoller bested him in the 100-yard dash. Wayne University tied with Michigan Normal for the 1936 State Intercollegiate Outdoor title largely because of the heroic efforts of Al Tolmich.

As a senior, Tolmich captured 28 first places for the Coach Holmes. In addition, he amassed three firsts at the Notre Dame relays and three more at the Armour games. At the ninth annual Armour Tech Relay Games at the University of Chicago field house, the versatile Wayne University star won the college division 70-yard dash and the 70-yard high and low hurdles to lead Wayne to the college title. His teammates Sam Schwartz and Don McElroy also performed well in the sprints. Connie Eizak took the shot put for Wayne, and Wellwood of Wayne took second in the high jump, and Roman Harkaway captured second in the 440-yard run.[67] Moreover, the little Detroit "timber topper" became the holder of the American indoor dirt track record for the 50-yard high-hurdles (6.3) and low-hurdles (5.6) at the Butler Relays.[68]

At the Texas Relays, Tolmich won the 100-yard dash, stepping off the distance in 9.7, his a personal best. He also went over the 120-yard high-hurdles in 14.3, which was within two-tenths of a second of Forrest Towns' world record. At the 1937 Penn Relays Tolmich pushed the world champion from the gun shot to the tape in placing second to Towns in the highs.

In 1937 Wayne University won most of its track meets. Wayne claimed victories over Western Teachers College, Butler University, and the University of Akron.[69] However, it was the accomplishments of a few outstanding track athletes and not the teams as a whole that gave Wayne University the reputation of being a strong track school. For example, at the 1935 Michigan Indoor Intercollegiate only six Wayne University track men scored points, while Michigan State College had fifteen men scoring points, Michigan Normal had twelve, and Western State Teachers had eleven.[70] The same pattern held throughout Coach Holmes's reign at Detroit City College/Wayne University. Team victories were not a common event for Wayne, where the training and track facilities were perpetually substandard, and there was rarely enough money to support a full track program. While David Holmes was a good coach, his won-lost record did not reflect his greatness.[71]

When Wayne University's eleven man track team headed for East Lansing to compete on Michigan State College's new track for the 1937 State Intercollegiate Championships, Coach Holmes was pessimistic about Wayne's title chances. With Don McElroy definitely out of the meet, because of a bruised leg muscle, Coach David L. Holmes indicated that his team's chances of capturing the championship were slim, as Wayne was not even represented in the distance events or the pole vault. The *Detroit Free Press* announced, "Wayne's title burden now falls on Allan Tolmich, the mercury-winged Tartar." "Al Tolmich has been the Jesse Owens of Michigan track for the past two years, and looks good enough to carry off the laurels in the two dashes, low-hurdles and broad jump." But, Coach Holmes feared that Tolmich could not gather in the title without more help than he was likely to get.[72] Coach Holmes' concerns proved justified. Wayne did not repeat as State track titlist.

Tolmich wound up his collegiate career by placing second in the highs at the NCAA Championships. Two weeks later he won the National AAU 110-meter high-hurdles Championship, breaking Forrest "Spec" Towns' two year lock on the event and beating Olympian Fritz Pollard and Roy Stanley in the bargain. Tolmich also won the 200-meter low-hurdles at the AAU meet in Milwaukee.[73]

Allan Tolmich credits Coach Holmes with much of his success as an intercollegiate runner. Holmes was calm and steady. "No theatrics, but a powerful motivator," according to Tolmich. Allan remembers Holmes as a master of technique, but willing to let success speak for itself rather than insist that thing always be done his way. Tolmich recalls that Coach Holmes had pamphlets with sequential drawings showing the athlete how to perform the technical aspects of each track and field event. He also sold those pamphlets to other coaches. It was not unusual to find copies of one or more of Holmes's pamphlets posted in the locker rooms of competing teams. Even at an advanced age, Holmes demonstrated how to do each aspect of the athlete's event. Even so, Holmes was pragmatic about changes to techniques. By contrast, Lloyd Olds, the Michigan Normal College coach and AAU official was rigid. Allan Tolmich and Lloyd Olds did not like each other, because Tolmich changed the way the high hurdles were run and ignored Olds' advice. Olds was a stickler for proper form, but Tolmich felt that the techniques Olds taught were more appropriate for a taller man than for a short fellow like himself. Tolmich was one of the first hurdlers to attack the race as if it was a dash, and to make technique secondary to winning when they came into conflict.

When Tolmich ran, the hurdles were very heavy and hitting one definitely slowed the runner. According to the rules of the time, one could not be credited with a meet record for the hurdles if you hit a hurdle. "We still dug holes for starting—no starting blocks." The placement of spikes was different. "When I beat Forest Towns, he hit a hurdle, but I would have won anyway." "When I was in Japan I had special white track shoes made. When I went into the Army, I gave those shoes to Lorenzo Wright." "Most of the other hurdlers were much taller than I was."[74]

Tolmich frequently drove to Ann Arbor during the indoor season to work out on the hurdles at Yost Fieldhouse. University of Michigan track coaches Charles B. Hoyt and Ken Doherty often treated Al as if he was a Wolverine. It was not unusual for Tolmich to ride the train to meets with the Michigan squad when no other Wayne University athlete was invited to participate in the meet, which frequently occurred during the indoor season. When Coach Holmes could not be present at the NCAA meet in California in 1937 because of budget problems, Coach Hoyt kept Tolmich from over committing himself by participating in too many events.[75]

On May 27, 1938, fifty members of the Wayne University Campus Club held a tribute for Tolmich. Coach David L. Holmes was the principal speaker.[76] It was a fitting tribute to one of the best athletes in the school's history.

On July 3, 1939 William Henderson, a Wayne University trackman, won the hop, step, and jump (46–9½) at the National AAU Junior

Championships in Nebraska, to earn All-American honors. Walter Arrington of Michigan State College placed second in the hop, step, and jump and was fourth in the broad jump at that meet.[77]

Track and Medicine Were Wayne's Claim to Fame

Looking back on their years at Wayne, more than one former student recalled, "When I was a student at Wayne University, we all knew that our school was nationally known for two things: its medical school and its track team."[78]

In 1940 Coach David L. Holmes earned $6,600 as an Associate Professor. It was the same salary extended to the Assistant Dean of the College of Education, and nine hundred dollars more than paid to the Dean of the College of Law. He was one of the highest paid faculty members at Wayne, but he also was one of the longest tenured employees of the University. The average instructional salary at Wayne University in 1940 ranged from $1,600, for starting instructors, to $3000 per year for associate professors.[79]

In 1940 Coach Holmes again fashioned a championship mile relay team. This team featured Bob Grant, Charles Doan, Lin Wright, and Bob Wingo. Bob Grant was on the winning Cooley High School 880-yard relay team at the Detroit Metropolitan League Indoor at Central High School gym.[80] In 1940 he attended Wayne University, where he joined speedsters Charles Doan, Bob Wingo, Tom Adams and Bob Luby.

Bob Luby, the son of a Jewish clothing storeowner, was born in Hamtramck. His family moved to Detroit in 1921–22. After losing his clothing store in the depression, Bob's father became an insurance salesman. On May 10, 1936, the *Detroit Sunday Times*, recognized Bob Luby, the Central High runner, in its "Prep Hall of Fame," when he defeated Jim Knight in the hurdles in a duel meet with Hamtramck High School. Luby weighted only 132 pounds in high school and 146 pounds in college. During the summers, starting in 1936, he worked in summer camps for children.

Bob Luby recalls that during the indoor track season in 1938 or 1939 the Wayne University track team was booked into a hotel in Chicago. When they refused to accept Negro members of Wayne team, Coach Holmes moved the entire team to a hotel that would accept all of them.[81]

When Luby graduated from Wayne in 1940, he substituted in the Detroit Public Schools before being hired as a full time elementary school teacher at Detroit's Columbian Primary School for the fall of 1941. Bob entered the U. S. Army Airforce in 1942 and served as a first lieutenant until 1946, in the Convalescent Rehabilitation program in Sedalia, Missouri. In 1951, he became an assistant principal at Alger Elementary School, then was shifted to Franklin School where Aretha Franklin was one of his students. In 1962, Bob became Divisional Director of Health, Physical Education, and Athletics in the Detroit Public Schools. He served in that position, and was also an adjunct professor at Wayne State, the University of Detroit and Mercy College until 1983, when he retired to become Physical Education Director at Interlocken Camp for the Arts. Later, he became Director of Development [fund raising] at Interlocken.[82]

In mid-February 1940 Wayne University sent eleven men to the Illinois Relays, the University of Michigan sent twenty-eight men, Michigan Normal sent ten, and Michigan State sent eight.[83] Wayne University won the college mile relay, and Michigan Normal placed second in that event.[84] Wayne University, however, generally did poorly in dual meets. For example, Michigan Normal defeated Wayne 60–44.[85]

On March 2, 1940 the Wayne University Tartars had a small group of trackmen who were making an impression on the track world. Charley Doan, Don Ainsworth, Bob Luby, and Warner Pressman all eclipsed Fred Alderman's record in the 300-yard dash record at the Michigan State Relays. In addition, Wayne University's speedy combination of Bob Wingo, Willie Henderson, Bob Luby, and Tom Adams captured the 440-yard relay meet and the Jenison Fieldhouse record.[86] In early March 1940, for the first time in its history, Wayne University competed as a member of the Central Collegiate Conference. Holmes took an eight-man team to South Bend. Captain Charles Doan, Bob Grant, Lin Wright and Bob Wingo were entered in the mile relay. Tom Adams was entered in the 60-yard dash and the 65-yard high-hurdles, Ralph Betker in the shot put, Art Seigel in the 880 and Brennan Clark in the pole vault.[87]

On April 26–27, 1940 Wayne University won a special mile-relay [college division] race at the Penn Relays. Lacking in manpower, Coach David L. Holmes had his Tartar trackmen doing double and triple duty when Wayne opened its indoor season against a vastly superior Butler University team in Indianapolis.[88] Again they lost the dual meet.

On February 22, 1941 Bob Wingo, Linwood Wright, Robert Grant and Wayne Hatfield ran the sprint medley relay and the 880-yard relay at the AAU Senior Indoor Championships held at Madison Square Garden. The following year, they placed third in the sprint medley relay

(1:58) and were "also rans" in the one-mile relay at the National AAU Senior Indoor Championships. They won flight four of the college mile relays (3:18.5) at the Penn Relays, and on June, 20, 1942 won the mile-relay (3:18.7) at the National AAU Senior Championships, earning All-American status. Bob Wingo also placed fourth in the 400-meter run (48.1) at the National AAU Senior Outdoor Championships.

In 1942 indoor season, Coach Holmes scheduled Kalamazoo and Albion colleges in an effort to both contain costs and get some wins for his Tartars. In meets against these weak opponents a single good track athlete could rack up enough points to overcome the lack of depth. For example, against Albion College Bob Wingo won the 40, 220, and 440-yard sprints, ran on the relay team, and also placed second in the low-hurdles and third in the high jump to earn 24 points, 19 of them individually. Thus, even though Lin Wright had to miss the meet because of his part-time job, Wayne University chalked up a victory.[89] The absence of a key runner and similar disappointments were common at an urban, commuter college, like Wayne, and complicated the work of Coach Holmes.

Wayne University at a Time of Suburbanization

After the Second World War metropolitan Detroit changed rapidly. In 1943 the city had 119 movie theaters, by 1986 there were only six. In 1950 the population of the City of Detroit was 1,850,000. In 1980 the population was scarcely a million, and would fall below a million by the end of the century. In 1950 the City of Detroit housed more than half the population of the metropolitan area. By 1980 it housed less than one-fourth the metropolitan area's families.[90] Detroit's infrastructure grew old and its housing stock was neglected. Its ethnic neighborhoods broke up and its families of European stock moved to the suburbs. The once magnificent city became a huge slum, with Wayne State University at its center.

The movement to the suburbs was fueled by new, moderate priced housing financed by the Veteran's Administration, and movement by whites away from African-Americans. The GI Bill also opened new educational opportunities for Blacks to attend college. As a result, an increasing number of Wayne's track stars were African-Americans.

A Detroit Cass Technical High School graduate recalled that after training to be a pilot at the rigidly segregated Tuskegee Air Base, he served in Italy for the duration of the war in Europe. When he got back home after the war, the only job he could get was shoveling coal at the Ford Motor Company steam plant. It proved to be very hard work, and so he looked around for an alternative way to make a living. He decided to enroll at Wayne University using his GI Bill benefits.[91]

After the war, vets were a majority in the school at Wayne University. Many vets were admitted despite sometimes-mediocre high school grades. Nonetheless, they were serious students and did well after their war experiences. A third of the veterans enrolled between 1946 and 1950 were African-Americans.[92]

Racial Change in Detroit and Elsewhere

In 1948 five of the eleven Detroit Metropolitan League track coaches were individuals trained by David L. Holmes. Four had attended Wayne University, and the other was Carl Holmes, David's brother.[93] Jimmy Russell at Northwestern High School, Don Cooper at Cass Tech, Leroy Dues at Miller High School, George Cairn at Cooley, and Carl L. Holmes were the most consistent winners in the league. Only one of these coaches, Leroy Dues, was African-American.

The hard times of the previous two decades had made high school coaching an extremely stable occupation. With thousands of people out of work, uncertain paychecks, and low-wages the security of a public school position was highly prized. The eleven Detroit Public School Metro League coaches had served in their positions for an average of thirteen years. Six had been on the job more than ten years,[94] despite the fact that Metropolitan League prep track facilities, long woefully inadequate, were at a new low. As the *Detroit Times* put it in the spring of 1949, "The league's one good running track, at Denby Field, will be taxed to the limit in the next two weeks. All of this season's metro championship competition, East and West Side meets, City semifinals, and finals, have been relegated to the East Side school out of sheer necessity."[95]

In 1948, at the time when integration of the U. S. Armed Forces was about to begin by order of President Truman, "nearly 7,500 seniors received high school diplomas from Detroit Public Schools the week of June 21, 1948." Approximately 12% of them were African-American students.[96] That summer, when Hubert Humphrey was battling the "Dixiecrats" to place a civil rights plank in the Democratic Party Platform, Lorenzo Wright won an Olympic gold medal in London.

In 1948, the "gentlemen's agreement" among Big Ten coaches to bar blacks from playing basketball in the conference was finally lifted.[97] In 1948–49, the GI Bill allowed the droplets of African-American men attending college to expand to a trickle, but professional jobs available to Negroes were still extremely limited. Parents asked young men, "Why go to college? You can become a postman without going to college." But, at Wayne University, Robert Wingo, Leon Wingo, Lorenzo Wright, L. Brown Jackson, Irving Petross, Junior, Elmer "Buddy" Coleman, and Allan Tellis were running on the track team and preparing for professional careers. In 1946, when Irving Petross entered Wayne University, only 2.5% of the student body were African-American men.

Likewise, when black track star Aaron Z. Gordon graduated from the University of Michigan in the spring of 1952, he was one of only 14 African-American men out of a graduating class of 3,000. Less than .5% of the class was African-American. Only two of the 14 African-Americans were athletes. Gordon was one of only four blacks from Detroit to graduate from the University of Michigan in 1952.[98] The situation at the University of Michigan had not changed since 1924, when only eight of 1,456 students graduating from the University of Michigan were black.[99] Moreover, African-Americans found that President Truman's Executive Order to integrate the armed services was being resisted by many white military officers.

For example, when Captain Aaron Z. Gordon found himself the ranking officer overseeing track and field athletes on June 17, 1953, in Jackson, Mississippi, he was confronted with a whites-only party at the officer's club. Since such gatherings were forbidden by the President's Executive Order, Captain Gordon ordered the party halted and sent the party-girls home. This move was fraught with danger. Less than a month earlier, the Hot Springs (Arkansas) minor league baseball team had been forced to forfeit a game in Jackson, Mississippi, when they tried to play a Negro pitcher.[100] On the following day, Captain Gordon qualified for the All-Army European tour, but instead of flying to Europe, found himself shipped to the front lines in Korea, during the Korean War, for having the audacity to enforce Army Regulations. For all intents and purposes, these events ended Dr. Gordon's track career. He was awarded a Bronze Star in Korea.[101] These young, black men from Michigan colleges, however, were destined to be among the next generation of track coaches and school administrators in the Detroit Public Schools.

Between 1949 and 1961, the percentage of black teachers in the Detroit Public Schools increased from about 5% to 21%. In 1956, the State Athletic Director declared, "We have just closed one of the greatest school years in athletics we have ever known in the State of Michigan." African-American athletes like Hayes Wendell Jones (Pontiac

Aaron Z. Gordon was the only USA citizen who was part of the world record setting University of Michigan distance medley relay team on February 3, 1952 and again on April 19, 1952. *(Photo courtesy of Aaron Gordon)*

Central HS) and Paul Wesley Jones (Pershing HS) were setting records in the hurdle events, and would go on to impress the world with their athletic prowess and leadership skills.[102] Concurrently, future Detroit Public School teachers John Telford, Allan W. Tellis, Mark H. Smith, Jr. and Billy Smith were making track history at Wayne State University. By 1963, black students would make up a majority of the students in the Detroit Public Schools.[103]

It was during these years-when the civil rights movement was propelling the market for black professionals-that the future leaders of the school system were being recruited. The pool of black males available for these opportunities was small, and the opportunities for athletic coaches to become administrators was better than average, because coaches were often selected to be assistant principals to deal with the school's trouble makers. Trackmen were the highest profile members of the African-American teacher-coaches in the pool from which the next generation of school leaders was selected.[104] In the late 1950's and early 1960's, while they waited for their opportunity to coach and administer, thirty Detroit teachers and former college track stars ran as members of the Detroit Track Club.[105]

The appointment of Dr. Norman Drachler as superintendent of the Detroit schools in the summer of 1966 came at a time of great change and growing unrest for Detroit and its schools. Indeed, in 1967, the civic unrest erupted in civil disturbances.[106]

Upon becoming Superintendent of the Detroit Public Schools, Dr. Drachler increased teaching and administrative opportunities for African-Americans. He appointed African-Americans to two deputy superintendent positions, and set about the task of doubling the number of African-Americans in other administrative positions. At the end of the 1970–71 school year, Dr. Drachler announced his retirement when the voters of Detroit denied the property tax increases needed to improve the schools.[107] Rather than preside over the decline of public education in Detroit, he accepted a leadership position at the Institution for Education at Washington University in the nation's capital.

Wayne Track and Field at Peak Performance

In 1947 Lorenzo Wright placed second in the long jump at the NCAA Championships and the AAU Junior Championships. In 1948 Wright won the long jump at the New York Athletic Club Games, the AAU indoor championships, the Penn Relays, and placed third at the NCAA Championships and second in the AAU Senior Championships.

On March 19, 1949 Elmer "Buddy" Coleman set the meet record and tied the American record for 70-yard dash (7.0) in a duel meet with Illinois Tech.[108] The 1949 Wayne University mile-relay team was ranked second in the USA.[109]

Al Tellis, Coach of Champions

Most Wayne University trackmen, however, were ordinary young men just trying to make a better life than their parents. One such trackman was Allan W. Tellis. Allan was born on the West Side of Detroit, Michigan on November 23, 1928, at a time when Cass Technical High School graduate and track superstar Eddie Tolan was stirring the hearts of Detroiters with his track feats at the University of Michigan. Allan started running to the store for his mother when he was seven years old or so. He would tell his mother, "Mama, I want to show you how fast I am." Later, he showed his playmates his speed when he out ran them in races around the block and in games of catch the runner, where he particularly excelled in long distance chases. Allan also practiced boxing in his back yard while a student at Columbian Primary School.[110]

Allan's father was born in Georgia and moved to Detroit during the 1920s. During the depression Mr. Tellis worked on the Works Project Administration (WPA). Later he got a job with the Wayne County Drain Commission and became active in the labor movement. Allan's mother was also born in Georgia, but had been brought up in Springfield, Massachusetts. His parents met in about 1926 in downtown Detroit near what is now Greek town. Allan remembers his father as intelligent, but uneducated. During the 1940s his mother attended night school and earned high school diploma. Later in life she got an Associates Degree.

In elementary and high school, Allan was an adequate but indifferent scholar. All of his teachers were white. Nevertheless, they taught him pride in his race with stories about Paul Robeson, W. E. Du Bois, and other African-American role models. He and his sister attended McMichaels Junior High School for a time, but were asked to leave when his older sister got into a fight with another student. Al completed junior high school at Winger. When he entered 10th grade at Northwestern High School in the fall of 1944, Allan went out for track because all of his friends were involved in sports. His track coach, Mr. Russell, was a nice man who was supportive of his track athletes, but gave little, if any, advice on the techniques of running. Al particularly liked running indoors on the boards during the winter track season, but became discouraged when Cooley High School's track team dominated the City League track meets. He wanted to quite track, but his mother insisted that he stick with the sport, and in his senior year Northwestern High School won the West Side track championship.

In 1946, Tellis won a first in the Wayne Relays. On March 28, 1947 he took second place in the Detroit indoor championships at Central High. As a half miler, Al ran 2:05 indoors and as fast as 2:06 outdoors.

On May 16 he placed second in the 880-yard run (2:08) at the West Side Championships of the Detroit Metropolitan League.[111] Six days later Al placed second in the half-mile run (2:06.2) in the Metro-League championships.[112] He also ran a quarter-mile on Northwestern High's mile relay team.

As a high school senior Al dreamed of attending Michigan State College and becoming a State Highway Patrol Police Officer, but in those years those opportunities were rarely, if ever, open to African-Americans. He did not have the money nor the grades necessary to attend Michigan State and was not a super-jock destined to get an athletic scholarship. So, after graduating from high school Allan went to work at the Ford Motor Company Rougue Plant. He ran from his job to the plant gate every day to maintain his running skills. Finally, in January 1949 Allan Tellis entered Wayne University on probation status. Instead of keeping up on his schoolwork, he fell in love, ignored his schoolwork, and flunked out of Wayne. He returned to work at the Ford Motor Company, and joined the National Guard.

In May 1950 Al got married and took the U. S. Post Office examination. When the Korean War broke out in August 1950, his National Guard unit was called to active duty. Al, along with his friend, John Conyers Jr. who later became a U.S. Congressman, was sent to Fort Lewis in the State of Washington. Thanks to the intervention of Michigan Governor G. Mennen Williams, his Michigan National Guard unit was not sent to Korea like the other units being trained at Fort Lewis. Instead, they were shipped to Germany.

While at Fort Lewis, Al Tellis saw an opportunity to avoid combat duty by trying out for the boxing team. He had excellent reflexes and good boxing techniques, and made the team. Shortly after that, however, during a boxing match Al Tellis had his jaw broken in two places, and spent several months in the hospital recovering. En route to Germany, Al continued to train by skipping rope and exercising. His preparations paid off. When his unit got to Germany there was a notice of tryouts for the U.S. Army's European track team. Allan made the team as a quarter-miler. The spot on the track team qualified Al for assignment to the Special Services Branch, where he helped to operate the bar at a military service center. He worked under an African-American officer from Detroit, known to the enlisted men as "Cocky" Glover. While he was in Europe, his wife divorced him.

Al Tellis excelled in both boxing and in track during his Army tour in Europe. He ran in the open 200-meter and 220-yard races, the 400-

meter hurdles, and the mile relay. His quarter-mile time was 50 seconds. He qualified to run in the all-European championships in Rome in 1951, where his mile-relay team won. Jesse Owens met and complimented Al on his race. Al had his picture taken with Jesse handing him the Team Championship trophy.

When Al was discharged from the Army in 1952, he went to work at the U.S. Post Office. In those days in the black community, the Post-Office was known as the "grave yard of degreed men." Because there were so few opportunities for college educated African-American men, degreed blacks often ended up working for the Postal Service. Proud of their education, they urged Al, who they called "young blood," to get a college education and helped *pull his coat* on how to select college professors, to study, and prepare for tests. Carl Washington, a college educated mail handler who later became a dentist, was particularly helpful. In 1953 at the urging of his fellow Postal workers, Al returned to college part-time, on the GI Bill. This time, he was more diligent in his studies. Al met his second wife at Wayne and married her in 1954.

Al's journey through Wayne University was not an easy one. At first he worked full-time at the post-office. Then, in 1954 became a partner in a Shrimp Hut franchise, which prospered until 1956 when it was doomed by over expansion. He also ran on the track team. In 1956 he was one of the team's leading broad jumpers.[113] His schedule was not conducive to high academic achievement. Nonetheless, Allan struggled through Wayne's College of Education, and made a significant contribution to the track team. In 1957, he was elected co-captain of the track team, ran in the Penn Relays, and did well in major college track meets throughout the mid-west. Coach David L. Holmes was an inspiration to Al, and contributed to his determination to graduate from college.

In violation of university recommendations, Al tried to student teach and work full time. This did not sit well with his student teacher supervisor, and he was pulled out of his first student teaching assignment. Drs. Russell and Mulhouser gave him a stern lecture and reassigned him to another school. To his surprise, his new student teacher-supervisor was "Cocky" Glover. This did not turn out as well as expected. Glover held his own prejudices, and gave Al a "C" in student teaching. Despite his anger, at what he believed to be a lower grade than he deserved, Tellis handled the situation with temperance and good judgement. This later allowed him to achieve his goal of obtaining a teaching certificate. In 1958 Al received his B. A. Degree, but was not issued a teaching certificate.

In 1959 and 1960 Mr. Tellis served as a volunteer assistant track coach under Lorenzo Wright at Detroit's Eastern High School. In 1963 Tellis resigned his position with the Post Office and took a position as a teacher with Wayne County Juvenile Home, and also began substitute teaching for the Detroit Public Schools. These experiences significantly improved Tellis' teaching skills. He related well with students and his high energy made him popular in the classroom. In 1964 he was asked to teach at the Moore School for [Delinquent] Boys. During this period of time, Mr. Tellis worked on his master's degree in education at Wayne State. In 1964 Dr. Russell approved his teaching certification. When he spoke to Dr. Russell he was told, "If you had asked me to sign this years ago, I would have refused to sign it." This experience taught Tellis the value of not burning his bridges. While teaching would later pay adequately, in 1964 more than half of all male teachers were forced to hold a second job, at least in the summers, to make ends meet.[114]

In the fall of 1965, Allan accepted a position at Burbank Primary School, which had only two black students. When he allowed the black students to square dance with white partners in gym class, the Principle called him into his office and told Mr. Tellis that "We rednecks don't like this sort of thing. I've asked the Board of Education to transfer you." Fortunately for Tellis, an old track buddy of his, Lorenzo C. Wright, received the transfer request, and Fred Martin, the Elementary Supervisor, assigned Tellis to Condon Junior High School, where he taught from early 1966 until 1970. Lorenzo Wright's wife was a close friend of Allan Tellis' sister. The two had been friends from early grade school onward, and Al Tellis had cautioned Lorenzo about her volatile temper before his marriage to her. In 1970, shortly before his death, Lorenzo Wright appointed Allan Tellis track coach at Pershing High School in Detroit.

While coach at Pershing High School, Tellis won three State Regional Boys Track Championships. He also coached a winning mile relay team that ran 3:19.5 at the National Indoor meet held in Cobo Hall. In 1972 this team was the first high school team in Michigan to break 3:20 outdoors at that distance. He restarted girl's track in the Detroit Public Schools, won the City Girl's Outdoor Championships in 1976, and placed second in the State Championships that year. Moreover, he produced three world class track stars in Darnell Hall, who won a gold medal in the Olympics; Ella Willis, who was a State Champion and an outstanding college runner; and Wendy Truvillion, six times All-American at Louisiana State University. When he retired the first time in 1993, he was a respected teacher and coach, whose track stars always did well academically and were good role models and community representatives.

George Gaines, Acting Director of Health

George Gaines was born on January 24, 1930 in Biloxi, Mississippi. In 1930, Harrison County was in the depths of economic depression, and there were few good jobs for Negroes in Biloxi, a Gulf coast town of 15,000 souls. Although his parents were not Catholic, his aunts and uncles were, and, at their urging, George was baptized at Our Mother of Sorrow Catholic Church. In 1932 the Gaines family took the Louisville and Nashville Railroad north, and ended up on the West Side of Detroit. George's father found a job as a waiter, and at age five George attended Wineg Primary School.[115]

George was not a good student and did not keep up with his classmates. He failed second grade and was later retained a half year in fourth grade as well. He also fell in with the wrong crowd and began getting into trouble. In 1943 when he was in sixth grade, George stole an automobile, was arrested, and spent a night in jail. The court placed George on probation and assigned his case to a probation officer. The social worker assigned to George's case made an indelible impression on him with his non-judgmental support and positive direction, and ultimately led directly to his decision to go to college to become a social worker.

In hopes of getting his son headed in a better direction, George's father, who was now a defense worker at the Ford Rouge Plant, made arrangements to send his son to Saint Benedict, a Moor Catholic boarding school in Milwaukee. It was a wise decision. The new circle of friends, smaller classes, and strict supervision had a beneficial effect. During the three years George spent at Saint Benedict, he improved his grades and began to participate in sports. He did particularly well in wrestling.

In 1946, George returned to school in Detroit as a freshman at Northwestern High School. He went out for football, but was too small to play and was cut the first day of practice. George noticed the cross-country team training, so joined that group. It turned out to be a good match. He enjoyed long-distance running and did well in cross-country. He and Stan Fields were an important part of the Northwestern

High School cross-country team that won three straight city champi-onships, against such fine runners as Miller High School's Aaron Z. Gordon. Stan won the City cross-country championship and George was fifth in the fall of 1948. George also lettered three years as a miler in track.

Track kept George Gaines out of trouble and headed him toward col-lege. Supportive parents, good role models, and strong spiritual roots were helpful, but he believes that it was the success and camaraderie experienced in track and field that was the mortar that kept it all together. His grades continued to be below average for a college bound student, and it was not until he was a senior in high school that he began to study seriously.

According to the 1949 *Northwester*, his high school's yearbook, "Georgie Gaines is one of those rare individuals whose personality is so pleasing that he is seemingly without an enemy. This good thing in a small package led the track team to victory as their capable captain, served as an officer of the "N" Club, held membership on the Class Day Committee, and offered his literary ability as a Colt staff member." George's track teammates included Stan McConner, Billy Smith, Allan Tellis, and Stan Fields.

When George graduated from high school in January 1949, 58% of his graduating class was African-American, but there was only one black teacher in the school. Despite raising his grade considerably in his sen-ior year, they were so marginal that he was denied admission to several colleges. Only his track skills and the influence of his father's friends, who prevailed on the admission's committee at Adrian College to give the young man a break, gained his admittance to college on probation.

Attending Adrian College, as a freshman, was once again the right decision. Small classes and the personal attention provided by the school's professors were extremely helpful to George's academic growth. In particular, an English teacher tutored him enough to gain the skills necessary to pass college English. She taught him to write essay tests and academic papers, vital skills that he lacked. His success as a distance runner continued at Adrian College, and now that he had established that he could do college level academic work, he was given a track scholarship at Wayne University.

In 1950, David L. Holmes, the track coach at Wayne University, was one of the best college track coaches in America and one of the few who took a personal interest in Detroit athletes. Despite the absence of a credible indoor track, or even a first class outdoor track, year in and year out Wayne University had some of the best track athletes in the country. George Gaines became an important part of the Wayne University track program from 1950 through the spring of 1953, when he graduated. When George first met with Coach Holmes, the Coach told him that "Running is the most natural thing a man can do." Holmes kept meticulous records on each runner. He knew what their spit times were and how they could best improve their times. He devised an individual training program for each of his runners.[116]

In 1950 George placed second in the two-mile run in a dual meet against the Bowling Green University freshmen.[117] The 1953 *Griffin*, the Wayne University yearbook, referred to George as "one of [the school's] top performers." He ran a half-mile leg on the two-mile relay team, a three-quarter mile leg on the distance medley team, and the one-mile and two-mile individual races. The two-mile run was his best event. An appearance in the Penn Relays in 1953 was one of the highlights of his track career. George was awarded three letters in both cross-country and track.

After graduating from Wayne University with a degree in Social Work, George was drafted by the U.S. Army, where he ran as a half miler for the First Army Track Team from 1953 until his discharge in 1955. His interest in and support of track and field competition continued for more than forty-five years.

After his discharge from the Army, George began his social work career at the Children's Aid Society of Detroit, and in 1957 was hired into the Tuberculosis Unit of the Wayne County Department of Social Services. In 1959 George began work on a Masters Degree in Social Work at Wayne State University. He completed his MSW in 1963, after serving an internship as a Psychiatric Social Worker at Wayne County General Hospital's Psychiatric Unit. In 1961 George was assigned to the Herman Kieffer Tuberculosis Hospital to assist in closing down the TB sanitarium, which was made obsolete by the discovery of isoniocin, which made ambulatory treatment of tuberculosis possible. George continued at this assignment until 1965, when Norbert Reinstein recruited him, as a program planner for the Wayne County Tuberculosis and Health Society. In the meantime, the civil rights movement was developing, and George became active in it. During that period he also became a health planner for Heart, Cancer and Stroke with the Wayne State University Medical School, a position he held until 1968.

In 1968 Murray Jackson, the founding President of Wayne County

Community College, hired Mr. Gaines. Murray and George had been friends, roommates and members of the Adrian College Track team in 1949, and now Murray was calling on an old friend to put together the health section of the new community college. It was a wonderful opportunity and George took full advantage of it. While working for the Community College, George became politically active with State Senator Coleman Young, a high school drop out who became active with the United Auto Workers and parlayed his labor union activism into a seat in the state legislature. As one of only a handful of African-American politicians in Michigan at that time, Coleman Young was a natural magnet for a young activist like George Gaines, who was now sporting an Afro hair style. George advised Coleman Young on health policy and worked on his campaigns.

When Coleman Young was elected Mayor of Detroit in 1973, George Gaines was appointed Deputy Director of the City of Detroit Health Department on September 16, 1974. Mayor Young specifically asked Gaines to oversee the substance abuse programs and to find alternatives to methadone maintenance for treating the growing number of African-Americans being addicted to hard drugs. To perform this task, Mr. Gaines enrolled in the University of Michigan School of Public Health, and in 1980 was awarded a Masters Degree in Public Health. On two occasions George Gaines was interim director of the City Health Department, and ran the Department for more than two years, albeit without the title. In 1992 he retired from the Health Department and became Executive Director of Detroit Central City Community Mental Health, Inc. George retired from that position in the summer of 1997, but remained active with the Detroit Blazers Track Club, where his daughter was a middle distance runner.[118]

"Bullet" Billy Smith

Billy Smith, five-foot, four inch sophomore at Northwestern High School was unbeaten in the high and low-hurdles in 1948.[119] According to the *Northwester, 1949*, "Speedy Bill Smith is a good thing in a small package. Smitty is a hurdles champ on the track team. He was on the football team, in the "N" Club, and his plans for the future also include an athletic career. Ambitious Billy will surely succeed with his wholesome manner and determined way."

The "half-pint" speedster attended Wayne University in the fall of 1949, and in the spring of 1950 Coach Holmes had a promising freshmen track team. Billy Smith had set the Detroit Metropolitan High School League record in the 880-yard relay (1:31.4) at the City Championships in 1948.[120] In 1949, as a high school senior, he had won the 120-yd low-hurdles (13.6) and the 120-yard high hurdles (15.4) championships in the Detroit Metropolitan League, despite an injured back.[121]

In a dual meet with the Bowling Green University freshmen in May 1950 Billy demonstrated his potential. He won the 100-yard dash (10.5), the 220-yard dash (23.5), the 120-yard high hurdles (16.7), and the broad jump (20' 3¾") and placed second in the 220-yard low-hurdles.[122] Billy's freshman class at Wayne included Walter Jenkins, George Gaines, and McCarty. On May 9 these four spearheaded a sound thumping of the Bowling Green frosh runners in Ohio, 83½ to 43½.[123]

It should be noted that the Wayne University and Bowling Green track teams were fairly even at that time. In 1948 the Wayne University freshmen defeated the Bowling Green University freshmen 79 to 52.[124] But in 1949 the B G freshmen beat the Wayne freshmen 72 to 49.[125] The 1950 Wayne freshmen team, however, never led to a great varsity squad. In 1951 Billy Smith placed third in the 60-yard dash at the Purdue Relays, won the 100-yard dash (10.4) and the 220-yard dash (22.5) at the Conference Championships in Peoria, and placed second in the broad jump (23–1) at the Central Collegiate Conference Open Meet in Milwaukee.

After his sophomore year at Wayne, Billy Smith joined the Army and did not return to school until 1956. While he was gone, Walter Jenkins concentrated on football and became a professional football player rather than the great track star he had the talent to become. Gaines and McCarty contributed but never starred as track athletes. Once in the Army, Billie won the 200-meter dash (21.3) at the All-Army European Championships in Nuremberg, West Germany in the fall of 1951.

In the summer of 1956 Billy Smith completed his enlistment and that fall returned to Wayne State University. In 1956 he set the unofficial world, indoor record for the 65-yard low hurdles (7.1) at the Central Collegiate Indoor Championships in Ypsilanti. In early April 1956 Billy missed a track meet at Central Michigan College, and had plans to leave college to help his family.[126] The incident was apparently the manifestation of a mood swing, and Coach Holmes helped Billy work through the situation. Two weeks later, Billy was on the winning the

880-yard relay team (1:27.2 wind aided) at the Ohio Relays, and ran at the Penn Relays, with less success.

"Bullet" Billy frequently won the dash events in Wayne's dual meets, and on December 28, 1957 he won the 60-yard low-hurdles (7.0) and placed second in the 220-yard dash (22.6) at the Chicago Holiday Meet held at University of Chicago Fieldhouse. Billy Smith graduated from Wayne State University in 1957.

He continued to run in 1958 as part of the Detroit Track Club. On January 11, 1958 Billy was second in the 220-yard dash (22.4) at the Chicago Invitational. In February his relay team was second in the Swedish 1,060-yard relay (1:57.1) at the Millrose Games, and earned a spot on a special National AAU team toured Asia. He won the 100-meter dash (10.9) and the 200-meter dash (21.6) at the Third Asian Games at Meiji Park in Tokyo, Japan. He also ran at the Malaya Games.[127]

During the 1960s Billy Smith became special education teacher and coach at Southwestern High School in Detroit. Before long, however, he experienced mental health problems, and self medicated with alcohol. After several difficult years, his wife left him. In the late 1960s, according to Bob Luby, his supervisor, Billie Smith had to be relieved from his coaching duties because he was unstable and, as a result, was not a good coach.[128] He ended up an addict at Harbor Light, and died of stroke and kidney failure on February 14, 1990 at age 50.[129]

Mark Smith, National Champion

Coach Holmes saw Mark Smith playing pick-up basketball at the Wayne University gymnasium and talked him into trying high jumping, and the long jump. Mark high jumped at a time when the landing areas were treacherous. He would often drop from a height of nearly seven feet onto sand or thinly padded concrete surfaces. As a result, Mark was plagued with hip and back injuries, and suffered from inconsistent results particularly in late season.

The NCAA adopted a new rule in 1936 to determine winners for the high jump and pole vault. These rules stated: "the competitor with the lower number of failures at the tying height shall be placed ahead of the competitor with a higher number of failures. If the tie still remains, the competitor with the lower total of failures until having cleared the tying height shall be placed ahead of the competitor with a higher total. If the tie remains, the competitor with the lower total of attempts until having cleared the tying height shall be placed ahead of the competitor with the higher total."[130]

On June 20, 1953 in Lincoln, Nebraska at the NCAA Finals, "Mark Smith, the big, green-clad Negro from Wayne (missed at 6–4 and 6–5) . . . scrambled over on his third effort. . . . Smith cleared 6' 8¼" on his third try. At 6' 9⅛" Smith nearly made it on his third try." He tied for the Championship with two others.[131] In 1953 he was named to the NCAA All-American team in high jump.[132] Mark taught health and physical in elementary school in Detroit Public Schools from 1956 until the summer of 1962. He received an MA degree at Wayne in 1962. From 1962 through 1968 Mark was a principal in the Highland Park Public Schools. In 1970 he earned a Ph. D. at Ohio State University in 1970 and was on the faculty of Wayne State University for 26 years. Dr. Smith became Associate Dean and Professor College of Education at Wayne State, and was inducted into the school's Hall of Fame in 1979.

Mark Smith once confided that he never heard Coach Holmes raise his voice or swear at an athlete.

He had a way of requesting that you do things in a way that made you want to run into brick walls to please him. He was a real gentleman. He wasn't at all political, and had a strict belief in British style amateurism. If he had been more political we probably would have had better athletic facilities, but I cannot fault him for his strongly held beliefs. He gave me more support than anyone except my parents. I have the utmost respect for Coach Holmes. I remember when Coach Holmes and I went to the National NCAA meet in Lincoln. It was very hot in Nebraska that June. We were having breakfast in the hotel coffee shop, when Don Canham came by our table and after saying his hellos, told us how hot it was outside, and expressed his concerns about how hard it would be to compete in the unseasonably hot weather. When Canham left, Coach Holmes leaned over to me and said, 'Don't pay any attention to him son. He's just trying to psych you out, to give his high jumper an advantage.' I am proud to say that Coach Holmes would never think of stooping to such a tactic.[133]

Unrealized Potential

Cliff Hatcher was born in Detroit on August 4, 1932, and grew up on Inverness Street in Pilgrim Village in the northwest area of the city. He attended Longfellow Primary School, Durfee Middle School, and Central High School. Cliff was one of only twenty or so black students at the predominately Jewish Central High School. His dad was legally blind and collected welfare. His mother worked as a maid. He had a twin brother, Clarence, who could not run, but was an All-City football player. Both boys weighed about 145 pounds in those years. Cliff found school studies easy—and English particularly easy, but usually did not study enough to get good grades. He was too busy acting like "Billy Big

Time," the school hero, to study. Cliff was on the basketball team, the cross-country team, and the track team. He referred to himself and his brother as "the poorest kids to attended Central High School in those years."

Cliff became interested in track when he was in junior high school. He loved baseball, but couldn't throw accurately. On the other hand, running was easy. It was natural, and he could run like the wind. He decided that if he wanted a future in sports, it would be in track rather than baseball or football. When Cliff was fourteen years old, he could already beat Central High's star sprinter, Alphonzo Sparks.

When he entered Central High in the autumn of 1948, he became one of the best runners on the cross-country team. He was All-City in cross-country all three years in high school, and as a senior broke the City record when he came in second in the City cross-country championships, three seconds behind the winner. In the spring of 1949, he was the school's half-miler and lost only one race—he came in second in the All-City meet, held May 26. The winner that day had a time of 2:02.2. He was undefeated in the half-mile his junior and senior years in high school, when he won a Metropolitan West Side meet on May 16, 1950 in 2:04.[134] He followed up the next day with a qualifying time for the City meet of 2:00.9.[135] He won the West Side finals in 2:00.6 on May 19,[136] before becoming the City Champion in the 880 on a blustery May 25 with a time of 2:01.6.[137]

As a senior at Central High School, Cliff started running the quarter mile so that he could compete on the relay team. On May 16, 1951, the lanky youngster with a smooth stride unofficially broke the City League record for the 440-yard run held by Stan McConner. He posted a blistering 49.4 in a triangular meet held at Sawyer Field. He also anchored the Central 880-yard relay team to a win and broad jumped 20–11.[138] On May 26 Cliff won the 880-yard run at the Wayne Relays.[139] On June 5, at Denby Field during the City Meet Preliminaries, Cliff won the quarter mile with a new City and state record (48.8).[140] Days later, he anchored the Central High 880-yard relay team to a second place finish in the City Championships, and won the 440 with a time of 49.2.[141]

When he graduated in 1951, Clifford Hatcher was a high school All-American in the 440. His time for the 440-yard dash was the fourth best scholastic time in the nation, and the best performance times in Michigan times were generally among the top five in the nation in nearly every event.[142] Several colleges recruited Cliff, but his low grades were a handicap. Cliff also was uncomfortable about leaving town, because of his girl friend, so he went to Wayne. His high school coach never once talked to him about going to college or things to consider when making a choice. When he entered Wayne University in the fall of 1951, Coach Holmes took the cross-country team to a resort on Manitoulin Island, Ontario, in Lake Huron to train. At that camp, Cliff pulled a hamstring and missed the entire cross-country season.

Normally a shy person, Cliff joined a fraternity. It helped him socially, but distracted from his studies. "I lived on the edge. I looked like I was a playboy, but I was a sick kid—I felt so much pressure to do well and I was not prepared for any of it." He dropped out of school. In the spring of 1952 Eddie Tolan came to Cliff's house in an attempt to help prepare Cliff to qualify for the Olympic tryouts. Eddie took Cliff to meet his mother and attempted to get Cliff in shape for the Olympic try-outs, but Cliff just could not focus on the task. Cliff later recalled, "I was mentally screwed up at the time." [143]

In the fall of 1952, Cliff returned to Wayne University. But, after the cross-country season, he dropped out of school for a year and a half. In 1953, when he was twenty-one years old, Cliff married his eighteen year old sweetheart and finally returned to school in the fall of 1954, still more interested in partying than in his education. When running on the small indoor track at Wayne University, he hit a corner of a wall and injured his leg badly. He became depressed, and attempted suicide. He took whole box of aspirins, slashed his own arm, stopped eating, and gave up on his marriage. After ten days in the psychiatric-ward at Detroit Receiving Hospital, Cliff dropped out of school again. "After going through a living hell," Cliff later reported, "I learned about how Bob Richards, the Olympic pole-vaulter who was on a national tour for Wheaties breakfast cereal, had busted up his left leg and had returned to competition. It motivated me to make a comeback."

In 1954 Cliff met college freshman, John Telford. In 1955 they ran together on Wayne's 880-yard and mile relay teams. On February 26 Cliff placed second in the 440-yard dash in a duel meet with Central Michigan College.[144] He also excelled in the 880.[145] In 1956, Cliff and John became roommates on the road and best friends. While John never had the natural ability given to Cliff, Telford had a strong work ethic and an inner drive that made him one of the best quarter-milers in the world. Telford, Hatcher, and Billy Smith made their mile relay team a consistent threat to set a track record, and John Telford became a NCAA Track All-American in 1957.

Cliff met Barbara Harris in 1957. She brought stability to his life. He married Barbara in 1962, they had two children, and he went on to be a business success. Although he did not finish college, in 1965 Cliff went into partnership in the haberdashery business with an old Jewish friend from high school. Over an eight-year period they came to own three stores, but, in 1972, they experienced financial problems that put them out of business. In 1980 Cliff purchased a storefront and started a party store. He later sold that business.

At the end of the century Cliff owned a home just a few houses away from where his mother was once a maid, was happily married for more than 35 years, and was an active member of the Lutheran Church, where he was a Church elder for a number of years. His daughter had a Master's Degree from the University of Michigan and managed a day care center. His son also was a college graduate and a success.

Cliff knew that he was a natural runner with extraordinary talent. "It was never really work for me, but I'm sorry to say I'm the man who never really ran his best race." Nevertheless, he was proud to have been a trackman at Wayne University.[146]

Fleeting Fame

John Perry Telford was born in Detroit on January 25, 1936. He was raised in a frame house in a poor, inner-city neighborhood. His mother had a two-year degree, and was a kindergarten teacher. She later completed a BA degree. His hard-drinking father had been born in Scotland, and worked in coal mining and metal fabricating when he was not fighting as an unranked welterweight. Well past his prime when John was born, "Scotty" Telford did not want to be a father, and expressed his views loudly, particularly when he was drunk. His drinking resulted in irregular employment, and forced John's mother to provide much of the family's financial support. Nevertheless, as an adult John often idealized his youth and his father's role in his life, recalling that "his father brought home KO Morgan, a champion Scottish pugilist, and knew Gordie Howe, who achieved immortality down the block on the Olympia's ice."

John was often left alone during his elementary school years, and was frequently isolated. When he showed an early interest in playing the violin, he was teased and found himself in fights to defend his interest in a "sissy" musical instrument. While he showed an early interest in reading and story telling, he also had a propensity to talk to his neighbors in school and to misbehave during air raid drills and the like.

John Telford, 1957 All-American, 440 yard dash. *(Photo: Wayne State University pubicity, courtesy of John Telford)*

John also had difficulty focusing on his schoolwork. Meanwhile, at home John was rarely given encouragement by his father, who abused him.

High School friend, Hiram Badia, reported that John was well liked by his peers at Denby High School, was a good student, and worked hard to achieve success in track. However, John's home life was far from normal. Hiram declared:

I wouldn't have changed parents with him for a million dollars. My dad helped teach me how to work with tools and fix things around the house. His father either belittled him or ignored him. Sometimes his father would ask me to fix something at their house, and he would make John sit and watch me while he berated John for being so stupid and awkward. I was so embarrassed for John that I avoided his father so John wouldn't be put in that position. There was none of the love and caring we had in our family. I think John's father hit him sometimes and almost never give him any encouragement.[147]

Yet, John appeared to seek his dead father's approval when he argued,

Nothing is more dramatic than an individual sport. They're more visceral than team sports. Boxing and quarter-miling exemplify life's struggle. I know because I ran 206 races, winning 174, most of them quarter mile sprints. I rank quarter miling with boxing because it's as far as the human body was built to sprint full out, and there is an element of art within that race. The art is to encounter the tape at the threshold of unconsciousness. It's unlike the 100-yard dash where natural talent is primary. In the quarter mile you have to know precisely what you're doing. A man without superior talent can still win by knowledge of pace, willingness to accept pain, strategy, and will.[148]

John's track career began in 1952 during his junior year at Denby High School, after being asked to leave Northwestern High School, due to a disciplinary infraction. At Denby, John ran the 100-yard dash in 10.4, the 220-yard dash in 22.5, and the 440 in 57. His personal best in the quarter-mile in high school was 51.3.[149] He also was the lead off runner on the school's medley relay team that won the East Side Detroit Metropolitan League Championship. John turned loneliness and sadness into a determination to prove himself—to succeed. Track helped to establish self-esteem and some measure of confidence. While John's track accomplishments in high school were noteworthy, they were not outstanding.[150] Coach Holmes was the only college coach to show an interest in him and offer John a track scholarship when he graduated from Denby High School in January 1954.

It was at Wayne University that John learned the discipline that allowed him to excel and to accomplish All-American status. Coach David L. Holmes became John's surrogate father, giving him the direction, recognition, and support he did not get from his real father. Although John was not a gifted runner, his determination and will to succeed were so strong that under the expert tutelage of Coach Holmes, he became one of the best quarter-milers in the world. His African-American teammates became his friends and support system, and John finally received the recognition he had longed for his entire life. Driven and energized by childhood difficulties and powered by a fine mind, John established bonds while on the track team at Wayne University that compelled him to risk all to stand with minorities, the underdog, the oppressed, and the friendless—all of whom he identified with himself. Success in track salvaged his life.

When Coach Holmes died at the age of 72, John later wrote:

> I was devastated and grieved heavily to the point of emotional disorientation, when my old friend and mentor died suddenly of a heart attack. I was scheduled for an invitational 440 on the West Coast, but stayed at home to serve as a pallbearer, along with Billy Smith and several other Holmes athletes. I agreed with Billy, when he said, 'I feel like my father died.'[151]

In 1955 John Telford began to distinguish himself as a Wayne University quarter-miler. Just three weeks before Bowling Green University was designated as one of the emergency medical bases for Toledo in case of a hydrogen bomb attack,[152] Telford won three events in a dual meet against the Bowling Green thinclads on the Whittaker field track 24 miles south of Toledo. On May 3, John won the 440-yard dash (49.0), the 880-yard relay (1:31.5), and the mile relay (3:25.7). Outstanding performances by Telford, Cliff Hatcher and Mark Smith were not enough to win the meet for Wayne University. They lost to the Bowling Green Falcons, who racked up eight first place wins and plenty of second and third place showings, primarily in the distance races, hurdles, and field events.[153]

The obstacles to success in track at Wayne University during the 1950s were daunting. The training facilities were virtually non-existent; the travel budget continued to be limited, and the college and community support was meager. Budgetary problems frequently complicated travel arrangements. For example, when the Wayne track team was scheduled to participate in a triangular meet on Saturday, February 25, 1956 in Mt. Pleasant, Michigan, they were unable to stay overnight because of the cost, so were obliged to travel to the meet by bus in an ice storm. Road conditions caused the team to arrive at the meet late. Wayne missed the first three events and was forced to compete without warming up. Nevertheless, John won the two events in which he was entered. Overall the team, however, did not fare as well.[154]

After placing second in the 440 (47.8) at the Central Collegiates and breaking Wayne University's varsity record in that event, Telford and

Coach Holmes flew to Berkeley, California in 1956 where John participated in the NCAA outdoor championships. He ran a 47.8 400-meter in the preliminaries, but he pulled a hamstring that ended his season in the semifinals.[155]

In 1957 John reached the pinnacle of his track career. The breakthrough came on February 16, 1957 when he won the 600-yard run at the Michigan State Relays at Jenison Fieldhouse in East Lansing. It was the first time that John had won a major meet against nationally ranked competition. However, even at the start of the outdoor track season, Telford was not listed among the top ten contenders in the quarter-mile. Yet, he steadily improved during the course of the season and he qualified for the NCAA finals in Austin, Texas, at the Central Collegiates in Milwaukee. In Texas, he surprised the track world by finishing second in the 440-yard dash, to become only the third Wayne University All-American following World War II. In those years only the first three place winners at the NCAA Championships were considered for All-American honors.

On June 22 he followed up his NCAA coup by finishing second to Reggie Pearman, a 33-year old New York City junior high school teacher, and defeating Olympic Champion Charley Jenkins for the second time in eight days. It was the most important race of John's life, because the first three place winners would have the opportunity for international competition. The *Track and Field News* called the meet at Dayton High School stadium in Ohio "the poorest National AAU meet in many years" because of inadequate officiating.[156] While Telford ran a superb race before 6,721 fans at the National AAU, his performance in the 440-yard dash was clouded by mismeasured lanes that caused the outcome to be disputed. At the halfway mark, Telford stormed along with Pearman and Charley Jenkins in a battle for the lead. John made a determined bid to match Pearman's closing burst, but he did not quite make it.[157] Some claimed, "This event should be declared no contest. As the race was actually run, the nine finalists ran around 2 curves from staggered starts . . . The staggers were wrong. Each runner in the race ran about 4 feet less than the man on his left. Reggie Pearman ran only 432 yards." Telford ran 430 yards and 2 feet, according to Cordner Nelson in *Track and Field News*, July, 1957.[158]

The *Track and Field News* evaluation of the race with all contestants running 440-yards placed Telford's time at 47.6 rather than 46.5 and put him in third place rather than second place. "One wag said, 'This is the first time in history that the AAU was conducted on a handicap basis.'" Nevertheless, Telford had a good season in 1957. That year, he logged one of the six fastest quarter-mile times (46.8) in the world.[159] John was declared an All-American by *Track and Field News*, who ranked him fourth in the USA in the 440.[160] Telford also was named to the NCAA 1957 All-America track team for the 440-yard dash.[161] David Owen, Ira Murchison and John Telford were the only Michigan track athletes on the world's best list for 1957.

While on the Amateur Athletic Union's European track tour, John Telford met Pope Pious XII at a private audience held for the United States team. Telford ran in Milan, Turin, and Ancona, Italy, and Lisbon, Portugal.[162]

In 1958 John Telford ran on the relay team with Jim Bibbs and Irving Petross that was second in the sprint medley relay [1,060-yards] (1:57.1) at the National AAU Senior Indoor Championships at Madison Square Garden. On May 30 he won the 440-yard dash (47.8) at the Michigan AAU Meet in Kalamazoo, and the 440-yard dash (48.6) at the Tri-State AAU Open in Fort Wayne two weeks later. He ended the year by winning the 600-yard run at Chicago Holiday meet on December 26.

On February 14, 1959 Telford won the 600-yard run (1:14.4) at the Junior National AAU Indoor Championships held at the University of Chicago fieldhouse. On June 14, 1960 Rex Cawley, representing the Detroit Athletic Club, defeated John, Detroit Track Club, in the 440-yard dash at the Dearborn Athletic Club Meet. Rex ran the quarter-mile in 46.8, and Telford ran the distance in 47.0.[163] In 1960 John was advised by physicians to discontinue running because of an acute case of asthma. He nevertheless tried a comeback in 1961, but failed to establish himself again as a world-class sprinter. In 1963 John was an assistant track coach at Southeastern High School in Detroit, where he helped to develop George Wesson.[164]

During his active years as a runner, All-American John Telford won 174 races. He was the runner-up in the 440-yard dash in the NCAA and AAU outdoor meets, competed on an American AAU team in Europe, and won the National Junior AAU Indoor Championship in the 600-yard run.[165] These were amazing achievements for a poor inter-city kid attending a commuter college. He ranks among the top 100 track and field athletes in the State's history and the top seven in the history of Wayne State University and its predecessor schools.

Telford taught and was assistant track coach, to Nick Cheolas, at Southeastern High School in Detroit from 1960–63. He also taught and was head track and cross-country coach at Finney High School in Detroit, while earning an Ed. D. at Wayne State University.[166] From

1970–72, John was Dean of Basic Education, Macomb County Community College.

In 1974 "Dr. John Telford, director of athletics for Berkley Schools, received special recognition for officiating in the NCAA track meets for 10 consecutive years."[167] After working in Berkley and Walled Lake, Telford became Assistant Superintendent at the Rochester Public Schools.

As Assistant Superintendent of the Rochester Public Schools, he integrated and promoted ethnic diversity within the faculty and administration of this large upper-middle class community. He also made the school curriculum friendlier to the Asian and other non-Christian minorities moving into parts of the school district. Furthermore, he expressed concern about the possible consequences of public gun policies on public school safety. In January 1990 Telford became embroiled in controversy when, for the third straight year, he pondered the future of public education in Rochester and published his opinions in a planning document he referred to as "Telford's Telescope." A part of John's difficulty was that he reproduced and distributed the "Telescope" with the Rochester Community School's logo and the names of the Board members, without the Board's consent or knowledge of its content. This difficulty was compounded by the openly liberal views he expressed in this politically conservative, suburban community. Among his most controversial comments were his Madisonian declarations that "certain rights cannot be trusted to a hoped-for fair-mindedness in ethnocentric residential enclaves with a very few minority-group members, and to the majoritarian impulses of governmental and other public officials."

A parent complained, "Telford expresses contempt for anyone who disagrees with him, anyone who hunts, anyone who still believes in a strong national defense, all Republican presidents of this century, and presumably the 90 percent of this community who voted for them."[168]

Dr. Telford retired from the Rochester Public Schools in 1992, but continued to teach in the Departments of Education at Oakland and Wayne State Universities. After a bit of turmoil in his personal life,[169] John became Executive Director of Detroit SNAP, an agency organized to reduce crime, make urban neighborhoods safer, and to provide support for senior citizens.[170] In the fall of 1999, he returned to teaching and coaching in an inner-city school and again began to find satisfaction and self-fulfillment in his work.[171] In the last year of the century he was Assistant Superintendent of the Detroit Public Schools.

With the help of Coach Holmes, Dr. Telford used his troubled childhood to fuel a tremendous drive for success in his academic studies as well as in track, and later in school management and reform. He wanted to prove himself and he did. His daughter, Katherine, graduated from Michigan State University in 1998.

A Hard Road to Travel

Coaching track at Wayne University was a hard road to travel. The training conditions handicapped the school's runners and made recruitment nearly impossible. Nearly all track meets had to be held out of town on a shoestring budget. On May 12, 1956 Wayne University held its first home meet in three years when it hosted and defeated the Western Reserve University track team in a Presidents Conference dual meet at Tartar Field.[172] Wayne University track All-American John Telford recalled the training conditions:

> Wayne . . . trackmen trained on an eighty-yard balcony track in the school's Old Main building. The rickety track [had] . . . narrow turns. . . . [It] was shiny with linoleum patches of various vintages. When [the Olympic champion and world-record holder] Mal Whitfield came to Detroit to visit his friend Lorenzo Wright, Wayne's 1948 Olympian . . . . Whitfield tried to take a workout on the track, but was unable to complete [it]. 'My feet hurt,' he was quoted as saying. Indeed, one boy [in my time] . . . broke his left tibia on [the track] . . . Another put his foot through [it] during a fast workout. . . . Shin splints . . . [afflicted] almost everyone who trained there. The turns were frequent. . . . You had to train on those turns to become able to negotiate them at top speed without going into a wall or out a widow.[173]

Holmes did not have a single winning track season from 1954 to his retirement in 1958. His teams consistently lost to rivals like Central Michigan College, Michigan Normal College, and Western Michigan College.[174] Nevertheless, Coach Holmes was highly regarded in Michigan and around the nation. In 1955 and 1956 a David L. Holmes trophy was awarded the winner of the mile run at the Chippewa Relays held at Central Michigan College.[175]

"Walter Reuther's University"

During the 1950s, when Wayne University was attempting to become a state university, legislators from the western and northern part of the state often referred to Wayne as "the red university" or "Walter Reuther's University."[176] Their bias against Wayne reflected intolerance toward the ethnic diversity and African-Americans living in Detroit. They particularly resented the political influence of the labor unions that often represented the interests of these groups. In 1956 southeastern Michigan legislators finally pressed the bill through the state legislature, and Governor G. Mennen Williams signed Public Act 183, adopting Wayne University into the State University system, into law on April 22. In the fall of 1956 Wayne University became Wayne State University.

State support did little to improve the schools under funded athletic program. In 1957 it was reported: "Coach David L. Holmes claims he doesn't have 'a real track team; only several good men.' His 'several good men' pulled off one of the most lopsided victories in school history Saturday by trampling Western Reserve, 97–29, in Cleveland."[177]

In the fall of 1957 Coach Holmes again found himself scouting among fall enrollees at Wayne State University for track prospects. In an effort to attract any able-bodied male students to the track program, the veteran coach held a meeting at 6 p.m. the Student Center to show films of the 1956 Olympics.[178] Richard A. Swanson was a freshman cross-country athlete in the fall of 1957 and would become a two-mile track star at Wayne State. He later became Wayne's third head track coach.

During the great depression, Richard's parents went broke farming in South Dakota. His mother attended one year of college, and had been a teacher in a one-room school. His family moved to Detroit in the 1930s and his father become a factory worker. Richard attended Cody High School. A few weeks after Dick started at Wayne in 1957, in an attempt to become the first college graduate in his family, his father died and his mother called Coach Holmes to ask Dick to come home. Coach Holmes informed Dick of the death, gave him a supportive talk, and drove him home. Holmes also arranged a partial wavier of tuition for Richard and a job working for him so that the young man could stay in school. When he returned to college a week later, Dick found himself woefully behind in geography, and his other subjects. The term ended with Cs in all his subjects, except for a D in geography. Consequently, he was ineligible to participate in track the following term.

Richard later reported that telling Coach Holmes that he was ineligible was the most difficult thing he ever did in his life. Yet, Coach Holmes responded with caring and understanding. This act of kindness persuaded Dick to change his major from business to physical education. After graduating from Wayne, he worked on his masters degree and taught elementary school physical education in the Detroit Public Schools for two years, while his wife completed her degree. Later, he received his Ph. D from Ohio State University, was on the faculty of Wayne State, and the University of San Francisco, before becoming a Dean at the University of North Carolina Greensboro. Richard was amazed at how well Coach Holmes fashioned winning track athletes from the neglected, rejected, and unrecruited.[179]

Coach Holmes more than provided himself worthy of adulation in his role as coach, mentor, and role model, but never approached that level of success as an athletic director and community leader. He was unable to grasp the realities of academic, community, and sports politics with enough clarity and resolve to gain the support needed to build adequate training facilities, tracks, and stadiums, or to obtaining appropriations for budgets large enough to sustained a national or even state-wide track and field presence. He never mobilized his loyal constituency into the power base needed to bring about change. As a result, his athletes were never given an even break when it came to national or international competition. Moreover, he allowed his athletes, who were generally from the under-classes of society, to be victims of the rules of amateurism that placed them at a perpetual disadvantage. It is, therefore, a marvelous tribute to both him and his athletes that Wayne University was able to leave such a prominent mark on the track history of state and nation during Holmes' tenure in Detroit.

According to Irving "Pete" Petross, Jr., Coach Holmes was almost always positive. He always made you feel like you meant something to him. Anytime you did something wrong, you felt like you were letting him down. He got things out of his athletes that other coaches would not have gotten. Trackmen coached by David L. Holmes won half of all the individual national championships captured by Wayne's male student-athletes during the twentieth century.

David L. Holmes, Jr. remembers sitting with his father in his room in a Philadelphia hotel eight years before the Civil Rights Act and noticing that the imitation leather on his chair was cracked and ripped. His father, however, thought it was a splendid hotel because it allowed his racially integrated team to stay and dine together.[180]

Although decidedly not a promoter or an entrepreneur, David L. Holmes did design "The Holmes Steel Folding hurdle" and the "Holmes Starting-Block." He held a stake in The Holmes Folding Hurdle Company, the firm that manufactured the hurdles. Touted as "easy to handle" and "the finest hurdle on the market," the Holmes hurdles were used at the Texas Relays, the Drake Relays, the Canadian Championships, and the National AAU Championships.[181] While this venture supplemented the coach's modest retirement benefits, it did not recompense him for the years of sacrifice or the many travel expenses that were not reimbursed during his 40 years of coaching.

When the new Wayne State University physical education building was constructed in 1965, it was named for Frederick C. Matthaei, a philanthropist. Some felt that Holmes had been slighted. John Telford and Lorenzo Wright argued that Coach Holmes worked and waited in vain for 40 years for this badly needed facility, and that his accomplishments deserved the recognition of his name on the complex.[182] Instead, the Wayne State University track program was soon eliminated.[183]

In 1980 Elliot Tabron put Wayne State back in the NCAA indoor track championships for the first time in four years. Tabron recalled, "I was hoping to qualify in the 60, but my start wasn't quite fast enough. So I moved up to the quarter because it was my chance to compete in the nationals." Tabron qualified by running 48.27 seconds to third place in the Central Collegiates in Ann Arbor. Tabron was at Wayne State because he did not run until his senior year in high school. He won the West Side Championship and placed second in the city meet, but his entry to the regional meet was sent in late and he was not allowed to compete in the regional or state meets.[184]

In December 1982 the Wayne State University Athletic Director all but eliminated the track program to save the football team, when the Board of Governors cut the football budget. The track program was stripped of its coach and budget, with the argument that the school lacked adequate facilities for the sport.[185] Thereafter, the track program suffered a slow agonizing death.[186]

12. Basking in the Sun: 1948–1965

During the period between 1948 and 1966 there were remarkable worldwide improvements in track and field performance. Some of the changes due to changes in diet and training techniques, while others are attributable to physical improvements in facilities, running shoes, and landing areas for jumpers. Outdoor running surfaces and indoor tracks changed considerably and had a profound affect on performance. These types of changes would continue to affect performance over the balance of the century.

Indoor tracks vary greatly in size and banking. Banked tracks are faster than unbanked tracks. Everything else being equal, a longer track is faster than a shorter track. Some tracks are 12 or more laps-to-the-mile banked tracks, some are 9 to 11 laps unbanked tracks, and 9 to 11 banked laps to the mile. Others have 8 laps or less to the mile. Surfaces also vary.[1]

At the NCAA Rules Committee Meeting in August 1963, the Committee added the 440-yard relay and the mile relay to their championship program. They also changed the rules so that all races not run in lanes were to employ a curved starting line so that all runners are equidistant from the start of the curve.[2]

Over the years the number of events at track meets grew. Some events were dropped, but the size of the program tended to grow. In 1888 the first AAU Outdoor Championships featured 17 events. The 32nd California Relays in Modesto in 1973 featured a 37-event program.[3] The 64th Annual Drake Relays had a 21-event program.[4] The 90th Annual Drake Relays had 93 events, 36 of them women's or girl's events.[5]

Without factoring in these types of changes, when the tenth best collegiate performance of the year was tracked over a ten-year period from 1947 to 1957, there was in significant improvement in every event from the 100-yard dash to the javelin throw.[6] The period between 1948 and 1966 was also the most productive era in the track history for Michigan athletes.

A 1964 study was made of 157 male Olympic track and field athletes who participated in the XVIII Olympiad and were in the final eight in one or more of the 20 track and field events (including the marathon but not the walks). The study revealed that the average age of male track athletes was 25½ years old, the average height was 5–10, and the average weight was 156 pounds. Field athletes were slightly older, 26¼ years old; some 3 inches taller on average, and about 35 pounds heavier. The age range for all athletes studied ranged from 19 years 4 months to 33 years 9 months. The range in heights was from 5–4¼ to 6–7. The range in weight was from 119 to 265 pounds. Older athletes participated in the discus and hammer throws and the 10,000-meter and marathon runs. The tallest athletes participated in discuss, shot put, high jump, broad jump, and decathlon. The heaviest in the shot put, discuss, hammer throw, javelin, and decathlon. The lightest athletes were in the distance runs.[7] This analysis reflected the growing interest in statistical analysis as a tool for improving track performance.

Between 1948 and 1966 fundamental changes took place in American athletics and the status of track and field in the sports hierarchy in Michigan. Prior 1950 when America's first credit card was issued, the State of Michigan could claim 39 track and field Olympians at eleven Olympiads and at least 35 world or American track and field record holders.[8] During the last half of the twentieth century, the United States participated in eleven Olympiads and Michigan could claim 28 track and field Olympians and 33 world or American record holders. There were about half as many male Olympians from Michigan during the last half of century than there had been during the first fifty years of the century. More dramatically, between 1966 and the end of the century Michigan could claim only one gold medal winner (two gold medals) and one world record holder, and he left the State at the age of fourteen to live in California. Michigan athletes won 25 Olympic gold medals, set 29 world records and 85 American records between 1900 and 1965. The University of Michigan, Wayne University, Michigan State, and Eastern Michigan athletes were the primary contributors to these records, although Michigan athletes attending Arizona State, the University of Oregon, Princeton, the University of Missouri, Northwestern University, and the University of Southern California also made their mark.

Michiganians set 15 world records and 44 American records between 1948 and 1966. The most prolific Michigan runner of this era was Hayes Jones from Pontiac and Eastern Michigan University. He set one world record and eight American records, between 1958 and 1964.

Henry Carr set six world records, Ira Murchison set three world records, Otis Davis set two world records, and Charles Fonville and Warren "Rex" Cawley set one each.[9] In addition, Elmer "Buddy" Coleman, Bill Porter, Aaron Z. Gordon, Willie Atterberry, Warren Druetzler, Jim Bibbs, Billy Smith, Irv Petross, Fred Johnson, John Bork, Irving Petross, Jerry Bashaw, Jerry Ashmore, Dick Pond, and Eugene Washington set or tied American records that in some cases were also considered unofficial world records. No other state in the union made a greater contribution to men's track and field during this 18-year period.

After the 1964 Olympics, however, American track and field, and particularly track and field in the State of Michigan lost its luster. The factors contributing the change no doubt included changes in athletic training, a lowering of the public profile for track and field relative to other sports, an accelerated emphasis on revenue generating sports by colleges and universities, the distracting conflicts unleashed by the civil rights movement, and the increased public acceptance of a variety of winter sports. Sometime during the 1960s high school coaches stopped requiring football and basketball players to participate in high school track as a method of training for their sport of choice.

During this period, the length of both the football and basketball seasons expand in both high schools and colleges. Equally as important, coaches began to introduce weight lifting and other year around training techniques that siphoned quality athletes away from participation in track and field. Greater per capita wealth made a variety of indoor sports more accessible to the American public, and drew fan support and athletes away from indoor track in places like Michigan. Hockey, figure skating, gymnastics, soccer, swimming, and wrestling each gained in participation and fan support, crowding indoor track off the sports pages and out of the public spotlight. Finally, television was unkind to track and field. It was more suited to football, basketball, gymnastics and figure skating than to track and field.

There was simply no way to capture the excitement of a track meet on the television screen. A track meet is a like a three-ring circus: there are usually a number of events taking place at the same time. The action is often fast, decisive and intense, but at times there are seemingly endless attempts to jump or throw with no immediate outcome. These are difficult characteristics to show on the screen. This explains why so much of Olympic television coverage for track and field events is devoted to profiles of the athletes rather than to sports action. It is an imposing challenge to transfer the thrill of being there to the screen, particularly if you are close to the action, as spectators are at the Drake and Penn Relays or at Cobo Hall.

Over the course of the twentieth century, alumni of the Detroit Public Schools set about 40 percent of the world and American track and field records set by Michiganians. The Detroit Public School alumni who held world records include: Ralph Craig, Bill Bonthron, Eddie Tolan, Allan Tolmich, Charles Fonville, Otis Davis, Henry Carr, and Quincy Watts.[10] For a variety of reasons, after 1965 the athletic program in the Detroit Public Schools turned out fewer track stars than in earlier years.

As the 1950s progressed into the 1960s, the growing black community in Detroit became increasingly resentful of being locked out of both mainstream politics and culture and became increasingly frustrated. Inevitably frustration led to the violence that peaked in the 1967 rebellion. The rich mosaic of African-American culture that sustained the black community with hope, charity, and bonds of friendship during the Jim Crow years, began to pull apart at the seams. In the face of growing disorder youth gangs began to flourish, and the athletic programs of the Detroit Public Schools, particularly the track program, began to suffer.[11] Equally important, athletic scholarships began to play a different role for African-Americans. In the 1960s, demands for year around training became more intense and intruded on the college athletes' efforts to gain the advantages of higher education. Prior to the Civil Rights Act of 1964, athletic scholarships were important in creating opportunities for African-American men to launch professional careers in education, the law, and civil service. After 1964, there were broader scholarship opportunities for African-Americans and athletic scholarships carried training demands that increasingly intruded on educational achievement.[12]

Michigan State Joins the Big Ten

When Michigan Agricultural College became Michigan State College in 1925, the school's nickname changed from the "Aggies" to the "Michigan Staters." However, the *Lansing State Journal* sports editor decided that the name was too cumbersome, and held a contest to change the name. The winner was "Spartans."[13]

In 1941 Michigan State College had an enrollment of 6,356 students. In 1945 enrollment had fallen to 3,651, with only 946 men enrolled. By 1953, however, the enrollment had increased to nearly

19,000 students, and in 1969 there were 39,948 students enrolled at Michigan State University.[14]

On Friday night May 23, 1947, in a driving rain, Michigan State College, featuring Jack Dianetti and Fred Daniel Johnson gained the first track and field victory over the University of Michigan in school history. Although Charley Fonville held up his end of the bargain, by setting the track record in the shot put, Michigan State won the meet. They achieved the victory by winning the last event of the night on the strength of Dianetti's strong anchor leg in the mile relay. However, a week later, when Dr. John A. Hannah, President of Michigan State College, appeared before the Big Nine faculty group to request entry to the Western Conference to replace the University of Chicago, Michigan State's application was rejected.[15]

In 1950, after more than two decades of attempts, Michigan State was admitted into the Big Ten Conference, and the State Legislature changed Michigan State College to Michigan State University. By the time the Spartans joined the Big Ten, they were already emerging as a cross-country and track powerhouse. Led by Roy Fehr, Michigan State won its first NCAA team championship in cross-country in 1939. In 1948 and 1949 Michigan State again won the NCAA cross-country championship. In 1948 Warren Druetzler gained All-American status by placing fifth in the national cross-country championships. In 1949 William Mack placed third in NCAA cross-country championships while leading State to its second straight national championship. In 1950 MSU placed second in the Big Ten outdoor track and field championships. Led by Henry Kennedy, who placed second and third in 1955 and 1956, MSU again captured the national NCAA cross-country title.

The 1950 Michigan State University track team had several extraordinary athletes, including Jack Dianetti, Fred Johnson, Warren Druetzler, William G. Mack, Don Makielski, Jesse Thomas, and Adolf Weinacker.

Jack "The Rochester Rocket" Dianetti

"Jack Dianetti was the best runner I have ever watched, and I participated in three Olympiads. He had a natural stride that was smooth, seemed effortless, and was beautiful to watch," Adolf Weinacker, a Michigan State cross-country teammate confided.[16] Jack Dianetti grew up in East Rochester, New York. He was the fastest teenage half-miler and miler in the country, and earned the nickname "the Rochester Rocket." He also was a crowd pleaser because of his sensational "kick" at the end of his races. Immediately out of high school and before attending college, "the Rochester Rocket" placed fourth in the 1,500-meter run at the National AAU Senior Championships in San Antonio, Texas on June 29, 1946.

Jack entered Michigan State College on September 22, 1946. He came to East Lansing prepared to make an immediate impact on the Michigan State track team. Prone to colds, the eighteen-year old college freshman was slowed by pneumonia. Nevertheless, during his freshman year he ran both the mile and the half-mile faster than any other teen-ager in track history up to that time.[17] He broke records as if they were dry macaroni spilled on the floor to be stepped on at will. On January 25, 1947 he helped set a meet record in the mile relay (3:27) in a dual meet with Ohio State University. On March 1 he set the Notre Dame gym record and the meet record for the 880-yard run (1:54.9) in a dual meet. On May 10 he set the American collegiate record for freshmen in the mile run (4:12.0) in a dual meet with Penn State University at State College, and in May he also set the Michigan State College varsity outdoor track record for the sprint medley relay (3:25.7). In June 1947 Dianetti became an All-American for the second straight year by placing second in the 880-yard dash (1:50.8) at the NCAA National Championships. He was ranked twelfth in the world in the 880-yard run that year.

As a college sophomore, Dianetti demonstrated that he could run distance as well as middle-distance races. He placed third in the IC4A cross-country championships, and fifth in the Ninth Annual NCAA Cross-country Championships held on November 24, 1947 in East Lansing. On May 29, 1948 Dianetti won the 880-yard run (1:53.2) and placed sixth in the mile run at the 72nd IC4A Championships held in Tri-borough Stadium, New York City. On June 19 he qualified for the Olympic trials by placing second in the 800-meter run (1:51.6) at the NCAA Championships in Minneapolis. At the final Olympic track and field try-outs at Dyche Stadium in Evanston, on July 9–10, 1948 Dianetti placed second in the second heat of the 800-meter preliminaries and placed fifth in the finals of the 800-meter run.

Some athletes consider the final Olympic trials as the most important of all track meets. Those who fail to make the team, sometimes by the barest of margins, suffer remorse and even depression. However, athletes lose for a variety of reasons. Some are too young, too old, or too inexperienced to be at their peak of performance. Some lose because they did not train as hard or as wisely as required, and some lose because they lacked the financial support or the coaching to compete on equal footing with their competitors. Individuals also lose because of illness or injuries, bad race strategy, or just plain bad luck. While it is not universally recognized, making the Olympic team is not the most important accomplishment of a track athlete's life. The ability to overcome and rise above troubles, to contribute to your family and others, to lead a spiritually balanced life, and to gain control of one's self are much greater accomplishments. No track athlete's career should be judged solely on whether or not he made the Olympic team.

In 1949 Jack Dianetti set the Michigan State varsity outdoor track record for the 880-yard run (1:52.8). In 1950 he helped set the indoor two-mile relay record at the Michigan AAU Indoor Relays, and the Michigan State University varsity track record for the mile relay. On May 19, 1950 he helped set the American collegiate record for the two-mile relay (7:31.8) at the Los Angeles Coliseum Relays. For some reason, Jack Dianetti failed to accomplish his dream of doing graduate work at the University of Southern California and running for the Los Angeles Track Club after graduating from MSU.[18]

William Gustav Mack from Palos Park, Illinois, attended Michigan State University as a physical education major from 1947 to 1950. On February 21, 1947 Mack was second in the 1,500-meter run (3:53) at the National AAU Senior Indoor Championships held in New York City. On June 21, 1947 he was third in the mile run at the NCAA Championships in Salt Lake City, and a week later he was second in the mile (4:15.8) at the National AAU Senior Championships.

At the 1948 Millrose Games, Mack was second in the mile run (4:15.7). In February he was third in the mile run at the Boston Knights of Columbus Games. Two weeks later he was third in the mile run (4:15.3) at the National AAU Senior Indoor Championships. In the summer he was fourth in the 1,500-meter run at the NCAA and third at the National AAU Senior Championships. On November 27 he won the AAU (31:10) cross-country championships. In March 1949 he set the Central Collegiate Conference record for the mile run (4:15.5), and on April 30, 1949 Mack helped win the four-mile relay (17:32.3) at the Drake Relays.[19]

On February 25, 1950 Mack set the meet record for the mile run (4:11) at the IC4A Indoor Championships, and on May 19 he helped set the world record for the two-mile relay (7:31.8) at the Los Angeles Coliseum Relays. In 1951 Mack was on the winning four-mile relay team (17:21.2) at the Drake Relays, and on February 9, 1952 he placed fifth in the mile run at the New York Athletic Club Games. On March 14, 1952 he was second in the mile run (4:12.5) at the Knights of Columbus Invitational Meet in the Cleveland Arena, and on March 22, 1952 he placed third in the mile-run (4:08.2) at the Olympic Carnival at Madison Square Garden.[20]

Middle-Distance Runner Extraordinary

Warren Oliver Druetzler was born June 8, 1929 in Chicago, and grew up in La Grange, Illinois. His father was a wedding consultant. In high school, Warren weighted 150 pounds and stood 6–1. In the spring of 1946 he was captain of the Lyon Township High School track team and placed third in the mile run at Illinois High School State Meet. In November 1946 set the state record in cross-country while winning the state cross-country championship. He was again captain of the track team in 1947 and set the state record in the mile run (4:23.1). He graduated from high school in June 1947.[21]

In the fall of 1948 Warren Druetzler was a 19-year old college sophomore, who weighed 165 pounds, and was on the Michigan State College cross-country team that scored the first grand slam in cross-country history. MSC won the team title in the IC4A, NCAA, and AAU Championship meets. Druetzler was fifth in the IC4A and NCAA cross-country championships, and, on November 27 placed third (30:01) in the AAU cross-country championship. Thus, he was a cross-country All-American in both the NCAA and the AAU. In the spring of his sophomore year, Druetzler placed second in the two-mile run (9:08.9) at the NCAA Outdoor Championships held at the Los Angeles Coliseum, and became a track and field All-American.[22]

In 1950 Warren turned his ankle warming up at the Purdue Relays on March 25 destroying an opportunity to break the distance medley relay record.[23] But, on May 19, 1950 Druetzler, Don Makielski, William G. Mack, and Jack Dianetti set the American collegiate record for the two-mile relay (7:31.8) at the tenth annual Los Angeles Coliseum Relays. Warren ran his half-mile leg in 1:52.[24]

Warren Druetzler also missed the AAU meet, because of ROTC training. He told Godner Nelson: 'I hope to run in the Olympics.' I thought he might be the next steeplechase champion, but he laughed about his disastrous fall at Fresno last summer, and said, 'No more steeplechase for me.'"[25] His comments regarding the steeplechase turned out to be premature.

In July 1950 Druetzler won the 1,500-meter run (3:51.4) in Stockholm, Sweden. At that time he was ranked seventh in the world at that event.[26] On November 28, 1950 he placed second in the cross-country (20:39) at the NCAA Cross-country Championships held in East Lansing.

In 1951, Druetzler set the Michigan State University varsity outdoor track record for the mile run (4:08.8), the four-mile relay (17:18.6), and the 3,000-meter steeplechase (9:19.6). On April 27 Druetzler, Don Makielski, William G. Mack, and James Kepford set a meet record winning the four-mile relay (17:21.2) at the Drake Relays.[27] On June 15 Druetzler won the mile run (4:08.8) at the 30th Annual NCAA Championships in Seattle.[28] In his victory in the NCAA Championships, Warren posted the best mile run time (4:08.8) in the USA that year.[29] He was again named to the NCAA All-America track team for the mile run.[30]

On July 8 he placed second in the 1,500-meter run (3:52.5) at the National AAU Senior Championships in Pasadena.[31] He was rewarded with a trip to Japan. In August 1951 Warren won the 1,500-meter run and the 3,000-meter steeplechase, and placed third in the 800-meter run (1:55.3) at an USA vs. Japan Meet held in Tokyo. He set stadium records for the 1,500-meter run (3:52.4) and the steeplechase (9:19.2) at that meet.[32] He earned a degree in Business Administration at MSU in 1951.

After graduating from Michigan State University, Druetzler entered the Army, where he was allowed to continue to train for the 1952 Olympics and participate in open meets despite the Korean War. On January 25, 1952 Druetzler placed second in the mile run at the *Los Angeles Times* Games, then flew east where he placed fifth in the mile run at the 45th Millrose Games the next day. On February 2 Druetzler was fourth in the mile run (4:14.1) at the Boston Athletic Association Indoor Meet, and on February 9 he was fourth the mile run (4:14.2) at the New York Athletic Club Games. A week later he won the mile run at the California AAU Indoor Meet in Berkeley. Then, on March 22 he won the mile-run (4:08.2), turning in the fastest mile of the indoor season at the Olympic Carnival in Madison Square Garden. The following weekend Druetzler won the Bankers Mile (4:09.7) at the Chicago Indoor Relays.[33]

On April 25–26, 1952 Druetzler represented Camp Lee at the Penn Relays. On a slow, rain soaked cinder track in Philadelphia, he placed third in the mile run (4:21.3). In May Druetzler was second in the 1,500-meter run (3:54.2) in the Coliseum Relays; won the 10,000-

meter run at the All-Service Finals; placed sixth in the Boardwalk mile (a wind blown 4:11.0) in Honolulu, and, despite a strong wind, won the 1,500-meter run (3:53.6) and the All-Services steeplechase (9:29) at the All-Army Championships in Berkeley, California.[34]

On June 21, 1952 Druetzler placed second in the 1,500-meter run at the National AAU Senior Championships in Long Beach. On June 27–28 he placed second in the 1,500-meter run (3:50.8), and having made the American Olympic team, scratched in the 3000-meter steeplechase, at the final Olympic tryouts in Los Angeles.[35]

On July 24, 1952 Druetzler won the second heat of the first round of the 1,500-meter run (3:51.4) and finished fourth in the semifinals (3:50.8) at the Olympic Games in Helsinki, Finland. On July 25 Druetzler placed twelfth in the finals of the 1500-meter run (3:56.0) at the Helsinki Olympics. Roger Bannister, who on May 6, 1954 would be the first person to break the four-minute mile barrier, placed fourth.[36]

After the Olympic Games, on July 31, 1952 Druetzler placed second in the 1,000-meter run (2:23.4) at Orcbro, Sweden. On August 4, 1952 he was part of the winning four-mile relay that set the American record for that event (16:52.6) in the British Empire vs. the USA duel meet, London, England.[36] The record stood until April 29, 1961, when it was broken at the Drake Relays by Western Michigan University. He also placed first or second in meets at Cologne, Dortmund, and Berlin, West Germany; Zurich and Boras, Switzerland; Vasteras and Uppsala, Sweden; and the US Army Meet in Luxembourg. On August 23 Druetzler was third in the two-mile run at the Highland Games in Edinburgh, Scotland.[37]

In 1953 Warren Druetzler continued to run as a member of the U. S. Army team. He ran at the Boston Knights of Columbus Meet, Millrose Games, the New York Athletic Club Meet, the South Atlantic AAU Meet, the New York Knights of Columbus Games, the New York PC Games, and the Los Angeles Coliseum Games.[38] On June 18 he ran for the U. S. Army Second Army team and won the mile run (4:14.6) and the three mile run and was second in the 880-yard run in Jackson, MS.[39] On June 26 he was second in the two-mile steeplechase (10:29.7) at the National AAU Senior Championships. On June 28 while with the U.S. Army, Druetzler set the American 2,900-meter medley relay record (6:58.9) at the AAU Relay Championships in Buffalo.[40] Warren was as on the All-Army team in 1953.

On February 6, 1954 Druetzler placed 5th in the mile run at the 47th Millrose Games in Madison Square Garden. During his seven years as a world-class runner, Warren Druetzler consistently ranked among the top ten milers in America.[41]

William Wehrwein, 600-Yard Man

Bill grew up in Roseville, a suburb of Detroit. He started to run the 440 as a junior at Roseville High School, where he set the school's quarter-mile and the 100-yard dash records. By the time he graduated from high school he was fourth in the state (49.3) 440-yard dash and his high school mile relay team held the state record (3:22.0)[42]

In the fall of 1967 Bill Wehrwein enrolled at Michigan State University where his high school friend and teammate, Pat Wilson was already on the track team.[43] His coach at MSU was Francis Dittrich.[44] In March 1968 Wehrwein ran in the 600-yard in the NCAA Indoor Championships at Cobo Arena, but was handicapped by a lack of experience on the board track. The 6–1 Wehrwein was a relatively slow starter, but picked up speed during the race. At the NCAA Indoor finals he got boxed in and did not place. Nevertheless, Coach Dittrich felt that, "Bill could be a great athlete in any sport he wanted to enter."[45]

Wehrwein, however, did make an immediate impact as a member of a record-setting mile relay team (3:08.3) that placed fifth at the NCAA outdoor championships. He was named to the NCAA All-America track team for 1968 for the mile relay.[46]

On February 2, 1969, when he was a sophomore, Bill set the Michigan State varsity record for the 300-yard dash (30.8).[47] More important, three weeks later in a duel meet with Ohio State University, he set the Jenison Fieldhouse record for the 600-yard run (1:08.6), breaking his own mark of 1:09.0 set two weeks earlier at the Michigan Relays.[48] The *Ann Arbor News* declared, "Wehrwein holds the world's best for that distance [600-yards] on an eight-lap unbanked track like Jenison Field-house."[49]

MSU Coach Dittrich recalled, "Wehrwein couldn't sleep before the Big Ten meet. His high-strung nature made him a tough competitor." But Bill, an amiable young man with an engaging smile, disputed this statement—in a way. "I never get to sleep before 2 a.m., after all, my first class is not until 11:30 a.m. I get a lot of sleep but I have a tough time falling off before 2 a.m. I'm really not nervous."[50] At the Big Ten Conference Indoor Championships in Champaign on February 28 and March 1, 1969, Wehrwein led all the way in the 600, posting a big victory by 1.5 seconds in 1:09.4. He followed with a 46.7 anchor leg in the mile relay that overcame a stride lead by Winzenried (47.0) to give

Michigan State a 3:13.4 mile relay victory over Wisconsin (3:14.0)."[51] Bill Wehrwein won the NCAA 600-yard run (1:09.8) championship in Detroit in March and was named to the 1969 NCAA Indoor All-America team.[52]

On April 21, 1969 Coach Dittrich demanded that Wehrwein cut his hair by Wednesday. When Bill showed up at practice Wednesday without a hair cut, Dittrich told him to turn in his gear if he was not going to comply with his request. Bill promptly handed the coach his gear. The following day Bill showed up at the Union where the team was boarding the bus to leave for the Drake Relays. He brought a "trim-comb" with him and told the coach he would trim his hair once they got to Iowa. However, Dittrich spurned the idea and refused to let him go.[53] On April 24, Wehrwein, the Spartan 600-yard indoor NCAA champion, was left behind as a "disciplinary measure" because he refused to get a haircut and shave, when his teammates flew to Des Moines.[54]

Wehrwein was one of several trackmen told to cut or trim their hair. All but Bill agreed. Wehrwein felt that the coach had no right to dictate standards of appearance for his athletes. Coach Fran Dittrich, on the other hand, would not let his star runner compete in the meet because the young man refused to get his hair cut. "We (MSU) have an image to uphold because we are known all over the U.S. for gentlemanly and neat appearance," Dittrich declared. "He didn't comply with regulations and he didn't go." Dittrich said Wehrwein would not compete in any more meets for the Spartans until he complied with the order to get a hair cut.[55] A three-way conversation involving Wehrwein, Dittrich and Asst. Athletic Director Burt Smith followed. Finally, Wehrwein agreed to attend practice sessions and showed up at practice [the following] Tuesday afternoon. His equipment was reissued at that time.[56] The compromised worked out forced Coach Dittrich to be a bit more flexible than he wanted to be regarding hair styles, and required Bill Wehrwein to trim his hair. Dire predictions about how the lack of discipline, reflected in long hair, would lead to a bad life turned out to be delusions.

The conflict reflected "baby" boomers concerns about authoritarian parental and teaching methods and the values being imposed on them. It also foreshadowed the value conflicts that would dominate politics for more than a generation. One view held that the "parent" must set the rules and maintain strict standards or a moral breakdown would follow. The other held that hair styling and attire were a matter of taste, not a question of morals to be dictated by elders. The dictatorial methods of coach Dittrich were going out of style, and were increasingly an impediment to recruiting top athletic talent. Interestingly enough, Bill went on to become a respected public school teacher in Chelsea, Michigan and an admired parent.

Bill's son, Daniel Noah Wehrwein, was born October 1, 1976. Dan became an All-State and All-American scholastic track star at Chelsea High School and a middle distance runner at Michigan State in 1995–6. On July 14, 1996 Dan wrote:

My dad was the biggest influence on my track and field career. He always wanted me to succeed in whatever I wanted to do. Once I decided to run, he always had faith that I would do the best I could. He is my hero and idol. He never gives up on me. He works hard and doesn't complain. He has reached a level of athletic [accomplishment] that very few have ever reached. He held a world record and is still a very down to earth guy.[57]

While Dan claimed no church affiliation, he was clearly raised in a loving environment with high moral standards.

On May 16–17, 1969 Bill Wehrwein won the 440-yard dash (46.2) at the Big Ten Outdoor Track Championships held in West Lafayette, and on June 14 he placed third in the 440-yard dash (45.7) [45.9 in the heats] at the NCAA Championships in Knoxville. Bill did not compete in the AAU Championships in Miami, Florida.[58]

On January 3, 1970, Spartan track star Bill Wehrwein was timed in 1:11.3, the same as the winning time, but was placed second by the judges. His second place finish in the invitational 600-yard run at the 7th Annual *Examiner* All-American Games at the Cow Palace in San Francisco was a strong opening for the new indoor season.[59] Later that year, Bill Wehrwein was named to the NCAA All-America indoor track team for his third place finish in the 600-yard run at the indoor championships in Detroit on March 14.[60]

A Short Man Makes a Big Contribution

James Bibbs was born on March 12, 1929 in Ecorse, Michigan. His parents worked hard to support their family. While neither of his parents was educated beyond sixth grade, they valued the benefits of a good education for their children. Jim grew up in Ecorse. He was a good student and an all-around athlete at Ecorse High School, as part of the Class of 1947. He was a sprinter and a broad jumper on a track team that contended for the State Class B track and field championship.

However, he was a particularly good baseball player, and was offered a Class A baseball contract with the New York Yankees. But, when he graduated from high school, Bibbs wisely felt that he should get a college education to fall back on before trying his hand at professional baseball.[61]

Influenced by several of his high school classmates, Bibbs decided to attend Michigan Normal, because it was nearby and affordable to someone who would have to work and pay his own way through college. Since baseball was not offered to freshmen at Michigan Normal College, track coach George Marshall induced Jim Bibbs to join the track team. An arduous worker, Bibbs had a good deal of success his freshman year. He ran well against such track stars as Lorenzo Wright and Fred Johnson, and soon became convinced that he had a future in track and field. In May 1949, during his sophomore year in college, Bibbs was the 100-yard and 200-yard champion at the Interstate Intercollegiate Athletic Conference championships.[62]

The following year (1950), he was a member of the Michigan Normal College championship 400-meter relay team. On April 28–29, 1950 his Michigan Normal College relay team, performing in the worst weather for the Drake Relays in 41 years, won the 880-yard college relay (1:28.3) and placed third in the mile relay.[63] On May 13 his Michigan Normal College relay team won the 880-yard relay in record setting time (3:20.4) at the First Annual Bowling Green Relays at Whittaker Track in Bowling Green, Ohio. His group also won the 440-yard relay (42.6) only to be disqualified for passing the baton outside the passing zone.[64] Two-weeks later on May 27,1950, he won the 100-yard dash (9.7) and 220-yard dash (21.3) at the Interstate Intercollegiate Athletic Conference championships in Normal, Illinois. He then went on to win the 440-yard relay (42.1), place third in 100-yard dash, and finish fifth in the 220-yard dash at the Central Collegiate Conference Meet at Marquette stadium on June 10. Jim Bibbs was named to the Interstate Intercollegiate Athletic Conference All-Conference Track Team in 1950 and again in 1951.[65]

In his senior year he won the 60-yard dash (6.2) at the Michigan AAU Indoor in Ann Arbor on January 27, 1951. In the preliminaries that afternoon, Bibbs tied the unofficial world record for the 60-yard dash with a 6.1 clocking.[66] A few weeks later, on February 23, he won the 60-yard dash (6.4) and tied for first in the high jump (5–10¾) in an indoor dual meet with the University of Michigan in Ann Arbor. Two weeks later he won the 45-yard dash at the Cleveland Knights of Columbus

Indoor Invitational in Cleveland. During the outdoor track season he became the 100-yard and 200-yard champion at the Interstate Intercollegiate Athletic Conference championships, and led the Eastern Michigan Warriors to the first of six consecutive Interstate Intercollegiate Athletic Association conference championships. He also won the 100-yard dash in the Central Collegiate Conference Outdoor Meet.

After earning a bachelor's degree from Eastern Michigan University in 1951, Bibbs began substitute teaching in the Detroit Public Schools and worked on a Masters Degree at Wayne University. In 1957–8, Jim helped John Telford, Billy Smith, and Irving Petross create the Detroit Track Club, and while running for the Club experienced considerable success. With the fervor of tent preachers, they gathered an impressive collection of former collegiate track stars from southeast Michigan. Armed with high hopes and a kitty of only $100, the Detroit Track Club survived for nearly a decade.[67] The Detroit Track Club played an important part in nursing women's track in Detroit from infancy to the international stage.

At the Michigan AAU Indoor Relays in Ann Arbor on January 31, 1958 Jim Bibbs was on the Detroit Track Club relay team that set the USA dirt track record for 880-yard relay (1:30.2). On February 22 he ran on the relay team with John Telford and Irving Petross that was second in the sprint medley relay [1,060-yards] (1:57.1) at the National AAU Senior Indoor Championships at Madison Square Garden. When the Detroit Track Club ran in the Michigan AAU Meet in Ann Arbor on April 26 he contributed to their relay team's win in the 440-yard relay (45.4). The same relay team won the 440-yard relay (43.4) at the Highland Games in Waterloo, Ontario on July 30.[68]

In the following indoor track season, he finished third in the 60-yard dash (6.3 in the semi-finals) at the Junior National AAU Indoor Championships at the University of Chicago fieldhouse. In that race, he set the 60-yard dash meet record (6.3) only to have the record broken a few minutes later by Al Jacobs of the University of Chicago Track Club.

In 1960, Jim stopped running and coached the Detroit Track Club team. He continued to teach and act as an assistant in track to Coach Irving Petross at Chadsey High School in Detroit. He earned an MA in Physical Education from Wayne State University, but still was not given a full-time teaching-coaching position until Ecorse High School hired him as athletic director and head track coach in 1964. In the summer of 1964 Bibbs also began coaching the Motor City woman's track team. His instruction contributed to the success of the Motor City women, who won five consecutive national women's relay championships from 1964 through 1967. In 1966 Bibbs was named the Michigan AAU Women's Track Coach of the Year.

It was at Ecorse High School that Jim Bibbs experienced his first significant success as a coach. His Ecorse High School track team won the Twin Valley Conference title and placed fourth place in the State Class B Championships in 1964. The following year they were third in the State Class B championships. In 1966, Ecorse High placed second in the State meet, and in 1967 they won the Class B State Championship. This success resulted in Jim Bibbs being named the outstanding Michigan coach of the year by the Michigan High School Coaches Association.

In 1967 Coach Bibbs was appointed to be a coach of the women's track team for the Pan-American Games. The trials for the team were held in Minneapolis on July 15–16 and the Pan-American Games were held in Winnipeg in early August, where the U. S. Women's team won 8 of 11 events. Bibbs also coached for the USA AAU team when it toured Europe in mid-August 1967.

In 1968 Biggie Munn hired Jim Bibbs to assist Fran Dittrich coach track at Michigan State University. At about the same time Jim and Martha Bibbs were married. The marriage had been preceded by an extended courtship. It was a happy marriage. He helped Martha raise five children. During that time he earned an Ed. D. at Wayne State University.

Bibbs would ultimately spend 28 years coaching in East Lansing. He was destined to serve under eight University Presidents and seven athletic directors. He was an assistant track coach from 1968 through 1975. In 1972 Michigan State won both the Big Ten Indoor and Outdoor Championships, and placed second in the NCAA Indoor Championships.

Athletic director Burt Smith named Bibbs acting head coach of the MSU track team in 1976. The following year he was made head coach. He remained in that position until his retirement at the close of the 1995–6 track season. While at Michigan State University, Jim Bibbs coached 26 All-Americans. His athletes captured 30 indoor and 22 outdoor titles in individual-events in the Big Ten Championships. His teams finished among the top teams in the Big Ten Conference meet fourteen times in twenty-years. Among the many great athletes he coached at MSU were All-Americans Herb Washington, Bill Wehrwein, Marshall Dill, Judi Brown, Eliot Tabron, Ann Pewe, Bob Cassleman, Ken Popejoy, and Paul Pinwinski.

Bibbs was inducted into the Eastern Michigan University Athletic Hall of Fame in 1973. In the spring of 1974 he was inducted into the Michigan Amateur Sports Hall of Fame. After retiring from Michigan State University, Bibbs became a volunteer coach at East Lansing High School and in 1998 his tutelage helped them win the Michigan Class A Championship.[69]

James Podoley, All-Around Athlete

James Podoley was born on September 16, 1933 and grew up on an 80-acre farm near Mount Morris, just a few miles north of Flint, Michigan. The family was of Czech descent. His mother did not speak English, and his father died when he was 12 years old. He had an older sister and two older brothers.[70]

His two older brothers got him interested in sports at an early age. Charles was twenty years older than Jim, and had spent much of his youth in Czechoslovakia. Nevertheless, Charles played baseball in the Cleveland Indians farm system. Joe was a solid, all-around athlete at Mt. Morris High School.[71] After high school, Joe attended Western Michigan College for two years before playing minor league baseball for Terra Haute, Indiana in the Three-I League.[72]

The boys built a crude quarter mile track on the farm and held track meets among themselves. They also played basketball and baseball almost continually until their father died, and as often as possible thereafter.

Jim was shy and modest. He worked hard to follow in his brother Joe's footsteps. He walked four miles to high school and four miles home every day until his senior year in high school. Jim made the varsity starting line-up in basketball as freshman in high school. As a sophomore he also ran and high jumped on the track team.[73] As a junior at Mt. Morris High School, Jim Podoley was a standout in track as well as basketball. He won the 180-yard low-hurdles (21.6) and the high jump (5–7¾), placed second in the 120-yard high-hurdles, and was on the third place medley relay in the Class B division at the Annual Genesee Country Track and Field Carnival held at Dort Field in Flint on May 12, 1950.[74]

When his brother went away to college, Jim was left with the primary responsibility of operating the family farm. He often went to school in the morning, skipped school in the afternoon to work on the farm, and returned for basketball practice. In the spring of 1951 Jim was expelled because the school principal at Mt. Morris mistakenly believed that Jim had organized a senior skip day. A family friend, who was on the school board at Otisville made arrangements of Jim to take final exams and graduate from Otisville High School[75]

After graduating from high school, Jim worked at the Pontiac Motor Company factory for a year and a half and also helped his mother operate their family farm. It became clear to Jim during that time that he wanted an easier life, which only a college education would allow. So, in January 1953 Podoley entered Central Michigan College with the goal of teaching physical education and coaching.[76]

Podoley was offered no inducement to attend Central Michigan College and was considered only a fair basketball prospect. He planned to go out for the basketball team as a walk-on, but was advised by Dan Rose, the basketball coach to save his eligibility and go out for indoor track to keep in shape. Podoley demonstrated his high jumping ability to the track coach in hopes of competing, and, when he cleared six feet, made the team. Over the course of the next two years, he competed in twelve different events, excelling in the sprints, hurdles, and the broad jump. For the next three years he would be named the Interstate Conference's most valuable track and field competitor. Jim never played college basketball.

While attending Central Michigan, Podoley continued to help his mother on the family farm, on weekends whenever possible. In the fall of 1953, he went out for football at Central. In high school he had played end, but Central Michigan converted him to halfback to take advantage of his speed. At six-two and 190 pounds, Podoley became a great, breakaway runner. In the 1953 and 1954 seasons he scored 29 touchdown, all but two of which were from more 25 yards out. During his four seasons of football at Central Michigan, he scored 51 touchdowns, the most ever scored by a Michigan athlete in a college career through the first 60 years of the twentieth century.[77] He achieved this record despite missing the first three games of the 1955 football season because he was training for the 1956 Olympic trials.

Podoley was named a second team Associated Press Little All-American in 1954 and 1956; was named an All-American by the Williamson Football ratings in 1955; and was a NAIA All-American in 1956.[78] He also appeared in the Blue-Gray and Senior Bowls in 1956–7. In the 1956 National Football League draft, Podoley was picked in the fourth round by the Pittsburgh Steelers and traded by previous agreement to the Washington Redskins.[79] He played 43 games at halfback and wide receiver for the Washington Redskins from 1957 through 1960.[80]

Podoley was the first Central Michigan University football player to have his number [62] retired.[81]

Starting with his first meet with the Chippewa track team, Podoley was consistently the high scorer. As a freshman, Podoley was named the outstanding athlete at the Interstate Intercollegiate Conference Track and Field Championships.

On March 20, 1954 Jim Podoley was awarded the trophy for being the outstanding athlete at the First Annual Walter J. Livingston Relays held at Dennison University in Grandville, OH. He won the broad jump, setting a fieldhouse and CMC record with a jump of 23–10½, and the 55-yard dash (6.0). He placed second in the 55-yard high-hurdles (7.3) and the 55-yard low-hurdles (6.7), and fourth in the sprint medley relay.[82] On May 15, mid-way through the outdoor track season, Podoley won the 100-yard dash (9.8), the high-hurdles (15.3), the 220-yard dash (22.0), the high jump (6–1½), and the broad jump (22–11½). He also finished second that day in the 220-yard low-hurdles in a duel meet with the University of Chicago at Stagg Field. Podoley set one school record and tied another. After only three semesters of track, the Czech superman held four CMC school records and had tied a fifth one.[83] On June 11 Podoley placed sixth in the 220-yard low-hurdles (23.4) at the NCAA National Championships in Ann Arbor.[84]

In 1955 the 170-pound Podoley led the Chippewa thinclads to an undefeated indoor track season. On May 12 Podoley won the 100 (10.0) and 220-yard dashes (21.6). He also won low-hurdles (23.9); tied for first in the high jump (6′), and was second in the high hurdles (15.2) and the broad jump in an outdoor duel meet with Michigan Normal College in Ypsilanti.[85] He performed equally well on May 20–21 when he won the 100-yard dash, the 220-yard dash, the broad jump, and the low-hurdles, then won the meet for Michigan Central over Michigan Normal by placing second in the high jump. Podoley personally won twenty-seven of his team's fifty-nine 11/15 points and was awarded the Lloyd W. Olds most valuable trackman award at the Interstate Intercollegiate Athletic Conference Meet in Macomb, Illinois.[86] It was Central Michigan's first conference track and field championship.[87]

In his final year of track eligibility in 1956, Podoley won the 220-yard dash (22.6) and the 220-yard low-hurdles (25.5), placed second in the 120-yard high-hurdles, third in the 100-yard dash, and fifth in the mile relay at the Interstate Intercollegiate Athletic Conference Championships held in Mt. Pleasant on May 18–19. He earned the Lloyd Olds award as the outstanding athlete for the fourth straight year, when his exploits helped Central Michigan win the conference championships for a second straight year.[88]

On May 29 Podoley ended his college track career by winning the 120-yard high-hurdles, the 220-yard dash, the 220-yard low-hurdles, and the high jump in a duel meet against Western Michigan College at Alumni Field. His first place finishes together with a second place in the 100-yard dash lead Central Michigan to a rare win over its arch rival from Kalamazoo. He set two school records and tied a third that afternoon.[89]

In April 1954 Jim Podoley entered his first decathlon, with almost no prior meet experience in the discus, shot put, and javelin. He won the Kansas Relays decathlon in record setting fashion on his first venture into the event. "I plan to drop football and attempt to make the cross country team," declared Jim Podoley in April 1954. He planned to work on the family farm that summer and work out from time to time at Central Michigan College. He had been offered an opportunity to train in California that summer, but lacked the funds necessary to accept the offer. His hope was to make the U.S. Olympic team in 1956.[90]

Jim returned to the Central Michigan campus ten days before the first of July to do some concentrated training before making the trip to Atlantic City.[91] In 1954, Jim Podoley placed fourth in the 36th Annual American AAU decathlon championships, July 2 and 3 at Athletic City, NJ. He held a commanding lead until he pulled a leg muscle in the pole vault, the second event of the second day. His injury hindered his pole vault jump, interfered with his javelin throw, and forced him to skip the 1,500-meter run. Rev. Richards won the event (6,501 points), Aubrey Lewis was second with 6,118 points, and Rafer Johnson was third with 5,874 points.[92]

On April 21, 1955 Podoley and his coach flew to Kansas for the Kansas Relays. On April 22–23 Podoley defended his Kansas Relays decathlon title. He improved on his 1954 metric mile time by 39 second (to 5:06.9), making this event the deciding factor in the event.[93] At the end of the track season, Podoley was honored for his athletic achievements by being given a Senior Varsity Club Award. On July 1 and 2 Podoley placed fourth to Reverend Bob Richards ahead of Syracuse star Jim Brown at the National AAU Championships held in Crawfordsville, Indiana.[94]

On February 17, 1956 Podoley suffered from a "rupture" in the leg nevertheless competed against Indiana University in Bloomington. He was third in the 60-yard dash and the 70-yard high-hurdles, but pulled another leg muscle and was put out of action for three weeks.[95] In mid-March, Podoley saw a bone, muscle, and joint specialist at the University of Michigan.[96] The tendon injury kept Podoley from defending his decathlon championship at the Kansas Relays in 1956.[97] Podoley missed track competition from early February until May 1.[98]

His bad luck continued when he suffered from a kidney infection a week before the Olympic trials. The infection blocked his efforts to make the Olympic team. His primary competitors in the decathlon were Milt Campbell, who had attended the University of Indiana in 1955; Rafer Johnson, who was attending UCLA; and Rev. Robert Richards. Campbell placed second in the 1952 Olympics in Helsinki, Finland, and Johnson won the decathlon at the 1955 Pan American Games. In 1955 Campbell dropped out of college and joined the U.S. Navy where he could train daily without interference from school studies or a need to earn a living.

On July 13–14, 1956 Podoley placed 12th in the decathlon (6, 082 points) at the AAU National Championship and U.S. Olympic trials at Wabash College in Crawfordsville, Indiana.[99] Suffering from the effects of a kidney infection, and facing fierce competition, Podoley was unable to perform at his best. Rafer Johnson, Milt Campbell, and Bob Richards won the three U.S.A. decathlon spots on the 1956 Olympic team. All three men scored over 7,000 points. Never before in the modern decathlon history had three men scored over 7,000 points in the same meet.

At the Melbourne Olympics, Milton Campbell, a 22-year old sailor from Plainfield, NJ, won the decathlon with 7,937 points or 7565, using the 1985 tables. World record holder Rafer Johnson was hampered by injury, yet placed second the decathlon with 7,587 points or 7,422 points using the 1985 tables. Bob Richards, the 1952 Olympic decathlon champion did not place in the 1956 Olympics.[100]

After playing professional football, Podoley acquired a State Farm Insurance Agency in Washington, DC.

David Meyers, Runner and Teacher

David Meyers was born in Mt. Pleasant, Michigan on January 19, 1937. He won the Michigan High School Class B State Track and Field Championships in the 220-yard dash, and was second in the 100-yard dash and the 880-yard relay in Ann Arbor on May 21, 1955 as a member of the Mt. Pleasant High School Oilers track team. A week later on May 28 he won the 100-yard dash (10.7), the 220-yard dash (23.7), and the

880-yard relay at the North Central Conference Championships held in Mt. Pleasant.[101]

After graduating from high school, he volunteered for the draft and served two years in the United State Army. He made the All-Army track team and spent the better part of his two-year hitch running track. After his tour of duty, David returned home and married his high school sweetheart. He considered attending Michigan State University, but attend Central Michigan because his wife had a good job in Mt. Pleasant. Dave received an athletic scholarship that covered tuition and books.

Training conditions at Central Michigan were only mediocre. Dave ran on an indoor dirt track that required 2½ laps for a quarter-mile. Yet, at Central Michigan College, Dave achieved All-American status in the quarter-mile and ran on one of the fastest mile relay teams in the nation. There were three good quarter-milers at Central Michigan during Dave's period of eligibility. Bob Water and Ken Blaylock helped make the Central mile relay team as good as any in the nation. In 1959 they won the college division mile relay at the Kansas Relays and the Drake Relays. The following year, an ice storm kept the University of Kansas from competing in the *Chicago Daily News* Relays, and Central Michigan University became a last minute entry in the mile relay. To the surprise of nearly everyone, Central Michigan defeated Villanova, the top ranked mile relay team in the nation. Later that year, Central again won the Kansas and Drake Relays College Division mile relays, and Dave Meyers became an All-American when he placed fourth in the 440-yard run at the NCAA finals in Berkeley, California.

After placing fourth in the AAU Championships, David stayed in California for the Olympic trials. It proved to be a poor decision. Working out without a coach, lonely for his wife and children, and not feeling well, Dave did not do well at the Olympic trials. It would have been far better if he had returned to Michigan to prepare. Dave drew lane 1, the worse draw possible starting position, and did not run well in the second round of trials. He did not make the American Olympic team.

In 1961 Dave taught in San Diego. However, sickness brought him and family back home to Mt. Pleasant, where he taught and coached for 13 years. In November 1999 Dave was inducted into the Central Michigan Athletic Hall of Fame.[102]

Western Michigan University Contributions to Track and Field

George Dales, one of the most successful track and cross-country coaches in the United States, attended Miami University of Ohio, and graduated with cum laude honors. He taught for three years at East High School in Cleveland and spent the 1938 school year doing graduate work at the University of Michigan. In 1939 he accepted the cross-country coaching job at Western Michigan Normal College (founded in 1903), when the school was not known as a track powerhouse.[103]

By the mid-1950s, Western Michigan was developing a strong reputation in both cross-country and track and field, in part because of the exploits of Ira Murchison. In 1956, the recently renamed Western Michigan College took twelfth place in the NCAA cross-country championships. Between 1956 and 1966 Western finished sixth and third twice, fifth once, second in 1964, and first in 1965. Dales' cross-country squads were not known to boast individual stars, but had great depth.

Western Michigan slowly gained prominence in track and field. Between 1958 and 1965 they won the Mid-American Conference outdoor championship every year, and took Central Collegiate Conference indoor honors in 1962, 1963 and 1964. They placed second in the Central Collegiate Conference indoor meet in 1965.[104]

Dales was named to the Drake Relays Hall of Fame in 1985 for his contribution to the Western Michigan University track program and its success at the Relays.[105]

"The Human Sputnik" Had Speed and Courage

Ira James Murchison was born February 6, 1933 in Chicago. At five feet four inches, Ira was one of the shortest great sprinters in history. He was known for his tremendous starts. Ira was a consistent high finisher in the sprints at major meets for a dozen years. In 1958 while at Western Michigan University he was the NCAA 100-yard Champion.[106] He set an Olympic gold record in Melbourne, twice held the official world record for the 100-meter dash, and, on December 1, 1956, helped to set the world record in the 400-meter relay (39.60). He was the first national track and field champion and track Olympian to attend Western Michigan University. Most important of all he was also a person of enormous personal courage and unquestioned character.

In May 1951, while at Phillips High School in Chicago, Ira Murchison won the Illinois State High School Championship in the 100 (9.6) and 220-yard dashes, and placed second in the 880-yard relay. After graduating from high school, he attended the University of Iowa on a track scholarship. On March 8, 1952 he placed third in the 60-yard dash at the Big Ten Indoor Finals in Champaign. The next day he placed third in the 50-yard dash at the Chicago Indoor Relays. During the out-door season, he was on the University of Iowa 440-yard relay team that won (41.5) that event at the Drake Relays. Moreover, he either won or placed second in the dashes in meets with Northwestern University, the University of Michigan, and the University of Minnesota. On June 7 he placed second in the 100-yard dash at the Central Collegiate Conference Open Meet in Milwaukee, and on June 20 he placed third in the second heat of the 100-meter-dash at the National AAU Senior Championships in Long Beach. He had less academic success, however, and flunked out of Iowa.[107]

Ira returned to Chicago, worked for the Chicago Catholic Youth Organization, and continued to run as an amateur. On March 13, 1953 he won the 60-yard dash (6.3) at the Central AAU Indoor Championships in Chicago, and in June 1953 placed seventh in the 100-yard dash (9.6) at the National AAU Senior Championships.

In 1953 Ira Murchison, "the Human Sputnik," returned to college. This time he chose Western Michigan University in Kalamazoo. On June 11–12, 1954 Murchison placed fifth in the semi-finals (10.1) of heat two and third in the semi-finals of the 220-yard dash (21.5) at the 33rd NCAA Championships in Ann Arbor. In June 1954 he represented the Chicago Catholic Youth Organization and won the 440-yard relay (40.8) at the AAU relays championships in Buffalo. In doing so, he became Western Michigan's first track and field All-American.[108]

In January 1955 Murchison ran in the Michigan AAU Indoor, and in February he ran indoor duel meets against Marquette University, Central Michigan University, Michigan State University and Northwestern University. He finished the 1955 indoor season by running in the Central Collegiate Indoor Championships, the *Milwaukee Journal* Indoor Relays, the Cleveland Knights of Columbus Relays, the *Chicago Daily News* Relays. On April 30, he helped Western Michigan finish third in the college sprint medley relay and fifth in the 880-yard relay at the Drake Relays. During the outdoor season Murchison won the 100-yard dash at the Mid-American Conference Meet and at Central Collegiate Championships.[109]

Again facing academic problems,[110] Ira entered the Army after the 1955 outdoor track season. It was a propitious move. As a member of the All-Army track team, Ira Murchison could give his full attention to preparing for the Olympic trials without distracting concerns about academic study and earning a living.

On June 1, 1956 Murchison tied the world record for the 100-meter dash (10.2) while winning at the Compton Relays. Four days later, he placed third in the 100-meter dash (10.5) at the All-Army Track Meet in Compton. On June 14–15 he participated in the 100-meter dash at the Inter-Services Meet in Los Angeles. Finally, on June 29–30 he placed second in the 100-meter dash (10.34) at the USA Olympic trial finals, and made the American Olympic team. It is unlikely that he could have achieved this feat if he had not been in the Army. At that time, Ira was 23 years old, 5–4 in height, with black hair, brown eyes, and weighed 145 pounds.[111]

On July 25 Murchison won the 100-meter dash (10.5) at the European Military Championships in Nuremberg, West Germany. The International Military Meet was held in West Berlin's Olympic Stadium August 3–5. On August 4, the storied Berlin Olympic Stadium, the arena for an Inter-Service meeting staged by the Conseil International du Sport Militaire, was the site of one of Ira Murchison's greatest feats.

Among the entries in the 100-meter dash were Willie Williams[112] and Ira Murchison. On the evening of August 3, the news from Berlin that Williams had been clocked at 10.1 in a preliminary heat of the 100-meter dash created quite a stir among metric-minded Europeans. Many forget that such a time was intrinsically of equal value to a 9.3 for the 100-yards, a mark that had been previously achieved on six occasions. The next day, in a semi-final, Murchison matched the 10.1 clocking.

Quite understandably the outcome of the finals was awaited with great interest.

On 5 August the famous track was washed by much rain, which let up just an hour before the decisive race. Little Ira Murchison, an explosive starter, held a minor lead in the initial stage, but Williams had an early pick-up. In the second half of the race, Williams gradually inched his way ahead and finally won by a foot. The winner's time was again 10.1, while Murchison was given 10.2. In none of the three 10.1 races did the wind creep over 1 meter per second. The times were therefore ratified as world records.[113]

Between October 15 and November 20 Murchison generally placed second or third in the 100-meter dash in Olympic team exhibitions. At the Melbourne Olympics on November 22 "the Human Sputnik" won the first heat of the qualifying round of the Men's 100-meter dash (10.5); and won the second heat of the second qualifying round (10.3) in Olympic record setting time.[114] On November 23 he won the first heat of the semi-finals for the Men's 100-meter dash (10.5). On November 24, however, he finished fourth in the finals of the men's 100-meter dash in a photo finish. After finishing fourth, Ira Murchison said, "I thought I was third, as I didn't see Hogan come up on the outside, I could not get any drive out of the track in the last 30 yards. I felt I could win, but it was my slowest race this year."[115]

On December 1 Ira was the lead-off member of the team of the winning 400-meter relay team (39.5) that set a world record at the Melbourne Olympics. After winning the 4 × 100-meter relay, he simply said. "I'm happy." Ted Waterford, a Melbourne promoter, pursued Ida to turn pro, but the little speedster decided to returned to Western Michigan to complete his education.[116]

Immediately after the Olympics, Ira Murchison was given an honorary discharge from the Army, and he returned to college at Western Michigan. As a gold metal winner, he was in great demand on the American indoor track circuit. On December 27 he won the 70-yard dash (7.1) at the Chicago Holiday Indoor Games, the first major indoor meet of the season. He won the 50-, 60-, or 70-yard dashes at the *Philadelphia Inquirer* Games, the *Washington Star* Meet, the Boston Athletic Association Games, the Chicago Indoor Open, the Michigan AAU Indoor, the Millrose Games, the National AAU Senior Indoor Championships, the Central Collegiate Conference Indoor Meet, the Livingston Relays, the *Milwaukee Journal* Relays, the *Chicago Daily News* Relays, and the Cleveland Knights of Columbus Meet. He also won sprints in indoor duel meets with Miami of Ohio, Central Michigan University, and MSU. The "the Human Sputnik" won events in more than fifty flights held at 15 meets over a three-month period.

There was no let down in the outdoor season. He placed second in the 100-yard dash (9.6) and the 440-yard relay at the Drake Relays, and was second in the 100-yard dash (9.3/9.4) at the NCAA Championships. In the second heat at the NCAA meet in Austin,

Ira Murchison was off to a legitimate but fantastically good start. He jumped to a lead of about 5 feet over the defending champ [Bob Morrow], and at 50 yards still held two of it. But the powerful Morrow, back in top form after some hard training, was coming. He collared his little Olympic teammate about 20 yards from the tape, or so most observers thought. Murchison, however, said he couldn't see Bobby at about 90 yard mark, and felt he didn't lose the race until the last five yards. So fast was Morrow traveling that the margin appeared to be nearly three feet at the end. Still Murchison was officially timed in 9.3 also, although it was not announced how many watches were on the second place man.[117]

In the finals of the 100-yard dash, Murchison again got a great, although less spectacular start than his earlier one. But this time Morrow also got off nicely, though still trailing the scooter from Western Michigan University. "Then Bobby Joe picked-up well, as usual . . ." Morrow won in 9.3 by 3 inches and Murchison was second.[118] A week later he placed third in the 100-yard dash at the 69th National AAU Championships in Dayton, Ohio. Ira Murchison was named to the NCAA and AAU 1957 All-America track teams for the 100-yard dash.[119]

Over the summer, Murchison toured Europe as a member of AAU Group IV. He won nine matches in Italy and Portugal, and on August 18 he won the 100-yard dash (9.4) at the National AAU Relays in Buffalo. In 1957 Murchison had the second best 100-yard dash mark (9.3) in the world, and the fourth fastest 100-meter mark (10.3) in the world.[120]

The following year, Coach George Dales was worried about Ira Murchison, who suffered a minor leg injury in national competition.[121] On April 26, 1958 Ira defeated Bobby Mitchell in the 100-yard dash at the Drake Relays in a wind-blown 9.5 dash.[122] In June Ira won the 100-yard dash at the NCAA Championships. The "the Human Sputnik" was confident of victory. "I always run better in the second heat. I felt if I could beat [Ray] Norton [of San Jose State College] out of the blocks I would win. He was my big worry. I think I made it out of the blocks before anybody."[123] Murchison's cocky confidence was illustrated when he went to a college party after a track meet in 1958 and was asked by a co-ed if he had been in the track meet that afternoon. He responded, "I was the track meet."[124]

In February 1960 Murchison underwent a serious intestinal operation.[125] The operation was much more serious than most people were allowed to know. In July 1960 the *Toronto Daily Star* provided unique insight in to what had happened:

Six months ago, Ira Murchison was released from a Chicago hospital following the third stage of a major operation, removal of an ulcerated colon. One of the world's great sprinters, his running days were said to be over. Co-holder of the world's 100-metre record (10.1), the 27-year old former U.S. Olympic runner immediately commenced training again. That was in February, and although doctors advised him to forget his career, he prepared for the Olympic trials. He failed to qualify last week at Stanford, but he did reach the semifinals.

Last night, the tiny five foot-four, 140 pound sprinter competed in the Canadian relay championships at Varsity stadium and did amazingly well. He's definitely a candidate for comeback of the year honors in track and field. Wearing a plastic sack connected to an artificial tube to replace the removed organ he was beaten by an eyelash in the 100-yard dash by Nate Adams of the Cleveland Striders club, who equaled the Canadian record of 9.6. Also Ira was a member of the University of Chicago track club team which finished second in both the 880-yard relay and the 440-yard event. 'My goal is to run the 100-yard in 9.2," said Ira, 'Then I'll retire.'[126]

In 1963 Ira Murchison was selected to represent the United States in the Pan American Games in Sao Paulo, Brazil. The track portion of the Games got underway on April 27, and ended on May 4, 1963. Murchison ran the 100-meter dash and the 400-meter relay.[127] Murchison won a bronze medal in the 100-meter-dash (10.5) and a gold medal in the 400-meter relay (40.4) at the Pan American Games.

Ira Murchison was the woman's track coach at Chicago State University from 1980 until 1997. He was an inspiration and role model to students at Chicago State University. The kids loved him. "He never said a bad word about anybody. He took a leave of absence due to his illness. He never gave up. He kept smiling and saying, 'I'll be back,'" "He's the one who taught Lou Brock[128] how to get off the block and steal bases." "Ira was cocky, confident, upbeat. He thought he could win any race he entered." When he died of cancer on March 28, 1994, his wife, a son; and a stepson survived him.[129] Ira Murchison was inducted into the Mid-American Conference Hall of Fame in 1990.

A Precarious Lead

John Bork, Jr. grew up in Monroe, Michigan. On April 24–25, 1959 Bork was a member the Western Michigan University relay team that won the college division sprint medley (3:24.8) at the Drake Relays. However, Bork gained his first national recognition in track in 1961 as a college senior. On February 25, 1961 he set the American indoor dirt track record for the 1,000-yard run (2:09.2) at Notre Dame's fieldhouse at the Central Collegiate Indoor Championships.[130]

On April 28–29 Bork scored a coup at the 52nd Drake Relays, with his outstanding third leg in the four-mile relay. Bork, a novice at miling but an exceedingly good quarter-miler, was content to trail Oregon State's Dale Story and follow his pace until the head of the backstretch, about 260 to 280 yards out.[131] At that point Bork started his kick, which was so strong that Bork left Story some thirty yards out when he passed the baton to Dick Pond. Bork ran his leg in 4:07.0 and was instrumental in WMU setting an American record for that event (16:50.4).[132]

In the distance medley relay John Bork made-up a 30-yard deficit with an outstanding 1:48.7 half-mile leg and held the lead when he passed the baton to Pond. As in the four-mile relay, his contribution to the team's 9:58.7 victory was the critical factor in Western Michigan's win. Bork was named the Outstanding Athlete of the 1961 Drake Relays.[133]

On June 3, 1961, toward the end of the season, Bork ran at the Central Collegiate Conference Championships. In the 880-yard run, Bork, whose previous best was 1:50.2, allowed Drake's Charles Durant to set the pace, then drew away on the last lap with Kirk Hagan of Kansas pulling up to take second away from fading Durant. Bork won half-mile run at the Central Collegiates, with a time of 1:49.0, earned a spot at the NCAA outdoor finals, and was named the top athlete at that meet.[134]

At the NCAA Finals on July 16–17 in Philadelphia, there were four qualifying heats in the 880-yard run, with four men from each heat qualifying for the semi-finals. John Bork won the second heat (1:50.6) and Ergas Leps, a European champion from Canada, who was attending the University of Michigan, won the third flight, while Drake University's Charles Durant won the fourth. Bork and Leps were paired in the same semi-final heat that was held two hours and thirty minutes after the preliminary heats. Leps, the blond headed Canadian, won that semi-final heat by a tenth of a second over Bork, but both qualified for the finals.

At the outset, of the finals, Charles Durant, a tall African-American college-senior, led in the field, but his quarter-mile pace was only 54. Yet, John Bork was not near the front as he had been in both his earlier heats, nor was Leps bringing up the rear as usual. Leps cut Durant's eight-yard lead to around three yards around the first curve of the final lap. When the field bunched going into the backstretch, Bork made his move. Running with his head off center and his arms pumping powerfully, Bork spurted around the entire field on the backstretch and widened the gap around the turn. Leps was caught napping, and did not set out after Bork until the Western Michigan star had a four yard lead. Bork's 46.9 quarter-mile speed and 4:07 mile run endurance were too much for the other runners. He pulled away to win by 10-yards with a time of 1:48.3, the third fastest half-mile time recorded in 1961.

As a sophomore Bork was a quarter-miler, as a junior he was an intermediate hurdler. He doubted his ability in the half-mile until early in the 1961 season. His finish in the NCAA Finals convinced everyone that he was a serious half-miler.[135]

A week later Bork ran in the National AAU Senior Finals in New York City. Several other Michigan athletes were participating in the

AAU Finals, including Ira Murchison, Hayes Jones, Paul Jones, Otis Davis, and John Telford. John Bork ran in the first heat of the first qualifying round of the half-mile run, and placed second with an energy saving 1:53.9. He also drew the first heat of the semi-finals, and placed third (1:52.2), just good enough to make the finals, where he was third best in the nation, among all comers. Later that year he traveled to New Zealand where he ran with a U.S. AAU team against the New Zealand national team.[136] He was only the second All-American and national track champion to attend Western Michigan.

After attending Western Michigan, Bork earned a Masters' Degree from Miami University of Ohio in 1963. He taught for a time before serving as a manufacturing and marketing director for athletic shoes in northern California. John married and at last report was the proprietor of Out West Flyfishers in Cupertino, CA.

Close, But No Cigar

Stan McConner was a very promising runner when he graduated from Detroit's Northwestern High School in January 1949, and enrolled at Adrian College. While in high school Stan ran the 440 in 49.8 and he had the endurance to run cross-country. On May 16, 1947 he won the 880-yard run (2:08) at the West Side Championships. Two days later he won the half-mile run (2:05.7) in the Metro-League championships held at Redford High. In 1948 Stan shattered a 21-year old city record in the quarter-mile set by John W. Lewis in 1927 to become the first Detroit school boy to run the distance under 50 seconds.[137]

After transferring to Eastern Michigan University, he was a teammate of sprinter Bob Parks. As a sophomore, Stan won the 440-yard dash (50.7) at the Michigan AAU Indoor Relays held at Yost Fieldhouse in Ann Arbor. As a junior, he was the critical cog on the school's relay teams. He ran on Eastern's mile relay, sprint medley relay, and two-mile relay teams. In the 1951 indoor season they won events at the Michigan State and Purdue Relays. He placed fourth in the 440-yard dash (48.5) at the Central Collegiate Conference Open Meet in Milwaukee.[138]

In 1952, as a college junior McConner placed third in the 440-yard dash at the Central Collegiate Conference Indoor Championships. On May 3 he won the 440-yard dash (48.5) in a duel meet with the University of Michigan. May 24 he won the 440-yard dash (50.5) and the mile relay (3:28.6), and placed second in the 220-yard dash and the 120-yard high-hurdles at the Interstate Intercollegiate Athletic Conference Championships. On May 30 he won the 440-yard dash (48.8) at the Central Collegiate Conference Championships. He ended the season and his college running career by placing third in the third heat of the 400-meter hurdles at the National AAU Senior Championships, and sixth in the first heat of the 400-meter hurdles at the final Olympic trials in Los Angeles.[139]

The Converted Basketball Player from Miller High School

Otis Crandell Davis was a good basketball player at Detroit's Miller High School, but never went out for track. After he graduated from high school in 1952, he enlisted in the Army for three years before enrolling at the University of Oregon on the GI Bill to get a college education and to play basketball. In 1956 Coach Bill Bowerman, the track coach of the Oregon Ducks and co-founder of Nike, discovered Otis Davis while watching basketball practice. Davis was unable to break into the starting line-up on the basketball team, but his jumping ability impressed Bowerman and he urged Davis to join the track team. Davis, now 26 years old, soon volunteered to run the sprints and Coach Bowerman converted him to a quarter-miler.[140]

"Otis Davis of Oregon, who started as a basketballer, turned to sprinting, and graduated into the quarter-mile, sped around two turns in 46.4 [at the] . . . Pacific Coast Conference Championships."[141] On May 23, 1959 Otis Davis not only won the 440-yard dash, he placed fourth in the 220-yard dash (21.5) at the Pacific Coast Conference Outdoor Championships in Seattle. On June 13, after going out too fast, Davis placed seventh in the 440-yard dash (47.3) at the NCAA Finals. In the rain on June 19 in Boulder, Colorado, he was third in the third heat of the 400-meter dash (46.9) and failed to make the finals at the National AAU Senior Championships.

After graduating from the University of Oregon, Otis Davis prepared for the Olympic trials by running for the Emerald Empire Athletic Association of Portland. On May 20, 1960 he won the 400-meter intermediate-hurdles (51.0) at the Coliseum Relays, and in early June Otis tuned up for the National AAU meet by winning the 400-meter dash (45.8) at the Emerald Empire AA Meet in Portland. At the National AAU Senior Championships in Eugene, Otis Davis earned a spot on the American Olympic team by winning the 400-meter dash (46.8). He proved that he was a serious threat to win a gold medal at the Rome Olympics when he won the 400-meter run (45.6) in a pre-Olympic meet held in Bern, Switzerland.[142]

In Rome on September 3, 1960, the beautiful, flag-rimmed Stadio Olimpico, had a sizable crowd, but not one large enough to fill the 75,000 available seats. The mostly European throng was generally knowledgeable and appreciative. The track and runways were excellent by the standards of the day, and, while the officiating was never perfect, it was acceptable. The weather was variable and changed unpredictably. "A severe heat wave broke in time for the start of the track program, but some days were fairly hot, cooling off rapidly when the sun dipped behind the golden statue to the West at about five o'clock. On September 5 a cloudburst cleared the stands.[143]

There were 52 athletes competing in the Olympic 400-meter dash, including more than 15 of the 25 or so men who had run the distance in less than 47 seconds. Nine first round heats were held in the morning. All of the favorites advanced to the second round, except the Finish 1956 bronze medalist in the event, Voitto Hellstten. In the afternoon the four heats of second round were held. The fourth heat, the heat in which Otis Davis ran, was the fastest and most closely contested. Otis Davis ran the final 100-meters in 11.4 to win in 45.9 with Mal Spence of South Africa, who had been rumored to be out of conditions, on his heals. Abdul Amu of Nigeria was third in the heat upsetting Jerzy Kowalski of Poland for the last spot in the semi-finals.

The semi-finals and the finals in the 400-meter run were held on September 5. This change helped improve times in this event. In the first heat of semi-finals, Davis floated the first furlong, made his move in the middle of the final turn, drove into the lead at 300-meters, and finished strongly in 45.5, a new personal best and an Olympic record. Carl Kaufmann, of Germany, won the other heat by holding off Mal Spence with a respectable time of 45.7.

For the first time since 1912, the 400-meter run Olympic finals in Rome were held on a different day than the semi-finals. On Tuesday, September 6 Kaufmann was in lane one, Earl Young (USA) was in lane 2, and Otis Davis was in lane 3, Spence, Singh, and Kinder rounded out the field. At the gun Spence went out quickest. He hit the 200-meter mark in 21.2. Otis Davis was in fourth place at that juncture. However, Davis accelerated dramatically, covering the next 100-meters in 10.8 seconds, and entered the final straight with a four yard lead over Brooklyn-born Carl Kaufmann, who was running for Germany. Kaufmann then made a sensational sprint, but Davis leaned forward at just the right moment and won by one-hundredth of a second, setting a new world record in the process.[144]

Certainly no one expected a race like this. Davis, who once told Coach Bill Bowerman, "You'll never make a runner out of me," exploded with joy when told he had won. "I can't believe it. I can't believe it," he said. "I was tired coming down the stretch. I started my kick a long ways from home, farther than I ever have. And it's a good thing I did. That Kaufmann was really coming fast at the end."[145]

On Wednesday September 7 at the Olympics in Rome four heats of the 4 × 400-meter relay were held to qualify for the semi-finals held later than day. On the following day, the finals of the event were held. The American team featured Jack Yerman, Earl Young, Glenn Davis, and Otis Davis. A light rain fell during the running of the finals. "The blue-shirted Americans started from lane four, flanked by the red, white and blue chest band of Great Britain. On the outside, in the new orange, pink and blue colors of the West Indies were the American college men who won the Pan American Games Championship the year before." Jack Yerman started for the U.S., and after his illness and subsequent poor showing in the 400 semi-finals, it was feared that he might lose the race for his team. But, he surged into the lead on the last turn, and piled up a needed seven-yard lead over fourth place Germany. Yerman ran the first leg in 46.2.

In the second leg of the relay, Manfred Kinder, the young German star, pressed his black-striped running shirt to within two-yards of Earl Young, and held on around the last curve, then gained another yard on Young. Kinder ran the leg in 44.9; Young ran it in 45.6.

The United States gained two precious yards on the baton pass to Glenn Davis. Davis chose to run a tactical race, waiting until Johannes Kaiser tried to pass on the backstretch, then holding him off. "With dangerous Carl Kaufmann running against erratic Otis Davis on the anchor leg, the U.S. needed a lead, and Glenn Davis poured it on in the stretch to pull away from a game Kaiser by five yards." The West Indies team was seven yards back.

The Americans gained another yard on the pass, and Otis Davis was off six yards ahead of Kaufmann. The great German, capable of running 400-meters under 45 seconds, moved up on the heels of Davis going into the last curve and it looked like his superior power could win the race. But barely past the middle of the curve, Davis made one of the quickest sprints in quarter-mile history. Almost instantly, surely before Kaufmann knew it, Davis added two yards to the lead, and before Kaufmann could rally, Davis added another yard. He now had a four-yard lead to hold down the stretch. The Brooklyn-born German was game, but could not cut the U.S. margin of victory. Thus, while the Germans sliced over a second off Jamaica's world record, they lost. The newly established world record was an impressive 3:02.2. Otis Davis ran the last 400-meters in 45.0: Kaufmann in 44.9. After the race Otis Davis said, "I just learned how to run in the last couple of races. I accelerated a little to make Kaufmann use his strength to catch me, then I floated. When he came up again, I'd accelerate, then float again. I figured he'd use up his power trying to catch me each time, then I'd turn on the kick and walk away."[146]

Analysis of Otis Davis' feats stirred the track and field discussions for several months following the 1960 Olympics.[147] Ken Doherty concluded that "Otis Davis probably won the Olympic 400 due to correct pacing: 11.1, 10.7, 10.8, 11.3." He went on to say, "I would like to make a study of 400-meter splits at each 100 and would be interested in hearing from anyone with this data."

Vince Reel, the coach at Claremont College and Milkha Singh's Olympic coach, had devised a strategy he believed would bring his runner the gold medal in the 400-meter run in Rome. Reel reported that,

as soon as we received the lane assignments Milkha and I began to make our tactical plans for the final. We eliminated Young and Kinder from our planning—isn't that something, not worrying about two men who ran 45.9—but that was our first move. Kaufmann and Milkha had run each other four or five times just before the Games and although Kaufmann won each time the distance between them kept diminishing until in their last race they were both clocked in the same time. So we figured that Kaufmann would be concerned with Milkha and would not consider himself a cinch to whip him. A second consideration with our plans for Kaufmann was the fact that he drew lane 1 and would be screened from Milkha in lane 5 for much of the race.

With Young in lane 2, our next consideration was the man we feared the most, Otis Davis in lane 3. Basic to all our thinking was the fact that Milkha possessed as much if not more speed than anyone in the race with the possible exception of Kaufmann. Davis we figured would be a 'follower' since he had drawn the third lane. Spence in lane four was the key to the race. We based this on the Commonwealth Games 440 where Milkha defeated Spence for the title. Spence in that race was in lane 1 with Singh on the outside. Spence let Milkha get too big a lead in the first 330 and then couldn't catch him in the final dash for the tape. This time, we thought Spence would not let Milkha build up that much of a lead—especially since he was in the closest lane.

Therefore our job was to control the race in such a manner that the field was practically even coming into the home straight and would then become a dash with inherent speed as the major factor. To do this, we planned to run the first 200 in 22.3 to 22.5 figuring that Spence would stay back of Milkha, that Davis would follow Spence and that Kaufmann would be keeping his eye on Davis, thereby slowing the entire field and giving Milkha a chance to take advantage of his speed.

The planning, of course, still worked for the first 200 with Spence following Milkha and Davis following Spence and Kaufmann behind Davis. The only trouble was that Milkha ran about 21.3 instead of 22.3 and the tactics were completely changed. As you know, when they came off the last turn, Davis had about three yards over Kaufmann and almost got caught; Spence had three yards over Milkha and almost got caught. So there went the best laid plans— and if they had worked the entire results might have been different. You won- der how many 'plans' were changed in the Games as races were run. If Milkha had held back that extra second would the others have still followed? We'll never know, but these are the things which make track the interesting challenge it is.[148]

On January 14, 1961 Davis' inexperience in track became evident. Coach Bill Bowerman thought that a match up between Otis Davis and Eddie Southern at the Oregon Invitational Indoor in Portland would produce a world record in the 500-yard indoor run. However, it was the first time running on the boards for both men, and they were con- fused by the stagger, lost count of the laps, and were beaten by little- known Rick Harder of Washington in the relatively slow time of 59.5.[149] Otis went to the Los Angeles Invitational Meet the following week and won the 500 by the time of 58.4. Otis retired from track after the 1961 indoor season to teach and coach.

In 1968 Otis Davis was hired by the U.S. Olympic Committee to be Director of Housing for the Mexico City Olympic Games.[150] In 1980 he was appointed Director of Recreation of the Sports Complex for the U.S. Military in Germany.[151]

In 1960, the year birth control pills were approved by the Federal Drug Administration for use, there were a half a million competitive runners actively involved in track and field, cross-country, or both sports. After football and basketball, track was the third most popular high school sport in the nation, and next to basketball it was the sec- ond most prevalent sport in America's secondary schools.[152] However, the landscape of sports activities was beginning to change, and track and field would suffer. At a time when Mao Zedong was advocating self-reliance and arduous struggle for China's youth, interest in track and field by American youth was declining. An increasing number of high school students were becoming "sideline sitters," and an increase in the average size in high schools was not helping the trend. In addi- tion, once upon a time there had been separate seasons for football, basketball, track and baseball. Those good old days are gone by 1967. Changes in training for football and basketball were siphoning talented athletes away from involvement in spring track, and the growing num- ber of sports, such as soccer and gymnastics, sponsored by suburban schools also had a negative impact on participation in track and field.

13. Walk Like a Duck

Torso leaning forward, elbows jerking back and forth, and legs flopping like marionettes, Charles Foster—with his white head gear—pressed hard, as he fought to qualify for the American Olympic team destined for Paris. Race-walking is a strange-looking sport. Popular since before the American Civil War, it often appears to the outsider as a graceless, goofy duck walk. But to the well informed, race-walking can be poetry in motion. Beyond the flying arms and flopping legs, the sport has grace and purpose.

The major requirement of race-walking is that one foot be in contact with the ground at all times. Thus, the race-walker should be gliding along. There should be no springing or jarring impacts, as the athlete uses his hips to cushion the impact of the foot hitting the ground. On a rudimentary level, walking is a normal human exercise. But to move at speeds faster than eight miles an hour, refinements in technique are needed. Race-walkers leans forward at about a 15-degree angle. They keep their legs fully straight, but relaxed, and must land each step on the heel of the foot and roll forward onto the toes. In 1924 the race-walker generally took long strides. Later it was discovered that short steps and rapid turnover resulted in faster times.

Charles A. Foster was a member of the Detroit YMCA track team for fully thirty years. Sponsored by the YMCA Athletic Club, the Y's track team participated at AAU meets in Michigan and Chicago. The Detroit YMCA also sponsored an occasional Olympic athlete, as it did when it paid Ralph Craig's expenses to Stockholm in 1912.[1]

The physical education department of the Detroit YMCA originated in 1876 when the Farmer Street Building opened with the Y's first gymnasium. Twelve years later the Detroit Y established an Athletic Club. The Athletic Club included an outdoor running track, a baseball diamond, and two tennis courts. Their Athletic Club's first indoor track meet was held in March 1904 at the Detroit Light Guard Armory.[2]

Charles Foster was already an active amateur race-walker in the September 1921, when he placed second in the three-mile walk at the

Central AAU Championships at Stagg Field in Chicago. In October 1921 he placed third in the National AAU Seven-mile Walk Championship at Glenn Park in Yonkers, New York.[3] In 1922, Foster was a clerk living at 8808 Mackinaw Avenue, Detroit.[4] Little else is known about this future Olympian.

When the first American amateur track and field championship was held in 1876, race-walking championships were held at three distances; the one-mile walk; the three-mile walk, and the seven-mile walk.[5] The 10-kilometer (10-K) walk made its appearance in the 1912 Olympics,[6] and the 50-kilometer (10-K) walk, which covers 31 miles and 120-yards, was added in 1929.

In 1932 American race-walking adopted the metric system. The standard walking distances became the 1,500-meter walk, 10-K walk, 15-K walk, 20-K-walk, 30-K walk, 40-K walk, and 50-K walk. In 1943 a National AAU 25-K Walk Championship was added, and, starting in 1949, a 35-K championship held. The 20-K walk was added to the Olympic program in 1956.

The first U.S. appearance in Olympic race-walking competition was George Bonhag's gold medal effort in the 1,500-meter walk at the 1906 Olympiad in Athens. Six years later, the American Olympic Committee sent four competitors to participate in the 10-K walk in Stockholm. None placed in the finals of that event. In 1920 the United States again sent a race-walking team to the Olympics in Antwerp, where the 3-K and 10-K distances were contested. The U.S. won a bronze medal in the 3-K walk and a silver medal in the 10-K walk. International Olympic Committee's plan for race-walking at the sixth Olympiad in Paris was limited to the 10-K walk.

As the Olympic trials for the 1924 games approached, Charles Foster, "one of the best walkers in the country," set his sights on making the U.S. team.[7] The regional trials were scheduled for May 30, 1924 in Ann Arbor. At that test of ability, Foster, wearing white headgear, as he usually did when he was race-walking,[8] lapped the entire field and took first place in the finals of the 10-K walk. His outstanding time of 49 minutes 21 seconds made it virtually certain he had earned a berth on the American Olympic team that would compete in Paris in July.[9] He sailed for Europe on June 16 as one of only two American race-walkers on the U.S. Olympic team.[10]

In Paris, Foster placed ninth in the second heat of the 10-K walk. He did not qualify for the finals. Nevertheless, it was a fine showing for his first venture in international competition. After the Olympics, Foster continued to race-walk for the next seventeen years.

Foster and his wife Kathryn lived at 3771 Brown Place, Detroit in 1928, and he worked as a shipping clerk at Woodward Washing Machine Company.[11] Because of his family and work responsibilities, Foster confined most of his competitive activities to Michigan. Between 1925and 1941, Charles Foster won ten State race-walking championships and placed second or third in three other state AAU meets. He also participated in at least five National AAU Walking Championships. In 1935 he placed sixth in the National AAU 50-K Walk Championship in Cincinnati. While never a national champion, he was a race-walker of national stature.

By March 1940 Foster was slowing down as a race-walker. A *Detroit Times* sports reporter wrote: "Foster, bald-headed and clad in trunks that hung to his knees completed tonight [at the Michigan AAU indoor meet], but was no match for the swift moving field."[12] Foster died in Plymouth, MI on November 20, 1970 at the age of 82. His accomplishments in race-walking were completely ignored in his obituary and, at the time of his death, forgotten by nearly everyone.[13]

College Drop-Out Makes Three Olympic Teams

The generation of race-walkers that came to prominence during the great depression included three champions who were not born in Michigan, but developed strong affiliations with the wolverine state. Ernest Crosbie was born in Ainwick, Northumberland, England on December 6, 1909. His father was a chief engineer aboard Canard Line steamships, but was dismissed when a hangover resulted in a missed assignment. The Crosbie family immigrated to New Jersey when Ernie was 3½ years old. After a short time in New Jersey, they moved to Baltimore, where his mother, Ida, took a job as a piano player in a silent movie theater, and Ernie started to school. Ernie was a precocious young man. He graduated from high school at the age of 15, and attended John Hopkins University for one year before dropping out of school because of clinical depression.[14]

Ernie took to fast walking because it made him feel better. He came to the attention of the track world in 1931–32 when he race-walked with the Baltimore Cross-country Club. On June 6, 1932 Ernest won the 50-K walk at the Olympic tryouts in Central Park in New York City. This feat qualified the teenager for the final Olympic trials in Palo Alto

Race-walker Ernest Crosbie onboard the *S S Manhattan* enroute to Hamburg, Germany to participate in the Nazi Olympics in Berlin. Ernie injured himself in a playful wrestling match during the voyage. He participated in the 1932, 1936 and 1948 Olympic Games. *(Photo Michigan State University Archives.)*

on July 16. Crosbie again won the event, and in August placed eighth in the 50-K walk at the Los Angeles Olympics.

At the Olympic games, Ralph Young, track coach and athletic director at Michigan State College, met Ernie and offered him assistance to attend Michigan State College. Ernie accepted the offer. After the Olympics, Crosbie returned to Baltimore and on September 3, 1932 placed second in the National AAU 50-K Walking Championship at the resort town of May Landing, NJ. In 1932, shortly after the National Championships, Ernest Crosbie enrolled as a freshman at Michigan State in East Lansing.[15] During his first year at State College, Ernie suffered repeated from bouts of depression, and dropped out of college again. He stayed in Michigan and continued to race-walk. In April 1934 and 1935, Crosbie represented the Detroit Track Club when he placed second in each case in the National AAU 50-K Walk Championship in Cincinnati. During this period of time, Ernie was employed by the Oldsmobile Division of General Motors in Lansing as a production engineer, and trained rigorously for the 1936 Olympics.

Returning home to Baltimore for a time in 1936, Crosbie won the National AAU 50-K Walk Championship and qualified for his second trip to the Olympic Games. General Motors' management helped him underwrite his trip by asking him to visit several of their plants in Germany. Ernie's trip to the Olympics gave them a unique opportunity to get a first hand account of how Nazi control was affecting their property in Germany.

Enroute to Germany Ernie was horsing around with a member of the wrestling team and cracked his ribs. In August 1936 Crosbie raced with bandages protecting his cracked ribs. Every step of the race was painful. Nevertheless, he completed the race, placing 26th in the 50-K walk at the Berlin Olympics. Because of the injury, his time was slower than it had been in Los Angeles four years earlier.

After the Olympics, Ernie returned to East Lansing and enrolled in some classes at Michigan State College. He met Rosalie Frutig at a college dance in March 1937. The bright, handsome young man smote her, and, after a short courtship, they planned to get married. However, when be became depressed and started acting strangely, she broke off the marriage plans. Crosbie returned to Baltimore and competed again in 1939, winning the National AAU 50-K Walking Championship. He lost all contact with Rosalie. Ernie's bouts with mental illness kept him out of the armed services during World War II, but he was hired by

Bethlehem Steel. After the war he walked on behalf of the Whitehorse Democratic Club in Baltimore.

In 1947 Ernie was hired by the Boeing Aircraft Corporation to be a process engineer at their plant in Wichita, Kansas. He completed a comeback in race-walking in 1948 at the age of 38, when he again won the National AAU 50-K Walk Championship. He was named to the 1948 AAU Men's Track and Field All-American team in the 50-K walk,[16] and on July 31,1948 placed twelfth in the 50-K race-walk (5:15:16) at the 14th Olympiad in London.[17] During his 17 years of national competition, Crosbie won four national championships.

In 1948, Rosalie wrote to Ernie congratulating him on making the Olympic team for the third time. Her letter rekindled their romance, and they were married on November 24, 1949, over the Thanksgiving holidays. They moved back to Lansing in December 1950. They had two children. Ernie could not keep a job, and life was difficult. He was diagnosed with manic-depressive disorder, a chronic illness that afflicted his mother, sister, and son. Many individuals who have manic-depressive disorder self-medicate with alcohol or opiates. Ernie did so with alcohol. In 1968 Ernie and his family moved to Traverse City. It was not until 1970 that Lithium was approved for treatment of bipolar disorder, before then there was no adequate treatment, and even Lithium had limited benefit for many patients. Ernie's bright potential came to a tragic end when he died in July 1979.[18]

Mill-Town Race-Walker Goes to College

The second depression era race-walker with a Michigan connection was Albert J. Mangan, who grew up in the New England mill-town of Lowell, Massachusetts. Like Ernest Crosbie, Albert Mangan broke onto the track scene in an Olympic year, when he placed second at the National AAU 50-K Walk Championship in Cincinnati and qualified for the American Olympic team. In Berlin, Al Mangan placed 21st in the 50-K walk, and the following year won the National AAU 50-K Walk Championship and participated in the National Senior AAU Outdoor Track and Field Championships in Milwaukee. He was named to the 1937 AAU Track and Field All-American team in the 50-K walk.[19]

In September 1937 Albert J. Mangan became a member of the Michigan State College Class of '41. He immediately joined Roy Fehr and others on the Michigan College cross-country team. On November 21, 1938 Al finished 41st at the first ever NCAA cross-country championship, which was held in East Lansing. On May 31, 1940 Mangan won the two-mile walk (15:15.6) at the Michigan AAU Championships held in Kalamazoo and set the Michigan State College varsity record and meet record for that event. On November 28, 1940 Al ended his college track career by placing 15th in the AAU Senior Cross-country Championship held in Detroit. In 1947, after serving in the armed services in World War II, Al Mangan had moved back to Lowell, MA.[20]

Not A Polish Ham

The third depression era Michigan race-walker was William Mihalo. Mihalo was the son of Polish immigrants. He grew up in the South Park area of Chicago, and became a race-walker for the Chicago Park District and the South Park Athletic Club. In June 1933 Bill Mihalo placed second in the 5-K walk at the National AAU Junior Championship held in Chicago.[21]

On June 10, 1934 William Mihalo was walking for the South Park Athletic Club and won the 5-K walk at the 33rd Annual Central AAU Championships in Chicago. As winner of that race, Mihalo qualified for the Polish-American track team that traveled to Warsaw and race-walked there on August 6.[22]

In 1935 Mihalo moved to Ogden Park, IL but continued to race-walk for the Chicago Park District team.[23] That year, four race-walking events were contested nationally: (1) the 3-K walk; (2) the 5-K walk; (3) the15-K walk; and (4) the 50-K walk.[24] On May 12, 1935 Mihalo placed seventh at the AAU National 50-K Walk Championship in Cincinnati. In June, he won the Central AAU 1,500-meter walk. John Ruban, representing the Detroit Track Club, won the 1,500-meter walk at the Michigan AAU Meet and placed fourth in the 3-K walk at the National AAU Championships in Nebraska. In 1936 and 1937 Mihalo continued to race-walk in and around Chicago.[25]

In 1938 William Mihalo apparently moved to Hamtramck, a Polish community near downtown Detroit.[26] The 1940 city directory lists William Mihalo (driver) and his wife Stella living at 12636 Charest Avenue, Hamtramck.[27]

It was in Hamtramck that William Mihalo began to blossom as a nationally-ranked race-walker. From 1939 to February 1940 Mihalo won sixteen straight walking races.[28] In 1939 Mihalo won the National AAU 50-K Walk and the National 10-mile Walk. In 1940 he coached the Hamtramck Boys Club track club and represented them in five State and national meets. On March 23 he won the mile walk in record setting time at the Michigan AAU Indoor meet at Yost Fieldhouse in Ann Arbor.[29] Mihalo won the National AAU 50-K Walk for the second straight year and placed second in the National AAU 10-K Walk. He was named to the AAU All-American track team for race-walking for 1940.[30] William Mihalo apparently stopped representing the Boys Club when officials became concerned about how he was supervising boys.[31]

In 1941 Mihalo won the Michigan AAU indoor mile walk and out-door two-mile walk. In 1942 he won the National AAU 20-K Walk Championship and the National 50-K Walk Championship. The fol-lowing year he won the National AAU 25-K Walk and, for the third year in four outings, the 50-K walk.

In April 1944 William Mihalo was a private in the U.S. Army sta-tioned at Fort Riley, Kansas. He was promoted to corporal by August.[32] In the Army, he continued to dominate American race-walking with national championships in the 25-K and 30-K Walks, and a third place finish in the 50-K Walk. In 1944, Mihalo was again named to the AAU All-American track team as a race-walker.[33] In 1945 he won the National 25-K Walk and the 40-K Walk.

The Golden Age of Detroit Race-Walking

Detroit had several good race walkers besides Mihalo in 1944. Auto-worker, Walter Fleming, representing Ford-UAW Union Local 600, won the National AAU 50-K Walk Championship (5:22.49.5),[34] placed fourth at the National AAU 15-K Walk Championship,[35] and placed second in the National AAU 40-K Walk Championship.[36] Walter Ome-lenchuk, Carl Peselk, and George Wieland placed fourth, fifth, and sixth at the National AAU 25-K Walk Championships.[37] George Wieland and Carl Paselk placed 3rd and 4th at the National AAU 40-K Walk Championship.[38]

Nor was Walter Fleming a flash in the pan. In 1946 he placed second in the National AAU 25-K Walk Championship held at Dearborn, Michigan,[39] and he placed fourth in the National AAU 50-K Walk.[40] On October 27, 1946 he placed second in the National AAU 40-K Walk held at Springfield, Ohio. On September 26, 1948 Fleming placed sixth (3:16.39) in the National AAU 30-K Walk held in Detroit.[41] Moreover, George Wieland of Detroit won (5:17.25) the National AAU 50-K Walk Championship held in Cincinnati on May 12, 1946; and Walter Ome-lenchuk of Detroit placed fifth in the 1947 National AAU 50-K Walk Championship.[42]

When he returned to civilian life in 1946, Mihalo continued his winning ways. He won the 25-K national race-walking championship six out of seven years from 1943 to 1950.[43] As reported in the *Detroit News*:

Bill Mihalo has won so many walking races that his associates began to take it for granted that he couldn't lose. Then last Sunday he finished third in the national AAU 50,000-meter championship event at Cincinnati. Mihalo says everybody sought him out to ask "What happened? Other suggested: "you're getting old" or "you ought to get a wheelchair." "I don't like to alibi," says Mihalo, "but I had a bad charley horse in my left leg the last six miles of the race. I'll make up for it in the 25-kilometer championship this month at Belle Isle. I'm going to break the record. The 25-kilometer event (15 miles, 940 yards, 10 inches) has AAU sanction and is sponsored by the Ford Motor Company. It will be held May 18.[43]

In 1947 William Mihalo was named AAU All-American in track.[44] He was again made an All-American in track for race walking in 1948 and 1949 by *Track and Field News*, making it five All-American team selections in eight years. In 1949, Mihalo claimed to have won his 30th national championship.[45]

According to Adolf Weinacker, Mihalo was a kind of a braggart, perhaps out of insecurity. Mihalo often pumped up his accomplishments and diminished those of others. He would even stoop to trickery to win. During a race walk in 1951 in Pittsburgh, Adolf passed Mihalo and was on his way to victory when Mihalo proposed that they walk together and make it a double victory for Detroit. However, Mihalo's reputation had proceeded him, and Adolf felt certain that if he had accepted the proposal Mihalo would take advantage of him by stepping forward at the end of the race to rob Adolf of the win. According to several contemporaries, "That was the kind of fellow Mihalo was."

No one, however, should demean Mihalo's accomplishments. While, he never qualified for the Olympics, in part because his best years as a race-walker occurred during the Second World War when the Olympic Games were suspended. William Mihalo won 21 senior AAU race-walking titles during his career, placing him fifth all-time among American race-walking champions.[46] Then, in 1952 he turned professional creating the World's Professional Walking Association. Competing in the world professional championships at Detroit in October 1952, Mihalo broke seven long-standing pro records established in the 1880s, lowering the standards at 6 through 12 miles. America amateur records are recognized at the first five distances at which Mihalo set the pro record, and in each instance Mihalo's performance was faster than the amateur record.[47] Later in life Mihalo moved to California, and people in Detroit lost contact with him.

On Sunday November 5, 1950 six Detroit walkers were in the field participating in the 50-K walk championship in Cincinnati. The Detroiters at the meet included Adolf Weinacker, Bill Mihalo, Chris Clegg, Walter Fleming, Walter Omelenchuck, and Erwin W. Erkfitz. The oldest entrant in the walk race was 81-year old Tom Brown, of Milwaukee. Other contestants included Canadian champions (H. Ferd Hayward and Peter Lambert), a Pittsburgh Olympian (John Deni), and John Wall from Baltimore.[48] The winner of the race was scheduled to represent the USA in the Pan American Games in Buenos Aires in February 1951. John Deni, a 1948 Olympian, won the event, yet the motor city contestants provided strong competition.

Erwin W. "Carrot Eater" Erkfitz, who was sponsored by Thompson Products of Detroit in 1952, was among the great Michigan race-walkers and unabashed self-promoters. In 1952 he placed sixth in the AAU 40-K Walk Championship held in Dearborn on April 6.[49] Erwin owned a health food store in Detroit and was a vegetarian. He was proud of his physical fitness and even wrote about health and fitness under the pen name, Earnest Endeavor. In 1959 Erwin got word that someone was offering a $10,000 prize for anyone who could break the record time for walking across the United States from Los Angeles to New York City. So, "Carrot Eater" put together a scheme to collect the prize. He persuaded a Nash Rambler dealer to donate the use of a car for the walk attempt, and made arrangements for the owner and inventor of ruppled-soled shoes to provide shoes and some underwriting for the trip.

Erkfitz started his trip from LA and averaged forty-four miles a day along U.S. Highways 66 and 40. When he arrived in New York City sixty-seven days later on Thanksgiving weekend, he discovered that the reward offer was a hoax. "Carrot Eater" did set the trans-continental American walk record and made an appearance on Dave Garroway's *Today Show*, but otherwise came home empty handed. Erkfitz later appeared on the television show *I've Got a Secret*, became President of the Michigan Organic Gardening Club, and became a distributor for Nature's Sunshine Products. He was also an active member of the International Walker's Association. He died in 1992 at the age of 81.[50]

Adolf Weinacker, who took up race-walking in 1946, also proved to be one of the nation's best practitioners of the sport.

Dr. Dolittle Does Everything

Because of adverse economic circumstances in post-World War I Germany, Adolf Weinacker's father, a butcher, immigrated to the United States in 1923. He brought his wife to America from Germany two years later. Adolf was born on October 29, 1928, one year before the American stock market crash. His younger brother was born in the early years of the depression.[51]

Adolf grew up during the great depression in a German-speaking family and entered high school during the Second World War. At the outset of the war, his parents were required to register as enemy aliens, because they had not yet completed naturalization requirements. Because they were registered aliens, they were not allowed to have binoculars, short-wave radios, or cameras. Adolf also was teased mercilessly during the War because of his first name and German heritage. On one occasion, when he was in ninth grade, his entire class stood up and said "Heil Hitler" when he walked into the classroom. The "Heil Hitler" joke followed Adolf into high school. Athletes from other Detroit high schools recall feeling sympathy for Weinacker because of the "Heil Hitler" references made by Eastern High School students as late as 1946.[52] While the jokes hurt his feelings, Adolf took the ribbing in good humor, and, despite their teasing, he remained popular with his classmates.

In high school Adolf became an All-City mile runner and a cross-country star for the Eastern High School "Indians," with their orange and black colors. He also earned a letter in swimming by competing in the breaststroke. Although he was not offered a scholarship or recruited by the track coach, he intended to run for the track and cross-country teams at Michigan State College when he attended college.

During the summer of 1946, Adolf worked for a veterinarian and kept in shape by running at Belle Isle. During one of his workouts, he happened on a small group of race-walkers, and became interested in what they were doing. One of the members of the group explained the heel-toe techniques of race-walking and told him that the short-distance (two-mile) Michigan State AAU race-walking championships would be held at Belle Isle on September 1.

"I decided to enter that race. It was a two-mile race. I was in good condition, and much to my surprise I came in third. After the race someone told me that there was going to be a ten-mile walking race in Dayton, Ohio, the following weekend, so I decided to enter it. In those days a handicap was allowed for newcomers and slower walkers in order to make the contests more interesting. I won that race, in Dayton. It was the last time I received a handicap." Three weeks later he won the national AAU-30-K title in Pittsburgh. Adolf traveled to these meets in his father's tiny Crosley automobile, the only vehicle his family could afford.[53]

"After I started attending Michigan State College, I continued to train and race-walk. It wasn't always easy." During his freshman year at Michigan State, Adolf worked in the dining room in one of the residence halls, participated in ROTC, ran cross-country, and was on the freshman swim team. "It was very difficult going to veterinary school and participating in athletics at Michigan State College. They gave me no breaks at all. My how things have changed at Michigan State."[54]

Adolf had no race-walking coach, and learned the tricks of the trade on his own, often the hard way. For example, he learned that it was wise to rub Vaseline under his arms and in his groin area to protect against chafing during a race. He also discovered that a piece of tape over the nipples would protect against the incessant rubbing of one's shirt across the chest caused by the arm swing needed to walk with speed. In another instance, he discovered that the wrong kind of meal before a race could be like taking on a load of lead weights. He particularly liked to pass other race-walkers going up hill. "There is nothing more psychologically intimidating than passing or being passed by a competitor when you're struggling uphill and they seem to have energy to spare."

In 1948 I had a good chance of making the Olympic team. Of course, in those days the Olympics were not the big deal they are now. The Olympic Trials for race-walking were scheduled in Cincinnati for May 16, 1948, during finals week at Michigan State. When I requested the opportunity to postpone my final exams until after the Olympic Trials, two of my professors refused to allow me to reschedule my final exams. One went so far as to say, 'Weinacker, you'll have to decide if you want to be an athlete or a veterinarian.'[55]

Adolf interpreted the professor's comments as a clear threat to flunk him out of veterinary school if he missed this exam. Adolf went to the Chairman of the Department to request help in dealing with the dilemma. Fortunately, the Department Chairman was more sympathetic to Adolf Weinacker's problem and persuaded the two hard nosed professors to allow Adolph to take a late exam, although it was implied that the make-up exam would be considerably harder than the normal exam. Adolf was a very good student, and passed his exams, after qualifying for the 1948 U.S. Olympic team. He later said, "I wasn't going to let them grind me down."

At the 1948 Olympics in London, Ernie Crosbie finished twelfth (5:15:16.0) and Weinacker placed sixteenth (5:30:14.0) in the 50-K race-walk. "It was a once-in-a lifetime experience to walk around the Wembley Stadium track before a packed crowd as a representative of the United States." He wore canvas Keds instead of the custom made kangaroo leather shoes worn by the more experienced, and better financed competitors. It was a hard lesson. Adolf ended the race with badly bruised toes from walking in inadequate shoes. At the Olympics, Adolf found that the Europeans pushed the envelope more than was allowed in American race-walking. In the U.S.A. unbroken contact with the ground was usually demanded, and a locked knee position was required to enforce this rule. In Europe, officials usually allowed bent knees and occasional "flying" or loss of continuous contact with the ground. This gave the Europeans an advantage in international competition when European judges were in charge.

After the Olympic games Adolf traveled with the Olympic team to Paris, where they competed. At that juncture, he was given permission to break from the group and was given a ticket to America. He then journeyed to Germany to find out if his relatives were still alive. On his way back to Rotterdam, where he was to catch his ship back to the U.S.A., he asked directions in German and was nearly lynched.

In the fall of 1948, Michigan State awarded Adolf an athletic scholarship for his Olympic achievements. The scholarships was withdrawn the following year, to make it available for a football player. Race-walking was given no respect because it was not a revenue generating sport. So, despite his world-class status as a race-walker, the Michigan State University Athletic Department would not consider continuing the scholarship.

In 1949 Weinacker won the National AAU 35-K, 40-K, and 50-K Walk Championships and was named an All-American in distance walking by *Track and Field News*.[56] The 22-year old Michigan State senior won six national race-walking championships in 1950. He won the AAU Seven Mile (15-K), 20-, 25-, 30-, 35-, and 40- kilometer Walk Championships.[57] On Sunday September 10, 1950 Weinacker walked the 22 miles from downtown Pittsburgh to Verona, Pennsylvania in three hours, 18 minutes and 40 seconds, defeating John Deni by nearly 10 seconds and Bill Mihalo by 17 minutes.[58]

Adolf won the National AAU 20-K Walk Championship on October 12 in Providence, Rhode Island. The 21-year-old veterinary student covered the 12.4 miles in one hour 40 minutes and 10.8 seconds. The flat, downtown course was rainy and wet during the competition. Bill Mihalo, who had won this event on no less than four occasions was disqualified five miles into the race for failing to observe walking techniques.[59] Ten days, later in Springfield, Ohio, the MSU student set a new course record in winning the National AAU 40-K Walk Championship. The course from Springfield to Urbana and back covered 24 miles, 1,054 yards. Detroit entrants dominated the race. Mihalo placed second, Walter Fleming placed fifth, Ray McGhee was sixth Erwin "Carrot Eater" Erkfitz was eighth and Don Shorupski placed 10th. All were from Detroit.[60] On Sunday November 5 Weinacker participated in, but took the wrong course [because he was misdirected], and was disqualified in the AAU 50-K Walk Championship held in Cincinnati.[61] Still, his unprecedented accomplishments that season were acknowledged on the front cover of *The Amateur Athlete*, December 1950.

As a student, Adolf was very active.[62] In 1950, Adolf received a degree from Michigan State University in Agricultural Science / Veterinarian Science. He was on the dean's list five times and was in the top eight percent of his graduating class.[63]

Immediately out of college he was recruited by the U.S. Department of Agriculture at $5,000 per year to go to Mexico to fight hoof and mouth disease. The job often required that he ride a horse over rugged terrain for eight to ten hours per day. After nine months of this work, he faced the draft, but was given an opportunity to be commissioned as an officer, if he enlisted. He chose to enlist in the U.S. Air Force as a veterinarian. He remained in the Air Force Veterinary Corps for eight years.

The role of a veterinarian in the U. S. Air Force varies considerably from posting to posting. At some postings the assignment is primarily sanitation inspection and the inspection of food preparation, while in others it involves the care and feeding of guard dogs or even animal research. Once in the Air Force, his commander discovered that he had been an Olympian in 1948, and Adolf was asked if he wanted to tryout for the 1952 Olympics. When he admitted that he wanted to return to the Olympics, every effort was made to give him a posting that would make training and preparation for the Olympics possible. He chose to be posted at Willow Run near Detroit. On April 6, 1952 Adolf placed fourth in the AAU 40-K Walk Championship in Dearborn. One month

later, on May 4, Adolf placed second at the AAU 50-K Walk Championship in Baltimore, and qualified for the Olympic Games in Helsinki.
At year's end he was named 1952 All-American track team.[64]

At Helsinki on July 21, 1952 he finished twenty-second in the 50-K
walk (5:01:00).[65] His time improved significantly from 1948 to 1952,
but the competition had improved at an even faster rate. While in Helsinki, Weinacker witnessed Emil Zatopeck of Czechoslovakia win the
"Woolworth double" and then run the marathon for the first time to
the thunderous chant of Za-to-pek, Za-to-pek. In 1991 Weinacker said,
"I still get goose bumps thinking about it."[66]

While in Helsinki, Weinacker also met Jesse Owens and Adi Dassler,
the founder of Adidas athletic shoes. Adi wanted to ask Owens, who
wore track shoes manufactured by Dassler in the 1936 Olympics, for
Jesse's advice on Dassler's newest shoe design and, because of
Weinacker's ability to speak German, Adolf was asked to act as an interpreter. The Michigan race walker later visited Adi Dassler in his home,
and learned of the Dassler family rivalry.[67] It seems that during the
closing months of the Second World War, Adi became friends with
American soldiers, who had moved into the Dassler home. Meanwhile,
his brother Rudi was interned in an American prisoner-of-war camp,
and resented his brother's failure to use his new connections with the
Allies to get him out of prison camp. Fueled by his resentments against
Adi, Rudi walked away from the family home and business in 1948 and
started his own shoe business, later named Puma. The Dassler Shoe
Company became Adidas. The Dassler brothers never spoke to one
another again, except in court, and were intense rivals.[68]

After the 1952 Olympics Weinacker returned to the United States
and won the AAU 25-K Walk Championship in Chicago on August 31
as a representative of the ESAF Veterinary Corps,[69] before being posted
to Japan. From there, he was sent on missions to the Philippines, India,
Korea, Hong Kong, Thailand, Macau, and Vietnam. By 1953–4 the
United States subsidized nearly 80% of French military expenditures in
French Indochina, and Vietnam pressure on Dien Bien Phu was fero-
cious.[70] During this period, Weinacker was sent to Vietnam to determine the feasibility of using guard dogs to protect American airplanes
with French markings being flown by Americans. He flew in civilian
clothing on commercial aircraft to Saigon, and from Saigon north to a
French airbase that was supplying Dien Bien Phu. What he discovered
along the way appalled him. It was dangerous to fly anywhere because
of ground fire. The outer defenses of the air base were virtually inde-

fensible, and South Vietnam soldiers resisted being sent to almost certain death at Dien Bien Phu. Moreover, there were no local veterinarians that could be recruited to support the use of guard dogs to safeguard the aircraft at the airbase. Adolf returned to Headquarters in Japan without a solution to the problems that turned out to have no American military solution.

In 1956 Adolf again qualified for the Olympic Games in the 50-K walk. In Melbourne, Australia he placed seventh (5:00:16.0), the best performance by an American in that event up to that time and one of the four best place finishes by an American in that event in the history of Olympic competition.[71]

While in the Air Force, Adolf met his wife Irene. A native of Pennsylvania who grew up near Penn State University, she was a Major in the Air Force Nursing Corps when Adolf met her. On July 7, 1957 Captain Adolf Weinacker placed second to Rudolph Haluza of the New York Pioneer Club in the National AAU 20-K Walk Championship held in Patterson Park in Baltimore, where he was stationed.[72] Over the course of his 14-year career in race-walking, Weinacker won 14 senior AAU race-walking titles.[73] He left the Air Force in 1960, after attending the Rome Olympics as a spectator, and joined the U. S. Public Health Service for a time. Finally, he returned to his old neighborhood to become an animal doctor because he had a lot of faith that the long-range prospects for Detroit were good. When asked what his wife thought about moving to Detroit, he admitted that they had never talked about it, then said, "Perhaps I should ask her. On the other hand, maybe I should let sleeping dogs lie," he quipped with a grin.

One friend, and a long-time cat and dog owner, referred to Dr. Weinacker as the Dr. Doolittle of Detroit, because he was more interested in healing than in making money. When asked about his profession, Dr. Weinacker said, "I'm a lucky man. I really like working with animals. I enjoy going to work every day."

In 1991, at the age of 63, Adolf ran four miles three to four times a week, and had run the *Detroit Free Press* Marathon three times.[74] In 1992 the Pegasus Athletic Club Walkers in Port Huron sponsored the first Weinacker Cup Race-Walking Championships between Michigan and Ontario. The Weinacker Cup races are still held in early June each year.

At age 70 he was still a sprite, active man who appears to be twenty-years younger than his chronological age. He has rich memories of Michigan track stars he admired, such as Erwin "Carrot Eater" Erkfitz and Jack Dianetti.[75]

Wayne State Hero

In June 1964 Goetz H. Klopfer, who was born in Baton Rouge, Louisiana and living in Birmingham, Michigan, was attending Wayne State University. According to friends, Goetz would often strap a knapsack to his back and walk seventeen miles to school. He and his two older brothers became active in Michigan race-walking circles in 1963–4.[76] In July 1965 Goetz won the two-mile walk at the Michigan AAU Outdoor Championships, and the following year he won the Michigan AAU championships in the one-mile, two-mile, four-mile, 15-K, and 12-mile walks.[77] Over the next eight years, Goetz would represent the United States in race-walking at two Olympic Games (Mexico City and Munich), two Pan-American Games (Winnipeg and Cali), and two World Racing-Cup Championships (Bad Saarow, England and Eschborn, West Germany). He also placed second in the National 50-K Walk Championship and the 20-K Walk on two occasions, placed fourth in the National 30-K Walk Championship.[78] In 1971 he lived in the San Francisco Bay area of California. He was inducted into the Wayne State University Sports Hall of Fame in 1984.

Lady Race-Walkers

Women's race-walking started in the 19th century, and world records for the women's 10-K walk have been kept since 1943. However, it was not until 1968 that the Women's World Cup, with individual and team championships for the 5-K walk, was initiated. Women's race-walking was finally introduced in 1971 as an AAU outdoor championship event and in 1973 as an indoor championship event, and did not become an Olympic event until 1992.[79]

Southeast Michigan produced the first two world-class American women race-walkers of the twentieth century: Lynn Olson and Jeanne Rautio Bocci. Jeanne Rautio was born in March 1943 in Calumet, Michigan, in the heart of the cooper mining area of the Upper Peninsula of Michigan. She graduated from Calumet High School in 1961 and moved to Detroit to attend Michigan Technical College. In 1964 Jeanne took up running for the Detroit Track Club, where Jim Bibbs and Hayes Jones coached her. Lacking leg speed, she generally ran the 880-yard run and the mile run, the longest distances sanctioned at that time. In the summer of 1964 she persuaded Goetz Klopfer to show her how to race-walk. In late June 1965 she entered her first race-walk, a one-mile walk, and won (10:37) the Michigan AAU Championship at that distance. A week later she won the State AAU two-mile walk (21:36) Championship, and the following week won the State AAU three-mile Championship (29:35). She finished the 1965 season by winning the women's division of the Mackinac Bridge Walk on Labor Day with a new state record for the event.[80]

Jeanne met Jerry Bocci in the course of her running and they started dating. Jerry had been a distance runner at Denby High School in Detroit and at Western Michigan University. In 1957–8 he had helped to found the Michigan Road Runners, which later became the Michigan Striders. Jerry encouraged Jeanne's running and race-walking, and in November 1965 they got married. Jeanne continued to compete for the Detroit Track Club until Hayes Jones moved to New York City and Jim Bibbs accepted a coaching position at Michigan State University. In 1969 she became an assistant coach for the Wolverine Parkettes and began to compete for them. She also attended Wayne State University, where she earned her BA degree in education. Her first child was born on January 1, 1970.

In the summer of 1970 Jeanne and Jerry attended the Olympic Training Camp in Bolder Colorado for three weeks. The following New Years eve, several of their friends from the training camp came to visit them, and they decided to hold a New Years Eve handicapped road race. About a dozen runners competed in that race in 1970, and Jeanne served a spaghetti dinner after the race. The following year friends and neighbors asked to be included in the race, and the participants doubled. By 1975 the New Years Eve run was drawing 250 runners and walkers, and the Bocci's were forced to move the event away from their house to Belle Isle. In 1992 Detroit Edison agreed to sponsor the New Years Eve Family Fun Run and the attendance grew to over 1,000. In 1999 the Blue Cross-Blue Shield Network assumed sponsorship of the run.

On July 9–10, 1971 Lynn Olson of the Wolverine Parkettes set an American outdoor record in the one-mile race-walk (7:53.8) at the National AAU Women's Championships in Bakersfield, CA.[81] It was the first time the event was held at the women's AAU outdoor championships. On June 18, 1972 her 29-year-old teammate, Mrs. Jeanne Rautio Bocci of Detroit, broke the American women's outdoor record for the one-mile walk (6:53.3). Two weeks later on July 2, while competing for the Wolverine Parkettes, Jeanne broke Lynn Olson's National AAU women's meet record for the 1,500-meter race-walk at the AAU National Senior Women's Outdoor Championships held at Kent State University's Stark County Branch in North Canton, Ohio. Jeanne logged

Jeanne Bocci at the 1988 National Race-walking 50-K Championships, February 21, 1988. *(Photo courtesy of Jeanne Bocci)*

a time of 6:59.1 and Lynn's time was 7:06.0 before a crowd of 6,500 spectators.[82] A week later Jeanne clipped off 1,500-meters in 6:50.4 to set the American standard for women at that distance.[83]

After her 1972 AAU victory in North Canton, Jeanne told an *Akron Beacon Journal* reporter, "When I'm in shape, which means not being

pregnant, I'm undefeated. Last year I was five months pregnant and
didn't compete in the AAU. I could've, but wouldn't have won. So
what's the sense of competing." When the reporter mused about the
chuckles that frequently start the second the women's race starts,
because of the duck-like waddle that nearly always accompanies walking very fast, Jeanne told him, "Sure, I hear the chuckles, but they don't
bother me. I couldn't care less. I just tell myself I'm in better shape than
any of the people laughing." She was no doubt correct. She ran four
miles every morning, and race-walked eight to ten miles every afternoon, depending on how much freedom her eight-month old daughter
and two-year old son allow her.[84] Five years later, in 1977, while race-
walking for the Motor City Striders, Jeanne Bocci won the first ever
National Women's 15-K Race-Walking Championship.[85]

In 1973, while she was attending Ferris State College, Lynn Olson
won the first National AAU women's indoors one-mile race-walking
championship on February 23rd at Madison Square Garden with a
7:37.0 performance.[86] In 1978 June McDonald of Detroit won the
National Women's 15-K Race-Walking Championship with a time of
1:27:10.[87]

Jeanne Bocci continued to set and hold race-walking records well
into her 40s. She coached track at Gross Point North High School during the 1980s. During that decade she won the walk division of the New
York marathon, placed eighth in the race-walk trials for the 1984
Olympic team, and set a women's world record for the 100-K walk. In
the mid-1990s she still held the American records for the 35-K and
40-K race-walks. On October 3, 1999 Jeanne won the national USA
Track Federation masters level one-hour walk (8,808 meters) in Worchester, Massachusetts.[88] At the turn of the century Jeanne was still walking and coaching. She was coaching the East Detroit High School Girl's
track team and dreaming of setting new records.

The Man from Milan

William Franklin Weigle was born on May 25, 1940. He started competing as a race-walker in 1971 at the age of 31 for the Colorado Track
Club.[89] On July 17, 1972 the six feet tall, 160 pounds Bill Weigle confided,

I had a lot of trouble training last fall and winter with tendonitis in the lower left
shin area. After consulting a podiatrist we found the only way to overcome the

problem was to correct for shortness in my left leg. I now wear shoes that have an extra ½ inch sole on the left foot and I have had no more leg problems.

When he was asked how he prepared himself mentally for competition Bill Weigle wrote:

At this point I'm still inexperienced in national competition. I just try to reassure myself that I'm only going to do my best when I start feeling pre-race tension. I always feel relaxed shortly before and during the race.

The individual aspects of my form aren't unlike those of other walkers, but I think maybe I concentrate a little harder on putting them all together than some others do. My primary objective has been to develop a form that for a given walking pace requires a minimum amount of muscular work. This involves things like keeping the body as low to the ground as possible by not pushing upon toes each stride, using the arms only for balance and rhythm in a free swinging manner, maintaining good pasting, straightening the leg as the leg as the heel touches the ground. The advantage of my style is that it is efficient enough to allow me to keep up with people who may be physically stronger than I am for very long races. The disadvantage is that speed comes a bit more slowly. But it is coming. Also, it's a good, legal form.

I try to use an even pace. Often I let someone else set the pace, if it's right and just concentrate on relaxation. The second half of my best races have always been faster.

The 1972 Olympic trials for the 50-K race-walk were the occasion for an unusual obstacle to victory. Larry Young, America's premiere distance walker, was wiggling along his inimitable style in 93-degree weather when a St. Bernard dog wandered onto the course and threatened to bite the only American walker to ever to win an Olympic medal. "I thought he was going to take my leg off," said Young. "I might have broken contract [with the ground] then, but I guess the judges gave me a little leeway."[90] The dog was apparently pulled off the course before Bill Weigle passed that point in the race, for he completed the race and finished second without incident.

When he qualified for the 1972 Olympic team, Bill Weigle was walking the 50-K speed walk for only the second time. In the Olympic trials, Bill Weigle was well back in the pack with eight other competitors for the first half of the race. Just after the halfway mark, Bill moved up to fifth, and at the 40-K mark he advanced to third place. In the final few miles he took over second place where he finished more than three minutes ahead of the third place finisher, Steve Hayden, a 28-year old junior high school mathematics teacher. Bill and his wife Pam Keller Weigle made their home in Milan, Michigan.[91] Pamela placed forth in the AAU Senior National Women's 5-K race walk in Bolder, Colorado in 1972.[92]

In 1973 Bill and Pam moved to Carmel, California. He competed in the Lugano Cup races. His goal was get his 50-K time under 4 hours and ten minutes and to gain experience in international race-walk competition over the next three years so that he could be a contender at the Montreal Olympics. He was training by walking 55 to 60 miles per week and running an additional 15 miles a week. His sustained walking was for 10 to 20 miles at a pace of 8:15 to 8:40 minutes per mile. He ran at a pace of 6:15 to 6:20 minutes per mile. His pace and the length of his workouts were longer than during the previous year.[93]

Bill Weigle ranked eighth in 1971 and was second among U.S. race-walkers in the 50-K race-walk in 1972 and 1973. He ranked eighth in the 20-K walk in 1973.[94]

Mexican race-walkers began to emerge as world leaders in the sport in the mid-1970s. Daniel Bautista, Raul Gonzales, Domingo Colin, Ernesto Canto, and Felix Gormez ranked among the best race-walkers in the world between 1974 and 1984.[95] During that period of time, Raul Gonzales, Enrique Vera, and Felix Gomez posted the fastest times in history for the 50-K walk.[96]

As Good as It Gets

Carl Schueler was born in Newburyport, Massachusetts on February 26, 1956, but spent his early years in Ann Arbor. He attended St. Thomas elementary school in Ann Arbor from third through ninth grade before his family moved to Silver Spring, Maryland. He became a serious student of race-walking while attending Frostburg State College in Maryland, when he suffered leg injuries while running on the track team. In 1976 Schueler was runner-up in the NAIA, and in 1980 he finished second in the 50-K walk at the Olympic trials (3:59.33). After the 1980 Olympics, he quit racing to attend graduate school and earn a Masters Degree at the University of Michigan. He resumed training in May 1983 and set a personal best of 1:29.04 for the 20-K walk and won the Athletic Congress 40-K championship that year. In 1984 he won the TAC championship at 35-K.[97] Schueler finished third in the 50-K walk (4:15.06) at the Olympic trials and qualified to represent the USA in that event at the 1984 Olympics in Los Angeles.

Schueler recalls, "I died out there. For one thing it was very hot, and I went out conservatively, but I got very dehydrated and my muscles tensed up on me. By the time we finished, it was 85 degrees in the hot sun; the road was newly asphalted. I just hung on to get third [beating the fourth place finisher by little more than a minute]."[98] Schueler was six feet tall and weighed 150 pounds. His fastest times were 1:25:04 for the 20-K walk in 1986 and 3:57.09 for the 50-K walk in 1987.[99]

"The first gold medal in the glamour sport [track] of the Summer Games was decided tonight [August 3, 1984] when Ernesto Canto of Mexico set an Olympic record in the 20-K walk (1:23:12.36). His countryman, Raul Gonzales, won the silver and Maurizio Damilano of Italy, the 1980 Olympic champion took the bronze."[100] The 50-K walk at the Los Angeles Olympics started at 8 am on Saturday August 11, 1984 to avoid the afternoon heat and smog. Carl Schueler placed sixth (3:59:46) in that race-walk, one of the highest finishes in that event by an American in the history of the Olympic Games.[101]

Carl Schueler ranked in the top 10 American 20-K race-walkers twelve times between 1978 and 1992. He ranked in the top 10 American 50-K race-walkers 11 times between 1978 and 1996. During his race-walking career, Schueler won fourteen National championships, and posted six of the fastest 20 times for 50-K ever walked by an American.[102]

The Seoul Man

Gary F. Morgan was born at St. Joseph Hospital in Pontiac, Michigan on January 7, 1960. He had two brothers and one sister, and was raised in Pontiac. His father, who grew-up in Port Huron, operated a hardware store, and later was a handyman and did building maintenance in Birmingham, Michigan. When Gary was14 or 15 years old, he was pudgy. At an AAU meet Detroit track club coach Betty Lou Robinson suggested to him that he try race-walking.

In 1975 Gary placed third in a regional race-walking meet, and in 1976 won the regional one-mile walk. Always active, he also became an Eagle Scout in 1976. In August of that year he participated in and clocked a respectable (8:05) at the AAU National Junior one-mile race-walking championships in Memphis, but became discouraged and gave up race-walking. Instead, he took up high school cross-country running and ran the mile in outdoor track to help rid his body of an extra 10–15 pounds. During this period, he also tried cross-country skiing. Gary graduated from Pontiac Central High School in 1978. After high school, Gary became an apprentice electrician at a General Motors (GM) plant in Pontiac and took classes at Oakland Community College. In November 1980 he grew a beard and joined the Wolverine Pacers

Athletic Club to fill up his spare time. He ran cross-country and marathon for Oakland Community College in 1981 and 1982.[103]

Coach Frank Alongi, an Italian Olympic distance runner[104] and race-walking coach, immigrated to Dearborn, Michigan in 1960. In 1980 he formed the Wolverine Pacers and intensified his promotion of race-walking. Frank charged only eight dollars for membership to his athletic club.[105] Starting in May all three sessions were held at Levagood Park in Dearborn. After some vigorous calisthenics, and several laps on their own, Frank provided individual instruction for walking faster and more efficiently.

These lessons improved Gary's race-walking style and he began to walk competitively again in 1981. On June 29 he won the 1,500-meter walk (6:16) at the International Freedom Festival Meet at the University of Windsor. In July Gary placed 13th (1:15.39) at the National 15-K Walk Championship in Niagara Falls. Later that year, the six-foot two inch, 175 pound Morgan won the State of Michigan 5-K Walk Championship and the State 10-K Walk Championship. In September 1981, Gary was still running cross-country for Oakland Community College.

As a result of his 1981 performances, Martin Rudlow invited Gary to the Olympic Race Walking Development Camp at the United States Olympic Training Center in Colorado Springs.[106] At this camp, Gary was introduced to many of the technical aspects of race walking. A number of issues, such as maintenance of appropriate heart rate to avoid fatigue, coordination of arm and leg movements, optimum stride and turnover of steps, were addressed for the first time in his career. Among other things, Gary discovered that his normal standing heart rate should be 43 to 45 beats per minute. When it gets above 50 he gets tired. This was a critical step in his development.

On March 28, 1982 Gary competed in his first indoor meet at Madison Square Garden. He finished fifth in the National two-mile walk. During his career he would race at Madison Square Garden 25 times, including 15 appearances at the Millrose Games, and 10 at the National Indoor Championships. When in New York City, he practiced the heel and toe in Central Park, and was frequently greeted with snickers and smirks for his efforts. No matter—he was used to it. Nevertheless, he preferred the quieter atmosphere in Michigan where he could commune with nature while training in near anonymity.[107]

Success did not come easily. Unlike most modern day world-class athletes, Gary had a full-time job, and could not be a full-time athlete. He was now a union electrician (Local 653) at G M's Pontiac Motors

Olympic race-walker Gary Morgan and Erwin "Carrot Eater" Erkfitz in 1990. Erkfitz walked across the USA in 1959 as a publicity stunt. *(Photo courtesy of Gary Morgan)*

and needed the job to support himself. Success came only after years of hard, relentless work. During those years, his body broke down on several occasions with bronchitis, strep throat, or both, interrupting training schedules and slowing down progress in conditioning. Gary mounted numerous comebacks after sickness or injuries. In addition to persistence, he needed luck to achieve his goals.

On the average day, when preparing for a meet, Gary's workout began at 5 a.m. In 1983, he ran three miles to start work at 6 a.m. At lunchtime, he ran an additional two miles, and after working eight hours, he ran three miles back home. Then, once he had changed clothes, he drove to a nearby Indian Springs Metropolitan Park and speed-walked the eight-mile loop once or twice. He sometimes finished the day with a swim of a mile or so. For recreation he liked to cross-country ski, bike, and roller blade. During workouts, when he really concentrated, his tongue stuck out of the corner of his mouth.[108] On average, Gary walked or ran 80 to 90 miles per week around Pontiac Township, or spinning around the track at Pontiac Central High School, and swam three nights a week in his effort to build stamina. He did not, however, time his workouts as closely as he would a decade later. During this period of time, Gary's mother was a consistent source of inspiration and encouragement. Gary explained, "I work off motivation and desire. Happiness comes from within. You must be self-motivated to be a champion and it has always been my intention to be a champion."

On May 5, 1984 placed third (21:02.4) in the 5-K Walk at the Jesse Owens Classic, Columbus, OH. As the Olympic trials approached, Gary told a *Oakland Press* reporter, "I'm not a favorite, but I've worked real hard. There are three or four guys way up there. After that, there is a whole group trying to move up. I'm in that group."[109] Gary did not make the Olympic team in 1984, but he proved that he was a good prospect for future Olympic teams. After the 1984 Olympic trials, Gary was asked to join the New York Athletic Club race-walking team. He did, and believes that it was one of the best moves he ever made. Their financial support for travel expenses made possible significant leaps forward in his career.

Gary did well in 1985. He moved to Clarkston. On June 15 he placed sixth in the U.S. Track and Field National 20-K Walk Championship in Indianapolis. He won his first National Championship in the 10-K at Niagara Falls. He also placed fourth in the 15-K Walk at the Olympic Festival in Baton Rouge on July 27. The race was held at 6 a.m. and Gary finished only one second out of third place. In September he participated in the triple duel track meet in Tokyo involving Japan, the USA, and the USSR. He placed second in the 20-K walk.

In the fall of 1986 Gary decided that he would rather be an Olympian than an engineer, so he shifted his energies away from school toward more vigorous training. When the victories did not piling up, he decided to ask Frank Alongi of Dearborn to help him improve his walking techniques. The following year he experienced a breakthrough. As he would later recall, "I didn't start making my best times until I was 27 years old." On July 16, 1987 Gary won the 20-K walk at the Olympic Festival in Raleigh-Durham. He also placed fourth at the National 20-K Walk at the USA/Mobil Outdoor Championships in San Jose, CA.[110] and qualified for the World Championships in Rome. While in Europe, Gary walked in races held in Germany, Italy (where he met the Pope), and Spain. On September 2 Gary placed 28th in the 20-K Walk (1:28:08) at the World Championships—a good showing. This tour was fun for Gary because of the team camaraderie, an element of international track-team tours that is increasingly missing. With the infusion of big bucks paid to a few track stars, there are fewer and fewer team tours, less time to train together, and the stars do not travel with the team. Instead, they fly in for their event, talk to almost no one, and leave immediately after they compete.

Race-walking is a difficult sport to master, and it has the lowest profile of all events in track and field. Like distance running, it takes endurance, but unlike running, it is both an athletic event and an art form. Participants must lock their knee on every stride and always have one foot in contact with the ground. An entrant is disqualified if a judge catches him making a mistake on three occasions. "It's all legs," Morgan explains. "You have to be stronger than a runner, and you have to be thinking all the time." "I love it. I love the competition and it keeps me in good shape."[111]

Gary continued to train by walking the eight-mile bike trail at the Metropark [on White Lake] four times a week and twice a week worked out with Frank Alongi in Dearborn. His style of training also was changing because he was working smarter and the whole idea behind how to race-walk had changed. "We no longer take long strides. We want short rapid strides now. The turnover is so rapid no one can tell whether or not both feet are off the ground. The idea is to be smooth. If you are smooth, you won't get disqualified." He also placed more emphasis on speed than he had in earlier years. He now trained with a stopwatch and used the mile markers to advantage. He usually walked at a rate of about 6:50 to 7:30 minutes per mile, and generally walked an average of 50-miles per week.[112]

After shifting into high gear in January 1988 Gary trained seriously for six months. On Saturday July 16 Gary Morgan won the 20-K walk at the U.S. Olympic trials in Indianapolis.

The heat was almost unbearable [averaging 98∞] but Gary Morgan of Clarkston mastered sweltering temperatures and his competitors as he won the 20-kilometer walk at the U. S. Track and Field trials at Indiana University Stadium. "I've been training in this type of weather north of Detroit the last couple of months, otherwise it would have done a number on me. I was real dehydrated the last couple of miles." Morgan had to be taken to the medical tent for about 30 minutes, but was fine. He beat a field of 26 race walkers. "I took the lead at about 7,500 meters. This was definitely the hottest weather we've ever competed in."[113]

Wearing a T-shirt that read "Seoul Man," Gary Morgan left for Los Angeles on August 31. After a weeks in Los Angeles., the entire Olympic team traveled to Tokyo. They arrived in Seoul, South Korea on September 15, and Morgan had to cool his heels in a hotel room for eight days before his Olympic event. He was the first American to cross the finish line in the 20-K walk, but only placed 37th.

When the Olympic team returned home, Gary attended a ceremony in the White House hosted by President Reagan, and an Olympic awards dinner put on by the New York Athletic Club. Finally, he traveled to Argentina to race-walk in the Pan-American Race-Walk Cup Championships.[114]

On June 19, 1989 Morgan, "the Seoul man," placed second (1:28:06) at the National 20-K Walk in Houston. On October 10 he won his first National Championship at the National two-hour walk (15 miles and 1,716 yards) held in Cambridge, MA. In 1989 he also placed 55th in the 20-K Walk (1:29:13) at the World Cup Race-Walking Championships, L'Hospitalel, Spain.

Gary achieved his personal best in the 20-K Walk (1:26:57) in July 1991, when he finished second at the Los Angeles Olympic Festival at Drake Stadium on the UCLA Campus. In September, he bettered the American record (20:33) for the 5-K Walk at the TAC National Racewalking Championships at Research Triangle Park in Raleigh-Durham. He closed the season with a $1,000 prize for winning the Step Ahead Stampede in Indianapolis on October 13th with a 20:38 time.[115]

Because race-walking is a very technical sport, expert assistance and specialized training are essential to the development of young race-walkers. The size of the stride must be tailored to the height of the walker and the length of his or her legs. Arm motion must be kept close to the body. Upper body posture is critical, hip motion, and the timing of the locked knee are key to being considered a legal walker, rather than a runner. Since Federal support for Olympic sports dried up at the end of the cold war, necessary assistance is missing for promising track athletes. As Gary puts it, "race-walking is the Rodney Dangerfield event of track and field. It gets no respect." A lot of guys don't want to pay the price to be a track champion these days. In 1983 267 runners met the American Olympic trial standards for the marathon. In 1999 only 27 met that standard. Running always hurts, too many fellows avoid pain these days." "People aren't healthy. What I do is work."

Another problem is the subjective aspect of race-walking. The timing of the straight knee is open to interpretation and the fast turnover of strides makes it difficult to detect if the walker has maintained contact with the ground. Short walkers often take 200 strides per minute, while taller walkers average closer to 175 strides per minute. Consequently little guys are more likely to get away with having both feet off the ground than taller walkers.

On February 28, 1992 Gary raced around the track at Madison Square Garden 34 times to win the 5-K Walk (19:55) at the United States Indoor Championships, proving once again that he was a champion. On June 22–6, 1992 Gary demonstrated that motivation and desire to win are critical when he placed 2nd in the 20-K walk (1:30:40) at the U.S. Olympic trials, Tad Gormley Stadium in New Orleans to qualify for the American Olympic team a second time. However, the rules changed and his times were not fast enough for him to qualify for the preliminaries at the Olympic Games in Barcelona. He was listed as an alternate on the 1992 U.S. Olympic Team.[116]

In late May 1993 Gary rebounded by winning the 5-K race walk at the annual Dexter-Ann Arbor First America Run on its twentieth anniversary. Gary liked the race so much that from then on he put the event on his racing calendar at the beginning of every year. For the next seven years he won this 5-K race walk.[117] On August 15 Gary won (2:02:31) the National 25-K Walk Championship at New York State University in Albany.

As the Olympic trials approached again in 1996, few gave Gary Morgan much of a chance to make the team. However, as Gary puts it, "when the Olympic trials come along, I'm ready to roll. Now it's time to do it. Others get nervous: I become determined. The bigger the race, the better I do." On June 21, 1996 at the U.S. Olympic trials in Atlanta, Gary placed third in the finals of the 20-K Walk (1:31.00), slightly over one minute behind the winner. While Gary qualified for the American Olympic team, his times were not fast enough to compete in the Olympics. But, in 1996 Gary carried the Olympic Torch when it came through Taylor, Michigan. It was one of the greatest thrills of his life. Later that year he made the Pan American Race-Walk Cup team and on September 19, 1996 traveled to the rainforests at Manaus, Brazil, where he placed eleventh in the 20-K Walk.

On April 21, 1998 the Quarter-Century Club honored Gary Morgan with the James M. Cooke Award as the New York Athletic Club's Man of the Year.[118] After speaking to the Quarter-Century Club, Gary said:

I want to be a champion. I love New York. New York is a riot. You can feel the electricity in the air. I'm pumped up when I'm in New York. I'm ready to go. You've got the crowd here. "The first thing I do when I come to New York is to take a lap of Central Park. I walk all over the City. I love it.

Race-walking and the New York Athletic Club have been great to me. A job is just a job, but race-walking is fulfilling for me. I love to travel. I have been to every state except North Dakota. I've been all over the world—to Canada, Japan, Finland, Scotland, Guatemala, Brazil, Argentina, Spain, England, France, Italy, and Russia. I've been most everywhere I want to go, all because of race-walking. The problem is that track and field is a dying sport. Only a few are benefiting. There is too much money for a few greedy people, while opportunity to develop new comers is being eliminated.

Ten days later Gary placed well (2:25.37) in the USATF National 30-K Championship in Albany, New York. In August he placed fifth in the 20-K walk at the Goodwill Games, Long Island. He was the top American finisher in that race.

In a the last minute decision after work on a Friday in mid-September 1998, the 38 year-old Gary Morgan decided to accompany Jerry and Jeanne Bocci, long time Michigan walkers, to the National 40-K Walk Championships. Gary and the Boccis drove all night to Fort Monmouth, New Jersey in a van, and all three entered the meet. Much to his surprise, Gary won the National 40-K Championship in his best personal time at that distance (3:21:48). Until then he had never considered himself capable of walking in world-class competition at distances over 35-K.

Encouraged by his success, he set out to train for the 50-K championships held in February 1999. At the National 50-K Walk Championships, Gary placed fifth with a personal record time of 4:15:0 5. This qualified him to walk in the World Cup Race in Mezidon, France. At the World Cup Race on May 2 he again posted a personal best at 50-K with a time of 4:13.13. This time qualified him for the United States track team that would race at the Pan-American Games in Winnipeg the following July, where he placed fourth.[119] An unplanned, spur-of-the-moment decision had catapulted him to new heights in his two-decade old track career.

On September 25–26 Gary won the National 5-K walk held in Kingsport, Tennessee. At Worcester Poly-Technical Institute in Worcester, MA on October 3 he won the national 2-hour walk by covering 25-K and 33-meters. He capped-off the year by dodging a heard of ten to 15 deer, that obstructed his path on Belle Isle, to win the *Detroit Free Press*/ Flagstar Bank Race-walk.[120]

When asked why he had taken up race-walking, Morgan said,

I like to eat too much, and I'm a health nut. I want to keep physically fit, so I exercise through active sports. I love to compete. I've got more heart than anybody has. All of us have good years and bad years, but don't quit! Even at 39 years of age, I have not hit my potential yet. Working out is fun for me. I like being outdoors. I have a true appreciation of nature which is fostered by being outside for my workouts. I don't take any drugs, not even an aspirin. Instead, I take a carefully determined set of vitamins and natural food supplements. Too many athletes drop dead 10 or 20 years after taking drugs. Those thing catch up with you.

As he grew older, Maurilio de Zolt, the Italian cross-country skier became Gary's role model. Zolt won a gold medal by helping the Italian four by 10-K cross-country ski team beat the Norwegians at the 1994 Olympic Games in Lillehammer, Norway when he was 43-years old. "Like Zolt, I too will be a champion after I am forty." In pursuit of that dream, Gary trained relentlessly to make the 50-K Olympic race-walk team.[121]

The Olympic trials were conducted in inclement weather that did not favor the 40-year-old walker, who was struggling with a bad foot and hip. His Olympic dream in the 50-K ended in Sacramento, California on Sunday February 13, 2000. Despite cold rain and gusting winds that ranged between 20 and 30 miles per hour, Gary finished the race. Thirty-two year-old Curt Clausen won the trial in the time of 3 hours, 56 minutes and 19 seconds. Gary Morgan walked the 31 plus miles in 47 degree weather in 4 hours, 37 minutes and 2 seconds and placed sixth, good enough to qualify him for the Pan-American Cup Races on April 8 in Mexico.[122]

On March 4 he placed fourth in the 5-K walk at the USA Track and Field Indoor Championships in Atlanta.[123] Finally, on April 16 he won his seventeenth national championship when he captured the 30-K National Championship in Flushing, MI.

The meets in Sacramento and Atlanta at the close of the century made it clear to those present that the officiating and meet conduct of national race-walking by USA Track and Field made a travesty of race-walking rules. A majority of participants, including the first three place winners were clearly engaged in a running trot. These participants did not lock their knee or keep one foot on the ground at all times as required by the rules, and these violations were completely ignored by the officials. It was part of an international trend that threatened to destroy this unique event.

Over his twenty-year race-walking career, Gary competed in Madison Square Garden twenty-five times and won six out of the first ten *Detroit Free Press* race-walk championships.[124] He won 17 national race walk championships.[125] He was the 1989 and 1992 Indoor Grand Prix Race-Walk winner, he qualified for three United States Olympic teams, and he represented the United States at the 1988 Olympics in Souel, South Korea. He competed on four Pan-American Race Walking Cup teams (1988, 1992, 1996 and 1998), two World Race-Walking Cup Championship teams (1989 and 1999), and at the World Track and Field Championships (1987). He was a three-time Olympic Festival medalist. He also competed at the Goodwill Games (1998) and the Pan American Games (1999). In 1998 Gary was the New York Athlete Club Athlete of the Year. Morgan was ranked in the top 10 American 20-K race-walkers nine times between 1985 and 1996.[126]

Michigan's Contribution

Race-walkers, with a Michigan connection, have played an important role in this unique sport during most of the twentieth century. Michigan has produced more champion race-walkers than any other state, with the possible exception of New York. The Olympic Games and National Champion race-walkers who have a Michigan connection include: Charles Foster, Ernest Crosbie, Albert Mangan, William Mihalo, Walter Fleming, Adolf Weinacker, Goetz Klopfer, Jeanne Bocci, William Weigle, Ward Freeman, Carl Schueler, and Gary Morgan. These Michigan walkers won no less than 82 national race-walking championships. They have participated in 11 Olympiads, 4 Pan-American Games, 2 World Championships, 2 Goodwill Games, 10 World Cups meets, 7 Pan American Race-walking cup matches, and a NAIA College Championship. Since 1971, Michigan connected race-walkers have placed in the *Track and Field News* top ten rankings for the 20-K walk 26 times and for the 50-K walk 18 times.[127]

14. Hurdling To Fame: Starring Hayes Jones And Rex Cawley

The earliest hurdle races governed by strict rules of any sort were held in the middle of the nineteenth century. They were run at the Scottish Highland Games in Liverpool in 1858. On July 27, 1859 the hurdles, featuring four hurdles, were run at the Wenlock Olympics in England, and the 440-yard hurdles were run at the London Olympics in 1866.[1]

The three classic distances in hurdling are the 110 meter (120 yards), the 200 meter (220 yard), and 400 meter (440-yards), which according to the height of the barriers—always ten for each race—are commonly referred to in athletics jargon as the 'highs', the 'lows', and the 'intermediates' respectively. It should be noted that the 200-meter hurdles have only been included in the Olympic program twice, 1900 and 1904. The lows, a typically American event for decades, were dropped from the NCAA outdoor program in 1962. The hurdles for this race are only 2 feet 6 inches (76 cm.) high, and tended to make it an additional event for sprinters.[2] In 1971 the low-hurdles were eliminated from indoor events.[3]

The hurdles for the 110-meters and 120-yards[4] are 3 feet 6 inches (1.06 meters) high and are placed at intervals of 10 yards (9.14 meters) from each other.[5] Initially and at the end there is a flat course of 15 yards (13.72 meters). The slight surplus for the metric event is added at the end. The English [or Scottish] origin of the high-hurdles event is well established.

The earliest barriers were solid sheep hurdles, 3 feet 6 inches in height and 'rigidly staked into the meadow'. Under such conditions pioneers were primarily concerned with making a safe clearance—however uneconomical. In going over the barriers, the body was almost erect and the legs were raised and bent as in a standing jump. Consequently the center of gravity remained far too high, and the action over the hurdles was slow. Either leg could be used as the lead leg, and the rhythm between hurdles was far from uniform . . . By the beginning of the 20th century, Americans became masters of the high-hurdles. Alvin Kraenzlein is considered the father of modern hurdlers. He was one of the first to adopt the straight-leg lead. "On 18 June 1898 in Chicago he won the AAU title race in 15.2, the official American record at the turn of the century." At the 1900 Paris Olympics, this powerful, barrel-chested six-footer won four events [in three days] including the high and low-hurdles. His 1898 low-hurdle record (23.6) stood for twenty-five years.[6]

No state in the USA assembled as many champion hurdlers during the twentieth century as Michigan. Starting with John McLean, the silver medal winner of the 110-meter high-hurdles at the 1900 Paris Olympics and ending with Central Michigan University's 1999 All-American Greg Richardson, Michigan produced 35 hurdling champions. Included in that mix are twenty-seven All-Americans, nine Olympians, thirteen AAU or NCAA champions, two NAIA champions, ten Drake Relays, Penn Relays or Millrose Games winners, and seven Big Ten Champions. The world-class hurdlers included John Garrels, Walter Fishleigh, Joe Malcomson, James B. Craig, Carl E. Johnson, William DeHart Hubbard, Edward O. Spence, Charles Beatty, Willis Ward, Robert Osgood, Harvey Woodstra, Al Tolmich, Charles Hlad, Fred D. Johnson, and Bill Porter in the first half of the century. In the last half of the century such champions as Clifton Cushman, Hayes Jones, Rex Cawley, Willie Atterberry, Eugene Washington, Bob Steele, Gerald Cerulla, Bill Tipton, Bob Cassleman, Eddie Brown, Tiberia Patterson, Tom Wilcher, and Alex Washington are on the list. Then, of course, we can not forget Olympians Debby Lansky La Plante, Kim Turner, and Judi Brown.

Over the course of 100-years, rules and equipment changes had an impact on the hurdling events. At the start of the twentieth century a contestant was disqualified for knocking down a hurdle. The rule was soon changed to allow one hurdle to be knocked down, but records in the three hurdle events were not accepted if a hurdle was knocked over, and knocking down two hurdles would still result in disqualification. On July 4, 1921 Gus Desch of Notre Dame University was deprived of a record in the 440-yard three-foot hurdles at the National Senior AAU Championships in Pasadena because he knocked down one hurdle.[7] The same happened to Morgan Taylor at the VIII Olympiad in Paris in 1924, when he set a world record in the 400-meter hurdles at Colombes Stadium in Paris, only to have it denied because he knocked down one hurdle.[8] In the 1924 Olympics George Guthrie of the USA finished third in the high-hurdles but was disqual-

ified for knocking over three hurdles. In 1932 Olympics in Los Angeles, Will Welscher of Germany placed fourth in high-hurdles but was
disqualified for knocking over four hurdles.[9]

By the mid-1960s hurdling records were no longer disqualified for
knocking down hurdles. Instead, for championship events, hurdles
were constructed that required a minimum of an eight-pound pulling
force to overturn under rigid specifications, because a hurdler may hit
every hurdle during a race without being disqualified. Thus a hurdler
was penalized in speed each time he hit a hurdle.[10] Later, the hurdles
were made lighter, and the penalty for hitting a hurdle became minimal.

When the low-hurdles were eliminated in 1962, the 330-yard hurdles race was retained on the dual meet schedule but it was no longer
permissible to substitute the 220-lows. However, where mutually
acceptable the 440-mediums could be substituted. All races not run in
lanes were required to employ a curved starting line so that all runners
were equidistant from the start of the curve.[11]

A "Beautiful Stylist" From Jackson, Michigan

The last great hurdler from the State of Michigan of the first half of the
century was William Franklin Porter III. Born in Jackson, Michigan on
March 24, 1926, Porter attended Western Michigan Normal from July
1944 to November 1945; then transferred to Northwestern University
where he graduated in 1948.

In the spring of 1946 Porter won the high-hurdles in meets against
the Universities of Wisconsin and Iowa. He dominated the 1947 Western Conference indoor season. The Jackson, Michigan timber topper
won the high-hurdles, the low-hurdles, or both in meets with the University of Chicago, the University of Iowa, Ohio State University and
the University of Wisconsin. At the Big Nine indoor meet on March 8,
1947, "Porter ran a perfect race in the high hurdles to tie the [Ameri-
can] record [for the 70-yard high-hurdles] of 8.5 seconds. Porter passed
the defending champion, George Walker of Illinois, just before the last
hurdle."[12] He went on to win the high-hurdles and place second in the
low-hurdles in the Big Nine outdoor championships. At the NCAA
championships, he placed second to Harrison Dillard in the high and
low-hurdles.

The six feet three inches tall Porter, peaked in 1948 just in time for
the Olympic games. At the Drake Relays he placed second in the low-
hurdles. On May 28 he won the won the 120-yard high (14.1) and
220-yard low hurdles (23.2) at the Big Nine Championships in Madi-

son. On June 11–12 he won the 120-yard high-hurdles (13.9), the 220-yard low-hurdles (23.1), the 440-yard shuttle hurdle relay (56.8), and the mile relay (3:14.1) at the Big Ten-Pacific Coast Inter-conference duel meet. The following week he placed second in the high-hurdles at NCAA Championships in Minneapolis. Finally, when the shift was made from 120-yards to 110-meters, he won the highs at the AAU Senior Championships in Milwaukee on July 3, and repeated his domination of that event at the final Olympic trials at Northwestern University on July 10.[13] The 110-meter hurdles are about one foot longer than 120-yard highs. The extra eleven inches of running seemed to help Porter.

At the London Olympics, Bill Porter, often referred to as a "beautiful stylist," won all three races in the 110-meter high-hurdles, and set the Olympic high-hurdle record (13.9). Here is Bill Porter's own story of the race:

I got off fast and I thought I had the race won. Then I hit the third hurdle and by the time we reached the sixth hurdle I was two yards behind Craig. Right then I thought he had me beat, but he made a mistake over the eighth hurdle and I had him for keeps. Record or not, it was a sloppily run race. I'm surprised it was that fast. My 14.1 semi-final somehow felt faster.[14]

William F. Porter was named All-American in the high-hurdles.[15] After college, he became an executive in a hospital supply business.[16] In 1959 he was inducted into the Drake Relays Hall of Fame.

The Most Versatile Runner in State History

Willie J. Atterberry, Sr. was born in Laurel, Mississippi on May 16, 1934. His step-father, Clemon Shropshile, was a shipping clerk. Willie moved to Detroit with his family just before World War II. In high school Atterberry, for all practical purposes, was a five-minute miler: A "mule aiming for the Kentucky Derby." Struggling academically and without a sense of direction, Willie dropped out of Eastern High and joined the Army in January 1953.[17]

It was in the Army that a personal transformation took place. It started in Korea with an Army mess sergeant. As Willie Atterberry recalls it, "when I learned that a place on the battalion track team was a ticket out of k.p. I saw running in a new light." Now, he had an enthusiasm for the sport he never before felt in high school. But, he found that in the middle distance Bob McMillen, the NCAA 880-yard champion from Occidental College blocked his way onto the team, so he tried the 440-yard dash, "the dead man's race."

In his first race, he ran the quarter-mile in 50 seconds flat. Two starts later, he was down to 48 seconds. That ended kitchen duty, and demonstrated how much powerful motivation can change a person's life. By year's end Willie Atterberry worked on the hurdles and set an Army record.[18] Success in track led to a G.E.D. high school diploma.

Upon completion of his tour of duty, Atterberry enrolled at Compton Junior College in California. At Compton, Willie set four National Junior College track records. On April 3, 1956 he set the record for the 880-yard run (1:52.1) at a meet in Glendale. On April 7 he set the record for the sprint medley relay (3:26.2) in a meet at Santa Ana. On May 4 he set the record for the mile-relay (3:15.7) in a meet in Riverside, and on May 12 he set the record for the two-mile relay in a meet in Fresno.[19] At the end of the summer, Atterberry finished fourth in 400-meter intermediate-hurdles at the U.S. Olympic trials. He just missed the 1956 Olympic team, despite recording the fastest fourth place time (51.2) in the history of the Olympic trials.[20] His showing made him an alternate for the team, but he did not make the trip to Melbourne.

Preferring to compete closer to home than in California, Willie wrote to Kark Schlademan, the track coach at Michigan State, and to Don Canham at the University of Michigan. Both offered him a scholarship, but Canham thought that his six months at Compton Junior College had cost Willie some eligibility and explained that he could only offer him a two year scholarship. Schlademan talked of three competitive years, which was correct. Atterberry became a Spartan.

Atterberry sat out of college competition for the 1956–7 academic year. He did, however, compete in AAU meets, and on a hot and humid April afternoon in Ohio State's huge stadium he broke the world out-door record (1:08.5) in the 600-yard run. His performance was unequalled either indoors or outdoors. Bill Wehrwein came close in 1969, but Atterberry's record stood for nearly twenty years.

One afternoon in a dual meet with Notre Dame in May 1958—when he was a college sophomore—the six-foot one inch, 150 pound Atter-berry won the mile (4:16) and the 220-yard dash (21.5) in a 20-minute stretch. In 1958, the tenth best American in the intermediate hurdles was more than one second faster than in 1957. While Willie was get-ting better, so was his competition. From June 26 through mid-July, 1958 Willie toured and competed in Germany and Switzerland with an AAU team of four athletes.[21] John Telford was the best man at his wed-ding. Because of poor grades in his medical technology course, Atterberry was ineligible for the 1959 track season at Michigan State University.[22] Atterberry discovered, as others did, that a demanding class schedules conflict with training. As one track athletes lamented, "My professors hate the fact that I'm on the track team. They don't make it easy. They keep telling me I need more time for my studies."[23]

In 1960 Atterberry won the Big Ten indoor track title in the 1,000-yard run (2:11.7) nipping Illinois middle distance runner Ted Beastall by just one second. In the Big Ten Outdoor Meet, he finished second in the 440 and third in the 220-yard dash.[24] However, Willie suffered a leg injury and was eliminated from heats at the NCAA meet.

Atterberry received a bachelor's degree in Medical Technology from Michigan State University in 1960. In 1961 Willie Atterberry moved to Los Angeles to become a medical technician for the Red Cross, and continued to run competitively.[25] In the summer of 1962 "Willie Atterberry, a lanky man with good speed (46.9 for the quarter) and plenty of stamina (1:50.0 for the half-mile) beat Salvatore Morale, the great hurdler from Teolo, Italy, in a race under terrible conditions. However, he showed little improvement in the intermediates between 1956 and 1962."[26] On July 10 Atterberry won the 440-yard intermediates (51.6) at the British National Track Championships and on August 20 he won the 400-meter hurdles and 400-meter run (46.7) at the Goteborg Games in Sweden.[27]

Atterberry was one of forty track and field athletes selected to represent the United States in the Pan American Games in Sao Paulo, Brazil.[28] On May 1 the former Spartan placed second for a silver medal in the 400-meter intermediate-hurdles (50.4) in Sao Paulo.

Jim Allen got sick, just as the USA vs. USSR Meet was scheduled to start in Moscow on July 20, 1963. The AAU put in an emergency call to Atterberry, and he came through in the clutch by winning the points that made the difference between the USA winning and losing the meet.[29]

Willie Atterberry told a reporter for *Track and Field News*,

In your last edition, you mention that I quit the LA Track Club. I didn't quit. I was kicked off by Bob Anderson, the new president of the LA Track Club. Bob wanted me to turn down my trip to Europe this summer. He told me that if I went I wouldn't run for the LATC in '64. It turned out to be the best trip of all for me. After two weeks in Finland my wife met me in London. From there we went to Germany for a couple of meets. When I was called to Russia to run for Jim Allen, I had to leave my wife in Amsterdam for three days. For the next two weeks my wife and I were spending our delayed honeymoon in Italy and France. To make matters worse, the LATC tour to Europe didn't go through. I've tried to get back with the LATC, but Mike tells me he does not want to be reasonable [have the option of not following his demands] for anyone who has a chance of making the Olympic team or anyone who will accept an AAU tour [over loyalty to his program].[30]

In 1963 Atterberry set his sights on making the Olympic team in the intermediate hurdles. His primary competitor, Rex Cawley felt that Atterberry was "very smooth but lacked speed." This was an inaccurate assessment. Atterberry was a 46.7 quarter-miler in 1962 and a 1:50 half-miler. Moreover, he had enough endurance to place ninth in the 1958 AAU steeplechase. Atterberry's 1964 ambition was, "to run several hurdle races down in the 49's next year. I plan to run in as many hurdle races as possible. Looking back over last year's times, my chances look pretty good. But I am worried as hell about next year; not about Allen or Cawley, but about the 'unknown.'"[31] Age and increased competitions were the unknown obstacle. Willie peaked in 1962, not in 1964.

In the finals of the intermediate hurdles at the Olympic semi-final trials held July 3–4, 1964 at Randalls Island, New York,

Willie Atterberry went out fast but by 150 yards Hardin was the decisive leader. Coming off the final turn, Billy Hardin hit the eighth hurdle and lost valuable ground." Jay Luck and Rex Cawley began to move up at that time. Off the ninth hurdle, Luck was clearly in the lead, and extended his lead to the tape. His time was only two-tenths of a second off the world record. Atterberry, who had run every race well all year but could not get his time under 50.5, was nosed out for sixth place. Atterberry said, "I'll keep running this summer if I get a trip to Europe. I hope they will advance me, particularly since I was so close to sixth. If I don" go on a trip, I'll hang it up for good.[32]

As the *Lansing Journal* reported,

Willie Atterberry sat in the depths of depression at New York City's Morningside Heights. The former Michigan State track star had just missed his third and, probably, his last chance at a berth on an U.S. Olympic track team. As he sat dejected in a dormitory at New York University he could only say hopefully, 'Maybe I'll run a fast time in Europe this summer and they'll let me run in September." "I was hoping I would have a bad year so I could quit, but I'm running faster than ever." Unfortunately for Willie every one else is running faster than ever, too. His time of 50.5 in New York was one of the best of his career, yet he was only seventh.[33]

Willie J. Atterberry demonstrated that he was one of the most versatile runners in U.S. track and field history. After working for the Red

Cross and a hospital as a specialist in medical technology, he worked for Property Management Services in Los Angeles from 1988 to the end of the century.[34]

Cedarville Silver

One of the 400-meter hurdlers who kept Willie Atterberry out of the 1960 Olympics was Clifton Emmett Cushman, who was born on June 2, 1938 in Cedarville, Michigan. Clifton attended the University of Kansas, where his versatility allowed him to run the mile (4:11.6) and to place sixth in the triple jump at the 1959 NCAA outdoor championships. In 1960 Cushman won the 400-meter intermediate hurdles at the NCAA championships, and placed third in that event at the final Olympic trials. Cliff took second in the intermediate hurdles at the Rome Olympics, and won the intermediates at the AAU championships in 1961.

Five years later, on September 25, 1966, Clifton Cushman was killed while serving in the armed services in Vietnam.[35]

A Frequent Flyer: Hayes Wendell Jones

Hayes Jones was born on August 4, 1938 in Starkville, Mississippi, the location of Mississippi State College. His father was a janitor and he had two aunts who were married and had relocated to Pontiac, Michigan. In 1940, Mr. Jones resigned from his janitorial job, and went north to Michigan, where he took a job in the foundry at Pontiac Motors. The rest of the Jones family moved to Pontiac in 1941, when Hayes Jones was three years old.[36]

When Hayes was in fourth grade he participated in the Kiwanis Club's "Little Olympics." This experience resulted in a lifetime interest in sports, and particularly in track and field. Hayes soon played half-back on his elementary school football team. When he moved on to Washington Junior High School, however, he was too small to play football or basketball, so he focused on track. Yet, he was slow in acquiring adult muscles, so he was not a good athlete. Relegated to third or fourth in every event he tried, and he tried them all, he decided to tryout for the cheerleading team when he reached high school so that he could be included with the athletes. While he still ran track, Hayes was not particularly good at any event.

Between his sophomore and junior year in high school Hayes asked the track coach if he could practice on the hurdles over the summer. The coach agreed to leave two hurdles in an unlocked shed at a school

Hayes Jones truly did work his way through college. Here he is washing dishes at an Eastern Michigan University dormitory to pay tuition since the school offered no athletic scholarships until the late 1960s. *(Photo Eastern Michigan U Archives)*

near the Jones home. That summer Hayes Jones practiced nearly every day, while his friends were enjoying themselves swimming and "horsing around" at Walled Lake.[37] Hard work and additional maturity paid off. On April 15, 1955 Hayes Jones won the high-hurdles (15.4) and the broad jump (19–2), and tied for first in the high jump (5–11) in a duel meet with Fordson High School.[38] Then on May 21 he won the high-hurdles at the Michigan High School Class A Championships.[39]

At Pontiac Central High School, Dean Wilson, a former Western Michigan University football and track star, coached Hayes Jones. In 1953, at the age of 27, after coaching track at Traverse City for three years, Wilson accepted the head coaching post at Pontiac Central. Almost immediately, Pontiac Central became a dominant power in Michigan high school track. The Chiefs won four straight State High School Championships (1955 through 1958) and repeated again in 1960. During this period Wilson coached eleven individual, State champions. Bill Tipton, Michigan high school and National Junior's high and low-hurdle champion, was one of his proteges.[40] On April 6, 1956 Hayes won the 65-yard high-hurdles (7.4; 8.0) and the 65-yard low-hurdles in record setting time at the Central Michigan Indoor Interscholastic Meet in Mt. Pleasant.[41] In May 1956 he won the 180-yard low-hurdles (19.4), the 120-yard high-hurdles (14.3), the high jump (6–2), and the broad jump (23–8¾) at the Michigan Class A High School Championships.

As a result of his dominant showing at the State Championships, several Michigan colleges with strong track programs recruited Hayes Jones. Head coaches from Western, Central, and Eastern Michigan Colleges, and the University of Michigan, as well as Ohio State University, expressed an interest in having him attend their school. Since the Jones family did not own an automobile, Hayes rejected the offers from Ohio State and Western Michigan out of hand, because his parents would be unable to see him compete. Coach Wilson recommended that Hayes attend a smaller college where he would not get lost in a big athletic program and where he could get special attention with his academic programs if he needed it.

When his parents met Coach George Marshall at Eastern Michigan College, that sealed the question of where he would go to college. They liked Coach Marshall. He was a strong father figure who seemed likely to do what was best for their son rather than what was best for his track program. Even though Eastern could not offer him a scholarship, they would guarantee a job that would pay board and room and books. Moreover, since they had church friends who had children at Eastern, his parents could get a ride to Ypsilanti to see their son run in meets. By contrast, they were suspicious of Coach Canham at the University of Michigan. They were afraid that while he could offer a scholarship and would showcase their son better than Eastern, their son's interests would not be the uppermost consideration at the University of Michigan.[42]

So, Hayes Jones attended Eastern Michigan College without a scholarship. He washed dishes and cleared tables at Jones Hall to pay for room and board, and his mother and father paid his tuition.[43] Later, Hayes purchased an automobile for his parents—their very first—to repay them for their love and help.

His freshmen track coaches at Eastern Michigan College were Walter Schoerke and Ray Lowry, a former track star at Eastern. They had difficulty determining whether or not Jones would be best served by specializing in one event. Jones ran the 120-yard high-hurdles in 13.6; 100-yard dash in 9.4; and the 220-yard low-hurdles in 22.9. He could also high jump 6–4½, and broad jump 25–1½. At Eastern College, under the direction of Head Coach George Marshall, Jones perfected the two arm style in hurdling, first developed by Thompson of Dartmouth, and in use at Eastern Michigan College for some 35 years. His form in the high-hurdles was flawless. Hayes majored in physical education with a minor in health. He was a good student, modest and unassuming, and very popular with faculty and students.[44]

As a freshman in college, Hayes Jones won the high hurdles at indoor meets with Marquette University, Central Michigan University, the University of Chicago, and at the Michigan AAU and the Denison University Relays. However, it was his encounters with Lee Calhoun and Milton Campbell at the *Chicago Daily News* Relays and the Knights of Columbus Meet in Cleveland that convinced Hayes that he was a world-class athlete himself. Calhoun and Campbell had just won gold medals at the Olympics in Melbourne.[45] At the *Chicago Daily News* relays Hayes Jones came in second, but he beat Campbell. In Cleveland Jones beat Calhoun.[46]

During the outdoor season, Jones won events at the Ohio Relays and the Interstate Intercollegiate Conference Championships. On April 27, 1957 he won the College Division 440-yard relay (41.7) at the Drake Relays. On June 22 he placed fourth in the 220-yard low-hurdles and fifth in the 120-yard high-hurdles at the National AAU Championships in Dayton, Ohio. His showing at the AAU meet was good enough to earn him a trip to Europe with AAU Tour Group I.

In Europe he won the high hurdles (14.3), the Swedish relay [sprint medley] (1:51.9), and the 4 × 100-meter relay (41.2) in Bordeaux, and the high hurdles (14.4) and the 4 × 100-meter relay in Paris, Nancy, Sochaux, and Lausanne, France. He also won the high-hurdles and placed second in the 100-meter dash (10.6) in Champagnole, France.

In December 1957 Hayes injured his ankle [at first it was reported as a broken bone], but recovered for the Michigan AAU Relays held in late January 1958.[47] As a college sophomore, Hayes Jones was the outstanding athlete of the Michigan AAU Relays on January 31, 1958 in Ann Arbor. He equaled meet records in both the high and low-hurdles and lost by only 6 inches to Ira Murchison in the 60-yd dash. In the 65-yard highs, Jones won his heat in 8.8, his semi in 8.0 and the finals in 7.9. In the lows he ran 7.4 for all three. He won 60-yard heats in 6.3 and 6.2 before losing to the national champion in 6.2.[48] On March 1, 1958 Hayes Jones won the 70-yard low-hurdles (7.6), the 60-yard dash (6.1), the 70-yard high-hurdles (8.3), and the high jump; he was second in the broad jump (23' 8") in a duel meet with Indiana University held in Ypsilanti. He accounted for 22 of Eastern Michigan's 54 points in their four point win over a strong Big Ten team.[49]

On February 22, 1958 Hayes Jones won the 60-yard high-hurdles at the National Senior AAU Indoor Championships held at Madison Square Garden. At that meet a college friend from New York attended the meet with his father and won several dollars betting on the relatively unknown Jones boy from Michigan. On June 21, 1958 Hayes Jones won the 120-yard high-hurdles at the National AAU Senior Championships at Memorial Stadium in Bakersfield, California.

Hayes Jones continued his winning ways in 1959. At about the time the first computer chip was being patented, he was named the outstanding men's performer at the Drake Relays.[50] In late August 1959 he won the high hurdles in the Pan-American Games, and in a duel meet with the USSR. He won the National AAU Indoor Championships in 1958, '60, and '61 and equaled the indoor low-hurdles record of 7.0. He was now established as one of fastest of the world's great hurdlers. He had run the 100-yard dash in 9.4 and the 220 in 20.9; the high-hurdles in 13.5; the low-hurdles in 22.5. He high jumped 6'4¼" and broad jumped 24'½".

At one point Jim Bibbs asked Eastern Michigan coach George Marshall how he instructed someone with the talent of Hayes Jones, hoping to learn some coaching tips for his own use. Marshall replied, "If you're lucky enough to get a kid as good as Hayes Jones, the best thing you can do is talk to him every morning to see how he feels and to ask him if he's happy. Keeping him healthy and happy is the best coaching you can do."[51]

At the USA vs. the Soviet Union duel meet in Philadelphia on July 18, 1959, the skies were clear, the temperature was 85 degrees and the humidity was 58% when the 110-meter high-hurdle race was called.

It was a real race. Fast-starting Hayes Jones was never quicker off the blocks. At five hurdles, he had a full meter on Olympic Champion Lee Calhoun. The latter is a truly great fighter and at this point he struck back. Though Jones was flying, Lee pulled even at the 8th barrier. The 20-year-old Eastern Michigan ace would not concede. Hayes, who sometimes fades at this juncture, dug in. He edged ahead and held that slight advantage as both men lunged for the tape. Calhoun, who had outleaned Jack Davis at Melbourne, was the loser. Official times showed 13.6 to 13.7, quite impossible. It was a virtual dead heat. Almost unnoticed, Anatoliy Mikhailov finished in 13.9—possibly a tenth or so generous. At 22, he's still young but a typical Russian—no basic speed. Form-wise, his bobbing head and lurching body do not contribute to an efficient hurdle action.[52]

H. W. Jones competed in only one NCAA track and field championship during his four years at Eastern. George Marshall had severe financial restraints and very limited travel funds. Moreover, since Eastern was a relatively small school, Hayes Jones did not find much competition from the hurdlers and sprinters in his conference. Instead, Coach Marshall arranged for Hayes Jones to compete in the AAU indoor and outdoor meets, even when it deprived Eastern of his participation in dual and triangular meets with conference rivals. Jones typically ran in all 12 of the AAU sanctioned indoor meets, while in college. In most cases, these meets paid the travel costs associated with his participation. This made it possible for Hayes to attend a small school with a good track and academic program, without foregoing his prospects for being an international track athlete and Olympic champion.[53]

On January 20, 1960 Hayes sprained his ankle, and missed the *Washington Evening Star* Games.[54] "Hayes Jones of Eastern Michigan continued unbeaten in the hurdles this season by again whipping Olympic champion Lee Calhoun and equaling the meet record of 7.1 for the 60-yard high-hurdles in the New York Knights of Columbus meet. Jones broke two yards on top and stayed that far ahead all the way to beat Calhoun for the sixth straight time."[55]

In 1960, Hayes stood 5'11" and weighed 169 pounds. At the Millrose Games in New York City Hayes came in third in the voting for the meets outstanding performer in 1960.[56] He opened his bid for a gold medal in the Rome Olympics by winning the high-hurdles at the Marine Corps Relays in Quantico, Virginia on April 16. His performance was one of the 18 meet records set in the first rainless version of the relays.[57] At 3 p.m. on Saturday July 2, Hayes Jones got off the blocks in a fast start in the finals of the 110-meter high-hurdles in the final Olympic trials at Stanford, California. He had a decided lead as he skimmed over the first hurdle, but he held it for less time than ever before. By the second barrier, the 27-year old Lee Calhoun was in front. As the hurdles clipped by, Calhoun poured it on, gaining a four-foot advantage. Hayes Jones, also a fierce competitor, stuck with the 1956 Olympic champion. His closing burst, however, failed to recover all the lost ground and the fast stepping Willie May caught Jones to tie for second place. Calhoun's 13.4 time tied the American record for the event, but the time did not seem that fast to Calhoun, who was pointing for a 13.3 to set the world record.[58]

At the Olympic Games in Rome, Lee Calhoun won the high-hurdles, Willie May placed second and Hayes Jones third. It is interesting to note that in later years these three and Charles "Deacon" Jones, the University of Iowa steeplechase champion who placed seventh in that event at the Rome Olympics, often would spend "Super Bowl Sunday" together swapping "war stories" about their days on the track circuit.[59]

At the USA vs. the USSR meet at Central Lenin Stadium in Moscow on July 15–16, 1961 Hayes Jones was the leadoff runner on an all-African-American relay team that set the world record in the 400-meter relay (39.1). They broke the world record by four seconds in front of 60,000 Russian fans against a Soviet team that set the European record that Saturday afternoon.[60]

On June 23, 1962 at the National AAU Championships in Walnut Creek, CA sports writers declared, "This was one of the greatest hurdle duels of all time."

Jerry Tarr had shown himself to be the equal of Hayes Jones by passing him at Modesto before he hit a hurdle, but Jones had said it would happen again when the pressure was on Tarr. Jones, the fastest man ever for the first two hurdles, put the pressure on Tarr from the start. Jones is usually a yard ahead of everybody at the first hurdle, and this was no exception. Tarr is usually a yard behind everybody, but this time he trailed only Jones by a yard. Later, he said 'I'm not a good starter, but tonight I got one of my best.'

Jones increased his lead to almost five feet at the second hurdle. Then Tarr began to gain. Slowly but definitely, he crept up to the flying Jones. At the ninth hurdle they were even, Tarr appeared sure to win. But it was not over.

Jones, who admits he needs endurance work, was still fast. Tarr gained little over the last 25 yards. To spectators he appeared to have a six-inch margin after the last hurdle, but both hurdlers tell it another way.

"I pulled even with him [Jones] as we landed after the last hurdle," Tarr said. "I leaned way forward as we hit the tape and barely made it." Jones agreed, "Tarr edged me from the last hurdle in. We both leaned for the tape, but he leaned better. He had more chest, I guess." Tarr was pointing for Jones. "Hayes Jones was rated number one in the world, and so he was the one man I wanted to beat. He has taken me to the cleaners five or six times and I wanted to get out of that rut. I would say I won on confidence and desire. I'm mighty happy." Jones groaned, 'I've got no excuses. I ran a perfect race."[61]

Hayes Jones was possibly the best starter of all time in the 110-meter hurdles. He was blessed with quick reactions and great leg speed. Jones matched Dillard's 'speed' (personal best, 9.4) for the 100 yards, and lowered the indoor record for the 60-yards high-hurdles to an almost unbelievable 6.9 (1962). Jones was just a bit taller than Dillard. His improvement after 1957 was slow but constant. "On momentous occasions, however, he had been outshone by Calhoun."[62]

Hayes Jones was the only American to run in all five of the USA vs. USSR meets. At the USA vs. USSR meet held on July 20–21, 1963, Hayes was keyed for the 110-meter high-hurdle race. He faced two solid competitors: teammate Blaine Lindgren and Russia's Anatoliy Mikhailov. When the gun fired, Hayes Jones knew he had false started and slowed up. Mikhailov went on to out-chest Lindgren at the tape. In the meantime, Jones had told the starter of his error and the recall gun was fired. Officials decided to re-run the race later in the day, despite whistling from Russian spectators. In the second race Jones again hesitated at about the second hurdle, apparently because he felt there was another false start, and was never in the race for first. Mikhailov had a good lean at the finish, and beat Lindgren in similar fashion, although there was a tenth of a second difference in the time. When asked what happened, Jones answered, "It was something unique. I jumped. I was guilty so I stopped. I turned and told the starter and he fired the recall."[63]

"Hayes made no alibis for finishing third in the hurdles ("It just wasn't my day."). Jim Dunaway of Track and Field News speculated that "Hayes lost confidence in the starter. . . . The runners were afraid of that starter. In fact, the meet started out with four false starts in the decathlon 100-meter. Certainly the start Jones got must have been one of his poorest ever. And Blaine Lindgren running with an injured foot, did well to run 13.9."[64]

The following January, competitors in the high-hurdles at the Maple Leaf Games held in Toronto on January 24 were elated to hear that the fog had made air travel from Detroit impossible. The joy, however, was short lived when Hayes and Paul Jones showed up at the meet. As *Track and Field News* reported:

> The Detroit airport was fogged in, so Hayes Jones [and Paul W. Jones] drove to Toronto. Despite the resulting fatigue, he [Hayes] streaked to a record-breaking 5.9 victory for his 50th consecutive high-hurdles victory.[65]

Hayes Jones' extended streak of indoor victories in the high-hurdles over several years is probably the greatest example of consistency in track history. It started after Jones lost his last indoor meet of the season to Lee Calhoun at the Cleveland Knights of Columbus meet in March 1959. His streak began with the start of the 1960 indoor season and ended when he retired from indoor track following the Baltimore All-Eastern Games in 1964. During that span he won first place in the hurdles in 55 consecutive meets. Jones competed in both high- and low-hurdle races in three, college dual meets in 1960 and won all three. So he won 58 hurdle victories in 55 consecutive meets.

Jones' performances were consistently outstanding. Of the eighteen major US meets being held annually at that time, Jones held meet records in 13 of them and was the co-holder of the hurdles record in the other five. When he bowed out of indoor hurdling, he held world records at three distances (50, 60, and 70 yards) and was co-holder at another (45 yards). At that time, he was the only man ever to break 7.0 seconds for the most common hurdle distance of 60-yards—first breaking it with a 6.9 at the *Chicago Daily News* Meet in 1962. Probably his most remarkable record was for the 60-yards, which was contested in 10 major meets. His 6.8 for this event is exceptionally good: only he and Milt Campbell had done 7.0 prior to Jones breaking this record in 1962.[66]

At the semi-final trials for the Olympics, held on Randalls Island on July 3–4, 1964, Hayes Jones equaled his lifetime best of 13.4, which was only a fifth of a second off the world record, in winning the 110-meter high-hurdles. Despite his supposed lack of conditioning, he got off to his typically fast start and widen his lead throughout the race. "The time surprised me because I'm really not in top condition yet. I guess I ran so fast because I was scared. I've got a lot of respect for Blaine Lindgren. He really sends the adrenaline pouring into my system," Hayes recalled. Lindgren, who had beaten Jones in their only two encounters before the AAU finals, finished second in 13.7. Usually he closed on Jones in the last 30 yards, but not this time.[67]

In the USA vs. USSR Meet at the Los Angeles Coliseum on July 25–26 Hayes Jones hit the last two hurdles and lost the highs by two feet to Blaine Lindgren. When asked about his performance Hayes responded, "This meet meant nothing to me. This is an Olympic year and that's all I'm interested in. I really just wanted to see what kind of shape I'm in, whether that 13.4 in the Olympic trials was just something I pulled out of a bag or if I'm really that sharp. I never did get straightened up after the start. So I was leaning forward a little off balance all the way. It finally got me to the point where I hit the last two hurdles—and that broke my stride."[68]

At the final Olympic trials held in the Los Angeles Coliseum on September 12 Hayes Jones was off in the lead as usual. However, at the first hurdle he was only a foot ahead of six foot one inch, 185-pound Willie Davenport, a 1962 high school graduate who had been in the Army for two years. Davenport ran close to Jones for seven hurdles, then pulled away. Davenport won and Hayes Jones was second. After the race, Davenport said, "I was surprised to win. I thought the best I could do was third. I took the lead over the last three hurdles. I'm naturally very happy. This is my all-time best."

Jones said, "I led over the first hurdle and then ran neck and neck with Davenport until the last three hurdles. I feel I ran a good race, but I'll have to go home and ponder what I did wrong. I believe we can score a sweep at Tokyo. Tokyo will be my last race."[69]

When the U.S. track team reached Tokyo, *Track and Field News* observed, "Hayes Jones is confident and hates to lose. He runs his best races in follow-up heats held the same day."[70] The preliminaries for the 110-meter high-hurdles were held on October 17, a sunny, mild day [73° F]. Willie Davenport injured his leg four days before the preliminary heats, and wore a big bandage on his left thigh for the first round heats. Despite the injury he qualified for the semi-finals by placing second in his heat. Blaine Lindgren and Hayes Jones of the United States also qualified for the semi-finals. Lindgren won his heat. Hayes Jones led all the way in his heat only to be nipped at the finish by Marcel Duriez of France, but still qualified from his heat.

When the semi-finals were run the following day, in the cold [57° F] and rain, it became obvious that at least a half dozen American high-hurdlers who did not make the Olympic team were fast enough to make the Olympic finals in the high-hurdles. But, Davenport lost whatever chance he had for a medal when his injury caused him to fall off balance on the fifth hurdle and trip on the 10th hurdle in the semi-finals. Lindgren won his semi-final heat defeating Jones by a tenth of a second. In the finals, however, Lindgren drew the pole lane—a position he disliked—and Jones ran in lane six. As usual, Jones was out fastest of all the competitors, and Lindgren was also out well. By the second hurdle there was little difference between the two Americans, although Jones was probably a foot or two ahead. At each hurdle, Lindgren inched up on Jones until they were virtually dead even at the seventh hurdle. At the eighth barrier, Lindgren may have edged ahead by inches, but as they approached the last hurdle, they were dead even again. Hayes Jones' superior speed gave him the gold medal by inches (13.6). Lindgren was clocked at 13.7), as was Anatoliy Mikhailov of the Soviet Union, who won the bronze medal.

Hayes Jones had finally won his gold medal. He had won and accomplished just about everything in hurdling over his ten-year track career. It was a very disappointing conclusion for Blaine Lindgren, who confessed, "It has been a long time since I cried, but I'm not ashamed to say I did after Jones beat me. What hurt was that I lost the race because of a stupid mistake. I started leaning for the tape too quickly but I'll never make the same mistake again." But Lindgren was high in his praise for Jones. "I don't want to take anything away from Jones, however. He ran a great race and deserved to win. He's a very fine hurdler. I really can't say enough good about him."[71]

Hayes lamented, "I might run indoors this season. I said I was through, but it's easy to get the bug again. But I'll never run outdoors again."[72] Hayes Jones, running for the Detroit Varsity Club, was named to the 1964 AAU All-American team for the 110-meter high-hurdles.[73]

Hayes pocketed his gold medal in the high-hurdles and retired from competition, but not from track. He did some coaching with girls and worked with the new NCAA indoor meet held in Detroit.[74] By the end of 1965 when he retired from running, Hayes held the world, American, and collegiate indoor track record for every hurdle event from 50 yards to 75 yards.[75]

Becoming an Olympian was no frivolous undertaking. It required incessant training, an internal drive and love of the sport strong enough to overcome injuries and defeat, and could even necessitate inventing intricate "head games" for oneself to sustain the effort and overcome the persistent pressure associated with becoming the best at your chosen endeavor. As a prerequisite to winning an Olympic gold medal, Hayes Wendell Jones spent nine years and ran in more than 400-heats in competitive men's track and field meets after becoming a high school state championship. Anyone who thought that being an amateur athlete was a part-time job did not compete during the second half of the century. Yet, the camaraderie, recognition, and opportunities available to a poor and disenfranchised young man, as a result of the experience, made that effort well worth the price for Hayes Jones.

In 1966 the Detroit Varsity Club sponsored an AAU sanctioned meet at Cobo Arena on Friday January 14. The meet director was Hayes Jones, and the meet was called the Motor City International Indoor Track Meet.[76] It sought to take advantage of the new board track at Cobo Arena, and to maintain the city's track and field heritage. Among the Detroit track greats who functioned as officials for that meet were: David J. Beauvais, Robert R. Luby, Charles E. Fonville, John Telford, Lorenzo Wright, Horace Coleman, Mark Smith, Leroy Dues, Billy Smith, Irving Petross, Aaron Gordon, Don McEwen, and Charles Eugene Beatty.[77]

Unfortunately, while the event was an artistic success, the meet lost money. Fewer than half of Cobo Arena's 9,500 seats were filled despite the appearance of champion sprinter Charlie Green and Olympic champions Ralph Boston, Wyomia Tyus, and Wilma Rudolph.[78]

Hayes Jones is a member of the USA Track and Field Hall of Fame and the Drake Relays Hall of Fame. In 1965 he was a sales representative for American Airlines. In the 1980s Jones was elected to the Pontiac Board of Education, and at the turn of the century he worked in community relations.

The Other Jones

Paul Wesley Jones was born in Detroit on November 22, 1938 and grew up in the motor city. In the spring of 1956, while a senior at Pershing High School, he won the Metropolitan League track championship in both the 120-yard low-hurdles and high-hurdles with times of 13.5 and 15.1. If it had not been for the extraordinary feats of Pontiac Central High School track star, Hayes Jones, Paul would have been the best scholastic hurdler in the state. Upon graduation in January 1957, he enrolled at Michigan Normal College, which was soon to become Eastern Michigan College. He lettered for two seasons in indoor and outdoor track on a team that won two Interstate Intercollegiate Athletic Conference titles. In 1957, Paul finished fifth in the high and low-hurdles at the National Association of Intercollegiate Athletics (NAIA) National Track Meet. Most of the season he ran behind Hayes Jones.

Paul dropped out of college in the fall of 1959, the year the first computer chip was patented. But, he continued to compete in track and field. In 1960 Paul rode his first airplane to the District of Columbia to run in the *Washington Star* Games. It was snowing, and he was scared almost out of his mind. When he got to the arena he expected to find a dirt or cinder track. He was surprised to find that he would be running on a wooden gym floor, just as he had done in high school.[79] He came within one spot of making the 1960 U.S. Olympic trials in the 110-meter high-hurdles. At the 72nd National AAU Championships held in Bakersfield, California, he finished fifth in the high-hurdles with a time of 14.2, after finishing third in the semi-finals and winning the third heat of the preliminaries at 14.6.

In the fall of 1961, Paul W. Jones enrolled at Wayne State University, where he earned letters in track in 1962 and 1963. While at Wayne State, he tied the Canadian National Indoor 50-yard high-hurdles record during a meet at the old Maple Leaf Gardens in Toronto. In 1963, he led a contingent to the Penn Relays, where he won the 120-yard high hurdles, and broke a 26-year-old Wayne University school record in that event held by Al Tolmich.[80] In 1962 Paul Jones and his good friend Hayes Jones drove together to Chicago to run in the *Chicago Daily New* Relays. When they got to Chicago they roomed together. Shortly before the limousine came to take them to the meet, Hayes Jones discovered that he had forgotten to bring a T-shirt to run in, so Paul loaned him an extra track shirt he had brought. That evening Hayes won the event and Paul placed third. Paul later quipped, "I am the only hurdler ever beaten to the finish line by his own T-shirt."[81]

After graduating from Wayne State University in 1963 with a Bachelor of Science in Health and Physical Education, Jones taught for three years in the Detroit Public Schools, and continued to compete in track, winning several regional team titles. At the 1964 Midwest AAU Meet in Dayton, he ran a personal best of 13.5 in the 110-meter high hurdles. He was inducted into the Wayne State University Athletic Hall of Fame.

Paul married and had two children. From 1967–74 he worked in sales with several corporations, including Shell Oil, Johnson & Johnson, and Hallmark Cards. In 1974 he joined the Human Resources Department of the Kellogg Company in Battle Creek. He retired in 1997 and moved to Southfield, Michigan.[82]

In 1964 the low-hurdles were completely phased out of intercollegiate competition. The 330-yard hurdles were retained on the duel meet schedule but it was no longer permissible to substitute the 220-lows hurdles for the 330-yard intermediate hurdles. However, where mutually acceptable the 440 mediums could be substituted for the 330-yard hurdles.[88]

"Rex" Cawley Went West to Seek Gold

Warren Rex Cawley was born in Highland Park, Michigan on July 6, 1940. He was a precocious runner. As a junior at Farmington High School, he won both the high and low hurdles at the Michigan High School Championships. In 1958 while still in high school, Rex took the initiative in organizing the Detroit's Suburban Track Club. His track club won gold watches by placing first in the junior sprint medley relay and setting a Canadian open record for that event (3:40.4) at the Canadian National Relay Championships in Toronto on July 4.[89]

As a high school senior, Rex won the 60-yard high-hurdles (7.5) at the National Junior AAU Indoor Championships held at the University of Chicago fieldhouse. In May 1959 he ran the 120-yard high-hurdles (13.9) [ran 13.6 wind aided] and ran the 120-yard low-hurdles (18.9) for Farmington High School in winning the State Championship for these events for the second straight year. His times were the second fastest times for a high school track runner in the USA that year. On June 19–20 shortly after high school graduation, at the National AAU Meet in Boulder, Colorado, Rex Cawley and the other contestants ran in the rain. The rain cut the crowd to an estimated 6,000 on Friday and 8,000 on Saturday, but did little damage to the competition. The asphalt runways and the dark gray cinder track stood up well. Cawley drew the sharp-curve inside lane for the finals of the 200-meter low-hurdles. "Running in the rain, [Charles] Tidwell was off fast and gained around the curve on the inexperienced Hayes Jones. But Jones, a yard and a half back into the stretch, almost caught the great Kansan, losing by less than half a foot in world record time of 22.6. Four yards back, running like a demon, was Cawley, beating out Gilbert for third spot."[90] Rex placed in three events-fifth in the 110-meter high hurdles (14.5), third in the 200-meter low hurdles (23.0), and sixth in the 400-meter intermediate hurdles (53.7). *Track and Field News* proclaimed Cawley "the best high school hurdler in the USA."[91]

His performance in the low-hurdles qualified him for All-American status and an AAU sponsored trip to Europe in July 1959. "This 19-

year-old phenom more than confirmed his recently acquired status as one of history's greatest all-round hurdlers." In the "highs" he ran a 13.9 in Oslo (7/31/59). In the "intermediates" he ran 51.6 in Goteborg (8/4/59) losing to Martini of Italy, whose 51.4 was a new national record. In the Oslo race, won by Martini in 51.6, Cawley just managed to nip former world record holder Yuri Lituyev of USSR (51.9). Rex's best time on the flat was 21.5 for 200-meter at Uddevalla, (8/5/59).[92]

Don Canham attempted to recruit "Rex" for the University of Michigan, but Cawley did not have sufficient academic standing. Canham then arranged for Rex to go to the University of Southern California, even paying his airfare to California for the site visit, just to keep him away from other Big Ten competitors.[93] According to *Track and Field News* "Southern California landed a better-than-usual crop of freshmen, headed by Warren "Rex" Cawley, prize plum of the lot. Already [with] international interest in all three hurdles, Cawley will undoubtedly spend a lot of time on the 400-meter hurdles with an eye toward Rome."[94] Cawley was a member of the USC Class of 1964.

On June 14, 1960 Cawley, representing the Detroit Athletic Club, defeated John Telford, of the Detroit Track Club, in the 440-yard dash at the Dearborn Track Club Meet. Rex ran the quarter-mile in 46.8, and Telford covered the distance in 47.0.[95] This race proved beyond doubt that Cawley had the speed to be a great 400-meter hurdler.

On Friday July 1 Rex Cawley ran second in the second heat of the intermediates to qualify for the finals at final Olympic trials at Stanford. Just over an hour later, he participated in the fastest 400-meter hurdle contest in the 40-year history of that event. Cawley, an exceptional 19-year-old, drew the second lane.

All seven of the finalists had run 51.1 or better in the preliminaries, setting the stage for one of the best hurdle races in history. Eddie Southern, a 22-year old, led the contestants over the first hurdle. At the halfway point of the race, he still led, but the schoolteacher, Glenn Davis, was beginning to move up from his lane one vantage spot. By the seventh hurdle, Cawley trailed the pack. On the straightaway, after eighth barrier, Davis galloped for home, pulling away from the pack slowly but irresistibly. His 49.5 time equaled his own meet and world record. Cawley, who ran last, did his personal best with a time of 50.6. It was the fastest seventh place in history, and only four others not in the race had ever run that fast in this event.[96]

In 1960 Rex Cawley was the best college, freshman track athlete in the world in the 440-yard dash (46.8) and the 400-meter hurdles (50.6); the second best in the low-hurdler, and the fourth best high-hurdler.[97] In June 1961 Rex was injured and could not compete at the NCAA Outdoor Championships. By 1962 *Track and Field News* considered Cawley one of the five best all around hurdlers in the world.[98]

At the AAWU Conference Meet in Berkeley, on May 25, 1963, Cawley contributed 10 points to the Trojan cause. He ran a victorious (46.7) 440-yard and followed it up with a win in the medium hurdles, "where he managed to look incredibly bad yet fast, as he clocked 51.5."[99] On June 15, 1963 at the NCAA Outdoor Championships in Albuquerque, Rex had one of the best double wins in the history of the sport. He won the 440-yard dash (46.1)[100] then won the intermediate-hurdles (49.6). Ulis Williams, a sophomore from Arizona State, ran with smooth speed, and led Cawley by three yards into the stretch in the 440-yard dash, but Cawley closed to win. Cawley ran five races in three days, yet did not miss a step. Trailing the leaders in the intermediate-hurdles by two yards heading into the stretch, Cawley suddenly unleashed an amazing kick, shooting past the two leaders in a matter of a few yards. He won the race going away.[101] Jack Shepard, of *Track and Field News* ranked this achievement as one of the top ten double wins in American track history.[102]

On June 21–22, 1963 Rex won the 440-yard intermediate-hurdles (50.4) at the National AAU Senior Championships in St. Louis. His time was the second fastest AAU time ever. Yet, Rex complained, "this track is too springy. It is murder on the hurdlers. When you come down it throws you too close to the hurdle, and you have to change your stride."[103] After the race he remarked, "I felt very strong and confident in the stretch, and gave a little extra lunge at the finish line. I learned that from Lee Calhoun. At the last hurdle he (Allen) was a couple of yards ahead of me, but I felt strong and confident, because this is how I planned my race."[104]

Going into the Olympic trials in 1964 American intermediate hurdlers were improving rapidly. Rex was six feet tall and weighed 165 pounds. He was seriously injured two years earlier, but recovered and was now improving to his earlier form. He was running the 440 in 46.2.[105]

Rex Cawley was definitely the best in 1963, and at 23 he is hardly over the hill, although the first year after collegiate competition ends is a crucial one. Cawley says, 'I hope to run consistent sub 50.0 races and occasionally go below 49.0. I will run cross-country this fall and work only on the hurdles next year with particular emphasis on my step. Up until now, I haven't trained much at all. I've been getting in shape in the meets. But this year will be different.[106]

On July 25, 1964 Rex ran the intermediate hurdles in the USA vs. USSR Meet at the Los Angeles Coliseum. He caught Billy Hardin at the eighth hurdle and finished in 49.5. After the race Cawley said,

I'm very surprised at the time. That 49.5 scares me a little. Maybe I'm too sharp when you consider I have to keep that sharpness all the way through October. I have done very little work on the hurdles since I ran 49.8 at the Olympic semis. So I must credit those tough 500 yard workouts I've been having with Ulis Williams for my strong finish.[107]

On September 13 at the final Olympic trials in the Los Angeles Coliseum, Rex broke the world record for the 400-meter hurdles (49.1).[108]

The preliminaries for the 400-meter hurdles at the Tokyo Olympics were held on October 14, the semi-finals the following day, and the finals on October 16.

With only 40 entries, only three races were needed. Five heats were run in the trials with the first three in each heat plus the fastest losing qualifying into the semi-finals the following day. The heats went according to form. In the first heat John Cooper of Great Britain looked extremely good as he won in 50.5, his best time of the year. . . . The second heat saw Rex Cawley, USA, break on top with Juan Dyrzka of Argentina running even until the 8th hurdle when Cawley pulled away to win in 50.8.

The weather was again good the next day. Cawley ran in lane five in the first heat of the semi-finals. Robert Frinolli of Italy was away well and led until the 9th hurdle when Cawley, who was in fourth place over the fifth hurdle, caught him and won looking over his shoulder in the stretch in 49.8. Two fine hurdlers from the heat, Jaakko Tuominen from Finland and Ferdinand Haas of Germany did not make the finals. In the second semi-final heat, Billy Hardin of the USA was shut out. He had hoped to emulate his father, Glenn Hardin, who won this event in 1936. Jay Luck of the USA did make it to the finals from the second heat.

On Friday, clear weather with a comfortable temperature of 68 degrees Fahrenheit greeted the finalists of the 400-meter intermediate hurdles. Rex Cawley drew lane six. Jay Luck was in lane three and John Cooper, of Great Britain, was in lane four.

Cawley was out of the blocks slowly, as Salvatore Morale and Roberto Frinolli of Italy lead for the first five hurdles. Luck and Cooper were also ahead of Cawley early in the race. Rex ran off-stride until the sixth hurdle. Rex started to move going into the turn and caught everyone except Frinolli between the 7th and 9th hurdles. He passed Frinolli going over the 9th hurdle and closed with his usual burst of speed to win easily in 49.6. Meanwhile, things were happening behind him. Frinolli struggled as his pursuers closed on him. Luck moved in the turn but hit the 8th hurdle and then lost his chance for second when he hit the 10th hurdle. Cooper and Morale also moved past Frinolli, and Cooper outran Morale for the silver medal.[109]

At the victory stand presentation, Cawley said he was most thrilled when two American trumpeters, Uan Rasey and Manny Klein, finished the Star Spangled Banner for the Japanese band.[110]

The 400-meter hurdles in 1964 were a far cry from the event that was first run in the 1900 Olympic Games in Paris. In 1964 contestants cleared ten three-foot high hurdles spaced 35-feet apart, after a 45-foot approach. The finish line was 40 feet from the finish line. In 1900, the "hurdles" were 30-foot long telephone poles, and there was a water jump just before the finish.[111]

On June 26, 1965 Rex won the 440-yard intermediate-hurdles (50.3) at the National AAU Senior Championships, and toured with the American AAU team that summer. At a meet in Kiev on August 1 "Rex Cawley, not exactly in his Tokyo form had to work hard in the 400-meter hurdles. He lacked rush and a last ditch dive eventually brought him slightly ahead of Vasiliy Anisimov."[112] Rex Cawley never matched 1964 but still was still the best intermediate hurdler in the world.[113]

Between 1964 and 1969 there were few remarkable 440-yard hurdlers. According to Rex Cawley, "Up to a couple of years ago, the intermediates weren't run on a regular basis. The race was usually found only in the national championships and a few relay and invitational meets. In the Olympic year, there were no opportunities whatsoever. But the inclusion of the intermediates in the collegiate program will really boost the performance in the near future." However, the problem also involved the wide range of talent required for success in this event. Cawley summed it up this way, "The ideal man would be a combination of Wilt Chamberlain's size. Tommie Smith's speed, Abebe Bikila's stamina, Lee Calhoun's hurdling technique and George Young's determination. Until such a man comes along, we'll have to look for a measure of each of these characteristics in slightly less magnificent proportions."

When asked whether to use 13 or 15 strides between hurdles, Cawley said,

I don't believe either method is inherently faster than the other. It depends on the man using it. A tall man chopping to 15 steps would tire quickly and look as ridiculous as a short man bounding along stretching to make 13. Whichever method is most comfortable and efficient for the athlete should be used. Sometimes a mixture of the two is best.[114]

At the time Rex Cawley stopped running at the end of the summer AAU tour in 1965, he was still the best intermediate hurdler in the history of the event.

Eugene Washington, Denied Equal Access in Texas

Eugene Washington was born on November 23, 1944 in La Porte, Texas. Gene's father, Henry, was a construction worker. Gene attended George Washington Carver High School in Baytown, Texas where he was an All-State football player for three years—two years as an end and one year as a quarterback. His football team won the state championship twice. Gene was holder of the Texas High School record for the 120-yard low-hurdles and All-State in track for three years. He also was a letter winner in baseball and basketball, All-State in Basketball, fifth in his graduating high school class, and a member of the National Honor Society.[115]

When he graduated from high school in 1963, Gene was denied admission at both the University of Houston and the University of Texas because of his color. Subsequently, Michigan State University, where he became an All-American football player, recruited him. In November 1965 the 209-pound 6-foot-2 Washington was named United Press International Midwest lineman of the week for scoring three touchdowns against Indiana. Coach Duffy Daugherty commended Gene Washington for his superior coordination and speed.[116]

Gene helped the Spartans win two Big Ten football titles and the 1966 national championship. He earned three letters and was an All-American in track 1965, when he was NCAA indoor 60-yard high-hurdles champion.[117] An academic All-American, Gene recalled,

The thing I'm most proud of, beyond my athletic achievements, are my education achievements. . . . I'm so thankful Michigan State got me out of the segregated South. I had enough of the separate drinking fountains and having to use the back door at restaurants. It's amazing that this country had that situation not too long ago. All these kids know today is an integrated environment and for that, they should feel fortunate and thankful.[118]

Spartan track coach Fran Dittrich picked Gene Washington as a co-captain of his 1966 indoor cinder squad, because he is academically sound and had strong leadership skills.[119] Responding to the challenge, Gene played an important part in helping the Spartans win their first Big Ten indoor track title. At the Big Ten indoor meet, "hurdling was the key to MSU's power, and the agreement between Washington and [Clint] Jones at least contributed to their sweep of this event." When

Gene and Clint qualified first and second in the hurdles, they switched lanes so that Gene always ran on the right of Clint. Gene was left-footed and Clint was right-footed. MSU coaches made certain that Gene was on the right so that when their leading legs when over the hurdles together their trailing legs, which often fling out to the opposite sides, would not get tangled and throw them both.[120]

In 1966 the MSU 480-yard high-hurdles relay team that included Gene Washington, Clinton Jones, and Bob Steele set the USA college record for the event at the Drake Relays. "But [the record was theirs] only after Nebraska's anchorman fell over the last hurdle while leading by two yards."[121]

There was a bizarre sidelight during the preliminary heat in the shuttle relay in 1966. Iowa State University finished second in their heat of the 480-yard hurdle relay, apparently winning a place in the finals, but alert observers in the press box were puzzled. They knew tall, dark-haired John Adams had led off for Iowa State; they also knew that an unidentified anchorman, also tall and dark haired, looked suspiciously like Adams. One thing was certain—the fourth runner was *not* the listed runner, Darryl Green. Officials asked Adams who led off: "Adams," said Adams Who anchored? Adams hesitated, then said, "I think it was Adams." He explained that Green hadn't showed up for the race, adding: 'I didn't know what else to do," said Adams, "so I ran the first leg and went back into the blocks at the other end and ran the anchor, too. "That last 120 yards was a lot longer than the first." It turned out that Green told Coach Bob Lawson just before the race that he had a sore leg. It was too late—and too much—for the coach. He sent Green home.[122]

In 1967 the Minnesota Vikings drafted Gene Washington in the first round, and signed with them on June 10.[123] He was All-Pro in 1969 and 1970, and played in the Super Bowl in 1970. "While I was with the Vikings, I worked at 3M on Monday, our off day. And I worked there before practice Tuesday through Friday. I knew it would be important to have a second career," said Washington. In the off-season between 1968 and 1972, Washington was an assistant director of student placement services at MSU, while he worked on a master's degree.

After his stint in professional football was over, he moved back to Minneapolis. He retired from pro-football because of a foot injury that required re-constructive surgery. Prior to retiring from pro-football, he coordinated the Dayton Department Store's Affirmative Action, College Relations, and Employee Relations Programs. After leaving football he became their Disability and Claims Administrator. In April 1976 he became Personnel Manager for the company's Distribution Center, and was promoted to Manager of Merchandise Distribution in June 1977. He served in that capacity until he was made Coordinator of Executive Recruitment and College Relations in August 1978. In April 1982 Gene became Personnel Manager and served in that capacity until May 1984.

In June 1984 Gene Washington became National Sales Manager and Director of Human Resources for the Lustrasilk Corporation, where he served until becoming Western Regional Sales Manager for the Fitness Equipment Division of the Toro Company. Finally, he returned to the 3M Company in 1988. While with 3M, he budgeted and managed a part of the 14 million dollars in contributions 3M Foundation annually gave to educational endeavors. In 1998, Washington became a manager in 3M's staffing and resource center in St. Paul, Minnesota.[124]

At the end of the century, his wife, Claudith, once a bank vice-president, was an elementary school teacher. The Washington's had three daughters.

Robert Edward Steele Triathlon Superstar

Robert E. "Bob" Steele was born on October 18, 1945 in Buffalo, New York to Glen R. and Edna Steele. Glen was an engineer. Bob graduated from Plymouth High School in Michigan in 1963. At that time Bob stood 6–2, weighed 165 pounds, and had red-blond hair and blue eyes. In high school he lettered two years in basketball and three years in track. Initially he majored in physical education, but received a bachelor's degree in History.[125]

During his first year at Michigan State University, Bob was part of a shuttle relay team that won the Michigan State Relays, the Ohio Relays, and the Drake Relays. He also helped the Spartans win their first Big Ten Track championship in the spring of 1965.

From a modest fourth place lifetime best of 52.5 in the 440-yard intermediate hurdles as late as the Drake Relays in 1966, Steele made significant improvements as a junior at State. He suddenly posted a 50.7 a month later to winning the Big 10 Championships. He slipped back to 52.6 the following week, but returned a 50.8 in capturing the Central Collegiates the first week in June. Then came the NCAA outdoor championships at Indiana University on June 17, where he won his heat in 51.4, took the semi-finals in 50.1, and became the national collegiate champion in 50.4. Each race was won by a big margin. He was the first Spartan runner to win an outdoor track title in six-years.[126]

Lacking confidence, he had to be encouraged to run in the AAU meet. Steele raced to a creditable third with his second best time of 50.3 but considered it a disappointment. In the summer of 1966 he toured Europe with the AAU team that received support from the U.S. State Department. Although the meet with the Soviet Union was cancelled at the last moment, he ran in the British Games in London, England on July 9, 1966. Later that summer he ran against the Polish National Team at Berkeley, California.[127]

Some considered his approach to track to be overly simple. When asked about his style and form, he would respond, "I run to win." Nevertheless, he had an aggressive attitude and little fear of the hurdles. He would shoot out of the blocks fast, charge over the timbers with an apparent lack of concern for missing his step, and bear down the homestretch with a considerable will to win. He did not conceal his desire to become an Olympic champion. A broken foot that sidelined him in 1965 was an obstacle in his path to Mexico City in 1968.

In 1966 Bob trained seven days a week, 10 months a year, and engaged in some lightweight weight lifting. He had plans to continue competing until he was 26 years old. In August he told a reporter, "I wish I had known earlier in the year that I was going to be running so well later—I could have worked harder."[128] Bob Steele was named to the NCAA Outdoor 1966 All-America track team for the 440-yard hurdles.[129]

Steele opened the 1967 outdoor season by winning the intermediate hurdles in 52.2 and running a leg of the winning mile relay team at the Michigan Federation meet in Ann Arbor.[130] On June 17 he won the 440-yard hurdles at the NCAA in Provo, Utah, becoming the first two time NCAA track champion in Michigan State University history.[131] Bob was named an NCAA Outdoor All-American for 1967 in the intermediate-hurdles.[132] On July 16–17 he placed third in the 400-meter hurdles (50.9) in the U.S. Pan American tryouts in Minneapolis, missing a berth on the USA squad by 3/10 of a second.[133] On August 20 he ran in the Toronto Exposition meet. He student taught at Warren High School the fall of 1967.[134]

In 1968 Bob Steele was ranked fourth in the USA in the 440-yard intermediate hurdles, and was in a good position to make the Olympic team.[135] However, he was off-form all track season.[136] On June 20–21 Bob placed seventh in 400-meter intermediates (52.7) at the National

AAU Senior Championships in Sacramento. In July during the High-land Games in Hamilton, Ontario, Bob Steele hit a hurdle, and broke his leg while running the 400-meter hurdles. The accident ended his dreams of making the Olympic team.[137]

After graduation in 1968, Steele competed in 30 countries, on a worldwide basis for nine years, and consistently ranked among the top ten or twelve 400-meter hurdlers in the world. In the summer of 1971, Bob and his wife Judy spent much of the summer touring Europe with the U.S. track team. Judy knew little about sports before she married Bob, but he noted with pleasure the enthusiasm with which she had adapted to the lifestyle of world class trackmen. She looked forward to another summer of travelling together.[138]

From 1970–73 Bob Steele ran for the Ann Arbor Track Club. In 1972 he entered the intermediate hurdles in both the Penn Relays and the Drake Relays which were being run the same day within three hours but some 973 miles apart. He opted to run at the Drake Relays in Des Moines.[139] Later that year he placed third in the intermediates at the tenth U.S. Track Federation Meet in Wichita.[140]

During the 1970s Bob Steele was a triathlon athlete. Between 1975 and 1978 he won two new cars and $1,500 in prizes from the Superstar Championship TV Program. In June 1977 when Bob was a 32-year-old elementary physical education teacher in East Lansing, he won $1,200 in the Brandywine Superstars Championship, covering seven iron-man events.[141] During that period, he was also City Adult Tennis Champion on several occasions.

In 1992 Robert Steele was nominated for the MSU Hall of Fame. At that time he had been a physical education teacher in the East Lansing Public Schools for 24 years. He initiated, coordinated, and maintained the Lansing Elementary Schools track and field day program for more than a quarter of a century. He attributed the following benefits to his attendance at MSU: his wife, his job training, his adult residency in East Lansing, worldwide travel, and his network of friends.[142] He lived in Lansing and taught elementary physical education in the East Lansing Public Schools for more than thirty years.

The Wyandotte Wonder

Gerald Edward "Jerry" Cerulla a five foot ten inch tall hurdler from Wyandotte [MI] High School ran in the 76th Annual AAU Senior Men's Outdoor Championships in New Brunswick, NJ on June 27–28, 1964. He placed fifth in the 110-meter high-hurdles (14.3) at the AAU Championships. On July 3–4 Jerry was seventh in the 110-meter high-hurdles (13.9) at the semi-final Olympic trials at Randalls Island. The race was so close that runner three through seven had the same time.[143]

That fall, Cerulla attended Utah State University and ran for them in 1965 and 1966. In March 1965 he placed third in the 60-yard high-hurdles (7.3) at the NCAA Division I Indoor Championships in Detroit. In June he was second in the 120-yard high-hurdles (13.9) at the NCAA Outdoor Championships at Berkeley. "Jerry Cerulla [Utah State University], a bull of a man with heavy legs and a shaved head, hit all ten hurdles in his semi-final while winning in 14.1, and he had trouble in the final, running only 13.9."[144] Nevertheless, he won All-American status. Starting in the 1960s, the first six-place NCAA finishers qualified as All-Americans.[145]

On March 11–12, 1966 Jerry tied the collegiate record for the 60-yard high-hurdles (7.2) while winning at the NCAA Indoor Championships. In May 1966 he was injured.[146] Despite the handicap, he was sixth in the semi-finals of the 120-yard high-hurdles[147] at the NCAA Outdoor Championships in Bloomington. Lonely and homesick, Cerulla transferred from Utah State to Eastern Michigan.

After "red shirting" himself in 1967, Cerulla failed to place in the semifinals of the 60-yard high-hurdles at the National Association of Intercollegiate Athletics (NAIA) indoor championships in Kansas City on January 19, 1968. Later that year he just missed making the U. S. Olympic team.

Doing God's Work

Joseph William Tipton was born in Pontiac, Michigan on May 17, 1949. Joseph William was called "Bill" almost as soon as he was born so as not be confused with his grandfather, Joseph Wesley Tipton. Bill went out for track when he entered junior high school, and was coached by Bob Kent. In 1962 at age 13, when he was in seventh grade, Bill Tipton ran the 60-yard low-hurdles in 9.4 and the 100-yard low-hurdles in 14.4. By age 15, when Bill was in ninth grade, he ran the 60-yard high-hurdles in 8.1 and the 120-yard high-hurdles in 16.7. His 100-yard low-hurdle time was 11.9.[148]

Bill Tipton attended Central High in Pontiac, where Dean Wilson was his coach. In 1966, as a junior he ran the 120-yard high-hurdles in 13.8 and the 180-yard low-hurdles in 18.9. In 1967 he was five feet ten inches tall and weighed 150-pounds. April 1967, according to EMU coach Bob Parks, "He led off Pontiac Central's 880-yard relay team in the Hurons Relays and gave his team about a 20-yard lead." Parks also noted, "He's a yard ahead of the other runners by the time he gets to the first hurdle. At the Mt. Pleasant indoor meet, he ran the 65-yard low hurdles in 7.1 seconds, which is Jones' varsity record here."[149] The high-hurdles are slightly higher in college than in high school—the high-hurdles in Michigan high school track are set at 39 inches, while those in college are 42 inches high. Low-hurdles are the same (30 inches high) in both high school and college.

Tipton was timed in 20.8 for 220-yards during a relay race in his senior year in high school. On May 27, 1967 he won the 120-yard high-hurdles (13.5) and the 180-yard low-hurdles (19.3) running into a 20-mile per hour head wind at the Michigan State Athletic Association Class A Championships in Saginaw. He tied the national scholastic record for the 120-yard high-hurdles (13.5).[150] In June he won the 120-yard high-hurdles at the Golden West Invitational in San Francisco, and on August 25–26 he won the 120-yard high-hurdles (13.4) and the 180-yard low-hurdles (18.3) around a curve at the third annual National Jaycee Junior Championships in Des Moines. Both were national interscholastic records around a curve. These feats made him one of the best high school track athletes in North America.

Tipton said of Coach Kent, "He is a great coach and shows interest in all his trackmen. He stimulated me to work harder, and the more I hurdle the more it becomes a passion with me to succeed." As for Dean Wilson, developer of countless great athletes at Central High School, Bill Tipton said, "His record should give you an indication of his talents. He has coached many great athletes and the *Detroit News* named him Coach of the Year for the State of Michigan."

Hayes Jones was Tipton's hero. When he was a junior in high school, he met Hayes Jones. "Just knowing that Hayes Jones had been a hurdler at Pontiac Central influenced my decision to be a hurdler." It also influenced his decision to attend Eastern Michigan University.

After deciding to attend Eastern, Bill trained with focus and intensity. His goal was to make an immediate impact on college track. Tipton explained, "I use the basic hurdle technique, but after practicing on the college hurdles I find that I have to carry my body weight forward a little more than usual. Plus, I have to hold my forward lean over the hurdle more." Tipton did 14.5 over the higher barriers in the AAU meet. Bill went on a concentrated weight-training program before the 1967 season, and said, "It seems to help my speed. I lift weights for my legs and upper body. I did leg-curls by lying on my stomach and lifting with the heels. This puts all the weight on the hamstrings." He trained five or six days a week for all but two weeks of the year and twice a day during the summer months. In the fall Bill joined the cross-country team to build endurance and won a letter in that sport. He concentrated on weights during the 1966–7 winter season and did over-distance work before working on his form over the barriers. Repetition work and sprints followed in the spring before he took up double workouts in the summer.[151]

When Bill arrived at EMU, he had problems adjusting to the three-inch change in the height of the high-hurdles. "Everything has to be technically right" to do well in the high-hurdles. He observed, "If you get a slow start against a good field, you're through."[152]

Young Bill Tipton was already an evangelist when he enrolled at EMU in 1967 in the midst of what many referred to as militant protests, "an irreligious society," and "a general lack of discipline." Bill, saw his participation in track—perhaps the most grueling, self-disciplining sport—as "the will of the Lord."

> "Track is a lonely battle," Tipton observed. "It's you and the pain and the hard work and the sweat." "I have a definite reason for running track. It has to do with my personal relationship with Jesus Christ. . . . Track gives me a personal opportunity to reach other people. . . . Track has opened up many doors for me," he said. "It has provided me with opportunities to speak at banquets and gatherings where I can get the word of God, as found in the Bible, out. I feel the Lord wanted me to come here and run. Most bible schools aren't track schools, but I may hit one after I graduate"[153]

In October 1967 Jerry Cerulla said, "I think my freshman teammate Bill Tipton could be a possibility to make the US Olympic team."[154] However, it did not work out that way. While he won the NAIA Indoor and NCAA Division II outdoor high hurdles, was second in the NAIA outdoor high hurdles, qualified for the NCAA Division I meet, and ran in the 1968 Olympic trials, he never achieved Division I NCAA All-American status, won the Drake or Penn Relays, or ran in international meets. To his credit, Tipton ran 13.7 in the outdoor high-hurdles and 7.1 in the indoor high-hurdles.[155] Moreover, he was the lead-off member of the Huron shuttle hurdle relay team with Alton Davis, Bob Lynn, Jerry Cerulla that set a American Collegiate indoor record for the 240-yard shuttle hurdle relay (28.84) in February 1968.[156]

The year the first man walked on the moon, 1969, Bill missed the track season because of an appendicitis operation. Hayes Jones called

Tipton at the hospital to encourage him. At that time, Bill acknowledged that making the Olympic track team takes "an act of God" and extreme training in a sport that offers little glory.[157] Bill Tipton was named to the NCAA All-America College Division outdoor track team for 1970 for the 120-yard high-hurdles[158] and was inducted into the Eastern Michigan Hall of Fame in 1986. Tipton became a minister in Plymouth and at the end of the century lived in Waterford, Michigan.[159]

A Late Bloomer

In eighth grade Bob Cassleman was a "little stubby guy" who had not grown up. As a result, he shunned track in the ninth grade. As a sophomore at Catholic Central High in Grand Rapids, Cassleman gave the sport another chance, but his team lost every event in the dashes and hurdles. Finally, Bob emerged as a 220-yard dash point winner. In his junior year at Catholic Central Cassleman pulled a leg muscle and was sidelined for the entire season. But, he rebounded in his senior year. Late in the spring campaign, he ran the 440-yard dash for his first time against East Christian High School in the remarkable time of 48.4. Prior to this performance Central Michigan University was the only college interested in him. However, with his 440 performance, several colleges, including Notre Dame, the University of Michigan, Michigan State, and the University of Southern California, set out to recruit him. After considerable deliberation, Cassleman chose MSU over Notre Dame because it offered him an opportunity to study hotel administration. He graduated from high school in 1970.[160]

Bob Cassleman recalled:

In high school I was what you would call a mediocre sprinter by college standards. It wasn't until halfway through my senior year that I showed any semblance of track talent. When I ran my first quarter I did it in 48.6. Still, no one gave me any attention because they thought it was a fluke. But after I ran a 48.6 the second time everyone took me seriously, even myself.[161]

At 6'1", 160-pounds, Cassleman was about ten pounds lighter and the same height as Wehrwein, and like Wehrwein had an exceptionally strong finishing kick over the last 100-yards. According to MSU track coach Fran Dittrich, "Wehrwein was a power runner, while Cassleman had good power but was much smoother."[162]

On February 13, 1971, during his freshman year at State, Cassleman ran the 600-yard in 1:08.8, just 2/10 of a second off the American indoor record set by Wehrwein in 1969.[163] "He has a fantastic attitude.

He can't stand to see anyone out in front of him. Cassleman has the potential to be one of the greatest in the world," observed MSU middle distance coach Jim Gibbard. However, his high school coach [Jerry Sieracki] noted, "It's corny to say this, but the best way to describe Bob is humble. He's not convinced he's good, that this is really happening to him. He's still living in a surprise world."[164] Even three years later Robert Cassleman considered "the win in the 660 to be one of my biggest thrills. Mark Winzenried from Wisconsin, who was the American record holder in the event and the Big Ten champ three years going was expected to run away with the race again. I wasn't given much of a chance. But I won."[165]

Cassleman spent much of his freshman, spring track season sidelined with mononucleosis. He ran the 440-intermediate hurdles at a couple of meets, but was not really in shape.[166] "During my freshman year, I still wasn't sure what my best event was. I didn't feel completely confident anywhere, but the intermediate hurdles gave me that satisfaction."[167]

The following year Bob Steele helped Cassleman with both his hurdling form and his mental attitude.[168] In 1972 Bob Cassleman was named to the NCAA Indoor All-American team in two events.[169] He won the intermediate hurdles and ran legs on the Spartan's winning mile and 440-yard relay teams at the Big Ten Championships. On June2–3, 1972 he placed second in the first heat of the semifinals of the intermediate-hurdles (50.3) but was disqualified after placing third (49.9) in the finals at the 51st Annual NCAA Championships in Eugene. The judges contended that Cassleman had dragged his trailing leg around, rather than over, three hurdles. Two other finalists were also disqualified. Cassleman contended that "the judging setup is ridiculous. I know I didn't do on the hurdles what they said I did. But, there's no way the judge could really tell from where he was."[170]

In his junior year at MSU, on February 10, 1973, Bob set a meet and Jenison Fieldhouse record for the 600-yard run (1:08.2) at the 50th Michigan State Relays. After the race Cassleman said, "This is the perfect track to have an outstanding race. I ran my own race according to plan and I always do better that way. This record really built my confidence.[171] That spring Cassleman reported, "I have a measure of confidence in what I can do now that I never had before. I'm much more optimistic about my chances [in the NCAA finals] than I was last year."[172] He was named to the NCAA indoor All-America team in the 600-yard run and to the 1973 outdoor All-America team in the intermediates.[173]

Bob Cassleman, who was also an All-American in track in 1974, felt that the NCAA Indoor Championships should be moved out of Detroit because the small track kept times down. "I think the national meet should be run on a 220 yard track." Cassleman added that he felt the meet is designed for spectators, not the athletes. "The smaller track at Cobo 'ties athletes up' resulting in slower times and destroying the competitiveness of the NCAA championships." Coach Bibbs explained that "in the middle distance events finalists have to compete in two heats instead of going head-to-head, and the competitive aspect is lost."[174]

In the preliminaries of the 1974 NCAA Outdoor Championships Cassleman hit a hurdle and fell. In his four years at State he took or shared in 13 Big Ten track titles.[175] As he neared graduation at State, Cassleman said, "I have no regrets about coming to MSU and I really have done almost everything I had hoped to accomplish." Titles and awards were not a Cassleman trademark. They resulted from hard work, dedication and being in the right place at the right time.[176]

On August 29, 1976 former Michigan State track star Bob Cassleman accepted a teaching position at Central Michigan University and joined the coaching staff of its track and cross-country teams.[177] He has since moved on.

Small School Striders

Two small college hurdlers deserve to be included among Michigan's great track athletes. Randy Williams, from Detroit Cooley High School, attended Kentucky State University from 1973 to 1978. Randy won the NCAA Division II 400-meter intermediate hurdles and placed third in intermediates at the Division I Championships. He also ran on a crack mile-relay team that placed second at the Penn Relays. Following graduation from Kentucky State, Randy coached track and joined the Detroit Police Department.[178]

Edward "Eddie" Brown, from Otisville, MI, came from a large family. He had nine brothers and sisters. As a senior at LakeVille High School, he excelled. In May 1979, Ed was timed at 37.1 in the 330-yard hurdles, 22.7 in the 220-yard dash, and leaped 23-¼.[179] At the Metro League Track and Field Meet at Lapeer East High School on May 23, Eddie won the long jump (21–1) and captured the 220-yard dash. However, he lost his favorite race, the 330-yard low-hurdles when he blew a 15-yard lead by tripping over the fifth hurdle and could only salvage a third place finish.[180] He was a state champion in the 300-

meter intermediate hurdles, but his grades were too low to qualify for college entrance.

Ed's younger brother, Ricky, was a good student with more than enough talent to attract college recruiters. Ricky ran the quarter mile in high school in 48:8, and Doug Hansen, the coach at Saginaw Valley College, was anxious to recruit him for his track team. Ricky asked if Coach Hansen could offer a package deal for him and his brother, Eddie. The coach said that Eddie would have to prove himself academically, and if he could do that, he would give him a scholarship as well. So the two brothers enrolled at Saginaw Valley, and both ran on the track team in Division 2 of the NCAA as freshmen. Ricky had a scholarship for the first year, but Eddie did not. The second year, Eddie qualified for a scholarship as well.[181]

As sophomores Ricky and Eddie Brown sparkled in the NCAA Division III outdoor track meet in Sacramento. Eddie won the 400-meter intermediate hurdles and Ricky finished fourth in the 800-meter run. They both earned All-American honors for their efforts. Eddie was the first Saginaw Valley State athlete to win an individual NCAA event. He set the National Association of Intercollegiate Athletics (NAIA) record for the 400-meter intermediate-hurdles (50.17) one-week earlier in Charleston, WV. Ricky set the Saginaw Valley State College varsity record for the 800-meter run (1:49.46) in qualifying for the NCAA finals.[182]

Eddie was always a strong team player. He frequently made personal sacrifices for the benefit of the team. For example, at the National Championships during his freshman year, the coach suggested that Eddie pass up participation in the triple jump because the event was scheduled right in the middle of the meet, and was likely to adversely affect Eddie's performance in other events. However, Eddie calculated that if the team was to have any chance of winning the national championship, they would need his points in the triple jump. So, he begged the coach to let him participate in that event, even if it interfered with his chances to set meet records in the hurdle events and mile relay—his best events.

Eddie had his best work ethic in a team setting. He was not a self-starter. But in a team setting, Eddie would give his all, particularly if the coach told him to pick up the pace when he was dropping off.

Eddie proved to be a more than adequate student. He never got into academic trouble in college, and while he was not at the top of his class, he was never ineligible. He proved that when he was properly focused and motivated, he could do the work. No doubt, his success in athletics, and his desire not to let the team down motivated him in his studies. He did not have a tutor, and all of his accomplishments were his own.

Saginaw Valley had an All-Michigan team in the period 1981–1984 when Eddie and Ricky were their stars. Their major competition at other schools tended to be against Kenyans, and athletes of other nations, who were the principal track athletes at other schools. Nonetheless, Saginaw Valley won several track and field national championships. In February 1983 Saginaw Valley's two-mile relay team, with Ricky and Eddie Brown on it, defeated the University of Michigan's two-mile relay team at the Michigan State Relays.[183] On March 12, 1983 Eddie became the first Saginaw Valley State College athlete to become a NCAA Division I All-American, when he placed sixth in the 440-yard dash (48.48) at the NCAA Indoor Championships in Pontiac.[184] Eddie represented the Nike team in European competition during the summer of 1983.

Eddie was a humble person who did not allow his personal success to make him feel self-important. Eddie's strength as a team player or a "we" person was also his weakness because, even though he had the talent, without team support he was unable to make the transition to world class competition after graduation. His times in the high-hurdles (13:70) and the intermediate hurdles (49:77) look as impressive fifteen years later as they did at the time they were clocked. He also triple jumped 51–1½. He was seven times national champion in the hurdles and was on two mile-relay teams that won national championships. He also set records in the shuttle hurdle relay and ran a very competitive quarter mile.

Eddie graduated from Saginaw Valley State College in 1984 and became owner of his own construction company in Flint. His brother, Ricky, was in charge of affirmative action at Kettering University in Flint at the end of the century.

Thomas "Heat Feet" Wilcher

Born in Detroit in 1964, Thomas Wilcher was one of seven children, and the only one with recognized athletic ability. At age 11, Tom was the fastest schoolboy in Detroit in the high hurdles, quarter mile, the 100-yard dash, and the 200-yard dash. He then began building his body for future track events with two hours of sprints and other exercises daily. As a junior and senior at Detroit Central High School he was the fastest high hurdler in the Detroit Public Schools, and set the junior national record for the high-hurdles. In 1982, as a senior, he was Detroit High School track champion in four events and Class A High School State Champion in three events.[185]

Wilcher wanted to break his own state high-hurdle record in 1982, but the starting gun went off quicker than he expected and he wasn't ready. When asked about what is the secret to his track success, he said, "Dedication and a little speed." His friends called him "heat feet," and he was proud of the nickname.[186]

He was given a football scholarship at the University of Michigan. In 1985–6 Thomas Wilcher was the first University of Michigan athlete to win a national indoor title when he won the NCAA 55-meter high-hurdles (7.21) in March 1986. He also won the 110-meter high-hurdles (13.75) at the Penn Relays in April 1986 and ran in the Olympic trials in 1988.[187] At the turn of the century, Tom was the track coach at Detroit's Cass Tech.

Tiberia Patterson

Tiberia Patterson only participated in one year of track at Redford High School and did not place at the Michigan high school track meet. Nevertheless, on April 24, 1993 Tiberia Patterson, who was attending Eastern Michigan University, won the high-hurdles (13.19) and placed third in the shuttle relay (59.92) at the Drake Relays.[188] The following year he broke the 55-meter and 60-meter high-hurdles varsity records (7.19/7.70) at Eastern that had been set by Hayes Jones in 1960, and set the 60-meter high-hurdles record for the MAC conference.[189] On April 30, 1994 Tiberia placed second in the high-hurdles finals (13.82) at the Drake Relays. He won the 1991, 1993 and 1994 MAC indoor 55-meter high-hurdles championships. In 1994 he became an All-American when he placed fourth in the 55-meter high-hurdles at the NCAA indoor meet.[190] He lived in Detroit at the turn of the century.

Greg Richardson

At the close of the twentieth century, Michigan produced an All-American hurdler in Greg Richardson. Greg was born December 27, 1976 and attended Everett High School in Lansing. His older sister was a high school and college hurdler. Greg followed in her footsteps. In 1995 he won the State High School Class A 110-meter high-hurdles championship with a 13.9 performance. Greg then won the Midwest Meet of

Interscholastic Champions in Fort Wayne. He then enrolled at Central Michigan, where his sister was still attending college.

In the spring of 1999 he won the high-hurdles at the Purdue Invitational Quadrangle Meet with a time of personal best of 13.67. Despite the death of his grandmother on the weekend of the Drake Relays, he placed third in the high-hurdles. He went on to win the Mid-American Outdoor high-hurdles championship with a 13.60 time. This qualified him for the NCAA Outdoor Championships in Boise, Idaho, where he placed third with a 13.59 run.[191]

During the twentieth century, Michigan athletes set 30 American AAU or NCAA hurdle records.

15. "A Foreign Invasion By Invitation of Don Canham" [1948–74]

During the 38 years between 1901 and 1949 in which the University of Michigan track team participated in the Big Ten Track and Field Championships, they won 20 outdoor championships, and 15 out of 29 indoor championships. They also placed second or third on nine occasions for the indoor championship, and on 14 occasions for the outdoor championship. In short, the University of Michigan placed lower than third only 3 times for the outdoor and seven times for the indoor championship over 38 years. When Don Canham, Wolverine indoor and outdoor high jump Big Nine Champion, was named track coach of the University of Michigan, the Wolverines were beginning to lose their iron-grip on Western Conference track and field.[1] The Wolverines had not won a Big Ten track and field championship since March 1945, the longest span of losses since the 1927–1930 dry spell.

Some attributed the problem to changes in the way colleges were recruiting track athletes. During the depression era recruiting was generally very low-key. Outstanding high school prospects were guided by their high school coach or were sent a letter or two by a college track coach, but little aggressive outreach and financial assistance was offered, beyond arranging a job. If a scholarship was awarded, the athletic department seldom did it. Except for a few football prospects, scholarships generally depended on a combination of financial need and academic accomplishment. However, with the GI Bill, recruitment became much more aggressive. Ken Doherty, the University of Michigan Coach at the close of World War II, like his mentors David L. Holmes and Charles B. Hoyt, was part of the old school when it came to recruiting. Doherty was a low-key recruiter. His idea of recruiting was to send a letter or two to an outstanding high school prospect. He also never understood or used public relations. That type of communications was difficult for him.[2]

Doherty did not get along with University of Michigan Athletic

Director Fritz Crisler. Fritz resented Ken because he was an extremely successful and popular coach. Moreover, Doherty kept a picture of Hoyt, who had left Michigan for Yale, hanging on his wall. This did not sit well with Crisler, who thought that the University of Michigan had the best athletic department in America, and could not abide anyone who would chose another program over his for any reason.[3]

In 1949, Doherty became the track coach at the University of Pennsylvania and moved to Swarthmore, PA. Before he left for Pennsylvania, Doherty advised against hiring Canham as his replacement, because he thought that Canham lacked the qualifications and experience to do the job well.[4] By Wolverine standards, Canham's first three years as head coach were a disaster. As he later admitted, "I made a few mistakes our first year."[5] His outdoor track team finished sixth in 1949 and 1950, and fourth in 1951. While his indoor record was somewhat better, he still placed seventh in 1949 and second in 1950 and 1951. Canham's only ray of hope was the performances of Donald S. McEwen, from Canada, and his strong distance medley relay team, of whom Aaron Z. Gordon was the only U.S. citizen.[6]

On February 4, 1950 McEwen won the two-mile run at the Michigan State Relays.[7] McEwen went on to win two national championships (1950 and 1951) in the two-mile run, and set the world record twice as part of Michigan's distance medley relay team. McEwen was the only Wolverine ever to win a NCAA championship for the two-mile.[8] Don McEwen was named to the 1951 NCAA All-American team.[9]

Canham's response to the relatively poor performance by his U.S. recruits was to recruit more Canadians. In 1952 Canham had six Canadian lettermen on his track team, an indication of his dependence on Canadian runners. In March of that year, Canham took his six Canadian-Wolverine track stars to the Canadian National indoor Championships in Montreal. They won five Canadian national indoor titles. McEwen won the mile and two-mile, Jack Carroll won the 500-yard run, and George Lynch won the 1000-yard run. John Moule was second in the junior mile, and Jeff Dooley was third in the 1000.[10] McEwen set the Canadian record for the two-mile run (9:04) at the meet.[11]

Track and Field News observed:

Fellow coaches are kidding Michigan's Don Canham, asking if he shouldn't adopt a new national anthem. They suggest 'The Maple Leaf Forever.' It so happens that Michigan, in the current influx of track stars from other countries, has welcomed a Canadian group that brings to nine the number of "M" competitors from north of the border. Also, and much more startling, is the fact that by their indoor feats, some of them promise to rival or even surpass the feats of the Wolverine's talented Don McEwen, twice NCAA two-mile champ.

Breaking into collegiate competition with the biggest splash was John Ross, a handsome sophomore from Oakville, Ontario. He astounded everyone, including Canham to some extent, by clocking a 4:12 mile on the relatively slow Michigan dirt track in a triangular meet February 4. The splits on Ross were something to talk about. He ran 62 seconds for the opening quarter, added another 62, [and] then became a little apprehensive when they shouted "2:04" at the half. He slowed noticeably, to a 66, added a slow 220 to start the final quarter. Then, feeling strong, he sprinted in for his 4:12.

"I could have done 4:10 easily," he said afterward. (Note: He did 4:09.4 in the Big Ten Indoor.)

Another sophomore, Jack Carroll of Toronto, looms as perhaps the best quarter-miler in the Big Ten. As a freshman, he won the Cleveland Knights of Columbus indoor 600, beating the Illinois half-mile record holder, Henry Cryer. This winter, Carroll has improved sharply. I watched him lead off Michigan's distance medley relay team when it knocked 4.3 seconds off its own American indoor record at the Michigan Relays. Carroll did 48.9. In the mile relay, Carroll ran the anchor leg and tied into Drake's Canadian star, Jim Lavery, to no avail. Both ran 48.2, the three-yard advantage for Lavery never wavering all the way. (Note: Carroll won the Big Ten 440 in 48.8).

Canham used a Canadian freshman, Johnny Moule, to lead off his two-mile relay combination. The boy did 1:57.5. Rayen Sordom added a 1:56.6 stint, McEwen went 1:56.1, and Ross laid on a fine anchor stint in 1:52.9. The time, 7:42, knocked over meet and fieldhouse marks.

One of Michigan's best Canadians, George Lynch, is a transfer from Illinois and is ineligible for a year because of it. However, he has been competing in an occasional AAU meet, and at the Massachusetts Knights of Columbus Games was a bang-up 9:14.9 second placer in the two-mile. Ross Coates, Freshman sprinter from Hamilton; Al Rankin letterman sprinter from Ottawa, and shot-putter Roy Pella from Sudbury, Ontario are other boys from the land of the Maple Leaf on the Michigan squad. Michigan also has Fritz Nilsson, gigantic sophomore weight man who competed for Sweden in the 1948 Olympics. Nilsson put the shot 53'6½" at the Michigan State College Relays, but his best event is the discus.[12]

Roland Nilsson, University of Michigan freshman from Sweden, won the shot put at the Michigan AAU Relays, January 27, 1951.[13] Nilsson was again named to Sweden's Olympic team in 1952.[14] Nilsson placed fifth in the shot put at the Helsinki Olympic Games.[15] Roland "Fritz" Nilsson from Svano, Sweden, became the first man to win the shot put and the discus three times in a row at the Penn Relays. Nilsson also was an All-American in those events in 1952, 1953 and 1954. He won the

Big Ten Indoor Championship in the shot put 1952–54; and the outdoor championship in the shot put 1952–54 and discus in 1953.

Both Charles Hoyt and Ken Doherty had sometimes hesitated to hold AAU-organized track meets on the Michigan campus because of the cost in time and money, but Canham told Lloyd Olds that he was interested in doing so.[16] In an effort to reward Canham's support for the AAU, Lloyd Olds, from neighboring Eastern Michigan University and a prominent AAU track official, arranged to have Canham accompany a team of AAU champions to Northern Europe. Canham used the trip to expand his efforts to recruit world class European track stars to Michigan to bolster his Wolverine track team. He also imported the idea of the "loopfilm" as a coaching aid. That idea launched his private company, School-Tech Inc. and ultimately made him a millionaire. As Canham reports the incident:

It was my coaching trips to Europe and the Caribbean that started foreign athletes coming to Michigan. Eeles Landstrom, the European pole vault champion, Fritz Neilsen, the Swedish discus champion, and Tom Robinson, the Bahamian four-time Olympian, were the first to arrive. Each year saw Michigan with foreign athletes, particularly from the Caribbean countries. Canada, due to proximity, has always had athletes on our teams. The first of note was Don McEwen in 1948. Since McEwen, more than 50 Canadians have competed in track for Michigan." In 1956 I had coached the Kenya and Uganda Olympic teams for the American State Department.[17]

Don's first book resulted from his European trip.[18] Canham, however, was not a great track coach. While he was as obsessive and determined as all great coaches, he never understood that great coaches do not impose their will on athletes. Instead, they find a way to vary their coaching techniques and methods of motivation so that the different strengths of their athletes can be maximized. Most of all, they have the innate sensitivity and intelligence to structure their coaching in such a way that it draws out character in all of its infinite variations and not try to build it. His excessive use of all-out time trials in daily practices caused many of his trackmen to leave too much of their energy on the practice track or tied up in physic distractions. This blanket approach was inconsistent with record breaking achievement.

Missed Opportunities

Canham's failure to recruit the most promising athletes from Michigan high schools or those from nearby states and developing their talent was also the subject of considerable controversy. It was not a question of whether or not Michigan was still producing talented runners. It was. Between 1950 and 1966 the State of Michigan produced All-Americans Mark Smith, Jr., James Podoley, Willie Atterberry, John Telford, Hayes Jones, David Meyers, John Bork, Henry Carr, Bob Steele, Dennis Holland, Jerry Cerulla, and Lou Scott. Canham did little to recruit any of these track stars, and several had the academic qualifications necessary for the University of Michigan. Moreover, track greats Warren Druetzler, Ira Murchison, and William Gustav Mack from nearby Illinois ran for Michigan Universities, but were never seriously considered by Canham for the University of Michigan.

In 1947 Michigan State miler, William G. Mack, from Palos Park, Illinois, was ranked third in the mile run in the USA by *Track and Field News*[19] In the fall of 1948 Mack was on the Michigan State College cross-country team that scored the first grand slam in cross-country history, winning the team title in the IC4A, NCAA, and AAU Championship meets. In March 1950, Bill Mack [class of '50] was listed as having the 16th fastest indoor mile run (4:09.6) in US track history.[20]

There were several American born athletes from Michigan who held there own against imported athletes. Seventeen-year-old Louis C. Scott of Detroit Eastern High School won the mile-and-a-half run at the *Globe and Mail* Meet in Toronto, Ontario on July 12, 1963, and came back fifty minutes later to win the mile run (4:17.7).[21] Scott, who had been coached by Lorenzo Wright, also won the July 5, 1964 National AAU Senior 25-K running Championship (1:20.35) in Ecorse, Michigan. Chris Murray of the University of Michigan placed second in that meet (1:21.2).[22] Lou, the third of six children, was born into a Methodist minister's family, and became determined to go to the Olympics as a four foot nine inch high school sophomore. The only college in Michigan to show an interest in him was Western Michigan, and they did not offer him a full scholarship. Lou attended Arizona State University in the fall of 1963,[23] and ran the 5-K in the 1968 Olympics.

In Canham's defense, during the 1960s the Big Ten Conference awarded athletic aid based on need, while other conferences offered scholarships that completely covered an athlete's costs. This discrepancy caused the conference to lose a number of good athletes to other conferences.

Coaches and track fans reacted negatively to Canham's recruitment strategy pointing out that he was breaking NCAA rules. "America is being invaded by foreign track stars enrolling in American universities," lamented *Track and Field News*. "There are at least 20 athletes here already. I'd like to point out that many American universities have a rule against inviting an athlete to enroll. The athlete must begin the action himself, by writing a letter to the university he desires to attend."[24] Canham had no qualms about breaking that rule.

In 1953 Canham recruited Peter "Cam" Gray from Hamilton, Ontario. Gray lettered at Michigan, 1954–56, and became an All-American in the 880 in 1955.[25] On March 4–5, 1955 he won the 880 (1:54.7) and the 1000-yard run (2:18.7) at the 45th Big Ten Indoor Championships held at East Lansing. On May 14, Gray won the mile relay and the two-mile relay at the second Big Ten Conference Relays in Evanston. Gray also won the 880 (1:51.4) and the mile relay (3:14.4) at the May 27–28 Big Ten Outdoor in Columbus. On June 4 he won the 880-yard run (1:54.1) and the mile relay (3:15.0) at CCC Outdoor in Milwaukee. Finally, he placed second in the 880 (1:50.3) at the 34th NCAA Outdoor Championships in Los Angeles on June 17–18. On June 21 he placed third in the 880 at the Big Ten vs. Pacific Coast Conference Duel Meet held in Berkeley, California. It was this type of performance that made Canham's reputation as a track coach. In 1956 Peter Gray won the 1,000-yard run (2:14.4) at the 46th Annual Big Ten Indoor Championships in East Lansing on March 2–3, but did not place at a major meet the balance of the season.[26]

Few of Canham's All-Americans were United States citizens. Of the 32 U of M trackmen who earned All-American honors during the twenty-year Canham coaching era, all but 9 were foreign nationals. One of the few American born All-Americans that Canham recruited in his first ten years as head track coach at the U of M was David Owen, who lettered from 1955 through 1957. Owen, a member of the Triangles, a club that promoted fellowship in the College of Engineering,[27] was named to the NCAA All-America track team for the shot put in 1956.[28] Owens was from Milwaukee and was also named to the NCAA 1957 All-American track team.[29] Owen was inducted into the Drake Relays Hall of Fame in 1959.

By 1966 a flood of Canadian, European, and Caribbean athletes were competing for American Colleges and Universities.[30] Among the foreign nationals who competed as track athletes at Michigan colleges and universities were University of Michigan stars—Tom Robinson, Eeles Landstrom, Ergas Leps, Kent Bernard, Cliff Nuttall, George Puce, Kevin Sullivan, Tania Longe, Nicole Forrester, and Maria Brown. Eastern Michigan University featured foreign nationals—Gordon Minty,

David Ellis, Tommy Asinga, Greg Rhymer, Tony Nelson, and Hasely Crawford. Henry Kennedy, Sevatheda Fynes and Selwyn Jones were among the foreign born track and field All-Americans at MSU.

Michigan State Foreign Born Champions

In 1955 and 1956 Scottish born, Henry Kennedy, who was born in Glasgow on August 20, 1932, was recruited from Toronto in 1954. On November 7, 1955 Henry Kennedy and MSU won the Big Ten cross-country championship. On November 14 he crossed the four-mile trek first, while leading his team to a win in the 47th IC4A cross-country championship at Van Cortlandt Park in New York City. Two weeks after that he placed second (19:57.5) and led MSU to its fifth national cross-country championship at the 17th Annual NCAA Cross-country Championship held at East Lansing. In 1956 Henry Kennedy again paced MSU in winning the Big Ten cross-country championship. Then he again placed first (24:01.8) and MSU won the IC4A cross-country championship. On November 26, 1956 Kennedy placed third (20:10) over the four mile course and MSU won its sixth national championship at the 18th NCAA Cross-country Championship.

Henry Kennedy was named to the NCAA All-America cross-country team for 1955 and 1956.[31] During the 1956 track season Henry Kennedy placed third in the four-mile relay at the Drake Relays, and won the steeplechase (9:16.5) at the NCAA Championships. His steeplechase performance set an NCAA record, and made him a track All-American.[32] Henry was Director of Canadian Studies at Central Florida University for more than twenty-five years before retiring.[33]

Selwyn Jones, the sturdy Canadian runner from Michigan State, ran the 10-K run in meet record time at the 1956 NCAA Outdoor Championships at Berkeley, CA. He also placed third in the 5-K run. Selwyn was named NCAA All-American for 1956 in both events.[34]

Eastern Michigan Foreign Nationals

One of the best foreign athletes to attend a Michigan university was Hasely Crawford, who was at Eastern Michigan. Crawford, from Trinidad, won the 300-yard dash at the Central Collegiate Conference indoor championships in March 1975, and became the NCAA indoor champion at Cobo Arena. That year, he was the 29th Annual Mid-American Conference Outdoor champion in the 100-yard dash and 440-yard dash (41.1), and at the 50th Central Collegiate Conference

Outdoor Championships, he won the 100-yard dash (9.4). On June 6 Crawford won the 100-yard dash (9.35) at the NCCA Championships. Hasely Crawford, representing Trinidad and Tobago, won the gold medal in the 100-meter dash (10.06) 1976 Olympic Games.

During the Cold War, it was common for the American Press to keep a comparative count of Olympic medals, especially in track and field. Between 1952 and 1972 the USA dominated the USSR in track and field,[35] but thereafter the gap narrowed significantly. There is little doubt that the decline in American track and field performance was connected to the relative neglect of American track and field athletes at many U. S. universities in favor of foreign recruits and revenue earning sports.

In 1974 when the University of Tennessee won the NCAA Outdoor Championship, *The Oakland Press* declared in a headline, "Vols win track title without a foreigner." It was the first time in four years that an American University had won the national championship without the help of foreign athletes. Even then, second place UCLA earned points from a French pole-vaulter, and the Texas-El Paso team was known as "the foreign legion." Indeed in 1974, foreign athletes scored 148 points or one-fourth of the total points earned in 53rd American national collegiate championship.[36]

The issue of foreign athletes at the NCAA Track and Field Championship continued to surface the following winter at the indoor championships in Detroit. The *New York Times* reported

The United States athletes won today, but not by much. Overshadowing the winning of a second consecutive team title by the University of Texas-El Paso . . . was the overwhelming influence of foreign competitors. They won nine of the 15 individual events and accounted for 45 per cent of the total individual points in the two-day meet. Even events long cherished as symbols of American pride, the 60-yard dash and one-mile run were won for the first time by foreigners. Hasely Crawford, a Trinidad Olympian who attends Eastern Michigan, bolted past Cliff Outlin of Auburn, the defending champion, in the last 26 yards and won the 60-yard dash by one foot in 6 seconds. Eamonn Coghlan, a Villanova junior from Dublin, and Wilson Waigwa, a Kenyan enrolled at UTEP, ran-away from a field of milers.[37]

Despite the prevalence of foreign athletes in American universities, a poll of NCAA coaches indicated that 65 per cent of them wanted to bar foreigners from competing for points in the NCAA national championships. The rich schools over-ruled the majority of the members of the association, and foreign nationals continued to dominate American track and field. Headlines in the sport section of the *Detroit News* on Sunday March 15, 1981 [p. 1-D] read, "Texas-El Paso Maintains its Supremacy in Track." Until the track team budget at the University of Texas-El Paso was cut by $56,000 for the 1982–3 school year, its "foreign legion" of track stars dominated American track and field. Texas-El Paso won the NCAA indoor meet in Detroit seven out of nine years between 1974–83. Eleven of the Texas-El Paso twelve 1982 NCAA indoor meet qualifiers were from Tanzania, Botswana, South Africa, Kenya, Jamaica, the Bahamas, Norway and Toronto. Several were world class runners before attending Texas-El Paso. Only shot putter Carlos Scott was from Texas.[38]

Coach Ted Banks, the man who assembled this international powerhouse, resigned when his budget at Texas El Paso was cut. He subsequently took a higher playing job with a shoe and equipment company involving far less travel, as he was no longer roaming the world looking for world-class track stars.[39]

The number of foreign athletes competing in the 1992 NCAA Outdoor Championships, including 14 of the 36 individual champions, continued to raise concerns among American sports fans and coaches about the role of foreign athletes in the track programs of American colleges and universities. Should American universities recruit foreign athletes for the purpose of winning American collegiate championships or should those scholarships be used to help develop American athletes? At some of the leading collegiate track powers, foreign athletes were regularly recruited. Washington State was famous for its Kenyan distance runners; Arkansas was known for its Irish and British middle-distance runners; Southern Methodist specialized in Scandinavian discus and hammer throwers.[40]

As Frank Gagliano, Georgetown University track coach put it; "We only have 14 track scholarships over a three-year period. How are we going to develop American athletes to be Olympic champions if we use the scholarships for foreign athletes, who in many cases are already far along in their development and can score in the NCAA meet even as freshmen?"[41]

A year later, officials at the USA Track and Field Championships met in Eugene met in a local hotel to discus what was wrong with their sport. "There was much too mull over: failing television ratings, the absence of head-to-head showdowns between international stars, and a European circuit that is siphoning off a lot of the top competition," explained one official.[42]

Nevertheless, the foreign influence on American track and field continued until the end of the century. On May 31, 1996 Neil Gardner from Jamaica, who was attending the University of Michigan, won the NCAA 400-meter intermediate hurdles and placed eighth in the 110-meter high-hurdles at the NCAA Championships.[43] The following year he won the 55-meter indoor hurdles at the NCAA Championships. Gardener was Big Ten Champion in the 400-meter intermediate hurdles in 1996 and 1997. He set the University of Michigan team record for the 400-meter intermediate hurdles (48.30) and is third on their all-time list for the Michigan varsity triple jump (50–7¼).[44] He represented Jamaica in the 1996 Olympics and made it to the semi-finals in the 400-meter intermediate hurdles. At Eastern Michigan University, Clement Churkwu placed second in the 200-meter dash (20.73) and James Nieto places third in the high jump (7–6) at the NCAA indoor championships in Indianapolis on March 6, 1999.[45] At the New York and Boston Marathons few Americans were among the top ten finishers over the last twenty years of the twentieth century.

In His Glory

In 1958 the University of Michigan began to use its foreign recruits to dominate Big Ten track. In March 1961 Canham's thinclads, lead by middle-distance runner Ergas Leps, hurdler Benjamin McRae, and high jumper/hurdler Dick Cephas, rolled up 69 points—39 points more than its nearest rival—to win his third straight Big Ten indoor title.[46]

On an airplane returning from Washington, D.C. in December 1964 *Detroit News* columnist "Doc" Greene asked "Biggie" Munn, the Athletic Director at Michigan State University, and Don Canham if they would be interested in sponsoring a nation-wide indoor track meet in Detroit. Canham responded, "Well, if somebody will buy a track, I'll run the meet." A week later Peter Clark, publisher of the *News*, asked Canham to come to Detroit to discuss the proposition. Canham called Walter Byers, executive director of the NCAA, and said, "Walter, how about starting an indoor track meet, the National Championships, in Detroit? I'll do all the work, and I think we can make it self-financing." Byers responded, "Go ahead. Give me some ideas. Give me some plans. And give me a financial breakdown." Canham met with Clark, and included promotion director Bob Reese and his assistant Jim Stower. The *News* agreed to buy a track that would fit into Cobo Arena and would give it to the City of Detroit.[47]

The track used for the National Collegiate Indoor Track Championships in Detroit was presented to the City of Detroit in 1965 by the *Detroit News*. DiNatale Floor Company of Boston specifically designed it for the Detroit's Convention Arena at a cost of more than $31,000. It was built of processed and aged Sitka spruce and supported by scaffold-type steel. It took two months to construct. The curve oval was 12 feet wide and 160 yards long (11 laps to the mile) measured one foot from the pole edge. The straightaway was 24 feet wide and approximately 70 yards long with an additional run-off length of 30 yards. A crew of 16 men, working 20-hours, was required to install the track. A civil engineer then measures the track and certifies the accuracy of each distance to be run before marking start and finish lines. A Bulova Phototimer was used to record the elapsed time of a race for each individual in the race. Photographs were taken by the Phototimer at the end of the race for the officials to interpret.[48]

In 1965 the United States Track Coaches Association, under the guiding force of Don Canham and his close friend Phil Diamond, promoted the nation's first NCAA National Indoor Track Championships. The meet was held in Detroit in March and was sponsored by the *Detroit News* as a public service. Canham drew on the large reservoir of Detroit track old timers to serve as meet officials.[49] For the next 14 years the meet was held at Cobo, with sellouts both for the Friday night and Saturday night competition. Record crowds followed when the meet was moved next door to Joe Louis Arena, and again when it moved to the Silverdome in Pontiac, where it drew 25,000 spectators two consecutive years. The Detroit meet was a success for twenty years, and successfully competed with the NCAA basketball tournament for fans. By 1967 ABC's Wide World of Sports was televising the action, and the meet was attracting over 360 track and field standouts from 93 universities.[50]

For 17 years Detroit was the center of international track as host to the climactic meet of the indoor season. Runners from Florida and Texas to Washington State strove to get to Detroit for the NCAA indoor championships, before starting over outdoors. In 1980 track and field in the United States took on strong international appearance when the NCAA adopted rules that limited record setting performances to those set using metric measurements.[51] In 1981 nearly 400 athletes arrived in Detroit to run on the board track at Joe Louis Arena. The Ivory Coast, South Africa, Belgium, the Netherlands, the Bahamas, Barbados, Jamaica and

Trinidad were among the countries typically represented. Track teams, however, were not great for downtown business. College runners were used to eating spaghetti, not known as a high profit meal.[52]

In 1982, after 17 successful years in Detroit, the NCAA indoor championship moved out of Detroit's Cobo Hall to the Pontiac Silverdome and was touted as the "Super Bowl of Track." A new plywood track was built and shipped from Albuquerque. It was bigger and faster than the old track and required fewer turns for distance races. Because of the basketball court at the other end of the dome, the 35-pound weight throw had to be held at Eastern Michigan University.[53]

When the NCAA moved the indoor track championships away from Detroit to Syracuse University, they experienced a significant drop in attendance. In 1984, the first year the meet was held outside metropolitan Detroit, the meet drew only 4,000 spectators and was little better in 1985.[54] Even when the NCAA indoor meet moved to Indianapolis, the attendance never matched the draw the meet had in Detroit.

The University of Michigan won more Big Ten track titles than any other conference member between the start of the century and 1967. During that period the Wolverines won 24 outdoor titles and 21 indoor titles. The runner-up, the University of Illinois, won 22 outdoor titles and 16 indoor track and field titles. The University of Chicago won three outdoor titles and three indoor titles, while the University of Iowa won 2 and 1, and Ohio State won two outdoor and three indoor titles. Don Canham brought twelve Big Ten crowns to Ann Arbor.[55] "Total performance" had special meaning within the context of Michigan's athletic traditions. Michigan thinclads started making their presence known on the national track and field scene in 1893, when A. O. Austin set the national record for the pole vault with a jump of 9–6.[56]

The University of Michigan won the 1959–62 Big Ten championships by using foreign nationals such as nine-time Big Ten champions Tom Robinson from the Bahamas and Ergas Leps from Canada, and single event champions Les Bird from Canada, Steve Willams, Bennie McRae, and Raymond Locke. However, the Wolverines did not win another outdoor Big 10 championship until after Jack Harvey assumed command of the track program in 1976.

When other colleges and universities began competing with Michigan for established foreign athletes, the talent flow to the U of M from abroad slowed down, and was not easily replaced because state and regional contacts and talent had been neglected. Between 1964 when

Michigan won the mile relay and 1973, when Michigan beat North Carolina Central in the sprint medley, the U of M did not win a single relay race at the Penn Relays.[57]

There were, of course, some talented American athletes on the Michigan track squad during the 1960s and 1970s. Among these were: Jack Harvey, Ron Kutschinski, Reggie Bradford, and Greg Meyer. Jack Harvey was Big 10 shot put champion in 1966–7 and in 1967 placed second in the NCAA indoor championships. He also won the shot put at the Penn Relays twice and the U.S. Track and Field championships once.[58]

The biggest American born star of the Don Canham era was Ron Kutschinski, if one considers Charles Fonville a carry over from the Doherty era.

Ron Kutschinski

Roland C. Kutschinski was born in Grand Rapids, Michigan and attended East Grand Rapids High School. In May 1966 he won the State Class A half-mile championship, and agreed to attend the U of M. At the University of Michigan, Ron trained on a dirt track. As a freshman, Ron ran the outdoor 660 in 1:17.5, a full second under the varsity mark. When he went to Madison Square Gardens on February 10, 1967, as part of the University of Michigan two-mile relay team, to compete in the U.S. Track and Field Invitational Meet, it was the first time he ever ran in a major indoor meet on the hardwood boards. Running on the tighter track often affects how a race is run. "You can't just whip off the last corner on the tighter track," Kutschinski observed after running a 1:51 half-mile.[59] On February 25 Kutschinski set the Yost Field House and varsity record for the 880-yard run (1:51.5), as Head Coach Don Canham barked off the time at the end of each lap, in a triangular meet with Indiana and Northwestern University. After the meet, Kutschinski said, "when I heard my 660 time I knew I had it." Speaking of his star runner, Canham said, "He's got everything: great speed, and a hell of a mental attitude. When he's out there on the track, he doesn't worry about anything or anybody. Ron's going to win his share. He has a very efficient way of running. He's very relaxed out there. Why, he was more relaxed on the last lap today than he was on the third one," Canham continued.[60]

Words of praise for Kutschinski came from more than one quarter. The sports editor for the *Michigan Daily* wrote "Ron Kutschinski is an athlete who knows what he wants . . . and he gets what he wants." Don McEwen, former Wolverine, thinclads' two-mile record holder, declared: "You classify track athletes as good or great. Kutschinski's one of the great ones. He is going to be one of the world's best."[61]

Despite the lingering effects of flu and bronchitis, Kutschinski was third in the 880-yard (1:51.1) on March 4 at the Big Ten indoor Championships in Madison. "I just ran a poor race," Kutschinski said. "They ran good ones. I thought the pace would be faster. When I tried to sprint at the end, I just didn't have it."[62]

At the Third Annual NCAA Indoor Championships in Detroit on March 15 the University of Michigan two-mile relay team took second place by virtue of an outstanding race by Ron Kutschinski. When Ron took the baton as the team's anchorman, Michigan was in fourth place. He brought the baton home in second place.[63] Kutschinski felt, "Running anchor is not much different from running individually. My job is to cross the finish line first, and that's that."[64] Kutschinski was named an indoor NCAA All-American for 1967 for the two-mile relay.[65]

In 1968 three days after Presidential candidate Robert F. Kennedy was shot and killed, Ron was voted the outstanding performer at the United States Track and Field Federation Championships in Houston after running a 1:47.1 half mile.[66] At that time, the American record for the 880 was 1:44.9, set by University of Kansas middle-distance runner Jim Ryan earlier in the year. However, Ryan was now suffering from mononucleosis and would not be at his peak for the Olympic trials.[67] This set of circumstances would benefit Kutschinski, who was just beginning to peak.

At the NCAA outdoor championships, none of the 1967 finalists made it to the finals of the half-mile. Ron Kutschinski was disqualified for allegedly colliding with Oregon State's John Lilly, who noticeably tripped at the 600-yard point. Despite being spiked, Ron managed to win his heat in 1:48.2—fastest of the five heats. Assistant coach Dave Martin protested without results but it's questionable whether Kutschinski's foot would have held up. Two of the nation's swiftest half-milers, Roy Shaw and Jim Baker of Harvard, did not compete.[68]

Because of the spiking injury at the NCAA meet, Ron Kutschinski had to petition to be included in the final Olympic trials held at Echo Summit, a mountain pass near the California-Nevada border close to South Lake Tahoe. Ron ran a strong 1:46.7 in an 800-meter practice race at the United States team's training site at Echo Summit. "Trailing the Wolverine across the finish line was Villanova's Dave Patrick, who was clocked in 1:46.9 and Wisconsin's Ray Arrington." This was the first time that Patrick had been beaten in the 800-meter run. Kutschinski's effort was not totally unexpected. He ran a very fast 1:47.1 in the 880-yard run earlier this year. If the standard seven-tenths of a second were subtracted from this time, it gave a 1:46.4 for the 800-meters.[69] Kutschinski's effort in late August was one of the fastest 800-meters run anywhere in the world in 1968, and raised his hopes of making the U.S. Olympic track team.

On September 9, 1968 Ron Kutschinski finished third in his 800-meter heat just ahead of the struggling Jim Ryun in the final Olympic trials. On September 11, in the finals the towheaded Kutschinski ran an aggressive race. He moved to second on the first backstretch and remained there until the final homestretch. In doing so he boxed Tom Farrell in behind him. However, in the homestretch Jim Ryun slowed abruptly, and Farrell dashed through the hole, took the lead and won handily in 1:46.5. Ryun, who simply had not had time since his illness for the necessary speed work, compounded his problem by running as wide as the third lane on some curves, adding about 15 yards to his distance. When Farrell and Wade Bell passed him in the homestretch, Kutschinski tied up but struggled past Mark Winzenried [University of Wisconsin] to take third place by a foot. Kutschinski fell after the finish and Winzenried helped him to his feet, but Ron suffered from exhaustion long after the race.[70]

The thin air at 7,377-feet above sea level had been withering. Ron had still not adjusted to running at high altitudes. Inexperience in international competition and the training time lost to the spiking injury also were serious impediments to success in Mexico City.[71] Yet, a total of only 69 American athletes from the field of 175 made the Olympic team for Mexico City Games, which began October 12, and Ron was one of those 69 athletes.[72]

On October 14 at the Olympic games Ron Kutschinski tied up and finished fifth in his semi-finals heat (1:47.3), missing the finals by two-tenths of a second.[73] Kutschinski remained the third fastest 800-meter contestant for the USA. He was named to the 1968 NCAA All-America indoor two-mile relay team.[74]

After the 1968 Olympic Games, Ron was tired and took an extended training break. When the University of Michigan indoor track season opened January 26, 1969 on a new $35,000 rubberized asphalt track, "Olympian Ron Kutschinski ran well for Michigan's relay teams, but obviously was not up to par."[75] On March 1 he placed third in the 1,000-yard run (2:07.9) at the Big Ten Indoor Championships at Champaign. University of Wisconsin athletes, Arrington and Winzenried finished ahead of him.[76] On March 14–15 Ron placed second in the 880-yard run (1:52.5) and was third in the two-mile relay (7:33.0) [his leg 1:51.0] at the NCAA Indoor Championships.[77] Kutschinski again was named to the 1969 NCAA Indoor All-America team for the 880-yard run and the two-mile relay.[78]

In June 1969 Ron Kutschinski did not qualify for the NCAA Championship finals in the 880-yard run in Knoxville[79] and soon afterward retired from competition.

16. Who Will Run Things?

The daily life of the track athlete, during the 1960s, was often dominated by an almost stifling routine of grinding work and overwhelming pressure. Nor was it easy to be the spouse of a track athlete. Baseball, basketball, and football players had a season with a beginning and an end, but track athletes engaged in a sport that never ends. Day after day, week after week, the training grind went on. When the outdoor season ended, cross-country or training for the indoor season began. The end of the indoor season meant it was time to begin training for the outdoor season. All of that in addition to study or working for a living.[1]

Still, many considered amateurism a state of mind. It was an attitude toward sport that recognized it is something other than a means of a livelihood or a life's work. Amateurism was expected to be a qualified commitment that acknowledges that the athlete will give his or her all for a few hours a day, but will spend the majority of the typical day on other endeavors.[2] Indeed, most trackmen did get their joy from competition and the satisfaction of doing their best in the slice of life they have reserved for the sport, and were not concerned with payment for participation. However, when the demands of training for national or international meets significantly interfered with a normal life, studies, or a job, most athletes believed that they were entitled to a subsidy to off-set their losses. Moreover, if their sport was considered entertainment, they felt they should be paid as entertainers. In the 1950s, Wes Santee, a noted middle-distance runner from Kansas, was one of the first to actively and openly challenge the hypocrisy of AAU reimbursement rules for track athletes.[3]

The basic conflicts of interests between the revenue producing athlete and the institutions that benefited from his athletic endeavors were as old as amateur sports. In 1925 the New England Association of the Amateur Athletic Union charged that the New York Metropolitan Association was using their monopoly on Paavo Nurmi's race schedule for the financial benefit of the New York Athletic Clubs.[4] As early as 1928 Major John L. Griffith, commissioner for athletics of the Western Conference [The Big Ten], expressed strong opposition to the linkage between the American Olympic Committee and the AAU. He felt that AAU domination over American amateur athletics and Olympic performance was deplorable and declared, "the AAU is an organization of 'cheap politicians.' They use intimidation, such as threats of disbarment of any athlete who competes in an amateur event not sanctioned by them."[5]

In 1948, almost immediately after Don Canham was named track coach at Michigan, Lloyd Olds invited Canham to become involved in the AAU. Between 1948 and 1953 Canham conducted the indoor and outdoor AAU championships at the University of Michigan, and received a quid pro quo from the AAU for his involvement.[6]

By the same token, the NCAA was not without sin. In June 1956 a series of charges were made that "phony" or "fake jobs" were being used at the University of California to subsidize athletes in violation of NCCA rules.[7]

Financing Track

Money was at the core of the conflict between the AAU and the NCAA. To understand this conflict it is important to understand the finances involved in a national championship track meet in 1962. The NCAA championships held in Eugene, Oregon that year attracted a larger crowd than usual, and the meet took in $47,933 and spent $19,137.70. The remaining funds—a record $28,795.30—went primarily toward travel expenses of the competing athletes with about 25% going to the NCAA for operational support. Under NCAA policy the host school receives no share of the profit and was responsible for any loss which might occur. The host school was repaid for certain expenses, but receives nothing for the many hours contributed by its athletic director, track coach and others, nor for overhead.

Receipts included $41,778 in ticket sales; $3495 in program sales; $1325 in program advertising; and $1335 for radio and television rights. Promotional expenses include entry blanks and preliminary announcements ($192.50), publicity folders and posters ($343.15), other advertising ($85.10), supplies ($203.45), clerical expense ($158.48), postage [including ticket sales] ($509.75), telephone and telegraph ($366.35), and meetings (committees, press, etc.) ($468.09.)

Games committee and official expenses: meet director ($300), starter ($50), assistant starter ($25), event manager ($100), travel expenses of Games Committee NCAA Rules Committee ($300). Games expenses: Awards, team trophies ($120.71), plaques and medals ($262.82); equipment, implements ($1754.24), [printing the] numbers [used to identify participants] ($206.60); motion pictures and supplies ($455.02): building and grounds expenses, supplies ($1844.77), labor ($1410.30); public address ($500.50); police and ushers ($868.75); program expenses & sellers' commissions ($699), printing ($2896.20), timer rental ($50).

NCAA treasurer ($2879.53), competitors for travel expenses ($19,224.20), NCAA treasurer ($3345.78), to competing institutions on a per man basis for point winners ($3345.78).[8]

It is clear that with the possible exception of the Olympic Games and an occasional international meet, track and field was not a big revenue sport. It is also clear that the sport depended heavily on volunteer workers and institutional support. In this context, the important perks of international travel, participation on the United State and International Olympic Committees, support from the U.S. State Department for special assignments and events, and media recognition were controlled by the AAU.

But, the AAU and the IOC also had their problems. While a small group of individuals at the top enjoyed luxurious meetings, power, and privilege, they could not finance the U.S. Olympic track and field team without exploiting the track athlete. It became common for the U.S. Olympic Committee to schedule a number of meets before and after the Olympic Games to generate enough revenue to underwrite expenses. Before the Rome Olympic Games, there were two meets at which the entire team was scheduled to participate, and another set of meets at which smaller groups of athletes were invited. Olympic team members were asked if they could stay over after the Games and about two-thirds indicated a desire to do so. On September 9 and 10, 1960 a full U.S. team participated in a meet held with Greece and Germany at night in Athens. Then, as many athletes as possible were invited to Israel for meets in Tel-Aviv and Jerusalem. On September 14 the entire U.S. team competed against the British Empire in a relay meet in London. Finally, invitations were received to send men to the following meets, with number of athletes in parenthesis:

Cologne, Germany, September 16 (6); Hanover, Sept. 17 (8); Wuppertal, Sept. 20 (12); Berlin, Sept. 24–25 (6–8); Amsterdam, Sept. 15 (10–15); Bern, Sept.

16–17 (8); Dublin, September 17–18 (4 mile relay and 6 others); Helsinki, Sept. 16 (6); Turku, Sept. 18 (6); Stockholm, Sept 16 (6); Goteborg, Sept. 18 (6); Malmo, Sept 20 or 21 (6); Lisbon, after the 14ᵗʰ (7); Monaco, Sept. 29 (6); Oct. 4 (6).[9]

The AAU Needed Reorganization

Reorganization of the AAU was long past due. A majority of high school graduates were now enrolling in community or junior colleges, colleges, or universities. Yet, these groups were not represented on the track committee of the AAU. The New York Athletic Club and the other elite athletic clubs had long since ceased to play the dominant role in track and field they had played before the great depression. And, with the suburban sprawl, groups like the Catholic Youth Organization, the Jewish Federation, and the YMCA were becoming less relevant to the development of young athletes, and public high school coaches were becoming more important to their development. Yet, traditional faith-based groups were still a part of the power structure of the AAU, reflecting long gone realities instead of the current situation.

The AAU was failing on several fronts. In the midst of the civil rights revolution, the AAU gives its official sanction to "whites only" meets, sanctioned meets that covertly practiced discrimination, and accepted an invitation for a white only team to compete in South Africa and sent such a team. In 1968 many black athletes boycotted the New York Athletic Club's annual AAU sanctioned indoor track meet because the NYCA did not admit Negroes to its membership.

AAU rules were often far from logical and their enforcement was frequently inconsistent. For example, when Lee Calhoun met with Dan Ferris, the head of the AAU, and AAU lawyers in 1958 to discuss his suspension for appearing on the TV program *Bride and Groom*. According to AAU lawyers, it did not matter that Calhoun got wedding presents, only that he got them on national television. If he had received the same presents in a different context, he would not have been barred from amateur competition for a year. The claim that Calhoun had capitalized on his athletic fame to receive the gifts was spurious, since the show's producers did not even know Calhoun was a track athlete and there was ample evidence to that effect.

The suspension was lifted when Calhoun and John Nagye, the chairman of the AAU Lake Erie Association in Cleveland raised between $35,000 and $40,000 for the AAU, but refused to turn it over until the deal was worked out.[10] In the end, the entire handling of the situation smelled foul.

In 1961–2 the National Collegiate Track Coaches Association (NCTCA) lead by its officers—President Oliver "Ollie" Jackson (a coach at Abilene Christian College); Vice President Bill Bowerman (the University of Oregon), and Secretary-Treasurer Phil Diamond (University of Michigan), and Diamond's ally, Don Canham—and with the assistance of the NCAA and Cordner Nelson, publisher of *Track and Field News*, became involved in forming the U.S. Track and Field Federation.[11] Several coaching associations in other sports had formed their own federations to go head-to-head with the AAU with the purpose of applying for international recognition. The move to form the U.S. Track and Field Federation escalated a bitter fight between the AAU and the NCAA that lasted for seventeen more years.

Track and Field News listed the failures of the AAU that lead to the proposed group:

1. Poor communications with both athletes and the public regarding track and field,
2. a lack of proper protection of U. S. athletes in international competition (such as failure to inform athletes of schedule changes),
3. failure to communicate rules changes in a timely manner, and aggressively represent the USA in setting rules for scoring at international meets,
4. invitations to compete abroad are withheld from athletes without their knowledge,
5. poor treatment of foreign athletes,
6. failure to make application for records for all American athletes who broke U. S. records, world records, or both
7. coaches inadequately represented in running the AAU (less than a third of those on the AAU track and field committee were track coaches),
8. little attempt was made to keep abreast of worldwide training, officiating, and meet conduct,
9. politics frequently played a role in selecting coaches, athletes, and managers for international meets and State Department sponsored trips,
10. development work for U.S. track athletes was inadequate,
11. racial segregation was condoned (The AAU gives its official sanction to "whites only" meets, to meets which covertly practiced discrimination, and accepted and sent a white only team to South Africa),
12. registration rules and sanction fees were inconsistent and irregular,
13. resisted and hindered the formation and operation of Road Running Clubs,
14. inadequately managed National championships,
15. was New York oriented,

16. AAU committees did not adequately represent the track and field constituency (the Catholic Youth Organization, Jewish Welfare Board, YMCA, and Athletic Clubs were represented, but not the NCAA or junior colleges), or generate enough manpower to manage track since it handled nearly 20 other sports including baton twirling, skin diving and synchronized swimming,

17. money collected from track was diverted to other sports, and

18. athletes were sometimes refused permission to accept foreign invitations solely because they were needed to participate in U.S. indoor season.[12]

They might well have added that expense monies for track athletes was woefully inadequate.

On September 30, 1961, Ken Doherty, former coach at the Universities of Michigan and Pennsylvania, past President of the NCTCA, and currently director of the Penn Relays, wrote an "Open Letter" regarding the proposed Track and Field Federation. His unselfish, reasoned moderation, favoring what was best for track and field, was applauded by nearly everyone. Doherty argued that "First and above all, we must be clear as to what the proposed Track and Field Federation of America stands for, not merely what and who it is against. The decisions we reach will determine our sport for the next hundred years. We can afford a year or so of delay while we plan with cool and careful deliberation."[13]

In January 1962 the new United States Track and Field Federation was formed and applied for recognition as the official representative of the USA in international track and field competition. A polling of track coaches indicated that an overwhelming number of coaches at all levels of the sport supported the new Federation.[14] The by-laws for the proposed Federation offered eight seats to colleges (the NCAA, NAIA, and junior colleges), eight seats to the AAU, four to the American Armed Forces, four to high schools, and two at-large.

The AAU predictably turned downed the Federation's offer and rallied its core supporters to fight the hostile take-over of their track and field functions. The U.S. Olympic Committee called for a compromise. For the most part, track athletes were uninvolved and confused. Most did not know that failing to keep their AAU card current could bar them from international competition if the Federation did not replace the AAU as the official international representative of the USA. A proposed USTFF championship meet was strongly opposed by the NAIA as well as the AAU.[15]

By March 1962 the U.S. Track and Field Federation had lost the first round of the struggle for control of the management of American track and field. The Federation had started with the support of the NCAA, the National Collegiate Track Coaches Association, and *Track and Field News*. It had hoped to win the support of the National Association of Intercollegiate Athletes (NAIA)—a group representing 465 small colleges, the American Armed Forces track program, the American High School Athletic Associations, and the American Junior College Athletic Association. Although several of these groups showed considerable interest, the AAU fended off the hostile takeover of their control of America's involvement in international track and field competition by making major revisions in its table of organization and membership on their governing committees. Long indifferent to both internal and external criticism, the AAU was forced to make changes, albeit modest ones to fend off the NCAA and its track coaches.[16]

Isolate and Destroy

Starting in 1965, many college athletes no longer participated in AAU meets.[17] The NCAA opposed college athletes participating in AAU meets and skipping the NCAA championships, so they began pressuring colleges and universities to keep senior division AAU athletes from using college facilities for training and competition. A few coaches, like the track coach at the University of Chicago, resisted but most caved into NCAA pressure. However, the AAU still controlled international athletic events and sponsored summer tours for track athletes, so many track stars continued to run in AAU championship meets, where the competition was stiffer than in the AAU because college graduates and other amateurs could participate. The Pan-American and Olympic Games were important to sustaining the AAU.[18]

In 1967 a Sports Arbitration Board was appointed by vice president Hubert Humphrey to attempt to arbitrate the dispute. Don Canham served on the board as a NCAA representative. The AAU never agreed that the committee had any authority in the matter. The board met several times under the leadership of Douglas MacArthur, Bobby Kennedy, and Hubert Humphrey, but failed to find a solution. In the end, the board was disbanded. Nevertheless, athletes and coaches continued to challenge the AAU definition of "amateurism."

The feud between the NCAA and the AAU often placed the athlete in the middle. The AAU would not allow athletes to participate in international meets, including the Olympics, if they did not belong to the AAU and follow their rules. On the other hand, the NCAA prohibited college athletes from taking part in AAU meets under threat of stripping athletes of their scholarships.[19] Finally, on May 17, 1971 the AAU and the NCAA held exploratory talks in Knoxville in hopes of finding a basis for settling the dispute. The conflict centered on who would control track and field competition in the USA.[20] The talks did not resolve anything.

A seven-member committee on "Eligibility for the United States Olympic Team" met in 1972 and proposed refinements to the definition of amateurism in hopes that these changes would be adopted for the 1976 Olympics. The committee recommended the following changes:

1. A person should not lose amateur status in one sport because he is a professional in another.
2. A former amateur may have that status reinstated if he meets certain requirements.
3. Coaching or teaching athletics in any sport does not change his amateur status unless such a job constitutes his primary vocation.
4. A person can remain an amateur and still (a) be paid expense money, (b) be reimbursed for income lost while away from a primary occupation because of training or competition, (c) receive payment for commercial endorsements as long as such activity doesn't involve participation in his sport, (d) receive scholarship aid, (e) receive accident or illness insurance in connection with training or competition, (f) accept prizes won in competition within the limits of the authority governing his sport, and (g) receive royalties from publications related to his sport.
5. An athlete is still an amateur if he signed a professional contract or agreement, but has received no payment.

Avery Brundage, head of the International Olympic Committee (IOC), was steadfastly against changing, in any way, Rule 26 on amateurism. His opposition prevented Olympians from receiving most types of compensation, except basic expenses, insurance, and scholarships, for their competition. Marcus Plant [NCAA President] observed that "Brundage is expected to retire after this year's Olympics. After he leaves the climate should be better for expecting changes by the IOC. If the president of the IOC is violently opposed to change, it is pretty hard to update Rule 26."[21]

In 1975, President Ford appointed the Commission of Olympic Sports, with Gerald B. Zornow, chairman of the board of Eastman Kodak, in charge. This Commission, with extensive behind the scenes work by Walter Byers, executive director of the NCAA, ended the control of the AAU over international track competition. It also ended efforts from the AAU to influence NCAA policies.[22]

They Forgot About the Athlete

Concern about the lack of support for American track and field athletes surfaced every four years as the Olympic Games approached. In June 1968 Lou Scott graduated from Arizona State University. He had run an average of 30 miles a day for nearly five years in preparation for the Olympic trials. He had a wife, a small child, a ten-year-old automobile with a full tank of gasoline, and a dream of running in the Olympics. Without a penny to his name, he drove to California with his family. Once in California his friends gave Lou and his family a place to stay and helped him get a job. The Scott family endured abject poverty to fill Lou's Olympic dream.[23]

In 1972 a 24-year old Vince Matthews, who ran on the 800-meter relay team in 1968 as part of the 15-man U.S. Olympic team, worked in the Brooklyn Neighborhood Youth Corps between 1968 and 1972 while he trained for the next Olympic trials. Matthews and Charles Turner, his coach, climbed fences at Boys High School after dark in order to find a suitable practice field. Turner, a Brooklyn bus driver, used the $2,500 he and his wife had saved for a house to sent Matthews and two other young men to the Olympic trials in Eugene. They were rewarded when Matthews earned the third spot in the 400-meter dash by beating Olympic champion Lee Evans to make the 15-man U.S. Olympic Track and Field team.[24] But, the sacrifices made to represent the United States seemed ridiculous in light of the money being made on the Olympics by television networks, media representatives, IOC members, sports equipment companies, and coaches.

There was a hand-printed sign on the bulletin board in Bean Hall in Eugene begging for assistance that read: "Help! Poverty Stricken Marathoner Will Need Way Home to Mass. (Had to pay own way here)." Penciled under this plea were the words, "So did everyone else." At the same time the Olympic team was advertising: "Be Proud: Be Part . . . Support Your United States Olympic Team."[25] The disconnect was as enormous as the myth that one could be a world class athlete without working at it as vigorously and with the kind of coaching and equipment support required by a professional when training for his or her sport.

Trackmen asked, "Where does the money for support of the Olympic Games go?" Many amateur athletes openly questioned the administration, operation and fiscal responsibility of the United States Olympic Committee. "I always thought the Olympic Committee didn't have much money," said Tom Derderian from South Deerfield, MA, who paid his own way to the Olympic trials and did not have the money to pay his way home. "I'm beginning to realize things are different. The Olympic officials won't admit how much money they have or give an accounting for what they have spent. They are certainly not spending it on the athletes."[26]

Increasingly track athletes were calling for an investigation of IOC money management. There also were concerns that the rules of amateurism resulted in unequal competition. They argued that charitable gifts are a tax deduction and therefore should be accounted for publicly. They also felt that athletes who are members of the armed services or belong to rich athletic clubs should not be given unfair advantages over athletes who receive no subsidies.

The Olympic Committee did not pay the expenses to the trials of any of the athletes who participated. While track clubs or colleges sponsor a majority of the 550 athletes attending the 10-day trials, nearly every athlete felt that the U.S. Olympic Committee should, at the every least, provide room and board while on site. After all, each had met qualifying standards to be invited to attend the trials. Athletes were asking "How much are we supposed to sacrifice to make the team?" Athletes attached to the various military services compounded the problem. They trained nearly full time, were fully supported, and received a salary. There also were track clubs that support athletes, but discriminated on the basis of race, ethnicity, or both.[27]

George Frenn, a U.S. Olympian in the hammer throw in 1972, felt that the AAU was more interested in promoting events than in training athletes. "They won't spend any money unless they're forced to. Our turnover in track is so enormous because the athletes, sooner or later, get fed up with the program. Over the long run, the only reason track and field survives is because of 'oddballs and weirdoes' who bear any burden and pay any price for the chance to compete."

In 1972 there were approximately 200 hammer throwers in the United States, each of whom followed a grueling schedule. Frenn, for example, lifted 600-pound weights three days each week.

That kind of heavy work does unbelievable destruction to the body. There's not a day I'm not in constant pain." He put up with the pain because he enjoyed the image of manliness and virility that was so closely associated with the sport. "It's an ego trip and show me a man who's not on an ego trip. What's so great about holding a record in the throw? Well, some impressive looking people have held it. Look at my body. I like pitting its strength against that of another man. You know, I hold a record in the 56-pound throw, otherwise known as the 4-stone throw. They were throwing the stone weight back in the time of Henry the Eighth. He threw the stone. It's a heavy nostalgic trip to sit-on the throne of the 4-stone throw.[28]

No American finished in the top eight in the hammer throw from1964 to 1992, except for a fifth place finish in 1984 when the Eastern Europeans did not compete. However, Al Feuerbach put the shot 70–9 at the Mount San Antonio Relays in Walnut Creek, CA on April 28, 1973.[29] In 1980 a Soviet put the shot 70 feet in the Olympic Games, and in 1988 four athletes bettered 70 feet. By then positive tests for excessive testosterone were relatively common in the weight throwing events.

Nothing Rhymes with Orange

Starting in the late 1950s Adidas introduced athletic shoes with nylon soles and molded rubber studs. These shoes were particularly advantageous in wet weather. In 1956 Adidas gave its track shoes to track and field Olympians, who wore them for a worldwide audience at the Melbourne games. This move turned out to be a major marketing coup. By 1964 eighty percent of the track and field winners and nearly all soccer players in the Olympic Games wore high quality, well-designed Adidas athletic shoes.[30] Puma countered with its own lightweight, durable athletic shoes, and began paying track stars under the table to wear their brand, and University of Oregon track Coach Bill Bowerman helped start Nike to compete in the lucrative athletic shoe market.[31]

At the 1968 Olympics in Mexico City, running shoe companies became embroiled in a battle for the favors of athletes, particularly Americans. Reports of large amounts of money being left in the track shoes of certain competitors were made to the International Olympic Committee, and several American athletes reportedly bought cars and clothes with their payoffs. No action was taken against either the athletes or the companies after the games.

The outrage in Mexico City prompted international officials to propose that starting in 1969 white shoes, without trademarks be worn in future Olympics and at major international meets. Shoe companies fought the plan, and the proposal was defeated. Under international rules athletes were allowed to receive a "reasonable amount of equipment" from companies.[32]

The Nike Phenomenon

Gillette, Wheaties, and Miller Lite beer used sports themes in their advertising for years before 1963 when Phil Knight founded Blue Ribbon Sports, the forerunner of Nike. But, no one combined sports, marketing, business, and pop culture in the dynamic manner of Nike. Nike's brilliant ad campaigns made track shoes and basketball shoes the footwear of choice for the last quarter of the century. By 1972 the Nike Athletic Shoe Company was one of the largest running-shoe manufacturers in the world. Based in Beaverton, Oregon, Nike was one of the first running-gear makers to understand the commercial value of promoting road races open to large fields of hobbyist athletes as well as to the elite racers. More importantly, they saw the importance of the goodwill gained by "investing back into the sport."

The Nike/Oregon Track Club sponsored their first marathon in September 1972. Held on a flat terrain with few hindering headwinds, the race was designed to insure fast times. It became an immediate success. Nike also sponsored the prestigious Athletics West track club, which bankrolled training and participation for world-class track and field athletes. Other shoe companies also started track teams. New Balance, Nike, Adidas, and other shoe companies began to pay some runners $14,000 a year simply to run in their shoes. By 1981, runners like Greg Meyer endangered their future participation in the Olympic Games by openly accepting $10,000 for winning the Cascade Run-off. At the same time, the European track circuit paid at least two runners $20,000 apiece per race, all under-the-table, of course, to run a series of mile runs.[33]

Athletic shoe companies often filled the gap left by the Olympic Committee. Gene White, a world-class high jumper, who contends that a representative from Adidas was prepared to offer him money if he wore the company's shoes in the American trials and again at Munich if he qualified for the Olympics.[34]

A touch of irony accompanies White's involvement. The 21-year-old black from Bristol, Pa., was serving a two-month to two-year sentence for forgery, and was granted a furlough by a judge and prison officials in order to try out for the American team.[35]

Steve Prefontaine

Between 1970 and May 31, 1975 when he was killed in an automobile accident, Steve Prefontaine set 14 American records at distances from 2-K to 10-K. He placed fourth in the 5-K run in the 1972 Olympics, when he was only 21-years old. While the part-time bartender, from a working-class background in Coos Bay, Oregon, never won an Olympic medal, his dedication, bold front-running style, and brash willingness to take on the sports establishment made him an American legend. He had little patience for the hypocrisy of the "amateur" system. He challenged the rules that limited an athlete's ability to earn a living and required them to seek permission to compete abroad. At a time when athletes received a scant $3 a day spending money, he turned down more than $100,000 to join the fledgling professional track tour. Prefontaine's forceful support was critical in the athletes' movement that culminated in the 1978 Amateur Sports Act, that gave athletes a say in the leadership of Olympic sports.[36]

In 1974 the International Olympic Committee, under the leadership of Lord Killanin, finally took steps to ease the amateur code espoused by Brundage.[37]

The International Track Association: Professional Track

On November 14, 1972, Michael O'Hara announced the formation of the International Track Association. He had previously founded the American Basketball Association and the World Hockey Association. The new track association was committed to giving runners above the board payments contingent on their performance in any given meet, rather than payments negotiated beforehand and paid under the table.

In 1973 professional track made its debut in New York City featuring John Carlos and professional football players, Bob Hayes, Rocky Thompson, and Eddie Bell. In 1975 David Wottle of Bowling Green State University in Ohio smashed the world professional indoor record for the 880-yard run at an International Track Association Meet in Atlanta.[38]

Cliff Buck, president of the United States Olympic Committee, said "speaking as an individual and not as president of the United States Olympic Committee, I think that as a natural reaction the pure amateur will refuse to compete in the Olympics against the pros." He expressed his opinion that "opening up the Olympics to professionals would spell the end of the movement." He went on to expose his ignorance of the true state of competition in the Olympics by arguing

The man who competes because he loves the sport would never have a chance against one [a pro] who spends his entire life working to perfect his physical skills. He'd know before he started that he wouldn't have a chance and thereby he would resent the intrusion of the pros. It follows that he would quit, and without the amateurs there would be no Olympics.

Buck was asked how he felt about athletes from communist countries, who, many contend, are the closest thing to professionals because they are Government-subsidized and spent all their time perfecting their skills with the ultimate goal the winning of international titles, such as the Olympics. Buck said

> I just don't believe all those stories. Sure, most Iron Curtain country athletes are subsidized, but to say flat out they are professionals, I just don't know. It's too hard to draw parallels between the United States and Russia, for instance, because of the great difference in our economies and the way we live.

Buck and other United States Olympic officials came under fire for not extending financial help to athletes participating in the Olympic trials. They spuriously argued that "such help would be a violation of amateurism."[39]

What Place for Criminals?

Bobby Lee Hunter and Gene White were athletes who were in State correctional facilities and were seeking places on the United States Olympic team in 1972, with the complete backing of the U. S. Olympic Committee. According to Clifford H. Buck, the president of the U.S. Olympic Committee, there were no specific legal restrictions against filing entries for athletes serving prison terms. In 1971 Hunter qualified for the U. S. Pan-American Games team and was issued a passport by the Department of State. The State of South Carolina, where Hunter was serving a sentence for manslaughter, arranged for a state correctional officer to accompany him to the games. In Cali, Colombia, Hunter lived with the other team members in the Pan-American Village. His conduct was exemplary. The correctional officer lived in a downtown hotel.[40]

President Ford Does Good

President Ford, who had been an amateur athlete at the University of Michigan, had a controlling interest in amateur sports. By 1975 it was becoming increasingly clear that amateur sports in the United States were fragmented, ill defined, and without a clear direction. It was generally acknowledged that there were now excellent athletes from Kenya, Uganda, East Germany and other countries that only a few years ago were nowhere to be found in the world's international athletic arenas. It was also lamented that Cuba had performed particularly well in the 1975 Pan-American Games. Moreover, it was generally felt that because of "continuing conflicts among organizations involved with amateur sports, there was declining performance by the United States in international competition." Consequently, President Ford impanelled a Commission on Olympic Sports. The charge to the commission stated: "other countries of the world have improved the quality and quantity of their participation in internationally competitive amateur sports at a rate far in excess of improvements made by the United States."[41]

On September 9, 1975 President Gerald Ford appointed and swore in the 22-members of the commission, which included four Senators, four Representatives and four well-known athletes. The commission opened hearings the day members were sworn in. On February 9, 1976 the commission made its preliminary report. Calling on memories of the defunct model of the Amateur Athletic Union, the report declared:

The [necessary] reform cannot come from within the existing structure. Rather, there seems to be a need for a single; comprehensive organization to provide the leadership necessary to effect change within the current system. We see this organization as concerned with all amateur sports rather than just those sports currently on the Olympic roster. . . . An unfortunate form of elitism [was identified as another source of trouble.] [The report expressed concern that] school sports programs have tended to emphasize already popular, mass-participation sports such as basketball, baseball, and football for their competitive and physical education programs. Conflicts for control of amateur sports in this country are diffusing public interest and financial support. It is not unusual, [the report said] to find one-third to one-half of the population of European countries engaged in regular sporting activity of one type or another. . . . Almost every country in the world supports its athletes and athletic programs out of the government treasury.[42]

In 1977 the University of Michigan hosted the Ann Arbor Federation Track Meet at Ferry Field, clearly declaring itself at odds with the AAU.[43] The seven-decade-old dispute between the AAU and the NCAA finally ended in 1978 when Congress passed legislation recommended by President Ford.

The Athletics Congress/USA

The Amateur Sports Act of 1978, required that all of America's national governing bodies for sports on either the Olympic or Pan American Games program have individual autonomy by November 1980. The Act also allowed the U. S. Olympic Committee to charge sponsors for exclusive rights to the word "Olympics" and the five Olympic rings. The principal affect of the act was that the Amateur Athletic Union, which had dominated American track and field for more than ninety years because it held the USA's international memberships for eight sports on the winter and summer games program, was forced out of sports governance within two years. This permitted each of these sports to operate independently and to be the United States member of its own international federation.

Track and field was the first of the sports to declare independence from the AAU. For more than a century, the term "athletics" was the term to cover the sports of track and field, race walking, cross-country, and road racing. Consequently, a new organization to be known as "The Athletics Congress/USA" (TAC), with membership in the International Amateur Athletic Federation (IAAF), was formally established in August 1979. The new organization was responsible for representing and protecting the interests of men and women from age ten to those over eighty years of age in participation in athletics. They would register athletes, establish and maintain the sports' rules of competition, hold National Championships, and select teams to represent the United States in international competition.[44]

A number of amateur sports organizations including the NCAA, the National Federation of State High School Associations, National Association of Intercollegiate Athletics, and the National Junior Collage Athletic Association became members of The Athletic Congress of the USA. By 1992 TAC had 56 member Associations that oversaw the sport at the local level, and offered more than 140 National Championships each year.

In 1980 the U. S. Olympic Committee instituted a reward system that paid athletes for medals won at the Olympics and world championships. This reward system was significantly improved in 1989. By 1992 any U.S. athlete who won a gold medal received $15,000. A silver medal winner was given $10,000; and a bronze medal winner was awarded $7,500. The U.S. Olympic Committee also gave money to national governing bodies (NGB) of each Olympic sport from sponsors based on an agreed on formula linked to team size and medals won over the past eight years. The money was used for coaching, free training facilities, room and board, complete health insurance, and direct, grant payments to athletes to defray basic living and training expenses. In 1996 USA Track and Field received $2.2 million from the U.S. Olympic Committee.[45]

With a few exceptions, the athletes who fill the 144 U.S. Olympic track and field slots every four years still found the money needed to train and compete at a world-class level difficult to come by. The new system was better than the AAU system for nearly all Olympic track and field competitors. But, while millions were being paid by television and corporate sponsors to underwrite the Olympic Games, little of that support found its way to the average Olympian, who was still pretty much on his or her own, except for shoe contracts.

At its Annual Meeting in 1992, The Athletic Congress of the USA was renamed USA Track & Field to more appropriately convey what the organization does to a generation unfamiliar with the original meaning of the term athletics.[46]

A Melancholy Sigh

While the 20-year feud between the AAU and the NCAA finally ended in August 1979 with the creation of The Athletic Congress/USA,[47] the basic conflict of interests between the revenue producing athlete and the institutions that benefited from athletic endeavors was largely ignored. College athletic departments continued to seek independence from university interference with their management of athletics. They complained that some university presidents confused control with management. The university president was to control and not manage day-by-day operations of athletic departments, but much was hidden in the daily operations that affects the role, status, and influence of college athletics, and that was often the way athletic departments like it. In 1983 the University of Michigan formed the Board of Intercollegiate Athletics to assert a measure of faculty control.

Athletic Directors, like Don Canham, were quick to criticize any effort to change or challenge the status quo. When the NCAA proposed a change in the scholarship formula that gave more emphasis to financial need in issuing athletic scholarships, Canham told an audience of coaches and athletic officials,

quite frankly [the NCAA scholarship formula] scares the hell out of me. We've got the best football and basketball programs ever put together. We've got it going. Let's not tamper with it. If we have to save money, let's do it other ways. Let's have a convention to determine how we're going to increase revenues, not cut costs.[48]

Canham promoted a system that depended on revenue producing sports to underwrite the entire intercollegiate athletic program, and penalized sports that did not produce adequate income to be self-supporting. In 1980 he charged $50 for a two-day clinic on sports promotion and marketing at which he implored his audience "not to kill the goose that laid the golden egg."[49] He urged the group to "promote football as hard as you can and within the rules of the NCAA, back your coaching staff to the nth degree. At Michigan, football goes a long way toward carrying the financial load for may other sports. Promote football as a spectacle, an event, without regard to last year's record."[50] Yet, under his plan football and basketball got the lion's share of the budget and minor sports, like track and field and all women's sports were short changed whenever there was not enough money to go around.

In 1987 the deep divisions in philosophy within the NCAA surfaced once again when the chancellor of the University of California at Berkeley, Ira Michael Heyman, called for fundamental changes that would reduce the commercialization of sports. He claimed that commercialization had corrupted the educational values of even those schools that run their programs honestly. "Even at the clean, successful programs, the commercialization of big-time sports—and the accompanying emphasis on winning—requires engaging in activities that are not good for our institutions or our students." He pointed out that some coaches are paid up to $500,000 a year, while tenured professors with international reputations as scholars and teachers earn less than one-fourth that amount. "This situation distorts values on many campuses."

Bo Schembechler retorted that "there is nothing inherently bad with the status quo." He went on to argue that "Revenue producing is not a sin. Bigness is not corruption. We [coaches] are not the enemy. I'm for cost cutting if you have to. I'm not for de-emphasis."[51]

Not everyone framed the issues the way Bo did. Warren Goldstein, co-author of *A Brief History of American Sports*, agreed with Ira Heyman. Goldstein put it this way:

> Let's say it straight out: Division I basketball and football are the true minor leagues for the National Basketball Association and the National Football League. Let's professionalize college sports, up front and cleanly, and end the cynicism, the pretense that any more ten percent to twenty percent of top-flight college athletes are genuine students. The National College Athletic Association, despite a raft of regulations, is next to useless because it has never had the will or the power to enforce genuine amateurism. It never will. The truth is that no powerful sports related interest group in America really wants truly amateur college sports. Not the TV networks, their sponsors, the fans, or

the alumni, and certainly not the colleges, who are making as much money as possible.[52]

Sports and Politics

Politics and sports are never far apart. In 1976 the American CIA and FBI assisted Canada with security preparations for the Olympic Games.[53] Following the Munich terrorist attack on and massacre of nine Israeli athletes, security became a major concern for those planning the Games.

It appears that, in some cases, success in track gives the track star the illusion that the individual can overcome nearly any obstacle to win against difficult odds and that group or community action is an unnecessary impingement on the individual. As a result, a number of white, track stars became politically active in conservative causes. Don Canham was a conservative Republican,[54] as was Bob Parks. Parks, for example, spoke out against President Carter's boycott of the 1980 Olympics. As Parks put it,

> I haven't supported the U.S. Olympic Committee with one dime since then [the 1980 boycott] because they gave in to that idiot Jimmy Carter. I wasn't going to vote for him anyway, but that sealed it. Truthfully, I think the only way you can eliminate the threat of terrorists is to hold the [Olympic] Games at a site behind the Iron Curtain. I don't like the idea of a permanent site there, but you won't have the problems . . . Los Angeles is kind of a kook town anyway. Behind the Iron Curtain the anti-anything groups don't have a say.

He also argued for maintaining national ties in the Olympic Games because the designations are half of the fun of it.[55]

In 1996 Jim Ryun, the Kansas track icon and the first high school student in the century to run the mile under four minutes (3:55.3), ran for and won the second Congressional District seat in Kansas as an ultra-conservative Republican.[56]

The NCAA moved its offices from Overland Park, Kansas to Indianapolis, the location of USA Track & Field.[57]

17. "Black Lightning" [1962–1973]

The U.S. track squads encountered problems in the 1948–60 Olympics because many of the athletes made the team in June and were not in top condition in late summer or late autumn. In 1964, the U.S. Olympic Committee decided to correct the situation. As in the past, six men from the NCAA and six from the AAU championships qualified for the Olympic trials at Randalls Island. The Randalls Island tryouts were held July 4–5. At that meet, six in each event were selected for a final tryout to be held in California the second week in September. Outstanding performers from the Armed Forces meet were added to the winners of the Randalls Island meet. The first three men in the California meet made the Olympic team.

The men who competed in the California meet were given at least a week to train at the site of the final Olympic trials and had their entire expenses paid by the Olympic Committee. Those who failed to qualify had their expenses back home paid by the Olympic Committee. Those who made the team remained together under the jurisdiction of their coaches and trained as a unit until they departed for Tokyo. Additional conditioning meets were held on the West Coast prior to departure in late September. Athletes were given ample time to accustom themselves to conditions in Japan.[1]

The prime candidates from Michigan for the Tokyo Olympics were Henry Carr, Hayes Jones, and Rex Cawley. Henry Carr was "black lightning," if such a thing ever existed. He was a mediocre starter, but was as fast and smooth a runner at 200 and 400-meters as anyone who ever has donned track shoes.

Sprinter Nonpareil

Henry Carr was born in Montgomery, Alabama on November 27, 1942. He attended Northwestern High School in Detroit. Before the age of 17, Carr ran the 100-yard dash in 9.7 and the 220-yards at 21.0 seconds. On June 4, 1960 he then won the 220-yard dash at the Detroit Metropolitan League Championships in the remarkable time of 20.6. After

Henry Carr graduated from Northwestern HS in Detroit before attending Arizona State University, where he set word records in the 200-meter dash and the 4 × 400-meter relay. He won two gold medals in record setting time at the Tokyo Olympics in 1964. *(Photo The Walter P. Reuther Library, Wayne State University)*

graduating from high school in 1961, he accepted an athletic scholarship at Arizona State University in Tempe.

Carr was a conscientious, fast, well-trained sprinter. While he never had a great love for the 100-meter, Henry was among the best in the USA, running that distance in 10.2. At the 200-meter he dominated America's collegiate track ranks in 1963 and 1964, often winning by wide margins. His long stride was so smooth and effortless, that he was the envy of runners everywhere. His comfortable wins at 200-meters suggested that the quarter-mile was his most natural race.

Carr was defeated only twice in the 220-yard dash in the two years prior to the 1964 Olympics, and broke the 200-meter world record three times and the mile relay record twice.[2] On March 19, 1963 Carr appeared to set the world record in the 220-yard dash (20.4) in a duel meet with Utah in Tempe. However, a later measurement showed the course to be 18 inches short.[3] Four days later, however, Carr set the world record in the 220-yard dash around a turn (20.3). A surveyor put in the staggers. Carr won the 220 by six yards. He also ran a 46.0 quarter and helped the Sun Devils set a national collegiate record for the mile relay (3:07.2) in a duel meet with the University of Southern California at Tempe. On April 27 the Arizona State University mile relay team set a world record (3:04.5) in that event at Walnut Creek, California. Then, on April 4, 1964 Carr again set the world record in the 220-yard dash (20.2) at Tempe. Carr also set Olympic records in the 200 meter run (20.3) and the 4 by 400-meter relay (3:00.7) in which he ran an anchor leg at 44.5.[4]

According to Bob Hayes, the Florida A & M sprinter, who was academically ineligible for the NCAA season, he and Henry Carr ran in the 220 at the Coliseum Relays on May 17, 1963 just to please the meet's promoter. "I wasn't in shape, and Henry and I ran it only eight minutes after the 100." Nevertheless Carr ran the 220 in 20.8, and then ran the anchor leg on won the mile relay team (3:05.2) in 45.4.[5]

At the National AAU Senior Championships in St. Louis on June 21–22, 1963 Carr, running for the Phoenix Athletic Club, tied for first with Paul Drayton in the 220-yard run (20.4 wind aided). Carr led the finalists around the turn and into the stretch, but Drayton, the two-time champion, was at his best while Carr was taped up above and below both knees with connecting tape on the sides because of his loose joints. Drayton gained steadily, but observers on the line thought Carr held him off by a few inches. The finish judges picked Carr. Lunging at the tape, Carr fell a few yards beyond. "My legs have been sore for two weeks," he said. "My knee just gave out after the race."[6]

Villanova coach Jim "Jumbo" Elliott saw the Bulova photo and protested Carr's victory. After hours of haggling, the finish judges could not decide unanimously that Carr had won because Drayton was partly hidden behind Carr. Finally, the matter was decided by referee Cap Haralson, who ruled it a dead heat. The time of 20.4 (20.69 on the Bulova) was wind-aided, and so was not a meet record."[7]

When asked about the controversial decision to call the 1963 AAU 220 a dead head Cap Haralson chairman of the AAU track and field committee explained,

As meet referee it was my duty to make the final decision on the close finish of the 220. I called the judges together, had them study the phototimer picture individually, and they voted four for Carr, three for Dayton. The picture showed Carr's hips ahead, but Dayton had the better lean and his neck, which is considered part of the torso, was even with Carr's. Their chests were even although Carr had twisted one shoulder ahead. After much consideration, study and thought I found I could rule nothing but a dead heat. I was concerned; too, with the wind reading for it didn't seem as if there were an excessive breeze. As there is some question on Carr's earlier 20.3—it may not be a full curve—this would be a world record if the wind question were cleared up. We have to give a lot of thought to the question of wind on a race on one curve. In this race we had a quartering wind, from the back and one side at the finish of the 220. But it blew against the runners on most of the first part of the race.[8]

Jim "Jumbo" Elliott adopted white tops for his runners following a similar incident in 1960 involving his Olympian Frank Budd. "Jumbo" felt that a white jersey showed up better on his African-American runners in photos taken in photo-finishes than a black shirt.[9] "Jumbo" Elliott would later coach America's premiere miler Marty Liquori, who was the nemesis of Ken Popejoy, the Michigan State University Big Ten Champion miler of the early 1970s.

On March 29, 1964 Henry Carr, the 6–3, 185-pound 20-year old runner, married his high school sweetheart, Glenda Nixon, in Detroit. Five days later, in a race in Tempe, an "out of shape" and injured Henry Carr stepped onto his favorite track for a challenge 220 race with Adolph Plummer in a duel meet between Arizona State and the Los Angeles Striders. However, before the challenge race Henry made up five yards against Plummer on the anchor leg of the 440-yard relay, and incurred a muscle injury to his thigh during the 100-yard dash. In that race, Carr was several yards behind Gerald Ashworth at 80 yard, then rallied to win by two-feet at the tape. Both men were timed at 9.5.

In the challenge race, Carr lined up in lane two with Plummer in lane one. Carr had one of his typical mediocre starts, but he led by four yards coming off the curve and increased his lead to nearly six at the finish. Plummer, the world 440-yard record holder, finished six-tenths back in 20.8. Afterwards Carr responded to questions about his world record breaking 20.2 run by saying that the feat surprised him. "I'm not in top condition yet," he confessed. "I thought the injury would be all right after the 100. The muscle felt tight before the start of the 220, but

I felt it pull in the race. I should have stopped then." Carr was pulled out of the mile relay. Only a small wind gauge, which registered a 1.1-mph wind velocity was used during the race. But world records had been accepted with similar wind gauges. His 20.2 clocking erased his own 20.3 world mark. He ran times of 20.5, 20.4 and 20.3 the previous season on this same track. At that time, no other person had ever legally run the 220-yard dash faster than 20.5.[10]

Carr had to share the spotlight that day with Charles Dumas, the 1956 Olympic Games high jump champion who had not jumped competitively since the 1960 Rome Games. Dumas, the first human ever to officially clear seven-feet in the high jump, came out of retirement in spectacular fashion, soaring 7'¼", a height he had previously bettered only once.

An Olympic year always creates close competition, and early season results seem more important as a forecast of the future. The Coliseum Relays in May provided exciting competition in almost every event. Top billing went to the race between Bob Hayes and Henry Carr at 200 meters. Hayes appeared to run away from Carr at the start, making up the stagger by mid-turn, but then Hayes began to fade as Carr's strength showed. Two yards back into the stretch, Carr caught Hayes, who tied up 30 yards from the tape and lost by two yards. Carr declared, "I'm going for broke at 200-meters in the Olympics. I won't even try the 100."[11]

As the 1964 Olympic trials approached, few track and field experts doubted that Henry Carr was the best 200-meter runner in the world. However, Carr was injured again in mid-June 1964, and there was concern that he might not recover in time for the final Olympic trials. There was also concern about the best use of his talent. Carr's competitors did not see him on the 100-meter team, although he would be a strong relay runner. Carr could also do well in the 400, but the Olympic schedule made a 200–400 double impossible in 1964 because these events were sandwiched in a way that precluded such a combination. Carr could, however, be used in the 1600-meter relay.[12]

On July 25–26 Henry Carr ran and won three events in the USA vs. the USSR meet held at the Los Angeles. He won the 200-meter run by five yards, and in the 1,600-meter relay he gained 20-yards on his opponent. When asked about his performance Henry Carr said,

I'm in three events in this meet but for the Olympics I'll be satisfied with one. I still have to make the team. Of course, I'll be available for relay duty—either 400 or 1600—anytime they want me. Right after this meet I'm going home and rest for a few weeks before picking up serious training. Right now I'm not both-ered by any of my earlier injuries. I'd say I'm about 90 percent from top form.[13]

At the final Olympic trials at the Los Angeles Coliseum on September 12 and 13 Henry Carr ran poorly in the 200-meter run. He leaped straight up at the start, was defeated by Paul Drayton, Richard Stebbins, and Bob Hayes. Henry barely beat John Moon for fourth place. The Olympic Committee decided to leave Carr on the team. There was spec-ulation that a poor start, marriage, a recent back injury, and the lack of incentive may have affected his performance.[14]

The Importance of Lane Assignments

Small things, like lane assignments, can determine the outcome of a race. At the Olympic trials in Eugene in late June 1972, competitors in the 200-meter and 400-meter dashes said, "No one likes running in lanes 1 and 2 in Eugene."

The lane assignment in the 200-meter dash around a curve was often a critical factor in who won this event. In seven NCAA 200-meter finals, the runner in the outside lane won five and the other two won from lane 6. Only 2 men out of 18 failed to qualify from lanes 6, 7 and 8, while 11 out of 16 failed from the three inside lanes. The three out-side lanes showed an average time four tenths of a second faster than the three inside lanes. At the final Olympic trials in 1960 Stone John-son had to run in the pole lane and could only run 20.8 after setting a world record of 20.5 in a heat.[15] In 1972 Lee Evans would agree. "It is almost impossible to win a 200-meter dash from lanes 1 and 2 in Eugene, and it is impossible to win a quarter mile race in lanes 1," according to Evans.[16]

Tokyo Olympics

The Tokyo Olympics saw the introduction of electric timing to the hun-dredth of a second as the official medium of measuring man's achieve-ments in the running events. Until then, electric timing devices were used only as a check or to adjust non-winning times.[17] The first round of 200-meter dash at the Tokyo Olympics was held on October 16, a sunny and mild day [67° F]. Paul Drayton, of the USA, won the first heat (20.9). Henry Carr, who had suffered from a bad back earlier in the season, came in second (21.1) to Heinz Schumann of Germany (21.0), in the seventh heat, raising fears about the condition of his back. Later that day, the second round of the preliminaries was held. Again, Drayton won the first heat (20.9), and this time Henry Carr won the second heat (21.0) defeating Schumann, denying him a place in the semi-finals. Carr slept poorly that night because of nervousness.

The semi-finals and the finals of the 200-meter dash were held the following day, which was also sunny and mild [73° F]. Drayton won the first semi-final heat (20.5) equaling the Olympic record, and in the other heat Henry Carr came into the stretch two yards back and drove into the first place to win (20.6). At this stage of the contest, Drayton continued to look like the best prospect to win the event.

The finals were held at 4:00 p.m. with a slight wind against the runners. Drayton was in lane five. Carr drew lane seven, and was unable to keep an eye on more than one runner. Everyone started well, but it soon became clear that USA runner Richard Stebbins was running poorly, and that Carr had nothing wrong with him. His long legs stretched out fully with power and great speed. He went into the stretch a full yard ahead and he increased his lead by another foot or so to win in the Olympic record time of 20.3. "I didn't think it was that fast," Carr said. "This was the easiest of my races." Drayton said, "I was surprised to come out of the turn behind him. If I had come out ahead I would have won." As it was, he had to drive ahead of Edwin Roberts (Trinidad) to win the silver medal.[18]

At the Tokyo Olympics, three heats were held on October 20 for the 4 × 400-meter relay, with the first two teams in each heat, plus the two fastest losers, advancing to the next day's final. The field scratched down to 17 teams, but since none of the strong teams had scratched, the heats were not re-drawn. The event was fast. It including 12 men who had bettered 46 seconds from a standing start.

In the first heat, the USA, running Henry Carr, Ollan Cassell, Mike Larrabee and Ulis Williams, cruised to an easy 20-yard win over the Russians in 3:05.3, with Carr blasting 45.8 off the blocks and Williams of Arizona State University anchoring in the team. Before the final, the American team huddled and suggested a new running order to coach Bob Giegengack. The team recommended that Ollan Cassell of the Houston Track Club lead off, followed by Mike Larrabee of the Los Angeles Striders, Ulis Williams and Henry Carr. Giegengack said;

I told them they could run 2:58 with Carr leading off. But they answered that the important thing was to make sure of the gold medals, and that they knew Carr could bring the baton home first no matter where he got it. I had to agree with them on both counts, so we made the change.

On October 21 at three o'clock, the eight leadoff men in the four by 400-meter relay went to their marks. The staggers looked extra-long, and they were: to avoid a traffic jam after the first exchange, the second-leg men were to continue in lanes for another 100 meters, breaking for the pole after three full turns had been run. The staggers therefore, amounted to a 200-meter stagger added to a 400-meter stagger. From the inside out, the order was Germany, U.S.A., Jamaica, Trinidad, USSR, France, Poland, Great Britain.

During the first leg the race divided into two sections. Great Britain's Tim Graham ran the second curve hard to put his team slightly ahead of Cassell who ran his leg for the United States in 46.0. Trinidad and Jamaica were close at hand at the exchange, with Russia leading the second group about 8 yards back. As the runners broke from their lanes in the backstretch, Adrian Metcalfe of Britain led Mike Larrabee by two yards, with Kent Bernard of Trinidad and Jamaican Mal Spence just behind them. Metcalfe stretched Great Britain's lead to five yards at 200-meters, at which point Larrabee stepped up his pace. Larrabee took the lead halfway down the stretch and handed Ulis Williams a 5-yard lead. Bernard also passed the tiring Metcalfe, and Mal Spence drew within a yard. Larrabee ran his leg in 44.8.

In a multi-team race, the team with the lead when the baton is passed often gains an extra yard or two on the other teams. This happened as Ed Roberts, taking the handoff in second place, lost two valuable yards running around Larrabee. The 200-meter bronze medalist from Trinidad quickly recovered, and went flying after Williams. He passed Williams on the backstretch, but not enough to cut in. Williams fought him off for the next 150 yards or so, finally pulling away only in the last 70 yards. Meanwhile, Malcolm Spence drove hard on around the last curve and came speeding down the straight to pass the surprisingly fast John Cooper (GB) and draw even with Roberts at the exchange. Ulis Williams ran his leg in 45.4: Mal Spence ran it in 45.2.

After handing Carr the baton with the 5-yard lead intact, Williams fell to the track in lane one, but his fall did not impede any of the other contenders. Behind Carr, George Kerr of Jamaica took the stick even with Trinidad's Wendell Mottley; Brightwell was another yard or so behind. Kerr caught Carr in the backstretch, but only for a second. Carr said, "I figured on running the first 200 just fast enough so Mottley would have to burn himself out to catch me." Henry then moved confidently away, pouring it on in the stretch to win. His superb 44.5 anchor leg brought America home about ten yards in front of Britain's Brightwell with a pulsating final clocking of 3:00.7, a new world record.[19] Robbie Brightwell, who had discovered the folly of trying to stay with Mottley over the first 200-meters, ran his own race this time and passed Kerr down the stretch and then nail Mottley of Trinidad-Tobago, diving past him at the tape to take second for Germany by inches. Thus three teams broke the great 1960 world record of 3:02.2 set by the American team of Jack Yerman, Earl Young, Glenn Davis and Otis Davis at the Rome Olympics, and a fourth missed it by a tenth of a second. Germany had the misfortune to run legs of 45.7, 45.9, and 45.6 and lose ground—lots of it—on every one. National records were set by all finalists except Germany and France, as well as by many of the non-qualifiers in the heats.[20]

Henry Carr was named AAU All-American for 1964 for the 200-meter dash and was placed on their 1964 All-College, All-American team for the 200-meter.[21]

Carr was probably a better 400-meter than 200-meter runner. He ran the 400 meters only eight times, and was never beaten. His long stride was smooth and effortless and he usually won races by a comfortable margin. After the Tokyo Olympics, at the age of 22 he quit track before hitting his prime as a runner. He and Bob Hayes decided to play professional football, as they were poor and saw no future chance for making a living in running. Bob Hayes, the 100-meter gold medal winner in Tokyo signed with the Dallas Cowboys of the NFL, while Carr played defensive back for the New York Giants for two years. Carr was dumped by the Giants, in part, because of his outspoken concerns about racism on the club. He was inducted as a member of the USA Track and Field Hall of Fame in 1999. Carr became a devout Christian and lay religious teacher, and still lived in Detroit at the end of the twentieth century.[22]

Distance Ace

Detroiter Louis Scott, who attended Arizona State University at the urging of Henry Carr, made a major contribution to America's distance running efforts by placing second in the 5-K run at the Pan-American Games in Winnipeg, Canada on August 3, 1967. He also placed third in the 5-K run (14:53.2) at the final U.S. Olympic trials in 1968. After college and running in the 1968 Olympics, he returned to Detroit to teach in the public schools.

The Base-stealer

Herb Washington was born on November 16, 1950 in Belzonia, Mississippi. His parents moved to Flint, Michigan when he was a young boy. Herb found his talent for running almost by accident. As an African-

American youngster, he and other kids ran races from corner to corner on their block and Herb seemed always to win. Even as a high school senior, Herb recognized the part track played in his life. "Track is something I look forward to every day, day after day. It has opened many new fields to me and has given me many new experiences that I otherwise would never have had." Herb was an outstanding high school football player. In 1968 he stood six-one in height and weighted 168 pounds.[23]

On March 1, 1968 while still in high school he won the 50-yard dash (5.3) at the Cleveland Knights of Columbus Indoor Meet and a week later was second in the 50-yard dash (5.1) at the United States Track Indoor Finals in Milwaukee. On March 23 Herb Washington tied the World, American, and scholastic records in the 50-yard dash (5.1) at the Highland Games, Hamilton Ontario, defeating Trinidad Olympian Ed Roberts in the process.[24] He capped his senior year in high school on May 25 by tying the State Class A record in the 100-yard dash (9.8) at the Michigan State Athletic Association High School Championships in East Lansing. On May 21, 1968 Herb signed a tender for an athletic scholarship with Michigan State.[25]

Herb Washington attributed his success at Flint Central High School to his coach, Carl Krieger. According to Herb, "He spent many hours working with me, teaching me the best techniques to achieve the best results." Krieger was also quick to praise Herb. "He's one of the finest young men I've ever met."[26]

That August the Soviet tanks invaded Czechoslovakia and brutally ended the promising economic reforms and increased freedom of the press that had flowered under the leadership of Alexander Dubcek.

In January 1968 new NCAA rules were approved to allowed freshmen to compete on varsity teams for the first time since the Korean War. Conferences were given the choice of whether or not to allow freshmen to compete.[27] Consequently, on January 25, 1969 Herb Washington was permitted to compete on the varsity track team at Michigan State as a college freshman. In January Herb won the 60-yard dash (6.2) at the Michigan Relays held in Yost Field House. Herb placed third in the NCAA indoors and was named to the 1969 NCAA Indoor All-America team for the 60-yard dash.[28] On April 19 he won the 100-yard dash (9.7) at the Ohio Relays.

Herb Washington starred in football as well as track at Michigan State. As a wide receiver, he was good enough to be drafted by the Baltimore Colts of the NFL and the Toronto Argonauts of the Canadian Football League.

In 1970 Herb won the 60-yard dash (6.0) at the Michigan Relays, the Western Michigan Relays, and the Michigan State Relays. He also won the 60-yard dash in a duel meets with the University of Illinois and the University of Michigan. On March 7 he won the 60-yard dash (6.0) at the 60th Big Ten Indoor Championships in East Lansing. On March 14 Herb set the meet record and tied the American record for the 60-yard dash (5.9) at the NCAA Indoor finals in Detroit. On March 21 he tied the world record in the 50-yard dash (5.1) at the Highlander Games, Hamilton, Ontario. Herb Washington was named to the NCAA indoor All-America track team for the 60-yard dash in 1970.[29] Washington finished the conference outdoor season by winning the 100-yard dash (9.5), placing third in the 440-yard relay, and placing fourth in the 220-yard dash at the 70th Big Ten Championships in Bloomington. On June 5–6 he won the 100-yard dash (9.4) and placed second in the 440-yard relay at the 45th Central Collegiate Conference Championships.[30]

In 1971 Herb continued to win the 60-yard dash at the Western Michigan Relays, the Michigan State Relays, and at the Big Ten Indoor Championships. On March 11–12 he placed second in the 60-yard dash at the NCAA Indoor finals in Detroit. He went on to the Drake Relays, where he placed third in the 100-yard dash, and second in the 440 and 880-yard relays. On May 28–29 he won the 100-yard dash (9.4) at the Big Ten Championships in Iowa City. Herb was again named to the 1971 NCAA Indoor All-America track team for the 60-yard dash.[31]

In his senior year at Michigan State, Herb won the 60-yard dash (6.1) at the NCAA Indoor finals, and on April 28, 1972 won the finals of the 100-yard dash (9.6), and placed fifth in the 100-meter (10.7) invitational at the Drake Relays. On May 27 Herb tied the Big Ten outdoor record for the 100-yard dash (9.4) set by Jesse Owens in 1935. That same day, at the Big Ten Championships in Champaign, Herb also set the Michigan State varsity 440-yard relay record (40.2).[32] On June 8–9 Herb ran in the NCAA Championships in Eugene. On June 30 Herb qualified for the semifinals of the 100-meter dash (10.0) at the U.S. Olympic trials, but did not make the American Olympic team. Still, as a sprinter, Herb was talented enough over the course of his track competition to beat Olympic medallists such as John Carlos and Valery Borzov. Herb was named to the NCAA Indoor All-American team for 1972 for the fourth straight year.[33]

In January 1973 Herb needed six hours of academic credit to graduate from MSU. The athletic Department allowed him to stay on, although his eligibility was over. He trained with the team, and ran in indoor meets around the country.[34] On January 26, 1973 Herbert Washington was second in voting for outstanding performer at the Millrose Games.[35] Herb also ran at the AAU Senior indoor championships in Madison Square Garden. The preliminaries for the 60-yard dash began at after lunch (at 1:25 p.m.) on Friday, February 23, 1973, and the semi-finals were run at 4:45 in the afternoon. The finals were scheduled for 8:25 in the evening.[36] Herb had two strong competitors at the AAU meet. Hasely Crawford was a sophomore at Eastern Michigan University. The 22-year-old Trinidad Olympian, had been a finalist in the 100-meter dash at the Munich, and was voted Trinidad's outstanding athlete. Valery Borzov of the Soviet Union, the Olympic 100-meter and 200-meter champion, was also in the race.

In the finals, Herb Washington, who considered himself the world's fastest human indoors, was guilty of a false start. "The false start killed me; it broke my concentration. I felt I never got control of the race," said Washington. The 6-foot 1¾-inch Crawford recounted, "Herb had me by about half a step at 20 yards. I caught him at 40 and put everything I had into the last 20." Borzov finished in third place, a foot behind Washington.[37]

After graduating from Michigan State, Washington worked part-time as a reporter with a television station in East Lansing. He also continued to compete in national and international track meets, and continued to weigh offers to play pro football, when Charley Finley called. Herb thought the call was a prank, and responded, "How are you Mr. Finley? This is Herb Washington, the world's fastest human." Finley said, "That's precisely why I'm calling you, Herb. How would you like to play some baseball?" Herb: "Mr. Finley, I'm not sure I'm following you. Sir, I haven't picked up a bat since high school." Finley: "Herb, it's not your bat I'm interested in, it's your legs. I want you to become a full-time pinch runner for us. Over the course of the season, I figure you could win a handful of games for us with your base-running."[38]

In February 1974 Herb Washington signed a $50,000 no-cut contract in Chicago with the Oakland A's. Charles Finley hired Herb to steal bases and games. Thus, Herb became the first designated base stealer in professional baseball. A week later reported to spring training and began learning the art of base stealing from Maury Wills. Herb Washington played a lot of sandlot baseball while he was growing up in Flint and was good at the sport. But he never dreamed that one day he would play in the major leagues. Herb recalled, "Track and baseball seasons overlapped, and I had to make a decision between the two. It really wasn't a difficult one. If you run a 50-yard dash that's just a tenth of a second off the world record when you are a high school sophomore, you kind of know what direction you want to go."[39]

Baseball purists thought the designated runner experiment was just another eccentric stunt. Herb also discovered very quickly that speed is only part of the base running equation. Deciphering a pitcher's pick-off move and gauging a catcher's arm were every bit as important as running speed. In 1974 Herb Washington scored the winning or tying run in ten of Oakland's 91 victories, and helped them reach the World Series. After winning a World Series ring, Herb was released midway through the 1975 season, to make room for an extra pitcher.

"Washington's career line for one and one-half seasons in Oakland reads: 104 games, 33 scored runs, 30 stolen bases, and zero at bats." Washington used the money he earned from baseball to purchase a McDonald's fast-food franchise in Rochester, New York. The fast-food entrepreneur now owns five restaurants in Rochester, and in 1993 was appointed by President Clinton to the Federal Reserve Board. He has also received honors for his extensive community service work.[40]

High School Athlete of the Year

Marshall Dill was born in Monroe, Louisiana on August 9, 1952. He attended junior high school in Texas, and high school at Northern High in Detroit. Dill ran the 100-yard dash in 9.9 at the age of 14. He was also a good student, and a member of the National Honor Society. Dill was named "High School Athlete of the Year" by *Track and Field News* in 1970. On May 23, 1970 Marshall Dill won the 100-yard dash (10.0) and the 220-yard dash (21.9) at the Class A Michigan High School Championships. The following year he repeated his double victory by winning the 100-yard dash (9.6) and the 220-yard dash (20.6) at the Class A Michigan High School Championships. Shortly after high school graduation, on June 20, 1971 Marshall Dill won the 100-yard dash (9.6) and the 220-yard dash (21.0) at the Golden West Invitational in Sacramento, California and was named the meet's outstanding athlete.[41]

At 6–2½ in height with a solid frame, Dill had been All-City and All-State as a halfback at Detroit Northern High School. When Marshall Dill enrolled at Michigan State, it was anticipated that he would play football, as well as run track. But, in the fall of 1971 Dill passed on freshman football to concentrate entirely on running in hopes of making the 1972 Olympic team. He was afraid that a football injury might ruin his chances of going to Munich.[42] Consequently, Marshall Dill's football career never worked out, but four years later his mind was still on football. "I think of football all the time. That's where money is for a trackman. If I am drafted by a pro team I won't even consider it . . . I'll just go and sign up."[43]

After a great indoor season in 1972, Dill slumped in the outdoor season. He experienced a tonsillectomy and some leg trouble. Nevertheless, he did win the Big Ten Outdoor 220.[44] On July 7 Marshall placed third in heat 2 to qualify for the finals of the 200-meter dash (21.3) at the U.S. Olympic trials. On July 8 he placed fourth in the finals of the 200-meter dash (20.6) at the U.S. Olympic trials. Dill missed the Olympic team by a fiftieth of a second.[45] While Dill did not make the Olympic team, on July 29 he won the 100-meter dash (10.2) and the 400-meter relay (39.6) at the USA vs. USSR Junior Meet in Sacramento. The meet was limited to athletes 19 years of age and under.[46] Dill was named to the 1972 NCAA Indoor All-American team.[47]

On May 25–26, 1973 Marshall Dill tied the meet record for the 100-yard dash (9.4), equaling the times run by Jesse Owen and Herb Washington, at the Big Ten Championships.[48] He also set the field record and tied the meet record for the 220-yard dash (20.7) at the 48th Central Collegiate Conference Championships. Dill was again named 1973, Track Indoor All-American in the 60-yard dash (p.60); and was named to the 1973 NCAA Outdoor All-America track team in the 220-yard dash.[49]

In the fall of 1973 Marshall Dill considered transferring to either the University of Southern California or the University of Tennessee. He felt that "everything [at MSU] is work, work, work and I don't like to do anything which constitutes no enjoyment for me." He felt that maybe the West Coast would offer more exposure and possibly would enhance his already illustrious track career. But, he decided against a move because he did not want to sit out of competition for a year.[50]

On May 17–18, 1974 Dill cruised to wins the 220-yard dash (20.9)[wind-aided] and 100-yard dash (9.5). He also placed second in the 440-yard relay (41.3) at the Big Ten Championships in Ann Arbor. "This was the easiest Big Ten meet I've ever been in, maybe the easiest meet of any kind," said Dill, who was unchallenged after Purdue's Larry Burton withdrew with a leg injury.[51] However, on May 25, 1974 at the Central Collegiate meet in Bowling Green, Ohio, he wasn't so lucky. On Friday May 24 in the 220-yard dash, Marshall strained a muscle in his left leg. The next day, he pulled up in the 100-yard dash and did not complete the race. "I hurt my leg yesterday in the 220 tri-als. It doesn't hurt that badly, but I didn't want to push myself because I want to be in good shape for the nationals" [which were just two weeks away].[52]

In 1974 Marshall Dill failed to qualify for the Munich Olympics, in large measure because of the injury. The next winter, when he was a senior, he was academically ineligible for the indoor track season.

> I knew my responsibility academically and I knew I didn't fulfill my respon-sibility and that was the penalty. It was just something I had to take care of myself. I was negligent. I knew last term that I had to hit the books or the same thing would happen this term. Still, I think I've been pretty successful. I've had fun and I guess that's the basic thing . . . to have fun. You know, anytime you win eight Big Ten championships, you've got to have had some fun along the way.
>
> I think being out of competition last term helped me in a way. I've been run-ning competitively almost 16 years now, all year long. I think maybe the layoff helped because I think I'm further along this spring than I normally am at this point. The thing I've really tried to do here . . . is find out what life is all about. Thanks to track, I've been all over the world and I've just tried to figure out where I fit in the scheme of things.[53]

While at Michigan State, Marshall Dill won 109 individual Big Ten track events and was the Conference's 220-yard outdoor championship four straight years. He won the 100-yard outdoor title his junior and senior years.[54] Dill also won the 100-yard dash at the Drake Relays three straight years: in 1973 (9.6), 1974 (9.3), and 1975 (9.6). He mar-ried (Carol) by 1976 and was inducted into the Drake Relays Hall of Fame in 1990.[55]

Fast, fearless and self-assured

Reggie Jones won the Michigan Class A High School 100 and 220-yard dashes as a junior at Saginaw High School. According to his coach, Claude Marsh, there was "none better" in high school track in Michi-gan.[56] As a senior, a sore hamstring bothered him much of the track sea-son. Nevertheless, Reggie won the 100 and the 220-yard dashes at the Saginaw Valley League Championships.[57] He also won the sprint med-ley relay, the 440-yard relay, and the 880-yard relay at the George Graves Relays at Midland on May 9, and was named the meet's most outstanding athlete award.[58] He then went on to win the Regional and State Class A Championships in those events.[59] At the Regional Cham-pionships, "there was a fellow here [at the meet] from [the University of] Tennessee so Reggie put on a little show for him," according to Coach Marsh.[60]

Reggie chose to attend the University of Tennessee during the years 1974–6. He made an immediate impact. At the Penn Relays on April 26–27, 1974 he was part of the winning 440-yard relay team (40.0). The following month Reggie won the 220-yard dash (20.8) and the 440-yard relay (40.3) at the Southeast Conference Outdoor Championships. On June 7–8 he won the 100-yard dash (9.18 w) and 220-yard dash (20.0) at the 53rd NCAA Championships in Austin. The events are described: "Moments later Tennessee asserted itself in spectacular fashion. Reggie Jones, a 20-year-old freshman from Saginaw, Michigan, beat San Diego States' Steve Williams who had been vying all spring for the title of the "world's fastest human." "I just wanted to show everyone Reggie can run too," said Jones. Reggie was voted the meet's outstanding performer.[61]

During the 1975 season, Reggie Jones got off to a rocky start. He placed third in the 60-yard dash at the 19th Southeastern Conference Indoor Championships, and on March 14–15 he placed fourth in the 60-yard dash at the NCAA Indoor Championships in Detroit. However, during the outdoor season he rebounded. At the Penn Relays, Jones tied for first in the 100-yard dash (9.4) and placed second in the 440-yard relay. In May he won the 220-yard dash (20.7) and the 440-yard relay (40.0) at the Southeast Conference Championships. Finally, on June 6–7 at the NCAA Championships in Provo, Utah he won the 220-yard dash (20.60) and placed third in the 100-yard (9.44) dash, to win All-American honors for his second straight year.[62]

On February 7, 1976 Reggie placed third in the 70-yard-dash (6.9) at the Mason-Dixon Games in Louisville. This did not bode well for his third appearance at the NCAA indoor championships. On March 13 Jones lamented, "I came out [of the blocks] crooked, and just couldn't catch 'em."[63] He placed third in the 60-yard dash at the 12th Annual NCAA Indoor Championships. However, he again performed better outdoors. Reggie won the 100-meter dash (10.2), the 400-meter relay (39.4), and the 800-meter relay (1:21.5) at the Penn Relays. The 800-meter performance was good enough to set the meet and the world record. On June 5 Jones anchored the winning the 400-meter relay and was second in the 100-meter dash (10.33) at the NCAA Championships in Philadelphia.[64]

On June 21, 1976 Reggie qualified for the semifinals in the 200-meter dash (20.86) at the U.S. Olympic trials, but did not demonstrate that he was one of the ten fastest sprinters in America that summer. He did not make the trip to Montreal in 1976 as part of the USA Olympic team. The unheralded performance of Dwayne Evans, a speedy 17-year old high school student from Phoenix was one reason Reggie missed the team. Evans won a bronze medal in the 200-meter run (20.43).[65] During his tenure at Tennessee, Reggie Jones earned All-American honors nine times. Twice indoors in the 60-yard dash (1975–6), and seven times outdoors (100-yard dash (1974, 75); 100-meter dash (1976); 220-yard dash (1974, 75): 440-yard relay (1974); 400-meter relay (1976).[66]

Wayne State University's Last Track and Field All-American

Eliot "Sweet ET" Tabron was born in Detroit. His father, Cleveland Tabron, was a mechanic. His mother, Elnora, was a social worker. His father played baseball as a young man, and his brother, Avery Tabron, ran track at Western Michigan University. Eliot attended Murray-Wright High School. He was nicknamed "E. T." for the Extra-Talented."[67]

E. T. did not run in high school track until his senior year, and then only ran in three track meets. He won the West Side Public League Championship in the 100-yard dash and placed second in the City Meet. However, Eliot did not get his entry into the Regionals in time, and did not make the state meet.[68] As a result, Wayne State and Eastern Michigan were the only schools to recruit him. Tabron selected Wayne State because they were the first to offer him a scholarship.[69] "Coach [Don] Sims kept calling me and saying, 'You're not going to let me down, now, are you?' I don't think I have." Tabron was put up at the Cass-Forest Apartments, but was not given get a full-ride until his sophomore year.

Eliot never ran the quarter mile in high school. Like anyone who runs, Tabron dreamed of being the fastest man on the track. He brought his time down from 9.8 seconds to 9.2 in the 100-yard dash, but he was relatively slow off the starting blocks. When it was clear that he could not make the NCAA Division I indoor championships in the 60-yard dash, Eliot turned to the quarter-mile. Sprinters often have to be dragged kicking and screaming into the quarter. "That was my feeling," Tabron said. "I did 47 seconds outdoors last year, and I've run a few in relays, but at first I refused. It hurts."[70] "I was afraid to [run the 440] because there's a lot of agony that 440 men go through. Your head hurts and you wheeze a lot. But my recovery period is starting to decrease."[71]

"My form has improved tremendously because of superior coaching at Wayne. It's still not up to par yet—I'm running off raw speed."[72] Tabron had another advantage beyond raw talent. "Tabron's the kind of guy who drives for the finish line in a close race," Coach Sims remarked. "He has that killer instinct."[73]

"It's hard to be good at Wayne State because of our poor facilities," he remarked. "But we have good coaching and make do with what we have. We're going to be a quality team, and I'm going to be part of it." Coach Sims says he doesn't know where his program would be without Tabron. "He's one of the few people I've recruited that has been able to handle Wayne's academic programs. I'm looking for quality people to build a program around and Eliot's the base right now . . . he's lean and mean, top-notch running machine."[74]

Eliot majored in accounting. He played in the high school band and was in the national honor society. He had a summer job with General Motors while at Wayne State University.[75] Traveling kept ET's interest in track. "I came to find that there was a lot of traveling involved. So that's what really kept me in track. I knew that the experience I'd get from traveling would help me."[76]

Tabron transferred to MSU in 1981 when the track program at Wayne State suffered major cutbacks, changing from a permanent program to a temporary sport. Tabron brought impressive credentials with him from Wayne State. He was twice All-American in the 100-meter and once in the 200-meter dash.[77] He placed second in the 100-meter dash at the NCAA-IAA Championships.

During the 1982 indoor season, Tabron was ineligible to compete and did not train consistently. "When I'm in condition I'm ready to tackle anyone in the Big Ten," Eliot quipped, but he was not yet at his peak. One of the keys to his success would be his ability to remain healthy. "After I run a series of events, my muscles contract. Right after the meet I have the trainer, stretch my muscles to insure against injury or tightness of the muscles."[78] At the Big Ten Championships on May 21–22 Eliot Tabron set the meet and conference record in the 400-meter run (45.32). The Michigan State 400-meter relay team, which was anchored by Tabron, came close to being crowned Big Ten Champions. The U of M team edged-out State by 9/100 of a second. This is the first time State ever placed second in the 400-meter relay at the Big Ten Championships. Mistakes in handoffs prevented State from winning.[79]

In the summer of 1982 Eliot toured with the U.S. national AAU team in Europe and the Far East. On July 9 he helped the 4 × 400 relay (3:01.09) win in a duel meet with at the Democratic Republic of Germany in Karl Marx Stadt in East Berlin. On August 5 he won the 400-meter run (46.10) at the Copenhagen Games in Denmark.

At the Central Collegiate Indoor Championships in Kalamazoo, on February 18–19, 1983, Eliot Tabron won the 400-yard dash (47.05) and the 1,600-meter relay (3:10.02). He ran his 400-meter leg in the relay in 47.1.[80] At the Drake Relays Tabron placed third in both the 1600-meter relay (3:03.68) and the University 800-meter relay (1:22.53). On May 28, 1983 E. T. won 400-meter run (45.17), the 400-meter relay (46.3), and the 1,600-meter relay at the 58th outdoor Central Collegiate Championships in Toledo. Tabron recounted his thoughts about the race:

It feels like everything is finally coming back together. I broke the track and meet records in the preliminaries on Friday with my 46.09. But I felt something was missing and I was doing something wrong. I couldn't understand why I wasn't running as well as I did last year. This confused me and baffled me. So I thought about it at night and got a good night's sleep. Finally, I told myself that relaxation is the key. I just kept telling myself to stay relaxed. When I ran, I ran fast but relaxed for the entire race. I found this enabled me to come in stronger at the finish.[81]

Eliot was named the outstanding performer at the 1983 Central Collegiate Meet.[82]

On June 5, 1983 Eliot Tabron placed third in 1,600-meter relay (3:02.51) and tenth in the 400-meter dash (46.41) at the NCAA Championships in Houston. He was also on the winning 1,600-meter relay team (3:01.24) and placed fourth in the 400-meter dash (45.82) at the XII World University Games in Edmonton, Alberta on July 10. He represented the USA at the DN Galan meet in Sweden on July 25. On August 6–14 Tabron ran in the First World Championships in Helsinki, Finland; and on August 14–29 he represented the USA in the 400-meter dash at the Pan American Games in Caracas.[83]

Eliot Tabron graduated from Michigan State in 1984, and was a member of the Bud Light Team that won the open mile relay (3:11.82) at the U.S. Olympic indoor Invitational at East Rutherford, New Jersey on February 11. On June 17 he was seventh in the sixth heat of the first round of the 400-meter dash (46.21) at the Olympic trials, Los Angeles, and thus did not qualify for the Olympic team.[84]

Quincy Dushawn Watts

Quincy Watts was born on June 19, 1970 to Rufus Watts, a post office employee, and Allitah Hunt. Quincy lived with his mother in Detroit until he was thirteen. At that time, his mother sent him to Los Angeles to live with his father, because she was concerned that he was getting involved with the wrong crowd in Detroit. The elder Watts recognized his son's potential as a runner and introduced him to John Smith, the sprint coach at UCLA. Smith was one of the fastest 400-meter runners in the world in the 1970s, and agreed to Coach Watts, an excellent basketball and football player as well as a good runner.

Quincy attended Taft High School in Woodland Hills, California. In 1986 and 87, Quincy won the 200-meter dash at the California State High School championships on consecutive years. In 1987 Watts also won the 100-meter dash in the State High School championships. That year, as a high school senior, Watts ran his first 440 yard dash. When Watts graduated from high school in 1987, he attended the University of Southern California, where he majored in communications.[85]

On June 6, 1992 Quincy, running for the University of Southern California, won the 400-meter run (44.00) at the NCAA finals in Austin. Quincy ran the fastest 400-meter time in the world in winning the national collegiate championship. It was the sixth fastest 400-meter run of all time.[86] Watts graduated from the USC with a bachelor's degree in communications in 1992.

At the U.S. Olympic trials in New Orleans on June 23–24, 1992 Watts won the third heat of the preliminary round of the 400-meter dash (45.47) and the first heat of the semifinal round of the 400-meter dash (43.97). He qualified third for the Olympic team at 400-meters. In late July Watts won the 400-meter run (43.50) at the Olympic Games in Barcelona, setting a new Olympic record in the process. On August 8 he was a member of the winning 1,600-meter relay team that set a world record (2:55.74) in that event, winning by 30-meters. Watts ran the fastest 400-meter leg in relay history (43.1) of that event.

Watts was the fifth African-American since 1956 to win the Olympic 400-meter championship. While Watts was all but forgotten in the U. S. after the 1992 Olympics, it was different in Europe. Nike chose him to star in a television commercial that was shown in several countries, in which a Viking king offers to trade his "super-cushioned wife" for Watts' "super-cushioned Air MAX shoes." Watts takes one look at the massive Viking woman and sprints away at full speed while the super-cushioned wife bellows "Quin-cy!" "Quin-cy!" became a very popular advertising slogans.[87]

At the U. S. Championships on June 19, 1993, Quincy was barely able to claim third place in a 400-meter group that included Butch

Reynolds, Michael Johnson, Andrew Valmon, and Darnell Hall. Michael Johnson set a new meet record with a 43.74 dash, Butch Reynolds was clocked at 44.12, and Quincy Watts ran a 44.24.[88]

Changes in Training

For most of the twentieth century, great runners achieved nearly the same level of performance. Modest improvements in running surfaces, shoes, technique, and training regiments account for nearly all of the variations in running speed until the introduction of performance enhancing drugs. Drugs that build muscle mass and quickness during training, rather than simply giving better outcomes on the day of performance, have threatened to transform individual sports of all kinds into human pharmaceutical experiments. As Amby Burfoot pointed out,[89] "genetic differences, which are likely to be linked to family or even tribal inheritance—but not to race—are important determinants of athletic success, but they do not account for the equally important attributes of drive, determination, persistence, and consistency of work ethic." Indeed, individual sports accomplishments are usually more about mastery over one's self than mastery of opponents.

Some events remained "white" events for years. For example, when Fred Hansen set a new world record in pole vault at the San Diego Pre-Olympic Meet on June 13, 1964 there were no African-American pole vaulters in world-class competition.[90] However, at the USA Indoor Championships held in Atlanta on March 4, 2000, Lawrence Johnson, an African-American who graduated from the University of Tennessee, won the pole-vault with a jump of 19 feet ¼ inches.[91]

18. The Things That Divide Us: The Continuing Struggle Against Unequal Treatment, 1967–1976

The barriers that divided black and white society in America were slow to disappear. In 1950 the enrollment of the Detroit Public Schools was largely segregated and rapidly becoming predominately an African-America. Twenty-five years later it was overwhelmingly African-American and still segregated despite a decade of efforts to promote integration.[1] Nor did racial attitudes change quickly. On May 2, 1957 the Louisiana Boxing Commission ruled that Ralph Dupas must furnish a copy of his birth certificate before he could box again in the state. While the 21-year old Dupas was educated in the white public schools, the fourth ranked lightweight boxer was accused of being a Negro.[2] In the same vain, Detroit was particularly slow to open opportunities for black professional athletes in team sports. In 1957 the *Kalamazoo Gazette* reported:

> The fact that the Detroit Tigers have never had a Negro player on the major league roster often has been touchy, but never a controversial subject . . . Thirteen major league clubs have had Negro players on the roster. Only Detroit and Boston in the American League and Philadelphia in the senior circuit have not.[3]

Nor was Detroit alone in its recalcitrant defiance of efforts to institute equal opportunities regardless of race, age or ethnic origin. In June 1964 Ole Miss [the University of Mississippi], founded in 1844, competed against Negro athletes for the first time in the school's history.[4]

In 1966 African-American men were being killed in Vietnam at rates that exceeded the average for all service men. While Negroes made up about 11% of the total fighting force in South Vietnam and 10% of all Americans, they accounted for 17.6% of all combat deaths. This means that African-Americans were being killed at a rate about 60% higher than their portion of servicemen in Southeast Asia,[5] suggesting that African-Americans were being disproportionately assigned to the most dangerous situations.

The racial outburst in Detroit in late June 1943 was finally surpassed with an outburst of civil disorder of July 1967 that shook the nation. The rebellion or riot, depending upon one's point of view, went on for days, and large sections of the city were looted or set on fire.

Many African-American athletes felt that instead of breaking down barriers, sports had set up false goals, perpetuated prejudices, and fostered inequalities. Most black athletes were "dissatisfied, disgruntled, and disillusioned." They complained that they were rarely roomed with white athletes, assigned to first-class seats, or permitted the same expectations as white athletes. Coaches invariably stereotyped them and treated them like subhuman. "We want a new attitude and a new set of accommodations that does not reflect the dreary intolerance we see in other aspects of American life," complained track athletes like Harry Edwards.[6]

The idea that institutions of higher learning were more tolerant of diversity than the community at-large did not reflect the experience of most black athletes on American campuses during the 1960s. Coaches and athletic directors generally held black athletes in rigid social check. While other students were accountable to their parents, the dean of students, their class advisor, and the dorm counselor, coach and athletic director held inordinate power over African-American athletes. These white men could pull an athletic scholarship for any whim, depriving the kid from a poor family any opportunity for an escape from the ghetto. Many coaches used this power not just paternalistically, but as a weapon. Their attitude was: "I got you here and it's my scholarship that is paying for your education."[7]

Harry Edwards, an East St. Louis discus thrower who set records while at San Jose State College in California, complained, "Black athletes aren't given athletic scholarships for the purpose of an education. Blacks are brought in to perform. Any education they get is incidental to their main job, which is playing sports."[8]

In truth, in the 1960s many Negro athletes were not prepared to attend college in the first place. Often they arrived at a university without ever having read a book from cover to cover. The problem started with the enormous gulf between the quality of the elementary schools attended by white children and those attended by African-American children. Moreover, instead of a support system that focused on learning, most black children were busy facing or reacting to the problems that confront the poor and deprived.

When the black athlete went to a white college, he entered a schizophrenic world where he was lionized on the field and ignored off it. One athlete complained that "All I got was four years of loneliness and alienation in the white man's world. I was expected to keep my mouth shut and perform valiantly in front of cheering white audiences."[9]

The biggest problem for the average African-American, college athlete in the 1960s was the English language. It was spoken one way in the white culture and another in the black. On campus the black athlete often wallowed in fear and confusion for a few weeks until a jock-strap alumni and campus counselors show them the shortcuts. These short cuts seldom lead to a degree. Most black athletes of the era athletes, including Wilt Chamberlain, Wayne Hightower, Gale Sayers, Walt Wesley, Bob Hayes and Henry Carr, did not graduate from college.

In spite of the Dr. Martin Luther King's willingness to face the ultimate sacrifice to promote economic and social equality in Memphis, the abysmal performance of the athletic department at Memphis State University between 1973 and 1986 testified to the lack of progress. During that 13-year period, only four of 38 basketball players graduated from the University and none of them was black.[10]

Coaches rarely made good guidance counselors, and were seldom empathetic to the problems faced by their Negro athletes. They were strong on "stay away from white women," but did not consider how isolated the black athlete was on a white college campus. The coach's racial attitudes were often strong and thinly disguised. For example, when white athletes messed up, a coach might call them a "jerk" or an "idiot", but when a black athlete messed up he would call them an "animal." Athletic directors were no better. For example, when the athletic director at the University of Texas at El Paso was asked about the status of his Black athletes he responded, "In general, the nigger athlete is a little hungrier, and we have been blessed with having some real outstanding ones. We think they've done a lot for us, and we think we've done a lot for them."[11]

It was true that a few African-American athletes gained opportunities not otherwise available to them. Harry Edwards, an outspoken advocate of a black athletic rebellion against the 1968 Olympics, was lifted out of the ghetto by the white sports establishment. Edwards was in several jails before San Jose State offered him an athletic scholarship when it was discovered that he could throw the discus farther than most of his contemporaries. *Sports Illustrated* pointed out that:

If it were not for sports Harry Edwards would be alongside his brother Donald, serving 25 years to life in the Iowa State Penitentiary for armed robbery, or following in the footsteps of his father, an alumnus of Pontiac State Penitentiary, or his mother, who once came home from a street brawl wearing 86 stitches.

Harry Edwards responded, "Any education black students get is incidental to the main job, which is playing sports. In most cases their college lives are educational blanks." Like it or not, Harry Edwards was right.

Aside from dealing with personal racial animosity, the most common complaints by African-American athletes were that they were expected to be significantly better than their white counterparts to be recruited. Moreover, at that time black athletes were not considered for careers as coaches, reporters, or sport casters once they had completed their athletic careers.[12] Black athletes felt that they were being dehumanized, exploited and discarded, and they were finally realizing that they must have some kind of life after they stopped competing in athletics.

Tom Randolph Leads a Protest at Western Michigan University

At the Western Michigan Relays, February 3, 1967 Coach Dale said of Tom Randolph, "He's good and he'll get even better," as Randolph flashed past a University of Michigan runner in his final stride in the mile relay to win the event for WMU.[13]

The following year Tom was point man on effort by black athletes at WMU to get improved conditions.[14] On May 15 the 30 African-American athletes at Western Michigan University, which had 13,000 students at the time, presented a request to University President Dr. James W. Miller and Athletic Director Joseph T. Hoy for "more equitable treatment." Sprinter, Tom Randolph, who was the spokesman for the group said, "this is not to be considered as any form of threat. We have no plans for any boycotts by black athletes."

The letter asked for realistic, constructive changes, such as more blacks in coaching positions, and more scholarships for blacks, better counseling, and better utilization of African-American personnel. On the same day four Negroes, three of them on the track team who won the 440-yard relay at the Kansas and Drake Relays, were suspended for the balance of the season "because of unfavorable attitudes and behaviors" for airing complaints.[15]

Later that year, Randolph was named to the NCAA All-America indoor track team for the 440-yard run and for the 1968 NCAA outdoor, University Division All-America team for the 440-yard relay.[16] Tom placed fifth in the 200-meter dash (20.1) and eighth in the 100-

meter dash (10.3) at the final Olympic trials at South Lake Tahoe, California on September 6–16, 1968. His time for the 200-meter run was the same as the third place finisher. He missed going to the Olympics by seven hundredths of a second.[17] In 1969 Tom Randolph was named to the NCAA Indoor All-America team for the 400-yard dash.[18]

We're Not Watermelon Eating Idiots

Despite the lowest unemployment rate in 15-years, the jobless rate for African-American workers in 1968 was double that for the rest of the workforce.[19] Reports of this kind lent tangible credence to the feelings borne of generations of experience that African- Americans were getting short changed and that something needed to be done about it now. Negro athletes at American universities presented demands ranging from appointment of African-American coaches to selection of a Negro girl cheerleader, and threatened boycotts. In only one case, however, were athletes at a major school staying away from drills. This was at the University of California at Berkeley, where 14 black football players boycotted spring practice. At the University of Kansas fifteen African-American football players boycotted spring training for two days on the grounds there were no Negro girls on the eight member 'pom pom' team, no Negro coach, no Negro history course and few Negro faculty members. The University of Kansas agreed to put an African-America girl on the "pom pom" team, to offer an African-American history class and to look for a good African-American professor. The Athletic Department at Kansas agreed to discuss hiring a African-American coach later. At the University of Oklahoma, black athletes were dropped from teams after an exchange of recriminations, but were later reinstated. Both white and Negro members of the team had presented grievances, but both sides apologized.

However, eleven African-American members of the track and field team at the University of Texas, El Paso were dropped after eight of them refused to participate in a meet at Brigham Young University, because of the attitude on the BYU campus, a Mormon Institution, that Negroes are an inferior people. When recriminations started, three additional black athletes at Texas El Paso stood by their teammates when they were faced with loss of their scholarships. All eleven trackmen were dismissed.

Six members of the Marquette University basketball team threatened to withdraw from school in a dispute over hiring of a Negro administrator. They were backed by three priests and stayed in school.

At Michigan State University 38 African-American athletes stood up for hiring Negro coaches and higher academic standards for black athletes. Michigan State hired an assistant football coach and agreed to hire a track coach [Jim Bibbs].[20] The action on academic standards was not so clear cut.

Anticipating problems, the University of Michigan hired Ken Burnley on June 18, 1968. Burnley was made assistant track coach for sprinters and hurdlers, and was the first African-American coach in school history. Burnley held degrees in physical education and special education and had been teaching at Ypsilanti East Junior High. He was still competing for the Ann Arbor Track Club.[21] On the same day Western Michigan University hired the first two fulltime Negro coaches in that school's history. One of the new hires was Fletcher Lewis, age 32, an assistant track coach, the other was an assistant football coach.[22]

Links to the Civil Rights Movement

The outspoken complaints by African-American athletes in 1967–8 had their root cause in the same dissatisfaction with apartheid that produced the sit-ins, freedom rides, and the riots in Watts, Detroit, Chicago and Newark. Black athletes were tired of being treated like a commodity, while being systematically excluded from normal campus life.

The hundredth anniversary celebration of the founding of the New York Athletic Club became the warm-up target of those who sought to make a major statement regarding civil rights by boycotting the Olympics, which were being held in the western hemisphere for the first time since 1932. The New York Athletic Club indoor track meet on February 15, 1968 was a high profile event and relatively easy to boycott. The meet was televised throughout the USA and clearly a showcase for Olympic hopefuls.

Boycott of the New York Athletic Club's indoor meet involved many individual African-American athletes and predominantly Negro schools such as Morgan State and Maryland State, but the boycott was not limited to black athletes. Villanova, the East's top track power, voted unanimously not to participate. The three service academies refused to participate by orders from the Department of Defense, and the Catholic High Schools Athletic Association coaches of New York's Public Schools Athletic League voted not to take part. In the meantime, the New York Athletic Club refused to comment on the charges of discrimination against Negroes and Jews.[23] Their position was that they were a private club with a limited membership roster and could not accommodate the needs of everyone.[24]

The boycott resulted in a significant decline in attendance and participation and gave notice that conditions had to change if African-American athletes were going to continue to participate in college and amateur sports. The New York Athletic Club had denied African-Americans membership, yet profited from their participation in their annual meet.[25] On the other hand, major indoor track meets were a marginal economic enterprise and the boycott ended the sponsorship of one of the premier indoor meets in the United States. Before the end of the century the New York Athletic Club sponsored a number of black athletes, including Olympic gold medalist, Antonio McKay.[26]

The University of Texas at El Paso track team went to the annual New York Athletic Club track meet despite a boycott. The UTEP track team which had several New York athletes supported the trip to New York in order to, "to visit our people with all expenses paid." The black athletes of UTEP crossed the Madison Square Garden picket line and performed despite intense pressure from Negro militants. But, the experience got these athletes thinking. The assassination of Martin Luther King ended their vacillation and brooding. It created a cohesive unit among the Negro UTEP trackmen. At an Easter week track meet against BYU, a Mormon school [the Book of Mormon specifies an inferior role for the Negro], most of the Black athletes decided not to participate.[27]

Spurred on by the success of the New York Athletic Club boycott, plans were made to boycott the 1968 Olympic Games in Mexico City. The idea for boycotting the Olympic Games had its origins in 1964 with the comedian and black human-rights activist, Dick Gregory.[28] In the fall of 1967 Tommie Smith, a 200-meter dash record holder from San Jose State College in California, told reporters that "Some black athletes have been discussing the possibility of boycotting the [Olympic] games to protest racial injustice in America." It seems reasonable to infer that steps by Western Michigan University in 1968 to hire its first fulltime Negro coaches, including track coach Fletcher Lewis, were influenced by treats of protest. Likewise, when Don Canham succeeded H. O. "Fritz" Crisler as Athletic Director the University of Michigan and elevated Ken Burnley, a former Wolverine sprinter, to a varsity-level coaching job, fear was involved.

The men's U.S. Olympic track and field trials in 1968 were unlike any ever before conducted by the U.S. Olympic Committee. Amid the pressures for Black athletes to boycott the Olympics and the anger following the assassinations of Martin Luther King Jr. and Robert Kennedy, the best U.S. men's track athletes withdrew to Echo Summit, a training camp and track literally carved out of the El Dorado National Forest near South Tahoe, CA. The site was selected because its altitude was nearly the same as that of Mexico City, and, unlike other years, the men's team was afforded a tranquil training atmosphere, with good food at no cost to the athletes. While many of the African-American runners suspected that the extended trials were held to weed out black runners, the Echo Summit training camp benefited nearly all those who attended. In the twilight years of amateur track, this training camp was a rare gift that resulted in the best showing ever made by the American men's Olympic track team. Overall, the 1968 team won twelve gold medals and set six world records and five additional Olympic records.[29]

At the Mexico City Olympics, sprinters Tommie Smith and John Carlos raised their hand in a Black power sign while the "Star-spangled Banner" played in honor of their medal winning performance in the 200-meter run. This act of defiance by Carlos and Smith sparked a controversy that can still generate heated discussion. They were kicked out of the Olympic Village, and were branded by some as traitors. This effort to focus on the inequalities in American life and the reaction of Brundage and the USOC forever overshadowed the accomplishments of the individuals and team.

Sixteen years later Carlos observed:

I'll always be John Carlos, the protester. The radical. . . . They said I was a Black Panther, a terrorist, a this or a that. I was nothing but a young American who believes in the ideals of America, freedom and justice for all, the land of the free. I don't regret what we did. Not in the least. It was an important statement. But it's too bad that I'm still struck with that label. . . . I'd still do something today. . . . But I wouldn't do what I did in '68. Today I know how to go behind a closed door, bang a table, raise some hell. I was young and idealistic then. I'm still idealistic, but I think I have a better idea of how things get done.[30]

If Carlos was wiser, it was experience that taught him. Life after the protest was not easy. He could not find a good job after the Olympics. He ran track for a while, played pro football in Canada, for a while, worked as a security guard, and bummed around. He ran up debts. Some took years to pay off. "I realized (the protest) would have impact," Carlos says, "but I had no idea of the intensity of it. I didn't know it would affect my whole life." It brought him grief: it brought him tragedy. Carlos' first wife committed suicide, and he's certain that the aftermath of Mexico City was the principal cause.

I couldn't find a job. I had a wife and two kids and I had to put some food on the table. I would go to college campuses and give speeches. We'd pass the hat and get money from the audience. At the same time when I was gone, someone would send letters—I don't know how, the government or some-body—saying, "You're home and Carlos is gone on the campus. He's a ladies' man and he's got women." Things to tear her head up, make her disen-chanted. . . . Eventually, she killed herself. It tore up the life of everyone involved. Tommie got divorced. It wasn't easy for him, either.

Smith also had trouble finding work. He and Carlos were rivals and never friends.[31]

A series of controversies regarding the 1,500-meter run disrupted the 1972 Olympic trials. Howell Michael, an African-American Marine lieutenant, was disqualified for bumping Reg McAfee on the final turn of the last lap in their heat. Both runners had qualified for the finals, but officials disqualified Lt. Michael.

The disqualification followed a stormy scene involving Willie Eash-man and his coach at Heyward State, Mal Andrews, who claimed that a series of redrawn heats and the readmittance of a runner previously disqualified (Jere Van Dyk) on July 6 had been "race-oriented." At one point, Andrews had to be restrained by several athletes and a police-man as he stormed and shouted on the track. "Something's definitely wrong," said Andrews, who had primed Eashman to become the first African-American to break 4 minutes in the mile. "We've got to look into this situation—right now." Later, at a far corner of the track, after consulting with a group of blacks that included Lee Evans and John Smith, a meeting of black athletes was called.[32]

In 1969 fourteen black athletes were kicked off the University of Wyoming football team for wearing black armbands to protest the racial practices of the Mormon Church in their game with Brigham Young University. They sued for damages. However, the courts said they had no standing for their suit.[33] Title IX of the Education Act passed in 1972 finally provided remedy to the racist actions of schools like Brigham Young and the University of Wyoming.

The Fall-Out Lasted for Years

The fall-out from the black boycotts continued for years. On February 23, 1972 a group of Michigan State's African-American athletes submitted a list of demands designed to improve their situation.[34] The following Saturday a protest by black students over conditions facing African-American students at MSU delayed the start of the Michigan State-Iowa basketball game.[35] In 1975 and 1983, an African-American track coach, George McGinnis, was suspended from coaching duties at Ferris State College. It was claimed that he falsified meal vouchers, mislead athletes about their eligibility, and changed the place of a Ferris runner from fourth to third in the 1982 invitational track meet at Ferris. After a five-year court battle, he was reinstated when Ferris agreed to an out-of-court settlement of a racial discrimination lawsuit. "During that go-around," McGinnis said, school officials "agreed to remove from my file more than 40 allegations. The athletic director . . . went around to everyone in the department from the secretaries to the janitors, and asked if they had any trouble with me. They scraped the bottom of the barrel to make me look bad and get rid of me."[36]

"After witnessing a player walkout to remove a basketball coach last December the Detroit Public School League is now in the throes of a boycott to reinstate a fired track coach." Dick Cole, the Cass Tech track and football coach, was relieved of his track duties on May 3, 1976. He was charged with misconduct stemming from an exchange of words the Cass Athletic Director at a track meet on April 18 at Pershing High School. Cass Athletic Director Sandra Smith claimed that Cole was disrespectful to her and members of the Northern High School coaching staff. Cole, a white coach, felt that the meet should have been cancelled because of cold weather. He also protested an illegal high jump and complained because meet officials forced his 880-relay team to run the entire race around the track in the outside lane. The Athletic Director, who was African-America, accused Cole of "making references to her race and sex." The all-black track team sided with the coach. Cole filed a grievance through the Detroit Federation of Teachers.[37]

Faced with a possible walkout by top American athletes, three [white] South African competitors were asked to withdraw from the National AAU Championships on June 15, 1972. The withdrawal request was made by the men's track and field committee following a meeting with a group of predominately African-American track stars. South Africa was barred from the Olympics because of its apartheid policy, but South African athletes had been competing in invitation meets in the USA and some were attending American colleges. Halberstadt, a student at Oklahoma State, won the NCAA 10,000-meter run in 1972. Van Reenen, a NCAA champion while at Washington State, was seeking legislative assistance to become an American citizen to qualify for the Olympics. While most of the athletes protesting the South African entries were blacks, several black athletes were sympathetic to the South Africans. They knew that Van Reenen and others did not share their government's view on apartheid. Nonetheless, since African-America athletes were not allowed to compete in South African meets, it was agreed that South African athletes would not be allowed to compete in the USA national championships.[38]

In 1976 African nations boycotted the Montreal Olympics over issues arising from South African apartheid. Lord Killanin, who was president of the International Olympic Committee from 1972 until 1980, like his predecessor, Avery Brundage, opposed tying politics to Olympic participation. Although Lord Killanin came to the Olympic presidency at the time African nations forced the IOC to expel white-dominated Rhodesia from the Munich Games, and was dealing with the aftermath of the massacre of Israeli Olympians, he was often insensitive to many of the legitimate complaints of people of color.[39]

Negro Colleges Track Stars Emerge

A United States Bureau of the Census study reported that blacks born in the South do economically better in northern cities based on 1970 census data.[40] This kind of news sparked renewed interest in black colleges, particularly black colleges in the South.

During a track season dominated by headlines about the exploits of west coast distance runner Steve Prefontaine, much more was happening in the sport. On February 3, 1973 Rodney Milburn, the high-hurdle Olympic champion who was attending Southern University, tied the world's indoor record for the 50-yard high-hurdles at the 33rd Annual Greater Cleveland Knights of Columbus Meet.[41]

Milburn was one of a growing number of black track stars emerging from predominantly African-American colleges. The following June the NCAA championships were held at Louisiana State University. Although Southern University was located only a few miles from LSU, the nation's best high-hurdler had never been invited to run on the track at LSU. As a result, Milburn did not make up his mind to attend the NCAA Championships until the last minute. Only after his friends had convinced him that his appearance could contribute to better relations between Southern University and LSU, did Milburn show up and establish a new meet record (13.1) for the high-hurdles at the NCAA championships.[42]

The Civil Rights Movement Gives Way to Higher Gasoline Prices

The decade of the 1970s brought America many of the excesses that characterized the balance of the century. A promising "War on Poverty" was undermined by America's escalation of the senseless intervention in the Vietnamese civil war. The expanding war in Vietnam eroded public support for American foreign policy and glamorized the uncivil behavior of protesters, who often broke the law. The "War on Poverty," while not a complete failure, was labeled a failure and soon gave way to the "War on Drugs." Because the "War on Poverty" failed to end either poverty or discrimination, it left many Americans disillusioned. Most African-Americans were angered by a nation, with apparently limitless potential, that was unable to or unwilling to significantly alter their lives after decades of "Jim Crow" discrimination. At the same time, many whites were disillusioned by increases in crime and welfare rolls.

The Nixon administration attributed growing public concern with crime and violence to an increased prevalence of drug use, and declared a "War on Drugs." After more than two decades of incarcerating black youth; diverting attention away from the needs of urban education, recreation, and youth employment; and ignoring addiction treatment, the "War on Drugs" increased cynicism, created a new prison industry, and contributed significantly to a loss of civil rights, but did little else.

The combined failure of the war in Vietnam, and efforts to end poverty and violent crime eroded public confidence in government's ability to solve pressing problems. The result was a generation that focused on itself. Whereas earlier generations understood life as a struggle involving sacrifice and obligations, the generation that grew up in the 1970s did not accept this view of life. They abandoned long-term commitments and looked for easier ways to make a living. The nation's well-to-do used America's accumulated wealth for self-indulgence with little concern about long-term consequences, while working-class families increasingly became two-income or single parent families, exposing their off-spring to neglect and undue peer group influences.

In contrast to the "me-first," immediate gratification so popular during this era, track and field demanded persistence, a commitment to hard work, and a willingness to defer rewards. This made track and field a better match for the old values than for the new ones. Perhaps, changing popular values contributed to the apparent decline in interest in the sport.

Amide continuing turmoil and war in the Middle East, in September 1972 at the Olympic Games in Munich, West Germany a group of terrorists known as Black September murdered eleven Israeli athletes, while Avery Brundage insisted that the games must continue. The economic dependence of the United States, Japan, and Western Europe were underscored during the decade by the creation of an oil cartel that precipitously increased the price of crude oil and cause an energy crisis in North America. The increase in heating and travel costs, in turn, had a major impact on the management and conduct of intercollegiate sports.

Ironically, in terms of race relations, before the end of the century many white athletes saw themselves as a minority on sports teams dominated by African-Americans who set the terms of play.[43]

19. "Women Running Things" [1924–1983]

The history of women's track and field in the United States is largely an untold story of opposition by official groups to strenuous recreational activities for women and more particularly to interscholastic and intercollegiate sports for women. Yet, it is also a rich heritage of unheralded success, unanticipated heroic performance, and undaunted courage. It is generally acknowledged that women's track in the United States began as part of the pedestrian race movement. Despite perceptions that physical activity would render women "manly, indelicate, and unsexed," by the mid-1870's, women walkers were competing for prize money worth up to $500.[1]

Few women attended high school or college in the nineteenth century and nearly all of them were from the homes of the well-to-do. Only 11,000 women were enrolled in American colleges and universities in 1870 and they and their peers were burdened by up to twenty-pounds of Victorian fashions that seriously endangered their health. As a result, the newly emerging women's physical education instructors in the few women's colleges were preoccupied with posture inspections and regulating diet, weight, exercise, and sleeping habits.

As the number of college women grew to 85,000 in 1900, women were gaining additional freedom. Middle-class women found attendance at Normal Colleges an attractive alternative to early marriage, and college girls discovered more vigorous forms of recreation.[2]

In 1891 Bryn Maur girls established the first Women's Athletic Association and university women at other colleges soon established women's athletic associations of their own.[3] Women's high jump competition was held at Bryn Maur College starting in 1892, but it was not until November 9, 1895, when the Vassar College Athletic Association held a meet with five events, that American college women had their first chance to participate in a track meet.[4] Between the formation of the Vassar Athletic Association on March 27, 1895 and the beginning of the twentieth century, five American women's colleges conducted track meets. Winthrop College in Rock Hill, South Carolina was the first woman's college in the twentieth century to add track and field as a competitive sport.

It was in the arena of women's basketball, however, that women's intercollegiate sports first surfaced as serious business. In a meeting at the 1899 Physical Training Conference in Springfield, Massachusetts, female physical educators established a basket ball committee. It was the first governing committee for women's college athletics.[5] In 1917 the Women's Basketball Rules Committee of the American Physical Education Association was renamed the Committee on Women's Athletics (CWA). In the 1950s the CWA became the National Association for Girls and Women's Sports (NAGWS). The Association of Intercollegiate Athletics for Women (AIAW) was formed as a subcommittee of NAGWA. In 1967 the Commission on Intercollegiate Athletics for Women (CIAW) was formed. CIAW became the AIAW in 1971 and served as the counterpart to the NCAA from 1971 through 1982.[6]

It was the second generation of college women that became the physical education teachers who would leave an indelible mark on twentieth century women's sports. By and large, they were from upper-class families, and shared that class' bias against professionalism in sports. They favored amateurism, and were influenced by control issues that were deeper than class-consciousness. Animosity developed early on between male and female coaches. Male dominated Board's of Education and University Regents prohibited the generation of teachers who taught during the first quarter of the twentieth century, from teaching after they married. Consequently, those who remained in the profession were frequently called "old maids," and were sometimes considered to be lesbians by male coaches, who, in turn, were called "testosterone driven, bullies" by female physical education teachers. Understandably, female physical education teachers came to hold strong feelings about the right of women to control women's sports.[7]

In the late nineteenth and early twentieth century, the public at-large frequently saw athletic competition as a means of reining in the unbridled sexual passion of young men. Male participation in sports was seen as an acceptable and reasonable outlet for their sexual energy and an expression of masculinity. There was a conscientious effort to balance "passive" scholarly activity with physical activity. Men who were not athletic were frequently targets of jokes and sexual innuendoes about being feminine.[8] Thus, it should come as little surprise that female physical education teachers sought to separate women's sports from men's sports, and to shun interscholastic and intercollegiate sports, which they felt were tainted by the professional influences of money and exploitation. They wanted to keep women's sports out of the corrupting control of men, and emphasized intramural over inter-scholastic and intercollegiate sports.

Despite the increased popularity of women's track and field, there was considerable resistance to inter-school competition and concern about the affects of athletic activity on women's health. To alleviate concerns about the negative affects of running on women's health, Dr. Harry Eaton Stewart, a physician and the physical education director at Wykeham Rise School for Girls in Washington, Connecticut, under-took research to determine the affects of vigorous exercise on heart and blood pressure. Stewart reported in the January 1916 issue of the *American Physical Education Review* that vigorous exercise in track improved women's health rather than endangered it. Nevertheless, in March 1917 the Women's Athletic Association of the Mid-West, with repre-sentatives from four Western Conference Universities, passed a resolu-tion opposing intercollegiate athletic competition.[9]

In 1918 the AAU appointed the first National Women's Track and Field Committee. Dr. Harry Eaton Stewart [who had become the ath-letic director of the New Haven Normal School of Gymnastics] was the only male member of the seven-person committee charged with administrating track and field for women.[10] In April 1922 the Board of Governor's of the AAU met in New York City with the supporters and advocates of women's athletics to set the date for the first women's AAU track and field championship.[11]

When the International Olympic Committee refused to recognize women's track and field as an Olympic event in 1920, the Federation of Sportive Feminine International (FSFI) was formed in 1922 to host an international women's track meet in suburban Paris. On May 13, 1922 at Oaksmere School in Mamaroneck, New York, Dr. Harry Stew-art sponsored the first significant women's track and field meet in the United States. The meet was held as tryouts for the American team that would represent the USA at the first Federation of Women's Sports International Meet at Pershing Stadium just outside Paris starting on August 18. Thirteen women qualified for the trip. Twelve members of the team sailed on the *Aquitania* on August 2, 1922. The Spalding Com-pany designed the first women's international competition outfits. Baggy bloomers were abandoned once and for all in favor of shorts, albeit long shorts. Even before Stewart's group sailed for France, oppo-sition to women engaging in international competition began to surface. The AAU refused to sanction the women's team, and in June 1922 the American Physical Education Association excluded Dr. Harry E. Stewart from their committee, and requested that the trip to Europe be canceled.[12]

Before the International meet started, Dr. Stewart pledged to promote international women's track and field in the United States and was chosen vice president of the Federation of Sportive Feminine International. A crowd of 20,000 watched the American girls place second in the meet. Lucile Godbold from Winthrop College was one of the outstanding athletes at the meet. Later, she became women's athletic director at Columbia College in New York City.[13]

Dead Janes oppose Swift Babies

When the girl's team returned to the States, opposition among leaders in women's physical education grew and they spoke out against the "evils" of competition. In late December 1922, the American Physical Education Association vehemently opposed the AAU's efforts to take control of women's athletics and continued to emphasized the "danger of competitive sports exploiting" girls and women to the detriment of their good health, and physical and social education. There also was an underlying concern that men would gain control of women's sports.

After the FSFI meet near Paris, the IOC, AAU, and the International Amateur Athletic Federation (IAAF) all took a sudden interest in women's track. The first national women's intercollegiate Telegraphic Track and Field Meet was held in the fall of 1922, eighty colleges throughout the United States participated. The first women's track meet also was conducted under the auspices of the AAU in 1922. It was held at Lewishon Stadium at City College in New York City. The first National Women's AAU Outdoor Track and Field Championship was not held until September 29, 1923.[14]

In 1923 the National Amateur Athletic Federation, which had been initiated by the U. S. War Department during the first World War, brought together leaders from military and men's intercollegiate sports to examine concerns about the high number of draftees rejected for physical reasons during the war. At that time, Secretary of War John W. Weeks and Secretary of the Navy Edwin Denby meet with Lou Henry Hoover, the wife of Secretary of Commerce Herbert Hoover, to discuss ways of establishing physical fitness standards for girls and women to accompany those being developed for men. After consulting with female physical education educators, Mrs. Herbert [Lou Henry] Hoover suggested that she call a Conference on Athletics and Physical Recreation for Women and Girls. The conference was held in Washington, DC on April 6–7, 1923.

Smarting from the possible loss of control over women's athletics to the AAU and opposed to women's sports becoming a marketable commodity, the CWA approved 16 resolutions that were distributed under the name of the Women's Division of the National Amateur Athletic Federation. The emphasis of the recommendations was on limiting inter-school athletic competition for women and girls. A resolution also was passed opposing international competition for women and girls. A majority of women's physical education teachers present wanted their committee to deliberate, investigate, legislate, promote, and control national sports for girls and women.[15]

This conference was a turning point for women's track and field in the United States. Several members of the American Physical Education Association showed their disapproval of the AAU's approach to women's track by withdrawing from the AAU Women's Athletic Committee or refusing to serve on it. The resulting split between the AAU and the American Physical Education Association created antagonisms that remained for half a century. Moreover, the Conference hardened positions and virtually stopped the growth of school-based girl's track and field in the United States until 1960, when the triumphs of Wilma Rudolph reactivated interest in the sport at the secondary school level.

Michigan Pioneers

Interest in girl's track and field in Michigan was particularly slow in developing. In 1911 the Grand Rapids Public Schools sponsored a playground festival with a field day for lower elementary school boys *and girls* in which a 50-yard dash was included. A few years later the Detroit Public Schools initiated a field day for all elementary students that functioned successfully until World War II. As was often the case, the Detroit Public Schools lead the rest of the state in adopting inter-scholastic women's sports. In 1924 the Detroit Public Schools initiated competitive track and field for high school girls. By 1926 the Greater Detroit Interscholastic League staged duel meets and a City Championship for girls in track, tennis and golf.[16] It was also in 1926 that the state produced its first women's track star. Florence Wolf of the VVV Girl's Athletic Club of Detroit placed fourth in the discus throw at the third annual AAU Women's Outdoor Championship held under a blazing sun in Philadelphia.[17] However, in the balance of the state, interest in girl's track was very limited until the early 1970s.

By 1922 Michigan Normal College in Ypsilanti was holding an annual women's indoor track meet for its students. In 1925, 300 young women took part in the meet, which—in truth—featured few track and field events.[18] In 1926 there were reports that both Western State Normal College in Kalamazoo and Battle Creek Normal School had a women's track team.

The 1928 Olympic games were the first in which women were allowed to participate in track and field competition. In the Ninth Olympiad in Amsterdam, Holland, there were only three track events and two field events for female athletes. Women ran the 100-meter dash, the 4 by 100-meter relay and the 800-meter run. Elizabeth Robinson won the 100-meter dash. Florence McDonald was sixth in the 800-meter run, and the U.S. women's relay team earned the silver medal. The 1928 women's high jump championship went to Canadian, Ethel Catherwood, while American women placed third (Mildred Wiley), fourth (Jean Shiley), and eighth (Catherine Maguire). Lillian Copeland won a silver medal for the USA in the discuss, and Maybelle Reichardt placed seventh in that event.[19]

The Michigan AAU Track and Field Committee took advantage of the interest generated by women's participation in track and field at the Olympics to promote women's track in Michigan. For the first time, they included two open women's events in the AAU State Outdoor Championships held on August 18, 1928. Fifteen women, representing the Detroit Turners and the Michigan Central Athletic Association, participated in the 50 and 100-yard dashes.[20]

Four years later, Dorothy Frances Anderson, a high school student from Highland Park, a suburb of Detroit, emerged as the second female track star from Michigan. Dorothy went by her middle name, Frances, because there were four girls on here block whose first name was Dorothy. D. Frances Anderson was born on May 7, 1912 and she had three brothers. Her father was born in Scotland and immigrated to Canada before moving to Detroit. Her desire to pal around with her brothers got her involved in sports, and she went out for track when she was in the ninth grade.[21] In June 1928 she set a Detroit City League girl's high jump record with a leap of 4–9.[22]

The 5 foot 11½ inch tall Miss Anderson attended Michigan Normal College in Ypsilanti to pursue her dream of becoming a physical education teacher. At Michigan Normal, she was on the championship field

Highland Park's Dorothy Frances Anderson placed fourth in the high jump at the trials for the 1932 Olympic team, while a student at Michigan Normal College. *(Photo Eastern Michigan U Archives)*

hockey and girl's basketball teams. She was President of the school's Women's Athletic Association, which was formed in 1925 to sponsor girl's on-campus, athletic activities. She was also a member of the Physical Education Club and the Kappa Gamma Phi Sorority.[23]

Encouraged by her high school experience and her practice jumps at Michigan Normal, and undeterred by warnings that taking part in athletics would put her motherhood at risk, she registered for the National Women's AAU Championships, which doubled as the U. S. Olympic trials.[24] Held at Northwestern University in Evanston on June 16, 1932, she placed fourth in the high jump (5 feet) to Mildred "Babe" Didrikson, missing the Olympic team by two inches.[25] Anderson recalls that the progress of the rounds was very slow because "Babe" was in so many events that they often had to wait for her to take her turn. But, Anderson and the other girls did not get mad, because "Babe" was so nice to each of them.

"In those days, we used the scissors kick jump because the rules more or less required it. 'Babe' had a different jumping style that was ruled illegal at the Olympic Games. If they had caught that problem in the trials, it is likely that I would have been in the 1932 Olympics, as the took the first three place winners and I tied for fourth."[26]

In her senior year at Normal, men's track coach Lloyd Olds made arrangements for her to participate in the National AAU Indoor Meet at Madison Square Garden. Anderson placed second in the high jump (5 feet 1/16 inch) at the National AAU Indoor on February 25, 1933. She concluded her national involvement in track and field on June 30, 1933 by participating in the high jump at the 46th Annual National AAU Outdoor Championships in Chicago.[27] Ms. Anderson graduated from Michigan Normal in 1933 with a teaching certificate in physical education. After substituting as an elementary school gym teacher in the Detroit Public Schools for more than three years, on November 11, 1936 she was hired as a gym teacher and swimming coach at Fordson High School in Dearborn.

During World War II, a Pennsylvania born welder who grew up in upstate New York, rented a room from Frances Anderson's mother. Ms. Anderson married the young man, becoming Mrs. Merena in August 1942. She stopped teaching in 1943 when she started raising a family. The two were still happily married after raising three daughters and living together 58 years.[28]

One-of-Twenty Children

Another Michigan women's track and field star did not emerge until 1955, when Anna Mae Sullifant of Ann Arbor ran the 100-yard dash against Wilma Rudolph at the National AAU Girl's Division Championships held in Ponca City, Oklahoma. It was the first national meet for both girls.[29]

The fifteen-year old Wilma Rudolph was the youngest of twenty children. She grew up in Clarksville, Tennessee. She had been a sickly child, and overcame double pneumonia, measles, mumps, chicken pox, scarlet fever and polio to become a runner. The track coach at Tennessee State University noticed Wilma when he was refereeing girl's basketball game in which she was leading her high school team to the finals of the state tournament. He offered her a full college athletic scholarship to run track at Tennessee State and asked her to attend a summer training program in 1955. It was as a result of this training program that Wilma Rudolph beat Anna Sullifant in the 100-yard dash in

Ponca City, Oklahoma.[30] Sullifant's career was completely over-shadowed by Wilma Rudolph's exploits.

In 1956, Wilma, now a freshman at Tennessee State and nicknamed "Skeeter," was named to the AAU Women's All-American track and field team. She was on the winning 400-meter relay team and placed second in the 200-meter dash at the National AAU Outdoor Women's Championships held in Philadelphia on August 18. A week later she qualified for the nineteen-woman Olympic track and field team bound for Melbourne. In late November 1956, Wilma finished third in the second heat of the 200-meter run, but did not make the finals. She did, however, win a bronze medal as part of the U.S. 400-meter relay team.[31]

In 1957 Wilma won the 75-yard dash, the 100-yard dash and the 300-yard medley relay when she lead Tennessee State University to the championship of the Girl's Division of the AAU.[32] Wilma sat out the 1958 track season when she had her first daughter, but returned in 1959 to dominate the sprints at the National AAU Indoor Women's Championships held in Washington, D.C. on January and the National Outdoor Championships held in Cleveland, Ohio on June 28. She was named to the AAU All-American team and was a member of the Pan-American Games team. Wilma won a gold and a silver medal at those games in Chicago in early September 1959.

In the summer of 1960 the 20-year old, 5–11, 135 pound Wilma Rudolph proved that she was the world's fastest female runner when she won three gold medals at the Olympics in Rome. She tied the world record in the semi-finals of the 100-meter dash and set Olympic records in the finals of the 100 and 200-meter dashes. Finally, Wilma anchored her Tennessee State team to a new, world record in the 400-meter relay. When she was asked which was her favorite gold medal, she answered without hesitation, "That's an easy question. It was the relay, because I won that with my Tennessee State Tigerbelle teammates, and we could celebrate together."[33]

Wilma's astounding performance drew worldwide attention to women's track and energized the sport. The heroine of the 1960 Rome Olympics had over 100 photographers chasing after her for pictures, and could not leave the athletic village without creating a mob scene. She also promoted racial justice when she insisted on the integration of the hometown parade and banquet celebration following her Olympic victories.[34]

Wilma Rudolph's popularity provided the leverage needed to integrate women's track with men's track and field. In 1961 women's sprint events were added to the program at both the Millrose Games and the New York Athletic Club indoor games. The Millrose Games introduced the women's 60-yard dash into their featured race card. The meet had long sponsored a club meet for women's relay teams in the New York area, but they had never before featured a world class women's race. Wilma Rudolph won the race, but officials of the Millrose Games did not feature a women's race again until 1965 when Judith Amoore, the world record holder in the 440, won a woman's 440 at the 58th Millrose Games. The first individual women's event in its 51 years history was held at the Drake Relays on April 29, 1961 when Wilma Rudolph was invited to run the 100-yard dash at the meet. The Olympic gold medal winner from Tennessee State University was politely turned away from several gates, with the admonition, "no girls allowed," before being allowed to enter the stadium for the women's events. Her performance was an outstanding, show-stopping run that trilled the 18,000 fans that filled the stadium.[35]

"Red's Girls"

Kenneth "Red" Simmons was a former Michigan Normal College and Detroit Police AA track star. While a member of the Detroit Police Department, "Red" pioneered in the use of weight training in track and field. He received bonus pay for running on the Police track team, and needed the extra money to support his growing family. As he aged, "Red" defied "expert" advice and successfully turned to weight lifting to extend his track career.

After retiring from the Detroit Police Department, "Red and his wife attended the Olympic games in Rome. Inspired by Wilma Rudolph's performance, but concerned by the relatively poor showing of the rest of American woman's track team, he decided to recruit and coach a woman's track team in Ann Arbor. At the time "Red" organized the Michigammes Track Club, there were few interscholastic track teams for high school girls in Michigan, and the University of Michigan did not have a woman's track team. "Red" was about to become a pioneer in the promotion of woman's track in Michigan.

"Red" asked his wife, who was a middle-school teacher, to identify the best female athletes at the school where she taught. At her suggestion, "Red" started his girl's track team by recruiting Francie Kraker. Francie proved to be an ideal choice. She had great athletic talent and the heart of a champion.

When she was a toddler, Francie Kraker had developmental prob-

Kenneth "Red" Simmons, the University of Michigan's first women's track coach, standing next to one of his prize students, Michigan's first female Olympian, Francie Kraker Goodrich. *(Photo University of Michigan, Sports Information)*

lems with her legs, and required medical attention and braces. She overcame these problems, and by the time she was in Junior High School agreed to run on "Red's" track team. Francie became "Red's" first project. "During the 70th annual national convention of the AAU in 1958, two running events were added to the Women's Outdoor championships for the 1959 season. These were the 440 and 880 yards runs.[36] Initially these events were confined to the women division and were not included in the girls' (14 to 17 years) championship program.[37] In 1964 the girl's division finally included an 880-yard run.

Francie was better a middle-distance runner than sprinter, so "Red" made her a half-miler. On July 10, 1964 their hard work paid off when Francie won the 880 (2:17.4) at the National AAU Girls Championships in Hanford, California and established the record for this new event. She was rewarded by being named to the AAU Girls' All-American track team.[38]

It is revealing to note that a major controversy was touched off after the women's 800-meter run was first held at Olympic Games in 1928, because several women collapsed in exhaustion after the race was run in the world record time of 2:16.8. The record stood for 16 years, and the women's 800-meter run was not held again in the Olympics until 1960 because it was felt that the distance was too strenuous for women.[39] Francis's time in 1964 would have placed her among the top fifteen women in the world that event in 1960.

Louise Gerrish of the Ann Arbor Anns also emerged as a national track star in the Girl's Division of the AAU in 1964. Louise placed third in the basketball throw at the Girl's Division Indoor Meet in March, and third in the javelin throw outdoors in Hanford.

Louise Garrish became an AAU Girl's Division All-American in 1965 when she won the javelin throw at the National AAU Girl's Division Championships in Columbus, Ohio. She continued to place in the javelin throw and basketball throw at national meets in 1966 and 1967.[40]

Growing interest in women's sports was reflected in the call for the first National Institute on Girl's Sports which was held in March 1964 in Greenville, SC.[41] The second National Institute was held at Michigan State University, September 26 to October 1, 1965, and "Red" Simmons was one of ten featured speakers at the second Institute.[42]

In 1965 the 1,500-meter run was included in AAU women's championship competition for the first time. On January 14, 1966 Francie placed third in the 880 (2:13.9) at the Motor City International meet at Cobo Arena in Detroit.[43] In late June 1966 Francie placed third in both the 880 (2:10.9) and the 1,500-meter run (4:37.3) at the National AAU Women's Championships in Frederick, Maryland.[44]

At the age twenty, when she was a college sophomore, Francie Kraker emerged as a world-class runner. On January 20, 1967 she finished second in the 880 (2:13.5) at the Los Angeles Times Invitational. Six days later, on Thursday January 26, Francie ran the woman's half-mile on the boards at the 60th annual Millrose Games. At that meet, she set a new 880 record (2:11.8).[45] According to Coach "Red" Simmons, "Francie ran the race exactly as planned. This is the first perfect race she has run, tacticwise. Her clockings were just about what we planned to run before the meet." Her performance at the Millrose Games unleashed a flood of invitations to participate in other meets.[46]

Two days later Francie set a new American indoor record for the women's 880-yard run (2:09.7) at the 78th annual Boston Athletic Association Indoor Meet. In that race, "Miss Kraker led early, yielded to [Olympian] Marie Mulder with three laps to go, regained the lead as the bell sounded the start of the last lap and won by eight yards. Miss Mulder tired badly and showed the effects of running 360 yards in the relay race only 20 minutes before."[47] And, on February 17, 1967 Francie set an American and world record for the 600-yard run (1:22.4) at the New York Athletic Club Indoor Meet.[48] The record stood until 1970. A photograph of this record-setting race can be found in the *Encyclopedia Britannica 1968 Annual*. On March 4 Kraker took two third places in the national AAU woman's meet in Oakland, CA. She ran the half-mile in 2:10.2 and the mile in 5:01. In the mile-run Francie had the same time as the second place runner, but "unfortunately, the girl next to Francie leaned forward at the tape. Their feet were even, but their top halves were not," according to Simmons.[49]

In 1968 Francie Kraker qualified for the US Olympic team and trained with the team at Echo Summit.[50] In October 1968 she was the third fastest 800-meter U.S. female performer (2:05.3) at the Mexico City Olympics. After the 1968 Olympics, Francie married Mister Johnson, a Boston salesman and photographer, dropped out of college, and moved to Boston.[51] She continued to run wearing a Michigammes uniform.

On February 27, 1970 Francie ran the half-mile at the National AAU Indoor Championships and won the national championship with a 2:10.2 performance. When she crossed the finish line, "Red" Simmons, her former coach, was one of the first persons to congratulate her.[52]

In 1972 the women's Olympic trials were held July 7–8 at Governor Thomas Johnson High School field in Frederick, Maryland. Running for the Liberty Athletic Club, Francie Kraker Johnson placed second in the 1,500-meter run (4:15.2), beating the Olympic qualifying-standard of 4:20.[53] As a result, Francie was invited to the U. S. Olympic training camp and was again a member of the US Olympic team.[54] The women's 1,500-meter run was held for the first time in 1972 as an Olympic event.

There were 36 competitors from 21 nations entered in the women's metric mile at Munich.[55] The first round heats were held on Monday September 4.[56] Francie Kraker ran in the second heat of the first round, and finished fourth with a respectable time of 4:14.7. Her performance qualified her for the semi-finals, making her one of the fastest 16 runners in the world in that event. In the semi-finals held on Thursday September 7, less than three days after nine Israeli Olympians and two trainers were killed by Palestinian terrorists, Francie finished eighth in her heat. In the semi-finals, 13 of the 17 women running the race broke the pre-Olympic world record.[57] Francie was not one of them, but her Olympic time of 4:12.7 was the second-fastest all-time woman's American performance for the 1,500-meter run at that point in time and was her personal best.[58] She continued to compete until 1975 and remained in the top-ten U.S.A. performances for that event for nearly a decade.

After divorcing her first husband, Francie returned from Wellsley, Massachusetts to the University of Michigan, where she completed her B. A. degree in 1974. In 1974 and 1975, Francie was a substitute teacher in secondary schools in New York and Michigan. In 1975–76 she was the coordinator of Women's Athletics and Head Women's cross-country and track and field coach at the University of Wisconsin-Milwaukee. In 1982 she became Head Women's cross-country and track and field coach at the University of Michigan, and in 1983 her track team won Michigan's first ever Big Ten Indoor Championship and was second in the outdoor championships, losing by only one point. Her cross-country team was runner-up in the NCAA Regional Championships and finished eighth in the National NCAA Championships.

Francie remarried, becoming Mrs. John Goodridge. In 1984, she accepted the position of head cross-country and track coach at Wake Forest University. In 1985 Francie was named NCAA Region III cross-country coach of the year, and in 1986 she was named Atlantic Coast Conference cross-country coach of the year. In November 1994 Francie was named to the University of Michigan Hall of Honor, and the following year to their Woman's Track and Field Hall of Fame.

A Penny for your Thoughts

Along with Francie Kraker, Penny Neer was one of "Red" Simmons' most successful projects. Penny Lou Neer was born in Hillsdale, Michigan on November 7, 1960. Her parents were Ronald and Ursula Neer. Penny's father is six-foot two and was a semi-pro basketball player in Germany, where he met Penny's mother while he was in the Air Force.

In 1992, the University of Michigan's Penny Neer became the State's first female, field athlete to make the Olympic team. *(Photo University of Michigan, Sports Information)*

Neer's mother, Ursula, is 5–10 and was on track teams in her native West Germany. "My mother," Neer said, "was the one who instilled in me a work ethic. She taught me to work hard, but also to have fun."

Penny's older sister, Laura, was All-State in track and attended to Hillsdale College on a combined volleyball and track scholarship. Her little brother, Rusty, was a 6–10 basketball player at a technical school in Fort Wayne.[59]

Penny recalls, "In high school I didn't want to throw the discus. My mother said, 'With big hands like that you've got to be able to throw far.' "I know those big hands must be good for something more than just basketball," her mother argued. Soon, Ursula Neer became her daughter's workout partner. "Being a small school, North Adams didn't even have a track. So I would throw behind our house and she would shag it and throw it back at me." Penny Neer said. "After awhile, I got to be pretty good." "I owe a lot to my mom and dad. They've always given me a lot of encouragement. They've always been for whatever I've decided."[60]

As a senior, Penny responded by winning the State Girl's High School Discus Championship. At that time Penny just stood in the circle and did not spin her body before throwing. Penny was All-State in basketball, and all-conference in volleyball, softball, and track. She was captain of the volleyball team and the leagues' outstanding girl's track athlete. Penny was selected for Girl's State, and was valedictorian of her class at North Adams High School.

"Red" Simmons first met Penny in June of 1978 at the state track meet. Penny was throwing the discus. She stood 6' tall and weighed 165 pounds, wore braids and had on high top sneakers. She had thrown well, and without even a hello, "Red" asked, "How about a track scholarship to Michigan?" Penny replied, "I am sorry, I cannot accept it." The disappointment was visible on "Red's" face. But when Penny explained that she was already going to the University of Michigan on an athletic scholarship to play basketball, he looked like it was Christmas morning. Later that month she placed eighth in the discus at the National AAU Junior Women's Meet.[61]

"When she got to the University of Michigan, neither she or her basketball coach thought she was going to be a great basketball player," Simmons said. "I convinced her she would make a better discus thrower. She had a hand half-again the size of mine; she was well coordinated, quick, smart and very coachable." As a freshman, she sold programs at the football games.[62] During the summers, while in college, she worked in a private nursing home and as a waitress. She and her sister also play softball for the OK Boilerettes of Albion.

When Penny first started to compete at Michigan, she threw the discus an average of only 130 feet. "Red" started by helping her establish her athletic objectives, then set about reinforcing and building on the values her parents had taught her: to have balance in life, value your family, to work hard, get an education, and strive toward goals. "Red" told Penny that she would be the first lady Wolverine to win a national track and field title, and be the team's first All-American. He also told her that someday she would make the Olympic team.

"Red" was a motivational genius. Early on, demonstrated pride in each team member. Before the days of team sweat suits, he even gave several members of the team their own maize and blue sweat suit. Penny recalls, "My ankles and wrists stuck out the ends, but I wore them until they were thin." All the while, Coach Simmons provided encouragement to his team members. Penny recalls, "He couldn't talk to me during competition," so "he had hand signals telling me what to do. He said, "You're the best" and "You're the berries". He said, "You can win this thing." But his favorite saying was "Chest out! Chin up! You're the Best!" It was because of the encouragement of Coach Simmons that Penny Neer threw the shot put as well as the discus. She disdained the shot put in college because "there's no finesse, no grace to that sport." "I didn't want to throw the shot put because it made my neck dirty. Or I would protest and say, "But they [her competitors] are so big!" And "Red" would respond, "But you are prettier. Go get em, Champ!"[63]

During Penny's sophomore year at Michigan, the assistant track coach taught her to spin as she threw the discus and increased her throw by about 20 feet. As a result, Penny won the Big Ten discus championship. When the team returned to Ann Arbor, "Red" presented Penny with a beautiful trophy. She found out later that he had taken one of your own trophies from the 1930's and replaced the plaque on it with a new one inscribed with Penny's name. He also sent her to the AIAW National Intercollegiate Championships in Eugene, paying for the trip out of his own pocket. When Penny got to Oregon, she had a migraine headache and performed poorly, placing 25th in the discus. Instead of being upset, "Red" said, "But did you have fun?" To "Red" that was what was important, that track should always be fun. As Penny Neer put it, "Many people focus on accomplishments, but Coach Simmons taught me that it is the journey we take toward reaching our goals that is important."

"Red" had a style all his own. When the women's team trained, he had nicknames for everyone, like "Miss Penny" and "Bonnie Woman," as well as nicknames for discus throws ("worm burner and rain maker"). He chuckled at good luck charms—a carved wooden whale and a rubber snake, and laughed at the adventures of his team members—like being stopped at the airport x-ray scanner because of a runner's lucky charms.[64]

"Red" was always searching for a better reward system. He set high goals, and expected the best. He told Penny that for every ten feet she improved in the discus, he would buy her a steak dinner. He paid for steak dinners at 140 feet, 150, 160 and so on. Penny was a real competitor. During the winter, she often shoveled snow to clear a place to throw and she also would practice in the rain.

Michigan did not earn a single point at the AIWA outdoor track championships in 1979 and 1980, "but [Athletic Director Don] Canham still had the confidence to send us to the nationals." Simmons who was pushing 72 years of age, was retiring as head coach of women's track and field at the University of Michigan at the close of the 1981 season and really wanted to take his team to the meet. "He was looked upon as a father figure by his athletes, and he knew it would not be easy walking out." Simons said he would "be associated with something around the university, I just don't know what yet. I don't want to be tied down to set hours."[65]

It was raining hard at the national AIAW championships at the University of Texas in Austin in June 1981. It thundered too. But the rain did not wash away the meet—only the dreams of a few competitors who were not able to perform well in the slippery, soggy conditions.

Because of the rain, "all the girls panicked," Penny explained. "They had on their special-made discus shoes. I just wore my high tops from basketball. All the girls laugh at me because I didn't lift weights, wear special shoes, or even wear my uniform. They wouldn't give me a track uniform until I turned in my basketball stuff and I hadn't done that before I left for the meet. But when it rained, my basketball shoes stuck to the cement surface, while their shoes slipped." Expected to finish no better than twelfth, she tossed the discus 163 feet, 7 inches-nearly 10 feet below her personal best—to finish fifth. Benefiting from the rain, she became the University of Michigan's first woman track All-American, since the first six finishers were automatically All-Americans.

Penny participated in both basketball and track during her first three years at Michigan. Finally, she decided not to play basketball in her senior year, and devoted her extra time to a track and weightlifting program designed to help her fare even better in the discus. The thought of weightlifting had her worried. She was concerned about keeping her well-proportioned figure. "I don't know if I should lift weights and put on the bulky weight and win or not lift weights and not win, but be able to put on a dress after competition. My mom and dad see some of the girls I have to compete against and they say, 'Oh, look at her!"

She met Michigan Athletic Director Don Canham for the first time in 1981. "He asked, 'Are you lifting weights?' Neer recalls. "I said no. He said, 'Good. Stay like that.'" Yet, others told her she could do wonders with a weight program. "Coaches came up to me and said, 'What weight program do you follow?' I said none. They said, 'Well, what DO you do?'[66]

Instead of lifting weights, she chopped wood and mowed lawns. Jack Harvey, the men's track coach, was after Penny to lift weights for a long time, but Penny was concerned that it would adversely affect her love life. "It'll affect my throwing, I'm sure, but I just don't know how it'll affect other things. I hope I won't need a new wardrobe. I could get up into the 200s and that's world-class caliber," Neer said. "But I'll have to change my attitude and start taking it seriously and not just go out and wing it and win."

Starting in high school, Neer was often able to go to a meet and win without much concentration or practice, but that changed as she entered tougher competition—like the U.S. Olympic Committee's National Sports Festival in July 1981 in Syracuse. During her last year at Michigan, Francie Kraker Goodrich was her track coach, but men's track coach Jack Harvey provided Penny's instruction in the discus.[67]

"There's an adventure to the discus," Penny declared. "There are so many different blocks involved to learn. I'll probably be 60 or 70 years old with a cane and still be throwing. I don't like shot put because it's a dirty event, you get mud all over you. Aside from the mud, there's not as much grace in shot put, the stretching and uncoiling of muscles isn't as great. There's no beauty in seeing a plain round shot go plop a few feet down the way. Ah, but a discus, now that soars majestically toward the horizon.

"Before meets, a lot of people ask what I do. When I tell them discus and shot put they say, 'But you've got a dress on' and I just say 'so what?"

"Penny's such a good person and she's a real athlete, not one of those 'steroid' ladies," Francie Goodridge observed. Coach Goodrich was referring to the illegal use of anabolic steroids by some track athletes. "She's a great competitor, takes work very seriously and loves it."[68] An interview with Penny reinforced Coach Goodrich's observations. Neer said that she has been offered bulk-building steroids, but refused them for several reasons.

I like how I look now. Everyday, they come up with something new it does to you [referring to the bad side-effects]. I want to be able to have kids and look normal. More and more, I'm hearing friends of mine who said they'd never take it but are. I'm really disappointed. They don't count themselves lucky and see what they can do with what they've got (naturally). But it's not you throwing. It's the drug. My goal is to see how far I can throw on my own. I hope to put on perhaps 10 pounds to increase my strength even more and I know I need work on her technique, but I gain confidence knowing that those who are already near their potential aren't throwing much farther than I am. The things I have to do are real defined. Other girls have already done them, and are turning every which way, seeking more distance. I really think I can do it. A 50-foot increase really sounds incredible, but since I started throwing, I've increased 100 feet.[69]

During her senior year at Michigan, Penny won her third Big Ten discus championship, and on June 12, 1982 became the University's first female athlete to win a national track and field championship. At the Association of Intercollegiate Athletics for Women [AIAW] Championships in College Station, Texas, Neer beat all comers with a throw of 184 feet 8 inches to win.

Penny stayed in Ann Arbor during the 1982–83 academic year. She worked at a sports shop and trained seven days a week, alternating throwing and lifting weights, preparing for the 1984 Olympic Trials.[70] In May 1983 she placed fifth in the discus at the Athletes Congress Meet. On July 4 she placed second at the National Sports Festival in Colorado Springs, and on July 10 she placed seventh in the discus at the XII World University Games in Edmonton, Canada. She finished the summer track season in August when she represented the United States at the Pan American Games in Caracas, Venezuela.

After the Pan-American Games, Penny was still in search of the 200-yard throw. Undeterred she insisted, "It will come, those women who have reached that level say it feels no different than throwing 180 or 190. It's just a matter of getting everything together under the right conditions." Discus throwers prefer a light wind coming toward them. A light wind provides lift and carries the discus higher and farther. A crosswind or a wind from behind can cause trouble.

She practiced without a coach, but was so familiar with her workout that she could pinpoint her own technical problems. "If I feel I need help, I'll just ask some one around the track to watch and see if they can help." As with so many great athletes, Penny competed against herself, trying to achieve a series of goals.[71]

Competing for the West Michigan Track Club, Penny Neer qualified for the finals of the Olympic tryouts held June 24, 1984. Her throw of 179–7 was well short the leaders in the event, who threw 20 feet farther. "It was not a real good throw," she acknowledged, but she did not give up her Olympic dream.[72] Always the optimist, "Red" Simmons told the press, "All she really needs is another year of weight training to increase her strength and a little more work on technique." Like many gifted athletes, Penny learned to analyze her losses and short-comings and turn them into positive experiences. She had a strong sense of accomplishment and kept athletics in perspective. "You can't take all this too seriously," Neer philosophized. "If it turns into a job, you've got to get out."[73]

With a degree in computer science in hand, Penny took a job as a systems analyst and production planner with Bose Corporation in Hillsdale, where her father had worked for thirty-years and was direc-tor of public utilities. Training became more difficult. While still ranked in the top ten women discus thrower in the United States she did not have a real training regimen. She trained when she could." Basically, she became a part-time athlete who trained and traveled on her own.[74] Nevertheless, on June 15, 1985 she placed second in the discus (185–2) at the USA/Mobile [TAC] Outdoor Championships in Indianapolis.

As the 1988 Olympics approached, Penny Neer stepped up her train-ing again. On June 15 she placed fourth in the discus (200 feet 11 inches) with the best marks by an American woman in 1988.[75] On June 17, 1988 she placed third in the discus (199.2 meters) at the TAC National Championships in Tampa. But, on July 21 she only placed eighth in the finals of the discus throw (177.1 meters) at the U. S. Olympic trials in Indianapolis. Penny was devastated. As she put it, "I had tried to make the team in 1984, and again in 1988. I didn't make it, and I became discouraged. I gave away my discs and shoes and wanted to give up." "Red" came to the rescue, he insisted that she be persistent. "Because of Coach Simmons's encouragement and support, I trained four more years and tried again in 1992. He made it possible for me to realize my potential to the fullest. He was there every step of the way for me."[76]

In June 2, 1990 she was on the comeback trail, placing second (191–2) at the Prefontaine Classic Meet, and third (186–7) twelve days later at the Track Athletic Congress (TAC) Championships at Cerritos College in Norwalk, California. The next year she placed third in the finals of the discus throw (190.1 meters) at the TAC National Outdoor Championships at Randalls Island. She placed 25th (176.0 meters) at the World Track and Field Championships in Tokyo.[77]

Penny trained at Hillsdale College in preparation for the 1992 Olympic trials in New Orleans. Everyone in town was pulling for her. Her co-workers at the Bose Corporation gave her a send off party when she left for the trials. Once at New Orleans, "I had to count on myself and just go out and do it," Neer said. Never was the difference between Neer and her competitors more noticeable than at the Olympic trials in Tad Gormley Stadium. "Every one of the other girls had coaches there," Neer said. "After every throw, they would look up in the stands and go up and try to find out what they did wrong. They had people there who had set up their weight-lifting regimen and training schedules. The last ten years, I haven't had a coach. It's just been me." At age 31, she finished third in the women's discus with a toss of 193–6, good enough to make the U. S. Olympic team for the first time.[78]

At last Penny Neer was bound for Barcelona. She had been working for this opportunity for fourteen years. She was acknowledged to be a down to earth, very personable, quality young woman—one of those people who is hard not to like. While Penny did not win a medal at the Olympics, she was a winner by all other measures. In 1994 when "Red Simmons was 83 years old and still competing in master's track," Neer said. " I still remember him yelling at me, 'Chin out, chest out,' when I was practicing."[79]

The AIAW Seeks to Govern Intercollegiate Women's Track

In 1969 the Division for Girls and Women's Sports of the American Association for Health, Physical Education, and Recreation, a national affiliate of the National Education Association began sponsoring a National Intercollegiate Track and Field Championship. On May 29–30, 1970 the second DGWA National Outdoor Championships were held at the University of Illinois Memorial Stadium in Champaign. Five young ladies from Michigan institutions for higher education participated in that meet. Wayne State University sent Pamela Bagian (220-meter hurdles and mile run), Eastern Michigan University sent Gloria Ewing and Susan Dudley (440-yard dash and 880-yard run), Central Michigan was represented by Karen Lehman (220-yard dash) and Joan Ludtke (javelin throw), and the University of Michigan was represented by Wonda Powell (880-yard run). The meet featured fifteen events, including the 880-yard relay.[80]

The following year the Association for Intercollegiate Athletics was formed out of the DGWS because of the rapid growth of women's intercollegiate sports during the 1960s. The first AIAW National Intercollegiate Outdoor Championships were held at Eastern Washington State College in Cheney, Washington on May 14–15, 1971.[81] No one from

Michigan, and few athletes from East of the Mississippi River, took part in the meet because of its remote location for these athletes. In 1974 Michigan State University sent six women athletes coached by Jim Bibbs to the meet. Western Michigan University had two javelin throwers in the meet: Marcia Karwas and Paula Nyman. By 1975 there were published entry standards for the AIAW meet.[82]

Detroit Girls Take Charge

Like "Red" Simmons, Hayes Jones, Jim Bibbs, and Richard Ford were early supporters and coaches of girl's track. After the Rome Olympics, Hayes Jones and Jim Bibbs became active coaches in women's track. By 1965 Hayes Jones had become chairman of the AAU women's track and field division.[83] Before becoming track coach at Michigan State, Jim Bibbs coached the Detroit Track Club girls, including such stars as Alfreda Daniels, Majorie Grimmett, and Lynn Smith. Richard Ford coached the Motor City Striders, whose women track stars included Cheryl Gilliam,[84] Delisa Walton, Myra Jones, and Kim Turner.

One of the first champions trained by Hayes Jones and Jim Bibbs was Karen Dennis. Karen was born in Detroit. In the late 1920s her father, Thad Dennis, ran on the same track team as Eddie Tolan, Eugene Beatty, and John W. Lewis.[85] Karen was discovered by Bibbs in the mid-1960s on a summer day at Belle Isle where Karen was participating in the Detroit Youth Games. She beat Bibb's best girl, but was disqualified for running out of her lane. Knowing that Karen was unset, Bibbs found out her first name and went searching for her. She was behind her dad's car crying. Bibbs offered to coach her and she accepted the offer. Karen attended Detroit's Chadsey High School. Because there was no girl's track team at her high school, between the ages of 13 and 18, she competed for the Detroit Track Club. Jim Bibbs coached her to four consecutive national AAU appearances, 1964 through 1967.[86] On July 9–10, 1964 Karen placed third in the 220-yard dash (25.3) and fourth in the 440-yard relay at the National AAU Girls Championships in Hanford, California. In 1965 she placed third in the 640-yard sprint medley relay at the National AAU Indoor Championships [February 19–20, 1965] and fourth in the 880-yard relay at the National AAU Girl's Outdoor Meet in Columbus, Ohio. In 1966 she placed second in the 1,060-yard medley relay at the National AAU Indoor Championships in Albuquerque, New Mexico, and third in the 440-yard relay at the National Outdoor Championships in Fredrick,

Maryland. She ended her competition for the Detroit Track Club on March 4, 1967 with a second place finish in the 220-yard dash (25.3) at the National AAU Indoor Championships in Oakland, CA.[87]

On January 14, 1966 Karen ran in the Motor City International at Cobo Arena in Detroit.[88] On January 21, 1967 Karen was third in the women's 60-yard dash (6.08) at the National Association of Intercollegiate Athletics (NAIA) Indoor Championships in Kansas City. Jim Bibbs was the women's track coach for the U.S. Pan-American team in the summer of 1967.[89]

After high school, Karen followed the path of Wilma Rudolph by enrolling at Tennessee State University. In 1968 she ran on the 440 and 880-yard relay teams, set a world record in the 640-yard indoor relay, and placed fifth in the 220 at the Olympic trials.[90] However, she then dropped out of school. She later said, "I was going through a growing up period." She put in a year at Wayne State University, then got pregnant and left her family to go out West. After her daughter Ebony was born in 1972, Karen returned to Detroit for the support of her family.

At the urging of Jim Bibbs, by then track coach at Michigan State, Karen returned to college in 1974. It was not easy. "It was really a struggle trying to run again." Dennis said later. "I think the pounding was just too severe for my feet and as a result I developed tendonitis. The only way to cure it is to just stay off the track, so about the only thing I could do was jog around the grass." By the 1975 outdoor season Dennis had sufficiently healed to win the women's AIAW National Intercollegiate Championship in the 200 meter dash (24.96) at Corvallis, Oregon in June and ease the aches.[91] Karen was named an All-American in the 220-yard dash for 1975. Much of the following year was lost again to injuries; nevertheless, Karen was awarded letters in track at Michigan State University in 1976 and 1977. By 1977 Karen Dennis had adopted the Nicherin Daishonin life philosophy, a form of Buddhism.

Karen Dennis received a B. A. degree in Public Affairs Management in 1977 and a Masters Degree in Physical Education in 1979. In 1977 Karen was named assistant coach for Women's Track and Field at the Michigan State, and was successful in recruiting within the State of Michigan. On September 9, 1981 she was made head coach for Women's Track and Field at MSU. She added cross-country head coaching duties to her responsibilities. At that time she said, "I've been in this program almost since its inception. I took a lot of pride in wearing the green and white, and I hope to instill that pride in the ladies I will be coaching."[92] She was a member of the NCAA Track Coaches Association, and the NCAA Track and Field Committee in 1985.

In 1992 Karen Dennis stated her primary goal as a track coach: "I want to win the nationals and I want to do it while providing more educational opportunities to young people from culturally deprived environments." It was unlikely that Dennis was going to win an NCAA track championship at MSU, that averaged 10 or 11 scholarships a year, while fully funded programs had 16 to spread over 19 outdoor events. Despite that disadvantage, which was most acute in the '80s when there were tight budgets for non-revenue sports, Dennis' program prospered. It was even inspired. In 1990 when the Spartan's women's team finished third in the Big Ten, two fully funded programs finished ahead of her and one behind her program. Of necessity, Karen was forced to focus on certain events, particularly sprints and hurdles. She developed All-Americans Judi Brown-King, Cheryl Gilliam, Odessa Smalls, Mary Shea and Molly Brennan. Karen almost cried every time she thought about leaving, and she did cry when she told her athletes. "I want to think that for some people's lives, I made a difference. That's what it's all about."[93]

Karen was concerned that MSU kept too many "at-risk" girls out of her program. "If we can get the kids into school, I can get them through and out of school, and with their degree of choice. But, I see my kids not able to get in here." Academic standards were getting tougher at MSU, and many student-athletes had to take courses that improved their grades rather than their career expectations. One of her athletes, for example, came to MSU to study nursing, but lacked the grades and studied to become a teacher. "With academic standards here, the kids have to change their goals to match what someone says is their academic ability."[94]

In 1990 the Spartans finished fourth in the Big Ten and Karen was named District IV coach of the year. In 1990 Karen Dennis was named Women's coach for the 1991 Pan American Games in Havana, Cuba.[95] During her 11 seasons at MSU, the women's team finished first in the Big Ten in 1982, second once and third four times. Karen, however, longed for more championships, and did not feel she was given the budget to achieve that goal.

She accepted a position as track coach at the University of Las Vegas. Dennis "was one of five coaches from women's programs to leave Michigan State between June 1992 and June 1993 to pursue other opportunities. For Karen it was the opportunity to be the best. "I like having the kind of budget that a track team needs to become national champion. Here [at UNLV] we have the budget to be contenders on the national level. We have the budget to recruit nationally. We have the budget to travel around the country and face the top teams. At UNLV the administration is committed to having all its sports programs consistently in the Top 20, not just football and men's basketball. I feel I can grow as a coach now that I have a fully funded program with all the resources. Toward the end, I felt stagnant at Michigan State. The way the playing field was set up, it was a great season if we finished third or even in the upper division. I couldn't live with that anymore. . . . [But,] I miss the changing of the seasons."[96]

In her first season she was named Division VIII coach of the year after guiding UNLV to the Big West Conference Championship and the number 17 ranking in the nation. In 1998 Karen was named as one of the U.S. Women's Olympic coaches for year 2000 Olympics. She was finally reaching her goal. She declared, "Making the Olympics is like trying to make it to heaven. Many are called, but few are chosen."[97]

Girl's Interscholastic Track Becomes a Reality in Michigan

The adoption of athletic programs for high school and college women did not occur without a struggle. During the 1970–72 track seasons, several Michigan girls achieved national prominence in women's track and field. Pam Bagian, competing for the Wolverine Track Club and the Wolverine Parkettes, placed third in the one-mile run (5:04.8) at the National AAU Indoor Championships at Madison Square Garden on February 27, 1970. The following year the Wolverine Parkettes placed second in the mile relay at AAU National Indoor Meet at Madison Square Garden. The race walkers Lynn Olson, Jeanne Bocci, and Pam Weigle won national honors, and Lynn Lovat placed fourth in the 3,000-meter run on July 1, 1972 at the National AAU Women's Outdoor Championships in Canton, Ohio. Still, few Michigan schools had interscholastic sports of any kind for girls.

Sue Parks, the daughter of Bob Parks—track coach at Eastern Michigan University and member of the Drake Relays Coaches Hall of Fame, also began to make her mark in 1970–71. Born in 1956 when Bob Parks was an assistant coach at Western Michigan University, Sue took to running early in her life. In 1970–71 she joined the Wolverine Track Club in Ann Arbor and on July 6–7, 1971 placed third in the 880-yard run (2:11.7) at the National AAU Junior Girls Championships in Bakersfield, CA. Two days later, she was part of the Wolverine Track Club relay team that took second in the two-mile relay (9:01.7) at the National AAU Senior Women's Championships. As a result, Sue Parks, who was just entering high school, qualified for the Pan-American Games women's track team.[98] She competed in the high jump at the Pan-American Games from July 30 to August 13, 1971 in Cali, Columbia, and placed seventh, with a jump of 5–3.[99]

In 1971–2 there was no girls' track team at Ypsilanti High School, so when she returned home from the Pan American Games it was hard for Sue to nourish her dream of making the American 1972 Olympic team. In response to Sue's dreams, the Parks family sued the Michigan State High School Athletic Association to permit Sue to run track on the boy's track team. As the lawsuit was being decided, she placed second in the women's mile at the Drake Relays.[100] The Park's family won the lawsuit and issued a court order which forced the State Athletic Board to give Sue and other girls in Michigan an equal opportunity to participate in high school sports.

On Saturday May 6, 1972—just four days after the death of J. Edgar Hoover and a week after the Drake Relays—Sue Parks made history when she ran the anchor leg on Ypsilanti High School's sprint medley relay as a member of the boy's track team at the Howell Relays. Their sprint medley team placed fourth out of nine teams.[101] The following Tuesday she did not fare so well. In a duel meet against Jackson High School at Shadford Field in Ypsilanti. Battling 25 to 30 mile-per-hour headwinds the slender, blond sophomore finished fifth out of five runners in the half-mile, with a slow 2:22 clocking. "I really feel bad," Miss Parks said. "I just didn't run well at all and I let the team down. I know I can do better than this. I've run a 2:10 before."[102]

Her teammate and team captain spoke up for her, after he won the race with a 2:03 clocking. "That wind was awfully tough for her," said Dane Fortney. "It slowed me down too. I'm really glad to have her on the team, though. Even if she doesn't place in a single meet, I think this is a good thing. She has already made a lot of difference in the morale of the team. Some of these guys who didn't really care much before really care much before are really killing themselves now, because they don't want to get beat by a girl. Besides, this could help her in making the Olympic team, too. I think it's a great thing."[103]

Sue did not make the Olympic team in 1972 or any other year. While she qualified for the 1972 Olympic trials held at Frederick, Maryland in both the 800-meter and 1,500-meter runs, she opted to run only in the 1,500-meter. She managed to make it to the finals in that event, but placed ninth with the mediocre time of 4:30.5.[104] She did, however, place second in the 880-yard run (2:17.7) and the high jump, and third in the 440-yard dash at the First Michigan Girls' State High School Championships on May 19, 1973. As a high school senior, Sue placed fifth running against Mary Decker in the Women's 1,000-meter run at the Millrose Games on January 25, 1974 and won the 880-yard-run (2:14.4) at the Second Michigan Girls' High School State Championship on June 1, 1974.[105]

After high school, Sue ran on the Eastern Michigan University women's track team. In 1976 she won the half-mile (2:21.2) at the Western Michigan Indoor Women's Invitational, and placed second in the 400-meter hurdles at the Central Michigan University Invitational, but generally she was not the standout she had been as a teen-ager. In 1977 she placed second in the 880-yard win (2:20.0) and third in the mile relay (4:12.0) at the Michigan State Women's Invitational. On January 28, 1983 Sue set the Finch Fieldhouse record for the 800-meter run (2:13.06) at an Eastern Michigan quadrangular meet at Central Michigan.[106]

During the late 1970s, when Sue Parks was in college, the Central Michigan University Lady Chippewas dominated women's track in the Mid-American Conference.[107] Sue Reimer, from Walled Lake Western, qualified for the AIAW pentathlon in 1978, set a MAC record in the heptathlon, and, as a college senior, participated in 13 events at the 1981 MAC conference outdoor meet. But, she made no real mark on the national women's track and field scene.[108] Likewise, Keela Yount qualified for the 1,500-meter run in the AIAW National Meet in Knoxville in 1978, but was unable to compete in the national championships because Central Michigan University had not budgeted the trip. Keela went on to be three-time women's track coach of the year in the Mid-American Conference, but left no mark on the national scene as an athlete.[109]

Keela Yount coached at Chesaning High School for a year before becoming an assistant track and cross-country coach at the University of Arkansas, where she earned a MS in exercise physiology.[110] In 1984 she was name head coach of the lady harriers at Central Michigan University, a position she held for twelve years.

Sue Parks became to coach cross-country at Huron High School in Ann Arbor, earned a Masters Degree in physical education from Eastern Michigan University, and become an assistant cross-country coach at the University of Michigan.[111] After a stint as assistant cross-country coach at MSU in 1987–8, Sue Parks was appointed Women's Track and Field Coach at Ball State University in Muncie, Indiana. Ms. Park's career reminded some of the Helen Reddy song, issued by Capital Records in 1973, "I am Woman, I can do anything."

Debbie Odden and Sue Latter were contemporaries of Sue Parks. Debbie and Sue Latter also participated in Michigan's first high school girl's track championship on May 19, 1973. Debbie was a senior at Oak Park High School in 1973. She was Northwest Suburban League champion in the 100-yard dash, long jump, and 440-yard relay. She placed second in the State Regional Meet and fourth in the State Meet in the long jump. Debbie went on to compete in track and field at Eastern Michigan University in the 220-yard dash and the broad jump. Each year she qualified for the AIAW national meet, but because of a lack of funds for women's track was unable to compete in the national championships until 1976 when she went to Manhattan, KS.[112]

At the first Michigan high school girls' track and field championships in 1973, a total of 359 girls from 117 Lower Peninsula schools took part. The Lincoln Park High School girls' team won the State Championship, and Walled Lake Western High School placed a close second. Sue Parks, the only girl entered by Ypsilanti High School, scored 20 points to earn fifth place at the meet for her school. Sue finished second in both the 880 and the high jump, and placed third in the 440-yard dash. Sue Latter of Clarkston also was an outstanding performer at Michigan's first girls' high school track championship. Miss Latter won the 880-yard run (2:17.7) and the 440-yard dash (51.7).[113] Sue Latter ran as an exhibition runner with the Clarkston boys' team in 1973 before winning the two state championships.[114]

Sue Latter was born to Fred and Katie Latter in 1957 and grew up in Independence Township near Clarkston, Michigan. In 1974, as in 1973, Clarkston High School had no girl's track team, so the four girls who went out for track at Clarkston High School in 1974 were placed on the boy's eligibility list. They ran as exhibition or non-scoring runners in some early meets, but did not compete as boys. Nevertheless, in mid-May 1974 Sue Latter was declared ineligible for the girl's regional meet by her High School principal and Allen Bush, the Executive Director of the Michigan High School Athletic Association, because she had been on the boy's eligibility list.[115] The decision was quietly reversed only after Frank Crowell, the Madison Heights Regional Meet manager, allowed Miss Latter to run and was backed by pressure from the *Oakland Press*. Miss Latter went on to place second in the 100-yard dash

(11.1) and the 220-yard dash (25.1) at the Girls High School Regional Meet in Madison Heights.[116] On June 1 she placed second in the 100-yard dash (11.3) and the 220-yard dash (25.2) at the Class A and B State Girls High School Champion-ship.[117] Sue Latter was named to the All-Oakland County track team in 1974.[118]

Sue graduated from Clarkston High School in 1974, and attended Michigan State University, where she obtained a Master's Degree in athletic administration. She won the 880-yard run (2:08.2) at the MSU Women's Invitational on May 7, 1977.[119] On June 9–11 Sue Latter won the 800-meter run (2:03.8) at the second combined men and women's AAU National Championships at UCLA. She was an All-American in the 800-meter run that year, and on September 2–4 placed fifth in the 800-meter run (2:05.0) at the first track and field World Cup Championships in Duesseldorf, West Germany. On January 21, 1978, Sue Latter set the MSU all-time performance record for the 1,000-meter run (2:52.10).[120]

She married a competitive runner, Ron Addison, who was three years older. Ron became a track and field promoter for the Nike Shoe Company, and they moved to Eugene, where Sue ran with the Athletics Club. "I never ran more than 70 miles a week and that was in the fall and winter. In the spring, I work more on speed and cut down to about 50 miles a week." The base work from the year before held over. In 1983 she won the 800-meter run (2:03.75) at the Drake Relays.[121]

In the track and field events for the United States Olympic team, trials are held to determine who makes the team. In this one-time elimination, bad luck or an off day can keep a premier athlete off the team. In the semifinal round of the 1,500-meter U.S. Olympic trials on June 22, 1984, Sue ran her personal best time (4:09) and qualified for the finals the following day. Her strategy for Sunday June 23 was stay with Mary Decker as long as she could. "If I die, I die, . . . when Gina (Jacobs) went with her I figured I might as well as well go along." Sue Addison closely followed American record holder Mary Decker and 1,500-meter favorite around the track for the second day. Addison, and everyone else, conceded the first two middle-distant running places on the Olympic team to Decker and Kim Gallagher, but Sue felt sure that she could get the third spot on the team.[122]

Sue Addison missed her chance to compete in the Olympic 1,500-meter run by a half a second. Addison was accidentally bumped from behind, 300-meters from the finish line, lost momentum and finished fifth. The top three in the final heat make the Olympic team. "I knew going into the race, Mary [Decker, her running partner at Nike West, who won the race] would not race the 1,500 in the games, so I knew fourth place would be good enough. I guess it wasn't meant to be. You can't sit around and be bitter. I can't say I was tripped. Of course I was disappointed, I cried for days after missing out."[123]

Congress Votes Equality for Women's Sports, But Women Lose Control of Women's Track

Before President Richard Nixon signed Title IX of the Education Amendments of 1972 prohibiting sexual discrimination in educational programs receiving federal funds, men were given preferential considerations for college admissions, scholarships, and loans. Women made up only 6 percent of students in professional schools, such as medicine, law, dental, and business-schools, and women held fewer than 20% faculty positions at co-educational colleges and universities. But, the most contentious area covered by Title IX was high school and college athletics. In 1972 financial support for female student-athletes was virtually non-existent and few high schools in Michigan, or elsewhere, offered girl's interscholastic track as a sport. Just five years earlier, the circus atmosphere created by the 55 year old tennis hustler Bobby Riggs, who enticed over 7,000 people to watch him play tennis against Margaret Court, had focused national attention on women's sports.[124]

The enactment of Title IX of the Federal Amendments to the Education Acts of 1972 significantly altered college athletics. Starting in 1970, the Association of Intercollegiate Athletics for Women (AIAW) staked itself out as the governing body for intercollegiate women's athletics. Despite limitations, academic women controlled the AIAW. Historically, the women's physical education department had controlled women's sports at the University level. Title IX would inevitably change the balance of power in women's sports. While Title IX allowed women leaders to demand greater resources and facilities for their programs, it also exposed them to competition from athletic departments that had more money and were controlled by men with a different philosophy of sports. For example, the AIAW prohibited athletic scholarships for women on the grounds that athletic scholarships commercialized sports and diminished the educational context women's physical education departments considered essential to intercollegiate sports.

Female athletes and their coaches did not universally accept the AIAW's position on athletic scholarships. Fern Kellmeyer, a physical education teacher and women's tennis coach at Marymont College, was one of those who challenged the AIAW and its "educational model" of intercollegiate competitive sports for women. In February 1973 she and others instituted a lawsuit against the NEA and the AIAW challenging their rule against athletic scholarships for women on the grounds that it was discriminatory. Her lawsuit, Kellmeyer, et al. vs. NEA, et al. was filed in the Federal Southern District in Florida.

In March 1973, when lawyers for the NEA brought the facts of the case before the AIAW Board of Directors, it was clear that their rule prohibiting athletic scholarships was untenable and must be dropped. In April the AIAW altered the discriminatory aspects of their rules.[125] The University of Miami in Coral Gables was one of the first "big-time sports colleges" to respond. In May 1973 that Florida institution awarded five athletic scholarships to women, and set aside ten more athletic scholarships for female, freshman athletes.[126]

The capitulation of the AIAW on athletic-scholarships opened the door to competition from the NCAA that favored the latter. Athletic-scholarships are generally financed by income from revenue producing sports. In the 1970s there were no women's sports that produced enough revenue to support their own cost of operation, much less show the profit needed for women's athletic scholarships. On the other hand, men's college football and basketball, along with the alumni endowments they generated, offered a substantial financial pool from which to draw. The male dominated NCAA, with its "commercial model" for intercollegiate sports, had been steadily winning the battle against the AAU within intercollegiate circles since 1921.

Within a decade the NCAA virtually annihilated the AIAW and women's control over women's intercollegiate sports. In a lawsuit initiated by the AIAW against the NCAA alleging that the NCAA diverted funds from men's sports to support women's intercollegiate athletics and thereby engaged in unfair competitive practices, the NCAA denied the charge. Yet, Don Canham gives credence to the AWAW charges by stating that men's revenue sports [football, basketball, and hockey] were asked to underwrite not only men's non-revenue sports but women's sports as well.[127]

On the eve of new regulations covering the distribution of funds to women's athletics in schools receiving Federal funds, the distribution was far from equitable. Susan A. Hager, Director of Women's Competitive Sports at Bowling Green University in Ohio complained, "we receive no grant-in-aid scholarships for female athletes, we have no money for recruiting, we are not allowed to charge admission to our events, and we have no whirlpool machines or other equipment of that kind. I believe the women on this campus deserve a better shake than they've gotten in the past."[128] What was true at Bowling Green was true all across Michigan and every other state in the union.

On February 28, 1975, Casper Weinberger, Secretary of Health, Education and Welfare, sent President Ford regulations, known as Title IX. These regulations were designed to create equal opportunities in college sports for men and women, while allowing schools and colleges flexibility in determining how best to provide such opportunities.[129] During a three-month period of review and comment, women's groups called the guidelines weak, while the NCAA called them too strong and a threat to major college sports.[130] Perhaps, they were the best politics would allow. President Ford signed the controversial anti-discrimination rules.

In 1976 some colleges and universities began the process of merging the management of men and women's intercollegiate sports.[131] On the afternoon of April 27, 1978 the effects of Title IX became apparent at the Penn Relays. While women had competed at the Relays since 1924, they had never before commanded a full afternoon for themselves. The stands were nearly empty on that raw, rainy afternoon.[132] Before long, Wayne State University and Cleveland State University were among the colleges that eliminated men and women's track from their athletic programs.[133] Ironically, support for track and field was declining at the very time that jogging was becoming one of the popular activities in the nation.[134]

It Was Not Easy To Get Men To Treat Women Equally

The University of Michigan Athletic Department began managing women's sports in 1973, but women's track and field was not instituted at the U of M until 1976. Even more amazing than their tardy entrance into women's track was the bitter fight at Michigan over whether or not to award female athletes the same "Block M" letter for women as was awarded to men for outstanding athletic performance.

From the time that it became inevitable that Title IX would force the University of Michigan to consider starting a women's track program, there was active opposition to women's intercollegiate sports being funded through the athletic department. The Alumni "M" Club President, William M. Mazer, Jr., with the tacit support of the male-dominated U of M Athletic Department, fought women's intercollegiate sports at every turn. Mazer wrote a letter to graduate alumni M club members stating, "I am sure you will realize how serious it would be for the yellow M to be awarded for synchronized swimming, softball and so forth. It would make the award worthless, in my opinion and obviously in the opinion of some of the coaches. . . ." Supportive letters from Football Coach Bo Schembechler and Head basketball coach John Orr were attached to his letter. Calling the Graduate M Club "a private organization," Mazer refused to answer questions from reporters.[135]

Women's athletic director Marie C. Hartwig was not silent. She said, "We can't believe they're doing it." The women's intercollegiate teams at the University of Michigan included field hockey, tennis, basketball, volleyball, competitive swimming and synchronized swimming. The debate became so heated that the issue was tabled at the April 1975 meeting of the 18-member Board in Control of Intercollegiate Athletics at the University.[136]

Women were finally awarded varsity letters in 1976, but the letters awarded to women were smaller and looked different than the varsity letters awarded to men. Moreover, women were not allowed membership in the M Club, an honorary organization for varsity letter-winners established in 1913, until 1993.[137]

Not only did University of Michigan athletic officials, lead by Bo Schembechler and Don Canham, seek to deny women the Block M athletic award and access to the M Club, but more importantly athletic scholarships. The National Organization for Women observed that the University of Michigan offered $700,000 in athletic scholarships to men and none to women. U of M President, Robben Fleming, said, "The main problem is where the money is coming from, whether from current revenue, new revenue, or men's athletic revenues." At the core of the problem was the men's athletic department's refusal to share money raised mostly from the school's football and basketball programs.[138]

From 1973 until 1981 women's sports at the University of Michigan were under the umbrella of the AIWA. It 1981 female athletes began to conduct championship competition in the NCAA. When women's events were combined into the NCAA indoor track and Field Championships, according to Don Canham "it doubled the size of the meet and reduced fan interest." When they moved the meet from Detroit after the 1985 meet at the Silverdome, it was unable to generate equal fan support elsewhere. The sponsorship of the *Detroit News* was critical to the popular success of the meet.[139] However, it is clear that his opposition to women's sports colored Canham's view.

By 1985, the University of Michigan athletic department came to support more than 20 different women's teams and spent $2 million a year on sports for women. At that time, women's sports at the University had almost no income. According to some, this situation increased pressure on men's football, basketball, and hockey programs to win at any cost to earn the income needed to carry the non-revenue producing sports. The reality was different. Despite tax-exempt status, donations, and state-support, athletic departments were rarely self-supporting and revenue sports never fully supported minor men's sports, much less women's sports.[140]

The invention of the sports bra was symbolic of the changes taking place. In the late 1970s two enterprising women sewed a pair of male jockstraps together to make the first spots bra. Twenty years later the marketplace was full of sports bras.[141]

The lady Chippewas at Central Michigan University functioned as a track club, independent of the intercollegiate varsity athletic program, from 1965 until 1974. Central Michigan nearly always had more women enrolled than men,[142] and consequently, in the years before athletic scholarships for women, had a larger pool of possible recruits than most rivals. Even after acceptance as a varsity sport, as late as March 1978, Central Michigan University did not recruit or offer athletic scholarships to female athletes for varsity sports. Fourteen track scholarships for women were allotted the first time at CMU in March 1978 for the 1978–79 academic year.[143] The path to equal treatment at the Mount Pleasant campus had already been a long one, despite the majority status of women at that University.

The transition that integrated men and women's track had not yet started in 1981, when women were officially affiliated with the Mid-American Conference. From 1946 until the 1980–81 academic year the Mid-American Conference was a men's only club. The decision to allow women to affiliate with the conference was finally made on May 17, 1980.[144] In 1981, the Men's MAC Outdoor Championship was held in Muncie and the Women's Outdoor was held the same week-end in Kalamazoo.[145] In 1984 the MAC men's and women's outdoor track Championships were still being held at different locations. The men's meet was held at Kent, Ohio and the women's meet at Ypsilanti.[146] However, some joint men and women's track meets were being scheduled in the MAC.[147] Women were included in the NCAA Men's Indoor Meet for the first time in March 1983.[148] The Big Ten men's and women's outdoor track meet also was held together for the first time in 1983.[149]

When asked for his reaction to the incorporation of women into the men's NCAA indoor meet, Southern California's an assistant track coach Ken Matsuda responded, "If they add to the meet and don't just detract from men's opportunities, fine. I don't think women's track has paid the price to be ready for this level of competition. . . . But, I think we have to accept the fact that it's here."[150] The track at the Silverdome was enlarged by three inches on the curves, to reassure runners rather than give them more room. A second runway was introduced so that women's and men's long jumping events could proceed simultaneously.[151] Races were scheduled every 10 minutes—barely time to introduce the runners, shooting the starter's gun and hustle them off the track to get ready for the next race. Meanwhile, two or three jumping and throwing events were under way constantly next to the track. The Silverdome was a busy and colorful sight.[152]

20. The Flowering of Women's Track in Michigan

Deby Lansky was born April 3, 1953 in Trenton, Michigan. She was the third of five children, and came from a very athletic family. Her father, Art Lansky, had been a Golden Gloves Champion nicknamed "Killer" Lansky. Two of her three brothers, John and Ron, played college sports. One played baseball at Eastern Michigan University and the other played football and hockey at MSU.[1] In 1967, when Deby was 14, her father noticed that she was a good sprinter and called around to several track clubs before signing her up with the Lincoln Park-Parkettes. After trying several different events, she discovered that she had a natural talent as a hurdler. She was good enough to try out for the 1968 Olympic team.[2]

Deby graduated from Taylor Center High School in June 1971.[3] She attended Eastern Michigan University in the fall of 1971, where she later met senior middle-distance runner, Fred La Plante from Toledo, Ohio. In the spring of 1972, Fred was running on a distance medley relay team that set the Drake Relays record and he placed in the mile run at NAIA National Championships. Deby and Fred began dating, but their mutual interest in track had nothing to do with the relationship at that time. Furthermore, Eastern Michigan did not yet have a formal women's track team, although an informal duel meet was held Eastern and Central Michigan women on March 23, 1972 in which Debbie and Sue Parks participated.[4]

In 1972 Deby again qualified for the Olympic trials. This time they were held in Frederick, Maryland on the Governor Thomas Johnson High School track. Deby was one of the three top seeds in the 100-meter hurdles, and appeared to have a solid chance of making the Olympic team. Instead, fourteen seconds after the gun went off starting the third heat at about 8 p.m. on Friday night July 7, she was depressed and dejected. She had placed ninth out of 14 hurdlers, and last in her heat.[5] Lacy O'Neal, a Washington, D.C. teacher who had dropped-out of track after failing to make the 1964 Olympic team, had tied the American record in the 100-meter hurdles with a 13.1 clocking in the heat Deby was expected to win.[6] Deby later said,

> I was so discouraged that I didn't get out of my heats, that when I got back to Taylor, I didn't want to do anything. . . . I hated track. I had no coach at the time. Nobody to push me. So I quit. Later I met Fred [La Plante]. At first we dated, then he was my coach and then he was my husband. . . . There are no problems with him coaching me.[7]

Deby rose to national prominence in track and field by a far different route than most women. Her route to success was not through intercollegiate track and field but open competition engineered, in large measure, by Deby and her husband, Fred.

After graduating from Eastern Michigan, Fred decided to move to Santa Barbara, California and try his hand at running on the track circuit. Once in California, he persuaded Deby to come out to California too with the expectation that Gary Powers would coach her. However, Powers took off before Deby reached Santa Barbara in April 1973, and Fred, who had always wanted to be a track coach, found himself coaching Ms. Lansky. The first meet Deby entered in California was the Mount Sac Relays. Before Deby tripped and fell on the sixth hurdle, she was very competitive. On the advice of one of the other coaches, Fred called Dick Hall at San Diego State University and made an appointment to spend a half a day with him picking up pointers on coaching the high-hurdles. That session proved to be very helpful.[8]

According to Fred, "Deby did not have great speed, but she was a good all-around athlete, a great technician of the art of hurdling, and was a fearless competitor. While she hated to practice and often tried to avoid training, she like playing the game and loved beating others in a competitive situation." The challenge for Fred was to find creative ways to get Deby to work out.

In 1974 Fred and Deby got married. They moved to Taylor, Michigan and Fred returned to Eastern Michigan University to study for a Masters Degree and work as an assistant track coach. The following year, Fred took a job as a middle school teacher and track coach. During this time he continued to coach Deby, who was working at the Detroit Metropolitan Airport. They held workouts with Hasley Crawford at the University of Michigan track in the evening when the track was not being used by their team. Since there was no underwriting available, it was difficult for Deby to enter meets, as they did not have the entrance fees or the money for travel. It was impossible for Fred to accompany her to meets. Nevertheless, Deby placed second in the national indoor championships, and was an alternate to the USA vs. USSR duel meet. The lack of recognition after placing second in the nationals fueled a desire to "show them she belonged." Deby placed fourth in the national outdoor championships that year.

Deby was very shy, but was strongly motivated. She got a rush from winning, and took competition personally. When she was running, she disliked her competitors. Fred had overcome being 33rd on a 33-man squad, to hold national meet records. While rarely the best, he was a winner. He ran the mile in 4:06 and the 880 in 1:59. Not world class, but very good. With average talent, he had to learn more than most to do so well.

In 1975 Deby won a silver medal in the 100-meter hurdles at the Pan-American Games in Mexico City. In February 1976, the 22-year old, curly-haired La Plante placed second in the Amateur Athletic Union indoor championships at Madison Square Garden. In May 1976, she was considered a very good bet to make the American Olympic track team for the twenty-first Olympiad in Montreal.[9] She did indeed make the U.S. Olympic team and ran in the semi-finals of the 100-meter hurdles at the Montreal Olympics.

In 1977, as a result of the failure of a school bond issue, Fred lost his teaching job in Taylor. That September, Fred and Deby moved to New York City, where Fred took a coaching job in track at Columbia University. Deby began running for the D.C. Striders. When she set a world record at the National AAU Indoor Championships on February 24, 1978, Deby was awarded the *Redbook* Trophy as the outstanding female performer.[10]

The following year Fred took a position as women's track coach at San Diego State University. At the age of 26 Deby enrolled at San Diego State. On May 26, 1979 she placed second to Ohio State University's Stephanie Hightower in the 100-meter hurdles at the AIAW Outdoor Championships held at Michigan State University. She was named to the college All-American team for her effort.[11] In Walnut, California on June 15–17, 1979, Deby set the American record for the 100-meter-hurdles (12.86) at the last national AAU Outdoor Championships ever held. Since 1923 the AAU had claimed to be the governing body for women's track.[12] Deby won the 100-meter hurdles at the Pan American Games in San Juan, Puerto Rico held July 1–15 and ran at the World Cup Championships held in Montreal on August 25–26. Her victories gained her a sponsorship from Adidas.

Deby came into the 1980 track season with high hopes of winning a medal at the up-coming Moscow Olympics. On May 24, 1980 she placed second to Ohio State University's Stephanie Hightower in the 100-meter hurdles at the AIAW Outdoor Championships in Eugene.[13] Despite a broken bone in her foot, she was on course for a medal in the Olympic Games. ABC scheduled Deby and Fred for an "Up-Close and Personal" segment. The filming caused friction when the TV crew demanded footage that distorted Fred's coaching style. These tensions heighten when President Carter called for a boycott of the Olympic Games. Deby felt her chance at an Olympic medal slipping away. She was 27 years old, and at her running peak. The 1984 Olympics would be too late for her. Stephanie Hightower was already challenging her. In the meaningless 1980 Olympic trials in Eugene, Deby tripped on a hurdle and separated her shoulder. The video picture of her fall was featured for several years on "the agony of defeat" images that frequently prefaced ABC sports events. Deby seriously considered giving up track for good.

When Deby decided to film the movie *Personal Best*, the relationship between her and Fred floundered and failed. Fred became head women's track coach at the University of Southern California, and later became the assistant men's track coach at the University of Michigan. Deby remarried. Now Deby Smith, she made a comeback in the women's hurdles after a layoff of three and one-half years. She won the 60-yard hurdles at the Sunkist Invitational in 7.54, only three-tenths of a second shy of her personal best.[14] She, however, failed to make the finals of the 1980 Olympic trials. At the turn of the century she was married to Bob Sweezey, had raised two children, and lived in West-chester, California.

Other Pioneers

Western Michigan University did not initiate women's varsity track and field until 1974. The first notable, female track-athlete at Western was Marcia Karwas from Pontiac, who was in the first group of track-women at the school. Marcia set the school's record in the javelin throw (193 feet 10 inches) and qualified for the national AIAW meet every year she was at Western.[15] As a college senior, she won the javelin throw and placed third in the discus and shot put at the Eastern Illinois University Invitational in Charleston.[16] She did not, however, achieve All-American status.

Western did not produce an All-American until Kay Barstow achieved that honor with a fifth place finish in the high jump in the

1979 AIAW Championships.[17] Kay prepped at Kalamazoo Central, where she won the Regional High School high jump championship with a 5–4 jump.[18] She qualified for the national championships in 1977 by winning the Eastern Illinois University Invitational with a jump of 5–6.[19] She still held the WMU indoor record for the high jump (5–9) 21 years later.

Some pioneers in women's track never made it big, but still made a contribution to the progress of the sport. Debbie Romsek from Concord, Michigan was the Girl's Class C-D State Champion in the 440 in 1975 was member of an outstanding mile-relay team at Bowling Green University.[20] In 1976 Debbie Romsek qualified for the AIAW Track and Field Championships held at Kansas State University, Manhattan, Kansas, and ran the 800-meter at the AIAW National Meet held May 26, 1978 in Knoxville.[21]

A Distance Runner Makes Her Mark

In June 1969 a seven year old Delisa Walton ran into the street and was hit by a car. She was rushed to the hospital with a broken right hip. "My hip was as big as my thigh," Delisa recalled. "They had to stretch it and put it in a slot—talk about pain. They put me in a cast from my toes to my chest. I was in it for two months. I couldn't even sit up. Then when I got out of that my appendix burst." But, according to Delisa, the worst was yet to come. When fall rolled around she was on crutches and was sent to a school for crippled children. "I cried everyday I went to that school," Delisa remembered. According to her doctor, Delisa could have been crippled for life. "At first the doctor said I might need a pin in my leg. Then he said I would walk with a limp forever. I told the doctor there was no way I was going back to that school. He said I could go to regular school on a trial basis. I broke my crutches on a sewer and tried walking without them. I guess I was hardheaded. The doctor said, "You're a very determined young lady." I was determined then and that's how I am now—determined to win. Later, Walton said, "I always wanted to be in the Olympics. I used to do my little therapy exercises and read Wilma Rudolph's book. She was a cripple and she overcame it. I knew I could do the same thing."[22]

Delisa started running for the Motor City Track Club at the age of 13. Between 1975 and 1979 Delisa spent most of her spare time running for the Track Club. Richard Ford, who had turned out a number of outstanding female track stars, was the coach of the club and he fed her dreams.[23] By the time she was a junior at Detroit's Mackenzie High

School in 1978, Delisa was already a mature runner with the grace of a gazelle. She was 5–7 and weighted 125 pounds, when she won the State Class A State High School 440-yard dash and the 880-yard run championships and was named to the All-State team.[24] Her winning time in the 880 was an amazing 2:09.7. However, she was a disappointing fourth in the Junior Nationals in Bloomington, Indiana.

The following year Delisa explained, "Last year when I came up against good competition I just froze. By being nervous and scared I got so tired. Running against women is a lot different than running against high school girls. I have to plan my race because there's a lot of pushing and shoving. As a senior in high school she finished sixth in the AAU national championships in Madison Square Garden. "It was hard even qualifying for the finals. I had to run just as hard in the heats as I did in the finals. Even if I finished last I knew I was the eighth best in the country. I was petrified, but I didn't want to be left too far behind." Increasingly she combines both speed and endurance. According to the *Detroit Free Press*, "She has All-American looks and an all-world smile."[25]

The April 1979 issue of *Seventeen Magazine* contained a four-page story on Delisa. The pictures were taken in late December 1978, when they asked her to come to New York for three days. January 3 they cut her hair. "I hated it. They said they were going to cut this much off [she said holding her fingers a half-inch apart]. When I looked up I was bald-headed. I was ready to pack up and come home. But they took me out to dinner at an expensive restaurant and I kind of forgot about it."[26]

Even before winning the Detroit Public League Championship and the State Girl's Class A Championship in the 440 and 880 for a second straight year, Delisa signed a letter of commitment to the University of Tennessee. A Detroit daily newspaper observed: "Walton's looks and bubbly personality will come in handy when she majors in communications at [the University] Tennessee. She says she would like to get into sports broadcasting. . . ."[27]

The Intercollegiate athletic program for women at the University of Tennessee, including their indoor and outdoor track program, officially began during the 1976–77 academic year. Delisa Walton made an almost immediate impact for the lady Volunteers. In May 22, 1980 she won the 800-meter run (2:04.88) and the 800-meter medley relay at the AIAW Outdoor Championships, Eugene and on June 14 she placed 7th in the 800-meter run (2:20.83) at the Athletic Congress Championships in Walnut, CA. She also qualified for the semifinals of the 800-

meter run (2:05.06) at the Olympic tryouts in Eugene on June 21, 1980. On June 22 she placed third in her semifinal heat (2:04.14) and on June 24 placed fourth in the 800-meter run in the finals of the Olympic Tryouts.[28] While she missed making the team, the boycott of the Moscow Olympics took much of the sting out of the failure.

The following March 1981 she won the 600-meter run at the AIAW Indoor Championships in Pocatello, Idaho. Her impact on Tennessee track continued. On May 16 she won the 400-meter run and the 800-meter medley relay at the Southeast Conference Outdoor Championships in Knoxville. On May 30 she was on the winning 1600-meter relay (3:31.70) and placed second in the 800-meter run (2:08.37) at the AIAW Outdoor Championships in Austin, Texas.[29]

At the University of Tennessee, Delisa Walton became the best friend of future Olympic gold-medalist Benita Fitzgerald. Benita was a 100-meter hurdler from Dale City, VA who was majoring in Industrial Engineering. Benita had unsuccessfully tried gymnastics, softball, and playing the violin before finding her niche in track. Later, after spending some time as an industrial engineer, Benita would become director of the United States Colorado Springs Olympic Training Center and oversee all the other U.S. Olympic Training Centers. During their sophomore and junior years in college, Delisa and Benita roomed together. Both married before their last year of college competition. Benita was the second American woman and the first African-American woman to win an Olympic gold medal in track.[30]

As a junior in college, Delisa Walton toppled the collegiate, American, and world record in the 600-yard run with a time of 1:17.38 at the AIAW National indoor championship.[31]

During the summer of 1982 she married Stanley Floyd. Stan was a sprinter, who had just graduated from the University of Tennessee. He had made the 1980 Olympic team, only to miss the Olympics because of the American boycott. In 1983 Stanley Floyd ran for Tiger International. He took fifth in the 60-yard dash and second in the one-mile club relay in the Millrose Games on January 28, 1983.[32]

In February 12, 1983 Delisa won the 800-meter run (2:03.24) at the Vitalis/U.S. Olympic Indoor Invitational Meet at the Meadowlands Arena in East Rutherford, NJ. A few days later on February 25 she won the 880-yard run (203.10) at the U.S.A./Mobil Indoor Championships at Madison Square Garden. At the NCAA Indoor Championships at the Pontiac Silverdome on March 11–12, Delisa Walton Floyd said it was both exciting and worrying to come home and run before her neighbors in Detroit. She told reporters:

It felt really good to be here. But it also was a lot of pressure. I felt like I had to run well. But once the races started, I didn't think about that anymore. [Most of her competition at Tennessee this year has been in major invitational meets, in which her husband, sprinter Stanley Floyd, also runs.] It's nice to run without him being at the same meet. 'Stanley's races usually come earlier than mine. If he doesn't do well, then I feel like I have to make up for it. And if he runs well, I feel like I have to do just as well.[33]

This was the first time Delisa had run in Detroit since high school in the spring of 1979. She won the 600-yard run (1:12.21) and anchored the University of Tennessee mile-relay team to a world record (3:37.08). Delisa ran the fastest leg of the record setting mile relay, 52.9 seconds for the 440. The mile-relay race was so fast that even the third place Morgan State team broke the American record.[34]

Delisa Walton Floyd was an All-American at Tennessee in each year of competition from 1980 through 1983, and continued to run after graduation. Payment for track competition was just opening up, and Delisa could earn $1,000 to $2,000 for an American meet, but was paid up to $25,000 for a meet in Europe.[35] On June 17, 1984 she was fifth in the first heat of the semifinals of the 800-meter run (2:00.94) at the Olympic trials in Los Angeles, and failed to make the Olympics.

Despite the disappointment, Delisa continued to run competitively. On June 27, 1987 she placed second in the 800-meter run (1:59.20) at the USA/Mobil Outdoor Championships in San Jose, California. In 1988 Delisa finally became an Olympian. On July 19, 1988 she placed second in the finals of the 800-meter run (1:59.20) at the U.S. Olympic trials in Indianapolis. In Seoul, Korea she was fifth in the 800.[36]

On August 29, 1991 Delisa Floyd, the 30-year old two-time national champion at 800-meters champion—now living in Houston, Texas— became the first athlete to fail a drug test at the World Championships in Tokyo. Officials of the International Amateur Athletic Federation announced that Floyd's urine sample, taken after the semifinals on Sunday August 25 by random selection, had traces of amphetamines, a banned substance. Floyd finished last in her race. She was suspended for four years, effectively ending her track career. She left Tokyo to return to the USA immediately after being confronted. Stanley, her husband, said she was stunned by the test, and that she had taken no banned substances.[37]

Delisa appealed her four-year suspension complaining that the United States Olympic Committee's own drug hotline had assured her that she was taking a harmless carbohydrate supplement not on any prohibited substances list. Track's world governing body did not buy the story and turned down her appeal on May 31, 1992. A few days later she filed suit in Federal Court seeking to force the IOC. to lift the suspension and allow her to participate in the 1992 summer Olympics.[38] Her claim that she was taking a carbohydrate supplement that turned out to have "amphetamine qualities,"[39] also lost on appeal.

Stanley and Delisa continued to live in Houston, Texas for the balance of the century.

The University of Michigan's First Woman All-American Distance Runner

Suzanne "Sue" Frederick, Ann Arbor Huron High School class of 1979, was second to Delisa Walton in the Girls Class A High School 880-yard run in 1979. While Delisa Walton rose quickly to national prominence as a middle-distance runner, Sue Frederick was less than outstanding in her first two years at the University of Michigan. She did not obtain a national ranking until the spring of 1982, just before she married Mark Foster. On May 29, she placed third in the 1,500-meter run at the AIAW Outdoor Championships at Texas A & M. That fall she came under the tutelage of Coach Francie Kraker Goodridge, and the following track season Sue Frederick Foster became a force in Big Ten distance-running.[40]

In the spring of 1983 Sue wrote,

I am a senior student in the School of Education majoring in Leisure Studies with emphasis on Adult Fitness. Currently, I teach an internship in aerobic dance classes at the University of Michigan Dearborn Campus. I am also assisting in research on strength and movement limitations in quadriplegics who are interested in competitive rowing. I have a 3.4 grade average. My grades have improved over the past two years. My teammates voted me the co-captain of the track and field team. Prior to the Indoor Big Ten Championships I organized and held a potluck dinner at my house to help develop a strong team network. I budget my time to fit in two runs a day, school, and my husband. I also train during the summer. I am involved in ADARA, a campus-wide interactive society for leaders from various groups and organizations.[41]

Goodridge was a major factor in Foster's emergence as a track star. "When I first started coaching her I admired her," said Goodridge, a two-time Olympian. "If she was one of my competitors, she would have scared me because of the kind of pace she can carry." Under Kraker's guidance, Foster cut her time in the 1,500-meter run in 1983 from 4:29.00 to 4:11.50." Sue Foster won the 1,500-meter run (4:19.94) at the 1983 Big Ten Outdoor Championships in West Lafayette. This was followed by a striking performance at the Athletic Conference meet in October where Foster shattered (4:11.50) the 4:17.00 mark needed to qualify for the Olympic trials. When she graduated, Sue Foster held five, individual University of Michigan women's varsity track records.

"Suzanne Foster is so quiet and steady and consistent that it is possible to take her for granted. I wish that I could recycle Sue every four years because I don't know what I'll do without her! In my recruiting I am looking for young women who can match her character, determination, and excellence, and so her fine example continues," said coach Kraker.[42]

After Sue graduated in December 1983, she was ranked the fifth fastest for the metric-mile in USA. Just before her race for the NCAA 1,500-meter indoor championship in 1994, Foster recalls, "I was very confident until 15 minutes before the race. But by the time I got to the starting line I was almost ready to cry." Foster finished fourth. According to Coach John Goodridge, "That was the first race that Sue actually had a chance to win—for the first time she was a contender." Francie Kraker added, "She had moved into the big time so quickly after the Big Tens that she was not as experienced as some of the other girls. Experience will be a major hurdle for Foster, due to her rapid climb to the top. Experience counts a lot in the Olympics, but sometimes freshness counts even more. This could be an advantage for Sue. The emotional part may be her biggest problem. You can be as good as anyone else physically but psyche your self out." "It takes a lot of the pressure off already having qualified for the trials," said Foster. Sue trained daily for the Olympic trials. "Making the Olympics is a goal I've set for myself. If I don't it won't be the end of the world, but, I have a good shot at it if things go right."[43] Sue Foster did not make the Olympic team, but she did become women's cross-country coach at the University of Michigan in 1987.[44]

Michigan State University Star Loses in the Boycott

Diane Williams lettered at MSU in 1980. That year, on May 23, she placed fourth in the 100-meter dash (11.32) at the AIAW National Outdoor Championships at Hayward Field in Eugene, setting the MSU Women's Track team record for the 100-meter dash in the process. This qualified her for the Olympic tryouts.[45] On June 23 she placed sixth in the 100-meter dash (11.61) and was named to the 1980 United States Olympic team as a part of the 4 by 100-meter relay team.[46] However, when President Carter cancelled U.S. participation in the 1980 Moscow Olympics because of the Soviet invasion of Afghanistan, she lost her only opportunity to be an Olympian.

Ann Pewe, who was attending Michigan State University, won the 1,000-yard run and placed second in the mile run in a triangular meet with the U of M and CMU in early January 1981. In early April she placed third in the 1,500-meter run (4:35.7) at the Fifth Annual Western Michigan University Invitational, giving notice that she was a promising middle-distance runner.[47] In 1982 she anchored the winning 4 × 800-meter relay (8:47.2) and placed fourth in the 1,500-meter run (4:25.31) at the Drake Relays.[48] Finally, in June 1982 Ann earned All-American honors in the 3-K run.[49]

Eastern Michigan Builds a Women's Track Team

The addition of athletes like Ann Meachum did much to build the women's track program at Eastern Michigan University. Ann Meachum [Lohner] a long jumper; and sprinter (55-meter dash; 55-meter hurdles) graduated from St. Francis High School in Traverse City in 1978, after staring on the school's track team for four years. Ann attended EMU (1978–82), and set their freshman long jump record (19–5¼).[50]

The following year she placed 13th in the AIAW National Outdoor Championships in East Lansing with a jump of 19–1½.[51] On April 25, 1981 Ann started the outdoor season by placing second in the long jump (19–4½) at the Drake Relays.[52] Two-weeks later, on May 9 she won the long jump (19–3), placed second in the 200-meter dash (24.86), and fourth in the 100-meter hurdles (14.77) at the Midwest AIAW Championships in East Lansing. On May 16–17, 1981 she won the long jump (19–3¼) and the 400-meter relay (47.4) at the Mid-America Conference in Kalamazoo. Ann was a 1981 AIAW All-American.[53] In 1981 she set the indoor EMU varsity long jump record with a jump of 20–2½. This EMU record held up for the balance of the century. She married former EMU Assistant Track Coach Ray Lohner.

At many universities, women's track was given more latitude than men's track in building a team. In the Mid-American Conference, for example, women's track was allowed 20 grant-in-aid scholarships under AIAW rules, while men's track was limited to 8 grant-in-aid athletic scholarships.[54]

Still Going To Court to Gain Equality

The 1984 Olympics in Los Angeles was the first in which the women's marathon was held. However, Mary Decker and Grete Waitz had to file a sex discrimination lawsuit against the International Olympic Committee in the Superior Court of Los Angeles to draw attention to the committee's failure to approve 5- and 10-K races for women in the Olympics.[55]

Winning by a Hundredth of a Second

Kim Turner was born in Detroit on March 21, 1961.[56] Her mother was a substitute teacher in the Detroit Public Schools. While at Mumford High School, Kim set the state girl's high school record for the 110-yard low-hurdles in 1978 and in 1979 improved on that state record and set a national scholastic record for that event.[57] Turner helped Mumford win the Detroit Public School League Track Championship.

One week after winning the Michigan Class A low-hurdles championship, Kim graduated from high school on June 9, 1979. That Friday night Detroit Public School League seniors held a "Swing-out" and Kim, "like any normal red-blood American girl, had the time of her life celebrating." The following afternoon, running into a strong headwind, she won the second annual *Free Press* Girls Invitational Meet at Warren Fitzgerald High. She ran the 110-yard hurdles in 13.9 seconds, three-tenths of a second off her national record but eight-tenths of a second better than the meet record.[58]

"Boy, that wind was something," Turner said after the race. "It started about the fifth hurdle, it just hit me. I just said, "Wow." And then Judi [Brown of East Lansing] was right on my tail and I had to move it. I ran well enough to win, but I sure am tired. Last night we were all out in our cars with pom-poms. I probably shouldn't have run here, but I really wanted to."[59]

Turner attended the University of Texas-El Paso. "I really wanted to get away from home," she said, "and besides, Carmen Rivers and Kim Watts (both from Detroit Mackenzie) and Rochelle Collins (Detroit Immaculate) are already down there. The Olympics is my goal. I think 1984 will be my year, I'm not quite ready yet. I'd like to win there, but even making the team would be a big deal for me.[60]

Kim Turner was an All-American and a national champion at Texas-El-Paso. Going into the Olympic trials in 1984, Kim was listed as having the second fastest time in the 100-meter hurdles (13.07) for the year to-date.[61] At the Olympic trials in Los Angeles on June 23, Turner ran the 100-meter hurdles in just a shade over 13 seconds, but there appeared to be a four-way tie for first place, and only three places on the Olympic team. Turner had to wait almost a half-hour for the results, as track officials agonized over a photo finish. "As for the agonizing half-hour wait for results after the race, Turner moaned: "I almost had about three or four heart attacks. I'm so impatient anyway. I just wished they'd give us a place, anything to ease the tension." Three hurdlers came in at 13.13, but American record holder and four-time national champion, Stephanie Hightower was left off the team. "I guess we all got an extra burst of energy at the end," said Kim Turner, who was declared the winner of the heat in 13.12, a time that was only one-hundredth of a second faster than the next three finishers. "The good Lord must have been looking over me because I was expecting to come in fourth. I'm just happy to be here."[62]

Kim Turner was one of the athletes featured in a *Ebony magazine* special on "The 1984 Olympics."[63] She won a bronze medal in the Los Angeles Olympics. After college she ran as a member of the Los Angeles Mercurettes. She also got married and had a child. As late as 1992, she was one of the leading runners on the Mobile Outdoor Grand Prix circuit.[64]

"Sweet" Judi Brown

Judi Brown was part of the emergence of Michigan women's track stars in the late 1970s. Judith L. "Judi" Brown was born in Milwaukee, and grew up in Indiana. Her father, Mitchen, was an engineer and her mother, Margaret, was a teacher. Her favorite sports were volleyball and basketball. She was not that interested in track, but when her family moved to East Lansing for her senior year in high school there was no volleyball team, so she played basketball and went out for track. If there had been a volleyball team, she never would have run track.[65] Judi did not take running seriously she was until a high school senior.[66]

In her first year in track Judi was second in the 110-yard low-hurdles (14.7) and was second in the 440-yard dash (55.9) at the Girl's Class A State High School Championships in Brighton on June 2, 1979. A week later she won the 440-yard run (57.1) and placed second to Kim Turner in the 110-yard low hurdles (14.1) at the *Free Press* Girl's Invitational Track Meet at Fitzgerald Public School in Warren. These performances earned her an athletic scholarship at Michigan State University.

At Michigan State, Judi specialized in the 400-meter hurdles. The women's intermediate hurdles are 30 inches high, compared to 36 inches for men. As Jackie Joyner-Kersee would later learned the hard way, it takes a long time to learn how to run the 400-meter hurdles.[67] Judi began to shin during her junior year at State. In February 1982 she won the 4×220-yard relay (1:41.26) and the 440-yard run (56.35) at the Big Ten Indoor Championships. At the Drake Relays on April 23, she placed seventh in the 400-meter hurdles (1:02.03), and in May she won the 400-meter hurdles (59.77) at the Big Ten Outdoor Championships.[68]

However, her senior year in college started as a disaster. She worked hard to qualify for the national NCAA indoor championships at the Pontiac Silverdome by winning the Big Ten 60-yard high-hurdles and the 440-yard dash, only to be disqualified for false starts in the preliminaries of the 440-yard dash. She was also disqualified in the intermediates on April 29, 1983 at the Drake Relays. Finally, on May 7 at the Ohio Relays in Columbus Judi won the intermediates and set a track record.[69] Then, she won the intermediates in the Big Ten Outdoor Championships, and on June 3, 1983 she ran in the finals of the 400-meter hurdles at the NCAA Outdoor Championships in Houston.[70]

Because Judi had been disqualified at the Drake Relays earlier that year for improper form, over the first three hurdles she concentrated on her form. After the third hurdle, she realized the rest of the field was way ahead. "I suddenly realized how fast everyone else had gone out, and I thought, how am I going to get back into this race? I just decided to keep plugging away and see who I could catch-up." By the final curve, Judi was in third place and then, finally, only American record-holder Sharriefa Barksdale of Tennessee was ahead of her. Then she had an out-of-body experience. "My body reacted before my mind did," and she surged ahead. Judi's winning time was her best ever (56.44). "The abilities we have are so mortal, so short-lived, that we have to do the most we can with what we have," Judi later philosophized.[71] She had run one of the greatest comeback races in women's track.

The victory at the NCAA outdoor nationals started a string of outstanding performances that made 1983 truly memorable for Judi. On June 19 she placed second in the 400-meter hurdles (56.51) at the USA Outdoor Championships in Indianapolis. On June 26 she won the intermediates at the TAC International Games in the Los Angeles Memorial Coliseum, and on July 3–4 Judi placed fifth in the intermediates at the

National Sports Festival in Colorado Springs.[72] She finished the season with a second place finish in the intermediates at the World University Games in Edmonton, Canada on July 10, and won gold medals in the intermediates and the mile relay at the Pan American Games in Caracas, Venezuela in mid-August. Juli Brown set the 400-meter hurdles record (56.32) for the Pan American Games.[73] She also ran in the DN Galan meet in Sweden in July 1983 and the first World Track and Field Championships in Helsinki, August 6–14, 1983.[74]

Judi earned a degree in speech and audiology from MSU in 1983. She was a letter winner all four years at Michigan State, and was team captain 1983. That year she was named "Big Ten Suzy Favor Female Athlete of the Year," "the George Alderton Athlete of the Year" (presented to the top male and female athlete at Michigan State), and "the MSU Sportswoman award" (presented to the female student-athlete who best combined athletic and academic achievement). During her four years at MSU Judi was an All-American on three occasions. She gained All-American status for the indoor distance medley relay in 1981and earned it twice in the 1983 NCAA outdoor championships—once in the 4 × 400-meter relay and the other in the 400-meter hurdles.[75]

On September 28, 1983 more than 70 people gave Ms. Brown a standing ovation when she stood at the lectern in the Spartan Room off Cross Roads Cafeteria on the MSU campus. She was being given a send off before leaving for Irvine, California to begin training for the Olympic trials. During her four-years at MSU she won 12 Big Ten titles (6 of them individually), a NCAA title, and earned two Pan-American Games gold medals.[76]

Once in California, world-record holder, Edwin Moses, helped Judi improve her hurdling technique.[77] While they were not exactly buddies, Moses was very helpful. "He basically trains like a half-miler. Well, I hate the half, that's the part I didn't follow." But her new strength enabled her to run an evenly paced race. She could now run the 400-hurdles faster than she ran that distance on the flat in high school.[78]

As Brown prepared for the 1984 Olympic trials, she was coached by former Polish Olympic long jump, gold medalist Elzbieta "Ella" Krzesinski, who had an immeasurable effect on her. Going into the Olympic trials Judi was listed as having the fifth fastest time in the 400-meter hurdles (56.40) for the year to-date.[79] This meant that she was an underdog for a place on the Olympic team. On June 9 at the USA-Mobil Track and

Field Championships in San Jose, CA, Juli smashed the America 400-meter hurdles record with a clocking of 54.99.[80] On June 21 she surprised many by winning the finals of the 400-meter hurdles (54.93) at the Olympic trials. Consequently, she would now run her favorite event in the first Olympics in which this women's event was held.

Judi did not attend the opening ceremonies for the Los Angeles Olympics. They were held eight days before the preliminaries for her event. Furthermore, she also avoided a tiring two-and-a-half hour wait outside the Coliseum before the parade of athletes. She explained, "If I'd gone there that early, I know I'd have gotten distracted. Instead, I ran on Sunday, Monday and Wednesday. And I didn't leave for LA until Friday. I didn't even watch any of the events on television. I didn't want to know what was happening."[81]

In the finals of the 400-meter hurdles, Judi was assigned lane eight. "That was the worst possible place I could have been," she told a reporter.[82] As a notoriously slow starter, the disadvantage was impossible to overcome. Unable to see the rest of the field of runners, Judi did less than her very best. On August 8 she finished second (55.20) to Nawal El Mouthwa-Kel of Morocco. "I lost. You win the gold—nothing else. When you leave with the silver, it means you lost the gold." Twelve years later, the Olympic silver medal sat neglected in her sock drawer.[83]

Judi Brown began doing free lance motivational and fitness speaking in 1983. She also worked for Nike, Inc in Beaverton, Oregon from 1983–88. On September 7, 1985 she set the American record for the 400-meter hurdles (54.38) at the IAAF Mobile Grand Prix track finals in Rome, Italy.[84] From 1984 through 1988 she was the Volunteer and Program Development Coordinator for the Lane County Relief Nursery in Eugene. She was elected to the Juvenile Services Commission in Lane County, Oregon, and served in that position from 1986–88.

Juli's husband, Garland King, was an analyst for Dun & Bradstreet. She met Garland, who was from Dayton, Ohio, in January 1984 on a blind date arranged by her sister-in-law. Her sister-in-law's brother roomed with Garland at Virginia's Hampton Institute.[85] Judi got married in 1985.

After marriage, Judi spent her spare time [three times a week]

working with community agencies [a nursery century for abused children] to help the children of abused and abusive parents, of drug-addicted parents, and of parents who for other reasons cannot cope with their world or their children. 'I don't know how it all evolved,' King said. 'I guess it's curiosity, but I've always befriended the social misfits. My first dog, I picked out the ugliest puppy in the litter. I remember baby-sitting kids who no one else wanted to baby-sit because they were so bad. I remember being friends with a girl named Cynthia in the third grade who was slightly retarded. She was the butt of everybody's jokes. I was sure she faced the same kind of thing at home, I didn't think it was right.

Judi and her husband adopted a methadone baby, whose mother was working as a prostitute to support a drug habit. King also learned that the woman was well known to the local police as a drug dealer. Judi and Garland adopted the child because she did not want a pregnancy to interrupt her training.[86]

On June 27, 1987 Judi Brown-King set a meet record in winning the National Championship in the 400-meter hurdles.[87] In late-July she ranked second in overall points in the Mobil [world-wide] Grand Prix.[88] On August 11–12 Judi experimented with her stride in winning the gold medal for the 400-meter hurdles at the Pan-American Games. Ordinarily she used a 14-step stride in which she alternated her lead foot over each hurdle. At the Pan-American Games in Indianapolis she switched to a 15-step stride in which she led with the same foot over each hurdle in the belief that shorter steps would increase her speed.[89] She had problems with her digestive system, but not her new stride. She set the Pan American Games, Stadium, and American record (54.23) for the event at the Pan American meet held in Indianapolis.[90] In the 1987 World Championships in Rome, Juli was sick, nervous and dehydrated and ran what she called "the worst race of my life."

"I'll be disappointed if I don't win a gold medal at the 1988 Olympics in Seoul, but not devastated," she said with surety. "Even though I'm training hard, another part of me is still a success. I know I'm not a failure."[91] Judi did not make the 1988 Olympic team, but she was *Sports Illustrated* Sportsman of the Year Award in 1987. She was inducted into the Michigan State Athletic Hall of Fame in 1995. She was also the national TAC championship four times, a World Cup silver medalist, and a National Track gold medalist. Most of all, she was not a failure.

Other Michigan Women Who Qualified for the Olympic Trials

Annette Bohach, grew up in Muskegon Heights in western Michigan, and went to North Muskegon High School. She placed first in shot put and set the meet record (45–5½) and was second in the discus (124–7) at the *Free Press* Girls Invitational held on June 9, 1979. In 1980 she attended the University of Indiana. Annette placed eighth in the shot put at the NCAA indoor finals on March 12, 1983. She was also in 1984

Olympic trials. On June 18, 1988 she placed sixth in the shot put (54–4¾) at the TAC National Championships in Tampa for the Western Michigan Track Club, but also failed to make the Olympic team on her second try.

Maria Shoup was born May 15, 1963 and attended Custer High School in Walhalla, Mason County, Michigan. In April 1979 she ran the 110-yard low-hurdles (15.0), 440-yard dash (60.0) and the 880-yard run (2:27.0) to qualify in three events for the State High School Girl's Class D State Track Championships. On June 2 she won, and set the state record for, the 200-meter hurdles at the State High School Championships.[92] On June 9 she was seventh in the 880-yard dash (2:53.4) at the *Free Press* Girls Invitational.

On May 30, 1981 Maria won and set the state record for the 200-meter low-hurdles (28.84). She also won the long-jump (18.5 meters), placed second in the 100-meter hurdles (15.04), and placed fourth in the 1,600-meter relay (4:14.44) at the Michigan Class D Girl's State High School Championships in Caro.[93]

Shoup attended Western Michigan University where on May 21, 1983 she ran at the Mid-American Conference Outdoor Championships in Bowling Green, and set the WMU woman's track team record for the 400-meter relay (47.27).[94] On May 5, 1984 she ran in a quadrangular meet against Eastern Michigan, Central Michigan, and Kent State Universities at the Olds/Marshall Track in Ypsilanti. That year she set the WMU Kanley track record for the 3,200-meter relay (8:59.5), the 1,600-meter relay (3:45.1), and the WMU woman's track team record for the 500-meter dash (1:13.2). She also set the WMU woman's track team record for the 400-meter hurdles (57.97), and the 400-meter relay (46.87). On May 18–19 she ran in the Mid-American Conference Championships, and on June 18 she was seventh in the 4th heat of the 400-meter intermediate-hurdles (60.15) at the Olympic trials.[95]

In 1985 Maria Shoup set the WMU woman's track record for the 600-yard dash (1:21.89), the 240-yard shuttle hurdle relay, and the 100-meter hurdles (14.2). On May 17–18 she became the first woman to win three individual events in the women's Mid-American Conference meet. She also was on a winning relay team. Shoup, a physical education major from a village near Ludington, was the workhorse of the meet. She was entered in six events. "Six events is a load, I admit that, but I just worry about one at a time. For the most part, they're spaced far enough apart that I can get some rest." She won the 100-

meter high-hurdles (14.02), 400-meter run (54.94), 400-meter hurdles (58.96), and the 1,600-meter relay (3:47.68). She also ran on the unsuccessful 400-meter relay, and ran in, but did not place in, the 200-meter run. Her efforts gave the Western Michigan University the Mid-American Conference Women's Outdoor Championships.[96] Shoup was named Female Track Athlete of the Year at the meet.[97] After graduating from Western, Maria married Maurice Holbrook, a former pole vaulter, and coached women's track at Ludington High School.[98]

Juli Ravary graduated from tiny Erie Mason High School located near Toledo, Ohio, and attended Central Michigan University. CMU, founded in 1849, was in the midst of a growth spurt that was taking the school from 3,000 students in the 1955–6 academic year to 16,500 students in 1989–90 academic year.[99] During the indoor season, Ravary threw the shot put and frequently placed third or better in that event in conference meets.[100] Her best event, however, was the javelin throw. In 1984 she won the Mid-American Conference javelin throw (156–2).[101] In 1985 Ravary placed fourth in the javelin throw with a throw of 154–9 at the Drake Relays.[102] She capped off the season by setting the Mid-American Conference record in the javelin at the conference meet in Kalamazoo on May 17 with a throw of 163–9, eclipsing the previous mark by nearly 12 feet.[103]

Money, Always a Lack of Money

On May 23, 1973 Fred Thompson, the coach of the all-women Atoms track team in Brooklyn, told a U.S. Senate hearing that he had no money to send his 15 women team to California in June for the national championships. He needed $7,500 to send his potential Olympic qualifiers to California.[104] The Atoms, along with women's teams in Chicago Parks Association, the Cleveland Parks, Boston, and the Los Angeles, were among the pioneer teams in women's track.

According to NCAA statistics, between 1981 and 1991 the total number of female athletic participants increased by 25 percent, to 92,778. The number of male athletes increased only 4.3 percent to 177,156 athletes during the same period. Title IX forced intercollegiate athletics to reform. It focused attention on college budgets, which reflected considerable abuse.[105] Of course, strengthening women's teams, in some ways, reduced men's opportunities. Title IX created a new environment that had the effect of reducing men's track and field to the status of a minor sport. The budget restrictions and expense distribution between male and female sports it imposed encouraged sports with large popular followings, such as football and basketball, to steal limited resources from track at a time when hockey, swimming, soccer, and gymnastics were gaining in popularity and scrambling for funds. Personnel costs increased for three reasons: (1) more coaches were required to recruit and train athletes, (2) coaches for woman's teams were required to have equal levels of staff support and office equipment, and (3) schools needed to prove that they had tried to offer sports that meet the interests and abilities of the under-represented sex.[106]

Title 1X, barring sexual discrimination at schools receiving Federal money, was a landmark victory for women's sports, but it had an unanticipated byproduct. As participation in organized women's athletics rocketed from 300,000 to 3 million student-athletes, thousands of new coaches were needed to direct women's sports. As a consequence, the percentage of female head coaches of women's teams fell from 90% in 1972 to 47.4% 28 years later. In 1998 just 18% of head coaches in women's college track were women.[107] Despite the high percentage of male coaches, vague school policies, and a lack of certainty over what constitutes an improper relationship or contact, relatively few male coaches were reported for sexual harassment or inappropriate relationships with female athletes. There were, however, a number of situations where greater sensitivity on the part of male coaches, when dealing with female athletes, would have benefited all concerned.[108]

From 1972 until his retirement, Don Canham opposed Title IX. While in favor of women's athletic competition, he protested against the rules that called for parity. He championed big time men's football and basketball and felt that Title IX hurt minor sports. "No consideration was given to the difference between getting a new program off the ground and maintaining an established 100-year-old program." "We had 120 or 130 athletes turn out for football alone, 50 or 60 for track, and to come up with equal numbers for women couldn't be done by waving a magic wand or a regulation." HEW confused "financial proportionality" with equal opportunity, Canham claimed. Title IX made male "walk-ons" a thing of the past, he argued, and many colleges dropped a number of minor sports.[109]

In 1975 an economic recession brought about by rising energy prices caused by the OPEC oil cartel created economic pressures on athletic programs in colleges of all sizes. These pressures came at the same time that athletic programs for women were being expanded. The economic pinch fueled the anger of many male athletic directors against Title IX directives. It also contributed to changes in both recruiting and scheduling. Central Michigan University decided not to recruit out of state, curtailed out of state games for non-revenue producing sports, and carefully weighed all the factors before sending a team or players to post-season competition.[110] Don Canham and other Big Ten Athletic Directors advocated reducing travelling squads, cutting rising expenses by curtailing off-campus recruiting, and limiting the number of campus visits by prospective recruits. Canham argued, "It's either that or lose all sports, but at the same time we want to protect our revenue-producing sports."[111] These types of austerity decisions accelerated the decline of track at Michigan colleges and universities.

Donna Gets a Second Chance

Donna Donakowski attended Dearborn Riverside High School. Her brothers were University of Michigan All-American distance runners Gerard A. Donakowski and William J. Donakowski. Her school was too small to have a girl's track team, but in her senior year Riverside Rebel cross-country coach Mark Shoshanian entered Donna in the Girl's Class C Regional Meet in Capac. Donna turned out to be the talk of the meet. She easily won the half-mile run in a personal best time of 2:17. Then she ran the mile and the two-mile runs with about a half hour between events, and won both.[112]

Two weeks later Donna single-handedly took the fourth place team trophy in the Girl's Class C State Track Championship in Bangor, Michigan. She won and set meet records in the 1,600-meter run (5:00.3), the 800-meter run (2:16.3), and the 3,200-meter run (11:17.2). Her coach bragged, "She did something that people won't see for a long time. She was super. Plus she only had about 15 minutes rest between the last two events." In the 3,200-meter run Donna pulled away from the pack on the sixth lap and won by ten seconds. After the race, she received a standing ovation from the crowd.[113]

Dennis Craddock, the men and women's head track and cross-country coach at the University of Virginia, recruited Donna on a track scholarship.[114] Soon after arriving at Charlottesville in the fall of 1983, Donna incurred an injury and was red-shirted.[115] Before long she was unhappy with Virginia and the Cavalier track program, quit college, and returned home. In the summer of 1985 Eastern Michigan's new women's track, Coach Bob Maybouer, saw Donna working at a Burger

King. He asked her if she would like to run for Eastern and she accepted his offer.[116] It turned out to be a lucky chance meeting for both parties.

On February 1, 1986 Donna won the mile run (4:43.01) at the Wolverine Open in Ann Arbor. That spring she won the 3-K run (9:32.45) and the 5-K run (16:42.16), and placed second in the 1,500-meter run (4:26.45) at the Mid-American Conference Outdoor Championships in Oxford, Ohio, setting the MAC outdoor meet record for the 3-K run (9:32.45) in the process. In November 1987 she set EMU record for cross-country (16:47.50), and in February 1988 Donna set the EMU varsity and MAC conference record for the indoor mile run (4:41.44). In May 1988 she won the 5-K run (16:59.85) and placed second in the 1,500-meter run (4:28.53) at the Mid-American Conference Outdoor Championships in Mt. Pleasant. That month she also set EMU record for the outdoor 3-K run (9:14.44), and on June 3 placed sixth in the 3-K run (9:16.37) at the NCAA Division I Outdoor Championships to achieve All-American honors.[117]

One of Donna's teammates at Eastern Michigan was Andrea Bowman. When Andrea graduated from Livonia's Churchill High School in June 1983, she went virtually unnoticed by college track coaches. While Andrea had finished fifth in the 800-meter run at the State High School Class A Championships, she ranked low as a future middle-distance runner. Nonetheless, Brian McKenna, former Michigan Track Club coach, suggested to Bob Maybouer, the women's track coach at Saginaw Valley State College that he take a chance on Andrea. The Cardinal coach signed her to a late letter of commitment. "She was our third or fourth best half-miler after our fall program," coach Maybouer recalled. "She was a very smooth runner. One of the smoothest runners we've ever had. She was very graceful."[118]

On February 26, 1984 Andrea finished fifth in the 600-meter run (1:30.3) at the NAIA National Indoor Meet to earn All-American honors. She also ran an 880-leg on their winning two-mile relay team (9:20.6). On March 31, a cold rainy day, she broke the Saginaw Valley State College 880-yard record (2:12.76) while placing second at Purdue University.[119] In 1985, when coach Maybouer took over the women's track program at Eastern Michigan University, Andrea transferred to Eastern, and stayed through the 1988 season.

On February 1, 1986 Andrea placed second the 1,000-meter run at the Wolverine Open in Ann Arbor. In 1987 she qualified for the NCAA Championships in Baton Rouge, where she placed fifth in her preliminary heat.[120] On July 20, 1988 she placed sixth in the second heat of the 1,500-meter run (4:23.83) at the U.S. Olympic trials in Indianapolis. The next day she was 14th in first heat of the semifinals of the 1,500-meter run (4:29.30).[121] After graduating from college, Andrea was elected to the Eastern Michigan University Hall of Fame.

Andrea married P. J. Osika, Michigan High School Class A State 800-meter champion from Waterford Kettering High School in 1983 and Eastern Michigan University half-miler.[122]

From England to Iowa By Way of Detroit

Vivien McKenzie was born in London, England on April 27, 1964 to American parents. Her parents separated while she was in high school. At age 18, Vivien lived with her mother Nora Edison McKenzie, a nurse. Her father, an Army veteran, was an auto mechanic.

Vivien started running for Coach Richard Ford of the Motor City Track Club when she was twelve years old. She ran with Delisa Walton and Kim Turner, among others. Because of her parent's separation, Vivien was shifted from school to school. She won state track championships at West Bloomfield High in 1979, Mumford High School in 1981, and Detroit Chadsey in 1982. She also played basketball and volleyball. She was five foot six inches tall and weighted 135 pounds when she graduated from Chadsey High School in June 1982.

When she started at the University of Iowa, she majored in computer science. Later, she changed her major to broadcast and film. Vivien won the Big Ten Outdoor Track 100-meter championship her first three years at Iowa. She also won the 55-meter dash at the Big Ten Indoor Championships in 1984.[123]

Vivien had her best year in 1985. She won the 55-meter dash and took third in the 300-meter dash at the Big Ten Conference Indoor Championships. At the Kansas Relays on April 20 she finished second in the 100-meter dash (11.45) setting a University of Iowa women's varsity record in that event. She also qualified for both the NCAA and TAC national championships. After the meet Vivien explained, "I'm benefiting from an injury-free indoor season. Last year I strained a hamstring during the indoor season and it really affected me in the outdoor meets. This year everything's going along very positively." She added, "I'm in a very positive frame of mind. I feel very strong and it's mostly due to the great workouts we've been having. It helps a lot to work out with the caliber of people that I get to run with here at Iowa."

The University of Iowa's Vivien McKenzie was one of half-dozen, female runners from Michigan to earn All-American status for out of state universities during the 1980s. *(Photo University of Iowa Sports Information)*

Vivien was one of three exceptional sprinters on the Hawkeye roster in 1985. Elaine Jones, a senior from Detroit was also on the team.[124]

On Saturday May 18, 1985 during the preliminaries for the 100-meter dash Vivien McKenzie set a new conference, stadium and meet record for the 100-meter dash at the Big Ten Outdoor Championships held at Northwestern University. The next day she won her third straight Big Ten Outdoor 100-meter championship. She finished second to Odessa Smalls in the 200-meter dash. According to Vivien, "It feels really good being a three-time champion. The Big Ten keeps getting better and better and I'm glad. It really makes it fun to win."[125] She was named University of Iowa's most valuable women's track athlete for 1985. On the final day of the meet a gusting 20-mile-an-hour wind blew a large cardboard box onto the track as the ladies came down the homestretch during the women's 4 × 100 relay. Although a catastrophe was avoided, the event signaled the blowout the Wisconsin women would achieve in dominating the rest of the meet.[126]

Vivien McKenzie participated on the North squad's 400-meter relay team at the National Sports Festival in Baton Rouge held July 24 through August 4, 1985.

Michigan Track Stars Continue to Head South

In 1979, Tonya Lowe helped lead the Flint Northern Vikings to five straight duel meet victories and first place in the Spartan, the Central Michigan University, and the Mott Relays.[127] The Vikings also went on to win the Flint City, the Saginaw Valley Conference, the Regional High School, and the Class A State High School Championships that year.[128] On occasion, these victories were accomplished under adverse conditions. For example, The Vikings outpointed the combined total of their two closest rivals, despite temperatures in the mid-40s and a bone-chilling wind that swept the field.[129]

Tonya was only a junior, yet she won three events at the Saginaw Valley Conference Meet in 1979. She also won three events at the Regionals in Lansing on May 19 and her times over the course of the season were among the best in the state. Her time in the 100-yard dash was 11.4. She ran the 110-yard hurdles in 14.8 seconds; the 220-yard dash in 25.5 seconds; the 440-yard dash 57.8 seconds; and in the Mile relay 3:59.0.[130]

Tonya attended the University of Kentucky. While at Kentucky, she was twice Southeast Conference champion in the hurdles. In 1984 she was 60-meter indoor champion (7.84) and 100-meter outdoor conference champion (13.35). She was an All-American three times. She gained that honor in the 1982 NCAA indoor championships for the 60-meter hurdles, and in 1983 and 1984 NCAA outdoor championships for the 100-meter hurdles. Tonya Lowe was one of the first women's track and field All-American at the Kentucky [there were none before the 1982 indoor season.]. She was SEC "Athlete of the Year" in 1984. At the end of the century she still held the University of Kentucky women's 100-meter hurdles record (13.35). She graduated in 1984, and became a pharmacist in Charlotte, NC.[131]

Kathi Harris was born in Pontiac on January 2, 1964, and grew up in Walled Lake, Michigan. She was a standout in the 800-meter run at Walled Lake Central High School, but was talented enough for the heptathlon. As a high school sophomore, Kathi Harris won the Inter-Lakes League championship in the quarter-mile, the regional 880-yard championship, and placed fifth in the 880-yard run at the State Class A Meet. She was named to the All-Oakland County track team.[132]

In 1981 the *Oakland Press* declared, "Kathi Harris . . . is the county's most versatile athlete. She has leaped 5–6 in the high jump; has run 5:27.1 in the mile; has gone 60.0 in the 440 and has done 15.3 in the 110-yard hurdles. She was Inter-Lakes League champion in the 440 and 880 and took Oakland County and regional titles in the 880. Her best time was 2:16.9." She was again named to the All-Oakland County track team for the 880-yard run.[133]

Kathi enrolled at the University of Tennessee in the fall of 1982 before the AIAW allowed athletic scholarships and she did not qualify for a scholarship on the basis of need. Her parents even had to pay the entire cost of her visits to the campus to check out the track program. During her first year at Tennessee, she was being groomed for the heptathlon, but preferred to run the half-mile. Hampered by a foot inflammation that wiped-out most of her freshman year, she ended up on crutches during the indoor season. Kathi did manage to run two races—an indoor half-mile in Florida where she clocked a 2:11, and the Dogwood Relays where she placed fourth with a 2:09.[134]

Kathi understood that if she ran well at the Dogwood Relays, she would accompany the team to the Penn Relays to run a half-mile, but was left home. Feeling ignored, she quite the team and sat out her entire sophomore year. In 1985 she returned to the track, placing third in the 800-meter run at the NCAA indoor championships in Syracuse and sixth in the 800-meter and second in the four by 400-meter relay at the NCAA outdoor championships. When the coach only offered to pay for her books in her senior year, she was insulted and transferred to Louisiana State University.

The University of Tennessee retaliated by refusing to release her for athletic competition in 1986, so Kathi sat out another year of competition, but was given a manager's scholarship by LSU. In 1987 while she completed a degree in finance, Kathi ran for LSU without a scholarship. She was again plagued by foot injuries, but contributed to the first LSU women's NCAA national track and field championship.[135]

After graduating from LSU, Kathi continued to live in Baton Rouge, and ran on the international track circuit.[136] In 1988 she was quoted saying, "I've only run six races this year." "My ex-boy friend is from the Netherlands and he is helping me train."[137] On July 18 she placed sixth in the finals of the 800-meter run (2:01.86) at the U.S. Olympic trials in Indianapolis. After the 1988 Olympic trials, Kathi retired from running, got married, and had a child. However, she still had the running bug. After giving birth to a daughter in 1993, she started running again to "to burn off some weight." Beginning in January 1995 she began training in earnest for a shot at the Atlanta Olympics.

In 1996 Kathi came close to an Olympic spot. On June 14 she was fourth in heat 2 of the first round of the 800-meter run (2:02.69) at the U.S. Olympic trials in Atlanta. The next day she placed second in the first heat of the semi-finals with a 2:00.99; and placed fourth in the finals with an amazing 1:59.28, just missing the final Olympic slot.

On June 14, 1997 Kathi won the USA Track and Field 800-meter championship beating Jill McMullen and Delisa Walton-Floyd, among others.[138] Her victory at the national championships earned her an August trip to the world championships in Greece, where she ended up 18th in the 800-meter.

On May 30–31 she opened the 1998 outdoor track season by placing second in the 800-meter run (2:00.10) at the Prefontaine Classic. Three weeks later she placed fifth in the 800-meter run (2:01.53) at the USA Track Federation Outdoor Championships in New Orleans. Kathi ran fifteen races in Europe in 1998, including a personal best for the year (1:59.98) when she won the 800-meter in Stuttgart, Germany on August 8. In 1995 she was ranked fifth in the USA. As late as April 25, 1999 she placed second in the 800-meter run (2:01.35) at the Grand Prix Meet, Rio de Janeiro, Brazil.[139] On June 12, 1999 she placed second in the 800-meter run (2:00.91) at the Pontiac Grand Prix in Raleigh, NC. On June 24, 1999 Kathi placed second in the 800-meter run (2:05.07) in the first heat of the first round of the U.S. Outdoor Championships. On June 27, 1999 she placed third in the finals of the 800-meter run (2:00.71) at the U.S. Outdoor Championships. Her hopes for a place on the 2000 Olympic team were still alive, but later faded.

Michele Morris started running when she was in junior high. Her father had an interest in running, and later was a track coach at Redford High School. At first, Michele was an average runner. Several other girls were faster, but she worked hard, and "had the tenacity of a pit bull," according to her junior high school coach.[140]

In her freshman year in high school, Michele began to blossom as a runner. The first evidence of her new found speed showed up when the boys and girls trained together, and she started to beat several young men in wind sprints. She placed third in the State High School Class B Championships as a freshman. According to her high school coach, Bernard Wells, Michele went to the rest room just before the 220-yard finals, and nearly missed her start time. She ran without proper preparation and might have won the event with better planning.

In both 1980 and 1981, Michele went undefeated in duel meets, won the conference 440-yard and 880-yard relays, and captured the 220-yard dash at the *Detroit Free Press* Invitational.[141] On May 31, 1980 Michele placed third in the 200-meter dash (24.9) at the Michigan Girl's High School Class B Championships in Sturgis.[142] The following year she placed second in the 200-meter dash (25.3) and fifth in the 400-meter relay at the Oakland County Girl's Meet held at Walled Lake Central High School.[143] At the State Class B Meet in Sturgis, on May 30, 1981 she won the 200-meter dash (25.3), placed third in the 400-meter run (57.6) and the 800-meter relay (1:43.9).[144] Michele Morris was selected for the second team All-Oakland County track team in the 220-yard dash by the sports department of the *Oakland Press*.[145]

During her senior year, Ms. Morris was clocked at 11.4 for the 100-yard dash [12.1 for 100-meters], 24.7 for the 200-meter dash, 56.8 for the 400-meter dash [60.3 in the 440].[146] On May 23, 1982 Michele won the 220-yard dash (25.4) and the 440-yard dash (58.0), and placed second in the mile relay at the Michigan High School Class B Regional Championships in Warren. On June 3, 1982 she won the 200-meter dash (25.62) and the 800-meter relay (1:55.90) and placed second in the 400-meter dash (56.94) at the Oakland Country Girl's Track Championships.[147] On June 6, 1982 she won the 200-meter dash (24.7) and the 880-yard relay (1:44.8), and placed second in the 440-yard dash (57.3) at the Michigan Girl's High School Class B State Championships in Grand Rapids.[148]

While at Oak Park High, Michele set school track records in seven events: the 100-meter dash, the 200-meter dash, the 400-meter dash, the long jump, the 400-meter relay, the 800-meter relay, and the 1,600-meter relay. Six of those records still stood 20 years later. Only her long jump record has been eclipsed. Michele set all of those records before Lady Diana Spencer married Prince Charles. Her achievements were more durable than Princess Diana's marriage, and even outlived the Princess.

Despite her supportive family and B average at a strong academic high school, Michigan universities did not actively recruit Michele Morris. She attend Louisiana State University, where she became a seven times All-American. In 1987, she was on the LSU's first women's NCAA national championship track team. She did not, however, leave LSU with a diploma when her eligibility ended. In 2000 she had one child and lived in Farmington, Michigan where she managed an apartment complex.

Wendy Truvillion, a 400-meter and 800-meter runner from Detroit's Pershing High School, also became a six-time track All-American at LSU. Wendy was the fourth of seven children. Her mother was an active softball player and her older sister, Terry, was an All-American basketball player, who coached at Pershing High School, before becoming Principal at McNair Technical School in Detroit. Wendy began running for the MG Pacers Track Club in the fifth grade, and in junior high school ran for Coach Harry Weaver, who started the Detroit Cheetahs Track Club and was active at the Hawthorn Recreation Center.[149]

Wendy ran her first high school meet as a freshman for Coach Al Tellis. As a junior and senior she placed second in the 800-meter run at the Class A Michigan Girl's State High School Championships in 1981 and 1982.[150] Wendy had a 3.4 grade average and was recruited by Karen Dennis at Michigan State, as well as by the University of Michigan, Stanford University, Indiana University, the University of Richmond, Old Dominion, and Louisiana State University. She chose LSU because they sent videotape of the campus and it was a long way from Detroit.

Wendy and Michele Morris entered LSU at the same time. As freshmen they ran together on the 4 × 400-meter relay team that qualified for the national NCAA meet, but did not attend the meet. Wendy was elected team captain for each year for the balance of her college eligibility. As a college junior she was an indoor track All-American in the 500-meter run and the 4 × 400-meter relay, and an outdoor track All-American in the 4 × 400-meter relay. Her relay team won the National outdoor championship in 1985. As a college senior she an indoor All-American in the 4 × 400-meter relay in 1986 and as a "red shirt" senior in 1987 she was an indoor All-American in the 4 × 400 relay and an outdoor All-American in the 4 × 400-relay. LSU won the National team championship in 1987. A pulled hamstring muscle kept her from a possible All-American showing in the 400-meter hurdles in 1987. Wendy ran internationally for the American AAU team in the summers of 1985 and 1987.

In August 1987 Wendy married Derek Harper, a University of Michigan Big Ten Champion long-jumper and relay sprinter in 1982 and 84. They were divorced in 1991. Wendy was an assistant track coach at Georgia Tech University from 1988 to 1993, and head women's track coach at Georgia Tech from 1993 through 1995. In January 1996 she became assistant track coach at Penn State University until moving back to Georgia in 1997, where at the close of the century she coached the Quick Silver Track Club and taught at an academy.[151]

Among the other Michigan women who found track success in Southern Universities were Charlotte Williams from Detroit, who competed for Mississippi State University; Tere Stouffer from Royal Oak's Shrine of the Little Flower, who competed at the University of Tennessee in the 10-K run, and Laura Matson, a middle-distance runner from Bloomfield Hills Andover High School, who set the national scholastic record for the 1,600-meter run (4:39.4) and ran for the University of Florida.[152]

Going the Distance at Michigan

Susan Beth Schroeder was born on December 20, 1963 in Napoleon, Ohio to Peter and Joann Schroeder Her father was a maintenance worker; her mother was a nurse who was trained at Henry Ford Hospital in Detroit. Sue played basketball and ran in both cross-country and track in high school. She was All-league in cross-country and track all four years of high school. She was All-State in cross-country for three-years, and All-State in track two years. She was also a member of the national honor society. She stood 5–5 and weighed 102 pounds when she was a junior in college. Her college objectives were to prepare to teach German and to coach track.[153]

Sue was a walk-on at the University of Michigan, and emerged as their finest female distance-runner. On January 26, 1985 she set the meet and University of Michigan record for the 1,500-meter run (4:24) at the Can-American Invitational in Windsor, Ontario. On June 8, 1985 she set the University of Michigan women's record for the 5-K run (15:42.7) when she placed second at the NCAA finals in Austin.[154] Sue also set the Ferry Field record for the 5-K run (16:29.23) in 1985. In 2000 she still held the women's varsity outdoor record for the 3-K (9:11.2) and 5-K runs (15:42.70), together with the women's indoor varsity records for the 1,500-meter (4:22.40) and the 3-K run (9:09.45).[155]

Sue won All-American honors in cross-country and indoor track in 1984. In May 1985 she was awarded the prestigious Marie Hartwig Award for being Michigan's outstanding female athlete of the year. Her grade point in 1985 was 3.9 0n a 4.0 scale for her three years at Michigan. She was on the President's list as an outstanding student.[156]

On February 1, 1986 Schroeder set University of Michigan varsity, meet, and fieldhouse records for the 3-K run (9:13.61) at the Wolverine Open. Despite the need to start the meet an hour late because of treacherous road conditions, Sue did not let the delay stop her from qualifying for the NCAA Indoor meet. Sue recalled, "I was shooting for 9:25 so I was surprised. I was 4:59 at the mile and felt good so . . . the 3,000 I think is my best event. I'd like to think I'm going to get faster. The type of workouts I've done are not the type that would make me peak. I haven't done any speed work at all." Assistant coach Sue Parks added, "I thought she would qualify, but I didn't think she would run 9:13. Her training hasn't been that hard yet."[157] In February 1986, Sue was the Big Ten's Woman Track Athlete of the Month. As captain of the U of M women's track team, she won every race she competed in that month, and broke two school records.[158]

On June 7, 1986 Sue Schroeder placed second in the finals of the 5-K run (15:44.27) at the NCAA women's outdoor championships in Indianapolis. After the meet Sue said, "I was happy but a little disappointed at the same time. Near the end of the race I began to move up, but she [Stephanie Herbst of Wisconsin] had a last spurt of energy. It was pretty close."[159]

Schroeder was the first Michigan University female to earn All-American honors five times.[160] Sue was an academic All-Big Ten athlete three years, and was inducted into the Women's Academic Hall of Honor at the University in 1986. She also was awarded the Big Ten Medal of Honor in 1986 for highest demonstration of scholarship and athletic abilities. She was a GTE At-Large Academic second team All-American three times. She was awarded the Marie Hartwig and the James B. Angell Scholarship while at Michigan. She was a twice captain of both the cross-country and track teams.

State Concentrates on Sprinters

Odessa Smalls was born in South Carolina on May 8, 1964. She grew up in the Bedford-Stuyversant area of Brooklyn. Her father worked in the newsroom of Channel 5. She attended high school at Eastern District HS (NYC) and ran track for Coach Conrad Ford, who died on May 13, 1985. At the time of Coach Ford's death, Odessa recalled, "He made me have faith in myself." Small was offered scholarships from 42 colleges and universities, and chose Michigan State University after nearly signing with Iowa.[161] Smalls would not have qualified academically for MSU in 1990.[162] According to Odessa,

When I came here I was kind of scared. But Karen [Dennis], Coach [Jim] Bibbs and Coach [Bruce] Waha are all so much like family to me I'm not scared anymore. They treat you as more than an athlete. If I have some kind of problem and need to talk to one of them, I can call any time day or night and they'll be there. The other people on the team are such a big support to me, too."[163]

Odessa majored in Criminal Justice. She was named All-American three times and "Most Valuable Player" for the MSU women's track team in 1986.

Shirley Evans was on the sixth place MSU sprint medley relay team in 1989 at the Drake Relays.[164] Shirley attended Detroit Country Day High School, where she won the State Class C 100 and 200-meter Championships in 1987.[165] She qualified for the finals of the 100-meter dash at the Drake Relays in 1991 with a 12.32 clocking and was on the MSU 4 × 100 relay team that made the finals.[166] The following day she placed 7th in the finals of 100-meter dash (12.11) and the relay team did the same (47.01).[167] Shirley was 8th in the second heat of the semi-finals of the Women's 100-meter dash (11.70) at the National AAU Championships on May 31, 1991. Her 1992 indoor performance for 55-meters (6.98) was the second fastest in school history and she was the fastest in school history for 200-meters (23.78). At 100-meter outdoors she was third fastest in school history. In 1992 she was Big Ten outdoor champion in the 200-meter dash and indoor and outdoor champion in the 4 × 400-meter relay.[168]

The University of Michigan Finally Recruits a Detroit Area Black Woman

For much of the twentieth century Michigan colleges and universities were homogeneous institutions at which female students of color were an unusual sight. It is believed that the first African-American woman was admitted to the U of M in 1877, but as late as 1925 African-American students at the University were required to live in segregated housing.[169] In 1952, only 14 of 3,000 graduating seniors at the University were African-Americans.[170] While the rate at which females of color were admitted to Michigan increased over the next two decades, African-American and Asian women were rarely found on the athletic fields at the U of M before 1980.

Joyce Louise Wilson was born on March 1, 1964 in Seattle, Washington. Her father, Percy Wilson, was a career Army man, who became a welder when he retired from military service. Her mother was a press operator. Both of parents had athletic skills, but little experience in formal athletic competition. Joyce had male cousins who were college athletes. She attended high school at Tower High School in Warren, where she ran track, and played basketball and volleyball. In 1982, she was an honor roll student, did well in nurses aide competition, and was the state 440-yard champion.[171]

In 1984 Wilson was ranked 13th in the world in the 600-yard run by *Track and Field News*. Joyce and Sue Schroeder were members of the two-mile relay team that set the Big Ten Conference record (8:44.42) in 1984 and still held it 15 years later. Joyce was an indoor track All-American in 1984. In 1984 Joyce set the University of Michigan varsity indoor record for the 400-meter dash (54.82) and the following years she set the varsity outdoor record (52.64). Both records have stood for 15 years.[172] She had flu during the Big Ten indoor championships in 1984.

Joyce Wilson graduated from Michigan with a bachelor's degree in nursing in 1988. After graduation, she became a volunteer assistant girl's track coach at Huron High School in Ann Arbor. When Kelly Byrd left Huron High School to become the Women's Track Coach at the University of Georgia, Wilson took over the program at Huron HS. She married in 1988, and had a daughter in 1991.[173]

State Recruits a Distance Runner of Note

Mary Shea was born in Johnson City, New York on December 20, 1965. Her family was Roman Catholic. They moved to Hudson, Ohio[174] when she attended grade school. Her father, James Shea, was a Director of Human Resources. Her mother, Mary, was a housewife.

Mary started running in eighth grade. "Some of my friends were running track, so I decided to do it, too. I was always fast when I was younger, so I figured track was the thing to do."[175] "I didn't like it at first because it was hard." She added that once her skill level improved her interest in the sport increased.[176] In high school, she ran an average of 30 miles a week, and became All-State in the 3,200-meter relay and in cross-country. She ranked fourth in the state in cross-country and was co-captain of her high school girl's cross-country team.

Most people who saw Mary Shea's bright smile or encounter her gregarious personality did not guess that once she heard the crack of the starter's gun, a fierce competitive streak took over. "I get this force in me to make my body go through all the pain."[176] Long-distance running has to be developed. A distance runner has to learn to accept pain while refusing to acknowledge it mentally.

Mary worked at Sea World of Ohio during the summers while in college. As a college student-athlete she ran an average of 70-miles a week. Success begets success. According to track coach Karen Dennis, "She's the finest distance-runner we have. She's very conscientious and dedicated, not only to athletics but to academics. She's an overachiever. She has very high goals and is willing to work to achieve those goals."[177] Shea was Big Ten 10-K run champion in 1987, and placed seventh in that year's NCAA outdoor track and field championships. Her showing in the 10-K run earned her All-American honors that year. In 1988 she was a NCAA All-American in cross-country.

Shea enjoyed the camaraderie of cross-country competition because there are fewer members on the team. "The night before a race we just relax. We get up really early, at least five hours before the race, and eat a tiny bit. If the race is later in the day, we go for a morning jog to loosen up. An hour before the race, we run the course for our warm-up."[178]

Shea graduated from MSU in December 1988 with a degree in finance. "I came close to getting a job, but I'm kind of glad I didn't," she said. Domino's Pizza Inc. made a name for itself by sponsoring Michigan-based athletes. They paid for basic equipment and race entry fees. She put off a career to join the Domino's professional track team, and study sports administration. However, an Achilles heel injury hampered her running most of the 1989 indoor season.[179]

Scapegoat

Judi Brown was one of Karen Dennis' athletes at MSU in the early 1980s. In 1985 Judi was the winter term commencement speaker at Michigan State University.[180] While training in Oregon, Judi worked for Nike as a coach, and began learning that role.[181] Judi and Karen became friends after Judi's career ended and she had moved on to Oregon to train for both the 1984 and 1988 Olympic games.[182] From March 1989 until June 1990 Judi worked as project director for independent schools, for the Boys Club of Greater Dallas, Texas.

Judi took good care of her health and continued to be physically fit. She told a Michigan magazine, "I watch what I eat pretty closely. I don't eat much red meat and I take vitamins. I drink lots of juices and try to concentrate on eating fruits and vegetables."[183] "I don't indulge. I'm blessed with a lot of energy. I'm very health conscious, and I don't eat sweets. I run a couple of times a week. I walk. I take the steps rather than the elevator.[184]

When Karen Dennis decided to leave MSU for Nevada-Las Vegas, she told Judi and suggested that Judi might be considered for her job. "I talked it over with my husband and we decided that it was something worth going after." On August 3, 1992, while living in Roulette, Texas, Judi submitted her application to become head coach of the MSU woman's track team. At that time Judi was working as a supervisor of travel relations for American Express, and was a member of the board of directors of the Athletic Congress.[185] In early fall, four finalists were chosen from a large number of applicants. Judi was one of them. She flew to East Lansing for a day-long interview. On October 21 MSU athletic director Merrily Dean Baker called to tell Judi, "We've decided you're the best choice for the women's track job. The job is yours."[186]

At age 31, after competing all over the world, Judi Brown King jumped at this chance to coach track, move closer to her family, and give back to her alma mater. Later that fall she was hired. Judi felt that there are a lot of things she would bring to the MSU women's track team. "I have had access to a variety of coaching techniques, and have experienced competition at all levels," she declared.[187] She wanted to build some summertime track and field programs for area youngsters that would help produce revenue, and encourage community involvement. "We can produce a quality team just by using kids from Michigan. There is plenty of talent in this state. We just have to identify it and then get kids in here and start training them." "In Oregon, up to 2,000 people would attend [track] meets because the community was so involved," King said. "Same thing in Florida where the program gets great community support."[188]

Judi took over the head coaching post on November 5, 1992 and began her first season as a track coach at MSU began on January 15, 1993 with a duel meet against Central Michigan University. Unlike the football, basketball and hockey coaches at MSU, non-revenue coaches are hired essentially on a year-to-year basis. Women's track was considered a low priority. "This is a Big Ten tail-ender because other schools, like Illinois, Wisconsin and Ohio State, place emphasis in the area and provide more funding." Judi was expected to do some significant fund raising to get more money for scholarships.[189]

As head women's track coach, Judi Brown worked with about 32 students on her first team and about 85 percent of them were "walk-ons," receiving no financial aid of any kind. Her Spartans work out in Jenison Fieldhouse when the weather is poor, five days a week for two hours a day.[190] "Running is such an individual sport that I need to deal with each runner on a one-on-one basis most of the time. Each runner needs a special touch and I try to give it to each and every one of my ladies."[191] Like most college coaches, her duties required more than on-track activity. She was a counselor to those struggling in school and helped develop mental frameworks for producing consistent, top-notch efforts. Running can produce tremendous emotional duress, especially when competitive times are not good enough to win.[192]

Judi Brown was named assistant coach on the United States Olympic Festival North squad to be held July 8–10, 1994 in St. Louis.[193] She put her heart and soul into the women's track and field program at State, yet in January 1997 she was offered up as a sacrificial lamb for minor violations of the NCAA rules. At a time when the coaches of revenue-generating sports, and their alumni allies, at nearly every major university were surreptitiously flaunting the rules in significant ways, it was nearly the height of hypocrisy for the Michigan State athletic department and the NCAA to bring charges against Coach Judi Brown.

After a nine-month investigation, which included at least five interviews with Brown, the NCAA investigator claimed six violation of NCAA rules. Individually none of the charges went beyond knit picking. She was charged with allowing one of her runners make a free long-distance call to her parents to get insurance information following a minor automobile accident. She was charged with allowing two second team members to stay in her room when their other accommodations fell through, rather than leave them stranded without a safe place to spend the night. She was cited for the absence of some receipts, because she stayed at a friend's house during two different recruiting trips. And, she allowed more than one person to volunteer as a coach for a short time.[194]

The entire incident smelled of over-kill aimed at distracting the public attention away from more serious problems with the NCAA oversight of big time college athletics.

Michigan State University Carried On

Despite the firing of Judi Brown, the MSU track program carried on with a few stars. Stephanie Leigh Dueringer, a distance-runner (5-K and 10-K runs), was born in Champaign, Illinois on July 14, 1975. She attended high school at Champaign Centennial. A Roman Catholic, she was the daughter of William and Janet Dueringer. Her father was an attorney and her mother a nurse anesthetist. Her childhood idol was University of Wisconsin distance-runner, Suzy Favor Hamilton. Stephanie attended from Michigan State University (1993–97), where she majored in Exercise Science. At State she was three times Academic All-Big Ten, All-Big Ten in cross-country, and All-American in track. She was also a recipient of the Dr. James Feurig Award, and was captain of the 1997 track team. Immediately following graduation, she did graduate work and was the MSU undergraduate student assistant coach.[195]

On March 8, 1997 Stephanie set the MSU indoor record in the 5-K run (16:29.72) at the NCAA indoor championships, and on April 24, 1999 placed fifth in the 5-K run (16:43.06) at the Drake Relays.[196]

Chandra Renee "Cee" Burns was also a MSU track star. Born in Detroit on August 4, 1975, Chandra attended Northern High School. As a junior, she placed second in the 200-meter dash at the Class A State Championships. As a senior, she won all three dashes in the Detroit Metropolitan League Championships in 1993, and won the 200 and 400-meter dashes at the Class A State Championships.[197]

When Chandra attended Michigan State (1994–97), she won the 200-meter dash (23.91) and set the MSU record for the women's 400-meter dash (53.78) at the Big Ten Indoor Championships on February 25, 1996. At the 1996 Big Ten Outdoor Championships she won the 200 (23.30) and the 400-meter dashes (51.89), and went on to place eighth in the 400-meter run (52.70/54.90) at the NCAA Women's Outdoor Championships. Chandra placed sixth in the first heat of the quarterfinals of the 400-meter run (53.51) at the U.S. Olympic trials in Atlanta.[198]

The following year, Chandra won the 400-meter dash (54.01) at the indoor Cannon IV Classic, in Indianapolis placed second in the 400-meter dash (54.81) and fifth in the 200-meter dash (24.97) at the Big Ten Indoor Championships in Champaign. That spring, she placed second in the 4 by 100-meter relay at the Big Ten Outdoor Championships at the University of Illinois. She also placed fifth in the Special 400-meter run (53.94) at the Drake Relays, and on June 4 she placed sixth in the semifinals of the 400 (58.16) and sixth in the 200-meter dashes (23.38) in the semifinals at the NCAA Division I Track and Field Championships. A week later she placed seventh in the 400-meter dash (51.71) and advanced to the semi-finals of the USA Outdoor Championships. On August 28 she placed seventh in the 400-meter run (51.71) and advanced to the semifinals in the 200-meter dash (23.38) at the World University Games in Sicily, Italy. All in all, Chandra Burns was a noteworthy All-American.[199]

Small Colleges Also Excelled at Women's Track

Starting in 1986 Nancy Meyer built a women's cross-country and track program that led tiny Calvin College to eleven straight conference titles, ten straight Great Lakes regional championships, and six top four finishes in NCAA Division III. She was Regional coach of the year five times, and in 1998 was named NCAA Division III coach of the year.[200] From 1992 through 1996 Betsy Haverkamp won consistently for Nancy Meyer teams.

In high school, Betsy Haverkamp was the 1992 Michigan Girl's High School Class B State Champion in cross-country. She was recruited and given offers of athletic scholarships by Hillsdale College and the University of Michigan. She was also recruited by non-scholarship Calvin College. Betsy chose to attend Calvin College as a matter of personal preference. "That's where I wanted to go deep inside," she later told a reporter.[201]

Betsy Haverkamp was an education major with an emphasis in Spanish. In college she carried a 3.61 grade point, and had what her assistant cross-country coach called a "perma-grin." Despite the big smile, she was a fierce competitor. Haverkamp was a Division III cross-country All-American four times. In doing so she became only the fifth Division III female athlete to accomplish that feat. She was also All-MIAA first team every year in college, and the conference's most valuable cross-country athlete in 1996. In track she was a Division III All-American on three occasions. In 1995 she was third in the 5,000-meter run at the NCAA Division III Championships. In 1997 Betsy won the Division III National Championship in the 3-K and placed second in 5-K run. She earned all-MIAA conference honors in track each of the three years she ran track, and set new Calvin College records in the 1,500-meter (4:38.76), the 3-K (9:52.72), and the 5-K run (16:54.20). In 1997 she was named the MIAA co-MVP in track and field.[202]

When asked why she was involved in track without a scholarship for her efforts she responded: "I just love to run and compete. I look at running as a talent that God has given me and I try to use that talent to the best of my ability." As a sophomore, Betsy earned All-American honors in track by placing third in the 5-K run in a driving rainstorm.

Betsy missed the 1996 track season because she was studying in Spain. She enjoyed the experience, and came back with a new attitude

toward life in general, not to mention an increased vigor toward training. During the 1996 cross-country season, Ms. Haverkamp earned
GTE First Team Academic All-American honors.[203]

As the 1997 Division III NCAA National approached Betsy confided,
"It has always been a dream of mine to win a national title and I'm just
going to go out and run the best I can and hope it happens." However,
four weeks before the meet she pulled a hamstring and it was questionable whether or not she would be able to run in the nationals. But
through her hard work and the guidance of her coaches Brian Diemer
and Al Hoekstra, she was ready.

On Friday evening, May 24, 1997, Betsy faced Meredith Unger from
Haverford College in Massachusetts, who carried the fastest time in the
country in the 3-K run into the race. "We talked with Betsy during the
warm-ups that if she went through a period of doubt with two or three
laps to go, that somehow, somewhere on the lap, she'd find a little
extra," Diemer recalled. With 800-meters to run in the race, both
Haverkamp and Unger were among a pack of five runners who had
pulled away from the field of 11 runners. Unger then moved out to a
50-meter lead over Haverkamp. It stayed that way until the 200-meter
mark, when Haverkamp made her move. By the final turn, Betsy had
pulled even with Unger. From there, she made the best sprint of her
life. "I figured I'd give it everything I had. I wanted this (national title),"
Haverkamp remembered. Coach Diemer added, "Somewhere on the
last lap, Betsy dug down from the deepest part of her body and pulled
the race out." Haverford added, "Things didn't go as I planned, but I got
what I wanted. I want to thank God for giving me the ability to run, my
coaches, teammates, parents and all those who supported me. With out
them this wouldn't have been possible."[204]

Betsy won the 3-K run in the time of 9:57.62. For Coach Hoekstra,
the race brought back memories of the Diemer's effort in the 1992 U.S.
Olympic Trials when he won the 3-K steeplechase. "After everything
Betsy has been through with her hamstring injury, that was one of the
greatest athletic achievements I've ever seen with the way she came
back in the final 300 meters to win. . . . You can't possibly be more
proud of an athlete than when they come back from adversity and then
come through like a champion."

The next day she placed second in the 5-K run at the NCAA Division
III Outdoor Championships in La Crosse, Wisconsin. Calvin College
coach Brian Diemer was impressed by Haverkamp's effort. "It was a
tremendous performance by Betsy this weekend," said Diemer. "For

Betsy to go out and win the 3,000 the way she did last night put her into some serious oxygen debt, and yet she still came back 20 hours later to finish second in a hard 5,000 which was just incredible."

While at Calvin College, Haverkamp participated in a number of volunteer activities. She tutored inner city children through Eastern Avenue Christian Reformed Church. She played the flute with a musical group that performed at several retirement homes, and served as a volunteer at Kent Community Hospital and Wedgewood Acres.

In 1997 she was named NCAA "Woman of the Year" for the state of Michigan. After graduation from Calvin College, Betsy Haverkamp became a Spanish teacher at South Christian High School, her alma mater.[205]

Perhaps it is fair to say that Mindy Ramsey, from Saginaw Valley State College was the last great Michigan small college track star of the twentieth century. Despite torn ligaments in her right shoulder, she won the NCAA Division II shot put title and placed second in the discus on May 27–28, 2000.[206]

The University of Michigan Closed the Century with a Winner

Kathryn E. McGregor was born in Willoughby, Ohio on September 2, 1977. She had two brothers. Her mother, Nanci, attended Ursuline College. Her father, William McGregor, ran on the varsity track team from 1970–1974 and was team captain in 1973–4 at John Carroll College. "My dad was a runner in high school. He was a sprinter, mostly. I started running because of him, he's always been there and been more involved. Back in high school, I wouldn't know anything, because he would know everything. If I need to know a time or something about a race or something about someone else, he would know everything, so I just kind of didn't worry about anything. I'm still kind of like that. I'm not really big about talking about running, I just do it."[207]

Kati attended Willoughby South High School, which was a member of the Greater Cleveland Conference. She was a member of the National Honor Society, and was a cross-country and track star all four years. In the fall of 1991 as a freshman Kati was conference, district, and regional cross-country champion. She placed seventh in the State cross-country meet. The following spring Katie was undefeated in the 800, the 1,600, and the 3,200-meter runs. She won the state meet in the 3,200-meter relay and placed second in the 1,600-meter run.

McGregor recalled, "As I got older, I was the only one of my pack of friends that ran. We were all athletes, but we all did different sports. I had to get up and run early in the day so I could spend the rest of the day with my friends. I put the time in, but I would do it early in the morning or late at night, so it wouldn't interfere with anything else I could do throughout the day. It was a priority of mine, because I did what I had to do on my own time, and no one else really knew about it."[208]

As a high school junior, McGregor became the first runner in Northeast Ohio and the entire state to win Division I 800, 1,600 and 3,200 meter runs. Her decision to run all three events at the state meet was considered foolhardy by many coaches and athletes. Katie, however, was not afraid to reach for greatness. She placed third in the 800, and second in the 1,600-meter run, but was disqualified in the 3200-meter run after finishing third. She bumped another runner in the final 200-meters of the race. "I think the call was a good one. I cut someone off, and I deserved it," she told a writer for the *Willoughby News-Herald*. Her times in all three events were the best for any female runner in northeast Ohio.[209] Her willingness to accept responsibility won her more respect than winning the race would have achieved.

In 1995 McGregor enrolled in the College of Literature, Science and Arts at the University of Michigan. From the beginning of her college track career, she felt that tough workouts helped her performance in meets. "No matter how hard we work in practice, I don't consider whether it's going to hurt or help my racing," McGregor said. "I think it would help more than anything—the harder you workout in practice, the faster you go in a race."[210]

As a sophomore at Michigan McGregor finished third in the 3-K and fourth in the 5-K at the Big Ten outdoor championships, but was disappointed that the University of Michigan women finished second in the meet. "We did just about anything anyone could ask for, and we got a slap in the face," McGregor said.[211] She qualified for NCAA Outdoor championships in both the 3-K and the 5-K. She chose to run the 5-K because "I have a lot of room for improvement in it. I've only run it twice this year, and I was basically running it by myself. We're going to go there and run with a high level of competition—unbelievably good runners. Hopefully we'll just go along with them, finish as fast as we can and come out winners."[212] McGregor came through in strong fashion. She finished eighth with a time of 16:16.05, beating her previous career-best time by more than 13 seconds.[213]

Katie McGregor rose out of an unheralded past to take fifth at the 1997 NCAA cross-country championship. When she was interviewed about her strong showing she said, "Fifth place doesn't even really mean anything to me. I was looking at a picture from the race the other day and I saw people that finished right behind me and right in front of me and it's just amazing that I had even gotten that place." "I still don't keep track of times or yards or who my competition is. But I think that I've had the influence of a lot of good teammates. I'm really competitive and I always want to be the best. I've never really said I can't be the best, so that's just what I want to keep doing, just keep improving, as long as I'm healthy and keep feeling the way I do. Still, I don't think of myself as one of the big dogs. I thought it was just crazy that I got fifth last year [November 1997] at cross [country]. And when we won the DMR [distance medley relay on March 14, 1998 at the NCAA Women's Indoor] and I won the 5000 indoors, it was just unbelievable. I never even thought in a million years that would be me."[214]

McGregor also won the 3-K run at the NCAA Women's Indoor Championships in 1998.[215] In November 1998 she became the first national champion in cross-country in U of M history when she defeated pre-race favorite Amy Skieresz of Arizona. In Lawrence, Kansas, McGregor caught Amy in the final 500-meters of the race and put her away to capture the title in 16:47.21. Katie ran in eight cross-country meets in 1998 and won seven of them, including the Big Ten Conference and NCAA Great Lakes Regional Championships.[216] As a senior she was awarded the Honda National Sports Award for women's cross-country and was nominated for "Michigan's Best Sports Figure in 1998."[217]

As the century ended, foreign athletes influenced women's track as in men's track. At the University of Michigan, Canadian Nicole Forrester won the high jump at the Drake Relays in 1998[218] and was a strong force at national meets in 1999.

Western and Eastern Michigan Universities Also Contributed at the End of the Century

Virgie Bullie of Eastern Michigan University made a considerable contribution to Michigan track in 1988. On April 30, 1988 she placed third in the finals of the sprint relay (1:40.52) and sixth in the 400-meter relay (46.05) and the 1,600-meter relay at the Drake Relays. On May 21, 1988 she won the 100 (11.72) and the 200-meter dashes (23.55), the 1,600-meter relay (3:39.40), and the 400-meter relay (45.69) at the Mid-American Conference Outdoor Championships held at Mt. Pleasant. On July 22, 1988 she placed sixth in the second round of the 200-meter run (24.56) at the U. S. Olympic trails.[219]

Joy Inniss from Eastern Michigan also achieved All-American status by placing fifth in the triple jump at the NCAA Division I Indoor Championships in Indianapolis in March 1993.[220] Inniss was Mid-American Champion nine times. She won the MAC 1,600-meter relay four times and the MAC triple jump three times.[221]

In 1993 Jill Kristen Stamison, from Lake Bluff, Illinois, became the third Western Michigan University woman to earn All-American honors when she finished third in the 800-meter run at the 1993 NCAA indoor championships in Indianapolis and fourth in the outdoor championships in New Orleans.[222] After she graduated from Western in 1993, Jill ran for Nike North. She placed fifth in the 400-meter dash (55:42) at the Drake Relays on April 29, 1995.[223] On September 16, 1995 she married Paul McMullen at the Church of St. Mary in Lake Forest, Illinois. The following year she qualified for the 1996 Olympic trials in the 800-meter run. Slowed by an injury to the Achilles tendon, she placed third in her heat of the preliminary round of the Olympic trials in Atlanta.[224]

On June 13, 1997 Jill placed third in the 800-meter run (2:00.81) at the USA Outdoor Championships. A month later, she earned $1,750 by winning the 15th Annual Golden Mile Run in record setting time (4:32) at the Cherry Festival in Traverse City. She ended that season in August by competing in the World Championships in Athens, Greece.[225] In the last year of the century Jill won the 800-meter invitational (2:08.81) at the Drake Relays.[226]

Another Western Michigan University track-lady who deserves mention is Jamie Strieter from New Prairie High School in Rolling Prairie, Indiana, who was National Honor Society member and salutatorian of her high school class. In 1997, when she placed sixth in the javelin throw (150–1) at the Drake Relays, Jamie was a NCAA provisional qualifier in the javelin throw. She won the javelin throw at the Mid-American Conference Championships in 1996, 1997, and 1998. She also placed third in the shot put at these meets, and placed second in the javelin (165–1) at the Drake Relays in 1998.[227]

Carrie Gould started track at Burton Bendle High School in suburban Flint, where she was the Michigan High School Class C cross-country champion in 1992 and 1993 and the Class C 3,200-meter track and Field champion in 1993. In 1994 she transferred to Flint Powers Catholic High School and was ineligible for the state meet that year because of the transfer. In 1995 she nearly missed the State Meet because of illness. Before the May 20, 1995 regional meet, she con-

Jamie Strieter. Western Michigan University, 1995–8; MAC javelin champion. *(photo credit: Chuck Comer)*

tacted an unknown illness, which made it difficult for her to breathe and caused dizziness. If she had missed the regional, she would not have qualified for the state meet. "I didn't even go to school the day before," Gould later said. "I'd stand up and pass out. I only ran because it was the regionals."

She not only ran well enough to qualify for the state meet, but won the 1600 and 3200. "It was one of the most amazing things to see her come back and run the two-mile," Powers coach Jim Neumann said. "I would have bet the mortgage she wouldn't do it. She said she'd do it and blew the competition away. She just doesn't like to lose."

On June 3 at Midland High School Gould became the first Flint-area girl to win the 1,600 and 3,200-meter runs in a State Class B Meet. These two victories, combined with a Class B cross-country title for Powers in the fall of 1994, made Gould unbeaten in six career races at state meets. "I wasn't as psyched [for the 3,200-meter run] as I was for the mile," said Gould. "My legs were really fresh before the mile. After the mile, it took everything out of me. I surprised myself."[228]

Carrie attend Eastern Michigan University, where on May 15–17, 1997 she placed second in the 3-K run (9:49.29) and forth in the 1,500-meter run (4:39.54) at the Mid-American Conference Championships held at Kent State University. At the Mid-American Conference Indoor Championships held at Bowling Green University in 1999, Carrie won the 3-K run (10:02.54) and the distance medley relay (11:40.20), and was named to the All-Conference team. On April 23, 1999 Gould won the 10-K run (34:28.33) at the Drake Relays.[229] In February 2000 Carrie won the women's distance medley relay (11:39.08) and the 5-K run (17:08.30), and placed forth in the 10-K run at the Mid-American Conference Indoor Championships.[230] She placed third in the 10-K at the Drake Relays on April 28, 2000.[231]

An Overview of Women's Sports Thirty Years After Title IX

Female athletes did not generate much excitement following the passage and implementation of Title IX. Perhaps this can be attributed to the virtual absence of newspaper coverage of women's sports during the 1970s, when it was nearly impossible to find the results of women's track meets or any other women's sports event in any newspaper in the country. While the law outlawed all forms of discrimination on the basis sex in educational institutions receiving federal funding, it did not force male sports writers to cover women's sports nor did it require sports fans to attend women's meets or to generate interest in women's sports. Consequently, the law initially appears to have contributed more to preparing women to play a greater role in the American economy than in creating a new market for athletic endeavors. The gender pay gap between the average earnings for women doing the same jobs as men narrowed slowly. Between 1975 and 1997, women gained 15 percent on men's wages for the same tasks, but were still paid 26 percent less than men.[232]

In 1972, seven percent of the law degrees and nine percent of medical degrees went to women. In 1999 nearly half of all new lawyers and 40 percent of new doctors were women. In 1976, women earned 6 percent of baccalaureate engineering degrees, twenty-three years later 19 percent were earned by women. Title IX fostered an explosion of interest in new women's gymnastics and skating clubs, as well as soccer, basketball and softball leagues. However, Title IX only marginally increased interest in women's track and field.[233] It also generated considerable political opposition to equal rights for women among conservatives.

The Ronald Reagan administration staunchly opposed equal rights for women throughout the 1980s and was generally insensitive to women's issues, including efforts to promote women's track and field.[234] In March 1988 Congress was forced to override Reagan's veto of the Civil Rights Restoration Act made necessary when a Supreme Court decision, the Grove City College case, virtually eliminated Title IX. Without the Restoration Act, the legal underpinnings for equality in funding women's athletics would have been destroyed.[235] Nevertheless, interest in women's sports did develop to the point where 90,000 fans attended the finals of the Women's World Cup Soccer Match in the Rose Bowl on July 10, 1999.[236] This interest was also reflected in an increased number of domestic track meets and improved domestic television exposure for women's track.[237] The number of women participating in intercollegiate sports increased substantially in the 1990s. During the 1997–8 school year, women comprised 40 percent of all participants in Division I athletics, up from 31 percent in the 1995–6 school year. Money spent on recruiting, scholarships and coaches' salaries also increased proportionately for women.

It is significant that the University of Michigan was performing better on title IX than most of its Division I rivals. In the 1998–9 academic year their athletic program was nearing gender equality in athletic participation, with 48.2 percent of its athletes being women and 38 percent of expenditures earmarked for women. At Michigan State 45.4 percent of the athletes were women and 32 percent of expenses went to women's athletics.[238]

It was slowly dawning on the country that girls have a right to prepare for interesting work and economic independence, and the same right as boys to develop as mentally and emotionally sound individuals. Track was contributing to both of these goals, as well as to the enjoyment of the body to which each of us is born.

21. "True Individualism in an Era of Team Sports" [1970-2000]

Between **1974 and 1980** economic changes challenged the financial base of collegiate athletics. Male athletic directors blamed the problem on the "requirements of equal funding for women's athletics under Title IX." But, the changes were more fundamental. Beginning in 1973 and extending through 1983, the Organization of Petroleum Exporting Countries (OPEC) engineered enormous increases in oil prices that resulted in basic economic changes. At the University of Michigan, the athletic budget, excluding women's sports, was climbing faster than the university's operating-budget. Overall, the increased cost of intercollegiate athletics was caused by rapidly rising energy prices, which affected the cost of travel, shipping, heating and cooling. The result was increased operating costs for both the college and its athletic programs. Colleges were forced to raise the price of tuition, and this increased the cost of grant-in-aid scholarships, which comprised a significant portion of athletic department budgets. Concurrently, the number of grant-in-aid scholarships purchased by the athletic department increased as the result of Title IX. Clearly, athletic scholarships for women did not create the economic crisis in collegiate sports, but they did add to it.

The response to Title IX at most colleges and universities, between 1975 and the end of the twentieth century was reprehensible. Instead of expanding the number of full or partial scholarships so that women and men had equal opportunities, most Division I schools cut men's athletic scholarships in non-revenue sports, so that they could keep the total number of women's athletic scholarships low. This strategy was ruinous for men's track and field, baseball, wrestling, and a variety of other inter-collegiate sports. Concurrently, athletic departments expanded the number of scholarships for male athletes in revenue generating sports. The number of football scholarships permitted in NCAA Division I athletic programs rose from 55 to 85. This strategy exacerbated long-term problems for athletic departments.

College athletics truly was a big business. Athletic fund-raising was elevated to an ingenious art form, generating as much as $100-million a year among the 105 Division I-A schools in 1985. According to NCAA reports, 12% of the budgets at Division I schools comes from booster contributions.[1]

Revenue and Sports

On July 1, 1968 Donald B. Canham was appointed to succeed Herbert O. Crisler as the fifth Athletic Director in University of Michigan history. Canham, born on April 27, 1918, attended the University of Michigan from 1937 until 1941, and received a bachelor's degree in physical education, history and science.

When Don Canham became Athletic Director at Michigan he assumed responsibility for a business enterprise that faced a $250,000 operating deficit. Rather than cutting back on expenses, Canham completed the transformation of college athletics from a student activity into an entertainment product. As Athletic Director, Canham made the University of Michigan Athletic Department a commercial juggernaut directly linked to entertainment industry. He was a pioneer in the development of merchandising and licensing agreements.

The first sports licensing agreement was signed by the Chicago Cubs with the Warsaw Company to produce ceramic ashtrays in 1928. By 1965, royalties from licensees had become an important revenue stream for professional football.[2] In an effort to eliminate the operating deficit, Canham began marketing football tickets through Hudson's Department Stores and then undertook a direct mail promotion and advertising campaign, as if he was promoting a Florida land development. It was a course of action "not tried before by any [academic] institution." He also included souvenir offers for coffee cups, pennants, playing cards, jackets and T-shirts displaying Michigan logos along with ticket applications. It was an idea he had picked up at UCLA, but placed under the control of the Athletic Department at Michigan, rather than the college bookstore. The Athletic Department was soon in the souvenir and premium sports ware business "big time." They designed the block M and learned about how to license, register and copyright their logos. Canham even ran marketing seminars for other colleges and Universities.[3] During Canham's reign, the University of Michigan had the largest intercollegiate athletic program in the nation.[4]

Canham incorporated the University of Michigan Athletic Department. The move was justified on the basis of self-support. Canham argued:

We cut our own grass, shovel our own snow, put on roofs, and negotiate with unions. Our budget is $15 million. We're borrowing $3 million to build a new swimming pool. The university will not be liable for that debt. We will. In 1985 the University of Michigan athletic department had about 130 full-time employees, including a travel agent, mechanics, carpenters and engineers, as well as several hundred part-time people who work at sporting events. Its 12 buildings, including Michigan Stadium, which has a seating capacity of 101,701, are located on an area near the main campus known as the 'athletic campus' and are valued at more than $200 million.[5]

Canham said that the University of Michigan Athletic Department had spent $10 million on renovating existing facilities in recent years and the annual maintenance costs about $100,000. Because the Athletic Department was a separate legal entity, it paid the university $40,000 a year to administer its payroll. The Athletic Department also paid full tuition for students receiving athletic scholarships. Far from getting assistance from the university, the Athletic Department was charged by the university an ever-increasing amount for services. Athletics paid for patrolling, groundskeeping, paving, and insurance for their facilities. The rewards were also great, however. A sold-out home football game could bring in as much as $1.5 million. By 1985, the sale of the team logo also was becoming a major source of revenue at many colleges and universities.[6] In the 1998–9 fiscal year the University of Michigan ranked second among colleges and universities in the United States in the sale of licensed merchandise.[7]

However, there was a downside to Canham's approach to college athletics. The insatiable appetite of an increasingly prosperous mass audience for unscripted entertainment made college athletics a commercial product vulnerable to over exposure, showboat exhibitionism by athletes, conflicts of interest by self-centered celebrity coaches, and intense pressure from mass media and commercial enterprises that had little interest in what is best for the athlete or the university.[8] Moreover, Canham's autocratic, command and control management style subverted the academic constraints that are vital to the objectives of a world class university and gave the false impression that his compartmentalized athletic department was self-supporting. Finally, for all intents and purposes, during Canham's tenure as athletic director, the University of Michigan became a one-sport program [football], to the detriments of both track and field and gender equality. Between 1964 and 1989 the University of Michigan did not earn a national championship in any sport.

Separation Anxiety

The separation of athletics from other university functions usually reflect a decision by universities not to subsidize their athletic programs. Indeed, there are often state policies barring subsidies. As a result, athletic programs have to make money to survive. Since football and basketball are the most profitable sport at most schools, they are under the most pressure to win. "Show me a football program that doesn't win and I'll show you an athletic department with no money," Don Canham told a group of athletic directors. In 1980, 61% of the 187 universities in Division I and I-AA reported average profits from their football program of $1 million or more.

The myth that college football and basketball underwrote the cost of inter-collegiate sports was only true for a very small, elite group of colleges and universities.[9] At most institutions of higher education, football and even basketball lose money. In the Mid-American Conference, for example, all twelve universities lost money on football in 1998–99, and ten of twelve schools lost money on men's basketball.[10]

Initially, the top fifty division I colleges and universities used increased football revenues to cover rising costs.[11] But, at most colleges and universities—such as those in the Mid-American Conference—smaller stadiums and the limited drawing power of football at that level of play could not generate enough increased revenue to solve the money pinch. Consequently, nearly all colleges demanded that non-revenue earning sports, like track and field, trim their budgets. At many colleges, minor sports were dropped to balance the athletic budget.[12]

At most division I schools, including Michigan and Michigan State, rising costs placed added pressure on revenue earning sports to generate income. Recruiting abuses, which were already rampant, escalated during this period, according to the *New York Times*.[13] Competition for the best football and basketball players in the nation was intense and frequently involved gifts, lures and favors far beyond legal limits. The destructive atmosphere created by placing so much emphasis on revenue generation by men's intercollegiate football and basketball programs was exposed by Title IX. Some athletic directors, like Don Canham, claimed that a ruling for equal scholarships and equal equipment for women "would destroy football, which pays the bills."[14] However, a closer examination indicated it was the structure of system, and not equal opportunities for women that created the crisis. The system was seriously flawed and an invitation to abuse.

The need to win, in order to balance ever-escalating athletic department budgets, led to growing concerns about inadequate academic standards and improper payments to athletes. The large sums of money involved caused both temptation and pressure to feed the "win at any cost" mentality.[15] As intercollegiate sports grew in popularity and profitability, recruiting systems became more sophisticated. In 1985, more than a million young boys played organized sports, and there was a proliferation of sports camps run by college coaches and professional athletes.[16] In addition to the athletic department, the primary beneficiaries of football profits were football programs and football coaches. For example, the University of Michigan football team received $1.4 million for playing in the Orange Bowl on January 1, 2000, but spent $16,949 more than they made.[17]

In 1989 the highly respected United States General Accounting Office released a survey that found that at NCAA's 287 Division I institutions—the schools with the largest athletic programs—the average graduation rates for student athletes were higher than for all students at the school. However, it also found the average graduation rate for basketball and football players at those institutions was lower than for other student athletes. Frank Deford, a former senior editor of *Sports Illustrated* magazine and sports commentator, told a House Education and Labor subcommittee there was much too much emphasis on athletics. "Big-time collegiate athletics degrade higher education in this country. Big-time athletics is competing with education . . . and our education system is deteriorating. . . . Big-time college athletics is soiling education." Robert Atwell, President of the American Council on Education, agreed:

The major problem with college athletics is the pressure to make money. It is a vicious cycle in which schools have to make money to spend on more things and on and on. If one had to point to a single factor among the many that have corrupted college sports, it would be money. If we want to encourage academics over athletics we should have shorter seasons for football, basketball and baseball, and eliminate athletic scholarships and rely entirely on need-based aid.[18]

Between 1993 and 1999, athletic department expenses increased 70 percent and their income only increased 30 percent. The University of Michigan became so dependent on licensed merchandise sales that an unexpected decline in revenue from that source caused the University of Michigan Athletic Department to hire a commercial finance firm to help solve its financial problems. In the 1998–99 fiscal year, the University of Michigan reported a $2-million deficit on its $46-million budget.[19]

Rampant commercialism in college sports led University of Michigan President-Emeritus Duderstadt to suggest that a return to single platoon football was needed to restore the balance in intercollegiate sports programs in American Universities. Duderstadt maintained that this change would reduce the cost of intercollegiate sports substantially because it would eliminate more than half of the football scholarships and coaching expenses needed to operate the sport that was the engine behind the imbalance.[20] Although it had endowment generating benefits, football usually was not a revenue generating sport at most colleges and universities, because of the expenses football incurs. At the vast majority of colleges and universities, basketball generated the most surplus revenue for athletic departments.

The Era of Team Sports

It has been asserted that in the 1970s the American counterculture of the 1960s became the dominant culture of the so-called "baby-boomers," or the children born in the decade following World War II. Some believe that this group rejected external control, competition, and participation in formal organizations. "Baby-boomers," the argument went, generally were indifferent to formal roles and more interested in process than in outcome, and in group cooperation and participation than in individual achievement.[21] If true, this transition favored team sports such as basketball, soccer, football, and hockey over individual sports such as track and field, wrestling, swimming, and gymnastics.

This intriguing notion might be used to explain the decline in interest in track and field that occurred after 1965, but it does not explain why the track program at Eastern Michigan University flourished or why American women's track exploded in popularity.

Eastern Michigan University, Track Powerhouse Under Coach Parks

In the late 1950s, Michigan Normal College President Eugene B. Elliot took a stand against all athletics. He did all he could to weaken the existing intercollegiate athletic programs. During this period, the track team was forced to drop out of the Central Collegiate Conference. As a consequence, the Alumni Track Club used its influence to get Dr. Elliot dismissed as President of the College. When Dr. Harold Sponberg replaced Elliot due in part from pressure from the track club, the Eastern Michigan University track program regained national prominence.

In 1966 EMU looked to hire a new coach to replace ailing George Marshall. Despite considerable opposition, EMU allowed Marshall to select Bob Parks, as his assistant and heir apparent. Parks was a former Michigan Normal sprinter, who was an assistant track coach at Western Michigan University. In June 1967, Marshall went into the hospital and Parks stepped in as head coach. In 1970 Eastern rejoined the Central Collegiate Conference. In 1972 EMU qualified 27 track athletes for the college division NCAA outdoor track and field championships in Ashland, Ohio and won Eastern Michigan University's first national championship.[22]

Bob Parks: Don't Wish for It: Work for It

At a time when team sports dominated fan attention, and when teamwork was emphasized in every aspect of life from work to marriage and child rearing, the primary proponent of individualism in American life was still track and field. The track athlete practices alone, worries alone, and finally performs alone. The individual is supreme, and bears personal responsibility for turning in a good effort. Sure, there is a team score and there are outdoor and indoor championships, but even winning such a title is more a measure of which coach can get the most from the sum total of the individual efforts of his squad.

By this yardstick, coach Bob Parks was surely one of the great coaches of individuals in an era of team sports. On May 25–27, 1972 coach Parks took his Eastern Michigan College Hurons to the National College Division track and field championships in Ashland, Ohio. It was to be the last college division track meet for Eastern Michigan because the school was scheduled to step up to university status in the fall. According to Dennis Lustig of the *Cleveland Plain Dealer*, the Eastern Michigan swan song at Ashland was a happening.[23] Eastern Michigan dominated the meet as few others have ever dominated a major track and field championship.

The 611 athletes from 115 colleges and universities at the meet were stunned by Eastern Michigan's savage assault on the record books. Led by Bob Parks' crew, athletes at the Ashland meet set 14 new marks. The Huron's great distance runner, Gordon Minty—a 24-year old sophomore from London, England—was particularly impressive in successfully defending his titles in the 5- and 10-K runs by winning each them in record time. Minty's 29:29.6 in the 10-K stood as the Division II record for more than a decade. However, his (28:51.3) 10-K effort at the 51st Annual NCAA Division I Outdoor Championships in Eugene only gave him second place at that meet. Even when Eastern Michigan athletes did not win they pressed their opponents. Eastern Michigan miler, Fred La Plante, finished a half-second behind Garry Bentley of South Dakota, and Bill Cartwright of Eastern Michigan lost to Rod Jackson of Eastern Illinois in the 400-meter intermediate hurdles by 4/10 of a second.

When the meet was over, Eastern Michigan scored 93 points: their nearest rival accumulated only 49 points. Eighteen College Division All-Americans certificates were awarded to Eastern Michigan athletes, while no other team was awarded more than six.[24] Eastern Michigan track stars set three new meet records, and pressed runners in two other events to record performances to beat them. The meet was indeed a true "happening."

In 1972 Eastern became a NCAA Division I competitor and that fall joined the Mid-American Conference. Eastern Michigan University achieved its first MAC track championship in the spring of 1974.

A Very Quiet Man Who Ran Very Fast

Stanley Vinson graduated from Chauncy High School in 1971, where he won the 440-yard dash (48.0) at the Class A State High School Championships. He attended Eastern Michigan University that fall, where he was an instant star. In February 1972 Stan won the 600-yard run in the Millrose Games, and on March 8, the Eastern Michigan freshman was seventh in the 600-yard run and fourth in the mile relay at the NCAA Indoor Championships at Cobo Arena.[25]

During the outdoor season, Vinson placed fifth in the 880-yard relay (1:26.8) and helped Eastern win the distance medley relay (9:43.4) and place fifth in the college division, mile relay (3:11.2) at the Drake Relays. In May Stan played an important role in Eastern Michigan's winning the National College Division NCAA Track and Field Championship. He was on the winning the mile relay (3:09.7) and placed fourth in the 400-meter run (46.5) at that meet at Ashland College. On June 8–9, 1972 he placed fifth in heat 3 of the 400-meter run (46.8) at the NCAA Division I Outdoor Championships.

Stan was a very quiet young man. He trained hard, was humble, and only became aggressive when he stepped on the track. At the indoor meets at Eastern Michigan University, the balcony at the indoor track would fill up with the dorm guys whenever Stan ran. When he got the baton in a relay race, Stan would raise his fist in a black power salute. Just before the last 200-meters of the race he would again raise his fist in a black power salute, as he took off for the closing portion of the race.

After he won, as he invariably did by "toasting" his opponents with his relentless, driving finish, Stan would again become the mild-mannered, meek student. Stan was stronger than he was fast, but he could move pretty good too. Bob Parks created an atmosphere that fostered personal athletic development. Parks expected you to do well. He loved time trials.[26]

In 1974 Stan won the 600-yard run (1:11.2) and the mile relay at the 67th Millrose Games, and placed second in the 600-yard run (1:11.3) at the National AAU Indoor Championships at Madison Square Garden.[27] In March he won the 400-meter dash (48.3) and the 2,000-meter medley relay (4:19.4) at the Russia vs. USA meet at the Brothers Znamenskiy Indoor Meet in Moscow, Russia. A week later Vinson won the 600-yard run (1:10.1) at the Tenth National NCAA Division I Indoor Championships.[28]

In the Spring of 1974 Stan placed third in the sprint medley relay (3:24.6) and placed third in the 440-yard Invitational (46.2) at the Drake Relays. In June he reached the semifinals of the 440-yard dash at the 53rd NCAA Championships in Austin. A week later he won the 440-yard dash (46.7) at the 12th U. S. Track and Field Federation Meet.[29]

In February 1975 Stan placed fourth in the 600-yard run (1:11.6) at the National AAU Senior Indoor Championships. In March he placed second in the 440-yard dash (48.4) at the USA vs. USSR Indoor duel meet in Richmond, Virginia, and won the 600-yard run (1:10.2) at the NCAA Division I Indoor Championships in Detroit. In early April Bob Parks kept four of his best runners, including Stan Vinson and Hasley Crawford, home from an early April duel meet with Bowling Green University. Thirty-one degree temperatures and gusting winds of up to 40 miles per hour caused safety problems that made him unwilling to risk the health of his star athletes.[30] In late April Vinson placed third in the open 440-yard dash (47.1) and in the university sprint medley relay (3:20.4) at the Drake Relays.

Stan Vinson was "one of the best indoor 400 men and relay anchorman ever" to attend Eastern Michigan.[31] In the 1972 Stan was named a College Division NCAA All-American.[32] It was the first of his six All-American awards. Vinson won 15 Mid-American Conference and Central Collegiate Conference titles and had 20 top three finishes. Some of his best marks included: 200 meters (21.44), 300-yards (30.94), 400-meters (46.94), 800 meters (1:48.72), and the triple jump (50–6½).

After graduating from Eastern Michigan University, Stan Vinson ran for the Florida Track Club, the Washington D.C. Striders, and the University of Chicago Track Club. July 4, 1975 he won the 400-meter dash (45.8) in the USA vs. Soviet Union match meet, Kiev, U. S. S. R.[33] Victories against Poland, Czechoslovakia, and West Germany followed. On July 18–19, 1975 Stan won the 400-meter run (45.4) at the USA-Pan-African Games in Los Angeles.[34]

In 1976 he won the 500-yard run (55.7), and the mile relay (3:11.0) at the Mason-Dixon Games, and the 500-meter run (1:02.6) at the Olympic Invitational in Madison Square Garden. On February 27, 1976 while competing for the Florida Track Club, Vinson was second in the 600-yard run (1:10.2) at the National AAU Senior Indoor Championships.[35] On March 6 Stan won the 400-meter run (47.69) and the 2,000-meter relay (4:19.6) at the USA vs. USSR Senior Indoor Meet in Leningrad. He placed third in the 1,600-meter relay [ran his leg in 45.4] at the Penn Relays, and on June 22, 1976 qualified for the semifinals in the 400-meter dash (46.35) at the U.S. Olympic trials,[36] but did not make the team. The slowest American Olympic qualifier ran a 44.75.

Despite missing the Olympic team, Stan Vinson continued to compete. In 1977 he lived in Silver Springs, Maryland and ran for the D.C. Striders. Stan was third in the 600-yard run (1:10.3) and third in the mile-relay (3:12.6) at the National AAU Senior Indoor Championships. He was second in the 440-yard dash (48.9) and won the sprint medley relay (3:02.2) at the USA-USSR-Canada indoor meet in Toronto. As part of the D.C. Striders relay he team won the sprint medley special (3:18.8) at the Penn Relays, and on May 25–26 won the 400-meter run (45.82) at the 15th U. S. Track and Field Federation Championships. Stan was fifth in the 400-meter run and second in the mile relay (3:38.62) at the 1977 National AAU Outdoor Championships in Los Angeles.[37] On June 20–1 he won the 400-meter run (46.07) at the USA vs. European track tour meet [Italy, Great Britain, USA] in Turin, Italy.

The high-mark of his illustrious track career occurred when he anchored the USA relay team to a new American and world indoor record in the 1,600-meter relay (3:08.9) on March 14, 1978 in the USA vs. Europe track meet, Milan, Italy.

In 1978 Stan became a fireman in Chicago. At the end of the century, he was a Fire Inspector in Chicago. As an active member of Jehovah's Witnesses, he refused membership in the EMU Hall of Fame.[38]

Bronze Medal Olympian

Earl Jones was born in Inkster, Michigan on July 11, 1964.[39] Earl was an outstanding middle-distance runner at Taylor Center High School.

On May 30, 1981 he won the 880-yard run (1:54.6) and placed second in the mile run (4:16.4) at the Class A High School Championships held in Flint. Going into the State High School Championships in 1982, Earl was ranked the best the 880-yard runner (1:52.9), second best in the mile runner (4:17.1), and fourth in the 440-yard runner (48.6) in the Detroit metropolitan area.[40] On June 5 Earl lived up to expectations when he won the 800-meter (1:52.7) and the 1,600-meter run (4:18.1), and placed third in the 1,600-meter relay (3:18.0) at the Class A State Championships.[41] Earl graduated from Taylor Center High School in June 1982.[42]

In 1983 as a freshman at Eastern Michigan, Earl lost in the semi-finals of the mile run and placed seventh in the two-mile relay at the NCAA Indoor Championships in Pontiac. At the Drake Relays Jones placed third in heat 2 of the 1,600-meter relay (3:10:44) and fourth in the finals of the 3,200-meter relay (7:23.92). He placed second in the 1,500-meter run (3:40.64) at the NCAA Outdoor Championships, to earn All-American status. On June 19 Earl placed twelfth in the 1,500-meter run (3:46.78) at the USA Outdoor Championships in Indianapolis.[43]

In 1984 Earl Jones set a new 1,500-meter Mid-American Conference record at the Conference outdoor meet in Bowling Green, Ohio. But, Coach Parks noted that he had trouble coming back in the 800-meter forty minutes later, so in 1984 he had concerns about entering in both races again. Nevertheless, he entered Earl in both events again, and also had him run on the mile relay team. Jones won all three events.[44]

On June 1, 1984 Earl Jones was second in the 800-meter run (1:45.79) at the NCAA National Championships in Eugene.[45] After spending two years at Eastern Michigan, Earl Jones moved to the West Coast for the summer to run for the Santa Monica Track Club. On June 5, Jones was listed as having the third fastest time in the 800-meter run (1:45.79) for the year to-date.[46]

On Monday June 18, 1984 Earl Jones qualified for the finals of the 800-meter Olympic trials by placing second with a time of 1:46.33.[47] A crowd of 21, 081, the largest ever to witness an Olympic track trials, watched Earl Jones, a 19-year old from Inkster, Michigan, lead all the way in the 800-meter finals. Earl ran the first 400-meters in the exceptionally fast time of 50.15, and at the finish just held off the lunging Johnny Gray. Jones set the American record for the 800-meter run with the astounding time of 1:43.74. This was the first time four men bettered 1:44 in one race. Only seven men in the world had ever run the distance faster than Jones.[48] The strategy for the race was fashioned by Coach Bob Parks, who felt that Earl needed a fast breakout to make the U. S. Olympic team.[49]

In August 1984 Earl Jones placed third to Joaquim Carvalho Cruz of Taguatinga, Brazil who trained in the USA and was clocked at the Olympic record time of 1:43.00.[50] Jones earned a bronze medal in the time of 1:43.83.

On May 18, 1985 Jones won the 800-meter run (1:49.29), the 1,500-meter run (3:47.33), and the 1,600-meter relay (3:08.95) at the Mid-American Conference Championships in Kalamazoo. He was named co-athlete of the year at that Meet.[51] In 1985 Eastern Michigan University had the second fastest 1,600-meter relay team in the nation on a 200-meter track, but did not qualify for the NCAA indoor meet because ten teams qualified at a single meet running on oversized tracks. He did, however, place third at the 800-meter at the U.S. Championships.[52]

On February 14, 1986 Jones won the 1,000-meter run (2:20.18) at the Wanamaker-Millrose Games. In May he won the 800-meter run (1:47.08) at the Jesse Owens Classic in Columbus, and in June he took fifth in the TAC.[53] On July 5 he won the 800-meter run (1:44.70) at the Bislett Games Grand Prix in Oslo, Norway. He ran his personal best in the 800-meter at Zurich and for the 1,500-meter run at Hengelo, Netherlands. He was third in the standings for the 800-meter run in the International Amateur Athletic Federation Mobil Outdoor Grand Prix through Sunday July 6, 1986.[54] In 1986 Earl was involved in an automobile accident, and never fully recovered from what did not seem at the time like career-ending injuries.[55]

Eastern Michigan Marches On

In 1981 the NCAA and the Big Ten allowed 14 grant-in-aid athletic scholarships in men's track, while the Mid-American Conference only allowed 8 full-grant-in-aid scholarships in men's track.[56] Despite the handicap, Coach Parks managed to win year after year against opponents with better grant-in-aid programs. From 1972 through the end of the century Eastern Michigan finished first or second at every MAC outdoor track championship, except for 1979 and 1980, when they finished fourth and third, respectively. They won all but two MAC indoor championships from 1974 to the end of the century meet held February 25–26, 2000. In 1981 and 1985, they placed second.

During his tenure at Eastern, which ended with the close of the century, Parks won three NAIA indoor championships, 11 Central Collegiate indoor championships and 17 Mid-American Conference indoor titles. In indoor track he coached 150 individual MAC champions, 115 individual CCC champions, and 14 NCAA Division and NAIA national champions. Outdoors, he won 17 MAC titles, 13 CCC titles, two NAIA national titles, and the 1972 NCAA Division II national championship. He coached 141 individual MAC champions, 95 individual CCC champions, 17 NAIA, NCAA Division I and II national champions. In 1990, he was named NCAA Division I National Indoor Coach of the Year. He also coached the 1987 U.S. track team that competed against England and Northern Ireland.[57]

One of Park's trackmen observed:

There was no place Bob Parks draws the line to extend opportunity for his athletes. He gives every athlete on his squad a chance to prove himself, and will go out of his way to get all his trackmen a chance to run in a meet. Many of Park's athletes did not like his Holland, Michigan political beliefs, and tried to prove him wrong, but they still liked Bob Parks the man.[58]

Eastern Michigan had a track Olympian in every Olympiad starting in 1960. EMU Olympians include: Hayes Jones, David Ellis, Hasley Crawford, Tony Nelson, Earl Jones, Tommy Asinga, Paul McMullen, Greg Rhymer, and Clement Cukwa.

A 1981 article by an *Ypsilanti Press* reporter spoke to the subject.

Year after year, season after season, several things are certain. Taxes are due in April, death is due any darn time it's ready, and Eastern Michigan's men's track team is a winner. Bob Parks and his Huron track team always hold up their part of the deal. Nevertheless, "Eastern is sometimes a hard place to recruit to with all the bad raps like it being a suitcase college," Parks said. "We've just got a great tradition with the guys we've had in the Olympics and the great indoor facilities we have. Our kids don't set any limits for themselves because all they have to do is look at what was ahead of them. Every year I see the NCAA qualifying standards and think we'll never get anybody there, and every year we keep getting kids breaking them. Once a program tastes success things just tend to keep getting better. You have to touch all the bases. You can't leave anything to chance. You need to keep up on recruiting, on your alumni, with public relations. You have to check it all. It's easier once you get rolling and then it's easier to keep it going. We get kids here now as walk-ons that other schools are offering two-thirds scholarships to. The EMU track program has become its own little 'family' with each succeeding generation having a previously successful group ahead of it to live up to. And the best thing about it all? They love it. They love the atmosphere, the feeling of being part of something close, the feeling of winning. It's something that's not hard to get used to.

As former EMU assistant coach Ray Lohner put it. "You've got to have the right coach at the right time in the right situation. Bob Parks is the right coach for Eastern Michigan.[59]

On Saturday May 2, 1990 Bob Parks was at the Drake Relays with his track team. After the meet they drove back to Ypsilanti from Iowa and arrived home at 5 a.m. Sunday morning. Yet, without failure he honored his usual 9:30 a.m. office hours on Monday where he met a reporter from the *Ann Arbor News*. Parks, who was originally from Howell, Michigan, told the Ann Arbor reporter that after 37 years in the profession—24 of which were spent at Eastern Michigan University—he still loves coaching track.

When Bob Parks is talking track, he is a fountain of knowledge bubbling over with enthusiasm. "I love this school and I love working with the kids. I don't even mind the recruiting, but I'm not a phony. I'm always going to tell it like it is."

The track gospel according to Parks is simple. There's a place for any athlete, regardless of talent who is willing to work hard. 'I'm like a dinosaur in this sport in that respect, and I've been doing it differently for a long time. A lot of teams like to have one big shooter, but that's not what this sport is about. I believe in the team concept.'" If you're working, and you're going to practice, he'll bend over backwards for you. If you do what he asks, he'll help you out the rest of the way," said one of his athletes. "He added, "We have a little joke among the guys on the team. We say, 'Who cares what Parks thinks? We still think you're a good runner." "Parks never sugar coats anything. He tells you flat out what he thinks."

Gary Bastien said, "He takes guys and makes the right moves, and they turn out better. I'm a good example of that kind of guy. I was a good pole-vaulter in high school, and in any other [college] program I'd have been stuck doing that. But he saw something in me." Bastien, who grew up in Grandville, Michigan and moved to Saline, Michigan. [In 1980 Gary Bastien of Eastern Michigan University won the decathlon at the Drake Relays, and after graduation from EMU, became one of the nation's best decathlon athletes.]

Fred La Plante, a former Huron runner, added, "Parks is always focused on high expectations. It doesn't matter what your talent level, if you screw up, you'll know about it. But he gives attention to people at the high and low end of the program."

EMU's tradition of track excellence was in place when Parks took over the program in 1967. "The tradition doesn't mean that much to a kid looking at the school, but it means a lot to the kids on the team," according to Parks. "The kids rise to another level because they think they're supposed to. They see the pictures on the wall, and want to be there." Parks attributes his success to his ability to adapt to the often unforgiving ways of intercollegiate athletics. For example, he's learned how to divide eight scholarships—six less than the maximum allowed by the NCAA—to help as many athletes as possible. "I've changed with the times long enough to stay afloat," Parks says. "That explains my longevity. But my basic philosophy has stayed the same."

"People who don't even know me think I'm a genius. Others think that I'm a dodo head. I'm neither, I'm fortunate to have been at the right school for me. I can operate in this environment."[60]

Those who opposed the appointment of Bob Parks as track coach in 1966 obviously had a defective crystal ball.

Yankees Running for the Tennessee Volunteers

Of course, Eastern Michigan University was not the only institution of higher education to feature notable track teams during the 1970s and 80s. Few schools had a better track program than the University of Tennessee. The Tennessee Volunteers participated in their first conference level track meet in 1895, and were participants in the first Southeastern Intercollegiate Athletic Association track meet held on May 15, 1896. By the start of the twentieth century, eight of the thirteen Southeastern Conference (SEC) charter members had track programs.

The Southeastern Intercollegiate Athletic Association became the Southeastern Conference in 1966. Between 1966 and 1987 the University of Tennessee won the SEC outdoor track and field championship 19 out of 21 years and placed second in 1979. They won the SEC indoor championship 14 out of 21 years and placed second five times during that period. Tennessee also placed in the top ten of the NCAA outdoor track and field championship 13 times during those 21 years, and produced 74 individual outdoor All-Americans and 53 indoor track and field All-Americans.[61] Among those who made this remarkable record possible were five All-Americans from Michigan: Doug Brown from St. Claire Shores; Reggie Jones from Saginaw; Sam Jones from Highland Park; Dave Krafsur from Southfield Lathrup; and Doug Tolson from Westland. During the 1990s, Chad Smith, a decathlete from Ypsilanti High School, would also become an All-American at the University of Tennessee. In addition to these All-Americans several other Michigan runners ran for the Volunteers including Bob Dickie from Grand Blanc.

From a Family of Ten

Doug Brown was one of ten children, and one of the best American track athletes in the last half of the twentieth century.[62] He was born and grew up in St. Claire Shores, Michigan and attended Notre Dame

Catholic High School in Harper Woods. Doug set records in the mile run while in high school track.[63] On May 15, 1969 Doug Brown won the mile run (4:18.4) at the Class A Regional Championships in Warren. The following year he again won the mile run (4:13.75) at the Michigan Regional Championships.[64]

The University of Tennessee recruited Doug and transformed him into a distance runner. As a freshman, Doug set the SEC record for the 3-mile run in 1971 (14:05.6).[65] He also placed third in the six-mile run at the NCAA outdoor championships to win All-American honors, and was a cross-country All-American in 1972 and 1973.

In June 1972 Brown placed third in the 3,000-meter steeplechase at NCAA outdoor Championships. On July 2 he placed second in the finals of the 3,000-meter steeplechase (8:31.8) at the U.S. Olympic trials, to qualify for the USA Olympic team. On September 1 Doug placed ninth in the steeplechase (8:41.2) in the third heat of round one at the Olympic Games in Munich, Germany.

After his Olympic experience, Doug won the two-mile run (8:43.9) at the SEC indoor championships, and placed fifth in the mile run at the NCAA indoor in Detroit. Then, he won the steeplechase (8:43) at the 1973 Penn Relays. Doug Brown helped the Tennessee Volunteers win their tenth consecutive Southeastern Conference Championship in 1973 at Auburn by winning three events—the steeplechase (9:00.6), the three-mile run (13:58.8), and the six-mile run (28:58.8). He was the first athlete in a decade to be a triple winner at the Southeast Conference Meet.[66] On June 9 he went on to win the steeplechase (8:28.1) at the NCAA Outdoor Championships in Baton Rouge.

In 1974 Doug again won the SEC two-mile indoor and was awarded the Tony Wilson Memorial Trophy at the SeaRay Relays as the outstanding athlete in the running events. For good measure, he won the steeplechase at the Gatorade Classic on May 11, setting the Tom Black track record (8:23.2) in the process.[67] At the SEC outdoor championships, Doug again won the three-mile, the six-mile, and the steeplechase. He had a damaged toe going into the NCAA Championships in Austin.[68] Nevertheless, on June 7–8 he won the steeplechase at the NCAA Championships. In his collegiate career Doug Brown won All-American honors a truly remarkable seven times.

After graduating from the University of Tennessee, Doug stayed in Knoxville and ran for the Knoxville Track Club. On February 7, 1976 he placed second in the 5,000-meter run (14:05) at the Mason-Dixon Games in Louisville. That summer, he won the steeplechase (8:27.4) at the Olympic trials in Eugene on June 27. On July 25 he placed 14th in the steeplechase (8:33.25) at the Montreal Olympics.[69]

Two years later, Doug placed second in the steeplechase (8:30.1) at the National AAU Senior Outdoor Championships in Westwood, California, while running for Nike West. On June 15–16, 1980 Doug Brown won the steeplechase (8:26.2) at the Athletics Congress National Championships in Walnut, California.[70] On June 28 Brown placed second in the steeplechase (8:20.60) at the U.S. Olympic tryouts.[71] He qualified for the U. S. Olympic team and had a good enough time to rank in the top ten in the world, but the U.S.A. cancelled its participation in the Olympics by President Carter because of the Soviet invasion of Afghanistan. In 1984 Doug Brown was an administrator for the Athletics West Track Club for Nike.

Highland Park High School's Best

Sam James was "the best trackman ever produced at Highland Park High School." As a junior in high school, Sam placed third in the mile run (4:15.7) at the Class A State Championships. As a senior, he won the State three-mile (14:45) cross-country championship. He also won the two-mile run (9:19.3) at the Huron Relays in Ann Arbor, the mile run (4:17.8) at the Spartan Relays in East Lansing, and the two-mile run (9:14.9) at the Detroit Central Relays, before winning the 2-mile run (9:04.7) at the State Class A Championships. Sam was Vice-President of his high school class, had a 3.2 scholastic average, and was a member of the National Honor Society.[72]

Sam enrolled at the University of Tennessee in the fall of 1976. As a freshman, Sam James won the 800-meter run (1:50.9) and the two-mile relay (7:33.3) at the SEC Indoor Championships. In April 1977 he was part of the winning 6-K relay team (15:09.4) at the Penn Relays. He also set four records that year. He established the university's freshman indoor record for the 880-yard run (1:50.9). He also was a member of the relay teams that set Tennessee varsity records for the two-mile relay (7:21.58), the 6-K relay (15:09.3), and the four-mile relay (16.15.5); and Tom Black Track records for the four-mile relay. On June 17–18 Sam won the 1,500-meter run (3:47.77) at the National AAU Junior Men's Meet in Knoxville to become an AAU All-American.

In May 1978 Sam James won the steeplechase at the SEC Outdoor Championships. The following year he won the two-mile relay (7:32.52) at the SEC Indoor Championships. He also won the 1500-

meter run and the steeplechase (3:43.51) at the SEC Outdoor Championships, and in June 1979 placed fifth in the steeplechase at the NCAA Outdoor Championships to earn All-American status.

In March 1980 Sam James won the 800-meter run (1:52.95) at the SEC Indoor Championships, and placed second in the distance medley relay (9:43.56) at the NCAA Indoor Championships to become an All-American for the fourth time. In May 1980 Sam won the steeplechase (8:38.3) at the SEC Championships, and was given the Jon Young Memorial Captain's Award by Tennessee.[73]

Westland Wanderer

Doug Tolson from Wayne Memorial High School in Westland was the Michigan high school cross-country champion his junior and senior years. In the fall of 1981 Tolson enrolled at the University of Tennessee, where he immediately won a letter in cross-country. Doug was second in the SEC cross-country meet in the fall of 1982, and earned All-American honors in cross-country with a 26th place finish at the NCAA finals. Tolson was one of the captains of the University of Tennessee track team in 1983. He won the three-mile run (13:42.92) at the SEC Conference Indoor Championships in Baton Rouge on February 25–26, 1983. Doug qualified for the NCAA outdoor championships in by winning 10-K run at the Dogwood Relays on April 13–14, 1983. He also ran a 3:51.65 1,500-meter at the Kentucky Relays in April 1983.[74]

Doug Tolson was SEC indoor three-mile champion in 1984. That fall he was the SEC individual cross-country champion and was again a cross-country All-American. In 1985 he again won the SEC three-mile indoor and was an All-American in track as part of the NCAA sixth place, Tennessee metric distance medley relay team. Doug followed up with the SEC 10-K outdoor championship. The three-time All-American his track career at Tennessee by winning the 5-K run at the SEC indoor meet in 1986 and in 1988 he placed 12th in the 5-K-run at the USA Track and Field Championships and ran in the Olympic trials.[75]

Dave Krafsur from Southfield Lathrup also ran track at the University of Tennessee. In high school Krafsur placed second in the two-mile run at the 1982 Class A state meet, and placed second in the Mid-west Meet of Champions in Fort Wayne. The Fort Wayne race earned the call from the University of Tennessee. In 1983 as a sophomore at Tennessee in 1983, he ran the 5-K and 10-K. Krafsur finished fourth in the two-mile (9:02.55) at the SEC indoor championships. He ran a 14:32.48 in the 5-K at the Southern Methodist University Relays on

March 17, 1983.[76] In the fall of 1985 Krafsur was a cross-country All-American.[77]

Michigan State University's Sub-Four Minute Miler

During the 1960s and 70s MSU challenged the University of Michigan as the track kingpin of the Big Ten. During those two decades, MSU produced twenty All-Americans and five NCAA champions [Gene Washington, Robert Steele, Bill Wehrwein, Herb Washington, and Ken Popejoy], whereas the University of Michigan did not produce a single national champion and relatively few All-Americans who were citizens of the USA.

One of MSU's national champions was Kenneth Lee Popejoy. Ken was born to a Methodist family in Elmhurst, Illinois on December 9, 1950. His father, Charles Popejoy, was a Big Ten miler at Purdue University in 1933 who ran against Glen Cunningham twice and won the Big Ten two-mile championship before became a lawyer. His mother, Catherine, was a housewife. Ken's family moved to Glen Ellyn, Illinois before he attended junior high school.

When Ken was in junior high school and only 4 feet 11 inches tall and weighed a ponderous 85 pounds, his father bet him $25 dollars that he couldn't stick it out two weeks on the cross-country team. "I really used to drag myself home at night, but I didn't want to lose that bet. I didn't have 25 bucks and didn't want to cut that many lawns or wash that many cars." Popejoy could do little else but run. He tried the pole vault but couldn't lift the pole. He tried basketball and said, "I was okay as long as nobody was covering me. I could throw the ball in the basket, but if somebody was on me, I was through. Baseball? Well, I always batted last and was afraid of the ball. And as for football . . . well, I wasn't that sadistic to even try it except in the corner lots with the kids."[78] When he found his father's medals and scrapbook, he decided to become a runner to be like his dad.

Ken attended and graduated from Glenbard West High School. He was co-captain of his high school cross-country team. He also was All-Conference and All-District in track for three years, and All-State for two years. He was a member of the National Honor Society and the Math Club, and was awarded the American Legion Citizenship Award.[79]

When a young man is less than 5 foot ten tall and weighs less than a hundred pounds in junior high school, he does not have much of a future in athletics unless he is a runner. So, Ken Popejoy became a runner and used the discipline he acquired to become a standout prep runner, a stellar collegiate star, and to acquire a law degree. His high school coach was Jim Arnold, who in 1951 became the first freshman ever to earn a track letter at Michigan State University. Under his guidance, Popejoy lowered his mile time from 4:36 as a freshman to 4:09 as a senior, when he finished second to Steve Prefontaine at the Golden West meet in California. His high school coach "didn't influence me at all to go to Michigan State. He was like a second father to me. He left the decision up to me."[80]

When Ken enrolled at Michigan State, following in the footsteps of his high school coach, he still looked less than full-grown. In 1970, Popejoy became the second freshman (after Jim Arnold) to win a track letter. During his freshman year in college, Ken Popejoy experienced a reoccurring knee-joint injury that interfered with his training and competition. "I hope he doesn't have an operation. The injury was a tremendous disappointment to him," his father confessed.[81]

On March 12, 1971 he finished third (4:09) in the mile run at the NCAA indoor track championships in Detroit. On March 5 Ken finished fifth in the mile run (4:10.6) at the Big Ten Indoor Championships.[82]

Ken was a thin 5–8, 125-pound runner. Like his father, Ken ran both cross-country and middle-distance track events. When a reporter stated: "Simply put, it's amazing that a little guy can run so fast . . . as he has to take more strides than his competitors." This brought a smile to Ken's face. "'I guest that's true, but it also gives me an edge,' he said. 'I can change speeds, change the pace, quicker than most guys. They usually have to power up or power down. I can do it in a couple of strides.'" "Yes, I dream of Munich, but I know that there are about 25 outstanding milers in the country. My aim is to at least make it to the Olympic trials. After that, who knows what'll happen." Popejoy had run 3:58 and 3:59 in workouts but had not been able to overcome the psychological barrier of the four-minute mile in competition. "I'm getting there. . . . I'm not scared like I used to be," he said. "I feel I've got the ability to do it, but that isn't always what counts. It's what you have upstairs that's important, too." Roger Bannister—psychological. He had the mind to do it when nobody else did."[83]

On April 22, 1972 Ron Cool, Bob Cassleman, Rob Cool, and Ken Popejoy won the University Division distance medley relay (9:41.6) at the Kansas Relays in Lawrence. All week long there had been talk about Kansas State trying to break the world record in the distance medley relay, and once the race started Michigan State's position seemed hopeless. When Ken took the baton he was in fourth place, 30-yards behind Jerome Howe, who had anchored Kansas State to second place in the NCAA indoor and who had run a 3:57.9 relay leg that spring. Ken's task appeared to be hopeless.

"All I thought about was second place. I didn't even think about catching Howe, But we went through the half mile in two minutes and all at once he started coming back to me. So I followed him and kicked in the last 220 yards," Popejoy later recounted. "At Kansas, of course, everyone hates Kansas State, so the crowd was really cheering." Ken ran the final quarter mile in 56.9 seconds, and finished with a mile leg of 3:59.4. At that time, only one Big Ten runner—Lee LaBadie of Illinois who did it in a duel meet in 1971—had ever run a sub-four minute mile in a regular race. Michigan State beat Kansas State with a time of 9:41.6.[84]

Popejoy was named 1970 cross-country All-American and 1971 NCAA Indoor All-America track team for the mile run.[85] He also was named to the 1972 NCAA Indoor All-America track team.[86] However, on July 7, 1972 at the Olympic trials in Eugene, Ken placed fifth in the semi-finals of the metric mile with a time of 3:48.8. Only a select few runners such as Jim Ryun, Jerome Howe [Kansas State], Reggie McAfee, and David Wottle ran faster.[87] Popejoy was a "kicker," who startled his rivals with bursts of speed, but could not out sprint men like Dave Wottle.

David Wottle ran for Canton, Ohio's Lincoln High School and attended Bowling Green University, a Mid-American Conference rival of Eastern Michigan University. In 1972 he pointed toward making the U. S. Olympic team as a 1,500-meter runner, and entered the Olympic trials 800-meter run as an insurance policy, thinking that he did not have enough foot speed to win a medal at that event. To his surprise, he tied the world record (1:44.3) in the finals of the 800-meter trials held in Eugene on Saturday night July 1.[88] Wottle went on to win a gold medal at the Munich Olympic Games. After graduating from college he returned to Canton to coach track and cross-country at Walsh College. In 1977 he took a similar job at Bethany College in West Virginia.[89]

Ken Popejoy was married in December 1972, but was not leading a normal married life because his wife was attending the University of Illinois. Their married life would not take on a more normal appearance in June when they both received their sheepskins.[90] Until Saturday May 5, 1973, Ken Popejoy had a frustrating indoor and outdoor season, and was giving serious thought to abandoning his oft-times spectacular track career. However, on that day he shocked himself out of the doldrums by running the finest mile (3:57) in Big Ten history at MSU's Ralph Young Field in a duel meet against Notre Dame. Popejoy's performance was the second best by a collegian in the U.S. in 1973— only Steve Prefontaine was better, 3:55—and the 18th fastest in American history.

All Ken had intended to do that Saturday was give his self-esteem a little shot in the arm. "I was hoping to be respectable—do something in the 4:02 to 4:04 range—but I wasn't trying for anything spectacular. After the first lap (his time was two seconds faster than he had expected) it dawned on me that I had nothing to lose, so I thought, why not try. I really didn't feel any fatigue or pressure until the last 220 yards or so, but by then I just knew I had it. It's really quite a feeling, and I'm glad I could do it".[91] After the race Ken said, "I always thought that I was capable of running a 3:57 mile, but I'm still trying to believe I did it." "I called my dad [in Glen Ellyn] and he said, "You hang up and call me back in an hour because I'm not going to believe it." I told him, "I'm still trying to believe it myself."[92] Latter his dad said, "whatever else the season may bring you've accomplished something that you'll always remember.'"[93]

A week later he again ran a sub-four minute mile. This time he ran 3:57.3. "With the win at the King games, my confidence is at an all-time high. I know now that I can run two types of races. I can strike out fast like I did in the Notre Dame meet or I can lay back and then use my kick like I did this weekend." At the Martin Luther King Games, Popejoy overtook McAfee in the last 50 yards, once again validating his finishing kick. "Previously I would be tight before a race and it sometimes would work against me. However, of late I have just been running my own race and it's this relaxed atmosphere that is making the difference."[94] Ken ran his May 12, 1973 sub-four minute mile at the King Games with quarter-mile lap times of 58.7, 60.8, 60.0, and 57.5.

In mid-May 1973 Ken Popejoy reflected on his sub-four minute miles:

It's a very surprising and rewarding feeling to run a mile under four minutes. . . . My workouts have not been as hard as last year but I've been running more relaxed. . . . I've had excellent communication with Coach Jim Gibbard this season. During my four years at MSU I've had my ups and downs so I decided to talk things out with him and we've talked pretty well.

The only time I really had the feeling that I was going under four minutes was three weeks ago when I ran 3:57 flat. The first time and the third time I didn't think I was under four minutes. But against Notre Dame I thought of it the whole last lap. It was like dreaming the last lap. It was very exciting for me because I've wanted to do it for so long.

Last year there was noticeable drain of energy or strength when I was attempting to go under four minutes but none of my races this year have been exhausting. The 3:57 flat was one of the easiest races I've run at Michigan State. It's a matter of how your mind copes with it. Usually you can run the first half mile at the pace you want. It's the third quarter that the fatigue starts to jump on you. You have to make a conscious effort to pick it up. You can't just keep the same speed because you'll really be slowing down. That's when you really have to push it. When you get to the last lap, you know you're in good shape. It's a good mental feeling.

It's never been a painful thing to me physically to run a mile. It's been a very tiring experience to run any kind of mile at a good pace, no matter what kind of shape you're in. But this pain thing . . . too many people think you're having physical pain like putting a needle in you or something. It really isn't that way. Your body is drained when it's over but it's a good feeling, it's not a painful feeling.

The idea of lungs bursting within the chest of a miler has not part of my experience. But that's not to say other runners haven't had that experience. It's a matter of pushing yourself to that point of fatigue. I've never pushed myself to that point. It takes conditioning—physically and mentally—to run a sub-four minute mile. You've got to be in the top kind of shape to do it and your mind has to be really to do it. When you begin to feel tired you'll give up if you're not on top of the situation mentally. I train nine months a year. I don't run during the summer. I like to get away from the sport so I don't get as tired of it. But I run six-mile cross-country during the fall and I'll run 50 or 60 miles a week from January to June. It takes 30 or 35 hours a week of my time. I've kept a running log ever since I began running in my freshman year in high school. I've run approximately 22,000 miles. I figure I have about 3,000 more miles to get once around the world (laughing). It's kind of weird when you think of all the miles you've run and the time you've put in. It's an investment . . . if you enjoy it.

It takes a special kind of person to subject himself to a track program. Distance men have to learn to pace ourselves. It's a thing we feel different from sprinters. We have to know the limits of our bodies . . . how much you can push it, where you can push it. You're out there running from four minutes to 30 minutes. It's like working out a family budget. You have to know when to expand yourself and when to rest. It's a challenge to work your body at a limit.

I choose a mile or two-mile instead of a quarter or a half-mile because it fits my ability best. A lot of that depends on where your ability is. I'm no Herb Washington in the sprints and I'm no Steve Prefontaine when it comes to six miles. If you're a distance runner you've always been a distance runner. I'm a miler. I know my ability is best put in the mile.

I think to an extent you have to be somewhat weird to excel in track, as society looks at you. Of course, the definition of weird depends on who's looking at you. I guess you have to be weird to spend 30 or 35 hours a week running.

If you're going to college that doesn't leave you much time for anything else. I don't do much else, besides study and run.

There have been times when I've looked back and wondered if I'd have preferred the life of goofin' around with the boys. But I think it has been worth the effort I've put into running.

The pro-track tour does not interest me personally. I would not find money a motivating factor to run. . . . The only reason I run is that I enjoy it and when I stop enjoying it, money won't make me enjoy it. I'll be out of the sport when I stop enjoying it.[95]

Going into the Big Ten Outdoor Championships, Popejoy knew he would be facing his archrival, Mike Durkin of the University of Illinois. Ken thought,

Durkin has one of the best heads in the country for running. . . . I've never had the killer instinct he has. He never says anything to me, just looks daggers at me and then runs. I just hope I can get my head and body together and run a good race. I didn't want to get senioritis too bad this year and I think the bad race at Drake woke me up a little.[96]

On May 19, 1973 he won the mile run (3:59.2) at the 73rd Big Ten Outdoor Championships in Minneapolis. After winning the Big Ten mile championships, Popejoy told reporters, "Finally winning this championship means more to me than breaking 3:58 the last two weeks, or anything else I've ever won. For once, I didn't come in scared. After those good times the last two weeks, I was very confident. I had told someone last week that Durkin always looks daggers at me. So Friday he came up and pointed his fingers out from his eyes and said, 'daggers.' That's about the only thing he has ever said to me, but I thought I had him if he had been upset that much. I decided I would concentrate on breaking four minutes and let everyone else see if they could keep up," added Popejoy, who in the past had tended to rely on his finishing sprint. This time he took the lead after one lap and kept pulling away. Durkin couldn't keep up with the pace and dropped out after three laps.

"John Clark of Iowa and I had talked about the race on Friday. We both said we wanted a fast pace, so he agreed to take the lead for the first lap and then I would take over. I hate to make arrangements like that, but it worked out well for both of us." Clark placed second in 4:03, a personal best.

After running 4:15 at the Drake Relays I never thought I would be this fast now. I sort of gave up then and just wanted to finish out the season. But the next week I ran 3:57 and just destroyed my mind. I had been thinking of 4:02

or something like that. It shows how important mental preparation is. This year I have done less work and not as fast work in practice, but I haven't destroyed myself during the week. So I have come into the races confident and relaxed. I was very tired after winning at the Martin Luther King Games a week ago, but I still did my workouts, including 10 quarter-miles at a 60-second pace on Tuesday. After that I eased up and got my strength back for this week-end.[97]

On May 26, 1973 Ken placed second in the 880-yard run (1:47.9) to future Olympic gold medal winner Dave Wottle at the 48th Central Collegiate Conference Championships in East Lansing. That same day in East Lansing, Missouri's Charles McMullen thrilled the crowd with a 3:59.7 mile.[98] On May 27 Ken won the mile run (3:58.4) at the Vons Classic Invitational Meet in Los Angeles.

In May 1973 Ken Popejoy had set a NCAA record for the mile by running five consecutive sub-four minute miles in competition. On June 10, he was awarded a $1,000 postgraduate scholarship by the NCAA for his outstanding performances in the mile run.[99] Ken graduated with a 3.25 average with a major in pre-law. He told an interviewer, "From about the time I was eight years old the most important thing in my life has been to become a lawyer. Now, when I should be on the verge of achieving that goal, I find that I can't get into law school." Three law schools rejected him. Not, however, because of any deficiency on his part. The supply of law students simply exceeded the capacity of many law schools. Finally, he was admitted at Illinois Institute of Technology's Chicago-Kent College of Law.[100]

On December 21, 1974 Ken ran in the invitational mile run at the University of Chicago's Holiday Indoor Track Meet.[101]

By 1975, Ken was ranked ninth in the world in the 1,500-meter run (3:38.4).[102] He was then an attorney working in Wheaton, Illinois. The running bug almost killed Popejoy in 1985. He entered the Chicago marathon. He covered the first 20 miles in 1 hour 51 minutes. "I was passing people left and right and then it was like I got hit head-on by a Mack truck," said Popejoy. "I finished in 2:34, but spent four and one-half hours in the hospital tent. They put 4½ bags of IV fluid in me."[103]

Starting in 1981 Ken Popejoy began volunteering his time as an assistant coach for tiny North Central College (enrollment 1,300) in Naperville, now one of the best Division III teams in the country. "It's been ideal," Popejoy said. "I'm strictly volunteer. I'm kind of in that 'in-between' phase of being a coach and one of the guys." "It probably costs me $10,000 a year to come down here to do this. I could be back putting in extra hours at the office to make the 'big bucks,' but money can't buy the moments I've experienced here working [on track]." He never received a penny as an assistant coach; he was intrinsically motivated, and he did it because it loved the sport.[104]

Ken Popejoy won the Masters 800-meter run at the Drake Relays in 1991 (1:56.64), 1992 (1:57.39), 1993 (1:58.08), and 1994 (1:58.36). He was inducted into the Drake Relays Hall of Fame in 1997.[105]

Jumping Seven Feet

In 1971 Mike Bowers, representing the Ann Arbor Track Club at age 26, won the open high jump at the Drake Relays, setting a new meet record with a jump of 7-½.[106] One of his protegees, Mel Embree, who attended Ann Arbor Huron High School, became Harvard University's high jump record holder. Embree attended Harvard from 1972 through 1976. In February 1973 Embree placed fourth in the high jump (6–9) at the 52nd Annual IC4A Indoor Championships held in the Jadwin Gymnasium in Princeton, NJ. That spring he placed fifth in the high jump (6–8) at the 97th Annual IC4A Outdoor Championships.[107]

In March 1975 Embree reached seven feet when won the high jump at the Indoor Heptagonal Track Meet in Ithaca, New York. A week later, he topped seven feet when he placed second in the high jump (7–1) at the IC4A Indoor Championships. On March 14–15 he tied for sixth in the high jump (6–11) at the NCAA Division I Indoor Championships in Detroit, to earn All-American honors. In the spring he again topped seven feet in winning the high jump (7–1½) at the Heptagonal Outdoor Championships, and tied for sixth place in the high jump (6–10) at the NCAA Division I Outdoor Championships in Provo, Utah, again earning All-American status.[108]

In 1976 Embree won the high jump (7–2) in a duel meet with Yale, setting the Harvard Stadium high jump record. On May 15 won the high jump (7–3) and set the meet record at the Heptagonal Championships to complete his collegiate track career.[109]

Mike Winsor from Fulton High School, Middleton, Michigan was an outstanding high jumper at Central Michigan University. In 1973, while in high school at Houghton-Middleton, he won the Class C State High School high jump championship held at Mount Pleasant with a jump of 6–4.[110] As a college freshman, he jumped 7–5 and was in the NCAA national indoor championships. He jumped 7 feet in the preliminary round, and tied for sixth. He bowed out at 6–11 in the final round for seventh place. At the time it was the highest national indoor finish for a CMU track athlete. "Really, I choked," said Winsor. "I wasn't thinking and didn't adjust myself to correct the errors I was making. After I was done jumping, I realized what I had been doing wrong." World record holder Dwight Stone set the indoor record (7–7) at the meet.[111] Winsor did, however, win the high jump championship (7–1) and set a meet record at the Mid-American Conference Outdoor Championships in Oxford, Ohio on May 27, 1976 and qualified for the finals of the Olympic trials in 1976.[112]

In 1978 Mike Winsor of Central Michigan University placed second in the high jump (7–1¾) at the Drake Relays.[113] He won the MAC outdoor high jump championship with a jump of 7–2.[114] In 1979 Mike Winsor placed third in the MAC Outdoor Championships with a jump of 6–8¾.[115] In 1980 he won the high jump (7–1¾) at the MAC outdoor championships held on May 16–17 in De Kalb, Illinois.[116]

Paul "Pie" Piwinski, Sr. was born on November 3, 1961 in Warren, Michigan, the son of Thaddeus and Shirley Piwinski. His father was an engineer with General Motors and his mother was a Registered Nurse. He was a Michigan All-State high school Track athlete in the high jump in 1978.[117] Indeed, he was All-State in the high jump for three consecutive years, and a scholastic All-American. He lettered in football, basketball, and track at Warren Cousino High School. He was Co-captain of the track team his junior and senior years. He stood 6–4 and weighted 180 pounds when he was 20 years old. His father had not been an athlete, and Paul's interests centered on restoration of old cars, water skiing, and billiards.[118]

At Michigan State University, Paul set the meet and Jenison Fieldhouse record for the high jump at the Michigan State Relays on February 5, 1983. His 7–5 jump is still the Michigan State University varsity high jump record at the end of the century. Later that indoor season, Piwinski won the Big Ten high jump championship with a jump of 7–1¾. "Pie" also was a NCAA indoor All-American in 1983. He won the 58th Annual Central Collegiate Conference high jump championship and set a track record with a 7–3 jump at Toledo, Ohio on May 28.[119] Paul majored in business marketing and became a marketing representative for Anheuser-Busch's Olympic Job Opportunity Program after graduating from MSU.

The Javelin Throw

In 1976 Ron Parisl, a student athlete at Western Michigan University, won the javelin throw at the Drake Relays with a throw of 74.24 meters or 243–7.[120] On May 15, 1976 he won the javelin throw in a duel meet with Central Michigan University.[121] Ron won the MAC Championship in the javelin on May 21, 1976 with a throw of 240 feet.[122] He won the MAC outdoor javelin championship on May 29, 1978 with a throw of 228–8.[123] Ron won the javelin (226–7) at the MAC outdoor championships held on May 16–17, 1980 in De Kalb, IL.[124]

During the 1980s performance in field events exploded. At the UCLA Invitational in Los Angeles on May 14, 1983 Tom Petranoff of Northridge, CA set the world record in the javelin with a throw of 327–2. He broke the record of Hungarian Ferene Paragi by nearly ten feet before a crowd of 15,000 fans.[125] On April 14, 2000 Damon Page of Eastern Michigan won the collegiate javelin championship at the SeaRay Relays with a throw of 198–7.[126]

Noteworthy Performances

Michigan State's Ricky Flowers, from Saginaw, was the individual star of the 1979 Big Ten Championships held in Ann Arbor. Ricky set the Big Ten record for the 400-meter dash (46.13) at the 79th Big Ten Outdoor Championships.[127] On April 29, 1983 Jeffrey Drenth of Central Michigan University won the Invitational 5,000-meter run (13:49.10) at the Drake Relays.[128]

Western Michigan University senior track star, John Winterbottom, who was a graduate of North Farmington High School, placed second in the open 200-meter run and second as part of the WMU 3,200-meter relay team at the Domino Pizza Relays in Tallahassee, Florida in 1986.[129]

The University of Michigan Track Program Rebounds: The Jack Harvey Era

When Jack Harvey took over the maize and blue track program in 1975, it was suffering from recruiting problems that carried over from the Canham era. Jack Harvey coached the University of Michigan track team for the last 26 years of the twentieth century. During that span he coached 47 All-Americans, seven national champions, and three Olympians. His most noteworthy of his U.S. stars were: Greg Meyer, William and Gerard Donakowski, Mike Shea, Brian Diemer, Tom Wilcher, John Scherer, Brad Barquest, Brad Darr, Trinity Townsend, and John Mortimer.

The Last American to Win the Boston Marathon

Jack Harvey's first outdoor All-American was Gregory A. Meyer, a native of Grand Rapids. Although Greg Meyer was a very good distance runner at the University of Michigan 1974–77, he was not a great runner. He was the first Michigan native runner to break the four-minute mile,[130] but otherwise made little impact on Michigan running until he started doing marathons. He did not set a single University of Michigan record and his name can not be found among their top performers.[131] He won only one letter in cross-country, and was an All-American only once, with a fifth place finish in the NCAA steeplechase in June 1976. Ron Addison, who would be Sue Latter's husband, placed third in the steeplechase that year.

On May 28, 1976 Greg placed second in the steeplechase at the Central Collegiate Conference Championships at Kanley Field in Kalamazoo. Ed Grabowski of Eastern Michigan placed third (8:53.2) just behead of him.[132] In 1977 Meyer won the Big Ten Conference outdoor 10-K run championship. After graduating from Michigan he took a job in metropolitan Boston, moved to Holliston, Massachusetts, and began training with Bill Rodgers, winner of four previous Boston Marathons [1975, 1978, 1979, and 1980]. In 1978 the Greater Boston Track Club had four men running the marathon in 2 hours 11 minutes or less. By contrast, going into the Olympic trials in the year 2000, only two runners in the USA bettered the Olympic A qualifying standard of 2 hours 14 minutes and the only Olympic marathon qualifier at the trials, Rod DeHaven, ran the 26.2 miles in 2:15. 30.[133]

Greg Meyers made his first attempt to win the Boston Marathon on Monday April 20, 1981. It was only his third marathon and he was pitted against Bill Rodgers, and Toshihiko Seko, the Japanese national marathon champion. Consequently, Meyer was not considered among the major contenders to win the world's premier long-distance running event. Still, before the race, Meyer told a reporter that "there were only ten runners in the race that are better than me." As if to prove it, shortly after the Wellesley checkpoint about 14 miles into the 26 mile 385 yard course, Greg took a ten-yard lead in an effort to "bust open the race and go for the whole ball of wax."[134]

His relentless pace soon began to exact its toll on the competition. Bill Rodgers had trouble breathing and had a weird feeling in his chest, yet he pushed on in attempt to keep up with Meyer. At 15 miles Rodgers faded to sixth place behind Meyer, with Seko hanging on to second place. But, on the hills with a slower cadence and using different muscles, Rodgers began to loosen up and he found it easier to run. He caught up with Meyer and Seko at about 18 miles and ran with them and Craig Virgin, from Lebanon, Illinois and the only American ever to win the World Cross-country Championship. At the twenty-three mile mark, Seko made his move and won the race in record setting time (2:09:04). Virgin placed second and Rodgers took third. Greg Meyer faded to eleventh, but still posted a very respectful 2:13:07.[135]

Greg skipped the 1982 Boston Marathon, but returned in 1983 better prepared. He had rounded into condition by running and winning the ten-mile Cherry Blossom Run in Washington, DC and the 10-Kilometer Colonial Relays. While running with the Greater Boston Track Club, he had also practiced Coach Bill Squire's surge technique. He entered the April 18, 1983 Boston Marathon absolutely convinced he would win, and he did what he planned to do. Downhill into Newton Lower Falls Benji Durden, an ardent science fiction reader from Georgia, lead by a considerable distance, but Meyer caught up with Durden halfway up Heartbreak Hill and left him in the dust, passing the 20-mile mark in a world-record pace. Meyer ran 4:49 from mile 21 to 22 and 5:09 from 22 to 23. The Michigan man cruised the last mile waving to the crowd, missed his chance to set the meet record.[136] Nevertheless, he ran the fourth-best time for the distance ever run by an American.

Greg Meyer was the last American runner in the twentieth century to win the Boston Marathon.[137] In the last Boston Marathon of the twentieth century, the first Michigan runner to finish was Matt Smith from Holland, Michigan, who placed forty-first.[138] At that time, the 44 year old Greg Meyer was working in the development office at the University of Michigan.[139]

Three-time Olympian

Brian Diemer was born in Grand Rapids on October 10, 1961. He grew up in the Grand Rapids suburbs, and began his athletic career when he went out for the cross-country team in the tenth grade at Cutlerville Christian High School. According to Shirley Diemer, Brian's mother, "He wanted to be a golfer, not a steeplechaser." When Brian was in tenth grade, "they needed more runners for the cross-country team and Brian's friends told the coach to talk to Brian," his mother remembers. "He ran with the team and stayed up front with the seniors. And he was running in tennis shoes, not running shoes. We knew then that he had ability."[140] He was soon the best runner on the team. He graduated from Grand Rapids South Christian High School with the class of 1979. In his senior year in high school he won the state cross-country championship. Diemer received a scholarship to the University of Michigan, where Greg Meyers and William J. Donakowski had put distance running on the map.[141] Bill Donakowski's younger brother, Gerard enrolled at the University of Michigan in 1980.

In 1980, 1981, and 1982 Brian honed his running skills. In 1981 Diemer won the Big Ten Conference steeplechase and in 1982 he ran the outdoors 5-K in 13:47.15. In 1982 Brian and Mike Shea earned All-American honors in the distance medley relay with a second place finish at the NCAA indoor meet. Gerard Donakowski won the Big Ten indoor three-mile run, but otherwise neither Diemer nor Donakowski made a major break through on the national track and field scene.[142]

Diemer's break through in college came during the 1983 indoor season when he ran a mile in 3:59 in a duel meet against Michigan State University and the two-mile in 8:30 at the NCAA Indoor at the Silverdome. Diemer became the second Michigan born trackman to run a sub-four minute mile, and his two-mile run performance earned him third place and individual All-American status at the national NCAA indoor championships. "I started increasing my mileage and I could just feel myself getting stronger."[143] Gerard Donakowski also became an All-American at the 1983 NCAA indoor meet with a fourth place performance in the two-mile run.

On May 20, 1983 teammates Brian Diemer and Gerard Donakowski attempted to cross the finish line together in the 10-K run at the Big Ten Championships in West Lafayette. The Accutrak timer, however, found five-hundredths of a second difference and gave the victory to Donakowski in 30 minutes 11.92 seconds. Throughout the race they were never much farther apart. Diemer said, "Neither one of us would be as good without the other to train with."[144]

In June, Diemer won the steeplechase at the NCAA outdoor championships. The 3,000-meter steeplechase is unlike any other track event. It is about 200-meters short of two miles—or 7½ laps around the 400-meter track. But on each lap, the runners must negotiate four hurdle-like barriers and a combination hurdle-water jump. It requires the speed of a miler, the strength of a 10-K runner and the flexibility and technique of a hurdler. The barriers steal the runner's strength and disrupt his rhythm.[145] The track and field steeplechase was first contested at the London Olympic Games on August 2, 1866 in the original Crystal Palace. The first steeplechase was only a half-mile long.[146]

Brian recalls, at the NCAA Division I Championships on June 3,

I stayed in the pack most of the race. Then with a quarter of a mile to go, I took the lead to try to shake up the group, but not to run away with it yet. Most of the top guys went with me and some of them passed me. With 150 yards to go,

Gerard Donakowski, one of three All-American runners in his family, and future Olympian, Brian Diemer, at the 1993 NCAA Indoor Championships. Diemer placed third and Donakowski forth in the meet's two-mile run. *(Photo University of Michigan, Sports Information)*

I accelerated into the water jump and gained about 10 yards. My momentum took me out of the water pit faster and that's how I won. We had planned it that way. I knew I had to make my move at the [final] hurdle [situated at the bank of a 10-foot long water pool]. He [Coach Warhurst] studies the other runners. He knows his runners inside and out and he knows our potential. He's an excellent coach. At times I felt I wasn't qualified to run in this field of national contenders. After all, I had run the steeplechase only three times during the regular season. Most of the guys run it every week. But once I got here, I didn't feel that way.[147]

His time was 10 seconds faster than his previous personal best.

On June 9, 1983 Diemer was named the recipient of the Big Ten Medal of Honor as the outstanding senior student-athlete given for academic excellence, athletic achievement and leadership. He had an overall 2.95 GPA in the School of Natural Resources and a 3.48 his senior year. He was the first male Michigan runner since 1957 to win a national track championship. Earlier in the academic year he became an All-American in cross-country. While running for the blue and maize, he was a four time All-American.[148]

When Diemer made it to the semifinals of the World Championships in Helsinki in 1983, he recalls, "It was my first taste of big time international competition. It was pretty scary at first. But they run just like we do. Maybe they elbow a little more. They're a little bit rougher."[149]

Brian Diemer maintained his relationship with his high school sweetheart, Kerri Laudenbach. After graduating from college in December 1983 with a degree in environmental design, Brian married her. He also joined his father's landscaping business, Everett's Landscaping and Snowplowing in Grand Rapids.[150] He worked as much as 30 to 35 hours a week in his father's landscaping business. For most runners living in Grand Rapids would have been a mistake. Too far from good coaching and training partners, and mired in snow in the winter, his chances of making the 1984 Olympic team did not look good. But as Doug Brown a former Olympic steeplechaser from St. Claire Shores and later the administrator of the Athletics West track club in Eugene, Oregon put it, "Brian Diemer is an exceptional young man. He's very intelligent, cooperative and mature."[151]

Diemer soon proved his self- discipline and his commitment to running. Despite the snow and the need to drive to Ann Arbor once a week to confer with his old U of M track coach, Ron Warhurst, Brian worked out a training schedule that allowed him to peak at just the right time. As he revealed to a Detroit reporter,

When I'm on the track, all of my concentration is on the race. But when I'm training or not racing, I'm not thinking about track. Most people probably don't even know I run. My work, probably more than my running, is my passion.[152]

Brian's income was supplemented by a consulting contract with the Nike. He was also a member of Athletics West, the Nike-sponsored elite track team.

At the Olympic trials on June 19, 1984 in the first round of the steeplechase, Diemer coasted to a 8:37.67 third place in his heat, just enough to move on. "Physically, I'm right where I want to be," he said. "But you have to have a good week to make the [Olympic] team."[153] On June 21 Brian won the first heat of the semifinals of the steeplechase (8:24.44) at the Olympic trials in Los Angeles. "We figured our heat would be tougher to qualify in. It turned out that way." "Staying fresh and running a smart race are my priorities."[154] "The race went out a little faster than I wanted it to, and that hurt." Two nights later, however, on June 23 in the finals of the steeplechase it did not show. The finals in the steeplechase trials boiled down to a duel between Diemer and six-time national champion and American record holder Henry Marsh. The battle began in earnest a few hundred yards before the final obstacle, the water jump, when Marsh made his move.

Diemer remembers, "I didn't want to get spooked into thinking I had to make up ground. I actually had to slow down to get outside a group of runners [before the water jump]." Diemer did just that, but by the time the pack got to the water jump he had a firm hold on second place and a return trip to Los Angeles. He did not catch Marsh, but then he did not slow up, either. Brian broke his personal-best record by five seconds.[155]

"I dreamed about that exact race last night," said Diemer, who took it slow at the start, running as far back as eighth place. "It's pretty much happened the way I hoped it would. I was hoping to give Marsh a run for his money, but that was close enough right there, I guess. The important thing is that I came home strong. You have to come home strong. That's where you're going to lose it, from the last dry barrier on."[156] Diemer finished second (8:17.00) at the Olympic trials.

After the U.S. Olympic track and field trials in Los Angeles, Brian returned to Grand Rapids to train. He found the support and encouragement at home that was vital to his success.[157] He went on to win a bronze medal at the Los Angeles Olympics.

Diemer came up short in the steeplechase at the 1988 Olympics. It seems likely that the presence of the Eastern European athletes, who boycotted the 1984 summer Olympic Games, was the most important factor in his inability to make the finals in his event. After all, Brian was 26 years old, and nearing the peak of his most productive period as a distance runner. Brian's mother, Linda, had no doubt that "what makes Brian special is his determination. Whatever he sets his mind to, he does it. He follows through until it is done," she declared. Still, Diemer could not emerge from the shadow of Henry Marsh, America's best steeplechaser.[158] Moreover, in the semifinals of the steeplechase in Seoul, South Korea on September 7, 1988, Diemer faltered.

I was in good position for most of the race, but my legs just didn't have any energy left. I just ran out of gas. Naturally, I'm disappointed because I wanted to make it to the finals again. But I'm not disappointed with my effort. I obviously wasn't at the top, but I gave 133 percent. There are some boys here who are ready to run. My muscles were cramped up and tired. Because of that, I wasn't feeling as confident as I should have for this race. . . . The [1992 Games] are a long way off, but I'm already thinking about them. I want to prove that I can get back with the best in the world.[159]

In 1991 Diemer placed fifth in the steeplechase at the World Championships.[160] In 1992 at age 31 Brian was coaching cross-country at Calvin College. He suffered from a stress fracture on April 15 and was unable to train for two months. He thought his chances of making the a third Olympic team were gone. Despite the setback, Diemer qualified for the Olympic trials in New Orleans. He made the U.S. Olympic team with the fastest steeplechase time (8:16.56) by an American in 1992.[161] At the Olympic training camp in Narbonne, France, Diemer was named captain of the U.S. Olympic men's track and field team.[162] He placed seventh in the steeplechase at Barcelona.

On June 18, 1993 Brian placed third in the steeplechase at the USTF Outdoor Championships and again qualified for the World Championships.[163] When Brian stopped running competitively, he had an Olympic bronze medal in his possession, but winning the Big Ten medal of honor for academic and athletic prowess his senior year at Michigan ranks right up there with it, he declared.[164] In 1996 Brian and his wife were living at Caledonia, Michigan.

Out of the East

John Otto Scherer was born in Silver Springs, Maryland on November 3, 1966. His father, J. Otto Scherer was an engineer: His mother, Carol, was a nurse, turned homemaker. At Glenelog High School in Dayton, Maryland, John played soccer and ran in both track and cross-country. He also enjoyed sailing. He was athlete of the year in his high school, and was a member of the National Honor Society. He always prayed to God before running a race.[165]

However it is important to remember, as one athlete put it, "sometimes it is comforting [for us to think we] know where God is, and it is easy to fall into the trap of thinking that God is going to favor us [in an athletic contest] because of our faith. But, God takes no sides in athletic contests."[166]

In the fall of 1984 John Scherer was given an Alumni Scholarship valued at $1500 to attend the University of Michigan. He majored in Aerospace Engineering. He initially ran track as a walk-on and earned a track letter in the spring of 1986. That fall John received a track scholarship that he kept through the winter of 1987, when he was named a James B. Angell Scholar.[167]

During the 1987 cross-country season, John Scherer was a steady runner. During the entire season he won all but three races. His worse showing was at the Big Ten Cross-country Championships, where the entire team did poorly and he placed ninth. Michigan's cross-country team was only allowed to go to the NCAA District Championships when their petition stating that their team might have suffered from food poisoning at the Big Ten Championships was accepted. On November 14 Scherer won the 10-K cross-country (30:04. 64) at the NCAA District IV Championships and qualified his team for the national championships. On November 23 John Scherer pulled a surprise by finishing second (29:20.56) at the National NCAA Cross-country Championships held at the University of Virginia.[168]

On May 21, 1988 in front of a crowd of 1,275 at Ferry Field, John Scherer pulled away in the final half-mile to win the 10-K title at the Big Ten Championships. The heat of the day caused a delay of one hour in the 10-K run, the final event of the first day. The heat did not cause any problem for Scherer who finished in 29:23.15, four seconds ahead of the second place finisher. Early in the race, Scherer ran in eighth place, and slowly moved past three more runners until a pack of five emerged two miles into the race. "I felt pretty comfortable for almost five miles," said Scherer. "I was relaxed. We were on qualifying speed for the first three miles, but they relaxed a little about halfway through [the race]. I didn't want to lead. I have to run tomorrow (in the 5-K) so I didn't want to run any faster than I had to. Tomorrow's just whatever's left."[169]

At the 10-K run (a 6.21 mile contest) in the NCAA Championships on June 3, 1988, after almost a half-hour of racing, the two runners from schools only six miles apart finished almost exactly together. Scherer finished first in 28:50:39 with Don Johns from Eastern Michigan University second at 28:50:48. There was no love lost between the two track programs. John Scherer remembered:

We've run a lot against each other. There's not a lot of tension there. I was in a good situation during the race. The last 100 meters was the toughest I've ever run. To win here was a good feeling. The crowd was great. I was really motivated by all the clapping. My adrenaline was pumping, especially when Johns passed me toward the end.[170]

Scherer began the race in back of the pack, and moved steadily throughout the race before taking the lead in the eighteenth lap. Scherer led for two laps, before being passed Johns and Bob Kempainen of Dartmouth. Scherer was able to stay close to the leaders and on the final lap he made his move to take the lead. Johns followed, trailing him right to the wire, but unable to pass the charging Sherer. The race down the final stretch was so close that Johns actually passed his Wolverine rival in the final meters, only to be nosed out when Scherer made a lunge like a sprinter at the tape. But the result was not apparent at the line and, according to Johns, Scherer thought it was Johns who had won.[171] U of M Assistant track Coach Ron Warhurst said, "John [Sherer] ran a very smart and controlled race. He moved when he had to and picked up the pace when it was necessary."[172] It was the first time a U of M athlete won an NCAA outdoor national championship since Brian Diemer won the steeplechase in 1983.[173] Sherer missed qualifying for the 1988 Olympic trials by .05 seconds.

Jon Scherer graduated Summa cum laude (3.760 grade point) in December 1988. He was invited into two honor societies: Sigma Gamma Tau (Aerospace Engineering) and Tau Beta Pi (Engineering). After receiving a BS Degree in Engineering, Scherer enrolled in the Rackham School of Graduate Studies, where he studied gas dynamics in the Department of Engineering until the spring of 1990. Scherer was captain of the cross-country team in 1988 and co-captain of the track team in 1989. He also was NCAA indoors 5-K champion and outdoors 10-K champion in 1989. On August 20, 1989 Scherer placed eighth in the 10-K run (29:05.22) at the World University Games in Duisburg, West Germany.[174]

In March 1991, John Scherer finished fifth in the 3-K at the World Indoor Track Championship at Seville. It was his international debut. His time of 7:45 was :03 behind champion Frank O'Mara of Ireland. The previous weekend in Scotland, Scherer helped the United States beat Great Britain in a dual meet by placing second in a tactical 3-K race. Scherer was working on a doctorate at the time.[175]

In 1993 John ran for Nike North and placed fourth in the 5-K run (13:46.53) at the USTF Outdoor Championships. He missed making the USA delegation to the World Championships by less than 2 seconds.[176]

Out of the West

Brad Barquist was born to Norman and Shirley Barquist in Portland, OR, on February 24, 1968. His family moved to Bainbridge Island, Washington, where he attended Interlake High School in Bellevue. On May 1986 Barquist won the Washington State High School one-mile and two-mile runs. Brad was steered to the University of Michigan by

Fred La Plante, then women's coach at University of Southern California. Fred's brother-in-law was Brad's high school coach.[177]

When Brad entered the University of Michigan in September 1986, he was 5–11 and weighed 132 pounds. He majored in communications and dreamed of winning a gold medal at the Olympics. Brad did not have a significant impact on the Big Ten until 1988. On February 26–27, 1988 he placed third in the 3-K (8:12.45) and fourth in the 5-K run (14:17.26) at the Big Ten Indoor Championships.[178]

On March 1989, the year the Berlin Wall fell and the World Wide Web was invented, Barquist became an All-American when he placed third in the 3-K run at the NCAA indoor finals. In May 1989 he again placed third in the 3-K (8:00.63) at the NCAA Championships. On July 26, 1996 Barquist achieved his dream of running in the Olympic Games as part of team USA, where he placed sixteenth in the second heat of the 10-K run at (29:11.20) the Atlantic Olympic Games.[179]

The four-time All-American continued to run following the Olympic Games.[180] On June 13, 1997 Brad placed sixth in the 10-K run (29:11.79) at the USA Outdoor Championships in Indianapolis.

Pole Vaulting

In 1992 Brad Darr became the first Michigan athlete since 1978 to win the Big Ten pole vault championship. Between 1970 and 1992 the rules governing the pole vault had changed significantly. Starting in 1970 the pole was allowed to pass under the bar in a successful vault. In 1976 the crossbar construction was made more stable, and in 1979 the size of the pole was increased and vaulters were finally allowed to use resin on their hands and on the pole.[181]

Brad Darr was introduced to pole vaulting by his father. "My father was a pole vaulter," Darr admitted. "We had mattresses and used bamboo poles in the back yard. My high school coach Brian Evenson was a tremendous help. I was really surprised I got my track scholarship out of high school." Darr was an all-around athlete in high school. He leaped 6–1 in the high jump and 21–0 in the long jump as well as sub-15 seconds in the high hurdles, 40.7 in the low hurdles, and 52 seconds in the 400. He was also an all-state defensive back on the football team.[182]

Darr believed that the trick to a successful pole vault is to envision it first. A vision quest. "See yourself holding the pole, sprinting down the 120-foot runway. Approach, plant, vault, release . . . clear." "Picture it, do it. Like playing out a dream." Unfortunately, Darr's vision was not always crystal clear. At the Big Ten Championships one week following his record-setting jump at Eastern Michigan University, although favored to win, Darr never cleared a bar. He remembered a horrible, lonely moment:

I got to the runway for my first jump and, I don't know, I just blanked out. I couldn't think of my vault, I couldn't visualize what I wanted to do. It was just me, my pole and that bar. The seven-pound pole felt like it weighed 20 pounds. The 120-foot runway looked a mile long. The bar, set at the normally non-threatening height of 16–10 appeared to be 20 feet high. You are always jumping against yourself. I love the sport, I really do. But there are times when the desire is just not there. I guess I had a little burnout going. It's time to get done with school [he was to graduate in May], find a job and start my life, although making the Olympic Trials has always been my ultimate goal.[183]

Darr did not make the Olympic team. He was, however, an All-American pole vaulter in 1991 and 1992, when he placed fourth and sixth in the NCAA indoor championships. He also set the Central Collegiate Championship pole vault record with a 17–10 jump. At the end of the century, Darr was an assistant track coach at the University of Michigan.

Fast as the Wind

Like Bruce Jenner, Darnell Hall is learning impaired, but acknowledges that he is a lucky man. He inherited good running genes and a supportive family. He grew-up in a Detroit Public Housing Project and had plenty of opportunities to steer away from the straight and narrow. But, his parents, Nelson and Dana, kept him involved in sports. His maternal grandfather, Jette Byrd, was one of the Detroit Metro League's better sprinters during the late 1940s, and his father, Nelson Hall, was a high school pole-vaulter. They made sure that Darnell stayed active with the Detroit Police Athletic League (PAL) sports program. Starting at the age of eight, he ran track and played baseball in the spring and summer, football in the fall and basketball in the winter. He was not an immediate success. "I wasn't good until my junior year of high school."[184]

Darnell attributes his success, however, attributes his success to his neighborhood friends and classmates.

You know, what the real key to my success was? The guys who were doing wrong—the guys who were selling drugs and who dropped out of school—they were the ones who made me walk in the right direction. They encouraged me not to follow in their direction. If I needed some money, they gave it to me, instead of me going out there trying to make a hustle, selling drugs, whatever. Evidently they saw something in me I didn't see in me. As I was growing up and maturing, I realized [what could have happened], and I appreciate it, because I could have been selling drugs or in a gang or probably dead.[185]

Darnell Hall went to Detroit's Pershing High School, but did not run until his junior year when his friends from the PAL program convinced him to join them on the track team. At Pershing he was coached by Wayne University track letterman, Al Tellis, who helped shape Darnell's natural talents into championship form.[186] In June 1989 he won the Class A 400-meter state championship. On June 2, 1990, as a high school senior, Hall won the 400-meter run (47.56) and placed second in the 800-meter relay (1:20.03) at the State Class A Championships in Midland.[187]

Handicapped by his learning disability, Darnell did not have good enough grades or SAT exams to qualify for entrance into a four-year college, so he attended Blinn Junior College in Texas, noted for its superb track and field program. In the now-defunct program, Darnell improved to a world-class level of performance. After his second season at Blinn, Hall placed sixth in the 400-meter run in the Olympic trials and made the 1992 United States Olympic team as a 1,600-meter relay team alternate. He was the youngest member of the 1992 U.S. Olympic men's track team.[188] Darnell won a gold medal for his work in getting the U.S. team through the heats. He promptly had the Olympic rings tattooed on his arm. "I never grew up thinking that I was going to be in the Olympics," Darnell recalled. "I just turned my life around in one year."[189]

Finished at Blinn Junior College, Darnell faced a decision about what to do next. Unable to transfer to a Division I school because of poor grades, Hall chose to compete professionally. The program at Blinn prepared him physically and mentally for "running with the big boys." His plan was to return to Detroit and prepare for the Atlanta Olympics under his father's direction. In 1993 and 1994 he stayed in the mix. In 1994 Hall ran for the Reebok Racing Club,[190] and won the USA Track and Field 400-meter indoor championship in Atlanta.

In 1995 he ran for the Powerade Athletic Club. That year, he captured the World Indoor 400-meter title, placed third in that event at the USA Track and Field Outdoor Championships, and set his personnel record of 44.34 in the 400-meter dash. At the World Outdoor Championships in Sweden, Darnell had the bad luck of drawing lane one and mismanaged the race in his attempt to compensate for that disadvantage. He tied up near the finish and placed sixth. He later explained, "The 400 is all strategy. My thing was the first 200—if I didn't have a good start, I wouldn't have a good race. The last 200, with the big bear on your back, always came down to heart—who wanted it the most."[191] He was a member of the 1995 World Champion American 4 × 400-meter relay team.

Darnell went into the 1996 Olympic trials in Atlanta in the best shape of his life. He had gone to Europe and finished second in all four races he ran. He was considered by most track insiders to be a good bet for a silver medal, but, in the first heat—after running 250-meters—his right hamstring cramped and he ended up walking to the finish line. The disappointment of missing the 1996 Olympics plunged Hall into a depression, and he began drinking. It took intervention by his running buddies from PAL to jolt him back to reality.[192]

In 1998 Hall was fourth in the 500-meter dash (1:04.12) at the Millrose Games, and placed 6th in heat 4 of the 400-meter run (45.80), but was again injured in the semifinals in the 200-meter run of the USA Track and Field National Championships in New Orleans. His Asics shoe contract, which paid $50,000 a year, plus travel and expenses, expired in late 1998, and he began to wonder what he would do after his sport's career. With a wife, Kenyettia Weber-Hall, and six-year old daughter to think about, Darnell Hall—Detroit's last great sprinter of the twentieth century—stopped running and joined the Detroit Police Department. In the last year of the century he took over the Department's Police Athletic League Track Program. "PAL was where my track career started, and now this is my way of giving back. . . . Everyone around me, it seems, wants me to run [in the 2000 Olympics]. But I'm doing what I want to do. I know what it takes to be an Olympic champion—the sacrifices—and at this stage of my life, it's not worth it."[193]

Trinity Townsend

Trinity was born on February 7, 1974 in Winona, Mississippi. His father was Travis Townsend; his mother Joann Odneal. As a child, Trinity made a habit of running where he needed to be. "Every day I would miss the bus, and would have to run as fast as I could to make to school in time to beat the bell. It was a half mile, oddly enough." Trinity credits his high school coach, Mark Belrose at Muskegon Heights High School [Michigan], with introducing him to real training and made him see his potential.

In college, Trinity stood 5–8 and weighted 146 pounds, had had size 12 feet. He specialized in the 400-meter dash much of his running career, and did not try the 800-meter run until he was a senior at the

University of Michigan. Townsend was an NCAA indoor All-American in the distance medley relay in 1995 and 1996, and an outdoor All-American in the 800-meter run in 1996.

Following college, he became a full-time high school English teacher in Ypsilanti. Despite the difficulty, he continued to run. "Train and teach, that's all I do. Everyday is the same. I get up at 6 a.m. teach until 3:30 p.m., practice from 4 to 7, go to a computer lab to check papers and plan my teaching, then I go home to eat and sleep. I believe I can be the best half-miler in the country. I have the tools, and I have the training. Mentally, there can't be many who are tougher, teaching full-time in addition to training. I challenge anybody to try my life."[194]

Townsend discovered that the 800 is a tough race. You used to be able to go out slow and kick. Now the whole race has become a sprint.[195] The Michigan Association of USA Track & Field gave Townsend its "Open Men's Track and Field Athlete of the Year" award on March 18, 2000. On June 10, 2000 Townsend won the 800-meter (1:47.24) at the First Michigan International Meet in Plymouth.[196]

The McMullens

Doug and Theresa McMullen met at Ferris State University, fell in love, and got married.[197] Theresa grew up in a military family and longed for a stable environment where she and Doug could establish deep roots and raise a family. Doug's hometown of Cadillac, a resort community of 10,000 to 12,000 people, proved to be just such a place. Their oldest child, Paul, was born on February 19, 1972 in Cadillac, and he and his younger brother Phil and his sister Sarah were raised in Cadillac and attended the public schools in that community. Paul grew up to be an Olympian, Phil became an All-American decathlete, and Sarah turned out to be a better than average tennis player.[198]

Doug McMullen attributes the interest of his two sons in track to the family's summer cottage in Le Roy, MI. Doug figures that because the family spent their summers at the cottage on Wells Lake, the boys could not play baseball with their friends. When they got to high school Paul and Phil did not have the hitting and fielding skills of many of their classmates and therefore were forced to chose track over baseball as their spring sport.[199]

Paul McMullen's first love in high school sports was football. He enjoyed hitting people on the football field and, as many good football players do, even tried to hurt them. He played tight end on offense, linebacker on defense, punted and returned punts and kickoffs for

Cadillac High School. Paul particularly enjoyed running back kicks. Like a runaway freight train he returned a kickoff 89 yards for a touchdown during the homecoming game his senior year. His coach, Paul Verska, felt that McMullen was the best player he had ever coached. According to Verska, "He could probably have played Division I college football."[200]

Not everyone understood Paul's enthusiasm or his desire to crunch the opposition. The cross-country coach at Cadillac High School remembers that "Paul was quite immature in high school and [at times] was arrogant. He would often deride his teammates by gloating, when he beat them. He did not really have much success [in track] until his senior year. Track Coach Tom Pierson had a much better impression of Paul [than I.] Paul has since matured a great deal and seems to want to be a nice guy now and acknowledges he wasn't always the best person."[201] What a lot of people considered arrogance, Paul considered confidence.[202]

In high school Paul dreamed of becoming a professional football player. He went out for track for the first time to keep in shape for football. He did not put track ahead of football until he won the State Class B mile run championship in 1989.[203] Nevertheless, as a junior in high school he did well in tack. On April 29, 1989 Paul placed second in the 1,600-meter run (4:44.6) and the 1,600-meter relay (3:38.7) at the Gladwin Invitational.[204] That May 9 he won the mile run (4:50.06) and the two-mile relay (9:21.91) in a duel meet with Benzie Central High School in Cadillac.[205] A week later he won the mile (4:36.77) and placed third in the 800-meter at the North Central Conference Meet. Finally, on May 20, 1989 ran the mile at the Class B Regional Meet held on the Sanford Meridian High School Track.[206]

Paul's personal best in the mile run that track season (4:36.77) put him in fourth in the North Central Region, and was more than 10 seconds slower than Mark Smith's school record for the mile run set in 1979.[207] During his junior and senior year's in high school Paul lost 17 half-mile races to the same runner, Kris Eggle. But, he persisted and in his senior year he finally beat Kris. "The first time I beat him, I knew it was my real beginning," Paul recalls, "At the age of 17 I realized that my football record wasn't glorious and by this time I was running. Also, I knew by then that God had given me a gift; so it was at this time I made my commitment to running."[208]

On May 19, 1990 Paul led the Cadillac High School boys track team to the Class B Regional Championships at the Remus-Chippewa Hills

High School. Paul came away from that meet with individual first place wins in the 400-meter (51.1), the 800-meter (1:57.8), and the 1,600-meter runs (4:28.9). His coach, Tom Pierson, said, "That's the toughest triple you can run. The weather was a factor, but his off-season strength and conditioning program paid off for him."[209] On June 2 at the State Class B Championships, Paul won the mile run (4:19.9), and placed second in both the 800 meter run (1:55.9) and the 3200-meter relay (8:05.7).[210]

In addition to running and playing football, Paul earned as much as $100 a week mowing lawns. He loved mowing lawns. He liked the smell of the freshly cut-grass, the summer heat, and the sweat rolling down his back.[211]

He doesn't Look like a Runner

Eastern Michigan University was the only school to recruit Paul, and Coach Parks only offered him a $600 partial athletic scholarship for his freshmen year.[212] Paul was considered by most college coaches "too big to be a runner." Even Bob Parks could not get excited. "He just did not look like a miler."[213] At 6–2, he ultimately became the largest of the world's top 100 runners.[214] In 1990 Paul was sponsored by the Cadillac Rotary Club to participate in the International Sports Tour Glasnost '90 Games in Moscow. He went house to house requesting donations to help pay for the trip. Paul won four first places in those games. He went on to attend Eastern Michigan where he soon bonded with Coach Parks, who was noted for both his knowledge of track and field and his ability to motivate his runners.

According to some reports, during his freshman year at Eastern Michigan Paul horsed around and generally acted immature.[215] He experienced a collapsed arch running cross-country at 195 pounds and was red shirted for track that year.[216]

The following year Coach Parks placed Paul on the 4 × 800-meter relay team at the Central Collegiate Conference indoor meet in March 1992, and Paul responded by running his personal best.[217] Paul also won the 1,500-meter at the Central Collegiates, and placed second in the MAC 1,500-meter run. While watching an advertisement for the upcoming 1992 Olympics, Paul told his grandfather, David H. McMullen, that he was setting his sites on making the 1996 Olympic team. Paul attended the Olympic trials in 1992 as a spectator. At the trials, he told coach La Plante that he would be running in the 1996 Olympics. It seemed to Fred more like a hollow boast than a prediction.[218]

As a sophomore, Paul placed third in the 1,500-meter run (3:44.85) at the University of Tennessee Invitational, won the 1,500-meter run (3:42.56) at the Drake Relays, won a Mid-American Conference Championship in the 1,500-meter, and was an All-American in the 4 × 800 relay. He placed eighth in the NCAA 1,500-meter run in New Orleans, but was disqualified in the preliminary heats at the USTF Outdoor Championships in Eugene on June 18, 1993. The 1993 season suggested that Paul had potential, and he was learning that life has its ups and downs. Fortunately for Paul, he was about to experience a natural high.

Love and Marriage

Paul saw Jill Stamison for the first time at a cross-country meet in East Lansing in September 1993. She was a student athlete at Western Michigan University, and an All-American half-miler. His mother remembers, "I was watching this runner who looked like Wonder Woman, and Paul said 'Look at her. How beautiful.'"[219] "When I saw her, I was hit by a bolt of lightning!" Paul recalls.[220] Four months later they saw Jill again at an indoor track meet, and Paul asked his mother to take her picture. Paul had learned through a friend from Cadillac who was attending Western Michigan University that Jill had a hometown boy friend, and he was afraid to approach her. He carried her picture around for weeks and told people, "This is the girl I'm going to marry" long before asking her for a date. Even then, he only asked for a date after feeling out the situation through mutual friends.[221]

Paul hitchhiked and stowed away on the Amtrak train because he did not have any money so that he could visit Jill.[222] Paul's track career and his personal reputation among competitors improved markedly after he started dating Jill. Paul married Jill Kristen Stamison on at 6:30 on the evening of September 16, 1995 at the Church of St. Mary in Lake Forest, Illinois.

A Good Day, Except for Getting Beat.

On March 11, 1995 Paul became the third Michigan born man to run a sub-four minute mile. At the NCAA Indoor Championships in March, Paul ran two sub four-minute miles, one in the mile-run (3:58.21) and the other in the distance-medley relay, and lost both races. He came in third in the mile run and second in the relay.[223] In April 1995 Paul McMullen won the 1,500-meter run (3:42.56) at the Drake Relays.

The following month Paul received a degree in General Business, with an emphasis in accounting, from Eastern Michigan U. His brother

Phil, a business student, would soon emerging as a decathlon star at Western Michigan U.[224]

Paul began his run for the Olympics in 1995. On April 8 he was awarded the Tony Wilson Memorial Trophy in 1995 for the outstanding athlete in running events at the SeaRay Relays, when he broke the meet record in the 1,500-meter run (3:39.40) and anchored a winning 4 × 1,600-meter relay team.[225] On April 29 Paul was named the outstanding men's performer at the Drake Relays, after winning those same events.[226] He went on to break the track record for the 1,500-meter at the Central Collegiate Conference Championships at Notre Dame, win three events and set a conference record in the 800-meter run at the Mid-American Conference Championships in Kalamazoo.

At the national college track championships in Knoxville, there was an exciting race between Kevin Sullivan and Paul for the metric mile championship. Brian Hyde from William and Mary College set the initial pace with a brisk 800-meters at 1:58 and then opened a 10-meter lead down the straightaway with a lap to go. But, 10-meters was not a serious lead for the two gentlemen from the North. The University of Michigan's Kevin Sullivan, who had come from 40-yards back to win the NCAA indoor mile crown, ran the final lap in 54 seconds. He passed Hyde with 200-meters left, with Paul close on his heels. Sullivan crossed the finish line in 3:37.57 a comfortable 10 meters ahead of the second place McMullen. Hyde drifted back to seventh place.[227]

Turning Professional

After placing second in the metric mile in the NCAA Outdoor Championships, Paul won the national championship in the 1,500-meter run at the United States Track and Field Championships in Sacramento, surprising the favored Steve Holman.[228] Following the National Championships, Paul signed a professional contract with the Asics Shoe Company. Winning the national championship in the 1,500-meter qualified the Eastern Michigan graduate for the World Championships in Goteborg, Sweden.

On August 8, 1995 in Goteborg, Paul fell down in the semi-finals with 500-meters left in the race. Undaunted, he scrambled to his feet and ran the last 400-meters in 52 seconds to qualify for the finals. The next day Paul called Bob Parks from Europe. "Coach, I'm going to win." McMullen did not win his first international championship, but he did try. He lead Noureddine Morceli, the best miler in the world, for 1,000-meters before fading to tenth.[229] From that time on, Paul measured his progress "on the level of the planet" rather than on a national level.[230]

While running in Europe for Asics, Paul improved his 1,500-meter time by nearly five seconds. He beat the Olympic qualifying time in Lausanne, Switzerland in July and ran his personal best (3:34.45) in Cologne, Germany in August. Yet, Paul never lost his bearings. He told his hometown newspaper, "The last thing I am doing is forgetting where I came from. I grew up on those streets and I am a better athlete for running around that lake."[231]

A Rivalry Develops

While in college, Paul had two primary rivals in the 1,500-meter and mile runs: Kevin Sullivan, a Canadian attending the University of Michigan, and 1992 Olympian Steve Holman, from Georgetown University. In 1995 Paul won the 1,500-meter run at the U.S. Track and Field Championships in Sacramento, defeating Steve Holman, among others. Bob Wischnia wrote in *Track and Field News*, "It's hard to figure how Holman, one of the most intelligent runners, could blow last year's USATF final so badly and finish fifth." Nevertheless, Steve ended the year ranked fourth in the world, while Paul was ranked twelfth.[232] Holman and McMullen were "a study contrasts," according to half-miler Richard Kenah, Holman's college roommate. "Paul feeds on emotion, while Steve is an introverted thinker."[233]

Steve Holman won the metric mile in 3:38.39 at the NCAA Outdoor Championships in Austin, Texas in June 1992. The Arlington, Virginia collegiate had improved steadily during his four years at Georgetown University.[234] No American runner had won a gold medal in the 1,500-meter run since 1908, and none had been ranked best in the world in the 1,500 for twenty years.[235] As America's leading miler, it seemed that Steve Holman might have that opportunity, if he continued to improve as he had during the previous four years.

In 1992 Steve made the Olympic team, and over the next three years ran successfully in Europe. In 1994 he placed third in the mile run at Goodwill Games in St. Petersburg, Russia with the respectable time of 3:52.77.[236] He even ran well in the 3-K, taking fourth in the USTF Indoor Championships at the Georgia Dome in Atlanta in March 1995.[237] Most important of all, he sat on the ruling committee of track and field for the Olympics, pursuant to the 1978 Amateur Sports Act.[238]

By contrast, Paul McMullen was considered by many to be cocky and a little erratic. Driven by emotion, he was sometimes guided more by his feeling than by his brains. As Paul told a *Chicago Tribune* reporter, "I have a football mentality." He proudly defied the stereotype of the waif-like distance runner. Like Steve Prefontaine, McMullen had a working class mentality, never gave up, was as confrontational as a professional wrestler, and was as aggressive as a hockey player. A month before the Olympic trials, Paul had so much excess energy, he wanted to do something that was completely the opposite of running but in a physical area, so for 20 minutes he wrestled with former Iowa State All-American wrestler and Eastern Michigan University Wrestling coach, "Willie" Gadson. "Willie put a serious whipping on me," Paul later admitted.[239]

Go, Paul, Go!

Going into the U.S. Olympic trials, the competition for places on the U.S. Olympic track and field team was fierce. Paul McMullen suffered a pair of ankle sprains early in the track season and missed nearly three months to these injuries. The setbacks meant that Paul was not quite at his peak going into the Olympic trials. He was working out with in Ann Arbor with Kevin Sullivan, who would be running for Canada. In early June, Paul, Jill, and Coach Bob Parks headed to Atlanta so that Paul could get acclimated to running in southern weather.[240]

Track and Field News called the upcoming competition "trial by fury." Every competitor knew the stark reality, "finish in the top three or wait four years to try again." No politics: no verdicts behind closed doors. Bob Wischnia, writing in *Track and Field News*,[241] saw the key match-up in the 1,500-meter run as Steve Holman against himself, with Paul McMullen as someone else to watch. He predicted "Holman's much too smart and too good to make the same mistake he made last year [in the USATF Championships]. Holman needs to win the Trials for his confidence—and win impressively."

Despite being the fastest U.S. miler and performing well in Europe, Holman usually struggled against McMullen. At the international level running often was a lot more mental than at lower levels of competition. As Paul puts it, "You sure as hell don't have time for self-doubt at this level." While some runners warm up together, joking around to relieve tension, McMullen compounds tension. He won't even make eye contact, let alone grant them a nod or a smile. "I'm certainly much more aggressive than most of them that way," he said. "But I want to let them know that, today, it's business."[242]

Run in the Atlanta Sun

With encouragement from coach Bob Parks, Paul McMullen approached the Olympic trials by posturing to position himself physiologically. "I am being extremely serious about this race. I plan coming across first in my heat," McMullen told a news conference before the first round preliminaries. "I want to send a message that I am here to kick butt and not mess around. I want to control the last 700-meters." When asked about the affects of the temperature, that was expected to be in the 90 degree range at race time, Paul said, "I enjoy the heat."[243]

On June 17 Steve Holman won the second heat of the 1,500-meter preliminary round, and Paul placed second in the third heat of that round.[244] Paul said he ran fairly easy. He wasn't trying to win the race, just advance to the next round. Bob Parks was not altogether happy about how Paul ran the first round race. Parks told a reporter, "I really wouldn't have minded if he ran hard in the first round because of the three day rest [until the semi-finals.] He probably ran easier than maybe what I would have preferred. We wanted him to send a message, which I don't think he did. But that is immaterial at this point."[245]

In the semi-final round, Paul was in the same heat as Steve Holman. Brian Hyde was also in that heat, and jumped out into the lead. Holman followed. McMullen then caught up with Holman and boxed-in the Georgetown miler. McMullen later reported, "Steve had no control of the race. He had to stay patient until there was an opening. I did not open the box." After 1,000-meters, Holman became frustrated and started shoving Hyde and others to assure a spot in the finals. As it got down to the final lap, Holman went to the outside, running in the fifth lane. "Steve had to work a lot to get out of the box," McMullen recounted. Holman won the heat, but at a high price. At the same time, Paul ran a conservative race and saved his energy for the finals the following day.[246]

Paul had achieved Bob Park's objective. He had frustrated his principal opponent by making his life as difficult as possible, while saving his energy for the race that counted. As Parks put it that evening, "Both Paul and Holman have the same agenda in the finals—go out and run 3:36 or 3:37. They are the only two guys in the field that can do this. A slow race in the finals could be trouble for Paul, but Holman would definitely be in trouble. McMullen can run any kind of race; he has shown he can run a fast race, and he can run a slower race," Parks observed. "Paul is an unusual kid; he's a thinker and sometimes that is bad, you can think too much. One advantage he does have is he can run it any ol' which way. He can kick pretty good, or he can run a hot pace from the gun." Parks expected Holman to try and get the lead early and set a hot pace. "But," he predicted "The 1,500 is just short enough that people are bumping, trying to make a move or cut in front of somebody at the right time or at the wrong time. We have got to react to what other people do. If they do this or if that happens, we have to do this or that. You just don't know what they're going to do."[247]

In the finals of the Olympic trials for the 1,500-meter run the temperature was over 100 degrees Fahrenheit on the track. Michael Cox took the lead and McMullen, running in the second lane, held onto second. Paul later said, "I didn't want to be in the lead, but I wanted to be right on his shoulder, in striking position. I relaxed a little bit." With about 800-meters to go McMullen pushed the pace and got into position to take the lead in the final lap. In the meantime, Holman was mired back in the pack. The race was turning out to be a relatively slow one, the pack was tight, and the unexpected was happening to Steve Holman. Coming around the last corner, McMullen tried to out kick those trailing him, but the race stayed tight. Coming down the straightaway, six or seven men had a shot at the first three places that would guarantee them a ticket to the Olympics, provided that they met the Olympic qualifying time. "I wanted to be the first to the finish line. I just wanted to keep running and I was telling myself 'don't lose faith,'" Paul recalls. With three meters to go he leaned in and that was it. He had pulled it off. The man from Cadillac was going to the Olympic games, but Steve Holman was saying home. Steve finished thirteenth, near the back of the pack.[248]

When Paul won the Olympic trials the *Detroit Free Press* told its readers, "EMU's McMullen has the guts to win" in a bump and run contest. McMullen, the ex-football player could take and elbow or three and bully his way to victory.[249] When Holman failed to make the 1996 U.S. Olympic team, Jason Pyrah, one of the runners who made the Olympic team, referred to Holman as "a head case." Paul's wife, Jill, weighed in calling Holman a "choker."[250] Holman consulted a sports psychologist soon after the Olympic trials. He recalls, "For a while it [losing the Olympic trials] was something I was ashamed of, but everyone has struggles. Its how you deal with them."[251]

On the Monday following the 1,500 final trials, Paul McMullen told the assistant editor of his hometown newspaper, "I have more getting in shape to do. I definitely can do better and hard work starts [today] and Tuesday. I bet Bob Parks has a workout for me."[252] At 8 p.m. on the Fourth of July, Paul held a Public workout at the Cadillac High School track. At the workout, he ran a sub-four minute mile, followed by a 15-minute recovery period. Then he ran an 800-meters, and after a second

15-minute recovery period he ran 400-meters. Thousands of his family's friends and neighbors turned out to urge their hometown hero to "Go Paul Go." His family and the local Rotary Club sold 1,800 T-shirts that yielded $4,000 to underwrite Paul's Atlantic Olympic expenses.[253] The entire town seemed to rally behind Paul and became invested in his run for the Gold.

Some believed that an athlete must use performance-enhancing drugs to qualify for a modern Olympic team. Paul and his family say "not so." Paul said, "Reaching my Olympic dream meant I had to become focused. I had to stop eating ranch-flavored potato chips, going out late at night with my girl friend, and risking my body on activities like water-skiing barefoot." "I worked hard, mighty hard for the chance to represent my community and my country at the Olympics."[254] "My parents are a perennial source of support for me. It means a lot when they are at a track meet."

At the Atlanta Olympics

It had been 28 years since an American had medaled in the 1,500-meter race at the Olympics.[255] The odds were against Paul breaking that string of losses, in what nearly everyone agreed was going to be one of the most competitive races in modern track and field. During the Olympic trials, McMullen spent a lot of time in the second lane. Coach Parks did not want to see that happen in the finals. "You lose about 11 feet a turn when you run in the second lane. Over the course of a lap, you lose about seven yards." It wasn't something Parks was wild about. In a fast 1,500-meter race, 24-yards is a lot of ground to make up.

Parks had coached an athlete participating in every summer Olympics since 1968. Unlike 1,500-meter races in the European circuit, Olympic races at that distance are less likely to be all-out speed races. This gave Paul a shot at a medal.

On Monday morning July 29 Paul ran in the fifth heat of the first round of the 1,500-meter run at the Atlanta Olympics. When the race started Paul was in the back of the pack, pacing himself. On the third lap Paul started to make his move. He passed eight runners and moved into third place. When he came around the last bend, Paul was relaxed and finished second with a time of 3:39.94, clinching a berth in Thursday's semifinals.[256] The next day, Paul mowed the lawn for two hours to relax. He wanted to go to the Hootie and the Blowfish Concert, but decided not to squander his opportunity to win an Olympic medal.[257]

The two heats of the semifinals were held at about 7 p.m. on August 1. The fastest 12 runners would advance to the finals. Wearing electric pink shoes, Paul moved into eighth place shortly after the starter's pistol signaled the start of the race. Early in the first lap McMullen moved up to third position, but by the end of the first lap he was back in the pack at ninth. Paul dropped back to last place early in the second lap and remained there for the remainder of lap. At 800-meters his time was 1:58. In the third lap, Paul started moving up in the pack until he was running fifth, but his kick failed him in the final lap. McMullen finished ninth in his heat and nineteenth overall, failing to make the finals.[258] Since Paul was the only American to make it to the semifinals, the United States was not represented in the finals of the metric mile.

After losing, Paul skipped the pageantry of the closing ceremonies. As he put it, "I'm looking out for my best interest of keeping sane. I just want to go home and see my dog." "We have to decide where to go from here training-wise. Right now I'm not at the level I would like to be." He was still young for a 1,500-meter runner and could look forward to as much as eight years of competitive running.[259]

A Good Deed Gone Bad

After the 1997 Penn Relays, Paul felt like the fun had gone out of running. "Where was that high school attitude that I had for so long?" He asked himself. "I couldn't find it anymore.[260]

Paul always enjoyed mowing lawns. Mowing the lawn was just one of the ways he distanced himself from the pressures of competition. His wife read to unwind; Paul mowed the lawn.[261] He mowed his neighbor's grass free and without being asked. "There's something about finishing one row and starting another. It's kind of hypnotic," Paul admitted. When its all over [track and field] he told friend, he would like to own his own lawn care business.[262] It was even claimed that McMullen volunteered to trim untidy lawns while racing in England, France and even in Atlanta during the Olympics.[263] It was his way of avoiding the "lobby lizards," the guys who sit in the lobbies where all the athletes stay when there is a track meet and constantly talk about track and field.[264]

On the afternoon of June 3, 1997—ten days before he was to compete in the U.S. Outdoor Championships for his third straight title in the 1,500-meter run—McMullen mangled his right foot in a lawn mower while helping an elderly, Ypsilanti widow by mowing her lawn. As Paul recalls it, "I had finished mowing on this steep bank, which was about

45 degrees. I should have shut the mower off. Instead, while I was going down the hill, I slipped on the grass. My right foot went out from under me."[265] The mower rolled back over his right foot, shearing the running shoes he was wearing, cutting off parts of his second and third toes and broke and mangling the big toe. He lost 80 percent of the second toe and 70 percent of the third toe.[266] "The mower was set on high. I didn't let go of the mower and my foot got caught under it. I screamed."[267] It was the damage to his big toe that was the most worrisome.[268]

Paul experienced fear in its most vivid form. "My career passed before my eyes. I was calm, but I knew it was bad. I thought it was all over, just like that. When I was alone in the hospital, sure I asked, 'why me?" McMullen admitted. "I didn't feel right again until I could walk on my own."[269]

Paul was rushed to St. Joseph's Hospital in Ann Arbor, where Dr. Michael Masini, a Notre Dame graduate and former Fighting Irish football player, performed surgery.[270] Immediately after the operation, Dr. Masini did not think Paul would be a world class runner again. Others repeated that judgement. Paul countered their skepticism by selling T-shirts that read: "Dream Big and Work Hard."[271]

"Not many milers consider losing two toes to a lawn mower a career boost. But that's what happened to Paul McMullen. Instead of blaming the lawn mower, Paul contacted the Toro Company and asked them to hire him as a spokesman for consumer safety.[272] In early March 1998 Toro sent Paul a free lawn mower and made him a product safety spokesman.[273] Paul McMullen became the only runner in the world with an endorsement deal with a lawn-mower company. Some runners found peace on mountaintops, Paul found it mowing lawns.[274]

Paul was running again three months after the accident. In July 1997, he reported, "I still have some pain, but I'm healing pretty well. The doctors say my balance won't be affected because my big toe will be OK. I'll have to get some orthopedics because the slightest little glitch in your stride can screw up a whole bunch of things. But I'll be fine: I'll be back."[275]

McMullen looks for positives in every situation, and he found some concerning his foot injury. "My life was just going too fast. I was travelling all over the country. I was living out of a suitcase most of the time. Something had to give. The time at home (in Ypsilanti) really helped. I needed that."[276]

Paul worked as a dishwasher in a Ypsilanti restaurant while recuperating from the loss of his toes. "I had nothing to do, and I didn't want to feel sorry for myself. It was probably stupid to be on my [injured] foot so much, but it gave me great perspective. Being at the bottom of the totem pole was humbling for me," Paul recalled. He trained in the summer of 1997 by cycling. Physical therapist Gary Grey was the first to tell Paul that he would race again.[277] He rode his bike about 10-K (6.2 miles) a day. Jill joked with Paul to keep his spirits up.[278] She told him, "Now you can get a discount on a pedicure!" She changed his dressings. "She never wavered [in her support for me], and never allowed me to think anything negative," Paul recalled. He dealt with regular blood blisters before the thin skin, stretched over the savaged toe bones, toughened.[279] He resumed running on Labor Day [1997]. His right shoe was now a half-size smaller than his left. He didn't use orthotics. He performed foot-strengthening exercises to compensate for the missing toe.[280]

In October 1997 he started training with the Eastern Michigan University cross-country team. "The first two weeks were the toughest of my career," he said. "I thought I'd never run like I did before. I struggled so bad. I was way, way back in workouts. I was exhausted. I had to swallow tremendous pride. I don't think I talked to Jill for two weeks.[281] "It was scary to run again. My body was still adjusting slowly to my plant foot. When I push off, there's nothing there. There's no support from the toes next to the big one."[282] When he was running 1,000-meter intervals during his workouts in October and the other runners were crushing him, Paul, who never enjoys losing, threw a tantrum and wanted to quit. He took off his shoe and threw it. The always alert and composed Coach Parks casually asked Paul, "Are you done yet?" Paul yelled, "No, I'm not done." Parks responded, "Paul, did you think this was going to be easy? It's going to be the toughest thing you've done. Get your head out of your butt, get off the ground and quit feeling sorry for yourself." The ever coachable McMullen, put his shoes back on and "gutted out" the workout.[283]

Back on the Track with Eight Toes Racing Ahead

Paul's Asics contract expired on December 31, 1997 and was renewed for two years, but most of the financial rewards in the renewal were based on incentives. "That's fine," McMullen said. "It would be better for the sport if we were rewarded for performance instead of getting appearance fees."[284]

On January 24, 1998, Paul entered his first race following the accident. The race took place at the University of Michigan Track and Tennis Building. There is a fierce rivalry between Eastern Michigan University and the University of Michigan. Coach Parks has a sign in is office that asks and answers the question, "How do you get to Ann Arbor?" His sign says, "Just go West and follow the smell." The rivalry was particularly strong when Paul and the University of Michigan's Kevin Sullivan faced each other regularly when both were in college. During the January race, a University of Michigan coach taunted Paul, yelling "Hey, no toes, better be careful with lawn mowers." At first Paul was furious, but later he used the taunt for motivation.[285] In the end, the usually volatile McMullen benefited from these experiences. He used the taunt for personal motivation. It gave him "more emotional fire."[286]

Paul lost 10 pounds and changed his mental state of mind. "You become very thankful when you lose your gift and then it's given back. You begin to trust God more, like there's another power at play here."

On Friday February 13, 1998, Paul ran the Wanamaker Mile at the Chase Millrose Games and finished second to Laban Rotich of Kenya, with an exceptionally fast time of 3:57.46 for a tight indoor track. Paul later told a reporter, "My body has slowly adjusted to the difference in my foot plant . . . I couldn't be more ecstatic about my progress."[287] Jill's congratulations: "You just set a world record for a guy with eight toes." McMullen hugged Jill and said, "I'm loving her more. It's kind of mushy." "When your spirit is taken care of and your heart is taken care of, then you can let your body go. I've become a lot more carefree about racing. Running has become more fun and less risky."[288] Later, he told New York track writers, "If you're going to run a good race, you have to get good position. The pace felt quite comfortable because I used to run 800-meter races. Rotich is human. That's what I got from racing him. He never completely broke me mentally. Maybe he let me stay that close, I don't know."[289]

At the Drake Relays Paul continued to have a great comeback season. On April 24, Paul led more than half of the 800-meter run, only to lose a close race. Yet, he ran the 800-meters in 1:49.33, a good time. The next day, Paul trailed Terrance Herrington by two meters with a lap to go in the open mile run, and came back to win (3:59.12). Paul recounted, "I didn't start fast enough and didn't get the time I wanted, but it was a great race and that's what track's all about—two runners running shoulder to shoulder to the finish with the fans screaming." McMullen's time was the fastest in the world that spring.[290]

On April 30, 1998 a mere 8,874 people [only 6,474 paid fans] saw the USA Indoor Track and Field Championships in Atlanta's Georgia

Dome. Paul McMullen's recovery was to be fully tested at this meet. He would run against long time rival Steve Holman, who had posted the fastest time in the mile run (3:50.40) of any American in the past five years. "I told myself," Paul McMullen recounted, "This guy is going to run a lot different than before—he's going to give a shot. I just zeroed in on the back of his head, on his number [number 220]. I had a change in the game plan. But I wanted to stay right there and be able to make my run later." Near the start of the bell lap, McMullen passed Holman and won the race by a meter or so. After he crossed the finish line, Paul turned a cartwheel on the track to celebrate his victory. One sports writer quipped that McMullen still had Holman's number.[291]

After his victory lap, Paul spoke about the rivalry with Holman, trying to put it in a new perspective. "Steve is the best miler in the country." "There's been a mellowing of my killer instinct. I don't know if I'm ready to step out and start a friendship with Steve, but I'll treat him with respect. I think our rivalry is good for track, but it's time to leave certain stuff to the boxers and football players. Runners are more reserved. It fits the sport better."[292] Yet, it was clear to many outside observers that both Steve's speed and Paul's toughness were needed for North Americans to compete successfully with the Kenyans, who had the advantage of living and training at high-altitudes and thereby gaining the advantage of extra oxygen-carrying capacity in their blood.

Paul did not forget where he came from. After winning the USA National Indoor Mile Championship in Atlanta, he returned to Cadillac to tell the Rotary Club, "I want you to know how much I appreciate your support. I have a lot of fun running and my goal is to take it all the way. It's coming along well.[293]

On June 21 Paul McMullen ran in the 1,500-meter run at the USA Track and Field National Championships in New Orleans. With temperatures in the shade approaching 103 degrees Fahrenheit and 116 degrees in the sun, Paul was running last at the 800-meter mark, and Steve Holman was leading the race when Paul made his move. Paul was nearing the lead when someone clipped his heel. Paul stumbled, nearly fell and found himself back in the pack, again. With victory out of his reach, Paul set sights on rival Steve Holman, whom he regularly beat at major meets. Paul closed furiously, passing Holman a step before the finish line for third place with the time of 3:39:46. Jason Pyrah won the race.[294] Jason Pyrah would become Paul McMullen's training partner in January 1999.[295]

By the summer of 1998 the 26 year old Paul had made a full recovery from his lawn mower accident the year before. On July 11 he ran the Golden Mile before an estimated 10,000 people at the Traverse City Cherry Festival in a sizzling 3:56.2 to set a new course record. He ran the first quarter-mile in 60-seconds and every split after that was faster. "I really fed off the crowd. I got as close to the people as I could. I could feel their excitement. I could hear them yelling in my ear. It was great. I never dreamed I'd come back this quickly. But thanks to the support of my family, my coach and the community, I was competing again in eight months. It was a painful trip. Thankfully, it was shorter than expected." McMullen received $1,750 for the victory: $1000 for winning and a $750 bonus for running under 4 minutes. He donated his bonus check to the Grand Traverse Area Catholic Schools.[296]

The Struggle to Stay Focused

In December 1998 Paul and Jill McMullen leased their house in Ypsilanti. In early January they packed up their clothes and a few household items; put their three year old, 150 pound English bull mastiff, Chugalug in the car; and headed to California in a snow storm.[297] Their mission was to work with Tom Craig who was also guiding Regina Jacob's career. Paul would be on a full-time training regimen and working out with Jason Pyrah. His hope was to prepare himself for the European season and move up enough to win a medal in the 2000 Olympics.[298]

On April 24, 1999 Paul placed second in the one-mile men's special invitational run (4:04.60) at the 90th Drake Relays in Des Moines. In the third lap Paul McMullen slowed and lost the race to Mark Houser in the last half of the final lap of the race.[299] The Drake Relays was to be symptomatic of the problems for Paul in 1999. Tom Craig did not give Paul enough attention, and the Eastern Michigan runner could not duplicate his 1998 accomplishments without more direction. Frustrated, he and Jill moved back to Ypsilanti in the summer of 1999 and went back to the care of coach Parks.[300]

At the Millrose Games on February 4, 2000 Paul went out too fast in an effort to gain position, again ran out of energy, and finished last.[301] On March 4, 2000 he ran a perfect race for the first half-mile but visibly lacked the energy to hold the pace necessary to maintain his second place position. Paul finished sixth (4:03.62). Jason Pyrah won the USA Indoor mile championship in 3:57.83, and the next three place winners also ran sub-four minute miles.[302] Paul recovered by running second in the 1,500-meter (3:44.03) at the SeaRay Relays on April 14 to keep his dream of returning to the Olympics alive, only to have them die later.[303]

For the Love of the Sport

Paul McMullen loves track. He enjoys the speed, the tactics, and the strategy. But most of all he enjoys the adulation that comes from success. "I don't think about beating people. I set my sights on standards I want to reach. I'm always pushing my body. My faith and belief in my gift of running takes me beyond the normal pain threshold as I train and compete. I have to watch the ground. I can't afford to twist an ankle because if I do, it's like a flat tire on a race car."[304] There seems to be two philosophies of running. Paul appears to belong to the "just do it" and "then fix it" group, while Steve Holman appears to belong to the "do the right thing, the right way the first time" group. One approach is action oriented, the other depends on thinking before action. Neither approach is right or wrong. Both reflect personality and each can lead to a championship.

It is difficult to reach and maintain world class status in track and field even for those with a gift for running, jumping, or throwing. It is a particularly difficult for to become one of the best 20 middle-distance runners in a world of 6 billion people.

Brother Phil

Paul McMullen's younger brother Phil charted his own path to the upper ranks of American track and field by means of the decathlon. When Phil attended Western Michigan University in 1995, he had never competed in six of the ten events included in the decathlon. "Obviously, I was at a disadvantage, when I came to college, but my body was starting from scratch," Phil said. "I may have brought bad habits to college if I would have done a bunch of the events in high school." He had never done the pole vault, shot put, high hurdles, long jump, javelin, 100-meter dash or 1500-meter before enrolling in college. The six foot two inch, 200-pound Phil McMullen did not brag. He was a confident athlete who put in countless hours training for the most grueling event in a track meet. The decathlon is the 100, long jump, shot put, high jump and 400 on the first day and the 110 high-hurdles, discus, pole vault, javelin, and 1,500 on the second day.[305]

The break through to significant national ranking in the decathlon took place at the Sea Ray Relays in Knoxville on April 9–11, 1998 when he won the event with 8,009 points. According to Jack Shaw, Western Michigan's track coach, "Phil is a great second-day decathlete. The first day is a speed day and he doesn't do as well in the speed events as in the skill and distance events."

At the SeaRay Relays Phil came forward in the pole vault and the 1,500-meter run. Phil recalled, "My brother Paul showed up during the pole vault and that's always a big influence on me. It kind of gave me a boost. We said a little prayer before the 1,500-meter and that helped.[306] Phil vaulted 16 feet ½ inch, placing him fifth on Western Michigan's all-time pole vault list. Both Phil and his brother Paul have a super-loud whistle that you can hear everywhere. By pre-arrangement,

Paul was at the start line and was going to whistle if I was off my pace at the end [of the 1,500-meter run at the SeaRay]. With about 300-meters to go, he was whistling like crazy and I kept thinking, 'I'm going, I'm going. . . .' It's 45 degrees and it's dark already.

Nevertheless, Phil came through.[307]

Phil likes the Michael Johnson quote, "talent plus opportunity times hard work equals success. Talent is fixed, opportunity is something you're given, but you control hard work." "When I step on the track, I'm going to show you everything I've got. . . . I busted my butt ever since I got here to get to where I'm at and learn all those things. . . . Javelin is still tough [for me] and I have the most room for improvement in this event."[308]

Phil had developed a championship mindset. On April 23–24, 1998 he placed second in the decathlon at the Penn Relays. Then, at the Mid-American Conference outdoor Championships in Akron's athletic complex, Phil competed in thirteen events. He won his fourth consecutive MAC decathlon championship, with 7,821 points. On the first day Phil ran a 11.23 100-meter dash and achieving a personal best in the high jump (6–6). He followed that up with a second day that included: the 110-meter high-hurdles (15.18), the discus (187–4), pole vault (15–5), the javelin (174–6), and the 1,500-meter run (4:25.0). He also participated in the open pole vault, placing eighth with a jump of 15–5¾; the discus—where he failed to place, and the 4 × 400-meter relay that was disqualified for an improper baton pass.[309]

Tragically, the night the meet ended, Phil twisted an ankle and spoiled his chances of winning the NCAA decathlon championship two weeks later. Still, University of Akron Coach Dennis Mitchell called Phil "the best athlete in the country right now."[310] After the NCAA Championships in Buffalo, Phil joined the Indianapolis Invaders track team. On June 20, 1998 at the USA Track and Field National Championships in New Orleans, Phil finished sixth in the decathlon (7,947 points) and was only 134 points shy of qualifying for the Goodwill Games.[311] "He will be a hero of this city in the future," his brother Paul predicted.[312]

Phil sat out the entire 1999 track season after undergoing foot surgery. Starting in the fall of 1999, under the guidance of coaches for the Indiana Invaders, Phil adopted an entirely new style of training. "I started focusing more on speed and explosiveness—explosive movements," Phil related. "Those changes made a large impact. I've beaten my [personal record] in the long jump by over a foot. In the shot put, I've changed my technique from the spin to the glide."[313] On March 3–4, 2000 his new training style paid-off when he placed second in the Men's Heptathlon (5,828 points) at the USA Indoor Track and Field Championships, Georgia Dome in Atlanta. He rallied from sixth place after the third event on day one to move up to third place at the end of the day, after the high jump. On the second day he placed fourth in the high-hurdles, tied for second in the pole vault (16-¾), and placed second in the 1,000-mter run.[314]

Following the indoor championships, Phil targeted the decathlon at the SeaRay Relays in early April with the expectation of meeting the Olympic-qualifying standard of 7,900 points. On April 13, 2000 Phil set a new Sea Ray Meet record for the decathlon with 8,097 points and qualified for the Olympic trials in July.[315] He finished fourth in the Olympic trials.

University of Michigan Middle Distance Runner

John, son of Jack and June Mortimer, was born on March 18, 1976 in Londonderry, New Hampshire. In fifth grade, at the age of eleven, he set out to win a mile run held for the fifth and sixth grade students in his hometown. When the race was over, he had placed second to a bigger and faster sixth grader. The next year John came back and won that race. "That race [as a sixth grader] kind of got me started," John later said. In Junior high school he became a state cross-country champion, and retained that title throughout high school. In both 1994 and 1995, while in high school, he was national champion in the indoors two-mile run. In 1995, he was also national runner-up in the Footlocker National Cross-country Invitational, and he was a national scholastic All-American four times.

John Mortimer was an outstanding student. In high school he was a four-time honor roll recipient. With Mortimer's strong academic credentials and track/cross-country achievements, one would have expected that the New Hampshire track star would be on the target list of recruits for the University of Michigan. However, this was not the case. John Mortimer selected the University of Michigan because it has a well-regarded academic program in architecture as well as a good running program. He called Michigan cross-country coach Ron Warhurst, and asked to come to Michigan to look at the school. Once Mortimer visited Michigan, a couple of members of the track team inspired to want to be a part of their team, and once Warhurst realized how good Mortimer was he offered him a scholarship.[316]

As a freshman at the University of Michigan, in the fall of 1995, Mortimer found immediate success on the cross-country team. He earned All-American status with a 37th place finish at the NCAA Championships, and was named Big Ten freshman cross-country man of the year. According to coach Warhurst, "He was mature coming in. Distance running is a head trip, and it takes more than natural ability . . . he was able to overcome adversity quickly." It helped that he trained with Kevin Sullivan, the U of M All-American from Brantford, Ontario.

In his sophomore year, Mortimer flourished as a runner. He won the Big Ten and NCAA District cross-country championships. He missed the indoor track season because of pneumonia,[317] but rallied for the outdoor track season. During the outdoor track season, he won the steeplechase at the Arkansas Invitational, the Jesse Owen Classic, the Texas Relays, and the Big Ten Championships. He was second in the 10-K at the Raleigh Relays and won the 10-K run at the Big Ten Championships. He was third in the 5-K run in the Penn Relays, and was fifth in the steeplechase at the USA Track and Field Championships. Finally, he was awarded the honor of Big Ten athlete of the year. John represented the U of M at the World University Games in Sicily in 1996.[318]

Mortimer was red-shirted halfway through the 1997 indoor track season because of pneumonia. During the outdoor season, Mortimer led the Michigan men's track team to a third-place finish at the Big Ten Championships with a tremendous individual performance. Twenty-eight of Michigan's 97 points came from Mortimer, who placed first in the 10-K and steeplechase, and second in the 5-K. His total dominance was the most impressive thing about his performance. Mortimer casually checked his watch as he crossed the finish line of the 10-K. Mortimer placed second in his last event, the 5-K, when fatigue was taking its toll.[319] Mortimer was named the most valuable athlete at the meet, and was an Academic All-Big Ten in track in 1997.[320]

Mortimer was seeded ninth in the steeplechase going into the national NCAA outdoor meet in 1997. He finished third.[321] John gained international experience when he competed and finished ninth in the World University Games in Sicily, Italy on August 29, 1997. He had 10 days on the island before he had to compete, so had an opportunity to do some sightseeing.[322]

In the fall of 1997 Mortimer finished eleventh in the NCAA cross-country Championships and once again earned All-American status. At the NCAA Indoor Championships in mid-March 1998 Mortimer, who was well known for his endurance, but lacking a strong finishing kick, placed fifth in the 5-K run. His finish earned him All-American standing for the fourth time.[323] On May 22–24, 1998 Mortimer won the steeplechase (8:50.77) and the 10-K (30:17.00) and placed fourth in the 5-K at the 98th Annual Big Ten Outdoor Championships[324] He placed second in the steeplechase and seventh in the 5-K at the NCAA outdoor championships.

John Mortimer represented America in the steeplechase at the Goodwill Games in New York City on July 20 and placed seventh. Mortimer sat out the NCAA regional cross-country championships in Terre Haute in November because of a leg injury.[325] He finished 31st in the NCAA cross-country national championships in Kansas on November 21. He battled injuries for several weeks, and underwent surgery to repair torn meniscus in his right knee prior to the indoor track season.[326]

In 1998–9 John Mortimer and Katie McGregor shared a house while students at the University of Michigan. According to Katie, "It was not like a boyfriend/girlfriend thing." She characterized Mortimer was a student of the sport. He kept tabs on all sorts of all things and got her a lot more involved in the running world. He also got her to think about what she wanted to become and where she wanted to go. "He's someone who is very goal oriented. I'm more serious because of him. He knows where he's going and he's very dedicated, so he's been a good influence. I'm also really competitive with him. If he gets all these awards or he gets attention, I want that too. But he got me to realize the options, the things I can do with my running."[327]

Mortimer and his teammates did volunteer work at Mott Children's Hospital in 1998. He was also a "Big Brother" to Ann Arbor youth. According to his coach, "John's a wonderful runner, but he's a better person."[328] Like so many track athletes, the Ann Arbor runners were proving their individuality in an era of team sports.

22. "Sports as Entertainment Replaces Athletic Competition: Track Is No Longer Connecting With The Masses"

Between 1960 and November 1999, world population doubled. It took until 1800 for the world population to reach one billion. If a billion people were spaced 15 inches apart, they would form a straight line from the earth to the moon. World population reached two billion in 1930, three billion in 1960, and six billion in 1999.[1] Population growth, in turn, has brought worldwide increased population density and has driven the need for more infrastructure development. The presence of more people inevitably results in the demand for more clean water, food, clothing, houses, schools, fossil fuels, places of worship, shopping centers, roads, and recreation areas. Increased population also means more energy use, traffic jams, air and water pollution, and conflicts. It is likely to result in less open space and, on a worldwide basis, lower per capita incomes.

Population size and density also will impact participation in sports and recreational activities, popular tastes in sports, and the demand for sports training facilities, sports venues, and coaching. Perhaps population should also affect the awards given at international track and field competitions. Does it not seem logical that with quadruple the nations participating and a doubling of the competitors between 1924 and 1996, the Olympics Games might find it advantageous to start giving medals to the first five places in each event, rather than rewarding just the first three places?

During the last third of the twentieth century, radio and television, popular music, the internet, and peer group influences began to replace parental, village or neighborhood, and religious guidance in the establishing the interests, tastes, fashions, and values of young people. Without fundamental changes in child rearing practice or greater emphasis on and investment in community recreation this phenomenon is likely to continue for some time. Peer driven popular culture has seriously undermined the popularity of track and field and has tolerated the health risks, such as obesity, associated with the lack of physical activity, and will continue to do so until adolescents become more physically active.

It Wasn't News If It Wasn't In The Newspaper

For more than a century, the media has influenced the relationship between sports and the public. From the day the sports page of the newspaper was invented by William Randolph Hearst's *New York Journal* in 1895, public interest in athletics has been shaped by what is reported. In the 1920s sports coverage in daily newspapers reached the space generally accorded to this section of the paper for the balance of the century. Prior to the mid-1950s, spectator sports and newspapers had a symbiotic relationship. Newspaper coverage of sports increased fan interest and fan interest in sports sold newspapers.

Radio and Television Change What Is News

Between 1955 and 1990 the coverage of sports events and athletes changed dramatically. The broadcast media—television in particular—contributed significantly to the change. Radio and television began to pay for the broadcast rights for major collegiate sports. In doing so, they began to contribute to the economic package used to support collegiate sports programs. Because of this economic leverage, TV reporters and deadlines took precedence over newspaper coverage, forcing newspaper to alter the content of the articles they published. Play-by-play reports became old news before they were printed, and more emphasis was placed on analysis (opinion) and less on factual reporting. TV and radio created media competition with newspapers that altered coverage in various ways. Newspapers of record disappeared. In the past, it had been possible to follow the progression of important events in newspapers. This was no longer the case.

Competition from television news killed the afternoon newspaper. It promoted sensationalism and bigger headlines to get people's attention. It further eroded factual coverage, led to saturation coverage of big events, and elimination of much minor sport coverage. It also encouraged an adversarial relationship between newspaper reporters and coaches and athletes, making the latter less willing to share personal information. Finally, as television promoted the rise of sports, such as tennis, figure skating, gymnastics, professional football, professional basketball, hockey, and wrestling, newspapers expanded coverage too, and the resulting competition for space almost completely eliminated coverage of track and field.

Simultaneously, travel options reduced the time required to reach the sites for out-of-town meets. This reduced the time available to sports writers to get to know coaches and athletes personally and in depth. It shifted the interviews to the locker room, until locker room interviews were replaced by more controlled news conferences. Sports information directors became more functionary and more focused on revenue generating sports than in the past, and so even this avenue of publicity for track and field dried up.[2]

In 1965 track and field was a major sport with front-page sports coverage. At the end of the twentieth century, track and field was not even on the radar screen as one of the top ten fan supported sports. It ranked well below NASCAR, golf, soccer, wrestling, figure skating, bowling, and tennis.[3] Responsibility for the decline of track in the United States can be spread over a wide area. Professional basketball was a major culprit. It nearly single handedly drove track out of Madison Square Garden, grabbed coverage from track on sports pages, and diverted fan interest. The increased popularity of hockey, touring ice shows and circuses also contributed to the loss of indoor track venues and fan support. But, most of all, between 1960 and 1990 coverage of track by the media had fundamentally changed.

Competing Against the Circus Within the TV Set

As early as 1960 there were complaints that the Olympic Games had become too big and too impersonal. Suggestions were put forth that the games be divided into four divisions—one each for water sports, team spots, track and field and winter sports.[4] However, efforts to replicate the Olympic experience and build on its following with a National Sports Festival failed. In 1985 the twelve-day festival held in Baton Rouge, Louisiana, which included competition in gymnastics, cycling, wrestling and other Olympic sports as well as track and field, lost $1.3 million. The festival drew only 210,000 fans—90,000 short of break even.[5]

Does Track and Field Need a Heart Transplant?

One of the problems facing track and field was that it was not as compatible with television as football and basketball. It was easy to transform live performances of football and basketball into entertainment: it was not easy to do so with track and field. Television could alter play in both football and basketball to make room for advertisements, and it could use its cameras to highlight action with close-ups, slow-motion shots, and replays. By contrast, competitive running and walking are continuous activities. They can not be broken up without destroying the compelling aspects of the competition.

Another way in which track and field and television are incompatible is that the sprints are too fast for live TV. Sprints are often measured to the thousandths of a second to determine a winner. At the NCAA indoor championships in Fayetteville, Arkansas on March 10, 2000 Clemson University senior Shawn Crawford set the U.S. record in the 200-meter run of 20.26 seconds. However, Florida's John Capel had the same time, so the times were taken to thousandths of a second to determine the winner and record holder. Crawford was awarded the record with a time of 20.252, while Capel had a time of 20.257.[6] This incident illustrates the difficulty of televising live what the human eye cannot see, unless there is a slow motion camera. More importantly, field events appear to be too disjointed in real time to be of interest to an audience reared on action movies and video games. Without a large fan base, most networks repackage track for a mass audience, thereby replacing sport with entertainment. During the XXIV summer Olympic Games in Sydney, NBC devoted more televised time to commercials, features about the personal lives of star athletes, and in-studio banter than to actual sports competition.[7]

Like horse racing, much of the fun in track and field for spectators comes in handicapping competitors. This requires an informed audience with access to detailed information. Just as batting averages, earned run averages, and the like, are vital to baseball fans, performance records, split times, and race records are key to track and field fans. Yet, after 1965 this kind of information became increasingly difficult for track fans to obtain. Between 1958 and 1968 *Track and Field News* filled this need, but after Cordner Nelson stepped aside as publisher of *Track and Field News*, the publication no longer met that need. Even most important, media guides and track meet programs became less informative.

Despite the growing emphasis on sports as entertainment, track and field kept its hold on competitors remarkably well. In 1996 there were nearly 10,000 men and women track and field competitors at the Atlantic Olympic Games.[8] Running enthusiasts seemed to understand intuitively that winning and losing are not as important as the passion of pursuit of something you enjoy.

In 1888 the national indoor track and field championships started in the original Madison Squire Garden, a former horse barn used by the New York and Harlem Railroad. Except for a rare visit to places like Buffalo, Chicago, Louisville, Albuquerque, Oakland, and Philadelphia, the national indoor was held at Madison Square Garden. However, in 1994, after several years of half-empty seats at the Garden, the national indoor championship was moved to the Georgia Dome in Atlanta. The reason given for the move was a new 200-meter banked track with Mondo, a plastic-like surface, that was a faster track than the Garden's 146-meter, tight banked-board oval. Nevertheless, the move was far from successful in terms of building a fan base for the sport. The 73,000 seats as the Georgia Dome made even a large crowd seem small, and Atlanta simply did not have the population base or the fan interest to match that of the "Big Apple."[9]

At the last national indoor championships of the twentieth century held at the Georgia Dome in Atlanta, there were five Michigan athletes participating: Gary Morgan, Phil McMullen, Paul McMullen, Chad Smith, and Katie McGregor, placing the State of Michigan in the top quartile of contributors to the meet. Phil McMullen placed second (5828 points) and Chad Smith, who attended Ypsilanti High School and the University of Tennessee, placed third (5755 points) in the Men's heptathlon. Gary Morgan placed fourth in the 5-kilometer walk, Paul McMullen placed sixth in the mile run (4:03.62), and Katie McGregor placed sixth in the 3-K run (9:09.30). Katie placed tenth in the 5-K run USATF Outdoor Championship held on June 3, 2000 in Albany.[10]

These results suggest that despite a lack of publicity and public awareness regarding track and field, Michigan was still a stronghold of the sport at the end of the twentieth century, although the center of gravity had clearly shifted to the South and West. Perhaps influenced by the location of the meet, California, Texas, Tennessee, North Carolina, South Carolina, Florida, Ohio, and Indiana all sent more athletes to the meet than Michigan.

The training requirements and skills necessary to win in world-wide competition are so demanding that they are nearly impossible to achieve without significant subsidies, particularly for the period after an athlete left college and before he or she reached peak performance. Craig Masback, the chief executive of USA Track and Field, admitted that the sport in America simply was not getting the level of financial support needed for that task. As a result, by international standards at the end of the twentieth century, America distance-running, and particularly marathoning, was at its low point. The winning time in the men's Olympic trials in 2000 was the slowest since 1972. The richest and one of the largest countries in the world qualified only one man and one woman for the marathon in Sydney Olympics, and neither any chance of winning a medal.[11] Moreover, the last summer Olympics of the twentieth century was the first since 1896 in which Michigan did not send a single track athlete.

Style Over Substance

In 1979 the metric system replaced the British measurement system in U.S. track meets. The belief, put foreword by Don Canham, that track declined because coaches miscalculated the public relations disaster brought about by the switch to the metric system, appears to be, at best, a minor factor in the decline of interest in the sport. The contention that the magic of the four-minute mile was not replaced by the 1,500-meter run, and the argument that few can relate to jumps measured in meters has some merit. Moreover, the fact that duel meets have been dropped, foreign nationals have been allowed to dominate American intercollegiate track, and coaches have allowed the team aspects of the sport to disappear are interesting arguments but have little to do with the decline of the sport.

How the Emphasis on Revenue Impacted Track and Field

One of the most accurate measures of the perceived value of track and field, in the modern world of sport entertainment, is the average salary paid to the head coach of a college sport. Using this measure, track and field does not fare very well. According to information collected from the budgets of Michigan's 12 or so publicly supported State colleges and universities, on average, the coaches of football, basketball, hockey, swimming, volleyball, wrestling, and women's softball, baseball, and field hockey are paid more than track coaches.[12]

It is clear that the revenue sports dominate hiring and payroll considerations in intercollegiate athletics, even when revenue results do not match the promised return on investment. The head football coach at the University of Michigan received $763,000 in fiscal year 1998–99 and the head football coach at Michigan State made $697,330, but was offered a five year, $6-million contract to coach at Louisiana State University.[13] By contrast, the 41 coaches and assistant coaches who guide men and women's track and cross-country in the 15 state supported colleges and universities of the State of Michigan received aggregate earnings of only $1,268,200. This is less than these two head football coaches took home.

Moreover, the average coaching salary for track and field ranks below that paid to the head coaches for field hockey, swimming, wrestling, or volleyball. Even Coach Bob Parks, the dean of track coaches in the state received only $54,478 for coaching both men's track and cross-country. The salary scale tells the whole story of the decline in status of intercollegiate track and field over the course of the twentieth century. Once the sport of the rich and powerful, track and field struggles to stay ahead of soccer, tennis, golf, and rowing as an intercollegiate sport.

The Risks Created by Sports Entertainment

When college athletic departments and television networks conspired to make college sports entertainment rather than athletic contests, they opened a Pandora's box of potential problems. They placed sports at the fickle mercies of the market, robbing such activities of much of the fun and free help that traditionally helped to underwrite these endeavors. They also made athletes employees without the protections or rewards of most employees, while excusing the promoters of the responsibilities of normal business expenses. For example, "if scholarship athletes were recognized as the paid entertainers they became, the college sports industry would be subject to unrelated business income taxes, antitrust scrutiny and demands by the players for a bigger share of the revenue." In turn, workman's compensation, disability insurance, and protection from hazardous working conditions would cover athletes. Many believe that the NCAA became an economic cartel that cynically manipulated the concept of amateurism to serve its financial interests.[14]

By 1986, a number of elite track stars, like Carl Lewis, were beginning to bypass NCAA events. They renounced remaining college eligibility to gain the freedom to compete when and where they gain the most advantage and to accept money for running.[15] The NCAA rules forbid anyone on scholarship to be paid for a job and forbid any college athlete from taking money or prizes from any source. Thus, scholarship athletes without family money had no acceptable source of money for clothing, a car, and incidentals. Non-collegians could accept prize and appearance money and endorsement fees as long as the money was placed in a trust fund supervised by The Athletic Congress (TAC) or later by Track & Field USA's governing body. College rules forbid receiving money even for a trust fund, though some track athletes did receive appearance money under the table.

College coaches were interested in duel meets and would run their best athletes in two or three events. This risked injury and drained energy, placing star athletes at a disadvantage in national and international competition. Track stars were learning to pace themselves. One college runner confided:

People expect me to run faster and faster. I think it's more important to get through a race without injury. When you're hurt, you think before a race, "I don't want to get hurt again." Well, I don't want to think negative thoughts like that. I understand more now. I'm a better runner. I'm more patient, more controlled, with running, with everything.[16]

The business side of athletics undermined support for track in another way. Highly ranked runners increasingly avoided competition with other highly ranked runners for fear of diminishing their marketability if they lost. Sebastian Coe and Steve Ovett avoided racing each other. Ovett even used his status in Europe to keep Steve Scott, the American record holder out of his event, and Noureddine Morceli, the 1996 Olympic gold medalist from Algeria demanded veto power over his competitive field. Michael Johnson withdrew from so many big meets when faced with possible loss, with claims of injuries, that he caused many skeptics to doubt whether he was injured.[17] The financial consequences of winning or losing became so significant that any highly ranked track athlete might find it advantageous to avoid racing if he or she did not feel at the top of their talent. Since every track athlete wins sometimes and loses at other times, there is a persistent temptation of good athletes to scratch at the last hour. The failure of track stars to run at advertised events seriously undermines fan support for the sport.

The Limits of Pro-Track

The conflict of interests between the revenue producing athlete and the institutions that benefited from athletic endeavors surfaced again with efforts to establish a professional track circuit. Those promoting an end to what they called "phony amateurism" argued that all world class athletes are professionals and it was time to legitimize their status. The professional track circuit became much more popular in Europe than in North America. For a fifteen-year period, from 1980 to 1995, the Mobile Grand Prix attempted, without much success, to generate interest in professional track. A hand full of super-stars made a very good living running most of the meets on the European circuit and adding a few American meets, but, after intercollegiate track, the majority of runners and field athletes found it necessary to hold a paying job as well as participate in track.

Some even became creative in their efforts to support themselves as trackmen. For example, Ryan Vierra, a native of California and former All-American shot-putter, joined the Highland Games circuit to support himself as a weight thrower. He became the world champion in the caber and sheaf tosses, and earned just under than $30,000 a year competing in the 30 or so Scottish festivals around North America. Most men on the Scottish festival circuit, however, "had a real job back home." Like Vierra, they were former field athletes who were not Scottish and had nowhere else to turn to keep competing after college.[18]

Kicking the Gong Around

In 1968 a new International Olympic Committee (IOC) ruling required that the top six place winners in the Olympics be tested for steroids. Drug use by athletes was not new. Alcohol abuse by athletes is as old as sport itself. In 1924, Hans Liljekvist, a Swedish modern pentathlon contestant, was disqualified for drinking too much alcohol, and a Danish runner died in the Rome Olympics of 1960 after taking a stimulant. However, about 1952, when Soviet Union weightlifters began to use testosterone supplements to help in muscle development, drug use in athletic competition took on a new meaning. Anabolic steroid use followed in 1958. At Tokyo in 1964, there was nearly conclusive evidence that a British shot putter took anabolic steroids.[19]

The fact that athletes could now manipulate their hormones to enhance their athletic performance aroused enormous concern because it was feared that athletes might be doing irreparable harm to both themselves and to "sport." The IOC, however, was slow to act, and failed to include anabolic steroids and testosterone among the banned substances at their 1967 meeting. By 1969, the used of anabolic steroids moved into the main stream of American sport fan consciousness.[20]

Several experts correctly argued that delaying the ban on such drugs was helping to promote their use. At the 1972 Olympics, Jay Sylvester, a member of the U.S. Track team, made an unofficial poll of all track and field contestants in Munich and found that two-thirds of them had used some form of anabolic steroid in their preparation for the games. Fifteen years later, steroid use was still a persistent problem.[21]

There can be little doubt that the use and reported use of anabolic steroids harmed track and field as a sport. A controversial physician who prescribes steroids claimed that "more than a dozen Olympic athletes who used banned anabolic steroids have won medals during the

1984 Games, but they escaped detection because they stopped taking the drugs several months before the Games." Some Olympic competitors used human growth hormones, drugs for which there was no accurate detection tests. An article on steroid use in a April 1997 issue of *Sports Illustrated*, claimed that more than 90% of world class Olympic athletes were using performance-enhancing drugs.[22]

To be more specific about performance-enhancing drugs, it is edifying to explore blood doping. There are several ways to raise the hemoglobin levels of blood to enhance its oxygen carrying capacity for distance running. One can train at high altitudes or spend time in a chamber with low oxygen levels. A shot of erythropoietin (EPO) will also raise hemoglobin levels, as will blood doping or banking one's own red blood cells for a week or more and then injecting them back into the body shortly before the race. None of these practices seriously endangers an athlete's health or causes long term side effects. Indeed, each of these efforts to enhance performance is no more risky than the stress and deprivation normally involved in training for a sport. The ethical issues associated with performance-enhancing drugs are not as simple as often portrayed.[23]

"Blood doping" surfaced as an ethical problem in track and field in the 1976 Olympics in Montreal, when Lasse Viren of Finland won the "Woolworth double" and placed fifth in the marathon. Viren demonstrated extraordinary resilience down the homestretch in the 5-K run. Fourth place finisher, Ron Dixon of New Zealand charge that "He has got that extra blood in him." While blood doping was not illegal, and it was never proven that an extra pint of blood gave Lasse Viren his extraordinary stamina, most of his competitors believed that Viren was "cheating."[24] The issue of "blood doping" came up again in 1980 when a series of tests demonstrated that blood doping improved performance for distance-runners.[25]

At the 1983 Pan-American Games in Caracas, the International Olympic Committee stripped 11 athletes from six countries of medals. Six athletes from five countries were disqualified from the Pan-American Games for drug use in August 1987, and three other athletes were said to have used substances that could hide the use of steroids.[26]

In February 1989, Olympic sprinter Evelyn Ashford made an emotional plea for an end to the use of performance-enhancing drugs by some of her fellow female track stars.

I want my sport to live forever. I don't want it to die. But if something is not done about drugs, it will die. It's bad, and it's getting worse.

Ashford declined to name the athletes she believed had used steroids to enhance their performance, but she said they were well known among track athletes. She said that mandatory testing, which is now limited to major meets, is easy to beat, and that the only way to curb the use of steroids would be to institute mandatory, year-round testing, including blood tests.[27]

By the mid-1990s, international track athletes preferred human growth hormones to steroids, like prednisone, for development of muscle-mass and EPO for red blood cell accumulation to benefit oxygen carriage for distance runners. Neither could be detected by urine test. They could only be detected by blood testing not done by the IOC.[28]

In May 1992, Lyle Alzado, a professional football player, died of brain cancer at the age of 43. He attributed his fatal illness to steroid use, although there was no evidence that steroid use contributed to his death. Nevertheless, Alzado's fears about the consequences of his own use of steroids placed a further shadow over track and field, a sport often associated with rampant steroid use.[29]

Steroids were not the only drugs that concerned the general public. Cocaine use provoked a mental breakdown by former world heavyweight boxer Joe Louis in the mid-1960s.[30] National Football League Hall of Fame quarterback Bart Starr's son, Bret Starr, died from a severe cocaine use in Tampa Bay,[31] and nearly every news broadcast revealed the name of some sports star or entertainment celebrity who was caught using mood altering drugs. The blending of sports and entertainment added to the public perception that a significant number of athletes were abusing marijuana, cocaine, or other controlled substances.

By 1990, the "war on drugs," started in the Nixon Presidency and greatly expanded by the Reagan Administration, fueled fears of steroid used by high school athletes. Despite a lack of evidence that steroid use was a problem among Michigan's high school athletes, the Michigan legislature passed a law in 1989 requiring the state health department to distribute steroid warning notices for community gyms, health clubs and training centers.[32]

The disconnect between excessive worry over performance-enhancing drugs and uncritical applause for the other ways of boosting an athlete's performance—from high-technology running shoes to chains of stores devoted to dietary supplements—worried some sports fans. If the goal is "to preserve what is beautiful and admirable in sports and to ensure that all athletes compete on a level playing field", the solution involves more than monitoring the use of performance-enhancing drugs, they argued.[33] Drugs are chemicals that change the body, but so are special training diets, and what about special shoes or specifically engineered racing clothes, flexible fiberglass poles for vaulting, and oxygen tanks for rapid recovery between races?

Running Shoes and other Improvements in Equipment

In 1984 Adidas dominated the world sporting goods market with annual sales of $2.2 billion. Adidas churned out over 250,000 pairs of sports shoes a week. Most of the buyers were not athletes, but were sports fans influenced by the shoes worn by champions. When Horst Dassler, the son of Adolf Dassler, died of cancer on April 10, 1987, over eighty per cent of the medal winners at the Olympic games wore Adidas shoes.[34] Horst had refined the process of influencing athletes and athletic organization for the benefit of his company to a fine art. His death opened the door to a realignment of the sport products market.

Competition for the lucrative sport's product market was already underway before 1987. A new running shoe with twelve plastic ridges on the sole developed by Puma, the West German shoe manufacturer, made its American debut at the Penn Relays in late April 1972. A distributor for Puma said two and a half years of research and over $200,000 had been spent trying to develop a shoe for synthetic surfaces to replace the conventional six-spiked track shoe. Dubbed "the Claw" because of its teeth-like ridges, these new shoes were well received. "You don't feel anything sticking into the ground and coming up, like you do with spikes," one runner told the weekly luncheon of the Track Writers' Association of New York. "The shoes don't stick in the track, they just respond." The athletes don't have to expend the energy of having a spike dig in. Sprinter John Carlos used a controversial Puma track shoe, with 68 tiny brush spike on the sole, at the final United States trials proceeding the Olympic Games in Mexico City. He clocked an amazing 19.7 seconds for 200-meters, but the record was disallowed because the shoe had not been approved.[35]

According to exercise physiologist William Kraemer, formerly of Ball State University, "compression garments made of Lycra and similar materials boost athletic performance and the staying power of muscles." Compression shorts will not help an athlete jump higher or farther, but they will help flush away lactic acid and will help eliminate chafing for long distance runners.[36]

At the close of the twentieth century, a Calgary company was testing ceramic cleats in unusual shapes that compress the track instead of puncturing it. In addition, MIT scientists were developing tiny sensors that beep when runners should adjust their stride for best results.[37]

Lack of Action by the IOC

The International Olympic Committee summoned an international conference that met in Lausanne, Switzerland in early February 1999 after a doping scandal at the Tour de France in the summer of 1998. The main IOC proposal was for creation of a worldwide agency to conduct drug testing in and out of competition, refine analysis of urine and blood samples, and educate the young against using sports drugs. The IOC's position was undermined by revelations that IOC members took bribes to determine the locations of Olympic Games.

After three days of debate at the drug summit, the IOC adopted a watered-down declaration on doping. While Juan Antonio Samaranch, the IOC president, said the declaration brought 'hope for the athletes of the world, hope for the fans and hope for human dignity,' the 15-nation European Union rejected the Olympic committee's leadership and did not approve the declaration as the meeting came to a close. The support of the United States for the pronouncement was lukewarm.

At the same time, the American position on doping fell under attack again. Richard Pound, an IOC vice president from Canada, criticized the United States' attitude toward doping, pointedly noting that Mark McGwire, who used a supplement banned by the Olympics while setting the home run record last summer, had become a national hero. "The closer you are to the Olympic movement, the more you are concerned about doping," Pound declared. "The farther away you are, the less you care. All of a sudden you are in Mark McGwire land, and this is a national hero all souped up."[38]

The Olympic committee's efforts to push through an antidoping program that it would control failed. It backed off actually creating an anti-doping agency and imposing mandatory two-year drug sanctions. The resolution that was adopted only established a committee for the IOC to work with national governments that would within three months form a council that would elect a president, appoint a staff and begin work by the 2000 Summer Games in Sydney, Australia. Tony Banks, the British Minister of Sport, who has been prominent in the attack on Samaranch and the IOC, said some of the provisions of the resolution were "both minimalist and permissive. These issues are bigger than the IOC," he said. American drug-czar, General Barry R. McCaffrey felt, "it was a good first step." He was interested in a worldwide, independent antidoping agency, stiffer sanctions for athletes caught using drugs, and the will of international sports to step up research into detecting currently undetectable performance-enhancing substances.[39]

Still, efforts to detect drug use moved forward. On March 25, 2000 it was announced that researchers at the Australian Institute of Sport had a valid blood test for detecting the use of erythropoietin (EPO) and would use it in cycling and the triathlon.[40]

Overall, at the end of the twentieth century, the failure to stop the use of performance enhancing drugs was seriously undermining public support for track and field. Roger Bannister, the 71-year-old former track superstar, was among those who favored more blood testing to limit the problems caused by the use of performance enhancing drugs.[41]

"Caviar-Loving" Freeloaders

The personal privileges and private advantages accorded to the members of the IOC continued, unknown to the general public, and virtually unchallenged by the sports community for nearly a century.[42] Controlled by a self-perpetuating oligarchy who traveled the world like kings, the IOC and the U.S. Olympic Committee pursued elitist and ethnocentric policies that harmed countless athletes of color and of Jewish heritage, and reinforced the destructive aspects of both nationalism and colonialism. These policies frequently resulted in particular harm to athletes from disadvantaged families, poor nations, or both. During the last third of the century, IOC policies frequently benefited multi-national corporations such as Adidas, Coca-Cola, Seiko, and Mars.

Although there were plenty of signs of corruption in the Olympic movement as early as 1987, it was not until a local newspaper in Salt Lake City, Utah revealed that IOC members had solicited and received personal gifts totaling more than $1 million that the private, entrepreneurial nature of the Olympic movement came under significant public scrutiny. The idea that IOC members sought bribes in return for their votes, when selecting the sites for the Olympics Games, was abhorrent to most sports fans. U.S. Olympic Committee officials were forced to appoint an independent commission chaired by former Senator George J. Mitchell. That commission made four recommendations. One of the recommendations would place the IOC under the authority of the Foreign Corrupt Practices Act, which would make an aggressive program of cash payments and gift-giving illegal.[43]

Some saw the IOC as "caviar-loving" freeloaders. Without making significant changes in their closed-door club or its policies, the IOC and the Salt Lake City winter Olympic host committee restated their objective of raising an unprecedented amount of money from corporate sponsors to conduct another entertainment spectacular with athletes as bit players.[44]

Corruption among the IOC members led some corporate sponsors of the Olympic Games, like the John Hancock Mutual Life Insurance Company, to withdraw their support for the Games in the year 2000 and to cancel advertising on NBC during TV coverage of the games.[45] However, at a crucial time, Detroit's General Motors stepped forward to reaffirm its financial support for the Olympics by signing a $1 billion contract to advertise during NBC coverage of the 2000, 2002, and 2004 Games. In making this move, GM reaffirmed its belief that the alliance between American corporations and the Olympic entertainment complex was still alive and well. GM obviously felt that their was business advantage to be gained by being the only American, domestic automobile company to advertise on telecasts throughout a significant part of the United States.[46] The John Hancock Insurance Company soon rediscovered that it had a vested interest in maintaining the Olympic Games as an entertainment extravaganza and rejoined those supporting the Games that would be run pretty much as usual.

When the United States Olympic Committee chose a successor to oversee the scandal-pocked Salt Lake City 2002 Winter Olympic project, they put business ahead of sports in selecting a chief executive officer. "The first thing we wanted was someone with experience running a large, complex organization, and somebody who's an agent of change. This is a voluntary, nonprofit organization, but it's so big, it's like a large corporation." The new chairman, Norman P. Blake Jr., recently chief executive officer for the Promus Hotel Corporation, announced, "I'm attracted to making sure the U.S. Olympic Committee staff is of equal quality to the athletes." The U.S. Olympic Committee's budget for current quadrennium is $441 million. In the 1976–80 quadrennium it was $13 million.[47]

Progress in Human Performance

One of the achievements of the twentieth century was to establish that running has a special place, an equal place, for woman. By the end of the century, there were woman's races and equipment. At races, women had their own award categories, and sometimes they race only against themselves. Races that awarded financial prizes usually had separate and equal money structures for men and women.[48]

Track and field was also much more ecumenical than it had been a century before. In 1900 twenty-six nations participated in the track and field events at the Olympic Games in Paris. In 1996 197 nations competed in the Olympic Games in Atlanta.[49] In the New York City Marathon held on November 7, 1999, none of the top ten finishers in either the men's or top nine in the women's division were Americans. Five men were from Kenya, while Italy, Spain, Portugal, Morocco, and Ecuador each produced one of the top 10 men. In the women's Marathon Adriana Fernandez from Mexico won, two Kenyans, a German, Italian, Russian, two Romanian, and a Brazilian topped Zofia Wieciorkowska from Stratford, Connecticut.[50] The same pattern continued at the last Boston Marathon of the century, where Kenyans won five of the first six places and Africans won the first nine places. The first American born runner came in twenty-fourth.[51]

While the improvements in performance by track and field athletes were remarkably modest over the course of 100-years, records were still being broken at the close of the twentieth century. On March 24, 2000 Michael Johnson smashed the world 300-meter dash record at the Friday night Engen Grand Prix meet in Pretoria, South Africa, with an astounding 30.85 performance.[52] On the other hand, the long jump record has only been broken twice in 30 years. Perhaps some records were approaching the upper limits of human possibilities.

Champions Are Raised, Not Born

As newspaper and television coverage of track and field declined, the sport experienced a lack of interest by young people whose culture was being defined by television and music. For more than a century, boys wanted to participate in sports to establish their masculinity. Now, this form of motivation was losing some of its lure.

More recently, girls began to play sports for peer acceptance. However, external motivation does not always bode well for running, which usually relies on task orientation and internal motivation. The problem with external pressure, as the motivation for running, is the sport's implicit isolation. Because of this isolation, there is a strong likelihood of an externally motivated child dropping out of the sport when he or she becomes discouraged or loses the external support of parents, mentors, or peers. For many young people, parents and coaches make running seen more like work than fun. Unfortunately, some coaches are verbally abusive or ignore all but the most promising athletes. Others focused on comparisons, rather than on bringing the best out in each young runner. Moreover, poor coaching introduce weight lifting and other forms of work-like drudgery before the young runner can see the personal value of these activities or develop the self-motivation for these tasks. In short, the sport's low profile, shortage of good coaching, and hostile play environment were, all too often, poisoning interest in the sport.

Few head coaches are good educators. Many are successful recruiters, good judges of talent, great trainers, decent administrators, or even accomplished politicians and/or entrepreneurs. But, few are as committed to the life success of their athletes as they are to a 40-yard dash time, a bench press number, or the potential for scoring points at the conference meet. It is a fortunate student-athlete who, during their formative years, selects the right coach—one who will guide them beyond athletic success to life success. It is more fortunate still when the athletic department at the school they attend allows such coaches to survive.

One of the lasting legacies of amateurism is the way it discriminates against athletes from low-income families. Unless an athlete is lucky enough to have considerable athletic and academic ability and is blessed with both patience and committed personal support from family and friends, most student-athletes will find it difficult to achieve both academically and athletically at a Division I NCAA University. Few student-athletes, who originate in poor or uneducated families, matriculate the system without getting scarred. The odds against the success of a student-athlete are tremendous. Unrealistic time demands by coaches and athletic schedules, the chances of injury, the lack of money, and distractions of all sorts impede the path toward a degree.[53] But, for those who succeed in translating their talent into something that transcends sports success, the journey is worth the trip. The maturity, vitality, life force, and blessed restlessness that make life valuable come most readily to those who possess the spirit that allows them strive to be their best in both mind and body.

Let's Light This Candle

We know that regular doses of exercise can hide a multitude of dietary sins, but in today's world it seems like there is a conspiracy to keep kids buried in sedentary activities. At home there is the TV, most likely cabled into dozens of channels, the VCR, and a Nintendo-like game system waiting for them. Then there is the computer, offering a non-exercising trip down the information highway or into a world of hi-tech games. With these beckoning, a ride around the neighborhood on the bicycle, a game of football or driveway basketball apparently does not seem appealing. A drive through nearly any urban areas will show few kids getting exercise of any kind. Even traditional exercise-inducing chores like mowing the lawn, raking the leaves, or shoveling the sidewalk can now be done without sweating, by using a snow blower, leaf blower, power mower, or weed whacker made to ease life and leave our flesh unmuscled.

Every year, high school coaches find a number of students whose first year in cross-country is also the first time they have ever exercised on a regular basis. Their desire is strong but their muscles are weak and oftentimes they develop injuries because they over using their muscles. Somehow we need to find a way to get kids a daily shot of exercise. . . . Some school districts offer no gym classes at all. This is a generation of kids that needs to be rescued.[54]

Running is a relatively inexpensive activity. Sure, with all of the high-tech equipment and clothing available today, it can be costly. But it does not need to be. Just put on a T-shirt, a pair of shorts, and some tennis shoes, and step out the door and start running.

Oddly enough, the minimal need for athletic supplies in track and field has become a handicap in the promotion of the sport. Athletic suppliers have become an important source of lobbying for spots: the more equipment involved the more active the lobbying. Because track requires little equipment, it gets less lobbying promotion than football, hockey, and basketball, sports that have larger purchasing and market potential.[55] Running, however, supports the work of health and diet. With millions of Americans concerned about their weight, the sport should have a natural base of support.[56]

Once revered as much for his manly image as his on-the-field performance, the male athlete is receiving increased scrutiny for his off-the-field behavior with women. Studies of assaults on college campuses indicate that athletes are involved in a disproportionate number of rapes and other sexual assaults. Although exact figures on such crimes by athletes are difficult to obtain anecdotal evidence from counselors and rape treatment recovery programs indicate that sexual assault is a serious problem for a fair number of athletes. Some believe that athletes develop aggressiveness and a sense of entitlement that encourages inappropriate behavior.[57]

It is important to note that while aerobic exercise releases endorphins that mitigate against bio-chemical imbalances that contribute to depression, it does not cure mental illness. A number of runners have demonstrated courage in overcoming personal problems to excel despite depression, anxiety disorders, obsessive compulsive behavior, paranoid delusions, and even antisocial personality problems.

The most publicized case was Kathy Ormsby, a middle-distance at North Carolina State, who attempted suicide during the National NCAA Outdoor championships in Indianapolis in June 1986. On June 4, 1986 a thunderstorm and occasional lightning delayed the start of the meet for almost three hours.[58] During the women's 10-K run, Kathy Ormsby bolted from the race, ran out of the stadium, and jumped off a bridge. She ended up permanently paralyzed from a multiple spine fracture in the thoracic region.[59] But, several Michigan track athletes, including Clark Haskins, William Watson, Billy Smith, Cliff Hatcher, and Ernest Crosbie were great track stars, despite experiencing emotional problems of one kind or another during their life.

The swiftest is not always the most intellectually the most gifted, or are they the dumb. Several great runners experience academic problems, although as a group track athletes have better academic records than most other athletes. Moreover, brave individuals, like Marla Runyan who became the first legally blind athlete ever to qualify for the Olympic games, have demonstrated that track is a equal opportunity sport.[60]

Lessons Learned At the Dawn of the New Millennium

All too often, sports stories create myths and promote hero worship. This is a dangerous tradition. It blurs reality and impairs the judgement of athletes, sports fans, and historians. Offering realistic portraits of great track and field athletes does not diminish their value as role models. Instead, it is important for everyone to learn that each of us, with our individual strengths and weaknesses, has a hero within us that can be tapped if we have the will and the judgement to overcome our doubts and call on our strengths for the right purposes.

The foremost lesson to be learned from a history of track and field is that sports are a part of life, not the purpose of life. Sports need to be kept in perspective, and the great coaches understand that they have a role in helping their athletes keep this point of view. A person does not have to be perfect to be a great athlete. Great athletes, like all of us, are a mixture of virtues and vices, talents and weaknesses, learned skills and the absence of well-developed skills. Athletes, like all of us, are the lucky or unlucky victims of circumstances and situations. Some are born with great problems as well as great talent.

Many of the lessons learned in sports, and particularly track and field—as contrasted with commercialized entertainment—are transferable to the rest of life. Understanding the importance of having clear and positive goals, discovering that success is not always dependent on external approval, and realizing that failure, injury, and disappointment are prevalent obstacles too important achievements are examples of lessons that are transferable. Most important, discovering the joy of pursuing a passion to the point of personal best is the greatest reward of all.

Finally, as John Donne, the early 17th century English, metaphysical poet recognized—and Ernest Hemingway acknowledged in his classic 1940 novel *For Whom The Bell Tolls*—"No man is an island entire of itself. . . ." None of us achieves anything entirely on our own. We learn from and depend on others in ways too numerous to cite here, and it is important that we acknowledge and repay our debt to others and the community at large. Specifically, we have a moral obligation to inspire hope, to affirm our common humanity by supporting community institutions, and to give of ourselves to others in gratitude for the blessings that have been rendered to us over the years.

Notes

Prologue

1. *Detroit Free Press*, June 20, 1888, p. 8.
2. "How Tracks Were Built 50 Years Ago from A.A.U. Handbook of 1888," *The Amateur Athlete for December, 1938*, pp. 16, 52.
3. *Ibid.*
4. *Detroit Free Press*, June 20, 1888, p. 8.
5. *Ibid.*, September 18, 1888, p. 1
6. This is the origin of the term the term, "starting from scratch."
7. *Detroit Free Press*, August 29, 1888, p. 8.
8. *Ibid.*, September 7, 1888, p. 8 and September 16, 1888, p. 4.
9. *Ibid.*, September 19, 1888, p.8.
10. *Ibid.*
11. *Ibid.*
12. *Detroit Free Press*, September 18, 1888, p. 8.
13. *Ibid.*, September 19, 1888, p. 8.
14. *Ibid.*, September 20, 1888, p. 8.
15. *Ibid.*
16. John McClelland, "Athletics vs. Sport in Early Modern Europe," Paper presented at NASSH, Banff, Alberta, May, 2000.
17. Benjamin G. Rader, *American Sports: From the Age of Folk Games to the Age of Spectators*. New Jersey: Prentice-Hall, Inc., 1983. Pp. 38–40.
18. Raymond Krise and Bill Squires, *Fast Tracks: The History of Distance Running*: Battleboro, VT: The Stephen Greene Press, 1982, p.7 and Tom Derderian, *Boston Marathon*. Champaign, IL.: Human Kinetics, 1996, p. xvii.
19. Derderian, *op. cit.*, 1996, p. xvii.
20. Gerald Redmond, *The Caledonian Games in Nineteenth-Century America*. Rutherford, N. J.: Fairleigh Dickinson University Press, 1971, pp. 39–45.
21. Interview with Abe Rosenkrantz who won a handicap race at a Caledonian indoor track meet in New York City in 1931.
22. S. W. Pope, *Patriotic Games*. New York: Oxford University Press, 1997, p. 20.
23. Michael Oriard, *Reading Football*. Chapel Hill: University of North Carolina Press, 1993, p. 190–200.
24. *Spalding's Official Athletic Almanac, 1928*. New York: American Sports Publishing Co., 1928, pp. 127–130.
25. On November 11, 1868 the club held an amateur indoor meet. See Frank G. Menke, *The Encyclopedia of Sports*. 1953 edition. New York: A. S. Barnes and Company, Inc., 1953, p. 889.
26. An area later used for the foundations of the Harlem Bridge.
27. *Spalding's Official Athletic Almanac, 1928*. New York: American Sports Publishing Co., 1928, pp. 127–130.
28. Menke, p. 889 and Rader, p. 56.
29. Kenneth Greenberg, "When Sprinters Wore Tights," *Track and Field News*, November 1948, p. 8.

30. Gerald R. Gems, *Windy City Wars: Labor, Leisure, and Sport in the Making of Chicago*. Lanham, Maryland: Scarecrow Press, 1997, p. 25.
31. In 1905 the Irish-American Athletic Club held a track meet on Sunday, but was denied the ability charge admission to the meet because of blue laws. Their creative solution was to sell meet programs at the same price as normally charged for admission and to make it difficult to watch the meet without a program. The Law and Order Society attempted to stop the meet, but the police, many of whom were Irish, allowed it to continue. See *The New York Times*, April 24, 1905, p. 6.
32. *Detroit Free Press, June 9, 1895, p.7.*
33. *The Toronto Globe*, August 10, 1935, p. 6.
34. *Program for the 63ʳᵈ Millrose Games*, January, 30, 1970, pp. 12–14.
35. *64ᵗʰ Millrose Games Program*, January 29, 1971, p. 15.
36. R. L. Quercetani, *A World History of Track and Field Athletics, 1864–1964*. London: Oxford University Press, 1964, pp. 1–2.
37. C. G. Wood of Great Britain was credited with a 21.8 in 1886. See Menke, *op. cit.*, p. 952.
38. Quercetani, *op. cit.*, pp. 3.
39. *Chicago Tribune*, May 8, 1898, p. 7.
40. *Detroit Athletic Club News*, September 1991, p. 40 and *Detroit Free Press*, June 30, 1892; July 3, 1892; and July 24, 1892.
41. *New York Times*, April 29, 1973, section V, p. 4.
42. Quercetani, *op. cit.*, pp. 269.
43. Derderian, *op. cit.*, 1996, p. xxi.
44. David C. Young, *The Modern Olympics: A Struggle for Revival*. Baltimore, MD: Johns Hopkins University Press, 1996. P. 30.
45. *Ibid.*, P. 146–7.
46. *New York Times*, June 24, 1976, p. 40.
47. *Detroit Free Press*, August 13, 1897, p. 7.

Chapter 1

1. Bliss Perry, *The Amateur Sprit*. New York: Houghton, Mifflin and Company, 1904, p. 25.
2. Harold A. Harris, *Sport in Britain: Its Origin and Development*. London: Stanley Paul, 1975, p. 49; also see Derek Birley, *A Social History of English Cricket*. London, UK: Aurum Press, 1999.
3. See David C. Young, *The Modern Olympics: A Struggle for Revival*. Baltimore, MD: Johns Hopkins University Press, 1996.
4. Pope, *op. cit.*, p. 22.
5. *Ibid.*, p. 23. It is interesting to note that Walter Camp was doing exactly what he was preaching against.
6. *Ibid.*, p. 19.
7. "General Athletics," *Outing*, Vol. 6, number 5, May 1886, p. 251.
8. *Detroit Free Press*, August 29, 1888, p. 8.
9. The bankrupted University of Chicago had

been located on land donated by Stephen A. Douglas, Abraham Lincoln's long-time adversary. See Harold M. Mayer and Richard C. Wade, *Chicago: Growth of a Metropolis*. Chicago: University of Chicago Press, 1969, p. 102. "Boola Boola" was a nonsense song made up by Allan M. Hirsh, Yale class of 1901, in the fall of 1900 on the eve of the Harvard-Yale football game, It was sung by Yale fans after beating Harvad and came to symbolize Ivy League fan exuberance and sport boosterism.

10. For more details on the Rockefeller-Harper struggles to build the University of Chicago see Ron Chernow, *Titan: The Life of John D. Rockefeller, Sr.* New York: Random House, 1998. Pp. 309–329.

11. Lawrence R. Veysey, *The Emergence of the American University*. Chicago: University of Chicago Press, 1965, p. 326. Hal A. Lawson and Alan G. Ingham, "Conflicting Ideologies Concerning the University and Intercollegiate Athletics: Harper and Hutchins at Chicago, 1892–1950," *Journal of Sport History*, vol. 7, no. 3, winter 1980, p. 41–2.

12. Robin Lester, *The Rise, Decline, and Fall of Big-Time Football at Chicago*. Urbana: University of Illinois Press, 1995, p. 20. There is convincing research, published in 2000 in *The Journal of Contemporary Economics* by Thomas A. Rhoads and Shelby Gerking, showing that over the past 15 years athletic performance has had little positive, long-term impact on alumni and other philanthropic giving to colleges and universities, and rarely benefits anyone beyond the athletic department. Hence, although still widely accepted, William Rainy Harper's theory about philanthropic giving to institutions of higher education no longer appears to be valid.

13. *Detroit Free Press*, April 23, 1905, p. 13.

14. *Ibid.*, June 2, 1895, p.7.

15. *Ibid.*, June 16, 1895, p. 7.

16. Krise and Squires, *op. cit.*, p. 31.

17. Phil Pack, *100 Years of Michigan Athletics*. Ann Arbor: University of Michigan, 1918.

18. Charles Baird, "A Brief History of Ferry Field," *Michiganensian*, 1907, p. 191.

19. *Ibid.*

20. *The Michigan Daily*, April 28, 1904, p. 1.

21. W. R. Kirn, "Our "Fitz", *Michiganensian*, 1905, pp. 177–8.

22. *Detroit Free Press*, May 27, 1900, Part I, p. 7.

23. The Carnegie Report on college athletics undertaken in 1926 and published in 1929 cites the use of interscholastic athletic events as a favorite recruiting device. See Howard J. Savage, *American College Athletics*, Bulletin 23. New York: Carnegie Foundation for the Advancement of Teaching, 1929, pp. 63, 242.

24. *Chicago Tribune*, June 10, 1904, p. 8.

25. See John M. Carroll, *Red Grange and the Rise of Modern Football*. Urbana: University of Illinois Press, 1999, p. 52.

26. *Detroit Free Press*, April 23, 1905, p. 13.

27. *Ibid.*, June 17, 1897, p. 6.

28. Archives, University of Michigan, Bentley Historical Library.

29. Letters from Louis Elbel and pictures in the Bentley Michigan Historical Collection, and *The Michigan Alumnus*, vol. V, no. 8, May 1899, pp. 338–9.

30. *Ann Arbor News*, February 16, 1984.

31. *Grand Rapids Press*, September 17, 1995.

32. *The University of Michigan Daily*, March 13, 1901, p. 1

33. For evidence see *The University of Michigan Daily*, October 3, 1900, p. 1 and John Kenneth Doherty, *Track and Field Omnibook* 4th ed. Los Alto, California: Tafnews, [1976] 1985, pp. 3–4.

34. For examples of weather delayed practice see *The University of Michigan Daily* , p. 1; May 3, 1901, p. 1; May 28, 1901, p. 2 and May 1, 1903.

35. *Ibid.*, March 3, 1903, p. 1.

36. *Ibid.*, May 22, 1901, p. 1.

37. Necrology File, Bentley Historical Library, University of Michigan.

38. *Chicago Tribune*, June 3, 1900, p. 17.

39. *Detroit Free Press*, June 9, 1900, p. 6.

40. Mark Dyreson, *Making the American Team: Sport, Culture, and the Olympic Experience*. Urbana: University of Illinois Press, 1998, p. 60–61.

41. *Ibid.*, p. 62.

42. *New York Times*, June 24, 1900, p. 8.

43. Dyreson, p. 63. Ann Arbor businessmen sent four-trackmen to Paris: John McLean, Charles Dvorak, Howard Hayes (who placed second in the 800-meter handicap race), and Clark Leiblee.

44. Bill Mallon, *The 1900 Olympic Games*. Jefferson, NC: McFarland & Co., Inc., 1998, pp. 45, 52, and 63.

45. John Frederick McLean married Vassar graduate Georgiana Grant in 1910 and fathered three children. He died on June 4, 1955. See Necrology File, Bentley Historical Library, University of Michigan.

46. Bill Mallon and Ian Buchanan, *Quest for Gold: The Encyclopedia of American Olympians*. New York: Leisure Press, 1984, p. 294–5.

47. *Chicago Tribune*, June 3, 1900, p. 17 and *Detroit Free Press*, May 26, 1901, Part 1, p. 10.

48. *Detroit Free Press*, June 10, 1900, p. 10.

49. David Wallechinsky, *The Complete Book of the Summer Olympics* (1996 edition) Boston: Little, Brown and Company, 1984, 1996, p. 122.

50. *The University of Michigan Daily*, March 6, 1901, p. 2.

51. *Ibid.*, February 27, 1901, p. 3.

52. *Detroit Free Press*, May 26, 1901, Part 1, p. 10.

53. *Ibid.*, June 13, 1901, p. 10.

54. *Ibid.*, June 16, 1901, p. 7.

55. Margaret Leech, *In The Days of McKinley*. New York: Harper & Brothers, 1959, p. 592.

56. *University of Michigan Daily*, June 4, 1901, p. 2.

57. *Detroit Free Press*, September 12, 1903, p. 10.

58. *The University of Michigan Daily*, March 17, 1901, p. 1.

59. Gems, *op. cit.*, pp. 25–29.

60. See *The University of Michigan Daily*, 1898–1910.

61. *The Detroit News Tribune*, June 2, 1903, p. 10 and July 2, 1905, p. 10; Hartmut Keil and John B. Jentz, eds., *German Workers in Industrial Chicago, 1850–1910*. DeKalb: Northern Illinois University Press, 1983, and Gems, *Ibid.*, p. 32.

62. *Detroit Free Press*, May 22, 1901, p. 10.

63. Dyreson, *op. cit.*, p.75.

64. *Ibid.*, p.60–76.

65. Murray Sperber, *Shake Down the Thunder: The Creation of Notre Dame Football*. New York: Henry Holt and Company, 1993, p. 42 and 210.

66. *The New York Times*, March 19, 2000, p. 38.

67. *Chicago Tribune*, May 22, 1898, p. 6.

68. Necrology File, Bentley Historical Library, University of Michigan.

69. *The University of Michigan Daily*, January 17, 1901, p. 1.

70. *Detroit Free Press*, May 26, 1901, Part 1, p. 10.

71. *Spalding's Official Athletic Almanac, 1905*, pp. 91–99.

72. *Detroit Free Press*, June 16, 1901, p. 7.

73. *Michigan Daily News*, May 13, 1902, p. 1.

74. Necrology File, Bentley Historical Library, University of Michigan.

75. *Ibid.*

76. See Jack Lessenberry, "A Maize and Blue Olympic Century," *Michigan History Magazine*, September/October 1997, p. 76. For meet results see *The University of Michigan Daily*, April 24, 1901, p. 1.

77. *Ibid.*, May 24, 1904, p.1.

78. *Who's Who in American Sports.* Washington, DC: National Biographical Society, Inc., 1928. And Reid M. Hanley, *Who's Who in Track and Field.* New Rochelle, New York: Arlington House, 1973, p. 59.

79. *The Amateur Athlete*, September 1931, p. 10.

80. *Detroit Free Press, August 17, 1905*, p. 9.

81. *The Amateur Athlete*, September 1931, p. 10.

82. *The New York Times*, April 28, 1906, p. 12.

83. *Detroit Times*, July 23, 1920, p. 6.

84. *The Amateur Athlete*, September 1931, p. 10.

85. Virginius Dadney, *Mr. Jefferson's University*. Charlottesville: University Press of Virginia, 1984, pp. 118–9.

86. *Charlottesville Daily Progress*, January 22, 1955.

87. *The Amateur Athlete*, September 1931, p. 10.

88. Archie Hahn, *How to Sprint.* Chicago: American Sports Publishing Co., 1925.

89. Hanley, *op. cit.*, p. 59, and R. L. Quercetani, *op. cit.*, pp. 6.

90. See *Who's Who in American Sports.* Washington, DC: National Biographical Society, Inc., 1928 and *Charlottesville Daily Progress*, January 22, 1955.

91. *Charlottesville Daily Progress*, January 22, 1955.

92. Necrology File, Bentley Historical Library, University of Michigan.

93. *Detroit Free Press*, May 19, 1901, Part 1, p. 10.

94. *Detroit Times*, May 25, 1901.

95. *Detroit Free Press*, June 7, 1903, p. 9.

96. *Chicago Tribune*, June 10, 1904, pp. 9–10; *Michiganensian*, 1904, p. 173, and *Spalding's Official Athletic Almanac, 1905*, pp. 101.

97. Necrology File, Bentley Historical Library, University of Michigan.

98. *Detroit Free Press*, June 6, 1903, p. 10.

99. *Ibid.*, May 31, 1903, p. 10.

100. *The Michigan Daily*, March 10, 1904, p. 1.

101. *Michiganensian*, 1904, p. 170.

102. Necrology File, Bentley Historical Library, University of Michigan.

103. *The Michigan Daily News*, May 18, 1902, p. 1.

104. *Chicago Tribune*, June 5, 1904, pp. 9–10.

105. *Detroit Free Press*, April 23, 1905, p. 13.

106. Necrology File, Bentley Historical Library, University of Michigan.

107. *Detroit Free Press*, July 22, 1905, p.5.

108. *Wyandotte News Herald*, October 26, 1956.

109. *The Michigan Daily*, March 1, 1904, p. 1.

110. *Ibid.*, March 10 and 18, 1904, p. 1.

111. Fitzpatrick was quite aware of the intercollegiate rules, since he had been unable to take Archie Hahn to the Eastern Intercollegiate meet in 1901, because Archie had not been enrolled a full year before the meet. *The University of Michigan Daily*, May 21, 1901, p. 1.

112. *Ibid.*, March 27, 1904, p. 1.

113. *The Michigan Daily*, April 27, 1904, p. 1.

114. *Chicago Tribune*, June 5, 1904, pp. 9–10.

115. *Michiganensian*, 1905, p. 170.

116. *Detroit Free Press*, August 8, 1905, p. 9.

117. *Ibid.*, August 20, 1905, p. 11.

118. *The Michigan Daily*, January 14, 1905, p. 3.

119. Wallechinsky, *op. cit.*, p. 144, and *Detroit News Tribune*, July 16, 1905, p. 8.

120. *Detroit Free Press*, August 14, 1905, p. 8.

121. See William H. Fries, "Athletics at Detroit University School," *Detroit News*, November 11, 1939 and an interview with E. L. Knickerbocker in the *Detroit News*, October 7, 1941.

122. Wellington V. V. Grimes, "A History of the Detroit University School." Ann Arbor, MI: Bentley Historical Library, University of Michigan Department of History honors papers, August 1944, pp. 1–5 and an interview with Liggett School Archivist Jean Dautenhoff.

123. Interview with Jesse Bernstein [Barnes], who attended University School from 1918 through 1921.

124. Archives Liggett School, 1996.

125. *The University of Michigan Daily*, May 24, 1903, p. 1.

126. *Ibid.*, May 18, 1902, p. 1.

127. *Ibid.*, May 29, 1904, p. 1 and 4.

128. *Detroit Free Press*, August 10, 1905, p. 9.

129. *The Michigan Daily*, April 30, 1907, p. 1.

130. *Pasadena Star News*, December 21 and 26, 1948.

131. Wallechinsky, *op. cit.*, p.114.

132. *Pasadena Star News*, December 21 and 26, 1948 and Necrology File, Bentley Historical Library, University of Michigan.

133. *The Detroit Blue Book 1901–02.* Detroit: The Elite Publishing Company, 1901, p. 300.

134. R. L. Polk & Co., *Detroit City Directory, 1908*, p. 1614.

135. See *Detroit Free Press*, May 26, 1909 and June 11, 1909.

136. *Spalding's Official Athletic Almanac, 1910.*

137. Keith McClellan, *The Sunday Game.* Akron, OH: University of Akron Press, 1998, p. 137.

138. *Polk's Detroit City Directory, 1927–28*, p. 1561.

139. *Detroit Free Press*, April 23, 1905, p. 13.

140. Beatrice Notley, "The Administration of James B. Angell." Ann Arbor, MI: Bentley Historical Library, University of Michigan Department of History honors papers, August 1949.

141. Rader, *op. cit.*, p. 139. Yost often said one thing and acted in an opposite manner. On January 20, 1922 Yost told a room full of University of Michigan alumni that he "deplored recruiting of athletes," declaring that "such action tends to make a youth's athletic ability a marketable commodity rather than a source of recreation." Players "should be satisfied to play the game for its own sake." "Sacrifice and wholehearted devotion to a cause should not be marred. See *Cleveland Plain Dealer*, January 21, 1922.

142. Beatrice Notley, "The Administration of James B. Angell." Ann Arbor, MI: Bentley Historical Library, University of Michigan Department of History honors papers, August 1949.

143. Don Canham, *From the Inside: A Half-Century of Michigan Athletics*. Ann Arbor: Olympia Sports Press, 1996, p. 29–31.

144. *The Michigan Daily*, March 23, 1913, p. 4. President Angell resigned February 17, 1909.

145. *Ibid.*, March 23, 1913, p. 4.

146. *Ibid.*, February 27, 1913, p. 1.

147. *32nd Annual Millrose Games Program*, February 4, 1939, p. 19.

148. As an indication of his commitment to excellence, in 1933 Keene Fitzpatrick gave one of the Wingate Memorial Lectures on "A System of General Training." See *The Amateur Athlete*, February 1934, pp. 10–12. In that lecture, Keene Fitzpatrick advocated competitive athletics for high school and preparatory school boys, but felt that their competition should be limit two running events. He also recommended eight to nine hours of sleep "in a well ventilated rooms" and a balanced diet for growing boys. He spoke out strongly against over-eating. Fitzpatrick said, "I think I'd be safe in saying that 35 per cent of the people that die today die from over-eating, that is the cause of bringing on something that hurries their death." "Another thing is the bathing. Where it is possible to bathe after competition that should be encouraged all the time."

"Fitz" recommended running on grass often to build endurance and save legs and knees.

149. *The Michigan Daily*, November 17, 1912, p. 3.

150. *Ibid.*, February 11, 1913, p. 1.

151. Canham, *op. cit.*, p. 34.

152. *Chicago Tribune*, February 26, 1921, p. 9.

153. *The Michigan Daily News*, September 23, 1902, p. 4.

154. Interviews with Aaron Gordon and other African-American, University of Michigan graduates who earned degrees before 1952.

155. Sperber, *op. cit.*, p. 133.

156. Sperber, *op. cit.*, 1993, p. 30–33.

157. *Michigan Daily*, February 24, 1939, p. 1.

158. *Ibid.*, p. 210.

159. *Ibid.*, p. 210–11.

160. Canham, *op. cit.*, p. 128.

161. Rockne and Ralph Young played pro-football together in 1916–17 at Fort Wayne.

162. See Murray Sperber, *Onward to Victory: The Crisis that Shaped College Sports*. New York: Henry Holt and Company, 1998.

163. *Detroit Free Press*, October 8, 1999, p. 1.

164. *New York Times*, December 19, 1999, p. 52.

Chapter 2

1. Harold Faulkner, *The Quest for Social Justice, 1898–1914*. (1931).

2. Wallechinsky, *op. cit.* 1996, p. xvi.

3. Dyreson, *op. cit.*, 1998, pp. 129–130.

4. *Ibid.*, p. 134–5.

5. *Detroit Free Press*, April 30, 1905, p. 11.

6. *Melange, 1907*. Lafayette College Yearbook, p. 170.

7. *Melange, 1908*. Lafayette College Yearbook, p. 189.

8. *The Michigan Daily*, January 21, 1969, p. 8.

9. Archives Lafayette College, August 4, 1999.

10. *Melange, 1911*. Easton, PA: Yearbook for Lafayette College, 1910, p. 207.

11. *Harrisburg Patriot*, June 1, 1908, pp. 1 and 3 and *Melange, 1910*. Easton, PA: Yearbook for Lafayette College, 1909, p. 211.

12. *Philadelphia Inquirer*, May 30, 1909, p. 9.

13. Wallechinsky *op. cit.*, 1996, p. 131, 140.

14. Quercetani, *op. cit.*, pp. 135.

15. Derderian, *op. cit.*, p. xvii and 38. Louis Tewanima ran in the Boston Marathon in 1909, pp. 47–48.

16. Krise and Squires, *op. cit.*, pp. 6–7.

17. *Detroit Free Press*, July 1, 1888, p. 4.

18. Wallechinsky, *op. cit.*, p. 25.

19. *Ibid.*, p. 71.

20. Dyreson, *op. cit.*, 1998, pp. 136; and Pope, *op. cit.*, p. 45–47.

21. Lewis H. Carlson and John J. Fogarty, *Tales of Gold*. Chicago: Contemporary Books, Inc., 1987, p. 54. I should be noted that the great hammer thrower, Harold Connolly turned down the honor of carrying the U.S. flag in the opening ceremonies of the 1968 Olympics because he did not approve of the long standing tradition of not dipping the flag when passing the host country's head of state. See William O. Johnson, Jr., *All That Glitters is Not Gold: An Irreverent Look at the Olympic Games*. New York: G. P. Putnam's Sons, 1972, p.128–129 and Bob Burns, "Magic Mountain," *Chicago Tribune*, July 3, 2000, Section 3, p. 8.

22. Hanley, *op. cit.*, p. 122. Rose is a member of the Helms Hall of Fame.

23. Quercetani, *op. cit.*, pp. 269.

24. Wallechinsky, *op. cit.*, pp. 144, 149, 154, 184.

25. Sheridan went on to win the discus in the 1906 and 1908 Olympics.

26. *Detroit News Tribune*, July 16, 1905.

27. *Detroit Free Press*, August 8, 1905, p. 9.

28. *The Detroit News*, September 8, 1907.

29. *Chicago Tribune*, July 16, 1908.

30. R. L. Quercetani, "Athletes of the Century," *Track and Field News*, October 1963, p. 14 and Quercetani, *op. cit.*, 1964, pp. 269.

31. Mallon and Buchanan, *op. cit.*, p. 286–7.

32. *Chicago Tribune*, July 14, 1908.

33. While the USA took second place, Dull was not among the top three United States runners and did not qualify for a silver medal. *Chicago Tribune*, July 16, 1908.

34. *Chicago Tribune*, July 18, 1908. The University of Michigan could claim seven track Olympians in the 1908 London Games: Ralph Rose, John Garrels, John Neil Patterson Gayle Dull, William Coe, Harry L. "Spider" Coe, and Horace Ramey.

35. *Philadelphia Inquirer*, May 30, 1909, p. 9.

36. Necrology File, Bentley Historical Library, University of Michigan.

37. Necrology File, Bentley Historical Library, University of Michigan.

38. See *Who's Who in American Sports*. Washington, DC: National Biographical Society, Inc., 1928.

39. *Milwaukee Sentinel*, September 20, 1960, p. 10.

40. See *Philadelphia Inquirer*, April 29, 1894, p. 8; *The New York Times*, April 30, 1900, p. 10 and April

29, 1906, p. 9; and *The Philadelphia Inquirer*, April 6, 1909, p. 10.

41. *The Michigan Daily*, January 21, 1969, p. 8.

42. Quercetani, 1964, pp. 7.

43. Wallechinsky, *op. cit.*, pp. 52 and 59; Quercetani, *op. cit.*, 1964, pp. 135.

44. Nurmi, whose initial training took place between 1918 and 1920 while a member of the Finnish Army, also won the 1,500-meter run and the individual cross-country in 1924 and placed second in the 3,000-meter steeplechase in 1928. Ritola won the 3,000-meter steeplechase and placed second in the individual cross-country in 1924 for a grand total of 14 medals for the two Finns.

45. Thorpe, whose Indian name was "Bright Path," was a member of the Sac and Fox tribe.

46. Thorpe's personal best in the high jump was 6' 5".

47. Quercetani, *op. cit.*, 1964, pp. 316.

48. *Chicago Tribune*, May 20, 1983, Section 4, pp. 1 ff.

49. Six Olympians represented the State of Michigan in 1912: Ralph Craig, Ralph Rose, Carroll Haff, Frank Nelson, Avery Brundage, and Richard Leslie Byrd.

50. *Dau's Blue Book 1917, Detroit*. New York, 1917, p. 94.

51. *Detroit in History and Commerce*. Detroit: Rogers & Thorpe, Publishers, 1891.

52. *Detroit News, April 25, 1909*.

53. *Harrisburg Patriot*, June 8, 1908.

54. *Philadelphia Inquirer*, May 30, 1909, p. 9.

55. *History of the Class of 1910, Yale College*. New Haven, Connecticut: Yale University, 1910, p. 255

56. *History of the Class of 1910, Yale College*. New Haven, Connecticut: Yale University, 1917, p. 224.

57. *History of the Class of 1910, Yale College*. New Haven, Connecticut: Yale University, 1926, p. 220.

58. R. L. Polk, *Detroit City Directory, 1927–28* , p. 74.

59. *History of the Class of 1910, Yale College*. New Haven, Connecticut: Yale University, 1935, p. 150.

60. *History of the Class of 1910, Yale College*. New Haven, Connecticut: Yale University, 1950, p. 149; and 1960, p. 73.

61. *Chicago Tribune*, June, 1909. [look up date & page]

62. *The Adrian Daily Times*, May 21, 1912, p. 1.

63. *The [Adrian] College World*, June 4, 1912, p. 3, 8 and notes from Howard Dahlquist, local historian, Milford, Illinois.

64. *The Adrian Daily Times*, May 13, 1912, p. 6.

65. *The Adrian Daily Times*, May 21, 1912, p. 1.

66. *Ibid*.

67. *The Adrian Daily Times*, May 31, 1912, p. 1.

68. *The [Adrian] College World*, June 4, 1945, p. 3.

69. *The [Adrian] College World*, June 4, 1945, p. 3 and "Memories of the Last Olympic Games," *The Literary Digest*, vol. 66, July 1920, p.96.

70. Wallechinsky, *op. cit.*, p. 182.

71. *The [Adrian] College World*, June 4, 1945, p. 3, 8.

72. Necrology File, Bentley Historical Library, University of Michigan.

73. *Philadelphia Inquirer*, May 30, 1909, p. 9.

74. Hanley, *op. cit.*, p. 36.

75. *Ibid*.

76. William O. Johnson, *All That Glitters is Not Gold: An Irreverent Look at the Olympic Games* (New York: G. P. Putnam's Sons, 1972, p. 137–8.

77. Three of the eight men to win this Olympic double are graduates of the University of Michigan Hahn, Craig and Tolan, and all but Valery Borzov was a North American.

78. *The Fifth Olympiad: The Official Report of the Olympic Games of Stockholm, 1912*. Issued by the Swedish Olympic Committee, Edited by Erick Bergvall. Translated by Edward Adam Ray. Stockholm: Wahlstrom and Wildstrand, 1912.

79. William O. Johnson, *All That Glitters is Not Gold: An Irreverent Look at the Olympic Games*. New York: G. P. Putnam's Sons, 1972, p. 137–8.

80. *Track and Field News*, March 1962, p. 9.

81. Reported in *Spaulding's Athletic Almanac*, also see *Michigan Daily*, January 24, 1913, p. 1.

82. See *Who's Who in American Sports*. Washington, DC: National Biographical Society, Inc., 1928.

83. Necrology File, Bentley Historical Library, University of Michigan.

84. *The Michigan Daily*, March 23, 1913, p. 4.

85. *Ibid.*, May 4, 1913, p. 1.

86. *Chicago American*, July 5, 1913.

87. Necrology File, Bentley Historical Library, University of Michigan.

88. *Chicago American*, July 5, 1913.

89. *The Michigan Daily*, February 17, 1914, p. 1.

90. *Current Biography, 1948*, p. 75; Maynard Brichford, "Avery Brundage: Chicago Businessman," *Journal of the Illinois State Historical Society*, vol. 91, no. 4, Winter 1996, pp. 218–232; *Who Was Who in America, vol VI, 1974–76*. Chicago: Marquis Who's Who, Inc., 1976, pp. 58–59; and Johnson, *op. cit.*, pp. 78–79.

91. *Chicago Tribune*, June 6, 1909 and September 18, 1910.

92. *Current Biography, 1948*, p. 75 and Brichford, *op. cit.*

93. Wallechinsky, 1996 edition, p. 164–5, 186.

94. "Bill Would Clear Name of Thorpe," *Chicago Daily News*, March 20, 1943, p. 18. Brundage's response is in *Current Biography, 1948*, p. 80.

95. *Chicago Tribune*, April 28, 1918, Part 2, p. 1.

96. *Ibid.*, February 27, 1918, Part 2, p. 2.

97. *New York Times*, July 5, 1921, p. 18.

98. Krise and Squires, *op. cit.*, p.46. North and South America were considered a single land mass by Baron de Coubertin.

Chapter 3

1. Andre Siegfried, *America Comes of Age*. New York: Harcourt, Brace and Company, 1927, p. 161–2.

2. Preston W. Slosson, *The Great Crusade and After, 1914–28*. New York: The Macmillan Company, 1930, p. 219.

3. *Ibid.*, p. 136.

4. *The University of Michigan Daily*, March 3, 1903, p. 1.

5. *Detroit Times*, May 14, 1924, p. 18.

6. Slosson, *op. cit.*, p. 184.

7. Siegfried, *op. cit.*, p. 168.

8. *Detroit News*, June 10, 1927, p. 40.

9. *Ibid.*, July 7, 1929, Sports p. 8.

10. Mark Sullivan, *Our Times: The United States, The Twenties*, vol. VI. New York: Charles Scribner's Sons, 1935, p. 159–60.

11. Slosson, *op. cit.*, p. 81.

12. Sullivan, *op. cit.*, p. 212.

13. Slosson, *op. cit.*, pp. 170–2.

14. *Ibid.*, p. 321–4.

15. *Detroit Times*, April 24, 1924, p. 22.

16. Slosson, *op. cit.*, p. 329.

17. *The Michigan Daily*, April 20, 1921, p. 1.

18. M. J. Moses, "The Cost of College," *Good Housekeeping,*" Vol. LXXXV, no. 5, 1927, pp. 247–8.

19. *Detroit Times*, June 5, 1926, p. 12.

20. Jesse Abramson, "Track and Field," *Sport's Golden Age: A Close-up of the Fabulous Twenties*. Ed. Allison Danzig and Peter Brandwein. New York: Harper & Brothers, 1948, p. 136–7 and Wallechinsky, *op. cit.*, p. 4. Paddock set the World record in the 100-yard dash (9.6), the 100-meter dash (10.4), the 200-meter dash (20.8) and the 220-yard dash (20.8) in 1921. He also set the American record for the 110-yard (10.2) and the 300-yard dashes (30.2) in 1921. See Menke, *op. cit.*, p. 951, 959.

21. Hanley, *op. cit.*, p. 127.

22. *The Savitar*, University of Missouri Yearbook, 1916, p. 145.

23. *The Savitar*, University of Missouri Yearbook, 1918, p. 91, 307.

24. *Millrose Games Program*, January 31, 1948, pp. 51–52.

25. *Spaulding's Official Athletic Almanac*, 1928, p. 214.

26. *Millrose Games Program*, February 5, 1944.

27. University of Missouri Archives, Commencement, 1921; Enrollment, 1921–22, p. 345.

28. *Chicago Tribune*, June 6, 1915.

29. Necrology File, Bentley Historical Library, University of Michigan.

30. Wallechinsky, *op. cit.*, p. 179.

31. Mallon and Buchanan, *op. cit.*, p. 294.

32. *Detroit Free Press*, September 14, 1932.

33. *The Michigan Daily*, March 10, 1921, p. 1.

34. *Ibid.*, March 4 and 5, 1921, p. 3; 1.

35. Sullivan, *op. cit.*, p. 212.

36. Siegfried, *op. cit.*, pp. 70–90.

37. *Chicago Tribune*, March 5, 1921, p. 12. The "all-around" was comparable to the decathlon.

38. *Ibid.*, March 6, 1921, Part 2, page 2.

39. *The Michiganensian*, 1921, p.320.

40. *The Michigan Daily*, March 10, 1921, p. 3.

41. *Ibid.*, May 8 and 22, 1921 and *Chicago Tribune*, June 19, 1921.

42. *The Michigan Daily*, May 14, 1922.

43. *Chicago Tribune*, June 18, 1922.

44. Quercetani, *op. cit.*,1964, pp. 248–49.

45. *Chicago Tribune*, March 20, 1921, Part 2, p. 1.

46. Arthur R. Ashe, Jr., *A Hard Road to Glory: A History of the African-American Athlete 1919–1945* New York: Warner Books, An Amistad Book, 1988, pp. 79–80; and *Detroit Free Press*, September 17, 1922.

47. Quercetani, *op. cit.*, 1964, pp. 249 and Wallechinsky, *op. cit.*, p. 131.

48. *New York Times*, June 25, 1976, p. 25.

49. Hubbard had an A-average.

50. See John Behee, *Hail to the Victors! Black Athletes at the University of Michigan*. Ann Arbor: Ulrich's Books, Inc., 1974.

51. Canham, *op. cit.*, p.187.

52. *Chicago Tribune*, September 9, 1922, p. 11.

53. *90th* Annual Drake Relays Program, April 23–24, 1999, p. 95.

54. *New York Times*, June 25, 1976, p. 25 and Young, *op. cit.*, p. 146.

55. Quercetani, *op. cit.*, 1963, p. 14 and *New York Times*, June 25, 1976, p. 25.

56. *Spaulding Amateur Athletic Union Athletic Almanac for 1927* (1927), p. 6–7.

57. Mallon and Buchanan, *op. cit.*, p. 310.

58. Hanley, *op. cit.*, p. 127.

59. *Detroit News*, July 15, 1928, part 4, p. 5.

60. *New York Times*, June 25, 1976, p. 25.

61. See *Cleveland Plain Dealer*, June 24, 1976.

62. Kenneth Doherty, *Track and Field Omnibook*. Los Angeles, CA.: Tafnews Press, Book Division of Track and Field News, Inc., 1976, p. 3.

63. *The Toronto Globe*, July 14, 1924, p. 13.

64. *Ibid.*, June 16, 1924, p. 11.

65. *New York Times*, June 16 and July 8, 1924.

66. Wallechinsky, *op. cit.*, p. 18.

67. Carlson and Fogarty, *op. cit.*, p. 56.

68. *Millrose Games Program*, February 5, 1944.

69. Quercetani, *op. cit.*,1964, pp. 1–2.

70. Kenny Greenberg, *Track and Field News*, March 1952, p. 7.

71. *Chicago Tribune*, May 1, 1927, Section 2, page 2.

72. Wallechinsky, *op. cit.*, p. 19.

73. Mallon and Buchanan, *op. cit.*, p. 340–1.

74. *Detroit Times, April 26*, p. 13; April 27, 1924, Part 3, p. 1.

75. Wallechinsky, *op. cit.*, p. 6, 25–7.

76. *Millrose Games Program*, January 31, 1948, pp. 51.

77. Ellen Phillips, *The VIII Olympiad, Paris 1924*. Los Angeles: World Sport Research & Publications, Inc, 1996, p. 47–52.

78. Quercetani, *op. cit.*,1964, pp. 1–2.

79. Philips, *op. cit.*, p. 52.

80. Wallechinsky, *op. cit.*, pp. 6–7.)

81. Aljean Harmetz, "A Star Sprinter Looks Back to '24," *New York Times*, August 9, 1984, p. B15.

82. *Ibid.*

83. Al Le Coney, "My Most Exciting Race!" The J. Alfred Le Coney Papers, Special Collections, Lafayette College.

84. Bureau of Engraving and Printing, U.S. Department of the Treasury news release, July 2, 1996.

85. *Detroit Times*, April 24, 1925, p. 29.

86. Wallechinsky, *op. cit.*, p. 123.

87. *Detroit Times*, April 24, 1925, p. 29.

88. *The Viking* [the Northern High School Yearbook], June 1923.

89. Necrology File, Bentley Historical Library, University of Michigan.

90. *Who's Who in American Sports*, 1928, *op. cit.*

91. *The Toronto Globe*, June 9 and 19, 1924.

92. *Ibid.*, July 10, 1928, p. 10.

93. *Ibid.*, July 26, 1928, p. 1.

94. *Ibid.*, July 30, 1928, p. 1.

95. *Ibid.*, August 1, 1928, p. 10.

96. *Ibid.*, August 6, 1928, p. 8.

97. Necrology File, Bentley Historical Library, University of Michigan.

98. *Detroit Free Press*, April 6, 1925, p. 15.

99. Recollections of Gordon T. Hill, Class of 1926, *Wayne State Alumni Magazine*, April 1988, pp. 22–23, Archives Wayne State University.

100. *Detroit Free Press*, April 7, 1925, p. 19.

101. Hill, *op. cit.*, pp. 22–23, Archives Wayne State University, and *Detroit Free Press*, April 17, 1988.

102. *Detroit Times,* April 26, 1925, p. 13.

103. Analysis from Sixth Annual NCAA Outdoor Track and Field Championship program in the Lee Bartlett collection.

104. *Chicago Tribune,* June 12, 1927, Sports Section, p. 3.

105. *Ibid.,* February 27, 1927, Section 2, p. 1. For a brief profile of J. K. Doherty see Joseph M. Turrini, "Michigan's Forgotten Trackman," *Michigan History Magazine,* vol. 83, no. 2, March/April 1999, pp. 46–53.

106. Hoyt grew up in Greenfield, Iowa and graduated from Grinnell College in 1917. Hoyt coached at Sioux City High School before coming to the University of Michigan in 1923 as a football trainer. He became an assistant track coach before being elevated to the head track coach position in 1930.

107. *Spaulding Official Amateur Athletic Almanac for 1929,* p. 5–6.

108. Interview with Kenneth "Red" Simmons, July 13, 1998.

109. Ken Doherty admitted that his sons were more interested in music than in athletics.

110. *University of Michigan Track and Field Media Guide,* 1937, 1940, and 1948.

111. *Modern Track and Field.* Englewood Cliffs, NJ: Prentice-Hall, Inc., 1953, 1963.

112. *Track and Field Omibook.* Los Alto, California: Tafnews, 1985 (4th ed.).

113. *The Amateur Athlete,* February 1958, p. 28.

114. Held in Philadelphia in 1959.

115. *Philadelphia Inquirer,* April 21, 1996; and Hal Bateman, U. S. Track and Field Federation.

116. *Detroit Free Press,* May 19, 1923.

117. *Detroit News,* May 24, 1923.

118. Meet programs. See the Program for the meet held on February 27, 1937

119. Necrology File, Bentley Historical Library, University of Michigan.

120. *Detroit News,* May 25, 1924.

121. *Detroit Free Press,* June 1, 1924.

122. *Chicago Tribune,* May 1, 1927, Section 2, page 2.

123. Michigan State University, Intercollegiate Athletics Hall of Fame Candidate's Application Form filled out by Fred Alderman, 1992.

124. *The New York Times,* September 21, 1998 and *The Chattanooga Times,* September 21, 1998.

125. Thomas J. Fleming, *West Point: The Men and Times of the United States Military Academy.* New York: William Morrow, 1969, p. 311–12.

126. Mark Dyreson, "Ballyhoo and Social Capital: The Olympic Games of 1928 and American Culture," presented at the 1999 North American Society for Sport History Conference, May 22, 1999, p. 11.

127. Carlson and Fogarty, *op. cit.,* p. 57.

128. *Millrose Games Program,* January 31, 1948, pp. 51–52.

129. See Carlson and Forgarty, *op. cit.,* pp. 59–68 for the recollections of Raymond Barbuti on the incident. During World War, Lieutenant Ray Barbuti served in the U.S. Army Air Force. *Millrose Games Program,* February 6, 1943.

130. See Mallon and Buchanan, *op. cit.*

131. *Fifth Business.* Toronto, Ontario: Penguin Books, 1970, p. 24.

132. Not everyone was bothered by this behavior. The dapper and persuasive Major William Kennelly, President of the New York Athletic Club from 1926 to 1932, vigorously supported MacArthur's handling of the Olympic team. See Bob Considine and Fred G. Jarvis, *A Portrait of the NYAC: The First Hundred Years.* London: The Macmillan Company, 1969, p. 90–1.

133. William Manchester, *American Caesar: Douglas MacArthur, 1880–1964.* New York: Dell Publishing Co., 1978, p. 164.

134. MacArthur's racial prejudices would surface several times in his career. William Porter Gale, General Mac Arthur's director of his guerrilla operation in the Philippines during the second World War, was later the founder of the Christian Defense League, an anti-Semitic and anti-black militant hate group. See *Intelligence Report.* Published by the Southern Poverty Law Center. Winter 1998, issue 89, p.8. More on Mac Arthur's anti-Semitic and racist views see Joseph W. Bendersky, *The "Jewish Threat": Anti-Semetic Politics of the U.S. Army.* New York: Basic Books, 2000, p. 201–204.

Thurgood Marshall also discovered the evil harmful side of MacArthur's racism during the Korean War. In 1950 reports began to surface that African-American servicemen were being charged with cowardice and failure to obey orders on the battlefield in disproportionately high numbers. When Thurgood Marshall, an ardent anti-Communist, decided to handle the appeal of one such soldier, he was confronted by MacArthur's refusal to allow Thurgood access to records. Thurgood discovered that MacArthur had contacted J. Edgar Hoover to deny Marshall military clearance to see the records, based on Marshall alleged pro-Communist tendencies. Thurgood was required to get President Truman's support to overrule MacArthur, and found that there were indeed two standards of justice in MacArthur's theater of operation. He had one standard for white servicemen and a higher one for African-American servicemen. Juan Williams, *Thurgood Marshall: American Revolutionary.* New York: Random House, 1998, pp. 170–173; also see Stanley Weintraub, *MacArthur's War.* New York: The Free Press, 2000.

135. One of the real heroes in the 1928 Olympics was Clarence H. DeMar of Melrose, Massachusetts who ran in the marathon. While he did not place in top 10 in 1928, in 1924 he won a bronze medal. De Mar placed second in the Boston Marathon in 1910 and won it in 1911, 1922, and five additional times. He ran in every Boston Marathon from 1922–54. In May 1957 he had advanced cancer and following a colostomy ran the New England 30-K championship, placing 21st. He died on June 15, 1958 at the age of 70. See Derderian, *op. cit.,* p. 257.

136. Young, *op. cit.,* pp. 6, 21 and 26.

137. *Union City 1975 Bicentennial Book,* p. 61–2.

138. Union City Society for Historic Preservation, *News Letter,* Issue xiv, Winter, 1998.

139. 8 feet 6¼ inches and 8 feet 10¼ inches.

140. 98 feet 5 inches and 119 feet 9 inches long.

141. *Detroit Free Press,* June 5, 1927, Part 2, p. 27.

142. Wallechinsky, *op. cit.,* p. 145.

143. *Detroit News,* May 25, 1924, Sports, p. 2.

144. The details above were taken from Lee Bartlett's diary, held by his daughter Cheryle Proctor, Union City, MI.

145. "Adidas," *International Directory of Company Histories*. Editor, Tina Grant. Detroit: St. James Press, 1996. Volume 14, Pp. 6–9.

146. The winning throw by Finland's Matti Jarvinen was 238 feet 6 inches. *Battle Creek Enquirer and Evening News*, August 4 and 6, 1932.

147. *The Sou'Wester, 1924.*

148. *Michigan Daily*, April 28, 1929, p. 1.

149. *Chicago Tribune*, July 3, 1932, part 2, p. 4.

150. *Spaulding's Official Athletic Almanac for 1933*, p. 2–3.

151. *Spaulding's Official Athletic Almanac for 1934*, p. 4–5.

152. *Detroit News*, June 13, 1935.

153. *Spaulding's Official Athletic Almanac for 1937*, p. 5.

154. Wallechinsky, *op. cit.*, p. 35.

155. This count does not include Edward Lansing Gordon, Jr., who graduated from the University of Iowa, won a gold medal in the long jump at 1932 Olympics and spent the later years of his life in Detroit, where he died in September 1971.

Chapter 4

1. *American Legacy*, vol. 5, no. 4, winter 2000, p. 18.

2. Ashe, *op. cit.*, p. 73.

3. Richard Bak, *Joe Louis: The Great Black Hope*. Dallas, Tx: Taylor Publishing Co., 1996.

4. Behee, *op. cit.*

5. *Detroit Free Press*, May 18, 1909, Roxborough remained on the team.

6. Bak, *Op. Cit.*, p. 38; also see his obituary, *Detroit News*, December 19, 1975.

7. Jeffrey Mirel, *The Rise and Fall of an Urban School System: Detroit 1907–81*. Ann Arbor: The University of Michigan Press, 1993.

8. *The Coldwater Daily Reporter*, January 29, 1925, p. 4.

9. *The Detroit Evening Times*, July 10, 1929, p. 10.

10. *Ibid.*

11. See, Keith McClellan, "John Roesink's Mack Park." Unpublished manuscript, 1997; and Richard Bak, *Turkey Stearnes and the Detroit Stars: The Negro Leagues in Detroit, 1919–1933*. Detroit: Wayne State University Press, 1994.

12. *Chicago Tribune*, June 5, 1927.

13. *The Detroit Times*, June 8, 1927.

14. Now Eastern Michigan University.

15. In 1928 the Regional Olympic Trials for the States of Illinois, Indiana, and Michigan were held on June 29–30 at the University of Detroit Stadium. See *Detroit Times*, April 29, 1928, part 2, p. 2.

16. *Ypsilanti Press*, February 26, 1931, p. 6.

17. *Spalding's Official Athletic Almanac for 1930 and 1931*, pp. 6–8.

18. *Chicago Tribune*, July 3, 1932, part 2, p. 4.

19. Interview with Kenneth "Red" Simmons, who was a personal friend of John Lewis, July 13, 1998.

20. *Detroit Free Press*, May 24 and 31, 1925.

21. See *Brown and Gold*,[Western State Teacher's College Yearbook] *1929*, p. 70, 248.

22. See *Brown and Gold, 1931*, p. 56 and 149.

23. WMU Alumni Office, 1983.

24. Some have reported that he was born in Denver.

25. *Detroit Free Press*, May 13, 1936, p. 23.

26. *Chicago Tribune*, June 4, 1927, p. 17.

27. *Ibid.*, June 5, 1927, II, p. 1.

28. *Michigan Daily*, May 12, 1929, p. 1.

29. Quercetani, *op. cit.*, 1964, pp. 8.

30. *The* [Lansing] *State Journal*, April 24, 1930.

31. *Des Moines Register*, April 24, 1999, p. 1A and 7A.

32. *Ibid.*, p. 1 and 7A.

33. *The Amateur Athlete*, January 1932, p. 13; *Spaulding's Official Athletic Almanac for 1931*, p. 18.

34. Behee, *op. cit.*

35. *Battle Creek Enquirer and Evening News*, August 4, 1932.

36. J. P. Abramson, "Electrical Timer," *The Amateur Athlete*, December 1932, p. 7.

37. Johnson, *op. cit.*, p. 180–181.

38. *The Amateur Athlete for December 1932*, p. 7.

39. *Spaulding's Official Athletic Almanac for 1933*, p. 2–3.

40. *The Ypsilanti Daily Press*, January 24, 1933, p. 3. For more see Donald Potts, "World's Fastest Humans: Eddie Tolan," *Track and Field News*, December 1948, p. 2.

41. "Blacks in Detroit," *Detroit Free Press*, December 1980.

42. *The Michigan Daily* January 24, 1933, p. 1.

43. *Chicago Tribune*, June 24, 1933, p. 17.

44. *Detroit News*, July 2, 1933.

45. *Ibid.*, May 18, 1934.

46. *The Toronto Globe*, March 7, 1935, p. 8.

47. *Chicago Tribune*, July 3, 1932, part 2, p. 4.

48. *Butler Collegian*, March 24 and 27. 1933, p. 1.

49. See Mirel, *op. cit.*, 1993, p. 192.

50. See *The Detroit Times*, April 28, 1949, p. c-47. Charles Fonville set the world record in the shot put in 1948. See David Baldwin, *Track and Field Record Holders: World, Olympic and American Marks 1946 through 1995*. Jefferson, NC: McFarland & Co., 1996, p. 277.

51. *The Michigan Daily*, January 20, 1929, p. 3.

52. *Who's Who Among Black Americans (3rd ed.)*, 1981, p. 90.

53. *Ann Arbor News*, September 13, 1949.

54. Necrology File, Bentley Historical Library, University of Michigan.

55. *Ypsilanti Daily Press*, February 4, 1939, p. 5.

56. *The Detroit Free Press* and *The Detroit Times*. Three tracks were built, Belle Isle, Codd Field, and Goldberg, in 1921. Later a track was built at Northwestern HS (*Detroit Times*, April 30, 1921, p. 11.) Little else was done for a decade. See *The Detroit Times*, April 24, 1924, p. 22 for evidence of overcrowded athletic fields.

57. Lewis L. Forsythe, *Athletics in Michigan High Schools: The First Hundred Years*. New York: Prentice-Hall, Inc., 1950, p. 185–6.

58. Determined from pictures provided by Orlin Jones, Pershing HS, Class, January, 1951 and Detroit City-Champion 120-yard high hurdles, June 1950. Persing High School, one of Detroit's largest schools, was built in 1929 and spent more than 20 years without a gym, requiring the indoor track in the halls. *Detroit Times*, April 7, 1948, p. C-53

59. These observations were gained from the *Centralite*, the yearbook for Central High School in Detroit, years 1912, 1933, 1939, 1940, 1951, 1959, 1964, and 1970.

60. These observations are made based on research from the *Viking*, the Detroit Northern High School yearbook, years 1922, 1923, 1924, 1930, 1940, 1948, 1959, and 1970.

61. When January and June classes are combined there were about 600 graduating students per year.

62. These observations are made based on research from the Northwestern High School Yearbook, *The Northwester*, years 1922, 1924, 1929, 1930, 1948, 1949, and 1959.

63. Mirel, 1996.

64. Behee, op. cit., p. 95. Miller High School fielded a track team, but had no track.

65. For more see *New York Times*, December 5, 1999, p. A21.

Chapter 5

1. Eastern Michigan University, *The Alumnus*, Fall, 1971, p. 4.

2. Later re-named Roosevelt High School.

3. Dr. L. W. Olds, "The History of Michigan's Physical Education Council," March 1, 1951, Eastern Michigan University Archives.

4. *The Adrian Daily Times*, May 6, 1912, p. 6.

5. *Ibid.*, May 5, 1913, p. 8.

6. *Eastern College Focus*, Winter 1986 in Eastern Michigan University Archives. Some reports have Olds making the innovation in 1912 or 1914–5, but these reports are clearly inaccurate. For reports of earlier innovation see *Detroit News*, and June 15, 1976; *NRTR Journal*, March–April 1975.

7. *The Laguna Beach*[CA] *News Post*, November 12, 1975, p. 13.

8. *Normal College News*, July 13, 1937 and *Eastern Echo*, March 15, 1999, p. 8.

9. *Aurora*, 1925 [Michigan Normal College Yearbook], p. 288.

10. *Daily Ypsilanti Press*, April 23, 1925, p. 4.

11. *Detroit News*, June 12, 1927.

12. Interview with Kenneth "Red" Simmons, July 30, 1998.

13. See Dorothy Clarke Wilson, *Handicap Race: The Inspiring Story of Roger Arnett*. New York: McGraw-Hill and Company, 1967; *Ypsilanti Press*, August 9, 1969; Eastern Michigan University, *Alumni Newsletter*, April 1968, p. 9; and Arnett's hand written inscription in Dr. Olds' copy of *Handicap Race*.

14. *Chicago Tribune*, June 5, 1927, Part 2, p. 1.

15. The *Detroit Times*, June 1, 1928, p. 27.

16. *Aurora*, 1930.

17. *The Amateur Athlete*, January 1932, p. 13; and *Spaulding's Official Athletic Almanac for 1931*, p. 18.

18. Interview with Kenneth "Red" Simmons, July 13, 1998.

19. The *Ypsilanti Daily Press*, January 24, 1933, p. 3; and *Spaulding's Official Athletic Almanac for 1933*, p. 19.

20. Letter in the Archives of Eastern Michigan University, p. 2–3.

21. *Chicago Tribune*, July 3, 1932, part 2, p. 4.

22. *The Milwaukee Journal*, July 14, 1932, p.6.

23. *The Ypsilanti Daily Press*, January 24, 1933, p. 3 and interview with Kenneth "Red" Simmons, 1998.

24. *Spaulding's Official Athletic Almanac for 1934*, p. 4–5.

25. *Detroit News*, April 29, 1933, p. 16.

26. The 1933 *Aurora*.

27. Now Kingston School.

28. *Ann Arbor News*, December 3, 1982, p. A1.

29. Interview with Kenneth "Red" Simmons, July 30, 1998.

30. Interview with Kenneth "Red" Simmons, July 30, 1998 and the author's personal observations, 1998–99.

31. *Worchester Evening Post*, November 28, 1929 and *Worchester Sunday Telegram*, December 7, 1930, section 3, p. 6.

32. *Spaulding's Official Athletic Almanac, 1931*, pp. 4–6 and 102.

33. *Detroit Free Press*, June 26, 1932.

34. Interview with William Zepp, Sr., August 5 and 23, 1998.

35. Ibid.

36. *Ypsilanti Daily Press*, January 31, 1935, p. 6.

37. *Ibid.*, February 4, 1935, p. 3.

38. *The Amateur Athlete*, January 1934, p. 15.

39. *Ypsilanti Daily Press*, February 11, 1935, p. 3.

40. *Ibid.*, February 23, 1935, p. 3.

41. *Ibid.*, February 25, 1935, p. 3.

42. *Ibid.*, March 11, 1935, p. 3.

43. *Los Angeles Times*, June 23, 1935, part II, p. 12.

44. *Milwaukee Journal* June 27, 1936, p. 1.

45. *Ibid.*, June 27, 1936, p. 2.

46. Interview with William Zepp, Sr. and Jr. August 5 and August 23, 1998.

47. *Spalding's Official Athletic Almanac for 1931*.

48. *Spalding's Official Athletic Almanac for 1935*, p. 43–45.

49. *Spalding's Official Athletic Almanac for 1937*, p. 64.

50. *Detroit Free Press*, February 14, 1937; February 28, 1937; and April 25, 1937.

51. *Ibid.*, February 21, 1937 and May 16, 1937.

52. Eastern Michigan University Alumni Directory, 1982, p. 276.

53. *Ypsilanti Press*, February 26, 1963.

54. *Eastern Michigan Alumni Directory, 1991*. White Plains, NY: Harris Publishing Co., 1992 and *Eastern Michigan Alumni Directory, 1999*.

55. Later to be Poland.

56. Interview with Abe Rosenkrantz, July 13, 1998.

57. "Put your ass on the table" or "put your money where your mouth is."

58. Interview with Abe Rosenkrantz, July 13, 1998.

59. *Ypsilanti Daily Press*, January 31, 1935, p. 6.

60. *Ibid.*, February 4, 1935, p. 3.

61. *New York Times*, February 3, 1935, Part 4, p. 1 and *Ypsilanti Daily Press*, February 4, 1935, p. 3.

62. *Ypsilanti Daily Press*, February 11, 1935, p. 3.

63. *Detroit Free Press*, February 10, 1935, p. 3-Sports Section.

64. *Ypsilanti Daily Press*, February 23, 1935, p. 3.

65. *Ibid.*, March 18, 1935, and recollections of Abraham Rosenkrantz, interviewed July 13, 1998.

66. Recollection and scrapbook of Hugo Apt, Oak Park, MI. August, 1998 and April 12, 1999.

67. Recollections of Hugo Apt, Oak Park, MI. April 12, 1999.

68. *Milwaukee Journal*, June 28, 1936, Sports, p. 3.

69. *Detroit Free Press*, June 3, 1936, p. 19.

70. *Encyclopedia of Jews in Sports*. New York: Bloch Publishing Company, 1965, pp.495, 499.

71. Interviewed with Abe Rosenkrantz July 13, 1998 and December 20, 1998.

72. *Normal College News*, July 21, 1938, p. 1.

73. Eastern Michigan University Archives.

74. *Ypsilanti Daily Press*, February 17, 1941, p. 5.

75. *Ibid.*, February 21, 1941, p. 5.

76. *Ibid.*, March 6 (p. 6), March 7 (p. 6), and March 10, 1941, p. 5.

77. In 1943 Hlad ran the hurdles at the Chicago Daily News Relays wearing a University of Chicago track shirt, but did not place. See *Chicago Daily News*, March 19, 1943, p. 29, and March 22, 1943, p. 19.

78. *Normal College News*, February 4, 1940.

79. *Bee Gee News*, June 17, 1949, p. 4.

80. *Ibid.*, May 16, 1950, p. 4.

81. *Northwester, 1949.*

82. *Official AAU Track and Field Handbook, 1953–4*, p. 110. Stan attended Adrian College for one year before enrolling at Eastern Michigan U.

83. *Ibid.*, p. 3 and *AAU Official Track and Field Handbook, 1956–7*, p. 13.

84. *Ann Arbor News*, November 8, 1962.

85. *Ypsilanti Press*, February 26, 1963; and *Ann Arbor News*, December 3, 1982, p. A1.

86. *Ann Arbor News*, December 3, 1982, p. A1.

Chapter 6

1. *Detroit Free Press*, February 24, 1999, p. 8-B.

2. *Amateur Athlete*, July-August, 1933, p. 17.

3. *The Michigan Daily*, February 12, 1925, p.6.

4. *Ibid.*, April 5, 1925, p. 6.

5. *Ypsilanti Press*, June 14, 1931. Wuesthoff coached the Swiss Olympic track team in 1948 and at Denby HS from 1932–1950. *Detroit Times*, April 21, 1949, p. C-33.

6. Saturday August 28, 1926, Meet Program in the Lee Bartlett collection.

7. Fifth Annual Ohio Relays Program, April 21, 1928.

8. *Detroit Tribune*, May 22, 1954.

9. Interview with Aaron Z. Gordon on August 12, 1998. Eddie Gaines was a mentor to Aaron when he was the young man was in high school. At that time, Gaines told Aaron some of his life story.

10. *Toronto Globe*, July 24, 1934, p. 9.

11. *Ibid.*, July 25, 1934, p. 9.

12. *Ibid.*, July 26, 1934, p. 10.

13. *Ibid.*, August 1, 1935, pp. 9–10.

14. *Ypsilanti Daily Press*, February 11, 1935; *Detroit News*, June 14, 1936; and *Coldwater Daily Reporter*, July 31, 1936, p. 8.

15. Wallechinsky, *op. cit.*, p. 184.

16. *Detroit Free Press*, July 5, 1928.

17. *Ibid.*, February 10, 1935, p. 3-Sports Section.

18. Interview with Kenneth "Red" Simmons, July 30, 1998.

19. *The Toronto Globe*, July 26, 1934, p. 10.

20. Interview with Kenneth "Red" Simmons, July 30, 1998.

21. *Detroit News*, May 21, 1933.

22. *Spaulding's Official Athletic Almanac for 1939.*

23. *Detroit Free Press*, May 18, 1924, p. 22.

24. *Spalding's Official Athletic Almanac for 1937*, pp. 62–3.

25. *Los Angeles Times*, July 4, 1937, Part II, p. 12.

26. *Detroit Times*, March 24, 1940, part 2, p. 3.

27. *AAU Handbook, 1945.*

28. *Detroit Free Press*, March 21, 1937, p. 3-Sports Section.

29. *Ibid.*, February 10, 1935, p. 3-Sports Section.

30. *Ibid.*, March 21, 1937, p. 3-Sports Section.

31. University of Michigan Bentley Library, Athletic Department Box 2, track media guide 1960.

32. Interview with Kenneth "Red" Simmons, July 30, 1998. One of the first articles on weight lifting in track appeared in *Track and Field News*, June 1954, p. 8. The pioneers in this art Al Hershey, Jim Reynolds, Otis Chandler, and "Red" Simmons.

33. *The Michigan Daily*, February 18, 1933, p. 1.

34. *Ibid.*, May 12, 1933, p. 1.

35. *Ibid.*, May 21, 1933, p. 1.

36. *Detroit Times*, March 3, 1940, part 2, p. 1.

37. *The Amateur Athlete*, January 1934. P. 6.

38. J. P. Abramson, "I. C. 4-A Meet," *The Amateur Athlete*, June 1933, 5 and 10.

39. *The Amateur Athlete*, January 1934. P. 6.

40. *Spaulding's Official Athletic Almanac for 1934*, p. 4–5.

41. J. P. Abramson, "I. C. 4-A Meet," *The Amateur Athlete*, June 1933, 5 and 10.

42. Quercetani, *op. cit.*, 1964, pp. 106.

43. Bonthron was now running for the New York Athletic Club.

44. *New York Times*, February 3, 1935, Section 4, p. 1.

45. *Detroit Free Press*, February 17, 1935, p. 1-Sport section.

46. *Ibid.*, February 24, 1935, p. 1-Sports Section.

47. Hanley, *op. cit.*, 1973, p. 22.

48. *Detroit Times*, February 22, 1941, p. 9.

49. *Ibid.*, May 20, 1934 and *Milwaukee Journal*, June 30, 1934.

50. *New York Times*, February 3, 1935.

51. *Chicago Tribune*, March 1935 and *Toronto Globe*, March 1935.

52. *Des Moines Register*, April 1935; *Detroit News*, May 19, 1935; *Detroit Free Press*, May 26, 1935; *Los Angeles Times*, June 23, 1935; *Spaulding Official Athletic Almanac for 1936.*

53. *New York Times*, February 23, 1936; *The Amateur Athlete*, April 1936, p. 4; *Detroit Free Press*, May 17, 1936, Sports, p. 1.

54. *Spaulding's Official Athletic Almanac for 1937*, pp. 62–3.

55. *Detroit Free Press*, May 14, 1937, p. 24.

56. *Chicago Daily News*, March 27, 1939, pp. 17–18.

57. Interview with Kenneth "Red" Simmons, July 30, 1998.

58. *AAU Handbook, 1943.*

59. Louis Ruchames, *Race, Jobs, and Politics: The Story of the FEPC*. New York: Columbia University Press, 1953, p. 50.

60. Robert Shogan and Tom Craig, *The Detroit Race Riot: A Study in Violence*. Philadelphia: Chilton Books, 1964, p. 32.

61. Harvard Sitkoff, "The Detroit Race Riot of 1943," *Michigan History*, vol. 53, Fall 1969, p. 188.

62. Shogan and Craig, *op. cit.*, p. 34–89.

63. *Ibid.*, p. 230.

64. See *Detroit Times*, September 24, 1944, part 2, p. 2.

65. *Track and Field News*, September 1955, p. 12;

Chicago Tribune, June 3, 1956, part 2, p. 4; and interviews with his Wayne University track and field teammates at Detroit Track Old-timers Reunion, 1998.

66. *Detroit Free Press*, February 24, 1999, p. 8-B.

67. *New York Times*, July 10, 1972, p. 43.

68. Not all trackmen who became policemen participated on the Department's track team. George Wesson won the Michigan Class A State High School Championship in the 440-yard dash and went unbeaten in 14 starts, while attending Johnson C. Smith College in Charlotte, NC for one semester, before joining the U.S. Navy. See *The Detroit News*, April 4, 1964, p. 3-B. He later ran for Michigan State University before becoming a detective with the Wayne County Sheriff's Department.

Chapter 7

1. *Lockport Union-Sun*, May 21, 1934.

2. *Ibid.*, April 28, 1935.

3. *Detroit News*, February 21, 1934.

4. *Ann Arbor News*, April 20, 1935.

5. *Lockport Union-Sun*, February 28, 1934 and *Detroit News*, February 21, 1934.

6. Interview with Mrs. Evelyn Alix, West Bloomfield Township, Oakland County, Michigan, October 28, 1999.

7. *Ann Arbor News*, January 28, 1934.

8. *Ibid.*, February 5, 1934.

9. *The Michigan Daily*, February 18, 1934.

10. *Ibid.*, February 25, 1934.

11. *Detroit News*, February 21, 1934.

12. *Lockport Union-Sun*, February 28, 1934.

13. *The Michigan Daily*, March 4, 1934.

14. *Detroit News*, March 11, 1934.

15. *Detroit Free Press*, February 29, 1935 and *The Michigan Daily*, March 3, 1935.

16. *Chicago Tribune*, March 11, 1934 and *Michigan Daily*, March 11, 1934, p. 1.

17. *The Michigan Daily*, April 21, 1934.

18. *Ibid.*, May 19, 1934.

19. *Ann Arbor News*, April 20, 1935.

20. *Detroit News*, March 10, 1935.

21. *Detroit Times*, March 25, 1935. The Butler Relays was a major indoor track event held in late March from 1933 through 1942.

22. Autographs collected by Neree Alix enroute to Los Angeles, April 6–7, 1935.

23. Interview with Mrs. Evelyn Alix, October 28, 1999.

24. Itinerary for the University of Michigan Track Team, April 5 to 16, 1935 in Alix scrapbook.

25. *Detroit News*, April 14, 16 and 17, 1935.

26. *Ann Arbor News*, April 18, 1935.

27. Analysis with input from marathon runner Dr. Robert K. Moore, MD, October 1999. In 1935 it was believed that the break resulted from an unusual muscle contraction. See University of Michigan Bentley Library, Athletic Department Box 39, *Track and Field Media Guide, 1937*. This explanation is highly unlikely.

28. *Ann Arbor News*, April 18, 1935.

29. *The Michigan Daily*, April 30, 1935 and *Lockport Union-Sun*, May 15, 1935.

30. *Detroit News*, April 20, 1935 and *Detroit Times*, April 20, 1935.

31. *The Michigan Daily*, April 30, 1935.

32. *Ibid.*, May 1, 1935.

33. *Detroit News*, December 5–6, 1935.

34. *The Michigan Daily*, December 20, 1935.

35. *Detroit News*, December 28, 1935.

36. *Lockport Union-Sun*, March 5, 1937 and *Detroit Free Press*, March 6, 1937, p. 17.

37. University of Michigan Bentley Library, Athletic Department Box 39, *Track and Field Media Guide, 1937*.

38. *Los Angeles Times*, April 17, 1937, Part II, p. 12.

39. In a duel meet with the University of Illinois in Champaign on May 15, 1937 all three Michigan two-milers finished together in a show of solidarity. See *Detroit Free Press*, May 16, 1937 p. 2-Sports Section.

40. *Los Angeles Times*, July 4, 1937, Part II, p. 12.

41. *Lockport Union-Sun*, May 13, 1937.

42. *Detroit News*, April 18, 1942.

43. *Kansas City Star*, November 23, 1942 and interview with Mrs. Neree Alix, Oct 28, 1999.

44. *The Inter-Lake News*, January 28, 1954; March 28, 1963, p. 17; *Pontiac Press*, March 20, 1956, p. 22.

45. *The Inter-Lake News*, January 28, 1954 and May 5, 1956.

46. *Ibid.*, March 13, 1954.

47. *Detroit News*, July 10, 1963; *Pontiac Press*, July 10, 1963, p. 1 and August 8, 1963, p. 1, and *The Inter-Lake News*, July 29, 1964.

48. *The Birmingham Eccentric*, August 15, 1963, p. 3-A, incorrectly referred to Neree as Tony.

49. *Birmingham Observer and Eccentric*, December 2, 1978.

50. *The Oakland Press*, December 1, 1978, p. B-3 and *Birmingham Observer and Eccentric*, December 2, 1978.

51. *NCAA Track and Field Official Handbook, Rules and Records*. New York: American Sports Publishing Co., 1934, p. 96.

52. See *Detroit Times*, May 23, 1931.

53. *Detroit Times*, May 24, 1931, part 2, p. 1.

54. *Spaulding's Official Athletic Almanac for 1931*, p. 18 and *The Amateur Athlete*, January 1932, p. 13.

55. *The Milwaukee Journal*, June 12, 1932, 11.

56. *Chicago Tribune*, July 3, 1932, part 2, p. 4.

57. *The Milwaukee Journal*, July 14, 1932, p.6.

58. *Ibid.*, July 17, 1932, p.2.

59. *Detroit News*, June 2, 1935, Sports, p. 4.

60. *The Amateur Athlete*. November 1933, p.3.

61. *Detroit News, April 30, 1933* and the *90th* Annual Drake Relays Program, April 23–24, 1999, p. 94.

62. *Ibid.*, May 11, 1933, p. 32.

63. *The Michigan Daily*, May 20, 1933, p. 1.

64. *Detroit News*, May 21, 1933 and *Chicago Tribune*, May 21, 1933.

65. *The Grand Rapids Press*, May 25, 1933, p. 22.

66. *Chicago Tribune*, June 18, 1933.

67. *NCAA Track and Field Official Handbook. 1933*. New York: American Sports Publishing Co., 1934, p. 7.

68. *Detroit Free Press*, May 20, 1934.

69. Canham, *cp. cit.*, p. 187–8.

70. *Detroit Free Press*, August 10, 1999, p. 7A.

71. *The Michigan Daily*, March 3, 1935, p. 1.

72. Archives, University of Michigan.

73. *Ibid.*

74. "Blacks in Detroit," *Detroit Free Press*, December 1980.

75. Alexander Keyssar, *The Right to Vote: The Con-*

tested History of Democracy in the United States. New York: Basic Books, 2000; and J. Williams, *op. cit.*, pp. 93–112.

76. *Detroit News*, June 2, 1935, Sports, p. 4.

77. *Ibid.*, December 31, 1983, p. 7A.

78. *Ibid.*, December 31, 1983, p. 7A.

79. Letter from Barbara Woodstra, July 29, 1998.

80. Undated news clipping found in the Woodstra scrapbook. June 4–5, 1938 he tied the IC4A record for the 120-yard high-hurdles (14.4) at the Eastern Intercollegiate [IC4A] Championships, New York City. *Intercollegiate Association of Amateur Athletes of America Official Handbook, 1940*. New York American Sports Publishing Company, 1940, p. 121.

81. *Grand Rapids Herald*, June 5, 1938 and Michigan State College Commencement Bulletin, June 13, 1936.

82. Undated news clipping in the Woodstra scrapbook.

83. Donald H. Woodstra was inducted into U. S. Army in April 1941. He was sent to Officers Training School, and received his commission in February 1943. Shortly after that he was shipped to North Africa and served under George Patton. He was awarded a Silver Star for gallantry in action on the Italian battlefront. Later, he made Captain and was wounded in action. After the war, Don went back to work for Michigan Lithography. He became President of Modern Lithography before retiring. For Paul's war record see Michigan State University Archives, UA 10.2, folder box 434, folder 3, Alumni records, 1947.

84. *Michigan Hall of Honor* Booklet, October 21, 1983.

85. University of Michigan Bentley Library, Athletic Department Box 2, 1937 Track and Field Media Guide.

86. *New York Times*, July 5, 1936.

87. *University of Michigan Track and Field Guide*, 1937.

88. *The Michigan Daily*, February 14, 1937 and *Indianapolis Star*, March 24, 1937.

89. Quercetani, *op. cit.*, 1964, pp. 189.

90. *Los Angeles Times*, June 20, 1937.

91. *Michigan Hall of Honor* Booklet, October 21, 1983.

92. *Detroit Free Press*, February 6, 1940, p. 17.

93. Reports that Coach Holmes picked Tolmich out of a gym glass made in the *Detroit Free Press*, May 16, 1937, Sports Section, p. 6 are untrue according to Allan Tolmich in an interview, October 31, 1999.

94. "Olympic Games Program Hurts 2 Detroit Athletes," by John McManis, *The Detroit News*, June 5, 1936, p. 28.

95. *Detroit News*, May 24, 1936, p. 1.

96. *Detroit Free Press*, May 16, 1937, p. 11. For more on the Spanish Civil War, see Stanley G. Payne, *Spain's First Democracy: The Second Republic, 1931–36*. Madison, Ws: The University of Wisconsin Press, 1993.

97. Interview with Bob Luby March 25, 1998.

98. *Detroit Free Press*, May 13, 1937, p. 24.

99. *Ibid.*, March 14, 1937.

100. *Detroit Free Press*, March 21, 1937, p. 3-Sports Section.

101. *Ibid.*, April 18, 1937, p. 3.

102. *Ibid.*, April 24, 1937, p. 6.

103. *Los Angeles Times*, June 17, 1937, Part II, p.

13 and interview with Al Tolmich, October 31, 1999.

104. *Ibid.*, July 16, 1937, Part II, p. 12.

105. *Ibid.*, and June 19, 1937, Part II, p. 13.

106. *Ibid.*, June 20, 1937, Part II, p. 14.

107. *Ibid.*, July 2, 1937, Part I, p. 14 and July 4, 1937, Part II, p. 7.

108. *Spaulding's Official Athletic Almanac for 1938*, p. 8.

109. *The Amateur Athlete*, February, 1938, p. 3. Forrest "Spec" Towns became the head track coach at the University if Georgia after World War II. See *Atlanta Journal*, May 23, 1972, p. 3-D.

110. Interview with Allan Tolmich October 31, 1999.

111. See *Amateur Athlete*, August 1937, p. 5.

112. *Spaulding's Official Athletic Almanac for 1939*, p. 8–9 and *Spaulding's Official Athletic Almanac for 1940*, p. 6–7.

113. Bernard Postal, Jesse Silver, and Roy Silver, *Encyclopedia of Jews in Sports*. New York: Bioch Publishing Co., 1965, p. 486, 490–1, 496.

114. Interview with Allan Tolmich, October 31, 1999.

115. *Millrose Games Program*, February 3, 1940, p. 12.

116. *Detroit Free Press*, February 6, 1940, p. 17.

117. See *Detroit Times*, February 11, 1940.

118. *Ibid.*, February 22, 1940, p. 22.

119. *Detroit Free Press*, February 25, 1940, Sports p. 1.

120. *Spaulding's Official Athletic Almanac for 1941*, p. 4; and *Cleveland Plain Dealer*, March 16, 1941.

121. *Michigan Daily*, March 5, 1939, p. 7.

122. *Detroit Free Press*, March 7, 1937, Sports Section, p. 4.

123. *Ibid.*, May 9, 1937, Sport Section, p. 7.

124. *Grand Rapids Press*, June 18, 1934.

125. *Detroit Free Press*, May 9, 1937, Sport Section, p. 7.

126. *Ibid.*, March 7, 1937, Sports Section, p. 4.

127. *Ibid.*

128. *Ibid.*

129. *Los Angeles Times*, June 27, 1937, p. 12.

130. *Detroit Free Press*, May 24, 1939, p. 22.

131. *The Michigan Daily*, March 5, 1939, p. 7.

132. *Ibid.*, April 25, 1939, p. 3.

133. *Detroit Free Press*, May 1, 1939, p. 14.

134. *University of Michigan Track and Field Media Guide, 1940*.

135. *Detroit Free Press*, June 1, 1940, Sports, p. 6.

136. *Ibid.*, February 6, 1940, p. 17.

137. See Frank Zarnowski, *Olympic Glory Denied: A Final Opportunity for Glory Restored*. Glendale Publishing, 1996, pp. 237–137. *Spaulding's Official Athletic Almanac for 1941*, p. 4; *Grand Rapids Press*, June 17, 1940, p. 10.

138. Interviews with Aaron Gordon and Ken "Red" Simmons, 1998 and Behee, *op. cit.*; Zarnowski, *op. cit.*, pp. 147–48.

139. *Detroit Free Press*, March 3, 1973 and an interview with K. "Red" Simmons, July 30, 1998.

Chapter 8

1. The medieval Christian Church had an uncompromising, non-pluralistic, and intolerant view of the moral basis of society. It held that

because of the defiant opposition to the otherwise universally accepted concept of God, the Jews had violated the moral order of the world. The very existence of the Jewish religion defiled all that was sacred, and the Jew was the self-willed agent of the Devil. For more on this subject see Daniel Jonah Goldhagen, *Hitler's Willing Executioners: Ordinary Germans and the Holocaust.* New York: Alfred A. Knopf, 1996, Chapter 2 and Joshua Trachtenberg, *The Devil and the Jews: The Medieval Conception of the Jew and Its Relation to Modern Anti-Semitism.* Philadelphia: Jewish Publication Society of America, 1983.

2. Stanley G. Payne, *Spain's First Democracy: The Second Republic, 1931–1936.* Madison: University of Wisconsin Press, 1993, p. 6, 12, 45.

3. *Ibid.,* p. 3.

4. *Ibid.,* p. 46–8, 379–80.

5. Patrick J. Buchanan, *A Republic Not an Empire.* Washington, D.C.: Regnery Publishing, Inc., 1999, p. 276. The practices of the Stalin era that included terrorism, forced labor and concentration camps fueled these concerns. See Anne Applebaum, "Inside the Gulag," *The New York Review of Books,* Volume XLVII, No. 10, June 15, 2000, pp. 33–35; and "Stalin's Henchman [Lavrenty Beria] Deserved to Die: Court," *Canadian National Post,* May 30, 2000, p. A14. In 1936–37 both the Catholic Church and the British government went to great lengths to avoid seeing the dangers of the Fascist threat in Spain. In December 1936 they chose to turn a blind eye when Nazi Germany sent arms to Franco marked "Christmas Decorations" in violation of neutrality declarations. See Jill Edwards, *The British Government and the Spanish Civil War, 1936–1939.* London, 1979, p. 47.

6. William L. Shirer, *The Rise and Fall of the Third Reich.* New York: Simon and Schuster, 1960, p. 38, 43.

7. Goldhagen, *op. cit.,* p. 42, 53–5.

8. *Ibid.,* p. 3.

9. John Cornwell, *Hitler's Pope.* New York: Viking Press, 1999, p. 166. Michael Phayer, *The Catholic Church and the Holocaust, 1930–1965.* Bloomington, IN: Indiana University Press, 2000 for the record of the Church's role in the holocaust beyond that of Pius XII. Without effective Church leadership, Catholic clergy acted ambiguously, some saved Jews, others helped murder them, and the majority simply stood by while the murder of Jews and gypsies took place. Also see, Susan Zuccotti, *Under His Very Windows: The Vatican and the Holocaust in Italy.* New York: Yale U Press, 2001.

10. Siegfried, *op. cit.,* p. 3 and 15.

11. U. S. Department of Commerce, Bureau of the Census, *Religious Bodies: 1936,* volume I. Washington, D.C.: U. S. Printing Office, 1941, pp. 17–22.

12. *Ibid.,* pp. 35, 44, 51, and 55.

13. *Ibid.,* pp. 67, 72, and 395.

14. Bob Greene, "Some Rays of Light in a Darkened World," *Michigan Jewish History,* volume 39, fall 1999, p. 20. Anti-Semitism in the USA was pervasive. A series of polls from 1938 to 1946 indicated that over half of the American population perceived Jews as greedy, overly aggressive, and dishonest. About 45% said they would support an anti-Jewish movement. See *Jews in the Mind of America.* (ed.) Charles Stember (1966), pp. 53–62.

15. *Detroit Jewish News,* December 31, 1999, pp. 18–19.

16. Conot, *American Odyssey,* pp. 153–155.

17. *Ibid.,* pp. 207–210.

18. Keith McClellan, "The Morrison Electric: Iowa's First Automobile," *Annals of Iowa,* Vol. XXXVI, No. 8, Spring 1963, pp. 561–568; and Keith McClellan, unpublished manuscript on the automobiles exhibited at the World Columbian Exhibition, 1964.

19. Daniel J. Boorstin, *The Americans: The National Experience.* New York: Random House, 1965, pp. 30–34.

20. Keith McClellan, "A History of Chicago's Industrial Development," *Mid-Chicago Economic Development Study,"* Vol. III. Center for Urban Studies, University of Chicago, Mayor's Committee for Economic Development, February, 1966, pp. 22–24.

21. J. V. Compton, *The Swastika and the Eagle: Germany's Myopic View of America in the Fatal Years Before World War II.* Boston: Houghton Mifflin Co., 1967, pp. 7–9, 19.

22. William L. Shirer, *The Rise and Fall of the Third Reich,* 1960, p. 149. One does not have to look far to find continuing evidence of the popularity of Hitler's message. In November 1999, *Mien Kampf* was one of the most popular books in Germany, despite a law banning its publication and sale in the country, according to Amazon. Com and the German, publishing giant Bertelsmann. See *Detroit Jewish News,* December 3, 1999, p. 97.

23. *The Detroit News,* January 31, 1999, p. 14A. For more information see the writings of University of Michigan medical historian Martin Pernick.

24. Greene, *op. cit.,* p.20.

25. Cornwell, *op. cit.,* p. 331. It should be recognized that in contrast to Bishop Sheen and the others listed, the liberal Catholic weekly *Commonweal* spoke out in favor of opening America to Jewish refugees before Pearl Harbor, when such support was rare.

26. Doris Kearns Goodwin, *No Ordinary Time.* New York: Simon & Schuster, 1994, p. 164 and PBS, The American Experience: Eleanor Roosevelt, January 10, 2000.

27. Philip A. Klinkner with Roger M. Smith, *The Unsteady March: The Rise and Decline of Racial Equality.* Chicago: University of Chicago Press, 1999, pp. 138–139.

28. *The Coldwater Daily Reporter,* August 8, 1936, p. 2.

29. Lynching owes its name to Charles Lynch, a Virginia farmer who administered a rough justice to outlaws and Tories during the American Revolution. From 1882 to 1968 the U.S. Bureau of the Census recorded the lynching of 4,742 blacks, often as the result of little more than the suspicion of some crime or act of perceived act of disrespect. See *New York Times,* February 13, 2000, section 4, p. 3. When the song "Strange Fruit," with its haunting lyrics about lynching, was written in the late 1930s, there was only one integrated night club in New York City. See David Margolick, *Strange Fruit: Billie Holiday, Café Society and An Early Cry for Civil Rights.* New York: Running Press, 2000.

30. For more on this subject see Joseph W. Bendersky, *The "Jewish Threat": Anti-Semitic Policies of the American Army.* Cambridge, MA: Basic Books, 2000.

31. Ulysses Lee, *The United States Army in World War II, Special Studies: The Employment of Negro Troops.*

Washington, D.C.: Government Printing Office, 1966, p. 44.

32. Klinkner with Smith, *op. cit.*, pp. 152–4: and Goodwin, *op. cit.*, p. 165.

33. *Ibid.*, p. 149–150.

34. *Ibid.*, p. 159.

35. "Adidas," *International Directory of Company Histories*. Editor, Tina Grant. Detroit: St. James Press, 1996. Volume 14, Pp. 6–9.

36. Margaret Lambert, "A Jewish Athlete and the Nazi Olympics of '36," *New York Times*, February 3, 1980, p. V-2.)

37. *New York Times*, Obituaries, June 6, 1999, p. 50.

38. Cornwell, *op. cit.* P. 166. It should be noted that Cardinal Pacelli's Reich Concordat also left some Roman Catholic priests, such as the Rev. Josef Spieker of Cologne in harm's way. After delivering a sermon in October 1934 declaring that "Germany has only one Fuehrer. That is Christ," Spieker was arrested, jailed, acquitted at a trial for insufficient evidence, immediately rearrested and placed in solitary confinement, before being sent to a concentration camp. In 1936 he was retried for abusing his religious office, found guilty and sentenced to 15 months in prison. In 1937 he was deported to Chile. All of this happened without intervention by the Catholic Church hierarchy on his behalf. See Eric A. Johnson, *Nazi Terror*. New York: Basic Books, 2000.

For more on German-Jewish sports clubs see, Arnd Kruger, "Once the Olympics a through, we'll beat up the Jew": German Jewish Sports 1898–1938," *Journal of Sport History*, vol. 26, no. 2, Summer 1999, pp. 353–375.

39. *Detroit News*, April 22, 1927, p. 47; and *Current Biography, 1948*, p. 79.

40. An original copy of the Nuremberg Laws with Hitler's signature is available at the Huntington Library in Pasadena, CA. Also see *New York Times*, July 4, 1999, Section 4, p. 7 for the exact wording of the laws.

41. Kruger, *op. cit.*, p. 357.

42. *The Toronto Globe*, July 16, 1935, p. 1.

43. Duff Hart-Davis, *Hitler's Games: The 1936 Olympics* New York: Harper & Row, Publishers, 1986.

44. *New York Times*, February 21, 1999, Section 8, pp. 1 and 10.

45. *Current Biography, 1948*, p. 75.

46. *Ibid.*, p. 111.

47. William J. Baker, *Jesse Owens: An American Life*. New York: The Free Press, 1986, p. 50, 63.

48. *Ibid.*, pp. 69–71.

49. Best in the USA. See *Spaulding's Official Athletic Almanac for 1931*, p. 18.

50. *Milwaukee Journal*, June 28, 1936, Sports, p. 1.

51. Krise and Squires, *op. cit.*, pp. 6–7.

52. "Nigger", "jiggaboo", and "crow" were common derogatory names. William Randolph Hearst's Detroit newspaper, *The Detroit Times*, on occasion referred to African-Americans as coons. For example, see *Detroit Times*, April 24, 1925, p. 29. Hearst had pro-fascist views, and even paid Adolf Hitler and Benito Mussolini to write special articles promoting their views in his newspapers. See David Nasaw, *The Chief: The Life of William Randolph Hearst*. New York: Houghton Mifflin, 2000. Ironically, as the magnitude of the Jewish holocaust was beginning to be under-

stood, the Hearst newspapers rallied to support of the last remnants of European Jewry, declaring that the Hearst newspapers "have always been the fore of the nation's press in exposing the unfortunate plight of the Jews." See *Detroit Sunday Times*, September 10, 1944, part 1, p. 10. Hearst also held strong anti-Asian views which influenced reporting on Asian-Americans. See Thomas C. Leonard, "Hearst 101," *Columbia Journalism Review*, July/August 2000, pp. 54–55.

53. Carlson and Fogarty, *op. cit.*, p. 146.

54. Charles H. Williams, "Negro Athletes in the Eleventh Olympiad," *The Southern Workman*, LXVI (1937), pp. 45–59.

55. *The Coldwater Daily Reporter*, July 30, 1936, p. 6.

56. Carlson and Fogarty, *op. cit.*, p. 150.

57. *Report of the American Olympic Committee: Games of the XIth Olympiad, Berlin, Germany, August 1–16, 1936* (Edited by Frederick W. Rubien). New York: American Olympic Committee, 1937, p. 5.

58. Carlson and Fogarty, *op. cit.*, p. 152.

59. *Ibid., p. 150–154.*

60. Harry Edwards, *The Revolt of the Black Athlete*. New York: The Free Press, 1969, p. 171–4.

61. Carlson and Fogarty, *op. cit.*, p. 129.

62. Baker, *op. cit.*, p. 102–103.

63. *Ibid.*, p. 45.

64. Johnson, *op. cit.*, p. 177–184. Also see April 12, 1933 correspondence between Sigfrid Edstrom, an IOC member, and Avery Brundage for evidence of the anti-Semitic views of these two IOC members. Brundage Papers, Archives, University of Illinois.

65. *The Coldwater Daily, August 8, 1936, p. 2.* Marty Glickman contended that he had learned that Brundage "believed that it was enough humiliation for Germany to have black Americans winning gold medals, but having Jews on the gold medal victory stand was too much." See *New York Times*, January 7, 2001, p. 25.

66. Carlson and Fogarty, *op. cit.*, p. 171. Lawson Robertson participated in the 1906 Olympics in Athens. He tied for second in the standing high jump, placed third in the standing long jump, and fifth in the pentathlon. See Wallechinsky, *op. cit.*, pp. 182–3, 186.

67. *Detroit Free Press*, April 25, 1937 and *Los Angeles Times*, June 17, 1937, Part II, p. 13.

68. *Detroit Free Press*, March 7, 1937.

69. *Spaulding's Official Athletic Almanac for 1938*, p. 9.

70. *The Amateur Athlete*, February 1938, p. 3.

71. *Millrose Games Program*, February 3, 1940, p. 12.

72. Marty Glickman with Stan Isaac, *The Fastest Kid on the Block*. Syracuse: Syracuse University Press, 1996, p. 33. Marty Glickman died on January 3, 2001 at Lenox Hill Hospital in New York at age 83.

73. Letter from C. S. Bartlett to Lee M. Bartlett, July 22, 1936 and interviews with his daughter is Cheryl Proctor on August 29 and September 27, 1998.

74. Letter from Lee F. Kinney of Union City to Lee M. Bartlett, July 15, 1936.

75. *Milwaukee Journal*, June 27, 1936, p. 8 and June 28, 1936, Sports, p.1–3.

76. Luis Bolin, "Flight Into History," *Reader's Digest*, 1958, pp. 120–125.

77. Alan Bullock, *Hitler, A Study in Tyranny*. New York: Harper & Row, 1962 (1964), p. 349–50. See Richard Whelan, *Robert Capa: A Biography*. New York: Alfred A. Knopf, 1985 for details on the fighting in Spain.

78. Battle Creek *The Enquirer News* August 30, 1936.

79. *Coldwater Daily Reporter*, September 3, 1936, p. 1.

80. Johnson, *op. cit.*, p. 28–29.

81. Adolf Hitler, "Schlussrede auf dem Reichsparteitag 1937."

82. Richard D. Mandell, *The Nazi Olympics*. New York: The Macmillan Company, 1971, p. 291–2.

83. *Toledo Blade*, May 14, 1978, p. D5.

84. Stuart Cameron [United Press Sports Editor], "Four Thousand Athletes . . .", *The Coldwater Daily Reporter*, July 31, 1936, p. 8.

85. *The Coldwater Daily Reporter*, July 30, 1936, p. 6.

86. A. Scott Berg, *Lindbergh*. New York: G. P. Putnam's Sons, 1998, p. 361–362. Lindbergh's mother grew up in Detroit, graduated from Detroit Central High School and the University of Michigan (1899), and taught at Cass Technical High School from 1923 through 1942.

87. *Coldwater Daily Reporter* September 17, 1936, p. 1.

88. In 1943 Lee married Durstha Eleanor Buller, who was a few years younger. Durstha had been born into a railroad worker's family in Sturgus, Michigan. She lived in Union City during her school years, and then moved with her family to Three Rivers, Michigan. Lee and Durstha had Lee Marion Bartlett, Jr. in 1947 Lee Jr. live in Dayton, Ohio in 1999. Their daughter Cheryl was born in 1952. Lee Bartlett owned a summer cottage on Union Lake near Union City, and spent summers there from 1940 forward. Lee died on Halloween day 1972: Durstha died in 1977.

Lee Bartlett's Albion school record for the javelin throw (216–9) held up until April 11, 1987, when Dan Pekrul from Saline, Michigan established a new Albion College record with a throw of 219–4 at the Northwestern Relays. On May 29, 1987 Pekrul won the NCAA Division III national championship in Naperville, Illinois for the javelin with a throw of 223–5. See *Battle Creek Enquirer*, Sunday May 31, 1987, p. 5C. Pekrul, a physical education major, was especially happy that he broke the record after the javelin was changed. Under the new rules, the javelin does not fly as far as it did before the rule change, since they moved the center of mass back on the javelin, changing the weight distribution, thus shortening the length of throws for world-class javelin athletes.

89. *The Michigan Daily*, February 26, 1939, p. 1. It also should be noted thatin Germany on November 9–10, 1938, Kristallnacht, "the Night of Broken Glass," 7,500 Jewish-owned shop were looted, 192 synagogues were burned, 171 apartments in which Jews lived were burned, and 36 Jews were killed. See Jacob Shtull, *Kristallnacht Reader: Essays and Addresses*, 1983.

90. *Michigan Daily*, February 24, 1939, p. 1.

91. *New York Times*, June 7, 1986, p. 49.

92. Jack Scott, *Athletics for Athletes*. Oakland, Ca.: Other Ways Press, 1969.

93. Mandell, *op. cit.*, p. xii-xiii.

94. *Ibid.*, p. xi, xiv.

95. Note that Archie Williams hurt his leg in Sweden and ruined his track career. Carlson and Fogarty, *op. cit.*, p. 156.

96. Jesse Owens also had an infant son. *Coldwater Daily Reporter*, July 31, 1936, p. 8.

97. Baker, *op. cit.*, pp. 133–135.

98. *Coldwater Daily Reporter*, September 3, 1936, p. 1.

99. *Los Angeles Times*, June 1, 1997, p. C-6.

100. Personal recollections, Keith McClellan and conversations with Dr. Walter U. Miller, MD.

101. Mack died March 12, 2000. His wife of 45 years survived him, and was interviewed on National Public Radio, March 15, 2000.

102. For more on this subject see Maurice Isserman and Michael Kazin, *America Divided*. New York: Oxford University Press, 2000.

103. For more on this issue see Neal Gabler, *An Empire of Their Own: How the Jews Invented Hollywood*. Also see the 1998 A & E film, "Hollywoodism, Jewish Moguls, and the American Dream."

Chapter 9

1. London's Amateur Athletic Club (AAC) was later transformed into the British Amateur Athletic Association. The Henley rule got its name because it was first used in the Henley Regatta.

2. Young, *op. cit.*, p. 41.

3. *Ibid.*, pp. 61 and 193.

4. See David C.Young, *Olympic Myth of Greek Amateur Athletics*. Chicago: Ares Publishers, 1984, pp. 18–26.

5. Slosson, *op. cit.*, p. 271.

6. *Detroit News*, June 24, 1978, p. 2B. This subject is discussed more thoroughly in Chapter 16.

7. *Detroit Free Press*, June 28, 1895, p. 7.

8. *Ibid.*, July 3, 1895, p. 7.

9. *Track and Field News*, October 1963, p. 9.

10. *Spalding's Official Athletic Almanac, 1928*. New York: American Sports Publishing Co., 1928, pp. 127–130.

11. *The Amateur Athlete*, January, 1934, p. 15.

12. *Ibid.*, p. 15.

13. Each school enters one athlete each per event, making four entrants.

14. *Track and Field News*, October 1963, p. 9.

15. It should be noted that as late as 1999 applicants from private schools with the same qualifications as those from state schools were 25 times more likely to gain admission to Oxford and Cambridge. Despite educating only 7% of the children of the United Kingdom, private schools supplied 52% of all entrants to Oxford in 1999. See *New York Times*, June 3, 2000, p. A25, and Andrew Adonis and Stephen Pollard, *A Class Act: The Myth of Britain's Classless Society*. London: Hamish Hamilton, 1997.

16. *The Amateur Athlete*, December 1935, p. 6.

17. Johnson, *op. cit.*, p. 78–88; *Current Biography, 1948*, p. 75 and Hanley, *op. cit.*, p. 26.

18. *Current Biography, 1948*, p. 81.

19. *Ibid.*, p. 83.

20. *Current Biography, 1948*, p. 83.

21. *Ibid.*, p. 83.

22. Johnson, *op. cit.*, p. 82.

23. *Chicago Tribune*, June 24, 1933, p. 17.
24. *Detroit Free Press*, March 27, 1937, p. 13.
25. *The Michigan Daily, March 6, 1945*, p. 3.
26. Carlson and Fogarty, *op. cit.*, p. 338–9.
27. Johnson, *op. cit.*, 1972, p. 82.
28. *Current Biography, 1948*, p. 85.
29. *Ibid.*, p. 77.
30. *Detroit News*, April 29, 1932, p. 33.
31. Johnson, *op. cit.*, 1972, p. 78.
32. *Current Biography, 1948*, p. 75.
33. Aljean Harmetz, "A Star Sprinter Looks Back to '24," *New York Times*, August 9, 1984, p. B15.
34. *AAU Official Track and Field Handbook, 1945*. New York: The Amateur Athletic Union, 1945, p. 173.
35. Krise and Squires, *op. cit.*, p.46.
36. Interview with Kenneth "Red" Simmons, 1998.

Chapter 10

1. Goodwin, *op. cit.*, p. 63.
2. Michael J. Bennett, *When Dreams Came True: The G. I. Bill and the Marking of Modern America*. Washington, D.C. Brassey's Inc., 1996, p. 20, 171, and 242.
3. Telephone interview with Roy Fehr, April 26, 1998.
4. *Detroit News*, May 18, 1934.
5. *The Oak, May 1935*, Royal Oak High School Yearbook, p. 7, 25.
6. Morgantown newspaper clipping in the Woodstra collection, March 27, 1937.
7. *The* [Lansing] *State Journal*, April 24, 30, 1937.
8. *Ibid.*, May 14 and 15, 1937. P.31.
9. *Intercollegiate Association of Amateur Athletes of America 1939 Guide*. New York: American Sports Publishing Co., 1939, p. 73.
10. *Official NCAA Track and Field Guide, 1939*. New York: American Sports Publishing Co., 1939, p. 111.
11. Telephone interview with Roy Fehr, April 26, 1998.
12. Held on February 14, 1940.
13. Walter Arrington was the only African-American on the Michigan State College track team in 1940.
14. For performance data see Lyman L. Frimodig and Fred W. Stabley, *Spartan Saga: A History of Michigan State Athletics*. East Lansing, MSU, 1971, p. 207–209, 216. Roy was a member of the American Institute of Chemical Engineers, the Varsity Club, the track team, and the cross-country team. See *1940 Wolverine*. Yearbook for Michigan State College, 1940.
15. See Michigan State University Archives, UA 10.2, folder box 434, folder 3, Alumni records, 1947.
16. See *George A. Dondero High School Alumni Directory 1997* (Norfolk, VA: Bernard C. Harris Publishing Co., 1997, p. 68.
17. Interview with Dorothy Lamont Fehr, April 26, 1998.
18. Telephone Interview with Roy and Dorothy Fehr, April 26, 1998.
19. See *The Michigan Daily, March 8, 1942, p. 3* and *Michiganensian, 1916*, pp. 326–330.
20. *Chicago Daily News*, March 24, 1941, p. 20.
21. *The Michigan Daily*, February 21, 1942, p. 3;

February 28, 1942, p. 3; March 8, 1942, p. 3; and "Nazis Exterminate Jews," *Chicago Daily News*, March 16, 1942, p. 4.: Chicago Relay Results, *Chicago Daily News*, March 21, 1942, p. 19. For more on Jewish extermination and U.S. knowledge of these efforts during this period see David S. Wyman, *The Abandonment of the Jews*. New York: Pantheon Books, 1984, pp. 19–41.
22. *Des Moines Register*, April 26, 1942; *Detroit Free Press*, May 17, 1942, part 2, p. 4. and Canham, *op. cit.*, 1996, p. 144–50.
23. *Chicago Tribune*, February 14, 1943, part 2, p. 1–2; March 7, 1943 Part 2, p. 3.; Official *NCAA Track and Field Guide, 1944*. New York: American Sports Publishing Co., 1944. For 1943 Penn Relay results see *Detroit Times*, April 25, 1943, part 2, p. 3.
24. *Track and Field News*, March 1950, p. 6; and *AAU Official Track and Field Handbook, 1945*, New York: The Amateur Athletic Union, 1945, p. 10 for All-American status, and 40 for 600-yard AAU indoor championship.
25. See *Chicago Daily News*, March 20, 1944, p. 16 for relay results.
26. *The Michigan Daily*, March 6, 1945, p.3.
27. Canham, *op. cit.*, p. 144–50. Ufer was on the Board of Directors of Don Canham's company, School-Tech Inc., from 1960 to 1981.
28. *New York Times*, February 4, 1945; *Chicago Daily News*, March 16, 1945, p. 30, March 17, 1945, p. 10, and March 19, 1945, p. 17. *The Michigan Daily*, March 24, 1946, p.3. For more on Ross see *Michiganensian, 1947*, p. 122.
29. James Greenleaf Umstattd, *The Odyssey of Jim Umstattd*. Austin, Texas: The Whitley Company, 1977.
30. *Ibid.*
31. *Detroit Free Press*, June 11, 1939.
32. *Ibid.*, June 4, 1938.
33. *Official NCAA Handbook for Track and Field, 1936*. New York: American Sports Publishing Co., 1939, p. 126.
34. *Detroit Free Press* June 18, 1939.
35. Joe B. Frantz, *The Forty-Acre Follies*. Austin, Texas: Texas Monthly Press, Inc., 1983.
36. *Detroit Times*, April 28, 1941, p. 19.
37. Bentsen was a future U.S Senator, Secretary of the Treasury, and vice-presidential candidate. Dolph Briscoe was a future Governor. Mac was a member of the Pi Kappa Alpha fraternity, the T-Association, the Student Association, Phi Beta Kappa, and the track team. See *The Cactus, 1942* University of Texas Student Publications, Inc., 1942.
38. Archives, University of Texas.
39. Catherine Houston graduated from Austin H S, attended Mount Vernon College in Washington, D.C., and earned a BA from the University of Texas. The couple was married at St. David's Episcopal Church on January 10, 1945.
40. Archives, University of Texas.
41. *Austin American Statesman*, March 16, 1988.
42. See *1939–40 Directory Michigan State College*. Published by NWS, 1939 and *1940–41 Directory*.
43. Federal Works Agency, Works Projects Administration, *Cosmopolitan Education: A History of Hamtramck High School*. Detroit: Inland Press, 1940, p. 42.
44. *The National Directory of High School Coaches*,

1980–81 edition. Edited by John Allen Dees. Montgomery, Alabama: Athletic Publishing Co., 1980, p. 236.

45. Information from a telephone interview with Bob Wingo, April 9, 1998.

46. Archives, Wayne State University, New Detroit profile. Interview with Irving Petross, June 1998.

47. *AAU Official Track and Field Handbook*. New York: The Amateur Athletic Union, 1948, p.44.

48. *Track and Field News*, vol. 1, no. 2, March 1948, p.1.

49. *Track and Field News*, December 1948, p. 8.

50. 7.45 meters.

51. *Track and Field News*, August 1948, p. 4.

52. Red Smith, *The Red Smith Reader*. New York: Random House, 1982, pp. 21–23.

53. Interviews with Irving Petross, Allan Tellis, and Bob Wingo.

54. For more on the origins of African track programs see John Bale and Joe Sang, *Kenyan Running*. Newbury Park, Essex, UK: Frank Cass Publishers, 1997. For coaching assignments see, *The National Directory of High School Coaches*, 1965 edition. Edited by Cliff Harper. Washington, D.C.: Athletic Publishing Co., 1965, p. 152–3.

55. Bennett, *op. cit.*, p. 192, 242.

57. *Ibid.*, p. 24, 280, and 287.

58. There is a "substantial body of empirical evidence that a racially diverse student body promotes racial tolerance, improves academic performance, breaks down barriers among individuals of different races, and contributes to the robust exchange of ideas." See *NEA Today: The Magazine of the National Education Association*, vol. 18, no. 3, November 1999, p.20.

59. *The Detroit Times*, April 24, 1949, part 3, page 2.

60. *Ibid.*, May 1, 1949, part 3, page 1.

61. *Bee Gee News*, May 16, 1950, p. 4.

62. L. Wright graduated from Wayne University in 1951.

63. Robert Wingo graduated from Wayne in 1947.

64. Interview with Irving Petross. June 25, 1997.

65. *Chicago Tribune*, February 9, 1947, Part 2, p. 1.

66. See *Amateur Athlete*, June 1947, p. 13.

67. *Track and Field News*, February 1949.

68. *Ibid.*, December 1949, p. 3.

69. *Ibid.*, August 1949, p.8. For more on Johnson see *Wolverine, 1950*, p. 300.

70. Godner Nelson, "Track Talk," *Track and Field News*, April 1950, p. 4.

Chapter 11

1. Sidney Glazer, *Detroit: A Study in Urban Development*. New York: Bookman Publishing Co., 1965, p. 78.

2. "Americans First: How the People of Detroit are Making Americans of Foreigners, 1916," *Detroit*. Edited by Melvin G. Holli. New York: New Viewpoints-Division of Franklin Watts, 1976, p. 135.

3. See David A. Levine, *Internal Combustion: The Races in Detroit, 1915–26*. Westport, Conn.: Greenwood Press, 1976, pp. 26–27.

4. John Reginald Belleffeur, *Higher Education for the Many: The Realization and Abridgment of Extended Educational Access, in Detroit and at Wayne University, 1917–1961*. Ph. D. dissertation, Department of Education, University of Michigan, 1981, p. 29–30.

5. Robert Conot, *American Odyssey: A Unique History of America Told Through the Life of a Great City*. New York: William Morrow & Co. 1974, p. 83.

6. Don Lochbiler, *Detroit's Coming of Age*. Detroit: The Detroit News-Wayne State University Press, 1973, pp. 273–276.

7. *Ibid.*, p. 64–66.

8. Belleffeur, *op. cit.*, 1981, p. 238.

9. Much of information about Coach Holmes came from interviews with his son David L. Holmes, Jr. on May 31, 1998 and July 28, 1999 and his paper "A Coaches' Son: Growing Up in the Ethos of Muscular Christianity and Amateur Athletics in Detroit." Presented at the North American Association of Sports Historians, University of Windsor, Windsor, Ontario, May 31, 1998.

10. Detroit Junior College later became City College of Detroit. See Wayne State University, Athletic Hall of Fame Induction Ceremony Program, 1976 and 1987.

11. Leslie Hanawalt, *Place of Light: The History of Wayne State University*. Detroit: Wayne State University Press, 1968, p. 173.

12. Wayne State University, Hall of Fame, Induction Ceremony Program, 1978.

13. David L. Holmes, Jr., *op. cit.*, 1998.

14. For more on this subject see Summer Sanders, *Champions Are Raised, Not Born* (1998); Rick Wolff, *Good Sports* (1998); Daniel Gould, University of North Carolina; and Institute for Study of Youth Sports at Michigan State University.

15. *Detroit Times*, April 24, 1924, p. 22. The track facilities within the Detroit Metropolitan League were woefully inadequate throughout nearly all of the twentieth century. See *Detroit Times*, April 7, 1949, p. C-53; May 15, 1949, part 3, p. 4 and interview with Allan Tellis, October 9, 1997.

16. The internal nickname for Detroit City College was the Griffins, but the newspaper frequently referred to their athletic teams as "the Munies." In 1927, its nickname was changed to the Tartars. Near the end of the century the Tartars became the Warriors.

17. *Detroit Times*, May 4, Part 3, p. 1 and May 9, 1924, p. 30.

18. Now Western Michigan University. *Detroit Free Press*, May 8, 1924, p. 18.

19. *Detroit Free Press*, May 8, 1924, p. 18.

20. *Detroit Times*, May 9, 1924, p.30.

21. *Detroit Free Press*, May 18, p. 20 and June 1, 1924, Sports, p. 1 and 3.

22. Wayne State University, Hall of Fame, Induction Ceremony Program, 1986.

23. *Ibid.*, 1988.

24. See *The Detroit Times*, April 9, 1949.

25. *The Beacon, 1924*, yearbook of Western High School, Detroit.

26. *Chicago Tribune*, June 13, 1926, part 2, p.1 and 3.

27. *Detroit News*, June 5, 1927, part 4, p. 2.

28. *Spalding Official Athletic Almanac*, p. 213 and *Detroit News*, June 13, 1927, p. 28.

29. *Detroit Times*, July 8, 1928, part 2, p. 3.

30. J. K. Doherty, *Track and Field Omnibook*. Los Angeles, 1976, p. 11.

31. *Spaulding's Official Athletic Almanac*, 1928, p. 185.

32. *Detroit News*, June 18, 1927, p. 7.

33. *Detroit Times*, July 8, 1928, part 2, p. 1.

34. *The Michigan Daily*, May 24, 1925, p. and 3.

35. *Chicago Tribune*, June 10, 1928, part 2, page 4.

36. *Detroit Times*, May 19, 1929, part 2, p. 4.

37. Hanawalt, *op. cit.*, p. 189.

38. *The Beacon, 1925*, yearbook of Western High School, Detroit.

39. *The Michigan Daily*, March 20, 1927, pp. 1 and 6.

40. *Spaulding Almanac*, 1929, p. 185.

41. *Detroit News*, May 5, 1928, p. 12.

42. Ohio Relays Meet Program, Bartlett Collection; and *Detroit Times*, May 5, 1929, Part 2, p. 2.

43. *Detroit Times*, May 19, 1929, Part 2, p. 4.

44. Wayne State University, Hall of Fame, Induction Program, 1978.

45. *Detroit Times*, April 13, 1949, p. 32-C.

46. Interview with his son, David L. Holmes, Jr., July 28, 1999.

47. David L. Holmes, "Plenty of Room Above," *The Amateur Athlete*, June 1934, p. 4 ff.

48. *Detroit News*, April 21, 1933, p. 29.

49. *Ibid.*, May 7, 1933.

50. *Ibid.*, April 30, 1933.

51. *Ibid.*, May 7, 1933.

52. Hanawalt, *op. cit.*, p. 191.

53. Victor G. Reuther, *The Brothers Reuther and the Story of the UAW*. Boston: Houghton Mifflin Co., 1976, pp. 58–65.

54. Hanawalt, *op. cit.*, p. 183.

55. *Ibid.*, p. 183, 220–221, 259; and Willis F. Dunbar, *The Michigan Record in Higher Education*. Detroit: Wayne State University Press, 1963, p. 307.

56. *Detroit Free Press*, February 6, 1940, p. 17.

57. *Ibid.*

58. *Detroit Free Press*, May 16, 1937, Sports Section, p. 6.

59. *Ibid.*, April 11, 1948, p. 10–11.

60. *Detroit Free Press*, February 10, 1935, p. 3-Sports Section. In 1936 King set a meet high jump record (6-3_) at the State Intercollegiate meet in Ann Arbor. See *Detroit Free Press*, May 17, 1936, Sports, p. 1.

61. Interview with Allan Tolmich, October 31, 1999.

62. *Detroit Free Press*, May 16, 1937, Sports Section, p. 6.

63. *Ypsilanti Daily Press*, February 24, 1933, p. 5 and *Detroit News*, May 21, 1933, p. 8.

64. *Detroit News*, May 17, 1936, p. 4 and *National AAU Senior Track and Field Championships Program*, Chicago, June 30, 1933. Participated for the Great Lakes Mutual team.

65. Interview with Al Tolmich, October 31, 1999.

66. *Akron Beacon Journal*, May 9, 1937.

67. *Detroit Free Press*, March 21, 1937, Sports Section, p. 1.

68. *Ibid.*, May 16, 1937, Sports Section, p. 6.

69. *Ibid.*, February 24, 1937; May 2, 1937; May 9, 1937: and May 16, 1937.

70. *Ibid.*, February 17, 1935, p. 3.

71. Coach Holmes had a mediocre team record in track over his 40 years at Wayne University. He was 50 and 47 in outdoor meets and 38–38 in indoor meets. See *The 12th* Annual Athletic Hall of Fame induction ceremony booklet, March 7, 1987.

72. *Detroit Free Press.*, May 9, 1937, Sports Section, p. 5 and May 13, 1937, p. 24.

73. *Los Angeles Times*, June 20, 1937, Part II, p. 14; and, July 4, 1937, Part II, p. 12.

74. Interview with Allan Tolmich, October 31, 1999.

75. *Ibid.*

76. See *Detroit Free Press*, May 27, 1938, p. 21.

77. National AAU Record book, 1940.

78. Interview with Lenore Strobel by David L. Holmes, Jr. in 1997 a view shared by Allan Tolmich in 1999.

79. *Budget of the Board of Education, City of Detroit for 1941–42.* Board of Education, December 1940, p. 58–75.

80. *Detroit Times*, March 19, 1939, part 2, p. 1.

81. Telephone interview with Bob Luby, March 25, 1998.

82. *Ibid.*

83. *Detroit Free Press*, February 17, 1940.

84. *Ibid.*, February 18, 1940 Sports section, p. 1.

85. *Ibid.*, February 22, 1940, p. 15.

86. *Detroit Times*, March 3, 1940, part 2, page 3.

87. *Ibid.*, March 7, 1941, p. 25.

88. *Ibid.*, February 8, 1941, p. 11.

89. *Detroit Free Press*, February 22, 1942, p. 4.

90. *Ibid.*, December 1, 1999, p. A3.

91. Bennett, *op. cit.*, p. 22–3.

92. *Ibid.*, p. 254. A three year study published in 1927 indicated that the scholastic averages of track and field letter winners at the University of Michigan were superior to those of non-athletes and those of football and basketball players. See *Michigan Daily* February 26, 1927, p. 2. It seems likely that this tendency continued during the last half of the century.

93. See *The Detroit Times*, April 7–9, 13–15, 19–22, 28 and May 4, 1949.

94. *Ibid.*

95. *The Detroit Times*, May 15, 1949, part 3, p. 4.

96. *Detroit Free Press*, June 5, 1948, p. 17.

97. Behee, *op. cit.*, 1974.

98. Determined from the 1952 University of Michigan college yearbook.

99. Behee, *op. cit.*, 1974, p. 14.

100. *Detroit Free Press*, May 21, 1953, p. 25. It also should be noted that enforcement of laws still favored whites over blacks in most of the South. See Gail Williams O'Brien, *The Color of the Law: Race, Violence, and Justice in the Post-War South.* Chapel Hill: University of North Carolina Press, 1999.

101. Interview with Dr. Aaron Z. Gordon, February 7, 1998.

102. *The Detroit Times*, June 10, 1956, part 4, p.3.

103. Mirel, *op. cit.*,1996.

104. In support of this observation, during the last year of the twentieth century, Kenneth S. Burnley, a University of Michigan trackman, 1962–64, from Mumford High School Class of 1960, became Superintendent of the Detroit Public Schools. See *Detroit Free Press*, May 5, 2000, p. 1A. As assistant track coach in 1968, Burnley was the first African-American coach in University of Michigan history. See Chapter 18.

105. *Detroit Free Press*, June 1960.

106. Dr. Drachler was born on May 20, 1912 in Russia [the Ukraine] and brought to Detroit as a youngster when his father accepted a job teaching at Sholem Aleichem Institute. Norm began teaching in his father's school in 1929 at the age of 17 and in the Detroit Public Schools in 1937, after receiving a degree from Wayne University. He became an assistant principal in 1946, five years before receiving his Ph.D. from the University of Michigan and being named an elementary school principal. In 1957 he was chosen as director of research for the Citizens Committee headed by George Romney that was studying school needs. He was appointed Detroit's assistant superintendent in 1960. See Obituary, *Detroit Jewish News*, May 26, 2000, pp. 137–8.

107. "Dr. Norman Drachler Detroit Public Schools, 1966–71," *Michigan Jewish History*, Vol. 37, Sept. 1997, pp.16–7.

108. See *Chicago Tribune*, March 20, 1949, The *Detroit Times*, April 28, 1949, p. c-47; and Merke, *op. cit.*, p. 962.

109. *Track and Field News*. December 1949, p. 6. One of the often forgotten Tartar athletes of the era was James Polk, a triple jumper who qualified for the 1948 Olympic trials. See *Detroit Free Press*, August 15, 2000, p. 5B. He was orphaned in 1935 and enlisted in the Navy when he graduated from Northwestern HS where he was a champion boxer. After college he became a carpenter and building inspector for the City of Detroit.

110. Interview with Allan Tellis, October 9, 1997.

111. *Detroit Free Press*, May 17, 1947, p. 10.

112. *Ibid., May 23, 1947, p. 21.*

113. See *Mt. Pleasant Daily Times-News*, February 24, 1956.

114. *Atlanta Constitution*, June 6, 1964, p. 14.

115. Interview with George Gaines, August 26, 1997.

116. Interview with George Gaines, March 22, 2000.

117. *Bee Gee News*, May 12, 1950, p. 4.

118. Interview with George Gaines, August 26, 1997.

119. *Detroit Free Press*, May 22, 1948, p. 14.

120. *Ibid.*, May 27, 1948, pages 21, 25.

121. *The Detroit Times*, May 13, 1949, p. C-26.

122. *Bee Gee News*, May 12, 1950, p. 4.

123. *Ibid.*

124. *Ibid.*, May 19, 1948, p. 6.

125. *Ibid.*, June 17, 1949, p. 3.

126. See *Mt. Pleasant Daily Times-News*, April 2, 1956.

127. See *Amateur Athlete*, August 1958 and obituary *The Detroit News*, February 28, 1990, p. 4B.

128. Interview with Bob Luby, March 25, 1998.

129. *Detroit News*, February 28, 1990, p. 4B.

130. *NCAA Official Intercollegiate Track and Field Guide, 1937*. New York: American Sports Publishing Co., 1937.

131. *Track and Field News*, July 1953.

132. *Griffin, 1954*.

133. Interview with Mark Smith on June 9, 1998.

134. *Detroit Free Press*, May 17, 1950, p. 19.

135. *Ibid*, May 18, 1950, p. 25.

136. *Detroit Free Press*, May 20, 1950, p. 15.

137. *Ibid.*, May 26, 1950, p. 26.

138. *Ibid.*, May 17, 1951, p. 30.

139. *Ibid.*, May 27, 1951, p. C-2.

140. *Ibid.*, June 6, 1951, p. 24.

141. *Ibid.*, June 9, 1951, p. 16.

142. *Official NCAA Track and Field Guide, 1952*, p. 121, 124–25.

143. Interview with Cliff Hatcher, September 28, 1997.

144. *CM Life*, March 4, 1955, p. 3.

145. See the *Bee Gee News*, May 6, 1955, p. 3 for evidence of Cliff's 880-yard run prowess.

146. Interviewed Cliff Hatcher on September 28, 1997.

147. Interview with Hiram Badia, Richmond, MI, December 27, 1998.

148. *Rochester Hills Reminder*, January 22, 1990, p.1.

149. *Detroit News*, May 11, 1963, p. 3-B.

150. Letter from David L. Holmes, Wayne State University, to *Track and Field News*, September 23, 1957 from the archives of the Track and Field Hall of Frame, Butler University.

151. Unpublished writings by John Telford on his track career, 1997.

152. *Bee Gee News*, May 25, 1955, p. 1.

153. *Ibid.*, May 6, 1955, p. 3.

154. *Mt. Pleasant Daily Times-News*, February 27, 1956.

155. Interview with John Telford, June 10, 1998.

156. *Track and Field News*, July 1957, p. 1.

157. *New York Times*, June 23, 1957, p. S-1.

158. Nelson's finding were confirmed by Pincus Sober, chairman of the AAU track and field committee, in his official report on the Dayton meet. As a result the times for the 220-yard and 440-yard dashes were not accepted as records for these events, but since the athletes were not responsible for the errors, their place standings were permitted to stand. See *Track and Field News*, November 1957, p. 11.

159. *The Amateur Athlete*, March 1958, p. 6.

160. *Track and Field News* November, 1957.

161. *Official NCAA Track and Field Guide, 1958*. New York: The National Collegiate Athletic Bureau, 1958, p.18–19.

162. *Wayne State University Summer Collegian*, August 6, 1957, p. 1.

163. *Track and Field News*, August 1960, p. 9.

164. *Detroit News*, May 11, 1963, p. 3-B.

165. *The South End*, May 14, 1984, p. 8.

166. *The National Directory of High School Coaches*, 1965 edition. Edited by Cliff Harper. Washington, D.C.: Athletic Publishing Co., 1965, p. 152–3.

167. *The Daily Tribune* [Royal Oak], March 8, 1974.

168. *Rochester Hills Reminder*, January 22, 1990, p.1.

169. *Oakland Press*, November 20, 1997; *Clarion-Eccentric*, November 30, 1997; and *Oakland Press*, March 18, 1998.

170. *Detroit News*, February 3, 1999, p. 35.

171. *The Prospector*, February 15, 2000, p. 5D.

172. *Detroit Free Press*, May 13, 1956.

173. John Telford, *The Longest Dash*. Los Angeles: Tafnews Press, 1971.

174. See *Central Michigan Life* 1954–1959 for support of this statement.

175. *Central Michigan Life*, Aril 13, 1956, p. 3.

176. Bellefeur, *op. cit.*, 1981, p. 354.

177. *Wayne University Daily Collegian*, May 14, 1957, p. 3.

178. *Ibid.*, October 15, 1957, p. 3.

179. Interview with Richard Swanson, May 25, 1998.

180. Interview with his son, David L. Holmes, Jr., July 28, 1999.

181. The Holmes Folding Hurdle Co. brochure, 1958.

182. Letter to the editor, *Detroit News*, 1965 from Telford scrapbook.

183. *Detroit News*, March 16, 1986, p. 2C.

184. *Ibid.*, February 24, 1980.

185. *The South End*, December 14, 1982, p.1 and 6.

186. *Ibid.*, February 13, 1984, p. 8; *Michigan Chronicle*, August 17, 1985; and *Detroit Free Press*, April 19, 1986.

Chapter 12

1. See Ken Doherty, "Interval Training," *Track and Field News*, March 1956, pp. 11–13. See *Track and Field News*, December 1966, p.11 for variations in indoor tracks. Madison Square Garden replaced its sold its plywood and rubber track in 1978 to Virginia Tech University in Blacksburg, Virginia for $15,000. A new track of that type, without a synthetic surface would have cost $125,000. A fortuitous telephone call about invitations to the Garden told Virginia Tech that the old track was being replace and could be purchased. The problem was how to get the old track down to Blacksburg. "It was a nightmare. I thought it would take a tractor-trailer. It took five. Then the fork lift broke while we were unloading it, and we had to do it by hand. We had 55 or 60 guys on the team out there working all day. We still put it up each year and take it down," said Russ Whitenack. Five women qualified on that track for the National Collegiate Athletic Association Championships in 1983. See *New York Times*, January 27, 1983, p. B14.

2. *Track and Field News*, August 1963, p. 21.

3. *New York Times*, May 27, 1973, p. 11.

4. *Ibid.*, April 29, 1973, part V, p. 4.

5. 90th Annual Drake Relays Program, April 23–24, 1999, Des Moines, IA.

6. *Track and Field News*, November 1957, p. 11.

7. R. L. Quercetani, "Olympic Finalists: Olympic Age Analysis," *Track and Field News*, December 1964, p. 15.

8. America's first credit card was issued by Diners Club in February 1950. See *The New York Times*, March 12, 2000, Section 3, p. 11. See Appendix, Chart 5 for American and world record holders from Michigan.

9. David Baldwin, *Track and Field Record Holders: World, Olympic and American Marks 1946 Through 1995*. Jefferson, NC: McFarland & Co., 1996, p. 144, 152, 155, 228, 277.

10. Southeast Michigan Public Schools accounts for more than half of these record setters. This designation adds such stars as Hayes Jones, Rex Cawley, Jim Bibbs, John Bork, William Wehrwein, Herb Washington, Doug Brown, Debby La Plante, and Bob Wingo.

11. See Carl S. Taylor, *Dangerous Society*. East Lansing: Michigan State University Press, 1990 and Suzanne E. Smith, *Dancing in the Street: Motown and the Cultural Politics of Detroit*. Cambridge: Harvard University Press, 2000.

12. Graduation rates for black, male athletes at the University of Michigan and Michigan State University were lower than the university average at both schools during much of this period. See *Detroit Free Press*, December 2, 2000, p. B1. Also see "It Takes Guts to Put Classes Above Athletics," *New York Times*, December 3, 2000, P. 45 for more on this issue. It has been argued that NCAA policies initiated in the 1950s transformed scholarship athletes into university employees reducing the academic value of scholarships for athletes. See Allen L. Sack and Ellen, J. Staurowsky, *College Athletes for Hire*. Westport, CT: Praeger, 1998. In 1997 only 31% of African-American college basketball players graduated from college, see James J. Duderstadt, *Intercollegiate Athletics and the American University*. Ann Arbor: The University of Michigan Press, 2000, p. 199.

13. *Michigan State Cross Country/Track and Field Guide, 1996–7.*

14. *The Michigan State University Alumni Association, 1988*, p. xv. For performance highlights see Lyman L. Frimodig and Fred W. Stabley, *op. cit.*, p. 207–209, 216.

15. *Detroit Free Press*, May 24, 1947, p. 11; and May 31, 1947, p. 10.

16. Interview with Adolf Weinacker, June 1, 1998.

17. *Track and Field News*, December 1948, p. 1.

18. Godner Nelson, "Track Talk," *Track and Field News*, April 1950, p. 4.

19. *Track and Field News*, February 1948, p. 6; March 1948, p. 4, April 1948, p. 4, November 1948, p. 4; March 1949, p. 3; and April 1949, p. 6. Frimodig and Stabley, *op. cit.*, p. 208–209, 216.

20. *Track and Field News*, May 1950, p. 2; February 1952, p. 8; March 1952, p. 8; *Des Moines Register*, April 28, 1951; *New York Times*, March 23, 1952.

21. Michigan State College Sports Information records.

22. *Track and Field News*, November 1948, p. 4; June 1949, p. 8.

23. *Track and Field News*, March 1950, p. 6.

24. *Track and Field News*, May 1950, p. 1–2. Donald J. Makielski graduated from MSU in 1951 with a degree in agricultural marketing. He married Hildur S. Sangren, an MSU home economics major in the class of 1952. In 1988 they lived in Ann Arbor. See *The Michigan State University Alumni Association, 1988*, p. 254.

25. *Track and Field News, March 1950*, p. 4.

26. *Track and Field News*, December 1950, p. 3.

27. *Michigan Daily*, April 28, 1951, p. 6.

28. *Official NCAA Track and Field Guide, 1952*, p. 18.

29. *Track and Field News*, July 1951.

30. *Official NCAA Track and Field Guide, 1952*. New York: The National Collegiate Athletic Bureau, 1952, p. 20.

31. *Official AAU Track and Field Guide, 1952.*

32. *Track and Field News*, August 1951, p. 5.

33. *Ibid.*, January 1952, p. 2; March 1952, p. 1; *Chicago Daily News*, March 31, 1952, p. 22.

34. *Track and Field News*, April 1952, p. 1; May 1952, p. 7; June 1952, p. 10.

35. *AAU Official Track and Field Handbook, 1953–4*, p. 12.

36. *Track and Field News*, August 1952, 6–7. Many track experts, including Bruitus Hamiton track coach of the University of California, and the Boston miler, Gil Dodds, had asserted that a "four-minute mile is not physically possible." See *Chicago Daily News*, March 17, 1943, p. 27 and March 19, 1945, p. 16.

36. *Track and Field News*, September 1952, p. 3. Druetzler ran his leg in 4:09.6, which was faster than Roger Bannister's leg for the British.

37. *Ibid.*

38. *Track and Field News*, March 1953, p. 7.

39. *The Jackson Journal*, June 19, 1953, p. 6.

40. *Official AAU Track and Field Handbook, 1956–7*, p. 26.

41. *Track and Field News*, January 1956, p. 16.

42. *Detroit News*, March 11, 1969 and *Mt. Clemens Macomb Daily*, February 10, 1969.

43. Spartan Sports Services, April 30, 1968.

44. While an undergraduate during the 1930s, Dittrich had been an NCAA All-American in the triple jump and the long-jump, and was an alternate on the 1936 U.S. Olympic team. Dittrich was inducted into the Drake Relays Hall of Fame as a coach on April 24, 1999.

45. *Detroit News*, March 11, 1969.

46. *Official Collegiate Track and Field Guide, 1969*. Phoenix, AZ: College Athletics Publishing Service, 1968, p. 64.

47. *Michigan State News*, February 6, 1969 and Michigan State University Sports Information files, 1999.

48. *The Lansing State Journal*, February 23, 1969.

49. *The Ann Arbor News*, February 13, 1970, p. 15. *The Lansing Journal* claimed that Wehrwein had set an American and unofficial world record for the 600-yard run. However, Spartan runner Willie Atterberry, Sr. had posted a faster time for the 600-yard run (1:08.5) in Columbus, Ohio on April 20, 1957. It appears that Atterberry's time was run outdoors, and hence both deserve the record for that distance.

50. *Detroit News*, March 11, 1969.

51. *Track and Field News*, March 1969, p. 5.

52. *Official Collegiate Track and Field Guide, 1970*. Phoenix, AZ: College Athletics Publishing Service, 1969, p. 67.

53. *Michigan State News*, April 30, 1969.

54. *Detroit Free Press*, April 25, 1969.

55. *Michigan State News*, April 28, 1969.

56. *Ibid.*, April 30, 1969.

57. Michigan State University, Sports Information Track and Field Questionnaire, January 14, 1996 and June 14, 1996.

58. *Track and Field News*, July 1969.

59. *Michigan State News*, January 7, 1970.

60. *Official Collegiate Track and Field Guide, 1971*. Phoenix, AZ.: College Athletic Publishing Service, 1970, p. 57. Incidently, Bill's second son, Chris, also became a MSU runner. After graduating from MSU Chris moved to Pinkney, Michigan. Over Memorial Day week-end, on May 29, 1999, at the age of 23, Chris Wehrwein won the men's 10-kilometer run (30:47) finishing 13 seconds ahead of the runner-up at the twenty-seventh annual Dexter-Ann Arbor Run. See *Michigan Runner*, vol. 21, no. 2, summer 1999, p. 14.

61. Interview with Jim Bibbs on July 23, 1998.

62. *Track and Field News*, May, 1949, p. 10.

63. *Track and Field News*, April, 1950, p. 1.

64. *Bee Gee News*, May 16, 1950, p. 4.

65. Undated and untitled newspaper articles in Jim Bibbs scrapbook.

66. *Track and Field News*, January 1951, p. 3. On March 3, 1951 at the 24th annual Central Collegiate Conference meet at Notre Dame, Bibbs was credited with running the 60-yard dash in 6.1. See *Chicago Tribune*, March 4, 1951, part 2, p. 4. However, the *Official NCCAA Track and Field Guide, 1952* (p. 86) lists his time as 6.2 because that was his time in the finals.

67. *Detroit Free Press, May 20, 1958.*

68. Records of the Detroit Track Club, John Telford scrapbook and memorabilia.

69. Interview with Jim Bibbs on July 23, 1998.

70. His sister, Anne, graduated from Mt. Morris High School in 1940. She became Mrs. Naymik in 1946 and moved to Ann Arbor. *Morris-Sonian*. Mt. Morris High School Yearbook, 1940, 1945, and 1946. His brother Joe graduated from Mt. Morris High School in 1946. See *Morris-Sonian*. Mt. Morris High School Yearbook, 1946.

71. He lettered in football, basketball, track, and baseball. He played center and linebacker on the football team, was co-captain and All-Regional in basketball, and pitched on the baseball team. In addition, Joe was in the glee club, the class play, the French Club, and the operetta, and the student council. See *Morris-Sonian*. Mt. Morris High School Yearbook, 1945 and 6.

72. Interview with Jim Podoley, October 25, 1999.

73. *Morris-Sonian*. Mt. Morris High School Yearbook, 1948 and 9.

74. *Flint Journal*, May 13, 1950, p. 8.

75. Interview with Jim Podoley, October 25, 1999.

76. *Ibid.*

77. The record was tied by Nate Clark of Hillsdale College in 1956.

78. *CM Life*, January 18, 1957, p. 1.

79. CMU Sports Information files.

80. *The Pro Football Encyclopedia*. New York: Macmillan Books, 1997, p. 708.

81. *CM Life*, January 18, 1957, p. 1.

82. *Central Michigan Life*, March 26, 1954, p. 3.

83. *Ibid.*, May 21, 1954, p. 5.

84. Archives of University of Michigan Athletic Department, Track and Field, 1954, Bentley Historical Library.

85. *Detroit Free Press* (p.32) and the *Mt. Pleasant Daily Times-News* (p.9), May 13, 1955.

86. *Detroit Free Press*, May 22, 1955, p. C-2.

87. The members of the league were: Central Michigan, Michigan Normal, Eastern Illinois, Northern Illinois, Southern Illinois, Illinois Normal, and Western Illinois.

88. Central Michigan University Sports Information files and *Mt. Pleasant Daily Times-News*, May 21, 1956.

89. *Central Michigan Life*, June 1, 1956, p. 3.

90. *Ibid.*, April 30, 1954, p. 5.

91. *Ibid.*, July 1, 1954, p. 1.

92. *Ibid.*, July 8, 1954, p. 3.

93. *CM Life*, April 29, 1955, p. 4.

94. *Mt. Pleasant Daily Times News*, May 25, 1955 and *Track and Field News*, August 1955, p. 10.

95. *Mt. Pleasant Daily Times-News*, February 18, 1956.

96. *Mt. Pleasant Daily Times-News*, March 24, 1956.

97. *Central Michigan Life*, July 12, 1956, p. 1.

98. *Ibid.*, May 4, 1956, p. 3.

99. *Ibid.*, June 19, 1956, p. 3.

100. Wallechinsky, *op. cit.*, p. 170.

101. Telephone interview with David Meyers, October 4, 1999.

102. *Ibid.*

103. During World War II he received a fellowship in the Naval Aviation V-5 program and spent three years as chief athletic specialist in the Navy.

104. *Track and Field News*, December 1965, p. 9.

105. *90th Annual Drake Relays Program*, April 23–24, 1999, p. 17.

106. Hanley, *op. cit.*, 1973, p. 102.

107. *The Western Herald*, January 24, 1958, p.7.

108. *AAU Track and Field Handbook, 1955.*

109. *The Western Herald*, January 21, 1955, p. 6: *Detroit Free Press*, May 1, 1955, p. D-1: and Western Michigan University Sports Information.

110. *The Western Herald*, January 24, 1958, p.7.

111. *Track and Field News*, September 1956, p. 15.

112. Willie Williams was born in Gary, Indiana, on September 1931.

113. Quercetani, *A World History of Track and Field Athletics, op. cit.*, 1964, pp. 36–7, also see *New York Times*, August 5, 1956, Section 5, p. 1.

114. See *New York Times*, November 23, 1956.

115. *Track and Field News*, December 1956, p. 2.

116. *Kalamazoo Gazette*, March 15, 1957.

117. *Track and Field News*, July 1957, p. 2.

118. *Ibid.*

119. *Official NCAA Track and Field Guide, 1958.* New York: The National Collegiate Athletic Bureau, 1958, p.18–19.

120. *The Amateur Athlete*, March 1958, p. 6.

121. *The Western Herald*, February 14, 1958, p. 6.

122. *Track and Field News*, April, 1958, p.1.

123. *San Francisco Examiner*, June 15, 1958, p. 13.

124. From an interview with Jim Bibbs, July 23, 1998. Bibbs was with Ira that evening in 1958.

125. *Track and Field News*, April 1960.

126. *Toronto Daily Star*, July 9, 1960, p. 30.

127. *Track and Field News*, March 1963, p. 23.

128. Former all-time stolen base leader while with the Chicago Cubs and St. Louis Cardinals.

129. See *Chicago Tribune*, March 31, 1994.

130. *Track and Field News*, March 1961, p. 5.

131. An area of the track frequently referred to as the Wes Santee Corner at Drake Stadium.

132. *Track and Field News*, May 1961, p. 5.

133. *Ibid.*

134. *Ibid.*, June 1961, p.8.

135. *Ibid.*, July 1961, p.1.

136. *Ibid.*, p.7. *Western Michigan University Alumni Directory*. Montgomery, AL: College and University Press, 1982, p. 84.

137. *Detroit Free Press*, May 17, 1947, p. 10; May 27, 1948, p. 21 and 25; June 19, 1948, p. 19; and *Detroit Times*, April, 1949, p. 32-c.

138. *Track and Field News*, January 1950, p. 1;

February 1950, p. 6; *Chicago Tribune*, March 4, 1951, part 2, p. 4; *The Michigan Daily*, May 20, 1951, p. 6

139. *Official NCAA Track and Field Guide, 1953*, p. 36; and *Official AAU Track and Field Handbook, 1953–4*, p. 86, 110.

140. Interview with William H. Freeman, a former Oregon track athlete, May 28, 2000, Banff, Canada.

141. *Track and Field News*, May, 1959, p. 3.

142. *Ibid.*, August 1960, p. 9; September 1960, p. 5 and 13.

143. *Track and Field News*, September 1960, p. 1.

144. Don Potts, "Davis, Kaufmann Run 44.9," *Track and Field News*, September 1960, p.5; Wallechinsky, p. 29; and Baldwin, *op. cit.*, p. 150.

145. Potts, *op. cit.*, p. 5.

146. *Track and Field News*, September 1960, p. 13.

147. Baldwin, *op. cit.*, p. 152 and 155.

148. *Track and Field News*, January 1961, p. 20.

149. *Track and Field News*, January 1961, p. 3.

150. Harry Edwards, *The Revolt of the Black Athlete*. New York: The Free Press, 1969, p. 110.

151. Mallon and Buchanan, *op. cit.*, p. 294–5.

152. *Track and Field News*, March 1961, p. 24.

Chapter 13

1. *The Adrian Daily Times*, July 8, 1912, p. 1.

2. A. G. Studer, *One Hundred Years with Youth: The Story of the Detroit YMCA: 1852–1952*. Detroit: Privately Printed by the YMCA, 1953, pp. 98–99.

3. *AAU Handbook, 1922.*

4. *Polk's Detroit City Directory*. Detroit: R. L. Polk & Co., 1922, p. 991.

5. The seven-miles is approximately 15-kilometers. The Seven-mile walk was dropped in 1878 reinstated in 1879, dropped again in 1885, added again in 1912.

6. The 10-kilometer walk was dropped in 1932, only to be reintroduced on the Olympic program in 1948.

7. *Detroit Times*, May 18, 1924, Part 3, p. 4.

8. *The Amateur Athlete*, June 1937, p. 6 and picture in *Detroit Times*, June 1, 1924.

9. *Detroit News*, May 31, 1924, p.12.

10. *Detroit Times*, June 16, 1924, p. 16.

11. *Polk's Detroit City Directory*. Detroit: R. L. Polk & Co., 1929, p. 896.

12. *Detroit Times*, March 24, 1940, part 2, p. 2.

13. *Farmington Observer*, November 21, 1970.

14. Interview with Rosalie Frutig Crosbie, September 2, 1999.

15. *Directory Michigan State College, 1932–33.*

16. *AAU Official Track and Field Handbook, 1949–50.* New York: The Amateur Athletic Union, 1949, p. 9–10.

17. *Ibid.*, p. 38.

18. Interview with Rosalie Frutig Crosbie, September 2, 1999.

19. *Spaulding's Official Athletic Almanac for 1938*, p. 8.

20. See Michigan State University Archives, UA 10.2, folder box 434, folder 3, Alumni records, 1947.

21. *Spaulding's Official Athletic Almanac for 1933.*

22. *Chicago Tribune*, June 8, 1934, p. 28; June 10, 1934, Part 2, p. 5; and June 11, 1934, p. 21; and *Amateur Athlete for July, 1934*, p. 14.

23. *National AAU Championships, Nebraska Memorial Stadium* Meet Program, July 3–4, 1935.

24. *Spalding Athletic Almanac for 1936*, pp. 90 and 112.

25. *The Amatuer Athlete for August 1937*, p. 4.

26. Note: in 1937 his brother, Joseph Mihalo, a clerk, was the only Mihalo listed in Hamtramck and Detroit. R. L. Polk & Co., Detroit City Directory, 1937, p.1318.

27. R. L. Polk & Company, Detroit City Directory. Detroit, 1940. In 1940, Charles Wright of Lansing, Michigan placed 6th in the National AAU 50-K Walk Championship held in Cincinnati on May 15.

28. *Detroit Free Press*, February 24, 1940, p. 16.

29. *Detroit Times*, March 21, 1940, p. 19 and March 24, 1940, part 2, p. 3.

30. *Spaulding's Official Athletic Almanac for 1941*, p. 4.

31. Interviews with contemporaries who did not wish to be cited, summer 1999.

32. *AAU Official Track and Field Handbook, 1945*. New York: The Amateur Athletic Union, 1945, p. 40.

33. *Ibid.*, p. 10.

34. The 50-K Walk championship was held in Cincinnati May 14, 1944.

35. Held in Clove Lake, Staten Island, New York on April 30, 1944.

36. Held in Springfield, Ohio October 29, 1944.

37. Held in Dearborn, Michigan on April 23, 1944.

38. Held in Springfield, Ohio. See *AAU Official Track and Field Handbook, 1945*. New York: The Amateur Athletic Union, 1945, p. 40.

39. Held on April 28, 1946.

40. Held on May 12, 1946 in Cincinnati.

41. *AAU Official Track and Field Handbook, 1949–50*. New York: The Amateur Athletic Union, 1949, p. 38.

42. Held in Cincinnati on April 27, 1947.

43. *1997 USA Race Walking Handbook* edited by Bob Bowman. Indianapolis, Indiana: USA Track and Field Media Information Office, 1997, p. 70.

43. *Detroit News*, May 4, 1947, Part 2, p. 3.

44. *AAU Official Track and Field Handbook, 1948*. New York: The Amateur Athletic Union, 1948, p. 10.

45. *Track and Field News*, December 1948, p. 8 and December 1949, p. 3. *Detroit Times*, May 13, 1949, p. 26-c.

46. *1997 USA Race Walking Handbook*, 1997, p. 80.

47. Menke, 1953, p.888.

48. *Detroit News*, November 2, 1950.

49. *AAU Official Track and Field Handbook, 1953–4*. New York: AAU, 1953, p.100.

50. *Detroit News*, March 25, 1992, p. 15-D and *Detroit Free Press*, March 26, 1992, p. 2-B; and interview with Frank Soby of Detroit, November 23, 1999.

51. Interviews with Adolf Weinacker, June 1, 20, 22 and 25, 1998. Much of what follows is from those interviews and from an article in the *Detroit Free Press*, September 27, 1991, p. 9.

52. Interviews with Tommy Sledge, Richard Brown, Aaron Gordon, Stan Fields, and Al Tellis, fall 1998.

53. In 1945 the Crosley Corporation announced its intent to produce small cars powered with four-cylinder lightweight engines after the war. They produced their first small cars in 1946 and continued to produce small cars until July 1952. Some new car models sold for as little as $1,000. *Automobiles of America*. Detroit: Wayne State University Press, 1962, pp. 46–52.

54. Interview with Adolf Weinacker, June 1, 1998.

55. Interview with Adolf Weinacker, June 22, 1998.

56. *Track and Field News*, December 1949, p. 3.

57. *Official AAU Track and Field Handbook, 1953–54*. New York: AAU, 1953, p. 9, 100.

58. *Iron Mountain News*, September 11, 1950.

59. *Owosso Argus Press*, October 13, 1950.

60. *Lansing State Journal* and *The St. Joseph Herald-Press*, October 23, 1950.

61. *Detroit News*, November 2, 1950 and interview recollections.

62. In 1947 he was secretary of the dorm council and during his last two years at Michigan State he was President of the Dormitory General Council. He also was a member of student council, secretary of the Varsity Club, and a member of three honorary societies (Alpha Psi, Phi Zeta, and Phi Kappa Phi.)

63. Sports Information records and *The Spartan*, December 1950, Vol. 13, no. 7, p. 26.

64. *Official AAU Track and Field Handbook, 1953–54*. New York: AAU, 1953, p. 9, 100.

65. *Ibid.* p. 35.

66. *Detroit Free Press*, September 27, 1991, p. 9. Emil Zatopek died on November 22, 2000 at the age of 78. See *Lexington [KY] Herald-Leader*, November 23, 2000, p. C6.

67. Interview with Adolf Weinacker, June 22, 1998.

68. Editor, Tina Grant, *op. cit.*, Volume 14, pp. 6–9.

69. *Official AAU Track and Field Handbook, 1953–54*, p. 100.

70. Frances Fitzgerald, *Fire in the Lake*. New York: Random House, 1972, p. 91.

71. *1997 USA Race Walking Handbook*, p. 102–3.

72. *Detroit Free Press*, July 8, 1957.

73. *1997 USA Race Walking Handbook*, p.80.

74. *Detroit Free Press*, September 27, 1991, p. 9.

75. Interview with Adolf Weinacker, June 1998.

76. Interview with Jerry Bocci, November 24, 1999.

77. Undated newspaper clippings from Jeanne Bocci's scrapbook.

78. *1997 USA Race Walking Handbook*.

79. *Ibid.*, and Wallechinsky, 1996, p. 219.

80. Interview with Jeanne Bocci, November 24, 1999, and newspaper clippings from her scrapbook.

81. Louise Mead Tricard, *American Women's Track and Field: A History, 1895 through 1980*. Jefferson, NC: McFarland & Co., 1996, p. 536.

82. *Akron Beacon Journal*, July 3, 1972, p. B7.

83. Tricard, *op. cit.*, p. 539, 541.

84. *Akron Beacon Journal*, July 3, 1972, p. B7.

85. *1997 USA Race Walking Handbook*, p. 84.

86. *Ibid.*, p. 82.

87. *Ibid.*, p. 84.

88. *Michigan USA Track & Field*, Winter 1999–2000, p. 5.

89. U.S. Olympic Team Member Questionnaire," Track and Field News correspondence, Rare Book and Special Collections, Butler University. The quotes in the following paragraphs are from this questionnaire.

90. *New York Times*, July 5, 1972, p. 48.

91. *The Booster and Milan Leader*, July 19, 1972, vol. 91, no. 29, p. 1.

1692 Notes

92. Tricard, *op. cit.*, p. 554.
93. Questionnaire filled out by Bill Weigle for Track and Field News, March 3, 1973, Rare Book and Special Collections, Butler University.
94. *1997 USA Race Walking Handbook*, pp. 19, 23–24.
95. *Ibid.*, pp. 9–14.
96. *Ibid.*, pp. 33–34. In the mid-1990s, these records would be surpassed by French walkers.
97. Archives, Sport Information, University of Michigan.
98. *Ibid.*
99. *1997 USA Race Walking Handbook*.
100. *New York Times*, August 4, 1964, p. 15.
101. *Ibid.*, August 12, 1984, Section V, p. 10.
102. *1997 USA Race Walking Handbook*, pp19–26, 42–3, 80.
103. Interviews with Gary Morgan, his father, and sister, several times in 1999.
104. He ran the 5,000-meters in 1948 and 1956.
105. During the winter months club members meet in the Canfield gym in Dearborn on Tuesdays and Thursdays at 6:30 p.m. and on Saturdays at 10 a.m.
106. He was there the week of August 15–22, 1981.
107. *The Winged Foot*, May 1998, p. 14.
108. *Detroit News*, August 1, 1983, p. G-6.
109. *Oakland [Press] Sunday Magazine*, June 4, 1984.
110. *New York Times*, June 28, 1987, p. 59.
111. *The Clarkston (Michigan) News*, August 31, 1988, p. 19 and *Oakland Press*, July 18, 1988, p. C-5.
112. *Oakland Press*, July 17–18, 1988.
113. *Oakland Press*, July 17, 1988, p. B-1.
114. *The Clarkston (Michigan) News*, November 9, 1988, p. 19.
115. *Indianapolis News*, October 14, 1991.
116. In October Gary participated in the 20-K Walk at the Pan American Race Walking Cup Championships, Guatemala City, but was disqualified for having both feet off the ground during the race.
117. *Michigan Runner*, Vol. 21, no. 2, Summer, 1999, p.14.
118. *The Winged Foot*, April 1998, p. 8.
119. *Washington Post*, July 30, 1999, p. D9.
120. *Detroit Free Press*, October 18, 1999, p. 10D.
121. *Oakland Press*, January 30, 2000.
122. USA Track and Field Net, February 14, 2000.
123. *Atlanta Constitution*, March 5, 2000, p. E-21.
124. Interview with Gary Morgan and *Detroit Free Press*, October 18, 1999, p. 10D.
125. Morgan's national championships include the 5-kilometer [indoor (once) and outdoor (3 times)], the 10-kilometer (3 times), the 25-kilometer (twice), the 30-kilometer (twice), the 40-kilometer (once), and the two hour distance (five times).
126. *1997 USA Race Walking Handbook*, pp.19–22.
127. *1997 USA Race Walking Handbook*.

Chapter 14

1. Young, *op. cit.*, pp. 26, 30, and 36.
2. Quercetani, *op. cit.*, 1964, pp. 184–5.
3. *Official Collegiate Track and Field Guide, 1971.*

Phoenix, AZ.: College Athletic Publishing Service, 1970, p.2 of Official Track & Field Rules, p. 2.
4. The English distance of 120-yards is 10¾ inches or 27 cm. shorter than the 110-meter race.
5. USA high school high hurdles, except for a few states such as Ohio, are 3" lower than those used in college.
6. Quercetani, *op. cit.*, 1964, pp. 184–5.
7. *New York Times*, July 5, 1921, p. 18.
8. Phillips, *op. cit.*, p. 46.
9. Wallechinsky, *op. cit.*, pp. 84–5.
10. *1967 National Collegiate Indoor Track Championships, March 10–11, Meet Program*, pp. 28.
11. *Track and Field News*, August 1963, p. 21.
12. *Chicago Tribune*, March 9, 1947.
13. *Ibid.*, July 11, 1948.
14. *Track and Field News*, August 1948, p. 4.
15. *AAU Official Track and Field Handbook, 1949–50.* New York: The Amateur Athletic Union, 1949, p. 9–10. He also was named an All-American in track by *Track and Field News*, December 1948, p. 8.
16. Hanley, *op. cit.*, 1973, p. 116.
17. Bob Pille, "Willie-come-lately," *Detroit Free Press*, May 8, 1960.
18. *Detroit Free Press*, May 8, 1960.
19. *Official NCAA Track and Field Guide, 1957.* New York: The National Collegiate Athletic Bureau, p. 79.
20. *Track and Field News*, July 1956, p. 3.
21. *The Amateur Athlete*, July 1958, p.7.
22. *Track and Field News*, April 1959, p. 6; and *Detroit Free Press*, May 8, 1960.
23. *New York Times*, June 2, 1989, p.11.
24. *Lansing State Journal*, March 10, 1987.
25. *Ibid.*, July 3, 1964.
26. Quercetani, *op. cit.*, 1964, pp. 210.
27. *Track and Field News*, August 1962, p. 8.
28. *Ibid.*, March 1963, p. 23.
29. *Ibid.*, August 1963, p. 4.
30. *Ibid.*, December 1963, p. 18.
31. Cordner Nelson, "Who in Intermediates?" *Track and Field News*, December 1963, p. 17.
32. *Track and Field News*, July, 1964, p. 17.
33. *Lansing State Journal*, July 3, 1964.
34. *The Michigan State University Alumni Association Directory of Members, 1988*, p. 14.
35. Mallon and Buchanan, *op.*, p. 292–3.
36. Interview with Hayes Jones, June 1997 and February 28, 2000.
37. Interview with Hayes Jones, February 28, 2000.
38. *Detroit Free Press*, April 16, 1955, p. 15.
39. *Ibid.*, May 22, 1955, p. C-2.
40. *The Ypsilanti Press*, January 18, 1968, p. 12.
41. *Mt. Pleasant Daily Times-News*, April 7, 1956.
42. Interview with Hayes Jones, February 28, 2000.
43. U. S. Government Printing Office, *Hearings Before the Committee on Commerce, United States Senate, Eighty-ninth Congress, First Session on The Controversy in Administration of Track and Field Events in the United States*, August 16–27, 1965, pp. 103–109.
44. Lloyd W. Olds, "Sensation Hayes Jones Aiming at 1960 Olympics," *The Amateur Athlete*, July, 1958, p.20.
45. Calhoun in the high-hurdles and Campbell in the decathlon.

46. Interview with Hayes Jones, February 28, 2000.

47. *Track and Field News* March 1958, p.12.

48. *Ibid.*, vol. 10, no. 3, Feb. 1958, p. 5.

49. *Ibid.*, March 1958, p.12; His performance was also acknowledged as one of the noteworthy indoor track performances of all time in the *USA 1971–72 Official AAU Track and Field Handbook*, 1971, p. 59.

50. *90th Annual Drake Relays Program*, April 23–24, 1999, p. 30.

51. Interview with Jim Bibbs, July 23, 1998.

52. *Track and Field News*, volume 12, number 7, August 1959.

53. U. S. Government Printing Office, *Hearings, op. cit.*, August 16–27, 1965, pp. 103–109.

54. *Track and Field News*, January 1960, p. 4.

55. *Ibid.*, February 1960, p. 6. Calhoun had been forced to sit out the 1958 season after being suspended for receiving gifts on the television game show *Bride and Groom*.

56. *Millrose Games Program*, January 25, 1974, p. 10.

57. *Track and Field News*, April 1960.

58. *Ibid.*, July 1960, p. 6.

59. Interview with Hayes Jones, February 28, 2000. Lee Calhoun died June 22, 1989 at the age of 56.

60. *Track and Field News*, August 1961, p. 1.

61. *Ibid.*, July 1962.

62. Quercetani, *op. cit.*, 1964, pp. 196.

63. *Track and Field News*, August 1963, p. 2.

64. *Ibid.*, August 1963, p. 4.

65. *Track and Field News*, January 1964, p. 23.

66. Steve Gould, "55 Straight for Hayes Jones," *Track and Field News*, March 1964, p. 16. Also see Baldwin, *op. cit.*, 1996, p. 224.

67. *Track and Field News*, July 1964, p. 16.

68. *Ibid.*, August 1964, p. 4 and 23.

69. *Ibid.*, September 1964, p. 29.

70. *Ibid.*, p. 14.

71. *Ibid.*, October/November 1964, p. 16.

72. *Ibid.*, December 1964, p. 21.

73. *The A.A.U. Official 1965 Track and Field Handbook*. NY: The Amateur Athletic Union of the U. S, 1965, p. 14.

74. *Track and Field News*, December 1965, p. 9.

75. *Ibid.*, p. 15.

76. *Detroit News*, January 12, 1966, p. 3D and January 15, 1966, p. 1B.

77. Motor City International Indoor Track Meet Program, January 14, 1966.

78. *Detroit News*, January 15, 1966, p. 1B.

79. Interview with Paul W. Jones, February 13, 1999.

80. *Track and Field News*, May 1963, p. 7.

81. Interview with Paul Jones, February 13, 1999.

82. Twenty-second Annual Induction, *Wayne State University Athletic Hall of Fame*, April 26, 1997; and *Detroit Times*, May 29, 1956, p. 19, June 1, 1956, p. 26, June 8, 1956, p. 26, June 10, 1956, Part 4, p. 3. Interview with Paul W. Jones, February 13, 1999.

88. *Track and Field News*, August 1963, p. 21.

89. *The Toronto Globe and Mail*, July 5, 1958, p. 27.

90. *Track and Field News*, vol. 12, number 6, July 1959, p.1-ff.

91. *Ibid.*, August 1959, p. 14.

92. *Ibid.*, September, 1959.

93. Interview with Kenneth "Red" Simmons, July 30, 1998.

94. *Track and Field News*, December 1959, p. 3.

95. *Ibid.*, August 1960, p. 9.

96. *Ibid.*, July 1960, p. 4.

97. *Ibid.*, November 1960, p. 16.

98. *Ibid.*, February 1961, p. 20 and March 1962, p. 21.

99. *Ibid.*, June 1963, p. 6.

100. Rex Cawley ran a 46.0 in the semi-finals.

101. *Track and Field News*, July 1963, p. 9.

102. *Ibid.*, November 1967, p. 10.

103. *Ibid.*, July 1963, p. 5.

104. *Ibid.*, p. 23.

105. *Ibid.*, September 1964, p.15.

106. Cordner Nelson, "Who in Intermediates?", *Track and Field News*, December 1963, p. 17.

107. *Track and Field News*, August 1964, p. 4 and 24.

108. *Ibid.*, September 1964, p. 28. Also see Baldwin, *op. cit.*, p. 228.

109. Silver medalist John Cooper died in a Turkish Air Lines plane crash over France on March 3, 1974 at the age of 33.

110. *Track and Field News*, October/November 1964, p. 17.

111. Wallechinsky, *op. cit.*, p. 88.

112. *Track and Field News*, August 1965.

113. *Ibid.*, December 1965, p. 21.

114. *Ibid.*, May 1969, p. 16.

115. Michigan State University, Spartan Sports Service Information, 1963.

116. *Lansing Journal*, November 17, 1965.

117. *Detroit News*, March 14, 1966, p. 5D.

118. *Lansing State Journal*, October 28, 1998.

119. *State News*, January 18, 1966.

120. *Detroit News*, March 6, 1966, p. 6D.

121. *Track and Field News*, April 1966. Clinton Jones was recruited from Cleveland, Ohio in 1963. See *Track and Field News*, October 1963, p. 10.

122. *Drake Relays 75 Years of Excellence*, Edited by Robert H. Spiegel, Drake University, 1984 p. 31.

123. *Detroit Free Press*, June 11, 1967.

124. Gene Washington Resume in MSU Sport Information files.

125. Robert E. Steele file at MSU Sport Information.

126. *Mt. Clemens Macomb Daily*, June 23, 1966.

127. *Detroit Free Press*, May 26, 1967.

128. *Track and Field News*, September 1966, p. 19.

129. *Official National Collegiate Athletic Association Track and Field Guide, 1967*. Phoenix, AZ: College Athletics Publishing Service, 1967, *p. 11.*

130. *State News*, April 15, 1961.

131. *Lansing State Journal*, June 25, 1967.

132. *Official National Collegiate Athletic Association Track and Field Guide, 1968*. Phoenix, AZ: College Athletics Publishing Service, 1968, *p. 21.*

133. *Grand Rapids Press*, August 20, 1967.

134. *Ibid.*

135. *Track and Field News*, June 1968, 37.

136. *Ibid.*, June 1968, p. 9.

137. MSU Sports Information files.

138. *Lansing State Journal*, April 25, 1977.

139. *New York Times*, April 28, 1972, p. 50.
140. *Ibid.*, May 28, 1972, Section 5, p. 4.
141. *Lansing State Journal*, June 28, 1977.
142. MSU Sports Information files.
143. *Track and Field News*, July 1964, p. 16.
144. *Ibid.*, July 1965.
145. *Detroit Free Press*, June 4, 1988.
146. *Track and Field News*, June 1966, p. 3.
147. Cerulla ran 14.1 in the heats and 14.3 in the semi-finals.
148. *Ypsilanti Press*, April 27, 1967.
149. *Ibid.*
150. *Official Collegiate Track and Field Guide, 1970.* Phoenix, AZ: College Athletics Publishing Service, 1969, p. 86.
151. *Track and Field News*, September 1967, p. 12.
152. *Ypsilanti Press*, May 2–3, 1970, p. 13.
153. *Ibid.*
154. *Track and Field News, October* 1967, p. 16.
155. *Eastern Michigan University 1997 Men's Track and Field Media Guide.* One of Tipton's contemporaries at EMU was Arthur Gillespie, who later became track coach at Detroit's Northern HS, see *Detroit Free Press*, October 7, 2000, p. 11A.
156. *Detroit News*, May 21, 1986, p.10 F.
157. *Ypsilanti Press*, May 2–3, 1970, p. 13.
158. *Official Collegiate Track and Field Guide, 1971.* Phoenix, AZ.: College Athletic Publishing Service, 1970, p. 20.
159. *Detroit News*, May 21, 1966, p. 10-F; and Interview with Fred La Plante, July 15, 1999.
160. *The Grand Rapids Press*, March 7, 1971, p. 4-F.
161. *State News*, May 15, 1974.
162. Michigan State University, Department of Information Services, February 18, 1971.
163. *Ibid.*
164. *The Grand Rapids Press*, March 7, 1971, p. 4-F.
165. *State News*, May 15, 1974.
166. *Ibid.*, April 20, 1972.
167. *Ibid.*, May 15, 1974.
168. *Ibid.*, April 20, 1972.
169. *Official Collegiate Track and Field Guide, 1973*, p.60.
170. *Lansing State Journal*, June 3, 1973.
171. Michigan State University, Department of Information Services, February 13, 1973.
172. *Lansing State Journal*, June 3, 1973.
173. *Official Collegiate Track and Field Guide, 1974.* Shawnee Mission, KS: NCAA Publishing Serv., 1973, p. 18, 60.
174. *Detroit News*, March 12, 1974 and *The* [Royal Oak, MI.] *Daily Tribune*, March 12, 1972.
175. *Michigan State News*, June 28, 1974.
176. *Ibid.*, May 15, 1974.
177. *Mt. Pleasant Daily Times-News*, August 30, 1976.
178. Interviewed Randy Williams, March 22, 2000.
179. *Flint Journal*, May 22, 1979, p. C-5.
180. *Ibid.*, May 24, 1979, p. C-5.
181. Interviews with Doug Hansen and Ricky Brown, 1999.
182. *Flint Journal*, May 30, 1982, p. E-7.
183. *Lansing State Journal*, February 6, 1983, p. C3.
184. *Saginaw News*, March 13, 1983, p. F4.
185. *Detroit News*, June 2, 1982, p. 4-E and June 6, 1982, p. 12-D.

186. *Ibid.*
187. *Detroit News*, May 21, 1986, p.F1 and F8. July 23, 1988 Wilcher placed 4th in heat 3 of the 110-meter hurdles (13.79) at the Olympic Trials, Indianapolis. See *New York Times*, July 23, 1988.
188. *Des Moines Register*, April 25, 1993.
189. *2000 Mid-American Conference Indoor Track & Field Championships Meet Program.*
190. *Eastern Michigan University 1997 Men's Track and Field Media Guide*, p. 21.
191. His performance in Boise made him an All-American and qualified him for the 2000 Olympic trials.
On January 29, 2000, at the Central Collegiate Indoor Championships in Mt. Pleasant he set the new Jack Skoog Track record (7.86) for the 60-meter high-hurdles (Eye-witness and interview with Greg Richardson, January 29, 2000.) On March 10, 2000 Greg placed seventh in the 60-yard high-hurdles (7.90) at the NCAA Division I National Championships in Fayetteville, Arkansas (*New York Times*, March 12, 2000, p. 39). On April 29 he placed fifth in the 110-meter high hurdles (13.99) at the Drake Relays (*Des Moines Register*, April 30, 2000, p. 5C.)

Chapter 15

1. Don Canham was high jump Big Ten Champion in 1940 and 1941. His brother Robert Canham was a pole-vaulter for the University of Michigan in 1941, but did not earn a letter. Robert went on to become a surgeon. The owner of a construction company, who was a Wolverine fan, paid Don's tuition. Don worked in a fraternity helping serve meals and worked part-time for his room while in college, See Canham, *op. cit.*, p. 7–8 and *Detroit Free Press*, February 25, 1940, Sports Section, p. 3.
2. Canham, *op. cit.*, p. 65.
3. *Ibid.*, p. 65.
4. *Ibid.*
5. *Ibid.*, p. 66.
6. *Michigan Daily*, February 13, 1951, p. 3. A year later when they reset the record, Gordon was still the only U.S. citizen on the relay team. *Michigan Daily*, April 19, 1952, p. 3. For more on Gordon see *The Prospector*, Southwestern High School newspaper, February 15, 2000, p. 5D.
7. *Track and Field News, February* 1950, p. 6.
8. *University of Michigan Men's Track and Field Media Guide, 1998*, p. 41–43.
9. *Official NCAA Track and Field Guide, 1952.* New York: The National Collegiate Athletic Bureau, 1952, p. 20.
10. *Track and Field New*, March 23, 1952 p. 5.
11. *Toronto Star*, May 30, 1961, p. 20.
12. Jack Clowser, "Canadians Star for Michigan Squad," *Track and Field New*, March 1952, p. 7.
13. *Track and Field News, February* 1951, p. 6.
14. *Ibid., January* 1952, p. 11.
15. Wallechinsky, *op. cit.*, p. 146.
16. Canham's claim that Hoyt and Doherty had refused to hold AAU-organized track meets on the Michigan campus is untrue. AAU meets were held at Yost Fieldhouse in February 1933–35 and March 23, 1940 and March 19, 1941. The claim was made in Canham, *op. cit.*, p. 66.
17. Canham, *op. cit.*, p. 70–1.

18. See Don Canham and Tyler Micoleau, *Field Techniques Illustrated*, New York: The Ronald Press Company, 1952.

19. *Track and Field News*, February 1948, p. 6.

20. *Ibid.*, March 1950, p. 6.

21. *Ibid.*, August 1963, p. 7.

22. *The A.A.U. Official 1965 Track and Field Handbook*. NY: The Amateur Athletic Union of the US, 1965, p. 14, 82.

23. Interview with Louis C. Scott, December 7, 2000 and *Track and Field News*, October 1963, p. 10.

24. *Ibid.*, *May* 1951, p. 9.

25. *Official NCAA Track and Field Guide, 1956*. NY: The National Collegiate Athletic Bureau, 1956, p.18.

26. *Official NCAA Track and Field Guide, 1957*. NY: The National Collegiate Athletic Bureau, 1957, p.54.

27. *Michiganensian, 1956, p.289.*

28. *Official NCAA Track and Field Guide, 1957*, p.16.

29. *Official NCAA Track and Field Guide, 1958.* NY: The National Collegiate Athletic Bureau, 1958, p.18–19.

30. See, for example, the "Indoor Report," *Track and Field News*, February 1966, p. 9.

31. *Official NCAA Track and Field Guide, 1956*, p. 58; *Official NCAA Track and Field Guide*, p.16.

32. *Official NCAA Track and Field Guide, 1957*, p.16.

33. MSU Sports Information, February 28, 2000.

34. *Official NCAA Track and Field Guide, 1957*, p. 12, 16.

35. *New York Times*, July 11, 1976, p. 15.

36. *The Oakland Press*, June 10, 1974, p. C-5.

37. *New York Times*, March 16, 1975, p. V-1.

38. *Detroit News*, March 5, 1982, p. 4-C.

39. *Ibid.*

40. *New York Times*, June 8, 1992, p. C-9.

41. *Ibid.*, June 8, 1992, p. C-9.

42. *Ibid.*, June 19, 1993, p. 29.

43. *Oakland Press*, June 1, 1996, p. B-9. The U of M women's track team also came to rely on foreign-born athletes, See *The Michigan Daily*, April 14, 1997, p. 7-B.

44. *University of Michigan Men's Track and Field Media Guide, 1999*, p. 37–40.

45. *New York Times*, March 7, 1999, p. 36.

46. *Track and Field News*, March 1961, p. 10.

47. Canham, *op. cit.*, p. 70–1.

48. *1967 National Collegiate Indoor Track Championships, March 10–11*, meet program, p. 28.

49. *Ibid.*, pp. 2, 5, 8.

50. *Michigan Daily*, March 14, 1967, p. 7.

51. *NCAA Track and Field Guide*, 1980.

52. *Detroit News*, March 12, 1981, p. 1-B and 5-B.

53. *Ibid.*, March 11, 1982, p. 6-D.

54. *Ibid.*, March 9, 1985, p. 2D. In 1984, the *Detroit News* reported Friday night attendance at Carrier Dome in Syracuse to be 1,304 and the Saturday attendance was estimated to be 12,000 in an arena that seated 55,000. *Detroit News*, March 11, 1984, p. p. 14-C. It appears that most of the estimated crowd of 12,000 was unpaid.

55. *Michigan Daily*, March 8, 1967, p. 18.

56. *Ibid.*

57. *New York Times*, April 29, 1973, section v, p. 4.

58. *1998 U of Michigan Men's Track & Field Media Guide*, pp. 35–42.

59. *The Michigan Daily*, February 9, 1967, p. 7.

60. *Ibid.*, February 26, 1967, p. 6.

61. *Ibid.*

62. *Ibid.*, March 7, 1967, p.7.

63. *Ibid.*, March 17, 1967, p.7.

64. *Ibid.*, February 9, 1967, p.7.

65. *Official National Collegiate Athletic Association Track and Field Guide, 1968*, Phoenix, AZ: College Athletics Publishing Service, 1968, p. 67.

66. *The Michigan Daily*, June 11, 1968, p. 6.

67. *The Michigan Daily*, June 21, 1968.

68. *Track and Field News*, June 1968, p. 9.

69. *Ann Arbor News*, September 5, 1968, p. 2.

70. *Track and Field News*, September 1968, p. 36.

71. *Track and Field News*, September 1968, p. 7.

72. *Ann Arbor News* September 9, p. 16, September 11, p 24, and September 12, 1968, p.28.

73. *Track and Field News*, October/November 1968, p. 11–12.

74. *Official Collegiate Track and Field Guide, 1969.* Phoenix, AZ: College Athletics Publishing Service, 1968, p. 64.

75. *The Michigan Daily*, January 25 and 26, 1969, p. 6 and 8.

76. *Track and Field News*, March 1969, p. 5.

77. *Track and Field News*, March 1969, p. 6.

78. *Official Collegiate Track and Field Guide, 1970.* Phoenix, AZ: College Athletics Publishing Service, 1969, p. 67.

79. *Track and Field News*, July 1969, p. 7.

Chapter 16

1. See Frank Dolson, *Always Young*. New York: World Publications, 1975.

2. See Phil Coleman, *Sports Illustrated*, March 6, 1961.

3. See *Detroit Times*, April 26, 1956, p. 28. Joseph M. Turrini, Archivist for the United Federation of Teachers in New York City and Wayne State University Ph.D. candidate, has studied Santee's influence on subsequent challenges to and changes in AAU policies.

4. *Daily Ypsilanti Press*, March 2, 1925, p. 4.

5. *Battle Creek Enquirer and Evening News*, April 16, 1928, p. 10.

6. Canham, *op. cit.*, p. 68–9, 76–77.

7. *Chicago Tribune*, June 1, 1956, Part 4, p. 1.

8. *Track and Field News*, September 1963, p. 17.

9. *Ibid*, August 1960, p. 20.

10. Carlson and Fogarty, *op. cit.*, p. 339–40.

11. *Track and Field News*, September 1961, p. 1 and 14; and October 1961, p. 1, 12–14. Also Canham, *op. cit.*, p. 76.

12. *Track and Field News*, September 1961, p. 15. Also "The End of the AAU," *Sports Illustrated*, Sept. 25, 1961.

13. *Track and Field News*, October 1961, p.13–14.

14. *Ibid.*, p. 1.

15. *Ibid.*, January 1962, p. 14.

16. *Ibid.*, March 1962, p. 21.

17. *Ibid.*, June 1965, p. 9.

18. Interview with Jim Bibbs, July 23, 1998.

19. *Atlanta Journal*, May 17, 1971, p. 2-C.

20. *Ibid.*

21. *Ypsilanti Press*, May 11, 1972, p. 26.

22. Canham, *op. cit.*, p. 76–78.

23. Interview with Louis C Scott, December 7, 2000.

24. *New York Times*, July 11, 1972, p. 31.

25. *Ibid.*, July 9, 1972, p. V-5.

26. *Ibid.*

27. *Ibid.*

28. *Ibid.*, April 29, 1973, p. V-4.

29. *Ibid.*, p. V-7.

30. Editor, Tina Grant, *op. cit.*, Volume 14, Pp. 6–9.

31. J. B. Strasser and Laurie Becklund, *Swoosh: The Unauthorized Story of Nike and the Men Who Played There*. New York: Harcourt Brace Jovanovich, 1991; and "Fabled Track Coach Bill Bowerman Dies," *The [Portland] Oregonian*, December 26, 1999.

32. *New York Times*, July 3, 1972, p.11.

33. Krise and Squires, *op. cit.*, p. 265–6.

34. *New York Times*, July 3, 1972, p. 11.

35. *Ibid.*, July 2, 1972, p. V-5; and July 3, 1972, p. 11.

36. *Ibid.*, June 4, 1995, p. V-9. For more on Prefontaine see Joseph M. Turrini, *"Fire on the Track: The Steve Prefontaine Story*, 1995, and *Prefontaine*, 1997." *Journal of Sport History*, Vol. 25, no. 2, summer 1998, pp. 321–323.

37. Lord Michael Morris Killanian, *My Olympic Years*. NY: Morrow, 1983, p. 85–92; and *The New York Times*, April 26, 1999 (obituary).

38. *New York Times*, June 3, 1973; *Toledo Blade*, June 1, 1975, p. 2D.

39. *New York Times*, June 3, 1973.

40. *Ibid.*, July 2, 1972, p. V-5.

41. *Ibid.*, February 8, 1976, p. V-1, 6.

42. *Ibid.*, February 8, 1976, p. V-1.

43. *The Ypsilanti Press*, May 8, 1977, p. 3B.

44. Information provided by Hal Bateman, USA Track and Field, March 2000.

45. *The Washington Post National Weekly Edition*, May 20–26, 1996, p. 8.

46. Information provided by Hal Bateman, USA Track and Field, March 2000.

47. *Detroit News*, June 24, 1978, p. 2B.

48. *Toledo Blade*, May 25, 1976, p. 33.

49. Don Canham liked traveling in the fast lane. He made big money in training films and sports equipment while coaching track at the University of Michigan. See *Toledo Blade*, May 17, 1981, p. D-1.

50. *Toledo Blade*, May 11, 1980, p. D-5.

51. *New York Times*, June 30, 1987, p. D-29.

52. *The Washington Post National Edition*, September 23–30, 1996, p. 25.

53. *Detroit News*, May 19, 1974, p. 2-D.

54. Canham, *op. cit.*, p. 205.

55. *Ypsilanti Press*, May 10, 1984, p. B-1.

56. For Ryun's sub- four minute mile see *Sports Illustrated*, vol 92, no. 26, June 26, 2000, p. 37. The feat was duplicated by only two other prep runners, Tim Danielson (1966) and Marty Liquori (1967), during the balance of the century. On January 20, 2001 U of M recruit Alan Webb, ran a 3:59 mile indoor at the New Balance Games in NYC. *Detroit Free Press*, Jan 24, 2001, p. 6-C and *Detroit News* November 5, 1996 and conversations with Michigan Congressional representatives.

57. *Michigan Daily*, June 4, 1997, p. 14.

Chapter 17

1. *Track and Field News*, October 1963, p. 9.

2. *Ibid.*, September 1964, p. 5. For Carr's birth information see James A. Page, *Black Olympian Medalists*. Englewood, CO.: Libraries Unlimited, 1991, p. 21.

3. *Track and Field News.*, April 1963, p. 1.

4. Baldwin, *op. cit.*, p. 144.

5. *Track and Field News*, June 1963, p. 23.

6. *Ibid.*, p. 2.

7. *Ibid.*

8. *Ibid.*, July 1963, p. 23.

9. A story told by Jim Elliott at a Track Coaches Seminar, 1973.

10. *Track and Field News*, April, 1964, p. 1–2.

11. Cordner Nelson, "Villanova Runs Record 7:19," *Track and Field News*, May 1964, p. 7.

12. Cordner Nelson, "Newcomers Rising in Sprints," *Track and Field News*, May, 1964, p. 15.

13. *Track and Field News*, August 1964, p. 4 and 24.

14. *Ibid.*, September 1964.

15. *Ibid.*, August 1960, p. 20.

16. *New York Times*, June 25, 1972, Section 5, p. 4.

17. Quercetani, *op. cit., 1964*, pp. 45.

18. *Track and Field News*, October/November 1964, p. 15.

19. *The A.A.U. Official 1965 Track and Field Handbook* . NY: The Amateur Athletic Union of the US, 1965, p. 22.

20. *Track and Field News*, October/November 1964, p. 35.

21. *The A.A.U. Official 1965 Track and Field Handbook* , p. 14–15.

22. *Track and Field News*, December 1964, p. 15; *Track and Field News*, December 1965, p. 21; *Detroit Free Press*, 1999. For more on his football career see, "NFL Olympians," *Super Bowl Program XVIII*, January 22, 1984, p. 99. More than 20 Olympic track medalists have played professional football.

23. *Track and Field News*, April 1968, p. 11.

24. *Ibid.*, p. 4–5.

25. *Flint Journal* May 21, 1968.

26. *Track and Field News*, April 1968, p. 11.

27. *Ibid.*, February 1968, p.10.

28. *Official Collegiate Track and Field Guide, 1970*. Phoenix, AZ: College Athletics Publishing Service, 1969, p. 67.

29. *Official Collegiate Track and Field Guide, 1971*. Phoenix, AZ.: College Athletic Publishing Service, 1970, p. 57.

30. *Official Collegiate Track and Field Guide, 1970*.

31. *Official Collegiate Track and Field Guide, 1972*. Phoenix, AZ: College Athletics Publishing Service, 1971, p. 60.

32. *New York Times*, May 20, 1973, Part V, P. 3.

33. *Official Collegiate Track and Field Guide, 1973*, p.60.

34. *The Detroit News*, January 10, 1973, p. 7D.

35. *Millrose Games Program*, January 25, 1974, p. 10.

36. *New York Times*, February 23, 1973, p. 26.

37. *Ibid.*, February 24, 1973, p. 22.

38. Scott Pitoniak, "Herb Washington," *The National Pastime*, no. 17, 1997, pp. 95–97.

39. See Rhonda Sanders, *Bronze Pillars*. Flint: Flint Journal. 1995, p.232–233.

40. Pitoniak, *op. cit.*, pp. 95–97.

41. *Detroit Free Press*, June 21, 1971.

42. *Detroit News*, November 1971 and *Detroit Free Press*, May 13, 1975.

43. *Detroit Free Press*, May 13, 1975.

44. *The Detroit News*, January 10, 1973, p. 7D.

45. *New York Times*, July 9, 1972.

46. *Ibid.*, July 30, 1972, Section 5, p. 6.

47. *Official Collegiate Track and Field Guide, 1973,* p.60.

48. *New York Times*, May 20, 1973, Part V, P. 3.

49. *Official Collegiate Track and Field Guide, 1974.* Shawnee Mission, KS: NCAA Publishing Service, 1973, p. 18.

50. *Michigan State News*, January 8, 1973.

51. *Detroit News*, May 19, 1974, p. D-1.

52. *Ibid.*, May 26, 1974, p. 6-C.

53. *Detroit Free Press*, May 13, 1975.

54. *Ibid.*, May 18, 1975, p.3F.

55. *Ibid.*, April, 24, 1990 and *90th Annual Drake Relays Program*, April 23–24, 1999, p. 67 and 21.

56. *Saginaw News*, May 3, 1973, p. D2.

57. *Ibid.*, May 12, 1973, p. B1.

58. *Ibid.*, May 8, 1973, p. B9.

59. *Ibid.*, May 20, 1973, p. D3.

60. *Ibid.*, May 12, 1973, p. B1.

61. *Official Collegiate Track and Field Guide, 1975.* Shawnee, Kansas: NCAA Publishing Service, 1974.

62. University of Tennessee Sports Information.

63. *New York Times*, March 14, 1976, V-6.

64. University of Tennessee Sports Information.

65. Wallechinsky, *op. cit.*, p. 22.

66. University of Tennessee Track Media Guide, 1998.

67. *Lansing State Journal*, February 6, 1983, p. C1.

68. *Detroit News*, February 24, 1980.

69. *State News*, April 21, 1982.

70. *Detroit News*, February 24, 1980.

71. *Michigan Chronicle*, March 15, 1980.

72. *Ibid.*

73. *The South End*, April 14, 1981, p.5.

74. *Michigan Chronicle*, March 15, 1980.

75. MSU Sports Information Questionnaire, 1981.

76. *State News*, April 21, 1982, p. 7.

77. *Ibid.*

78. *Ibid.*

79. *State News*, May 25, 1982.

80. Spartan Sports Service, February 22, 1983.

81. *State News*, May 31, 1983.

82. Track and Field Records, Sports Information, Central Michigan University.

83. *Lansing State Journal*, June 6, 1983, p. 3C; *State News, July 11, 1983; Spartan Sports Service*, news release, September 1983.

84. Los Angeles Times, February 12, 1984, Part III, p. 17; *New York Times*, June 18, 1984, p. C4and June 19, 1984, p. A24.

85. Adam R. Hornbuckle, "Quincy Watts," *African-American Sports Greats: A Biographical Dictionary.* Edited by David L. Porter. Westport, CT: Greenwood Press, 1995, pp. 363–365.

86. *New York Times*, June 7, 1992, p. V-10.

87. Wallechinsky, *op. cit.*, p. 33.

88. *New York Times*, June 20, 1993, p. V-4 and V-10.

89. "White Men Can't Run," *The Best American Sports Writing, 1993.* Ed. Frank Deford. Boston: Houghton Mifflin Company, 1993.

90. *Atlanta Constitution*, June 15, 1964, p. 17.

91. *Ibid.*, March 5, 2000, p. E-21.

Chapter 18

1. *Detroit News*, June 16, 1976, p. 8A.

2. *Kalamazoo Gazette*, May 2, 1957, p. 23.

3. *Ibid.*, March 13, 1957.

4. *Atlanta Constitution*, June 1, 1964, p. 9.

5. *Michigan Daily*, February 15, 1967, p.3.

6. Jack Olsen, "The Cruel Deception," *Sports Illustrated*, June 29, 1968, vol. 29, no. 1, pp. 15–27.

7. Jack Olsen, "Pride and Prejudice," *Sports Illustrated*, July 6, 1968, vol. 29, no. 2, pp. 20 ff.

8. Olsen, "The Cruel Deception," *op. cit.*, p.16.

9. *Ibid.*, pp.15–27.

10. *New York Times*, May 31, 1986, p. 48.

11. Olsen, "The Cruel Deception," *op. cit.*, p. 15–17.

12. Jack Olsen, "In the Back of the Bus," *Sports Illustrated*, July 22, 1968, vol. 29, no. 4, pp. 34.

13. *The Michigan Daily*, February 4, 1967, p. 7.

14. *Ibid.*, May 16, 1968, p. 8.

15. *Ibid.*, May 16, 1968, p. 8.

16. *Official Collegiate Track and Field Guide, 1969.* Phoenix, AZ: College Athletics Publishing Service, 1968, p. 64.

17. *Ibid.*, p. 24.

18. *Official Collegiate Track and Field Guide, 1970.* Phoenix, AZ: College Athletics Publishing Service, 1969, p. 67.

19. *The Michigan Daily*, May 9, 1968, p.7.

20. *Ibid.*, May 18, 1968, p.6.

21. *Ibid.*, June 19, 1968, p.1.

22. *Ibid.*, May 18, 1968, p.6.

23. *Track and Field News*, February 1968, p.10.

24. Bob Considine and Fred G. Jarvis, *A Portrait of the NYAC: The First Hundred Years.* London: The Macmillan Company, 1969, p. 152–3.

25. Edwards, *op. cit.*, p. 67–9.

26. Fred G. Jarvis, *Steadfast and Changing: The New York Athletic Club from 1968 to 1993.* New York: New York Athletic Club, 1993, p. 27.

27. Jack Olsen, "In an Alien World," *Sports Illustrated*, vol. 29, no. 3, July 15, 1968.

28. *Ibid.*, p. 41.

29. Bob Burns, "Magic Mountain," *Chicago Tribune*, July 3, 2000, Section 3, p. 8.

30. Mike Littwin, "Guess Who's Coming to the L. A. Olympics," *Los Angeles Times*, February 12, 1984, Part III, p. 3.

31. *Ibid.*

32. *The New York Times*, July 8, 1972.

33. *Atlanta Journal*, May 15, 1971.

34. *Ann Arbor News*, February 24, 1972, p. 25.

35. *Ibid.*, February 27, 1972, p. 27.

36. *Detroit News*, March 2, 1983, p. 5F.

37. *Ibid.*, May 4, 1976, p. 3D.

38. *New York Times*, June 16, 1972, p. 29.

39. *Ibid.*, April 26, 1999 (obituary).

40. *Saginaw News*, May 3, 1973, p. C2.

41. *New York Times*, February 4, 1973, section V, p. 1.

42. *Ibid.*, June 9, 1973, p. 26.

43. "The Shoe is on the Other Foot," *The Washington Post National Weekly Edition*, May 26, 1997, p. 6.

Chapter 19

1. Tricard, *op. cit.*, pp. 5–6.

2. Barbara Miller Solomon, *In the Company of*

Educated Women: A History of Women and Higher Education in America. New Haven, CT: Yale University Press, 1985, p. 58.

3. *The American Woman in Sport*. Edited by Ellen W. Gerber, Jan Felshin, Pearl Berlin, and Waneen Wyrich. Reading, MA: Addison-Wesley Publishing Company, 1974, p. 62.

4. Tricard, *op. cit.*, p. 21.

5. Joan S. Hult, "The Governance of Athletics for Girls and Women: Leadership by Women Physical Educators, 1899–1949," *A Century of Women's Basketball: From Frailty to Final Four*. Edited by Joan S. Hult and Marianna Trekell. Reston, VA: AAHPERD, 1991. P. 55.

6. Joan S. Hult, "The Story of Women's Athletics: Manipulating a Dream 1890–1985," *Women and Sports: Interdisciplinary Perspectives*. Edited by D. Margaret Costa and Sharon R. Guthrie. Champaign, IL: Human Kinetics Publishers, 1994, Chapter 6.

7. See *New York Times*, October 24, 1999, p. 37 for more on the enduring problem with stereotype labeling. "Because the phrase lesbian coach has a negative connotation in mainstream America as well as in the overall sports world, it affects the way female sports are reported and athletes are perceived."

8. Todd Crosset, "Masculinity, Sexuality, and the Development of Early Modern Sport," *Sport, Men, and the Gender Order: Critical Feminist Perspective*. Edited by Michael A. Messner and Donald F. Sabo. Champaign, IL: Human Kinetics Publishers, 1990. P. 52.

9. Tricard, *op. cit.*, pp. 60–66.

10. *1919 Spalding's Official Athletic Almanac*.

11. Doris H. Pieroth, *Their Day in the Sun: Women of the 1932 Olympics*. Seattle: University of Washington Press, 1996, p. 1.

12. Allen L. Sack and Ellen J. Staurowsky, *College Athletes for Hire*. Westport, CT: Praeger, 1998. P.65–66 and Tricard, *op. cit.*, p. 85.

13. Tricard, *op. cit.*, pp. 68–81.

14. Only twelve teams, nearly all from Philadelphia, New York, and New Jersey, sent teams to the first National Women's AAU Meet held in Newark, New Jersey in 1923. Tricard, *op. cit.*, p. 85, 88.

15. "Women's Division: National Amateur Athletic Federation Platform," *Women and Athletics*. New York: A. S. Barnes and Company, 1930, pp. 3–4.

16. *Detroit Times*, May 5, 1929, Part 2, p. 3.

17. Tricard, *op. cit.*, p. 109.

18. *Daily Ypsilanti Press*, February 24, 1925, p. 4.

19. Wallechinsky, *op. cit.*, 1996, pp. 188, 200, 212–3, 219, and 228.

20. *Detroit News*, August 15, 1928, p. 25.

21. Interview with Dorothy Frances Anderson Merena, April 17, 2000.

22. *Detroit Times*, June 8, 1928.

23. *Aurora, 1933*, pp. 93, 262.

24. Doris H. Pieroth, *Their Day in the Sun: Women of the 1932 Olympics*. Seattle: University of Washington Press, 1996, p. 1.

25. Tricard, *op. cit.*, p. 184.

26. Interview with Dorothy Frances Anderson Merena, April 17, 2000.

27. *Ypsilanti Daily Press*, February 27, 1933, p. 3. Anderson did not place in the June 1933 meet, Tricard, *op, cit.*, p. 213–4.

28. Interview with Dorothy Frances Anderson Merena, April 17, 2000.

29. Tricard, *op. cit.*, p. 350.

30. See Ed Temple, *Only the Pure in Heart Survive*. Nashville, TN: Broadman Press, 1980. Also see Kathleen Krull, *Wilma Unlimited*. Orlando, FL: Harcourt Brace & Company, 1996. This children's book was named the best book of the year by the *School Library Journal*. Wilma Rudolph retired from running in 1962. She became a second grade teacher and a high school track coach. Wilma died in 1994 at the age of 54.

31. Wilma Rudolph, *Wilma*. New York: New American Library, 1977.

32. Tricard, *op. cit.*, pp.374–5.

33. *The Olympians' Guide to Winning the Game of Life*. Compiled by Bud Greenspan. Los Angeles: General Publishing Group, 1977, p. 12. Wilma's 200-meter dash record (22.9) stood until 1972 when Alice Annum, a 21-year old University of Tennessee freshman, broke it (22.8) at the AAU outdoor finals in North Canton, Ohio. See *New York Times*, July 2, 1972, Section 5, p. 7.

34. Tricard, *op. cit.*, pp. 409–19.

35. *Drake Relays 74 years of Excellence, op. cit.*, p. 14.

36. In Olympic and Pan American years, these events would be contested as national championships in 400 and 800 meters.

37. *The Amateur Athlete*, February 1958, p. 28.

38. *The A.A.U. Official 1965 Track and Field Handbook*. NY: The Amateur Athletic Union of the U S, 1965, p. 203, 183.

39. Wallechinsky, *op. cit.*, 1996, p. 200.

40. Tricard, *op. cit.*, pp. 472, 480–81, 484.

41. "Girl's Sport Institute in South Carolina," *Journal of Health, Physical Education and Recreation*, May 1964, p. 93.

42. Tricard, *op. cit.*, pp. 490–1.

43. Meet Program and *Detroit News*, January 15, 1966.

44. Tricard, *op. cit.*, p. 494.

45. *New York Times* January 27, 1967.

46. *The Ann Arbor News* January 27, 1967, p. 20.

47. *New York Times* January 29, 1967, Section 5, pp. 1 and 6.

48. *The Michigan Daily*, February 21, 1967.

49. *Ibid.*, March 8, 1967.

50. *The Ann Arbor News*, September 9, 1968, p. 18.

51. *Ibid.*, February 15 and 28, 1970, p. 15/13.

52. *Ibid.*, February 28, 1970, p. 13.

53. *Frederick Post*, July 8, 1972, p. B1 and *New York Times*, July 9, 1972, Section 5, p. 5 and July 10, 1972, p. 41. Note that only the winners of the eleven events automatically qualified for the women's Olympic team in 1972. The second and third place finishers only made the team if they bettered Olympic standards for the event. Different rules applied for men. See *Akron Beacon Journal*, July 9, 1972, p. B2 and *Frederick Post*, July 10, 1972, p. B1.

54. *Frederick Post*, July 10, 1972, p. B1.

55. Wallechinsky, *op. cit.*, p. 203.

56. *New York Times* September 4, 1972, p. 10.

57. Wallechinsky, *op. cit.*, p. 203.

58. Tricard, *op. cit.*, p. 546.

59. *Jackson Citizen Patriot*, August 8, 1983, p. C1.

60. *Detroit Free Press*, August 2, 1983.

61. *Go Blue*, September, 1981, p. 30–31.

62. *Ibid.*

63. *Jackson Citizen Patriot*, June 25, 1992 and Penny's personal recollections at the retirement of

Kenneth "Red" Simmon. University of Michigan Sports Information, Neer file, January 1994.

64. *Ibid.*

65. U-M Sports Information Archives.

66. Neer file, University of Michigan, Sports Information, January 1994.

67. *Ann Arbor News*, May 26, 1982.

68. *Ibid.*

69. *Jackson Citizen Patriot*, August 8, 1983, p. C4.

70. *Detroit Free Press*, August 2, 1983.

71. AZ News July 27, 1983 by Wayne DeNeff.

72. *Ann Arbor News*, June 24, 1984.

73. University of Michigan, Sports Information, Neer file.

74. *Detroit Free Press*, June 17, 1992.

75. *Los Angeles Times*, June 16, 1988, part II, p. 15.

76. Notes from a speech by Penny Neer, January 1994 on the occasion of Red Simmons' induction into the Michigan Woman's Track and Field Hall of Fame.

77. *Los Angeles Times*, June 3, 1990 and June 15, 1990. New York Times, June 16, 1991 and University of Michigan Sports Information, August 1991.

78. *Jackson Citizen Patriot*, June 25, 1992 and *Ann Arbor News*, July 25, 1992.

79. Notes from a speech by Penny Neer, January 1994.

80. AIAW Archives at the University of Maryland McKeldin Library.

81. This meet is also referred to as the third DGWS meet.

82. AIAW Archives at the University of Maryland McKeldin Library.

83. U. S. Government Printing Office, *Hearings op. cit.*, pp. 103–109.

84. *Lansing State Journal*, May 21, 1979. Cheryle graduated from Cass Tech High School in Detroit and MSU in East Lansing. Note: On February 23, 1973 the Motor City Police Athletic League 640-yard girl's relay team placed second at the National AAU Indoor Championships at Madison Square Garden.

85. Thad died in 1979.

86. *Detroit Free Press, September 6, 2000, p. C-2 and Michigan State News*, March 3, 1977.

87. *Los Angeles Times*, March 5, 1966.

88. Meet Program Bulletin, 1966.

89. Tricard, *op. cit.*, p. 505.

90. *Lansing State Journal*, May 16, 1979.

91. AIAW Archives, University of Maryland McKeldin Library; and *Michigan State News*, March 3, 1977, in her the MSU Sports Information folder.

92. *Detroit Free Press*, September 10, 1981.

93. *Lansing State Journal*, July 24, 1992.

94. *Lansing State Journal*, July 24, 1992.

95. *Detroit Free Press*, July, 13, 1990.

96. *Lansing State Journal*, December 25, 1993.

97. *Detroit Free Press*, May 17, 2000, p. 1D.

98. Tricard, *op. cit.*, p. 537–539.

99. *Ibid.*, p. 540.

100. *Des Moines Register*, April 30, 1972.

101. *Ypsilanti Press*, May 2, 1972, p. 1 and May 8, 1972, p. 2-B.

102. *Ibid.*, May 10, 1972, p. 25.

103. *Ibid.*, May 10, 1972, p. 25.

104. *Fredrick Post*, July 7–8, 1972, p. B1.

105. *New York Times*, January 26, 1974; and *Oakland Press*, June 2, 1974.

106. Files in Sports Information, Central Michigan University.

107. For evidence see the files in Sport Information, CMU and *CM Life*, April 12, 1876, p. 8; February 6, 1978, p. 10; Feb 13, 1978, p. 13; Feb. 20, 1978, p. 15; May 1, 1978, p. 15; and May 8, 1978, p. 14; *The BG News*, April 6, 22 and 29, 1975; April 7, 1976; and April 1977.

108. *The Oakland Press*, June 15, 1981, p. B-2.

109. *Central Michigan University Chippewas Women's Track and Field Media Guide, 1998–9*, p. 14–15.

110. *Central Michigan University 1991 Women's Track & Field and Cross Country* Media Guide.

111. *Michigan Daily*, February 3, 1986; *The Ann Arbor News*, November 7, 1985, p. B6.

112. *Ann Arbor News*, May 16, 1976, p. 42.

113. *Detroit News*, May 20, 1973, p. 6-D.

114. *The Oakland Press*, May 17, 1974, C1.

115. *Ibid.*, May 17, 1974, C1.

116. *Ibid.*, May 18, 1974, p. B-1.

117. *Ibid.*, June 2, 1974.

118. *Ibid.*, June 15, 1974, p. C-3.

119. *Lansing State Journal*, May 8, 1977, p. D-7.

120. Michigan State University Sports Information archives.

121. *Drake Relays 75 Years of Excellence*, Edited by Robert H. Spiegel, Drake University, 1984 p. 92.

122. *Ann Arbor News*, June 23, 1984.

123. *The Clarkston (MI.) News*, August 1, 1984, p. 20.

124. *Ann Arbor News*, May 6, 1973, p. 33.

125. Minutes of the AIAW meeting, Archives, University of Maryland.

126. *New York Times*, May 23, 1973, p. 57.

127. Canham, *op. cit.*, p. 249–50. For more on the Kellmeyer lawsuit see Ying Wu, "'Kellmeyer' the Lawsuit that Ruined Women's Control of Intercollegiate Athletics for Women?" Paper presented at the Twenty-seventh Annual Convention of the North American Society for Sport History, Penn State University, May 22, 1999.

128. *The BG News*, February 13, 1975, p. 6.

129. *New York Times*, March 1, 1975, p. 16.

130. *Ibid.*, June 1, 1975, Section V, p. 3.

131. *The BG News*, April 15, 1976, P. 6.

132. *New York Times*, June 25, 1992, p. B 13.

133. *Ibid.*, June 26, 1992, p. B11.

134. *Time Magazine*, December 27, 1982, p. 70.

135. *The Ypsilanti Press*, May 29, 1975, p. 1B.

136. *Ibid.*, May 29, 1975, p. 1B.

137. *Detroit Free Press*, August 24, 1999, p. E-1. In 1999, Marissa Pollick, from Huntington Woods, Michigan and twice captain of the U of M women's tennis team in the mid-1970s, became the first woman president of the M Club. In 1999 the club's female membership was still less than 10 percent of the total membership estimated at 2,000.

138. *Toledo Blade*, May 24, 1976, p. 23.

139. Canham, *op. cit.*, p. 71.

140. See *The New York Times*, June 8, 1986, p. 8 S for the assertion that revenue sports were expected to cover all intercollegiate sport costs. See James J. Duderstadt, *Intercollegiate Athletics and the American University*. Ann Arbor: The University of Michigan Press, 2000, pp. 51, 126–8 for the rebuttal.

141. *Newsweek*, December 14, 1998, p. 96.

142. *CM Life*, June 20, 1979, p. 6. Men did out-

number women at CMU by 73 students in 1956. See *Central Michigan Life*, September 28, 1956, p. 1.

143. *Central Michigan Life*, March 1, 1978, p. 1; and March 3, 1978, p. 4.

144. *CM Life*, February 27, 1980, p. 13.

145. *Ypsilanti Press*, May 17, 1981.

146. *Ibid.*, May 19, 1984, p. 2B.

147. *Ibid.*, May 6, 1984, p. 3B.

148. *Detroit News*, March 11, 1983, p. 2-C.

149. *Chicago Tribune*, May 23, 1983, p. 8, Section 4.

150. *Detroit News*, May 12, 1983, p. 3-B.

151. *Ibid.*

152. *Detroit News*, May 11, 1983, p. 3-C and May 12, 1983, p. 3-B.

Chapter 20

1. *Taylor Public Schools Alumni Directory, 1996.* Norfolk, VA.: Bernard C. Harris Publishing Co., Inc., 1996, p, 134 and an interview with Fred La Plante, July 15, 1999.

2. From an undated 1979 newspaper interview in the archives of the University of Maryland AIAW collection involving the 1979 AIAW Outdoor Meet in East Lansing, Michigan, probably *Detroit News*, May 24, 1979, p. D4.

3. *Taylor Public Schools Alumni Directory, 1996*, p. 134.

4. Central Michigan University Sports Information files.

5. *Frederick Post*, July 7, 8, and 10, 1972.

6. *Akron Beacon Journal*, July 8, 1972, p. B3 and *Frederick Post*, July 7, 8, 1972.

7. *Detroit News*, May 24, 1979, p. D4.

8. Much of the information on Deby Lansky La Plante came from an interview with Fred La Plante on July 15, 1999.

9. *The Ann Arbor News*, May 20, 1976, p.53.

10. Baldwin, *op. cit.*, p. 66.

11. AIAW Records, University of Maryland Archives.

12. Tricard, *op. cit.*, p. 630.

13. AIAW Records, University of Maryland Archives.

14. *Los Angeles Times*, January 21, 1984, Section III, p. 13.

15. *Kalamazoo Gazette*, May 16, 1977, p. C-4.

16. *Ibid.*, May 1, 1977, p. D-2.

17. *Ibid.*, May 16, 1977, p. C-4 and Western Michigan University, *1997–98 Track & Cross Country Yearbook*, p. 14.

18. *Kalamazoo Gazette*, May 23, 1976, p. E-2.

19. *Ibid.*, May 1, 1977, p. D-2.

20. *Oakland Press*, June 3, 1974, p. C-6 and *The BG News*, April 7, 1976, p. 9; April 13, 1976, p. 6.

21. AIAW Meet Program, May 25–27, 1978, University of Tennessee, Knoxville.

22. *Detroit Free Press*, June 6, 1979, p.7-D.

23. *Ibid.*

24. *Detroit News*, June 17, 1978, p. 3-B.

25. *Detroit Free Press*, June 6, 1979, p.7-D.

26. *Ibid.*

27. *Ibid.*

28. *Los Angeles Times*, May 23, 1980; June 15, 1980; June 22, 1980; and University of Tennessee Sports Information.

29. University of Tennessee Sports Information.

30. Interview with Benita Fitzgerald Mosley on July 8, 1999, in Marquette, Michigan.

31. The meet was held on Saturday March 13, 1982 in the University of Northern Iowa Dome. See *Des Moines Register*, March 14, 1982.

32. *New York Times*, January 29, 1983.

33. *Detroit News*, March 13, 1983, p. 10-C.

34. *Detroit News*, March 13, 1983, p. 1C.

35. Interview with Benita Fitzgerald Mosley on July 8, 1999, in Marquette, Michigan.

36. Wallechinsky, *op. cit.*, p. 202.

37. *New York Times*, August 30, 1991, p. B-11.

38. *Ibid.*, June 7, 1992, Section 8, p. 7.

39. *Ibid.*, June 6, 1992, p. 34.

40. Foster's written application for the Marie Hartwig Award, 1983.

41. *Ibid.*

42. Archives, Sport's Information, University of Michigan, 1983.

43. *Michigan Daily*, January 25, 1984, p.8.

44. *The Ann Arbor News*, November 15, 1987.

45. AIAW Archives, University of Maryland and Michigan State University Women's Track and Field Guide, 1998.

46. *New York Times*, June 30, 1980, p. C11. In 1988 Diane Williams was still in the hunt for an Olympic berth. She placed 4th in the first heat of the semi-finals of the 100-meter dash, *New York Times*, July 18, 1988, p. c-9.

47. CMU Sports Information files.

48. *Des Moines Register*, April 25, 1982, p. 4-D.

49. *MSU Women's Track and Field Media Guide*, 1998.

50. Eastern Michigan University Sports Information.

51. AIAW Archives, University of Maryland.

52. *Des Moines Register*, April 25, 1981, p.4-D.

53. Eastern Michigan University Sports Information.

54. *Toledo Blade*, May 17, 1981, p. D-1 and 8.

55. *Detroit News*, August 12, 1983, p. 2-C.

56. Page, *op. cit.*, p. 117.

57. *Detroit Free Press*, June 10, 1979, p. 7-E.

58. *Ibid.*

59. *Ibid.*

60. *Ibid.*

61. *Los Angeles Times*, June 5, 1984, Part III, p. 9.

62. *Ann Arbor News*, June 24, 1984.

63. *Ebony, October, 1984*

64. *New York Times*, June 8, 1992, p. C-10.

65. *Lansing Magazine*, April, 1993, p. 34–37.

66. *Michigan State News*, September 29, 1983.

67. *New York Times*, June 1, 1989, p. B9.

68. Des Moines Register, April 24, 1982 and MSU Sports Information files.

69. The Bowling Green *Daily Sentinel-Tribune*, May 9, 1983, p. 16.

70. *Los Angeles Times*, June 4, 1983

71. *MSU Today*, Summer 1983.

72. Misplaced hurdles threw Judi off stride at the National Sports Festival in Colorado Springs on July 1, 1983 adversely affecting her performance at that meet. *Detroit News*, July 2, 1983.

73. *Grand Rapids Press*, August 11, 1987.

74. *The State News*, July 25, 1983, p. 6.

75. MSU Sports Information, 1998.

76. *Michigan State News*, September 29, 1983.

77. *State News*, September 29, 1983.

78. *Track and Field News*, July 1984.

79. *Los Angeles Times*, June 5, 1984, Part III, p. 9.

80. *Lansing State Journal*, June 10, 1984, p. 1C and Baldwin, *op. cit.*, p. 74.

81. *Ibid.*, July 27, 1996 and Baldwin, *op. cit.*, p. 74.

82. *Ibid.*, July 27, 1996.

83. *Ibid.*, July 27, 1996.

84. *Ibid.*, September 8, 1985 and Baldwin, *op. cit.*, p. 74.

85. *Detroit News*, Sunday Special, July 22, 1984 and *Grand Rapids Press*, August 13, 1987.

86. *New York Times*, June 12, 1988, Section 8, p. 5; and *Detroit Free Press*, May 8, 1988.

87. *New York Times*, July 26, 1987, p. 59.

88. *Ibid.*, July 26, 1987, p. V-11.

89. *Grand Rapids Press*, August 11, 1987.

90. *Ibid.*, August 13, 1987 and Baldwin, *op. cit.*, p. 74.

91. *New York Times*, June 12, 1988, Section 8, p. 5.

92. *Grand Rapids Press*, June 3, 1979.

93. *Traverse City Record-Eagle*, May 31, 1981.

94. Mid-American Conference Meet Program, 2000.

95. Western Michigan University, Sports Information and *New York Times*, June 19, 1984.

96. *Toledo Blade*, May 19, 1985, p. D11 and *The Chicago Tribune*, May 19, 1985, Section 4, p.12.

97. *Chicago Tribune*, May 19, 1985, Section 4, p. 12.

98. Interview with Derek Shoup, February 26, 2000.

99. *Central Michigan Life*, September 28, 1956, p. 1 and *Central Michigan University 1990 Women's track and Field and Cross Country* Media Guide.

100. CMU Sports information files, January 27, 1984 and February 22, 1985.

101. *Toledo Blade*, May 20, 1984, p. D2.

102. *Des Moines Register*, April 27, 1985.

103. *Toledo Blade*, May 18, 1985, p. 15.

104. *New York Times*, May 24, 1973, p. 59.

105. *Ibid.*, June 21, 1992, Section 8, p.1–2.

106. *Ibid.*, June 22, 1992.

107. *Ibid.*, March 7, 1999, pp. 1 and 16.

108. *Ibid.*

109. Canham, *op. cit.*, p. 247–50.

110. *Ypsilanti Press*, May 15, 1975, p. 4B.

111. *Ibid.*, p. 2B.

112. *Dearborn Times-Herald*, May 26, 1983, p. 3-D. Gerard placed 8th in the finals of the 10,000-meter run at the Olympic Trials in 1988. See *New York Times*, July 19, 1988, p. A-24.

113. *Ibid.*, June 9, 1983, p. 4-C.

114. Craddock coached the University of Virginia to consecutive ACC track and field titles in 1983 and 1984, and won two women's national cross-country championships and a national indoor track championship before Donna enrolled at the school. See *The Cavalier Daily*, April 25, 1984, p. 10.

115. *The Cavalier Daily*, October 28, 1983, p. 7.

116. Sports Information, Eastern Michigan University, May 1999.

117. *Ibid.*

118. *Livonia Observer*, April 26, 1984.

119. *Ibid.*

120. *Results of the NCAA Finals June 3–6, 1987,*

Louisiana State University, Bernie Moore Track, Baton Rouge, LA.

121. *New York Times*, July 21, 1988, p. B-8.

122. *Oakland Press*, July 14, 1988, p. B-5. P. J. Osika placed second in the 3,200-meter relay at the Drake Relays in 1984 (*Des Moines Register*, April 28, 1984), and won the 1,500-meter run (3:44.4) at the Drake Relays in 1987 (*Des Moines Register*, April 26, 1987.) He also won the 1987 MAC Outdoor 1,500-meter (3:46.77), and ran in the preliminary round of the 1,500-meter at the NCAA championships in Baton Rouge.

123. University of Iowa Sports Information, 1999.

124. *The University of Iowa, Office of Public Information*, April 22, 1985.

125. *The University of Iowa, Office of Public Information*, May 20, 1985.

126. *Chicago Tribune*, May 20, 1985, Section 3, p. 5.

127. *Flint Journal*, May 3, 1979, p. C-2.

128. *Noroscope*, Flint Northern High School Yearbook, 1980, p.221.

129. *Flint Journal*, May 25, 1979, p. D-2.

130. *Flint Journal*, May 10, 1979, p. C-2; May 20, 1979, p. C-2; and May 25, 1979, p. D-4.

131. University of Kentucky, Athletic Department, Sports Information.

132. *Oakland Press*, June 15, 1980, *p. B-4.*

133. *Oakland Press*, July 7, 1981, p. B3-B4.

134. Interview with Kathi Harris-Rounds, November 23, 1999 and *Knoxville Sentinel-News*, April 10, 1983

135. Interview with Kathi Harris-Rounds, November 23, 1999.

136. *Oakland Press*, July 16, 1988, p. B-11.

137. *Ibid.*, July 17, 1988, p. B-1; and July 19, 1988, p.C-7.

138. *Los Angeles Times*, June 15, 1997, p. C-14.

139. *New York Times*, April 26, 1999, p. 7D.

140. Interview with Bernard Wells, March 17, 1999 at Oak Park High School.

141. *Revoir*, Oak Park High School Yearbook, 1982, p.139.

142. *Oakland Press*, June 1, 1980, p. B1.

143. *Oakland Press*, May 22, 1981, p. B4.

144. *Oakland Press*, May 31, 1981, p. B4.

145. *Oakland Press*, July 7, 1981, p. B3-B4.

146. See Oak Park High School records and *Oakland Press*, June 9, 1982, p. B6.

147. *Oakland Press*, June 4, 1982, p. B4.

148. *Oakland Press*, June 7, 1982, p. B4.

149. Interview with Wendy Truvillion, March 20, 2000.

150. *Oakland Press*, May 31, 1981, p. B4 and interview with Wendy, March 20, 2000.

151. Interview with Wendy Truvillion, March 20, 2000.

152. Interview with Allan Tellis, April 12, 2000; and *The Oakland Press*, June 9, 1986, p. C-5.

153. University of Michigan Sports Information, 1984.

154. University of Michigan Sports News, Sports Information, 1985.

155. Michigan Women's Track and Field Media Guide, 1999.

156. Michigan Sports News, Sports Information Department, June 10, 1985.

157. *Ann Arbor News,* February 3, 1986.
158. *Ann Arbor News,* March 5, 1986.
159. *Michigan Daily,* June 13, 1986.
160. Michigan Sports News, Sports Information Department, June 11, 1986.
161. *Lansing State Journal,* May 16, 1985.
162. *Lansing State Journal,* July 24, 1992.
163. *Lansing State Journal,* May 16, 1985.
164. *Des Moines Register,* April 29, 1989.
165. *Flint Journal,* May 31, 1987, p. D-6.
166. *Des Moines Register,* April 27, 1991.
167. *Des Moines Register,* April 28, 1991.
168. *MSU Women's Track and Field Guide,* 1998, pp. 14–15.
169. Ruth Bordin, *Women at Michigan,* 1998.
170. Determined from the 1952 University college yearbook.
171. University of Michigan Sports Information Office form completed by J. L. Wilson in 1983.
172. *University of Michigan Women's Track and Field Media Guide, 1999.*
173. *The Wolverine,* November 14, 1994, p. 25.
174. Hudson is located between Cleveland and Akron, OH.
175. *Lansing State Journal,* May 16, 1989.
176. *State News,* October 7, 1988, p. 16.
176. *State News,* May 15, 1987.
177. *State News,* October 10, 1986.
178. *State News,* October 7, 1988, p. 16.
179. *Lansing State Journal,* May 16, 1989.
180. Judith B. King Resume, 1991 in MSU Sports Information file.
181. *Lansing Magazine,* April, 1993, p. 34–37.
182. *Ibid.,* p. 34.
183. *Ibid.,* p. 37.
184. *Lansing State Journal,* April 15, 1994.
185. Letter from Judi Brown King to Ms. Baker, Director of Athletics, Michigan State University.
186. *Lansing Magazine,* April, 1993, p. 34–37.
187. *Michigan State News,* November 23, 1992.
188. *Lansing Magazine,* April, 1993, p. 34–37.
189. *Ibid.*
190. *Ibid,*
191. *Lansing State Journal,* February 5, 1993.
192. *Lansing Magazine,* April, 1993, p. 34–37.
193. MSU Press Release, July 5, 1994.
194. *Detroit News,* January 17, 1997 and February 6, 1997; *Lansing State Journal,* January 16, 17 and 19, 1997; *Michigan State News.* January 19, 1997.
195. *Michigan State University Women's Track and Field Guide, 1998.* P. 3–4.
196. *Ibid.,* p. 10; *Des Moines Register,* April 25, 1998.
197. *Detroit Free Press,* May 22, 1993; and May 30, 1993.
198. *Lansing State Journal,* August 5, 1997; p. 1C and 4C, and *Atlanta Constitution,* June 18, 1996.
199. Michigan State University Sports Information, 1997.
200. Sports Information, Calvin College, 1999.
201. Calvin College Alumni Magazine, 1997.
202. Sports Information files, Calvin College, 1999.
203. *Ibid.*
204. *Ibid.*
205. *Ibid.*
206. *Detroit Free Press,* June 2, 2000, p. 5D.

207. Trackwire Interview, 1998.
208. *Ibid.*
209. *Willoughby News-Herald,* June 21, 1994.
210. *Michigan Daily,* May 14, 1997, p. 13.
211. *Ibid.,* May 28, 1997, p. 12.
212. *Ibid.,* June 4, 1997, p. 15.
213. *Ibid.,* June 11, 1997, p. 13.
214. 10–6-98 katie mcgregor the trackwire interview.
215. *New York Times,* December 27, 1998, Sports Section p. 34.
216. University of Michigan Sports Information Archives.
217. *Detroit Free Press,* December 29, 1998, p. 8E.
218. *Des Moines Register,* April 25, 1998.
219. Central Michigan University Sports Information files and *New York Times,* July 23, 1988.
220. *New York Times,* March 14, 1993, p. V-8.
221. CMU Sports Information files.
222. *New York Times,* March 14, 1993, p. V-8; *Western Michigan University Track & Cross Country Yearbook, 1997–8,* p. 14; and interview with Theresa McMullen, September 3, 1999.
223. *Des Moines Register,* April 30, 1995.
224. *Cadillac Evening News,* June 17, 1996, p. B-1.
225. *Traverse City Record-Eagle,* July 13, 1997, p. 1-C.
226. *Cedar Rapids* [IA] *Gazette,* April 30, 2000.
227. *Des Moines Register,* April 26, 1997 and April 25, 1998; *Western Michigan University Track & Cross Country Yearbook, 1997–8,* p. 6–7.
228. *Flint Journal,* June 4, 1995, p. C-1 and C-4.
229. *Des Moines Register,* April 24, 1999.
230. *Ann Arbor News,* February 26 and 27, 2000.
231. *Cedar Rapids* [IA] *Gazette,* April 29, 2000, p. 7C.
232. *The Detroit News,* September 5, 1999, p. 4-C.
233. *Detroit Free Press,* July 9, 1999, p. 9A.
234. *The Daily Cavalier,* September 1, 1983, p. 2.
235. *New York Times,* February 3, 1989, p. B15.
236. *Ibid.,* July 11, 1999, p. 1A.
237. *Ibid.,* September 5, 1999, p. 32-V.
238. David A. Markiewicz, "School Achieving Gender Equality, But Too Slowly, NCAA Study Shows," *Detroit Free Press,* October 26, 1999, p. 3E.

Chapter 21

1. *New York Times,* June 11, 1986, p. 27.
2. *New York Times,* December 19, 1999, p. 52.
3. Canham, *op. cit.,* p. 81, 101–122.
4. *New York Times,* June 11, 1986, p. 275.
5. *Ibid.,* June 8, 1986, p. 8 S.
6. *Ibid.,* June 8, 1986, p. 8 S.
7. *Detroit Free Press,* October 8, 1999, p. 7A. The University of Tennessee ranked first in 1999.
8. For more see, James J. Duderstadt, *Intercollegiate Athletics and the American University.* Ann Arbor: The University of Michigan Press, pp. 19–23, 50–51, 126–8.
9. Grantland Rice first made the case that football revenue helps to support other sports in 1925. See *Literary Digest,* October 1925, p. 57–8.
10. *Detroit News,* December 19, 1999, pp. 2D, 12D.
11. *New York Times,* March 16, 1975, p. V-1.
12. *Toledo Blade,* May 17, 1981, p. D-1 and 8.
13. In March 1974 the *New York Times* surveyed

college sports and found "a slave market" in recruiting prompted by the need to "win at any cost." One year later the *Times* did a follow-up study and found that recruiting abuses remained. See *New York Times*, March 16, 1975, p. V-1.

14. *Toledo Blade,* May 11, 1980, p. D-5.

15. *The New York Times,* June 8, 1986, p. 8 S.

16. *Ibid.,* June 9, 1986, p. 37, C4.

17. *The Oakland Press,* March 26, 2000, p. B-2.

18. *Cadillac Evening News,* May 19, 1989, p. B-2.

19. *Detroit Free Press,* November 30, 1999, p. E2.

20. Interview on the Todd Mundt Show Public Radio, September, 1998.

21. *Social Problems in Athletics: Essays in the Sociology of Sports.* Edited by Daniel M. Landers. Urbana: University of Illinois Press, 1976, p. 185–193.

22. *The Ypsilanti Press,* May 26, 1972, p. 17.

23. *Official Collegiate Track and Field Guide, 1973.* Phoenix, Az: College Athletics Publishing Service, 1972, p. 21.

24. *Ibid.,* p. 18.

25. *New York Times,* February 1972; *Detroit News,* March 9, 1972.

26. Interview with Fred La Plante, July 15, 1999.

27. *Millrose Games Program, January 25, 1974,* p. 57 and 67; *Amateur Athlete, 1974.*

28. George (1903–1946) and Seraphim (1906–42) Znamenskiy were middle and distance runners and national record holders for the USSR and Second World War heros. *Amateur Athlete, 1974.*

29. *Des Moines Register,* April 24, 1974; and April 25, 1974, p. 2D; *Amateur Athlete. 1974; Official Collegiate Track and Field Guide, 1975,* p. 17, 48,55.

30. *The BG News,* April 7, 1975, p. 8.

31. Eastern Michigan University 1997 Men's Track and Field Media Guide, p. 23.

32. *Official Collegiate Track and Field Guide, 1973.* Phoenix, AZ: College Athletics Publishing Service, 1972, p.18.

33. *New York Times,* July 5, 1975, p. 14.

34. Detroit News, July 2, 1975, p. 1D; July 19, 1975.

35. *New York Times,* February 8, 1976, section V, p. 7; *Amateur Athlete Yearbook 1976,* p. 34

36. *Amateur Athlete Yearbook 1976,* p. 35; and *New York Times,* June 23, 1976, p. 30.

37. *Amateur Athlete Yearbook 1977,* p. 40.

38. *Amateur Athlete Yearbook 1978,* p. 53; Interview with Stan's mother and the Sport's Information Office, Eastern Michigan University, May 1999.

39. Page, *op. cit.,* p. 61.

40. *Detroit News,* June 3, 1982, p. 5-E.

41. *Detroit News,* June 6, 1982.

42. *Taylor Public Schools Alumni Directory, 1996.* Norfolk, VA.: Bernard C. Harris Publishing Co., Inc., 1996, p. vii.

43. *Ibid.*

44. *Ypsilanti Press, May 17, 1984,* p. B-1 and May 20, 1984, p. B-2.

45. *Los Angeles Times,* June 2, 1984.

46. *Ibid.,* June 5, 1984, Part III, p. 9. Earl was profiled in "The 1984 Olympics," *Ebony,* October 1984. Also see *The Ann Arbor News,* January 10, 1985, p. D4.

47. *Ypsilanti Press,* June 19, 1984.

48. *New York Times,* June 20, 1984, p. B-7.

49. *Ypsilanti Press,* June 21, 1984.

50. Wallechinsky, *op. cit.,* 1996, p. 39.

51. *Chicago Tribune,* May 19, 1985, Section 4, p. 12 and *Ann Arbor News,* February 19, 1989, p. D-2.

52. *Detroit News,* March 9, 1985, p. 2D and *New York Times,* June 17, 1985, p. C-10.

53. *Toledo Blade,* May 13, 1990, p. 7-B

54. *New York Times,* July 6, 1985, p. 8-Sports; July 8, 1986, p. B10.

55. *Chicago Tribune,* March 8, 1998, Section 3, p. 11.

56. *Toledo Blade,* May 17, 1981, p. D-1 and 8.

57. *Eastern Echo,* March 15, 1999, p. 8 and MAC and CCC records.

58. Interview with Fred La Plante, July 15, 1999.

59. *Ypsilanti Press,* May 21, 1984, p. B-1.

60. *Ann Arbor News,* May 4, 1990, p. D1 and 4.

61. University of Tennessee Track Media Guide, 1998.

62. *The Ann Arbor News,* June 10, 1973, p. 35.

63. *Macomb Daily,* May 18, 1970, p. 3-D.

64. *Ibid.*

65. *Atlanta Journal,* April 9, 1972, p. 11-D.

66. *New York Times,* July 3, 1972, p. 11; July 6, 1972, p. 50; and May 20, 1973, Section V, P. 3.

67. University of Tennessee Track Media Guide, 1998.

68. *Oakland Press,* June 3, 1974, p. C-4.

69. *New York Times,* February 8, 1976, Section V, p.7; June, 25, 1976, p. A18; July 11, 1976, special section, p. 14

70. *The World Almanac, 1981,* p. 860.

71. *Los Angeles Times, June 29, 1980.*

72. *Detroit News,* May 1, 1976, p. 3B and *Detroit Free Press,* April 10, 19; May 2: June 6, 1976.

73. University of Tennessee Track Media Guide, 1998.

74. *Livonia Observer Eccentric,* April 26, 1984, p. 21 and the University of Tennessee Track Media Guide, 1998.

75. Univ. of Tennessee Track Media Guide, 1998; *New York Times,* June 19, 1988, Section 8, p. 8; July 21, 1988, p. B8.

76. *Livonia Observer Eccentric,* April 26, 1984, p. 21.

77. University of Tennessee Track Media Guide, 1998, p. 38.

78. "Spartan Miler Pint-sized Star," by Joe Falls, *Detroit Free Press,* February 10, 1972.

79. MSU Sports Information Questionnaire, 1969.

80. *Detroit Free Press,* May 20, 1973.

81. Archives, MSU Sports Information.

82. *Detroit News,* March 13, 1971; *Lansing Journal,* March 5, 1971.

83. Falls, *op. cit., Detroit Free Press,* February 10, 1972.

84. *Detroit News,* April 28, 1972.

85. *Official Collegiate Track and Field Guide, 1972.* Phoenix, AZ: College Athletics Publishing Serv., 1971, p. 60, 68.

86. *Official Collegiate Track and Field Guide, 1973,* p.60.

87. *Akron Beacon Journal,* July 8, 1972, p. B4.

88. *Ibid.,* July 3, 1972, p. B5.

89. *Ibid.,* March 10, 1977, p. C7.

90. *The State Journal,* May 13, 1973.

91. *Ibid.*

92. *Chicago Tribune*, May 12, 1973, Section 2, p. 3.

93. *The State Journal*, May 13, 1973.

94. *Michigan State News*, May 15, 1973, p. 10.

95. Curt Sylvester, "Questions to Spartan Star Ken Popejoy," *Detroit Free Press*, May 20, 1973. The interview has been edited.

96. *Chicago Tribune*, May 12, 1973, Section 2, p.3.

97. *Detroit News*, May 20, 1973.

98. *Ann Arbor News*, May 27, 1973, p.27–28.

99. *Detroit Free Press*, July 10, 1973.

100. *The State Journal*, May 13, 1973 and *Michigan State News*, May 15, 1973, p. 10.

101. Press release from Illinois Institute of Technology, University Relations, December 10, 1974.

102. *The NCAA News*, September 16, 1985, p. 8.

103. *Chicago Tribune*, March 6, 1988.

104. *The NCAA News*, September 16, 1985, p. 8.

105. *90th* Annual Drake Relays Program, April 23–24, 1999, p. 31 and 21.

106. *Drake Relays 75 Years of Excellence*, p. 48.

107. *Official Collegiate Track and Field Guide, 1974.*

108. *Official Collegiate Track and Field Guide, 1976.*

109. *Official Collegiate Track and Field Guide, 1977.*

110. *Saginaw News*, May 20, 1973 p. F2.

111. *Central Michigan Life*, March 24, 1976, p. 6-B and *Detroit News*, June 7, 1976, p. 4-C.

112. *Toledo Blade*, May 23, 1976, p. C-6 and *New York Times*, June 27, 1976, p.V-4.

113. *Des Moines Register*, April 30, 1978, p. 6-D.

114. *Toledo Blade*, May 21, 1978, p. E-7.

115. *Ibid.*, May 20, 1979, p. D-5.

116. *Ibid.*, May 18, 1980, p. D-6.

117. *Detroit News*, June 16, 1978, p. 4-D.

118. Michigan State University Sports Information Questionnaire, 1980.

119. Central Michigan University Track and Field files, Sports Information.

120. *Des Moines Register*, April 24, 1976.

121. *Kalamazoo Gazette*, May 16, 1976, p. E-2.

122. *Toledo Blade*, May 23, 1976, p. C-6 and *Kalamazoo Gazette*, May 23, 1976, p. E-2.

123. *Toledo Blade*, May 21, 1978, p. E-7.

124. *Ibid.*, May 18, 1980, p. D-6.

125. *The Daily-Sentinel*, May 16, 1983, p. 15.

126. *The New York Times*, April 16, 2000, p. 39.

127. *Toledo Blade*, May 20, 1979, p. D-6.

128. *Des Moines Register*, April 30, 1983.

129. *Livonia Observer*, April 3, 1986, p. 4-D.

130. *Detroit Free Press*, June 7, 2000, p. 6D. Kevin Sullivan, former University of Michigan middle distance runner from Canada, ran the fastest outdoor mile run (3:55.82) on a track in the State of Michigan in the twentieth century on June 10, 2000 in Plymouth at the First Annual Michigan International Meet.

131. *University of Michigan Men's Track and Field Guide, 1998* and *1999*.

132. *Kalamazoo Gazette*, May 29, 1976, p. A-12.

133. *Detroit Free Press*, May 4, 2000, p. 9D and *New York Times*, May 8, 2000, p. D2.

134. Derderian, *op. cit.*, p. 433.

135. *Ibid.*, pp. 433–435.

136. *Ibid.*, pp. 452–454. Also see Hal Higdon, *A Century of Running: Celebrating the 100th Anniversary of the Boston Athletic Association Marathon*. Emmaus, PA: Rodale Press, Inc., 1995, p. 161.

137. *ESPN 1998 Sports Almanac*, p. 713.

138. *The New York Times*, April 18, 2000, p. A-29.

139. *Detroit Free Press*, May 4, 2000, p. 9D.

140. *Detroit Free Press*, August 28, 1988.

141. Bill Donakowski from Dearborn placed fourth in the indoor 2-mile run and the 10-K outdoor for All-American honors in 1978. See *University of Michigan Men's Track and Field Guide, 1998*.

142. *University of Michigan Men's Track and Field Guide, 1998.*

143. *Chicago Tribune*, May 22, 1983, Section 3, p. 5.

144. *Ibid.*

145. *Detroit Free Press, June 22, 1984.*

146. Young, *op. cit.*, 1996, pp. 36–37.

147. *Ann Arbor News*, June 6, 1983.

148. University of Michigan Sports Information, June 9, 1983.

149. *Detroit Free Press*, June 22, 1984.

150. *Ibid.*

151. *Ann Arbor News*, August, 1984.

152. *Detroit Free Press*, June 22, 1984.

153. *The Ann Arbor News*, June 20, 1984, p. C4.

154. *Ibid.*, June 23, 1984.

155. *Ibid.*, June 24, 1984, p. C3.

156. *Ibid.*

157. *Ibid.*, August 1984.

158. *Detroit Free Press*, August 28, 1988.

159. *Ann Arbor News*, September 9, 1988, p. C4.

160. *Detroit Free Press*, July 16, 1992.

161. *Ibid.*, July 16, 1992; *Ann Arbor News*, July 25, 1992.

162. *Ann Arbor News*, July 21, 1992.

163. *New York Times*, June 19, 1993, p. 30.

164. *Grand Rapids Press*, September 17, 1995.

165. For more on Scherer's strong Christian beliefs see *Michigan Daily*, April 5, 1989.

166. *Chicago Tribune*, April 22, 1999, p. 8, section 4.

167. University of Michigan Sports Information files.

168. *Ann Arbor News*, November 24, 1987.

169. *Ibid.*, May 22, 1988; and *Detroit News*, May 22, 1988, B-5.

170. *Ann Arbor News*, June 13, 1988, p. D-4.

171. *Ibid.* and University of Michigan Sports Information news release.

172. *The Michigan Daily*, June 10, 1988 and University of Michigan, Athletic Media Relations, June 7, 1988.

173. *Ann Arbor News*, June 4, 1988; and *Detroit Free Press*, June 4, 1988.

174. Sherer file at the University of Michigan Sports Information office.

175. *Ann Arbor News*, March 15, 1991.

176. *New York Times*, June 20, 1993, p. V-10.

177. La Plant's second wife's sister's husband. Interview with Fred La Plante, July 15, 1999.

178. Barquist file at the University of Michigan Sports Information office.

179. *Ibid.*, *New York Times*, June 18, 1996, p. B-14; July 27, 1996, p. 35.

180. *University of Michigan Men's Track and Field Guide, 1998.*

181. *Official Collegiate Track and Field Guide, 1971, 1977, 1981.*

182. *Ann Arbor News*, May 18, 1990, p. B2.

183. *Ibid.*, March 13, 1992.

184. U. S. A. Track and Field on the Web, 1999; and *Detroit Free Press*, May 3, 2000, pp. 1E and 5E.

185. U. S. A. Track and Field on the Web, 1999.

186. Interview with Al Tellis, 1998 and *Detroit Free Press*, May 3, 2000, pp. 1E and 5E.

187. *Traverse City Record-Eagle*, June 3, 1990, p. 3-C.

188. *Ann Arbor News*, July 25, 1992 and *Detroit Free Press*, May 3, 2000, p. 5E.

189. U. S. A. Track and Field on the Web, 1999.

190. *New York Times*, March 5, 1994.

191. *Detroit Free Press*, May 3, 2000, p. 5E.

192. *Ibid.*

193. *Ibid.*

194. U. S. A. Track and Field on the Web, 1999.

195. *New York Times*, February 5, 1999, p. C-22.

196. Run Michigan.com!

197. *Cadillac Evening Post*, January 6, 1999, p. C-1.

198. For more on Sarah see *Cadillac Evening News*, August 27, 1996, p. B-1.

199. Interview with Doug McMullen, September 1, 1999.

200. Tom Henderson, "A cut Above," *Runner's World*, vol. 33, no. 7, July 1998, pp. 80–83.

201. Letter from Dan Foley, one of Paul's high school teachers, January 3, 1999.

202. *Ann Arbor News*, July 16, 1996, p. D-1.

203. *South Bend Observer*, February 11, 1998, p. 16.

204. *Cadillac Evening News*, May 1, 1989, p. B-1.

205. *Ibid.*, May 10, 1989, p. B-1.

206. *Ibid.*, May 20–21, 1989, p. B-1.

207. *Ibid.*, Mark Smith became an All-American cross-country and distance runner at Eastern Michigan University.

208. *Traverse City Record Eagle*, April 1, 1998, p. 1-A and 3-A; *Listen Magazine*, June 1998, pp. 27–29.

209. *Ibid.*, May 20, 1990, p. 6-C.

210. *Traverse City Record-Eagle*, June 3, 1990, p. 3-C.

211. Henderson, *Runner's World*, July 1998, pp. 80–83.

212. *Track and Field News*, March 1998, p. 56.

213. Henderson, *Runner's World*, July 1998, pp. 80–83.

214. *Traverse City Record-Eagle*, April 1, 1998, p. 3-A.

215. Interview with Fred La Plante, July 15, 1999.

216. *Traverse City Record-Eagle*, April 1, 1998, p. 3-A, and interview with Doug McMullen, September 1, 1999.

217. *South Bend Observer*, February 11, 1998, p. 16.

218. Interview with Fred La Plante, July 15, 1999.

219. *Cadillac Evening Post*, January 6, 1999, p. C-1.

220. *South Bend Observer*, February 11, 1998, p. 16.

221. *Cadillac Evening Post, January 6, 1999, p. C-1* and an interview with Theresa McMullen, September 1, 1999.

222. *South Bend Observer*, February 11, 1998, p. 16.

223. *Indianapolis Star*, March 12, 1995.

224. Interview with Doug and Theresa McMullen, September 3, 1999 and *Ann Arbor News*, July 16, 1996, p. D-1.

225. *Cadillac Evening News*, July 3–4, 1996, p. B-3.

226. *90th Annual Drake Relays Program*, April 23–24, 1999, p. 30.

227. *New York Times*, June 4, 1995, p. V-5, V-10.

228. *Cadillac Evening News*, July 3–4, 1996, p. B-3.

229. Henderson, *Runner's World*, July 1998, pp. 80–83.

230. *Ann Arbor News*, July 16, 1996, p. D-2.

231. *Cadillac Evening News*, July 3–4, 1996, p. B-3.

232. *Track and Field News*, May, 1996, p. 64.

233. *Sports Illustrated*, March 9, 1998.

234. *New York Times*, June 8, 1992, p. C-9–10.

235. *Ibid.*, p. V-9.

236. *Ibid.*, July 27, 1994, p. B-6.

237. *Ibid.*, March 5, 1995.

238. *Ibid.*, June 4, 1995, p. V-9.

239. *Chicago Tribune*, March 8, 1998, Section 3, p. 11.

240. *Cadillac Evening News*, May 16, 1996, p. B-1.

241. *Track and Field News*, May, 1996, p. 64.

242. *Ann Arbor News*, July 16, 1996, p. D-1

243. *Cadillac Evening News*, June 17, 1996, p. B-1.

244. *Ibid.*, June 18, 1996, p. B-1.

245. *Ibid.*, June 21, 1996, p. B-1 and B-3.

246. *Ibid.*, June 22–23, 1996, p. B-1.

247. *Ibid.*, June 21, 1996, p. B-3 and June 22–23, 1996, p. B-1.

248. *Ibid.*, June 24, 1996, p. A-1.

249. *Detroit Free Press*, June 24, 1996.

250. *Grand Rapids Press*, June 24, 1996, p. C-8.

251. *Sports Illustrated*, March 9, 1998.

252. *Cadillac Evening News*, June 24, 1996, p. B-1.

253. *Ibid.*, July 4, 1996, p. A-1 and July 5, 1996, p. B-3.

254. Undated article in the McMullen family scrape book, 1998.

255. Jim Ryun placed second in 1968. Wallechinsky, *op. cit.*, pp.47–51.

256. *Cadillac Evening News*, July 30, 1996, p. A-1, A-3.

257. *Ibid.*, August 1, 1996, p. A-1.

258. *Ibid.*, August 2, 1996, p. A-1and A-3.

259. *Ibid.*, August 3–4, 1996, p. A-1and A-3.

260. *Ibid.*, April 27, 1998, p. B-1.

261. *Ann Arbor News*, July 16, 1996, p. D-1.

262. *Kalamazoo Gazette*, February 26, 1998.

263. *Sports Illustrated*, March 9, 1998.

264. *Ann Arbor News*, July 16, 1996, p. D-2.

265. *Kalamazoo Gazette*, February 26, 1998.

266. *Chicago Tribune*, March 8, 1998, Section 3, p. 11.

267. *Kalamazoo Gazette*, February 26, 1998.

268. *Chicago Tribune*, March 8, 1998, Section 3, p. 11.

269. *Traverse City Record-Eagle*, July 13, 1997, p. C-1.

270. *Kalamazoo Gazette*, February 26, 1998 and *South Bend Observer*, February 11, 1998, p. 16.

271. *Traverse City Record-Eagle*, April 1, 1998, p. 3-A.

272. National Public Radio report, March 1997.

273. *Chicago Tribune*, March 8, 1998, Section 3, p. 1.

274. Henderson, *Runner's World*, July 1998, pp. 80–83.

275. *Traverse City Record-Eagle*, July 13, 1997, p. C-1.

276. *Ibid.*, July 13, 1997, p. C-1.

277. *Chicago Tribune*, March 8, 1998, Section 3, p. 11.

278. *Kalamazoo Gazette*, February 26, 1998.

279. *Track and Field News*, March 1998, p. 56.

280. *USA Today*, March 2, 1998, p. 14-C.

281. *Ibid.*

282. *Kalamazoo Gazette*, February 26, 1998.

283. *Chicago Tribune*, March 8, 1998, Section 3, p. 11; and Henderson, *op. cit.*, pp. 80–83.

284. *Chicago Tribune*, March 8, 1998, Section 3, p. 11.

285. *Ibid.*

286. On January 24, 1998 Paul won the 800-meter run (1:50.22) at the University of Michigan Open Invitational.

287. *New York Times*, February 17, 1998, p. C-8.

288. *USA Today*, March 2, 1998, p. 14-C.

289. *New York Times*, February 17, 1998, p. C-8.

290. *Des Moines Register*, April 26, 1998, p. 4-D and *90th Annual Drake Relays Program*, April 23–24, 1999, p. 75.

291. *The Atlanta Journal-Constitution*, March 1, 1998 and *Sports Illustrated*, March 9, 1998.

292. Henderson, *op. cit.*, pp. 80–83 and *Sports Illustrated*, *March 9, 1998*.

293. *Traverse City Record-Eagle*, April 1, 1998, p. 3-A.

294. *New Orleans Times-Picayune*, June 22, 1998, p. D-2; and Tom Henderson, "Team McMullen turns nationals into a family affair," *The Detroit News*, June 24, 1998, p. 6F.

295. Interview with Doug McMullen, September 1, 1999.

296. *Traverse City Record-Eagle*, July 9, 1998 and July 12, 1998, p. C-1.

297. Interview with Theresa McMullen, September 1, 1999.

298. Interview with Doug McMullen, September 1, 1999.

299. Author's eye witness and *Quad-City Times*, April 25, 1999, 10 S.

300. *Detroit Free Press*, February 4, 2000, p. 4E.

301. Interview with Bob Parks, February 5, 2000.

302. *The Atlanta Journal-Constitution*, March 5, 2000, p. E21.

303. *The New York Times*, April 16, 2000, p. 39.

304. *Listen Magazine*, June 1998, pp. 27–29.

305. *Kalamazoo Gazette*, April 22, 1998.

306. *Ibid.*, April 16, 1998, p. D-7.

307. *Ibid.*, April 22, 1998.

308. *Ibid.*

309. *Kalamazoo Gazette*, May 23 and 24, 1998; *Akron Beacon Journal*, May 22, 1998, pp. D-1 and D-5.

310. *Akron Beacon Journal*, May 21, 1998, p. E-1.

311. *New Orleans Times-Picayune*, June 21, 1998, p. D-2.

312. *Traverse City Record-Eagle*, April 1, 1998, p. 3-A.

313. *Detroit Free Press*, March 9, 2000, p. 4E.

314. *Official USA Indoor Championships Results*, Georgia Dome, March 4, 2000.

315. *Official Records of the Sea Ray Relays*, April 14, 2000.

316. *The Michigan Daily*, October 27, 1998, p. 9 and University of Michigan Sports Information files.

317. *The Michigan Daily*, February 26, 1997, p. 12.

318. University of Michigan Sports Information files.

319. *Michigan Daily*, May 28, 1997, p. 12.

320. *Michigan Daily*, June 4, 1997, p. 15.

321. *Michigan Daily*, June 11, 1997, p. 13.

322. *Michigan Daily, August 13, 1997*, p. 15 and September 4, 1997, 15 A.

323. The Michigan Daily Online, March 15, 1998.

324. *University of Michigan Men's Track and Field Guide, 1999*, p. 33.

325. *Michigan Daily*, November 16, 1998, p. 3B.

326. University of Michigan Sports Information Archives.

327. 10–6-98 katie mcgregor the trackwire interview.

328. Chris Langrill, "Leader of the People," *The Michigan Daily*, October 27, 1998. Pp. 9–10 and University of Michigan 1998 Men's Track and Field Guide, p. 21.

Chapter 22

1. *MetroTimes*, August 25–31, 1999, p. 14–15.

2. For more information on this subject see Cindy Horchem, "The Relationships Between Midwestern Sportswriters and Their Primary Sources During the Big Eight Era: A Multi-Case Study," Proceeding of the Northern Michigan University Inaugural Conference on Sports and Society, July 8–10, 1999. Also see, Robert W. McChesney, "Media Made Sport: A History of Sports Coverage in the United States," *Media, Sports, and Society: Research on the Communication of Sport*, ed. Lawrence A. Wenner, Beverly Hills, CA: Sage Publications, pp. 49–69

3. *The Detroit News*, February, 6, 2000, p. 1-D.

4. *Track and Field News*, March 1961, p. 24.

5. *Chicago Tribune*, August 6, 1985, Section 3, p. 2.

6. *Detroit Free Press*, March 11, 2000, p. 2B.

7 Mark Danner, "The Lost Olympics," *The New York Review of Books*, volume XLVII, number 17, November 2, 2000, p. 67.

8. Track and Field USA, March 2000.

9. *New York Times*, March 1, 1994, p. B-15.

10. Official Results, USA Track and Field Indoor Championships, Atlanta, March 4, 2000. *Detroit Free Press*, June 7, 2000, p.6D.

11. *New York Times*, May 8, 2000, p. D2. One of the promising young American marathoners at the end of the century was Clint Verran, 1993 Lake Orion High School and 1998 Eastern Michigan University graduate, who placed 11th in the Olympic trials. See *Detroit Free Press*, May 10, 2000, p. 14D. Another is Dathan Ritzenheim of Rockford, Michigan and the North Kent Running Club, who set the State HS titles in the 1,600 (4:08.08) and 3,200-meter runs. See *Detroit Free Press*, June 7, 2000, p. 6D. He shattered the Michigan prep 5000-meter run (14:13) record on June 10, 2000 missing the Olympic standard by only 25 seconds, and won the two-mile run (8:48.06) by 50-meters at the Foot Locker National Interscholastic Championship in Raleigh, NC on June 16, 2000. See *New York Times*, June 18, 2000, sports p. 29 and *Sports Illustrated*, vol. 92, no. 26, June 26, 2000, p. 40. On November 4, 2000 Dathan Ritzenhein set the State Class A cross-country record (5K) with a time of 14:10.4. See *Detroit News*, November 5, 2000, p. 8c. He also won the year 2000 Foot Locker Division I National Cross-country Championship in Orlando

(14:35) and committed to attend the University of Colorado. See *Detroit Free Press*, January 4, 2001, p. 9D. The most promising Michigan 400-meter specialist at the end of the century was Godfrey Herring from Pontiac Northern, who was attending Middle Tennessee State University. He won the 400-meter at the 2000 Sea Ray Relays in 45.59 and qualified for the Olympic trials. See *The Oakland Press*, June 18, 2000, p. B-2.

12. The following average salaries were paid to coaches at Michigan's state colleges and universities in 1999:

Athletic Directors	$ 83,566
Head Football Coaches	189,245
Head Football Coach (excluding The U of Michigan and MSU)	62,180
Assistant football coaches, U of M	99,681
Assistant football coaches MSU	83,475
Assistant football coaches, MAC	43,374
Head Men's basketball coaches	156,011
Head Women's basketball coaches	67,830
Head coach men's hockey	100,414
Head coach swimming	62,243
Head coach volleyball	58,044
Head coach wrestling	57,443
Head coach women's softball	55,096
Head coach men's baseball	53,979
Head coach women's field hockey	53,037
*Head coach track and/or cross-co.	49,778
Head coach gymnastics	48,646
Head coach soccer	41,235

Source: Calculated from data published in *The Detroit News*, November 28, 1999, pp. 6A-7A.

13. *The Detroit News*, November 28, 1999, pp. 6A-7A and *Detroit Free Press*, November 30, 1999, p. A1.

14. Allen L. Sack, "Getting Up Close and Personal with Under-the-Table Payments," *The New York Times*, May 19, 2000, p. 38. James L. Shulman and William G. Bowen, *The Game of Life: College Sports and Educational Values*. Princeton, NJ: Princeton University Press, 2001 agree with Sack's assessment of the NCAA.

15. *New York Times*, June 1, 1986, Section 8, p. 6.

16. *New York Times*, June 1, 1990, p. A24.

17. *New York Times*, July 4, 1999. P. 23V.

18. *The Atlanta Journal-Constitution*, October 18, 1998, p. D-11.

19. *Track and Field News*, April 1969, p.13.

20. See Bil Gilbert, "Drugs in Sport," *Sports Illustrated*, June 23, 1969 p. 71 and June 30, 1969, p. 42.

21. Terry Todd, "Anabolic Steroids: The Gremlins of Sport," *Journal of Sport History*, volume 14, number 1, spring 1987, pp. 87–107.

22. *Sports Illustrated*, vol. 86, no. 15, April 14, 1997, pp 70–71 ff. Also, see *Los Angeles Times*, January 29, 1984 on Drug use by Olympic athletes.

23. This line of thinking was suggested by Gina Kolata, "Slippery Slope on the Playing Field," *New York Times*, July 11, 1999, Section IV, p. 18.

24. *New York Times*, August 1, 1976, p. V5.

25. *New York Times*, May 4, 1980, p. V-3.

26. *New York Times*, August 18, 1987, p. 1, D24; and August 19, 1987, p. D25.

27. *New York Times*, February 3, 1989, p. B15.

28. An interview with an Olympian who does not wish to be identified.

29. Bowling Green *Daily Sentinel Tribune*, May 15, 1992, p. 19.

30. *New York Times*, June 3, 1972, p. 23.

31. *Oakland Press*, July 14, 1988, p. B-1.

32. *Traverse City Record-Eagle*, May 19, 1990, p. 9-A.

33. Thomas Murray and Don Catlin, *Journal of the American Medical Association*, July 17, 1996, vol.276, number 3, pp. 231–237.

34. Vyv Simson and Andrew Jennings, *Dishonored Games: Corruption , Money & Greed at the Olympic*. New York: Shapolsky Publishers, 1992, p. 22.

35. *New York Times*, May 2, 1972, p. 55.

36. *Des Moines Register*, April 24, 1999, p. 2 T.

37. *Newsweek*, January 1, 2000, Vol. CXIV, No. 26, p. 80.

38. *New York Times*, February 5, 1999, p. C-20.

39. *Ibid.*

40. *New York Times*, March 26, 2000, p. 41.

41. See *New York Times*, May 7, 2000, p. 43.

42. For more detail see, Simson and Jennings, *op. cit.*, 1992.

43. *New York Times*, March 4, 1999, p. C-23, 26.

44. *New York Times*, May 16, 1999, p. 38.

45. *Ibid.*

46. *Oakland Press*, May 12, 1999, p. C-1.

47. *New York Times*, February 5, 2000, p. B19.

48. Ron Marinucci, "Running is an equal opportunity activity," *The Oakland Press*, April 4, 1999, p. B12.

49. *The 1998 ESPN Information Please Spots Almanac*. New York: Hyperion Press, 1997, p. 648.

50. *Detroit News*, November 8, 1999, p. 8-F.

51. *The Oakland Press*, April 18, 2000, p. B-7.

52. *The Oakland Press*, March 25, 2000, p. B-2.

53. See *New York Times*, May 16, 1999, p. 39 for the views of two successful student-athletes.

54. David Foley, "Kids are Growing and Slowing," *On Running*, Michigan Runner, January/February, 1996.

55. *New York Times*, June 10, 1986, p. B9.

56. *Ibid.*, June 18, 1990, p. C11.

57. *Ibid.*, June 3, 1990, section 8, pp. 1 and 4.

58. *Ibid.*, June 5, 1986, p. D25.

59. *Ibid.*, June 6, 1986, p. A25; June 7, 1986, p. 45.

60. *Ibid.*, July 17, 2000, p. D-3.

THE 100 BEST MALE TRACK AND FIELD ATHLETES FROM MICHIGAN IN THE TWENTIETH CENTURY

1. Charles Dvorak	UM	1900–04	Pole Vault • Silver Medal Olympics
2. Archie Hahn[†]	UM	1900–06	100 meter* • Gold Medal Olympics
3. Ralph Rose[†]	UM	1904–12	Shot Put* • Discus Gold, Silver Olympics
4. Fred Schule	UM	1904	Hurdles • Gold Medal Olympics
5. John C. Garrels	UM	1908	Hurdles • Gold Medal Olympics
6. John N. Patterson	UM	1906–8	High Jump • AAU Champ, Olympics
7. Joe Malcomson	DUS/STC	1909	Hurdles • AAU Champion
8. Frank T. Nelson	Yale	1910/12	Pole Vault • Silver Medal Olympics
9. Ralph C. Craig[†]	UM	1912	100 & 200 meter • Gold Metal Olympics
10. Richard Leslie Byrd	Adrian	1912	Discus, Standing high jump • Olympic Silver
11. Carroll B. Haff	UM	1912/3	440 • Olympic team
12. A. W. Kohler	UM	1913–4	Hammer • IC4A Champion
13. C. E. Johnson	UM	1918–20	Broad jump • Olympic Silver
14. Ivan Dresser	Cornell	1920	3-K • Olympic Gold
15. Jackson V. Scholz[†]	MO	1920	100 & 200 meter* • Gold Medal Olympics
16. Howard B. Hoffman	UM	1922	Discuss, Javelin • NCAA Champ in 2 events
17. James K. Booker	UM	1924	Pole Vault • Bronze Olympics
18. William DeHart Hubbard[†]	UM	1924	Broad Jump* • Gold Olympics

709

19. Charles Foster	YMCA	1924	Racing walk • Olympic team
20. George "Buck" Hester	UM	1924	100 & 200 meter • Olympic team
21. Philip M. Northrup	UM	1925	Pole Vault, discuss • NCAA Champ 2 events
22. Edward O. Spence	WU	1926	Hurdles • NCAA Champ; All-American
23. J. Ken Doherty†	WU	1928	Decathlon • Bronze Olympics
24. John W. Lewis	WU	1928	440 • Olympic team
25. Fred Alderman	MSU	1928	dashes/relays* • Olympic Gold
26. Thomas "Eddie" Tolan†	UM	1928/32	100 & 200 meter* • Olympic Gold
27. Wilford H. Ketz	UM	1928	Hammer • Drake Relays, NCAA Champ
28. Holly Campbell	UM	1930	Hammer • All-American
29. Bill Streng	WU	1931	220 dash • All-American
30. Clark Chamberlain	MSU	1931	2 mile run • NCAA & USA-British Champ
31. Lee M. Bartlett	Albion	1929	Javelin* • Olympic team
32. Clark Haskins	Detroit Police	1930–40	56 lbs weight • AAU Champion
33. Eugene Beatty	EMU	1932	400 meter hurdles • All-American
34. William Zepp	EMU	1932	2-mile run • All-American; AAU Champ
35. Thomas C. Ottey	MSU	1932–4	10-K run • Olympic team
36. Ernest Crosbie	MSU	1932–48	50-K walk • Olympic team
37. William Bonthron†	Princeton	1934	1,500-meters* • Sullivan Trophy
38. Willis Ward	UM	1934	Hurdles • All-American
39. George Huber	Detroit Police	1935	Discus, Weight throw • AAU Champion
40. Allan Tolmich	WU	1935	Hurdles* • All-American

41.	Abe Rosenkrantz	EMU	1935–6	880-yard run • Maccabee Games
42.	Albert Mangan	MSU	1936	50-K walk • Olympic Team
43.	Sam Stoller	UM	1936	100 meters • Olympic Team
44.	Bob Osgood	UM	1936	400-meter hurdles • All-American
45.	Harvey H. Woodstra	MSU	1938	Hurdles • All-American
46.	Bill Watson	UM	1939	Decathlon /Shot Put* • All-American
47.	William Mihalo		1940	50-K walk • All-American
48.	Don Canham	UM	1940	High Jump • All-American
49.	Roy B. Fehr	MSU	1940	2 mile run • All-American
50.	Charles Hlad	EMU	1941	Hurdles • All-American
51.	James McNutt Umstattd	Texas	1941	Medley relay* • Drake, Kansas, & Texas Relays
52.	Robert F. Wingo	WU	1942	400 meters • All-American
53.	Bob Ufer	UM	1943–5	440-yard run • All-American
54.	H. Ross and Bob Hume	UM	1944	Mile-run • NCAA Champs
55.	Herbert O. Barten	UM	1948	800-meter • Olympian
56.	Bill Porter	NWU	1948	110-meter high hurdles • Olympic Gold
57.	Charles Fonville	MU	1948	Shot put* • All-American
58.	Lorenzo Wright	WU	1948	Broad jump/100 meter • Olympic Gold
59.	Adolf Weinacker	MSU	1948–56	50-K walk • Olympic team
60.	Fred Johnson	MSU	1949	Broad jump • All-American
61.	Warren Druetzler	MSU	1952–6	Mile* • Olympic team
62.	James Podoley	CMU	1955	Decathlon • 4th in AAU
63.	Mark H. Smith, Jr.	WU	1956	High jump • NCAA Champion

64. David G. Owen	UM	1956	Shot put • All-American, Nat'l Champ
65. John Telford	WU	1957	440 • All-American; ran for AAU in Europe
66. Ira Murchison	WMU	1957	100 yd dash* • All-American. Gold Olympics
67. Hayes Jones†	EMU	1958	Hurdles* • Olympic Bronze, '60; Gold, '64
68. Willie Atterberry	MSU	1958	440-yards* • All-American, Pan-Am Games
69. Otis Davis	UO	1960	400 meter* • 2 Olympic Gold medals
70. Clifton Cushman	U of KS	1960	400-meter hurdles • Sliver Medal Olympics
71. David Meyers	CMU	1960	440 yards • All-American
72. John Bork	WMU	1961	880 yards* • NCAA Champion
73. Henry Carr†	AzSt	1964	200 meter* • 2 Olympic Gold
74. Warren Rex Cawley	USC	1964	400 meters* • Olympic Gold
75. Eugene Washington	MSU	1965	110-yard high-hurdles • All-American
76. Bob Steele	MSU	1966–7	440 Hurdles* • All-American
77. Louis Scott	AzSt	1968	5-K • Olympic team, Pan Am Games
78. Ronald C. Kutschinski	UM	1968	800 meter • Olympic team
79. Goetz Klopfer	WSU	1968/72	50-K walk • Olympic team
80. William Wehrwein	MSU	1969	600-yards • All-American
81. Herb Washington	MSU	1970	100-yard dash* • All-American
82. Marshall Dill	MSU	1971	300-yards • Pan-American Games
83. Stan Vinson	EMU	1972–5	600-yards* • Pan-African Games
84. Doug Brown	Univ. of TN	1972	Steeplechase • Olympic team

85. William Weigle	—	1972	50-K walk • Olympic team
86. Ken Popejoy	MSU	1972–3	mile run • Pan-American Games
87. Bob Cassleman	MSU	1974	600-yards • All-American
88. Reggie Jones	U of TN	1975	220-yards • All-American 9 times
89. Sam James	U of TN	1977–80	Steeplechase; medley relay • All-American (4)
90. Carl Schueler	Frostburg/UM	1980–4	50-K walk • Olympic team
91. Eddie Brown	Saginaw Valley	1981–4	400-meter hurdles • All-American
92. Elliott Tabron	WU/MSU	1983	440-yards • World Games
93. Brian Diemer	UM	1983	Steeplechase • Olympic Bronze
94. Greg Meyer	UM	1983	Boston Marathon winner
95. Earl Jones	EMU	1984	800 meters • Olympic Bronze
96. Gary Morgan	OCC	1984/99	20-K walk • Olympic team
97. John Sherer	UM	1989	10-K run • All-American
98. Darnell Hall	Blinn	1992	400 meters • Olympic Gold
99. Brad Barquist	UM	1996	10-K run • Olympic team
100. Paul McMullen	EMU	1992–6	1,500 meter run • Olympic team

*World and or American record

†U.S. Track and Field Hall of Fame Member

Note: Foreign national runners who competed for Michigan Colleges and Universities are excluded.

Compiled by Keith McClellan, September, 1998

FORTY-FIVE NOTABLE MICHIGAN WOMEN
TRACK AND FIELD STARS

1. Florence Wolf — VVV Girl's A C of Detroit — 1926 — discus • Fourth in National AAU

2. Dorothy Frances Anderson [Merena] — EMU — 1932 — H J • 2nd AAU Indoor; 4th Olympic trials

3. Anna Mae Sullifant — UM — 1955 — 100 yd. • 4th National AAU, Girls Div.

4. Louise Gerrish — Ann Arbor Anns — 1964–6 — Javelin • AAU, Girls' Div. All-American

5. Karen Dennis — Detroit T C/MSU — 1964 — 220 yards • 3rd AAU, Girls Div.; Olympic coach

6. Francie Kraker Goodridge — MU — 1964–8 — 600 meters* • All-America, Olympic team

7. Sue Parks — EMU — 1972–8 — 1,500-meter run • Pan Am. Games, Olympic Trials

8. Deby La Plante — SDSU — 1976–9 — 100 meter hurdles* • Olympic team

9. Jeanne Bocci — DTC — 1972–88 — Race walker • USA Cup Team

10. Sue Latter Addison — MSU — 1975–8 — 880 and mile • All-American, Olympic trials

11. Debbie Romsek — BGU — 1976–80 — 440 and 880 • Mac Champ

12. Sue Reimer — CMU — 1978–81 — Pentathlon • MAC Champ

13. Keela Yount — CMU — 1978–81 — 1,500-meter and 2-K run • MAC Champ

14. Diane Williams — MSU — 1980 — 100-meter dash • Olympic team

15. Sue Fredrick Foster — UM — 1981–3 — 1,500-meter run • Olympic trials

16. Penny Neer — UM — 1981, 92 — Discus • Olympic team

714

17. Ann Meachum [Lohner]	EMU	1979–82	Long jump • All-American
18. Sue Schroeder	UM	1982–6	1,500-meter run • All-American
19. Joyce Wilson	UM	1983–7	400-meter • Olympic trials
20. Delisa Walton [Floyd]	TN	1984/88	800 meters • All-American, Olympics
21. Kim Turner [McKenzie]	Texas	1984	100 meter hurdles • Olympic Bronze
22. Judi Brown [King]	MSU	1984	400 meter hurdles • Olympic Silver
23. Vivian McKenzie	U. of Iowa	1984	100-meter dash • Olympic trials
24. Juli Ravary	CMU	1982–5	Javelin throw, shot put • MAC Champ
25. Anne Pewe	MSU	1980–84	3-K • All-American
26. Annette Bohach	Indiana U	1983–4	Shot put • All-American
27. Michele Morris	LSU	1984	200-meter/400-meter dash • Olympic trials
28. Wendy Truvillion	LSU	1984–87	4 × 400/500-meter dash • All-Am. Six times
29. Maria Shoup	WMU	1984–88	400-meter hurdles • Olympic trials
30. Tonya Lowe	U of Ky	1984	100-meter hurdles • Olympic trials
31. Odessa Smalls	MSU	1984–87	220-yd • All-American
32. Donna Donakowski	EMU	1985–88	3-K, 5-K, 10-K • All-American
33. Virgie Bullie	EMU	1986–8	200-meter dash, • All-American
34. Mary Shea	MSU	1986	10-K run • Olympic trials
35. Andrea Bowman	EMU	1988	1,500-meter run • Olympic trials
36. Kathi Harris-Rounds	LSU	1988–96	800-meter • Olympic trials
37. Joy Inniss	EMU	1991–94	Triple-jump • All-American

38. Jill Stamison [McMillen]	WMU	1993	800-meter run • All-American, World Games
39. Stephanie Dueringer	MSU	1994–97	5-K • All-American
40. Betsy Haverkamp	Calvin C	1996	3-K, 5-K • All-American
41. Chandra Burns	MSU	1996	400-meter dash • All-Am., Olympic trials
42. Jamie Strieter	WMU	1996–8	Javelin • MAC Champ
43. Katie McGregor	UM	1996–9	1,500-& 5 K • All-American
44. Carrie Gould	EMU	1998–99	5-K and 10-K • Drake Relays Champ
45. Mindy Ramsey	SVSC	2000	shot put and discus • NCAA Div. II Champ

UNITED STATES TRACK AND FIELD OLYMPIANS FROM MICHIGAN

1900

Charles Dvorak, pole vault, placed second in the special pole vault

John McLean, 110-meter high-hurdles (2nd); also in 200-meter low-hurdles, 800-meter run, handicap long jump (2nd), standing triple jump (6th), running triple jump (8th), and long jump (placed 6th).

Howard Hayes, 800-meter handicap race, placed second.

Clark Leiblee, 100-meter dash, made semi-finals.

1904

Charles Dvorak, pole vault, won and set an Olympic record (OR).

Archie Hahn, 60-meter dash, 100-meter dash, 200-meter dash-won all three events and set an Olympic record in the 200-meter dash and tied the record in the 60-meter dash.

Ralph Rose, shot put (won, world record and OR), discus (tied for first), hammer throw (3rd), International tug-of war (2nd), and 56-pound weight throw (6th).

Fred Schule, 110-meter high-hurdles, won; 200-meter low-hurdles (placed 5th)

William Coe, shot put, placed second.

1906

Archie Hahn, 100-meter dash, won.

1908

Ralph Rose, shot put (won), discus, tug-of-war.

John Garrels, shot put (second), 110-meter high-hurdles (second), discus.

Gayle Dull, three-mile team race (placed 10th), 3,200-meter steeplechase.

Harry L. "Spider" Coe, 800-meter run, 1,500-meter run, 400-meter dash.

Horace Ramey, 400-meter dash, 800-meter run.

William Coe, shot put (4th), tug-of-war.

John Neil "Pat" ["Pinky"] Patterson, high jump (7th).

1912

Ralph Rose, shot put (2nd), shot put combined (won), hammer throw (9th), and discus (11th).

Richard Byrd, discus (2nd), standing high jump (4th), and standing broad jump (6th).

Ralph Craig, 100-meter dash (won), 200-meter dash (won).

Carroll Haff, 400-meter dash (5th).

Frank T. Nelson, pole vault (2nd).

Avery Brundage, decathlon (did not finish), pentathlon (6th).

1920
Ivan Dresser, 3,000-meter team-race (won).
Jackson V. Scholz, 100-meter dash (4th), 4 × 100-meter relay (won in OR.)
Carl Johnson, long jump (2nd).

1924
Jackson V. Scholz, 100-meter dash (2nd), 200-meter dash (won tied OR).
William De Hart Hubbard, long jump (won), hop, skip and jump.
James K. Brooker, pole vault (3rd).
Charles Foster, 10-kilometer walk.
George "Buck" Hester, 100-meter dash, 200-meter dash.

1928
Jackson V. Scholz, 200-meter dash (4th).
William De Hart Hubbard, long jump (11th).
George "Buck" Hester, 100-meter dash, 200-meter dash, 4 × 100-meter relay.
J. Kenneth Doherty, decathlon (3rd).
John W. Lewis, 4 × 400-meter relay.
Fred P. Alderman, 4 × 400-meter relay (won set world record and OR).
Lee M. Barrett, javelin throw.

1932
Lee M. Barrett, javelin throw.(5th)
Thomas Eddie Tolan, 100-meter dash (won, OR), 200-meter dash (won, OR).
Edwin "Ned" Turner, 800-meter run (5th)
Tom Ottey, 10,000-meter run.
Ernest Crosbie, 50-kilometer walk (8th).

1936
Lee M. Barrett, javelin throw.(11th)
Ernest Crosbie, 50-kilometer walk
Albert Mangan, 50-kilometer walk.
Sam Stoller, 4 × 100-meter relay (Did not run.)

1948
Ernest Crosbie, 50-kilometer walk.
Herbert O. Barten, 800 m. (placed 4th)
Adolf Weinacker, 50-kilometer walk, (placed 16th).
Bill Porter, 110-meter high-hurdles, (won, set OR).
Lorenzo Wright, long jump (4th), 4 × 100-meter relay (won).

1952
Adolf Weinacker, 50-kilometer walk, placed 22nd.
Warren Druetzler, 1,500-meter run, placed 12th.

1956
Adolf Weinacker, 50-kilometer walk, placed 7th.
Ira Murchison, 100-meter dash (4th), 4 × 100-relay (won, set world record and OR).

<u>1960</u>
Hayes Jones, 110-meter high-hurdles (3rd).
Otis Davis, 400-meter dash (won, set world and OR), 4 × 400 relay (won, set the world record and OR).
Clifton Cushman, 400-meter intermediate hurdles (2nd).

<u>1964</u>
Hayes Jones, 110-meter high-hurdles (won).
Henry Carr, 200-meter dash (won, set the OR), 4 × 400 relay (won, set the world record and OR)
Warren "Rex" Cawley, 400-meter Intermediate hurdles (won).

<u>1968</u>
Ron Kutschinski, 1,500-meter run (13th overall).
Goetz Klopfer, 50-kilometer walk (10th).
Francie Kraker, women's 800-meter run.
Lou Scott, 5,000-meter run

<u>1972</u>
Goetz Klopfer, 50-kilometer walk (19th).
Doug Brown, 3,000-meter steeplechase (10rd in his first round heat).
William Weigle, 50-kilometer walk, (placed 17th).
Francie Kraker, women's 1,500-meter run, (8th).

<u>1976</u>
Deby La Plante, 100-meter high-hurdles (semi-finals).
Doug Brown, 3,000-meter steeplechase, (14th).

<u>1980</u> (Boycott)   Diane Williams, 4 × 100-meter relay.

<u>1984</u>
Earl Jones, 800-meter run, (3rd).
Brian Diemer, 3,000-meter steeplechase, (3rd).
Kim Turner, 100-meter high-hurdles, (3rd).
Judi Brown, 400-meter hurdles, (2nd).
Carl Schueler, 50-kilometer walk, (6th).

<u>1988</u>
Brian Diemer, 3,000-meter steeplechase, (18th).
Carl Schueler, 50-kilometer walk, (23rd).
Gary Morgan, 20-kilometer walk, (37th).
Delisa Walton, 800-meter run, (5th).

<u>1992</u>
Brian Diemer, 3,000-meter steeplechase, (7th).
Carl Schueler, 50-kilometer walk, (23rd).
Darnell Hall, 4 × 400 relay (ran in preliminary races, the team won this event).

Quincy Watts, 400-meter run, (won, set OR), 4 × 400-meter relay (won, set the world record and the OR).
Penny Neer, women's discus, (8th).

1996
Brad Barquest, 10,000-meter run, (placed 16th in the second heat).
Paul McMullen, 1,500-meter run, (placed 19th overall.)

Total United States Track and Field Olympians with Michigan Roots: 67
Michigan Olympians before 1950: Men, 39   Women, 0
Michigan Olympians since 1950:   Men, 21   Women, 7

Olympic Gold medal winners before 1965: 25
Olympic Gold medal winners since 1965: 1 (Quincy Watts, who moved to California before high school).

Men's 100-Meter Dash

Jackson Scholz	September 16, 1920	10.6
Eddie Tolan	August 8, 1929 (10.4); August 1, 1932	10.3
Ira Murchison	June 1, 1956	10.2
Ira Murchison	August 4, 1956	10.1

Men's 200-Meter Dash

Archie Hahn	August 31, 1904	21.6
Henry Carr	March 23, 1962 (20.3); April 4, 1964	20.2

Men's 400-Meter Dash

Otis Davis	September 6, 1960	44.9

Men's 1,500-Meter Run

Bill Bonthron	June 30, 1934	3:48.8

Men's 400-Meter Intermediate Hurdles

Warren "Rex" Cawley	September 13, 1964	49.1

Men's Long Jump

William DeHart Hubbard	June 13, 1925	25 feet 10¾

Men' Shot Put

Ralph Rose	August 31, 1904	48 feet 7 inches
Ralph Rose	August 21, 1909	51 feet 0 inches
Charles Fonville	April 17, 1948	58 feet ¼ inches

Men's 4 × 100-meter Relay

Ira Murchison	December 1,1956	39.60
Hayes Jones	July 15, 1961	39.10

Men's 4 × 400-meter Relay

Fred Alderman	August 4, 1928	3:14.2
Otis Davis	September 8, 1960	3:02.37
Henry Carr	October 17, 1964	3:00.7
Quincy Watts	August 8,1992	2:55.74

Men's 75-yard Dash

Archie Hahn	March 11, 1905	7.6
Jackson Scholz	March 6, 1922	7.6

Men's 100-yard Dash

Archie Hahn	September 1901	9.8
DeHart Hubbard	May 9, 1925	9.6
T. Eddie Tolan	May 25, 1929	9.5

Men's 220-yard Dash

Ralph Craig	March 28, 1910 and May 15, 1911	21.2
Henry Carr	March 23, 1963	20.3
Henry Carr	April 4, 1964	20.2

Men's 70-yard High-Hurdles (Indoors)

Allan Tolmich	February 24, 1940	8.4

Men's Mile-Relay

Jackson Scholz	July 4, 1929	3:17.0
Henry Carr	March 23, 1963	3:07.2
Henry Carr	April 27, 1963	3:04.5

Men's Decathlon, 100-meter run and discus

William Watson	June 16, 1940	(10.8) (151–3¾) 7,523 points

Women's 600-meter Run

Delisa Walton [Floyd]	March 14, 1981 Pocatello, Idaho	(1:26.56)

American AAU Records—Men

40-yard high-hurdles (indoors) (5.2)	Ralph Craig, Ann Arbor, March 25, 1911
40-yard dash	John W. Lewis, NY City, Feb. 1930
45-yard high-hurdles (indoors) (5.4)	Charles Hlad, Cleveland, Mar. 27, 1942
50-yard dash (indoors) (5.2)	Jackson Scholz, Kansas City, March 15, 1918
50-yard dash (indoors) (5.2)	DeHart Hubbard, Detroit, April 6, 1925
50-yard dash (indoors) (5.1)	Herbert L. Washington, Hamilton, Ontario March 23, 1968 & March 21, 1970
50-yard high-hurdles (indoors, dirt track) (6.2)	Allan Tolmich, Indianapolis, Feb. 12, 1937
50-yard high-hurdles (indoors) (6.0)	Hayes Jones, Philadelphia, Feb. 12, 1960
50-yard high-hurdles (indoors) (5.9)	Hayes Jones, Cleveland, March 18, 1960; Milwaukee, March 11, 1961; Toronto, Jan. 24, 1964
60-yard dash (indoors) (6.2)	DeHart Hubbard, Ann Arbor, March 28, 1925

60-yard dash (indoors) (6.1)	Sam Stoller, Chicago, March 14, 1941
60-yard dash (indoors) (6.1)	Jim Bibbs, South Bend, March 3, 1951
60-yard dash (indoors) (6.1)	Ira Murchison, New York City, February 9, 1957
60-yard dash (indoors) (5.9)	Herb L. Washington, Detroit, March 14, 1970
60-yard dash (indoors) (5.8)	Herb L. Washington, East Lansing, Feb. 12, 1972
60-yard low-hurdles (indoors, dirt track) (6.8)	Fred Johnson, West Lafayette, March 27, 1948
60-yard high-hurdles (indoors) (7.2)	Charles Held, New York City, Feb. 7, 1942
60-yard high-hurdles (indoors) (7.0)	Hayes Jones, New York City, January 30, 1960
60-yard high-hurdles (indoors) (6.9)	Hayes Jones, Milwaukee, March 10, 1962
60-yard high-hurdles (indoors) (6.8)	Hayes Jones, Baltimore, February 29, 1964
60-yard high-hurdles (indoors) (6.1)	Eugene Washington, Detroit, March 12, 1965
65-meter high-hurdles (indoors) (8.3)	Allan Tolmich, N Y City, February 22, 1941
65-yard low-hurdles (indoors) (7.1)	Billy Smith, Ypsilanti, March 3, 1956
70-yard dash (indoors) (7.4)	Jackson Scholz, N Y City, February 10, 1920
70-yard dash (indoors) (7.0)	Elmer "Buddy" Coleman, Chi., Mar. 19, 1949
70-yard high-hurdles (indoors, dirt) (8.5)	Bill Porter, Champaign, March 8, 1947
70-yard high-hurdles (indoors) (8.2)	Hayes Jones, Louisville, Jan. 28, 1961
70-yard high-hurdles (indoors) (8.0)	Hayes Jones, Louisville, February 17, 1961
120-yard high-hurdles (14.0)	Robert Osgood, Ann Arbor, May 22, 1937
110-meter high-hurdles (13.4)	Hayes Jones, New York City, July 27, 1964
200-meter low-hurdles (23.5)	Allan Tolmich, Buffalo, July 3, 1939
440-yard dash (indoors) (48.1)	Bob Ufer, Chicago, March 6, 1943
440-yard hurdles (49.6)	"Rex" Cawley, Albuquerque, June 15, 1963
600-yard run (indoors) (1:11)	Bob Ufer, NY City, Feb. 21, 1944 [unsanctioned-improper start]

600-yard run (outdoors) (1:08.5)	Willie Atterberry, Sr., Columbus, April 20, 1957
600-yard run (indoors) (1:08.6)	William Wehrwein, East Lansing, Feb. 23, 1969
800-meters (1:43.74)	Earl Jones, Los Angeles, June 19, 1984
1,000-yard run (indoors, dirt) (2:09.2)	John Bork, Jr., South Bend, Feb. 25, 1961
2,000-meter run (5:22.6)	Warren Druetzler, Stockholm, Aug. 16, 1950
3,000-meter steeplechase (8:19.3)	Doug Brown, Baton Rouge, June 13, 1978
400-yard relay (37.5)	Eddie Tolan, Chicago, August 27, 1930
880-yard relay (indoors, dirt) (1:30.2)	Jim Bibbs, Irv Petross, Billy Smith, Ann Arbor, January 31, 1958
800-meter relay (1:21.5)	Reggie Jones, et al., Philadelphia, April 23–24, 1976
Sprint medley relay (3:24.0)	James "Mac" Umstattd, Austin, TX, April 5, 1941
Sprint medley relay (3:23.2)	James "Mac" Umstattd, Des Moines, April 27, 1941
1,600-meter relay (3:24.9)	Bob Wingo, Linwood Wright, Bob Grant, Wayne Hatfield, New York City, June 20, 1942
1,600-meter relay, indoors (3:08.9)	Stan Vinson anchored the USA relay team, Milan, Italy, March 14, 1978
2,900-meter medley relay (6:58.9)	Warren Druetzler, Buffalo, NY, June 28, 1953
2-mile medley relay (7:25.8)	Jackson Scholz, New York City, Sept. 26, 1921
Two-mile relay (indoors, dirt) (7:40.9)	H. Ross Hume, John Roxborough, Dave Matthews, Bob Ufer, West Lafayette, April 12, 1943
2½ mile Medley Relay (9:56.3)	Aaron Z. Gordon, Columbus, April 19, 1952.
4-mile Relay (16:52.6)	Warren Druetzler, London, August 4, 1952
4-mile Relay (16:50.4)	Jerry Bashaw, Jerry Ashmore, John Bork, Jr., and Dick Pond, Des Moines, April 29, 1961
Men's Decathlon (7784 pts.)	J. Kenneth Doherty, Denver, July 4, 1929
Javelin (216–7)	Lee M. Bartlett, Evanston, July 2, 1932

American Collegiate Records

60-yard high-hurdles (7.2 tied)	Gerald "Jerry" Cerulla Detroit, March 11–12, 1966
100-yard dash (9.8)	De Hart Hubbard, Chicago, June 13, 1925
220-yard low-hurdles (23.5)	Edward O. Spence, Chicago, June 12, 1926
220-yard low-hurdles (23.4)	Edward O. Spence, Chicago, June 11, 1927
240-yard shuttle hurdle relay (28.84)	Bill Tipton, Alton Davis, Bob Lynn, Jerry Cerulla, Big Rapids, MI., February 20, 1968
300-yard dash (Indoors) (31.2)	Fred Alderman, Champaign, IL., Feb. 25, 1926
480-yard high-hurdles relay (57.4)	Gene Washington, Clint Jones, and Bob Steele, Des Moines, April 30, 1966
3,000-meter steeplechase (8:28.1)	Doug Brown, Baton Rouge, June 9, 1973
2-mile relay (8:00.0)	Carroll Haff, Philadelphia, April 26, 1913
2-mile relay (7:31.8)	Don Makielski, Warren Druetz-ler, William G. Mack, Jack Dianetti, May 19, 1950
2½ mile medley relay (9:56.3)	Aaron Z. Gordon, East Lansing, February 3, 1951.
2½ mile medley relay (9:56.3)	Aaron Z. Gordon, Columbus, April 19, 1952.
4-mile relay (17:08.6)	Aaron Z. Gordon, Ypsilanti, May 6, 1952.
Javelin (202–3)	Howard B. Hoffman, Chicago, June 17, 1922
Javelin (216–7)	Lee M. Bartlett, Chicago, June 9, 1928

American Records-Women

60-yard hurdles (indoor) (7.53)	Deby La Plante, New York City, February 14, 1978
60-meter hurdles (indoor) (8.25)	Deby La Plante, Milan, Italy, March 14, 1978
70-yard hurdles (indoor) (8.8)	Deby La Plante, Louisville, February 7, 1976
100-meter hurdles (12.86)	Deby La Plante, Walnut Creek, June 16, 1979
400-meter hurdles (54.99)	Judi Brown [King], San Jose, June 9, 1984
400-meter hurdles (54.93)	Judi Brown-King, Los Angeles, June 21, 1984

400-meter hurdles (54.38)	Judi Brown [King], Rome, Italy, Sept. 7, 1985
400-meter hurdles (54.23)	Judi Brown [King], Indianapolis, Aug. 12, 1987
500-meter run (1:11.7)	Delisa Walton [Floyd], Louisville, Feb. 9, 1980
600-meter run (1:26.56)	Delisa Walton [Floyd], Pocatello, March 14, 1981
600-yard run (1:17.38)	Delisa Walton [Floyd], Cedar Falls, March 13, 1982

Index